Algorithmic Game Theory

Over the last few years, there has been explosive growth in the research done at the interface of computer science, game theory, and economic theory, largely motivated by the emergence of the Internet. *Algorithmic Game Theory* develops the central ideas and results of this new and exciting area.

More than 40 of the top researchers in this field have written chapters whose topics range from the foundations to the state of the art. This book contains an extensive treatment of algorithms for equilibria in games and markets, computational auctions and mechanism design, and the "price of anarchy," as well as applications in networks, peer-to-peer systems, security, information markets, and more.

This book will be of interest to students, researchers, and practitioners in theoretical computer science, economics, networking, artificial intelligence, operations research, and discrete mathematics.

Noam Nisan is a Professor in the Department of Computer Science at The Hebrew University of Jerusalem. His other books include *Communication Complexity.*

Tim Roughgarden is an Assistant Professor in the Department of Computer Science at Stanford University. His other books include *Selfish Routing and the Price of Anarchy.*

Éva Tardos is a Professor in the Department of Computer Science at Cornell University. Her other books include *Algorithm Design.*

Vijay V. Vazirani is a Professor in the College of Computing at the Georgia Institute of Technology. His other books include *Approximation Algorithms.*

Algorithmic Game Theory

Edited by

Noam Nisan

Hebrew University of Jerusalem

Tim Roughgarden

Stanford University

Éva Tardos

Cornell University

Vijay V. Vazirani

Georgia Institute of Technology

CAMBRIDGE
UNIVERSITY PRESS

CAMBRIDGE
UNIVERSITY PRESS

32 Avenue of the Americas, New York NY 10013-2473, USA

Cambridge University Press is part of the University of Cambridge.

It furthers the University's mission by disseminating knowledge in the pursuit of education, learning and research at the highest international levels of excellence.

www.cambridge.org
Information on this title: www.cambridge.org/9780521872829

First published 2007
Reprinted 2008 (twice)

A catalogue record for this publication is available from the British Library

Library of Congress Cataloguing in Publication data
Algorithmic game theory / edited by Noam Nisan...[et al.]; foreword by Christos Papadimitriou.
p. cm.
Includes index.
ISBN-13: 978-0-521-87282-9 (hardback)
ISBN-10: 0-521-87282-0 (hardback)
1. Game theory. 2. Algorithms. I. Nisan, Noam. II. Title.
QA269.A43 2007
519.3 – dc22 2007014231

ISBN 978-0-521-87282-9 Hardback

Contents

Foreword *page* xiii
Preface xvii
Contributors xix

I Computing in Games

1 Basic Solution Concepts and Computational Issues **3**
Éva Tardos and Vijay V. Vazirani
1.1 Games, Old and New 3
1.2 Games, Strategies, Costs, and Payoffs 9
1.3 Basic Solution Concepts 10
1.4 Finding Equilibria and Learning in Games 16
1.5 Refinement of Nash: Games with Turns and Subgame Perfect Equilibrium 18
1.6 Nash Equilibrium without Full Information: Bayesian Games 20
1.7 Cooperative Games 20
1.8 Markets and Their Algorithmic Issues 22
Acknowledgments 26
Bibliography 26
Exercises 26

2 The Complexity of Finding Nash Equilibria **29**
Christos H. Papadimitriou
2.1 Introduction 29
2.2 Is the NASH Equilibrium Problem NP-Complete? 31
2.3 The Lemke–Howson Algorithm 33
2.4 The Class PPAD 36
2.5 Succinct Representations of Games 39
2.6 The Reduction 41
2.7 Correlated Equilibria 45
2.8 Concluding Remarks 49
Acknowledgment 50
Bibliography 50

3 Equilibrium Computation for Two-Player Games in Strategic and Extensive Form **53**
Bernhard von Stengel
3.1 Introduction 53
3.2 Bimatrix Games and the Best Response Condition 54
3.3 Equilibria via Labeled Polytopes 57
3.4 The Lemke–Howson Algorithm 61
3.5 Integer Pivoting 63
3.6 Degenerate Games 65
3.7 Extensive Games and Their Strategic Form 66
3.8 Subgame Perfect Equilibria 68
3.9 Reduced Strategic Form 69
3.10 The Sequence Form 70
3.11 Computing Equilibria with the Sequence Form 73
3.12 Further Reading 75
3.13 Discussion and Open Problems 75
Bibliography 76
Exercises 77

4 Learning, Regret Minimization, and Equilibria **79**
Avrim Blum and Yishay Mansour
4.1 Introduction 79
4.2 Model and Preliminaries 81
4.3 External Regret Minimization 82
4.4 Regret Minimization and Game Theory 88
4.5 Generic Reduction from External to Swap Regret 92
4.6 The Partial Information Model 94
4.7 On Convergence of Regret-Minimizing Strategies to Nash Equilibrium in Routing Games 96
4.8 Notes 99
Bibliography 99
Exercises 101

5 Combinatorial Algorithms for Market Equilibria **103**
Vijay V. Vazirani
5.1 Introduction 103
5.2 Fisher's Linear Case and the Eisenberg–Gale Convex Program 105
5.3 Checking If Given Prices Are Equilibrium Prices 108
5.4 Two Crucial Ingredients of the Algorithm 109
5.5 The Primal-Dual Schema in the Enhanced Setting 109
5.6 Tight Sets and the Invariant 111
5.7 Balanced Flows 111
5.8 The Main Algorithm 115
5.9 Finding Tight Sets 117
5.10 Running Time of the Algorithm 118
5.11 The Linear Case of the Arrow–Debreu Model 121
5.12 An Auction-Based Algorithm 122
5.13 Resource Allocation Markets 124

5.14 Algorithm for Single-Source Multiple-Sink Markets 126
5.15 Discussion and Open Problems 131
Bibliography 132
Exercises 133

6 Computation of Market Equilibria by Convex Programming 135
Bruno Codenotti and Kasturi Varadarajan
6.1 Introduction 135
6.2 Fisher Model with Homogeneous Consumers 141
6.3 Exchange Economies Satisfying WGS 142
6.4 Specific Utility Functions 148
6.5 Limitations 150
6.6 Models with Production 152
6.7 Bibliographic Notes 155
Bibliography 156
Exercises 158

7 Graphical Games 159
Michael Kearns
7.1 Introduction 159
7.2 Preliminaries 161
7.3 Computing Nash Equilibria in Tree Graphical Games 164
7.4 Graphical Games and Correlated Equilibria 169
7.5 Graphical Exchange Economies 176
7.6 Open Problems and Future Research 177
7.7 Bibliographic Notes 177
Acknowledgments 179
Bibliography 179

8 Cryptography and Game Theory 181
Yevgeniy Dodis and Tal Rabin
8.1 Cryptographic Notions and Settings 181
8.2 Game Theory Notions and Settings 187
8.3 Contrasting MPC and Games 189
8.4 Cryptographic Influences on Game Theory 191
8.5 Game Theoretic Influences on Cryptography 197
8.6 Conclusions 202
8.7 Notes 203
Acknowledgments 204
Bibliography 204

II Algorithmic Mechanism Design

9 Introduction to Mechanism Design (for Computer Scientists) 209
Noam Nisan
9.1 Introduction 209
9.2 Social Choice 211
9.3 Mechanisms with Money 216
9.4 Implementation in Dominant Strategies 222

9.5 Characterizations of Incentive Compatible Mechanisms 225
9.6 Bayesian–Nash Implementation 233
9.7 Further Models 238
9.8 Notes 239
Acknowledgments 240
Bibliography 241

10 Mechanism Design without Money 243
James Schummer and Rakesh V. Vohra
10.1 Introduction 243
10.2 Single-Peaked Preferences over Policies 244
10.3 House Allocation Problem 253
10.4 Stable Matchings 255
10.5 Future Directions 262
10.6 Notes and References 263
Bibliography 264
Exercises 264

11 Combinatorial Auctions 267
Liad Blumrosen and Noam Nisan
11.1 Introduction 267
11.2 The Single-Minded Case 270
11.3 Walrasian Equilibrium and the LP Relaxation 275
11.4 Bidding Languages 279
11.5 Iterative Auctions: The Query Model 283
11.6 Communication Complexity 287
11.7 Ascending Auctions 289
11.8 Bibliographic Notes 295
Acknowledgments 296
Bibliography 296
Exercises 298

12 Computationally Efficient Approximation Mechanisms 301
Ron Lavi
12.1 Introduction 301
12.2 Single-Dimensional Domains: Job Scheduling 303
12.3 Multidimensional Domains: Combinatorial Auctions 310
12.4 Impossibilities of Dominant Strategy Implementability 317
12.5 Alternative Solution Concepts 321
12.6 Bibliographic Notes 327
Bibliography 327
Exercises 328

13 Profit Maximization in Mechanism Design 331
Jason D. Hartline and Anna R. Karlin
13.1 Introduction 331
13.2 Bayesian Optimal Mechanism Design 335
13.3 Prior-Free Approximations to the Optimal Mechanism 339
13.4 Prior-Free Optimal Mechanism Design 344

13.5 Frugality 350
13.6 Conclusions and Other Research Directions 354
13.7 Notes 357
Bibliography 358
Exercises 360

14 Distributed Algorithmic Mechanism Design 363
Joan Feigenbaum, Michael Schapira, and Scott Shenker
14.1 Introduction 363
14.2 Two Examples of DAMD 366
14.3 Interdomain Routing 370
14.4 Conclusion and Open Problems 379
14.5 Notes 380
Acknowledgments 381
Bibliography 381
Exercises 383

15 Cost Sharing 385
Kamal Jain and Mohammad Mahdian
15.1 Cooperative Games and Cost Sharing 385
15.2 Core of Cost-Sharing Games 387
15.3 Group-Strategyproof Mechanisms and Cross-Monotonic Cost-Sharing Schemes 391
15.4 Cost Sharing via the Primal-Dual Schema 394
15.5 Limitations of Cross-Monotonic Cost-Sharing Schemes 400
15.6 The Shapley Value and the Nash Bargaining Solution 402
15.7 Conclusion 405
15.8 Notes 406
Acknowledgments 408
Bibliography 408
Exercises 410

16 Online Mechanisms 411
David C. Parkes
16.1 Introduction 411
16.2 Dynamic Environments and Online MD 413
16.3 Single-Valued Online Domains 417
16.4 Bayesian Implementation in Online Domains 431
16.5 Conclusions 435
16.6 Notes 436
Acknowledgments 437
Bibliography 437
Exercises 439

III Quantifying the Inefficiency of Equilibria

17 Introduction to the Inefficiency of Equilibria 443
Tim Roughgarden and Éva Tardos
17.1 Introduction 443

17.2 Fundamental Network Examples 446
17.3 Inefficiency of Equilibria as a Design Metric 454
17.4 Notes 456
Bibliography 457
Exercises 459

18 Routing Games **461**
Tim Roughgarden
18.1 Introduction 461
18.2 Models and Examples 462
18.3 Existence, Uniqueness, and Potential Functions 468
18.4 The Price of Anarchy of Selfish Routing 472
18.5 Reducing the Price of Anarchy 478
18.6 Notes 480
Bibliography 483
Exercises 484

19 Network Formation Games and the Potential Function Method **487**
Éva Tardos and Tom Wexler
19.1 Introduction 487
19.2 The Local Connection Game 489
19.3 Potential Games and a Global Connection Game 494
19.4 Facility Location 502
19.5 Notes 506
Acknowledgments 511
Bibliography 511
Exercises 513

20 Selfish Load Balancing **517**
Berthold Vöcking
20.1 Introduction 517
20.2 Pure Equilibria for Identical Machines 522
20.3 Pure Equilibria for Uniformly Related Machines 524
20.4 Mixed Equilibria on Identical Machines 529
20.5 Mixed Equilibria on Uniformly Related Machines 533
20.6 Summary and Discussion 537
20.7 Bibliographic Notes 538
Bibliography 540
Exercises 542

21 The Price of Anarchy and the Design of Scalable Resource Allocation Mechanisms **543**
Ramesh Johari
21.1 Introduction 543
21.2 The Proportional Allocation Mechanism 544
21.3 A Characterization Theorem 551
21.4 The Vickrey–Clarke–Groves Approach 559
21.5 Chapter Summary and Further Directions 564

21.6 Notes 565
Bibliography 566
Exercises 567

IV Additional Topics

22 Incentives and Pricing in Communications Networks **571**
Asuman Ozdaglar and R. Srikant
22.1 Large Networks – Competitive Models 572
22.2 Pricing and Resource Allocation – Game Theoretic Models 578
22.3 Alternative Pricing and Incentive Approaches 587
Bibliography 590

23 Incentives in Peer-to-Peer Systems **593**
Moshe Babaioff, John Chuang, and Michal Feldman
23.1 Introduction 593
23.2 The p2p File-Sharing Game 594
23.3 Reputation 596
23.4 A Barter-Based System: BitTorrent 600
23.5 Currency 601
23.6 Hidden Actions in p2p Systems 602
23.7 Conclusion 608
23.8 Bibliographic Notes 608
Bibliography 609
Exercises 610

24 Cascading Behavior in Networks: Algorithmic and Economic Issues **613**
Jon Kleinberg
24.1 Introduction 613
24.2 A First Model: Networked Coordination Games 614
24.3 More General Models of Social Contagion 618
24.4 Finding Influential Sets of Nodes 622
24.5 Empirical Studies of Cascades in Online Data 627
24.6 Notes and Further Reading 630
Bibliography 631
Exercises 632

25 Incentives and Information Security **633**
Ross Anderson, Tyler Moore, Shishir Nagaraja, and Andy Ozment
25.1 Introduction 633
25.2 Misaligned Incentives 634
25.3 Informational Asymmetries 636
25.4 The Economics of Censorship Resistance 640
25.5 Complex Networks and Topology 643
25.6 Conclusion 646
25.7 Notes 647
Bibliography 648

26 Computational Aspects of Prediction Markets **651**
David M. Pennock and Rahul Sami
26.1 Introduction: What Is a Prediction Market? 651
26.2 Background 652
26.3 Combinatorial Prediction Markets 657
26.4 Automated Market Makers 662
26.5 Distributed Computation through Markets 665
26.6 Open Questions 670
26.7 Bibliographic Notes 671
Acknowledgments 672
Bibliography 672
Exercises 674

27 Manipulation-Resistant Reputation Systems **677**
Eric Friedman, Paul Resnick, and Rahul Sami
27.1 Introduction: Why Are Reputation Systems Important? 677
27.2 The Effect of Reputations 680
27.3 Whitewashing 682
27.4 Eliciting Effort and Honest Feedback 683
27.5 Reputations Based on Transitive Trust 689
27.6 Conclusion and Extensions 693
27.7 Bibliographic Notes 694
Bibliography 695
Exercises 696

28 Sponsored Search Auctions **699**
Sébastien Lahaie, David M. Pennock, Amin Saberi, and Rakesh V. Vohra
28.1 Introduction 699
28.2 Existing Models and Mechanisms 701
28.3 A Static Model 702
28.4 Dynamic Aspects 707
28.5 Open Questions 711
28.6 Bibliographic Notes 712
Bibliography 713
Exercises 715

29 Computational Evolutionary Game Theory **717**
Siddharth Suri
29.1 Evolutionary Game Theory 717
29.2 The Computational Complexity of Evolutionarily Stable Strategies 720
29.3 Evolutionary Dynamics Applied to Selfish Routing 723
29.4 Evolutionary Game Theory over Graphs 728
29.5 Future Work 733
29.6 Notes 733
Acknowledgments 734
Bibliography 734
Exercises 735

Index 737

Foreword

As the Second World War was coming to its end, John von Neumann, arguably the foremost mathematician of that time, was busy initiating two intellectual currents that would shape the rest of the twentieth century: game theory and algorithms. In 1944 (16 years after the minmax theorem) he published, with Oscar Morgenstern, his *Games and Economic Behavior*, thus founding not only game theory but also utility theory and microeconomics. Two years later he wrote his draft report on the EDVAC, inaugurating the era of the digital computer and its software *and its algorithms*. Von Neumann wrote in 1952 the first paper in which a polynomial algorithm was hailed as a meaningful advance. And, he was the recipient, shortly before his early death four years later, of Gödel's letter in which the P *vs.* NP question was first discussed.

Could von Neumann have anticipated that his twin creations would converge half a century later? He was certainly far ahead of his contemporaries in his conception of computation as something dynamic, ubiquitous, and enmeshed in society, almost organic – witness his self-reproducing automata, his fault-tolerant network design, and his prediction that computing technology will advance in lock-step with the economy (for which he had already postulated exponential growth in his 1937 Vienna Colloquium paper). But I doubt that von Neumann could have dreamed anything close to the Internet, the ubiquitous and quintessentially organic computational artifact that emerged after the end of the Cold War (a war, incidentally, of which von Neumann was an early soldier and possible casualty, and that was, fortunately, fought mostly with game theory and decided by technological superiority – essentially by algorithms – instead of the thermonuclear devices that were von Neumann's parting gift to humanity).

The Internet turned the tables on students of both markets and computation. It transformed, informed, and accelerated markets, while creating new and theretofore unimaginable kinds of markets – in addition to being itself, in important ways, a market. Algorithms became the natural environment and default platform of strategic decision making. On the other hand, the Internet was the first computational artifact that was not created by a single entity (engineer, design team, or company), but emerged from the strategic interaction of many. Computer scientists were for the first time faced with an object that they had to feel with the same bewildered awe with which economists have always approached the market. And, quite predictably, they turned to game theory for inspiration – in the words of Scott Shenker, a pioneer of this way of thinking who has contributed to this volume, "the Internet is an equilibrium, we just have to identify the game." A fascinating fusion of ideas from both fields – game theory and algorithms – came into being and was used productively in the effort to illuminate the mysteries of the Internet. It has come to be called algorithmic game theory.

The chapters of this book, a snapshot of algorithmic game theory at the approximate age of ten written by a galaxy of its leading researchers, succeed brilliantly, I think, in capturing the field's excitement, breadth, accomplishment, and promise. The first few chapters recount the ways in which the new field has come to grips with perhaps the most fundamental cultural incongruity between algorithms and game theory: the latter predicts the agents' equilibrium behavior typically with no regard to the ways in which such a state will be reached – a consideration that would be a computer scientist's foremost concern. Hence, algorithms for computing equilibria (Nash and correlated equilibria in games, price equilibria for markets) have been one of algorithmic game theory's earliest research goals. This body of work has become a valuable contribution to the debate in economics about the validity of behavior predictions: Efficient computability has emerged as a very desirable feature of such predictions, while computational intractability sheds a shadow of implausibility on a proposed equilibrium concept. Computational models that reflect the realities of the market and the Internet better than the von Neumann machine are of course at a premium – there are chapters in this book on learning algorithms as well as on distributed algorithmic mechanism design.

The algorithmic nature of mechanism design is even more immediate: This elegant and well-developed subarea of game theory deals with the design of games, with players who have unknown and private utilities, such that at the equilibrium of the designed game the designer's goals are attained independently of the agents' utilities (auctions are an important example here). This is obviously a computational problem, and in fact some of the classical results in this area had been subtly algorithmic, albeit with little regard to complexity considerations. Explicitly algorithmic work on mechanism design has, in recent years, transformed the field, especially in the case of auctions and cost sharing (for example, how to recover the cost of an Internet service from customers who value the service by amounts known only to them) and has become the arena of especially intense and productive cross-fertilization between game theory and algorithms; these problems and accomplishments are recounted in the book's second part.

The third part of the book is dedicated to a line of investigation that has come to be called "the price of anarchy." Selfish rational agents reach an equilibrium. The question arises: exactly how inefficient is this equilibrium in comparison to an idealized situation in which the agents would strive to collaborate selflessly with the common goal of minimizing total cost? The ratio of these quantities (the cost of an equilibrium over the optimum cost) has been estimated successfully in various Internet-related setups, and it is often found that "anarchy" is not nearly as expensive as one might have feared. For example, in one celebrated case related to routing with linear delays and explained in the "routing games" chapter, the overhead of anarchy is at most 33% over the optimum solution – in the context of the Internet such a ratio is rather insignificant and quickly absorbed by its rapid growth. Viewed in the context of the historical development of research in algorithms, this line of investigation could be called "the third compromise." The realization that optimization problems are intractable led us to approximation algorithms; the unavailability of information about the future, or the lack of coordination between distributed decision makers, brought us online algorithms; the price of anarchy is the result of one further obstacle: now the distributed decision makers have different objective functions. Incidentally, it is rather surprising that economists had not studied this aspect of strategic behavior before the advent of the Internet. One explanation may be that, for economists, the ideal optimum was never an available option; in contrast, computer scientists are still looking back with nostalgia to the good old days when artifacts and processes could be optimized exactly. Finally, the chapters on "additional topics" that conclude the book (e.g., on peer-to-peer systems and information markets) amply demonstrate the young area's impressive breadth, reach, diversity, and scope.

Books – a glorious human tradition apparently spared by the advent of the Internet – have a way of marking and focusing a field, of accelerating its development. Seven years after the publication of *The Theory of Games*, Nash was proving his theorem on the existence of equilibria; only time will tell how this volume will sway the path of algorithmic game theory.

Paris, February 2007 Christos H. Papadimitriou

and unfortunately absorbed by its rapid growth. Viewed in the context of the historical development of research in algorithms, this line of investigation could be called "the third compromise." The realization that optimization problems are intractable led us to approximation algorithms; the unavailability of information about the future, or the lack of coordination between distributed decision makers, brought us online algorithms; the price of anarchy is the result of one further obstacle: now the distributed decision makers have different objective functions. Incidentally, it is rather surprising that economists had not studied this aspect of strategic behavior before the advent of the Internet. One explanation may be that, for economists, the ideal optimum was never an available option; in contrast, computer scientists are still looking back with nostalgia to the good old days when artifacts and processes could be optimized exactly. Finally, the chapters on "additional topics" that conclude the book (e.g., on peer-to-peer systems and information markets) amply demonstrate the young area's promise of breadth, relevance, diversity, and scope.

[illegible] – human traditional [illegible] sparked by the advent of the Internet – have a way of [illegible] and focusing a field's development. Seven years after the publication of *The Theory of Games*, Nash was proving his theorem on the existence of equilibria; only time will tell how this volume will sway the path of algorithmic game theory.

Paris, February 2007 Christos H. Papadimitriou

Preface

This book covers an area that straddles two fields, algorithms and game theory, and has applications in several others, including networking and artificial intelligence. Its text is pitched at a beginning graduate student in computer science – we hope that this makes the book accessible to readers across a wide range of areas.

We started this project with the belief that the time was ripe for a book that clearly develops some of the central ideas and results of algorithmic game theory – a book that can be used as a textbook for the variety of courses that were already being offered at many universities. We felt that the only way to produce a book of such breadth in a reasonable amount of time was to invite many experts from this area to contribute chapters to a comprehensive volume on the topic.

This book is partitioned into four parts: the first three parts are devoted to core areas, while the fourth covers a range of topics mostly focusing on applications. Chapter 1 serves as a preliminary chapter and it introduces basic game-theoretic definitions that are used throughout the book. The first chapters of Parts II and III provide introductions and preliminaries for the respective parts. The other chapters are largely independent of one another. The authors were requested to focus on a few results highlighting the main issues and techniques, rather than provide comprehensive surveys. Most of the chapters conclude with exercises suitable for classroom use and also identify promising directions for further research. We hope these features give the book the feel of a textbook and make it suitable for a wide range of courses.

You can view the entire book online at
www.cambridge.org/us/9780521872829
username: agt1user
password: camb2agt

Many people's efforts went into producing this book within a year and a half of its first conception. First and foremost, we thank the authors for their dedication and timeliness in writing their own chapters and for providing important feedback on preliminary drafts of other chapters. Thanks to Christos Papadimitriou for his inspiring Foreword. We gratefully acknowledge the efforts of outside reviewers: Elliot Anshelevich, Nikhil Devanur, Matthew Jackson, Vahab Mirrokni, Herve Moulin, Neil Olver, Adrian Vetta, and several anonymous referees. Thanks to Cindy Robinson for her invaluable help with correcting the galley proofs. Finally, a big thanks to Lauren Cowles for her stellar advice throughout the production of this volume.

Noam Nisan
Tim Roughgarden
Éva Tardos
Vijay V. Vazirani

Contributors

Ross Anderson
Computer Laboratory
University of Cambridge

Moshe Babaioff
School of Information
University of California, Berkeley

Avrim Blum
Department of Computer Science
Carnegie Mellon University

Liad Blumrosen
Microsoft Research
Silicon Valley

John Chuang
School of Information
University of California, Berkeley

Bruno Codenotti
Istituto di Informatica e
Telematica, Consiglio
Nazionale delle Ricerche

Yevgeniy Dodis
Department of Computer Science
Courant Institute of Mathematical
Sciences, New York University

Joan Feigenbaum
Computer Science Department
Yale University

Michal Feldman
School of Business Administration
and the Center for the Study of Rationality
Hebrew University of Jerusalem

Eric Friedman
School of Operations Research
and Information Engineering
Cornell University

Jason D. Hartline
Microsoft Research
Silicon Valley

Kamal Jain
Microsoft Research
Redmond

Ramesh Johari
Department of Management Science
and Engineering
Stanford University

Anna R. Karlin
Department of Computer Science
and Engineering
University of Washington

Michael Kearns
Department of Computer
and Information Science
University of Pennsylvania

Jon Kleinberg
Department of Computer Science
Cornell University

Sébastien Lahaie
School of Engineering
and Applied Sciences
Harvard University

Ron Lavi
Faculty of Industrial Engineering
and Management, The Technion
Israel Institute of Technology

Mohammad Mahdian
Yahoo! Research
Silicon Valley

Yishay Mansour
School of Computer Science
Tel Aviv University

Tyler Moore
Computer Laboratory
University of Cambridge

Shishir Nagaraja
Computer Laboratory
University of Cambridge

Noam Nisan
School of Computer Science
and Engineering
Hebrew University of Jerusalem

Asuman Ozdaglar
Department of Electrical
Engineering and Computer
Science, MIT

Andy Ozment
Computer Laboratory
University of Cambridge

Christos H. Papadimitriou
Computer Science Division
University of California, Berkeley

David C. Parkes
School of Engineering
and Applied Sciences
Harvard University

David M. Pennock
Yahoo! Research
New York

Tal Rabin
T. J. Watson Research Center
IBM

Paul Resnick
School of Information
University of Michigan

Tim Roughgarden
Department of Computer Science
Stanford University

Amin Saberi
Department of Management
Science and Engineering
Stanford University

Rahul Sami
School of Information
University of Michigan

Michael Schapira
School of Computer Science
and Engineering
The Hebrew University of Jerusalem

James Schummer
M.E.D.S.
Kellogg School of Management
Northwestern University

Scott Shenker
EECS Department
University of California, Berkeley

R. Srikant
Department of Electrical and Computer Engineering and Coordinated Science Laboratory, University of Illinois at Urbana-Champaign

Siddharth Suri
Department of Computer Science
Cornell University

Éva Tardos
Department of Computer Science
Cornell University

Kasturi Varadarajan
Department of Computer Science
University of Iowa

Vijay V. Vazirani
College of Computing
Georgia Institute of Technology

Berthold Vöcking
Department of Computer Science
RWTH Aachen University

Rakesh V. Vohra
M.E.D.S.
Kellogg School of Management
Northwestern University

Bernhard von Stengel
Department of Mathematics
London School of Economics

Tom Wexler
Department of Computer Science
Cornell University

PART ONE

Computing in Games

CHAPTER 1

Basic Solution Concepts and Computational Issues

Éva Tardos and Vijay V. Vazirani

Abstract

We consider some classical games and show how they can arise in the context of the Internet. We also introduce some of the basic solution concepts of game theory for studying such games, and some computational issues that arise for these concepts.

1.1 Games, Old and New

The Foreword talks about the usefulness of game theory in situations arising on the Internet. We start the present chapter by giving some classical games and showing how they can arise in the context of the Internet. At first, we appeal to the reader's intuitive notion of a "game"; this notion is formally defined in Section 1.2. For a more in-depth discussion of game theory we refer the readers to books on game theory such as Fudenberg and Tirole (1991), Mas-Colell, Whinston, and Green (1995), or Osborne and Rubinstein (1994).

1.1.1 The Prisoner's Dilemma

Game theory aims to model situations in which multiple participants interact or affect each other's outcomes. We start by describing what is perhaps the most well-known and well-studied game.

Example 1.1 (Prisoners' dilemma) Two prisoners are on trial for a crime and each one faces a choice of confessing to the crime or remaining silent. If they both remain silent, the authorities will not be able to prove charges against them and they will both serve a short prison term, say 2 years, for minor offenses. If only one of them confesses, his term will be reduced to 1 year and he will be used as a witness against the other, who in turn will get a sentence of 5 years. Finally if they both confess, they both will get a small break for cooperating with the authorities and will have to serve prison sentences of 4 years each (rather than 5).

Clearly, there are four total outcomes depending on the choices made by each of the two prisoners. We can succinctly summarize the costs incurred in these four outcomes via the following two-by-two matrix.

P1 \ P2	Confess	Silent
Confess	4, 4	1, 5
Silent	5, 1	2, 2

Each of the two prisoners “P1” and “P2” has two possible strategies (choices) to “confess” or to remain “silent.” The two strategies of prisoner P1 correspond to the two rows and the two strategies of prisoner P2 correspond to the two columns of the matrix. The entries of the matrix are the costs incurred by the players in each situation (left entry for the row player and the right entry for the column player). Such a matrix is called a *cost matrix* because it contains the cost incurred by the players for each choice of their strategies.

The only stable solution in this game is that both prisoners confess; in each of the other three cases, at least one of the players can switch from “silent” to “confess” and improve his own payoff. On the other hand, a much better outcome for both players happens when neither of them confesses. However, this is not a stable solution – even if it is carefully planned out – since each of the players would be tempted to defect and thereby serve less time.

The situation modeled by the Prisoner’s Dilemma arises naturally in a lot of different situations; we give below an ISP routing context.

Example 1.2 (ISP routing game) Consider Internet Service Providers (ISPs) that need to send traffic to each other. In routing traffic that originates in one ISP with destination in a different ISP, the routing choice made by the originating ISP also affects the load at the destination ISP. We will see here how this situation gives rise to exactly the Prisoner’s dilemma described above.

Consider two ISPs (Internet Service Providers), as depicted in Figure 1.1, each having its own separate network. The two networks can exchange traffic via two transit points, called peering points, which we will call C and S.

In the figure we also have two origin–destination pairs s_i and t_i each crossing between the domains. Suppose that ISP 1 needs to send traffic from point s_1 in his own domain to point t_1 in 2nd ISP’s domain. ISP 1 has two choices for sending its traffic, corresponding to the two peering points. ISPs typically behave selfishly and try to minimize their own costs, and send traffic to the closest peering point,

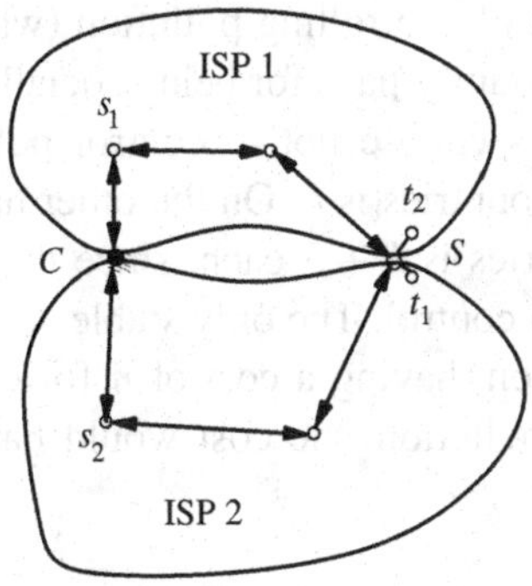

Figure 1.1. The ISP routing problem.

as the ISP with the destination node must route the traffic, no matter where it enters its domain. Peering point C is closer, using this peering point ISP 1 incurs a cost of 1 unit (in sending traffic along 1 edge), whereas if it uses the farther peering point S, it incurs a cost of 2.

Note that the farther peering point S is more directly on route to the destination t_1, and hence routing through S results in shorter overall path. The length of the path through C is 4 while through S is 2, as the destination is very close to S.

The situation described for ISP 1 routing traffic from s_1 to t_1 is in a way analogous to a prisoner's choices in the Prisoner's Dilemma: there are two choices, one is better from a selfish perspective ("confess" or route through peering point C), but hurts the other player. To make our routing game identical to the Prisoner's Dilemma, assume that symmetrically the 2nd ISP needs to send traffic from point s_2 in his domain to point t_2 in the 1st ISP's domain. The two choices of the two ISPs lead to a game with cost matrix identical to the matrix above with C corresponding to "confess" and S corresponding to remaining "silent."

1.1.2 The Tragedy of the Commons

In this book we will be most concerned with situations where many participants interact, and such situations are naturally modeled by games that involve many players: there are thousands of ISPs, and many millions of traffic streams to be routed. We will give two examples of such games, first a multiplayer version of the Prisoner's Dilemma that we will phrase in terms of a pollution game. Then we will discuss the well-known game of Tragedy of the Commons.

Example 1.3 (Pollution game) This game is the extension of Prisoner's Dilemma to the case of many players. The issues modeled by this game arise in many contexts; here we will discuss it in the context of pollution control. Assume that there are n countries in this game. For a simple model of this situation, assume that each country faces the choice of either passing legislation to control pollution or not. Assume that pollution control has a cost of 3 for the country, but each country that pollutes adds 1 to the cost of all countries (in terms of added health costs, etc.). The cost of controlling pollution (which is 3) is considerably larger than the cost of 1 a country pays for being socially irresponsible.

Suppose that k countries choose not to control pollution. Clearly, the cost incurred by each of these countries is k. On the other hand, the cost incurred by the remaining $n - k$ countries is $k + 3$ each, since they have to pay the added cost for their own pollution control. The only stable solution is the one in which no country controls pollution, having a cost of n for each country. In contrast, if they all had controlled pollution, the cost would have been only 3 for each country.

The games we have seen so far share the feature that there is a unique optimal "selfish" strategy for each player, independent of what other players do. No matter what strategy the opponent plays, each player is better off playing his or her selfish strategy. Next, we will see a game where the players' optimal selfish strategies depend on what the other players play.

Example 1.4 (Tragedy of the commons) We will describe this game in the context of sharing bandwidth. Suppose that n players each would like to have part of a shared resource. For example, each player wants to send information along a shared channel of known maximum capacity, say 1. In this game each player will have an infinite set of strategies, player i's strategy is to send x_i units of flow along the channel for some value $x_i \in [0, 1]$.

Assume that each player would like to have a large fraction of the bandwidth, but assume also that the quality of the channel deteriorates with the total bandwidth used. We will describe this game by a simple model, using a benefit or payoff function for each set of strategies. If the total bandwidth $\sum_j x_j$ exceeds the channel capacity, no player gets any benefit. If $\sum_j x_j < 1$ then the value for player i is $x_i(1 - \sum_j x_j)$. This models exactly the kind of trade-off we had in mind: the benefit for a player deteriorates as the total assigned bandwidth increases, but it increases with his own share (up to a point).

To understand what stable strategies are for a player, let us concentrate on player i, and assume that $t = \sum_{j \neq i} x_j < 1$ flow is sent by all other players. Now player i faces a simple optimization problem for selecting his flow amount: sending x flow results in a benefit of $x(1 - t - x)$. Using elementary calculus, we get that the optimal solution for player i is $x = (1 - t)/2$. A set of strategies is stable if all players are playing their optimal selfish strategy, given the strategies of all other players. For this case, this means that $x_i = (1 - \sum_{j \neq i} x_j)/2$ for all i, which has a unique solution in $x_i = 1/(n + 1)$ for all i.

Why is this solution a tragedy? The total value of the solution is extremely low. The value for player i is $x_i(1 - \sum_{j \neq i} x_j) = 1/(n + 1)^2$, and the sum of the values over all payers is then $n/(n + 1)^2 \approx 1/n$. In contrast, if the total bandwidth used is $\sum_i x_i = 1/2$ then the total value is 1/4, approximately $n/4$ times bigger. In this game the n users sharing the common resource overuse it so that the total value of the shared resource decreases quite dramatically. The pollution game above has a similar effect, where the common resource of the environment is overused by the n players increasing the cost from 3 to n for each players.

1.1.3 Coordination Games

In our next example, there will be multiple outcomes that can be stable. This game is an example of a so-called "coordination game." A simple coordination game involves two players choosing between two options, wanting to choose the same.

Example 1.5 (Battle of the sexes) Consider that two players, a boy and a girl, are deciding on how to spend their evening. They both consider two possibilities: going to a baseball game or going to a softball game. The boy prefers baseball and the girl prefers softball, but they both would like to spend the evening together rather than separately. Here we express the players' preferences again via payoffs (benefits) as follows.

Girl \ Boy	B	S
B	6 / 5	1 / 1
S	2 / 2	5 / 6

.

Clearly, the two solutions where the two players choose different games are not stable – in each case, either of the two players can improve their payoff by switching their action. On the other hand, the two remaining options, both attending the same game, whether it is softball or baseball, are both stable solutions; the girl prefers the first and the boy prefers the second.

Coordination games also arise naturally in many contexts. Here we give an example of a coordination game in the context of routing to avoid congestion. The good outcomes in the Battle of the Sexes were to attend the same game. In contrast, in the routing game, good outcomes will require routing on different paths to avoid congestion. Hence, this will be an "anticoordination" game.

Example 1.6 (Routing congestion game) Suppose that two traffic streams originate at proxy node O, and need to be routed to the rest of the network, as shown in Figure 1.2. Suppose that node O is connected to the rest of the network via connection points A and B, where A is a little closer than B. However, both connection points get easily congested, so sending both streams through the same connection point causes extra delay. Good outcomes in this game will be for the two players to "coordinate" and send their traffic through different connection points.

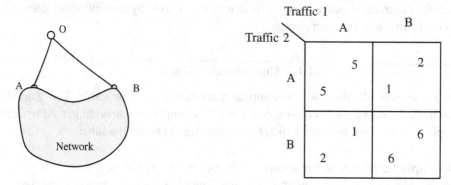

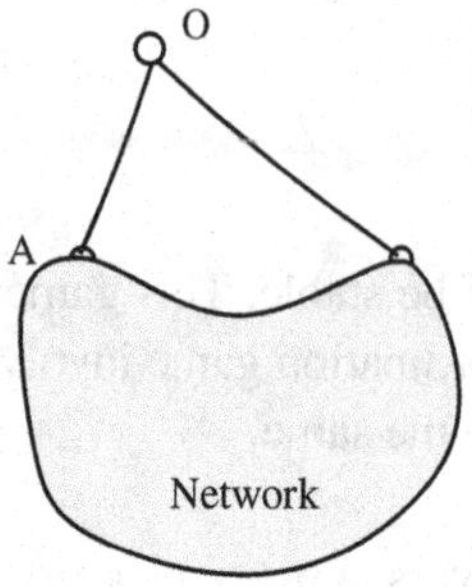

Traffic 2 \ Traffic 1	A	B
A	5, 5	1, 2
B	2, 1	6, 6

Figure 1.2. Routing to avoid congestion and the corresponding cost matrix.

We model this situation via a game with the two streams as players. Each player has two available strategies – routing through A or routing through B – leading to four total possibilities. The matrix of Figure 1.2 expresses the costs to the players in terms of delays depending on their routing choices.

1.1.4 Randomized (Mixed) Strategies

In the games we considered so far, there were outcomes that were stable in the sense that none of players would want to individually deviate from such an outcome. Not all games have such stable solutions, as illustrated by the following example.

Example 1.7 (Matching pennies) Two payers, each having a penny, are asked to choose from among two strategies – heads (H) and tails (T). The row player wins if the two pennies match, while the column player wins if they do not match, as shown by the following payoff matrix, where 1 indicates win and -1 indicated loss.

1 \ 2	H	T
H	1, -1	-1, 1
T	-1, 1	1, -1

One can view this game as a variant of the routing congestion game in which the column player is interested in getting good service, hence would like the two players to choose different routes, while the row player is interested only in disrupting the column player's service by trying to choose the same route. It is easy to see that this game has no stable solution. Instead, it seems best for the players to randomize in order to thwart the strategy of the other player.

1.2 Games, Strategies, Costs, and Payoffs

We have given examples of games and discussed costs, payoffs, and strategies in an informal way. Next we will define such a game more formally. The games we considered above were all *one-shot simultaneous move games*, in that all players simultaneously chose an action from their set of possible strategies.

1.2.1 Defining a Simultaneous Move Game

Formally, such a game consists of a set n of *players*, $\{1, 2, \ldots, n\}$. Each player i has his own *set of possible strategies*, say S_i. To play the game, each player i selects a strategy $s_i \in S_i$. We will use $s = (s_1, \ldots, s_n)$ to denote the *vector of strategies* selected by the players and $S = \times_i S_i$ to denote the set of all possible ways in which players can pick strategies.

The vector of strategies $s \in S$ selected by the players determine the outcome for each player; in general, the outcome will be different for different players. To specify the game, we need to give, for each player, a *preference ordering* on these outcomes by giving a complete, transitive, reflexive binary relation on the set of all strategy vectors S; given two elements of S, the relation for player i says which of these two outcomes i weakly prefers; we say that i *weakly prefers* S_1 to S_2 if i either prefers S_1 to S_2 or considers them as equally good outcomes. For example, in the matching pennies game the row player prefers strategy vectors in which the two pennies match and the column player prefers those in which the pennies do not match.

The simplest way to specify preferences is by assigning, for each player, a value to each outcome. In some games it will be natural to think of the values as the payoffs to players and in others as the costs incurred by players. We will denote these functions by $u_i : S \rightarrow \mathbf{R}$ and $c_i : S \rightarrow \mathbf{R}$, respectively. Clearly, costs and payoffs can be used interchangeably, since $u_i(s) = -c_i(s)$.

If we had defined, for each player i, u_i to be simply a function of s_i, the strategy chosen by player i, rather than s, the strategies chosen by all n players, then we would have obtained n independent optimization problems. Observe the crucial difference between this and a game – in a game, the payoff of each player depends not only on his own strategy but also on the strategies chosen by all other players.

1.2.2 Standard Form Games and Compactly Represented Games

To develop an algorithmic theory of games, we need to discuss how a game is specified. One option is to explicitly list all possible strategies, and the preferences or utilities of all players. Expressing games in this form with a cost or utility function is called the *standard form* or matrix form of a game. It is very convenient to define games in this way when there are only 2 players and the players have only a few strategies. We have used this form in the previous section for defining the *Prisoner's Dilemma* and the *Battle of the Sexes*.

However, for most games we want to consider, this explicit representation is exponential sized in the natural description of the game (possibly bigger or even infinite). Most games we want to consider have many players, e.g., the many traffic streams or the many ISPs controlling such streams. (In fact, in Part III of this book, we will even encounter games with infinitely many players, modeling the limiting behavior as the number of players gets very large.) For an example, consider the pollution game from Subsection 1.1.2, where we have n players, each with two possible strategies. There are 2^n possible strategy vectors, so the explicit representation of the game requires assigning values to each of these 2^n strategies. The size of the input needed to describe the game is much smaller than 2^n, and so this explicit representation is exponentially larger than the description of the game.

Another reason that explicit representation of the payoffs can be exponentially large is that players can have exponentially many strategies in the natural size of the game. This happens in routing games, since the strategy space of each player consists of all possible paths from source to destination in the network. In the version of the *Tragedy of the Commons*, we discussed in Section 1.1.2 players have infinite strategy sets, since any bandwidth $x \in [0, 1]$ is a possible strategy.

Such exponential (and superexponential) descriptions can sometimes be avoided. For example, the payoff may depend on the number of players selecting a given strategy, rather than the exact subset (as was the case for the pollution game). The routing congestion game discussed in Chapter 18 provides another example, where the cost of a chosen path depends on the total traffic routed on each edge of the path. Another possibility for compact representation is when the payoff of a player may depend on the strategies chosen by only a few other players, not all participants. Games with such locality properties are discussed in detail in Chapter 7.

1.3 Basic Solution Concepts

In this section we will introduce basic solution concepts that can be used to study the kinds of games we described in the previous section. In particular, we will formalize the notion of stability that we informally used in discussing solutions to some of the games.

1.3.1 Dominant Strategy Solution

The *Prisoner's Dilemma* and the *Pollution Game* share a very special property: in each of these games, each player has a unique best strategy, independent of the strategies played by the other players. We say that a game has a *dominant strategy solution* if it has this property.

More formally, for a strategy vector $s \in S$ we use s_i to denote the strategy played by player i and s_{-i} to denote the $(n-1)$-dimensional vector of the strategies played by all other players. Recall that we used $u_i(s)$ to denote the utility incurred by player i. We will also use the notation $u_i(s_i, s_{-i})$ when it is more convenient. Using this notation, a strategy vector $s \in S$ is a *dominant strategy solution*, if for each player i, and each alternate strategy vector $s' \in S$, we have that

$$u_i(s_i, s'_{-i}) \geq u_i(s'_i, s'_{-i}).$$

It is important to notice that a dominant strategy solution may not give an optimal payoff to any of the players. This was the case in both the *Prisoner's Dilemma* and the *Pollution Game*, where it is possible to improve the payoffs of all players simultaneously.

Having a single dominant strategy for each player is an extremely stringent requirement for a game and very few games satisfy it. On the other hand, *mechanism design*, the topic of Part II of this book, aims to design games that have dominant strategy solutions, and where this solution leads to a desirable outcome (either socially desirable, or desirable for the mechanism designer). We illustrate this, using the simple example of Vickrey auction.

1.3.2 Vickrey Auction: Designing Games with Dominant Strategy Solutions

Perhaps the most common situation in which we need to design a game is an auction. Suppose that we are faced with designing an auction to sell a valuable painting. To model this situation as a game, assume that each player (bidder) i has a value v_i for the painting. His value or payoff for not winning it is 0, and his payoff for winning it at a price of p is $v_i - p$. The strategy of each player is simply his bid. What is a good mechanism (or game) for selling this painting? Here we are considering single-shot games, so assume that each player is asked to state his bid for the painting in a sealed envelope, and we will decide who to award the painting to and for what price, based on the bids in the envelopes.

Perhaps the most straightforward auction would be to award the painting to the highest bidder and charge him his bid. This game does not have a dominant strategy solution. A player's best strategy (bid) depends on what he knows or assumes about the strategies of the other players. Deciding what value to bid seems like a hard problem, and may result in unpredictable behavior. See Section 1.6 for more discussion of a possible solution concept for this game.

Vickrey's mechanism, called *second price auction*, avoids these bidding problems. As before, the painting is awarded to the bidder with highest bid; however, the amount he is required to pay is the value of the second highest bid. This second price auction has the remarkable property that each player's dominant strategy is to report his true value as bid, independent of the strategies of the rest of the players! Observe that even if his true value happens to be very high, he is in no danger of overpaying if he reports it – if he wins, he will pay no more than the second highest bid.

Let us observe two more properties of the Vickrey auction. First, it leads to the desirable outcome of the painting being awarded to the bidder who values it most. Indeed, the larger goal of mechanism design is often to design mechanisms in which the selfish behavior of players leads to such a socially optimal outcome. For example, when the government auctions off goods, such as the wireless spectrum auctions, their goal is typically not to make as large a profit as possible, but rather to get the spectrum in the hands of companies that have the best technology to offer to customers.

Another nice feature of a dominant strategy game, such as Vickrey auction, is that it is extremely simple for the players to play such a game, since each player's optimal strategy is independent of other players' choices. In fact, one can implement all dominant strategy games by simply asking all players for their valuation functions and letting the game designer "play" the game for them. This is called the *revelation principle* (see Chapter 9). (In this book, we will not consider the complex issue of how players arrive at their own valuation function.) Unfortunately, in many contexts the valuation function of a player can be very complex and direct revelation may lead to extensive, maybe even exponential, communication (see Chapter 11). Another problem with direct revelation mechanisms is that they assume the presence of a central trusted party. Chapter 8 shows how cryptographic techniques can help a group of players implement such a mechanism or game without a trusted party.

1.3.3 Pure Strategy Nash Equilibrium

Since games rarely possess dominant strategy solutions, we need to seek a less stringent and more widely applicable solution concept. A desirable game-theoretic solution is one in which individual players act in accordance with their incentives, maximizing their own payoff. This idea is best captured by the notion of a Nash equilibrium, which, despite its shortcomings (mentioned below), has emerged as the central solution concept in game theory, with extremely diverse applications. The Nash equilibrium captures the notion of a stable solution, discussed in Section 1.1 and used in the *Tragedy of the Commons* and the *Battle of the Sexes* – a solution from which no single player can individually improve his or her welfare by deviating.

A strategy vector $s \in S$ is said to be a *Nash equilibrium* if for all players i and each alternate strategy $s_i' \in S_i$, we have that

$$u_i(s_i, s_{-i}) \geq u_i(s_i', s_{-i}).$$

In other words, no player i can change his chosen strategy from s_i to s_i' and thereby improve his payoff, assuming that all other players stick to the strategies they have chosen in s. Observe that such a solution is self-enforcing in the sense that once the players are playing such a solution, it is in every player's best interest to stick to his or her strategy.

Clearly, a dominant strategy solution is a Nash equilibrium. Moreover, if the solution is strictly dominating (i.e., switching to it always strictly improves the outcome), it is also the unique Nash equilibrium. However, Nash equilibria may not be unique. For example, coordination games have multiple equilibria.

We already know that Nash equilibria may not be optimal for the players, since dominant strategy solutions are Nash equilibria. For games with multiple Nash equilibria, different equilibria can have (widely) different payoffs for the players. For example, by a small change to the payoff matrix, we can modify the *Battle of the Sexes* game so that it still has two stable solutions (the ones in which both players go to the same activity); however, both players derive a much higher utility from one of these solutions. In

Part III of this book we will look more carefully at the quality of the best and worst equilibria in different games.

The existence of multiple Nash equilibria makes this solution concept less convincing as a prediction of what players will do: which equilibrium should we expect them to play? And with independent play, how will they know which equilibrium they are supposed to coordinate on? But at least a Nash equilibrium is stable – once proposed, the players do not want to individually deviate.

1.3.4 Mixed Strategy Nash Equilibria

The Nash equilibria we have considered so far are called *pure strategy* equilibria, since each player deterministically plays his chosen strategy. As illustrated by the *Matching Pennies* game, a game need not possess any pure strategy Nash equilibria. However, if in the matching pennies game, the players are allowed to randomize and each player picks each of his two strategies with probability $1/2$, then we obtain a stable solution in a sense. The reason is that the expected payoff of each player now is 0 and neither player can improve on this by choosing a different randomization.

When players select strategies at random, we need to understand how they evaluate the random outcome. Would a player prefer a choice that leads to a small positive utility with high probability, but with a small probability leads to a large negative utility? Or, is it better to have a small loss with high probability, and a large gain with small probability? For the notion of mixed Nash equilibrium, we will assume that players are risk-neutral; that is, they act to maximize the *expected payoff*.

To define such randomized strategies formally, let us enhance the choices of players so each one can pick a probability distribution over his set of possible strategies; such a choice is called a *mixed strategy*. We assume that players independently select strategies using the probability distribution. The independent random choices of players leads to a probability distribution of strategy vectors s. Nash (1951) proved that under this extension, every game with a finite number of players, each having a finite set of strategies, has a Nash equilibrium.

Theorem 1.8 *Any game with a finite set of players and finite set of strategies has a Nash equilibrium of mixed strategies.*

This theorem will be further discussed and proved for the two player case in Chapter 2. An important special case of 2 player games is zero-sum games, games in which the gain of one player is exactly the loss of the other player. Nash equilibria for these games will be further discussed in Section 1.4.

1.3.5 Games with No Nash Equilibria

Both assumptions in the theorem about the finite set of players and finite strategy sets are important: games with an infinite number of players, or games with a finite number of players who have access to an infinite strategy set may not have Nash equilibria. A simple example of this arises in the following pricing game.

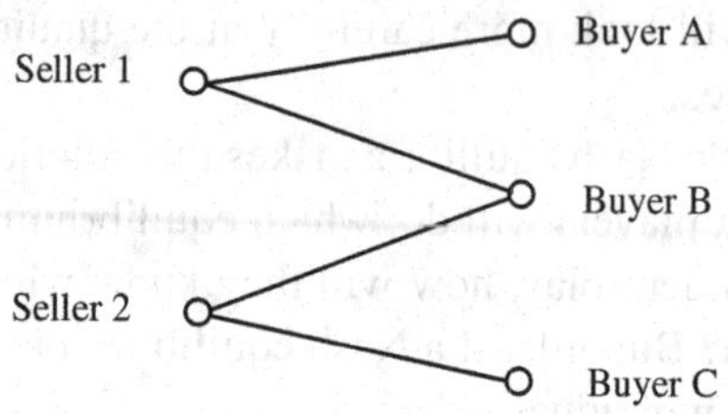

Figure 1.3. Sellers 1 and 2 are selling identical products to buyers A, B, and C.

Example 1.9 (Pricing game) Suppose two players sell a product to three possible buyers, as shown in Figure 1.3. Each buyer wants to buy one unit of the product.

Buyers A and C have access to one seller only, namely 1 and 2, respectively. However, buyer B can buy the product from any of the two sellers. All three buyers have a budget of 1, or have maximum value 1 for the item, i.e., will not buy the product if the price is above 1. The sellers play a pricing game – they each name a price p_i in the interval [0, 1]. Buyers A and C buy from sellers 1 and 2, respectively. On the other hand, B buys from the cheaper seller. To fully specify the game, we have to set a rule for breaking ties. Let us say that if both sellers have the same price, B buys from seller 1. For simplicity, we assume no production costs, so the income of a seller is the sum of the prices at which they sold goods.

Now, one strategy for each seller is to set a price of $p_i = 1$, and guarantee an income of 1 from the buyer who does not have a choice. Alternatively, they can also try to compete for buyer B. However, by the rules of this game they are not allowed to price-discriminate; i.e., they cannot sell the product to the two buyers at different prices. In this game, each player has uncountably many available strategies, i.e., all numbers in the interval [0, 1]. It turns out that this game does not have a Nash equilibrium, even if players are allowed to use mixed strategies.

To see that no pure strategy equilibrium exists, note that if $p_1 > 1/2$, player 2 will slightly undercut the price, set it at $1/2 < p_2 < p_1$, and have income of more than 1, and then in turn player 1 will undercut player 2, etc. So we cannot have $p_1 > 1/2$ in an equilibrium. If $p_1 \leq 1/2$, the unique best response for player 2 is to set $p_2 = 1$. But then player 1 will increase his price, so $p_1 \leq 1/2$ also does not lead to an equilibrium. It is a bit harder to argue that there is also no mixed strategy equilibrium in this game.

1.3.6 Correlated Equilibrium

A further relaxation of the Nash equilibrium notion was introduced by Aumann (1959), called correlated equilibrium. The following simple example nicely illustrates this notion.

Example 1.10 (Traffic light) The game we consider is when two players drive up to the same intersection at the same time. If both attempt to cross, the result is a fatal traffic accident. The game can be modeled by a payoff matrix where crossing successfully has a payoff of 1, not crossing pays 0, while an accident costs -100.

1 \ 2	Cross	Stop
Cross	-100 -100	0 1
Stop	1 0	0 0

This game has three Nash equilibria: two correspond to letting only one car cross, the third is a mixed equilibrium where both players cross with an extremely small probability $\epsilon = 1/101$, and with ϵ^2 probability they crash. The first two equilibria have a payoff of 1. The last one is more fair, but has low expected payoff (≈ 0.0001), and also has a positive chance of a car crash.

In a Nash equilibrium, players choose their strategies independently. In contrast, in a correlated equilibrium a coordinator can choose strategies for both players; however, the chosen strategies have to be stable: we require that the each player find it in his or her interest to follow the recommended strategy. For example, in a correlated equilibrium the coordinator can randomly let one of the two players cross with any probability. The player who is told to stop has 0 payoff, but he knows that attempting to cross will cause a traffic accident.

Correlated equilibria will be discussed in detail in Section 2.7. Formally, this notion assumes an external correlation device, such as a trusted game coordinator, or some other physical source. A correlated equilibrium is a probability distribution over strategy vectors $s \in \times_i S_i$. Let $p(s)$ denote the probability of strategy vector s, where we will also use the notation $p(s) = p(s_i, s_{-i})$ when talking about a player i. The distribution is a correlated equilibrium if for all players i and all strategies $s_i, s_i' \in S_i$, we have the inequality

$$\sum_{s_{-i}} p(s_i, s_{-i}) u_i(s_i, s_{-i}) \geq \sum_{s_{-i}} p(s_i, s_{-i}) u_i(s_i', s_{-i}).$$

In words, if player i receives a suggested strategy s_i, the expected profit of the player cannot be increased by switching to a different strategy $s_i' \in S_i$. Nash equilibria are special cases of correlated equilibria, where the distribution over S is the product of independent distributions for each player. However, correlation allows a richer set of equilibria as we will see in Section 2.7.

1.4 Finding Equilibria and Learning in Games

In this section we consider two closely related issues: how easy is it to find an equilibrium, and does "natural game play" lead the players to an equilibrium? Ideally, a perfect solution concept is one which is computationally easy to find, and also easy to find by players playing independently.

1.4.1 Complexity of Finding Equilibria

The complexity of finding Nash and correlated equilibria will be discussed in detail in Chapters 2 and 3. Here we give a short overview. We then discuss two-player zero-sum games in more detail and show that for such games a Nash equilibrium can be found efficiently using linear programming. It turns out that even general two-player games have a character different from that of games with three or more players. For example, two-player games where payoffs are rational numbers always admit a solution with rational probabilities, and this is not true for games with three or more players. Games with two players will be discussed in greater detail in Chapter 3.

We will discuss the complexity of finding Nash equilibrium in Chapter 2. NP-completeness, the "standard" way of establishing intractability of individual problems, does not seem to be the right tool for studying the complexity of Nash equilibria. Instead, we will use PPAD-completeness (see Chapter 2 for the definition). The problem of finding a Nash equilibrium is PPAD-complete even for two-player games in standard form.

In contrast, we will see in Section 2.7 that correlated equilibria are computationally easier. Correlated equilibria form a convex set and hence can be found in polynomial time for games defined explicitly via their payoff matrices, and finding a correlated equilibrium is polynomially solvable even in many compactly represented games. However, finding an "optimal" correlated equilibrium is computationally hard in many natural classes of compactly represented games.

1.4.2 Two-Person Zero-Sum Games

Here we consider two-player zero-sum games in more detail. A two-player game is a *zero-sum game* if the sum of the payoffs of the two players is zero for any choice of strategies. For such games it is enough to give the payoffs of the row player. Let A be the matrix of these payoffs, representing the winnings of the row player and the loss of the column player.

Recall from Theorem 1.8 that a Nash equilibrium of mixed strategies always exists. We will use this fact to show that an equilibrium can be found using linear programming. Consider a pair of probability distributions p^* and q^* for the row and column players that form a Nash equilibrium. The expected value paid by the column player to the row player can be expressed as $v^* = p^* A q^*$ (if we think of p^* as a row vector and q^* as a column vector).

A Nash equilibrium has the property that even if the players know the strategies played by the other players (the probability distribution they are using), they cannot be better off by deviating. With this in mind, consider a strategy p for the row player. The expected payoffs for different strategies of the column player will be pA. Once

p is known, the column player will want to minimize his loss, and play strategies that correspond to the minimum entries in pA. So the best publicly announced strategy for the row player is to maximize this minimum value. This best public strategy can be found by solving the following linear program:

$$v_r = \max v$$
$$p \geq 0$$
$$\sum_i p_i = 1$$
$$(pA)_j \geq v \text{ for all } j,$$

where we use $(pA)_j$ to denote the jth entry of the vector pA. The optimum value v_r is the row player's maximum safe value, the maximum value he or she can guarantee to win by playing a mixed strategy p that will be known to the column player.

How does v_r and the Nash value v^* compare? Clearly $v_r \leq v^*$, since the row player, can guarantee to win v_r, so must win at least this much in any equilibrium. On the other hand, an equilibrium is a strategy that is stable even if known to the opponent, so it must be the case that the column player is in fact selecting the columns with minimum value p^*A, so we must have $v^* \leq v_r$, and hence $v_r = v^*$.

Similarly, we can set up the analogous linear program to get the value v_c, the column player's minimum safe value, the minimum loss the column player can guarantee by playing a mixed strategy q that will be known to the row player:

$$v_c = \min v$$
$$q \geq 0$$
$$\sum_j q_j = 1$$
$$(Aq)_i \leq v \text{ for all } i.$$

where we use $(Aq)_i$ to denote the ith entry of the vector Aq. We can argue that $v^* = v_c$ also holds. Hence we get that $v_c = v_r$, the row players' maximum guaranteed win is the same as the column players' minimum guaranteed loss. This will imply that the optimal solutions to this pair of linear programs form a Nash equilibrium.

Theorem 1.11 *Optimum solutions for the above pair of linear programs give probability distributions that form a Nash equilibrium of the two-person zero-sum game.*

PROOF Let p and q denote optimum solutions to the two linear programs. We argued above that $v_c = v_r$. If the players play this pair of strategies, then the row player cannot increase his win, as the column player is guaranteed by his strategy not to lose more than v_c. Similarly, the column player cannot decrease his loss, as the row player is guaranteed to win v_r by his strategy. So the pair of strategies is at equilibrium. □

Readers more familiar with linear programming will notice that the two linear programs above are duals of each other. We established that $v_r = v_c$ using the existence of a Nash equilibrium from Theorem 1.8. Linear programming duality also implies that the two values v_r and v_c are equal. Once we know the values are equal, the proof of Theorem 1.4.2 shows that the optimal solutions form a Nash equilibrium, so linear programming duality yields a proof that a Nash equilibrium exists in the special case of zero-sum two-person games.

1.4.3 Best Response and Learning in Games

It would be desirable for a solution concept to satisfy a stronger condition than simply being polynomial computable: it should be the case that natural game playing strategies quickly lead players to either find the equilibrium or at least converge to an equilibrium in the limit.

Maybe the most natural "game playing" strategy is the following "best response." Consider a strategy vector s, and a player i. Using the strategy vector s player i gets the value or utility $u_i(s)$. Changing the strategy s_i to some other strategy $s_i' \in S_i$ the player can change his utility to $u_i(s_i', s_{-i})$, assuming that all other players stick to their strategies in s_{-i}. We say that a change from strategy s_i to s_i' is an *improving response for player i* if $u_i(s_i', s_{-i}) > u_i(s)$ and *best response* if s_i' maximizes the players' utility $\max_{s_i' \in S_i} u_i(s_i', s_{-i})$. Playing a game by repeatedly allowing some player to make an improving or a best response move is perhaps the most natural game play.

In some games, such as the *Prisoner's Dilemma* or the *Coordination Game*, this dynamic leads the players to a Nash equilibrium in a few steps. In the *Tragedy of the Commons* the players will not reach the equilibrium in a finite number of steps, but the strategy vector will converge to the equilibrium. In other games, the play may cycle, and not converge. A simple example is matching pennies, where the payers will cycle through the 4 possible strategy vectors if they alternate making best response moves. While this game play does not find a pure equilibrium (as none exists) in some sense we can still say that best response converges to the equilibrium: the average payoff for the two players converges to 0, which is the payoff at equilibrium; and even the frequencies at which the 4 possible strategy vectors are played converge to the probabilities in equilibrium (1/4 each).

Results about the outcome of such game playing strategies will be discussed in Chapter 4. We will see that best response behavior is not strong enough to guarantee convergence in most games. Instead, we will consider improving response type "learning" strategies that react to the frequencies played so far, rather than just to the current game play. We will show that in the special case of 2-player zero-sum games such natural game playing does converge to a Nash equilibrium. In general, even learning strategies do not converge to Nash equilibria, instead they converge to the larger region of correlated equilibria.

1.5 Refinement of Nash: Games with Turns and Subgame Perfect Equilibrium

Nash equilibria has become the central solution concept in game theory, despite its shortcomings, such as the existence of multiple equilibria. Since the emergence of this concept in the 1950s, there have been many refinements considered that address the selection of the "right" equilibrium concept. Here we will consider one such refinement for games with turns.

Many games have multiple turns of moves. Card games or board games all have turns, but games modeling many economic situations also have this form: a service provider sets up a basic service (turn 1) and then users decide to use the service or decide not to (turn 2).

How does Nash equilibrium extend to games with turns? We can reduce such games to simultaneous move games by having each player select a "full strategy" up front, rather than having them select moves one at a time. By a "full strategy" we mean a strategy for each turn, as a function of the state of the game. One issue with such strategies is that they tend to become rather large: a full strategy for chess would state the next move for any possible sequence of previous moves. This is a huge set in the natural description of the game in terms of the rules of chess. Games with turns is another example of a compactly represented game. We will see more on how to work with this type of compactly represented games in Chapter 3.

Here our focus is to point out that in this context the notion of Nash equilibrium seems a bit weak. To see why, consider the following simple game.

Example 1.12 (Ultimatum game) Assume that a seller S is trying to sell a good to buyer B. Assume that the interaction has two steps: first seller S offers a price p, and then buyer B reacts to the price. We assume the seller has no value for the good, his payoff is p if the sale occurs, and 0 otherwise. The buyer has a value v for the good, so his payoff is $v - p$ if he buys, and 0 if he does not. Here we are considering a full information game in which seller S is aware of the buyer's value v, and hence we expect that the seller offers price p just under v, and the buyer buys. (Ignore for now the issue of what happens if the price is exactly v.)

This game allows the first player to lead, and collect (almost) all the profit. This game is known as the *ultimatum game* when two players S and B need to divide up v amount of money. The game allows the first player S to make an "ultimatum" (in the form of a price in our context) on how to divide up the money.

To think about this game as a one-shot simultaneous move game, we need to think of the buyer's strategy as a function or the offered price. A natural strategy is to "buy if the price is under v." This is indeed an equilibrium of the game, but the game has many other equilibria. The buyer can also have the strategy that he will buy only if the price p is at most some smaller value $m \leq v$. This seems bad at first (why leave the $v - p$ profit on the table if the price is in the range $m < p < v$), but assuming that the buyer uses this alternate strategy, the seller's best move is to offer price $p = m$, as otherwise he makes no profit. This pair of strategies is also a Nash equilibrium for any value m.

The notion of subgame perfect equilibrium formalizes the idea that the alternate buyer strategy of buying only at $p \leq m$ is unnatural. By thinking of the game as a simultaneous move game, the difference between the two players in terms of the order of moves, is diminished. The notion of *subgame perfect* Nash equilibrium has been introduced to strengthen the concept of Nash, and make the order of turns part of the definition. The idea is to require that the strategy played is Nash, even after any prefix of the game is already played. We will see more about subgame perfect equilibrium as well as games with turns in Chapters 3 and 19.

1.6 Nash Equilibrium without Full Information: Bayesian Games

So far we talked about equilibrium concepts in full information games, where all players know the utilities and strategies of all other players. When players have limited information, we need to consider strategies that are only based on the available information, and find the best strategy for the player, given all his or her available information. Such games will be discussed in more detail in Section 9.6.

One source of limited information can come from not knowing properties and preferences of other players, and hence not knowing what strategies they will select. It is easiest to understand this issue by considering a game of cards, such as bridge. In such a game the players have information about the probability distribution of the other players' cards, but do not know exactly what cards they have. A similar information model can also be used to model many other situations. We illustrate this by the Bayesian first price auction game.

Example 1.13 (Bayesian First Price Auction) Recall the first price auction: all players state a bid, and the winner is the player with maximum bid, and has to pay his bid value as the price. What are optimal strategies for players in this auction? If the valuations of all players are common knowledge, then the player with maximum valuation would state the second valuation as his bid, and win the auction at the same (or slightly bigger) price as in the second price auction. But how should players bid if they do not know all other players' valuations? Naturally, their bids will now depend on their beliefs about the values and knowledge of all other players.

Here we consider the simple setup where players get their valuations from independent probability distributions, and these distributions are public knowledge. How should player i bid knowing his own valuation v_i, and the distribution of the valuation of the other players? Such games are referred to as Bayesian games, and are discussed in Section 9.6. For example, it is shown there that the unique Nash equilibrium in the case when player valuations come from independent and identical distributions is a nice analog of the second price auction: player i, whose own valuation is v_i, should bid the expected second valuation conditioned on v_i being the maximum valuation.

1.7 Cooperative Games

The games we talked about so far are all non-cooperative games – we assumed that individual players act selfishly, deviate alone from a proposed solution, if it is in their interest, and do not themselves coordinate their moves in groups. Cooperative game theory is concerned with situations when groups of players coordinate their actions.

First, in Section 1.7.1 we define the concept of strong Nash equilibrium, a notion extending the Nash equilibrium concept to cooperative situations.

Then we consider games with *transferable utility*, i.e., games where a player with increased utility has the ability to compensate some other player with decreased utility. When considering games with transferable utility the main concern is to develop solution concepts for formalizing fair ways of sharing a value or dividing up a cost in a cooperative environment. There have been many different notions of fairness proposed. In Section 1.7.2 we will briefly review two of them. We refer the reader to Chapter 15 for a more in-depth discussion of these two and other concepts.

1.7.1 Strong Nash Equilibrium

The closest notion from cooperative game theory to our discussion thus far is the concept of strong Nash equilibrium introduced by Aumann (1974). Consider a game and a proposed solution, a strategy for each player. In a cooperative game we assume that some group A of players can change their strategies jointly, assuming that they all benefit. Here we are assuming that the game has nontransferable utility, which means that in order for a coalition to be happy, we need to make sure that the utility of each member is increasing (or at least is not decreasing).

We say that a vector of strategies forms a *strong Nash equilibrium* if no subset A of players has a way to simultaneously change their strategies, improving each of the participant's welfare. More formally, for a strategy vector s and a set of players A let s_A denote the vector of strategies of the players in A and let s_{-A} denote the vector of strategies of the players not in A. We will also use $u_i(s_A, s_{-A})$ for the utility for player i in the strategy s. We say that in a strategy vector s a subset A of players has a *joint deviation* if there are alternate strategies $s'_i \in S_i$ for $i \in A$ forming a vector s'_A, such that $u_i(s) \leq u_i(s'_A, s_{-A})$ for all $i \in A$, and for at least one player in A the inequality is strict. A strategy vector s is *strong Nash* if no subset A has a joint deviation.

The concept of strong Nash is very appealing, for strong Nash equilibria have a very strong reinforcing property. One problem with this concept is that very few games have such equilibria. A nice example of a game with strong Nash equilibria is the game version of the stable marriage problem where boys and girls form pairs based on preference lists for the other sex. For a proposed matching, the natural notion of deviation for this game is a pair deviating (a couple who prefer each other to their current partners). This game will be reviewed in detail in Chapter 10. Chapter 19 considers network formation games, and will discuss another class of games where coalitions of size 2 (pairs) are the natural units causing instability of a solution.

1.7.2 Fair Division and Costsharing: Transferable Utility Games

When utility is transferable, we can think of the game as dividing some value or sharing a cost between a set of players. The goal of this branch of game theory is to understand what is a fair way to divide value or cost between a set of participants. We assume that there is a set N of n participants, or players, and each subset A of players is associated with a cost $c(A)$ (or value $v(A)$). We think of $c(A)$ as a cost associated with serving the group A of players, so $c(N)$ is the cost of serving all N players. The problem is to divide this cost $c(N)$ among the n players in a "fair" way. (In case of dividing a value $v(A)$, we think of $v(A)$ as the value that the set A can generate by itself.)

A *cost-sharing* for the total cost $c(N)$ is a set of cost-shares x_i for each player $i \in N$. We assume that cost-sharing needs to be *budget balanced*; i.e., we require that $\sum_{i \in N} x_i = c(N)$. One of the key solution concepts in this area is that of a *core*. We say that the cost-sharing is in the core if no subset of players would decrease their shares by breaking away from the whole set. More formally, we say that the cost-share vector c is *in the core* if $\sum_{i \in A} x_i \leq c(A)$ for all sets A. A violation of this inequality precisely corresponds to a set A of players who can benefit by breaking away.

Given a notion of fair sharing, such as the core, there are a number of important questions one can ask. Given a cost function c, we want to know whether there is a cost-sharing x that is in the core. In Chapter 15 we will see that there are nice ways of characterizing problems that have a nonempty core. We will also be concerned with the complexity of finding a cost-sharing in the core, and deciding whether the core is nonempty. The computational complexity of determining whether the core is empty has been extensively studied for many fundamental games. If the core is empty or finding a solution in the core is an intractable problem, one can consider a relaxed version of this notion in which subsets of players secede only if they make substantial gains over being in the whole set N. We will discuss these ideas in Chapter 15.

Here we briefly review a very different proposal for what is a "fair" way to share cost, the Shapley value. One advantage of the Shapley value is that it always exists. However, it may not be in the core, even for games that have nonempty core.

Example 1.14 (Shapley Value) Shapley value is based on evaluating the marginal cost of each player. If we order the player set N as $1, \ldots, n$ and use the notation that $N_i = \{1, \ldots, i\}$ then the marginal cost of player i is $c(N_i) - c(N_{i-1})$. Of course, this marginal cost depends on the order the players are considered. The *Shapley value* assigns cost-share x_i to player i that is the expected value of this marginal cost over a random order of the players.

In Chapter 15 we will show that the Shapley value can be characterized as the unique cost-sharing scheme satisfying a number of different sets of axioms.

1.8 Markets and Their Algorithmic Issues

Some of the most crucial regulatory functions within a capitalistic economy, such as ensuring stability, efficiency, and fairness, are relegated to pricing mechanisms, with very little intervention. It is for this reason that general equilibrium theory, which studied equilibrium pricing, occupied a central place within mathematical economics.

From our viewpoint, a shortcoming of this theory is that it is mostly a nonalgorithmic theory. With the emergence of numerous new markets on the Internet and the availability of massive computational power for running these markets in a centralized or distributed manner, there is a need for a new, inherently algorithmic theory of market equilibria. Such algorithms can also help understand the repercussions to existing prices, production, and consumption caused by technological advances, introduction of new goods, or changes to the tax structure. Chapters 5 and 6 summarize recent work along these lines.

Central to ensuring stability of prices is that there be parity between the demand and supply of goods. When there is only one good in the market, such an *equilibrium price* is easy to determine – it is simply the price at which the demand and supply curves intersect. If the price deviates from the equilibrium price, either demand exceeds supply or vice versa, and the resulting market forces tend to push the price back to the equilibrium point. Perhaps the most celebrated result in general equilibrium theory, due to Arrow and Debreu (1954), shows the existence of equilibrium prices in a very general model of the economy with multiple goods and agents.

It turns out that equilibria for several fundamental market models can be captured as optimal solutions to certain nonlinear convex programs. As a result, two algorithmic approaches present themselves – combinatorial algorithms for solving these convex programs and convex programming based approaches. These are covered in Chapters 5 and 6, respectively.

1.8.1 An Algorithm for a Simple Market

In this section, we will give a gist of the models and algorithms studied using a very simple market model. Consider a market consisting of a set A of divisible *goods* and a set B of *buyers*. We are specified for each buyer i, the amount $m_i \in \mathbf{Z}^+$ of money she possesses, and for each good j, the amount $a_j \in \mathbf{Z}^+$ of this good. Each buyer i *has access to* only a subset, say $S_i \subseteq A$ of the goods. She is indifferent between goods in S_i, but is interested in maximizing the total amount of goods obtained. An example of such a situation is when identical goods are sold in different markets and each buyer has access to only a subset of the markets; such a model is studied in Chapter 7. Without loss of generality we may assume that $m_i \neq 0$, $a_j \neq 0$, for each buyer i, $S_i \neq \emptyset$, and for each good j, there is a buyer i such that $j \in S_i$.

Once the prices $p_1, \ldots, p_n$ of the goods are fixed, a buyer i is only *interested in* the cheapest goods in S_i, say $S_i' \subseteq S_i$. Any allocation of goods from S_i' that exhausts her money will constitute her *optimal basket of goods* at these prices.

Prices are said to be *market clearing or equilibrium prices* if there is a way to assign to each buyer an optimal basket of goods so that there is no surplus or deficiency of any of the goods i.e., demand equals supply. It turns out that equilibrium prices are unique for this market; see Chapter 5 for a proof in a more general setting.

We will need the following notations and definitions. Define a bipartite graph $G = (A, B, E)$ on vertex sets A and B as shown on Figure 1.4. The edge (j, i) connects a good j to a buyer i such that $j \in S_i$. Because of the assumptions made, each vertex in G has non zero degree. For $S \subseteq A$ of goods, let $a(S)$ denote the total amount of goods in S, i.e., $a(S) = \sum_{j \in S} a_j$. For a subset $T \subseteq B$ of buyers, let $m(T) = \sum_{i \in T} m_i$ denote the total money possessed by buyers in T.

The algorithm given below is iterative and always assigns uniform prices to all goods currently under consideration. For a set S of goods, let $\Gamma(S)$ denote the set of buyers who are interested in goods in S; $\Gamma(S) = \{i \in B \mid S_i \cap S \neq \emptyset\}$. This is the

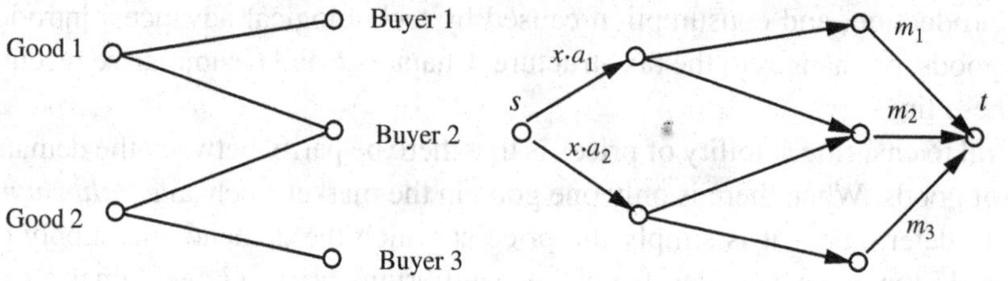

Figure 1.4. The graph G on the left and the corresponding max-flow network N.

neighborhood of S in G. We say that a uniform price x is *feasible* if

$$\forall S \subseteq A, \;\; x \cdot a(S) \leq m(\Gamma(S)),$$

i.e., the total cost of S is at most the total money possessed by buyers interested in goods in S. With respect to a feasible x, we will say that set $S \subseteq A$ is *tight* if $x \cdot a(S) = m(\Gamma(S))$. The importance of feasibility is established by the following lemma.

Lemma 1.15 *A uniform price of x on all goods is feasible if and only if all goods can be sold in such a way that each buyer gets goods that she is interested in.*

PROOF One direction is straightforward. If there is a subset $S \subseteq A$ such that $x \cdot a(S) > m(\Gamma(S))$ then goods in S cannot all be sold at price x since buyers interested in these goods simply do not have enough money.

To prove the other direction, we will use network N (see Figure 1.4) obtained from the bipartite graph G for computing allocations of goods to buyers. Direct the edges of G from A to B and assign a capacity of infinity to all these edges. Introduce source vertex s and a directed edge from s to each vertex $j \in A$ with a capacity of $x \cdot a_j$. Introduce sink vertex t and a directed edge from each vertex $i \in B$ to t with a capacity of m_i.

Clearly, a way of selling all goods corresponds to a feasible flow in N that saturates all edges going out of s. We will show that if x is feasible, then such a flow exists in N. By the max-flow min-cut theorem, if no such flow exists, then the minimum cut must have capacity smaller than $x \cdot a(A)$. Let S be the set of goods on the s-side of a minimum cut. Since edges (j, i) for goods $j \in S$ have infinite capacity, $\Gamma(S)$ must also be on the s-side of this cut. Therefore, the capacity of this cut is at least $x \cdot a(A - S) + m(\Gamma(S))$. If this is less than $x \cdot a(A)$ then $x \cdot a(S) > m(\Gamma(S))$, thereby contradicting the feasibility of x. □

If with respect to a feasible x, a set S is tight, then on selling all goods in S, the money of buyers in $\Gamma(S)$ will be fully spent. Therefore, x constitutes market clearing prices for goods in S. The idea is to look for such a set S, allocate goods in S to $\Gamma(S)$, and recurse on the remaining goods and buyers.

The algorithm starts with $x = 0$, which is clearly feasible, and raises x continuously, always maintaining its feasibility. It stops when a nonempty set goes tight. Let x^* be the smallest value of x at which this happens and let S^* be the maximal tight set (it is easy to see that S^* must be unique).

We need to give procedures for finding x^* and S^*. Observe that x^* is the largest value of x at which $(s, A \cup B \cup t)$ remains a min-cut in N. Therefore, x^* can be computed via a binary search. After computing x^*, compute the set of nodes that can reach t in the residual graph of this flow. This set, say W, is the t-side of the (unique) maximal min-cut in N at $x = x^*$. Then, $S^* = A - W$, the set of goods on the s side of this cut.

At prices x^*, buyers in $\Gamma(S^*)$ will have no surplus money left and increasing x any more will lead to infeasibility. At this point, the algorithm fixes the prices of goods in S^* at x^*. It computes a max-flow in N for $x = x^*$, as suggested by Lemma 1.15. This flow gives an allocation of goods in S^* to buyers in $\Gamma(S^*)$, which fully spends all the money $m(\Gamma(S^*))$. The same flow also shows that x^* is feasible for the problem for goods $A - S^*$ and buyers $B - \Gamma(S^*)$.

In the next iteration, the algorithm removes S^* and $\Gamma(S^*)$, initializes the prices of the goods in $A - S^*$ to x^*, and raises prices until a new set goes tight. The algorithm continues in this manner, iteratively finding prices of sets of goods as they go tight. It terminates when all goods have been assigned prices.

Lemma 1.16 *The value x^* is feasible for the problem restricted to goods in $A - S^*$ and buyers in $B - \Gamma(S^*)$. Furthermore, in the subgraph of G induced on $A - S^*$ and $B - \Gamma(S^*)$, all vertices have nonzero degree.*

PROOF In the max-flow computed in N for $x = x^*$, the flow going through nodes in S^* completely uses up the capacity of edges from $\Gamma(S^*)$ to t. Therefore, all the flow going through nodes in $A - S^*$ must exit via nodes in $B - \Gamma(S^*)$. Now, the first claim follows from Lemma 1.15. Furthermore, a good $j \in A - S^*$ must have nonzero degree to $B - \Gamma(S^*)$. Finally, since each buyer $i \in (B - \Gamma(S^*))$ has nonzero degree in G and has no edges to S^*, it must have nonzero degree to $A - S^*$. □

Theorem 1.17 *The above-stated algorithm computes equilibrium prices and allocations in polynomial time.*

PROOF At termination, all goods are assigned prices and are therefore fully sold. By the second claim in Lemma 1.16, when the algorithm terminates, each buyer must be in the neighborhood of one of the tight sets found and therefore must be allocated goods in return for her money. We need to show that each buyer gets her optimal bundle of goods. Let S^* be the first tight set found by the algorithm. Since S^* was a maximal tight set at x^*, prices must strictly rise before a new set goes tight in the second iteration. Therefore, prices are monotone increasing across iterations and all goods in $A - S^*$ are assigned higher prices than x^*. Since each buyer $i \in \Gamma(S^*)$ is allocated goods from S^* only, she was given an optimal bundle. Now, the claim follows by induction.

Clearly, the algorithm will execute at most $|A|$ iterations. The time taken for one iteration is dominated by the time required for computing x^* and S^*. Observe that $x^* = m(\Gamma(S^*))/a(S^*)$, i.e., its numerator and denominator are polynomial sized integers. Therefore binary search for finding x^* will take polynomial time. □

Acknowledgments

We would like to thank Christos Papadimitriou, Bernhard von Stengel, Tim Roughgarden, and Rakesh Vohra for their extremely valuable critiques and suggestions on an early draft of this chapter. We also thank Ramesh Johari and Tim Roughgarden for suggesting the ISP routing version of the Prisoners' Dilemma in Section 1.1.

Bibliography

K.K. Arrow and G. Debreu. Existence of an equilibrium for competitive economy. *Econometrica*, 22:265–290, 1954.

R.J. Aumann. Acceptable points in general cooperative *n*-person games. In: *Contributions to the Theory of Games IV*, Princeton University Press, 1959.

R.J. Aumann. Subjectivity an correlation in randomized strategies. *J. Math. Econ.*, 1:67–96, 1974.

D. Fudenberg and J. Tirole. *Game Theory*, MIT Press, 1991.

D. Gale and L.S. Shapley. College admissions and the stability of marriage. *American Mathematical Monthly*, 69:9–15, 1962.

A. Mas-Colell, M. Whinston, and J. Green. *Microeconomic Theory*, Oxford Press, 1995.

D. Monderer and L. Shapley. Potential games. *Games and Economic Behavior* 14:124–143, 1996.

J. Nash. Noncooperative games. *Annals of Mathematics*, 54:289–295, 1951.

M. Osborne and A. Rubinstein. *A Course in Game Theory*, MIT Press, 1994.

Exercises

1.1 Give a finite algorithm for finding a Nash equilibrium for a game with two players defined by a game matrix. Your algorithm may run in exponential time.

1.2 Consider a two-player game given in matrix form where each player has n strategies. Assume that the payoffs for each player are in the range [0, 1] and are selected independently and uniformly at random. Show that the probability that this random game has a pure (deterministic) Nash equilibrium approaches $1 - 1/e$ as n goes to infinity. You may use the fact that $\lim(1 - 1/n)^n = 1/e$ as n goes to infinity.

1.3 We have seen that finding a Nash in a two-person zero-sum game is significantly easier than general two-person games. Now consider a three-person zero-sum game, that is, a game in which the rewards of the three players always sums to zero. Show that finding a Nash equilibrium in such games is at least as hard as that in general two-person games.

1.4 Consider an n person game in which each player has only two strategies. This game has 2^n possible outcomes (for the 2^n ways the n players can play), therefore the game in matrix form is exponentially large. To circumvent this, in Chapter 7 we will consider a special class of games called graphical games. The idea is that the value (or payoff) of a player can depend only on a subset of players. We will define a dependence graph G, whose nodes are the players, and an edge between two players i and j represents the fact that the payoff of player i depends on the strategy of player j or vice versa. Thus, if node i has k neighbors, then its payoff depends only on its own strategy and the strategies of its k neighbors.

Consider a game where the players have 2 pure strategies each and assume that the graph G is a tree with maximum degree 3. Give a polynomial time algorithm to decide if such a game has a pure Nash equilibrium. (Recall that there are 2^n possible pure strategy vectors, yet your algorithm must run in time polynomial in n.)

1.5 Consider an n player game in which each player has 2 strategies. For this problem, think of the strategies as "on" and "off." For example, the strategy can be either to participate or not to participate in some event. Further more, assume that the game is symmetric, in that all players have the same payoff functions, and that the payoff for a player depends only on the strategy of the player and the number of people playing strategy "on." So the game is defined by $2n$ values: $u_{on}(k)$ and $u_{off}(k)$, which denote the payoff for playing the "on" and "off" strategies, assuming that k of the other players chose to play "on" for $k = 0, \ldots, n-1$.

Give a polynomial time algorithm to find a correlated equilibrium for such a game. Note that the input to this problem consists of the $2n$ numbers above. As usual, polynomial means polynomial in this input length. You may use the fact that linear programming is solvable in polynomial time.

1.6 Consider a 2-person game in matrix form. Assume that both players have n pure strategies. In a Nash equilibrium a player may be required to play a mixed strategy that gives nonzero probability to all (or almost all) of his pure strategies. Strategies that mix between so many pure options are hard to play, and also hard to understand. The goal of this problem is to show that one can reach an almost perfect Nash equilibrium by playing strategies that only choose between a few of the options.

We will use p^j to be the probability distribution for player j, so p_i^j is the probability that player j will use his ith pure strategy. The support of a mixed strategy p^j for player j is the set $S^j = \{i : p_i^j > 0\}$, i.e., the set of different pure strategies that are used with nonzero probability. We will be interested in solutions where each player has a strategy with small support.

For a given $\epsilon > 0$, we will say that a set of mixed strategies p^1, p^2 is ϵ-approximate Nash if for both players $j = 1$ or 2, and all other strategies $\bar{p}^j$ for this player, the expected payoff for player j using strategy $\bar{p}^j$ is at most ϵM more than his expected payoff using strategy p^j, where M is the maximum payoff.

Show that for any fixed $\epsilon > 0$ and any 2-player game with all nonnegative payoffs, there is an ϵ-approximate Nash equilibrium such that both players play the following simple kind of mixed strategy. For each player j, the strategy selects a subset $\hat{S}_j$ of at most $O(\log n)$ of player j's pure strategies, and makes player j select one of the strategies in $\hat{S}_j$ uniformly at random. The set $\hat{S}_j$ may be a multiset, i.e., may contain the same pure strategy more than once such a strategy is more likely to be selected by the random choice). The constant in the $O(.)$ notation may depend on the parameter ϵ.

Hint: Consider any mixed Nash strategy with possibly large support, and try to simplify the support by selecting the subsets $\hat{S}_j$ for the two players based on this Nash equilibrium.

1.7 The classical Bertrand game is the following. Assume that n companies, which produce the same product, are competing for customers. If each company i has a production level of q_i, there will be $q = \sum_i q_i$ units of the product on the market.

Now, demand for this product depends on the price and if q units are on the market, price will settle so that all q units are sold. Assume that we are given a "demand-price curve" $p(d)$, which gives the price at which all d units can be sold. Assume that $p(d)$ is a monotone decreasing, differentiable function of d. With this definition, the income of the firm i will be $q_i\, p(q)$. Assume that production is very cheap and each firm will produce to maximize its income.

(a) Show that the total income for a monopolistic firm, can be arbitrarlly higher than the total income of many different firms sharing the same market. Hint: this is true for almost all price curves; you may want to use, e.g., $p(d) = 1 - d$.

(b) Assume that $p(d)$ is twice differentiable, monotone decreasing, and $p''(d) \leq 0$. Show that the monopolistic income is at most n times the total income of the n competing companies.

1.8 Let V denote a set of n agents, labeled $1, 2, \ldots, n$. Let 0 denote the root node and for any subset $S \subseteq V$, S^+ denote the set $S \cup \{0\}$. Let $G = (V^+, E)$ be a complete, undirected graph with edge costs $c : E \to Z^+$ which satisfy the triangle inequality. For a subset $S \subseteq V$, let $c(S)$ denote the cost of a minimum spanning tree in the subgraph of G induced on S^+. The spanning tree game asks for a budget balanced cost-sharing method for minimum spanning tree that lies on the core.

Consider the following cost-sharing method for sharing the cost of building a minimum spanning tree in G among the n agents. Find any minimum spanning tree, say T, and root it at vertex 0. Define the cost of agent i to be the cost of the first edge on the unique path from i to 0 in T. Clearly, this cost-sharing method is budget balanced; i.e., the total cost retrieved from the n agents is precisely the cost of a minimum spanning tree in G. Show that this cost-sharing method is in the core, i.e., for any subset $S \subseteq V$, the total cost charged to agents in S is at most the cost they would incur if they were to directly connect to the root, i.e., $c(S)$.

CHAPTER 2

The Complexity of Finding Nash Equilibria

Christos H. Papadimitriou

Abstract

Computing a Nash equilibrium, given a game in normal form, is a fundamental problem for Algorithmic Game Theory. The problem is essentially combinatorial, and in the case of two players it can be solved by a pivoting technique called the Lemke–Howson algorithm, which however is exponential in the worst case. We outline the recent proof that finding a Nash equilibrium is complete for the complexity class PPAD, even in the case of two players; this is evidence that the problem is intractable. We also introduce several variants of succinctly representable games, a genre important in terms of both applications and computational considerations, and discuss algorithms for correlated equilibria, a more relaxed equilibrium concept.

2.1 Introduction

Nash's theorem – stating that every finite game has a mixed Nash equilibrium (Nash, 1951) – is a very reassuring fact: Any game can, in principle, reach a quiescent state, one in which no player has an incentive to change his or her behavior. One question arises immediately: Can this state be reached in practice? Is there an *efficient algorithm* for finding the equilibrium that is guaranteed to exist? This is the question explored in this chapter.

But why should we be interested in the issue of computational complexity in connection to Nash equilibria? After all, a Nash equilibrium is above all a conceptual tool, a prediction about rational strategic behavior by agents in situations of conflict – a context that is completely devoid of computation.

We believe that this matter of computational complexity is one of central importance here, and indeed that the algorithmic point of view has much to contribute to the debate of economists about solution concepts. The reason is simple: If an equilibrium concept is not efficiently computable, much of its credibility as a prediction of the behavior of rational agents is lost – after all, there is no clear reason why a group of agents cannot be simulated by a machine. Efficient computability is an important modeling perequisite for solution concepts. In the words of Kamal Jain, "If your laptop cannot find it, neither can the market."[1]

2.1.1 Best Responses and Supports

Let us thus define NASH to be the following computational problem: Given a game in strategic form, find a Nash equilibrium. Since Nash calls for the computation of a real-valued distribution for each player, it seems *primae facie* to be a quest in continuous mathematics. However, a little thought reveals that the task is *essentially combinatorial*.

Recall that a mixed strategy profile is a Nash equilibrium if the mixed strategy of each player is a *best response* to the mixed strategies of the rest; that is, it attains the maximum possibly utility among all possible mixed strategies of this player. The following observation is useful here (recall that the *support* of a mixed strategy is the set of all pure strategies that have nonzero probability in it).

Theorem 2.1 *A mixed strategy is a best response if and only if all pure strategies in its support are best responses.*

To see why, assume for the sake of contradiction that a best response mixed strategy contains in its support a pure strategy that is not itself a best response. Then the utility of the player would be improved by decreasing the probability of the worst such strategy (increasing proportionally the remaining nonzero probabilities to fill the gap); this contradicts the assumption that the mixed strategy was a best response. Conversely, if all strategies in all supports are best responses, then the strategy profile combination must be a Nash equilibrium.

This simple fact reveals the subtle nature of a mixed Nash equilibrium: Players combine pure best response strategies (instead of using, for the same utility, a single pure best response) in order to create for other players a range of best responses that will sustain the equilibrium!

Example 2.2 Consider the *symmetric game* with two players captured by the matrix

$$A = \begin{pmatrix} 0 & 3 & 0 \\ 0 & 0 & 3 \\ 2 & 2 & 2 \end{pmatrix}$$

A game with two players can be represented by two matrices (A, B) (hence the term *bimatrix game* often used to describe such games), where the rows of A are the strategies of Player 1 and the columns of A are the strategies of Player 2, while the entries are the utilities of Player 1; the opposite holds for matrix B. A bimatrix game is called *symmetric* if $B = A^T$; i.e., the two players have the same set of strategies, and their utilities remain the same if their roles are reversed.

In the above symmetric game, consider the equilibrium in which both players play the mixed strategy $(0, 1/3, 2/3)$. This is a *symmetric* Nash equilibrium,

[1] One may object to this aphorism on the basis that in markets agents work in *parallel*, and are therefore more powerful than ordinary algorithms; however, a little thought reveals that parallelism cannot be the cure for exponential worst case.

because both players play the same mixed strategy. (A variant of Nash's proof establishes that every symmetric game, with any number of players, has a symmetric equilibrium – it may also have nonsymmetric ones.) We can check whether it is indeed an equilibrium, by calculating the utility of each strategy, assuming the opponent plays $(0, 1/3, 2/3)$: The utilities are 1 for the first strategy, and 2 for the other two. Thus, every strategy in the support (i.e., either of strategies 2 and 3) is a best response, and the mixed strategy is indeed a Nash equilibrium. Note that, from Player 1's point of view, playing just strategy 2, or just strategy 3, or any mixture of the two, is equally beneficial to the equilibrium mixed strategy $(0, 1/3, 2/3)$. The only advantage of following the precise mix suggested by the equilibrium is that it motivates the other player to do the same.

Incidentally, in our discussion of Nash equilibria in this chapter, we shall often use the simpler two-player case to illustrate the ideas. Unfortunately, the main result of this section says that two-player games are not, in any significant sense, easier than the general problem.

It also follows from these considerations that finding a mixed Nash equilibrium means finding the right supports: Once one support for each player has been identified, the precise mixed strategies can be computed by solving a system of algebraic equations (in the case of two players, linear equations): For each player i we have a number of variables equal to the size of the support, call it k_i, one equation stating that these variables add to 1, and $k_i - 1$ others stating that the k_i expected utilities are equal. Solving this system of $\sum_i k_i$ equations in $\sum_i k_i$ unknowns yields k_i numbers for each player. If these numbers are real and nonnegative, and the utility expectation is maximized at the support, then we have discovered a mixed Nash equilibrium.

In fact, if in the two-player case the utilities are integers (as it makes sense to assume in the context of computation), then the probabilities in the mixed Nash equilibrium will necessarily be rational numbers, since they constitute the solution of a system of linear equations with integer coefficients. This is not true in general: Nash's original paper (1951) includes a beautiful example of a three-player poker game whose only Nash equilibrium involves irrational numbers.

The bottom line is that *finding a Nash equilibrium is a combinatorial problem:* It entails identifying an appropriate support for each player. Indeed, most algorithms proposed over the past half century for finding Nash equilibria are combinatorial in nature, and work by seeking supports. Unfortunately, none of them are known to be efficient – to always succeed after only a polynomial number of steps.

2.2 Is the Nash Equilibrium Problem NP-Complete?

Computer scientists have developed over the years notions of complexity, chief among them *NP-completeness* (Garey and Johnson, 1979), to characterize computational problems which, just like NASH and SATISFIABILITY,[2] seem to resist efficient solution. Should we then try to apply this theory and prove that NASH is NP-complete?

[2] Recall that SATISFIABILITY is the problem that asks, given a Boolean formula in conjunctive normal form, to find a satisfying truth assignment.

It turns out that NASH is a very different kind of intractable problem, one for which NP-completeness is not an appropriate concept of complexity. The basic reason is that *every game* is guaranteed to have a Nash equilibrium. In contrast, in a typical NP-complete problem such as SATISFIABILITY, the sought solution may or may not exist. NP-complete problems owe much of their difficulty, and their susceptibility to NP-completeness reductions, to precisely this dichotomy.[3] For, suppose that NASH is NP-complete, and there is a reduction from SATISFIABILITY to NASH. This would entail an efficiently computable function f mapping Boolean formulae to games, and such that, for every formula ϕ, ϕ is satisfiable if and only if any Nash equilibrium of $f(\phi)$ satisfies some easy-to-check property Π. But now, given any unsatisfiable formula ϕ, we could guess a NASH equilibrium of $f(\phi)$, and check that it does not satisfy Π: This implies NP = coNP!

Problems such as NASH for which a solution is guaranteed to exist require much more specialized and subtle complexity analysis – and the end diagnosis is necessarily less severe than NP-completeness (see Beame et al., 1998; Johnson et al., 1988; Papadimitriou, 1994 for more on this subject).

2.2.1 NASH *vs* Brouwer

In contemplating the complexity of NASH, a natural first reaction is to look into Nash's proof (1951) and see precisely how existence is established – with an eye towards making this existence proof "constructive." Unfortunately this does not get us very far, because Nash's proof relies on *Brouwer's fixpoint theorem,* stating that every continuous function f from the n-dimensional unit ball to itself has a fixpoint: a point x such that $f(x) = x$. Nash's proof is a clever reduction of the existence of a mixed equilibrium to the existence of such a fixpoint. Unfortunately, Brouwer's theorem is well-known for its nonconstructive nature, and finding a Brouwer fixpoint is known to be a hard problem (Hirsch et al., 1989; Papadimitriou, 1994) – again, in the specialized sense alluded to above, since a solution is guaranteed to exist here also.

Natural next question: Is there a reduction in the opposite direction, one establishing that NASH is precisely as hard as the known difficult problem of finding a Brouwer fixpoint? The answer is "yes," and this is in fact a useful alternative way of understanding the main result explained in this chapter.[4]

2.2.2 NP-Completeness of Generalizations

As we have discussed, what makes NP-completeness inappropriate for NASH is the fact that Nash equilibria always exist. If the computational problem NASH is twisted

[3] But how about the traveling salesman problem? Does it not always have a solution? It does, but this solution (the optimum tour) is hard to verify, and so the TSP is not an appropriate comparison here. To be brought into the realm of NP-completeness, optimization problems such as the TSP must be first transformed into decision problems of the form "given a TSP instance and a bound B, does a tour of length B or smaller exist?" This problem is much closer to SATISFIABILITY.

[4] This may seem puzzling, as it seems to suggest that Brouwer's theorem is also of a combinatorial nature. As we shall see, in a certain sense indeed it is.

in any one of several simple ways that deprive it from its existence guarantee, NP-completeness comes into play almost immediately.

Theorem 2.3 (Gilboa and Zemel, 1989) *The following are NP-complete problems, even for symmetric games: Given a two-player game in strategic form, does it have*

- *at least two Nash equilibria?*
- *a Nash equilibrium in which player 1 has utility at least a given amount?*
- *a Nash equilibrium in which the two players have total utility at least a given amount?*
- *a Nash equilibrium with support of size greater than a given number?*
- *a Nash equilibrium whose support contains strategy s?*
- *a Nash equilibrium whose support does not contain strategy s?*
- *etc., etc.*

A simple proof, due to (Conitzer and Sandholm, 2003), goes roughly as follows: Reduction from SATISFIABILITY. It is not hard to construct a symmetric game whose strategies are all literals (variables and their negations) and whose Nash equilibria are all truth assignments. In other words, if we choose, for each of the n variables, either the variable itself or its negation, and play it with probability $\frac{1}{n}$, then we get a symmetric Nash equilibrium, and all Nash equilibria of the game are of this sort. It is also easy to add to this game a new pure Nash equilibrium (d, d), with lower utility, where d (for "default") is a new strategy. Then you add new strategies, one for each clause, such that the strategy for clause C is attractive, when a particular truth assignment is played by the opponent, only if all three literals of C are contradicted by the truth assignment. Once a clause becomes attractive, it destroys the assignment equilibrium (via other strategies not detailed here) and makes it drift to (d, d). It is then easy to establish that the Nash equilibria of the resulting game are precisely (d, d) plus all satisfying truth assignments. All the results enumerated in the statement of the theorem, and more, follow very easily.

2.3 The Lemke–Howson Algorithm

We now sketch the Lemke–Howson algorithm, the best known among the combinatorial algorithms for finding a Nash equilibrium (this algorithm is explained in much more detail in the next chapter). It works in the case of two-player games, by exploiting the elegant combinatorial structure of supports. It constitutes an alternative proof of Nash's theorem, and brings out in a rather striking way the complexity issues involved in solving NASH. Its presentation is much simpler in the case of symmetric games. We therefore start by proving a basic complexity result for games: looking at symmetric games is no loss of generality.

2.3.1 Reduction to Symmetric Games

Define SYMMETRIC Nash to be the following problem: Given a symmetric game, find a symmetric Nash equilibrium. As noted above, Nash proved in his original paper that such equilibrium always exists. Here we establish the following fact, which was actually first pointed out before Nash's paper, in Gale et al., 1950 essentially with the same proof, for the case of two-player zero-sum games:

Theorem 2.4 *There is a polynomial reduction from* NASH *to* SYMMETRIC NASH.

Thus the symmetric case of Nash is as hard as the general one.

We shall describe the reduction for the two-player case, the proof for any fixed number of players being a straightforward generalization. Suppose that we are given a two-player game described by matrices A and B; without loss of generality, assume that all entries of these matrices are positive (adding the same number to all entries of A or B changes nothing). Consider now the symmetric game consisting of this matrix: $C = \begin{pmatrix} 0 & A \\ B^T & 0 \end{pmatrix}$ and let (x, y) be a symmetric equilibrium of this game (by x we denote the first m components of the vector, where m is the number of rows of A, and by y the rest). It is easy to see that, for (x, y) to be a best response to itself, y must be a best response to x, and x must be a best response to y. Hence, x and y constitute a NASH equilibrium of the original game, completing the proof.

Incidentally, the problem of finding *any* Nash equilibrium in a symmetric game is also equivalent to NASH (and in fact via the same reduction above, can you see why?). But how hard is it to find a *nonsymmetric* Nash equilibrium in a symmetric game? It cannot be easier than NASH (can you see why the same reduction above proves this?) but it could be harder — for example, it could be NP-complete.

2.3.2 Pivoting on Supports

So, let us concentrate on finding a NASH equilibrium in a symmetric two-player game with $n \times n$ utility matrix A, assumed with no loss of generality to have nonnegative entries and in addition no column that is totally zero. Consider the convex polytope P defined by the $2n$ inequalities $Az \leq 1, z \geq 0$ (it turns out that these inequalities are important in identifying mixed Nash equilibria, because, intuitively, when an inequality from $A_i x \leq 1$ is tight, the corresponding strategy is a best response). It is a nonempty, bounded polytope (since $z = 0$ is a solution, and all coefficients of A are nonnegative while no column is zero). Let us assume for simplicity that the polytope P is also *nondegenerate*, that is, every vertex lies on precisely n constraints (every linear program can be made nondegenerate by a slight perturbation of its coefficients, so this is little loss of generality). We say that a strategy i is *represented* at a vertex z if at that vertex either $z_i = 0$ or $A_i z = 1$ or both – that is, if at least one of the two inequalities of the polytope associated with strategy i is tight at z.

Suppose that at a vertex z all strategies are represented. This of course could happen if z is the all-zero vertex – but suppose it is not. Then for all strategies i with $z_i > 0$ it must be the case that $A_i z = 1$. Define now a vector x as follows:

$$x_i = \frac{z_i}{\sum_{i=1}^{n} z_i}.$$

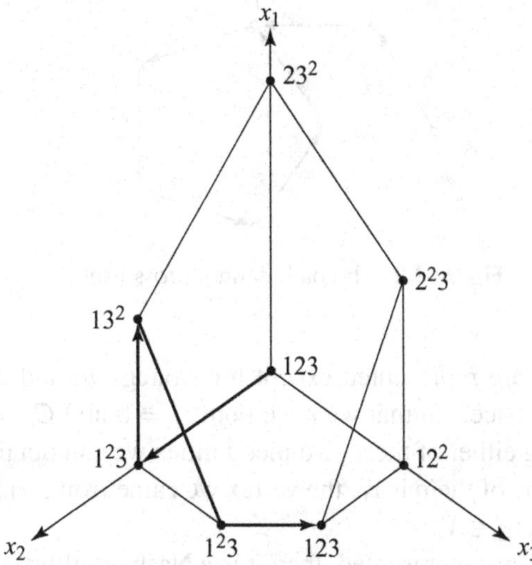

Figure 2.1. The Lemke–Howson algorithm can be thought of as following a directed path in a graph.

Since we assume $z \neq 0$, the x_i's are well defined, and they are nonnegative numbers adding to 1, thus constituting a mixed strategy. We claim that x is a symmetric NASH equilibrium. In proof, just notice that x satisfies the necessary and sufficient condition of a Nash equilibrium (recall Theorem): Every strategy in its support is a best response.

Let us apply this to the symmetric game of Example 2.2, with utility matrix

$$A = \begin{pmatrix} 0 & 3 & 0 \\ 0 & 0 & 3 \\ 2 & 2 & 2 \end{pmatrix}.$$

The polytope P is shown in Figure 2.1; it is nondegenerate because every vertex lies on three planes, and has three adjacent vertices. The vertices are labeled by the strategies that are represented there (ignore the exponents ^{2} for a moment). The only vertices where all strategies are represented are the vertex $z = (0, 0, 0)$ and the vertex $z = (0, 1/6, 1/3)$ – notice that the latter vertex corresponds to the NASH equilibrium $x = (0, 1/3, 2/3)$.

So, any vertex of P (other than $(0, 0, 0)$) at which all strategies are represented is a Nash equilibrium. But how do we know that such a vertex exists in general? After all, not all choices of n tight constraints result in vertices of a polytope. We shall develop a pivoting method for looking for such a vertex.

Fix a strategy, say strategy n, and consider the set V of all vertices of P at which all strategies are represented *except possibly for strategy n*. This set of vertices is nonempty, because it contains vertex $(0, 0, 0)$, so let us start there a path $\langle v_0 = 0, v_1, v_2, \ldots \rangle$ of vertices in the set V. Since we assume that P is nondegenerate, there are n vertices adjacent to every vertex, and each is obtainable by relaxing one of the tight inequalities at the vertex and making some other inequality tight. So consider the n vertices adjacent to $v_0 = (0, 0, 0)$. In one of these vertices, z_n is nonzero and all other variables are zero, so this new vertex is also in V; call it v_1.

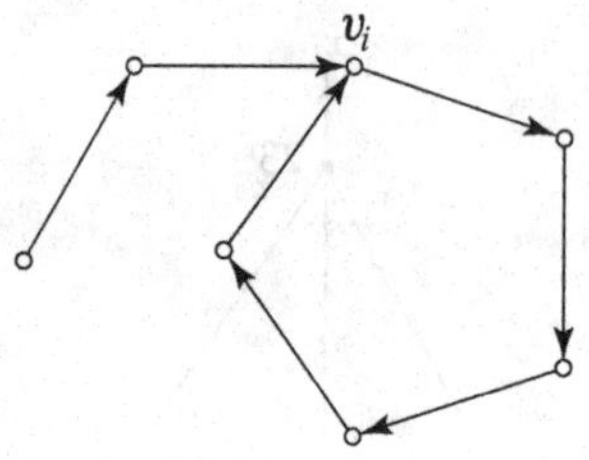

Figure 2.2. The path cannot cross itself.

At v_1 all strategies are represented except for strategy n, and in fact one strategy $i < n$ is "represented twice," in that we have both $z_i = 0$ and $C_i z = 1$. (We represent this by i^2). By relaxing either of these two inequalities we can obtain two new vertices in V adjacent to v_1. One of them is v_0, the vertex we came from, and the other is bound to be some new vertex $v_2 \in V$.

If at v_2 all strategies are represented, then it is a Nash equilibrium and we are done. Otherwise, there is a strategy j that is represented twice at v_2, and there are two vertices in V that are adjacent to v_2 and correspond to these two inequalities. One of these two vertices is v_1 and the other is our new vertex v_3, and so on. The path for the example of Figure 2.1 where strategy $n = 3$ is the one that may not be represented, is shown as a sequence of bold arrows.

How can this path end? No vertex v_i can be repeated, because repeating v_i (see Figure 2.2) would mean that there are *three* vertices adjacent to v_i that are obtainable by relaxing a constraint associated with its doubly represented strategy, and this is impossible (it is also easy to see that it cannot return to 0). And it cannot go on forever, since P is a finite polytope. The only place where the process can stop is at a vertex in V, other than 0 (a moment's thought tells us it has to be different from 0) that has no doubly represented strategy – that is to say, *at a symmetric Nash equilibrium!*

This completes our description of the Lemke–Howson algorithm, as well as our proof of Nash's theorem for two-player, nondegenerate games.

2.4 The Class PPAD

Let us dissect the existence proof in the previous section. It works by creating a graph. The set of vertices of this graph, V, is a finite set of combinatorial objects (vertices of P, or sets of inequalities, where all strategies are represented, with the possible exception of strategy n). This graph has a very simple "path-like" structure: All vertices have either one or two edges incident upon them – because every vertex $v \in V$ has either one or two adjacent vertices (depending on whether or not strategy n is represented in v). The overall graph may be richer than a path – it will be, in general, a set of paths and cycles (see Figure 2.3). The important point is that there is definitely at least one known endpoint of a path: the all-zero vertex. We must conclude that there is another endpoint, and this endpoint is necessarily a Nash equilibrium of the game.

We must now mention a subtle point: *the paths are directed.* Looking at a vertex in V, we can assign a direction to its incident edge(s), at most one coming in and at most

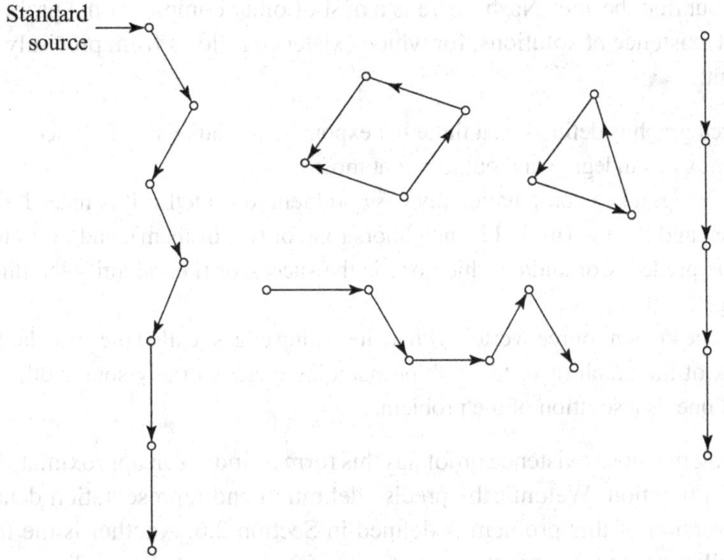

Figure 2.3. A typical problem in PPAD.

one going out, and do this in a way that is consistent from one vertex to another. In our three-dimensional example of Figure 2.1 the rule for asigning directions is simple: Going in the direction of the arrow, we should have a face all vertices of which are labeled 3 on our right, and a face all vertices of which are labeled 1 on our left. In games with more strategies, and thus a polytope of a higher dimension, there is a similar but more complicated (and more algebraic) "orientation rule." So, the graph in the proof of Nash's Theorem is a directed graph with all outdegrees and indegrees at most one.

What we mean to say here is that the existence proof of Nash's theorem (for the two-player symmetric, nondegenerate case, even though something similar holds for the general case as well) has the following abstract structure: A directed graph is defined on a set of nodes that are easily recognizable combinatorial objects (in our case, vertices of the polytope where all strategies, with the possible exception of strategy n, are represented). Each one of these vertices has indegree and outdegree at most one; therefore, the graph is a set of paths and cycles (see Figure 2.3). By necessity there is one vertex with no incoming edges and one outgoing edge, called a *standard source* (in the case of two-player Nash, the all-zero vertex). We must conclude that there must be a sink: a Nash equilibrium. In fact, not just a sink: notice that a source other than the standard (all-zero) one is also a Nash equilibrium, since all strategies are represented there as well. Another important point is that there is an efficient way, given a vertex in the graph to find its two adjacent vertices (or decide that there is only one). This can be done by simplex pivoting on the doubly represented variable (or on variable n, if it is represented).

Any such proof suggests a simple algorithm for finding a solution: start from the standard source, and follow the path until you find a sink (in the case of two-player NASH this is called the Lemke–Howson algorithm). Unfortunately, this is not an efficient algorithm because *the number of vertices in the graph is exponentially large*. Actually, in the case of two-player NASH there are examples of games in which such paths are exponentially long (Savani and von Stengel, 2004).

It turns out that, besides Nash, there is a host of other computational problems with guaranteed existence of solutions, for which existence follows from precisely this type of argument:

- A directed graph is defined on a finite but exponentially large set of vertices.
- Each vertex has indegree and outdegree at most one.
- Given a string, it is a computationally easy problem to (a) tell if it is indeed a vertex of the graph, and if so to (b) find its neighbors (one or two of them), and to (c) tell which one is the predecessor and/or which one is the successor (i.e., identify the direction of each edge).
- There is one known source (vertex with no incoming edges) called the "standard source."
- Any sink of the graph (a vertex with no outgoing edges), or any source other than the standard one, is a solution of the problem.

One problem whose existence proof has this form is finding an approximate Brouwer fixpoint of a function. We omit the precise definition and representation details here; a stylized version of this problem is defined in Section 2.6. Another is the following problem called HAM SANDWICH: Given n sets of $2n$ points each in n dimensions, find a hyperplane which, for each of the n sets, leaves n points on each side. There are many other such problems (see Papadimitriou, 1994). For none of these problems do we know a polynomial algorithm for finding a solution.

All these problems comprise the complexity class called PPAD.[5] In other words, PPAD is the class of all problems, whose solution space can be set up as the set of all sinks and all nonstandard sources in a directed graph with the properties displayed above.

Solving a problem in PPAD is to telescope the long path and arrive at a sink (or a nonstandard source), fast and without rote traversal – just as solving a problem in NP means narrowing down to a solution among the exponentially many candidates without exhaustive search. We do not know whether either of these feats is possible in general. But we do know that achieving the latter would imply managing the former too. That is, P = NP implies PPAD = P (proof: PPAD is essentially a subset of NP, since a solution, such as a Nash equilibrium, can be certified quickly if found).

In the case of NP, we have a useful notion of difficulty – NP-completeness – that helps characterize the complexity of difficult problems in NP, even in the absence of a proof that P $\neq$ NP. A similar manoeuvre is possible and useful in the case of PPAD as well. We can advance our understanding of the complexity of a problem such as NASH by proving it *PPAD-complete* – meaning that all other problems in PPAD reduce to it. Such a result implies that we could solve the particular problem efficiently if and only if *all* problems in PPAD (many of which, like BROUWER, are well-known hard nuts that have resisted decades of efforts at an efficient solution) can be thus solved.

Indeed, the main result explained in the balance of this chapter is a proof that NASH is PPAD-complete.

[5] The name, introduced in Papadimitriou (1994), stands for "polynomial parity argument (directed case)." See that paper, as well as Beame et al. (1998) and Daskalakis et al. (2006), for a more formal definition.

2.4.1 Are PPAD-Complete Problems Hard?

But why do we think that PPAD-complete problems are indeed hard? PPAD-completeness is weaker evidence of intractability than NP-completeness: it could very well be that PPAD $=$ P $\neq$ NP. Yet it is a rather compelling argument for intractability. If a PPAD-complete problem could be solved in polynomial time, then all problems in PPAD (finding Brouwer and Borsuk-Ulam fixpoints, cutting ham sandwiches, finding Arrow-Debreu equilibria in markets, etc., many of which have resisted decades of scrutiny, see Papadimitriou (1994) for a more complete list) would also be solved. It would mean that any local combinatorial description of a deterministic simplex pivoting rule would lead to a novel polynomial algorithm for linear programming. Besides, since it is known (Hirsch et al., 1989) that any algorithm for finding Brouwer fixpoints that treats the function as a black box must be exponential, PPAD $=$ P would mean that there is a way to find Brouwer fixpoints by delving into the detailed properties of the function – a possibility that seems quite counterintuitive. Also, an efficient algorithm for a PPAD-complete problem would have to defeat the *oracles* constructed in Beame et al. (1998) – computational universes in which PPAD $\neq$ P – and so it would have to be extremely sophisticated in a very specific sense.

In mathematics we must accept as a possibility anything whose negation remains unproved. PPAD could very well be equal to P, despite the compelling evidence to the contrary outlined above. For all we know, it might even be the case that P $=$ NP – in which case PPAD, lying “between” P and NP, would immediately be squeezed down to P as well. But it seems a reasonable working hypothesis that neither of these eventualities will actually hold, and that by proving a problem PPAD-complete we indeed establish it as an intractable problem.

2.5 Succinct Representations of Games

Computational problems have inputs, and the input to NASH is a description of the game for which we need to find an equilibrium. How long is such a description?

Describing a game in strategic form entails listing all utilities for all players and strategy combinations. In the case of two players, with m and n strategies respectively, this amounts to describing $2mn$ numbers. This makes the two-player case of NASH such a very neat and interesting computational problem.

But we are interested in games because we think that they can model the Internet, markets, auctions – and these have far more than two players. Suppose that we have a game with n players, and think of n as being in the hundreds or thousands – a rather modest range for the contexts and applications outlined above. Suppose for simplicity that they all have the same number of strategies, call it s – in any nontrivial game s will be at least two. *Representing the game now requires ns^n numbers!*

This is a huge input. No user can be expected to supply it, and no algorithm to handle it. Furthermore, the astronomical input trivializes complexity: If s is a small number such as 2 or 5, a trivial efficient algorithm exists: *try all combinations of supports.* But this algorithm is “efficient” only because the input is so huge: For fixed s, $(2^s)^n$ is polynomial in the length of the input, ns^n . . .

Conclusion: In our study of the complexity of computational problems for games such as NASH we must be especially interested in games with many players; however, only *succinctly representable* multiplayer games can be of relevance and computational interest.

And there are many such games in the literature; we start by describing one of the latest arrivals (Kearns et al., 2001) that happens to play a central role in our story.

2.5.1 Graphical Games

Suppose that many players are engaged in a complex game; yet, the utility of each player depends on the actions of very few other players. That is, there is a directed graph $(\{1, 2, \ldots, n\}, E)$, with vertices the set of players, and $(i, j) \in E$ only if the utility of j depends on the strategy chosen by i (j's utility depends, of course, on the strategy chosen by j). More formally, for any two strategy profiles s and s' if $s_j = s'_j$, and, for all $(i, j) \in E$ we have $s_i = s'_i$, then $u_j(s) = u_j(s')$. A *graphical game*, as these are called, played on a graph with n nodes and indegree at most d, and s choices per player, requires only ns^{d+1} numbers for its description – a huge savings over ns^n when d is modest. (For more on graphical games, see Chapter 7.)

For a simple example, consider a directed cycle on 20 players, where the utilities are captured by the game matrix A of example 2.2. That is, if a player chooses a strategy $i \in \{1, 2, 3\}$ and his predecessor in the cycle chooses another strategy j, then the utility of the first player is C_{ij} (the utility of the predecessor will depend on the strategy played by *his* predecessor). Ordinarily, this game would require 20×3^{20} numbers to be described; its graph structure reduces this to just a few bytes.

Can you find a NASH equilibrium in this game?

2.5.2 Other Succinct Games

There are many other computationally meaningful ways of representing some interesting games succinctly. Here are some of the most important ones.

(i) *Sparse games*. If very few of the ns^n utilities are nonzero, then the input can be meaningfully small. Graphical games can be seen as a special case of sparse games, in which the sparsity pattern is captured by a graph whose vertices are the players.

(ii) *Symmetric games*. In a symmetric game the players are all identical. So, in evaluating the utility of a combination of strategies, what matters is *how many* of the n players play each of the s strategies. Thus, to describe such a game we need only $s\binom{n+s-1}{s-1}$ numbers.

(iii) *Anonymous games*. This is a generalization of symmetric games, in which each player is different, *but cannot distinguish between the others*, and so again his or her utility depends on the partition of the other players into strategies. $sn\binom{n+s-1}{s-1}$ numbers suffice here.

(iv) *Extensive form games*. These are given as explicit game trees (see the next chapter). A strategy for a player is a combination of strategies, one for each vertex in the game tree (information set, more accurately, see the next chapter for details) in which the player has the initiative. The utility of a strategy combination is that of the leaf reached if the strategies are followed.

(v) *Congestion games.* These games abstract the network congestion games studied in Chapters 18 and 19. Suppose that there are n players, and a set of *edges* E. The set of strategies for each player is a set of subsets of E, called *paths*. For each edge $e \in E$ we have a *congestion function* c_e mapping $\{0, 1, \ldots, n\}$ to the nonnegative integers. If the n players choose strategies/paths $P = (P_i, \ldots, P_n)$, let the *load* of edge e, $\ell(P)$ be the size of the set $\{i : e \in P_i\}$. Then the utility of the ith player is $\sum_{e \in P_i} c_e(\ell(P))$.

(vi) There is the even more succinct form of *network congestion games*, where E is the set of edges of an actual graph, and we are given two vertices for each player. The strategies available to a player are all simple paths between these two nodes.

(vii) *Local effect games.* These are generalizations of the congestion games, see Leyton-Brown and Tennenholtz 2003.

(viii) *Facility location games.* See Chapter 19.

(ix) *Multimatrix games.* Suppose that we have n players with m strategies each, and for each pair (i, j) of players an $m \times m$ utility matrix A^{ij}. The utility of player i for the strategy combination $s_1, \ldots, s_n)$ is $\sum_{j \neq i} A^{ij}_{s_i, s_j}$. That is, each player receives the total sum of his or her interactions with all other players.

2.6 The Reduction

In this section we give a brief sketch of the reduction, recently discovered in Daskalakis et al. (2006) and Goldberg and Papadimitriou (2006) and extended to two-player games in Chen and Deng (2005b), which establishes that NASH is PPAD-complete.

2.6.1 A PPAD-Complete Problem

The departure point of the reduction is BROUWER, a stylized discrete version of the Brouwer fixpoint problem. It is presented in terms of a function ϕ from the three-dimensional unit cube to itself. Imagine that the unit cube is subdivided into 2^{3n} equal cubelets, each of side $\epsilon = 2^{-n}$, and that the function need only be described at all cubelet centers. At a cubelet center x, $\phi(x)$ can take four values: $x + \delta_i, i = 0, \ldots, 3$, where the δ_is are the following tiny displacements mapping the center of the cubelet to the center of a nearby cubelet: $\delta_1 = (\epsilon, 0, 0)$ $\delta_2 = (0, \epsilon, 0)$, $\delta_3 = (0, 0, \epsilon)$, and finally $\delta_0 = (-\epsilon, -\epsilon, -\epsilon)$. If x is the center of a boundary cubelet, then we must make sure that $\phi(x)$ does not fall outside the cube – but this is easy to check. We are seeking a "fixpoint," which is defined here to be any internal cubelet corner point such that, among its eight adjacent cubelets, all four possible displacements $\delta_i, i = 0, \ldots, 3$, are present.

But how is the function ϕ represented? We assume that ϕ is given in terms of a *Boolean circuit*, a directed acyclic graph of AND, OR, and NOT gates, with $3n$ bits as inputs (enough to describe the cublet in question) and two bits as outputs (enough to specify which one of the four displacements is to be applied). This is a computationally meaningful way of representing functions that is quite common in the complexity theory literature; any function ϕ of the sort described above (including the boundary checks) can be captured by such a circuit. And this completes the description of BROUWER, our starting PPAD-complete problem: Given a Boolean circuit describing ϕ, find a fixpoint of ϕ. We omit the challenging proof that it is indeed PPAD-complete (see Daskalakis et al., 2006).

2.6.2 The Plan

But how should we go about reducing this problem to Nash? We shall start by reducing Brouwer to an intermediate graphical game with many players. All these players have just two strategies, 0 and 1; therefore, we can think of any mixed strategy of a player as a number in [0, 1] (the probability he or she assigns to strategy 1). Three of these players will be thought of as choosing three numbers that are the coordinates of a point in the cube. Others will respond by analyzing these coordinates to identify the cubelet wherein this point lies, and by computing (by a simulation of the circuit) the displacements δ_i at the cubelet and adjacent cubelets. The resulting choices by the players will incentivize the three original players to change their mixed strategy – *unless the point is a fixpoint of* ϕ, in which case the three players will not change strategies, and the graphical game will be at a Nash equilibrium!

2.6.3 The Gadgets

To carry out this plan, we need certain devices – commonly called "gadgets" in the reduction business – for performing basic arithmetic and logical operations. That is, we need to define certain small graphical games with players that are considered as inputs and another player as output, such that in any Nash equilibrium the mixed strategy of the output player (thought of as a real number between 0 and 1) stands in a particular arithmetical or logical relation with the inputs (again, thought of as numbers).

Consider, for example, the *multiplication game*. It has four players, two input players a and b, an output player c, and a middle player d. The underlying directed graph has edges $(a, d), (b, d), (c, d), (d, c)$; i.e., one of these four players affects the utility of another if and only if there is an edge in this list from the former to the latter. The players have two strategies each, called 0 and 1, so that any mixed strategy profile for a player is in fact a real number in [0, 1] (the probability with which the player plays strategy 1). The utilities are so constructed that in any Nash equilibrium of this game, the output is always the product of the two inputs – all seen as numbers, of course: $c = a \cdot b$ (here we use a to represent not just player a, but also its value, i.e., the probability with which he plays strategy 1). To specify the game, we need to describe the utilities of the output and middle player (the utilities of the inputs are irrelevant since they have no incoming edges; this is crucial, because it allows the inputs to be "reused" in many gadgets, without one use influencing the others). If the middle player d plays 1 (recall that all nodes have two strategies, 1 and 0), then its utility is 1 if both inputs play 1, and it is 0 zero otherwise. Thus, if the two input players play 1 with probabilities a and b (recall that these are the "values" of the two inputs), and the middle player plays 1, then his utility is exactly $a \cdot b$. If on the other hand the middle player plays 0, then its utility is 1 if the output player plays 1, and it is 0 otherwise. Finally, the output player gets utility 1 if the middle player plays 1, and -1 if he plays 0.

Thus, the output player is motivated to play 1 with probability c, which is as high as possible, in order to maximize the utility from the middle player's playing 1 – but not so high that the middle player is tempted to play 0, as he would whenever $c > a \cdot b$. Thus, at equilibrium, c must be exactly $a \cdot b$, and the multiplication gadget works!

In a similar manner we can construct gadgets that add and subtract their inputs (always within the range $[0, 1]$, of course), or perform certain logical operations. For example, it is a trivial exercise to design a gadget with two nodes, an input x and an output y, such that $y = 1$ if $x > \frac{1}{2}$ and $y = 0$ if $x < \frac{1}{2}$ (notice that, importantly, the output of this comparator is undetermined is $x = \frac{1}{2}$). It is also easy to design gadgets that perform AND, OR, and NOT operations on their inputs (the inputs here are assumed to be *Boolean*, that is to say, pure strategies).

2.6.4 The Graphical Game

Using these devices, we can put together a graphical game whose Nash equilibria reflect accurately the Brouwer fixpoints of the given function ϕ.

The graphical game is huge, but has a simple structure: There are three players, called the *leaders*, whose mixed strategies identify a point (x, y, z) in the unit cube. These leaders are inputs to a series of comparators and subtractors which extract one by one the n most significant bits of the binary representation of x, y, and z, thus identifying the cubelet within which the point (x, y, z) lies. A system of logical gadgets could then compute the outputs of the given circuit that describes ϕ, when the inputs are the $3n$ extracted bits, repeat for the neighboring cubelets, and decide whether we are at a fixpoint.

But there is a catch: As we pointed out above, our comparators are "brittle" in that they are indeterminate when their input is exactly half. This is of necessity: It can be shown (see Daskalakis et al., 2006) that nonbrittle comparators (ones that behave deterministically at half) cannot exist! (It turns out that, with such comparators, we could construct a graphical game with no Nash equilibrium ...) This has the effect that the computation described above is imprecise (and, in fact, in an unpredictable manner) when the point (x, y, z) lies exactly on the boundary of a cubelet, and this can create spurious equilibria. We must somehow "smoothen" this discontinuity.

This is accomplished by a more complicated construction, in which the calculation of ϕ is carried out not for the single point (x, y, z) but for a large and very fine grid of points around it, with all results averaged.

Once the average displacement $(\Delta x, \Delta y, \Delta z)$ near (x, y, z) has been calculated, its components are added to the three leaders, completing the construction of the graphical game. This way the loop is closed, and the leaders (who had heretofore no incoming edges) are finally affected – very indirectly, of course – by their own choices. We must now prove that the Nash equilibria of this game correspond precisely to those points in the unit cube for which the average displacement is the zero vector. And from this, establish that the average displacement is zero if and only if we are near a fixpoint.

2.6.5 Simulating the Graphical Game by Few Players

We have already established an interesting result: Finding a Nash equilibrium in a graphical game is PPAD-complete. It is even more interesting because the underlying directed graph of the game, despite its size and complexity, has a rather simple structure: It is *bipartite*, and all vertices have indegree *three* or less. It is bipartite because all gadgets are bipartite (the inputs and the outputs are on one side, the middle nodes on the other; the logical gadgets can be redesigned to have a middle node as well); and the way the gadgets are put together maintains the bipartite property. Finally, the middle nodes of the gadget are the ones of maximum indegree – three.

The challenge now is to simulate this graphical game by one with finitely many players. Already in Goldberg and Papadimitriou (2006) and Daskalakis et al. (2006), a simulation by four players was shown, establishing that Nash is PPAD-complete even in the four-player case. The idea in the simulation is this: Each of the four players "represents" many nodes of the graphical game. How players are represented is best understood in terms of a particular undirected graph associated with the graphical game, called the *conflict graph*. This graph is defined on the vertices of the graphical game, and has an edge between two nodes u and v if in the graphical game either (a) there is an edge between u and v, in either direction, or (b) there are edges from both u and v to the same node w. This is the *conflict graph* of the game; it should be intuitively clear that eventualities (a) and (b) make it difficult for the same player to represent both u and v, and so coloring the conflict graph and assigning its color classes to different players makes sense. The crucial observation is that *the conflict graph of the graphical game constructed in the reduction is four-colorable.*

So, we can assign to each of four players (think of them as "lawyers") all nodes (call them "clients") in a color class. A lawyer's strategy set if the union of the strategy sets of his clients, and so the clients can be represented fairly if the lawyer plays the average of their mixed strategies. Since the clients come from a color class of the conflict graph, the lawyer can represent them all with no conflict of interest (he or she should not represent two players that play against one another, or two players who both play against a third one). But there is a problem: A lawyer may neglect some clients with small payoffs and favor (in terms of weights in his mixed strategy) the more lucrative ones. This is taken care of by having the four lawyers play, on the side, a generalization of the "rock-paper-scissors game," at very high stakes. Since this game is known to force the players to distribute their probabilities evenly, all clients will now be represented fairly in the lawyer's mixed strategy; the four-player simulation is complete.

These results, up to the four player simulation, first appeared in the beginning of October 2005 (Goldberg and Papadimitriou, 2006; Daskalakis et al., 2006). It was conjectured in Daskalakis et al. (2006) that the 3-player case of Nash is also PPAD-complete, whereas the 2-player case is in P. Indeed, a few weeks later, two independent and very different simulations of the graphical game by *three* players appeared (Chen and Deng, 2005b; Daskalakis and Papadimitriou, 2005) thus proving the first part of this conjecture. The proof in Daskalakis and Papadimitriou (2005) was local, and worked by modifying the gadgets so that the conflict graph became three-colorable; this approach had therefore reached its limit, because for the graphical game to work the conflict graph must contain triangles. It was again conjectured in Daskalakis and Papadimitriou (2005) that the two-player case can be solved in polynomial time. In contrast, the proof in Chen and Deng (2005b) was more ad hoc and nonlocal, and was therefore in a sense more open-ended and promising.

A month later, a surprisingly simple two-player simulation was discovered (Chen and Deng, 2005a), thus establishing that even the two-player case of Nash is PPAD-complete! The intuitive idea behind this new construction is that many of the "conflicts of interest" captured in the conflict graph (in particular, the (b) case of its definition) happen to be unproblematic in this particular game: The two input nodes of a gadget cannot effectively "conspire" to improve their lot – and thus they could, in principle, be represented by the same (carefully programmed) lawyer. Thus, only two players are needed, corresponding to the two sides of the bipartite graphical game. The construction is now in fact a little more direct: there is no graph game, and the two players are constructed ab initio, with the gadgets, as well as the side game of rock–paper–scissors, built in.

2.6.6 Approximate Equilibria

Incidentally, this side game of rock–paper–scissors is the source of another difficulty that permeates all these proofs, and which we have not yet discussed: It only guarantees that the lawyers *approximately* balance the interests of their clients; as a result, the whole reduction, and the argument at each stage of the construction, must be carried out in terms of *ϵ-approximate Nash equilibria.* An ϵ-approximate Nash equilibrium is a mixed strategy profile such that no other strategy can improve the payoff *by more than an additive* ϵ. (Notice that an ϵ-approximate Nash equilibrium may or may not be near a true Nash equilibrium.) It is easy to see, in retrospect, that this use of approximation is inherently needed: Two-player games always have rational Nash equilibria, whereas games with more players may have only irrational ones. Any simulation of the latter by the former must involve some kind of approximation.

Now that we know that computing Nash equilibria is an intractable problem, computing approximate equilibria emerges as a very attractive compromise. But can it be done in polynomial time? The reduction described so far shows that it is PPAD-complete to compute ϵ-approximate Nash equilibria when ϵ is exponentially small (smaller than the side of the cubelet in the initial Brouwer problem, or 2^{-cn} for some $c > 0$, where n is the number of strategies). Starting from an n-dimensional version of Brouwer, the result can be strengthened up to an ϵ that is an inverse polynomial, (n^{-c}) (Chen et al., 2006).

There are some positive algorithmic results known for approximate Nash equilibria: $\frac{1}{2}$-approximate Nash equilibria are very easy to compute in two-player games (Daskalakis et al., in press) and an ϵ-approximate Nash equilibrium can be found in less than exponential time (more specifically, in time $n^{\frac{\log n}{\epsilon^2}}$) in arbitrary games (see Lipton et al., 2003). Discovering polynomial algorithms for computing ϵ-approximate Nash equilibria for ϵ between these values – possibly for arbitrarily small constant $\epsilon > 0$ – remains an important open problem.

2.7 Correlated Equilibria

Consider the symmetric game (often called *chicken*) with payoffs

$$\begin{pmatrix} 4 & 1 \\ 5 & 0 \end{pmatrix}$$

The payoffs are supposed to capture the situation in which two very macho drivers speed toward an intersection. Each has two options: Stop or go. There are two pure equilibria (me and you) and the symmetric mixed equilibrium (1/2, 1/2). These three Nash equilibria create the following three probability distributions on the pure strategy profiles: $\begin{pmatrix} 0 & 1 \\ 0 & 0 \end{pmatrix} \begin{pmatrix} 0 & 0 \\ 1 & 0 \end{pmatrix} \begin{pmatrix} \frac{1}{4} & \frac{1}{4} \\ \frac{1}{4} & \frac{1}{4} \end{pmatrix}$

Consider however the following distribution: $\begin{pmatrix} 0 & \frac{1}{2} \\ \frac{1}{2} & 0 \end{pmatrix}$. It is not a Nash equilibrium; in fact, it is easy to see that there are no two mixed strategies for the two players that generate this distribution (in algebraic terms, the matrix is not of rank one). However, it *is* a rational outcome of the game, in the following more sophisticated sense: Suppose that a trusted third party draws from this distribution, and recommends to each player to play according to the outcome. (Coming back to the drivers story, this solution, randomizing between (stop, go) and (go, stop) is tantamount to a traffic signal.) If the lower left box is chosen, e.g., the recommendation is that Player 1 go and Player 2 stop (i.e., green light for Player 1). What is remarkable about this distribution of recommendations is that it is *self-enforcing*: If either player assumes that the other will follow the recommendation, his best bet is to actually follow the recommendation!

This motivates the following definition (Aumann, 1974): A *correlated equilibrium* is a probability distribution $\{p_s\}$ on the space of strategy profiles that obeys the following conditions: For each player i, and every two different strategies j, j' of i, conditioned on the event that a strategy profile with j as is strategy was drawn from the distribution, the expected utility of playing j is no smaller than that of playing j':

$$\sum_{s \in S_{-i}} (u_{sj} - u_{sj'}) p_{sj} \geq 0. \qquad (CE)$$

(Naturally, we also require that $p_s \geq 0$ and $\sum_s p_s = 1$.) Here by S_{-i} we denote the strategy profiles of all players except for i; if $s \in S_{-i}$, sj denotes the strategy profile in which player i plays j and the others play s. Notice that the inequalities express exactly the requirement that, if a strategy profile is drawn from the distribution $\{p_s\}$ and each player is told, privately, his or her own component of the outcome, and if furthermore all players assume that the others will follow the recommendation, then the recommendation is self-enforcing.

Notice also the following: If $p^i, i = 1, \ldots, n$, is a set of mixed strategies of the players, and we consider the distribution p_s induced by it ($p_s = \prod_i p^i_{s_i}$) then the inequalities (CE) state that *these mixed strategies constitute a mixed Nash equilibrium!* Indeed, for each i, j, j', equation (CE) states in this case that, if j is in i's support, then it is a best response. (If strategy j is not in the support, then the inequality becomes a tautology, $0 \geq 0$; if it is in the support, then we can divide by its probability the whole inequality, and the resulting inequality says that j is best response.) We conclude that any Nash equilibrium is a correlated equilibrium. In other words, the correlated equilibrium is a generalization of the Nash equilibrium, allowing the probabilities on the space of strategy profiles to be correlated arbitrarily. Conversely, Nash equilibrium is the special case of correlated equilibrium in which p_s's are restricted to come from a product (uncorrelated) distribution.

For example, in the drivers game, the (CE) inequalities are as follows:

$$(4-5)p_{11}+(1-0)p_{12}\geq 0$$
$$(5-4)p_{21}+(0-1)p_{22}\geq 0$$
$$(4-5)p_{11}+(1-0)p_{21}\geq 0$$
$$(5-4)p_{12}+(0-1)p_{22}\geq 0$$

A crucial observation now is that the (CE) inequalities are *linear* in the unknown variables $\{p_s\}$, and thus the system (CE) can always be solved efficiently by linear programming. In fact, we know that these inequalities always have at least one a solution: The Nash equilibrium that is guaranteed to exist by Nash's theorem.

To restate the situation in terms of our concerns in this chapter, *the correlated equilibrium is a computationally benign generalization of the intractable* NASH *equilibrium.* We can find in polynomial time a correlated equilibrium for any game. In fact, we can find the correlated equilibrium that optimizes any linear function of the $\{p_s\}$'s, such as the expected sum of utilities. For example, in the drivers game, we can optimize the sum of the players' expected utilities by maximizing the linear objective $8p_{11}+6p_{12}+6p_{21}$ over the polytope defined by the inequalities above. The optimum correlated equilibrium is this: $\begin{pmatrix}\frac{1}{3} & \frac{1}{3}\\ \frac{1}{3} & 0\end{pmatrix}$ – a traffic light that is red for both one third of the time.

2.7.1 Correlated Equilibria *vs* Nash Equilibria: The Whole Picture

The polytope defined by the (CE) inequalities in the case of the drivers game is shown in Figure 2.4 (the fourth dimension, $p_{22}=1-p_{11}-p_{12}-p_{21}$, is suppressed in the geometric depiction). Every point in this polytope is a correlated equilibrium. There are two pure Nash equilibria (N1 and N2) and one symmetric mied one (N3). The "traffic light" correlated equilibrium C1 $=\begin{pmatrix}0 & \frac{1}{2}\\ \frac{1}{2} & 0\end{pmatrix}$ and the optimum one C2 $=\begin{pmatrix}\frac{1}{3} & \frac{1}{3}\\ \frac{1}{3} & 0\end{pmatrix}$ are also shown. *Notice that the three Nash equilibria are vertices of the polytope.* This is no coincidence.

Theorem 2.5 *In any nondegenerate two-player game, the Nash equilibria are vertices of the (CE) polytope.*

Naturally, not all vertices of the (CE) polytope will be Nash equilibria, but at least one will be. In other words, in two-player games every Nash equilibrium is the optimum correlated equilibrium for some linear function – unfortunately, guessing this function is apparently not easy.

To recapitulate, Nash equilibria are correlated equilibria satisfying the further constraint that they are the product distribution of some pair of mixed strategies. It is this single additional constraint that makes the problem of finding a Nash equilibrium so much harder. It is apparently a very nonconvex constraint (think of it as a curved surface in Figure 2.4, "touching" the (CE) polytope at three of its vertices). In contrast, for three or more players there are games in which the NASH equilibria are not vertices

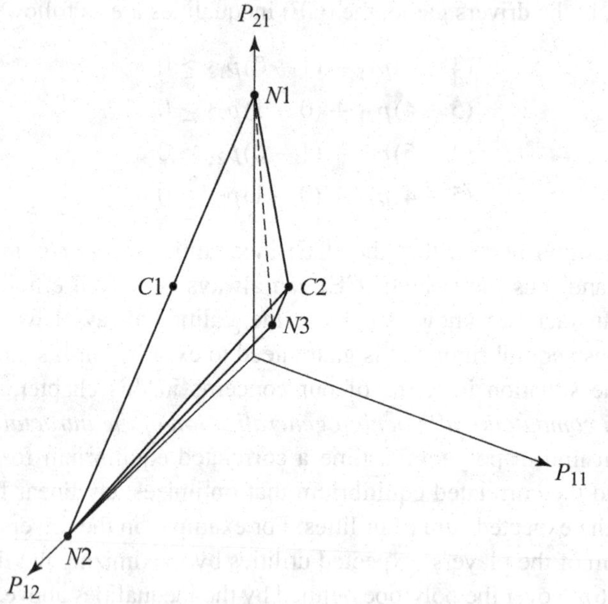

Figure 2.4. The three Nash equilibria (N1, N2, N3) of the drivers' game are vertices of the polytope of the correlated equilibria. Two other correlated equilibra are shown (C1, C2).

of the (CE) polytope; e.g., it is easy to see that any game with integer utilities that has only irrational Nash equilibria must be of this sort.

2.7.2 Correlated Equilibria in Succinct Games

But as we observed in Section 2.5, polynomial-time algorithms whose input is a game, such as the linear programming algorithm for finding correlated equilibria, make a mockery of complexity theory when the number of players is reasonably high. This brings us to the following important question: Can we find correlated equilibria efficiently when the game is represented succinctly?

There are some very interesting – and very natural – "learning" algorithms for *approximating* correlated equilibria, reviewed in Chapter 4 of this book. These algorithms work by simulating repeated play of the game, in which the various players change their strategies according to how much they "regret" previous decisions. Certain sophisticated ways of doing this are guaranteed to reach a point that is quite close to the (CE) polytope. To arrive at a distance ϵ, from the (CE) polytope, $\frac{1}{\epsilon^c}$ iterations are required, where c is some small constant depending on the particular method. But the question remains, can we find a point of the (CE) polytope in polynomial time?

Recently, there have been some interesting results on this question; to state them we need to introduce some definitions. We say that a succinctly representable game is *of polynomial type* if the number of players, as well as the number of strategies of each player, in a game represented by a string of length n is always bounded by a polynomial in n. For such a game, the *expected utility problem* is this: Calculate the expected utility of each player, if for each player i the given mixed strategy p^i played. It turns out that solving this problem is enough for the correlated equilibrium problem to be solved:

> **Theorem 2.6 (Papadimitriou, 2005)** *In any succinctly representable game of polynomial type for which the expected utility problem can be solved in polynomial time, the problem of finding a correlated equilibrium can be solved in polynomial time as well. Consequently, there is a polynomial-time algorithm (polynomial in the length of the description of the game) for finding a correlated equilibrium in sparse, symmetric, anonymous, graphical, congestion, local effect, facility location, and multimatrix games (among many others, recall the definitions in Section 2.5).*

But how about the slightly more demanding problem of finding, not just any correlated equilibrium, but the one that optimizes a given linear objective of the probabilities? A much less sweeping result is available here.

> **Theorem 2.7 (Papadimitriou and Roughgarden, 2005)** *The problem of optimizing a linear function over correlated equilibria can be solved in polynomial time for symmetric games, anonymous games, and graphical games for which the underlying graph is of bounded treewidth.*

In contrast, it is NP-hard to find the optimum-correlated equilibrium in general graphical games and congestion games, among others (Papadimitriou and Roughgarden, 2005).

2.8 Concluding Remarks

The computational complexity of equilibrium concepts deserves a central place in game theoretic discourse. The proof, outlined in this chapter, that finding a mixed Nash equilibrium is PPAD-complete raises some interesting questions regarding the usefulness of the Nash equilibrium, and helps focus our interest in alternative notions (most interesting among them the approximate Nash equilibrium discussed in the end of Section 2.6).

But there are many counterarguments to the importance of such a negative complexity result. It only shows that it is hard to find a Nash equilibrium in some very far-fetched, artificial games that happen to encode Brouwer functions. Of what relevance can such a result be to economic practice?

The same can be said (and has been said, in the early days) about the NP-completeness of the traveling salesman problem, for example. And the answer remains the same: The PPAD-completeness of NASH suggests that any approach to finding Nash equibria that aspires to be efficient, as well as any proposal for using the concept in an applied setting, should explicitly take advantage of computationally beneficial special properties of the games in hand, by proving positive algorithmic results for interesting classes of games. On the other hand (as has often been the case with NP-completeness, and as it has started to happen here as well; Abbott et al., 2005; Codenotti et al., 2006), PPAD-completeness proofs will be eventually refined to cover simpler and more realistic-looking classes of games. And then researchers will strive to identify even simpler classes.

An intractability result such as the one outlined in this chapter should be most usefully seen as the opening move in an interesting game.

Acknowledgment

Many thanks to Bernhard von Stengel for several useful suggestions.

Bibliography

T. Abbott, D. Kane, and P. Valiant. On the complexity of two-player win-lose games. *Proc. 2005 FOCS*.

R.J. Aumann. Subjectivity and correlation in randomized strategies. *J. Math. Econ.*, 1:67–96, 1974.

P. Beame, S. Cook, J. Edmonds, R. Impagliazzo, and T. Pitassi. The relative complexity of NP search problems. *J. Comput. Syst. Sci.*, 57(1):13–19, 1998.

X. Chen and X. Deng. 3-NASH is PPAD-Complete. *Electronic Colloquium on Computational Complexity*, 134, 2005a.

X. Chen and X. Deng. Settling the complexity of 2-player Nash-equilibrium. *Electronic Colloquium on Computational Complexity*, 134, 2005b; *Fdns. Comp.* 2006, to appear.

X. Chen, X. Deng, and S. Teng. Computing Nash equilibria: Aprroximation and smoothed complexity. FOCS 2006, pp. 603–612, 2006.

B. Codenotti, M. Leoncini, and G. Resta. Efficient computation of Nash equilibria for very sparse win-lose games. *Electronic Colloquium on Computational Complexity*, 12, 2006.

V. Conitzer and T. Sandholm. Complexity results about Nash equilibria. In: *Proc. 18th Int. Joint Conf. Artificial Intelligence*, pp. 765–771, 2003.

C. Daskalakis, P.W. Goldberg, and C.H. Papadimitriou. The complexity of computing a Nash equilibrium. *Symp. on Theory of Computing*, 2006, pp. 71–78.

C. Daskalakis, A. Mehta, and C.H. Papadimitriou. A note on approximate Nash equilibria. In: *Proc. 2006 Workshop on Internet Network Economics*, in press.

C. Daskalakis and C.H. Papadimitriou. Three-player Games are Hard. *Electronic Colloquium on Computational Complexity*, 139, 2005.

F.S. Evangelista and T.E.S. Raghavan. A note on correlated equilibrium. *Intl. J. Game Theory*, 25(1):35–41, 2005.

D. Gale, H.W. Kuhn, and A.W. Tucker. On symmetric games. In: H.W. Kuhn and A.W. Tucker, editors, *Contributions to the Theory Games,* 1:81–87. Princeton University Press, 1950.

M.R. Garey and D.S. Johnson. *Computers and Intractability: A Guide to the Theory of NP-Completeness*, Freeman, 1979.

I. Gilboa and E. Zemel. Nash and correlated equilibria: Some complexity considerations. *Games Econ. Behav.*, 1989.

P.W. Goldberg and C.H. Papadimitriou. Reducibility between equilibrium problems. *Symp. on Theory of Computing*, 2006, pp. 62–70.

S. Hart and D. Schmeidler. Existence of correlated equilibria. *Math. Operat. Res.,* 14(1):18–25, 1989.

M. Hirsch, C.H. Papadimitriou, and S. Vavasis. Exponential lower bounds for finding brouwer fixpoints. *J. Complexity*, 5:379–416, 1989.

D.S. Johnson, C.H. Papadimitriou, and M. Yannakakis. How easy is local search? *J. Comput. Syst. Sci.*, 37(1):79–100, 1988.

M. Kearns, M. Littman, and S. Singh. Graphical models for game theory. In: *Proc. Conf. on Uncertainty in Artificial Intelligence*, 2001, pp. 253–260.

K. Leyton-Brown and M. Tennenholtz. Local-effect games. *Intl. Joint Conf. Artificial Intelligence*, 2003, pp. 772–780.

R.J. Lipton, E. Markakis, and A. Mehta. Playing large games using simple strategies. *ACM Electronic Commerce*, 2003, pp. 36–41.

J. Nash. Noncooperative games. *Ann. Math.*, 54:289–295, 1951.

C.H. Papadimitriou. On the complexity of the parity argument and other inefficient proofs of existence. *J. Comput. Syst. Sci.*, 48(3):498–532, 1994.

C.H. Papadimitriou. Computing correlated equilibria in multi-player games. *Symp. on Theory of Computing*, 2005, pp. 49–56.

C.H. Papadimitriou and T. Roughgarden. Computing equilibria in multi-player games. *Symp. on Discrete Algorithms*, 2005, pp. 82–91.

R. Savani and B. von Stengel. Exponentially many steps for finding a Nash equilibrium in a Bimatrix Game. *Proc. of 45th Fdns. on Comp. Science*, pp. 258–267, 2004.

B. von Stengel. Computing equilibria for two-person games. *Handbook of Game Theory with Economic Applications*, Vol. 3, R. J. Aumann and S. Hart, eds. Elsevier, Amsterdam, pp. 1723–1759, 2002.

CHAPTER 3

Equilibrium Computation for Two-Player Games in Strategic and Extensive Form

Bernhard von Stengel

Abstract

We explain algorithms for computing Nash equilibria of two-player games given in strategic form or extensive form. The strategic form is a table that lists the players' strategies and resulting payoffs. The "best response" condition states that in equilibrium, all pure strategies in the support of a mixed strategy must get maximal, and hence equal, payoff. The resulting equations and inequalities define polytopes, whose "completely labeled" vertex pairs are the Nash equilibria of the game. The Lemke–Howson algorithm follows a path of edges of the polytope pair that leads to one equilibrium. Extensive games are game trees, with information sets that model imperfect information of the players. Strategies in an extensive game are combinations of moves, so the strategic form has exponential size. In contrast, the linear-sized sequence form of the extensive game describes sequences of moves and how to randomize between them.

3.1 Introduction

A basic model in noncooperative game theory is the *strategic form* that defines a game by a set of strategies for each player and a payoff to each player for any strategy profile (which is a combination of strategies, one for each player). The central solution concept for such games is the *Nash equilibrium*, a strategy profile where each strategy is a *best response* to the fixed strategies of the other players. In general, equilibria exist only in *mixed* (randomized) strategies, with probabilities that fulfill certain equations and inequalities. Solving these constraints is an algorithmic problem. Its computational complexity is discussed in Chapter 2.

In this chapter, we describe methods for finding equilibria in sufficient detail to show how they could be implemented. We restrict ourselves to games with *two players*. These can be studied using *polyhedra*, because a player's expected payoffs are linear in the mixed strategy probabilities of the other player. Nash equilibria of games with more than two players involve expected payoffs that are products of the other players' probabilities. The resulting polynomial equations and inequalities require different approaches.

For games in strategic form, we give the basic "best response condition" (Prop. 3.1, see Section 3.2), explain the use of polyhedra (Section 3.3), and describe the Lemke–Howson algorithm that finds one Nash equilibrium (Section 3.4). An implementation without numerical errors uses integer pivoting (Section 3.5). "Generic" games (i.e., "almost all" games with real payoffs) are nondegenerate (see Definition 3.2); degenerate games are considered in Section 3.5.

An *extensive* game (defined in Section 3.7) is a fundamental model of dynamic interactions. A game tree models in detail the moves available to the players and their information over time. The nodes of the tree represent game states. An *information set* is a set of states in which a player has the same moves, and does not know which state he is in. A player's strategy in an extensive game specifies a move for each information set, so a player may have exponentially many strategies. This complexity can be reduced: *Subgames* (see Section 3.8) are subtrees so that all players know they are in the subgame. Finding equilibria inductively for subgames leads to *subgame perfect* equilibria, but this reduces the complexity only if players are sufficiently often (e.g., always) informed about the game state. The *reduced* strategic form applies to general games (see Section 3.9), but may still be exponential. A player has *perfect recall* if his information sets reflect that he remembers his earlier moves. Players can then randomize locally with *behavior strategies*. This classic theorem (Corollary 3.12) is turned into an algorithm with the *sequence form* (Sections 3.10 and 3.11) which is a strategic description that has the same size as the game tree.

We give in this chapter an exposition of the main ideas, not of all earliest or latest developments of the subject. Section 3.12 summarizes the main references. Further research is outlined in Section 3.13.

3.2 Bimatrix Games and the Best Response Condition

We use the following notation throughout. Let (A, B) be a bimatrix game, where A and B are $m \times n$ matrices of payoffs to the row player 1 and column player 2, respectively. This is a two-player game in strategic form (also called "normal form"), which is played by a simultaneous choice of a row i by player 1 and column j by player 2, who then receive payoff a_{ij} and b_{ij}, respectively. The payoffs represent risk-neutral utilities, so when facing a probability distribution, the players want to maximize their expected payoff. These preferences do not depend on positive-affine transformations, so that A and B can be assumed to have nonnegative entries, which are rationals, or more simply integers, when A and B define the input to an algorithm.

All vectors are column vectors, so an m-vector x is treated as an $m \times 1$ matrix. A *mixed strategy* x for player 1 is a probability distribution on rows, written as an m-vector of probabilities. Similarly, a mixed strategy y for player 2 is an n-vector of probabilities for playing columns. The *support* of a mixed strategy is the set of pure strategies that have positive probability. A vector or matrix with all components zero is denoted by $\mathbf{0}$, a vector of all ones by $\mathbf{1}$. Inequalities like $x \geq \mathbf{0}$ between two vectors hold for all components. $B^\top$ is the matrix B transposed.

Let M be the set of the m pure strategies of player 1 and let N be the set of the n pure strategies of player 2. It is useful to assume that these sets are disjoint, as in

$$M = \{1, \ldots, m\}, \qquad N = \{m + 1, \ldots, m + n\}. \tag{3.1}$$

Then $x \in \mathbb{R}^M$ and $y \in \mathbb{R}^N$, which means, in particular, that the components of y are y_j for $j \in N$. Similarly, the payoff matrices A and B belong to $\mathbb{R}^{M\times N}$.

A *best response* to the mixed strategy y of player 2 is a mixed strategy x of player 1 that maximizes his expected payoff $x^\top Ay$. Similarly, a best response y of player 2 to x maximizes her expected payoff $x^\top By$. A *Nash equilibrium* is a pair (x, y) of mixed strategies that are best responses to each other. The following proposition states that a mixed strategy x is a best response to an opponent strategy y if and only if all pure strategies in its support are pure best responses to y. The same holds with the roles of the players exchanged.

Proposition 3.1 (Best response condition) *Let x and y be mixed strategies of player 1 and 2, respectively. Then x is a best response to y if and only if for all $i \in M$,*

$$x_i > 0 \implies (Ay)_i = u = \max\{\, (Ay)_k \mid k \in M\}. \tag{3.2}$$

PROOF $(Ay)_i$ is the ith component of Ay, which is the expected payoff to player 1 when playing row i. Then

$$x^\top Ay = \sum_{i\in M} x_i\,(Ay)_i = \sum_{i\in M} x_i\,(u - (u - (Ay)_i)) = u - \sum_{i\in M} x_i\,(u - (Ay)_i).$$

So $x^\top Ay \le u$ because $x_i \ge 0$ and $u - (Ay)_i \ge 0$ for all $i \in M$, and $x^\top Ay = u$ if and only if $x_i > 0$ implies $(Ay)_i = u$, as claimed. □

Proposition 3.1 has the following intuition: Player 1's payoff $x^\top Ay$ is linear in x, so if it is maximized on a face of the simplex of mixed strategies of player 1, then it is also maximized on any vertex (i.e., pure strategy) of that face, and if it is maximized on a set of vertices then it is also maximized on any convex combination of them. The proposition is useful because it states a finite condition, which is easily checked, about all pure strategies of the player, rather than about the infinite set of all mixed strategies. It can also be used algorithmically to find Nash equilibria, by trying out the different possible supports of mixed strategies. All pure strategies in the support must have maximum, and hence equal, expected payoff to that player. This leads to equations for the probabilities of the opponent's mixed strategy.

As an example, consider the 3×2 bimatrix game (A, B) with

$$A = \begin{bmatrix} 3 & 3 \\ 2 & 5 \\ 0 & 6 \end{bmatrix}, \qquad B = \begin{bmatrix} 3 & 2 \\ 2 & 6 \\ 3 & 1 \end{bmatrix}. \tag{3.3}$$

This game has only one pure-strategy Nash equilibrium, namely the top row (numbered 1 in the pure strategy set $M = \{1, 2, 3\}$ of player 1), together with the left column (which by (3.1) has number 4 in the pure strategy set $N = \{4, 5\}$ of player 2). A pure strategy equilibrium is given by mixed strategies of support size 1 each, so here it is the mixed strategy pair $((1, 0, 0)^\top, (1, 0)^\top)$.

The game in (3.3) has also some mixed equilibria. Any pure strategy of a player has a unique pure best response of the other player, so in any other equilibrium, each player must mix at least two pure strategies to fulfill condition (3.2). In particular, player 2 must be indifferent between her two columns. If the support of player 1's mixed strategy x is $\{1, 2\}$, then player 1 can make player 2 indifferent by $x_1 = 4/5$, $x_2 = 1/5$, which is the unique solution to the equations $x_1 + x_2 = 1$ and (for the two columns of B) $3x_1 + 2x_2 = 2x_1 + 6x_2$. In turn, (3.2) requires that player 2 plays with probabilities y_4 and y_5 so that player 1 is indifferent between rows 1 and 2, i.e., $3y_4 + 3y_5 = 2y_4 + 5y_5$ or $(y_4, y_5) = (2/3, 1/3)$. The vector of expected payoffs to player 1 is then $Ay = (3, 3, 2)^\top$ so that (3.2) holds.

A second mixed equilibrium is $(x, y) = ((0, 1/3, 2/3)^\top, (1/3, 2/3)^\top)$ with expected payoff vectors $x^\top B = (8/3, 8/3)$ and $Ay = (3, 4, 4)^\top$. Again, the support of x contains only pure strategies i where the corresponding expected payoff $(Ay)_i$ is maximal.

A third support pair, $\{1, 3\}$, for player 1, does not lead to an equilibrium, for two reasons. First, player 2 would have to play $y = (1/2, 1/2)^\top$ to make player 1 indifferent between row 1 and row 3. But then $Ay = (3, 7/2, 3)^\top$, so that rows 1 and 3 give the same payoff to player 1 but not the maximum payoff for all rows. Secondly, making player 2 indifferent via $3x_1 + 3x_3 = 2x_1 + x_3$ has the solution $x_1 = 2$, $x_3 = -1$ in order to have $x_1 + x_3 = 1$, so x is not a vector of probabilities.

In this "support testing" method, it normally suffices to consider supports of equal size for the two players. For example, in (3.3) it is not necessary to consider a mixed strategy x of player 1 where all three pure strategies have positive probability, because player 1 would then have to be indifferent between all these. However, a mixed strategy y of player 1 is already uniquely determined by equalizing the expected payoffs for two rows, and then the payoff for the remaining row is already different. This is the typical, "nondegenerate" case, according to the following definition.

Definition 3.2 A two-player game is called *nondegenerate* if no mixed strategy of support size k has more than k pure best responses.

In a *degenerate* game, Definition 3.2 is violated, for example, if there is a pure strategy that has two pure best responses. For the moment, we consider only nondegenerate games, where the player's equilibrium strategies have equal sized support, which is immediate from Proposition 3.1:

Proposition 3.3 *In any Nash equilibrium (x, y) of a nondegenerate bimatrix game, x and y have supports of equal size.*

The "support testing" algorithm for finding equilibria of a nondegenerate bimatrix game then works as follows.

Algorithm 3.4 (Equilibria by support enumeration) *Input:* A nondegenerate bimatrix game. *Output:* All Nash equilibria of the game. *Method:* For each $k = 1, \ldots, \min\{m, n\}$ and each pair (I, J) of k-sized subsets of M and N, respectively, solve the equations $\sum_{i\in I} x_i b_{ij} = v$ for $j \in J$, $\sum_{i\in I} x_i = 1$, $\sum_{j\in J} a_{ij} y_j = u$, for $i \in I$, $\sum_{j\in J} y_j = 1$, and check that $x \geq \mathbf{0}$, $y \geq \mathbf{0}$, and that (3.2) holds for x and analogously y.

The linear equations considered in this algorithm may not have solutions, which then mean no equilibrium for that support pair. Nonunique solutions occur only for degenerate games, because a linear dependency allows to reduce the support of a mixed strategy. Degenerate games are discussed in Section 3.6 below.

3.3 Equilibria via Labeled Polytopes

To identify the possible supports of equilibrium strategies, one can use "best response polytopes" that express directly the inequalities of best responses and nonnegative probabilities.

We first recall some notions from the theory of (convex) polyhedra. An *affine combination* of points $z_1, \ldots, z_k$ in some Euclidean space is of the form $\sum_{i=1}^k z_i \lambda_i$, where $\lambda_1, \ldots, \lambda_k$ are reals with $\sum_{i=1}^k \lambda_i = 1$. It is called a *convex combination* if $\lambda_i \geq 0$ for all i. A set of points is *convex* if it is closed under forming convex combinations. Given points are *affinely independent* if none of these points are an affine combination of the others. A convex set has *dimension d* if and only if it has $d + 1$, but no more, affinely independent points.

A *polyhedron* P in $\mathbb{R}^d$ is a set $\{z \in \mathbb{R}^d \mid Cz \leq q\}$ for some matrix C and vector q. It is called *full-dimensional* if it has dimension d. It is called a *polytope* if it is bounded. A *face* of P is a set $\{ z \in P \mid c^\top z = q_0\}$ for some $c \in \mathbb{R}^d$, $q_0 \in \mathbb{R}$ so that the inequality $c^\top z \leq q_0$ holds for all z in P. A *vertex* of P is the unique element of a zero-dimensional face of P. An *edge* of P is a one-dimensional face of P. A *facet* of a d-dimensional polyhedron P is a face of dimension $d - 1$. It can be shown that any nonempty face F of P can be obtained by turning some of the inequalities defining P into equalities, which are then called *binding* inequalities. That is, $F = \{z \in P \mid c_i z = q_i,\ i \in I\}$, where $c_i z \leq q_i$ for $i \in I$ are some of the rows in $Cz \leq q$. A facet is characterized by a single binding inequality which is *irredundant*; i.e., the inequality cannot be omitted without changing the polyhedron. A d-dimensional polyhedron P is called *simple* if no point belongs to more than d facets of P, which is true if there are no special dependencies between the facet-defining inequalities.

The "best response polyhedron" of a player is the set of that player's mixed strategies together with the "upper envelope" of expected payoffs (and any larger payoffs) to the *other* player. For player 2 in the example (3.3), it is the set $\overline{Q}$ of triples (y_4, y_5, u) that fulfill $3y_4 + 3y_5 \leq u, 2y_4 + 5y_5 \leq u, 0y_4 + 6y_5 \leq u, y_4 \geq 0, y_5 \geq 0$, and $y_4 + y_5 = 1$. The first three inequalities, in matrix notation $Ay \leq \mathbf{1}u$, say that u is at least as large as the expected payoff for each pure strategy of player 1. The other constraints $y \geq \mathbf{0}$ and $\mathbf{1}^\top y = 1$ state that y is a vector of probabilities. The best response polyhedron $\overline{P}$ for player 1 is defined analogously. Generally,

$$\begin{aligned} \overline{P} &= \{(x, v) \in \mathbb{R}^M \times \mathbb{R} \mid x \geq \mathbf{0},\ \mathbf{1}^\top x = 1,\ B^\top x \leq \mathbf{1}v\}, \\ \overline{Q} &= \{(y, u) \in \mathbb{R}^N \times \mathbb{R} \mid Ay \leq \mathbf{1}u,\ y \geq \mathbf{0},\ \mathbf{1}^\top y = 1\}. \end{aligned} \tag{3.4}$$

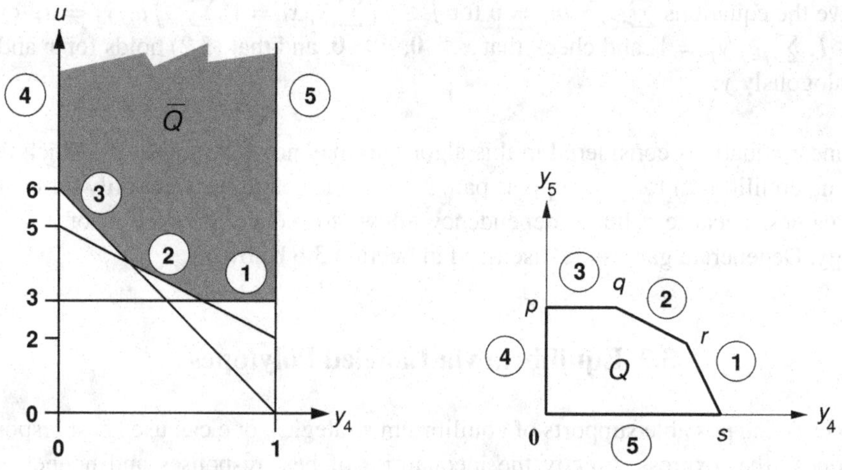

Figure 3.1. Best reponse polyhedron $\overline{Q}$ for strategies of player 2, and corresponding polytope Q, which has vertices $\mathbf{0}$, p, q, r, s.

The left picture in Figure 3.1 shows $\overline{Q}$ for our example, for $0 \leq y_4 \leq 1$, which uniquely determines y_5 as $1 - y_4$. The circled numbers indicate the facets of $\overline{Q}$, which are either the strategies $i \in M$ of the other player 1 or the own strategies $j \in N$. Facets 1, 2, 3 of player 1 indicate his best responses together with his expected payoff u. For example, 1 is a best response when $y_4 \geq 2/3$. Facets 4 and 5 of player 2 tell when the respective own strategy has probability zero, namely $y_4 = 0$ or $y_5 = 0$.

We say a point (y, u) of $\overline{Q}$ has *label* $k \in M \cup N$ if the kth inequality in the definition of $\overline{Q}$ is binding, which for $k = i \in M$ is the ith binding inequality $\sum_{j \in N} a_{ij} y_j = u$ (meaning i is a best response to y), or for $k = j \in N$ the binding inequality $y_j = 0$. In the example, $(y_4, y_5, u) = (2/3, 1/3, 3)$ has labels 1 and 2, so rows 1 and 2 are best responses to y with expected payoff 3 to player 1. The labels of a point (x, v) of $\overline{P}$ are defined correspondingly: It has label $i \in M$ if $x_i = 0$, and label $j \in N$ if $\sum_{i \in M} b_{ij} x_i = v$. With these labels, an equilibrium is a pair (x, y) of mixed strategies so that with the corresponding expected payoffs v and u, the pair $((x, v), (y, u))$ in $\overline{P} \times \overline{Q}$ is *completely labeled*, which means that every label $k \in M \cup N$ appears as a label either of (x, v) or of (y, u). This is equivalent to the best response condition (3.2): A missing label would mean a pure strategy of a player, e.g., i of player 1, that does not have probability zero, so $x_i > 0$, and is also not a best response, since $\sum_{j \in N} a_{ij} y_j < u$, because the respective inequality i is not binding in $\overline{P}$ or $\overline{Q}$. But this is exactly when the best response condition is violated. Conversely, if every label appears in $\overline{P}$ or $\overline{Q}$, then each pure strategy is a best response or has probability zero, so x and y are mutual best responses.

The constraints (3.4) that define $\overline{P}$ and $\overline{Q}$ can be simplified by eliminating the payoff variables u and v, which works if these are always positive. For that purpose, assume that

$$A \text{ and } B^\top \text{ are nonnegative and have no zero column.} \tag{3.5}$$

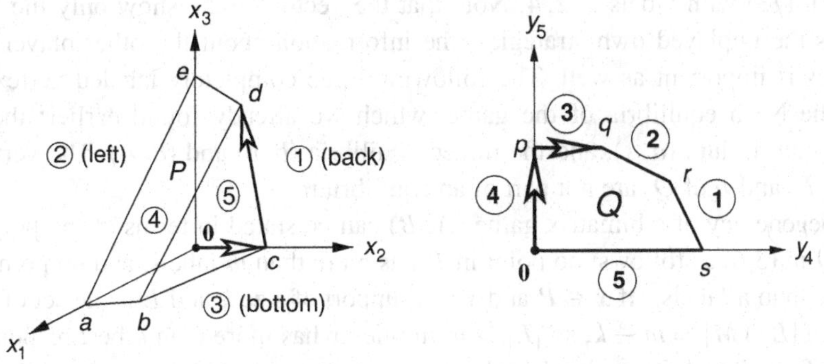

Figure 3.2. The best response polytopes P (with vertices $\mathbf{0}$, a, b, c, d, e) and Q for the game in (3.3). The arrows describe the Lemke–Howson algorithm (see Section 3.4).

We could simply assume $A > \mathbf{0}$ and $B > \mathbf{0}$, but it is useful to admit zero matrix entries (e.g., as in the identity matrix); even negative entries are possible as long as the upper envelope remains positive, e.g., for a_{34} (currently zero) in (3.3), as Figure 3.1 shows.

For $\overline{P}$, we divide each inequality $\sum_{i \in M} b_{ij} x_i \le v$ by v, which gives $\sum_{i \in M} b_{ij}(x_i/v) \le 1$, treat x_i/v as a new variable that we call again x_i, and call the resulting polyhedron P. Similarly, $\overline{Q}$ is replaced by Q by dividing each inequality in $Ay \le \mathbf{1}u$ by u. Then

$$\begin{aligned} P &= \{x \in \mathbb{R}^M \mid \ x \ge \mathbf{0},\ B^\top x \le \mathbf{1}\}, \\ Q &= \{y \in \mathbb{R}^N \mid Ay \le \mathbf{1}, \quad\ y \ge \mathbf{0}\}. \end{aligned} \tag{3.6}$$

It is easy to see that (3.5) implies that P and Q are full-dimensional polytopes, unlike $\overline{P}$ and $\overline{Q}$. In effect, we have normalized the expected payoffs to be 1, and dropped the conditions $\mathbf{1}^\top x = 1$ and $\mathbf{1}^\top y = 1$. Nonzero vectors $x \in P$ and $y \in Q$ are multiplied by $v = 1/\mathbf{1}^\top x$ and $u = 1/\mathbf{1}^\top y$ to turn them into probability vectors. The scaling factors v and u are the expected payoffs to the other player.

The set $\overline{P}$ is in one-to-one correspondence with $P - \{\mathbf{0}\}$ with the map $(x, v) \mapsto x \cdot (1/v)$. Similarly, $(y, u) \mapsto y \cdot (1/u)$ defines a bijection $\overline{Q} \to Q - \{\mathbf{0}\}$. These bijections are not linear, but are known as "projective transformations" (for a visualization see von Stengel, 2002, Fig. 2.5). They preserve the face incidences since a binding inequality in $\overline{P}$ (respectively, $\overline{Q}$) corresponds to a binding inequality in P (respectively, Q) and vice versa. In particular, points have the same *labels* defined by the binding inequalities, which are some of the $m + n$ inequalities defining P and Q in (3.6). An equilibrium is then a completely labeled pair $(x, y) \in P \times Q - \{(\mathbf{0}, \mathbf{0})\}$, which has for each label $i \in M$ the respective binding inequality in $x \ge \mathbf{0}$ or $Ay \le \mathbf{1}$, and for each $j \in N$ the respective binding inequality in $B^\top x \le \mathbf{1}$ or $y \ge \mathbf{0}$.

For the example (3.3), the polytope Q is shown on the right in Figure 3.1 and in Figure 3.2. The vertices y of Q, written as $y^\top$, are $(0, 0)$ with labels 4, 5, vertex $p = (0, 1/6)$ with labels 3, 4, vertex $q = (1/12, 1/6)$ with labels 2, 3, vertex $r = (1/6, 1/9)$ with labels 1, 2, and $s = (1/3, 0)$ with labels 1, 5. The polytope P is shown on the left in Figure 3.2. Its vertices x are $\mathbf{0}$ with labels 1, 2, 3, and (written as $x^\top$) vertex $a = (1/3, 0, 0)$ with labels 2, 3, 4, vertex $b = (2/7, 1/14, 0)$ with labels 3, 4, 5, vertex $c = (0, 1/6, 0)$ with labels 1, 3, 5, vertex $d = (0, 1/8, 1/4)$ with labels 1, 4, 5, and

$e = (0, 0, 1/3)$ with labels $1, 2, 4$. Note that the vectors alone show only the "own" labels as the unplayed own strategies; the information about the other player's best responses is important as well. The following three completely labeled vertex pairs define the Nash equilibria of the game, which we already found earlier: the pure strategy equilibrium (a, s), and the mixed equilibria (b, r) and (d, q). The vertices c and e of P, and p of Q, are not part of an equilibrium.

Nondegeneracy of a bimatrix game (A, B) can be stated in terms of the polytopes P and Q in (3.6) as follows: no point in P has more than m labels, and no point in Q has more than n labels. (If $x \in P$ and x has support of size k and L is the set of labels of x, then $|L \cap M| = m - k$, so $|L| > m$ implies x has more than k best responses in $L \cap N$.) Then P and Q are simple polytopes, because a point of P, say, that is on more than m facets would have more than m labels. Even if P and Q are simple polytopes, the game can be degenerate if the *description* of a polytope is redundant in the sense that some inequality can be omitted, but nevertheless is sometimes binding. This occurs if a player has a pure strategy that is weakly dominated by or payoff equivalent to some other mixed strategy. Nonsimple polytopes or redundant inequalities of this kind do not occur for "generic" payoffs; this illustrates the assumption of nondegeneracy from a geometric viewpoint. (A strictly dominated strategy may occur generically, but it defines a redundant inequality that is never binding, so this does not lead to a degenerate game.)

Because the game is nondegenerate, only vertices of P can have m labels, and only vertices of Q can have n labels. Otherwise, a point of P with m labels that is not a vertex would be on a higher dimensional face, and a vertex of that face, which is a vertex of P, would have additional labels. Consequently, only vertices of P and Q have to be inspected as possible equilibrium strategies.

Algorithm 3.5 (Equilibria by vertex enumeration) *Input:* A nondegenerate bimatrix game. *Output:* All Nash equilibria of the game. *Method:* For each vertex x of $P - \{\mathbf{0}\}$, and each vertex y of $Q - \{\mathbf{0}\}$, if (x, y) is completely labeled, output the Nash equilibrium $(x \cdot 1/\mathbf{1}^\top x, y \cdot 1/\mathbf{1}^\top y)$.

Algorithm 3.5 is superior to the support enumeration Algorithm 3.4 because there are more supports than vertices. For example, if $m = n$, then approximately 4^n possible support pairs have to be tested, but P and Q have less than 2.6^n many vertices, by the "upper bound theorem" for polytopes. This entails less work, assuming that complementary vertex pairs (x, y) are found efficiently.

Enumerating all vertices of a polytope P, say, is a standard problem in computional geometry. The elegant *lrs* (lexicographic reverse search) algorithm considers a known vertex, like $\mathbf{0}$ for P in (3.6), and a linear objective function that, over P, is maximized at that vertex, like the function $x \mapsto -\mathbf{1}^\top x$. For any vertex of P, the simplex algorithm with a unique pivoting rule (e.g., Bland's least-index rule for choosing the entering and leaving variable) then generates a unique path to $\mathbf{0}$, defining a directed tree on the vertices of P with root $\mathbf{0}$. The algorithm explores that tree by a depth-first search from $\mathbf{0}$ which "reverts" the simplex steps by considering recursively for each vertex x of P the edges to vertices x' so that the simplex algorithm pivots from x' to x.

3.4 The Lemke–Howson Algorithm

Algorithms 3.4 and 3.5 find all Nash equilibria of a nondegenerate bimatrix game (A, B). In contrast, the Lemke–Howson (for short LH) algorithm finds one Nash equilibrium, and provides an elementary proof that Nash equilibria exist. The LH algorithm follows a path (called LH path) of vertex pairs (x, y) of $P \times Q$, for the polytopes P and Q defined in (3.6), that starts at $(\mathbf{0}, \mathbf{0})$ and ends at a Nash equilibrium.

An LH path alternately follows edges of P and Q, keeping the vertex in the other polytope fixed. Because the game is nondegenerate, a vertex of P is given by m labels, and a vertex of Q is given by n labels. An edge of P is defined by $m - 1$ labels. For example, in Figure 3.2 the edge defined by labels 1 and 3 joins the vertices $\mathbf{0}$ and c. *Dropping* a label l of a vertex x of P, say, means traversing the unique edge that has all the labels of x except for l. For example, dropping label 2 of the vertex $\mathbf{0}$ of P in Figure 3.2 gives the edge, defined by labels 1 and 3, that joins $\mathbf{0}$ to vertex c. The endpoint of the edge has a new label, which is said to be *picked up*, so in the example label 5 is picked up at vertex c.

The LH algorithm starts from $(\mathbf{0}, \mathbf{0})$ in $P \times Q$. This is called the *artificial equilibrium*, which is a completely labeled vertex pair because every pure strategy has probability zero. It does not represent a Nash equilibrium of the game because the zero vector cannot be rescaled to a mixed strategy vector. An initial free choice of the LH algorithm is a pure strategy k of a player (any label in $M \cup N$), called the *missing label*. Starting with $(x, y) = (\mathbf{0}, \mathbf{0})$, label k is dropped. At the endpoint of the corresponding edge (of P if $k \in M$, of Q if $k \in N$), the new label that is picked up is *duplicate* because it was present in the other polytope. That duplicate label is then dropped in the other polytope, picking up a new label. If the newly picked label is the missing label, the algorithm terminates and has found a Nash equilibrium. Otherwise, the algorithm repeats by dropping the duplicate label in the other polytope, and continues in this fashion.

In the example (3.3), suppose that the missing label is $k = 2$. The polytopes P and Q are shown in Figure 3.2. Starting from $\mathbf{0}$ in P, label 2 is dropped, traversing the edge from $\mathbf{0}$ to vertex c, which is the set of points x of P that have labels 1 and 3, shown by an arrow in Figure 3.2. The endpoint c of that edge has label 5 which is picked up. At the vertex pair $(c, \mathbf{0})$ of $P \times Q$, all labels except for the missing label 2 are present, so label 5 is now duplicate because it is both a label of c and of $\mathbf{0}$. The next step is therefore to drop the duplicate label 5 in Q, traversing the edge from $\mathbf{0}$ to vertex p while keeping c in P fixed. The label that is picked up at vertex p is 3, which is now duplicate. Dropping label 3 in P defines the unique edge defined by labels 1 and 5, which joins vertex c to vertex d. At vertex d, label 4 is picked up. Dropping label 4 in Q means traversing the edge of Q from p to q. At vertex q, label 2 is picked up. Because 2 is the missing label, the current vertex pair (d, q) is completely labeled, and it is the Nash equilibrium found by the algorithm.

In terms of the game, the first two LH steps amount to taking a pure strategy (given by the missing label k, say of player 1) and considering its best response, say j, which defines a pure strategy pair (k, j). If this is not already an equilibrium, the best response i to j is not k, so that i is a duplicate label, and is now given positive probability in addition to k. In general, one possibility is that a duplicate label is a new best response which in the next step gets positive probability, as in this case. Alternatively, the duplicate label is a pure strategy whose probability has just become zero, so that it no longer needs to be maintained as a best response in the other polytope and the path moves away from the best response facet.

Algorithm 3.6 (Lemke–Howson) *Input:* Nondegenerate bimatrix game. *Output:* One Nash equilibrium of the game. *Method:* Choose $k \in M \cup N$, called the *missing label*. Let $(x, y) = (\mathbf{0}, \mathbf{0}) \in P \times Q$. Drop label k (from x in P if $k \in M$, from y in Q if $k \in N$). **Loop:** Call the new vertex pair (x, y). Let l be the label that is picked up. If $l = k$, terminate with Nash equilibrium (x, y) (rescaled as mixed strategy pair). Otherwise, drop l in the other polytope and repeat.

The LH algorithm terminates, and finds a Nash equilibrium, because $P \times Q$ has only finitely many vertex pairs. The next vertex pair on the path is always unique. Hence, a given vertex pair cannot be revisited because that would provide an additional possibility to proceed in the first place.

We have described the LH path for missing label k by means of alternating edges between two polytopes. In fact, it is a path on the product polytope $P \times Q$, given by the set of pairs (x, y) of $P \times Q$ that are *k-almost completely labeled*, meaning that every label in $M \cup N - \{k\}$ appears as a label of either x or y. In Figure 3.2 for $k = 2$, the vertex pairs on the path are $(\mathbf{0}, \mathbf{0})$, $(c, \mathbf{0})$, (c, p), (d, p), (d, q).

For a fixed missing label k, the k-almost completely labeled vertices and edges of the product polytope $P \times Q$ form a graph of degree 1 or 2. Clearly, such a graph consists of disjoints paths and cycles. The endpoints of the paths are completely labeled. They are the Nash equilibria of the game and the artificial equilibrium $(\mathbf{0}, \mathbf{0})$. Since the number of endpoints of the paths is even, we obtain the following.

Corollary 3.7 *A nondegenerate bimatrix game has an odd number of Nash equilibria.*

The LH algorithm can start at any Nash equilibrium, not just the artificial equilibrium. In Figure 3.2 with missing label 2, starting the algorithm at the Nash equilibrium (d, q) would just generate the known LH path backward to $(\mathbf{0}, \mathbf{0})$. When started at the Nash equilibrium (a, s), the LH path for the missing label 2 gives the vertex pair (b, s), where label 5 is duplicate, and then the equilibrium (b, r). This path cannot go back to $(\mathbf{0}, \mathbf{0})$ because the path leading to $(\mathbf{0}, \mathbf{0})$ starts at (d, q). This gives the three Nash equilibria of the game as endpoints of the two LH paths for missing label 2.

These three equilibria can also be found by the LH algorithm by varying the missing label. For example, the LH path for missing label 1 in Figure 3.2 leads to (a, s), from which (b, r) is subsequently found via missing label 2.

However, some Nash equilibria can remain elusive to the LH algorithm. An example is the following symmetric 3×3 game with

$$A = B^\top = \begin{bmatrix} 3 & 3 & 0 \\ 4 & 0 & 1 \\ 0 & 4 & 5 \end{bmatrix}. \qquad (3.7)$$

Every Nash equilibrium (x, y) of this game is symmetric, i.e., $x = y$, where $x^\top$ is $(0, 0, 1)$, $(1/2, 1/4, 1/4)$, or $(3/4, 1/4, 0)$. Only the first of these is found by the LH algorithm, for any missing label; because the game is symmetric, it suffices to consider the missing labels 1, 2, 3. (A symmetric game remains unchanged when the players are exchanged; a symmetric game has always a symmetric equilibrium, but may also have nonsymmetric equilibria, which obviously come in pairs.)

3.5 Integer Pivoting

The LH algorithm follows the edges of a polyhedron, which is implemented algebraically by *pivoting* as used by the simplex algorithm for solving a linear program. We describe an efficient implementation that has no numerical errors by storing *integers* of arbitrary precision. The constraints defining the polyhedron are thereby represented as linear equations with nonnegative *slack* variables. For the polytopes P and Q in (3.6), these slack variables are nonnegative vectors $s \in \mathbb{R}^N$ and $r \in \mathbb{R}^M$ so that $x \in P$ and $y \in Q$ if and only if

$$B^\top x + s = \mathbf{1}, \qquad r + Ay = \mathbf{1}, \tag{3.8}$$

and

$$x \geq \mathbf{0}, \quad s \geq \mathbf{0}, \quad r \geq \mathbf{0}, \quad y \geq \mathbf{0}. \tag{3.9}$$

A binding inequality corresponds to a zero slack variable. The pair (x, y) is completely labeled if and only if $x_i r_i = 0$ for all $i \in M$ and $y_j s_j = 0$ for all $j \in N$, which by (3.9) can be written as the orthogonality condition

$$x^\top r = 0, \qquad y^\top s = 0. \tag{3.10}$$

A *basic* solution to (3.8) is given by n *basic* (linearly independent) columns of $B^\top x + s = \mathbf{1}$ and m basic columns of $r + Ay = \mathbf{1}$, where the *nonbasic* variables that correspond to the m respectively n other (nonbasic) columns are set to zero, so that the basic variables are uniquely determined. A basic *feasible* solution also fulfills (3.9), and defines a vertex x of P and y of Q. The labels of such a vertex are given by the respective nonbasic columns.

Pivoting is a change of the basis where a nonbasic variable *enters* and a basic variable *leaves* the set of basic variables, while preserving feasibility (3.9). We illustrate this for the edges of the polytope P in Figure 3.2 shown as arrows, which are the edges that connect $\mathbf{0}$ to vertex c, and c to d. The system $B^\top x + s = \mathbf{1}$ is here

$$\begin{array}{rcl} 3x_1 + \phantom{\boxed{6}}2x_2 + 3x_3 + s_4 \phantom{{}+s_5} &=& 1 \\ 2x_1 + \boxed{6}\,x_2 + x_3 \phantom{{}+s_4} + s_5 &=& 1 \end{array} \tag{3.11}$$

and the basic variables in (3.11) are s_4 and s_5, defining the basic feasible solution $s_4 = 1$ and $s_5 = 1$, which is simply the right-hand side of (3.11) because the basic columns form the identity matrix. Dropping label 2 means that x_2 is no longer a nonbasic variable, so x_2 enters the basis. Increasing x_2 while maintaining (3.11) changes the current basic variables as $s_4 = 1 - 2x_2$, $s_5 = 1 - 6x_2$, and these stay nonnegative as long as $x_2 \leq 1/6$. The term $1/6$ is the *minimum ratio*, over all rows in (3.11) with positive coefficients of the entering variable x_2, of the right-hand side divided by the coefficient. (Only positive coefficients bound the increase of x_2, which applies to at least one row since the polyhedron P is bounded.) The minimum ratio test determines uniquely s_5 as the variable that leaves the basis, giving the label 5 that is picked up in that step. The respective coefficient 6 of x_2 is indicated by a box in (3.11), and is called the *pivot element*; its row is the pivot row and its column is the pivot column.

Algebraically, pivoting is done by applying row operations to (3.11) so that the new basic variable x_2 has a unit column, so that the basic solution is again given by the right-hand side. *Integer* pivoting is a way to achieve this while keeping all coefficients of the system as integers; the basic columns then form an identity matrix multiplied by an integer. To that end, all rows (which in (3.11) is only the first row) except for the pivot row are multiplied with the pivot element, giving the intermediate system

$$\begin{array}{rl} 18x_1 + 12x_2 + 18x_3 + 6s_4 &= 6 \\ 2x_1 + 6x_2 + x_3 + s_5 &= 1 \end{array} \tag{3.12}$$

Then, suitable multiples of the pivot row are subtracted from the other rows to obtain zero entries in the pivot column, giving the new system

$$\begin{array}{rl} 14x_1 + \boxed{16}\, x_3 + 6s_4 - 2s_5 &= 4 \\ 2x_1 + 6x_2 + x_3 + s_5 &= 1. \end{array} \tag{3.13}$$

In (3.13), the basic columns for the basic variables s_4 and x_2 form the identity matrix, multiplied by 6 (which is pivot element that has just been used). Clearly, all matrix entries are integers. The next step of the LH algorithm in the example is to let y_5 be the entering variable in the system $r + Ay = \mathbf{1}$, which we do not show. There, the leaving variable is r_3 (giving the duplicate label 3) so that the next entering variable in (3.13) is x_3. The minimum ratio test (which can be performed using only multiplications, not divisions) shows that among the nonnegativity constraints $6s_4 = 4 - 16x_3 \geq 0$ and $6x_2 = 1 - x_3 \geq 0$, the former is tighter so that s_4 is the leaving variable. The pivot element, shown by a box in (3.13), is 16, with the first row as pivot row.

The integer pivoting step is to multiply the other rows with the pivot element, giving

$$\begin{array}{rl} 14x_1 + 16x_3 + 6s_4 - 2s_5 &= 4 \\ 32x_1 + 96x_2 + 16x_3 + 16s_5 &= 16. \end{array} \tag{3.14}$$

Subsequently, a suitable multiple of the pivot row is subtracted from each other row, giving the new system

$$\begin{array}{rl} 14x_1 + 16x_3 + 6s_4 - 2s_5 &= 4 \\ 18x_1 + 96x_2 - 6s_4 + 18s_5 &= 12 \end{array} \tag{3.15}$$

with x_3 and x_2 as basic variables. However, except for the pivot row, the unchanged basic variables have larger coefficients than before, because they have been multiplied with the new pivot element 16. The second row in (3.15) can now be divided by the previous pivot element 6, and this division is integral for *all* coefficients in that row; this is the key feature of integer pivoting, explained shortly. The new system is

$$\begin{array}{rl} 14x_1 + 16x_3 + 6s_4 - 2s_5 &= 4 \\ 3x_1 + 16x_2 - s_4 + 3s_5 &= 2. \end{array} \tag{3.16}$$

This is the final system because the duplicate label 4 (given by the variable s_4 that has just left) is dropped in Q, where the missing label 2 is picked up. The basic solution in (3.16) is vertex d of P with $x_3 = 4/16$, $x_2 = 2/16$, and labels (given by the nonbasic columns) 1, 4, and 5.

Integer pivoting, as illustrated in this example, always maintains an integer matrix (or "tableau") of coefficients of a system of linear equations that is equivalent to the original system $B^\top x + s = \mathbf{1}$, in the form

$$CB^\top x + Cs = C\mathbf{1}. \tag{3.17}$$

In (3.17), C is the inverse of the *basis matrix* given by the basic columns of the original system, multiplied by the *determinant* of the basis matrix (which is 6 in (3.13), and 16 in (3.16)). The matrix C is given by the (integer) cofactors of the basis matrix; the cofactor of a matrix entry is the determinant of the matrix when the row and column of that element are deleted. Each entry in (3.17) has a bounded number of digits (by at most a factor of $n \log n$ compared to the original matrix entries), so integer pivoting is a polynomial-time algorithm. It is also superior to using fractions of integers (rational numbers) because their cancelation requires greatest common divisor computations that take the bulk of computation time. Only the final fractions defining the solution, like $x_3 = 4/16$ and $x_2 = 2/16$ in (3.16), may have to be canceled.

3.6 Degenerate Games

The uniqueness of an LH path requires a nondegenerate game. In a degenerate game, a vertex of P, for example, may have more than m labels. When that vertex is represented as a basic feasible solution as in (3.17) this means that not only the m nonbasic variables are zero, but also at least one basic variable. Such a degenerate basic feasible solution results from a pivoting step where the leaving variable (representing the label that is picked up) is not unique.

As an example, consider the 3×2 game

$$A = \begin{bmatrix} 3 & 3 \\ 2 & 5 \\ 0 & 6 \end{bmatrix}, \qquad B = \begin{bmatrix} 3 & 3 \\ 2 & 6 \\ 3 & 1 \end{bmatrix}, \tag{3.18}$$

which agrees with (3.3) except that $b_{15} = 3$. The polytope Q for this game is the same as before, shown on the right in Figure 3.2. The polytope P is the convex hull of the original vertices $\mathbf{0}, a, c, d, e$ shown on the left in Figure 3.2, so vertex b has merged with a. The new facets of P with labels 4 and 5 are triangles with vertices a, d, e and a, c, d, respectively.

In this example (3.18), the first step of the LH path for missing label 1 would be from $(\mathbf{0}, \mathbf{0})$ to $(a, \mathbf{0})$, where the two labels 4 and 5 are picked up, because vertex a has the four labels 2, 3, 4, 5 due to the degeneracy. If then label 4 is dropped in Q, the algorithm finds the equilibrium (a, s) and no problem occurs. However, dropping label 5 in Q would mean a move to (a, p) where label 3 is picked up, and none of the two edges of P that move away from the facet with label 3 (which are the edges from

a to d and from a to e) would, together with p, be 1-almost completely labeled, so the algorithm fails at this point.

Degeneracy can be resolved by *perturbing* the linear system *lexicographically*, which is well known from linear programming. Assume that the system $B^\top x + s = \mathbf{1}$, say, is changed to the perturbed system $B^\top x + s = \mathbf{1} + (\varepsilon^1, \ldots, \varepsilon^n)^\top$. After any number of pivoting steps, this system has the form

$$CB^\top x + Cs = C\mathbf{1} + C(\varepsilon^1, \ldots, \varepsilon^n)^\top \tag{3.19}$$

for some invertible matrix C. The corresponding unperturbed basic feasible solution may have a zero basic variable, which is a row of $C\mathbf{1}$, but for sufficiently small $\varepsilon > 0$ it is positive if and only if in that row the first nonzero entry of the matrix C is positive; this is the invariant maintained by the algorithm, using a more general "lexico-minimum" ratio test. No actual perturbance is required, and C is already stored in the system as the matrix of coefficients of s, as seen from (3.19).

Degenerate games may have infinite sets of equilibria. In the example (3.18), vertex a of P, which represents the pure strategy $(1, 0, 0)^\top$ of player 1, together with the entire edge that joins vertices r and s of Q, defines a *component* of Nash equilibria, where player 2 plays some mixed strategy $(y_4, 1 - y_4)$ for $2/3 \le y_4 \le 1$. However, this equilibrium component is a convex combination of the "extreme" equilibria (a, r) and (a, s). In general, even in a degenerate game, the Nash equilibria can be described in terms of pairs of vertices of P and Q. We write conv U for the convex hull of a set U.

Proposition 3.8 *Let (A, B) be a bimatrix game, and $(x, y) \in P \times Q$. Then (x, y) (rescaled) is a Nash equilibrium if and only if there is a set U of vertices of $P - \{\mathbf{0}\}$ and a set V of vertices of $Q - \{\mathbf{0}\}$ so that $x \in \text{conv}\, U$ and $y \in \text{conv}\, V$, and every $(u, v) \in U \times V$ is completely labeled.*

Proposition 3.8 holds because labels are preserved under convex combinations, and because every face of P or Q has the labels of its vertices, which are vertices of the entire polytope; for details see von Stengel (2002, Thm. 2.14).

The following algorithm, which extends Algorithm 3.5, outputs a complete description of all Nash equilibria of a bimatrix game: Define a bipartite graph on the vertices of $P - \{\mathbf{0}\}$ and $Q - \{\mathbf{0}\}$, whose edges are the completely labeled vertex pairs (x, y). The "cliques" (maximal complete bipartite subgraphs) of this graph of the form $U \times V$ then define sets of Nash equilibria conv $U \times$ conv V whose union is the set of all Nash equilibria. These sets are called "maximal Nash subsets." They may be nondisjoint, if they contain common points (x, y). The connected unions of these sets are usually called the (topological) *components* of Nash equilibria.

3.7 Extensive Games and Their Strategic Form

A game in strategic form is a "static" description of an interactive situation, where players act simultaneously. A detailed "dynamic" description is an *extensive* game where players act sequentially, where some moves can be made by a *chance* player, and where each player's *information* about earlier moves is modeled in detail. Extensive games are

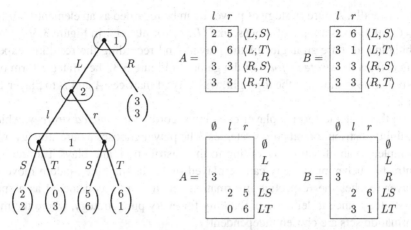

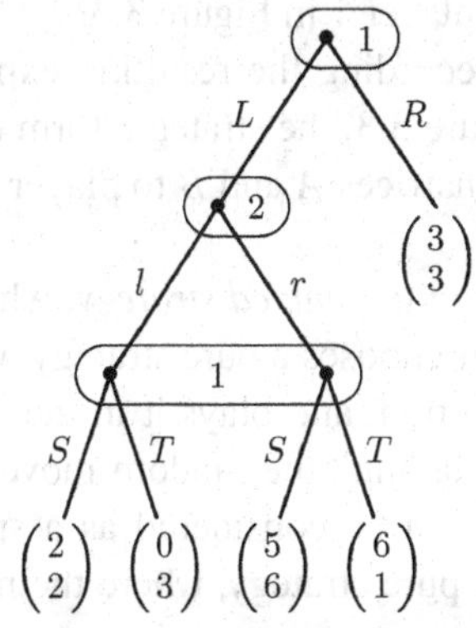

$$A = \begin{array}{c} \\ \end{array}\begin{array}{cc} l & r \\ \hline 2 & 5 \\ 0 & 6 \\ 3 & 3 \\ 3 & 3 \end{array} \begin{array}{l} \\ \langle L,S\rangle \\ \langle L,T\rangle \\ \langle R,S\rangle \\ \langle R,T\rangle \end{array} \qquad B = \begin{array}{cc} l & r \\ \hline 2 & 6 \\ 3 & 1 \\ 3 & 3 \\ 3 & 3 \end{array} \begin{array}{l} \\ \langle L,S\rangle \\ \langle L,T\rangle \\ \langle R,S\rangle \\ \langle R,T\rangle \end{array}$$

$$A = \begin{array}{ccc} \emptyset & l & r \\ \hline & & \\ & & \\ 3 & & \\ & 2 & 5 \\ & 0 & 6 \end{array} \begin{array}{l} \\ \emptyset \\ L \\ R \\ LS \\ LT \end{array} \qquad B = \begin{array}{ccc} \emptyset & l & r \\ \hline & & \\ & & \\ 3 & & \\ & 2 & 6 \\ & 3 & 1 \end{array} \begin{array}{l} \\ \emptyset \\ L \\ R \\ LS \\ LT \end{array}$$

Figure 3.3. Left: A game in extensive form. Top right: Its *strategic form* payoff matrices A and B. Bottom right: Its *sequence form* payoff matrices A and B, where rows and columns correspond to the sequences of the players which are marked at the side. Any sequence pair not leading to a leaf has matrix entry zero, which is left blank.

a fundamental representation of dynamic interactions which generalizes other models like repeated and multistage games, or games with incomplete information.

The basic structure of an extensive game is a directed *tree*. The nodes of the tree represent game *states*. Trees (rather than general graphs) are used because then a game state encodes the full history of play. Only one player moves at any one state along a tree edge. The game starts at the root (initial node) of the tree and ends at a leaf (terminal node), where each player receives a *payoff*. The nonterminal nodes are called *decision nodes*. A player's possible *moves* are assigned to the outgoing edges of the decision node.

The decision nodes are partitioned into *information sets*. All nodes in an information set belong to the same player, and have the same moves. The interpretation is that when a player makes a move, he only knows the information set but not the particular node he is at. In a game with *perfect information*, all information sets are singletons (and can therefore be omitted). We denote the set of information sets of player i by H_i, information sets by h, and the set of moves at h by C_h.

Figure 3.3 shows an example of an extensive game. Moves are marked by upper-case letters for player 1 and by lowercase letters for player 2. Information sets are indicated by ovals. The two information sets of player 1 have move sets $\{L, R\}$ and $\{S, T\}$, and the information set of player 2 has move set $\{l, r\}$. A play of the game may proceed by player 1 choosing L, player 2 choosing r, and player 1 choosing S, after which the game terminates with payoffs 5 and 6 to players 1 and 2. By definition, move S of player 1 is the same, no matter whether player 2 has chosen l or r, because player 1 does not know the game state in his second information set.

At some decision nodes, the next move may be a *chance* move. Chance is here treated as an additional player 0, who receives no payoff and who plays according to a known *behavior strategy*. A behavior strategy of player i is given by a probability distribution on C_h for all h in H_i. (The information sets belonging to the chance player are singletons.) A *pure strategy* is a behavior strategy where each move is picked deterministically. A pure strategy of player i can be regarded as an element $\langle c_h \rangle_{h \in H_i}$ of $\prod_{h \in H_i} C_h$, that is, as a tuple of moves, like $\langle L, S \rangle$ for player 1 in Figure 3.3.

Tabulating all pure strategies of the players and recording the resulting expected payoffs defines the *strategic form* of the game. In Figure 3.3, the strategic form of the extensive game is shown at the top right, with payoff matrices A and B to player 1 and player 2.

Given the strategic form, a player can play according to a *mixed strategy*, which is a probability distribution on pure strategies. The player chooses a pure strategy, which is a complete plan of action, according to this distribution, and plays it in the game. In contrast, a behavior strategy can be played by "delaying" the random move until the player reaches the respective information set. It can be considered as a special mixed strategy since it defines a probability for every pure strategy, where the moves at information sets are chosen independently.

We consider algorithms for finding Nash equilibria of an extensive game, with the tree together with the described game data as input. The strategic form is bad for this purpose because it is typically exponentially large in the game tree. As described in the subsequent sections, this complexity can be reduced, in some cases by considering *subgames* and corresponding *subgame perfect* equilibria. The *reduced* strategic form of the game is smaller but may still be exponentially large. A reduction from exponential to linear size is provided by the *sequence form*, which allows one to compute directly behavior strategies rather than mixed strategies.

3.8 Subgame Perfect Equilibria

A *subgame* of an extensive game is a subtree of the game tree that includes all information sets containing a node of the subtree. Figure 3.3 has a subgame starting at the decision node of player 2; the nodes in the second information set of player 1 are not roots of subgames because player 1 does not know that he is in the respective subtree. In the subgame, player 2 moves first, but player 1 does not get to know that move. So this subgame is equivalent to a 2×2 game in strategic form where the players act simultaneously. (In this way, every game in strategic form can be represented as a game in extensive form.)

The subgame in Figure 3.3 has a unique mixed equilibrium with probability $2/3$ for the moves T and r, respectively, and expected payoff 4 to player 1 and $8/3$ to player 2. Replacing the subgame by the payoff pair $(4, 8/3)$, one obtains a very simple game with moves L and R for player 1, where L is optimal. So player 1's mixed strategy with probabilities $1/3$ and $2/3$ for $\langle L, S \rangle$ and $\langle L, T \rangle$ and player 2's mixed strategy $(1/3, 2/3)$ for l, r define a Nash equilibrium of the game. This is the, here unique, *subgame perfect* equilibrium of the game, defined by the property that it induces a Nash equilibrium in every subgame.

Algorithm 3.9 (Subgame perfect equilibrium) *Input:* An extensive game. *Output:* A subgame perfect Nash equilibrium of the game. *Method:* Consider, in increasing order of inclusion, each subgame of the game, find a Nash equilibrium of the subgame, and replace the subgame by a new terminal node that has the equilibrium payoffs.

In a game with perfect information, every node is the root of a subgame. Then Algorithm 3.9 is the well-known, linear time *backward induction* method, also sometimes known as "Zermelo's algorithm." Because the subgame involves only one player in each iteration, a deterministic move is optimal, which shows that any game with perfect information has a (subgame perfect) Nash equilibrium where every player uses a pure strategy.

In games with imperfect information, a subgame perfect equilibrium may require mixed strategies, as Figure 3.3 demonstrates.

3.9 Reduced Strategic Form

Not all extensive games have nontrivial subgames, and one may also be interested in equilibria that are not subgame perfect. In Figure 3.3, such an equilibrium is the pure strategy pair $(\langle R, S\rangle, l)$. Here, player 2 is *indifferent* between her moves l and r because the initial move R of player 1 means that player 2 never has to make move l or r, so player 2 receives the constant payoff 3 after move R. If play actually reached player 2's information set, move l would not be optimal against S, which is why this is not a subgame perfect equilibrium. Player 2 can, in fact, randomize between l and r, and as long as l is played with probability at least 2/3, $\langle R, S\rangle$ remains a best response of player 1, as required in equilibrium.

In this game, the pure strategies $\langle R, S\rangle$ and $\langle R, T\rangle$ of player 1 are overspecific as "plans of action": the initial move R of player 1 makes the subsequent choice of S or T *irrelevant* since player 1's second information set cannot be reached after move R. Consequently, the two payoff rows for $\langle R, S\rangle$ and $\langle R, T\rangle$ are identical for both players. In the *reduced strategic form*, moves at information sets that cannot be reached because of an earlier own move are identified. In Figure 3.3, this reduction yields the pure strategy (more precisely, equivalence class of pure strategies) $\langle R, *\rangle$, where $*$ denotes an arbitrary move. The two (reduced as well as unreduced) pure strategies of player 2 are her moves l and r.

The reduced strategic form of Figure 3.3 corresponds to the bimatrix game (3.18) if $\langle R, *\rangle$ is taken as the first strategy (top row) of player 1. This game is *degenerate* even if the payoffs in the extensive game are generic, because player 2, irrespective of her own move, receives constant payoff 3 when player 1 chooses $\langle R, *\rangle$.

Once a two-player extensive game has been converted to its reduced strategic form, it can be considered as a bimatrix game, where we refer to its rows and columns as the "pure strategies" of player 1 and 2, even if they leave moves at unreachable information sets unspecified.

The concept of subgame perfect equilibrium requires fully specified strategies, rather than reduced strategies. For example, it is not possible to say whether the Nash equilibrium $(\langle R, *\rangle, l)$ of the reduced strategic form of the game in Figure 3.3 is subgame perfect or not, because player 1's behavior at his second information set is unspecified. This could be said for a Nash equilibrium of the full strategic form with two rows $\langle R, S\rangle$ and $\langle R, T\rangle$. However, these identical two rows are indistinguishable computationally, so there is no point in applying an algorithm to the full rather than the reduced strategic form, because any splitting of probabilities between payoff-identical strategies would be arbitrary. If one is interested in finding subgame perfect equilibria, one should use Algorithm 3.9. At each stage of that algorithm, the considered games have by definition no further subgames, and equilibria of these games can be found using the reduced strategic form or the sequence form.

A player may have *parallel* information sets that are not distinguished by own earlier moves. These arise when a player receives information about an earlier move by another player. Combinations of moves at parallel information sets cannot be reduced, which causes a multiplicative growth of the number of reduced strategies. In general, the reduced strategic form can therefore still be exponential in the size of the game tree.

3.10 The Sequence Form

In the reduced strategic form, pure strategies are only partially specified, by omitting moves at information sets that cannot be reached because of an own earlier move. In the *sequence form*, pure strategies are replaced by an even more partial description of *sequences* which specify a player's moves only along a *path* in the game tree. The number of these paths, and therefore of these sequences, is bounded by the number of nodes of the tree. However, randomizing between such sequences can no longer be described by a single probability distribution, but requires a system of linear equations.

A *sequence* of moves of player i is the sequence of his moves (disregarding the moves of other players) on the unique path from the root to some node t of the tree, and is denoted $\sigma_i(t)$. For example, for the leftmost leaf t in Figure 3.3 this sequence is LS for player 1 and l for player 2. The empty sequence is denoted $\emptyset$. Player i has *perfect recall* if and only if $\sigma_i(s) = \sigma_i(t)$ for any nodes $s, t \in h$ and $h \in H_i$. Then the unique sequence $\sigma_i(t)$ leading to any node t in h will be denoted σ_h. Perfect recall means that the player cannot get additional information about his position in an information set by remembering his earlier moves. We assume all players have perfect recall.

Let β_i be a behavior strategy of player i. The move probabilities $\beta_i(c)$ fulfill

$$\sum_{c \in C_h} \beta_i(c) = 1, \qquad \beta_i(c) \geq 0 \quad \text{for } h \in H_i\,,\;\; c \in C_h. \tag{3.20}$$

The *realization probability* of a sequence σ of player i under β_i is

$$\beta_i[\sigma] = \prod_{c \text{ in } \sigma} \beta_i(c). \tag{3.21}$$

An information set h in H_i is called *relevant* under β_i if $\beta_i[\sigma_h] > 0$, otherwise *irrelevant*, in agreement with irrelevant information sets as considered in the reduced strategic form.

Let S_i be the set of sequences of moves for player i. Then any σ in S_i is either the empty sequence $\emptyset$ or uniquely given by its last move c at the information set h in H_i, that is, $\sigma = \sigma_h c$. Hence,

$$S_i = \{\emptyset\} \cup \{\sigma_h c \mid h \in H_i,\; c \in C_h\}.$$

This implies that the number of sequences of player i, apart from the empty sequence, is equal to his total number of moves, that is, $|S_i| = 1 + \sum_{h \in H_i} |C_h|$. This number is linear in the size of the game tree.

Let β_1 and β_2 denote behavior strategies of the two players, and let β_0 be the known behavior of the chance player. Let $a(t)$ and $b(t)$ denote the payoffs to player 1 and player 2, respectively, at a leaf t of the tree. The probability of reaching t is the product of move probabilities on the path to t. The expected payoff to player 1 is therefore

$$\sum_{\text{leaves } t} a(t)\, \beta_0[\sigma_0(t)]\, \beta_1[\sigma_1(t)]\, \beta_2[\sigma_2(t)]\,, \tag{3.22}$$

and the expected payoff to player 2 is the same expression with $b(t)$ instead of $a(t)$. However, the expected payoff is nonlinear in terms of behavior strategy probabilities $\beta_i(c)$ since the terms $\beta_i[\sigma_i(t)]$ are products by (3.21).

Therefore, we consider directly the realization probabilities $\beta_i[\sigma]$ as functions of *sequences* σ in S_i. They can also be defined for mixed strategies μ_i of player i, which choose each pure strategy π_i of player i with probability $\mu_i(\pi_i)$. Under π_i, the realization probability of σ in S_i is $\pi_i[\sigma]$, which is equal to 1 if π_i prescribes all the moves in σ and zero otherwise. Under μ_i, the realization probability of σ is

$$\mu_i[\sigma] = \sum_{\pi_i} \mu_i(\pi_i)\pi_i[\sigma]. \tag{3.23}$$

For player 1, this defines a map x from S_1 to $\mathbb{R}$ by $x(\sigma) = \mu_1[\sigma]$ for $\sigma \in S_1$. We call x the *realization plan* of μ_1 or a realization plan for player 1. A realization plan for player 2, similarly defined on S_2 by a mixed strategy μ_2, is denoted y. Realization plans have two important properties.

Proposition 3.10 *A realization plan x of a mixed strategy of player 1 fulfills $x(\sigma) \geq 0$ for all $\sigma \in S_1$ and*

$$x(\emptyset) = 1, \qquad \sum_{c \in C_h} x(\sigma_h c) = x(\sigma_h) \quad \text{for all } h \in H_1. \tag{3.24}$$

Conversely, any $x\colon S_1 \to \mathbb{R}$ with these properties is the realization plan of a behavior strategy of player 1, which is unique except at irrelevant information sets. A realization plan y of player 2 is characterized analogously.

For the second property, two mixed strategies are called *realization equivalent* if they reach any node of the tree with the same probabilities, given any strategy of the other player. We can assume that all chance probabilities $\beta_0(c)$ are positive, by pruning any tree branches that are unreached by chance.

Proposition 3.11 *Two mixed strategies μ_i and μ'_i of player i are realization equivalent if and only if they have the same realization plan, that is, $\mu_i[\sigma] = \mu'_i[\sigma]$ for all $\sigma \in S_i$.*

These two propositions (to be proved in Exercise 3.13) imply the well-known result by Kuhn (1953) that behavior strategies are strategically as expressive as mixed strategies.

Corollary 3.12 (Kuhn's theorem) *For a player with perfect recall, any mixed strategy is realization equivalent to a behavior strategy.*

Proposition 3.10 characterizes realization plans by nonnegativity and the equations (3.11). A realization plan describes a behavior strategy uniquely except for the moves at irrelevant information sets. In particular, the realization plan of a *pure* strategy (that is, a realization plan with values 0 or 1) is as specific as a reduced pure strategy.

A realization plan represents all the relevant strategic information of a mixed strategy by Proposition 3.11. This compact information is obtained with the linear map in (3.23). This map assigns to any mixed strategy μ_i, regarded as a tuple of mixed strategy probabilities $\mu_i(\pi_i)$, its realization plan, regarded as a tuple of realization probabilities $\mu_i[\sigma]$ for σ in S_i. The simplex of mixed strategies is thereby mapped to the polytope of realization plans defined by the linear constraints in Proposition 3.10. The vertices of this polytope are the realization plans of pure strategies. The number of these vertices may be exponential. However, the number of defining inequalities and the dimension of the polytope is linear in the tree size. For player i, this dimension is the number $|S_i|$ of variables minus the number $1+|H_i|$ of equations (3.24) (which are linearly independent), so it is $\sum_{h\in H_i}(|C_h|-1)$.

We consider realization plans as vectors in $x \in \mathbb{R}^{|S_1|}$ and $y \in \mathbb{R}^{|S_2|}$, that is, $x = (x_\sigma)_{\sigma\in S_1}$ where $x_\sigma = x(\sigma)$, and similarly $y = (y_\tau)_{\tau\in S_2}$. The linear constraints in Proposition 3.10 are denoted by

$$Ex = e, \quad x \geq \mathbf{0} \qquad \text{and} \qquad Fy = f, \quad y \geq \mathbf{0}, \tag{3.25}$$

using the *constraint* matrices E and F and vectors e and f. The matrix E and right-hand side e have $1+|H_1|$ rows, and E has $|S_1|$ columns. The first row denotes the equation $x(\emptyset) = 1$ in (3.24). The other rows for $h \in H_1$ are the equations $-x(\sigma_h) + \sum_{c\in C_h} x(\sigma_h c) = 0$.

In Figure 3.3, the sets of sequences are $S_1 = \{\emptyset, L, R, LS, LT\}$ and $S_2 = \{\emptyset, l, r\}$, and in (3.25),

$$E = \begin{bmatrix} 1 & & & & \\ -1 & 1 & 1 & & \\ & -1 & & 1 & 1 \end{bmatrix}, \quad e = \begin{bmatrix} 1 \\ 0 \\ 0 \end{bmatrix}, \quad F = \begin{bmatrix} 1 & & \\ -1 & 1 & 1 \end{bmatrix}, \quad f = \begin{bmatrix} 1 \\ 0 \end{bmatrix}.$$

Each sequence appears exactly once on the left-hand side of the equations (3.24), accounting for the entry 1 in each column of E and F. The number of information sets and therefore the number of rows of E and F is at most linear in the size of the game tree.

Define the *sequence form payoff* matrices A and B, each of dimension $|S_1| \times |S_2|$, as follows. For $\sigma \in S_1$ and $\tau \in S_2$, let the matrix entry $a_{\sigma\tau}$ of A be defined by

$$a_{\sigma\tau} = \sum_{\text{leaves } t \,:\, \sigma_1(t)=\sigma,\ \sigma_2(t)=\tau} a(t)\, \beta_0[\sigma_0(t)]\,. \tag{3.26}$$

The matrix entry of B is this term with b instead of a. An example is shown on the bottom right in Figure 3.3. These two matrices are *sparse*, since the matrix entry for a pair σ, τ of sequences is zero (the empty sum) whenever these sequences do not lead to a leaf. If they do, the matrix entry is the payoff at the leaf (or leaves, weighted with chance probabilities of reaching the leaves, if there are chance moves). Then by (3.22), the expected payoffs to players 1 and 2 are $x^\top Ay$ and $x^\top By$, respectively, which is just another way of writing the weighted sum over all leaves. The constraint and payoff matrices define the *sequence form* of the game.

3.11 Computing Equilibria with the Sequence Form

Realization plans in the sequence form take the role of mixed strategies in the strategic form. In fact, mixed strategies x and y are a special case, by letting E and F in (3.25) be single rows $\mathbf{1}^\top$ and $e = f = 1$. The computation of equilibria with the sequence form uses linear programming duality, which is also of interest for the strategic form.

Consider a fixed realization plan y of player 2. A best response x of player 1 is a realization plan that maximizes his expected payoff $x^\top(Ay)$. That is, x is a solution to the linear program (LP)

$$\text{maximize } x^\top(Ay) \text{ subject to } Ex = e, \ \ x \geq \mathbf{0}. \tag{3.27}$$

This LP has a *dual* LP with a vector u of unconstrained variables whose dimension is $1 + |H_1|$, the number of rows of E. This dual LP states

$$\text{minimize } e^\top u \text{ subject to } E^\top u \geq Ay. \tag{3.28}$$

Both LPs have feasible solutions, so by the strong duality theorem of linear programming, they have the same optimal value.

Consider now a *zero-sum game*, where $B = -A$. Player 2, when choosing y, has to assume that her opponent plays rationally and maximizes $x^\top Ay$. This maximum payoff to player 1 is the optimal value of the LP (3.27), which is equal to the optimal value $e^\top u$ of the dual LP (3.28). Player 2 is interested in minimizing $e^\top u$ by her choice of y. The constraints of (3.28) are linear in u and y even if y is treated as a variable. So a *minmax* realization plan y of player 2 (minimizing the maximum amount she has to pay) is a solution to the LP

$$\underset{u,\,y}{\text{minimize}} \ e^\top u \text{ subject to } Fy = f, \ \ E^\top u - Ay \geq \mathbf{0}, \ \ y \geq \mathbf{0}. \tag{3.29}$$

The dual of this LP has variables v and x corresponding to the primal constraints $Fy = f$ and $E^\top u - Ay \geq \mathbf{0}$, respectively. It has the form

$$\underset{v,\,x}{\text{maximize}} \ f^\top v \text{ subject to } Ex = e, \ \ F^\top v - A^\top x \leq \mathbf{0}, \ \ x \geq \mathbf{0}. \tag{3.30}$$

It is easy to verify that this LP describes the problem of finding a *maxmin* realization plan x (with maxmin payoff $f^\top v$) for player 1.

This implies, first, that any zero-sum game has an equilibrium (x, y). More importantly, given an extensive game, the number of nonzero entries in the sparse matrices E, F, A, and the number of variables, is linear in the size of the game tree. Hence, we have shown the following.

Theorem 3.13 *The equilibria of a two-person zero-sum game in extensive form with perfect recall are the solutions to the LP* (3.29) *with sparse payoff matrix A in* (3.26) *and constraint matrices E and F in* (3.25) *defined by Prop.* 3.10. *The size of this LP is linear in the size of the game tree.*

A best response x of player 1 against the mixed strategy y of player 2 is a solution to the LP (3.27). This is also useful for games that are not zero-sum. By strong duality, a feasible solution x is optimal if and only if there is a dual solution u fulfilling $E^\top u \geq Ay$ and $x^\top(Ay) = e^\top u$, that is, $x^\top(Ay) = (x^\top E^\top)u$ or equivalently

$$x^\top(E^\top u - Ay) = 0. \tag{3.31}$$

Because the vectors x and $E^\top u - Ay$ are nonnegative, (3.31) states that they are *complementary* in the sense that they cannot both have positive components in the same position. This characterization of an optimal primal-dual pair of feasible solutions is known as *complementary slackness* in linear programming. For the strategic form, this condition is equivalent to the best response condition (3.2).

For player 2, the realization plan y is a best response to x if and only if it maximizes $(x^\top B)y$ subject to $Fy = f$, $y \geq \mathbf{0}$. The dual of this LP has the vector v of variables and says: minimize $f^\top v$ subject to $F^\top v \geq B^\top x$. Here, a primal-dual pair y, v of feasible solutions is optimal if and only if, analogous to (3.31),

$$y^\top(F^\top v - B^\top x) = 0. \tag{3.32}$$

Considering these conditions for both players, this shows the following.

Theorem 3.14 *Consider the two-person extensive game with sequence form payoff matrices A, B and constraint matrices E, F. Then the pair (x, y) of realization plans defines an equilibrium if and only if there are vectors u, v so that*

$$\begin{aligned} Ex = e,\ \ x \geq \mathbf{0}, \quad & Fy = f,\ \ y \geq \mathbf{0}, \\ E^\top u - Ay \geq \mathbf{0}, \quad & F^\top v - B^\top x \geq \mathbf{0} \end{aligned} \tag{3.33}$$

and (3.31), (3.32) *hold. The size of the matrices E, F, A, B is linear in the size of the game tree.*

The conditions (3.33) define a *linear complementarity problem* (LCP). For a game in strategic from, (3.8), (3.9), and (3.10) define also an LCP, to which the LH algorithm finds one solution. For a general extensive game, the LH algorithm cannot be applied to the LCP in Theorem 3.14, because u and v are not scalar dual variables that are easily eliminated from the system. Instead, it is possible to use a variant called *Lemke's algorithm.* Similar to the LH algorithm, it introduces a degree of freedom to the system, by considering an additional column for the linear equations and a corresponding variable z_0 which is initially nonzero, and which allows for an initial feasible solution where $x = \mathbf{0}$ and $y = \mathbf{0}$. Then a binding inequality in $r = E^\top u - Ay \geq \mathbf{0}$ (or $s = F^\top v - B^\top x \geq \mathbf{0}$) means that a basic slack variable r_σ (or s_τ) can leave the basis, with x_σ (respectively, y_τ) entering, while keeping (3.10). Like in the LH algorithm, this "complementary pivoting rule" continues until an equilibrium is found, here when the auxiliary variable z_0 leaves the basis.

3.12 Further Reading

A scholarly and more comprehensive account of the results of this chapter is von Stengel (2002). The best response condition (Proposition 3.1) is due to Nash (1951). Algorithm 3.4 is folklore, and has been used by Dickhaut and Kaplan (1991). Polyhedra are explained in Ziegler (1995). Shapley (1974) introduced distinct labels as in (3.1) to visualize the LH algorithm. He labels subdivisions of the mixed strategy simplices, ignoring the payoff components in $\overline{P}$ and $\overline{Q}$ in (3.4). We prefer the polytope view using P and Q in (3.6), which simplifies the LH algorithm. Moreover, this view is useful for constructing games with many equilibria (von Stengel, 1999) that come close to the upper bound theorem for polytopes (Keiding, 1997; McMullen, 1970) , and for games with exponentially long LH paths (Savani and von Stengel, 2006).

Algorithm 3.5 is suggested in (Kuhn, 1961; Mangasarian, 1964; Vorob'ev, 1958). The *lrs* method for vertex enumeration is due to (Avis, 2005; Avis and Fukuda, 1992). An equilibrium enumeration that (implicitly) alternates between $\overline{P}$ and $\overline{Q}$ is Audet et al. (2001). It has been implemented with integer pivoting (like *lrs*) by Rosenberg (2004).

The LH algorithm is due to Lemke and Howson (1964). Shapley (1974) also shows that the endpoints of an LH path are equilibria of different *index*, which is an orientation defined by determinants, explored further in von Schemde (2005). A recent account of integer pivoting is Azulay and Pique (2001). Proposition 3.8 is due to Winkels (1979) and Jansen (1981).

Extensive games with information sets are due to Kuhn (1953). Subgame perfection (Selten, 1975) is one of many *refinements* of Nash equilibria (von Damme, 1987). Main ideas of the sequence form have been discovered independently by (Koller and Megiddo, 1992; Romanovskii, 1962; von Stengel, 1996). Lemke's algorithm (Lemke, 1965) is applied to the sequence form in Koller et al. (1996); von Stengel et al. (2002).

A recent paper, with further references, on algorithms for finding equilibria of games with more than two players, is Datta (2003).

3.13 Discussion and Open Problems

We have described the basic mathematical structure of Nash equilibria for two-player games, namely polyhedra and the complementarity condition of best responses. The resulting algorithms should simplify the analysis of larger games as used by applied game theorists. At present, existing software packages (Avis, 2005; Canty, 2003; McKelvey et al., 2006) are prototypes that are not easy to use. Improved implementations should lead to more widespread use of the algorithms, and reveal which kinds of games practitioners are interested in. If the games are discretized versions of games in economic settings, enumerating all equilibria will soon hit the size barriers of these exponential algorithms. Then the LH algorithm may possibly be used to give an indication if the game has only one Nash equilibrium, or Lemke's method with varying starting point as in von Stengel et al. (2002). This should give practical evidence if these algorithms have usually good running times, as is widely believed, in contrast to the extremal examples in Savani and Stengel (2006). An open theoretical question is if LH, or Lemke's algorithm, has expected polynomial running time, as it is known for the simplex method, for suitable probabilistic assumptions on the instance data.

The computational complexity of finding one Nash equilibrium of a two-player game, as discussed in Chapter 2, is open in the sense that not even a subexponential algorithm is known. Incremental or divide-and-conquer approaches, perhaps using the polyhedral structure, require a generalization of the equilibrium condition, because equilibria typically do not result from equilibria of games with fewer strategies. At the same time, such an approach must not maintain the entire set of Nash equilibria, because questions about that set (such as uniqueness, see Theorem 2.3) are typically NP-hard.

Extensive games are a general model of dynamic games. The condition of perfect recall leads to canonical representations and algorithms, as described. Special types of extensive games, like repeated games and Bayesian games, are widely used in applied game theory. Finding equilibria of these models – where that task is difficult – should give a focus for further research.

Bibliography

C. Audet, P. Hansen, B. Jaumard, and G. Savard. Enumeration of all extreme equilibria of bimatrix games. *SIAM J. Sci. Comput.* 23, 323–338, 2001.

D. Avis and K. Fukuda. A pivoting algorithm for convex hulls and vertex enumeration of arrangements and polyhedra. *Disc. Comp. Geometry* 8, 295–313, 1992.

D. Avis. User's Guide for lrs. Available at: http://cgm.cs.mcgill.ca/~avis, 2005.

D.-O. Azulay and J.-F. Pique. A revised simplex method with integer Q-matrices. *ACM Trans. Math. Software* 27, 350–360, 2001.

C. Bron and J. Kerbosch. Finding all cliques of an undirectred graph. *Comm. ACM* 16, 575–577, 1973.

M.J. Canty. *Resolving Conflict with Mathematica: Algorithms for Two-Person Games.* Academic Press, Amsterdam, 2003.

R.S. Datta. Using computer algebra to compute Nash equilibria. *Proc. 2003 Int. Symp. Symbolic and Algebraic Computation*, ACM, 74–79, 2003.

J. Dickhaut and T. Kaplan. A program for finding Nash equilibria. *Math. J.* 1:4, 87–93, 1991.

M.J.M. Jansen. Maximal Nash subsets for bimatrix games. *Naval Res. Logistics Q.* 28, 147–152, 1981.

H. Keiding. On the maximal number of Nash equilibria in an $n \times n$ bimatrix game. *Games Econ. Behav.* 21, 148–160, 1997.

D. Koller and N. Megiddo. The complexity of two-person zero-sum games in extensive form. *Games Econ. Behav.* 4, 528–552, 1992.

D. Koller, N. Megiddo, and B. von Stengel. Efficient computation of equilibria for extensive two-person games. *Games Econ. Behav.* 14, 247–259, 1996.

H.W. Kuhn. Extensive games and the problem of information. In: *Contributions to the Theory of Games II*, eds. H. W. Kuhn and A. W. Tucker, Ann. Math. Studies 28, Princeton Univ. Press, Princeton, 193–216, 1953.

H.W. Kuhn. An algorithm for equilibrium points in bimatrix games. *Proc. National Academy of Sciences of the U.S.A.* 47, 1657–1662, 1961.

C.E. Lemke. Bimatrix equilibrium points and mathematical programming. *Manag. Sci.* 11, 681–689, 1965.

C.E. Lemke and J.T. Howson, Jr. Equilibrium points of bimatrix games. *J. SIAM* 12, 413–423, 1964.

O.L. Mangasarian. Equilibrium points in bimatrix games. *J. SIAM* 12, 778–780, 1964.

R.D. McKelvey, A. McLennan, and T.L. Turocy. Gambit: Software Tools for Game Theory. Available at: http://econweb.tamu.edu/gambit, 2006.

P. McMullen. The maximum number of faces of a convex polytope. *Mathematika* 17, 179–184, 1970.

J.F. Nash. Non-cooperative games. *Ann. Math.* 54, 286–295, 1951.

I.V. Romanovskii. Reduction of a game with complete memory to a matrix game. *Soviet Math.* 3, 678–681, 1962.

G.D. Rosenberg. Enumeration of all extreme equilibria of bimatrix games with integer pivoting and improved degeneracy check. CDAM Res. Rep. LSE-CDAM-2005-18, London School of Economics, 2004.

R. Savani and B. von Stengel. Hard-to-solve bimatrix games. *Econometrica* 74, 397–429, 2006.

R. Selten. Reexamination of the perfectness concept for equilibrium points in extensive games. *Int. J. Game Theory* 4, 22–55, 1975.

L.S. Shapley. A note on the Lemke–Howson algorithm. *Mathematical Programming Study 1: Pivoting and Extensions*, 175–189, 1974.

E. van Damme. *Stability and Perfection of Nash Equilibria*. Springer, Berlin, 1987.

A. von Schemde. *Index and Stability in Bimatrix Games*. Springer, Berlin, 2005.

B. von Stengel. Efficient computation of behavior strategies. *Games Econ. Behav.* 14, 220–246, 1996.

B. von Stengel. New maximal numbers of equilibria in bimatrix games. *Disc. Comp. Geometry* 21, 557–568, 1999.

B. von Stengel. Computing equilibria for two-person games. In: *Handbook of Game Theory with Economic Applications*, eds. R.J. Aumann and S. Hart, Elsevier, Amsterdam, 3, 1723–1759, 2002.

B. von Stengel, A.H. van den Elzen, and A.J.J. Talman. Computing normal form perfect equilibria for extensive two-person games. *Econometrica* 70, 693–715, 2002.

N.N. Vorob'ev. Equilibrium points in bimatrix games. *Theory of Probability and its Applications* 3, 297–309, 1958.

H.-M. Winkels. An algorithm to determine all equilibrium points of a bimatrix game. In: *Game Theory and Related Topics*, eds. O. Moeschlin and D. Pallaschke, North-Holland, Amsterdam, 137–148, 1979.

G.M. Ziegler. *Lectures on Polytopes*. Springer, New York, 1995.

Exercises

3.1 Prove the claim made after Algorithm 3.4 that nonunique solutions to the equations in that algorithm occur only for degenerate games.

3.2 Show that in an equilibrium of a nondegenerate game, all pure best responses are played with positive probability.

3.3 Give further details of the argument made after Algorithm 3.6 that LH terminates. A duplicate label of a vertex pair (x, y) can be dropped in either polytope. Interpret these two possibilities.

3.4 Why is every pure strategy equilibrium found by LH for a suitable missing label?

3.5 Show that the "projection" to polytope P, say, of a LH path from (x, y) to (x', y') in $P \times Q$ is also a path in P from x to x'. Hence, if (x, y) is an equilibrium, where can x be on that projected path?

3.6 Verify the LH paths for the example (3.7).

3.7 Apply integer pivoting to the system $r + Ay = \mathbf{1}$ in the example, omitted after (3.13).

3.8 After (3.14), what is the multiplier in the "suitable multiple of the pivot row"? Give formulas for the update rules of the tableau.

3.9 Draw the polytope P for the game (3.18), and verify that the described naive use of LH fails.

3.10 Implement the lexico-minimum ratio test for the system (3.19) using the data in (3.17); you need a suitable array to identify the order of the basic variables.

3.11 Adapt a clique enumeration algorithm for graphs such as (Bron and Kerbosch, 1973) to find all maximal Nash subsets (see at the end of Section 3.6).

3.12 Consider an extensive game with a binary game tree of depth L (and thus 2^L leaves), where the two players alternate and are informed about all past moves except for the last move of the other player (see von Stengel et al., 2002). How many reduced strategies do the players have?

3.13 Prove Proposition 3.10, using (3.20), (3.21), and (3.23). Prove Proposition 3.11.

3.14 Write down the LCP of Theorem 3.14 for the game in Figure 3.3. Find all its solutions, for example with a variant of Algorithm 3.4.

CHAPTER 4

Learning, Regret Minimization, and Equilibria

Avrim Blum and Yishay Mansour

Abstract

Many situations involve repeatedly making decisions in an uncertain environment: for instance, deciding what route to drive to work each day, or repeated play of a game against an opponent with an unknown strategy. In this chapter we describe learning algorithms with strong guarantees for settings of this type, along with connections to game-theoretic equilibria when all players in a system are simultaneously adapting in such a manner.

We begin by presenting algorithms for repeated play of a matrix game with the guarantee that against any opponent, they will perform nearly as well as the best fixed action in hindsight (also called the problem of *combining expert advice* or minimizing *external regret*). In a zero-sum game, such algorithms are guaranteed to approach or exceed the minimax value of the game, and even provide a simple proof of the minimax theorem. We then turn to algorithms that minimize an even stronger form of regret, known as *internal* or *swap* regret. We present a general reduction showing how to convert any algorithm for minimizing external regret to one that minimizes this stronger form of regret as well. Internal regret is important because when all players in a game minimize this stronger type of regret, the empirical distribution of play is known to converge to *correlated* equilibrium.

The third part of this chapter explains a different reduction: how to convert from the *full information* setting in which the action chosen by the opponent is revealed after each time step, to the *partial information* (bandit) setting, where at each time step only the payoff of the selected action is observed (such as in routing), and still maintain a small external regret.

Finally, we end by discussing routing games in the Wardrop model, where one can show that if all participants minimize their own external regret, then overall traffic is guaranteed to converge to an approximate Nash Equilibrium. This further motivates price-of-anarchy results.

4.1 Introduction

In this chapter we consider the problem of repeatedly making decisions in an uncertain environment. The basic setting is we have a space of N actions, such as what route to use to drive to work, or the rows of a matrix game like {rock, paper, scissors}. At each time step, the algorithm probabilistically chooses an action (say, selecting what route to take), the environment makes its "move" (setting the road congestions on that day), and the algorithm then incurs the loss for its action chosen (how long its route took). The process then repeats the next day. What we would like are adaptive algorithms that can perform well in such settings, as well as to understand the dynamics of the system when there are multiple players, all adjusting their behavior in such a way.

A key technique for analyzing problems of this sort is known as regret analysis. The motivation behind regret analysis can be viewed as the following: we design a sophisticated online algorithm that deals with various issues of uncertainty and decision making, and sell it to a client. Our algorithm runs for some time and incurs a certain loss. We would like to avoid the embarrassment that our client will come back to us and claim that in *retrospect* we could have incurred a much lower loss if we used his simple alternative policy π. The regret of our online algorithm is the difference between the loss of our algorithm and the loss using π.

Different notions of regret quantify differently what is considered to be a "simple" alternative policy. *External regret*, also called the problem of *combining expert advice*, compares performance to the best single action in retrospect. This implies that the simple alternative policy performs the same action in all time steps, which indeed is quite simple. Nonetheless, external regret provides a general methodology for developing online algorithms whose performance matches that of an optimal static offline algorithm by modeling the possible static solutions as different actions. In the context of machine learning, algorithms with good external regret bounds can be powerful tools for achieving performance comparable to the optimal prediction rule from some large class of hypotheses.

In Section 4.3 we describe several algorithms with particularly strong external regret bounds. We start with the very weak greedy algorithm, and build up to an algorithm whose loss is at most $O(\sqrt{T \log N})$ greater than that of the best action, where T is the number of time steps. That is, the regret per time step drops as $O(\sqrt{(\log N)/T})$. In Section 4.4 we show that in a zero-sum game, such algorithms are guaranteed to approach or exceed the value of the game, and even yield a simple proof of the minimax theorem.

A second category of alternative policies are those that consider the online sequence of actions and suggest a simple modification to it, such as "every time you bought IBM, you should have bought Microsoft instead." While one can study very general classes of modification rules, the most common form, known as *internal* or *swap* regret, allows one to modify the online action sequence by changing every occurrence of a given action i by an alternative action j. (The distinction between internal and swap regret is that internal regret allows only one action to be replaced by another, whereas swap regret allows any mapping from $\{1, \ldots, N\}$ to $\{1, \ldots, N\}$ and can be up to a factor N larger). In Section 4.5 we present a simple way to efficiently convert any external regret minimizing algorithm into one that minimizes swap regret with only a factor N increase in the regret term. Using the results for external regret this achieves a swap regret bound of $O(\sqrt{TN \log N})$. (Algorithms for swap regret have also been developed from first principles—see the Notes section of this chapter for references—but this procedure gives the best bounds known for efficient algorithms.)

The importance of swap regret is due to its tight connection to correlated equilibria, defined in Chapter 1. In fact, one way to think of a correlated equilibrium is that it is a distribution Q over the joint action space such that every player would have zero internal (or swap) regret when playing it. As we point out in Section 4.4, if each player can achieve swap regret ϵT, then the empirical distribution of the joint actions of the players will be an ϵ-correlated equilibrium.

We also describe how external regret results can be extended to the *partial information model*, also called the *multiarmed bandit* (MAB) problem. In this model, the online algorithm only gets to observe the loss of the action actually selected, and does not see the losses of the actions not chosen. For example, in the case of driving to work, you may only observe the travel time on the route you actually drive, and do not get to find out how long it would have taken had you chosen some alternative route. In Section 4.6 we present a general reduction, showing how to convert an algorithm with low external regret in the full information model to one for the partial information model (though the bounds produced are not the best known bounds for this problem).

Notice that the route-choosing problem can be viewed as a general-sum game: your travel time depends on the choices of the other drivers as well. In Section 4.7 we discuss results showing that in the Wardrop model of infinitesimal agents (considered in Chapter 18), if each driver acts to minimize external regret, then traffic flow over time can be shown to approach an approximate Nash equilibrium. This serves to further motivate *price-of-anarchy* results in this context, since it means they apply to the case that participants are using well-motivated self-interested *adaptive* behavior.

We remark that the results we present in this chapter are not always the strongest known, and the interested reader is referred to the recent book (Cesa-Bianchi and Lugosi, 2006) that gives a thorough coverage of many of the the topics in this chapter. See also the Notes section for further references.

4.2 Model and Preliminaries

We assume an adversarial online model where there are N available actions $X = \{1, \ldots, N\}$. At each time step t, an online algorithm H selects a distribution p^t over the N actions. After that, the adversary selects a loss vector $\ell^t \in [0, 1]^N$, where $\ell_i^t \in [0, 1]$ is the loss of the i-th action at time t. In the *full information model*, the online algorithm H receives the loss vector ℓ^t and experiences a loss $\ell_H^t = \sum_{i=1}^N p_i^t \ell_i^t$. (This can be viewed as an expected loss when the online algorithm selects action $i \in X$ with probability p_i^t.) In the *partial information model*, the online algorithm receives $(\ell_{k^t}^t, k^t)$, where k^t is distributed according to p^t, and $\ell_H^t = \ell_{k^t}^t$ is its loss. The loss of the i-th action during the first T time steps is $L_i^T = \sum_{t=1}^T \ell_i^t$, and the loss of H is $L_H^T = \sum_{t=1}^T \ell_H^t$.

The aim for the *external regret* setting is to design an online algorithm that will be able to approach the performance of the best algorithm from a given class of algorithms $\mathcal{G}$; namely, to have a loss close to $L_{\mathcal{G},\min}^T = \min_{g \in \mathcal{G}} L_g^T$. Formally we would like to minimize the external regret $R_{\mathcal{G}} = L_H^T - L_{\mathcal{G},\min}^T$, and $\mathcal{G}$ is called the *comparison class*. The most studied comparison class $\mathcal{G}$ is the one that consists of all the single actions, i.e., $\mathcal{G} = X$. In this chapter we concentrate on this important comparison class, namely, we want the online algorithm's loss to be close to $L_{\min}^T = \min_i L_i^T$, and let the external regret be $R = L_H^T - L_{\min}^T$.

External regret uses a fixed comparison class $\mathcal{G}$, but one can also envision a comparison class that depends on the online algorithm's actions. We can consider modification rules that modify the actions selected by the online algorithm, producing an alternative strategy which we will want to compete against. A *modification rule* F has as input the history and the current action selected by the online procedure and outputs a (possibly different) action. (We denote by F^t the function F at time t, including any dependency on the history.) Given a sequence of probability distributions p^t used by an online algorithm H, and a modification rule F, we define a new sequence of probability distributions $f^t = F^t(p^t)$, where $f_i^t = \sum_{j:F^t(j)=i} p_j^t$. The loss of the modified sequence is $L_{H,F} = \sum_t \sum_i f_i^t \ell_i^t$. Note that at time t the modification rule F shifts the probability that H assigned to action j to action $F^t(j)$. This implies that the modification rule F generates a different distribution, as a function of the online algorithm's distribution p^t.

We will focus on the case of a finite set $\mathcal{F}$ of memoryless modification rules (they do not depend on history). Given a sequence of loss vectors, the regret of an online algorithm H with respect to the modification rules $\mathcal{F}$ is

$$R_{\mathcal{F}} = \max_{F \in \mathcal{F}} \{L_H^T - L_{H,F}^T\}.$$

Note that the external regret setting is equivalent to having a set $\mathcal{F}^{\text{ex}}$ of N modification rules F_i, where F_i always outputs action i. For *internal regret*, the set $\mathcal{F}^{\text{in}}$ consists of $N(N-1)$ modification rules $F_{i,j}$, where $F_{i,j}(i) = j$ and $F_{i,j}(i') = i'$ for $i' \neq i$. That is, the internal regret of H is

$$\max_{F \in \mathcal{F}^{\text{in}}} \{L_H^T - L_{H,F}^T\} = \max_{i,j \in X} \left\{ \sum_{t=1}^{T} p_i^t (\ell_i^t - \ell_j^t) \right\}.$$

A more general class of memoryless modification rules is *swap regret* defined by the class $\mathcal{F}^{\text{sw}}$, which includes all N^N functions $F : \{1, \ldots, N\} \to \{1, \ldots, N\}$, where the function F swaps the current online action i with $F(i)$ (which can be the same or a different action). That is, the swap regret of H is

$$\max_{F \in \mathcal{F}^{\text{sw}}} \{L_H^T - L_{H,F}^T\} = \sum_{i=1}^{N} \max_{j \in X} \left\{ \sum_{t=1}^{T} p_i^t (\ell_i^t - \ell_j^t) \right\}.$$

Note that since $\mathcal{F}^{\text{ex}} \subseteq \mathcal{F}^{\text{sw}}$ and $\mathcal{F}^{\text{in}} \subseteq \mathcal{F}^{\text{sw}}$, both external and internal regret are upper-bounded by swap regret. (See also Exercises 4.1 and 4.2.)

4.3 External Regret Minimization

Before describing the external regret results, we begin by pointing out that it is not possible to guarantee low regret with respect to the overall optimal *sequence* of decisions in hindsight, as is done in competitive analysis (Borodin and El-Yaniv, 1998; Sleator and Tarjan, 1985). This will motivate why we will be concentrating on more restricted comparison classes. In particular, let $\mathcal{G}_{\text{all}}$ be the set of all functions mapping times $\{1, \ldots, T\}$ to actions $X = \{1, \ldots, N\}$.

Theorem 4.1 *For any online algorithm H there exists a sequence of T loss vectors such that regret $R_{\mathcal{G}_{\text{all}}}$ is at least $T(1 - 1/N)$.*

PROOF The sequence is simply as follows: at each time t, the action i_t of lowest probability p_i^t gets a loss of 0, and all the other actions get a loss of 1. Since $\min_i\{p_i^t\} \leq 1/N$, this means the loss of H in T time steps is at least $T(1 - 1/N)$. On the other hand, there exists $g \in \mathcal{G}_{\text{all}}$, namely $g(t) = i_t$, with a total loss of 0. □

The above proof shows that if we consider all possible functions, we have a very large regret. For the rest of the section we will use the comparison class $\mathcal{G}_a = \{g_i : i \in X\}$, where g_i always selects action i. Namely, we compare the online algorithm to the best single action.

4.3.1 Warmup: Greedy and Randomized-Greedy Algorithms

In this section, for simplicity we will assume that all losses are either 0 or 1 (rather than a real number in [0, 1]), which will simplify notation and proofs, although everything presented can be easily extended to the general case.

Our first attempt to develop a good regret minimization algorithm will be to consider the greedy algorithm. Recall that $L_i^t = \sum_{\tau=1}^{t} \ell_i^\tau$, namely the cumulative loss up to time t of action i. The `Greedy` algorithm at each time t selects action $x^t = \arg\min_{i \in X} L_i^{t-1}$ (if there are multiple actions with the same cumulative loss, it prefers the action with the lowest index). Formally:

`Greedy` Algorithm
Initially: $x^1 = 1$.
At time t: Let $L_{\min}^{t-1} = \min_{i \in X} L_i^{t-1}$, and $S^{t-1} = \{i : L_i^{t-1} = L_{\min}^{t-1}\}$.
Let $x^t = \min S^{t-1}$.

Theorem 4.2 *The* `Greedy` *algorithm, for any sequence of losses has*

$$L_{\texttt{Greedy}}^T \leq N \cdot L_{\min}^T + (N - 1).$$

PROOF At each time t such that `Greedy` incurs a loss of 1 and $L_{\min}^t$ does not increase, at least one action is removed from S^t. This can occur at most N times before $L_{\min}^t$ increases by 1. Therefore, `Greedy` incurs loss at most N between successive increments in $L_{\min}^t$. More formally, this shows inductively that $L_{\texttt{Greedy}}^t \leq N - |S^t| + N \cdot L_{\min}^t$. □

The above guarantee on `Greedy` is quite weak, stating only that its loss is at most a factor of N larger than the loss of the best action. The following theorem shows that this weakness is shared by any deterministic online algorithm. (A deterministic algorithm concentrates its entire weight on a single action at each time step.)

Theorem 4.3 *For any deterministic algorithm D there exists a loss sequence for which $L_D^T = T$ and $L_{\min}^T = \lfloor T/N \rfloor$.*

Note that the above theorem implies that $L_D^T \geq N \cdot L_{\min}^T + (T \bmod N)$, which almost matches the upper bound for Greedy (Theorem 4.2).

PROOF Fix a deterministic online algorithm D and let x^t be the action it selects at time t. We will generate the loss sequence in the following way. At time t, let the loss of x^t be 1 and the loss of any other action be 0. This ensures that D incurs loss 1 at each time step, so $L_D^T = T$.

Since there are N different actions, there is some action that algorithm D has selected at most $\lfloor T/N \rfloor$ times. By construction, only the actions selected by D ever have a loss, so this implies that $L_{\min}^T \leq \lfloor T/N \rfloor$. □

Theorem 4.3 motivates considering randomized algorithms. In particular, one weakness of the greedy algorithm was that it had a deterministic *tie breaker*. One can hope that if the online algorithm splits its weight between all the currently best actions, better performance could be achieved. Specifically, let Randomized Greedy (RG) be the procedure that assigns a uniform distribution over all those actions with minimum total loss so far. We now will show that this algorithm achieves a significant performance improvement: its loss is at most an $O(\log N)$ factor from the best action, rather than $O(N)$. (This is similar to the analysis of the randomized marking algorithm in competitive analysis.)

Randomized Greedy (RG) Algorithm

Initially: $p_i^1 = 1/N$ for $i \in X$.

At time t: Let $L_{\min}^{t-1} = \min_{i \in X} L_i^{t-1}$, and $S^{t-1} = \{i : L_i^{t-1} = L_{\min}^{t-1}\}$.
Let $p_i^t = 1/|S^{t-1}|$ for $i \in S^{t-1}$ and $p_i^t = 0$ otherwise.

Theorem 4.4 *The* Randomized Greedy (RG) *algorithm, for any loss sequence, has*

$$L_{\text{RG}}^T \leq (\ln N) + (1 + \ln N) L_{\min}^T .$$

PROOF The proof follows from showing that the loss incurred by Randomized Greedy between successive increases in $L_{\min}^t$ is at most $1 + \ln N$. Specifically, let t_j denote the time step at which $L_{\min}^t$ first reaches a loss of j, so we are interested in the loss of Randomized Greedy between time steps t_j and t_{j+1}. At time any t we have $1 \leq |S^t| \leq N$. Furthermore, if at time $t \in (t_j, t_{j+1}]$ the size of S^t shrinks by k from some size n' down to $n' - k$, then the loss of the online algorithm RG is k/n', since each such action has weight $1/n'$. Finally, notice that we can upper bound k/n' by $1/n' + 1/(n' - 1) + \cdots + 1/(n' - k + 1)$. Therefore, over the entire time-interval $(t_j, t_{j+1}]$, the loss of Randomized Greedy is at most:

$$1/N + 1/(N-1) + 1/(N-2) + \cdots + 1/1 \leq 1 + \ln N.$$

More formally, this shows inductively that $L_{\text{RG}}^t \leq (1/N + 1/(N-1) + \cdots + 1/(|S^t| + 1)) + (1 + \ln N) \cdot L_{\min}^t$. □

4.3.2 Randomized Weighted Majority Algorithm

Although `Randomized Greedy` achieved a significant performance gain compared to the `Greedy` algorithm, we still have a logarithmic ratio to the best action. Looking more closely at the proof, one can see that the losses are greatest when the sets S^t are small, since the online loss can be viewed as proportional to $1/|S^t|$. One way to overcome this weakness is to give some weight to actions which are currently "near best." That is, we would like the probability mass on some action to decay gracefully with its distance to optimality. This is the idea of the *Randomized Weighted Majority* algorithm of Littlestone and Warmuth.

Specifically, in the Randomized Weighted Majority algorithm, we give an action i whose total loss so far is L_i a *weight* $w_i = (1-\eta)^{L_i}$, and then choose probabilities proportional to the weights: $p_i = w_i / \sum_{j=1}^N w_j$. The parameter η will be set to optimize certain trade-offs but conceptually think of it as a small constant, say 0.01. In this section we will again assume losses in $\{0, 1\}$ rather than $[0, 1]$ because it allows for an especially intuitive interpretation of the proof (Theorem 4.5). We then relax this assumption in the next section (Theorem 4.6).

`Randomized Weighted Majority (RWM)` Algorithm
Initially: $w_i^1 = 1$ and $p_i^1 = 1/N$, for $i \in X$.
At time t: If $\ell_i^{t-1} = 1$, let $w_i^t = w_i^{t-1}(1-\eta)$; else ($\ell_i^{t-1} = 0$) let $w_i^t = w_i^{t-1}$.
Let $p_i^t = w_i^t / W^t$, where $W^t = \sum_{i \in X} w_i^t$.

Algorithm `RWM` and Theorem 4.5 can be generalized to losses in [0, 1] by replacing the update rule with $w_i^t = w_i^{t-1}(1-\eta)^{\ell_i^{t-1}}$ (see Exercise 4.3).

Theorem 4.5 *For $\eta \le 1/2$, the loss of* `Randomized Weighted Majority (RWM)` *on any sequence of binary* $\{0, 1\}$ *losses satisfies*

$$L_{\text{RWM}}^T \le (1+\eta)L_{\min}^T + \frac{\ln N}{\eta}.$$

Setting $\eta = \min\{\sqrt{(\ln N)/T}, 1/2\}$ yields $L_{\text{RWM}}^T \le L_{\min}^T + 2\sqrt{T \ln N}$.

(Note: The second part of the theorem assumes T is known in advance. If T is unknown, then a "guess and double" approach can be used to set η with just a constant-factor loss in regret. In fact, one can achieve the potentially better bound $L_{\text{RWM}}^T \le L_{\min}^T + 2\sqrt{L_{\min} \ln N}$ by setting $\eta = \min\{\sqrt{(\ln N)/L_{\min}}, 1/2\}$.)

PROOF The key to the proof is to consider the total weight W^t. What we will show is that anytime the online algorithm has significant expected loss, the total weight must drop substantially. We will then combine this with the fact that $W^{T+1} \ge \max_i w_i^{T+1} = (1-\eta)^{L_{\min}^T}$ to achieve the desired bound.

Specifically, let $F^t = (\sum_{i:\ell_i^t=1} w_i^t)/W^t$ denote the fraction of the weight W^t that is on actions that experience a loss of 1 at time t; so, F^t equals the expected loss of algorithm `RWM` at time t. Now, each of the actions experiencing a loss of 1 has its weight multiplied by $(1-\eta)$ while the rest are unchanged. Therefore, $W^{t+1} = W^t - \eta F^t W^t = W^t(1-\eta F^t)$. In other words, the proportion of the weight removed from the system at each time t is exactly proportional to the expected loss of the online algorithm. Now, using the fact that $W^1 = N$ and using our lower bound on W^{T+1} we have

$$(1-\eta)^{L^T_{\min}} \le W^{T+1} \;=\; W^1 \prod_{t=1}^{T} (1-\eta F^t) \;=\; N \prod_{t=1}^{T} (1-\eta F^t).$$

Taking logarithms,

$$\begin{aligned} L^T_{\min} \ln(1-\eta) &\le (\ln N) + \sum_{t=1}^{T} \ln(1-\eta F^t) \\ &\le (\ln N) - \sum_{t=1}^{T} \eta F^t \\ &\quad \text{(Using the inequality } \ln(1-z) \le -z) \\ &= (\ln N) - \eta L^T_{\mathrm{RWM}} \\ &\quad \text{(by definition of } F^t) \end{aligned}$$

Therefore,

$$\begin{aligned} L^T_{\mathrm{RWM}} &\le \frac{-L^T_{\min}\ln(1-\eta)}{\eta} + \frac{\ln(N)}{\eta} \\ &\le (1+\eta)L^T_{\min} + \frac{\ln(N)}{\eta}, \\ &\quad \text{(Using the inequality } -\ln(1-z) \le z + z^2 \text{ for } 0 \le z \le \tfrac{1}{2}) \end{aligned}$$

which completes the proof. □

4.3.3 Polynomial Weights Algorithm

The `Polynomial Weights (PW)` algorithm is a natural extension of the RWM algorithm to losses in [0, 1] (or even to the case of both losses and gains, see Exercise 4.4) that maintains the same proof structure as that used for RWM and in addition performs especially well in the case of small losses.

`Polynomial Weights (PW)` Algorithm
Initially: $w_i^1 = 1$ and $p_i^1 = 1/N$, for $i \in X$.
At time t: Let $w_i^t = w_i^{t-1}(1 - \eta \ell_i^{t-1})$.
Let $p_i^t = w_i^t / W^t$, where $W^t = \sum_{i \in X} w_i^t$.

Notice that the only difference between PW and RWM is in the update step. In particular, it is no longer necessarily the case that an action of total loss L has weight $(1-\eta)^L$. However, what *is* maintained is the property that if the algorithm's loss at time t is F^t, then exactly an ηF^t fraction of the total weight is removed from the system. Specifically, from the update rule we have $W^{t+1} = W^t - \sum_i \eta w_i^t \ell_i^t = W^t(1-\eta F^t)$ where $F^t = (\sum_i w_i^t \ell_i^t)/W^t$ is the loss of PW at time t. We can use this fact to prove the following.

Theorem 4.6 *The* `Polynomial Weights (PW)` *algorithm, using* $\eta \le 1/2$, *for any* $[0, 1]$*-valued loss sequence and for any k has,*

$$L^T_{\texttt{PW}} \le L^T_k + \eta Q^T_k + \frac{\ln(N)}{\eta},$$

where $Q^T_k = \sum_{t=1}^T (\ell^t_k)^2$. *Setting* $\eta = \min\{\sqrt{(\ln N)/T}, 1/2\}$ *and noting that* $Q^T_k \le T$, *we have* $L^T_{\texttt{PW}} \le L^T_{\min} + 2\sqrt{T \ln N}$.[1]

PROOF As noted above, we have $W^{t+1} = W^t(1 - \eta F^t)$, where F^t is PW's loss at time t. So, as with the analysis of RWM, we have $W^{T+1} = N \prod_{t=1}^T (1 - \eta F^t)$ and therefore

$$\ln W^{T+1} = \ln N + \sum_{t=1}^{T} \ln(1 - \eta F^t) \le \ln N - \eta \sum_{t=1}^{T} F^t = \ln N - \eta L^T_{\texttt{PW}}.$$

Now for the lower bound, we have

$$\begin{aligned}
\ln W^{T+1} &\ge \ln w^{T+1}_k \\
&= \sum_{t=1}^{T} \ln\left(1 - \eta \ell^t_k\right) \\
&\quad \text{(using the recursive definition of weights)} \\
&\ge -\sum_{t=1}^{T} \eta \ell^t_k - \sum_{t=1}^{T} \left(\eta \ell^t_k\right)^2 \\
&\quad \text{(using the inequality } \ln(1-z) \ge -z - z^2 \text{ for } 0 \le z \le \tfrac{1}{2}) \\
&= -\eta L^T_k - \eta^2 Q^T_k .
\end{aligned}$$

Combining the upper and lower bounds on $\ln W^{T+1}$ we have:

$$-\eta L^T_k - \eta^2 Q^T_k \le \ln N - \eta L^T_{\texttt{PW}},$$

which yields the theorem. □

4.3.4 Lower Bounds

An obvious question is whether one can significantly improve the bound in Theorem 4.6. We will show two simple results that imply that the regret bound is near optimal (see Exercise 4.5 for a better lower bound). The first result shows that one cannot hope to get sublinear regret when T is small compared to $\log N$, and the second shows that one cannot hope to achieve regret $o(\sqrt{T})$ even when $N = 2$.

Theorem 4.7 *Consider* $T < \log_2 N$. *There exists a stochastic generation of losses such that, for any online algorithm* $R1$, *we have* $E[L^T_{R1}] = T/2$ *and yet* $L^T_{\min} = 0$.

[1] Again, for simplicity we assume that the number of time steps T is given as a parameter to the algorithm; otherwise, one can use a "guess and double" method to set η.

PROOF Consider the following sequence of losses. At time $t = 1$, a random subset of $N/2$ actions gets a loss of 0 and the rest gets a loss of 1. At time $t = 2$, a random subset of $N/4$ of the actions that had loss 0 at time $t = 1$ gets a loss of 0, and the rest (including actions that had a loss of 1 at time 1) gets a loss of 1. This process repeats: at each time step, a random subset of half of the actions that have received loss 0 so far gets a loss of 0, while all the rest gets a loss of 1. Any online algorithm incurs an expected loss of 1/2 at each time step, because at each time step t the expected fraction of probability mass p_i^t on actions that receive a loss of 0 is at most 1/2. Yet, for $T < \log_2 N$ there will always be some action with total loss of 0. □

Theorem 4.8 *Consider $N = 2$. There exists a stochastic generation of losses such that, for any online algorithm R2, we have $E[L_{R2}^T - L_{\min}^T] = \Omega(\sqrt{T})$.*

PROOF At time t, we flip a fair coin and set $\ell^t = z_1 = (0, 1)$ with probability 1/2 and $\ell^t = z_2 = (1, 0)$ with probability 1/2. For any distribution p^t the expected loss at time t is exactly 1/2. Therefore any online algorithm $R2$ has expected loss of $T/2$.

Given a sequence of T such losses, with $T/2 + y$ losses z_1 and $T/2 - y$ losses z_2, we have $T/2 - L_{\min}^T = |y|$. It remains to lower bound $E[|y|]$. Note that the probability of y is $\binom{T}{T/2+y}/2^T$, which is upper bounded by $O(1/\sqrt{T})$ (using a Sterling approximation). This implies that with a constant probability we have $|y| = \Omega(\sqrt{T})$, which completes the proof. □

4.4 Regret Minimization and Game Theory

In this section we outline the connection between regret minimization and central concepts in game theory. We start by showing that in a two-player constant sum game, a player with external regret sublinear in T will have an average payoff that is at least the value of the game, minus a vanishing error term. For a general game, we will see that if all the players use procedures with sublinear *swap-regret*, then they will converge to an approximate *correlated* equilibrium. We also show that for a player who minimizes swap-regret, the frequency of playing dominated actions is vanishing.

4.4.1 Game Theoretic Model

We start with the standard definitions of a game (see also Chapter 1). A game $G = \langle M, (X_i), (s_i)\rangle$ has a finite set M of m players. Player i has a set X_i of N actions and a loss function $s_i : X_i \times (\times_{j \neq i} X_j) \rightarrow [0, 1]$ that maps the action of player i and the actions of the other players to a real number. (We have scaled losses to [0, 1].) The joint action space is $X = \times X_i$.

We consider a player i that plays a game G for T time steps using an online procedure ON. At time step t, player i plays a distribution (mixed action) P_i^t, while the other players play the joint distribution P_{-i}^t. We denote by ℓ_{ON}^t the loss of player i at time t, i.e.,

$E_{x\sim P^t}[s_i(x^t)]$, and its cumulative loss is $L_{\text{ON}}^T = \sum_{t=1}^T \ell_{\text{ON}}^t$.[2] It is natural to define, for player i at time t, the loss vector as $\ell^t = (\ell_1^t, \ldots, \ell_N^t)$, where $\ell_j^t = E_{x_{-i}^t \sim P_{-i}^t}[s_i(x_j^t, x_{-i}^t)]$. Namely, ℓ_j^t is the loss player i would have observed if at time t it had played action x_j. The cumulative loss of action $x_j \in X_i$ of player i is $L_j^T = \sum_{t=1}^T \ell_j^t$, and $L_{\min}^T = \min_j L_j^T$.

4.4.2 Constant Sum Games and External Regret Minimization

A two-player constant sum game $G = \langle\{1, 2\}, (X_i), (s_i)\rangle$ has the property that for some constant c, for every $x_1 \in X_1$ and $x_2 \in X_2$ we have $s_1(x_1, x_2) + s_2(x_1, x_2) = c$. It is well known that any constant sum game has a well-defined *value* (v_1, v_2) for the game, and player $i \in \{1, 2\}$ has a mixed strategy which guarantees that its expected loss is at most v_i, regardless of the other player's strategy. (See Owen, 1982, for more details.) In such games, external regret-minimization procedures provide the following guarantee.

Theorem 4.9 *Let G be a constant sum game with game value (v_1, v_2). If player $i \in \{1, 2\}$ plays for T steps using a procedure* ON *with external regret R, then its average loss $\frac{1}{T}L_{\text{ON}}^T$ is at most $v_i + R/T$.*

PROOF Let q be the mixed strategy corresponding to the observed frequencies of the actions player 2 has played; that is, $q_j = \sum_{t=1}^T P_{2,j}^t / T$, where $P_{2,j}^t$ is the weight player 2 gives to action j at time t. By the theory of constant sum games, for any mixed strategy q of player 2, player 1 has some action $x_k \in X_1$ such that $E_{x_2\sim q}[s_1(x_k, x_2)] \leq v_1$ (see Owen, 1982). This implies, in our setting, that if player 1 has always played action x_k, then its loss would be at most $v_1 T$. Therefore $L_{\min}^T \leq L_k^T \leq v_1 T$. Now, using the fact that player 1 is playing a procedure ON with external regret R, we have that $L_{\text{ON}}^T \leq L_{\min}^T + R \leq v_1 T + R$. □

Thus, using a procedure with regret $R = O(\sqrt{T \log N})$ as in Theorem 4.6 will guarantee average loss at most $v_i + O(\sqrt{(\log N)/T})$.

In fact, we can use the existence of external regret minimization algorithms to prove the minimax theorem of two-player zero-sum games. For player 1, let $v_{\min}^1 = \min_{x_1 \in X_1} \max_{z \in \Delta(X_2)} E_{x_2 \sim z}[s_1(x_1, x_2)]$ and $v_{\max}^1 = \max_{x_2 \in X_2} \min_{z \in \Delta(X_1)} E_{x_1 \sim z}[s_1(x_1, x_2)]$. That is, $v_{\min}^1$ is the best loss that player 1 can guarantee for itself if it is told the mixed action of player 2 in advance. Similarly, $v_{\max}^1$ is the best loss that player 1 can guarantee to itself if it has to go first in selecting a mixed action, and player 2's action may then depend on it. The minimax theorem states that $v_{\min}^1 = v_{\max}^1$. Since $s_1(x_1, x_2) = -s_2(x_1, x_2)$ we can similarly define $v_{\min}^2 = -v_{\max}^1$ and $v_{\max}^2 = -v_{\min}^1$.

In the following we give a proof of the minimax theorem based on the existence of external regret algorithms. Assume for contradiction that $v_{\max}^1 = v_{\min}^1 + \gamma$ for some $\gamma > 0$ (it is easy to see that $v_{\max}^1 \geq v_{\min}^1$). Consider both players playing a regret

[2] Alternatively, we could consider x_i^t as a random variable distributed according to P_i^t, and similarly discuss the expected loss. We prefer the above presentation for consistency with the rest of the chapter.

minimization algorithm for T steps having external regret of at most R, such that $R/T < \gamma/2$. Let L_{ON} be the loss of player 1 and note that $-L_{\mathrm{ON}}$ is the loss of player 2. Let $L^i_{\min}$ be the cumulative loss of the best action of player $i \in \{1, 2\}$. As before, let q_i be the mixed strategy corresponding to the observed frequencies of actions of player $i \in \{1, 2\}$. Then, $L^1_{\min}/T \leq v^1_{\min}$, since for $L^1_{\min}$ we select the best action with respect to a specific mixed action, namely q_2. Similarly, $L^2_{\min}/T \leq v^2_{\min}$. The regret minimization algorithms guarantee for player 1 that $L_{\mathrm{ON}} \leq L^1_{\min} + R$, and for player 2 that $-L_{\mathrm{ON}} \leq L^2_{\min} + R$. Combining the inequalities we have:

$$T v^1_{\max} - R = -T v^2_{\max} - R \leq -L^2_{\min} - R \leq L_{\mathrm{ON}} \leq L^1_{\min} + R \leq T v^1_{\min} + R.$$

This implies that $v^1_{\max} - v^1_{\min} \leq 2R/T < \gamma$, which is a contradiction. Therefore, $v^1_{\max} = v^1_{\min}$, which establishes the minimax theorem.

4.4.3 Correlated Equilibrium and Swap Regret Minimization

We first define the relevant modification rules and establish the connection between them and equilibrium notions. For $x_1, b_1, b_2 \in X_i$, let $\mathrm{switch}_i(x_1, b_1, b_2)$ be the following modification function of the action x_1 of player i:

$$\mathrm{switch}_i(x_1, b_1, b_2) = \begin{cases} b_2 & \text{if } x_1 = b_1 \\ x_1 & \text{otherwise} \end{cases}$$

Given a modification function f for player i, we can measure the regret of player i with respect to f as the decrease in its loss, i.e.,

$$\mathrm{regret}_i(x, f) = s_i(x) - s_i(f(x_i), x_{-i}).$$

For example, when we consider $f(x_1) = \mathrm{switch}_i(x_1, b_1, b_2)$, for a fixed $b_1, b_2 \in X_i$, then $\mathrm{regret}_i(x, f)$ is measuring the regret player i has for playing action b_1 rather than b_2, when the other players play x_{-i}.

A *correlated equilibrium* is a distribution P over the joint action space with the following property. Imagine a correlating device draws a vector of actions $x \in X$ using distribution P over X, and gives player i the action x_i from x. (Player i is not given any other information regarding x.) The probability distribution P is a correlated equilibrium if, for each player, it is a best response to play the suggested action, provided that the other players also do not deviate. (For a more detailed discussion of correlated equilibrium, see Chapter 1.)

Definition 4.10 A joint probability distribution P over X is a *correlated equilibrium* if for every player i, and any actions $b_1, b_2 \in X_i$, we have that

$$E_{x \sim P}[\mathrm{regret}_i(x, \mathrm{switch}_i(\cdot, b_1, b_2))] \leq 0.$$

An equivalent definition that extends more naturally to the case of approximate equilibria is to say that rather than only switching between a pair of actions, we allow simultaneously replacing every action in X_i with another action in X_i (possibly the same action). A distribution P is a correlated equilibrium iff for any function $F : X_i \to X_i$ we have $E_{x \sim P}[\mathrm{regret}_i(x, F)] \leq 0$.

We now define an ϵ-correlated equilibrium. An ϵ-correlated equilibrium is a distribution P such that each player has in expectation at most an ϵ incentive to deviate. Formally,

Definition 4.11 A joint probability distribution P over X is an ϵ-correlated equilibria if for every player i and for any function $F_i : X_i \to X_i$, we have $E_{x\sim P}[\text{regret}_i(x, F_i)] \leq \epsilon$.

The following theorem relates the empirical distribution of the actions performed by each player, their swap regret, and the distance to correlated equilibrium.

Theorem 4.12 *Let $G = \langle M, (X_i), (s_i)\rangle$ be a game and assume that for T time steps every player follows a strategy that has swap regret of at most R. Then, the empirical distribution Q of the joint actions played by the players is an (R/T)-correlated equilibrium.*

PROOF The empirical distribution Q assigns to every P^t a probability of $1/T$. Fix a function $F : X_i \to X_i$ for player i. Since player i has swap regret at most R, we have $L^T_{\text{ON}} \leq L^T_{\text{ON},F} + R$, where L^T_{ON} is the loss of player i. By definition of the regret function, we therefore have

$$L^T_{\text{ON}} - L^T_{\text{ON},F} = \sum_{t=1}^{T} E_{x^t\sim P^t}[s_i(x^t)] - \sum_{t=1}^{T} E_{x^t\sim P^t}\left[s_i\left(F\left(x^t_i\right), x^t_{-i}\right)\right]$$

$$= \sum_{t=1}^{T} E_{x^t\sim P^t}[\text{regret}_i(x^t, F)] = T \cdot E_{x\sim Q}[\text{regret}_i(x, F)].$$

Therefore, for any function $F_i : X_i \to X_i$ we have $E_{x\sim Q}[\text{regret}_i(x, F_i)] \leq R/T$. □

The above theorem states that the payoff of each player is its payoff in some approximate correlated equilibrium. In addition, it relates the swap regret to the distance from equilibrium. Note that if the average swap regret vanishes then the procedure converges, in the limit, to the set of correlated equilibria.

4.4.4 Dominated Strategies

We say that an action $x_j \in X_i$ is ϵ-*dominated* by action $x_k \in X_i$ if for any $x_{-i} \in X_{-i}$ we have $s_i(x_j, x_{-i}) \geq \epsilon + s_i(x_k, x_{-i})$. Similarly, action $x_j \in X_i$ is ϵ-*dominated* by a mixed action $y \in \Delta(X_i)$ if for any $x_{-i} \in X_{-i}$ we have $s_i(x_j, x_{-i}) \geq \epsilon + E_{x_d\sim y}[s_i(x_d, x_{-i})]$.

Intuitively, a good learning algorithm ought to be able to learn not to play actions that are ϵ-dominated by others, and in this section we show that indeed if player i plays a procedure with sublinear swap regret, then it will very rarely play dominated actions. More precisely, let action x_j be ϵ-dominated by action $x_k \in X_i$. Using our notation, this implies that for any x_{-i} we have that $\text{regret}_i(x, \text{switch}_i(\cdot, x_j, x_k)) \geq \epsilon$. Let D_ϵ be the set of ϵ-dominated actions of player i, and let w be the weight that player i puts on actions in D_ϵ, averaged over time, i.e., $w = \frac{1}{T}\sum_{t=1}^{T}\sum_{j\in D_\epsilon} P_{i,j}^t$. Player i's swap regret is at least $\epsilon w T$ (since we could replace each action in D_ϵ with the action that dominates it). So, if the player's swap regret is R, then $\epsilon w T \le R$. Therefore, the time-average weight that player i puts on the set of ϵ-dominated actions is at most $R/(\epsilon T)$, which tends to 0 if R is sublinear in T. That is:

Theorem 4.13 *Consider a game G and a player i that uses a procedure of swap regret R for T time steps. Then the average weight that player i puts on the set of ϵ-dominated actions is at most $R/(\epsilon T)$.*

We remark that in general the property of having low *external* regret is not sufficient by itself to give such a guarantee, though the algorithms RWM and PW do indeed have such a guarantee (see Exercise 4.8).

4.5 Generic Reduction from External to Swap Regret

In this section we give a black-box reduction showing how any procedure A achieving good external regret can be used as a subroutine to achieve good swap regret as well. The high-level idea is as follows (see also Figure 4.1). We will instantiate N copies $A_1, \ldots, A_N$ of the external-regret procedure. At each time step, these procedures will each give us a probability vector, which we will combine in a particular way to produce our own probability vector p. When we receive a loss vector ℓ, we will partition it among the N procedures, giving procedure A_i a fraction p_i (p_i is our probability mass on action i), so that A_i's belief about the loss of action j is $\sum_t p_i^t \ell_j^t$, and matches the cost we would incur putting i's probability mass on j. In the proof, procedure A_i will, in some sense, be responsible for ensuring low regret of the $i \to j$ variety. The key to making this work is that we will be able to define the p's so that the sum of the losses of the procedures A_i on their own loss vectors matches our overall true loss. Recall the definition of an R external regret procedure.

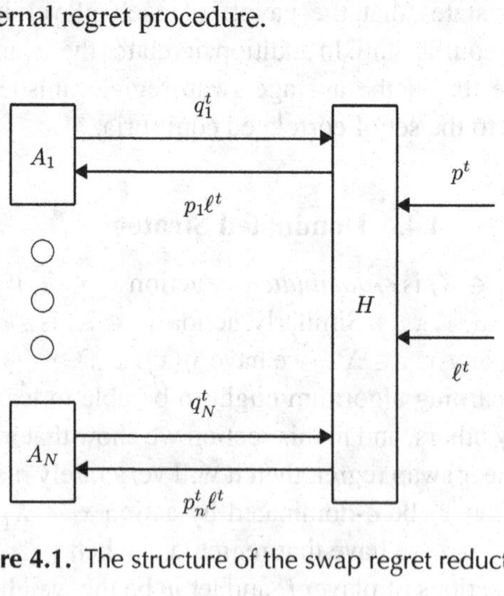

Figure 4.1. The structure of the swap regret reduction.

Definition 4.14 An R external regret procedure A guarantees that for any sequence of T losses ℓ^t and for any action $j \in \{1, \ldots, N\}$, we have

$$L_A^T = \sum_{t=1}^{T} \ell_A^t \leq \sum_{t=1}^{T} \ell_j^t + R = L_j^T + R.$$

We assume we have N copies $A_1, \ldots, A_N$ of an R external regret procedure. We combine the N procedures to one master procedure H as follows. At each time step t, each procedure A_i outputs a distribution q_i^t, where $q_{i,j}^t$ is the fraction it assigns action j. We compute a single distribution p^t such that $p_j^t = \sum_i p_i^t q_{i,j}^t$. That is, $p^t = p^t Q^t$, where p^t is our distribution and Q^t is the matrix of $q_{i,j}^t$. (We can view p^t as a stationary distribution of the Markov Process defined by Q^t, and it is well known that such a p^t exists and is efficiently computable.) For intuition into this choice of p^t, notice that it implies we can consider action selection in two equivalent ways. The first is simply using the distribution p^t to select action j with probability p_j^t. The second is to select procedure A_i with probability p_i^t and then to use A_i to select the action (which produces distribution $p^t Q^t$).

When the adversary returns the loss vector ℓ^t, we return to each A_i the loss vector $p_i \ell^t$. So, procedure A_i experiences loss $(p_i^t \ell^t) \cdot q_i^t = p_i^t (q_i^t \cdot \ell^t)$.

Since A_i is an R external regret procedure, for any action j, we have,

$$\sum_{t=1}^{T} p_i^t \left(q_i^t \cdot \ell^t\right) \leq \sum_{t=1}^{T} p_i^t \ell_j^t + R \tag{4.1}$$

If we sum the losses of the N procedures at a given time t, we get $\sum_i p_i^t (q_i^t \cdot \ell^t) = p^t Q^t \ell^t$, where p^t is the row vector of our distribution, Q^t is the matrix of $q_{i,j}^t$, and ℓ^t is viewed as a column vector. By design of p^t, we have $p^t Q^t = p^t$. So, the sum of the perceived losses of the N procedures is equal to our actual loss $p^t \ell^t$.

Therefore, summing equation (4.1) over all N procedures, the left-hand side sums to L_H^T, where H is our master online procedure. Since the right-hand side of equation (4.1) holds for any j, we have that for any function $F : \{1, \ldots, N\} \to \{1, \ldots, N\}$,

$$L_H^T \leq \sum_{i=1}^{N} \sum_{t=1}^{T} p_i^t \ell_{F(i)}^t + NR = L_{H,F}^T + NR$$

Therefore we have proven the following theorem.

Theorem 4.15 *Given an R external regret procedure, the master online procedure H has the following guarantee. For every function $F : \{1, \ldots, N\} \to \{1, \ldots, N\}$,*

$$L_H \leq L_{H,F} + NR,$$

i.e., the swap regret of H is at most NR.

Using Theorem 4.6, we can immediately derive the following corollary.

Corollary 4.16 *There exists an online algorithm H such that for every function* $F : \{1, \ldots, N\} \rightarrow \{1, \ldots, N\}$, *we have that*

$$L_H \leq L_{H,F} + O(N\sqrt{T \log N}),$$

i.e., the swap regret of H is at most $O(N\sqrt{T \log N})$.

Remark. See Exercise 4.6 for an improvement to $O(\sqrt{NT \log N})$.

4.6 The Partial Information Model

In this section we show, for external regret, a simple reduction from the partial information to the full information model.[3] The main difference between the two models is that in the full information model, the online procedure has access to the loss of every action. In the partial information model the online procedure receives as feedback only the loss of a single action, the action it performed. This very naturally leads to an *exploration versus exploitation trade-off* in the partial information model, and essentially any online procedure will have to somehow *explore* the various actions and estimate their loss.

The high-level idea of the reduction is as follows. Assume that the number of time steps T is given as a parameter. We will partition the T time steps into K blocks. The procedure will use the same distribution over actions in all the time steps of any given block, except it will also randomly sample each action once (the exploration part). The partial information procedure MAB will pass to the full information procedure FIB the vector of losses received from its exploration steps. The full information procedure FIB will then return a new distribution over actions. The main part of the proof will be to relate the loss of the full information procedure FIB on the loss sequence it observes to the loss of the partial information procedure MAB on the real loss sequence.

We start by considering a full information procedure FIB that partitions the T time steps into K blocks, $B^1, \ldots, B^K$, where $B^i = \{(i-1)(T/K)+1, \ldots, i(T/K)\}$, and uses the same distribution in all the time steps of a block. (For simplicity we assume that K divides T.) Consider an R_K external regret minimization procedure FIB (over K time steps), which at the end of block i updates the distribution using the average loss vector, i.e., $c^\tau = \sum_{t \in B^\tau} \ell^t / |B^\tau|$. Let $C_i^K = \sum_{\tau=1}^{K} c_i^\tau$ and $C_{\min}^K = \min_i C_i^K$. Since FIB has external regret at most R_K, this implies that the loss of FIB, over the loss sequence c^τ, is at most $C_{\min}^K + R_K$. Since in every block B^τ the procedure FIB uses a single distribution p^τ, its loss on the entire loss sequence is:

$$L_{\text{FIB}}^T = \sum_{\tau=1}^{K} \sum_{t \in B^\tau} p^\tau \cdot \ell^t = \frac{T}{K} \sum_{\tau=1}^{K} p^\tau \cdot c^\tau \leq \frac{T}{K} [C_{\min}^K + R_K].$$

At this point it is worth noting that if $R_K = O(\sqrt{K \log N})$ the overall regret is $O((T/\sqrt{K})\sqrt{\log N})$, which is minimized at $K = T$, namely by having each block

[3] This reduction does not produce the best-known bounds for the partial information model (see, e.g., Auer et al., 2002 for better bounds) but is particularly simple and generic.

be a single time step. However, we will have an additional loss associated with each block (due to the sampling) which will cause the optimization to require that $K \ll T$.

The next step in developing the partial information procedure MAB is to use loss vectors that are not the "true average" but whose expectation is the same. More formally, the feedback to the full information procedure FIB will be a random variable vector $\hat{c}^\tau$ such that for any action i we have $E[\hat{c}_i^\tau] = c_i^\tau$. Similarly, let $\hat{C}_i^K = \sum_{\tau=1}^K \hat{c}_i^\tau$ and $\hat{C}_{\min}^K = \min_i \hat{C}_i^K$. (Intuitively, we will generate the vector $\hat{c}^\tau$ using sampling within a block.) This implies that for any block B^τ and any distribution p^τ we have

$$\frac{1}{|B^\tau|}\sum_{t \in B^\tau} p^\tau \cdot \ell^t \;=\; p^\tau \cdot c^\tau \;=\; \sum_{i=1}^N p_i^\tau c_i^\tau \;=\; \sum_{i=1}^N p_i^\tau E[\hat{c}_i^\tau] \tag{4.2}$$

That is, the loss of p^τ in B^τ is equal to its expected loss with respect to $\hat{c}^\tau$.

The full information procedure FIB observes the losses $\hat{c}^\tau$, for $\tau \in \{1, \ldots, K\}$. However, since $\hat{c}^\tau$ are random variables, the distribution p^τ is also a random variable that depends on the previous losses, i.e., $\hat{c}^1, \ldots, \hat{c}^{\tau-1}$. Still, with respect to any sequence of losses $\hat{c}^\tau$, we have that

$$\hat{C}_{\text{FIB}}^K \;=\; \sum_{\tau=1}^K p^\tau \cdot \hat{c}^\tau \;\le\; \hat{C}_{\min}^K + R_K$$

Since $E[\hat{C}_i^K] = C_i^K$, this implies that

$$E\big[\hat{C}_{\text{FIB}}^K\big] \le E\big[\hat{C}_{\min}^K\big] + R_K \le C_{\min}^K + R_K,$$

where we used the fact that $E[\min_i \hat{C}_i^K] \le \min_i E[\hat{C}_i^K]$ and the expectation is over the choices of $\hat{c}^\tau$.

Note that for any sequence of losses $\hat{c}^1, \ldots, \hat{c}^K$, both FIB and MAB will use the same sequence of distributions $p^1, \ldots, p^K$. From (4.2) we have that in any block B^τ the expected loss of FIB and the loss of MAB are the same, assuming they both use the same distribution p^τ. This implies that

$$E\big[C_{\text{MAB}}^K\big] = E\big[\hat{C}_{\text{FIB}}^K\big].$$

We now need to show how to derive random variables $\hat{c}^\tau$ with the desired property. This will be done by choosing randomly, for each action i and block B^τ, an exploration time $t_i \in B^\tau$. (These do not need to be independent over the different actions, so can easily be done without collisions.) At time t_i the procedure MAB will play action i (i.e., the probability vector with all probability mass on i). This implies that the feedback that it receives will be $\ell_i^{t_i}$, and we will then set $\hat{c}_i^\tau$ to be $\ell_i^{t_i}$. This guarantees that $E[\hat{c}_i^\tau] = c_i^\tau$.

So far we have ignored the loss in the exploration steps. Since the maximum loss is 1, and there are N exploration steps in each of the K blocks, the total loss in all the exploration steps is at most NK. Therefore we have

$$\begin{aligned} E\big[L_{\text{MAB}}^T\big] &\le NK + (T/K)E\big[C_{\text{MAB}}^K\big] \\ &\le NK + (T/K)\big[C_{\min}^K + R_K\big] \\ &= L_{\min}^T + NK + (T/K)R_K. \end{aligned}$$

By Theorem 4.6, there are external regret procedures that have regret $R_K = O(\sqrt{K \log N})$. By setting $K = (T/N)^{2/3}$, for $T \geq N$, we have the following theorem.

Theorem 4.17 *Given an $O(\sqrt{K \log N})$ external regret procedure* FIB *(for K time steps), there is a partial information procedure* MAB *that guarantees*

$$L_{\text{MAB}}^{T} \leq L_{\min}^{T} + O(T^{2/3} N^{1/3} \log N),$$

where $T \geq N$.

4.7 On Convergence of Regret-Minimizing Strategies to Nash Equilibrium in Routing Games

As mentioned earlier, one natural setting for regret-minimizing algorithms is online routing. For example, a person could use such algorithms to select which of N available routes to use to drive to work each morning in such a way that his performance will be nearly as good as the best fixed route in hindsight, even if traffic changes arbitrarily from day to day. In fact, even though in a graph G, the number of paths N between two nodes may be exponential in the size of G, there are a number of external-regret minimizing algorithms whose running time and regret bounds are polynomial in the graph size. Moreover, a number of extensions have shown how these algorithms can be applied even to the partial-information setting where only the cost of the path traversed is revealed to the algorithm.

In this section we consider the game-theoretic properties of such algorithms in the Wardrop model of traffic flow. In this model, we have a directed network $G = (V, E)$, and one unit flow of traffic (a large population of infinitesimal users that we view as having one unit of volume) wanting to travel between two distinguished nodes v_{start} and v_{end}. (For simplicity, we are considering just the single-commodity version of the model.) We assume each edge e has a cost given by a *latency function* ℓ_e that is some nondecreasing function of the amount of traffic flowing on edge e. In other words, the time to traverse each edge e is a function of the amount of congestion on that edge. In particular, given some flow f, where we use f_e to denote the amount of flow on a given edge e, the cost of some path P is $\sum_{e \in P} \ell_e(f_e)$ and the average travel time of all users in the population can be written as $\sum_{e \in E} \ell_e(f_e) f_e$. A flow f is at Nash equilibrium if all flow-carrying paths P from v_{start} to v_{end} are minimum-latency paths *given* the flow f.

Chapter 18 considers this model in much more detail, analyzing the relationship between latencies in Nash equilibrium flows and those in globally optimum flows (flows that minimize the total travel time averaged over all users). In this section we describe results showing that if the users in such a setting are adapting their paths from day to day using external-regret minimizing algorithms (or even if they just happen to experience low-regret, regardless of the specific algorithms used) then flow will approach Nash equilibrium. Note that a Nash equilibrium is precisely a set of static strategies that are all no-regret with respect to each other, so such a result seems natural; however, there are many simple games for which regret-minimizing algorithms do *not* approach Nash equilibrium and can even perform much worse than any Nash equilibrium.

Specifically, one can show that if each user has regret $o(T)$, or even if just the average regret (averaged over the users) is $o(T)$, then flow approaches Nash equilibrium in the sense that a $1-\epsilon$ fraction of days t have the property that a $1-\epsilon$ fraction of the users that day experience travel time at most ϵ larger than the best path for that day, where ϵ approaches 0 at a rate that depends polynomially on the size of the graph, the regret-bounds of the algorithms, and the maximum slope of any latency function. Note that this is a somewhat nonstandard notion of convergence to equilibrium: usually for an "ϵ-approximate equilibrium" one requires that *all* participants have at most ϵ incentive to deviate. However, since low-regret algorithms are allowed to occasionally take long paths, and in fact algorithms in the MAB model *must* occasionally explore paths they have not tried in a long time (to avoid regret if the paths have become much better in the meantime), the multiple levels of hedging are actually *necessary* for a result of this kind.

In this section we present just a special case of this result. Let $\mathcal{P}$ denote the set of all simple paths from v_{start} to v_{end} and let f^t denote the flow on day t. Let $C(f) = \sum_{e\in E} \ell_e(f_e)f_e$ denote the cost of a flow f. Note that $C(f)$ is a weighted average of costs of paths in $\mathcal{P}$ and in fact is equal to the average cost of all users in the flow f. Define a flow f to be *ϵ-Nash* if $C(f) \leq \epsilon + \min_{P\in\mathcal{P}} \sum_{e\in P} \ell_e(f_e)$; that is, the average incentive to deviate over all users is at most ϵ. Let $R(T)$ denote the average regret (averaged over users) up through day T, so

$$R(T) \equiv \sum_{t=1}^{T}\sum_{e\in E} \ell_e\left(f_e^t\right) f_e^t - \min_{P\in\mathcal{P}} \sum_{t=1}^{T}\sum_{e\in P} \ell_e\left(f_e^t\right).$$

Finally, let T_ϵ denote the number of time steps T needed so that $R(T) \leq \epsilon T$ for all $T \geq T_\epsilon$. For example the RWM and PW algorithms discussed in Section 4.3 achieve $T_\epsilon = O(\frac{1}{\epsilon^2}\log N)$ if we set $\eta = \epsilon/2$. Then we will show the following.

Theorem 4.18 *Suppose the latency functions ℓ_e are linear. Then for $T \geq T_\epsilon$, the average flow $\hat{f} = \frac{1}{T}(f^1 + \cdots + f^T)$ is ϵ-Nash.*

PROOF From the linearity of the latency functions, we have for all e, $\ell_e(\hat{f}_e) = \frac{1}{T}\sum_{t=1}^{T} \ell_e(f_e^t)$. Since $\ell_e(f_e^t)f_e^t$ is a convex function of the flow, this implies

$$\ell_e(\hat{f}_e)\hat{f}_e \leq \frac{1}{T}\sum_{t=1}^{T} \ell_e\left(f_e^t\right) f_e^t.$$

Summing over all e, we have

$$\begin{aligned} C(\hat{f}) &\leq \frac{1}{T}\sum_{t=1}^{T} C(f^t) \\ &\leq \epsilon + \min_P \frac{1}{T}\sum_{t=1}^{T}\sum_{e\in P} \ell_e\left(f_e^t\right) \quad \text{(by definition of } T_\epsilon\text{)} \\ &= \epsilon + \min_P \sum_{e\in P} \ell_e(\hat{f}_e). \qquad \text{(by linearity)} \end{aligned}$$

□

This result shows the time-average flow is an approximate Nash equilibrium. This can then be used to prove that *most* of the f^t must in fact be approximate Nash. The key idea here is that if the cost of any edge were to fluctuate wildly over time, then that would imply that most of the users of that edge experienced latency substantially greater than the edge's average cost (because more users are using the edge when it is congested than when it is not congested), which in turn implies they experience substantial regret. These arguments can then be carried over to the case of general (nonlinear) latency functions.

4.7.1 Current Research Directions

In this section we sketch some current research directions with respect to regret minimization.

Refined regret bounds: The regret bounds that we presented depend on the number of time steps T, and are independent of the performance of the best action. Such bounds are also called *zero-order* bounds. More refined *first-order* bounds depend on the loss of the best action, and *second-order* bounds depend on the sum of squares of the losses (such as Q_k^T in Theorem 4.6). An interesting open problem is to get an external regret that is proportional to the empirical variance of the best action. Another challenge is to reduce the prior information needed by the regret minimization algorithm. Ideally, it should be able to learn and adapt to parameters such as the maximum and minimum loss. See Cesa-Bianchi et al. (2005) for a detailed discussion of those issues.

Large actions spaces: In this chapter we assumed the number of actions N is small enough to be able to list them all, and our algorithms work in time proportional to N. However, in many settings N is exponential in the natural parameters of the problem. For example, the N actions might be all simple paths between two nodes s and t in an n-node graph, or all binary search trees on $\{1, \ldots, n\}$. Since the full information external regret bounds are only logarithmic in N, from the point of view of information, we can derive polynomial regret bounds. The challenge is whether in such settings we can produce computationally efficient algorithms.

There have recently been several results able to handle broad classes of problems of this type. Kalai and Vempala (2003) give an efficient algorithm for any problem in which (a) the set X of actions can be viewed as a subset of R^n, (b) the loss vectors ℓ are linear functions over R^n (so the loss of action x is $\ell \cdot x$), and (c) we can efficiently solve the *offline* optimization problem $\text{argmin}_{x \in S}[x \cdot \ell]$ for any *given* loss vector ℓ. For instance, this setting can model the path and search-tree examples above.[4] Zinkevich (2003) extends this to *convex* loss functions with a projection oracle, and there is substantial interest in trying to broaden the class of settings that efficient regret-minimization algorithms can be applied to.

[4] The case of search trees has the additional issue that there is a rotation cost associated with using a different action (tree) at time $t + 1$ than that used at time t. This is addressed in Kalai and Vempala (2003) as well.

Dynamics: It is also very interesting to analyze the *dynamics* of regret minimization algorithms. The classical example is that of swap regret: when all the players play swap regret-minimization algorithms, the empirical distribution converges to the set of correlated equilibria (Section 4.4). We also saw convergence in two-player zero-sum games to the minimax value of the game (Section 4.4), and convergence to Nash equilibrium in a Wardrop-model routing game (Section 4.7). Further results on convergence to equilibria in other settings would be of substantial interest. At a high level, understanding the dynamics of regret-minimization algorithms would allow us to better understand the strengths and weaknesses of using such procedures. For more information on learning in games, see the book by Fudenberg and Levine (1998).

4.8 Notes

Hannan (1957) was the first to develop algorithms with external regret sublinear in T. Later, motivated by machine learning settings in which N can be quite large, algorithms that furthermore have only a logarithmic dependence on N were developed by Littlestone and Warmuth (1994), and extended by a number of researchers (Cesa-Bianchi et al., 1997; Freund and Schapire, 1997, 1999). In particular, the Randomized Weighted Majority algorithm and Theorem 4.5 are from Littlestone and Warmuth (1994) and the Polynomial Weights algorithm and Theorem 4.6 is from Cesa-Bianchi et al. (2005). Computationally efficient algorithms for generic frameworks that model many settings in which N may be exponential in the natural problem description (such as considering all s-t paths in a graph or all binary search trees on n elements) were developed in Kalai and Vempala (2000) and Zinkevich (2003).

The notion of internal regret and its connection to correlated equilibrium appear in Foster and Vohra (1998) and Hart and Mas-Colell (2000) and more general modification rules were considered in Lehrer (2003). A number of specific low internal regret algorithms were developed by a number of researcher (Blum and Mansour, 2005; Cesa-Bianchi and Lugosi, 2003; Foster and Vohra, 1997, 1998, 1999; Hart and Mas-Colell, 2003; Stoltz and Lugosi, 2005). The reduction in Section 4.5 from external to swap regret is from Blum and Mansour (2005).

Algorithms with strong external regret bounds for the partial information model are given in Auer et al. (2002) , and algorithms with low internal regret appear in Blum and Mansour (2005) and Cesa-Bianchi et al. (2006). The reduction from full information to partial information in Section 4.6 is in the spirit of algorithms of Awerbuch and Mansour (2003) and Awerbuch and Kleinberg (2004). Extensions of the algorithm of Kalai and Vempala (2003) to the partial information setting appear in Awerbuch and Kleinberg (2004), Dani and Hayes (2006) and McMahan and Blum (2004). The results in Section 4.7 on approaching Nash equilibria in routing games are from Blum et al. (2006).

Bibliography

P. Auer, N. Cesa-Bianchi, Y. Freund, and R.E. Schapire. The nonstochastic multiarmed bandit problem. *SIAM J. Comp.*, 32(1):48–77, 2002.

B. Awerbuch and R.D. Kleinberg. Adaptive routing with end-to-end feedback: Distributed learning and geometric approaches. In *Symp. on Theory of Computing*, pp. 45–53, 2004.

B. Awerbuch and Y. Mansour. Adapting to a reliable network path. In *PODC*, pp. 360–367, 2003.

A. Blum, E. Even-Dar, and K. Ligett. Routing without regret: On convergence to nash equilibria of regret-minimizing algorithms in routing games. In *Princ. Distributed Comp.*, 2006.

A. Blum and Y. Mansour. From external to internal regret. In *Conf. on Learning Theory*, 2005.

A. Borodin and R. El-Yaniv. *Online Computation and Competitive Analysis*. Cambridge University Press, 1998.

N. Cesa-Bianchi, Y. Freund, D.P. Helmbold, D. Haussler, R.E. Schapire, and M.K. Warmuth. How to use expert advice. *J. ACM*, 44(3):427–485, 1997.

N. Cesa-Bianchi and G. Lugosi. Potential-based algorithms in on-line prediction and game theory. *Mach. Learn.*, 51(3):239–261, 2003.

N. Cesa-Bianchi and G. Lugosi. *Prediction, Learning and Games*. Cambridge University Press, 2006.

N. Cesa-Bianchi, G. Lugosi, and G. Stoltz. Regret minimization under partial monitoring. *Math. of O.R.* (to appear), 2006.

N. Cesa-Bianchi, Y. Mansour, and G. Stoltz. Improved second-order bounds for prediction with expert advice. In *Conf. on Learning Theory*, 2005.

V. Dani and T.P. Hayes. Robbing the bandit: Less regret in online geometric optimization against an adaptive adversary. In *Symp. on Descrete Algorithms*, pp. 937–943, 2006.

D. Foster and R. Vohra. Calibrated learning and correlated equilibrium. *Games Econ. Behav.*, 21:40–55, 1997.

D. Foster and R. Vohra. Asymptotic calibration. *Biometrika*, 85:379–390, 1998.

D. Foster and R. Vohra. Regret in the on-line decision problem. *Games Econ. Behav.*, 29:7–36, 1999.

Y. Freund and R.E. Schapire. A decision-theoretic generalization of on-line learning and an application to boosting. *J. Comp. System Sci.*, 55(1):119–139, 1997.

Y. Freund and R.E. Schapire. Adaptive game playing using multiplicative weights. *Games Econ. Behav.*, 29:79–103, 1999.

D. Fudenberg and D.K. Levine. *The Theory of Learning in Games*. MIT Press, 1998.

J. Hannan. Approximation to bayes risk in repeated plays. In M. Dresher, A. Tucker, and P. Wolfe, editors, *Contributions to the Theory of Games*, 3:97–139, Princeton University Press, 1957.

S. Hart and A. Mas-Colell. A simple adaptive procedure leading to correlated equilibrium. *Econometrica*, 68:1127–1150, 2000.

A. Kalai and S. Vempala. Efficient algorithms for online decision problems. In *Conf. on Learning Theory*, pp. 26–40, 2003.

E. Lehrer. A wide range no-regret theorem. *Games Econ. Behav.*, 42:101–115, 2003.

N. Littlestone and M.K. Warmuth. The weighted majority algorithm. *Informat. Comput.*, 108:212–261, 1994.

H.B. McMahan and A. Blum. Online geometric optimization in the bandit setting against an adaptive adversary. In *Proc. 17th Annual Conference on Learning Theory*, pp. 109–123, 2004.

G. Stoltz and G. Lugosi. Internal regret in on-line portfolio selection. *Mach. Learn. J.*, 59:125–159, 2005.

G. Owen. *Game Theory*. Academic Press, 1982.

D. Sleator and R.E. Tarjan. Amortized efficiency of list update and paging rules. *Comm. ACM*, 28:202–208, 1985.

M. Zinkevich. Online convex programming and generalized infinitesimal gradient ascent. In *Proc. Intl. Conf. Machine Learning*, 928–936, 2003.

Exercises

4.1 Show that swap regret is at most N times larger than internal regret.

4.2 Show an example (even with $N = 3$) where the ratio between the external and swap regret is unbounded.

4.3 Show that the RWM algorithm with update rule $w_i^t = w_i^{t-1}(1-\eta)^{\ell_i^{t-1}}$ achieves the same external regret bound as given in Theorem 4.6 for the PW algorithm, for losses in [0, 1].

4.4 Consider a setting where the payoffs are in the range $[-1, +1]$, and the goal of the algorithm is to maximize its payoff. Derive a modified PW algorithm whose external regret is $O(\sqrt{Q_{max}^T \log N} + \log N)$, where $Q_{max}^T \geq Q_k^T$ for $k \in X_i$.

4.5 Show a $\Omega(\sqrt{T \log N})$ lower bound on external regret, for the case that $T \geq N$.

4.6 Improve the swap regret bound to $O(\sqrt{NT \log N})$. Hint: Use the observation that the sum of the losses of all the A_i is bounded by T.

4.7 **(Open Problem)** Does there exist an $\Omega(\sqrt{TN \log N})$ lower bound for swap regret?

4.8 Show that if a player plays algorithm RWM (or PW) then it gives ϵ-dominated actions small weight. Also, show that there are cases in which the external regret of a player can be small, yet it gives ϵ-dominated actions high weight.

CHAPTER 5

Combinatorial Algorithms for Market Equilibria

Vijay V. Vazirani

Abstract

Combinatorial polynomial time algorithms are presented for finding equilibrium prices and allocations for the linear utilities case of the Fisher and Arrow–Debreu models using the primal-dual schema and an auction-based approach, respectively. An interesting feature of the first algorithm is that it finds an optimal solution to a nonlinear convex program, the Eisenberg-Gale program.

Resource allocation markets in Kelly's model are also discussed and a strongly polynomial combinatorial algorithm is presented for one of them.

5.1 Introduction

Thinkers and philosophers have pondered over the notions of markets and money through the ages. The credit for initiating formal mathematical modeling and study of these notions is generally attributed to nineteenth-century economist Leon Walras (1874). The fact that Western economies are capitalistic had a lot to do with the overwhelming importance given to this study within mathematical economics – essentially, our most critical decision-making is relegated to pricing mechanisms. They largely determine the relative prices of goods and services, ensure that the economy is efficient, in that goods and services are made available to entities that produce items that are most in demand, and ensure a stable operation of the economy.

A central tenet in pricing mechanisms is that prices be such that demand equals supply; that is, the economy should operate at equilibrium. It is not surprising therefore that perhaps the most celebrated theorem within general equilibrium theory, the Arrow–Debreu Theorem, establishes precisely the existence of such prices under a very general model of the economy. The First Welfare Theorem,[1] which shows Pareto optimality of

[1] The First Welfare Theorem should come as a big surprise. On the one hand, a competitive equilibrium is arrived at when all agents actively pursue their self-interests (in a decentralized manner). On the other hand, the notion of Pareto optimality is an inherently centralized notion – it seeks maximal benefit for the society as a whole. The following quote from Adam Smith's classic work, *The Wealth of Nations*, 1776, is most illuminating: "It is not from the benevolence of the butcher, the brewer, or the baker, that we expect our dinner, but from their regard

allocations obtained at equilibrium prices, provides important social justification for this theory.

Although general equilibrium theory enjoyed the status of crown jewel within mathematical economics, it suffers from a serious shortcoming – other than a few isolated results, some of which were real gems, e.g., Eisenberg and Gale (1959) and Scarf (1973), it was essentially a nonalgorithmic theory. With the emergence of new markets on the Internet, which already form an important part of today's economy and are projected to grow considerably in the future, and the availability of massive computational power for running these markets in a distributed or centralized manner, the need for developing an algorithmic theory of markets and market equilibria is apparent. Such algorithms can also provide a valuable tool for understanding the repercussions of technological advances, new goods or changes to the tax structure on existing prices, production, and consumption.

A good beginning has been made over the last 5 years within algorithmic game theory, starting with the work of Deng et al. (2002). However, considering the fact that markets were an active area of study for over a century within mathematical economics, it is safe to say that we have only scratched the surface of what should be a rich theory.

Irving Fisher (see Brainard and Scarf, 2000) and Walras (1874) gave two fundamental market models that were studied extensively within mathematical economics. The latter model is also called the exchange model or the Arrow–Debreu model (Arrow and Debreu, 1954). In this chapter we will present combinatorial algorithms for both these models for the case of linear utility functions. A second approach that has emerged for computing equilibria for these models is the efficient solution of convex programs, since equilibrium allocations for both these models can be captured via convex programs; see Chapter 6 for this approach.

Two techniques have been primarily used for obtaining combinatorial algorithms for these models – the primal-dual schema (Devanur et al. 2002) and an auction-based approach (Garg and Kapoor, 2004). We will present algorithms for the Fisher and Arrow–Debreu models, using the first and second techniques, respectively.

An interesting aspect of the first algorithm was the extension of the primal-dual schema from its usual setting of combinatorially solving, either exactly or approximately, linear programs, to exactly solving a nonlinear convex program (see Section 5.5). The latter program, due to Eisenberg and Gale (1959), captures equilibrium allocations for the linear case of Fisher's model. Unlike complementary slackness conditions for linear programs, which involve either primal or dual variables, but not both, KKT conditions for a nonlinear convex program simultaneously involve both types of variables. The repercussions of this are apparent in the way the algorithm is structured.

In a different context, that of modeling and understanding TCP congestion control,[2] Kelly (1997) defined a class of resource allocation markets and gave a convex

to their own interest." . . . Each participant in a competitive economy is "led by an invisible hand to promote an end which was no part of his intention." Observe that the First Welfare Theorem is essentially a testament to the power of pricing mechanisms.

[2] In particular, Kelly's object was to explain the unprecedented success of TCP, and its congestion avoidance protocol due to Jacobson (1988), which played a crucial role in the phenomenal growth of the Internet and the deployment of a myriad of diverse applications on it. Fairness is a key property desired of a congestion avoidance protocol and Jacobson's protocol does seem to ensure fairness. Recent results show that if Jacobson's protocol is run on the end-nodes and the Floyd–Jacobson protocol (Floyd and Jacobson, 1993) is run at buffer queues,

program that captures equilibrium allocations for his model. Interestingly enough, Kelly's program has the same structure as the Eisenberg–Gale program (see also Chapter 22).

The *flow market* is of special significance within this framework. It consists of a network, with link capacities specified, and source – sink pairs of nodes, each with an initial endowment of money; allocations in this market are flows from each source to the corresponding sink. The problem is to find equilibrium flows and prices of edges (in the context of TCP, the latter can be viewed as drop rates at links).

Kelly's model attracted much theoretical study, partly with a view to designing next-generation protocols. Continuous time algorithms (though not having polynomial running time), for finding equilibrium flows in the flow market, were given by Kelly et al. (1998) (see also Wang et al., 2005, for more recent work along these lines). Soon after the appearance of Devanur et al. (2002), Kelly and Vazirani (2002) observed that Kelly's model esentially generalizes Fisher's linear case and stated, "Continuous time algorithms similar to TCP are known, but insights from discrete algorithms may be provocative."

With a view to answering this question, a systematic study of markets whose equilibria are captured by Eisenberg-Gale-type programs was undertaken by Jain and Vazirani (2006). In Section 5.14 we present, from this paper, a strongly polynomial algorithm for the special case of the flow market when there is one source and multiple sinks.

5.2 Fisher's Linear Case and the Eisenberg–Gale Convex Program

Fisher's linear case[3] is the following. Consider a market consisting of a set B of *buyers* and a set A of divisible *goods*. Assume $|A| = n$ and $|B| = n'$. We are given for each buyer i the amount e_i of money she possesses and for each good j the amount b_j of this good. In addition, we are given the utility functions of the buyers. Our critical assumption is that these functions are linear. Let u_{ij} denote the utility derived by i on obtaining a unit amount of good j. Thus if the buyer i is given x_{ij} units of good j, for $1 \le j \le n$, then the happiness she derives is

$$\sum_{j=1}^{n} u_{ij} x_{ij}.$$

Prices $p_1, \ldots, p_n$ of the goods are said to be *market clearing prices* if, after each buyer is assigned an optimal basket of goods relative to these prices, there is no surplus or deficiency of any of the goods. Our problem is to compute such prices in polynomial time.

First observe that w.l.o.g. we may assume that each b_j is unit – by scaling the u_{ij}'s appropriately. The u_{ij}'s and e_i's are in general rational; by scaling appropriately, they may be assumed to be integral. We will make the mild assumption that each good has

in the limit, traffic flows converge to an optimal solution of Kelly's convex program, i.e., they are equilibrium allocations, see Low and Lapsley (1999). Furthermore, Kelly used his convex programming formulation to prove that equilibrium allocations in his model satisfy proportional fairness (see Section 5.13), thereby giving a formal ratification of Jacobson's protocol.

[3] See Section 1.8 for a special case of this market and a simple polynomial time algorithm for it.

a *potential buyer*; i.e., a buyer who derives nonzero utility from this good. Under this assumption, market clearing prices do exist.

It turns out that equilibrium allocations for Fisher's linear case are captured as optimal solutions to a remarkable convex program, the Eisenberg–Gale convex program. Before stating the program, it will be instructive to list considerations that would be useful in deriving such a program.

Clearly, a convex program whose optimal solution is an equilibrium allocation must have as constraints the packing constraints on the x_{ij}'s. Furthermore, its objective function, which attempts to maximize utilities derived, should satisfy the following:

- If the utilities of any buyer are scaled by a constant, the optimal allocation remains unchanged.
- If the money of a buyer b is split among two new buyers whose utility functions are the same as that of b then sum of the optimal allocations of the new buyers should be an optimal allocation for b.

The money weighted geometric mean of buyers' utilities satisfies both these conditions:

$$\max \left(\prod_{i \in A} u_i^{e_i} \right)^{1/\sum_i e_i}.$$

Clearly, the following objective function is equivalent:

$$\max \prod_{i \in A} u_i^{e_i}.$$

Its log is used in the Eisenberg–Gale convex program:

$$\begin{aligned} \text{maximize} \quad & \sum_{i=1}^{n'} e_i \log u_i \\ \text{subject to} \quad & u_i = \sum_{j=1}^{n} u_{ij} x_{ij} \quad \forall i \in B \\ & \sum_{i=1}^{n'} x_{ij} \le 1 \quad \forall j \in A \\ & x_{ij} \ge 0 \quad \forall i \in B, \forall j \in A \end{aligned} \tag{5.1}$$

where x_{ij} is the amount of good j allocated to buyer i. Interpret Lagrangian variables, say p_j's, corresponding to the second set of conditions as prices of goods. By the Karush, Kuhn, Tucker (KKT) conditions, optimal solutions to x_{ij}'s and p_j's must satisfy the following:

(i) $\forall j \in A: \ p_j \ge 0.$
(ii) $\forall j \in A: \ p_j > 0 \Rightarrow \sum_{i \in A} x_{ij} = 1.$
(iii) $\forall i \in B, \forall j \in A: \frac{u_{ij}}{p_j} \le \frac{\sum_{j \in A} u_{ij} x_{ij}}{e_i}.$
(iv) $\forall i \in B, \forall j \in A: x_{ij} > 0 \Rightarrow \frac{u_{ij}}{p_j} = \frac{\sum_{j \in A} u_{ij} x_{ij}}{e_i}.$

From these conditions, one can derive that an optimal solution to convex program (5.1) must satisfy the market clearing conditions.

The Eisenberg and Gale program also helps prove, in a very simple manner, the following basic properties of equilibria for the linear case of Fisher's model.

Theorem 5.1 *For the linear case of Fisher's model:*

- *If each good has a potential buyer, equilibrium exists.*
- *The set of equilibrium allocations is convex.*
- *Equilibrium utilities and prices are unique.*
- *If all u_{ij}'s and e_i's are rational, then equilibrium allocations and prices are also rational. Moreover, they can be written using polynomially many bits in the length of the instance.*

PROOF Corresponding to good j there is a buyer i such that $u_{ij} > 0$. By the third KKT condition,

$$p_j \geq \frac{e_i u_{ij}}{\sum_j u_{ij} x_{ij}} > 0.$$

Now, by the second KKT condition, $\sum_{i \in A} x_{ij} = 1$. Hence, prices of all goods are positive and all goods are fully sold.

The third and fourth conditions imply that if buyer i gets good j then j must be among the goods that give buyer i maximum utility per unit money spent at current prices. Hence each buyer gets only a bundle consisting of her most desired goods, i.e., an optimal bundle.

The fourth condition is equivalent to

$$\forall i \in B, \forall j \in A : \frac{e_i u_{ij} x_{ij}}{\sum_{j \in A} u_{ij} x_{ij}} = p_j x_{ij}.$$

Summing over all j gives

$$\forall i \in B : \frac{e_i \sum_j u_{ij} x_{ij}}{\sum_{j \in A} u_{ij} x_{ij}} = \sum_j p_j x_{ij}.$$

This implies

$$\forall i \in B : \; e_i = \sum_j p_j x_{ij}.$$

Hence the money of each buyer is fully spent. This completes the proof that market equilibrium exists.

Since each equilibrium allocation is an optimal solution to the Eisenberg-Gale convex program, the set of equilibrium allocations must form a convex set.

Since log is a strictly concave function, if there is more than one equilibrium, the utility derived by each buyer must be the same in all equilibria. This fact, together with the fourth condition, gives that the equilibrium prices are unique.

Finally, we prove the fourth claim by showing that equilibrium allocations and prices are solutions to a system of linear equations. Let $q_j = 1/p_j$ be a new variable corresponding to each good j and let k be the number of nonzero x_{ij}'s in an equilibrium allocation. The system will consist of $k + n$ equations over $k + n$ unknowns, the latter being the n q_j's and the k the nonzero x_{ij}'s. The equations are corresponding to each good j, the equality given by the second KKT condition, and corresponding to each nonzero x_{ij}, the equality given by the fourth KKT condition. □

5.3 Checking If Given Prices Are Equilibrium Prices

Let $\boldsymbol{p} = (p_1, \ldots, p_n)$ denote a vector of prices. Let us first devise an algorithm for answering the following question: Is $\boldsymbol{p}$ the equilibrium price vector, and if so, find equilibrium allocations for the buyers.

At prices $\boldsymbol{p}$, buyer i derives u_{ij}/p_j amount of utility per unit money spent on good j. Clearly, she will be happiest with goods that maximize this ratio. Define her *bang per buck* to be $\boldsymbol{\alpha}_i = \max_j\{u_{ij}/p_j\}$. For each $i \in B$, $j \in A$, $\boldsymbol{\alpha}_i \geq u_{ij}/p_j$, with equality holding only if j is i's bang per buck good. If there are several goods maximizing this ratio, she is equally happy with any combination of these goods. This motivates defining the following bipartite graph, G. Its bipartition is (A, B) and for $i \in B$, $j \in A$, (i, j) is an edge in G iff $\boldsymbol{\alpha}_i = u_{ij}/p_j$. We will call this graph the *equality subgraph* and its edges the *equality edges*.

5.3.1 The Network $N(\boldsymbol{p})$

Any goods sold along the edges of the equality subgraph will make buyers happiest, relative to prices $\boldsymbol{p}$. Computing the largest amount of goods that can be sold in this manner, without exceeding the budgets of buyers or the amount of goods available (assumed unit for each good), can be accomplished by computing max-flow in the following network (see Figure 5.1). Direct edges of G from A to B and assign a capacity of infinity to all these edges. Introduce source vertex s and a directed edge from s to each vertex $j \in A$ with a capacity of p_j. Introduce sink vertex t and a directed edge from each vertex $i \in B$ to t with a capacity of e_i. The network is clearly a function of the prices $\boldsymbol{p}$ and will be denoted by $N(\boldsymbol{p})$.

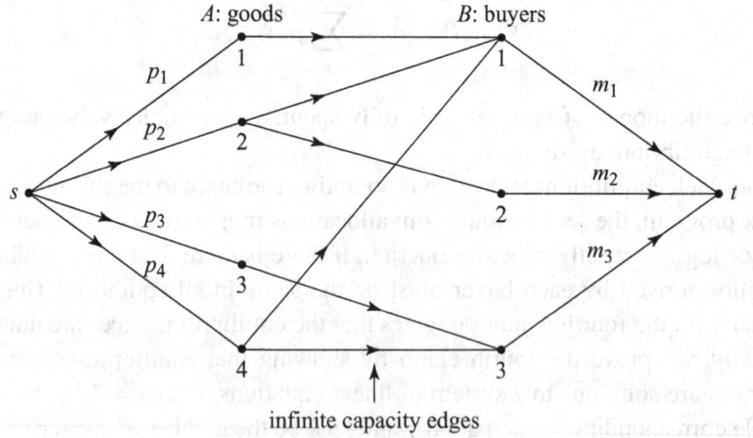

Figure 5.1. The network $N(p)$.

Corresponding to a feasible flow f in network $N(\mathbf{p})$, let us define the allocation of goods to the buyers to be the following. If edge (j, i) from good j to buyer i carries flow $f(j, i)$, then buyer i receives $f(j, i)/p_j$ units of good j.

The question posed above can be answered via one max-flow computation, as asserted in the following lemma. Its proof is straightforward and is omitted.

Lemma 5.2 *Prices* $\mathbf{p}$ *are equilibrium prices iff in the network* $N(\mathbf{p})$ *the two cuts* $(s, A \cup B \cup t)$ *and* $(s \cup A \cup B, t)$ *are min-cuts. If so, allocations corresponding to any max-flow in* N *are equilibrium allocations.*

5.4 Two Crucial Ingredients of the Algorithm

The algorithm starts with very low prices that are guaranteed to be below the equilibrium prices for each good. The algorithm always works on the network $N(p)$ w.r.t. the current prices $\mathbf{p}$. W.r.t. the starting prices, buyers have surplus money left. The algorithm raises prices iteratively and reduces the surplus. When the surplus vanishes, it terminates; these prices are equilibrium prices.

This algorithmic outline immediately raises two questions:

- How do we ensure that the equilibrium price of no good is exceeded?
- How do we ensure that the surplus money of buyers reduces fast enough that the algorithm terminates in polynomial time?

The answers to these two questions lead to two crucial ingredients of the algorithm: *tight sets* and *balanced flows*.

5.5 The Primal-Dual Schema in the Enhanced Setting

We will use the notation setup in the previous sections to describe at a high level the new difficulties presented by the enhanced setting of convex programs and the manner in which the primal-dual schema is modified to obtain a combinatorial algorithm for solving the Eisenberg–Gale convex program.

The fundamental difference between complementary slackness conditions for linear programs and KKT conditions for nonlinear convex programs is that whereas the former do not involve both primal and dual variables simultaneously in an equality constraint (obtained by assuming that one of the variables takes a nonzero value), the latter do.

As described in the previous section, the algorithm will start with very low prices and keep increasing them greedily, i.e., the dual growth process is greedy. Indeed, all known primal-dual algorithms use a greedy dual growth process – with one exception, namely Edmonds' algorithm for maximum weight matching in general graphs (Edmonds, 1965).

Now, the disadvantage of a greedy dual growth process is obvious – the fact that a raised dual is "bad," in the sense that it "obstructs" other duals that could have led to a larger overall dual solution, may become clear only later in the run of the algorithm. In view of this, the issue of using more sophisticated dual growth processes has received a lot of attention, especially in the context of approximation algorithms. The problem with such a process is that it will make primal objects go tight and loose and the number of such reversals will have to be upper bounded in the running time analysis. The impeccable combinatorial structure of matching supports such an accounting and in fact this leads to a strongly polynomial algorithm. However, thus far, all attempts at making such a scheme work out for other problems have failed.

In our case, even though the dual growth process is greedy, because of the more complex nature of KKT conditions, edges in the equality subgraph appear and disappear as the algorithm proceeds. Hence, we are forced to carry out the difficult accounting process alluded to above for bounding the running time.

We next point out which KKT conditions the algorithm enforces and which ones it relaxes, as well as the exact mechanism by which it satisfies the latter. Throughout the algorithm, we enforce the first two conditions listed in Section 5.2. As mentioned in Section 5.4, at any point in the algorithm, via a max-flow in the network $N(\boldsymbol{p})$, all goods can be sold; however, buyers may have surplus money left over. W.r.t. a balanced flow in network $N(\boldsymbol{p})$ (see Section 5.7 for a definition of such a flow), let m_i be the money spent by buyer i. Thus, buyer i's surplus money is $\gamma_i = e_i - m_i$. We will relax the third and fourth KKT conditions to the following:

- $\forall i \in B, \forall j \in A : \dfrac{u_{ij}}{p_j} \leq \dfrac{\sum_{j \in A} u_{ij} x_{ij}}{m_i}$.
- $\forall i \in B, \forall j \in A : x_{ij} > 0 \Rightarrow \dfrac{u_{ij}}{p_j} = \dfrac{\sum_{j \in A} u_{ij} x_{ij}}{m_i}$.

Consider the following potential function:

$$\Phi = \gamma_1^2 + \gamma_2^2 + \cdots + \gamma_{n'}^2.$$

We will give a process by which this potential function decreases by an inverse polynomial fraction in polynomial time (in each phase, as detailed in Lemma 5.21). When Φ drops all the way to zero, all KKT conditions are exactly satisfied.

Finally, there is a marked difference between the way this algorithm will satisfy KKT conditions and the way primal-dual algorithms for LP's do. The latter satisfy complementary conditions in *discrete steps*, i.e., in each iteration, the algorithm satisfies at least one new condition. So, if each iteration can be implemented in strongly polynomial time, the entire algorithm has a similar running time. On the other hand, the algorithm for Fisher's linear case satisfies KKT conditions *continuously* – as the algorithm proceeds, the KKT conditions corresponding to each buyer get satisfied to a greater extent.

Observe that at the start of the algorithm, the value of ϕ is a function not just of the number of buyers and goods but of the length of the input (since it depends on the money possessed by buyers). Therefore, even though a phase of the algorithm can be implemented in strongly polynomial time, the running time of the entire algorithm is polynomial and not strongly polynomial. Indeed, obtaining a strongly polynomial algorithm for this problem remains a tantalizing open problem (see Section 5.15).

5.6 Tight Sets and the Invariant

Let $\boldsymbol{p}$ denote the current prices within the run of the algorithm. For a set $S \subseteq A$ of goods, let $\boldsymbol{p}(S)$ denote the total value of goods in S; this is simply the sum of current prices of goods in S. For a set $T \subseteq B$ of buyers, let $m(T)$ denote the total money possessed by the buyers in T; i.e., $m(T) = \sum_{i \in T} e_i$. For $S \subseteq A$, define its *neighborhood in* $N(\boldsymbol{p})$,

$$\Gamma(S) = \{j \in B \mid \exists i \in S \text{ with } (i, j) \in N(\boldsymbol{p})\}.$$

Clearly, $\Gamma(S)$ is the set of buyers who are interested in goods in S at current prices.

We will say that S is a *tight set* if the current value of S exactly equals the money possessed by buyers who are interested in goods in S; i.e., $\boldsymbol{p}(S) = m(\Gamma(S))$. Under this circumstance, increasing prices of goods in S may lead to exceeding the equilibrium price of some good. Therefore, when a set of goods goes tight, the algorithm freezes the prices of all goods in S. As described in Section 5.7, when new edges enter the equality subgraph, the algorithm may unfreeze certain frozen goods and again start increasing their prices.

A systematic way of ensuring that the equilibrium price of no good is exceeded is to ensure the following Invariant.

Invariant: The prices $\boldsymbol{p}$ are such that the cut $(s, A \cup B \cup t)$ is a min-cut in $N(\boldsymbol{p})$.

Lemma 5.3 *For given prices* $\boldsymbol{p}$*, network* $N(\boldsymbol{p})$ *satisfies the Invariant iff*

$$\forall S \subseteq A : \boldsymbol{p}(S) \leq m(\Gamma(S)).$$

PROOF The forward direction is trivial, since under max-flow (of value $\boldsymbol{p}(A)$) every set $S \subseteq A$ must be sending $\boldsymbol{p}(S)$ amount of flow to its neighborhood.

Let us prove the reverse direction. Assume that $(s \cup A_1 \cup B_1, A_2 \cup B_2 \cup t)$ is a min-cut in $N(\boldsymbol{p})$, with $A_1, A_2 \subseteq A$ and $B_1, B_2 \subseteq B$ (see Figure 5.2). The capacity of this cut is $\boldsymbol{p}(A_2) + m(B_1)$. Now, $\Gamma(A_1) \subseteq B_1$, since otherwise the cut will have infinite capacity. Moving A_1 and $\Gamma(A_1)$ to the t side also results in a cut. By the condition stated in the Lemma, $\boldsymbol{p}(A_1) \leq m(\Gamma(A_1))$. Therefore, the capacity of this cut is no larger than the previous one and this is also a min-cut in $N(\boldsymbol{p})$. Hence the Invariant holds. □

The Invariant ensures that, at current prices, all goods can be sold. The only eventuality is that buyers may be left with surplus money. The algorithm raises prices systematically, thereby decreasing buyers' surplus money. When $(s \cup A \cup B, t)$ is also a min-cut in $N(\boldsymbol{p})$, by Lemma 5.2, equilibrium has been attained.

5.7 Balanced Flows

Denote the current network, $N(\boldsymbol{p})$, by simply N. We will assume that network N satisfies the Invariant; i.e., $(s, A \cup B \cup t)$ is a min-cut in N. Given a feasible flow f in N, let $R(f)$ denote the residual graph w.r.t. f. Define the *surplus* of buyer i, $\gamma_i(N, f)$, to be the residual capacity of the edge (i, t) with respect to flow f in network N,

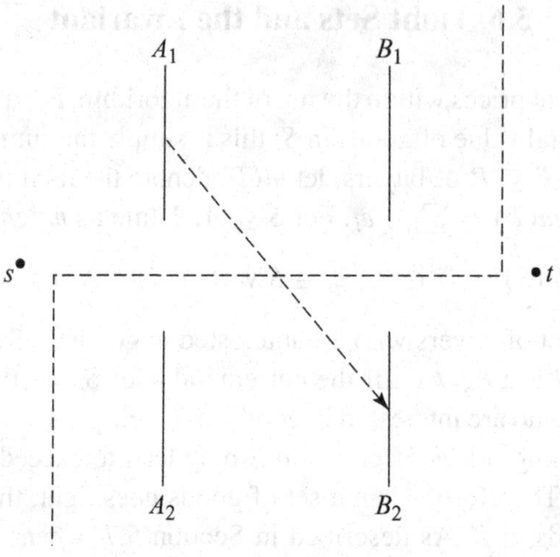

Figure 5.2. Min-cut in $N(p)$. There are no edges from A_1 to B_2.

i.e., e_i minus the flow sent through the edge (i, t). The *surplus vector* is defined to be $\gamma(N, f) := (\gamma_1(N, f), \gamma_2(N, f), \ldots, \gamma_n(N, f))$. Let $\|v\|$ denote the l_2 norm of vector v. A *balanced flow* in network N is a flow that minimizes $\|\gamma(N, f)\|$. A balanced flow must be a max-flow in N because augmenting a given flow can only lead to a decrease in the l_2 norm of the surplus vector.

Lemma 5.4 *All balanced flows in N have the same surplus vector.*

PROOF It is easy to see that if γ_1 and γ_2 are the surplus vectors w.r.t flows f_1 and f_2, then $(\gamma_1 + \gamma_2)/2$ is the surplus vector w.r.t the flow $(f_1 + f_2)/2$. Since the set of feasible flows in N is a convex region, so is the set of all feasible surplus vectors. Since a balanced flow minimizes a strictly concave function of the surplus vector, the optimal surplus vector must be unique. □

The following property of balanced flows will be used critically in the algorithm.[4]

Property 1: If $\boldsymbol{\gamma}_j(N, f) < \boldsymbol{\gamma}_i(N, f)$ then there is no path from node j to node i in $R(f) - \{s, t\}$.

Theorem 5.5 *A maximum-flow in N is balanced iff it satisfies Property 1.*

PROOF Let f be a balanced flow and let $\gamma_i(N, f) > \gamma_j(N, f)$ for some $i, j \in B$. Suppose, for the sake of contradiction, there is a path from j to i in $R(f) - \{s, t\}$.

In N, the only edge out of j is the edge (j, t). Since the path in $R(f)$ from j to i must start with a positive capacity edge which is different from edge (j, t), by flow conservation, the capacity of (t, j) must be positive in $R(f)$. Since $\gamma_i(N, f) > 0$, the edge (i, t) has a positive capacity in $R(f)$. Now, the edges (t, j) and (i, t) concatenated with the path from j to i gives us a cycle with positive residual capacity in $R(f)$ (see Figure 5.3). Sending a circulation of positive value along

[4] Unlike the previous sections, in Section 5.7, j will denote a buyer.

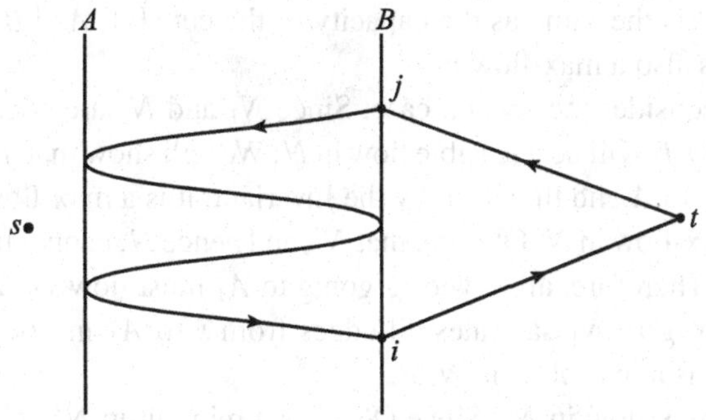

Figure 5.3. The circulation in $R(f)$ if Property 1 does not hold.

this cycle will result in another max-flow in which the residual capacity of j is slightly larger and that of i is slightly smaller; i.e., the flow is more balanced. This contradicts the fact that f is a balanced flow.

To prove the other direction, first observe that the l_2 norm of the surplus vector of a max-flow f satisfying Property 1 is locally optimum w.r.t. changes in pairs of components of the surplus vector. This is so because any circulation in $R(f)$ can only send flow from a high surplus buyer to a low surplus buyer resulting in a less balanced flow. Now, since l_2 norm is a strictly concave function, any locally optimal solution is also globally optimal. Hence, a max-flow f satisfying Property 1 must be a balanced flow. □

5.7.1 Finding a Balanced Flow

We will show that the following algorithm, which uses a divide and conquer strategy, finds a balanced flow in the given network N in polynomial time. As stated above, we will assume that this network satisfies the Invariant, i.e., $(s, A \cup B \cup t)$ is a min-cut in N.

Continuously reduce the capacities of all edges that go from B to t, other than those edges whose capacity becomes zero, until the capacity of the cut $(\{s\} \cup A \cup B, \{t\})$ becomes the same as the capacity of the cut $(\{s\}, A \cup B \cup \{t\})$. Let the resulting network be N' and let f' be a max-flow in N'. Find a maximal $s - t$ min-cut in N', say (S, T), with $s \in S$ and $t \in T$.

Case 1: If $T = \{t\}$ then find a max-flow in N' and output it – this will be a balanced flow in N.

Case 2: Otherwise, let N_1 and N_2 be the subnetworks of N induced by $S \cup \{t\}$ and $T \cup \{s\}$, respectively. (Observe that N_1 and N_2 inherit original capacities from N and not the reduced capacities from N'.) Let A_1 and B_1 be the subsets of A and B, respectively, induced by N_1. Similarly, let A_2 and B_2 be the subsets of A and B, respectively, induced by N_2. Recursively find balanced flows, f_1 and f_2, in N_1 and N_2, respectively. Output the flow $f = f_1 \cup f_2$ – this will be a balanced flow in N.

Lemma 5.6 *f is a max-flow in N.*

PROOF In the first case, i.e., $T = \{t\}$, the algorithm outputs a max-flow in N'. This flow must saturate the cut $(\{s\} \cup A \cup B, \{t\})$. However, since the capacity of this cut in N' is the same as the capacity of the cut $(\{s\}, A \cup B \cup \{t\})$, by the Invariant, this is also a max-flow in N.

Next let us consider the second case. Since N_1 and N_2 are edge-disjoint networks, $f = f_1 \cup f_2$ will be a feasible flow in N. We will show that f must saturate all edges from s to A and therefore by the Invariant, it is a max-flow.

Let g be a max-flow in N. Observe that N', and hence N, cannot have any edges from A_1 to B_2. Therefore, all flow of g going to A_1 must flow via B_1. Therefore, the restriction of g to N_1 saturates all edges from s to A_1 in N_1. Therefore, so must f_1 since it is a max-flow in N_1.

Let f' be a max-flow in N'. Since (S, T) is a min-cut in N', f' must saturate all edges from s to A_2. Furthermore, all flow of f' going to A_2 must flow via B_2, i.e., the restriction of f' to flow going through A_2 is a feasible flow in N_2. Since f_2 is a max-flow in N_2, it must also saturate all edges from s to A_2. Hence f saturates all edges from s to A in N, and is therefore a max-flow. □

Lemma 5.7 *f is a balanced flow in network N.*

PROOF We will show, by induction on the depth of recursion, that the max-flow output by the algorithm is a balanced flow in N. In the base case, the algorithm terminates in the first case; i.e., $T = \{t\}$, the surplus vector is precisely the amounts subtracted from capacities of edges from B to t in going from N to N'. Clearly, this surplus vector makes components as equal as possible, thus minimizing its l_2 norm.

Next assume that the algorithm terminates in the second case. By Lemma 5.6, f is a max-flow; we will show that it satisfies Property 1 and is therefore a balanced flow. By the induction hypothesis, f_1 and f_2 are balanced flows in N_1 and N_2, respectively, and therefore Property 1 cannot be violated in these two networks.

Let R be the residual graph of N w.r.t. flow f; we only need to show that paths in R that go from one part to the other do not violate Property 1. As already observed in the proof of Lemma 5.6, there are no edges from A_1 to B_2 in N, and therefore there are no residual paths from $j \in B_1$ to $i \in B_2$. There may however be paths going from $j \in B_2$ to $i \in B_1$ in R. We will show that for any two nodes $i \in B_1$ and $j \in B_2$, $\gamma_i(N, f) < \gamma_j(N, f)$, thereby establishing Property 1.

First observe that by the maximality of the min-cut found in N', all nodes in B_2 have surplus capacity > 0 w.r.t. flow f' in N' (all nodes having surplus zero must be in B_1). Therefore, the same amount, say X, was subtracted from the capac ity of each edge (i, t), $i \in B_2$, in going from network N to N'. We will show that $\gamma_i(N, f) > X$ for each $i \in B_2$. A similar proof shows that $\gamma_i(N, f) < X$ for each $i \in B_1$, thereby establishing Property 1.

Let L be the set of vertices in B_2 having minimum surplus w.r.t. f. Let K be the set of vertices in A_2 that are reachable via an edge from L in R. We claim that $\Gamma(K) = L$, because otherwise, there will be a residual path from $i \in L$ to $j \in B_2 - L$, thereby violating Property 1.

Let $c(K)$ denote the sum of capacities of all edges from s to vertices of K. Observe that all these edges are saturated in f' and this flow must leave via vertices of L. Let E_L denote the set of edges going from L to t. Let $c(L)$ and $c'(L)$ denote the sum of capacities of all edges in E_L in networks N and N', respectively. By the argument given above, $c'(L) > c(K)$.

Since X is subtracted from all edges in E_L in going from network N to N', $c(L) = c'(L) + |L|X$. The total surplus of the edges in E_L w.r.t. flow f is

$$c(L) - c(K) = c'(L) + |L|X - c(K) > |L|X.$$

Finally, since all edges in E_L have the same surplus, each has surplus $> X$. The lemma follows. □

Theorem 5.8 *The above-stated algorithm computes a balanced flow in network N using at most n max-flow computations.*

PROOF Clearly, the number of goods in the biggest piece drops by at least 1 in each iteration. Therefore, the depth of recursion is at most n. Next, observe that N_1 and N_2 are vertex disjoint, other than s and t, and therefore, the time needed to compute max-flows in them is bounded by the time needed to compute a max-flow in N. Hence, the total computational overhead is n max-flow computations. Finally, as shown in Lemma 5.7, the flow output by the algorithm is a balanced flow in N. □

5.8 The Main Algorithm

First we show how to initialize prices so the Invariant holds. The following two conditions guarantee this.

- The initial prices are low enough prices that each buyer can afford all the goods. Fixing prices at $1/n$ suffices, since the goods together cost one unit and all e_i's are integral.
- Each good j has an interested buyer, i.e., has an edge incident at it in the equality subgraph. Compute α_i for each buyer i at the prices fixed in the previous step and compute the equality subgraph. If good j has no edge incident, reduce its price to

$$p_j = \max_i \left\{ \frac{u_{ij}}{\alpha_i} \right\}.$$

If the Invariant holds, it is easy to see that there is a unique maximal tight set $S \subseteq A$. Clearly, the prices of goods in the tight set cannot be increased without violating the Invariant. On the other hand, the algorithm can raise prices of any subset of goods in $A - S$. The natural approach would now be to find a systematic way of increasing prices of goods in $A - S$ so that the total surplus money of the buyers decreases fast enough that the surplus vanishes in polynomial time. However, we do not know of any way of making this scheme work out.

Observe that the total surplus money of buyers is simply the l_1 norm of the surplus vector. Interestingly enough, if instead of l_1 norm, we use the l_2 norm of the surplus vector as our potential function, we can guarantee progress! The notion of balanced flows plays a crucial role in the algorithm, as detailed below. The starting idea is to define an *active subgraph* consisting of buyers having a lot of surplus money and the set of goods desired by such buyers. The prices of these goods only are raised – when a subset of these goods goes tight, the surplus of some of these buyers vanishes, thus leading to substantial progress. The problem is that as prices change, new edges enter the network $N(\boldsymbol{p})$, bringing other buyers into the active subgraph. How do we ensure that these buyers also have large surpluses? This crucial task is accomplished by Property 1 of balanced flows.

The iterative improvement steps follow the spirit of the primal-dual schema: The "primal" variables are the flows in the edges of $N(\boldsymbol{p})$ and the "dual" variables are the current prices. The current flow suggests how to improve the prices and vice versa.

A run of the algorithm is partitioned into *phases*, each phase ends with a new set going tight. Each phase is partitioned into iterations that are defined below.

A phase starts with computation of a balanced flow, say f, in the current network, $N(\boldsymbol{p})$. If the algorithm of Section 5.7 for finding a balanced flow terminates with $\delta = 0$, then by Lemma 5.2 the current prices and allocations are equilibrium prices and allocations and the algorithm halts. Otherwise, let δ be the maximum surplus of buyers w.r.t. f. Initialize I to be the set of buyers having surplus δ. Let J be the set of goods that have edges to I in $N(\boldsymbol{p})$. The network induced by $I \cup J$ is called the *active subgraph*. Throughout the phase, I' will consist of the set of buyers who have edges to goods in J but not to goods in $A - J$. These buyers are similar to those in I in that the prices of their desired goods will be raised; however, they do not have as large surpluses as buyers in I.

At this point, we are ready to raise prices of goods in J. However, we would like to do this in such a way that for each buyer $i \in (I \cup I')$, the set of goods she likes best, which are all in J, remains unchanged as prices increase. This can be accomplished by raising prices of goods in J in such a way that the ratio of any two prices remains unchanged. The rest of the algorithm for a phase is as follows.

Step $\diamond$: Multiply the current prices of all goods in J by variable x, initialize x to 1 and raise x continuously until one of the following two events happens. Observe that as soon as $x > 1$, buyers in $B - (I \cup I')$ are no longer interested in goods in J and all such edges can be dropped from the equality subgraph and $N(\boldsymbol{p})$.

- **Event 1:** If a subset $S \subseteq J$ goes tight, the current phase terminates and the algorithm starts with the next phase.
- **Event 2:** As prices of goods in J keep increasing, goods in $A - J$ become more and more desirable for buyers in I. If as a result an edge (i, j), with $i \in I$ and $j \in A - J$, enters the equality subgraph (see Figure 5.4). Add directed edge (j, i) to network $N(\boldsymbol{p})$ and compute a balanced flow, say f, in the current network, $N(\boldsymbol{p})$. If the balanced flow algorithm terminates in Case 1, halt and output the current prices and allocations. Otherwise, let R be the residual graph corresponding to f. Determine the set of all buyers that have residual paths to buyers in the current set I (clearly, this set will contain all buyers in I). Update the new set I to be this set. Update J to be the set of goods that have edges to I in $N(\boldsymbol{p})$. If there are any buyers in $B - (I \cup I')$ that have edges to goods in J but not to goods in $A - J$, move them into I'. Go to Step $\diamond$.
- **Event 3:** As prices of goods in J keep increasing, goods in $A - J$ become more desirable for buyers in I' as well. If as a result an edge (i, j), with $i \in I'$ and $j \in A - J$, enters the equality subgraph, add directed edge (j, i) to network $N(\boldsymbol{p})$ and move i from I' to $B - (I \cup I')$. Go to Step $\diamond$.

To complete the algorithm, we simply need to compute the smallest values of x at which Events 1, 2 and 3 happen, and consider the smallest of these. For Events 2 and 3, this is straightforward. We give an algorithm for Event 1 in the next section.

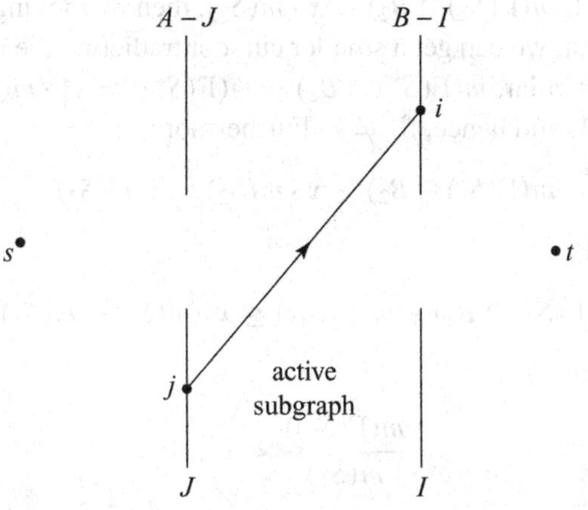

Figure 5.4. If Event 2 happens, edge (j, i) is added to $N(p)$.

5.9 Finding Tight Sets

Let $\boldsymbol{p}$ denote the current price vector (i.e., at $x = 1$). We first present a lemma that describes how the min-cut changes in $N(x \cdot \boldsymbol{p})$ as x increases. Throughout this section, we will use the function m to denote money of buyers or value of goods at prices $\boldsymbol{p}$. We will restrict attention to buyers in $I \cup I'$ and goods in J only. Therefore, it will be convenient to assume that $B = I \cup I'$ and $A = J$. Define

$$x^* = \min_{\emptyset \neq S \subseteq A} \frac{m(\Gamma(S))}{m(S)},$$

the value of x at which a nonempty set goes tight. Let S^* denote the tight set at prices $x^* \cdot \boldsymbol{p}$. If $(s \cup A_1 \cup B_1, A_2 \cup B_2 \cup t)$ is a cut in the network, we will assume that $A_1, A_2 \subseteq A$ and $B_1, B_2 \subseteq B$.

Lemma 5.9 *W.r.t. prices $x \cdot \boldsymbol{p}$:*

- *if $x \leq x^*$ then $(s, A \cup B \cup t)$ is a min-cut.*
- *if $x > x^*$ then $(s, A \cup B \cup t)$ is not a min-cut. Moreover, if $(s \cup A_1 \cup B_1, A_2 \cup B_2 \cup t)$ is a min-cut in $N(x \cdot \boldsymbol{p})$ then $S^* \subseteq A_1$.*

PROOF Suppose $x \leq x^*$. By definition of x^*,

$$\forall S \subseteq A : x \cdot m(S) \leq m(\Gamma(S)).$$

Therefore by Lemma 5.3, w.r.t. prices $x \cdot \boldsymbol{p}$, the Invariant holds. Hence $(s, A \cup B \cup t)$ is a min-cut.

Next suppose that $x > x^*$. Since $x \cdot m(S^*) > x^* \cdot m(S^*) = m(\Gamma(S^*))$, w.r.t. prices $x \cdot \boldsymbol{p}$, the cut $(s \cup S^* \cup \Gamma(S^*), t \cup (A - S^*) \cup (B - \Gamma(S^*)))$ has strictly smaller capacity than the cut $(s, A \cup B \cup t)$. Therefore the latter cannot be a min-cut.

Now consider the min-cut $(s \cup A_1 \cup B_1, A_2 \cup B_2 \cup t)$. Let $S^* \cap A_2 = S_2$ and $S^* - S_2 = S_1$. Suppose $S_2 \neq \emptyset$. Clearly $\Gamma(S_1) \subseteq B_1$ (otherwise the cut will have infinite capacity). If $m(\Gamma(S_2) \cap B_2) < x \cdot m(S_2)$, then by moving S_2 and $\Gamma(S_2)$ to the s side of this cut, we can get a smaller cut, contradicting the minimality of the cut picked. In particular, $m(\Gamma(S^*) \cap B_2) \le m(\Gamma(S^*)) = x^* \cdot m(S^*) < x \cdot m(S^*)$. Therefore $S_2 \ne S^*$, and hence, $S_1 \ne \emptyset$. Furthermore,

$$m(\Gamma(S_2) \cap B_2) \ge x \cdot m(S_2) > x^* m(S_2).$$

On the other hand,

$$m(\Gamma(S_2) \cap B_2) + m(\Gamma(S_1)) \le x^*(m(S_2) + m(S_1)).$$

The two imply that

$$\frac{m(\Gamma(S_1))}{m(S_1)} < x^*,$$

contradicting the definition of x^*. Hence $S_2 = \emptyset$ and $S^* \subseteq A_1$. □

Lemma 5.10 *Let $x = m(B)/m(A)$ and suppose that $x > x^*$. If $(s \cup A_1 \cup B_1, A_2 \cup B_2 \cup t)$ be a min-cut in $N(x \cdot \mathbf{p})$ then A_1 must be a proper subset of A.*

PROOF If $A_1 = A$, then $B_1 = B$ (otherwise this cut has ∞ capacity), and $(s \cup A \cup B, t)$ is a min-cut. But for the chosen value of x, this cut has the same capacity as $(s, A \cup B \cup t)$. Since $x > x^*$, the latter is not a min-cut by Lemma 5.9. Hence, A_1 is a proper subset of A. □

Lemma 5.11 *x^* and S^* can be found using n max-flow computations.*

PROOF Let $x = m(B)/m(A)$. Clearly, $x \ge x^*$. If $(s, A \cup B \cup t)$ is a min-cut in $N(x \cdot \mathbf{p})$, then by Lemma 5.9, $x^* = x$. If so, $S^* = A$.

Otherwise, let $(s \cup A_1 \cup B_1, A_2 \cup B_2 \cup t)$ be a min-cut in $N(x \cdot \mathbf{p})$. By Lemmas 5.9 and 5.10, $S^* \subseteq A_1 \subset A$. Therefore, it is sufficient to recurse on the smaller graph $(A_1, \Gamma(A_1))$. □

5.10 Running Time of the Algorithm

Let $U = \max_{i \in B, j \in A}\{u_{ij}\}$ and let $\Delta = nU^n$.

Lemma 5.12 *At the termination of a phase, the prices of goods in the newly tight set must be rational numbers with denominator $\le \Delta$.*

PROOF Let S be the newly tight set and consider the equality subgraph induced on the bipartition $(S, \Gamma(S))$. Assume w.l.o.g. that this graph is connected (otherwise we prove the lemma for each connected component of this graph). Let $j \in S$. Pick a subgraph in which j can reach all other vertices $j' \in S$. Clearly, at most $2|S| \le 2n$ edges suffice. If j reaches j' with a path of length $2l$, then $p_{j'} = ap_j/b$ where a and b are products of l utility parameters (u_{ik}'s) each. Since alternate edges of this path contribute to a and b, we can partition the u_{ik}'s in this subgraph into two sets such that a and b use u_{ik}'s from distinct sets. These considerations lead easily to showing that $m(S) = p_j c/d$ where $c \leq \Delta$. Now,

$$p_j = m(\Gamma(S))d/c,$$

hence proving the lemma. □

Lemma 5.13 *Consider two phases P and P', not necessarily consecutive, such that good j lies in the newly tight sets at the end of P as well as P'. Then the increase in the price of j, going from P to P', is $\geq 1/\Delta^2$.*

PROOF Let the prices of j at the end of P and P' be p/q and r/s, respectively. Clearly, $r/s > p/q$. By Lemma 5.12, $q \leq \Delta$ and $r \leq \Delta$. Therefore the increase in price of j,

$$\frac{r}{s} - \frac{p}{q} \geq \frac{1}{\Delta^2}.$$

□

Within a phase, we will call each occurrence of Events 1 and 2 an *iteration.*

Lemma 5.14 *The total number of iterations in a phase is bounded by n.*

PROOF After an iteration due to Event 2, at least one new good must move into the active subgraph. Since there is at least one good in the active subgraph at the start of a phase, the total number of iterations in a phase due to Event 2 is at most $n - 1$. Finally, the last iteration in each phase is due to Event 1. The lemma follows. □

Lemma 5.15 *If f and f^* are respectively a feasible and a balanced flow in $N(\boldsymbol{p})$ such that $\gamma_i(\boldsymbol{p}, f^*) = \gamma_i(\boldsymbol{p}, f) - \delta$, for some $i \in B$ and $\delta > 0$, then $\|\gamma(\boldsymbol{p}, f)^*\|^2 \leq \|\boldsymbol{\gamma}(\boldsymbol{p}, f)\|^2 - \delta^2$.*

PROOF Suppose we start with f and get a new flow f' by decreasing the surplus of i by δ, and increasing the surpluses of some other buyers in the process. We show that this already decreases the l_2 norm of the surplus vector by δ^2 and so the lemma follows.

Consider the flow $f^* - f$. Decompose this flow into flow paths and circulations. Among these, augment f with only those that go through the edge (i, t), to get f'. These are either paths that go from s to i to t, or circulations that go from i to t to some i_l and back to i. Then $\gamma_i(f') = \gamma_i(f^*) = \gamma_i(f) - \delta$ and for a set of vertices $i_1, i_2, \ldots, i_k$, we have $\gamma_{i_l}(f') = \gamma_{i_l}(f) + \delta_l$, s.t. $\delta_1, \delta_2, \ldots, \delta_k > 0$ and $\sum_{l=1}^{k} \delta_l \leq \delta$. Moreover, for all l, there is a path from i to i_l in $R(\boldsymbol{p}, f^*)$. Since f^* is balanced, and satisfies Property 1, $\gamma_i(f') = \gamma_i(f^*) \geq \gamma_{i_l}(f^*) \geq \gamma_{i_l}(f')$.

By Lemma 5.16, $\|\boldsymbol{\gamma}(\boldsymbol{p}, f')\|^2 \leq \|\boldsymbol{\gamma}(\boldsymbol{p}, f)\|^2 - \delta^2$ and since f^* is a balanced flow in $N(\boldsymbol{p})$, $\|\boldsymbol{\gamma}(\boldsymbol{p}, f^*)\|^2 \leq \|\boldsymbol{\gamma}(\boldsymbol{p}, f')\|^2$. □

Lemma 5.16 *If* $a \geq b_i \geq 0, i = 1, 2, \ldots, n$ *and* $\delta \geq \sum_{j=1}^{n} \delta_j$ *where* $\delta, \delta_j \geq 0, j = 1, 2, \ldots, n$, *then*

$$\|(a, b_1, b_2, \ldots, b_n)\|^2 \leq \|(a + \delta, b_1 - \delta_1, b_2 - \delta_2, \ldots, b_n - \delta_n)\|^2 - \delta^2.$$

PROOF

$$(a+\delta)^2 + \sum_{i=1}^{n} (b_i - \delta_i)^2 - a^2 - \sum_{i=1}^{n} b_i^2 \geq \delta^2 + 2a\left(\delta - \sum_{i=1}^{n} \delta_i\right) \geq \delta^2.$$

□

Let N_0 denote the network at the beginning of a phase. Assume that the phase consists of k iterations, and that N_t denotes the network at the end of iteration t. Let f_t be a balanced flow in N_t, $0 \leq t \leq k$.

Lemma 5.17 f_t *is a feasible flow in* N_{t+1}, *for* $0 \leq t < k$.

PROOF The lemma follows from the fact that each of the two actions, raising the prices of goods in J or adding an edge as required in Event 2, can only lead to a network that supports an augmented max-flow. □

Corollary 5.18 $\|\boldsymbol{\gamma}(N_t)\|$ *is monotonically decreasing with* t.

Let δ_t denote the minimum surplus of a buyer in the active subgraph in network N_t, for $0 \leq t < k$; clearly, $\delta_0 = \delta$.

Lemma 5.19 *If* $\delta_{t-1} - \delta_t > 0$ *then there exists an* $i \in H_{t-1}$ *such that* $\gamma_i(\boldsymbol{p}_{t-1}) - \gamma_i(\boldsymbol{p}_t) \geq \delta_{t-1} - \delta_t$.

PROOF Consider the residual network $R(\boldsymbol{p}_t, f)$ corresponding to the balanced flow computed at the end of iteration t. By definition of H_t, every vertex $v \in H_t \setminus H_{t-1}$ can reach a vertex $i \in H_{t-1}$ in $R(\boldsymbol{p}_t, f)$ and therefore, by Theorem 5.5, $\gamma_v(\boldsymbol{p}_t) \geq \gamma_i(\boldsymbol{p}_t)$. This means that minimum surplus δ_t is achieved by a vertex i in H_{t-1}. Hence, the surplus of vertex i is decreased by at least $\delta_{t-1} - \delta_t$ during iteration t. □

Lemma 5.20 *If* $\delta_{t+1} < \delta_t$ *then* $\|\boldsymbol{\gamma}(N_t)\|^2 - \|\boldsymbol{\gamma}(N_{t+1})\|^2 \geq (\delta_t - \delta_{t+1})^2$, *for* $0 \leq t < k$.

PROOF By Lemma 5.19, if $\delta_{t+1} < \delta_t$ then there is a buyer i whose surplus drops by $\delta_t - \delta_{t+1}$ in going from f_t to f_{t+1}. By Lemmas 5.15 and 5.17, we get the desired conclusion. □

Lemma 5.21 *In a phase, the l_2^2 norm of the surplus vector drops by a factor of*

$$\left(1 - \frac{1}{n^2}\right).$$

PROOF We will first prove that

$$\|\gamma(N_0)\|^2 - \|\gamma(N_k)\|^2 \geq \frac{\delta^2}{n}.$$

Observe that the left-hand side can be written as a telescoping sum in which each term is of the form $\|\gamma(N_t)\|^2 - \|\gamma(N_{t+1})\|^2$. By Corollary 5.18, each of these terms is non-negative. Consider only those terms in which the difference $\delta_t - \delta_{t+1} > 0$. Their sum is minimized when all these differences are equal. Now using Lemma 5.20 and the fact that $\delta_0 = \delta$ and $\delta_k = 0$, we get that

$$\|\gamma(N_0)\|^2 - \|\gamma(N_k)\|^2 \geq \frac{\delta^2}{k}.$$

By Lemma 5.14, $k \leq n$, giving the desired inequality.

The above-stated inequality and the fact that $\|\gamma(N_0)\|^2 \leq n\delta^2$ gives us

$$\|\gamma(N_k)\|^2 \leq \|\gamma(N_0)\|^2 \left(1 - \frac{1}{n^2}\right).$$

The lemma follows. □

Theorem 5.22 *The algorithm finds equilibrium prices and allocations for linear utility functions in Fisher's model using*

$$O(n^4(\log n + n \log U + \log M))$$

max-flow computations.

PROOF By Lemma 5.21, the square of the surplus vector drops by a factor of half after $O(n^2)$ phases. At the start of the algorithm, the square of the surplus vector is at most M^2. Once its value drops below $1/\Delta^4$, the algorithm achieves equilibrium prices. This follows from Lemmas 5.12 and 5.13 Therefore the number of phases is

$$O(n^2 \log(\Delta^4 M^2)) = O(n^2(\log n + n \log U + \log M)).$$

By Lemma 5.14 each phase consists of n iterations and by Lemma 5.11 each iteration requires n max-flow computations. The theorem follows. □

5.11 The Linear Case of the Arrow–Debreu Model

The Arrow–Debreu model is also known as the Walrasian model or the exchange model, and it generalizes Fisher's model. Consider a market consisting of a set A of agents and a set G of goods; assume $|G| = n$ and $|A| = m$. Each agent i comes to the market with an initial endowment of goods, $e_i = (e_{i1}, e_{i2}, \ldots, e_{in})$. We may assume w.l.o.g. that the total amount of each good is unit, i.e., for $1 \le j \le n$, $\sum_{i=1}^{m} e_{ij} = 1$. Each agent has linear utilities for these goods. The utility of agent i on deriving x_{ij} amount of good j, for $1 \le j \le n$, is $\sum_{j=1}^{n} u_{ij} x_{ij}$.

The problem is to find prices $\boldsymbol{p} = (p_1, \ldots, p_m)$ for the goods so that if each agent sells her initial endowment at these prices and buys her optimal bundle, the market clears; i.e., there is no deficiency or surplus of any good. An agent may have more than one optimal bundle; we will assume that we are free to give each agent any optiaml bundle to meet the market clearing condition.

Observe that a Fisher market with linear utilities, n goods, and m buyers reduces to an Arrow–Debreu market with linear utilities, $n + 1$ goods and $m + 1$ agents as follows. In the Arrow–Debreu market, we will assume that money is the $n + 1$'st good, the first m agents correspond to the m buyers whose initial endowment is the money they come to the market with and the $m + 1$'st agent's initial endowment is all n goods. The first m agents have utilities for goods, as given by the Fisher market and no utility for money, whereas the $m + 1$'st agent has utility for money only.

We define the following terms for the algorithm below. For agent i, let $a_i = \sum_{j=1}^{m} e_{ij}$. Let $a_{\min}$ be the minimum among a_i, $1 \le i \le m$. Denote by $p_{\max}$ the maximum price assigned to a good by the algorithm. Denote by $u_{\min}$ and $u_{\max}$ the minimum and maximum values of u_{ij} over all agents i and goods j.

5.12 An Auction-Based Algorithm

We will present an auction-based algorithm for the linear case of the Arrow–Debreu model. It will find an approximate equilibrium in the following sense. For any fixed $\epsilon > 0$, it will find prices $\boldsymbol{p}$ for the goods such that the market clears and each agent gets a bundle of goods that provides her utility at least $(1 - \epsilon)^2$ times the utility of her optimal bundle.

The algorithm initializes the price of each good to be unit, computes the worth of the initial endowment of each agent, and gives this money to each agent. All goods are initially fully unsold.

We will denote by $\boldsymbol{p} = (p_1, p_2, \ldots, p_n)$ the vector of prices of goods at any point in the algorithm. As $\boldsymbol{p}$ changes, the algorithm recomputes the value of each agent's initial endowment and updates her money accordingly. Clearly, at the start of the algorithm, the total surplus (unspent) money of all agents is n.

At any point in the algorithm, a part of good j is sold at price p_j and part of it is sold at $(1 + \epsilon) p_j$. The run of the algorithm is partitioned into iterations. Each iteration terminates when the price of some good is raised by a factor of $(1 + \epsilon)$. Each iteration is further partitioned into rounds. In a round, the algorithm considers agents one by one in some arbitrary but fixed order, say $1, 2, \ldots, m$. If the agent being considered, i, has no surplus money, the algorithm moves to the next agent. Otherwise, it finds i's optimal good, in terms of bang per buck, at current prices; say, it is good j. It then proceeds to execute the operation of *outbid*. This entails buying back good j from agents who have it at price p_j and selling it to i at price $p_j(1 + \epsilon)$. This process can end in one of two ways:

- Agent i's surplus money is exhausted. If so, the algorithm moves on to the next agent.
- No agent has good j at price p_j anymore. If so, it raises the price of good j to $p_j(1+\epsilon)$ by setting p_j to $p_j(1+\epsilon)$. The current iteration terminates and agents' moneys are updated because of this price rise.

When the current round comes to an end, the algorithm checks if the total surplus money with the buyers is at most $\epsilon a_{\min}$. If so, the algorithm terminates. Otherwise, it goes to the next round.

At termination, the algorithm gives the unsold goods to an arbitrary agent to ensure that the market clears. It outputs the allocations received by all agents and the terminating prices $\boldsymbol{p}$. Observe, however, that some of good j may have been sold at price $(1+\epsilon)p_j$ even though the equilibrium price of good j is p_j. Because of this descrepancy, agents will only get approximately optimal bundles. Lemma 5.25 will establish a bound on the approximation factor.

Lemma 5.23 *The number of rounds executed in an iteration is bounded by*

$$O\left(\frac{1}{\epsilon}\log\frac{np_{\max}}{\epsilon a_{\min}}\right).$$

PROOF Observe that if outbid buys a good at price p_j, it sells it at price $(1+\epsilon)p_j$, thereby decreasing the overall surplus. Therefore, in each round that is fully completed (i.e., does not terminate mid-way because of a price increase), the total surplus of agents is reduced by a factor of $(1+\epsilon)$. The total surplus at the beginning of the iteration is at most the total money possessed by all agents, i.e., $np_{\max}$. The iteration terminates (and in fact the algorithm terminates) as soon as the total surplus is at most $\epsilon a_{\min}$. Therefore, a bound on the number of rounds in an iteration is

$$\log_{1+\epsilon}\frac{np_{\max}}{\epsilon a_{\min}}.$$

□

Lemma 5.24 *The total number of iterations is bounded by*

$$O\left(\frac{n}{\epsilon}\log p_{\max}\right).$$

PROOF Each iteration raises the price of a good by a factor of $(1+\epsilon)$. Therefore the number of iterations is bounded by

$$n\log_{1+\epsilon}p_{\max}.$$

□

Lemma 5.25 *Relative to terminating prices, each agent gets a bundle of goods that provides her utility at least* $(1-\epsilon)^2$ *times the utility of her optimal bundle.*

PROOF The algorithm always sells an agent her optimal goods relative to current prices $\boldsymbol{p}$ (recall, however, that at the time of the sale, an agent is charged a price of $(1+\epsilon)p_j$ for good j). There are two reasons why an agent i may end up with a suboptimal bundle in the end. First, at termination, part of her money may remain unspent. Let M denote the total worth of i's initial endowment at terminating prices. Assume that she spent M_1 of this. Since the total surplus money left at termination is at most $\epsilon a_{\min}$, $M_1 \geq (1-\epsilon)M$.

The second reason is that some part of good j may have been sold at price $(1+\epsilon)p_j$ to agent i, even though the equilibrium price announced is p_j. Equivalently, we may assume that i gets her optimal goods at prices $\boldsymbol{p}$ for a fraction of her money. The latter is at least

$$\frac{M_1}{1+\epsilon} \geq \frac{(1-\epsilon)M}{1+\epsilon} \geq (1-\epsilon)^2 M$$

money. The lemma follows. □

Theorem 5.26 *The algorithm given above finds an approximate equilibrium for the linear case of the Arrow–Debreu model in time*

$$O\left(\frac{mn}{\epsilon^2}\log\frac{nv_{\max}}{\epsilon a_{\min} v_{\min}}\log\frac{v_{\max}}{v_{\min}}\right).$$

PROOF Observe that each good whose price is raised beyond 1 is fully sold. Since the total money of agents is the total worth of all goods at prices $\boldsymbol{p}$, the condition that the total surplus money of agents is at most $\epsilon a_{\min}$ must be reached before the price of all goods increases beyond 1. Hence at termination, the price of at least one good is 1.

Clearly, at termination, the ratio of maximum to minimum price of a good is bounded by $v_{\max}/v_{\min}$. Therefore, $p_{\max}$ is bounded by $v_{\max}/v_{\min}$. Each round is executed in $O(m)$ time. Now the bound on the total running time follows from Lemmas 5.23 and 5.24. □

5.13 Resource Allocation Markets

Kelly considered the following general setup for modeling resource allocation. Let R be a set of resources and $c\colon R \to \mathbf{Z}^+$ be the function specifying the available capacity of each resource $r \in R$. Let $A = \{a_1, \ldots, a_n\}$ be a set of agents and $m_i \in \mathbf{Z}^+$ be the money available with agent a_i.

Each agent wants to build as many *objects* as possible using resources in R. An agent may be able to use several different subsets of R to make one object. Let $S_{i1}, S_{i2}, \ldots, S_{ik_i}$ be subsets of R usable by agent a_i, $k_i \in \mathbf{Z}^+$. Denote by x_{ij} the number of objects a_i makes using the subset S_{ij}, $1 \leq j \leq k_i$; x_{ij} is not rquired to be integral. Let $f_i = \sum_{j=1}^{k_i} x_{ij}$ be the total number of objects made by agent a_i. We will say that

f_i, $1 \le i \le n$ is *feasible* if simultaneously each agent a_i can make f_i objects without violating capacity constraints on R.

Kelly gave the following convex program and showed that an optimal solution to it satisfies *proportional fairness*; i.e., if f_i^* is an optimal solution and f_i is any feasible solution, then

$$\sum_{i=1}^{n} \frac{f_i - f_i^*}{f_i^*} \le 0.$$

Intuitively, the only way of making an agent happier by 5% is to make other agents unhappy by at least a total of 5%.

$$\begin{aligned}
&\text{Maximize} && \sum_{a_i \in A} m_i \log f_i && \\
&\text{Subject to} && f_i = \sum_{j=1}^{k_i} x_{ij} && \forall a_i \in A \\
& && \sum_{(ij):r \in S_{ij}} x_{ij} \le c(r) && \forall r \in R \\
& && x_{ij} \ge 0 && \forall a_i \in A, 1 \le j \le k_i
\end{aligned} \tag{5.2}$$

This general setup can be used to model many situations. The following are examples of situations of a combinatorial nature.

(i) Market 1 (flow market): Given a directed or undirected graph $G = (V, E)$, E is the set of resources, with capacities specified. Agents are source-sink pairs of nodes, $(s_1, t_1), \ldots, (s_k, t_k)$, with money $m_1, \ldots, m_k$, respectively. Each $s_i - t_i$ path is an object for agent (s_i, t_i).

(ii) Market 2: Given a directed graph $G = (V, E)$, E is the set of resources, with capacities specified. Agents are $A \subset V$, each with specified money. For $s \in A$ objects are branchings rooted at s and spanning all V.

(iii) Market 3: Same as above, except the graph is undirected and the objects are spanning trees.

Using KKT conditions, one can show that an optimal solution to this convex program is an equilibrium solution. Let p_r, $r \in R$ be Lagrangian variables corresponding to the second set of conditions; we will interpret these as prices of resources. By the KKT conditions optimal solutions to x_{ij}'s and p_r's must satisfy the following equilibrium conditions:

(i) Resource $r \in R$ has positive price only if it is used to capacity.

(ii) Each agent uses only the cheapest sets to make objects.

(iii) The money of each agent is fully used up.

Since the objective function of convex program (5.2) is strictly concave, one can see that at optimality, the vector $f_1, \ldots, f_n$ is unique. Clearly, this also holds for every equilibrium allocation.

5.14 Algorithm for Single-Source Multiple-Sink Markets

In this section, we consider the special case of a flow market, Market 1, with a single source and multiple sinks. We will assume that the underlying graph is directed. In case it is undirected, one can use the standard reduction from undirected graphs to directed graphs – replace each undirected edge (u, v) with the two edges (u, v) and (v, u) of the same capacity.

Formally, let $G = (V, E)$ be a directed graph with capacities on edges. Let $s \in V$ be the source node and $T = \{t_1, \ldots, t_r\}$ be the set of sink nodes, also called terminals. Let m_i be the money possessed by sink t_i. The problem is to determine equilibrium flow and edge prices. The following example may help appreciate better some of the intricacies of this problem.

Example 5.27 Consider graph $G = (V, E)$ with $V = \{s, a, b, c, d\}$ and sinks b and d with \$120 and \$10, respectively. The edges are $(s, a), (s, c)$ having capacity 2, (a, b) having capacity 1, and $(a, d), (c, d), (c, b)$ having capacity 10 (see Figure 5.5). The unique equilibrium prices are $p_{(s,a)} = \$10$, $p_{(a,b)} = \$30$, $p_{(s,c)} = \$40$, and the rest of the edges have zero price. At equilibrium, flow on path s, a, d is 1, on s, a, b is 1, and on s, c, b is 2. Simulating the algorithm below on this example will reveal the complex sequence of cuts it needs to find in order to compute the equilibrium. Computing equilibrium for other values of money is left as an intersting exercise.

We will present a strongly polynomial algorithm for this problem which is based on the primal-dual schema; i.e., it alternately adjusts flows and prices, attempting to satisfy all KKT conditions. Often, primal-dual algorithms can naturally be viewed as executing an auction. This viewpoint is leads to a particularly simple way of presenting the current algorithm. We will describe it as an ascending price auction in which the buyers are sinks and sellers are edges. The buyers have fixed budgets and are trying to maximize the flow they receive and the sellers are trying to extract as high a price as possible from the buyers. One important deviation from the usual auction situation is

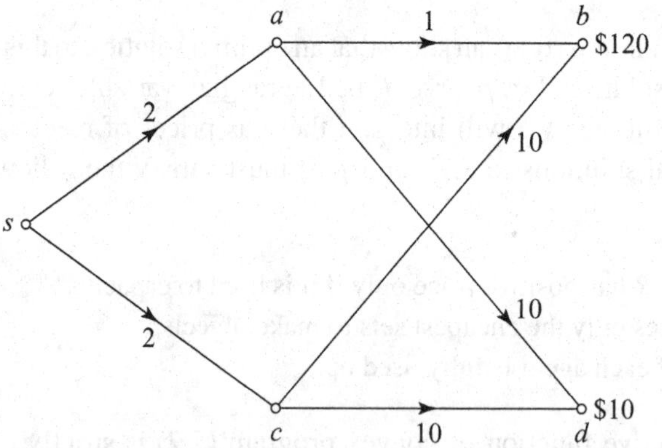

Figure 5.5. The network for Example 5.27.

that the sellers act in a highly coordinated manner – at any point in the algorithm, all edges in a particular cut, say $(S, \overline{S})$, raise their prices simultaneously while prices of the remaining edges remain unchanged. The prices of all edges are initialized to zero. The first cut considered by the algorithm is the (unique) maximal min-cut separating all sinks from s, say $(S_0, \overline{S_0})$.

Denote by rate(t_i) the cost of the cheapest $s - t_i$ path w.r.t. current prices. The flow demanded by sink t_i at this point is $m_i/\text{rate}(t_i)$. At the start of the algorithm, when all edge prices are zero, each sink is demanding infinite flow. Therefore, the algorithm will not be able to find a feasible flow that satisfies all demands. Indeed, this will be the case all the way until termination; at any intermediate point, some cuts will need to be oversaturated in order to meet all the demand.

The price of edges in cut $(S, \overline{S})$ is raised as long as the demand across it exceeds supply; i.e., the cut is oversaturated because of flow demanded by sinks in $\overline{S}$. At the moment that demand exactly equals supply, the edges in this cut stop raising prices and declare themselves sold at current prices. This makes sense from the viewpoint of the edges in the cut – if they raise prices any more, demand will be less than supply; i.e., the cut will be under-saturated, and then these edges will have to be priced at zero!

The crucial question is: when does the cut $(S, \overline{S})$ realize that it needs to sell itself? This point is reached as soon as there is a cut, say $(U, \overline{U})$, with $S \subset U$, such that the difference in the capacities of the two cuts is precisely equal to the flow demanded by sinks in $\overline{S} - \overline{U}$ (see Figure 5.6). Let $(U, \overline{U})$ be the maximal such cut (it is easy to see that it will be unique). If $U = V$, the algorithm halts. Otherwise, cut $(U, \overline{U})$ must be oversaturated – it assumes the role of $(S, \overline{S})$ and the algorithm goes to the next iteration.

Note that an edge may be present in more than one cut whose price is raised by the algorithm. If so, its price will be simply the sum of the prices assigned to these cuts.

Suppose that the algorithm executes k iterations. Let $(S_i, \overline{S_i})$ be the cut it finds in iteration i, $1 \leq i \leq k$, with $S_k = V$. Clearly, we have $S_0 \subset S_1 \subset \cdots \subset S_k = V$. Let T_i be the set of terminals in $S_i - S_{i-1}$, for $1 \leq i \leq k$. Let c_i be the set of edges of G in the cut $(S_i, \overline{S_i})$, for $0 \leq i < k$ and p_i be the price assigned to edges in c_i. Clearly, for each terminal $t \in T_i$, $rate(t) = p_0 + \cdots + p_{i-1}$, for $1 \leq i \leq k$.

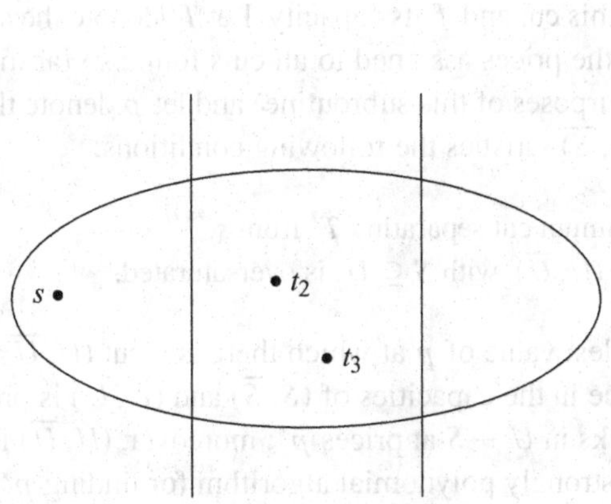

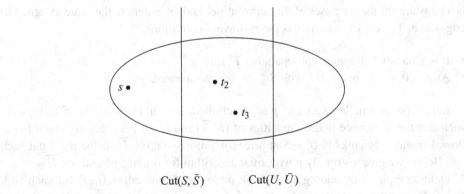

Figure 5.6. The total flow demanded by t_2 and t_3 equals the difference in capacities of cut $(S, \overline{S})$ and cut $(U, \overline{U})$.

Let G' denote the graph obtained by adding a new sink node t to G and edges (t_i, t) from each of the original sinks to t. Let the capacity of edge (t_i, t) be $m_i/\text{rate}(t_i)$. For convenience, even in G', we will denote $V - S$ by $\overline{S}$. It is easy to see that each of the cuts $(S_i, \overline{S_i} \cup \{t\})$ in G' has the same capacity, for $0 \leq i \leq k$, and each of these $k+1$ cuts is a mininimum $s - t$ cut in G'.

Let f' denote a maximum $s - t$ flow in G'. Obtain flow f from f' by ignoring flow on the edges into t. Then f is a feasible flow in G that sends $m_i/\text{rate}(t_i)$ flow to each sink t_i.

Lemma 5.28 *Flow f and the prices found by the algorithm constitute an equilibrium flow and prices.*

PROOF We will show that flow f and the prices found satisfy all KKT conditions.

- Since each of the cuts $(S_i, \overline{S_i} \cup \{t\})$, for $0 \leq i < k$ is saturated in G' by flow f', each of the cuts $c_0, c_1, \ldots, c_{k-1}$ is saturated by f. Hence, all edges having nonzero prices must be saturated.
- The cost of the cheapest path to terminal $t' \in T$ is rate(t'). Clearly, every flow to t' uses a path of this cost.
- Since the flow sent to $t' \in T$ is $m_i/\text{rate}(t')$, the money of each terminal is fully spent. □

Below we give a strongly polynomial time subroutine for computing the next cut in each iteration.

5.14.1 Finding the Next Cut

Let $(S, \overline{S})$ be the cut in G, whose price is being raised in the current iteration and let c be the set of edges in this cut and f its capacity. Let T' denote the set of sinks in $\overline{S}$. Let p' denote the sum of the prices assigned to all cuts found so far in the algorithm (this is a constant for the purposes of this subroutine) and let p denote the price assigned to edges in c. The cut $(S, \overline{S})$ satisfies the following conditions:

- It is a maximal minimum cut separating T' from s.
- At $p = 0$, every cut $(U, \overline{U})$, with $S \subseteq U$, is oversaturated.

Let p^* be the smallest value of p at which there is a cut $(U, \overline{U})$, with $S \subset U$, in G such that the difference in the capacities of $(S, \overline{S})$ and $(U, \overline{U})$ is precisely equal to the flow demanded by sinks in $U - S$ at prices p^*; moreover, $(U, \overline{U})$ is the maximal such cut. Below we give a strongly polynomial algorithm for finding p^* and $(U, \overline{U})$.

Define graph G' by adding a new sink node t to G and edges (t_i, t) for each sink $t_i \in \overline{S}$. Define the capacity of edge (t_i, t) to be $m_i/(p' + p)$ where m_i is the money of sink t_i (see Figure 5.7). As in Section 5.14 we will denote $V - S$ by $\overline{S}$ even in G'. The proof of the following lemma is obvious.

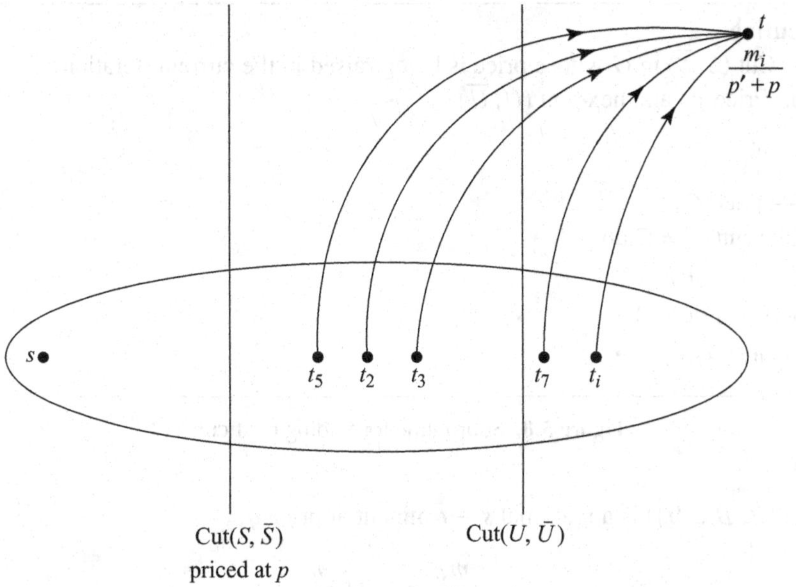

Figure 5.7. Graph G'.

Lemma 5.29 *At the start of the current iteration,* $(S, \overline{S} \cup \{t\})$ *is a maximal minimum* $s - t$ *cut in* G'. p^* *is the smallest value of* p *at which a new minimum* $s - t$ *cut appears in* G'. $(U, \overline{U} \cup \{t\})$ *is the maximal minimum* $s - t$ *cut in* G' *at price* p^*.

For any cut C in G', let $\text{cap}_p(C)$ denote its capacity, assuming that the prices of edges in c is p. For $p \geq 0$, define cut(p) to be the maximal $s - t$ min-cut in G' assuming that the price assigned to edges in c is p. For cut $(A, \overline{A} \cup \{t\})$, $A \subseteq V$, let price$(A, \overline{A} \cup \{t\})$ denote the smallest price that needs to be assigned to edges in c to ensure that $\text{cap}_p(A, \overline{A} \cup \{t\}) = f$; i.e., $(A, \overline{A} \cup \{t\})$ is also a min $s - t$ cut in G'; if $(A, \overline{A} \cup \{t\})$ cannot be made a minimum $s - t$ cut for any price p then price$(A, \overline{A} \cup \{t\}) = \infty$. Clearly, price$(A, \overline{A} \cup \{t\}) \geq p^*$. Observe that determining price$(A, \overline{A} \cup \{t\})$ involves simply solving an equation in which p is unknown.

Lemma 5.30 *Suppose* $p > p^*$. *Let* cut$(p) = (A, \overline{A} \cup \{t\})$, *where* $A \neq U$. *Let* price$(A, \overline{A} \cup \{t\}) = q$ *and* cut$(q) = (B, \overline{B} \cup \{t\})$. *Then* $B \subset A$.

PROOF Since we have assumed that $A \neq U$, it must be the case that $\text{cap}_p(A, \overline{A} \cup \{t\}) > f$. Therefore, $q = \text{price}(A, \overline{A} \cup \{t\}) < p$. Let c_A and c_B denote the capacities of $(A, \overline{A} \cup \{t\})$ and $(B, \overline{B} \cup \{t\})$ at price $p = 0$. Let m_A and m_B denote the money possessed by sinks in $(A - S)$ and $(B - S)$, respectively.

Since $(A, \overline{A} \cup \{t\})$ is a maximal $s - t$ mincut at price p,

$$c_A + \frac{m_A}{p} < c_B + \frac{m_B}{p}.$$

Subroutine

Inputs: Cut $(S, \overline{S})$ in G whose price is being raised in the current iteration.
Output: Price p^* and next cut $(U, \overline{U})$.

(i) $C \leftarrow (V, t)$
(ii) $p \leftarrow \text{price}(C)$
(iii) While $\text{cut}(p) \neq C$ do:
- **(a)** $C \leftarrow \text{cut}(p)$
- **(b)** $p \leftarrow \text{price}(C)$

(iv) Output (C, p)

Figure 5.8. Subroutine for finding next cut.

Since $(B, \overline{B} \cup \{t\})$ is a maximal $s - t$ mincut at price q,

$$c_B + \frac{m_B}{q} < c_A + \frac{m_A}{q}.$$

The two together imply

$$\frac{m_B - m_A}{q} < c_A - c_B < \frac{m_B - m_A}{p}.$$

First suppose that $A \subset B$. Clearly $m_A \leq m_B$. But this contradicts the last inequality since $q < p$.

Next, suppose that A and B cross. By the last inequality above, there must be a price, r, such that $q < r < p$ at which $\text{cap}_r(A, \overline{A} \cup \{t\}) = \text{cap}_r(B, \overline{B} \cup \{t\}) = g$, say. By the submodularity of cuts, one of the following must hold:

(i) $\text{cap}_r((A \cap B), \overline{(A \cap B)} \cup \{t\}) \leq g$. Since the money possessed by sinks in $(A \cap B) - S$ is at most m_B, at price q, $\text{cap}_q((A \cap B), \overline{(A \cap B)}\{t\}) < \text{cap}_q(B, \overline{B} \cup \{t\})$. This contradicts the fact that $(B, \overline{B} \cup \{t\})$ is a min-cut at price q.

(ii) $\text{cap}_r((A \cup B), \overline{(A \cup B)} \cup \{t\}) \leq g$. Since the money possessed by sinks in $(A \cup B) - S$ is at least m_A, at price p, $\text{cap}_p((A \cup B), \overline{(A \cup B)} \cup \{t\}) < \text{cap}_p(A, \overline{A} \cup \{t\})$. This contradicts the fact that $(A, \overline{A} \cup \{t\})$ is a min-cut at price p.

Hence we get that $B \subset A$. □

Lemma 5.31 *Subroutine 5.8 terminates with the cut $(U, \overline{U} \cup \{t\})$ and price p^* in at most r max-flow computations, where r is the number of sinks.*

PROOF As long as $p > p^*$, by Lemma 5.30, the algorithm keeps finding smaller and smaller cuts, containing fewer sinks on the s side. Therefore, in at most r iterations, it must arrive at a cut such that $p = p^*$. Since $\text{cut}(p^*) = (U, \overline{U} \cup \{t\})$, the next cut it considers is $(U, \overline{U} \cup \{t\})$. Since $\text{price}(U, \overline{U} \cup \{t\}) = p^*$, at this point the algorithm terminates. □

Theorem 5.32 *The algorithm given in Section 5.14 finds equilibrium edge prices and flows using $O(r^2)$ max-flow computations, where r is the number of sinks.*

PROOF Clearly, the number of sinks trapped in the sets $S_0 \subset S_1 \subset \cdots \subset S_k$ keeps increasing and therefore, the number of iterations $k \leq r$. The running time for each iteration is dominated by the time taken by subroutine (5.8), which by Lemma 5.31 is r max-flow computations. Hence the total time taken by the algorithm is $O(r^2)$ max-flow computations. By Lemma 5.28 the flow and prices found by the algorithm are equilibrium flow and prices. □

5.15 Discussion and Open Problems

Linear utility functions provided us with perhaps the easiest algorithmic questions that helped us commence our algorithmic study of market equilibria. However, such functions are much too restrictive to be useful. Concave utility functions are considered especially useful in economics because they model the important condition of decreasing marginal utilities as a function of the amount of good obtained. Furthermore, if the utility functions are strictly concave, at any given prices, there is a unique optimal bundle of goods for each agent. This leads to the following remarkable communication complexity fact: In such a market, it suffices to simply announce equilibrium prices – then, all agents can individually compute and buy their optimal bundles and the market clears!

On the other hand, concave utility functions, even if they are additively separable over the goods, are not easy to deal with algorithmically. In fact, obtaining a polynomial time algorithm for such functions is a premier open problem today. For the case of linear functions, the approach used in Section 5.8 – of starting with very low prices and gradually raising them until the equilibrium is reached – is made possible by the property of weak gross substitutability. This property holds for a utility function if on raising the price of one good, the demand of another good cannot go down. As a consequence of this property, the need to decrease the price of the second good does not arise.

Concave utility functions do not satisfy weak gross substitutability. Exercises 5.5 and 5.6 outline an approach that attempts to finesse this difficulty for the case of piecewise-linear, concave functions. Does this approach lead to an efficient algorithm for computing, either exactly or approximately, equilibrium prices for such functions? If so, one can handle a concave function by approximating it with a piecewise-linear, concave function. Alternatively, can one show that finding an equilibrium for such utility functions is PPAD-hard?

Considering the properties of the linear case of Fisher's model established in Theorem 5.1, one wonders whether its equilibrium allocations can be captured via a linear program. Resolving this, positively or negatively, seems an exciting problem. Another question remaining open is whether there is a strongly polynomial algorithm for computing equilibrium prices for this case. Finally, we would like to point to the numerous questions remaining open for gaining a deeper algorithmic understanding of Eisenberg–Gale markets (Jain and Vazirani, 2006).

Acknowledgments

I wish to thank Deeparnab Chakrabarty, Nikhil Devanur, Sergei Izmalkov, Kamal Jain and Kasturi Vardarajan for valuable discussions and comments on the writeup.

Bibliography

K. Arrow and G. Debreu. Existence of an equilibrium for a competitive economy. *Econometrica*, 22:265–290, 1954.

W.C. Brainard and H.E. Scarf. How to compute equilibrium prices in 1891. *Cowles Foundation Discussion Paper*, (1270) 2000.

X. Deng, C. Papadimitriou, and S. Safra. On the complexity of equilibria. In *Proc. ACM Symp. on Theor. Comp.*, 2002.

N. Devanur, C.H. Papadimitriou, A. Saberi, and V.V. Vazirani. Market equilibrium via a primal-dual-type algorithm. In *Proc. IEEE Annual Symp. Fdns. of Comp. Sci.*, 2002. To appear in *J. ACM*. Journal version available at: `http://www-static.cc.gatech.edu/vazirani/market.ps`.

N. Devanur and V.V. Vazirani. The spending constraint model for market equilibrium: Algorithmic, existence and uniqueness results. In *Proc. 36th Symp. on Theory of Computing*, 2004.

J. Edmonds. Maximum matching and a polyhedron with 0,1-vertices. *J. Res. Natl. Bur. Standards*, 69:125–130, 1965.

J. Edmonds. Optimum branchings. *J. Res. Natl. Bur. Standards, Section B*, 71:233–240, 1967.

E. Eisenberg and D. Gale. Consensus of subjective probabilities: The Pari-Mutuel method. *Annals Math. Stat.*, 30:165–168, 1959.

S. Floyd and V. Jacobson. Random early detection gateways for congestion avoidance. *IEEE/ACM Trans. Networking*, 1(1):397–413, 1993.

R. Garg and S. Kapoor. Auction algorithms for market equilibrium. In *Proc. 36th Symp. on Theory of Computing*, 2004.

V. Jacobson. Congestion avoidance and control. In *ACM SIGCOMM*, pp. 314–329, 1988.

K. Jain and V.V. Vazirani. Eisenberg-gale markets: Algorithms and structural properties. In *Proc. 39th Symp. on Theory of Computing*, 2007.

F.P. Kelly. Charging and rate control for elastic traffic. *Euro. Trans. on Telecomm.*, 8:33–37, 1997.

F.P. Kelly, A.K. Maulloo, and D.K.H. Tan. Rate control in communication networks. *J. Oper. Res. Soc.*, 49:237–252, 1998.

F.P. Kelly and V.V. Vazirani. Rate control as a market equilibrium. Unpublished manuscript 2002. Available at: `http://www-static.cc.gatech.edu/vazirani/KV.pdf`.

S. Low and D. Lapsley. Optimization flow control, 1: basic algorithm and convergence. *IEEE/ACM Trans. Networking*, 7(6):861–874, 1999.

C.S.J.A. Nash-Williams. Edge-disjoint spanning trees of finite graphs. *J. London Math. Soc.*, 36:445–450, 1961.

H. Scarf. *The Computation of Economic Equilibria (with collaboration of T. Hansen)*. Cowles Foundation Monograph No. 24., New Haven: Yale University Press, 1973.

W.T. Tutte. On the problem of decomposing a graph into n connected factors. *J. London Math. Soc.*, 36:221–230, 1961.

V.V. Vazirani. Spending constraint utilities, with applications to the Adwords market. Submitted to *Math. of Operations Research*, 2006.

L. Walras. *Éléments d'économie politique pure ou théorie de la richesse sociale (Elements of Pure Economics, or the theory of social wealth)*. Lausanne, Paris, 1874. (1899, 4th ed.; 1926, rev ed., 1954, Engl. transl.).

J. Wang, L. Li, S.H. Low, and J.C. Doyle. Cross-layer optimization in TCP/IP networks. *IEEE/ACM Trans. Networking*, 13:582–268, 2005.

Exercises

5.1 Give a strongly polynomial algorithm for Fisher's linear case under the assumption that all u_{ij}'s are 0/1 (the algorithm given in Section 1.8 is not strongly polynomial).

5.2 Let us extend Fisher's linear model to assume that buyers have utility for money (Vazirani, 2006). Let u_{i0} denote the utility accrued by buyer i for one unit of money. Now, each buyer's optimal bundle can also include money—effectively this is part of their own money which they prefer not to spend at current prices. The notion of equilibrium also generalizes—all goods need to be sold and all money needs to be either spent or returned as part of optimal bundles. Extend the algorithm given in Section 5.8 to this situation, still maintaining its polynomial running time.

5.3 Let us define a new class of utility functions, *spending constraint utility functions* for Fisher's model (Vazirani, 2006). As before, let A and B be the set of goods and buyers, respectively. For $i \in B$ and $j \in A$, let $r_j^i : [0, e(i)] \rightarrow \mathbf{R}_+$ be the *rate function* of buyer i for good j; it specifies the rate at which i derives utility per unit of j received, as a function of the amount of her budget spent on j. If the price of j is fixed at p_j per unit amount of j, then the function r_j^i/p_j gives the rate at which i derives utility per dollar spent, as a function of the amount of her budget spent on j.

Relative to prices $\boldsymbol{p}$ for the goods, give efficient algorithms for

(a) computing buyer i's optimal bundle,
(b) determining if $\boldsymbol{p}$ are equilibrium prices, and
(c) computing equilibrium allocations if $\boldsymbol{p}$ are equilibrium prices.

5.4 Prove that equilibrium prices are unique for the model of Exercise 5.3.

5.5 It turns out that there is a polynomial time algorithm for computing equilibrium prices and allocations for the utility functions defined in Exercise 5.3 (Devanur and Vazirani, 2004; Vazirani, 2006). The following is an attempt to use this algorithm to derive an algorithm for computing equilibrium prices for the case of piecewise-linear, concave utility functions for Fisher's model.

Let f_{ij} be the piecewise-linear, concave utility function of buyer i for good j; f_{ij} is a function of x_{ij}, the allocation of good j to buyer i. Let $\boldsymbol{p}$ be any prices of goods that sum up to the total money possessed by buyers (as before, we will assume that there is a unit amount of each good in the market).

Let us obtain spending constraint utility functions from the f_{ij}'s as follows. Let g_{ij} be the derivative of f_{ij}; clearly, g_{ij} is a decreasing step function. Define

$$h_{ij}(y_{ij}) = g\left(\frac{y_{ij}}{p_{ij}}\right),$$

where y_{ij} denotes the amount of money spent by i on good j. Observe that function h_{ij} gives the rate at which i derives utility per unit of j received as a function of the amount of money spent on j. Hence h_{ij} is precisely a spending constraint utility function. Let us run the algorithm mentioned above on these functions h_{ij}'s to obtain equilibrium prices, say $\boldsymbol{p}'$.

Show that $\boldsymbol{p} = \boldsymbol{p}'$ iff prices $\boldsymbol{p}$ are equilibrium prices for the piecewise-linear, concave utility functions f_{ij}'s (equilibrium prices for piecewise-linear, concave utility functions need not be unique).

5.6 **Open problem** (Devanur and Vazirani, 2004): Consider the process given in Exercise 5.3, which, given starting prices $\boldsymbol{p}$, finds new prices $\boldsymbol{p}'$. By the assertion made in Exercise 5.3, the fixed points of this process are precisely equilibrium prices for the piecewise-linear, concave utility functions f_{ij}'s.

Does this procedure converge to a fixed point, and if so, how fast? If it does not converge fast enough, does it converge quickly to an approximate fixed point, which may be used to obtain approximate equilibrium prices?

5.7 Consider the single-source multiple-sink market for which a strongly polynomial algorithm is given in Section 5.14. Obtain simpler algorithms for the case that the underlying graph is a path or a tree.

5.8 Observe that the algorithm given in Section 5.14 for Market 1 defined in Section 5.13 uses the max-flow min-cut theorem critically (Jain and Vazirani, 2006). Obtain a strongly polynomial algorithm for Market 3 using the following max–min theorem.

For a partition $V_1, \ldots, V_k$, $k \geq 2$ of the vertices of an undirected graph G, let C be the capacity of edges whose end points are in different parts. Let us define the edge-tenacity of this partition to be $C/(k-1)$, and let us define the *edge-tenacity* of G to be the minimum edge-tenacity over all partitions. Nash-William (1961) and Tutte (1961) proved that the maximum fractional packing of spanning trees in G is exactly equal to its edge-tenacity.

5.9 Next consider Market 2 defined in Section 5.13. For the case $|A| = 1$, a polynomial time algorithm follows from the following max–min theorem due to Edmonds (1967).

Let $G = (V, E)$ be a directed graph with edge capacities specified and source $s \in V$. The maximum number of branchings rooted out of s that can be packed in G equals $\min_{v \in V} c(v)$, where $c(v)$ is the capacity of a minimum $s - v$ cut.

Next assume that there are two agents, $s_1, s_2 \in V$. Derive a strongly polynomial algorithm for this market using the following fact from Jain and Vazirani (2006). Let F_1 and F_2 be capacities of a minimum $s_1 - s_2$ and $s_2 - s_1$ cut, respectively. Let F be $\min_{v \in V - \{s_1, s_2\}} f'(v)$, where $f'(v)$ is the capacity of a minimum cut separating v from s_1 and s_2. Then:

(a) The maximum number of branchings, rooted at s_1 and s_2, that can be packed in G is exactly $\min\{F_1 + F_2, F\}$.

(b) Let f_1 and f_2 be two nonnegative real numbers such that $f_1 \leq F_1$, $f_2 \leq F_2$, and $f_1 + f_2 \leq F$. Then there exists a packing of branchings in G with f_1 of them rooted at s_1 and f_2 of them rooted at s_2.

CHAPTER 6

Computation of Market Equilibria by Convex Programming

Bruno Codenotti and Kasturi Varadarajan

Abstract

We introduce convex programming techniques to compute market equilibria in general equilibrium models. We show that this approach provides an effective arsenal of tools for several restricted, yet important, classes of markets. We also point out its intrinsic limitations.

6.1 Introduction

The market equilibrium problem consists of finding a set of prices and allocations of goods to economic agents such that each agent maximizes her utility, subject to her budget constraints, and the market clears. Since the nineteenth century, economists have introduced models that capture the notion of market equilibrium. In 1874, Walras published the "Elements of Pure Economics," in which he describes a model for the state of an economic system in terms of demand and supply, and expresses the *supply equal demand* equilibrium conditions (Walras, 1954). In 1936, Wald gave the first proof of the existence of an equilibrium for the Walrasian system, albeit under severe restrictions (Wald, 1951). In 1954, Nobel laureates Arrow and Debreu proved the existence of an equilibrium under much milder assumptions (Arrow and Debreu, 1954).

The market equilibrium problem can be stated as a fixed point problem, and indeed the proofs of existence of a market equilibrium are based on either Brouwer's or Kakutani's fixed point theorem, depending on the setting (see, e.g., the beautiful monograph (Border, 1985) for a friendly exposition of the main results in this vein).

Under a capitalistic economic system, the prices and production of all goods are interrelated, so that the *equilibrium price* of one good may depend on all the different markets of goods that are available. Equilibrium models must therefore take into account a multitude of different markets of goods. This intrinsic large-scale nature of the problem calls for algorithmic investigations and shows the central role of computation.

Starting from the 60's, the intimate connection between the notions of fixed-point and market equilibrium was exploited for computational goals by Scarf and some coauthors, who employed path-following techniques to compute approximate equilibrium prices (Eaves and Scarf, 1976; Hansen and Scarf, 1973; Scarf, 1967, 1982). In their simplest form these methods are based upon a decomposition of the *price simplex* into a large number of small regions and on the use of information about the problem instance to construct a path that can be shown to terminate close to a fixed point. While the appropriate termination is guaranteed by the fixpoint theorems, the worst case running time of these algorithms turns out to be exponential.

Over the last few years, the problem of computing market equilibria has received significant attention within the theoretical computer science community. Inspired by Papadimitriou (2001), and starting with the work of Deng, Papadimitriou, and Safra (2003), theoretical computer scientists have developed polynomial time algorithms for several restricted versions of the market equilibrium problem.

In this chapter we focus on algorithms based on convex programming techniques. Elsewhere in this book (Vazirani, 2007), algorithms of a combinatorial nature are presented.

6.1.1 Definitions: Models and Equilibrium

We start by describing a model of the so-called *exchange economy*, an important special case of the model considered by Arrow and Debreu (1954). The more general one, which we will call the *Arrow-Debreu model*, includes the production of goods. We will deal with models with production in Section 6.6.

Let us consider m economic agents that represent traders of n goods. Let $\mathbf{R}^n_+$ denote the subset of $\mathbf{R}^n$ with all nonnegative coordinates. The j-th coordinate in $\mathbf{R}^n$ will stand for good j. Each trader i has a concave utility function $u_i : \mathbf{R}^n_+ \to \mathbf{R}_+$, which represents her preferences for the different bundles of goods, and an initial endowment of goods $w_i = (w_{i1}, \ldots, w_{in}) \in \mathbf{R}^n_+$. We make the standard assumption that u_i is non-satiable, that is, for any $x \in \mathbf{R}^n_+$, there is a $y \in \mathbf{R}^n_+$ such that $u_i(y) > u_i(x)$. We also assume that u_i is *monotone*, that is, $u_i(y) \geq u_i(x)$ if $y \geq x$. For the initial endowment of trader i, we assume that $w_{ij} > 0$ for at least one j. At given prices $\pi \in \mathbf{R}^n_+$, trader i will sell her endowment, and ask for the bundle of goods $x_i = (x_{i1}, \ldots, x_{in}) \in \mathbf{R}^n_+$ which maximizes $u_i(x)$ subject to the budget constraint[1] $\pi \cdot x \leq \pi \cdot w_i$. The budget constraint simply says that the bundles of goods that are available to trader i are the ones that cost no more than her income $\pi \cdot w_i$.

An equilibrium is a vector of prices $\pi = (\pi_1, \ldots, \pi_n) \in \mathbf{R}^n_+$ at which, for each trader i, there is a bundle $\bar{x}_i = (\bar{x}_{i1}, \ldots, \bar{x}_{in}) \in \mathbf{R}^n_+$ of goods such that the following two conditions hold:

(i) For each trader i, the vector $\bar{x}_i$ maximizes $u_i(x)$ subject to the constraints $\pi \cdot x \leq \pi \cdot w_i$ and $x \in \mathbf{R}^n_+$.

(ii) For each good j, $\sum_i \bar{x}_{ij} \leq \sum_i w_{ij}$.

[1] Given two vectors x and y, $x \cdot y$ denotes their inner product.

Let $\mathbf{R}^n_{++}$ be the set of vectors in R^n, whose components are strictly positive. For purposes of exposition, we will generally restrict our attention to price vectors in $\mathbf{R}^n_{++}$. When we violate this convention, we will be explicit about it.

For any price vector π, a vector $x_i(\pi)$, which maximizes $u_i(x)$ subject to the budget constraint $\pi \cdot x \leq \pi \cdot w_i$ and $x \in \mathbf{R}^n_+$, is called a *demand* of trader i at prices π. Observe that there is at least one demand vector, and that there can be multiple demand vectors. We will usually assume that there is exactly one demand vector at price π; that is, we have a demand function. This assumption holds if the utility function satisfies a condition known as *strict quasi-concavity*. Once again, we will be explicit when we will deal with exceptions, since for some common utility functions such as the linear ones, the demand is not a function but a *correspondence* or a *set valued function*.

The vector $z_i(\pi) = x_i(\pi) - w_i$ is called the *individual excess demand* of trader i. Then $X^k(\pi) = \sum_i x_{ik}(\pi)$ denotes the *market demand* of good k at prices π, and $Z^k(\pi) = X^k(\pi) - \sum_i w_{ik}$ the *market excess demand* of good k at prices π. The vectors $X(\pi) = (X^1(\pi), \ldots, X^n(\pi))$ and $Z(\pi) = (Z^1(\pi), \ldots, Z^n(\pi))$ are called *market demand* (or aggregate demand) and *market excess demand*, respectively. Observe that the economy satisfies *positive homogeneity*, i.e., for any price vector π and any $\lambda > 0$, we have $Z(\pi) = Z(\lambda\pi)$. The assumptions on the utility functions imply that for any price π, we have $\pi \cdot x_i(\pi) = \pi \cdot w_i$. Thus the economy satisfies *Walras' Law*: for any price π, we have $\pi \cdot Z(\pi) = 0$.

In terms of the aggregate excess demand function, the equilibrium can be equivalently defined as a vector of prices $\pi = (\pi_1, \ldots, \pi_n) \in \mathbf{R}^n_+$ such that $Z^j(\pi) \leq 0$ for each j.

6.1.2 The Tâtonnement Process

The model of an economy and the definition of the market equilibrium fail to predict any kind of dynamics leading to an equilibrium, although they convey the intuition that, in any process leading to a stable state where demand equals supply, a disequilibrium price of a good will have to increase if the demand for such a good exceeds its supply, and vice versa.

Walras (1954) introduced a price-adjustment mechanism, which he called *tâtonnement*. He took inspiration from the workings of the stock-exchange in Paris, and suggested a trial-and-error process run by a fictitious *auctioneer*. The economic agents receive a price signal, and report their demands at these prices to the auctioneer. The auctioneer then adjusts the prices in proportion to the magnitude of the aggregate demands, and announces the new prices. In each round, agents recalculate their demands upon receiving the newly adjusted price signal and report these new demands to the auctioneer. The process continues until prices converge to an equilibrium. In its continuous version, as formalized by Samuelson (1947), the tâtonnement process is governed by the differential equation system:

$$\frac{d\pi_k}{dt} = G_k(Z_k(\pi)), \quad k = 1, 2, \ldots, n, \tag{6.1}$$

where $G_k()$ denotes some continuous and differentiable, sign-preserving function, and $Z_k()$ is the market excess demand function for good k.

6.1.3 Approximate Equilibria

Since a price equilibrium vector that is rational exists only in very special cases, most algorithms actually compute an approximate equilibrium.

Definition 6.1 A bundle $x_i \in \mathbf{R}^n_+$ is a *μ-approximate demand,* for $\mu \geq 1$, of trader i at prices π if $u_i(x_i) \geq \frac{1}{\mu}u^*$ and $\pi \cdot x_i \leq \mu\pi \cdot w_i$, where $u^* = \max\{u_i(x)|x \in \mathbf{R}^n_+, \pi \cdot x \leq \pi \cdot w_i\}$.

A price vector π is a *strong μ-approximate equilibrium* ($\mu \geq 1$) if there are bundles x_i such that (1) for each trader i, x_i is the demand of trader i at prices π, and (2) $\sum_i x_{ij} \leq \mu \sum_i w_{ij}$ for each good j. A price vector π is a *weak μ-approximate equilibrium* ($\mu \geq 1$) if there are bundles x_i such that (1) for each trader i, x_i is a μ-approximate demand of trader i at prices π, and (2) $\sum_i x_{ij} \leq \mu \sum_i w_{ij}$ for each good j.

Definition 6.2 An algorithm that computes an approximate equilibrium, for any $\varepsilon > 0$, in time that is polynomial in the input size and $1/\varepsilon$ (resp., $\log 1/\varepsilon$) is called polynomial time approximation scheme (resp., polynomial time algorithm).

6.1.4 Gross Substitutability

In general, not only equilibria are not unique, but the set of equilibrium points may be disconnected. Yet many real markets do work, and economists have struggled to capture *realistic* restrictions on markets, where the equilibrium problem exhibits some structure, like uniqueness or convexity. The general approach has been to impose restrictions either at the level of individuals (by restricting the utility functions considered and/or by making assumptions on the initial endowments) or at the level of the *aggregate market* (by assuming that the composition of the individual actions is particularly well behaved).

The property of *gross substitutability* (GS) plays a significant role in the theory of equilibrium and in related computational results based on convex programming.

The market excess demand is said to satisfy gross substitutability (resp., weak gross substitutability [WGS]) if for any two sets of prices π and π' such that $0 < \pi_j \leq \pi'_j$, for each j, and $\pi_j < \pi'_j$ for some j, we have that $\pi_k = \pi'_k$ for any good k implies $Z^k(\pi) < Z^k(\pi')$ (resp., $Z^k(\pi) \leq Z^k(\pi')$). In words, GS means that increasing the price of some of the goods while keeping some others fixed can only cause an increase in the demand for the goods whose price is fixed.

It is easy to see that WGS implies that the equilibrium prices are unique up to scaling (Varian, 1992, p. 395) and that the market excess demand satisfies WGS when each individual excess demand does.

6.1.5 Special Forms of the Utility Functions

A utility function $u(\cdot)$ is *homogeneous* (of degree 1) if it satisfies $u(\alpha x) = \alpha u(x)$, for all $\alpha > 0$.

A utility function $u(\cdot)$ is *log-homogeneous* if it satisfies $u(\alpha x) = \log \alpha + u(x)$, for all $\alpha > 0$.

Three popular examples of homogeneous utility functions are as follows.

- The linear utility function, which has the form $u_i(x) = \sum_j a_{ij} x_{ij}$.
- The Cobb–Douglas function, which has the form $u_i(x) = \prod_j (x_{ij})^{a_{ij}}$, where $\sum_j a_{ij} = 1$.
- The Leontief (or fixed-proportions) utility function, which has the form $u_i(x) = \min_j a_{ij} x_{ij}$.

We now define the constant elasticity of substitution functional form (CES, for short), which is a family of homogeneous utility functions of particular importance in applications. A CES function is a concave function defined as

$$u(x_1, \dots, x_n) = \left(\sum_{i=1}^{n} \alpha_i x_i^{\rho} \right)^{\frac{1}{\rho}},$$

where the α_i's are the utility parameters, and $-\infty < \rho < 1$, $\rho \neq 0$, is a parameter representing the *elasticity of substitution* $1/1 - \rho$ (see Varian, 1992, p. 13).

CES functions have been thoroughly analyzed in Arrow et al. (1961), where it has also been shown how to derive, in the limit, their special cases, i.e., linear, Cobb–Douglas, and Leontief functions (see Arrow et al., 1961, p. 231). For $\rho \to 1$, CES take the linear form, and the goods are *perfect substitutes*, so that there is no preference for variety. For $\rho > 0$, the goods are *partial substitutes*, and different values of σ in this range allow us to express different levels of preference for variety. For $\rho \to 0$, CES become Cobb–Douglas functions, and express a perfect balance between substitution and complementarity effects. Indeed it is not difficult to show that a trader with a Cobb–Douglas utility spends a fixed fraction of her income on each good.

For $\rho < 0$, CES functions model markets with significant complementarity effects between goods. This feature reaches its extreme (*perfect complementarity*) as $\rho \to -\infty$, i.e., when CES take the form of Leontief functions.

6.1.6 Equilibrium vs Optimization

In 1960, Negishi showed that equilibrium allocations of goods for an exchange economy can be determined by solving a convex program where the weights of the function to be maximized are unknown (Negishi, 1960).

Negishi proved the following theorem.

Theorem 6.3 *Suppose that the initial endowment of each trader includes a positive amount of each good.*

Given positive welfare weights $\alpha_i, i = 1, \ldots, m$, *consider the convex program*

$$\text{Maximize} \quad \sum_i \alpha_i u_i(x_i)$$

$$\text{Subject to} \quad \sum_i x_{ij} \leq \sum_i w_{ij}, \text{for } 1 \leq j \leq n.$$

There exist $\alpha_i > 0$, $i = 1, \ldots, m$, *such that the optimal solutions* $\bar{x}_i$ *to the program above with these* α_i *are equilibrium allocations. That is, for some price vector* π, $\bar{x}_i = x_i(\pi)$ *for each* i.

In the proof of Negishi's theorem, the price vector π for a given set of welfare weights α_i is obtained from the dual variables in the Karush–Kuhn–Tucker characterization of the optimal solution to the convex program. Whenever the utility functions are log-homogeneous, the Karush–Kuhn–Tucker characterization implies that α_i is always equal to $\pi \cdot \bar{x}_i$. For the welfare weights that correspond to equilibrium, we must then have $\alpha_i = \pi \cdot w_i$.

Negishi's characterization of the equilibrium has inspired certain algorithmic approaches to compute it (Rutherford, 1999). It is also connected to some recent theoretical computer science work (Jain et al., 2003; Ye, in press).

6.1.7 The Fisher Model

A special case of the exchange model occurs when the initial endowments are *proportional*; i.e., when $w_i = \delta_i w$, $\delta_i > 0$, so that the relative incomes of the traders are independent of the prices. This special case is equivalent to *Fisher model*, which is a market of n goods desired by m utility maximizing buyers with fixed incomes. In the standard account of Fisher model, each buyer has a concave utility function $u_i : \mathbf{R}_+^n \to \mathbf{R}_+$ and an endowment $e_i > 0$ of *money*. There is a seller with an amount $q_j > 0$ of good j. An equilibrium in this setting is a nonnegative vector of prices $\pi = (\pi_1, \ldots, \pi_n) \in \mathbf{R}_+^G$ at which there is a bundle $\bar{x}_i = (x_{i1}, \ldots, x_{in}) \in \mathbf{R}_+^G$ of goods for each trader i such that the following two conditions hold:

(i) The vector $\bar{x}_i$ maximizes $u_i(x)$ subject to the constraints $\pi \cdot x \leq e_i$ and $x \in \mathbf{R}_+^n$.
(ii) For each good j, $\sum_i \bar{x}_{ij} = q_j$.

6.1.8 Overview

The rest of this chapter is organized as follows.

In Section 6.2, we analyze the Fisher model under the assumption that the traders are endowed with homogeneous utility functions, and present Eisenberg's convex program for computing an equilibrium in such models.

In Section 6.3, we consider exchange economies that satisfy weak gross substitutability, and show that, under such conditions, an important inequality holds, which implicitly gives a convex feasibility formulation for the equilibrium. We discuss algorithmic work that exploits this formulation.

In Section 6.4, we discuss convex feasibility formulations for exchange economies with some special and widely used utility functions, more precisely, linear and CES functions.

In Section 6.5, we expose the limitations of convex programming techniques, by presenting examples where convexity is violated (the equilibria are multiple and disconnected), and relating some of these examples to other equilibrium problems and to recently proven hardness results.

In Section 6.6, we discuss convex feasibility formulations for economies that generalize the exchange model by including production technologies.

Finally, in Section 6.7, we guide the reader through the bibliography.

6.2 Fisher Model with Homogeneous Consumers

Whenever the traders have homogeneous utility functions, the equilibrium conditions for Fisher model can be rewritten as the solution to the following convex program (Eisenberg's program), on nonnegative variables x_{ij}:

$$\text{Maximize } \sum_i e_i \log u_i(x_i)$$

$$\text{Subject to } \sum_i x_{ij} \leq q_j \quad \text{for each } j.$$

Recall that u_i is the i-th trader's utility function, e_i is the i-th trader's endowment of money, and q_j is the amount of the j-th good.

Notice that the program does not have variables corresponding to prices. The optimal solution to this program yields allocations for each trader that, at prices given by the Lagrangian dual variables corresponding to the optimal solution, are exactly the individual demands of the traders. We present a proof of this result for the case where the utility functions are differentiable.

Let $\bar{x}$ be an optimal solution to Eisenberg's program. Observe that $u_i(\bar{x}_i) > 0$ for each i. The Karush–Kuhn–Tucker necessary optimality theorem (Mangasarian, 1969, Chapter 7.7) says that there exist $\pi_j \geq 0$, for each good j, and $\lambda_{ij} \geq 0$, for each trader i and good j, such that

$$\pi_j \left(\left(\sum_i x_{ij} \right) - q_j \right) = 0 \quad \text{for each good } j, \tag{6.2}$$

$$\lambda_{ij} x_{ij} = 0 \quad \text{for each } i, j, \tag{6.3}$$

and

$$\frac{e_i}{u_i(\bar{x}_i)} \times \frac{\partial u_i(\bar{x}_i)}{\partial x_{ij}} = \pi_j - \lambda_{ij} \quad \text{for each } i, j. \tag{6.4}$$

For trader i, let us multiply the j-th equality in (6.4) by $\bar{x}_{ij}$, and add the resulting equalities. We obtain

$$\frac{e_i}{u_i(\bar{x}_i)}\sum_j \bar{x}_{ij}\frac{\partial u_i(\bar{x}_i)}{\partial x_{ij}} = \sum_j (\pi_j - \lambda_{ij})\bar{x}_{ij}.$$

Using 6.3 and Euler's identity $u_i(x_i) = \sum_j x_{ij}\frac{\partial u_i}{\partial x_{ij}}$ for the homogeneous u_i, this equality becomes

$$e_i = \sum_j \pi_j \bar{x}_{ij}.$$

At the price vector π, the bundle $\bar{x}_i$ thus exhausts the budget of trader i. Let $y_i \in \mathbf{R}^n_+$ be any bundle such that $\pi \cdot y_i \le e_i$. We proceed along the lines of the Karush–Kuhn–Tucker sufficient optimality theorem (Mangasarian, 1969, Chapter 7.2) to show that $u_i(\bar{x}_i) \ge u_i(y_i)$. Using the concavity of u_i,

$$\begin{aligned}
u_i(y_i) - u_i(\bar{x}_i) &\le \nabla u(\bar{x}_i)\cdot(y_i - \bar{x}_i)\\
&= \frac{u_i(\bar{x}_i)}{e_i}\sum_j(\pi_j - \lambda_{ij})(y_{ij} - \bar{x}_{ij})\\
&= \frac{u_i(\bar{x}_i)}{e_i}\left(\sum_j(\pi_j y_{ij} - \lambda_{ij}y_{ij}) - e_i\right)\\
&\le \frac{u_i(\bar{x}_i)}{e_i}\left(\sum_j \pi_j y_{ij} - e_i\right)\\
&\le 0.
\end{aligned}$$

We have shown that that $\bar{x}_i$ is a demand of trader i at price π. Turning now to market clearance, observe that (6.2) implies that $\sum_i \bar{x}_{ij} = q_j$ for any good j such that $\pi_j > 0$. For each good j such that $\pi_j = 0$, feasibility tells us that $\sum_i \bar{x}_{ij} \le q_j$; let us allocate the excess of any such good to trader 1. Slightly abusing notation, let $\bar{x}_1$ still denote the first trader's allocation. The bundle $\bar{x}_1$ continues to be a demand of trader 1 at price π, since the newly allocated goods have price zero and adding positive quantities of a certain good cannot decrease u_1. We have now satisfied all the requirements of an equilibrium.

6.3 Exchange Economies Satisfying WGS

We now consider exchange economies that satisfy WGS. In this scenario the following important Lemma holds.

Lemma 6.4 *Let $\hat{\pi}$ be an equilibrium price vector for an exchange economy that satisfies gross substitutability, and π be any nonequilibrium price vector. We then have $\hat{\pi} \cdot Z(\pi) > 0$.*

This lemma implies that the set of equilibrium prices forms a convex set by providing for any positive price vector π that is not an equilibrium price vector, a *separating hyperplane*, i.e., a hyperplane that separates π from the set of equilibrium prices. This is the hyperplane $\{x \in \Re^n \mid x \cdot Z(\pi) = 0\}$: indeed we have $\hat{\pi} \cdot Z(\pi) > 0$, whereas $\pi \cdot Z(\pi) = 0$, by Walras' law. To compute this separating hyperplane, we need to compute the demands $Z_j(\pi)$ at the prices π.

6.3.1 Computational Results

Lemma 6.4 tells us that if we start at price π, and move in the direction $Z(\pi)$, the Euclidean distance to the equilibrium $\hat{\pi}$ decreases. This observation is in fact the crux of the proof that a certain tâtonnement process converges to the equilibrium.

We now present a simple algorithm, which is a discrete version of the tâtonnement process, and prove that it converges to an *approximate equilibrium* in polynomial time for exchange markets satisfying WGS. For this, however, we will need to work with a transformed market.

Two Useful Transformations

We now describe a transformation that, given the exchange market M, produces a new market M' in which the total amount of each good is 1. The new utility function of the i-th trader is given by $u'_i(x_1, \ldots, x_n) = u_i(W_1 x_1, \ldots, W_n x_n)$, where W_j denotes $\sum_i w_{ij}$. It can be verified that, if $u_i()$ is concave, then $u'_i()$ is concave. The new initial endowment of the j-th good held by the i-th trader is $w'_{ij} = w_{ij}/W_j$. Let w'_i denote $(w'_{i1}, \ldots, w'_{in}) \in \mathbf{R}^n_+$. Clearly, $W'_j = \sum_i w'_{ij} = 1$.

The following lemma summarizes some key properties of the transformation.

Lemma 6.5

(i) *For any $\mu \geq 1$, $(x_{i1}, \ldots, x_{in})$ is a μ-approximate demand at prices $(\pi_1, \ldots, \pi_n)$ for trader i in M' if and only if the vector $(W_1 x_{i1}, \ldots, W_n x_{in})$ is a μ-approximate demand at prices $(\frac{\pi_1}{W_1}, \ldots, \frac{\pi_n}{W_n})$ for trader i in M.*

(ii) *For any $\mu \geq 1$, $(\pi_1, \ldots, \pi_n)$ is a weak μ-approximate equilibrium for M' if and only if $(\frac{\pi_1}{W_1}, \ldots, \frac{\pi_n}{W_n})$ is a weak μ-approximate equilibrium for M.*

(iii) *The excess demand of M' satisfies WGS if the excess demand of M does.*

We transform M' into another market $\hat{M}$ as follows. Let $0 < \eta \leq 1$ be a parameter. For each trader i, the new utility function and initial endowments are the same, i.e., $\hat{u}_i() = u'_i()$, and $\hat{w}_i = w'_i$. The new market $\hat{M}$ has one extra trader, whose initial endowment is given by $\hat{w}_{m+1} = (\eta, \ldots, \eta)$, and whose utility function is the Cobb–Douglas function $u_{m+1}(x_{m+1}) = \prod_j x_{m+1,j}^{1/n}$. A trader with this Cobb–Douglas utility function spends $1/n$-th of her budget on each good. Stated precisely, $\pi_j x_{m+1,j}(\pi) = \pi \cdot \hat{w}_{m+1}/n$.

Note that the total amount of good j in the market $\hat{M}$ is $\hat{W}_j = \sum_{i=1}^{m+1} \hat{w}_{ij} = 1 + \eta$.

Lemma 6.6 *(1) The market $\hat{M}$ has an equilibrium. (2) Every equilibrium π of $\hat{M}$ satisfies the condition $\frac{\max_j \pi_j}{\min_j \pi_j} \leq 2n/\eta$. (3) For any $\mu \geq 1$, a weak μ-approx equilibrium for $\hat{M}$ is a weak $\mu(1+\eta)$-approx equilibrium for M'. (4) $\hat{M}$ satisfies WGS if M' does.*

PROOF Statement (1) follows from arguments that are standard in microeconomic theory. Briefly, a quasi-equilibrium $\pi \in \mathbf{R}^n_+$ with $\sum_j \pi_j = 1$ always exists (Mas-Colell et al., 1995, Chapter 17, Proposition 17.BB.2). At price π the income $\pi \cdot \hat{w}_{m+1}$ of the $(m+1)$-th trader is strictly positive. This ensures that that $\pi_j > 0$ for each good j. But this implies (Mas-Colell et al., 1995, Chapter 17, Proposition 17.BB.1) that π is an equilibrium.

The proofs of the remaining statements are left as Exercise 6.4. The proof of (2) illustrates one crucial role that the extra trader plays. □

We define $\Delta = \{\pi \in \mathbf{R}^n_+ | \eta/2n \leq \pi_j \leq 1 \text{ for each } j\}$. Note that Lemma 6.6 implies that $\hat{M}$ has an equilibrium price in Δ. We define $\Delta^+ = \{\pi \in \mathbf{R}^n_+ | \eta/4n \leq \pi_j \leq 1 + \eta/4n \text{ for each } j\}$. For any $\pi \in \Delta^+$, we have $\frac{\max_j \pi_j}{\min_j \pi_j} \leq \frac{1+\eta/4n}{\eta/4n} \leq \frac{5n}{\eta}$.

Abusing notation slightly, we henceforth let $Z(\pi)$ and $X(\pi)$ denote, respectively, the excess demand vector and the aggregate demand vector in the market $\hat{M}$.

The Discrete Tâtonnement Process

We now state an algorithm for computing a weak $(1+\varepsilon)$-approximate equilibrium for $\hat{M}$. From Lemma 6.5 and Lemma 6.6 (applied with $\eta = \varepsilon$), this $(1+\varepsilon)$-approximate equilibrium for $\hat{M}$ will then be a $(1 + O(\varepsilon))$-approximate equilibrium for M. The algorithm assumes access to an oracle that can compute the excess demand vector of $\hat{M}$ at any given price vector in Δ^+. Such an oracle is readily constructed from an oracle for computing the excess demand for M.

Let π^0, the initial price, be any point in Δ. Suppose that we have computed a sequence of prices $\pi^0, \ldots, \pi^{i-1}$. We compute π^i as follows. If $\pi^{i-1} \notin \Delta^+$, we let π^i be the point in Δ closest to π^{i-1}. In other words, $\pi^i_j = \pi^{i-1}_j$ if $\eta/2n \leq \pi^{i-1}_j \leq 1$; $\pi^i_j = 1$ if $\pi^{i-1}_j > 1$; $\pi^i_j = \eta/2n$ if $\pi^{i-1}_j < \eta/2n$.

If $\pi^{i-1} \in \Delta^+$, we let

$$\pi^i = \pi^{i-1} + \frac{\delta}{(12n^2/\eta)^2} Z(\pi^{i-1}).$$

Analysis of Convergence

Lemma 6.4 is the building block upon which the proof of convergence of the (continuous) tâtonnement process is based. To prove the (fast) convergence of the discrete process just described, we need a more general result (Lemma 6.7 below). Together with Lemma 6.8, it says that if a vector $\pi \in \Delta^+$ is not a weak $(1+\varepsilon)$-approx equilibrium for $\hat{M}$, then the hyperplane normal to $Z(\pi)$ and passing through π separates π from all points within a certain distance of any equilibrium of $\hat{M}$ in Δ.

Lemma 6.7 *Let $\pi \in \Delta^+$ be a price vector that is not a weak $(1+\varepsilon)$-approximate equilibrium for $\hat{M}$, for some $\varepsilon > 0$. Then for any equilibrium $\hat{\pi} \in \Delta$, we have $\hat{\pi} \cdot Z(\pi) \geq \delta > 0$, where $1/\delta$ is bounded by a polynomial in n, $\frac{1}{\varepsilon}$, and $\frac{1}{\eta}$.*

PROOF We can assume that the goods are ordered so that $\frac{\pi_1}{\hat{\pi}_1} \leq \frac{\pi_2}{\hat{\pi}_2} \leq \cdots \leq \frac{\pi_n}{\hat{\pi}_n}$. Let α_s denote the quantity $\frac{\pi_s}{\hat{\pi}_s}$. For $1 \leq s \leq n$, let q^s denote the price vector $\min\{\alpha_s \hat{\pi}, \pi\}$, i.e., the componentwise minimum of $\alpha_s \hat{\pi}$ and π. Note that

$$q^s = (\pi_1, \ldots, \pi_{s-1}, \pi_s = \alpha_s \hat{\pi}_s, \alpha_s \hat{\pi}_{s+1}, \ldots, \alpha_s \hat{\pi}_n).$$

The first price q_1 in the sequence is an equilibrium price vector, being a scaling of $\hat{\pi}$ by α_1, and the last price vector q_n is π. For $1 \leq s \leq n-1$, let G_s^h denote the set of goods $\{1, \ldots, s\}$ and G_s^t denote the set of goods $\{s+1, \ldots, n\}$. If $\alpha_s < \alpha_{s+1}$, G_s^h is the subset of goods whose prices remain fixed during the s-th step, where we move from q^s to q^{s+1}, and G_s^t is the complement set.

Focusing on the s-th step, we have

$$\begin{aligned}
0 &= q^{s+1} \cdot Z(q^{s+1}) - q^s \cdot Z(q^s) \\
&= \sum_{j \in G_s^h} \pi_j \left(Z_j(q^{s+1}) - Z_j(q^s)\right) + \sum_{j \in G_s^t} \left(\alpha_{s+1} \hat{\pi}_j Z_j(q^{s+1}) - \alpha_s \hat{\pi}_j Z_j(q^s)\right) \\
&= \alpha_{s+1} \sum_j \hat{\pi}_j \left(Z_j(q^{s+1}) - Z_j(q^s)\right) + \sum_{j \in G_s^t} (\alpha_{s+1} - \alpha_s) \hat{\pi}_j Z_j(q^s) \\
&\quad - \sum_{j \in G_s^h} (\alpha_{s+1} \hat{\pi}_j - \pi_j) \left(Z_j(q^{s+1}) - Z_j(q^s)\right).
\end{aligned}$$

Applying weak GS to the price vectors q^s and $\alpha_s \hat{\pi}$, we see that $Z_j(q^s) \leq 0$ for $j \in G_s^t$. Applying weak GS to the price vectors q^s and q^{s+1}, we see that $Z_j(q^{s+1}) \geq Z_j(q^s)$ for $j \in G_s^h$. Noting that $\pi_j \leq \alpha_s \hat{\pi}_j \leq \alpha_{s+1} \hat{\pi}_j$ for $j \in G_s^h$, we have

$$\begin{aligned}
&\alpha_{s+1} \sum_j \hat{\pi}_j \left(Z_j(q^{s+1}) - Z_j(q^s)\right) \\
&\quad = \sum_{j \in G_s^h} (\alpha_{s+1} \hat{\pi}_j - \pi_j) \left(Z_j(q^{s+1}) - Z_j(q^s)\right) \\
&\qquad - \sum_{j \in G_s^t} (\alpha_{s+1} - \alpha_s) \hat{\pi}_j Z_j(q^s) \\
&\quad \geq \sum_{j \in G_s^h} (\alpha_{s+1} \hat{\pi}_j - \pi_j) \left(Z_j(q^{s+1}) - Z_j(q^s)\right) \\
&\quad \geq (\alpha_{s+1} - \alpha_s) \sum_{j \in G_s^h} \hat{\pi}_j \left(Z_j(q^{s+1}) - Z_j(q^s)\right).
\end{aligned}$$

That is,

$$\hat{\pi} \cdot (Z_j(q^{s+1}) - Z_j(q^s)) \geq \left(1 - \frac{\alpha_s}{\alpha_{s+1}}\right) \sum_{j \in G_s^h} \hat{\pi}_j \left(Z_j(q^{s+1}) - Z_j(q^s)\right) \quad (6.5)$$

Since the right-hand side is nonnegative, we have, for each $1 \le s \le n-1$,

$$\hat{\pi} \cdot (Z_j(q^{s+1}) - Z_j(q^s)) \ge 0. \tag{6.6}$$

Because $\pi = q^n$ is not a weak ε-approximate equilibrium for $\hat{M}$, we must have $\frac{\alpha_n}{\alpha_1} \ge 1 + \varepsilon/3$. (See Exercise 6.5.) So there is some value $1 \le k \le n-1$ so that $\frac{\alpha_{k+1}}{\alpha_k} \ge 1 + \varepsilon/6n$. We will show that the right-hand side of equation (6.5) is large for k.

We have $1 - \frac{\alpha_k}{\alpha_{k+1}} \ge \frac{\varepsilon/6n}{1+\varepsilon/6n} \ge \frac{\varepsilon}{12n}$.

We can lower bound that the increase in income of the $(m+1)$-th trader when we move from q^k to q^{k+1}:

$$\begin{aligned} q^{k+1} \cdot \hat{w}_{m+1} - q^k \cdot \hat{w}_{m+1} &\ge (q_n^{k+1} - q_n^k)\hat{w}_{m+1,n} = (\alpha_{k+1} - \alpha_k)\hat{\pi}_n \hat{w}_{m+1,n} \\ &\ge \frac{\varepsilon\alpha_k}{6n}\hat{\pi}_n \hat{w}_{m+1,n}. \end{aligned}$$

Recall that the $(m+1)$-th trader is a Cobb–Douglas trader with a utility function that ensures that she spends $\frac{1}{n}$th of her income on each good. As a result, we have

$$\begin{aligned} x_{m+1,1}(q^{k+1}) - x_{m+1,1}(q^k) &= \frac{q^{k+1} \cdot \hat{w}_{m+1}}{nq_1^{k+1}} - \frac{q^k \cdot \hat{w}_{m+1}}{nq_1^k} \\ &= \frac{1}{n\pi_1}(q^{k+1} \cdot \hat{w}_{m+1} - q^k \cdot \hat{w}_{m+1}) \\ &\ge \frac{\varepsilon\alpha_k \hat{\pi}_n \hat{w}_{m+1,n}}{6n^2\pi_1}. \end{aligned}$$

Since the market M' (the one without the $(m+1)$-th trader) satisfies weak GS and $1 \in G_s^h$, we have

$$\sum_{i=1}^m x_{i,1}(q^{k+1}) - \sum_{i=1}^m x_{i,1}(q^k) \ge 0.$$

Adding the two inequalities, we get $Z_1(q^{k+1}) - Z_1(q^k) \ge \frac{\varepsilon\alpha_k \hat{\pi}_n \hat{w}_{m+1,n}}{6n^2\pi_1}$. Plugging this into equation (6.5), and recalling that $Z_j(q^{k+1}) - Z_j(q^k) \ge 0$ for $j \in G_k^h$, we have

$$\begin{aligned} \hat{\pi} \cdot (Z_j(q^{k+1}) - Z_j(q^k)) &\ge \left(1 - \frac{\alpha_k}{\alpha_{k+1}}\right) \sum_{j \in G_k^h} \hat{\pi}_j \left(Z_j(q^{k+1}) - Z_j(q^k)\right) \\ &\ge \frac{\varepsilon^2 \alpha_k \hat{\pi}_n \hat{w}_{m+1,n}}{72n^3\pi_1}. \end{aligned}$$

Adding this inequality and the inequalities (6.6) for each $s \ne k$, we get

$$\hat{\pi} \cdot Z(\pi) = \hat{\pi} \cdot (Z(q^n) - Z(q^1)) \ge \frac{\varepsilon^2 \alpha_k \hat{\pi}_n \hat{w}_{m+1,n}}{72n^3\pi_1} = \delta.$$

It is easily verified that $1/\delta$ is bounded by a polynomial in n, $1/\varepsilon$, and $1/\eta$. □

Lemma 6.8 *For any* $\pi \in \Delta^+$, $||Z(\pi)||_2 \le 12n^2/\eta$.

PROOF

$$
\begin{aligned}
||Z(\pi)||_2 &\le \sum_j |Z_j(\pi)| \\
&\le \sum_j X_j(\pi) + \sum_j \hat{W}_j \\
&\le \frac{\max_k \pi_k}{\min_k \pi_k} \sum_j \hat{W}_j + \sum_j \hat{W}_j \\
&\le \frac{5n}{\eta} \sum_j \hat{W}_j + \sum_j \hat{W}_j \\
&\le \frac{10n^2}{\eta} + 2n \\
&\le \frac{12n^2}{\eta},
\end{aligned}
$$

where the third inequality follows from a simple calculation, the fourth inequality holds because $\pi \in \Delta^+$, and the fifth inequality holds because $\hat{W}_j \le 2$ for each j. □

We are now ready for the proof of correctness of the discrete tâtonnement process.

Theorem 6.9 *Let μ denote $\min\{\frac{\delta^2}{(12n^2/\eta)^2}, (\eta/4n)^2\}$. Within n/μ iterations, the algorithm computes a price in Δ^+ which is a weak $(1+\varepsilon)$-approximate equilibrium for $\hat{M}$. (Note that the bound on μ is polynomial in the input size of the original market M, $1/\varepsilon$, and $1/\eta$.)*

PROOF Let us fix an equilibrium π^* of $\hat{M}$ in Δ. We argue that in each iteration, the distance to π^* falls significantly so long as we do not encounter an approximate equilibrium in Δ^+. If $\pi^{i-1} \notin \Delta^+$, we have $|\pi_j^{i-1} - \pi_j^*| - |\pi_j^i - \pi_j^*| \ge 0$ for each j, while $|\pi_j^{i-1} - \pi_j^*| - |\pi_j^i - \pi_j^*| \ge \eta/4n$ for some j. From this it follows that

$$||\pi^* - \pi^{i-1}||^2 - ||\pi^* - \pi^i||^2 \ge (\eta/4n)^2.$$

Now suppose that $\pi^{i-1} \in \Delta^+$ and that π^{i-1} is not a weak $(1+\varepsilon)$-approx equilibrium for $\hat{M}$. By Lemma 6.7, $\pi^* \cdot Z(\pi^{i-1}) \ge \delta$. Since $\pi^{i-1} \cdot Z(\pi^{i-1}) = 0$ by Walras' Law, we have $(\pi^* - \pi^{i-1}) \cdot Z(\pi^{i-1}) \ge \delta$.

Let q denote the vector $\pi^i - \pi^{i-1} = \frac{\delta}{(12n^2/\eta)^2} Z(\pi^{i-1})$. We have

$$
\begin{aligned}
&(\pi^* - \pi^{i-1} - q) \cdot q \\
&\quad = (\pi^* - \pi^{i-1}) \cdot q - q \cdot q \\
&\quad = \frac{\delta}{(12n^2/\eta)^2} \left((\pi^* - \pi^{i-1}) \cdot Z(\pi^{i-1}) - \frac{\delta}{(12n^2/\eta)^2} ||Z(\pi^{i-1})||_2^2 \right) \\
&\quad \ge \frac{\delta}{(12n^2/\eta)^2} \left(\delta - \frac{\delta}{(12n^2/\eta)^2} 12n^2/\eta \right) \ge 0.
\end{aligned}
$$

Thus,

$$\begin{aligned}
&||\pi^* - \pi^{i-1}||^2 - ||\pi^* - \pi^i||^2 \\
&= ||\pi^* - \pi^{i-1}||^2 - ||\pi^* - \pi^{i-1} - q||^2 \\
&= (\pi^* - \pi^{i-1}) \cdot q + (\pi^* - \pi^{i-1} - q) \cdot q \\
&\geq (\pi^* - \pi^{i-1}) \cdot q \\
&= \frac{\delta}{(12n^2/\eta)^2}(\pi^* - \pi^{i-1}) \cdot Z(\pi^{i-1}) \\
&\geq \frac{\delta^2}{(12n^2/\eta)^2},
\end{aligned}$$

Suppose that every vector in the sequence $\pi^0, \dots, \pi^k$ is either not in Δ^+ or not a weak $(1+\varepsilon)$-approx equilibrium. We then have

$$||\pi^* - \pi^{i-1}||^2 - ||\pi^* - \pi^i||^2 \geq \min\left\{\frac{\delta^2}{(12n^2/\eta)^2}, (\eta/4n)^2\right\} = \mu,$$

for $1 \leq i \leq k$. Adding these inequalities, we get

$$k\mu \leq ||\pi^* - \pi^0||^2 - ||\pi^* - \pi^k||^2 \leq n.$$

□

Putting everything together, we can state the main result of this section.

Theorem 6.10 *Let M be an exchange market whose excess demand function satisfies WGS, and suppose that M is equipped with an oracle for computing the excess demand at any given price vector. For any $\varepsilon > 0$, the tâtonnement-based algorithm computes, in time polynomial in the input size of M and $1/\varepsilon$, a sequence of prices one of which is a weak $(1+\varepsilon)$-approx equilibrium for M.*

In order to actually pick the approximate equilibrium price from the sequence of prices, we need an efficient algorithm that recognizes an approximate equilibrium of M. In fact, it is sufficient for this algorithm to assert that a given price π is a weak $(1+2\varepsilon)$-approximate equilibrium provided π is a weak $(1+\varepsilon)$-approximate equilibrium. Since the problem of recognizing an approximate equilibrium is an explicitly presented convex programming problem, such an algorithm is generally quite easy to construct.

6.4 Specific Utility Functions

In many economic scenarios, the market is modeled by consumers having some specific utility functions. While in some cases this does not lead to a simplified computational problem, in other instances, the specific utility functions might expose a computationally useful structure. This turns out to be the case for linear utility functions, as well as for certain CES utility functions.

6.4.1 Convex Programs for Linear Exchange Economies

The equilibrium conditions for an exchange economy with linear utilities can be written as a finite convex feasibility problem. Suppose that the linear utility function of the i-th trader is $\sum_j a_{ij}x_{ij}$, and suppose that $w_{ij} > 0$ for each i, j.

Consider now the problem of finding ψ_j and nonnegative x_{ij} such that

$$\sum_k a_{ik}x_{ik} \geq a_{ij}\sum_k w_{ik}e^{\psi_k - \psi_j}, \quad \text{for each } 1 \leq i \leq m, 1 \leq j \leq n.$$

$$\sum_i x_i = \sum_i w_i.$$

Any solution to this program corresponds to an equilibrium obtained by setting $\pi_j = e^{\psi_j}$. The converse also holds, i.e., any equilibrium corresponds to a solution to this program.

We will discuss the ideas behind the derivation of the convex program above in the context of economies with production (Section 6.6).

6.4.2 Convex Programs for CES Exchange Economies

Demand of CES Consumers. We start by characterizing the demand function of traders with CES utility functions. Consider a setting where trader i has an initial endowment $w_i = (w_{i1}, \ldots, w_{in}) \in \mathbf{R}^n_+$ of goods, and the CES utility function $u_i(x_{i1}, \ldots, x_{in}) = (\sum_{j=1}^n \alpha_{ij}x_{ij}^{\rho_i})^{\frac{1}{\rho_i}}$, where $\alpha_{ij} > 0$, $w_{ij} > 0$, and $-\infty < \rho_i < 1$, but $\rho_i \neq 0$. If $\rho_i < 0$, we define $u_i(x_{i1}, \ldots, x_{in}) = 0$ if there is a j such that $x_{ij} = 0$. Note that this ensures that u_i is continuous over $\mathbf{R}^n_+$.

The demand vector for the i-th consumer is unique and is given by the expression

$$x_{ij}(\pi) = \frac{\alpha_{ij}^{1/1-\rho_i}}{\pi_j^{1/1-\rho_i}} \times \frac{\sum_k \pi_k w_{ik}}{\sum_k \alpha_k^{1/1-\rho_i}\pi_k^{-\rho_i/1-\rho_i}}. \tag{6.7}$$

The formula above can be derived using the Karush–Kuhn–Tucker conditions.

Efficient Computation by Convex Programming. Consider an economy in which each trader i has a CES utility function with $-1 \leq \rho_i < 0$. We show that the equilibria of such an economy can be characterized as the solutions of a convex feasibility problem.

Since the demand of every trader is well-defined and unique at any price, we may write the equilibria as the set $\pi \in \mathbf{R}_{++}$ such that for each good j, we have $\sum_i x_{ij}(\pi) \leq \sum_i w_{ij}$. Let $\rho = -1$, and note that $\rho \leq \rho_i$, for each i. Let $f_{ij}(\pi) = \pi_j^{1/(1-\rho)}x_{ij}(\pi)$, and $\sigma_j = \pi_j^{1/(1-\rho)}$. In terms of the σ_j's, we obtain the set of $\sigma = (\sigma_1, \ldots, \sigma_n) \in \mathbf{R}_{++}$ such that for each good j,

$$\sum_i f_{ij}(\sigma) \leq \sigma_j\left(\sum_i w_{ij}\right).$$

We now show that these inequalities give rise to a convex feasibility program. Since the right-hand side of each inequality is a linear function, it suffices to argue that the left-hand side is a convex function. The latter claim is established by the following proposition.

Proposition 6.11 *The function $f_{ij}(\sigma)$ is a convex function over $\mathbf{R}_{++}$.*

PROOF Clearly, it suffices to show that the constraint $f_{ij} \leq t$ defines a convex set for positive t. Using formula (6.7) for the demand, this constraint can be written as

$$\frac{\alpha_{ij}^{\frac{1}{1-\rho_i}}}{\sigma_j^{\frac{\rho_i-\rho}{1-\rho_i}}} \times \frac{\sum_k \sigma_k^{1-\rho} w_{ik}}{\sum_k \alpha_{ik}^{\frac{1}{1-\rho_i}} \sigma_k^{\frac{-\rho_i(1-\rho)}{1-\rho_i}}} \leq t.$$

Rewriting, and raising both sides to the power $1/(1-\rho)$, we obtain

$$\alpha_{ij}^{\frac{1}{(1-\rho)(1-\rho_i)}} \times \left(\sum_k \sigma_k^{1-\rho} w_{ik}\right)^{\frac{1}{1-\rho}} \leq t^{\frac{1}{1-\rho}} \sigma_j^{\frac{\rho_i-\rho}{(1-\rho_i)(1-\rho)}} v_i^{\frac{-\rho_i}{1-\rho_i}}, \tag{6.8}$$

where

$$v_i = \left(\sum_k \alpha_{ik}^{\frac{1}{1-\rho_i}} \sigma_k^{\frac{-\rho_i(1-\rho)}{1-\rho_i}}\right)^{\frac{1-\rho_i}{-\rho_i(1-\rho)}}. \tag{6.9}$$

The left-hand side of inequality 6.8 is a convex function, and the right-hand side is a concave function that is nondecreasing in each argument when viewed as a function of t, σ_j, and v_i, since the exponents are nonnegative and add up to one. Since $0 < \frac{-\rho_i(1-\rho)}{1-\rho_i} \leq 1$, the right-hand side of equality 6.9 is a concave function, in fact a CES function. It follows that the right-hand side of inequality 6.8 remains a concave function when v_i is replaced by the right-hand side of equality 6.9. This completes the proof. □

It is not hard to verify that the demand generated by an economy with CES utilities as above need not satisfy WGS. Indeed, the connectedness of the equilibria that is a corollary of the above convex feasibility formulation is an interesting new consequence.

6.5 Limitations

So far, we have presented efficient algorithms for restricted versions of the market equilibrium problem, which take advantage of the convexity of the set of equilibria. However, the set of equilibria in a general exchange economy does not even need to be connected. This implies that it is not possible to characterize the set of equilibria by a convex formulation.

In Section 6.5.1 we report an example that shows that CES exchange economies may present multiple disconnected equilibria, whenever $\rho < -1$. This suggests that it is unlikely that the results shown in Section 6.4.2 can be extended to encompass markets where some traders have CES utility functions with $\rho < -1$.

In Section 6.5.2 we outline some more general obstacles to the efficient solvability of the market equilibrium problem. More precisely, we give a tour of a number of recent computational complexity results which imply that Leontief exchange economies are hard for *PPAD*, a complexity class that contains a wealth of equilibrium problems. This shows that it is unlikely that the market equilibrium problem, even when restricted to exchange economies with Leontief consumers, can be solved in polynomial time.

6.5.1 Multiple Disconnected Equilibria

We describe a simple market with two traders and two goods that has multiple disconnected equilibria. The first trader has an initial bundle $w_1 = (1, 0)$ and the CES utility function $u_1(x, y) = ((ax)^\rho + y^\rho)^{1/\rho}$, where $a > 0$. The second trader has an initial bundle $w_2 = (0, 1)$ and the CES utility function $u_2(x, y) = ((x/a)^\rho + y^\rho)^{1/\rho}$. It is possible to show that for each $\rho < -1$ there is a sufficiently small value of a for which

(i) the vector $(1/2, 1/2)$ is an equilibrium price and
(ii) the vector $(p, 1 - p)$ is an equilibrium price for some $p < 1/2$, and the vector $(q, 1 - q)$ is not an equilibrium price for any $p < q < 1/2$.

This economy therefore does not admit a convex programming formulation in terms of some "relative" of the prices (such as the one given in Section 6.4.2 in terms of the σ_k) that captures *all* the price equilibria. Such a formulation implies that if $(p_1, 1 - p_1)$ is a price equilibrium and $(p_2, 1 - p_2)$ is a price equilibrium for some $p_1 < p_2$, then $(p_3, 1 - p_3)$ is also a price equilibrium for every $p_1 < p_3 < p_2$.

This example suggests that it may not be possible to extend convex programming techniques to encompass markets where some traders have a CES utility function with $\rho < -1$.

6.5.2 Hardness for the Class *PPAD*

The context of computation of equilibria calls for a complexity analysis conducted within the class *TFNP* of *total search problems*, i.e., problems whose set of solutions is guaranteed to be non empty. Nash Theorem guarantees that the problem of finding a Nash equilibrium in a noncooperative game in normal form is a total search problem. Arrow and Debreu Theorem gives sufficient conditions under which an exchange economy has an equilibrium. Therefore, under suitable sufficient conditions, the problem of finding a market equilibrium is a total search problem.

An important subclass of *TFNP* is the class *PPAD*, which is the class of total functions whose totality is proven by the following simple combinatorial argument: if a directed graph whose nodes have in-degree and out-degree at most one has a source, it must have a sink (see Chapter 2 of this book for more background, Papadimitriou, 2007).

This class captures a wealth of equilibrium problems, e.g., the market equilibrium problem as well as Nash equilibria for n-player games. Problems complete for this class include a (suitably defined) computational version of the Brouwer Fixed Point Theorem.

Consider exchange economies where m, the number of traders, is equal to the number of goods, and the i-th trader has an initial endowment given by one unit of the i-th good. The traders have a Leontief (or fixed-proportion) utility function, which describes their goal of getting a bundle of goods in proportions determined by m given parameters.

Given an arbitrary bimatrix game, specified by a pair of $n \times m$ matrices A and B, with positive entries, one can construct a Leontief exchange economy with $n + m$ traders and $n + m$ goods as follows.

Trader i has an initial endowment consisting of one unit of good i, for $i = 1, \ldots, n + m$. Traders indexed by any $j \in \{1, \ldots, n\}$ receive some utility only from goods $j \in \{n + 1, \ldots, n + m\}$, and this utility is specified by parameters corresponding to the entries of the matrix B. More precisely the proportions in which the j-th trader wants the goods are specified by the entries on the jth row of B. Vice versa, traders indexed by any $j \in \{n + 1, \ldots, n + m\}$ receive some utility only from goods $j \in \{1, \ldots, n\}$. In this case, the proportions in which the j-th trader wants the goods are specified by the entries on the jth column of A.

In the economy above, one can partition the traders in two groups, which bring to the market disjoint sets of goods, and are interested only in the goods brought by the group they do not belong to.

It is possible to show that the Nash equilibria of any bimatrix game (A, B) are in one-to-one correspondence with the market equilibria of such an economy, and that the correspondence can be computed in polynomial time. (For the Leontief economies under consideration, we need to get rid of the assumption – see the Introduction – that we will be concerned only with positive price equilibria. It is only then that they capture the complexity of bimatrix games.)

The problem of computing a Nash equilibrium for two-player nonzero sum games have been proven $PPAD$-complete. Combined with the game-market correspondence mentioned above, these hardness results imply that the problem of computing a market equilibrium, even when confined to the restrictive scenario of a special family of Leontief economies, is $PPAD$-complete.

6.6 Models with Production

In this section, we derive convex programs for certain economies that generalize the exchange model by including *constant returns to scale* technologies. The ideas for deriving these convex programs build on the ones developed for exchange economies with special utility functions. In a *constant returns* economy M, there are ℓ *producers*, as well as the m consumers and n goods of the exchange model. The k-th producer is equipped with a technology that is capable of producing some good, say o_k, using the n goods as input. The technology is specified by a concave function $f_k : \mathbf{R}^n_+ \rightarrow \mathbf{R}_+$ that is assumed to be homogeneous of degree 1. The interpretation is that given quantity

$z_j \geq 0$ of good j, for $1 \leq j \leq n$, the technology can produce up to $f_k(z_1, \ldots, z_n)$ units of good o_k.

At a given price vector $\pi = (\pi_1, \ldots, \pi_n) \in \mathbf{R}^n_+$, the producer will choose a technologically feasible production plan that maximizes her profit. That is, she will choose $z_1, \ldots, z_n \geq 0$ that maximizes the profit $\pi_{o_k} f_k(z_1, \ldots, z_n) - \sum_{j=1}^n \pi_j z_j$. Now if there is a choice of nonnegative $z_1, \ldots, z_n$ such that $\pi_{o_k} f_k(z_1, \ldots, z_n) - \sum_{j=1}^n \pi_j z_j > 0$, then using inputs $\alpha z_1, \ldots, \alpha z_n$, for $\alpha > 1$, she can obtain a profit of

$$\pi_{o_k} f_k(\alpha z_1, \ldots, \alpha z_n) - \sum_{j=1}^n \pi_j \alpha z_j = \alpha \left(\pi_{o_k} f_k(z_1, \ldots, z_n) - \sum_{j=1}^n \pi_j z_j \right).$$

Thus a profit-maximizing plan is not defined in this case. A profit-maximizing plan is defined if and only if no feasible plan can make a strictly positive profit. In such a case, a profit-maximizing plan is one that makes zero profit. In particular, the trivial choice $z_j = 0$, for $1 \leq j \leq n$, for which $f_k(z_1, \ldots, z_n) = 0$ is always a profit-maximizing plan whenever profit maximization is well defined.

It is useful to restate the above in terms of the unit cost function $c_k : \mathbf{R}^n_+ \rightarrow \mathbf{R}_+$. This is defined, at any given price vector $(\pi_1, \ldots, \pi_n) \in \mathbf{R}^n_+$, to be the minimum cost for producing one unit of good o_k. That is,

$$c_k(\pi) = \min \left\{ \sum_{j=1}^n \pi_j z_j | z_j \geq 0,\ f_k(z_1, \ldots, z_n) \geq 1 \right\}.$$

If $\pi_{o_k} > c_k(\pi)$, then profit maximization is undefined. If $\pi_{o_k} < c_k(\pi)$, then the only profit-maximizing plan is the trivial plan. If $\pi_{o_k} = c_k(\pi)$, the trivial plan, as well as any $(x_1, \ldots, x_n)$ such that $f_k(z_1, \ldots, z_n) c_k(\pi) = \sum_{j=1}^n \pi_j z_j$, is a profit-maximizing plan.

Each consumer is identical to the one in the exchange model: she has an initial endowment $w_i \in \mathbf{R}^n_+$ and a utility function u_i, which we now assume to be homogeneous. An equilibrium is a price vector $\pi = (\pi_1, \ldots, \pi_n)$ at which there is a bundle $x_i = (x_{i1}, \ldots, x_{in}) \in \mathbf{R}^n_+$ of goods for each trader i and a bundle $z_k = (z_{k1}, \ldots, z_{kn}) \in \mathbf{R}^n_+$ for each producer k such that the following three conditions hold: (i) For each firm k, profit maximization is well-defined at π and the inputs $z_k = (z_{k1}, \ldots, z_{kn})$ and output $q_{ko_k} = f_k(z_{k1}, \ldots, z_{kn})$ is a profit-maximizing plan; (ii) for each consumer i, the vector x_i is her demand at price π; and (iii) for each good j, the total demand is no more than the total supply; i.e., the market clears:

$$\sum_i x_{ij} + \sum_k z_{kj} \leq \sum_i w_{ij} + \sum_{k:j=o_k} q_{kj}.$$

Note that requirement (i) means that there is no feasible plan that makes positive profit. This rules out the trivial approach of ignoring the production units and computing an equilibrium for the resulting exchange model.

We now derive a convex program for certain kinds of utility and production functions. We first transform the economy M into an economy M' with m consumers, $n + m$ goods, and $l + m$ producers. For each consumer i, an additional good, which will be the $(n + i)$-th good, is added. The new utility function of the i-th consumer is $u'_i(x_1, \ldots, x_{n+m}) = x_{n+i}$; that is, the i-th consumer wants only good $n + i$. The new initial endowment w_i' is the same as the old one; that is $w_{ij}' = w_{ij}$ if $j \leq n$, and $w_{ij}' = 0$ if $j > n$. The first l producers stay the same. That is, for $k \leq l$, the k-th producer outputs good o_k using the technology described by the function $f_k'(z_1, \ldots, z_{n+m}) = f_k(z_1, \ldots, z_n)$. For $1 \leq i \leq m$, the $(l+i)$-th producer outputs good $n+i$ using the technology described by the function $f_{l+i}'(z_1, \ldots, z_{n+m}) = u_i(z_1, \ldots, z_n)$. It can be shown that there is a one-to-one correspondence between the equilibria of M and M'. We will therefore focus on characterizing the equilibria of M' – the simplicity of its consumption side will be of considerable help in this task.

6.6.1 Inequalities Characterizing Equilibrium

We begin by characterizing the equilibria for the market M' in terms of a system G of inequalities, in the following sets of nonnegative variables: (1) $\pi_1, \ldots, \pi_{n+m}$, for the prices; (2) $x_{i,n+i}$, for the demand of consumer i for the $(n+i)$-th good; (3) $z_k = (z_{k1}, \ldots, z_{kn}) \in \mathbf{R}_+^n$, standing for the inputs used by the k-th production sector; and (4) q_{ko_k}, for the output of the good o_k by the k-th producer.

$$\pi_{n+i} x_{i,n+i} \geq \sum_{j=1}^{n} \pi_j w_{ij}, \text{ for } 1 \leq i \leq m \tag{6.10}$$

$$q_{ko_k} \leq f_k(z_k), \text{ for } 1 \leq k \leq l+m \tag{6.11}$$

$$\pi_{o_k} \leq c_k(\pi_1, \ldots, \pi_n), \text{ for } 1 \leq k \leq l+m \tag{6.12}$$

$$\sum_k z_{kj} \leq \sum_i w_{ij} + \sum_{k:o_k=j} q_{kj}, \text{ for } 1 \leq j \leq n \tag{6.13}$$

$$x_{i,n+i} \leq q_{l+i,n+i} \text{ for } 1 \leq i \leq m \tag{6.14}$$

Here, $c_k()$ denotes the k-th producer's unit cost function, which depends only on the prices of the first n goods. Evidently, any equilibrium is a feasible solution to the system of inequalities G. What is not so evident is that any feasible solution of G is an equilibrium. To see this, we first note that the sets of inequalities (6.12) and (6.13) imply that no producer can make positive profit: we have $\sum_{j \leq n} \pi_j z_{kj} \geq \pi_{o_k} q_{ko_k}$ for each producer k. Adding up these inequalities, as well as the inequalities (6.10), we get a certain inequality that says that the cost of the consumer and producer demands is greater than or equal to the cost of the initial endowments and producer outputs. Whereas by multiplying each inequality in (6.13) and (6.14) by the corresponding price and adding up these inequalities, we get that the cost of the consumer and producer demands is less than or equal to the cost of the initial endowments and producer outputs.

This implies that the two costs must be equal. From this it follows that $\sum_{j \leq n} \pi_j z_{kj} = \pi_{o_k} q_{ko_k}$ for each producer k. Each production plan makes zero profit. Since (6.12) ensures that profit maximization is well defined, these are optimal production plans. Furthermore, we must have equality in (6.10): $x_{i,n+i}$ is the demand of good $n+i$ at price π. Since conservation of goods is guaranteed by (6.13) and (6.14), we conclude that any solution of G is an equilibrium.

6.6.2 Convex Programs for Specific Functions

Let us make the substitution $\pi_j = e^{\psi_j}$ in the system of inequalities above. This makes all the constraints convex, except possibly for the ones in (6.12). Whenever each inequality in the set (6.13) also becomes a convex constraint, we get a convex feasibility characterization of the equilibrium prices.

Let us first consider what happens to the constraint in (6.12) corresponding to a CES production function $f_k(z_1, \ldots, z_n) = (\sum_j a_{kj} x_j^{\rho})^{1/\rho}$, where $0 < \rho < 1$. The corresponding constraint is $\pi_{o_k} \le c_k(\pi) = (\sum_j a_{kj}^{\sigma} \pi_j^{1-\sigma})^{1/1-\sigma}$, where $\sigma = 1/(1-\rho)$ (we use a standard expression for the cost function corresponding to the CES production function f_k). Raising both sides to the power $(1-\sigma)$, and noting that $1-\sigma < 0$, this constraint becomes

$$\pi_{o_k}^{1-\sigma} \ge \left(\sum_j a_{kj}^{\sigma} \pi_j^{1-\sigma} \right).$$

It is now easy to see that the substitution $\pi_j = e^{\psi_j}$ turns this inequality into a convex constraint.

It is also easy to verify, using standard formulas for the cost functions, that the constraint in (6.12) corresponding to a linear or a Cobb–Douglas production function also becomes convex after the substitution $\pi_j = e^{\psi_j}$.

Thus, we obtain convex programs characterizing the equilibria in constant returns economies where the utility and production functions are linear, Cobb–Douglas, or CES with $\rho > 0$. The approach also works for a certain family of nested CES functions. Interestingly, the use of production technologies to simplifying the consumption side plays a key role in obtaining convex programs for pure exchange economies with nested CES utility functions.

6.7 Bibliographic Notes

The convex program of Section 6.2 is due to Eisenberg (1961). Generalizing an approach due to Eisenberg and Gale (1959) and Gale (1960) for linear utilities, Eisenberg (1961) shows how to write the equilibrium conditions for the Fisher model as the solution to a convex program whenever the traders have homogeneous utility functions.

Eisenberg's program can also be seen as following from Negishi's theorem. However Eisenberg establishes an arguably stronger result. Without loss of generality, assume $\sum_i e_i = 1$. Consider the *social utility function* $u : \mathbf{R}_+^n \to R$ that assigns to each $s \in \mathbf{R}_+^n$ the value

$$\max \left\{ \prod_{i=1}^{m} u_i(x_i)^{e_i} \mid x_i \in \mathbf{R}_+^n, \sum_i x_i \le s \right\}.$$

Eisenberg shows that u is homogeneous and concave, and that at any price vector π the market demand generated by the Fisher economy with m traders is identical to the demand of a single trader with utility function u and income 1.

Polterovich (1973) extends Eisenberg's program to a generalization of the Fisher model that includes production. Jain et al. (2005) generalize this result to quasi-concave, homothetic, utilities, and also consider economies of scale in production.

Lemma 6.4 of Section 6.3 has been proven by Arrow et al. (1959) under the stronger assumption of GS. It was later shown to generalize to markets which satisfy only WGS (Arrow and Hurwicz, 1960a, 1960b).

Polterovich and Spivak (1983) extended the characterization of Lemma 6.4 to scenarios where the demand is a set-valued function of the prices, which includes in particular the exchange model with linear utilities. This extension says that for any equilibrium price $\hat{\pi}$, and nonequilibrium price π, and any vector $z \in \mathbf{R}^n$ that is chosen from the set of aggregate excess demands of the market at π, we have $\hat{\pi} \cdot z > 0$.

The simple algorithm of Section 6.3.1, which is a discrete version of the tâtonnement process, is introduced and analyzed in Codenotti et al. (2005). Lemma 6.7 can also be used with the Ellipsoid method, as shown by Codenotti et al. (2005), to compute a weak $(1+\varepsilon)$-approximate equilibrium in polynomial time. That is, the dependence of the running time on $\frac{1}{\varepsilon}$ can be made polynomial in $\log \frac{1}{\varepsilon}$.

The simple algorithm of Section 6.3.1, which is a discrete version of the tâtonnement process, is introduced and analyzed in Codenotti et al. (2005).

The convex feasibility program of Section 6.4.1 is due to Nenakov and Primak (1983) and Jain (2004). For linear utilities, an equilibrium price vector whose components are small rational numbers exists. Jain (2004) proposes a variant of the Ellipsoid algorithm that, exploiting this, uses the separation hyperplane implied by the convex program to compute the equilibrium exactly in polynomial time. Ye (in press) presents an efficient interior-point algorithm that computes the exact equilibrium in polynomial time. The convex program of Section 6.4.2 has been introduced in Codenotti et al. (2005).

Section 6.5.1 describes a market with two traders and two goods that has multiple disconnected equilibria. Such example has been proposed by Gjerstad (1996).

The class PPAD introduced in Section 6.5.2 was defined by Papadimitriou (1994). The game-market correspondence was shown in Codenotti et al. (2006). The PPAD completeness of the computation of a Nash equilibrium for a bimatrix game is due to Chen and Deng (2005b). Chen and Deng's result came after a sequence of works, where first the $PPAD$-completeness of 4-player games (Daskalakis et al., 2005), and then of 3-player games (Chen and Deng, 2005a; Daskalakis and Papadimitriou, 2005) were proven.

The convex program of Section 6.6 has been introduced in Jain and Varadarajan (2006). We have not mentioned several other results on convex programs for production models. We refer the interested reader to Jain and Varadarajan (2006) and the references therein.

Bibliography

K.J. Arrow, H.D. Block, and L. Hurwicz. On the stability of the competitive equilibrium, ii. *Econometrica*, 27(1):82–109, 1959.

K.J. Arrow, H.B. Chenery, B.S. Minhas, and R.M. Solow. Capital–labor substitution and economic efficiency. *Rev. Econ. Stat.*, 43(3):225–250, 1961.

K.J. Arrow and G. Debreu. Existence of an equilibrium for a competitive economy. *Econometrica*, 22(3):265–290, 1954.

K.J. Arrow and L. Hurwicz. Competitive stability under weak gross substitutability: The euclidean distance approach. *Intl. Econ. Rev.*, 1:38–49, 1960a.

K.J. Arrow and L. Hurwicz. Some remarks on the equilibria of economic systems. *Econometrica*, 28:640–646, 1960b.

K.C. Border. *Fixed point Theorems with Applications to Economics and Game Theory*. Cambridge University Press, 1985.

X. Chen and X. Deng. 3-NASH is PPAD-complete. *Electronic Collog. Computational Complexity*, 2005a.

X. Chen and X. Deng. Settling the complexity of 2-player Nash-Equilibrium. *Electronic Collog. Computational Complexity*, 2005b.

B. Codenotti, B. McCune, S. Penumatcha, and K. Varadarajan. Market equilibrium for CES exchange economies: Existence, multiplicity, and computation. In *Proc. 25th Intl. Conf. Fdns. Software Tech. Theoretical Comp. Sci.*, pp. 505–516, 2005.

B. Codenotti, B. McCune, and K. Varadarajan. Market equilibrium via the excess demand function. In *Proc. 37th Annual ACM Symp. Theo. Comp.*, pp. 74–83, 2005.

B. Codenotti, S. Pemmaraju, and K. Varadarajan. On the polynomial time computation of equilibria for certain exchange economies. In *Proc. 16th Annual ACM-SIAM Symp. Disc. Algo.*, pp. 72–81, 2005.

B. Codenotti, A. Saberi, K. Varadarajan, and Y. Ye. Leontief economies encode nonzero sum two-player games. In *Proc. 17th Annual ACM-SIAM Symp. Disc. Algo.*, pp. 659–667, 2006.

C. Daskalakis, P. Goldberg, and C. Papadimitriou. The complexity of computing a Nash equilibrium. *Electronic Collog. Computational Complexity*, 2005.

C. Daskalakis and C. Papadimitriou. Three-player games are hard. *Electronic Collog. Computational Complexity*, 2005.

X. Deng, C. Papadimitriou, and S. Safra. On the complexity of price equilibrium. *J. Comp. Syst. Sci.*, 67(2):311–324, 2003. (Special Issue on Symp. Theory of Computing, 2002).

B.C. Eaves and H. Scarf. The solution of systems of piecewise linear equations. *Math. Oper. Res.*, 1(1):1–27, 1976.

E. Eisenberg. Aggregation of utility functions. *Mgmt. Sci.*, 7(4):337–350, 1961.

E. Eisenberg and D. Gale. Consensus of subjective probabilities: The pari-mutuel method. *Annals Math. Stat.*, 30:165–168, 1959.

D. Gale. *The Theory of Linear Economic Models*. McGraw Hill, 1960.

S. Gjerstad. Multiple equilibria in exchange economies with homothetic, nearly identical preference. University of Minnesota, Center for Economic Research, Discussion Paper 288, 1996.

T. Hansen and H. Scarf. *The Computation of Economic Equilibria*. Cowles Foundation Monograph No. 24., New Haven: Yale University Press, 1973.

K. Jain. A polynomial time algorithm for computing the Arrow–Debreu market equilibrium for linear utilities. In *Proc. 45th Annual Symp. Fdns. Comp. Sci.*, pp. 286–294, 2004.

K. Jain, M. Mahdian, and A. Saberi. Approximating market equilibria. In *Proc. RANDOM-APPROX*, pp. 98–108, 2003.

K. Jain and K. Varadarajan. Equilibria for economies with production: Constant-returns technologies and production planning constraints. In *SODA 06: Proc. 17th Annual ACM-SIAM Symp. Disc. Algo.*, pp. 688–697, 2006.

K. Jain, V.V. Vazirani, and Y. Ye. Market equilibria for homothetic, quasi-concave utilities and economies of scale in production. In *SODA 05: Proc. 16th Annual ACM-SIAM Symp. on Discrete Algorithms*, pp. 63–71, 2005.

O.L. Mangasarian. *Nonlinear Programming*. McGraw-Hill, 1969.

A. Mas-Colell, M.D. Whinston, and J.R. Green. *Microeconomic Theory*. Oxford University Press, 1995.

T. Negishi. Welfare economics and existence of an equilibrium for a competitive economy. *Metroeconomica*, 12:92–97, 1960.

E.I. Nenakov and M.E. Primak. One algorithm for finding solutions of the Arrow-Debreu model. *Kibernetica*, 3:127–128, 1983.

C.H. Papadimitriou. On the complexity of the parity argument and other inefficient proofs of existence. *J. Comp. Syst. Sci.*, 48:498–532, 1994.

C.H. Papadimitriou. Algorithms, games, and the Internet. In *Proc. 33rd Annual ACM Symp. Theo. Comp.*, pp. 749–753, 2001.

C.H. Papadimitriou. Algorithms for equilibria. In *Algorithmic Game Theory, Chapter 2*. Cambridge University Press, 2007.

V.M. Polterovich. Economic equilibrium and the optimum. *Matekon*, 5:3–20, 1973.

V.M. Polterovich and V.A. Spivak. Gross substitutability of point to set correspondences. *J. Math. Econ.*, 11(2):117–140, 1983.

T. Rutherford. Sequential joint maximization. In *J. Weyant Ed.* Energy and Environmental Policy Modeling. *Intl. Series Oper. Res. Mgmt. Sci.*, 18, 1999.

P.A. Samuelson. *Foundations of Economic Analysis*. Harvard University Press, 1947.

H. Scarf. The approximation of fixed points of a continuous mapping. *SIAM J. Appl. Math.*, 15(1):1328–1343, 1967.

H. Scarf. The computation of equilibrium prices: An exposition. In *Handbook of Mathematical Economics, Volume II*, pp. 1008–1061, 1982.

H. Varian. *Microeconomic Analysis*. W.W. Norton, 1992.

V. Vazirani. Combinatorial algorithms for market equilibria. In *Algorithmic Game Theory, Chapter 5*. Cambridge University Press, 2007.

A. Wald. On some systems of equations of mathematical economics. *Econometrica*, 19(4):368–403, 1951. Original version: Zeitschrift für Nationalökonomie, Vol. 7 (1936).

L. Walras. *Elements of Pure Economics, or the Theory of Social Wealth*. Richard Irwin, 1954. (Original version published in French in 1874).

Y. Ye. A path to the Arrow–Debreu competitive market equilibrium. *Math Progr.*. In press.

Exercises

6.1 Use the Karush–Kuhn–Tucker conditions to derive an explicit expression for the demand of a consumer with a Cobb–Douglas utility function. Also derive formula 6.7, the expression for the demand with a CES function.

6.2 Show that for an exchange economy with Cobb–Douglas utility functions, the positive equilirbium prices can be characterized as solutions to a linear feasibility program with variables for the prices. The number of constraints of the program must be polynomial in the number of traders and goods.

6.3 Prove that Lemma 6.4 implies that the set of equilibrium prices is convex.

6.4 Prove parts (2), (3), and (4) of Lemma 6.5.

6.5 Suppose that π and $\hat{\pi}$ are two price vectors such that $\max_j \frac{\pi_j}{\hat{\pi}_j} \leq (1+\varepsilon/3) \min_j \frac{\pi_j}{\hat{\pi}_j}$, and $\hat{\pi}$ is an equilibrium. Show that π is a weak $(1+\varepsilon)$-approximate equilibrium.

CHAPTER 7

Graphical Games

Michael Kearns

Abstract

In this chapter we examine the representational and algorithmic aspects of a class of graph-theoretic models for multiplayer games. Known broadly as *graphical games*, these models specify restrictions on the direct payoff influences among the player population. In addition to a number of nice computational properties, these models have close connections to well-studied graphical models for probabilistic inference in machine learning and statistics.

7.1 Introduction

Representing multiplayer games with large player populations in the normal form is undesirable for both practical and conceptual reasons. On the practical side, the number of parameters that must be specified grows exponentially with the size of the population. On the conceptual side, the normal form may fail to capture structure that is present in the strategic interaction, and which can aid understanding of the game and computation of its equilibria. For this reason, there have been many proposals for parametric multiplayer game representations that are more succinct than the normal form, and attempt to model naturally arising structural properties. Examples include congestion and potential games and related models (Monderer and Shapley, 1996; Rosenthal, 1973).

Graphical games are a representation of multiplayer games meant to capture and exploit locality or sparsity of direct influences. They are most appropriate for large population games in which the payoffs of each player are determined by the actions of only a small subpopulation. As such, they form a natural counterpart to earlier parametric models. Whereas congestion games and related models implicitly assume a large number of weak influences on each player, graphical games are suitable when there is a small number of strong influences.

Graphical games adopt a simple graph-theoretic model. A graphical game is described at the first level by an undirected graph G in which players are identified with vertices. The semantics of the graph are that a player or vertex i has payoffs that are entirely specified by the actions of i and those of its neighbor set in G. Thus G alone may already specify strong qualitative constraints or structure over the direct strategic influences in the game. To fully describe a graphical game, we must additionally specify the numerical payoff functions to each player – but now the payoff to player i is a function only of the actions of i and its neighbors, rather than the actions of the entire population. In the many natural settings where such local neighborhoods are much smaller than the overall population size, the benefits of this parametric specification over the normal form are already considerable.

But several years of research on graphical games has demonstrated that the advantages of this model extend well beyond simple parsimony – rather, they are computational, structural, and interdisciplinary as well. We now overview each of these in turn.

Computational. Theoretical computer science has repeatedly established that strong but naturally occurring constraints on optimization and other problems can be exploited algorithmically, and game theory is no exception. Graphical games provide a rich language in which to state and explore the computational benefits of various restrictions on the interactions in a large-population game. As we shall see, one fruitful line of research has investigated topological restrictions on the underlying graph G that yield efficient algorithms for various equilibrium computations.

Structural. In addition to algorithmic insights, graphical games also provide a powerful framework in which to examine the relationships between the network structure and strategic outcomes. Of particular interest is whether and when the local interactions specified by the graph G alone (i.e., the topology of G, regardless of the numerical specifications of the payoffs) imply nontrivial structural properties of equilibria. We will examine an instance of this phenomenon in some detail.

Interdisciplinary. Part of the original motivation for graphical games came from earlier models familiar to the machine learning, AI and statistics communities – collectively known as graphical models for probabilistic inference, which include Bayesian networks, Markov networks, and their variants. Broadly speaking, both graphical models for inference and graphical games represent complex interactions between a large number of variables (random variables in one case, the actions of players in a game in the other) by a graph combined with numerical specification of the interaction details. In probabilistic inference the interactions are stochastic, whereas in graphical games they are strategic (best response). As we shall discuss, the connections to probabilistic inference have led to a number of algorithmic and representational benefits for graphical games.

In this chapter we will overview graphical games and the research on them to date. We will center our discussion around two main technical results that will be examined in some detail, and are chosen to illustrate the computational, structural, and interdisciplinary benefits discussed above. These two case studies will also serve as natural vehicles to survey the broader body of literature on graphical games.

The first problem we shall examine is the computation of Nash equilibria in graphical games in which the underlying graph G is a tree (or certain generalizations of trees). Here we will discuss a natural two-pass algorithm for computing Nash equilibria requiring only the local exchange of "conditional equilibrium" information over the edges of G. This algorithm comes in two variations – one that runs in time polynomial in the representation size of the graphical game and computes (a compact representation of) *approximations* of all Nash equilibria, and another that runs in exponential time but computes (a compact representation of) all Nash equilibria *exactly*. We will discuss a number of generalizations of this algorithm, including one known as **NashProp**, which has close ties to the well-known belief propagation algorithm in probabilistic inference. Together these algorithms provide examples of the algorithmic exploitation of structural restrictions on the graph.

The second problem we shall examine is the representation and computation of the correlated equilibria of a graphical game. Here we will see that there is a satisfying and natural connection between graphical games and the probabilistic models known as Markov networks, which can succinctly represent high-dimensional multivariate probability distributions. More specifically, we shall show that any graphical game with graph G can have all of its correlated equilibria (up to payoff equivalence) represented by a Markov network with the same network structure. If we adopt the common view of correlated equilibria as permitting "shared" or "public" randomization (the source of the correlations) – whereas Nash equilibria permit only "private" randomization or mixed strategies – this result implies that the shared randomization can actually be distributed locally throughout the graph, and that distant parties need not be (directly) correlated. From the rich tools developed for independence analysis in Markov networks, it also provides a compact representation of a large number of independence relationships between player actions that may be assumed at (correlated) equilibrium. The result thus provides a good example of a direct connection between graph structure and equilibrium properties, as well as establishing further ties to probabilistic inference. We shall also discuss the algorithmic benefits of this result.

After studying these two problems in some detail, we will briefly overview recent research incorporating network structure into other game-theoretic and economic settings, such as exchange economies (Arrow-Debreu, Fischer and related models). Again the emphasis will be on computational aspects of these models, and on the relationship between graph structure and equilibrium properties.

7.2 Preliminaries

In this section we shall provide formal definitions for graphical games, along with other needed definitions, terminology, and notation. We begin with notions standard to classical multiplayer game theory.

A multiplayer game consists of n players, each with a finite set of *pure strategies* or actions available to them, along with a specification of the *payoffs* to each player. Throughout the chapter, we use a_i to denote the action chosen by player i. For simplicity we will assume a binary action space, so $a_i \in \{0, 1\}$. (The generalization of the results examined here to the multiaction setting is straightforward.) The payoffs to player i are given by a table or matrix M_i, indexed by the joint action $\vec{a} \in \{0, 1\}^n$. The value $M_i(\vec{a})$, which we assume without loss of generality to lie in the interval $[0, 1]$, is the payoff to player i resulting from the joint action $\vec{a}$. Multiplayer games described in this way are referred to as *normal form* games.

The actions 0 and 1 are the *pure strategies* of each player, while a *mixed* strategy for player i is given by the probability $p_i \in [0, 1]$ that the player will play 0. For any joint mixed strategy, given by a product distribution $\vec{p}$, we define the expected payoff to player i as $M_i(\vec{p}) = \mathbf{E}_{\vec{a}\sim\vec{p}}[M_i(\vec{a})]$, where $\vec{a} \sim \vec{p}$ indicates that each a_j is 0 with probability p_j and 1 with probability $1 - p_j$ independently. When we introduce correlated equilibria below, we shall allow the possibility that the distribution over $\vec{a}$ is not a product distribution, but has correlations between the a_i.

We use $\vec{p}[i : p'_i]$ to denote the vector (product distribution) which is the same as $\vec{p}$ except in the ith component, where the value has been changed to p'_i. A *Nash equilibrium (NE)* for the game is a mixed strategy $\vec{p}$ such that for any player i, and for any value $p'_i \in [0, 1]$, $M_i(\vec{p}) \geq M_i(\vec{p}[i : p'_i])$. (We say that p_i is a *best response* to the rest of $\vec{p}$.) In other words, no player can improve their expected payoff by deviating unilaterally from an NE. The classic theorem of Nash (1951) states that for any game, there exists an NE in the space of joint mixed strategies.

We will also use a straightforward (additive) definition for *approximate* Nash equilibria. An *ϵ-Nash equilibrium* is a mixed strategy $\vec{p}$ such that for any player i, and for any value $p'_i \in [0, 1]$, $M_i(\vec{p}) + \epsilon \geq M_i(\vec{p}[i : p'_i])$. (We say that p_i is an *ϵ-best response* to the rest of $\vec{p}$.) Thus, no player can improve their expected payoff by more than ϵ by deviating unilaterally from an approximate NE.

We are now ready to introduce the graphical game model. In a *graphical game*, each player i is represented by a vertex in an undirected graph G. We use $N(i) \subseteq \{1, \ldots, n\}$ to denote the *neighborhood* of player i in G – that is, those vertices j such that the edge (i, j) appears in G. By convention $N(i)$ always includes i itself as well. If $\vec{a}$ is a joint action, we use $\vec{a}^{\,i}$ to denote the projection of $\vec{a}$ onto just the players in $N(i)$.

Definition 7.1 A *graphical game* is a pair $(G, \mathcal{M})$, where G is an undirected graph over the vertices $\{1, \ldots, n\}$, and $\mathcal{M}$ is a set of n *local game matrices*. For any joint action $\vec{a}$, the local game matrix $M_i \in \mathcal{M}$ specifies the payoff $M_i(\vec{a}^i)$ for player i, which depends only on the actions taken by the players in $N(i)$.

Remarks. Graphical games are a (potentially) more compact way of representing games than standard normal form. In particular, rather than requiring a number of parameters that is exponential in the number of players n, a graphical game requires a number of parameters that is exponential only in the size d of the largest local neighborhood. Thus if $d \ll n$ – that is, the number of direct influences on any player is much smaller than the overall population size – the graphical game representation is dramatically smaller than the normal form. Note that we can represent any normal form game as a graphical game by letting G be the complete graph, but the representation is only useful when a considerably sparser graph can be found. It is also worth noting that although the payoffs to player i are determined only by the actions of the players in $N(i)$, *equilibrium* still requires *global* coordination across the player population – if player i is connected to player j who is in turn connected to player k, then i and k indirectly influence each other via their mutual influence on the payoff of j. How local influences propagate to determine global equilibrium outcomes is one of the computational challenges posed by graphical games.

In addition to Nash equilibrium, we will also examine graphical games in the context of *correlated equilibria (CE)*. CE (Aumann, 1974) generalize NE, and can be viewed as (possibly arbitrary) distributions $P(\vec{a})$ over joint actions satisfying a certain conditional expectation property.

The intuition behind CE can be described as follows. Imagine that there is a trusted party that faithfully draws a joint action $\vec{a}$ according to distribution P, and distributes to each player i only their private component a_i. If P is a product distribution, as in the NE case, then due to the independence between all players the revelation of a_i does not condition player i's beliefs over the play of others. For general P, however, this is not true. The CE condition asks that the expected payoff to i if he is "obedient" and plays a_i be at least as great the amount i could earn by "cheating" and deviating to play a different action. In other words, in Bayesian terms, despite the observation of a_i updating the posterior distribution over the other player actions from i's perspective, it is still payoff-optimal for i to play a_i. This leads to the formal definition below, in which for any given joint distribution $P(\vec{a})$ over player actions and $b \in \{0, 1\}$, we let $P_{a_i=b}$ denote the distribution on $\vec{a}$ conditioned on the event that $a_i = b$.

Definition 7.2 A *correlated equilibrium (CE)* for a two-action normal form game is a distribution $P(\vec{a})$ over actions satisfying

$$\forall i \in \{1, ..., n\}, \forall b \in \{0, 1\} : \mathbf{E}_{\vec{a}\sim P_{a_i=b}}[M_i(\vec{a})] \geq \mathbf{E}_{\vec{a}\sim P_{a_i=b}}[M_i(\vec{a}[i : \neg b])]$$

The expectation $\mathbf{E}_{\vec{a}\sim P_{a_i=b}}[M_i(\vec{a})]$ is over those cases in which the value $a_i = b$ is revealed to player i, who proceeds to "honestly" play $a_i = b$. The expectation $\mathbf{E}_{\vec{a}\sim P_{a_i=b}}[M_i(\vec{a}[i : \neg b])]$ is over the same cases, but now player i unilaterally deviates to play $a_i = \neg b$, whereas the other players faithfully play from the conditional distribution $P_{a_i=b}$. It is straightforward to generalize this definition to the multiaction case – again, we demand that it be optimal for each player to take the action provided by the trusted party, despite the conditioning information revealed by this action.

Remarks. CE offers a number of conceptual and computational advantages over NE, including the facts that new and sometimes more "fair" payoffs can be achieved, that CE can be computed efficiently for games in standard normal form (though recall that "efficiently" here means exponential in the number of players, an issue we shall address), and that CE are the convergence notion for several natural "no-regret" learning algorithms (Foster and Vohra, 1999). Furthermore, it has been argued that CE is the natural equilibrium concept consistent with the Bayesian perspective (Aumann, 1987; Foster and Vohra, 1997). One of the most interesting aspects of CE is that they broaden the set of "rational" solutions for normal form games without the need to address often difficult issues such as stability of coalitions and payoff imputations (Aumann, 1987). The traffic signal is often cited as an informal everyday example of CE, in which a single bit of shared information allows a fair split of waiting times (Owen, 1995). In this example, no player stands to gain greater payoff by unilaterally deviating from the correlated play, for instance by "running a light." This example also illustrates a common alternative view of CE, in which correlations arise as a result of "public" or "shared" random bits (in addition to the "private" random bits allowed in the standard mixed strategies or product distributions of NE). Here the state of the traffic light itself (which can be viewed as a binary random variable, alternately displayed as red and green to orthogonal streets) provides the shared randomization.

7.3 Computing Nash Equilibria in Tree Graphical Games

In this section, we describe the first and perhaps most basic algorithm exploiting the advantages of graphical game representation for the purposes of equilibrium computation. The case considered is that in which the underlying graph G is a tree. While obviously a strong restriction on the topology, we shall see that this case already presents nontrivial computational challenges, which in turn force the development of algorithmic tools that can be generalized beyond trees to obtain a more general heuristic known as.

NashProp. We first describe the algorithm **TreeNash** at a high level, leaving certain important implementation details unspecified, because it is conceptually advantageous to do so. We then describe two instantiations of the missing details – yielding one algorithm that runs in polynomial time and provably computes approximations of all equilibria, and another algorithm that runs in exponential time and provably computes all exact equilibria.

We begin with some notation and concepts needed for the description of **TreeNash**. In order to distinguish parents from children in the tree, it will be convenient to treat players/vertices symbolically (such as U, V, and W) rather than by integer indices, so we use M_V to denote the local game matrix for the player identified with player/vertex V. We use capital letters to denote vertex/players to distinguish them from their chosen actions, for which we shall use lower case. If G is a tree, we choose an arbitrary vertex as the root (which we visualize as being at the bottom, with the leaves at the top). Any vertex on the path from a vertex V to the root will be called *downstream* from V, and any vertex on a path from V to any leaf will be called *upstream* from V. Thus, each vertex other than the root has exactly one downstream neighbor (or child), and perhaps many upstream neighbors (or parents). We use $\mathrm{UP}_G(V)$ to denote the set of all vertices in G that are upstream from V, including V by definition.

Suppose that V is the child of U in G. We let G^U denote the subgraph induced by the vertices in $\mathrm{UP}_G(U)$ – that is, the subtree of G rooted at U. If $v \in [0, 1]$ is a mixed strategy for player (vertex) V, $\mathcal{M}^U_{V=v}$ will denote the subset of payoff matrices in $\mathcal{M}$ corresponding to the vertices in $\mathrm{UP}_G(U)$, with the modification that the game matrix M_U is collapsed by one index by fixing $V = v$. We can think of an NE for the graphical game $(G^U, \mathcal{M}^U_{V=v})$ as a *conditional* equilibrium "upstream" from U (inclusive) – that is, an equilibrium for G^U *given* that V plays v. Here we are simply exploiting the fact that since G is a tree, fixing a mixed strategy v for the play of V isolates G^U from the rest of G.

Now suppose that vertex V has k parents $U_1, \ldots, U_k$, and the single child W. We now describe the data structures sent from each U_i to V, and in turn from V to W, on the downstream pass of **TreeNash**. Each parent U_i will send to V a binary-valued "table" $T(v, u_i)$. The table is indexed by the *continuum* of possible values for the mixed strategies $v \in [0, 1]$ of V and $u_i \in [0, 1]$ of U_i, $i = 1, \ldots, k$. The semantics of this table will be as follows: for any pair (v, u_i), $T(v, u_i)$ will be 1 if and only if there exists an NE for $(G^{U_i}, \mathcal{M}^{U_i}_{V=v})$ in which $U_i = u_i$. Note that we will slightly abuse notation by letting $T(v, u_i)$ refer to both the entire table sent from U_i to V, and the particular value associated with the pair (v, u_i), but the meaning will be clear from the context.

Algorithm **TreeNash**

Inputs: Graphical game $(G, \mathcal{M})$ in which G is a tree.

Output: A Nash equilibrium for $(G, \mathcal{M})$.

(i) Compute a depth-first ordering of the vertices of G.

(ii) (**Downstream Pass**) For each vertex V in depth-first order:

- **(a)** Let vertex W be the child of V (or nil if V is the root).
- **(b)** For all $w, v \in [0, 1]$, initialize $T(w, v)$ to be 0 and the witness list for $T(w, v)$ to be empty.
- **(c)** If V is a leaf (base case):
  - **1.** For all $w, v \in [0, 1]$, set $T(w, v)$ to be 1 if and only if $V = v$ is a best response to $W = w$ (as determined by the local game matrix M_V).
- **(d)** Else (inductive case, V is an internal vertex):
  - **1.** Let $\vec{U} = (U_1, \ldots, U_k)$ be the parents of V; let $T(v, u_i)$ be the table passed from U_i to V on the downstream pass.
  - **2.** For all $w, v \in [0, 1]$ and for all joint mixed strategies $\vec{u} = (u_1, \ldots, u_k)$ for $\vec{U}$: If $V = v$ is a best response to $W = w, \vec{U} = \vec{u}$ (as determined by the local game matrix M_V), and $T(v, u_i) = 1$ for $i = 1, \cdots, k$, set $T(w, v)$ to be 1 and add $\vec{u}$ to the witness list for $T(w, v)$.
- **(e)** Pass the table $T(w, v)$ from V to W.

(iii) (**Upstream Pass**) For each vertex V in reverse depth-first ordering (starting at the root):

- **(a)** Let $\vec{U} = (U_1, \ldots, U_k)$ be the parents of V (or the empty list if V is a leaf); let W be the child of V (or nil if V is the root), and (w, v) the values passed from W to V on the upstream pass.
- **(b)** Label V with the value v.
- **(c)** (Non-deterministically) Choose any witness $\vec{u}$ to $T(w, v) = 1$.
- **(d)** For $i = 1, \ldots, k$, pass (v, u_i) from V to U_i.

Figure 7.1. Algorithm **TreeNash** for computing NE of tree graphical games.

Since v and u_i are continuous variables, it is not obvious that the table $T(v, u_i)$ can be represented compactly, or even finitely, for arbitrary vertices in a tree. For now we will simply assume a finite representation, and shortly discuss how this assumption can be met in two different ways.

The initialization of the downstream pass of the algorithm begins at the leaves of the tree, where the computation of the tables is straightforward. If U is a leaf and V its only child, then $T(v, u) = 1$ if and only if $U = u$ is a best response to $V = v$ (Step (ii) (c) of Figure 7.1).

Assuming for induction that each U_i sends the table $T(v, u_i)$ to V, we now describe how V can compute the table $T(w, v)$ to pass to its child W (Step (ii) (d)2 of Figure 7.1). For each pair (w, v), $T(w, v)$ is set to 1 if and only if there exists a vector of mixed strategies $\vec{u} = (u_1, \ldots, u_k)$ (called a *witness*) for the parents $\vec{U} = (U_1, \ldots, U_k)$ of V such that

(i) $T(v, u_i) = 1$ for all $1 \leq i \leq k$; and
(ii) $V = v$ is a best response to $\vec{U} = \vec{u}$, $W = w$.

Note that there may be more than one witness for $T(w, v) = 1$. In addition to computing the value $T(w, v)$ on the downstream pass of the algorithm, V will also keep a list of the witnesses $\vec{u}$ for each pair (w, v) for which $T(w, v) = 1$ (Step ii(d)2 of Figure 7.1). These witness lists will be used on the upstream pass.

To see that the semantics of the tables are preserved by the computation just described, suppose that this computation yields $T(w, v) = 1$ for some pair (w, v), and let $\vec{u}$ be a witness for $T(w, v) = 1$. The fact that $T(v, u_i) = 1$ for all i (condition (7.3) above) ensures by induction that if V plays v, there are upstream NE in which each $U_i = u_i$. Furthermore, v is a best response to the local settings $U_1 = u_1, \ldots, U_k = u_k$, $W = w'$ (condition (7.3) above). Therefore, we are in equilibrium upstream from V. On the other hand, if $T(w, v) = 0$, it is easy to see there can be no equilibrium in which $W = w$, $V = v$. Note that the existence of an NE guarantees that $T(w, v) = 1$ for at least one (w, v) pair.

The downstream pass of the algorithm terminates at the root Z, which receives tables $T(z, y_i)$ from each parent Y_i. Z simply computes a one-dimensional table $T(z)$ such that $T(z) = 1$ if and only if for some witness $\vec{y}$, $T(z, y_i) = 1$ for all i, and z is a best response to $\vec{y}$.

The upstream pass begins by Z choosing any z for which $T(z) = 1$, choosing any witness $(y_1, \ldots, y_k)$ to $T(z) = 1$, and then passing both z and y_i to each parent Y_i. The interpretation is that Z will play z, and is "instructing" Y_i to play y_i. Inductively, if a vertex V receives a value v to play from its downstream neighbor W, and the value w that W will play, then it must be that $T(w, v) = 1$. So V chooses a witness $\vec{u}$ to $T(w, v) = 1$, and passes each parent U_i their value u_i as well as v (Step (iii) of Figure 7.1). Note that the semantics of $T(w, v) = 1$ ensure that $V = v$ is a best response to $\vec{U} = \vec{u}$, $W = w$.

We have left the choices of each witness in the upstream pass unspecified or nondeterministic to emphasize that the tables and witness lists computed represent *all* the NE. The upstream pass can be specialized to find a number of specific NE of interest, including player optimum (NE maximizing expected reward to a chosen player), social optimum (NE maximizing total expected reward, summed over all players), and welfare optimum (NE maximizing expected reward to the player whose expected reward is smallest).

Modulo the important details regarding the representation of the tables $T(w, v)$, which we discuss next, the arguments provided above establish the following formal result.

Theorem 7.3 *Let* $(G, \mathcal{M})$ *be any graphical game in which* G *is a tree. Algorithm* **TreeNash** *computes a Nash equilibrium for* $(G, \mathcal{M})$*. Furthermore, the tables and witness lists computed by the algorithm represent all Nash equilibria of* $(G, \mathcal{M})$*.*

7.3.1 An Approximation Algorithm

In this section, we sketch one instantiation of the missing details of algorithm **TreeNash** that yields a polynomial-time algorithm for computing *approximate* NE for the tree game $(G, \mathcal{M})$. The approximation can be made arbitrarily precise with greater computational effort.

Rather than playing an arbitrary mixed strategy in [0, 1], each player will be constrained to play a *discretized* mixed strategy that is a multiple of τ, for some τ to be determined by the analysis. Thus, player i plays $q_i \in \{0, \tau, 2\tau, \ldots, 1\}$, and the joint strategy $\vec{q}$ falls on the discretized τ-grid $\{0, \tau, 2\tau, \ldots, 1\}^n$. In algorithm **TreeNash**, this will allow each table $T(v, u)$ (passed from vertex U to child V) to be represented in discretized form as well: only the $1/\tau^2$ entries corresponding to the possible τ-grid choices for U and V are stored, and all computations of best responses in the algorithm are modified to be approximate best responses.

To quantify how the choice of τ will influence the quality of the approximate equilibria found (which in turn will determine the computational efficiency of the approximation algorithm), we appeal to the following lemma. We note that this result holds for arbitrary graphical games, not only trees.

Lemma 7.4 *Let G be a graph of maximum degree d, and let $(G, \mathcal{M})$ be a graphical game. Let $\vec{p}$ be a Nash equilibrium for $(G, \mathcal{M})$, and let $\vec{q}$ be the nearest (in L_1 metric) mixed strategy on the τ-grid. Then $\vec{q}$ is a $d\tau$-NE for $(G, \mathcal{M})$.*

The proof of Lemma 7.4, which we omit, follows from a bound on the L_1 distance for product distributions along with an argument that the strategic properties of the NE are preserved by the approximation. We note that the original paper (Kearns et al., 2001) used a considerably worse L_1 bound that was exponential in d. However, the algorithm remains exponential in d simply due to the representational complexity of the local product distributions. The important point is that τ needs to depend only on the *local neighborhood* size d, not the total number of players n.

It is now straightforward to describe **ApproximateTreeNash**. This algorithm is identical to algorithm **TreeNash** with the following exceptions:

- The algorithm now takes an additional input ϵ.
- For any vertex U with child V, the table $T(u, v)$ will contain only entries for u and v multiples of τ.
- All computations of best responses in algorithm **TreeNash** become computations of ϵ-best responses in algorithm **ApproximateTreeNash**.

For the running time analysis, we simply note that each table has $(1/\tau)^2$ entries, and that the computation is dominated by the downstream calculation of the tables (Step (ii)(d) of algorithm **TreeNash**). This requires ranging over all table entries for all k parents, a computation of order $((1/\tau)^2)^k$. By appropriately choosing the value of τ in order to obtain the required ϵ-approximations, we obtain the following theorem.

Theorem 7.5 *Let $(G, \mathcal{M})$ be a graphical game in which G is a tree with n vertices, and in which every vertex has at most d parents. For any $\epsilon > 0$, let $\tau = O(\epsilon/d)$. Then* **ApproximateTreeNash** *computes an ϵ-Nash equilibrium for $(G, \mathcal{M})$. Furthermore, for* every *exact Nash equilibrium, the tables and witness lists computed by the algorithm contain an ϵ-Nash equilibrium that is within τ of this exact equilibrium (in L_1 norm). The running time of the algorithm is* *polynomial in* $1/\epsilon$, n *and* 2^d, *which is polynomial in the size of the representation* $(G, \mathcal{M})$.

7.3.2 An Exact Algorithm

By approximating the continuously indexed tables $T(u, v)$ in discretized form, the algorithm developed in Section 7.3.1 side-stepped not only the exact computation but also a fundamental question about the $T(u, v)$ – namely, do the regions $\{(u, v) \in [0, 1]^2 : T(u, v) = 1\}$ have any interesting geometric structure? It turns out the answer in the case of trees is affirmative, and can be used in developing an alternate instantiation of the general **TreeNash** algorithm of Section 7.3 – one that yields an algorithm for computing (all) *exact* equilibria, but in time that is exponential in the number of players n rather than only the degree d.

Although the details are beyond our scope, it is possible to show via an inductive argument (where again the leaves of G serve as the base cases) that in any tree graphical game, for any of the tables $T(u, v)$ defined by **TreeNash**, the region $\{(u, v) \in [0, 1]^2 : T(u, v) = 1\}$ can be represented by a finite union of (axis-aligned) rectangular regions in $[0, 1]^2$ (i.e., regions that are defined as products of closed intervals $[a, a'] \times [b, b']$ for some $0 \leq a \leq a' \leq 1, 0 \leq b \leq b' \leq 1$). The induction shows that the number of such regions multiplies at each level as we progress downstream toward the root, yielding a worst-case bound on the number of rectangular regions that is exponential in n.

This simple (if exponential in n) geometric representation of the tables $T(u, v)$ permits the development of an alternative algorithm **ExactTreeNash**, which is simply the abstract algorithm **TreeNash** with the tables represented by unions of rectangles (and with associated implementations of the necessary upstream and downstream computations).

Theorem 7.6 *There is an algorithm* **ExactTreeNash** *that computes an exact Nash equilibrium for any tree graphical game* $(G, \mathcal{M})$. *Furthermore, the tables computed by the algorithm represent all Nash equilibria of* $(G, \mathcal{M})$. *The algorithm runs in time exponential in the number of vertices of* G.

7.3.3 Extensions: NashProp and Beyond

At this point it is of course natural to ask what can be done when the underlying graph of a graphical game is not a tree. Remaining close to the development so far, it is possible to give an *heuristic* generalization of algorithm **ApproximateTreeNash** to the setting in which the graph G is arbitrary. This algorithm is known as **NashProp**, which we will now briefly sketch. By heuristic we mean that the algorithm is well-defined and will terminate on any graphical game; but unlike **ApproximateTreeNash**, the running time is not guaranteed to be polynomial in the size of the input graphical game. (In general, we should expect provably efficient algorithms for equilibrium computation to require *some* topological restriction, since allowing G to be the complete graph reduces to the classical normal form representation.)

Recall that the main computation at vertex V in **ApproximateTreeNash** was the computation of the downstream table $T(w, v)$ from the upstream tables $T(v, u_i)$. This assumed an underlying orientation to the tree that allowed V to know which of its neighbors were in the direction of the leaves (identified as the U_i) and which single neighbor was in the direction of the root (identified as W). The easiest way to describe **NashProp** informally is to say that each V does this computation once for *each* of its neighbors, each time "pretending" that this neighbor plays the role of the downstream neighbor W in **ApproximateTreeNash**, and the remaining neighbors play the roles of the upstream U_i. If all discretized table entries are initialized to the value of 1,[1] it easy to show that the only possible effect of these local computations is to change table values from 1 to 0, which in effect refutes conditional NE assertions when they violate best-response conditions. In other words, the tables will all *converge* (and in fact, in time polynomial in the size of the graphical game) – however, unlike in **ApproximateTreeNash**, the tables do not represent the set of all approximate NE, but a superset. This necessitates a second phase to the algorithm that employs more traditional search heuristics in order to find a true equilibrium, and it is this second phase that may be computationally expensive.

One of the merits of **NashProp** is that the first (table computation) phase can be viewed as an instance of constraint satisfaction programming (CSP), which in turn plays an important role in many algorithms for probabilistic inference in Bayesian networks, Markov networks, and related models. The **NashProp** algorithm was also inspired by, and bears a fair similarity to, the well-known belief propagation algorithm for Bayesian network inference. We shall see other connections to these models arise in our examination of correlated equilibria in graphical games, which we turn to now.

7.4 Graphical Games and Correlated Equilibria

Our second case study is an examination of graphical games and correlated equilibrium. As has already been noted, if we are fortunate enough to be able to accurately represent a multiplayer game we are interested in as a graphical game with small degree, the representational benefits purely in terms of parameter reduction may be significant. But this is still a rather cosmetic kind of parsimony. We shall see a much deeper variety in the context of correlated equilibrium.

The first issue that arises in this investigation is the problem of *representing* correlated equilibria. Recall that NE may be viewed as a special case of CE in which the distribution $P(\vec{a})$ is a product distribution. Thus, however computationally difficult it may be to find an NE, at least the object itself can be succinctly represented – it is simply a mixed strategy profile $\vec{p}$, whose length equals the number of players n. Despite their aforementioned advantages, in moving to CE we open a representational Pandora's Box, since even in very simple graphical games there may be correlated equilibria of essentially arbitrary complexity. For example, the CE of a game always include all mixture distributions of NE, so any game with an exponential number of NE can yield extremely complex CE. Such games can be easily constructed with very simple graphs.

[1] Note that in the description of **TreeNash** in Figure 7.1 it was more convenient to initialize the table values to 0, but the change is cosmetic.

More generally, whereas by definition in an NE all players are independent, in a CE there may be arbitrary high-order correlations.

In order to maintain the succinctness of graphical games, some way of addressing this distributional complexity is required. For this we turn to another, older graph-theoretic formalism – namely, undirected graphical models for probabilistic inference, also known as *Markov networks* (Lauritzen, 1996). We will establish a natural and powerful relationship between a graphical game and a certain associated Markov network. Like the graphical game, the associated Markov network is a graph over the players. While the interactions between vertices in the graphical game are entirely *strategic* and given by local payoff matrices, the interactions in the associated Markov network are entirely *probabilistic* and given by local potential functions. The graph of the associated Markov network retains the parsimony of the graphical game.

We will show that the associated Markov network is sufficient for representing *any* correlated equilibria of the graphical game (up to expected payoff equivalence). In other words, the fact that a multiplayer game can be succinctly represented by a graph implies that its entire space of CE outcomes can be represented graphically with comparable succinctness. This result establishes a natural relationship between graphical games and modern probabilistic modeling. We will also briefly discuss the computational benefits of this relationship.

7.4.1 Expected Payoff and Local Neighborhood Equivalence

Our effort to succinctly model the CE of a graphical game consists of two steps. In the first step, we argue that it is not necessary to model *all* the correlations that might arise in a CE, but only those required to represent all of the possible (expected payoff) outcomes for the players. In the second step, we show that the remaining correlations can be represented by a Markov network. For these two steps we respectively require two equivalence notions for distributions – *expected payoff equivalence* and *local neighborhood* equivalence. We shall show that there is a natural *subclass* of the set of all CE of a graphical game, based on expected payoff equivalence, whose representation size is linearly related to the representation size of the graphical game.

Definition 7.7 Two distributions P and Q over joint actions $\vec{a}$ are *expected payoff equivalent*, denoted $P \equiv_{\mathrm{EP}} Q$, if P and Q yield the same expected payoff vector: for each i, $\mathbf{E}_{\vec{a}\sim P}[M_i(\vec{a})] = \mathbf{E}_{\vec{a}\sim Q}[M_i(\vec{a})]$.

Note that merely finding distributions giving the same payoffs as the CE is not especially interesting *unless those distributions are themselves CE* – we want to preserve the strategic properties of the CE, not only its payoffs. Our primary tool for accomplishing this goal will be the notion of local neighborhood equivalence, or the preservation of local marginal distributions. Below we establish that local neighborhood equivalence both implies payoff equivalence and preserves the CE property. In the following subsection, we describe how to represent this natural subclass in a certain Markov network whose structure is closely related to the structure of the graphical game.

Expected payoff equivalence of two distributions is, in general, dependent upon the reward matrices of a graphical game. Let us consider the following (more stringent) equivalence notion, which is based only on the graph G of a game.

Definition 7.8 For a graph G, two distributions P and Q over joint actions $\vec{a}$ are *local neighborhood equivalent* with respect to G, denoted $P \equiv_{\mathrm{LN}} Q$, if for all players i, and for all settings $\vec{a}^{\,i}$ of $N(i)$, $P(\vec{a}^{\,i}) = Q(\vec{a}^{\,i})$.

In other words, the marginal distributions over all local neighborhoods defined by G are identical. Since the graph is always clear from context, we shall just write $P \equiv_{\mathrm{LN}} Q$. The following lemma establishes that local neighborhood equivalence is indeed a stronger notion of equivalence than expected payoff.

Lemma 7.9 *For all graphs G, for all joint distributions P and Q on actions, and for all graphical games with graph G, if $P \equiv_{LN} Q$ then $P \equiv_{EP} Q$. Furthermore, for any graph G and joint distributions P and Q, there exist payoff matrices $\mathcal{M}$ such that for the graphical game $(G, \mathcal{M})$, if $P \not\equiv_{LN} Q$ then $P \not\equiv_{EP} Q$.*

PROOF The first statement follows from the observation that the expected payoff to player i depends only on the marginal distribution of actions in $N(i)$. To prove the second statement, if $P \not\equiv_{\mathrm{LN}} Q$, then there must exist a player i and a joint action $\vec{a}^{\,i}$ for its local neighborhood which has a different probability under P and Q. Simply set $M_i(\vec{a}^{\,i}) = 1$ and $M_i = 0$ elsewhere. Then i has a different payoff under P and Q, and so $P \not\equiv_{\mathrm{EP}} Q$. □

Thus local neighborhood equivalence implies payoff equivalence, but the converse is not true in general (although there exists some payoff matrices where the converse is correct). We now establish that local neighborhood equivalence also preserves CE. It is important to note that this result does *not* hold for expected payoff equivalence.

Lemma 7.10 *For any graphical game $(G, \mathcal{M})$, if P is a CE for $(G, \mathcal{M})$ and $P \equiv_{LN} Q$ then Q is a CE for $(G, \mathcal{M})$.*

PROOF The lemma follows by noting that the CE expectation equations are dependent only upon the marginal distributions of local neighborhoods, which are preserved in Q. □

While explicitly representing *all* CE is infeasible even in simple graphical games, we next show that we *can* concisely represent, in a single model, all CE *up to local neighborhood (and therefore payoff) equivalence*. The amount of space required is comparable to that required to represent the graphical game itself, and allows us to explore or enumerate the different outcomes achievable in the space of CE.

7.4.2 Correlated Equilibria and Markov Nets

In the same way that graphical games provide a concise language for expressing local interaction in game theory, *Markov networks* exploit undirected graphs for expressing local interaction in probability distributions. It turns out that (a special case of) Markov networks are a natural and powerful language for expressing the CE of a graphical game, and that there is a close relationship between the graph of the game and its associated Markov network graph. We begin with the necessary definitions.

Definition 7.11 A *local Markov network* is a pair $M \equiv (G, \Psi)$, where

- G is an undirected graph on vertices $\{1, \ldots, n\}$;
- Ψ is a set of *potential functions*, one for each local neighborhood $N(i)$, mapping binary assignments of values of $N(i)$ to the range $[0, \infty)$:

$$\Psi \equiv \{\psi_i : i = 1, \ldots, n; \psi_i : \{\vec{a}^{\,i}\} \to [0, \infty)\},$$

where $\{\vec{a}^{\,i}\}$ is the set of all $2^{|N(i)|}$ settings to $N(i)$.

A local Markov network M defines a probability distribution P_M as follows. For any binary assignment $\vec{a}$ to the vertices, we define

$$P_M(\vec{a}) \equiv \frac{1}{Z}\left(\prod_{i=1}^{n} \psi_i(\vec{a}^{\,i})\right),$$

where $Z = \sum_{\vec{a}} \prod_{i=1}^{n} \psi_i(\vec{a}^{\,i}) > 0$ is the normalization factor.

Note that any joint distribution can be represented as a local Markov network on a sufficiently dense graph: if we let G be the complete graph then we simply have a single potential function over the entire joint action space $\vec{a}$. However, if d is the size of the maximal neighborhood in G, then the representation size of a distribution in this network is $O(n2^d)$, a considerable savings over a tabular representation if $d \ll n$.

Local Markov networks are a special case of Markov networks, a well-studied probabilistic model in AI and statistics (Lauritzen, 1996; Pearl, 1988). A Markov network is typically defined with potential functions ranging over settings of *maximal cliques* in the graph, rather than local neighborhoods. Another approach we could have taken is to transform the graph G to a graph G', which forms cliques of the local neighborhoods $N(i)$, and then used standard Markov networks over G' as opposed to local Markov networks over G. However, this can sometimes result in an unnecessary exponential blow-up of the size of the model when the resulting maximal cliques are much larger than the original neighborhoods. For our purposes, it is sufficient to define the potential functions over just local neighborhoods (as in our definition) rather than maximal cliques in G', which avoids this potential blow-up.

The following technical lemma establishes that a local Markov network always suffices to represent a distribution up to local neighborhood equivalence.

Lemma 7.12 *For all graphs G, and for all joint distributions P over joint actions, there exists a distribution Q that is representable as a local Markov network with graph G such that $Q \equiv_{LN} P$ with respect to G.*

PROOF The objective is to find a single distribution Q that is consistent with the players' local neighborhood marginals under P and is also a Markov network with graph G. For this we shall sketch the application of methods from probabilistic inference and maximum entropy models to show that the maximum entropy distribution Q^*, subject to $P \equiv_{\text{LN}} Q^*$, is a local Markov network. The sketch below follows the classical treatment of this topic (Berger et al., 1996; Lauritzen and Spiegelhalter, 1998; Dawid and Lauritzen, 1993) and is included for completeness.

Formally, we wish to show that the solution to the following constrained maximum entropy problem is representable in G:

$$Q^* = \text{argmax}_Q H(Q) \equiv \text{argmax}_Q \sum_{\vec{a}} Q(\vec{a}) \log(1/Q(\vec{a}))$$

subject to

(i) $Q(\vec{a}^{\,i}) = P(\vec{a}^{\,i})$, for all $i, \vec{a}^{\,i}$.

(ii) Q is a proper probability distribution.

Note first that this problem always has a unique answer since $H(Q)$ is strictly concave and all constraints are linear. In addition, the feasible set is nonempty, as it contains P itself.

To get the form of Q^*, we solve the optimization problem by introducing Lagrange multipliers $\lambda_{i,\vec{a}^{\,i}}$ (for all i and $\vec{a}^{\,i}$) for the neighborhood marginal constraints (Condition 7.4.2 above); let us call $\vec{\lambda}$ the resulting vector of multipliers. We also introduce a single Lagrange multiplier β for the normalization constraint (Condition (ii) above). The optimization then becomes

$$\begin{aligned} Q^* &= \text{argmax}_{Q,\vec{\lambda},\beta}\{L(Q,\vec{\lambda},\beta)\} \\ &\equiv \text{argmax}_{Q,\vec{\lambda},\beta}\left\{ H(Q) + \sum_{i\in[n]}\sum_{\vec{a}^{\,i}} \lambda_{i,\vec{a}^{\,i}}(Q(\vec{a}^{\,i}) - P(\vec{a}^{\,i})) \right. \\ &\quad \left. + \beta\left(\sum_{\vec{a}} Q(\vec{a}) - 1\right)\right\}, \end{aligned}$$

where $Q(\vec{a})$ is constrained to be positive. Here, L is the Lagrangian function.

A necessary condition for Q^* is that $\partial L/\partial Q(\vec{a})|_{Q=Q^*} = 0$, for all $\vec{a}$ such that $P(\vec{a}) > 0$. After taking derivatives and some algebra, this condition implies, for all $\vec{a}$,

$$Q^*_{\vec{\lambda}}(\vec{a}) = (1/Z_{\vec{\lambda}}) \prod_{v=1}^{n} I[P(\vec{a}^{\,i}) \neq 0] \exp(\lambda_{i,\vec{a}^{\,i}}),$$

where $I[P(\vec{a}^{\,i}) \neq 0]$ is an indicator function that evaluates to 1 iff $P(\vec{a}^{\,i}) \neq 0$. We use the subscript $\vec{\lambda}$ on $Q^*_{\vec{\lambda}}$ and $Z_{\vec{\lambda}}$ to explicitly denote that they are parameterized by the Lagrange multipliers.

It is important to note at this point that regardless of the value of the Lagrange multipliers, each $\lambda_{i,\vec{a}^{\,i}}$ is only a function of the $\vec{a}^{\,i}$. Let the dual function $F(\vec{\lambda}) \equiv L(Q^*_{\vec{\lambda}}(\vec{a}), \vec{\lambda}, 0)$, and let $\vec{\lambda}^*$ maximize this function. Note that those $\lambda_{i,\vec{a}^{\,i}}$ that correspond to $P(\vec{a}^{\,i}) = 0$ are irrelevant parameters since $F(\vec{\lambda})$ is independent of them. So for all i and $\vec{a}^{\,i}$ such that $P(\vec{a}^{\,i}) = 0$, we set $\lambda^*_{i,\vec{a}^{\,i}} = 0$. For all i, $\vec{a}^{\,i}$, we define the functions $\psi_i^*(\vec{a}^{\,i}) \equiv I[P(\vec{a}^{\,i}) \neq 0]\exp(\lambda^*_{i,\vec{a}^{\,i}})$. Hence, we can express the maximum entropy distribution Q^* as, for all $\vec{a}$,

$$Q^*_{\vec{\lambda}^*}(\vec{a}) = (1/Z_{\vec{\lambda}^*}) \prod_{i=1}^{n} \psi_i^*(\vec{a}^{\,i}),$$

which completes the proof. □

The main result of this section follows, and shows that we can represent any correlated equilibria of a graphical game $(G, \mathcal{M})$, up to payoff equivalence, with a local Markov network (G, Ψ). The proof follows from Lemmas 7.9, 7.10, and 7.12.

Theorem 7.13 *For all graphical games $(G, \mathcal{M})$, and for any correlated equilibrium P of $(G, \mathcal{M})$, there exists a distribution Q such that*

(i) *Q is also correlated equilibrium for $(G, \mathcal{M})$;*

(ii) *Q gives all players the same expected payoffs as P: $Q \equiv_{EP} P$; and*

(iii) *Q can be represented as a local Markov network with graph G.*

Note that the representation size for any local Markov network with graph G is linear in the representation size of the graphical game, and thus we can represent the CE of the game parsimoniously.

Remarks. Aside from simple parsimony, Theorem 7.13 allows us to import a rich set of tools from the probabilistic inference literature (Pearl, 1988; Lauritzen, 1996). For example, it is well known that for any vertices i and j and vertex set S in a (local) Markov network, i and j are conditionally independent given values for the variables in S if and only if S separates i and j – that is, the removal of S from G leaves i and j in disconnected components. This, together with Theorem 7.13, immediately implies a large number of conditional independences that must hold in any CE outcome. Also, as mentioned in the Introduction, Theorem 7.13 can be interpreted as strongly limiting the nature of the public randomization needed to implement any given CE outcome – namely, only "local" sources of random bits (as defined by G) are required.

7.4.3 Algorithms for Correlated Equilibria in Graphical Games

Having established in Theorem 7.13 that a concise graphical game yields an equally concise representation of its CE up to payoff equivalence, we now turn our attention to algorithms for *computing* CE. In the spirit of our results thus far, we are interested in algorithms that can efficiently exploit the compactness of graphical games.

It is well known that it is possible to compute CE via linear programming in time polynomial in the standard *noncompact* normal form. In this approach, one variable is introduced for every possible joint action probability $P(\vec{a})$, and the constraints enforce both the CE condition and the fact that the variables must define a probability distribution. It is not hard to verify that the constraints are all linear and there are $O(2^n)$ variables and constraints in the binary action case. By introducing any linear optimization function, one can get an algorithm based on linear programming for computing a single exact CE that runs in time polynomial in the size of the normal-form representation of the game (i.e., polynomial in 2^n).

For graphical games this solution is clearly unsatisfying, since it may require time exponential in the size of the graphical game. What is needed is a more concise way to express the CE and distributional constraints – ideally, linearly in the size of the graphical game representation. As we shall now sketch, this is indeed possible for tree graphical games. The basic idea is to express both the CE and distributional constraints entirely in terms of the local marginals, rather than the global probabilities of joint actions.

For the case in which the game graph is a tree, it suffices to introduce linear distributional constraints over only the local marginals, along with *consistency* constraints on the *intersections* of local marginals. We thus define the following three categories of local constraints defining a linear program:

Variables: For every player i and assignment $\vec{a}^{\,i}$, there is a variable $P(\vec{a}^{\,i})$.
LP Constraints:

(i) *CE Constraints:* For all players i and actions a, a',

$$\sum_{\vec{a}^{\,i}:a^i_i=a} P(\vec{a}^{\,i})M_i(\vec{a}^{\,i}) \geq \sum_{\vec{a}^{\,i}:a^i_i=a} P(\vec{a}^{\,i})M_i([\vec{a}^{\,i}[i:a']).$$

(ii) *Neighborhood Marginal Constraints:* For all players i,

$$\forall \vec{a}^{\,i}: \;\; P(\vec{a}^{\,i}) \geq 0; \;\; \sum_{\vec{a}^{\,i}} P(\vec{a}^{\,i}) = 1.$$

(iii) *Intersection Consistency Constraints:* For all players i and j, and for any assignment $\vec{y}^{\,ij}$ to the *intersection neighborhood* $N(i) \cap N(j)$,

$$\begin{aligned} P(\vec{a}^{\,ij}) &\equiv \sum_{\vec{a}^{\,i}:\vec{a}^{\,ij}=\vec{y}^{\,ij}} P(\vec{a}^{\,i}) \\ &= \sum_{\vec{a}^{\,j}:\vec{a}^{\,ij}=\vec{y}^{\,ij}} P_j(\vec{a}^{\,j}) \\ &\equiv P_j(\vec{a}^{\,ij}). \end{aligned}$$

Note that if d is the size of the largest neighborhood, this system involves $O(n2^d)$ variables and $O(n2^d)$ linear inequalities, which is linear in the representation size of the original graphical game, as desired. This leads to the following algorithmic result.

Theorem 7.14 *For all tree graphical games $(G, \mathcal{M})$, any solution to the linear constraints given above is a correlated equilibrium for $(G, \mathcal{M})$.*

Thus, for instance, we may choose any linear objective function $F(\{P(\vec{a}^{\,i})\})$ and apply standard efficient linear programming algorithms in order to find a CE maximizing F in time polynomial in the size of the graphical game. One natural choice for F is the social welfare, or the total expected payoff over all players:

$$F(\{P_i(\vec{a}^{\,i})\}) = \sum_i \sum_{\vec{a}^{\,i}} P_i(\vec{a}^{\,i})M_i(\vec{a}^{\,i}).$$

7.5 Graphical Exchange Economies

In the same way that the graph of a graphical game represents restrictions on which pairs of players directly influence each other's payoffs, it is natural to examine similar restrictions in classical exchange economies and other market models. In such models, there is typically some number k of goods available for trade, and n players or consumers in the economy. Each consumer has a utility function mapping bundles or amounts of the k goods to a subjective utility. (Settings in which the utility functions obey certain constraints, such as concavity or linearity, are often assumed.) Each consumer also has an endowment – a particular bundle of goods that they are free to trade. It is assumed that if prices $\vec{p} \in (\Re^+)^k$ are posted for the k goods, each consumer will attempt to sell their initial endowment at the posted prices, and then attempt to buy from other consumers that bundle of goods which maximizes their utility, subject to the amount of cash received in the sale of their endowment. A celebrated result of Arrow and Debreu (1954) established very general conditions under which an *equilibrium* price vector exists – prices at which all consumers are able to sell all of their intial endowments (no excess supply) and simultaneously able to purchase their utility-maximizing bundles (no excess demand). The result depends crucially on the fact that the model permits exchange of goods between any pair of consumers in the economy.

A natural graph- or network-based variant of such models again introduces an undirected graph G over the n consumers, with the interpretation that trade is permitted between consumers i and j if and only if the edge (i, j) is present in G.[2] The classical equilibrium existence result can be recovered – but only if we now allow for the possibility of *local* prices, that is, prices for each good–consumer pair. In other words, at equilibrium in such a *graphical economy*, the price per unit of wheat may differ when purchased from different consumers, due to the effects of network topology. In this model, rationality means that consumers must always purchase goods from the neighboring consumers offering the lowest prices.

As with graphical games, there are at least two compelling lines of research to pursue in such models. The first is computational: What graph topologies permit efficient algorithms for computing price equilibria? The second is structural: What can we say about how network structure influences properties of the price equilibria, such as the amount of price variation? Here we briefly summarize results in these two directions.

On the computational side, as with the **TreeNash** algorithm for computing NE in graphical games, it is possible to develop a provably correct and efficient algorithm for computing approximate price equilibria in tree graphical economies with fairly general utility functions. Like **ApproxTreeNash**, this algorithm is a two-pass algorithm in which information regarding *conditional* price equilibria is exchanged between neighboring nodes, and a discrete approximation scheme is introduced. It is complementary to other recent algorithms for computing price equilibria in the classical non-graphical (fully connected) setting under linearity restrictions on the utility functions (discussed in detail in Chapter 5.

[2] In the models considered to date, resale of purchased goods is not permitted – rather, we have "one-shot" economies.

On the structural side, it can be shown that different stochastic models of network formation can result in radically different price equilibrium properties. For example, consider the simplified setting in which the graph G is a bipartite graph between two types of parties, *buyers* and *sellers*. Buyers have an endowment of 1 unit of an abstract good called *cash*, but have utility only for *wheat*; sellers have an endowment of 1 unit of wheat but utility only for cash. Thus the only source of asymmetry in the economy is the structure of G. If G is a random bipartite graph (i.e., generated via a bipartite generalization of the classical Erdos–Renyi model), then as n becomes large there will be essentially *no* price variation at equilibrium (as measured, for instance, by the ratio of the highest to lowest prices for wheat over the entire graph). Thus random graphs behave "almost" like the fully connected case. In contrast, if G is generated according to a stochastic process such as preferential attachment (Barabasi and Albert, 1999), the price variation at equilibrium is unbounded, growing as a root of the economy size n.

7.6 Open Problems and Future Research

There are a number of intriguing open areas for further research in the broad topics discussed in this chapter, including the following.

- **Efficient Algorithms for Exact Nash Computation in Trees.** Perhaps the most notable technical problem left unresolved by the developments described here is that of efficiently (i.e., in time polynomial in the graphical game description) computing exact Nash equilibria for trees. This class falls between the positive results of Elkind et al. (2006) for unions of paths and cycles, and the recent PPAD-completeness results for bounded treewidth graphs (see Chapter 2).
- **Strategy-Proof Algorithms for Distributed Nash Computation.** The NashProp algorithm described here and its variants are clearly not strategy-proof, in the sense that players may have incentive to deviate from the algorithm if they are to actually realize the Nash equilibrium they collectively compute. It would be interesting to explore the possibilities for strategy-proof algorithms for graphical games.
- **Cooperative, Behavioral, and Other Equilibrium Notions.** Here we have described algorithms and structural results for graphical games under noncooperative equilibrium notions. It would be interesting to develop analogous theory for cooperative equilibria, such as how the coalitions that might form depend on graph topology. The recent explosion of work in behavioral game theory and economics (Camerer, 2003) is also ripe for integration with graphical games (and many other aspects of algorithmic game theory as well). For instance, one could investigate how the behavioral phenomenon of inequality aversion might alter the relationship between network structure and equilibrium outcomes.

7.7 Bibliographic Notes

Graphical games were introduced by Kearns et al. (2001) (abbreviated KLS henceforth). Related models were introduced at approximately the same time by Koller and Milch (2003) and La Mura (2000). Graph-theoretic or network models of interaction have a long history in economics and game theory, as surveyed by Jackson (2005); these models tend to be less general than graphical games, and there is naturally less explicit emphasis on computational issues.

The original KLS paper contained the algorithm and analyses of the tree-based algorithms examined in Section 7.1. The **NashProp** generalization of these algorithms is due to Ortiz and Kearns (2003). A follow-up to the KLS paper by the same authors (Littman et al., 2002) erroneously claimed an efficient algorithm for computing an *exact* NE in tree graphical games (recall that the KLS paper gave an efficient algorithm only for approximate NE in trees). The error was recently discovered and discussed by Elkind et al. (2006), who proved that in fact no two-pass algorithm can compute an exact equilibrium. The problem of efficiently computing an exact equilibrium in time polynomial in the size of a tree graphical game remains open.

The study of correlated equilibria in graphical games given in Section 7.4 is adapted from Kakade et al. (2003). Roughgarden and Papadimitriou (2005) and Papadimitriou (2005) gave more general algorithms for computing correlated equilibria in graphical games and other compact representations. It is interesting to note that while the Kakade et al. results show how all correlated equilibria (up to payoff equivalance) can be succinctly *represented* as a Markov networks, Papadimitriou's algorithm (2005) computes correlated equilibria that are mixtures of Nash equilibria and thus can be efficiently sampled. Intractability results for certain correlated equilibrium computations are given by Gilboa and Zemel (1989), as well as by Roughgarden and Papadimitriou (2005).

Other papers providing algorithms for equilibrium computation in graphical games include those of Vickrey and Koller (2002), who examine hill-climbing algorithms for approximate NE, as well as constraint satisfaction generalizations of **NashProp**; and Daskalakis and Papadimitriou (2006), who show close connections between the computation of pure NE and probabilistic inference on the Markov network models discussed in the context of correlated equilibria in Section 7.4.

Graphical games have also played a central role in striking recent developments establishing the intractability of NE computations in general multiplayer games, including the work by Daskalakis et al. (2006) and Goldberg and Papadimitriou (2006); these developments are discussed in detail in Chapter 29. Daskalakis and Papadimitriou also proved intractability results for computing NE in graphical games on highly regular graphs (Daskalakis and Papadimitriou, 2005), while Schoenebeck and Vadhan (2006) systematically characterize the complexity of a variety of equilibrium-related computations, including NE verification and existence of pure equilibria.

The formulation of the graphical exchange economy model summarized in Section 7.5, as well as the price equilibrium proof and algorithms mentioned, is due to Kakade et al. (2004). The result on price variation in different stochastic graph generation models is due to Kakade et al. (2005).

Recently a graph-theoretic generalization of classical evolutionary game theory has been introduced, and it has been shown that random graphs generally preserve the classical evolutionary stable strategies (Kearns and Suri, 2006); these results are discussed in some detail in Chapter 29.

Acknowledgments

I would like to give warm thanks to Michael Littman, Satinder Singh, Sham Kakade, John Langford, and Luis Ortiz for their permission to adapt material from our joint publications (Kakade et al., 2003; Kearns et al., 2001) for presentation in this chapter.

Bibliography

K. Arrow and G. Debreu. Existence of an equilibrium for a competitive economy. *Econometrica*, 22(3):265–290, 1954.

R.J. Aumann. Subjectivity and correlation in randomized strategies. *J. Math. Econ.*, 1, 1974.

R.J. Aumann. Correlated equilibrium as an expression of Bayesian rationality. *Econometrica*, 55, 1987.

A. Barabasi and R. Albert. Emergence of scaling in random networks. *Science*, 286:509–512, 1999.

A. Berger, S.D. Pietra, and V.D. Pietra. A maximum entropy approach to natural language processing. *Comp. Ling.*, 22(1), March 1996.

C. Camerer. *Behavioral Game Theory*. Princeton University Press, 2003.

C. Daskalakis, P. Goldberg, and C. Papadimitriou. The complexity of computing a Nash equilibrium. In *Proc. 38th ACM Symp. Theory of Computing*, pp. 71–78. ACM Press, 2006.

C. Daskalakis and C. Papadimitriou. The complexity of games on highly regular graphs. In *Proc. 13th Annual Euro. Symp. Algo.*, p. 71. Springer, Berlin, 2005.

C. Daskalakis and C. Papadimitriou. Computing pure Nash equilibria in graphical games via Markov random fields. In *Proc. 7th ACM Conf. on Electronic Commerce*, pp. 91–99. ACM Press, 2006.

A.P. Dawid and S.L. Lauritzen. Hyper Markov laws in the statistical analysis of decomposable graphical models. *Ann. Stat.*, 21(3):1271–1317, September 1993.

E. Elkind, L. Goldberg, and P. Goldberg. Graphical games on trees revisited. In *Proc. 7th ACM Conf. on Electronic Commerce*, pp. 100–109. ACM Press, 2006.

D. Foster and R. Vohra. Calibrated learning and correlated equilibrium. *Games Economic Behav.*, 1997.

D. Foster and R. Vohra. Regret in the on-line decision problem. *Games Econ. Behav.*, pp. 7–36, 1999.

I. Gilboa and E. Zemel. Nash and correlated equilibria: Some complexity considerations. *Games Econ. Behav.*, 1:80–93, 1989.

P. Goldberg and C. Papadimitriou. Reducibility among equilibrium problems. In *Proc. 38th ACM Symp. Theo. Comp.*, pp. 61–70. ACM Press, 2006.

M. Jackson. The economics of social networks. In *Adv. Economics and Econometrics, Theo. Appl.: Ninth World Congr. Econo. Soc.* Cambridge University Press, 2005.

S. Kakade, M. Kearns, J. Langford, and L. Ortiz. Correlated equilibria in graphical games. In *Proc. 4th ACM Conf. on Electronic Commerce*, pp. 42–47. ACM Press, 2003.

S. Kakade, M. Kearns, and L. Ortiz. Graphical economics. In *Proc. 17th Annual Conf. on Learning Theo.*, pp. 17–32. Springer, Berlin, 2004.

S. Kakade, M. Kearns, L. Ortiz, R. Pemantle, and S. Suri. Economic properties of social networks. In L. Saul, Y. Weiss, and L. Bottou, editors, *Adv. Neural Infor. Proc. Syst., 17*, pp. 633–640. MIT Press, 2005.

M. Kearns, M. Littman, and S. Singh. Graphical models for game theory. In *Proc. 17th Annual Conf. on Uncertainty in Artificial Intelligence*, pp. 253–260. Morgan Kaufmann, 2001.

M. Kearns and S. Suri. Networks preserving evolutionary equilibria and the power of randomization. In *Proc. 7th ACM Conf. Electronic Commerce*, pp. 200–207. ACM Press, 2006.

D. Koller and B. Milch. Multi-agent influence diagrams for representing and solving games. *Games Econ. Behav.*, 45(1):181–221, 2003.

P. La Mura. Game networks. In *Proc. 16th Conf. Uncertainty in Artificial Intelligence*, pp. 335–342. Morgan Kaufmann, 2000.

S. Lauritzen. *Graphical Models*. Oxford University Press, 1996.

S. Lauritzen and D. Spiegelhalter. Local computations with probabilities on graphical structures and their application to expert systems. *J. Royal Stat. Soc. B*, 50(2):157–224, 1988.

M. Littman, M. Kearns, and S. Singh. An efficient exact algorithm for singly connected graphical games. In *Adv. in Neural Inf. Proc. Syst. 14*. MIT Press, 2002.

D. Monderer and L. Shapley. Potential games. *Games Econ. Behav.*, 14:124–143, 1996.

J.F. Nash. Non-cooperative games. *Ann. Math.*, 54:286–295, 1951.

L. Ortiz and M. Kearns. Nash propagation for loopy graphical games. In S. Becker, S. Thrun, and K. Obermayer, editors, *Adv. Neural Inf. Proc. Syst. 15*, pp. 793–800. MIT Press, 2003.

G. Owen. *Game Theory*. Academic Press, UK, 1995.

C. Papadimitriou. Computing correlated equilibria in multi-player games. In *Proc. 37th ACM Symp. Theo. Comp.*, pp. 49–56. ACM Press, 2005.

C. Papadimitriou and T. Roughgarden. Computing equilibria in multi-player multi-player games. In *Proc. 16th ACM-SIAM Symp. Disc. Algo.*, pp. 82–91. SIAM, 2005.

J. Pearl. *Probabilistic Reasoning in Intelligent Systems*. Morgan Kaufmann, 1988.

R. Rosenthal. A class of games possessing pure-strategy Nash equilibria. *Intl. J. Game Theory*, 2:65–67, 1973.

G. Schoenebeck and S. Vadhan. The computational complexity of Nash equilibria in concisely represented games. In *Proc. 7th ACM Conf. Electronic Commerce*, pp. 270–279. ACM Press, 2006.

D. Vickrey and D. Koller. Multi-agent algorithms for solving graphical games. In *Proc. 18th Ntl. Conf. on Artificial Intelligence*, pp. 345–351. AAAI Press, 2002.

CHAPTER 8

Cryptography and Game Theory

Yevgeniy Dodis and Tal Rabin

Abstract

The Cryptographic and Game Theory worlds seem to have an intersection in that they both deal with an interaction between mutually distrustful parties which has some end result. In the cryptographic setting the multiparty interaction takes the shape of a set of parties communicating for the purpose of evaluating a function on their inputs, where each party receives at the end some output of the computation. In the game theoretic setting, parties interact in a game that guarantees some payoff for the participants according to the joint actions of all the parties, while the parties wish to maximize their own payoff. In the past few years the relationship between these two areas has been investigated with the hope of having cross fertilization and synergy. In this chapter we describe the two areas, the similarities and differences, and some of the new results stemming from their interaction.

The first and second section will describe the cryptographic and the game theory settings (respectively). In the third section we contrast the two settings, and in the last sections we detail some of the existing results.

8.1 Cryptographic Notions and Settings

Cryptography is a vast subject requiring its own book. Therefore, in the following we will give only a high-level overview of the problem of *Multi-Party Computation* (MPC), ignoring most of the lower-level details and concentrating only on aspects relevant to Game Theory.

MPC deals with the following problem. There are $n \geq 2$ parties $P_1, \ldots, P_n$ where party P_i holds input t_i, $1 \leq i \leq n$, and they wish to compute together a function $s = f(t_1, \ldots, t_n)$ on their inputs. The goal is that each party will learn the output of the function, s, yet with the restriction that P_i will not learn any additional information about the input of the other parties aside from what can be deduced from the pair (t_i, s). Clearly it is the secrecy restriction that adds complexity to the problem, as without it each party could announce its input to all other parties, and each party would locally compute the value of the function. Thus, the goal of MPC is to achieve the following two properties at the *same time*: correctness of the computation and privacy preservation of the inputs.

Two generalizations. The following two generalizations of the above scenario are often useful.

(i) *Probabilistic functions.* Here the value of the function depends on some random string r chosen according to some distribution: $s = f(t_1, \ldots, t_n; r)$. An example of this is the coin-flipping functionality, which takes no inputs, and outputs an unbiased random bit. Notice, it is crucial that the value r is not controlled by any of the parties, but is somehow jointly generated during the computation.

(ii) *Multioutput functions.* It is not mandatory that there be a single output of the function. More generally there could be a unique output for each party, i.e., $(s_1, \ldots, s_n) = f(t_1, \ldots, t_n)$. In this case, only party P_i learns the output s_i, and no other party learns any information about the other parties input and outputs aside from what can be derived from its own input and output.

The parties. One of the most interesting aspects of MPC is to reach the objective of computing the function value, but under the assumption that some of the parties may deviate from the protocol. In cryptography, the parties are usually divided into two types: *honest* and *faulty*. An honest party follows the protocol without any deviation. Otherwise, the party is considered to be faulty. The faulty behavior can exemplify itself in a wide range of possibilities. The most benign faulty behavior is where the parties follow the protocol, yet try to learn as much as possible about the inputs of the other parties. These parties are called *honest-but-curious* (or *semihonest*). At the other end of the spectrum, the parties may deviate from the prescribed protocol in any way that they desire, with the goal of either influencing the computed output value in some way, or of learning as much as possible about the inputs of the other parties. These parties are called *malicious*.

We envision an adversary $\mathcal{A}$, who controls all the faulty parties and can coordinate their actions. Thus, in a sense we assume that the faulty parties are working together and can exert the most knowledge and influence over the computation out of this collusion. The adversary can corrupt any number of parties out of the n participating parties. Yet, in order to be able to achieve a solution to the problem, in many cases we would need to limit the number of corrupted parties. We call this limit a threshold k, indicating that the protocol remains secure as long as the number of corrupted parties is at most k.

8.1.1 Security of Multiparty Computations

We are ready to formulate the idea of what it means to *securely* compute a given function f. Assume that there exists a *trusted party* who privately receives the inputs of all the participating parties, calculates the output value s, and then transmits this value to each one of the parties.[1] This process clearly computes the correct output of f, and also does not enable the participating parties to learn any additional information

[1] Note that in the case of a probabilistic function the trusted party will choose r according to the specified distribution and use it in the computation. Similarly, for multioutput functions the trusted party will only give each party its own output.

about the inputs of others. We call this model the *ideal model*. The security of MPC then states that a protocol is secure if its execution satisfies the following: (1) the honest parties compute the same (correct) outputs as they would in the ideal model; and (2) the protocol does not expose more information than a comparable execution with the trusted party, in the ideal model.

Intuitively, this is explained in the following way. The adversary's interaction with the parties (on a vector of inputs) in the protocol generates a *transcript*. This transcript is a random variable that includes the outputs of all the honest parties, which is needed to ensure correctness as explained below, and the output of the adversary $\mathcal{A}$. The latter output, without loss of generality, includes all the information that the adversary learned, including its inputs, private state, all the messages sent by the honest parties to $\mathcal{A}$, and, depending on the model (see later discussion on the communication model), maybe even include more information, such as public messages that the honest parties exchanged. If we show that *exactly* the same transcript distribution[2] can be generated when interacting with the trusted party in the ideal model, then we are guaranteed that no information is leaked from the computation via the execution of the protocol, as we know that the ideal process does not expose any information about the inputs. More formally,

Definition 8.1 Let f be a function on n inputs and let π be a protocol that computes the function f. Given an adversary $\mathcal{A}$, which controls some set of parties, we define $\mathrm{REAL}_{\mathcal{A},\pi}(t)$ to be the sequence of outputs of honest parties resulting from the execution of π on input vector t under the attack of $\mathcal{A}$, in addition to the output of $\mathcal{A}$. Similarly, given an adversary $\mathcal{A}'$ which controls a set of parties, we define $\mathrm{IDEAL}_{\mathcal{A}',f}(t)$ to be the sequence of outputs of honest parties computed by the trusted party in the ideal model on input vector t, in addition to the output of $\mathcal{A}'$. We say that π *securely computes* f if, for every adversary $\mathcal{A}$ as above, there exists an adversary $\mathcal{A}'$, which controls the same parties in the ideal model, such that, on any input vector t, we have that the distribution of $\mathrm{REAL}_{\mathcal{A},\pi}(t)$ is "indistinguishable" from the distribution of $\mathrm{IDEAL}_{\mathcal{A}',f}(t)$ (where the term "indistinguishable will be explained later).

Intuitively, the task of the ideal adversary $\mathcal{A}'$ is to generate (almost) the same output as $\mathcal{A}$ generates in the real execution (referred to also as the real model). Thus, the attacker $\mathcal{A}'$ is often called the *simulator* (of $\mathcal{A}$). Also note that the above definition guarantees correctness of the protocol. Indeed, the transcript value generated in the ideal model, $\mathrm{IDEAL}_{\mathcal{A}',f}(t)$, also includes the outputs of the honest parties (even though we do not give these outputs to $\mathcal{A}'$), which we know were correctly computed by the trusted party. Thus, the real transcript $\mathrm{REAL}_{\mathcal{A},\pi}(t)$ should also include correct outputs of the honest parties in the real model.

The inputs of the faulty parties. We assumed that every party P_i has an input t_i, which it enters into the computation. However, if P_i is faulty, nothing stops P_i from changing t_i into some t_i'. Thus, the notion of a "correct" input is defined only for honest parties.

[2] The requirement that the transcript distribution be exactly the same will be relaxed later on.

However, the "effective" input of a faulty party P_i could be defined as the value t_i' that the simulator $\mathcal{A}'$ (which we assume exists for any real model $\mathcal{A}$) gives to the trusted party in the ideal model. Indeed, since the outputs of honest parties look the same in both models, for all effective purposes P_i must have "contributed" the same input t_i' in the real model.

Another possible misbehavior of P_i, even in the ideal model, might be a refusal to give any input at all to the trusted party. This can be handled in a variety of ways, ranging from aborting the entire computation to simply assigning t_i some "default value." For concreteness, we assume that the domain of f includes a special symbol $\perp$ indicating this refusal to give the input, so that it is well defined how f should be computed on such missing inputs. What this requires is that in any real protocol we detect when a party does not enter its input and deal with it exactly in the same manner as if the party would input $\perp$ in the ideal model.

Variations on output delivery. In the above definition of security it is implicitly assumed that all honest parties receive the output of the computation. This is achieved by stating that $\text{IDEAL}_{\mathcal{A}',f}(t)$ includes the outputs of all honest parties. We therefore say that our current definition *guarantees output delivery*.

A more relaxed property than output delivery is *fairness*. If fairness is achieved, then this means that if at least one (even faulty!) party learns its outputs, then all (honest) parties eventually do too. A bit more formally, we allow the ideal model adversary $\mathcal{A}'$ to instruct the trusted party not to compute any of the outputs. In this case, in the ideal model either all the parties learn the output, or none do. Since $\mathcal{A}$'s transcript is indistinguishable from $\mathcal{A}'$'s this guarantees that the same fairness guarantee must hold in the real model as well.

Yet, a further relaxation of the definition of security is to provide only *correctness and privacy*. This means that faulty parties can learn their outputs, and prevent the honest parties from learning theirs. Yet, at the same time the protocol will still guarantee that (1) if an honest party receives an output, then this is the correct value, and (2) the privacy of the inputs and outputs of the honest parties is preserved.

Variations on the model. The basic security notions introduced above are universal and model-independent. However, specific implementations crucially depend on spelling out precisely the model where the computation will be carried out. In particular, the following issues must be specified:

(i) *The parties.* As mentioned above, the faulty parties could be honest-but-curious or malicious, and there is usually an upper bound k on the number of parties that the adversary can corrupt.

(ii) *Computational assumptions.* We distinguish between the computational setting and the information theoretic setting. In the information theoretic model we assume that the adversary is unlimited in its computing powers. In this case the term "indistinguishable" in Definition 8.1 is formalized by requiring the two transcript distributions to be either identical (so-called *perfect security*) or, at least, statistically close in their variation distance (so-called *statistical security*). On the other hand, in the computational setting we restrict the power of the adversary (as well as that of the honest parties). A bit more precisely, we assume that the corresponding MPC problem is parameterized by the *security parameter* λ, in which case (a) all the computation and communication shall be done in time polynomial in λ; and (b) the misbehavior strategies of the faulty parties are also restricted to be run in time polynomial in λ. Furthermore, the term "indistinguishability" in Definition 8.1 is formalized by *computational indistinguishability*: two distribution ensembles $\{X_\lambda\}_\lambda$ and $\{Y_\lambda\}_\lambda$ are said to be computationally indistinguishable, if for any polynomial-time distinguisher D, the quantity ϵ, defined as $|Pr[D(X_\lambda) = 1] - Pr[D(Y_\lambda) = 1]|$, is a "negligible" function of λ. This means that for any $j > 0$ and all sufficiently large λ, ϵ eventually becomes smaller than λ^{-j}.

This modeling of computationally bounded parties enables us to build secure MPC protocols depending on plausible computational assumptions, such as the hardness of factoring large integers, etc.

(iii) *Communication assumptions*. The two common communication assumptions are the existence of a *secure channel* and the existence of a *broadcast* channel. Secure channels assume that every pair of parties P_i and P_j are connected via an authenticated, private channel. A broadcast channel is a channel with the following properties: if a party P_i (honest or faulty) broadcasts a message m, then m is correctly received by all the parties (who are also sure the message came from P_i). In particular, if an honest party receives m, then it knows that every other honest party also received m.

A different communication assumption is the existence of *envelopes*. An envelope (in its most general definition) guarantees the following properties: a value m can be stored inside the envelope, it will be held without exposure for a given period of time, and then the value m will be revealed without modification. A *ballot box* is an enhancement of the envelope setting that also provides a random shuffling mechanism of the envelopes.

These are, of course, idealized assumptions that allow for a clean description of a protocol, as they separate the communication issues from the computational ones. These idealized assumptions may be realized by a physical mechanisms, but in some settings such mechanisms may not be available. Then it is important to address the question *if and under what circumstances* we can remove a given communication assumption. For example, we know that the assumption of a secure channel can be substituted with a protocol, but under the introduction of a computational assumption and a public key infrastructure. In general, the details of these substitutions are delicate and need to be done with care.

8.1.2 Existing Results for Multiparty Computation

Since the introduction of the MPC problem in the beginning of the 1980s, the work in this area has been extensive. We will only state, without proofs, a few representative results from the huge literature in this area.

Theorem 8.2 *Secure MPC protocols withstanding coalitions of up to k malicious parties (controlled by an attacker $\mathcal{A}$) exist in the following cases:*

(i) *Assuming that $\mathcal{A}$ is computationally bounded, secure channels, and a broadcast channel (and a certain cryptographic assumption, implied for example, by the hardness of factoring, is true), then:*

(a) *for $k < n/2$ with output delivery.*

(b) *for $k < n$ with correctness and privacy.*

(c) *additionally assuming envelopes, for $k < n$ with fairness.*

(ii) *Assuming that $\mathcal{A}$ is computationally unbounded:*

(a) *assuming secure channels, then for $k < n/3$ with output delivery.*

(b) *assuming secure and broadcast channels, then for $k < n/2$ with output delivery (but with an arbitrarily small probability of error).*

(c) *assuming envelopes, ballot-box and a broadcast channel, then for $k < n$ with output delivery.*

Structure of MPC protocols. A common design structure of many MPC protocols proceeds in three stages: commitment to the inputs, computation of the function on the committed inputs, revealing of the output. Below we describe these stages at a high level, assuming for simplicity that the faulty parties are honest-but-curious.

In the first stage the parties commit to their inputs, this is done by utilizing the first phase of a two-phased primitive called *secret-sharing*. The first phase of a (k, n)-secret-sharing scheme is the *sharing phase*. A dealer, D, who holds some secret z, computes n shares $z_1, \ldots, z_n$ of z and gives the share z_i to party P_i. The second phase is the *reconstruction phase,* which we describe here and utilize later. For the reconstruction, the parties broadcast their shares to recover z. Informally, such secret-sharing schemes satisfy the following two properties: (1) k, or fewer, shares do not reveal any information about z; but (2) any $k+1$ or more shares enable one to recover z. Thus, up to k colluding parties learn no information about z after the sharing stage, while the presence of at least $k+1$ honest parties allows one to recover the secret in the reconstruction phase (assuming, for now, that no incorrect shares are given).

The classical secret-sharing scheme satisfying these properties is the Shamir secret-sharing scheme. Here we assume that the value z lies in some finite field F of cardinality greater than n (such as the field of integers modulo a prime $p > n$). The dealer D chooses a random polynomial g of degree k with the only constraint that the free coefficient of g is z. Thus, $z = g(0)$. Then, if $\alpha_1, \ldots, \alpha_n$ are arbitrary but agreed in advance nonzero elements of F, the shares of party P_i is computed as $z_i = g(\alpha_i)$. It is now easy to observe that any $k+1$ shares z_i are enough to interpolate the polynomial g and compute $g(0) = z$. Furthermore, any set of k shares is independent of z. This is easy to see as for any value $z' \in F$ there exists a $(k+1)$st share such that with the given set of k shares they interpolate a polynomial g', where $g'(0) = z'$, in a sense making any value of the secret equally likely. Thus, properties (1) and (2) stated above are satisfied.

To summarize, the first stage of the MPC is achieved by having each party P_i invoke the first part of the secret-sharing process as the dealer D with its input t_i as the secret, and distribute the correct shares of t_i to each party P_j. If f is probabilistic, the players additionally run a special protocol at the end of which a (k, n)-secret-sharing of a *random and secret* value r is computed.

In the second stage the parties compute the function f. This is done by evaluating the pre–agreed-upon arithmetic circuit representing f over F, which is composed of addition, scalar-multiplication and multiplication gates. The computation proceeds by evaluating the gates one by one. We inductively assume that the inputs to the gates are shared in the manner described above in the secret-sharing scheme, and we guarantee that the output of the gate will preserve the same representation. This step forms the heart of most MPC protocols. The computation of the addition and scalar-multiplication gates are typically pretty straightforward and does not require communication (e.g., for the Shamir secret-sharing scheme the parties locally simply add or multiply by the scalar their input shares), but is considerably more involved for the multiplication gate and requires communication. For our purposes we will not need the details of the computation mechanism, simply assuming that this computation on shares is possible will suffice. Therefore, we can assume that at the end of the second stage the parties have a valid secret-sharing of the required output(s) of the function f. The most crucial observation is that no additional information is leaked throughout this stage, since all the values are always shared through a (k, n)-secret-sharing scheme.

Finally, in the last stage the parties need to compute their individual outputs of the function. As we have inductively maintained the property that the output of each gate is in the secret-sharing representation, then the same it true for the output gate of f. Thus, to let the parties learn the output s, which is the value of the function, the parties simply run the reconstruction phase of the secret-sharing scheme (as described above), by having each party broadcast its share of s.

8.2 Game Theory Notions and Settings

Strategic games. We assume that the reader is familiar with the basic concepts of strategic (or "one-shot simultaneous move") games, including the notions of Nash Equilibrium (NE) and Correlated Equilibrium (CE). In particular, recall from Chapter 1 that the class of NE corresponds to independent strategies of all the parties, while the class of CE – to arbitrary correlated strategies. However, in order to implement a given CE one generally needs a special "correlation device" – so-called *mediator* M – which will sample the prescribed strategy profile $s = (s_1, \ldots, s_n)$ for all the parties, and disclose privately only action s_i to each player P_i. In particular, it is very important that P_i does not learn anything about the recommended actions of the other parties, beyond what could be implied by its own action s_i. Finally, recall that one can achieve considerably higher payoffs by playing a well-selected CE than what is possible using any given NE, or even what can be achieved by taking any convex combination of NE payoffs.

Games with incomplete information. In games with incomplete information, each party has a private type $t_i \in T_i$, where the joint vector $t = (t_1, \ldots, t_n)$ is assumed to be drawn from some publicly known distribution. The point of such type, t_i, is that it affects the utility function of party P_i: namely, the utility u_i depends not only on the actions $s_1, \ldots, s_n$, but also on the private type t_i of party P_i, or, in even more general games, on the entire type vector t of *all* the parties. With this in mind, generalizing the notion of Nash equilibrium to such games is straightforward. (The resulting Nash equilibrium is also called *Bayesian*.)

Mediated games generalize to the typed setting, in which parties have to send their types to the mediator M before receiving the joint recommendation. Depending on the received type vector t, the mediator samples a correlated strategy profile s and gives each party its recommended action s_i, as before. We remark that the expected canonical strategy of party P_i is to honestly report its type t_i to M, and then follow the recommended action s_i. However, P_i can deviate from the protocol in two ways: (1) send a wrong type t_i' or not send a type at all to M, as well as (2) decide to change the recommended action from s_i to some s_i'. As a mediator may receive faulty types, a fully defined sampling strategy for the mediator should specify the joint distribution x for every type $t = (t_1, \ldots, t_n)$, even outside the support of the joint type distribution. Formally, x^t should be defined for every $t \in \prod_i (T_i \cup \{\perp\})$, where $\perp$ is a special symbol indicating an invalid type. (In particular, games of complete information can be seen as a special case where all $t_i = \perp$ and each party "refused" to report its type.) With this in mind, the generalization of CE to games with incomplete information is straightforward.

Aborting the game. We assume that the parties will always play the game by choosing an action $s_i \in S_i$ and getting an appropriate payoff $u_i(s)$. Of course, we can always model refusal to play by introducing a special action $\perp$ into the strategy space, and defining the explicit utilities corresponding to such actions. Indeed, many games effectively guarantee participation by assigning very low payoff to actions equivalent to aborting the computation. However, this is not a requirement; in fact, many games do not even have the abort action as parts of their action spaces. To summarize, aborting is not something which is inherent to games, although it could be modeled within the game, if required.

Extended games. So far we considered only strategic games, where parties move in "one-shot" (possibly with the help of the mediator). Of course, these games are special cases of much more general *extensive form* games (with complete or incomplete information), where a party can move in many rounds and whose payoffs depend on the entire run of the game. In our setting we will be interested only in a special class of such extensive form games, which we call *(strategic) games extended by cheap-talk*, or, in brief, *extended games*.

An extended game G^* is always induced by a basic strategic game G (of either complete or incomplete information), and has the following form. In the *cheap-talk (or preamble) phase*, parties follow some *protocol* by exchanging messages in some appropriate communication model. This communication model can vary depending on the exact setting we consider. But once the setting is agreed upon, the format of the cheap talk phase is well defined. After the preamble, the *game phase* will start and the parties simply play the original game G. In particular, the payoffs of the extended game are exactly the payoff that the parties get in G (and this explains why the preamble phase is called "cheap talk").

Correspondingly, the strategy x_i of party P_i in the extended game consists of its strategy in the cheap talk phase, followed by the choice of an action s_i that P_i will play in G. Just like in strategic games, we assume that the game phase must always go on. Namely, aborting the game phase will be modeled inside G, but only if necessary. However, the parties can always abort the preamble phase of the extended game, and prematurely decide to move on to the game phase. Thus, a valid strategy profile for the extended game *must* include instructions of which action to play if some other party refuses to follow its strategy, or, more generally, deviates from the protocol instructions during the cheap talk phase (with abort being a special case of such misbehavior).

Nash equilibrium of extended games. With this in mind, (Bayesian) Nash equilibrium for extended games is defined as before. We remark, however, that Nash equilibrium is known to be too liberal for extensive form games, as it allows for "unreasonable" strategy profiles to satisfy the definition of NE. For example, it allows for equilibrium strategies containing so-called "empty threats" and has other subtle deficiencies. Nevertheless, in order to keep our presentation simple, we will primarily restrict ourselves to the basic concept of NE when talking about extended games.

Collusions. All the discussion so far assumed the traditional *noncooperative* setting, where agents are assumed not to form collusions. In contrast, *cooperative game theory* tries to model reasonable equilibrium concepts arising in scenarios where agents are allowed to form collusions. However, traditional game-theoretic treatment of such equilibria are fairly weak. We will come back to this issue in Section 8.4.1, where we provide the definition of an equilibrium that we think is the most appropriate for our setting and has been influenced by the MPC setting.

8.3 Contrasting MPC and Games

As we can see, MPC and games share several common characteristics. In both cases an important problem is to compute some function $(s_1 \ldots s_n) = f(t_1, \ldots, t_n; r)$ in a private manner. However, there are some key differences summarized in Figure 8.1, making the translation from MPC to Games and vice versa a promising but nonobvious task.

Incentives and rationality. Game theory is critically built on incentives. Although it may not necessarily explain why parties participate in a game, once they do, they have a very well defined incentive. Specifically, players are assumed to be *rational* and only care about maximizing their utility. Moreover, rationality is common knowledge: parties are not only rational, but know that other parties are rational and utilize this knowledge when making their strategic decisions. In contrast, the incentives in the

Issue	Cryptography	Game Theory
Incentive	Outside the model	Payoff
Players	Totally honest or malicious	Always rational
Solution drivers	Secure protocol	Equilibrium
Privacy	Goal	Means
Trusted party	In the ideal model	In the actual game
Punishing cheaters	Outside the model	Central part
Early stopping	Possible	The game goes on!
Deviations	Usually efficient	Usually unbounded
k-collusions	Tolerate "large" k	Usually only $k = 1$

Figure 8.1. Differences between Crytography and game theory.

MPC setting remain external to the computation, and the reason the computation actually ends with a correct and meaningful output comes from the assumption on the parties. Specifically, in the MPC setting one assumes that there exist two diametrically opposite kinds of parties: *totally honest* and *arbitrarily malicious*. Thus, the settings are somewhat incomparable in general. On the one hand, the MPC setting may be harder as it has to protect against completely unexplained behavior of the malicious parties (even if such behaviors would be irrational had the parties had the utilities defined). On the other hand, the Game Theory setting could be harder as it does not have the benefit of assuming that some of the parties (i.e., the honest parties) blindly follow the protocol. However, we remark that this latter benefit disappears for the basic notions of Nash and correlated equilibria, since there one always assumes that the other parties follow the protocol when considering whether or not to deviate. For such basic concepts, we will indeed see in Section 8.4.2 that the MPC setting is more powerful.

Privacy and solution drivers. In the cryptographic setting the objective is to achieve a secure protocol, as defined in Definition 8.1. In particular, the main task is to eliminate the trusted party in a private and resilient way. While in the game theory setting the goal is to achieve "stability" by means of some appropriate equilibrium. In particular, the existence of the mediator is just another "parameter setting" resulting in a more desirable, but harder to implement equilibrium concept. Moreover, the privacy constraint on the mediator is merely a technical way to justify a much richer class of "explainable" rational behaviors. Thus, in the MPC setting privacy is the *goal* while in the game theory setting it is a *means to an end*.

"Crime and punishment". We also notice that studying deviations from the prescribed strategy is an important part of both the cryptographic and the game-theoretic setting. However, there are several key differences.

In cryptography, the goal is to compute the function, while achieving some security guarantees in spite of the deviations of the faulty parties. Most protocols also enable the participating parties to detect which party has deviated from the protocol. Yet, even when exposed, in many instances no action is taken against the faulty party. Yet, when an action, such as removal from the computation, is taken, this is not in an attempt to punish the party, but rather to enable the protocol to reach its final goal of computing the function. In contrast, in the game-theoretic setting it is crucial to specify exactly how the misbehavior will be dealt with by the other parties. In particular, one typical approach is to design reaction strategies that will negatively affect the payoffs of the misbehaving party(s). By rationality, this *ensures* that it is in no player's self-interest to deviate from the prescribed strategy.

We already commented on a particular misbehavior when a party refuses to participate in a given protocol/strategy. This is called *early stopping*. In the MPC setting, there is nothing one can do about this problem, since it is possible in the ideal model as well. In the Game Theory setting, however, we already pointed out that one always assumes that "the game goes on." That is, if one wishes, it is possible to model stopping by an explicit action with explicit payoffs, but the formal game is always assumed to be played. Thus, if we use MPC inside a game-theoretic protocol, we will have to argue – from the game-theoretic point of view – what should happen when a given party aborts the MPC.

Efficiency. Most game-theoretic literature places no computational limitations on the efficiency of a party when deciding whether or not to deviate. In contrast, a significant part of cryptographic protocol literature is designed to only withstand computationally bounded adversaries.

Collusions. Finally, we comment again on the issue of collusions. Most game-theoretic literature considers noncooperative setting, which corresponds to collusions of size $k = 1$. In contrast, in the MPC setting the case $k = 1$ is usually straightforward, and a lot of effort is made to make the maximum collusion threshold as high as possible. Indeed, in most MPC settings one can tolerate at least a linear fraction of colluding parties, and sometimes even a collusion of all but one party.

8.4 Cryptographic Influences on Game Theory

In this section we discuss how the techniques and notions from MPC and cryptography can be used in Game Theory. We start by presenting the notions of computational and k-resilient equilibria, which were directly influenced by cryptography. We then proceed by describing how to use appropriate MPC protocols and replace the mediator implementing a given CE by a "payoff-equivalent" cheap-talk phase in a variety of contexts.

8.4.1 New Notions

Computational equilibrium. Drawing from the cryptographic world, we consider settings where parties participating in the extended game are computationally bounded and we define the notion of *computational equilibriums*. In this case we only have to protect against *efficient* misbehavior strategies x_i. A bit more precisely, we will assume that the basic game G has constant size. However, when designing the preamble phase of the extended game, we can parameterize it by the security parameter λ, in which case (a) all the computation and communication shall be done in time polynomial in λ; and (b) the misbehavior strategies x_i are also restricted to be run in time polynomial in λ.

The preamble phase will be designed under the assumption of the existence of a computationally hard problem. However, this introduces a negligible probability (see Section 8.1.1) that within x_i the attacker might break (say, by luck) the underlying hard problem, and thus might get considerably higher payoff than by following the equilibrium strategy x_i^*. Of course, this can improve this party's expected payoff by at most a negligible amount (since the parameters of G, including the highest payoff, are assumed constant with respect to λ), so we must make an assumption that the party will not bother to deviate if its payoffs will increase only by a negligible amount. This gives rise to the notion of *computational Nash equilibrium*: a tuple of independent strategies $x_1^*, \ldots, x_n^*$ where each strategy is *efficient* in λ such that for every P_i and for every alternative *efficient* in λ strategy x_i, we have $u_i(x_i^*, x_{-i}^*) \geq u_i(x_i, x_{-i}^*) - \epsilon$, where ϵ is a negligible function of λ.

k-Resiliency. As we mentioned, the Game Theory world introduced several flavors of cooperative equilibria concepts. Yet, for our purposes here, we define a stronger type of such an equilibrium, called a *resilient* (Nash or Correlated) equilibrium. Being a very strong notion of an equilibrium, it may not exist in most games. Yet, we choose to present it since it will exist in the "Game Theory-MPC" setting, where we will use MPC protocols in several game-theoretic scenarios. The possibility of realizing such strong equilibria using MPC shows the strength of the cryptographic techniques. Furthermore, with minor modifications, most of the results we present later in the chapter extend to weaker kinds of cooperative equilibria, such as various flavors of a more well known *coalition-proof equilibrium*.[3]

Informally, resilient equilibrium requires protection against all coalitional deviations that strictly benefit even *one* of its colluding parties. Thus, no such deviation will be justifiable to *any* member of the coalition, meaning that the equilibrium strategies are very stable. A bit more formally, an independent strategy profile $(x_1^*, \ldots, x_n^*)$ is a *k-resilient Nash Equilibrium of G*, if for all coalitions C of cardinality at most k, all correlated deviation strategies x_C of the members of C, and *all* members $P_i \in C$, we have $u_i(x_C^*, x_{-C}^*) \geq u_i(x_C, x_{-C}^*)$. Thus, *no* coalition member benefits by x_C.

The notion of *k-resilient correlated equilibrium* is defined similarly, although here we can have two variants. In the *ex ante* variant, members of C are allowed to collude only *before* receiving their actions from the mediator: namely, a deviation strategy will tell each member of the coalition how to change its recommended action, but this would be done without knowledge of the recommendations to the other members of the coalition. In the more powerful *interim* variant, the members of the coalition will see the entire recommended action vector s_C^* and then can attempt to jointly change it to some s_C. Clearly, *ex ante* correlated equilibria are more abundant than *interim* equilibria. For example, it is easy to construct games where already 2-resilient *ex ante* CEs achieve higher payoffs than 2-resilient *interim* equilibria, and even games where the former correlated equilibria exist and the latter do not! This is true because the *ex ante* setting makes a strong restriction that coalitions cannot form after the mediator gave its recommended actions. Thus, unless stated otherwise, k-resilient CE will refer to the *interim* scenario.

Finally, we mention that one can naturally generalize the above notions to games with incomplete information, and also define (usual or computational) k-resilient Nash equilibria of extended games.

8.4.2 Removing the Mediator in Correlated Equilibrium

The natural question that can be asked is whether the mediator can be removed in the game theory setting, by simulating it with a multiparty computation. The motivation for this is clear, as the presence of the mediator significantly expands the number of equilibria in strategic form games; yet, the existence of such a mediator is a very strong and often unrealizable assumption.

Recall that in any correlated equilibrium x of a strategic game G (with imperfect information, for the sake of generality), the mediator samples a tuple of recommended action $(s_1, \ldots, s_n)$ according to the appropriate distribution based on the types of

[3] Informally, these equilibria prevent only deviations benefiting *all* members of the coalition, while resilient equilibria also prevent deviations benefiting even *a single* member.

the parties. This can be considered as the mediator computing some probabilistic function $(s_1, \ldots, s_n) = f(t_1, \ldots, t_n; r)$. We define the following extended game G^* of G by substituting the mediator with an MPC and ask whether the extended game is a (potentially computational) Nash equilibrium.

(i) In the preamble stage, the parties run an "appropriate" MPC protocol[4] to compute the profile $(s_1, \ldots, s_n)$. Some additional actions may be needed (see below).

(ii) Once the preamble stage is finished, party P_i holds a recommended action s_i, which it uses in the game G.

Meta-Theorem. Under "appropriate" conditions, the above strategies form a (potentially computational) Nash equilibrium of the extended game G^*, which achieves the same expected payoffs for all the parties as the corresponding correlated equilibrium of the original game G.[5]

As we discussed in Section 8.3, there are several differences between the MPC and the game theory settings. Not surprisingly, we will have to resolve these differences before validating the meta-theorem above. To make matters a bit more precise, we assume that

- x is an interim k-resilient correlated equilibrium[6] of G that we are trying to simulate. $k = 1$ (i.e., no collusions) will be the main special case.
- the MPC protocol computing x is cryptographically secure against coalitions of up to k malicious parties. This means the protocol is at least correct and private, and we will comment about its "output delivery" guarantees later.
- The objective is to achieve a (possibly computational) k-resilient Nash equilibrium x^* of G^* with the same payoffs as x.

Now the only indeterminant in the definition of G^* is to specify the behavior of the parties in case the MPC computation fails for some reason.

Using MPC with guaranteed output delivery. Recall that there exist MPC protocols (in various models) that guarantee output delivery for various resiliencies k. Namely, the malicious parties cannot cause the honest parties not to receive their output. The only thing they can do is to choose their inputs arbitrarily (where a special input $\perp$ indicates they refuse to provide the input). But since this is allowed in the mediated game as well, and k-resilient equilibrium ensures the irrationality of such behavior (assuming the remaining $(n - k)$ parties follow the protocol), we know the parties will contribute their proper types and our meta-theorem is validated.

Theorem 8.3 *If x is a k-resilient CE of G specified by a function f, and π is an MPC protocol (with output delivery) securely computing f against a coalition of up to k computationally unbounded/bounded parties, then running π in the preamble step (and using any strategy to select a move in case some misbehavior*

[4] Where the type of the protocol depends on the particular communication model and the capabilities of the parties.

[5] Note that the converse (every NE of G^* can be achieved by a CE of G) is true as well.

[6] As we already remarked, the techniques presented here easily extend to weaker coalitional equilibria concepts.

occurs) yields a k-resilient regular/computational NE of the extended game G^*, achieving the same payoffs as x.

Using fair MPC. In some instances (e.g., part i.*c* of Theorem 8.2) we cannot guarantee output delivery, but can still achieve fairness. Recall, this means that if at least one party P_i obtains its correct output s_i, then all parties do. However, it might be possible for misbehaving parties to cause everybody to abort or complete the protocol without an output.

In the case where the protocol terminates successfully, we are exactly in the same situation as if the protocol had output delivery, and the same analysis applies. In the other case, we assume that the protocol enables detection of faulty behavior and that it is observed that one of the parties (for simplicity, assume that it is P_n) deviated from the protocol. As the protocol is fair, the aborting deviation must have occurred before any party has any information about their output. The simplest solution is to restart the computation of x from scratch with all parties. The technical problem with this solution is that it effectively allows (a coalition containing) P_n to mount a denial of service attack, by misbehaving in every MPC iteration causing the preamble to run forever.

Instead, to make the extended game always finite, we follow a slightly more sophisticated punishment strategy. We restart the preamble without P_n, and let the $(n-1)$ remaining parties run a new MPC to compute the $(n-1)$-input function f' on the remaining parties' inputs and a default value $\perp$ for P_n: $f'(t_1, \ldots, t_{n-1}; r) = f(t_1, \ldots, t_{n-1}, \perp; r)$. Notice that in this new MPC n is replaced by $n-1$ and k replaced by $k-1$ (as P_n is faulty), which means that the ratio $\frac{k-1}{n-1} < \frac{k}{n}$, and, thus, f' can still be securely computed in the same setting as f. Also notice that P_n does not participate in this MPC, and will have to decide by itself (or with the help of other colluding members) which action to play in the actual game phase. In contrast, parties $P_1, \ldots, P_{n-1}$ are instructed to follow the recommendations they get when computing f', if f' completes. If not, then another party (say, P_{n-1}) must have aborted this MPC, in which case we reiterate the same process of excluding P_{n-1}, and so on. Thus, at some point we have that the process will end, as there is a finite number n of parties and we eliminate (at least) one in each iteration.

Next, we argue that the resulting strategy profile x^* forms a k-resilient Nash equilibrium of G^*. To see this, the fairness of the MPC step clearly ensures that the only effective misbehavior of a coalition of size $|C|$ is to declare invalid types $\perp$ for some of its members, while changing the real type for others. In this case, their reluctance to do so follows from the fact that such misbehavior is allowed in the mediated game as well. And since we assumed that the strategy profile x is a k-resilient correlated equilibrium of G, it is irrational for the members of the coalition to deviate in this way.

Using correct and private MPC: Case k = 1. We can see that the previous argument crucially relied on the fairness of the MPC. In contrast, if the MPC used only provides correctness and privacy, then the members of C might find their vector of outputs s'_C before the remaining parties, and can choose to abort the computation precisely when one of their expected payoffs $p'_i = \text{Exp}(u_i(s) \mid s_C = s'_C)$ when playing s'_C is less than the a priori value $p_i = \text{Exp}(u_i(s))$. In fact, even for two-players games of complete information, it is easy to construct a game G (e.g., the "Game of Chicken" in Chapter 1) where the above aborting strategy of the player who learns the output first will be strictly profitable for this player, even if the other player will play its "conditional" strategy suggested in the previous paragraph.

Nevertheless, we show that one can still use unfair (yet private and correct) MPC protocols in an important special case of the problem. Specifically, we concentrate on the usual coalition-free case $k = 1$, and also restrict our attention to games with complete information (i.e., no types). In this case, we show that if some party P_i deviates in the MPC stage (perhaps by aborting the computation based on its recommended action), the remaining parties P_{-i} can sufficiently punish P_i to discourage such an action. Let the *min–max* value v_i for party P_i denote the worst payoff that players P_{-i} can *jointly* enforce on P_i: namely, $v_i = \min_{z_{-i} \in \Delta(S_{-i})} \max_{s_i \in S_i} u_i(s_i, z_{-i})$.

Claim 8.4 *For any correlated equilibrium x of G, any P_i and any action s_i' for P_i in the support of x_i, $Exp(u_i(s) \mid s_i = s_i') \geq v_i$.*

PROOF Notice that since x is a CE, s_i' is the best response of P_i to the profile $\bar{x}_{-i}$ defined as x_{-i} conditioned on $s_i = s_i'$. Thus, the payoff P_i gets in this case is what others would force on P_i by playing $\bar{x}_{-i}$, which is at least as large as what others could have selected by choosing the *worst* profile z_{-i}. □

Now, in case P_i would (unfairly) abort the MPC step, we will instruct the other parties P_{-i} to punish P_i to its min–max value v_i. More specifically, parties P_{-i} should play the correlated strategy z_{-i}, which would force P_i into getting at most v_i. Notice, however, since this strategy is correlated, they would need to run another MPC protocol to implement z_{-i},[7] By the above claim, *irrespective of the recommendation s_i* that P_i learned, the corresponding payoff of P_i can only go down by aborting the MPC. Therefore, it is in P_i's interests not to abort the computation after learning s_i.

We notice that the above punishment strategy does not straightforwardly generalize to more advanced settings. For example, in case of coalitions it could be that the min–max punishment for P_1 tremendously benefits another colluding party P_2 (who poses as honest and instructs P_1 to abort the computation to get high benefits for itself). Also, in the case of incomplete information, it is not clear how to even define the min–max punishment, since the parties do not even know the precise utility of P_i!

8.4.3 Stronger Equilibria

So far we talked only about plain Nash equilibria of the extended game G^*. As we already commented briefly, Nash equilibria are usually too weak to capture extensive-form games. Therefore, an interesting (and still developing!) direction in recent research is to ensure much stronger and more stable equilibria that would simulate correlated equilibria of the original game.

Eliminating empty threats. One weakness of the Nash equilibrium is that it allows for the so-called empty threats. Consider, for example, the min–max punishment strategy

[7] Notice that there are no dishonest parties left, so any MPC protocol for the honest-but-curious case would work.

used above. In some games, punishing a misbehaving party to its min–max value is actually very damaging for the punishers as well. Thus, the threat to punish the misbehaving party to the min–max value is not credible in such cases, despite being an NE. In this case, eliminating such an empty threat could be done by modifying the punishment strategy to playing the worst Nash equilibrium of G for P_i (in terms of P_i's payoff) when P_i is caught cheating. Unlike the min–max punishment, this is no longer an empty threat because it is an equilibrium of G. However, it does limit (although slightly) the class of correlated equilibria one can simulate, as one can achieve only a payoff vector which is at least as large as the worst Nash equilibrium for each player. In addition, formally defining such so-called subgame-perfect or sequential equilibria has not yet been done in the computational setting, where most MPC protocols are analyzed.

Ex ante correlated equilibria. So far we only talked about simulating interim correlated equilibria, where colluding parties can base their actions after seeing all their recommendations. Another interesting direction is that of simulating *ex ante* correlated equilibria, where colluding parties can only communicate prior to contacting the mediator. To implement this physical restriction in real life, we need to design *collusion-free protocols*, where one has to ensure that no subliminal communication (a.k.a. *steganography*) is possible. This is a very difficult problem. Indeed, most cryptographic protocols need randomness (or entropy), and it is known that entropy almost always implies steganography. In fact, it turns out that, in order to build such protocols, one needs some physical assumptions in the real model as well. On a positive side, it is known that envelopes (and a broadcast channel) are enough for building a class of collusion-free protocols sufficient to simulate *ex ante* correlated equilibria without the mediator.

Iterated deletion of weakly dominated strategies. In Section 8.5.2 we will study a pretty general class of "function evaluation games," where the objective is to achieve Nash equilibrium that survives so-called *iterated deletion of weakly dominated strategies.*

Strategic and privacy equivalence. The strongest recent results regarding removing the mediator is to ensure (polynomially efficient) "real-life" simulation that guarantees an extremely strong property called *strategic and privacy equivalence*. Intuitively, it implies that our simulation gives exactly the same power in the real model as in the ideal model. As such, it precisely preserves all different types of equilibria of the original game (e.g., without introducing *new*, unexpected equilibria in the extended game, which we allowed so far), does not require the knowledge of the utility functions or an a priori-type distribution (which most of the other results above do), does not give any extra power to arbitrary coalitions, preserves privacy of the players types as much as in the ideal model, and has other attractive properties. Not surprisingly, strategic and privacy equivalence is very difficult to achieve, and requires some physical assumptions in the real model as well. The best known result is an extension of the MPC result ii.*c* in Theorem 8.2, and shows how to implement strategic and privacy equivalence assuming a broadcast channel, envelopes and a ballot box.

To summarize, MPC techniques are promising in replacing the mediator by cheap talk in a variety of situations. However, more work has to be done in trying to achieve stronger kinds of equilibria using weaker assumptions.

8.5 Game Theoretic Influences on Cryptography

The influence of Game Theory on Multiparty Computation has exemplified itself in modeling multiparty computation with a game-theoretic flavor by introducing *rational* parties with some natural utility functions into the computation. Once this is done, two main areas of investigation are as follows. First, we try to characterize the class of functions where it is in the parties' *selfish interest* to report their true inputs to the computation. We call such functions *noncooperatively computable* (NCC). Second, we can ask to what extent the *existing* MPC protocols (used to compute NCC functions) form an appropriate equilibrium for the extended game, where we remove the trusted mediator by cheap talk computing the same function. As we see, the answer will depend on the strength of the equilibrium we desire (and, of course, on the natural utilities we assign to the "function evaluation game" defined below). Furthermore, issues arising in the MPC "honest vs. malicious" setting also hold in the Game Theory "rational" setting, further providing a synergy between these two fields.

8.5.1 Noncooperatively Computable Functions

In order to "rationalize" the process of securely evaluating a given function f, we first need to define an appropriate *function evaluation game*. For concreteness, we concentrate on single-output functions $f(t_1, \ldots, t_n)$, although the results easily generalize to the n-output case. We also assume that each input t_i matters (i.e., for some t_{-i} the value of f is not yet determined without t_i).

Function evaluation game. We assume that the parties' types t_i are their inputs to f (which are selected according to some probability distribution D having full support). The action of each party P_i is its guess about the output s^* of f. The key question, however, is how to define the utilities of the parties. Now, there are several natural cryptographic considerations that might weight into the definition of party P_i's utility.

- *Correctness.* Each P_i wishes to compute f correctly.
- *Exclusivity.* Each P_i prefers others parties P_j not to learn the value of f correctly.
- *Privacy.* Each P_i wishes to leak as little as possible about its input t_i to the other parties.
- *Voyeurism.* Each P_i wishes to learn as much as possible about the other parties' inputs.

Not surprisingly, one can have many different definitions for a cryptographically motivated utility function of party P_i. In turn, different definitions would lead to different results. For concreteness, we will restrict ourselves to one of the simplest and, arguably, most natural choices. Specifically, we will consider only correctness and exclusivity, and value correctness over exclusivity. However, other choices might also be interesting in various situations, so our choice here is certainly with a loss of generality.

A bit more formally, recall that the utility u_i of party P_i depends on the true type vector t of all the parties, and the parties' actions $s_1, \ldots, s_n$. Notice that the true type vector t determines the correct function value $s^* = f(t)$, and parties' actions determine the boolean vector correct $= (\text{correct}_1, \ldots, \text{correct}_n)$, where $\text{correct}_i = 1$ if an only if $s_i = s^*$. In our specific choice of the utility function, we will assume that the utilities of each party depend only on the boolean vector correct: namely, which of the parties learned the output and which did not. Therefore, we will write $u_i(\text{correct})$ to denote the utility of party P_i. Now, rather than assigning somewhat arbitrary numbers to capture correctness and exclusivity, we state only the minimal constraints that imply these properties. Then, the correctness constraint states that $u_i(\text{correct}) > u_i(\text{correct}')$, whenever $\text{correct}_i = 1$ and $\text{correct}'_i = 0$. Similarly, exclusivity constraint states that if (a) $\text{correct}_i = \text{correct}'_i$, (b) for all $j \neq i$ we have $\text{correct}_j \leq \text{correct}'_j$, while (c) for some j actually $\text{correct}_j = 0$ and $\text{correct}'_j = 1$, then $u_i(\text{correct}) > u_i(\text{correct}')$. Namely, provided P_i has the same success in learning the output, it prefers as few parties as possible to be successful.

Noncooperatively computable functions. Having defined the function evaluation game, we can now ask what are the equilibria of this game. In this case, Nash equilibria are not very interesting, since parties typically have too little information to be successful with any nontrivial probability. On the other hand, it is very interesting to study correlated equilibria of this game. Namely, parties give their inputs t_i to the mediator M, who then recommends an action s_i^* for each party. Given that each party is trying to compute the value of the function f, it is natural to consider "canonical" mediator strategy: namely, that of evaluating the function f on the reported type vector t, and simply recommending each party to "guess" the resulting function value $s^* = f(t)$. Now, we can ask the question of characterizing the class of functions f for which this canonical strategy is indeed a correlated equilibrium of the function evaluation game. To make this precise, though, we also need to define the actions of the mediator if some party gives a wrong type to the mediator. Although several options are possible, here we will assume that the mediator will send an error message to all the parties and let them decide by themselves what to play.

Definition 8.5 We say that a function f is *noncooperatively computable* (NCC) with respect to utility functions $\{u_i\}$ (and a specific input distribution D) if the above canonical mediated strategy is a correlated equilibrium of the function evaluation game. Namely, it is in the parties' selfish interest to honestly report their true inputs to the mediator.

We illustrate this definition by giving two classes of functions that are never NCC. Let us say that a function f is *dominated* if there exists an index i and an input t_i, which determine the value of f irrespective of the other inputs t_{-i}. Clearly, for such an input t_i it is not in the interest of P_i to submit t_i to the mediator, as P_i is assured of $\text{correct}_i = 1$ even without the help of M, while every other party is not (for at least some of its inputs). Thus, dominated functions cannot be NCC. For another example, a function f is *reversible* if for some index i and some input t_i, there exists another input t'_i and a function g, such that (a) for all other parties' inputs t_{-i} we have $g(f(t'_i, t_{-i}), t_i) = f(t_i, t_{-i})$, and (b) for some other parties' inputs t_{-i} we have $f(t'_i, t_{-i}) \neq f(t_i, t_{-i})$. Namely, property (a) states that there is no risk in terms of correctness for P_i to report t'_i instead of t_i, while property (b) states that at least sometimes P_i will be rewarded by higher exclusivity. A simple example of such (boolean) function is the parity function: negating one's input always negates the outcome, but still in a manner easily correctable by negating the output back. Clearly, reversible functions are also not NCC.

In general, depending on the exact utilities and the input distribution D, other functions might also be non-NCC. However, if we assume that the risk of losing correctness is *always* too great to be tempted by higher exclusivity, it turns out that these two classes are the *only* non-NCC functions. (And, thus, most functions, like majority, are NCC.) More precisely, assume that the utilities and the input distribution D are such that for all vectors correct, correct$'$, correct$''$ satisfying $\text{correct}_i = \text{correct}'_i = 1$, $\text{correct}''_i = 0$, we have $u_i(\text{correct}) > (1-\epsilon)u_i(\text{correct}') + \epsilon u_i(\text{correct}'')$, where ϵ is the smallest probability in D. Namely, if by deviating from the canonical strategy there is even a minuscule chance of P_i not learning the value of f correctly, this loss will always exceed any potential gain caused by many other parties not learning the outcome as well. In this case we can show the following:

Theorem 8.6 *Under the above assumption, a function f is NCC if and only if it is not dominated and not reversible.*[8]

Collusions. So far we concentrated on the case of no collusions; i.e., $k = 1$. However, one can also define (a much smaller class of) *k-Non-Cooperatively Computable* (*k*-NCC) functions, for which no coalition of up to k parties has any incentive to deviate from the canonical strategy of reporting their true types. One can also characterize k-NCC functions under appropriate assumptions regarding the utilities and the input distribution D.

8.5.2 Rational Multiparty Computation

Assume that a given function f is k-NCC, so it is in the parties' own interest to contribute their inputs in the ideal model. We now ask the same question as in Section 8.4: can we replace the mediator computing f by a corresponding MPC protocol for f? Notice, by doing so the parties effectively run the cryptographic MPC protocol for computing f. Thus, a positive answer would imply that a given MPC protocol π securely computes f not only from a cryptographic point of view but also from a game-theoretic, rational point of view! Fortunately, since the function evaluation game is just a particular game, Theorem 8.3 immediately implies

Theorem 8.7 *If f is a k-NCC function (w.r.t. to some utilities and input distribution) and π is an MPC protocol securely computing f against a coalition of up to k computationally unbounded/bounded parties, then π is a k-resilient regular/computational Nash equilibrium for computing f in the corresponding extended game.*

From a positive perspective, this result shows that for the goal of achieving just a Nash equilibrium, current MPC protocols can be explained in rational terms, as long

[8] In fact, under our assumption that each party's input matters in some cases and D has full support, it is easy to see that every dominated function is also reversible.

as the parties are willing to compute f in the ideal model. From a negative perspective, the latter constraint nontrivially limits the class of functions f, which can be rationally explained, and it is an interesting open problem how to rationalize MPC even for non-NCC functions, for which the cryptographic definition still makes perfect sense.

Stronger equilibria. As another drawback, we already mentioned that the notion of Nash equilibrium is really too weak to capture the rationality of extensive-form processes, such as multiparty computation protocols. Thus, an important direction is to try achieving stronger kinds of equilibria explaining current MPC protocols, or, alternatively, design robust enough MPC protocols which would achieve such equilibria. In Section 8.4.3, we briefly touched on several *general* results in this direction (which clearly still apply to the special case of the function evaluation games). Here we will instead concentrate on the *specifics* of computing the function under the correctness and exclusivity preferences defined in the previous section, and will study a specific refinement of the Nash equilibrium natural for these utility functions.

To motivate our choice, let us see a particular problem with current MPC protocols. Recall, such protocols typically consist of three stages; in the first two stages the parties enter their inputs and compute the secret-sharing of the output of f, while the last stage consists of the opening of the appropriate output shares. Now we claim that the strategy of not sending out the output shares is always at least as good as, and *sometimes better* than, the strategy of sending the output shares. Indeed, consider any party P_i. The correctness of output recovery for P_i is not affected by whether or not P_i sent his own share, irrespective of the behavior of the other parties. Yet, not sending the share to others might, in some cases, prevent others from reconstructing their outputs, resulting in higher exclusivity for P_i. True, *along the Nash equilibrium path* of Theorem 8.7, such cases where the share of P_i was critical did not exhibit themselves. Still, in reality it seems that there is no incentive for any party to send out their shares, since this is never better, and *sometimes worse* than not sending the shares. This motivates the following definition.

Definition 8.8 We say that a strategy $s \in S_i$ is *weakly dominated* by $s' \in S_i$ with respect to S_{-i} if (a) there exists $s_{-i} \in S_{-i}$ such that $u_i(s, s_{-i}) < u_i(s', s_{-i})$ and (b) for all strategies $s'_{-i} \in S_{-i}$ we have that $u_i(s, s'_{-i}) \leq u_i(s', s'_{-i})$. We define *iterated deletion of weakly dominated strategies* (IDoWDS) as the following process. Let $\mathbf{DOM}_i(S_1, \ldots, S_n)$ denote the set of strategies in S_i that are weakly dominated with respect to S_{-i}. Let $S_i^0 = S_i$ and for $j \geq 1$ define S_i^j inductively as $S_i^j = S_i^{j-1} \backslash \mathbf{DOM}_i(S_1^{j-1}, \ldots, S_n^{j-1})$ and let $S_i^\infty = \bigcap_{j\geq 1} S_i^j$. Finally, we say that a Nash equilibrium $(x_1, \ldots, x_n)$ *survives IDoWDS*, if each x_i is fully supported within S_i^∞.

k-resilient Nash equilibria surviving IDoWDS are defined similarly.[9]

Now, the above discussion implies that the k-resilient Nash equilibrium from Theorem 8.7 does not survive IDoWDS. On a positive side, the only reason for that was that

[9] We notice that, in general, it matters in which order 1 removes the weakly dominated strategies. The specific order chosen above seems natural, however, and will not affect the results we present below.

the basic secret-sharing scheme where the parties are instructed to blindly open their shares does not survive IDoWDS. It turns out that the moment we fix the secret-sharing scheme to survive IDoWDS, the resulting Nash equilibrium for the function evaluation game will survive IDoWDS too, and Theorem 8.7 can be extended to Nash equilibrium surviving IDoWDS. Therefore, we will treat only the latter, more concise problem. We remark, however, that although a Nash equilibrium surviving IDoWDS is better than plain Nash equilibrium, it is still a rather weak concept. For example, it still allows for "empty threats," and has other undesirable properties. Thus, stronger equilibria are still very desirable to achieve.

Rational secret-sharing. Recall, in the (k, n)-secret-sharing problem the parties are given (random valid) shares $z_1, \ldots, z_n$ of some secret z, such that any k shares leak no information about z, while any $k+1$ or more shares reveal z. We can define the secret-sharing game, where the objective of each party is to guess the value of z, and where we assume that parties' utilities satisfy the correctness and exclusivity constraints defined earlier. In the extended game corresponding to the secret-sharing game, the parties can perform some computation before guessing the value of the secret. For our communication model, we assume that it is strong enough to perform generic multiparty computation, since this will be the case in the application to the function evaluation game. (On the other hand, we will need only MPC with correctness and privacy, and not necessarily fairness.) In addition, if not already present, we also assume the existence of a *simultaneous broadcast channel*, where at each round all parties can simultaneously announce some message, after which they atomically receive the messages of all the other parties. Our goal is to build a preamble protocol for which the outcome of all the parties learning the secret z will be a k-resilient Nash equilibrium for the extended game that survives IDoWDS.

As we observed already, the natural 1-round preamble protocol where each party is supposed to simply broadcast its share does not survive IDoWDS. In fact, a simple backward induction argument shows that any preamble protocol having an a priori fixed number of simultaneous broadcast rounds (and no other physical assumptions, such as envelopes and ballot boxes) cannot enable the parties to rationally learn the secret and survive IDoWDS. Luckily, it turns out that we can have *probabilistic* protocols with no fixed upper bound on the number of rounds, but which have a constant *expected* number of rounds until each party learns the secret. We sketch the simplest such protocol below. W.l.o.g. we assume that the domain of the secret-sharing scheme is large enough to deter random guessing of z, and also includes a special value denoted $\perp$, such that z is guaranteed to be different from $\perp$.

Let $\alpha \in (0, 1)$ be a number specified shortly. At each iteration $r \geq 1$, the parties do the following two steps:

(i) Run an MPC protocol on inputs z_i which computes the following probabilistic functionality. With probability α, compute fresh and random (k, n)-secret-sharing $z'_1, \ldots, z'_n$ of z, where party P_i learns z'_i. Otherwise, with probability $1-\alpha$ compute a random (k, n)-secret-sharing $z'_1, \ldots, z'_n$ of $\perp$, where party P_i learns z'_i.[10]

[10] This protocol is typically pretty efficient for the popular Shamir's secret-sharing scheme.

(ii) All parties P_i simultaneously broadcast z'_i to other parties.
(iii) If either the MPC protocol fails for even one party, or even one party fails to broadcast the value z'_i, all parties are instructed to abort.
(iv) Each party tries to recover some value z' from the shares received from the other parties. If the recovery fails, or at least one share is inconsistent with the final value z', the party aborts the preamble. Otherwise, if $z' = \bot$ the parties proceed to the next iteration, while in case $z' \neq \bot$ the parties stop the preamble and output z' as their guess for z.

Notice, by the privacy of the MPC step, no coalition C of up to k parties knows if the value z' is equal to z or $\bot$. Thus, in case this coalition chooses not to broadcast their shares, they will learn only the value z (while punishing all the other parties) with probability α, and not learn the value z forever with probability $1 - \alpha$. Thus, if α is small enough (depending on the particular utilities), the risk of not learning the secret will outweigh the gain of achieving higher exclusivity. Also, it is easy to see that no strategy of the above protocol is weakly dominated by another strategy, so the above Nash equilibrium survives IDoWDS.

The above protocol works for *any* k. However, it runs in expected $O(1/\alpha)$ iterations, which is constant, but depends on the specific utilities of the parties (and the value k). Somewhat more sophisticated protocols are known to work for not too large k, but have expected number of iterations which is independent of the utilities. These results are summarized without further details below.

Theorem 8.9 *Assume that the parties utilities satisfy correctness over exclusivity properties for the (k, n)-secret-sharing game. Then there exists k-resilient Nash equilibria for the extended game that survive IDoWDS and run in expected constant number of iterations r, where*

- *$k < n$, but r depends on the specific utilities.*
- *$k < n/2$, r is fixed, but the parties still need to know a certain parameter depending on the specific utilities.*
- *$k < n/3$, r is fixed, and no other information about the utilities is needed.*

8.6 Conclusions

As we have seen, the settings of MPC in cryptography and correlated equilibrium in game theory have many similarities, as well as many differences. Existing results so far started to explore these connections, but much work remains to be done. For example, can we use some flavors of MPC to remove the mediator, while achieving very strong types of Nash equilibria, but with more realistic physical and other setup assumptions? Or, can we use game theory to "rationalize" MPC protocols for non-NCC functions (such as parity), or to explain other popular cryptographic tasks such as commitment or zero-knowledge proofs? In addition, so far "rationalizing" MPC using game theory resulted only in more sophisticated protocols. Are there natural instances where assuming rationality will simplify the design of cryptographic tasks?

8.7 Notes

The multiparty computation problem (Section 8.1) was introduced in Yao (1982). The basic definitional and construction approaches were introduced by Goldreich et al. (1987), in particular the paradigm of a real/ideal execution. In Section 8.1.1 we follow the definitional framework of Canetti (2000), which is based on the works of Goldwasser and Levin (1990), Micali and Rogaway (1991), and Beaver (1991). The results mentioned in Theorem 8.2 are from the following: parts i.*a* and i.*b* from Goldreich et al. (1987), part i.*c* from Lepinski et al. (2004), part ii.*a* from Ben-Or et al. (1988) and Chaum et al. (1988), part ii.*b* from Rabin and Ben-Or (1989) and Beaver (1991), part ii.*c* from Izmalkov et al. (2005). The secret-Sharing protocol presented is Shamir's Secret-Sharing (1979). The notion of indistinguishability was introduced in Goldwasser and Micali (1984). For a more formal and in-depth discussion on multiparty computations see Goldreich (2004).

In Section 8.2 we present the classical results of Nash (1951) and Aumann (1974) for Nash and correlated equilibrium (respectively). The extension of correlated equilibrium to games with incomplete information is due to Forges (1986). The notion of extended games is from Barany (1992). For a broader game theory background, see the book by Osborne and Rubinstein (1999).

The comparison discussion between Game Theory and Cryptography, as it appears in Section 8.3, was initiated by Dodis et al. (2000) and later expanded by Feigebaum and Shenker (2002); yet here we further expand on these points. The related discussion was also carried out in many other works (Abraham et al., 2006; Barany, 1992; Lepinski et al., 2004; Izmalkov et al., 2005).

The notion of computational equilibrium which appears in Section 8.4.1 was introduced in Dodis et al. (2000). The work of Urbano and Vila (2002, 2004) also deals with the computational model, but does not explicitly define this notion. The importance of tolerating collusions was first addressed in our setting by Feigenbaum and Shanker (2002). For the k-resilient equilibrium we chose the formulation of Abraham et al. (2006), as we felt it best suited our presentation. For other related formulations, see the references in Abraham et al. (2006), and also a recent work of Lysyanskaya and Triandopoulos (2006). The results which appear in Section 8.4.2 appear in the following. Theorem 8.3 follows by combining results such as Dodis et al. (2000), Barany (1992), Ben-Porath (1998), Gerardi (2004), Urbano and Vila (2002, 2004) and Abraham et al. (2006). The result for using fair MPC appears in Lepinski et al. (2004). The introduction of a min-max punishment to deal with unfair MPC in the attempt to remove the mediator appears in Dodis et al. (2000). For some efficiency improvements to the protocol of Dodis et al. (2000), see the works of Teague (2004) and Attalah et al. (2006). The results which appear in Section 8.4.2 appear in the following. The worst equilibrium punishment technique was first applied to unmediated games by Ben-Porath (1998). The notion of collusion free protocols which is used to implement ex ante equilibria is from the work of Lepinski et al. (2005). The result of achieving strategic and privacy equivalence under physical assumptions is from Izmalkov et al. (2005).

The noncooperative computation formulation and some discussion used in Section 8.5.1 are introduced (for $k = 1$) by Shoham and Tennenholtz (2005), and expanded by McGrew et al. (2003). Theorem 8.6 is also from Shoham and Tennenholtz (2005), while the formulation of "correctness followed by exclusivity" utilities is from Halpern and Teague (2004). The results in Section 8.5.2 appear as follows: the introduction of rational secret-sharing surviving IDowDS and the impossibility result of reaching it in a fixed number of rounds are from Halpern and Teague (2004). The protocol for rational secret-sharing we present appears in Abraham et al. (2006) and (for $k = 1$) by Gordon and Katz (2006). Yet, a more complicated and less general solution along these lines appeared first (for $k = 1$) in Halpern and Teague (2004). Theorem 8.9 is from Abraham et al. (2006). For a different, but related "mixed MPC" model, see Lysyanskaya and Triandopoulos (2006).

Acknowledgments

We thank the following people for extensive discussions, explanations, and general advice: Ittai Abraham, Ran Canetti, Hugo Krawczyk, Matt Lepinski, Anna Lysyanskaya, Silvio Micali, abhi shelat, and Nikos Triandopoulos, and give special thanks to our coauthor Shai Halevi.

Bibliography

I. Abraham, D. Dolev, R. Gonen, and J. Halpern. Distributed computing meets game theory: Robust mechanisms for rational secret-sharing and multiparty computation. In *Princ. of Distributed Computing '06*, pp. 53–62. ACM Press, 2006.

M. Atallah, M. Blanton, K. Frikken, and J. Li. Efficient Correlated Action Selection. In *Financial Crypt.*, LNCS 4107:296–310. Springer, 2006.

R. Aumann. Subjectivity and correlation in randomized strategies. *J. Math. Econ.*, 1:67–96, 1974.

I. Barany. Fair Distribution Protocols or How the Players Replace Fortune. *Math. Oper. Res.*, 17(2):327–341, 1992.

D. Beaver. Secure multiparty protocols and zero-knowledge proof systems tolerating a faulty minority. *J. Cryptology*, 4(2):75–122, 1991.

M. Ben-Or, S. Goldwasser, and A. Wigderson. Completeness theorems for noncryptographic fault-tolerant distributed Computations. In *Proc. 20th Symp. on Theory of Computing* 88, pp. 1–10.

E. Ben-Porath. Correlation without mediation: Expanding the set of equilibrium outcomes by "cheap" pre-play procedures. *J. Econ. Theo.*, 80(1):108–122, 1998.

R. Canetti. Security and composition of multiparty cryptographic protocols. *J. Cryptology*, 13(1):143–202, 2000. Available at eprint.iacr.org/1998/018.

D. Chaum, C. Crepeau, and I. Damgard. Multiparty unconditionally secure protocols. In *Proc. 20th Symp. on Theory of Computing* 88, pp. 11–19.

Y. Dodis, S. Halevi, and T. Rabin. A cryptographic solution to a game theoretic problem. In *Crypto 2000*, pp. 112–130, 2000. LNCS No. 1880.

F.M. Forges. An approach to communication equilibria. *Econometrica*, 54(6):1375–85, 1986.

J. Feigenbaum and S. Shenker. Distributed algorithmic mechanism design: Recent results and future directions. In *Proc. 6th Intl. Wkshp. Disc. Algo. Meth. Mobile Comp. Comm.*, pp. 1–13. ACM Press, 2002.

D. Gerardi. Unmediated communication in games with complete and incomplete information. *J. Econ. Theo.*, 114:104,131, 2004.

O. Goldreich. *Foundations of Cryptography: Volume 2*. Cambridge University Press, 2004. Preliminary version http://philby.ucsd.edu/cryptolib.html/.

O. Goldreich, S. Micali, and A. Wigderson. How to play any mental game. In *Proc. 19th STOC*, pp. 218–229. ACM, 1987.

S. Goldwasser and L. Levin. Fair computation of general functions in presence of immoral majority. In *Crypto '90*, LNCS 537:77–93.

S. Goldwasser and S. Micali. Probabilistic encryption. *J. Comp. Syst. Sci.*, 28(2):270–299, April 1984.

S.D. Gordon and J. Katz. Rational secret-sharing, revisited. In *5th Conf. Sec. Crypto. Networks*, 2006. Updated version available at http://eprint.iacr.org/2006/142.

J. Halpern and V. Teague. Rational secret-sharing and multiparty computation. In *Proc. of 36th STOC*, pp. 623–632. ACM Press, 2004.

S. Izmalkov, M. Lepinski, and S. Micali. Rational secure computation and ideal mechanism design. In *Proc. of 46th Fdns. of Computer Science*, pp. 585–595, 2005.

M. Lepinksi, S. Micali, and A. Shelat. Collusion-free protocols. In *Proc. 37th Ann. ACM Symp. Theo. Comp.*, pp. 543–552. ACM Press, 2005.

M. Lepinski, S. Micali, C. Peikert, and A. Shelat. Completely fair sfe and coalition-safe cheap talk. In *PODC '04: Proc. 23rd Annual ACM Symp. Princ. Dist. Comp.*, pp. 1–10. ACM Press, 2004.

A. Lysyanskaya and N. Triandopoulos. Rationality and adversarial Behavior in Multi-Party Computation. In *Crypto 2006*, 2006.

R. McGrew, R. Porter, and Y. Shoham. Towards a general theory of non-cooperative computation (extended abstract). In *Theo. Aspects of Rationality and Knowledge IX*, 2003.

S. Micali and P. Rogaway. Secure computation. In *Crypto '91*, LNCS 576:392–404, 1991.

J. Nash. Non-cooperative games. *Annals of Math.*, 54:286–295, 1951.

M.J. Osborne and A. Rubinstein. *A Course in Game Theory*. MIT Press, 1999.

T. Rabin and M. Ben-Or. Verifiable secret-sharing and multiparty protocols with honest majority. In *Proc. 21st Symp. on Theory of Computing*, pp. 73–85. ACM, 1989.

A. Shamir. How to share a secret. *Comm. ACM*, 22:612–613, 1979.

Y. Shoham and M. Tennenholtz. Non-cooperative computation: Boolean functions with correctness and exclusivity. *Theor. Comput. Sci.*, 343(1–2):97–113, 2005.

V. Teague. Selecting correlated random actions. In *Financial Cryptography*, LNCS 3110:181–195. Springer, 2004.

A. Urbano and J.E. Vila. Computational complexity and communication: Coordination in two-player games. *Econometrica*, 70(5):1893–1927, 2002.

A. Urbano and J.E. Vila. Computationally restricted unmediated talk under incomplete information. *Econ. Theory*, 23:283–320, 2004.

A.C. Yao. Protocols for secure computations. In *Proc. Fdns. of Computer Science 82*, pp. 160–164, IEEE, 1982.

PART TWO

Algorithmic Mechanism Design

CHAPTER 9

Introduction to Mechanism Design (for Computer Scientists)

Noam Nisan

Abstract

We give an introduction to the micro-economic field of Mechanism Design slightly biased toward a computer-scientist's point of view.

9.1 Introduction

Mechanism Design is a subfield of economic theory that is rather unique within economics in having an engineering perspective. It is interested in designing economic mechanisms, just like computer scientists are interested in designing algorithms, protocols, or systems. It is best to view the goals of the designed mechanisms in the very abstract terms of *social choice*. A social choice is simply an aggregation of the preferences of the different participants toward a single joint decision. *Mechanism Design* attempts implementing desired social choices in a strategic setting – assuming that the different members of society each act *rationally* in a game theoretic sense. Such strategic design is necessary since usually the preferences of the participants are private.

This high-level abstraction of aggregation of preferences may be seen as a common generalization of a multitude of scenarios in economics as well as in other social settings such as political science. Here are some basic classic examples:

- **Elections:** In political elections each voter has his own preferences between the different candidates, and the outcome of the elections is a single social choice.
- **Markets:** Classical economic theory usually assumes the existence and functioning of a "perfect market." In reality, of course, we have only interactions between people, governed by some protocols. Each participant in such an interaction has his own preferences, but the outcome is a single social choice: the reallocation of goods and money.
- **Auctions:** Generally speaking, the more buyers and sellers there are in a market, the more the situation becomes close to the perfect market scenario. An extreme opposite

case is where there is only a single seller – an auction. The auction rules define the social choice: the identity of the winner.

- **Government policy:** Governments routinely have to make decisions that affect a multitude of people in different ways: Should a certain bridge be built? How much pollution should we allow? How should we regulate some sector? Clearly each citizen has a different set of preferences but a single social choice is made by the government.

As the influence of the Internet grew, it became clear that many scenarios happening there can also be viewed as instances of social choice in strategic settings. The main new ingredient found in the Internet is that it is owned and operated by different parties with different goals and preferences. These preferences, and the behavior they induce, must then be taken into account by every protocol in such an environment. The protocol should thus be viewed as taking the preferences of the different participants and aggregating them into a social choice: the outcome of the run of the protocol.

Conceptually, one can look at two different types of motivations: those that use economics to solve computer science issues and those that use computer science to solve economic issues:

- **Economics for CS:** Consider your favorite algorithmic challenge in a computer network environment: routing of messages, scheduling of tasks, allocation of memory, etc. When running in an environment with multiple owners of resources or requests, this algorithm must take into account the different preferences of the different owners. The algorithm should function well assuming strategic selfish behavior of each participant. Thus we desire a Mechanism Design approach for a multitude of algorithmic challenges – leading to a field that has been termed *Algorithmic Mechanism Design*.
- **CS for economics:** Consider your favorite economic interaction: some type of market, an auction, a supply chain, etc. As the Internet becomes ubiquitous, this interaction will often be implemented over some computerized platform. Such an implementation enables unprecedented sophistication and complexity, handled by hyperrationally designed software. Designing these is often termed *Electronic Market Design*.

Thus, both Algorithmic Mechanism Design and Electronic Market Design can be based upon the field of Mechanism Design applied in complex algorithmic settings.

This chapter provides an introduction to classical Mechanism Design, intended for computer scientists. While the presentation is not very different from the standard economic approach, it is somewhat biased toward a worst-case (non-Bayesian) point of view common in computer science.

Section 9.2 starts with the general formulation of the social choice problem, points out the basic difficulties formulated by Arrow's famous impossibility results, and deduces the impossibility of a general strategic treatment, i.e. of Mechanism Design in the general setting. Section 9.3 then considers the important special case where "money" exists, and describes a very general positive result, the incentive-compatible Vickrey–Clarke–Grove mechanism. Section 9.4 puts everything in a wider formal context of implementation in dominant strategies. Section 9.5 provides several characterizations of dominant strategy mechanisms. All the sections up to this point have considered dominant strategies, but the prevailing economic point of view is a Bayesian one that assumes a priori known distributions over private information. Section 9.6 introduces this setting and the notion of Bayesian-Nash equilibrium that fits it. All the treatment in this chapter is in the very basic "private value" model, and Section 9.7 shortly points out several extensions to the model. Finally, Section 9.8 provides bibliographic notes and references.

9.2 Social Choice

This section starts with the general social choice problem and continues with the strategic approach to it. The main message conveyed is that there are unavoidable underlying difficulties. We phrase things in the commonly used terms of political elections, but the reader should keep in mind that the issues are abstract and apply to general social choice.

9.2.1 Condorcet's Paradox

Consider an election with two candidates, where each voter has a preference for one of them. If society needs to jointly choose one of the candidates, intuitively it is clear that taking a *majority vote* would be a good idea. But what happens if there are three candidates? In 1785, The Marquis de Condorcet pointed out that the natural application of majority is problematic: consider three candidates – a, b, and c – and three voters with the following preferences:

(i) $a \succ_1 b \succ_1 c$
(ii) $b \succ_2 c \succ_2 a$
(iii) $c \succ_3 a \succ_3 b$

(The notation $a \succ_i b$ means that voter i prefers candidate a to candidate b.) Now, notice that a majority of voters (1 and 3) prefer candidate a to candidate b. Similarly, a majority (1 and 2) prefers b to c, and, finally, a majority (2 and 3) prefers c to a. The joint majority choice is thus $a \succ b \succ c \succ a$ which is not consistent. In particular for any candidate that is jointly chosen, there will be a majority of voters who would want to change the chosen outcome.

This immediately tells us that in general a social choice cannot be taken simply by the natural system of taking a majority vote. Whenever there are more than two alternatives, we must design some more complex "voting method" to undertake a social choice.

9.2.2 Voting Methods

A large number of different *voting methods* – ways of determining the outcome of such multicandidate elections – have been suggested. Two of the simpler ones are *plurality* (the candidate that was placed first by the largest number of voters wins) and Borda count (each candidate among the n candidates gets $n - i$ points for every voter who ranked him in place i, and the candidate with most points wins). Each of the suggested voting methods has some "nice" properties but also some problematic ones.

One of the main difficulties encountered by voting methods is that they may encourage *strategic voting*. Suppose that a certain voter's preferences are $a \succ_i b \succ_i c$, but he knows that candidate a will not win (as other voters hate him). Such a voter may be motivated to strategically vote for b instead of a, so that b is chosen which he prefers to c. Such strategic voting is problematic as it is not transparent, depends closely on the votes of the other voters, and the interaction of many strategic voters is complex. The main result of this section is the Gibbard–Satterthwaite theorem that states that this strategic vulnerability is unavoidable. We will prove the theorem as a corollary of Arrow's impossibility theorem that highlights the general impossibility of designing voting methods with certain natural good desired properties.

Formally, we will consider a set of alternatives A (the candidates) and a set of n voters I. Let us denote by L the set of linear orders on A (L is isomorphic to the set of permutations on A). Thus for every $\prec \in L$, $\prec$ is a total order on A (antisymmetric and transitive). The preferences of each voter i are formally given by $\succ_i \in L$, where $a \succ_i b$ means that i prefers alternative a to alternative b.

Definition 9.1

- A function $F : L^n \rightarrow L$ is called a *social welfare function.*
- A function $f : L^n \rightarrow A$ is called a *social choice function.*

Thus a social welfare function aggregates the preferences of all voters into a common preference, i.e., into a total social order on the candidates, while a social choice function aggregates the preferences of all voters into a social choice of a single candidate. Arrow's theorem states that social welfare functions with "nice" properties must be trivial in a certain sense.

9.2.3 Arrow's Theorem

Here are some natural properties desired from a social welfare function.

Definition 9.2

- A social welfare function F satisfies *unanimity* if for every $\prec \in L$, $F(\prec, \ldots, \prec) = \prec$. That is, if all voters have identical preferences then the social preference is the same.
- Voter i is a *dictator* in social welfare function F if for all $\prec_1 \ldots \prec_n \in L$, $F(\prec_1, \ldots, \prec_n) = \prec_i$. The social preference in a dictatorship is simply that of the dictator, ignoring all other voters. F is not a *dictatorship* if no i is a dictator in it.
- A social welfare function satisfies *independence of irrelevant alternatives* if the social preference between any two alternatives a and b depends only on the voters' preferences between a and b. Formally, for every $a, b \in A$ and every $\prec_1, \ldots, \prec_n, \prec'_1, \ldots, \prec'_n \in L$, if we denote $\prec = F(\prec_1, \ldots, \prec_n)$ and $\prec' = F(\prec'_1, \ldots, \prec'_n)$ then $a \prec_i b \Leftrightarrow a \prec'_i b$ for all i implies that $a \prec b \Leftrightarrow a \prec' b$.

The first two conditions are quite simple to understand, and we would certainly want any good voting method to satisfy the unanimity condition and not to be a dictatorship. The third condition is trickier. Intuitively, indeed, independence of irrelevant alternatives seems quite natural: why should my preferences about c have anything to do with the social ranking of a and b? More careful inspection will reveal that this condition in some sense captures some consistency property of the voting system. As we will see, lack of such consistency enables strategic manipulation.

Theorem 9.3 (Arrow) *Every social welfare function over a set of more than 2 candidates ($|A| \geq 3$) that satisfies unanimity and independence of irrelevant alternatives is a dictatorship.*

Over the years a large number of proofs have been found for Arrow's theorem. Here is a short one.

PROOF For the rest of the proof, fix F that satisfies unanimity and independence of irrelevant alternatives. We start with a claim showing that the same social ranking rule is taken within any pair of alternatives.

Claim (pairwise neutrality) Let $\succ_1, \ldots, \succ_n$ and $\succ'_1, \ldots, \succ'_n$ be two player profiles such that for every player i, $a \succ_i b \Leftrightarrow c \succ'_i d$. Then $a \succ b \Leftrightarrow c \succ' d$, where $\succ = F(\succ_1, \ldots, \succ_n)$ and $\succ' = F(\succ'_1, \ldots, \succ'_n)$.

By renaming, we can assume without loss of generality that $a \succ b$ and that $c \neq b$. Now we merge each $\succ_i$ and $\succ'_i$ into a single preference $\succ_i$ by putting c just above a (unless $c = a$) and d just below b (unless $d = b$) and preserving the internal order within each of the pairs (a, b) and (c, d). Now using unanimity, we have that $c \succ a$ and $b \succ d$, and by transitivity $c \succ d$. This concludes the proof of the claim.

We now continue with the proof of the theorem. Take any $a \neq b \in A$, and for every $0 \leq i \leq n$ define a preference profile π^i in which exactly the first i players rank a above b, i.e., in π^i, $a \succ_j b \Leftrightarrow j \leq i$ (the exact ranking of the other alternatives does not matter). By unanimity, in $F(\pi^0)$, we have $b \succ a$, while in $F(\pi^n)$ we have $a \succ b$. By looking at $\pi^0, \pi^1, \ldots, \pi^n$, at some point the ranking between a and b flips, so for some i^* we have that in $F(\pi^{i^*-1})$, $b \succ a$, while in $F(\pi^{i^*})$, $a \succ b$. We conclude the proof by showing that i^* is a dictator.

Claim Take any $c \neq d \in A$. If $c \succ_{i^*} d$ then $c \succ d$ where $\succ = F(\succ_1, \ldots, \succ_n)$.

Take some alternative e which is different from c and d. For $i < i^*$ move e to the top in $\succ_i$, for $i > i^*$ move e to the bottom in $\succ_i$, and for i^* move e so that $c \succ_{i^*} e \succ_{i^*} d$ – using independence of irrelevant alternatives we have not changed the social ranking between c and d. Now notice that players' preferences for the ordered pair (c, e) are identical to their preferences for (a, b) in π^{i^*}, but the preferences for (e, d) are identical to the preferences for (a, b) in π^{i^*-1} and thus using the pairwise neutrality claim, socially $c \succ e$ and $e \succ d$, and thus by transitivity $c \succ d$. □

9.2.4 The Gibbard–Satterthwaite Theorem

It turns out that Arrow's theorem has devastating strategic implications. We will study this issue in the context of social choice functions (rather than social welfare functions as we have considered until now). Let us start by defining strategic manipulations.

Definition 9.4 A social choice function f can be *strategically manipulated* by voter i if for some $\prec_1, \ldots, \prec_n \in L$ and some $\prec'_i \in L$ we have that $a \prec_i a'$ where $a = f(\prec_1, \ldots, \prec_i, \ldots, \prec_n)$ and $a' = f(\prec_1, \ldots, \prec'_i, \ldots, \prec_n)$. That is, voter i that prefers a' to a can ensure that a' gets socially chosen rather than a by strategically misrepresenting his preferences to be $\prec'_i$ rather than $\prec_i$. f is called *incentive compatible* if it cannot be manipulated.

The following is a more combinatorial point of view of the same notion.

Definition 9.5 A social choice function f is monotone if $f(\prec_1, \ldots, \prec_i, \ldots, \prec_n) = a \neq a' = f(\prec_1, \ldots, \prec'_i, \ldots, \prec_n)$ implies that $a' \prec_i a$ and $a \prec'_i a'$. That is, if the social choice changed from a to a' when a single voter i changed his vote from $\prec_i$ to $\prec'_i$ then it must be because he switched his preference between a and a'.

Proposition 9.6 *A social choice function is incentive compatible if and only if it is monotone.*

PROOF Take $\prec_1, \ldots, \prec_{i-1}, \prec_{i+1}, \ldots, \prec_n$ out of the quantification. Now, logically, "NOT monotone between $\prec_i$ and $\prec'_i$" is equivalent to "A voter with preference $\prec$ can strategically manipulate f by declaring $\prec'$" OR "A voter with preference $\prec'$ can strategically manipulate f by declaring $\prec$". □

The obvious example of an incentive compatible social choice function over two alternatives is taking the majority vote between them. The main point of this section is, however, that when the number of alternatives is larger than 2, only trivial social choice functions are incentive compatible.

Definition 9.7 Voter i is a *dictator* in social choice function f if for all $\prec_1, \ldots, \prec_n \in L$, $\forall b \neq a$, $a \succ_i b \Rightarrow f(\prec_1, \ldots, \prec_n) = a$. f is called a *dictatorship* if some i is a dictator in it.

Theorem 9.8 (Gibbard–Satterthwaite) *Let f be an incentive compatible social choice function onto A, where $|A| \geq 3$, then f is a dictatorship.*

Note the requirement that f is onto, as otherwise the bound on the size of A has no bite. To derive the theorem as a corollary of Arrow's theorem, we will construct a social welfare function F from the social choice function f. The idea is that in order to decide whether $a \prec b$, we will "move" a and b to the top of all voters' preferences, and then see whether f chooses a or b. Formally,

Definition 9.9

- Notation: Let $S \subset A$ and $\prec \in L$. Denote by $\prec^S$ the order obtained by moving all alternatives in S to the top in $\prec$. Formally, for $a, b \in S$, $a \prec^S b \Leftrightarrow a \prec b$; for $a, b \notin S$, also $a \prec^S b \Leftrightarrow a \prec b$; but for $a \notin S$ and $b \in S$, $a \prec^S b$.

- The social welfare function F that extends the social choice function f is defined by $F(\prec_1, \ldots, \prec_n) = \prec$, where $a \prec b$ iff $f(\prec_1^{\{a,b\}}, \ldots, \prec_n^{\{a,b\}}) = b$.

We first have to show that F is indeed a social welfare function, i.e., that it is antisymmetric and transitive.

Lemma 9.10 *If f is an incentive compatible social choice function onto A then the extension F is a social welfare function.*

To conclude the proof of the theorem as a corollary of Arrow's, it then suffices to show:

Lemma 9.11 *If f is an incentive compatible social choice function onto A, which is not a dictatorship then the extension F satisfies unanimity and independence of irrelevant alternatives and is not a dictatorship.*

PROOF OF LEMMAS 9.10 AND 9.11 We start with a general claim which holds under the conditions on f:

Claim: For any $\prec_1, \ldots, \prec_n$ and any S, $f(\prec_1^S, \ldots, \prec_n^S) \in S$.

Take some $a \in S$ and since f is onto, for some $\prec_1', \ldots, \prec_n'$, $f(\prec_1', \ldots, \prec_n') = a$. Now, sequentially, for $i = 1, \ldots, n$, change $\prec_i'$ to $\prec_i^S$. We claim that at no point during this sequence of changes will f output any outcome $b \notin S$. At every stage this is simply due to monotonicity since $b \prec_i^S a'$ for $a' \in S$ being the previous outcome. This concludes the proof of the claim.

We can now prove all properties needed for the two lemmas:

- Antisymmetry is implied by the claim since $f(\prec_1^{\{a,b\}}, \ldots, \prec_n^{\{a,b\}}) \in \{a, b\}$.
- Transitivity: assume for contradiction that $a \prec b \prec c \prec a$ (where $\prec = F(\prec_1, \ldots, \prec_n)$). Take $S = \{a, b, c\}$ and using the claim assume without loss of generality that $f(\prec_1^S, \ldots, \prec_n^S) = a$. Sequentially changing $\prec_i^S$ to $\prec_i^{\{a,b\}}$ for each i, monotonicity of f implies that also $f(\prec_1^{\{a,b\}}, \ldots, \prec_n^{\{a,b\}}) = a$, and thus $a \succ b$.
- Unanimity: If for all i, $b \prec_i a$, then $(\prec_i^{\{a,b\}})^{\{a\}} = \prec_i^{\{a,b\}}$ and thus by the claim $f(\prec_1^{\{a,b\}}, \ldots, \prec_n^{\{a,b\}}) = a$.
- Independence of irrelevant alternatives: If for all $i, b \prec_i a \Leftrightarrow b \prec_i' a$, then $f(\prec_1^{\{a,b\}}, \ldots, \prec_n^{\{a,b\}}) = f(\prec_1'^{\{a,b\}}, \ldots, \prec_n'^{\{a,b\}})$ since when we, sequentially for all i, flip $\prec_i^{\{a,b\}}$ into $\prec_i'^{\{a,b\}}$, the outcome does not change because of monotonicity and the claim.
- Nondictatorship: obvious. □

The Gibbard–Satterthwaite theorem seems to quash any hope of designing incentive compatible social choice functions. The whole field of Mechanism Design attempts escaping from this impossibility result using various modifications in the model. The next section describes how the addition of "money" offers an escape route. Chapter 10 offers other escape routes that do not rely on money.

9.3 Mechanisms with Money

In the previous section, we modeled a voter's preference as an order on the alternatives. $a \succ_i b$ implies that i prefers a to b, but we did not model "by how much" is a preferred to b. "Money" is a yardstick that allows measuring this. Moreover, money can be transferred between players. The existence of money with these properties is an assumption, but a fairly reasonable one in many circumstances, and will allow us to do things that we could not do otherwise.

Formally, in this section we redefine our setting. We will still have a set of alternatives A and a set of n players I (which we will no longer call voters). The preference of a player i is now given by a *valuation function* $v_i : A \rightarrow \Re$, where $v_i(a)$ denotes the "value" that i assigns to alternative a being chosen. This value is in terms of some currency; i.e., we assume that if a is chosen and then player i is additionally given some quantity m of money, then i's *utility* is $u_i = v_i(a) + m$, this utility being the abstraction of what the player desires and aims to maximize. Utilities of this form are called *quasilinear preferences*, denoting the separable and linear dependence on money.

9.3.1 Vickrey's Second Price Auction

Before we proceed to the general setting, in this subsection we study a basic example: a simple auction. Consider a single item that is auctioned for sale among n players. Each player i has a scalar value w_i that he is "willing to pay" for this item. More specifically, if he wins the item, but has to pay some price p for it, then his utility is $w_i - p$, while if someone else wins the item then i's utility is 0. Putting this scenario into the terms of our general setting, the set of alternatives here is the set of possible winners, $A = \{i\text{–wins} | i \in I\}$, and the valuation of each bidder i is $v_i(i\text{–wins}) = w_i$ and $v_i(j\text{–wins}) = 0$ for all $j \neq i$. A natural social choice would be to allocate the item to the player who values it highest: choose i–wins, where $i = \text{argmax}_j w_j$. However, the challenge is that we do not know the values w_i but rather each player knows his own value, and we want to make sure that our mechanism decides on the allocation – the social choice – in a way that *cannot be strategically manipulated.* Our degree of freedom is the definition of the payment by the winner.

Let us first consider the two most natural choices of payment and see why they do not work as intended:

- **No payment:** In this version we give the item for free to the player with highest w_i. Clearly, this method is easily manipulated: every player will benefit by exaggerating his w_i, reporting a much larger $w_i' \gg w_i$ that can cause him to win the item, even though his real w_i is not the highest.
- **Pay your bid:** An attempt of correction will be to have the winner pay the declared bid. However, this system is also open to manipulation: a player with value w_i who wins and pays w_i gets a total utility of 0. Thus it is clear that he should attempt declaring a somewhat lower value $w_i' < w_i$ that still wins. In this case he can still win the item getting a value of w_i (his real value) but paying only the smaller w_i' (his declared value), obtaining a net positive utility $u_i = w_i - w_i' > 0$. What value w_i' should i bid then?

Well, if i knows the value of the second highest bid, then he should declare just above it. But what if he does not know?

Here is the solution.

Definition 9.12 Vickrey's second price auction: Let the winner be the player i with the highest declared value of w_i, and let i pay the second highest declared bid $p^* = \max_{j \neq i} w_j$.

Now it turns out that manipulation never can increase any players' utility. Formally,

Proposition 9.13 (Vickrey) *For every $w_1, \ldots, w_n$ and every w'_i, Let u_i be i's utility if he bids w_i and u'_i his utility if he bids w'_i. Then, $u_i \geq u'_i$.*

PROOF Assume that by saying w_i he wins, and that the second highest (reported) value is p^*, then $u_i = w_i - p^* \geq 0$. Now, for an attempted manipulation $w'_i > p^*$, i would still win if he bids w'_i and would still pay p^*, thus $u'_i = u_i$. On the other hand, for $w'_i \leq p^*$, i would lose so $u'_i = 0 \leq u_i$.

If i loses by bidding w_i, then $u_i = 0$. Let j be the winner in this case, and thus $w_j \geq w_i$. For $w'_i < w_j$, i would still lose and so $u'_i = 0 = u_i$. For $w'_i \geq w_j$, i would win, but would pay w_j, thus his utility would be $u'_i = w_i - w_j \leq 0 = u_i$. □

This very simple and elegant idea achieves something that is quite remarkable: it reliably computes a function (argmax) of n numbers (the w_i's) that are each held secretly by a different self-interested player! Taking a philosophical point of view, this may be seen as the mechanics for the implementation of Adam Smith's *invisible hand*: despite private information and pure selfish behavior, social welfare is achieved. All the field of Mechanism Design is just a generalization of this possibility.

9.3.2 Incentive Compatible Mechanisms

In a world with money, our mechanisms will not only choose a social alternative but will also determine monetary payments to be made by the different players. The complete social choice is then composed of the alternative chosen as well as of the transfer of money. Nevertheless, we will refer to each of these parts separately, calling the alternative chosen the social choice, not including in this term the monetary payments.

Formally, a mechanism needs to socially choose some alternative from A, as well as to decide on payments. The preference of each player i is modeled by a valuation function $v_i : A \rightarrow \Re$, where $v_i \in V_i$. Throughout the rest of this chapter, $V_i \subseteq \Re^A$ is a commonly known set of possible valuation functions for player i.

Starting at this point and for the rest of this chapter, it will be convenient to use the following standard notation.

Notation Let $v = (v_1, \ldots, v_n)$ be an n-dimensional vector. We will denote the $(n-1)$-dimensional vector in which the i'th coordinate is removed by $v_{-i} = (v_1, \ldots, v_{i-1}, v_{i+1}, \ldots, v_n)$. Thus we have three equivalent notations: $v = (v_1, \ldots, v_n) = (v_i, v_{-i})$. Similarly, for $V = V_1 \times \cdots \times V_n$, we will denote $V_{-i} = V_1 \times \cdots \times V_{i-1} \times V_{i+1} \times \cdots \times V_n$. Similarly we will use t_{-i}, x_{-i}, X_{-i}, etc.

Definition 9.14 A (direct revelation) *mechanism* is a social choice function $f : V_1 \times \cdots \times V_n \to A$ and a vector of payment functions $p_1, \ldots, p_n$, where $p_i : V_1 \times \cdots \times V_n \to \Re$ is the amount that player i pays.

The qualification "direct revelation" will become clear in Section 9.4, where we will generalize the notion of a mechanism further. We are now ready for the key definition in this area, *incentive compatibility* also called *strategy-proofness* or *truthfulness.*

Definition 9.15 A mechanism $(f, p_1, \ldots, p_n)$ is called incentive compatible if for every player i, every $v_1 \in V_1, \ldots, v_n \in V_n$ and every $v_i' \in V_i$, if we denote $a = f(v_i, v_{-i})$ and $a' = f(v_i', v_{-i})$, then $v_i(a) - p_i(v_i, v_{-i}) \geq v_i(a') - p_i(v_i', v_{-i})$.

Intuitively this means that player i whose valuation is v_i would prefer "telling the truth" v_i to the mechanism rather than any possible "lie" v_i', since this gives him higher (in the weak sense) utility.

9.3.3 Vickrey–Clarke–Groves Mechanisms

While in the general setting without money, as we have seen, nothing nontrivial is incentive compatible, the main result in this setting is positive and provides an incentive compatible mechanism for the most natural social choice function: optimizing the social welfare. The social welfare of an alternative $a \in A$ is the sum of the valuations of all players for this alternative, $\sum_i v_i(a)$.

Definition 9.16 A mechanism $(f, p_1, \ldots, p_n)$ is called a Vickrey–Clarke–Groves (VCG) mechanism if

- $f(v_1, \ldots, v_n) \in \text{argmax}_{a \in A} \sum_i v_i(a)$; that is, f maximizes the social welfare, and
- for some functions $h_1, \ldots, h_n$, where $h_i : V_{-i} \to \Re$ (i.e., h_i does not depend on v_i), we have that for all $v_1 \in V_1, \ldots, v_n \in V_n$: $p_i(v_1, \ldots, v_n) = h_i(v_{-i}) - \sum_{j \neq i} v_j(f(v_1, \ldots, v_n))$.

The main idea lies in the term $-\sum_{j \neq i} v_j(f(v_1, \ldots, v_n))$, which means that each player is paid an amount equal to the sum of the values of all other players. When this term is added to his own value $v_i(f(v_1, \ldots, v_n))$, the sum becomes exactly the total social welfare of $f(v_1, \ldots, v_n)$. Thus this mechanism aligns all players' incentives with the social goal of maximizing social welfare, which is exactly archived by telling the truth. The other term in the payment $h_i(v_i)$ has no strategic implications for player i since it does not depend, in any way, on what he says, and thus from player i's point of view it is just a constant. Of course, the choice of h_i does change significantly how much money is paid and in which direction, but we will postpone this discussion. What we have just intuitively explained is as follows.

Theorem 9.17 (Vickrey–Clarke–Groves) *Every VCG mechanism is incentive compatible.*

Let us prove it formally.

PROOF Fix i, v_{-i}, v_i, and v_i'. We need to show that for player i with valuation v_i, the utility when declaring v_i is not less than the utility when declaring v_i'. Denote $a = f(v_i, v_{-i})$ and $a' = f(v_i', v_{-i})$. The utility of i, when declaring v_i, is $v_i(a) + \sum_{j\neq i} v_j(a) - h_i(v_{-i})$, but when declaring v_i' is $v_i(a') + \sum_{j\neq i} v_j(a') - h_i(v_{-i})$. But since $a = f(v_i, v_{-i})$ maximizes social welfare over all alternatives, $v_i(a) + \sum_{j\neq i} v_j(a) \geq v_i(a') + \sum_{j\neq i} v_j(a')$ and thus the same inequality holds when subtracting the same term $h_i(v_{-i})$ from both sides. □

9.3.4 Clarke Pivot Rule

Let us now return to the question of choosing the "right" h_i's. One possibility is certainly choosing $h_i = 0$. This has the advantage of simplicity but usually does not make sense since the mechanism pays here a great amount of money to the players. Intuitively we would prefer that players pay money to the mechanism, but not more than the gain that they get. Here are two conditions that seem to make sense, at least in a setting where all valuations are nonnegative.

Definition 9.18

- A mechanism is (ex-post) *individually rational* if players always get nonnegative utility. Formally if for every $v_1, \ldots, v_n$ we have that $v_i(f(v_1, \ldots, v_n)) - p_i(v_1, \ldots, v_n) \geq 0$.
- A mechanism has no positive transfers if no player is ever paid money. Formally if for every $v_1, \ldots, v_n$ and every i, $p_i(v_1, \ldots, v_n) \geq 0$.

The following choice of h_i's provides the following two properties.

Definition 9.19 (Clarke pivot rule) The choice $h_i(v_{-i}) = \max_{b\in A} \sum_{j\neq i} v_j(b)$ is called the Clarke pivot payment. Under this rule the payment of player i is $p_i(v_1, \ldots, v_n) = \max_b \sum_{j\neq i} v_j(b) - \sum_{j\neq i} v_j(a)$, where $a = f(v_1, \ldots, v_n)$.

Intuitively, i pays an amount equal to the total damage that he causes the other players – the difference between the social welfare of the others with and without i's participation. In other words, the payments make each player internalize the externalities that he causes.

Lemma 9.20 *A VCG mechanism with Clarke pivot payments makes no positive transfers. If $v_i(a) \geq 0$ for every $v_i \in V_i$ and $a \in A$ then it is also individually rational.*

PROOF Let $a = f(v_1, \ldots, v_n)$ be the alternative maximizing $\sum_j v_j(a)$ and b be the alternative maximizing $\sum_{j \neq i} v_j(b)$. To show individual rationality, the utility of player i is $v_i(a) + \sum_{j \neq i} v_j(a) - \sum_{j \neq i} v_j(b) \geq \sum_j v_j(a) - \sum_j v_j(b) \geq 0$, where the first inequality is since $v_i(b) \geq 0$ and the second is since a was chosen as to maximize $\sum_j v_j(a)$. To show no positive transfers, note that $p_i(v_1, \ldots, v_n) = \sum_{j \neq i} v_j(b) - \sum_{j \neq i} v_j(a) \geq 0$, since b was chosen as to maximize $\sum_{j \neq i} v_j(b)$. □

As stated, the Clarke pivot rule does not fit many situations where valuations are negative; i.e., when alternatives have costs to the players. Indeed, with the Clarke pivot rule, players always pay money to the mechanism, while the natural interpretation in case of costs would be the opposite. The spirit of the Clarke pivot rule in such cases can be captured by a modified rule that chooses b as to maximize the social welfare "when i does not participate" where the exact meaning of this turns out to be quite natural in most applications.

9.3.5 Examples

9.3.5.1 Auction of a Single Item

The Vickrey auction that we started our discussion with is a special case of a VCG mechanism with the Clarke pivot rule. Here $A = \{i\text{–wins} | i \in I\}$. Each player has value 0 if he does not get the item, and may have any positive value if he does win the item, thus $V_i = \{v_i | v_i(i\text{–wins}) \geq 0 \text{ and } \forall j \neq i,\ v_i(j\text{–wins}) = 0\}$. Notice that finding the player with highest value is exactly equivalent to maximizing $\sum_i v_i(i)$ since only a single player gets nonzero value. VCG payments using the Clarke pivot rule give exactly Vickrey's second price auction.

9.3.5.2 Reverse Auction

In a reverse auction (procurement auction) the bidder wants to *procure* an item from the bidder with lowest cost. In this case the valuation spaces are given by $V_i = \{v_i | v_i(i\text{–wins}) \leq 0 \text{ and } \forall j \neq i\ v_i(j\text{–wins}) = 0\}$, and indeed procuring the item from the lowest cost bidder is equivalent to maximizing the social welfare. The natural VCG payment rule would be for the mechanism to pay to the lowest bidder an amount equal to the second lowest bid, and pay nothing to the others. This may be viewed as capturing the spirit of the pivot rule since the second lowest bid is what would happen "without i."

9.3.5.3 Bilateral Trade

In the bilateral trade problem a seller holds an item and values it at some $0 \leq v_s \leq 1$ and a potential buyer values it at some $0 \leq v_b \leq 1$. (The constants 0 and 1 are arbitrary and may be replaced with any commonly known constants $0 \leq v_l \leq v_h$.) The possible outcomes are $A = \{\text{no–trade, trade}\}$ and social efficiency implies that trade is chosen if $v_b > v_s$ and *no-trade* if $v_s > v_b$. Using VCG payments and decreeing that no payments be made in case of *no-trade*, implies that in case of trade the buyer pays v_s and the seller is paid v_b. Notice that since in this case $v_b > v_s$, the mechanism subsidizes the trade. As we will see below in Section 9.5.5, this is unavoidable.

9.3.5.4 Multiunit Auctions

In a multiunit auction, k identical units of some good are sold in an auction (where $k < n$). In the simple case each bidder is interested in only a single unit. In this case $A = \{S\text{–wins} | S \subset I,\ |S| = k\}$, and a bidder's valuation v_i gives some fixed value v^* if i gets an item, i.e. $v_i(S) = v^*$ if $i \in S$ and $v_i(S) = 0$ otherwise. Maximizing social welfare means allocating the items to the k highest bidders, and in the VCG mechanism with the pivot rule, each of them should pay the $k + 1$'st highest offered price. (Losers pay 0.)

In a more general case, bidders may be interested in more than a single unit and have a different value for each number of units obtained. The next level of sophistication comes when the items in the auction are heterogeneous, and valuations can give a different value to each combination of items. This is called a combinatorial auction and is studied at length in Chapter 11.

9.3.5.5 Public Project

The government is considering undertaking a public project (e.g., building a bridge). The project has a commonly known cost C, and is valued by each citizen i at (a privately known) value v_i. (We usually think that $v_i \geq 0$, but the case of allowing $v_i < 0$, i.e., citizens who are hurt by the project is also covered.) Social efficiency means that the government will undertake this project iff $\sum_i v_i > C$. (This is not technically a subcase of our definition of maximizing the social welfare, since our definition did not assume any costs or values for the designer, but becomes so by adding an extra player "government" whose valuation space is the singleton valuation, giving cost C to undertaking the project and 0 otherwise.) The VCG mechanism with the Clarke pivot rule means that a player i with $v_i \geq 0$ will pay a nonzero amount only if he is pivotal: $\sum_{j \neq i} v_j \leq C$ but $\sum_j v_j > C$ in which case he will pay $p_i = C - \sum_{j \neq i} v_j$. (A player with $v_i < 0$ will make a nonzero payment only if $\sum_{j \neq i} v_j > C$ but $\sum_j v_j \leq C$ in which case he will pay $p_i = \sum_{j \neq i} v_j - C$.) One may verify that $\sum_i p_i < C$ (unless $\sum_i v_i = C$), and thus the payments collected do not cover the project's costs. As we will see in Section 9.5.5, this is unavoidable.

9.3.5.6 Buying a Path in a Network

Consider a communication network, modeled as a directed graph $G = (V, E)$, where each link $e \in E$ is owned by a different player, and has a cost $c_e \geq 0$ if his link is used for carrying some message. Suppose that we wish to procure a communication path between two specified vertices $s, t \in V$; i.e., the set of alternatives is the set of all possible $s - t$ paths in G, and player e has value 0 if the path chosen does not contain e and value $-c_e$ if the path chosen does contain e. Maximizing social welfare means finding the shortest path p (in terms of $\sum_{e \in p} c_e$). A VCG mechanism that makes no payments to edges that are not in p, will pay to each $e_0 \in p$ the quantity $\sum_{e \in p'} c_e - \sum_{e \in p - \{e_0\}} c_e$, where p is the shortest $s - t$ path in G and p' is the shortest

$s - t$ path in G that does not contain the edge e (for simplicity, assume that G is 2-edge connected so such a p' always exists). This corresponds to the spirit of the pivot rule since "without e" the mechanism can simply not use paths that contain e.

9.4 Implementation in Dominant Strategies

In this section our aim is to put the issue of incentive compatibility in a wider context. The mechanisms considered so far extract information from the different players by motivating them to "tell the truth." More generally, one may think of other, indirect, methods of extracting sufficient information from the participants. Perhaps one may devise some complex protocol that achieves the required social choice when players act strategically. This section will formalize these more general mechanisms, and the associated notions describing what happens when "players act strategically."

Deviating from the common treatment in economics, in this section we will describe a model that does not involve any distributional assumptions. Many of the classical results of Mechanism Design are captured in this framework, including most of the existing applications in computational settings. In Section 9.6 we will add this ingredient of distributional assumptions reaching the general "Bayesian" models.

9.4.1 Games with Strict Incomplete Information

How do we model strategic behavior of the players when they are missing some of the information that specifies the game? Specifically in our setting a player does not know the private information of the other players, information that determines their preferences. The standard setting in Game Theory supposes on the other hand that the "rules" of the game, including the utilities of all players, are public knowledge.

We will use a model of games with *independent private values* and *strict incomplete information.* Let us explain the terms: "independent private values" means that the utility of a player depends fully on his private information and not on any information of others as it is independent from his own information. *Strict incomplete information* is a (not completely standard) term that means that we will have no probabilistic information in the model. An alternative term sometimes used is "pre-Bayesian." From a CS perspective, it means that we will use a worst case analysis over unknown information. So here is the model.

Definition 9.21 A game with (independent private values and) strict incomplete information for a set of n players is given by the following ingredients:

(i) For every player i, a set of *actions* X_i.

(ii) For every player i, a set of *types* T_i. A value $t_i \in T_i$ is the private information that i has.

(iii) For every player i, a *utility function* $u_i : T_i \times X_1 \times \cdots \times X_n \rightarrow \Re$, where $u_i(t_i, x_1, \ldots, x_n)$ is the utility achieved by player i, if his type (private information) is t_i, and the profile of actions taken by all players is $x_1, \ldots, x_n$.

The main idea that we wish to capture with this definition is that each player i must choose his action x_i when knowing t_i but not the other t_j's. Note that the t_j's do not affect his utility, but they do affect how the other players behave. Thus the interplay between the different x_i's is more delicate than in "regular" games. The total behavior of player i in such a setting is captured by a function that specifies which action x_i is taken for every possible type t_i – this is termed a strategy. It is these strategies that we want to be in equilibrium.

Definition 9.22

- A strategy of a player i is a function $s_i : T_i \to X_i$.
- A profile of strategies $s_1, \ldots, s_n$ is an ex-post-Nash equilibrium if for every $t_1, \ldots, t_n$ we have that the actions $s_1(t_1), \ldots, s_n(t_n)$ are in Nash equilibrium in the full information game defined by the t_i's. Formally: For all i, all $t_1, \ldots, t_n$, and all x'_i we have that $u_i(t_i, s_i(t_i), s_{-i}(t_{-i})) \geq u_i(t_i, x'_i, s_{-i}(t_{-i}))$.
- A strategy s_i is a (weakly) dominant strategy if for every t_i we have that the action $s_i(t_i)$ is a dominant strategy in the full information game defined by t_i. Formally: for all t_i, all x_{-i} and all x'_i we have that $u_i(t_i, s_i(t_i), x_{-i}) \geq u_i(t_i, x'_i, x_{-i})$. A profile $s_1, \ldots, s_n$ is called a dominant strategy equilibrium if each s_i is a dominant strategy.

Thus the notion of ex-post Nash requires that $s_i(t_i)$ is a best response to $s_i(t_{-i})$ for every possible value of t_{-i}, i.e., without knowing anything about t_{-i} but rather only knowing the forms of the other players' strategies s_{-i} as functions. The notion of dominant strategy requires that $s_i(t_i)$ is a best response to any x_{-i} possible, i.e., without knowing anything about t_{-i} or about s_{-i}. Both of these definitions seem too good to be true: how likely is it that a player has a single action that is a best response to all x_{-i} or even to all $s_{-i}(t_{-i})$? Indeed in usual cases one does not expect games with strict incomplete information to have any of these equilibria. However, in the context of Mechanism Design – where we get to design the game – we can sometimes make sure that they do exist.

While at first sight the notion of dominant strategy equilibrium seems much stronger than ex-post Nash, this is only due to actions that are never used.

Proposition 9.23 *Let $s_1, \ldots, s_n$ be an ex-post-Nash equilibrium of a game $(X_1, \ldots, X_n; T_1, \ldots, T_n; u_1, \ldots, u_n)$. Define $X'_i = \{s_i(t_i) | t_i \in T_i\}$ (i.e. X'_i is the actual range of s_i in X_i), then $s_1, \ldots, s_n$ is a dominant strategy equilibrium in the game $(X'_1, \ldots, X'_n; T_1, \ldots, T_n; u_1, \ldots, u_n)$.*

PROOF Let $x_i = s_i(t_i) \in X'_i, x'_i \in X'_i$, and for every $j \neq i$ $x_j \in X'_j$. By definition of X'_j, for every $j \neq i$, there exists $t'_j \in T_j$ such that $s_j(t_j) = x_j$. Since $s_1, \ldots, s_n$ is an ex-post-Nash equilibrium, $u_i(t_i, s_i(t_i), s_{-i}(t_{-i})) \geq u_i(t_i, x'_i, s_{-i}(t_{-i}))$, and as $x_{-i} = s_{-i}(t_{-i})$ we get exactly $u_i(t_i, s_i(t_i), x_{-i}) \geq u_i(t_i, x'_i, x_{-i})$ as required in the definition of dominant strategies. □

9.4.2 Mechanisms

We are now ready to formalize the notion of a general – nondirect revelation – mechanism. The idea is that each player has some private information $t_i \in T_i$ that captures his preference over a set of alternatives A; i.e., $v_i(t_i, a)$ is the value that player i assigns to a when his private information is t_i. We wish to "implement" some social choice function $F : T_1 \times \cdots \times T_n \rightarrow A$ that aggregates these preferences. We design a "mechanism" for this purpose: this will be some protocol for interaction with the players, specifying what each can "say" and what is done in each case. Formally, we can specify a set of possible actions X_i for each player, an outcome function $a : X_1 \times \cdots \times X_n \rightarrow A$ that chooses an alternative in A for each profile of actions, and payment functions $p : X_1 \times \cdots \times X_n \rightarrow \Re$ that specify the payment of each player for every profile of actions. Now the players are put in a game with strict incomplete information and we may expect them to reach an equilibrium point (if such exists).

Definition 9.24

- A mechanism for n players is given by (a) players' type spaces $T_1, \ldots, T_n$, (b) players' action spaces $X_1, \ldots, X_n$, (c) an alternative set A, (d) players' valuations functions $v_i : T_i \times A :\rightarrow \Re$, (e) an outcome function $a : X_1 \times \cdots \times X_n \rightarrow A$, and (f) payment functions $p_1, \ldots, p_n$, where $p_i : X_1 \times \cdots \times X_n \rightarrow \Re$. The game with strict incomplete information induced by the mechanism is given by using the types spaces T_i, the action spaces X_i, and the utilities $u_i(t_i, x_1, \ldots, x_n) = v_i(t_i, a(x_1, \ldots, x_n)) - p_i(x_1, \ldots, x_n)$.
- The mechanism implements a social choice function $f : T_1 \times \cdots \times T_n \rightarrow A$ in dominant strategies if for some dominant strategy equilibrium $s_1, \ldots, s_n$ of the induced game, where $s_i : T_i \rightarrow X_i$, we have that for all $t_1, \ldots, t_n$, $f(t_1, \ldots, t_n) = a(s_1(t_1), \ldots, s_n(t_n))$.
- Similarly we say that the mechanism implements f in ex-post-equilibrium if for some ex-post equilibrium $s_1, \ldots, s_n$ of the induced game we have that for all $t_1, \ldots, t_n$, $f(t_1, \ldots, t_n) = a(s_1(t_1), \ldots, s_n(t_n))$.

Clearly every dominant strategy implementation is also an ex-post-Nash implementation. Note that our definition only requires that for *some* equilibrium $f(t_1, \ldots, t_n) = a(s_1(t_1), \ldots, s_n(t_n))$ and allows other equilibria to exist. A stronger requirement would be that all equilibria have this property, or stronger still, that only a unique equilibrium point exists.

9.4.3 The Revelation Principle

At first sight it seems that the more general definition of mechanisms will allow us to do more than is possible using incentive compatible direct revelation mechanisms introduced in Section 9.3. This turns out to be false: any general mechanism that implements a function in dominant strategies can be converted into an incentive compatible one.

Proposition 9.25 (Revelation principle) *If there exists an arbitrary mechanism that implements f in dominant strategies, then there exists an incentive compatible mechanism that implements f. The payments of the players in the incentive compatible mechanism are identical to those, obtained at equilibrium, of the original mechanism.*

PROOF The proof is very simple: the new mechanism will simply simulate the equilibrium strategies of the players. That is, Let $s_1, \ldots, s_n$ be a dominant strategy equilibrium of the original mechanism, we define a new direct revelation mechanism: $f(t_1, \ldots, t_n) = a(s_1(t_1), \ldots, s_n(t_n))$ and $p'_i(t_1, \ldots, t_n) = p_i(s_1(t_1), \ldots, s_n(t_n))$. Now, since each s_i is a dominant strategy for player i, then for every t_i, x_{-i}, x'_i we have that $v_i(t_i, a(s_i(t_i), x_{-i})) - p_i(s_i(t_i), x_{-i}) \geq v_i(t_i, a(x'_i, x_{-i})) - p_i(x'_i, x_{-i})$. Thus in particular this is true for all $x_{-i} = s_{-i}(t_{-i})$ and any $x'_i = s_i(t'_i)$, which gives the definition of incentive compatibility of the mechanism $(f, p'_1, \ldots, p'_n)$. □

Corollary 9.26 *If there exists an arbitrary mechanism that ex-post-Nash implements f, then there exists an incentive compatible mechanism that implements f. Moreover, the payments of the players in the incentive compatible mechanism are identical to those, obtained in equilibrium, of the original mechanism.*

PROOF We take the ex-post implementation and restrict the action space of each player, as in Proposition 9.23, to those that are taken, for some input type, in the ex-post equilibrium $s_1, \ldots, s_n$. Proposition 9.23 states that now $s_1, \ldots, s_n$ is a dominant strategy equilibrium of the game with the restricted spaces, and thus the mechanism with the restricted action spaces is an implementation in dominant strategies. We can now invoke the revelation principle to get an incentive compatible mechanism. □

The revelation principle does not mean that indirect mechanisms are useless. In particular, general mechanisms may be adaptive (multiround), significantly reducing the communication (or computation) burden of the players or of the auctioneer relative to a nonadaptive direct mechanism. An example is the case of combinatorial auctions studied in Chapter 11.

9.5 Characterizations of Incentive Compatible Mechanisms

In Section 9.3 we saw how to implement the most natural social choice function: maximization of the social welfare. The question that drives this section is: What other social choice functions can we implement? In economic settings, the main reasons for attempting implementations of other social choice functions are increasing the revenue or introducing some kind of fairness. In computerized settings there are many natural optimization goals and we would like to be able to implement each of them. For example, in scheduling applications, a common optimization goal is that of the "makespan" – completion time of the last job. This is certainly a social choice function that is very different than maximizing the total social welfare – how can it be implemented? Another major motivation for social choice functions that do not maximize social welfare comes from computational considerations. In many applications the set of alternatives A is complex, and maximizing social welfare is a hard computational problem (NP-complete). In many of these cases there are computationally efficient algorithms that *approximate* the maximum social welfare. Such an algorithm in effect gives a social choice function that approximates social welfare maximization, but is different from it. Can it be implemented?

Chapter 12 and parts of Chapter 11 address these issues specifically. This section limits itself to laying the foundations by providing basic characterizations of implementable social choice functions and their associated payments.

Because of the revelation principle, we can restrict ourselves again to look at incentive compatible mechanisms. Thus, in this section we revert to the notation used in Subsection 9.3.3: A mechanism $M = (f, p_1, \ldots, p_n)$ over domain of preferences $V_1 \times \cdots \times V_n$ ($V_i \subseteq \Re^A$) is composed of a social choice function $f : V_1 \times \cdots \times V_n \to A$ and payment functions $p_1, \ldots, p_n$, where $p_i : V_1 \times \cdots \times V_n \to \Re$ is the amount that player i pays. In the rest of the section we will provide characterizations of when such mechanisms are incentive compatible.

9.5.1 Direct Characterization

We start by stating explicitly the required properties from an incentive compatible mechanism.

Proposition 9.27 *A mechanism is incentive compatible if and only if it satisfies the following conditions for every i and every v_{-i}:*

(i) *The payment p_i does not depend on v_i, but only on the alternative chosen $f(v_i, v_{-i})$. That is, for every v_{-i}, there exist prices $p_a \in \Re$, for every $a \in A$, such that for all v_i with $f(v_i, v_{-i}) = a$ we have that $p(v_i, v_{-i}) = p_a$.*

(ii) *The mechanism optimizes for each player. That is, for every v_i, we have that $f(v_i, v_{-i}) \in \mathrm{argmax}_a(v_i(a) - p_a)$, where the quantification is over all alternatives in the range of $f(\cdot, v_{-i})$.*

PROOF (if part) Denote $a = f(v_i, v_{-i})$, $a' = f(v_i', v_{-i})$, $p_a = p(v_i, v_{-i})$, and $p_{a'} = p(v_i', v_{-i})$. The utility of i, when telling the truth, is $v_i(a) - p_a$, which is not less than the utility when declaring v_i', $v_i(a') - p_{a'}$, since the mechanism optimizes for i, i.e., $a = f(v_i, v_{-i}) \in \mathrm{argmax}_a(v_i(a) - p_a)$.

(Only-if part; first condition) If for some v_i, v_i', $f(v_i, v_{-i}) = f(v_i', v_{-i})$ but $p_i(v_i, v_{-i}) > p_i(v_i', v_{-i})$ then a player with type v_i will increase his utility by declaring v_i'.

(Only-if part; second condition) If $f(v_i, v_{-i}) \notin \mathrm{argmax}_a(v_i(a) - p_a)$, fix $a' \in \mathrm{argmax}_a(v_i(a) - p_a)$ in the range of $f(\cdot, v_{-i})$, and thus for some v_i', $a' = f(v_i', v_{-i})$. Now a player with type v_i will increase his utility by declaring v_i'. □

9.5.2 Weak Monotonicity

The previous characterization involves both the social choice function and the payment functions. We now provide a partial characterization that only involves the social choice function. In Section 9.5.5 we will see that the social choice function usually determines the payments essentially uniquely.

Definition 9.28 A social choice function f satisfies *Weak Monotonicity (WMON)* if for all i, all v_{-i} we have that $f(v_i, v_{-i}) = a \neq b = f(v'_i, v_{-i})$ implies that $v_i(a) - v_i(b) \geq v'_i(a) - v'_i(b)$.

That is, WMON means that if the social choice changes when a single player changes his valuation, then it must be because the player increased his value of the new choice relative to his value of the old choice.

Theorem 9.29 *If a mechanism $(f, p_1, \ldots, p_n)$ is incentive compatible, then f satisfies WMON. If all domains of preferences V_i are convex sets (as subsets of an Euclidean space) then for every social choice function that satisfies WMON there exists payment functions $p_1, \ldots, p_n$ such that $(f, p_1, \ldots, p_n)$ is incentive compatible.*

The first part of the theorem is easy and we will bring it completely, the second part is quite involved, and will not be given here. It is known that WMON is not a sufficient condition for incentive compatibility in general nonconvex (more precisely, nonsimply connected) domains.

PROOF (First part) Assume first that $(f, p_1, \ldots, p_n)$ is incentive compatible, and fix i and v_{-i} in an arbitrary manner. Proposition 9.27 implies the existence of fixed prices p_a for all $a \in A$ (that do not depend on v_i) such that whenever the outcome is a then bidder i pays exactly p_a. Now assume $f(v_i, v_{-i}) = a \neq b = f(v'_i, v_{-i})$. Since a player with valuation v_i does not prefer declaring v'_i we have that $v_i(a) - p_a \geq v_i(b) - p_b$. Similarly since a player with valuation v'_i does not prefer declaring v_i we have that $v'_i(a) - p_a \leq v'_i(b) - p_b$. Subtracting the second inequality from the first, we get $v_i(a) - v_i(b) \geq v'_i(a) - v'_i(b)$, as required. □

While WMON gives a pretty tight characterization of implementable social choice functions, it still leaves something to be desired as it is not intuitively clear what exactly the WMON functions are. The problem is that the WMON condition is a local condition for each player separately and for each v_{-i} separately. Is there a global characterization? This turns out to depend intimately on the domains of preferences V_i. For two extreme cases there are good global characterizations: when V_i is "unrestricted" i.e. $V_i = \Re^A$, and when V_i is severely restricted as to be essentially single dimensional. These two cases are treated in the next two subsections below. The intermediate range where the V_i's are somewhat restricted, a range in which most computationally interesting problems lie is still wide open. More on this appears in Chapter 12.

9.5.3 Weighted VCG

It turns out that when the domain of preferences is unrestricted, then the only incentive compatible mechanisms are simple variations of the VCG mechanism. These variations allow giving weights to the players, weights to the alternatives, and allow restricting the range. The resulting social choice function is an "affine maximizer":

Definition 9.30 A social choice function f is called an *affine maximizer* if for some subrange $A' \subset A$, for some player weights $w_1, \ldots, w_n \in \Re^+$ and for some outcome weights $c_a \in \Re$ for every $a \in A'$, we have that $f(v_1, \ldots, v_n) \in \text{argmax}_{a \in A'}(c_a + \sum_i w_i v_i(a))$.

It is easy to see that VCG mechanisms can be generalized to affine maximizers:

Proposition 9.31 *Let f be an affine maximizer. Define for every i, $p_i(v_1, \ldots, v_n) = h_i(v_{-i}) - \sum_{j \neq i}(w_j/w_i)v_j(a) - c_a/w_i$, where h_i is an arbitrary function that does not depend on v_i. Then, $(f, p_1, \ldots, p_n)$ is incentive compatible.*

PROOF First, we can assume wlog that $h_i = 0$. The utility of player i if alternative a is chosen is $v_i(a) + \sum_{j \neq i}(w_j/w_i)v_j(a) + c_a/w_i$. By multiplying by $w_i > 0$, this expression is maximized when $c_a + \sum_j w_j v_j(a)$ is maximized which is what happens when i reports v_i truthfully. □

Roberts' theorem states that for unrestricted domains with at least 3 possible outcomes, these are the only incentive compatible mechanisms.

Theorem 9.32 (Roberts) *If $|A| \geq 3$, f is onto A, $V_i = \Re^A$ for every i, and $(f, p_1, \ldots, p_n)$ is incentive compatible then f is an affine maximizer.*

The proof of this theorem is not trivial and is given in Chapter 12. It is easy to see that the restriction $|A| \geq 3$ is crucial (as in Arrow's theorem), since the case $|A| = 2$ falls into the category of "single parameter" domains discussed below, for which there do exist incentive compatible mechanisms beyond weighted VCG. It remains open to what extent can the restriction of $V_i = \Re^A$ be relaxed.

9.5.4 Single-Parameter Domains

The unrestricted case $V_i = \Re^A$ basically means that the valuation space has full dimensionality. The opposite case is when the space V_i is single-dimensional; i.e., there is a single real parameter that directly determines the whole vector v_i. There are several possible levels of generality in which to formalize this, and we will consider one of intermediate generality that is simple and yet suffices for most applications. In our setting each bidder has a private scalar value for "winning," with "losing" having value of 0. This is modeled by some commonly known subset of winning alternatives $W_i \subseteq A$. The main point is that all winning alternatives are equivalent to each other for player i; and similarly all losing outcomes are equivalent to each other. All the examples in Section 9.3.5 fall into this category. A simple example is an auction of one item where W_i is the single outcome where i wins. A more complex example is the setting of buying a path in a network (Subsection 9.3.5.6), where W_i is the set of all paths that contain edge i.

Definition 9.33 A single parameter domain V_i is defined by a (publicly known) $W_i \subset A$ and a range of values $[t^0, t^1]$. V_i is the set of v_i such that for some

$t^0 \leq t \leq t^1$, $v_i(a) = t$, for all $a \in W_i$ and $v_i(a) = 0$ for all $a \notin W_i$. In such settings we will abuse notation and use v_i as the scalar t.

For this setting it is quite easy to completely characterize incentive compatible mechanisms.

Definition 9.34 A social choice function f on a single parameter domain is called monotone in v_i if for every v_{-i} and every $v_i \leq v_i' \in \Re$ we have that $f(v_i, v_{-i}) \in W_i$ implies that $f(v_i', v_{-i}) \in W_i$. That is, if valuation v_i makes i win, then so will every higher valuation $v_i' \geq v_i$.

For a monotone function f, for every v_{-i} for which player i can both win and lose, there is always a *critical value* below which i loses and above which he wins. For example, in a second price auction the critical value for each player is highest declared value among the other players.

Definition 9.35 The critical value of a monotone social choice function f on a single parameter domain is $c_i(v_{-i}) = \sup_{v_i: f(v_i, v_{-i}) \notin W_i} v_i$. The critical value at v_{-i} is undefined if $\{v_i | f(v_i, v_{-i}) \notin W_i\}$ is empty.

We will call a mechanism on a single parameter domain "normalized" if the payment for losing is always 0, i.e., for every v_i, v_{-i} such that $f(v_i, v_{-i}) \notin W_i$ we have that $p_i(v_i, v_{-i}) = 0$. It is not difficult to see that every incentive compatible mechanism may be easily turned into a normalized one, so it suffices to characterize normalized mechanisms.

Theorem 9.36 *A normalized mechanism $(f, p_1, \ldots, p_n)$ on a single parameter domain is incentive compatible if and only if the following conditions hold:*

(i) *f is monotone in every v_i.*

(ii) *Every winning bid pays the critical value. (Recall that losing bids pay 0.) Formally, For every i, v_i, v_{-i} such that $f(v_i, v_{-i}) \in W_i$, we have that $p_i(v_i, v_{-i}) = c_i(v_{-i})$. (If $c_i(v_{-i})$ is undefined we require instead that for every v_{-i}, there exists some value c_i, such that $p_i(v_i, v_{-i}) = c_i$ for all v_i such that $f(v_i, v_{-i}) \in W_i$.)*

PROOF (If part) Fix i, v_{-i}, v_i. For every declaration made by i, if he wins his utility is $v_i - c_i(v_{-i})$ and if he loses his utility is 0. Thus he prefers winning if $v_i > c_i(v_{-i})$ and losing if $v_i < c_i(v_{-i})$, which is exactly what happens when he declares the truth.

(Only-if part, first condition) If f is not monotone then for some $v_i' > v_i$ we have that $f(v_i', v_{-i})$ loses while $f(v_i, v_{-i})$ wins and pays some amount $p = p_i(v_i, v_{-i})$. Since a bidder with value v_i is not better off bidding v_i' and losing we have that $v_i - p \geq 0$. Since a bidder with value v_i' is not better off bidding v_i and winning we have that $v_i' - p \leq 0$. Contradiction.

(Only-if part, second condition) Assume that some winning v_i pays $p > c_i(v_{-i})$ then, using Proposition 9.27, all winning bids will make the same payment, including a winning v_i' with $c_i(v_{-i}) < v_i' < p$. But such a bidder is better off losing which he can do by bidding some value $v^{\text{lose}} < c(v_{-i})$. In the other direction if v_i pays $p < c(v_{-i})$ then a losing v_i' with $c(v_{-i}) > v_i' > p$ is better of wining and paying p, which will happen if he bids v_i. □

Notice that this characterization leaves ample space for non-affine-maximization. For example we can implement social functions such as maximizing the euclidean norm $\text{argmax}_a \sum_i v_i(a)^2$ or maximizing the minimum value $\text{argmax}_a \min_i v_i(a)$. Indeed in many cases this flexibility allows the design of computationally efficient *approximation* mechanisms for problems whose exact optimization is computationally intractable – an example is given in Chapter 12.

9.5.5 Uniqueness of Prices

This section has so far focused on characterizing the implementable social choice functions. What about the payment functions? It turns out that the payment function is essentially uniquely determined by the social choice function. "Essentially" means that if we take an incentive compatible mechanisms with payments p_i and modify the payments to $p_i'(v_1, \ldots, v_n) = p_i(v_1, \ldots, v_n) + h_i(v_{-i})$ for an arbitrary function h_i that does not depend on v_i, then incentive compatibility remains. It turns out that this is the only leeway in the payment.

Theorem 9.37 *Assume that the domains of preference V_i are connected sets in the usual metric in the Euclidean space. Let $(f, p_1, \ldots, p_n)$ be an incentive compatible mechanism. The mechanism with modified payments $(f, p_1', \ldots, p_n')$ is incentive compatible if and only if for some functions $h_i : V_{-i} \to \Re$ we have that $p_i'(v_1, \ldots, v_n) = p_i(v_1, \ldots, v_n) + h_i(v_{-i})$ for all $v_1, \ldots, v_n$.*

PROOF The "if" part is clear since h_i has no strategic implications for player i, so we need only prove the only-if part. Assume that $(f, p_1', \ldots, p_n')$ is incentive compatible, and for the rest of the proof fix some i and some v_{-i}.

For every $a \in A$ denote $V^a = \{v_i \in V_i | f(v_i, v_{-i}) = a\}$. Using Proposition 9.27, the payment $p(v_i, v_{-i})$ is identical for all $v_i \in V^a$ and will be denoted by p_a. Similarly we denote $p_a' = p'(v_i, v_{-i})$ for some $v_i \in V^a$. It now suffices to show that for every $a, b \in A$, $p_a - p_b = p_a' - p_b'$.

For $a, b \in A$ we will say that a and b are *close* if for every $\epsilon > 0$ there exist $v_i^a, v_i^b \in V_i$ such that $||v_i^a - v_i^b|| = max_{c \in A}|v_i^a(c) - v_i^b(c)| \leq \epsilon$, and $f(v_i^a, v_{-i}) = a$ and $f(v_i^b, v_{-i}) = b$. We will first prove the required $p_a - p_b = p_a' - p_b'$ for close a, b. Fix $v_i^a, v_i^b \in V_i$ as in the definition of closeness. Since a bidder with type v_i^a does not gain by declaring v_i^b with payments p, we have that $v_i^a(a) - p_a \geq v_i^a(b) - p_b$, and since a bidder with v_i^b does not gain by declaring v_i^a we have that $v_i^b(a) - p_a \leq v_i^b(b) - p_b$. Putting together and rearranging we have that $v_i^a(b) - v_i^a(a) \leq p_b - p_a \leq v_i^b(b) - v_i^b(a)$. Similarly, by considering the mechanism with payments p' we have $v_i^a(b) - v_i^a(a) \leq p_b' - p_a' \leq v_i^b(b) - v_i^b(a)$. But now recall that $||v_i^a - v_i^b|| \leq \epsilon$ and thus the upper bound and the lower bound for $p_b - p_a$

and for $p'_b - p'_a$ are at most 2ϵ apart and thus $|(p_b - p_a) - (p'_b - p'_a)| \leq 2\epsilon$. Since ϵ was arbitrary $p_b - p_a = p'_b - p'_a$.

To show $p_b - p_a = p'_b - p'_a$ for general (not necessarily close) a and b, consider $B = \{b \in A | p_b - p_a = p'_b - p'_a\}$. Since $p_b - p_a = p'_b - p'_a$ and $p_c - p_b = p'_c - p'_b$ implies $p_c - p_a = p'_c - p'_a$ we have that no alternative in $A - B$ can be close to any alternative in B. Thus $V^B = \bigcup_{b \in B} V^b$ has positive distance from its complement $V^{A-B} = \bigcup_{b \notin B} V^b$ contradicting the connectedness of V. □

It is not difficult to see that the assumption that V_i is connected is essential, as for example, if the valuations are restricted to be integral, then modifying p_i by any small constants $\epsilon < 1/2$ will not modify incentive compatibility.

From this, and using the revelation principle, we can directly get many corollaries:

(i) The only incentive compatible mechanisms that maximize social welfare are those with VCG payments.

(ii) In the bilateral trade problem (Section 9.3.5.3) the only incentive compatible mechanism that maximizes social welfare and makes no payments in case of no-trade is the one shown there which subsidizes the trade. More generally, if a mechanism for bilateral trade satisfies ex-post individual rationality, then it cannot dictate positive payments from the players in case of no-trade and thus it must subsidize trade.

(iii) In the public project problem (Section 9.3.5.5) no ex-post individually rational mechanism that maximizes social welfare can recover the cost of the project. Again, the uniqueness of payments implies that if players with value 0 pay 0 (which is as much as they can pay maintaining individual rationality) then their payments in case of building the project must be identical to those obtained using the Clarke pivot rule.

In Section 9.6.3 we will see a similar theorem in the Bayesian setting, a theorem that will strengthen all of these corollaries as well to that setting.

9.5.6 Randomized Mechanisms

All of our discussion so far considered only deterministic mechanisms. It is quite natural to allow also randomized mechanisms. Such mechanisms would be allowed to produce a distribution over alternatives and a distribution over payments. Alternatively, but specifying slightly more structure, we can allow distributions over deterministic mechanisms. This will allow us to distinguish between two notions of incentive compatibility.

Definition 9.38

- A *randomized mechanism* is a distribution over deterministic mechanisms (all with the same players, types spaces V_i, and outcome space A).
- A randomized mechanism is incentive compatible in the *universal sense* if every deterministic mechanism in the support is incentive compatible.

- A randomized mechanism is incentive compatible in *expectation* if truth is a dominant strategy in the game induced by expectation. That is, if for all i, all v_i, v_{-i}, and v_i', we have that $E[v_i(a) - p_i] \geq E[v_i(a') - p_i']$, where (a, p_i), and (a', p_i') are random variables denoting the outcome and payment when i bids, respectively, v_i and v_i', and $E[\cdot]$ denotes expectation over the randomization of the mechanism.

It is clear that incentive compatibility in the universal sense implies incentive compatibility in expectation. For most purposes incentive compatibility in expectation seems to be the more natural requirement. The universal definition is important if players are not risk neutral (which we do not consider in this chapter) or if the mechanism's internal randomization is not completely hidden from the players. As we will see in Chapters 12 and 13 randomized mechanisms can often be useful and achieve more than deterministic ones.

We will now characterize randomized incentive compatible mechanisms over single parameter domains. Recall the single parameter setting and notations from Section 9.5.4. We will denote the probability that i wins by $w_i(v_i, v_{-i}) = Pr[f(v_i, v_{-i}) \in W_i]$ (probability taken over the randomization of the mechanism) and will use $p_i(v_i, v_{-i})$ to directly denote the expected payment of i. In this notation the utility of player i with valuation v_i when declaring v_i' is $v_i \cdot w(v_i', v_{-i}) - p_i(v_i', v_{-i})$. For ease of notation we will focus on normalized mechanisms in which the lowest bid $v_i^0 = t^0$ loses completely $w_i(v_i^0, v_{-i}) = 0$ and pays nothing $p_i(v_i^0, v_{-i}) = 0$.

Theorem 9.39 *A normalized randomized mechanism in a single parameter domain is incentive compatible in expectation if and only if for every i and every fixed v_{-i} we have that*

(i) *the function $w_i(v_i, v_{-i})$ is monotonically non decreasing in v_i and*

(ii) $p_i(v_i, v_{-i}) = v_i \cdot w(v_i, v_{-i}) - \int_{v_i^0}^{v_i} w(t, v_{-i})dt$.

PROOF In the proof we will simplify notation by removing the index i and the fixed argument v_{-i} everywhere. In this notation, to show incentive compatibility we need to establish that $vw(v) - p(v) \geq vw(v') - p(v')$ for every v'. Plugging in the formula for p we get $\int_{v^0}^{v} w(t)dt \geq \int_{v^0}^{v'} w(t)dt - (v' - v)w(v')$. For $v' > v$ this is equivalent to $(v' - v)w(v') \geq \int_{v}^{v'} w(t)dt$, which is true due to the monotonicity of w. For $v' < v$ we get $(v - v')w(v') \leq \int_{v'}^{v} w(t)dt$, which again is true due to the monotonicity of w.

In the other direction, combining the incentive constraint at v, $vw(v) - p(v) \geq vw(v') - p(v')$, with the incentive constraint at v', $v'w(v) - p(v) \leq v'w(v') - p(v')$, and subtracting the inequalities, we get $(v' - v)w(v) \leq (v' - v)w(v')$ which implies monotonicity of w.

To derive the formula for p, we can rearrange the two incentive constraints as

$$v \cdot (w(v') - w(v)) \leq p(v') - p(v) \leq v' \cdot (w(v') - w(v)).$$

Now by letting $v' = v + \epsilon$, dividing throughout by ϵ, and taking the limit, both sides approach the same value, $v \cdot dw/dv$, and we get $dp/dv = v \cdot dw/dv$.

Thus, taking into account the normalization condition $p(v^0) = 0$, we have that $p(v_i) = \int_{v^0}^{v_i} v \cdot w'(v)dv$, and integrating by parts completes the proof. (This seems to require the differentiability of w, but as w is monotone this holds almost everywhere, which suffices since we immediately integrate.) □

We should point out explicitly that the randomization in a randomized mechanism is completely controlled by the mechanism designer and has nothing to do with any distributional assumptions on players' valuations as will be discussed in the next section.

9.6 Bayesian–Nash Implementation

So far in this chapter we have considered only implementation in dominant strategies (and the very similar ex-post-Nash). As mentioned in Section 9.4 this is usually considered too strict a definition in economic theory. It models situations where each player has no information at all about the private information of the others – not even a prior distribution – and must operate under a "worst case" assumption. The usual working definition in economic theory takes a Bayesian approach, assumes some commonly known prior distribution, and assumes that a player that lacks some information will optimize in a Bayesian sense according to the information that he does have. The formalization of these notions, mostly by Harsanyi, was a major development in economic theory in the 1960s and 1970s, and is certainly still the dominant approach to handling lack of information in economic theory. In this section we will give these basic notions in the context of mechanism design, again limiting ourselves to settings with independent private values.

9.6.1 Bayesian–Nash Equilibrium

Definition 9.40 A game with (independent private values and) incomplete information on a set of n players is given by the following ingredients:

(i) For every player i, a set of *actions* X_i.

(ii) For every player i, a set of *types* T_i, and a prior distribution D_i on T_i. A value $t_i \in T_i$ is the private information that i has, and $D_i(t_i)$ is the a priori probability that i gets type t_i.

(iii) For every player i, a *utility function* $u_i : T_i \times X_1 \times \cdots \times X_n \to \Re$, where $u_i(t_i, x_1, \ldots, x_n)$ is the utility achieved by player i, if his type (private information) is t_i, and the profile of actions taken by all players is $x_1, \ldots, x_n$.

The main idea that we wish to capture with this definition is that each player i must choose his action x_i when knowing t_i but not the other t_j's but rather only knowing the prior distribution D_j on each other t_j. The behavior of player i in such a setting is captured by a function that specifies which action x_i is taken for every possible type t_i – this is termed a strategy. It is these strategies that we would want to be in equilibrium.

Definition 9.41 A strategy of a player i is a function $s_i : T_i \to X_i$. A profile of strategies $s_1, \ldots, s_n$ is a *Bayesian-Nash equilibrium* if for every player i and every

t_i we have that $s_i(t_i)$ is the best response that i has to $s_{-i}()$ when his type is t_i, in expectation over the types of the other players. Formally: For all i, all t_i, and all x_i': $E_{D_{-i}}[u_i(t_i, s_i(t_i), s_{-i}(t_{-i}))] \geq E_{D_{-i}}[u_i(t_i, x_i', s_{-i}(t_{-i}))]$ (where $E_{D_{-i}}[]$ denotes the expectation over the other types t_{-i} being chosen according to distribution D_{-i}).

This now allows us to define implementation in the Bayesian sense.

Definition 9.42 A Bayesian mechanism for n players is given by (a) players' type spaces $T_1, \ldots, T_n$ and prior distributions on them $D_1, \ldots, D_n$, (b) players' action spaces $X_1, \ldots, X_n$, (c) an alternative set A, (d) players' valuations functions $v_i : T_i \times A :\rightarrow \Re$, (e) an outcome function $a : X_1 \times \cdots \times X_n \rightarrow A$, and (f) payment functions $p_1, \ldots, p_n$, where $p_i : X_1 \times \cdots \times X_n \rightarrow \Re$.

The game with incomplete information induced by the mechanism is given by using the type spaces T_i with prior distributions D_i, the action spaces X_i, and the utilities $u_i(t_i, x_1, \ldots, x_n) = v_i(t_i, a(x_1, \ldots, x_n)) - p_i(x_1, \ldots, x_n)$.

The mechanism implements a social choice function $f : T_1 \times \cdots \times T_n \rightarrow A$ in the Bayesian sense if for some Bayesian–Nash equilibrium $s_1, \ldots, s_n$ of the induced game ($s_i : T_i \rightarrow X_i$) we have that for all $t_1, \ldots, t_n$, $f(t_1, \ldots, t_n) = a(s_1(t_1), \ldots, s_n(t_n))$.

In particular it should be clear that every ex-post-Nash implementation is by definition also a Bayesian implementation for any distributions D_i. In general, however, being a Bayesian implementation depends on the distributions D_i and there are many cases where a Bayesian–Nash equilibrium exists even though no dominant-strategy one does. A simple example – a first price auction – is shown in the next subsection. Just like in the case of dominant-strategy implementations, Bayesian implementations can also be turned into ones that are truthful in a Bayesian sense.

Definition 9.43 A mechanism is truthful in the Bayesian sense if (a) it is "direct revelation"; i.e., the type spaces are equal to the action spaces $T_i = X_i$, and (b) the truthful strategies $s_i(t_i) = t_i$ are a Bayesian–Nash equilibrium.

Proposition 9.44 (Revelation principle) *If there exists an arbitrary mechanism that implements f in the Bayesian sense, then there exists a truthful mechanism that implements f in the Bayesian sense. Moreover, the expected payments of the players in the truthful mechanism are identical to those, obtained in equilibrium, in the original mechanism.*

The proof is similar to the proof of the same principle in the dominant-strategy setting given in Proposition 9.25.

9.6.2 First Price Auction

As an example of Bayesian analysis we study the standard first price auction in a simple setting: a single item is auctioned between two players, Alice and Bob. Each has a private value for the item: a is Alice's value and b is Bob's value. While we already saw that a second price auction will allocate the item to the one with higher value, here we ask what would happen if the auction rules are the usual first-price ones: the highest bidder pays his bid. Certainly Alice will not bid a since if she does even if she wins her utility will be 0. She will thus need to bid some $x < a$, but how much lower? If she knew that Bob would bid y, she would certainly bid $x = y + \epsilon$ (as long as $x \leq a$). But she does not know y or even b which y would depend on – she only knows the distribution D_{Bob} over b.

Let us now see how this situation falls in the Bayesian–Nash setting described above: The type space T_{Alice} of Alice and T_{Bob} of Bob is the nonnegative real numbers, with t_{Alice} denoted by a and t_{Bob} denoted by b. The distributions over the type space are D_{Alice} and D_{Bob}. The action spaces X_{Alice} and X_{Bob} are also the non-negative real numbers, with x_{Alice} denoted by x and x_{Bob} denoted by y. The possible outcomes are {Alice-wins, Bob-wins}, with $v_{\text{Alice}}(\text{Bob-wins}) = 0$ and $v_{\text{Alice}}(\text{Alice-wins}) = a$ (and similarly for Bob). The outcome function is that Alice-wins if $x \geq y$ and Bob-wins otherwise (we arbitrarily assume here that ties are broken in favor of Alice). Finally, the payment functions are $p_{\text{Alice}} = 0$ whenever Bob-wins and $p_{\text{Alice}} = x$ whenever Alice-wins , while $p_{\text{Bob}} = y$ whenever Bob-wins and $p_{\text{Bob}} = 0$ whenever Alice-wins. Our question translates into finding the Bayesian–Nash equilibrium of this game. Specifically we wish to find a strategy s_{Alice} for Alice, given by a function $x(a)$, and a strategy s_{Bob} for Bob, given by the function $y(b)$, that are in Bayesian equilibrium, i.e., are best-replies to each other.

In general, finding Bayesian–Nash equilibria is not an easy thing. Even for this very simple first price auction the answer is not clear for general distributions D_{Alice} and D_{Bob}. However, for the symmetric case where $D_{\text{Alice}} = D_{\text{Bob}}$, the situation is simpler and a closed form expression for the equilibrium strategies may be found. We will prove it for the special case of uniform distributions on the interval [0, 1]. Similar arguments work for arbitrary nonatomic distributions over the valuations as well as for any number of bidders.

Lemma 9.45 *In a first price auction among two players with prior distributions of the private values a, b uniform over the interval* [0, 1], *the strategies $x(a) = a/2$ and $y(b) = b/2$ are in Bayesian–Nash equilibrium.*

Note that in particular $x < y$ if and only if $a < b$ thus the winner is also the player with highest private value. This means that the first price auction also maximizes social welfare, just like a second-price auction.

PROOF Let us consider which bid x is Alice's optimal response to Bob's strategy $y = b/2$, when Alice has value a. The utility for Alice is 0 if she loses and $a - x$ if she wins and pays x, thus her expected utility from bid x is given by $u_{\text{Alice}} = Pr[\text{Alice wins with bid } x] \cdot (a - x)$, where the probability is over the prior distribution over b. Now Alice wins if $x \geq y$, and given Bob's strategy $y = b/2$, this is exactly when $x \geq b/2$. Since b is distributed uniformly in [0, 1] we can readily calculate this probability: $2x$ for $0 \leq x \leq 1/2$, 1 for $x \geq 1/2$, and 0 for $x \leq 0$. It is easy to verify that the optimal value of x is indeed in the range $0 \leq x \leq 1/2$ (since $x = 1/2$ is clearly better than any $x > 1/2$, and since any

$x < 0$ will give utility 0). Thus, to optimize the value of x, we need to find the maximum of the function $2x(a - x)$ over the range $0 \leq x \leq 1/2$. The maximum may be found by taking the derivative with respect to x and equating it to 0, which gives $2a - 4x = 0$, whose solution is $x = a/2$ as required. □

9.6.3 Revenue Equivalence

Let us now attempt comparing the first price auction and the second price auction. The social choice function implemented is exactly the same: giving the item to the player with highest private value. How about the payments? Where does the auctioneer get higher revenue? One can readily express the revenue of the second-price auction as $min(a, b)$ and the revenue of the first-price auction as $max(a/2, b/2)$, and it is clear that each of these expressions is higher for certain values of a and b.

But which is better on the average – in expectation over the prior distributions of a and b? Simple calculations will reveal that the expected value of $min(a, b)$ when a and b are chosen uniformly in $[0, 1]$ is exactly 1/3. Similarly the expected value of $max(a/2, b/2)$ when a and b are chosen uniformly in $[0, 1]$ is also exactly 1/3. Thus both auctions generate equivalent revenue in expectation! This is no coincidence. It turns out that in quite general circumstances every two Bayesian–Nash implementations of the same social choice function generate the same expected revenue.

Theorem 9.46 (The Revenue Equivalence Principle) *Under certain weak assumptions (to be detailed in the proof body), for every two Bayesian–Nash implementations of the same social choice function f, we have that if for some type t_i^0 of player i, the expected (over the types of the other players) payment of player i is the same in the two mechanisms, then it is the same for every value of t_i. In particular, if for each player i there exists a type t_i^0 where the two mechanisms have the same expected payment for player i, then the two mechanisms have the same expected payments from each player and their expected revenues are the same.*

Thus, for example, all single-item auctions that allocate (in equilibrium) the item to the player with highest value and in which losers pay 0, will have identical expected revenue.

The similarity to Theorem 9.37 should be noted: in both cases it is shown that the allocation rule determines the payments, up to a normalization. In the case of dominant strategy implementation, this is true for every fixed type of the other players, while in the case of Bayesian–Nash implementation, this is true in expectation over that types of the others. The proofs of the two theorems look quite different due to technical reasons. The underlying idea is the same: take two "close" types, then the equations specifying that for neither type does a player gain by misrepresenting himself as the other type, put together, determine the difference in payments in terms of the social choice function.

PROOF Using the revelation principle, we can first limit ourselves to mechanisms that are truthful in the Bayesian–Nash sense. Let us denote by V_i the space of valuation functions $v_i(t_i, \cdot)$ over all t_i.

Assumption 1 Each V_i is convex. (Note that this holds for essentially every example we had so far. This condition can be replaced by path-connectedness, and the proof becomes just slightly messier.)

Take any type $t_i^1 \in T_i$. We will derive a formula for the expected payment for this type that depends only on the expected payment for type t_i^0 and on the social choice function f. Thus any two mechanisms that implement the same social choice function and have identical expected payments at t_i^0 will also have identical expected payments at t_i^1. For this, let us now introduce some notations:

- v^0 is the valuation $v(t_i^0, \cdot)$. v^1 is the valuation $v(t_i^1, \cdot)$. We will look at these as vectors (in $V_i \subseteq \Re^A$), and look at their convex combinations $v^\lambda = v^0 + \lambda(v_1 - v_0)$. The convexity of V_i implies that $v^\lambda \in V_i$ and thus there exists some type t_i^λ such that $v^\lambda = v(t_i^\lambda, \cdot)$.
- p^λ is the expected payment of player i at type t_i^λ: $p^\lambda = E_{t_{-i}} p_i(t_i, t_{-i})$.
- w^λ is the probability distribution of $f(t_i^\lambda, \cdot)$, i.e., for every $a \in A$ $w^\lambda(a) = Pr_{t_{-i}}[f(t_i^\lambda, t_{-i}) = a]$.

Assumption 2 w^λ is continuously differentiable in λ. (This assumption is not really needed, but allows us to simply take derivatives and integrals as convenient.)

Once we have this notation in place, the proof is easy. Note that under these notations the expected utility of player i with type t_i^λ that declares $t_i^{\lambda'}$ is given by the expression $v^\lambda \cdot w^{\lambda'} - p^{\lambda'}$. Since a player with type t_i^λ prefers reporting the truth rather than $t_i^{\lambda+\epsilon}$ we have that $v^\lambda \cdot w^\lambda - p^\lambda \geq v^\lambda \cdot w^{\lambda+\epsilon} - p^{\lambda+\epsilon}$. Similarly, a player with type $t_i^{\lambda+\epsilon}$ prefers reporting the truth rather than t_i^λ, so we have $v^{\lambda+\epsilon} \cdot w^\lambda - p^\lambda \leq v^{\lambda+\epsilon} \cdot w^{\lambda+\epsilon} - p^{\lambda+\epsilon}$. Re-arranging and putting together, we get

$$v^\lambda(w^{\lambda+\epsilon} - w^\lambda) \leq p^{\lambda+\epsilon} - p^\lambda \leq v^{\lambda+\epsilon}(w^{\lambda+\epsilon} - w^\lambda)$$

Now divide throughout by ϵ and let ϵ approach 0. $v^{\lambda+\epsilon}$ approaches v^λ, $(w^{\lambda+\epsilon} - w^\lambda)/\epsilon$ approaches the vector $dw^\lambda/d\lambda = w'(\lambda)$ and thus we get that $(p^{\lambda+\epsilon} - p^\lambda)/\epsilon)$ approaches $v^\lambda \cdot w'(\lambda)$, and thus the derivative of p^λ is defined and is continuous. Integrating, we get $p^1 = p^0 + \int_0^1 v^\lambda \cdot w'(\lambda) d\lambda$. □

Thus the revenue equivalence theorem tells us that we cannot increase revenue without changing appropriately the allocation rule (social choice function) itself. In particular, all the corollaries in Section 9.5.5 apply, in the sense of expectation, to all Bayesian–Nash implementations. However, if we are willing to modify the social choice function, then we can certainly increase revenue. Here is an example for the case of an auction with two bidders with valuations distributed uniformly in [0, 1]: Put a reservation price of 1/2, and then sell to the highest bidder for a price that is the maximum of the low bid and the reservation price, 1/2. If both bidders bid below the reservation price, then none of them wins. First, it is easy to verify that this rule is incentive compatible. Then a quick calculation will reveal that the expected revenue of this auction is 5/12 which is more than the 1/3 obtained by the regular second price or first price auctions. Chapter 13 discusses revenue maximization further.

9.7 Further Models

This chapter has concentrated on basic models. Here we shortly mention several model extensions that address issues ignored by the basic models and have received attention in economic theory.

9.7.1 Risk Aversion

All of our discussion in the Bayesian model assumed that players are risk-neutral: obtaining a utility of 2 with probability 1/2 is equivalent to obtaining a utility of 1 with probability 1. This is why we could just compute players' utilities by taking expectation. In reality, players are often risk-averse, preferring a somewhat lower utilities if they are more certain. A significant body of work in economic theory deals with formalizing and analyzing strategic behavior of such players. In our context, a particularly interesting observation is that the revenue equivalence principle fails and that with risk-averse bidders different mechanisms that implement the same social choice function may have different revenue. As an example it is known that first price auctions generate more revenue than second price auctions if the bidders are risk-averse.

9.7.2 Interdependent Values

We have considered only independent private value models: the types of the players are chosen independently of each other and each players' valuation depends only on his own private information. In a completely general setting, there would be some joint distribution over "states of the world" where such a state determines the valuations of all players. Players would not necessarily get as private information their own valuation, but rather each would get some "signal" – partial information about the state of the world – that provide some information about his own valuation and some about the valuations of others. Most of the results in this chapter cease holding for general models with interdependent values.

A case that is in the extreme opposite to the private value model is the "common value" model. In an auction of a single item under this model, we assume that the object in question has exactly the same value for all bidders. The problem is that none of them know exactly what this value is and each player's signal only provides some partial information. An example is an auction for financial instruments such as bonds. Their exact value is not completely known as it depends on future interest rates, the probability of default, etc. What is clear though is that whatever value the bonds will turn out to have, it will be the same for everyone. In such settings, an auction really serves as an information aggregation vehicle, reaching a joint estimate of the value by combining all players' signals. A common pitfall in such cases is the "winner's curse": if each bidder bids their own estimate of the object's common value, as determined from their own signal, then the winner will likely regret winning – the fact that a certain bidder won means that other signals implied a lower value, which likely means that the real value is lower than the estimate of the winner. Thus in equilibrium bidders must bid an estimate that is also conditioned on the fact that they win.

A commonly considered formalization that takes into account both a private value component and a common value component is that of affiliated signals. Roughly speaking, in such models each player gets a signal that is positively correlated (in a strong technical sense called affiliation) not only with his own value but also with the values of other players. In such settings, ascending English auctions are "better" (generate more revenue) than the non-adaptive second price auction (which is equivalent to an English auction in private value models): as the bidding progresses, each bidder gets information from the other bidders that increases his estimate of his value.

9.7.3 Complete Information Models

Our main point of view was that each player has its own private information. Some models consider a situation where all players have complete information about the game; it is only the mechanism designer who is lacking such information. A prototypical instance is that of King Solomon: two women, each claiming that the baby is hers. The women both know who the real mother is, but not King Solomon – he must design a mechanism that elicits this information from their different preferences. Several notions of implementation in such setting exists, and in general, mechanism design is much easier in this setting. In particular, many implementations without money are possible.

9.7.4 Hidden Actions

All of the theory of Mechanism Design attempts overcoming the problem that players have private information that is not known to the mechanism designer. In many settings a different stumbling block occurs: players may perform hidden actions that are not visible to the "mechanism." This complementary difficulty to the private information difficulty has been widely studied in economics and has recently started to be considered in computer science settings.

9.8 Notes

Most of the material in this chapter can be found in graduate textbooks on microeconomics such as Mas-Collel et al. (1995). The books (Krishna, 2002; Klemperer, 2004) on Auction theory contain more detail. As the Internet gained influence, during the 1990s, researchers in AI, computer networks, and economics started noticing that mechanism design can be applied in computational settings. This was put forward in a general way in Nisan and Ronen (2001) who also coined the term Algorithmic Mechanism Design.

The earliest work on voting methods including that of Condorcet and Borda goes back to the late 18th century, appropriately around the time of the French Revolution. The modern treatment of social choice theory originates with the seminal work of Arrow (1951), where Arrow's theorem also appears. Over the years many proofs for Arrow's theorem have been put forward; we bring one of those in Geanakopolos (2005). The Gibbard-Satterthwaite theorem is due to Gibbard (1973) and Satterthwaite (1975). The computational difficulty of manipulation of voting rules was first studied in Bartholdi et al. (1989).

The positive results in Mechanism Design in the quasi-linear setting originate with the seminal work of Vickrey (1961), who, in particular, studied single-item auctions and multiunit auctions with downward sloping valuations. The public project problem was studied by Clarke (1971), who also suggested the pivot rule, and the general formulation of what is now called VCG mechanisms appears in Groves (1973). The Bilateral Trade problem was studied in Myerson and Satterthwaite (1983), and the application of buying a path in a network was put forward in Nisan and Ronen (2001).

The general framework of Mechanism Design and its basic notions have evolved in microeconomic theory mostly in the 1970s, and mostly in the general Bayesian setting that we only get to in Section 9.6. Among the influential papers in laying out the foundations are Vickrey (1961), Clarke (1971), Groves (1973), Satterthwaite (1975), Green and Laffont (1977), Dasgupta et al. (1979), and Myerson (1981).

Early papers in algorithmic Mechanism Design, such as Nisan and Ronen (2001) and Lehmann et al. (2002), pointed out the necessity and difficulty of implementing social choice functions other than welfare maximization, due to other optimization goals or due to computational hardness. Characterizations of incentive compatible mechanisms have been previously obtained in economic theory as intermediate steps on the way to theorems with clear economic motivation. The discussion here tries to put it all together independently of particular intended applications. The weak monotonicity condition is from Bikhchandani et al. (2006) and the sufficiency of this condition in convex domains is from Saks and Yu (2005). The affine-maximization characterization in complete domains is from Roberts (1979), and Lavi et al. (2003) attempts generalization to other domains. The uniqueness of pricing is the analog of the revenue equivalence theorem in the Bayesian setting which is due to Myerson (1981); Green and Laffont (1977) showed it in the dominant strategy setting for welfare maximizing social choice functions. The corollary of the impossibility of budget-balanced bilateral trade appears in Myerson and Satterthwaite (1983) in the Bayesian setting.

The Bayesian setting is currently the main vehicle of addressing lack of information in economic theory, and this development has mostly happened during the 1960s, with the main influence being the seminal work of Harsanyi (1968). As mentioned previously, most of development of the field of Mechanism Design noted above was in this setting. The revenue equivalence theorem, the form of the expected payment in single-parameter domains, as well as an analysis of revenue-maximizing auctions is from Myerson (1981).

Risk-averse bidders in (reverse) auctions are analyzed by Holt (1980). Auctions in the common value model are analyzed in Wilson (1977) and Milgrom (1981). The general model of interdependent valuations with affiliated signals was studied in Milgrom and Weber (1982). Mechanism Design in complete information models is discussed in Maskin (1985) and Moore and Repullo (1988).

Acknowledgments

I thank Shahar Dobzinski, Dana Fisman, Jason Hartline, Orna Kupferman, Ron Lavi, Ariel Procaccia, and James Schummer for comments on earlier drafts of this chapter.

Bibliography

K. Arrow. *Social Choice and Individual Values*. Yale University Press, 1951.

J. Bartholdi, III, C. Tovey, and M. Trick. Computational difficulty of manipulating an election. *Soc. Choice Welfare*, 6(3):227–241, 1989.

S. Bikhchandani, S. Chatterji, R. Lavi, A. Mu'alem, N. Nisan, and A. Sen. Weak monotonicity characterizes deterministic dominant strategy implementation. *Econometrica*, 74(4), 2006.

E.H. Clarke. Multipart pricing of public goods. *Public Choice*, 17–33, 1971.

P. Dasgupta, P. Hammond, and E. Maskin. The implementation of social choice rules: Some general results on incentive compatibility. *Rev. Econ. Stud.*, (46):185–216, 1979.

J. Geanakopolos. Three brief proofs of arrow's impossibility theorem. *Econ. Theor.*, 26(1):211–215, 2005.

A. Gibbard. Manipulation of voting schemes: a general result. *Econometrica*, 41:587–601, 1973.

J. Green and J.J. Laffont. Characterization of satisfactory mechanism for the revelation of preferences for public goods. *Econometrica*, 427–438, 1977.

T. Groves. Incentives in teams. *Econometrica*, 617–631, 1973.

J.C. Harsanyi. Games with incomplete information played by 'bayesian' players, parts i ii and iii. *Mgmt. Sci.*, 14, 1967–68.

C. Holt. Competitive bidding for contracts under alternative auction procedures. *J. Political Econ.*, 88:433–445, 1980.

P. Klemperer. *Auctions: Theory and Practice*. Princeton University Press, 2004.

V. Krishna. *Auction Theory*. Academic Press, 2002.

R. Lavi, A. Mu'alem, and N. Nisan. Towards a characterization of truthful combinatorial auctions. In *FOCS*, 2003.

D. Lehmann, L.I. O'Callaghan, and Y. Shoham. Truth revelation in approximately efficient combinatorial auctions. *JACM* 49(5), 577–602, Sept. 2002.

A. Mas-Collel, W. Whinston, and J. Green. *Microeconomic Theory*. Oxford University Press, 1995.

E. Maskin. The theory of implementation in nash equilibrium. In *Soc. Goals and Soc. Org.: Essays in Honor of Elisha Pazner*, 1985.

P. Milgrom. Rational expectations, information acquisition, and competitive bidding. *Econometrica*, 49:921–943, 1981.

P.R. Milgrom and R.J. Weber. A theory of auctions and competitive bidding. *Econometrica*, 50(5):1089–1122, 1982.

J. Moore and R. Repullo. Subgame perfect implementation. *Econometrica*, 56:1191–1220, 1988.

R. B. Myerson. Optimal auction design. *Math. Oper. Res.*, 6(1):58–73, 1981.

R.B. Myerson and M. Satterthwaite. Efficient mechanisms for bilateral trading. *J. Economic Theory*, (28):265–281, 1983.

N. Nisan and A. Ronen. Algorithmic mechanism design. *Games Econ. Behav.*, 35:166–196, 2001.

K. Roberts. The characterization of implementable choice rules. In *Aggregation and Revelation of Preferences*, J-J. Laffont (ed.), North Holland Publishing Company, 1979.

M. Saks and L. Yu. Weak monotonicity suffices for truthfulness. In *EC*, 2005.

M.A. Satterthwaite. Strategy-proofness and arrow's condition: Existence and correspondence theorems for voting procedures and social welfare functions. *J. Economic Theory*, 187–217, 1975.

W. Vickrey. Counterspeculation, auctions and competitive sealed tenders. *J. Finance*, 8–37, 1961.

R. Wilson. A bidding model of perfect competition. *Rev. Econ. Stud.*, 44:511–518, 1977.

CHAPTER 10

Mechanism Design without Money

James Schummer and Rakesh V. Vohra

Abstract

Despite impossibility results on general domains, there are some classes of situations in which there exist interesting dominant-strategy mechanisms. While some of these situations (and the resulting mechanisms) involve the transfer of money, we examine some that do not. Specifically, we analyze problems where agents have single-peaked preferences over a one-dimensional "public" policy space; and problems where agents must match with each other.

10.1 Introduction

The Gibbard–Satterthwaite Theorem (Theorem 9.8) is a Procrustean bed[1] that is escaped only by relaxing its assumptions. In conjunction with the Revelation Principle (Proposition 9.25), it states that on the *general domain* of preferences, only dictatorial rules can be implemented in dominant strategies (if the range contains at least three alternatives). In this chapter we escape Procrustes by examining dominant strategy implementation on *restricted* domains of preferences.[2]

In most applications it is clearly unreasonable to assume that agents' preferences are completely unrestricted, as was assumed in the voting context of Section 9.2.4. For instance, in situations involving the allocation of goods, including money, one can safely assume that each agent prefers to receive more money (or other goods). As can be seen in the following chapters, the ability for agents to make monetary transfers allows for a rich class of *strategy-proof* rules.

Nevertheless there are many important environments where money cannot be used as a medium of compensation. This constraint can arise from ethical and/or institutional

[1] Procrustes was a giant that lived by one of the roads that led to Attica. He boasted of a bed whose length exactly matched the size of its occupant. What he neglected to mention was that this remarkable feature was obtained by either stretching or butchering his guest to fit the bed.

[2] Other avenues of escape not discussed here include randomization, making preferences common knowledge, and using weaker notions of implementation.

considerations: many political decisions must be made without monetary transfers; organ donations can be arranged by "trade" involving multiple needy patients and their relatives, yet monetary compensation is illegal. In this chapter we focus on a few examples of just this kind.

Before proceeding with the examples, we formalize the idea that dominant-strategy implementation is a weaker concept on restricted domains of preferences. In general, a decision problem can be described by these parameters: a set of agents $N = \{1, 2, \ldots, n\}$, a set of alternatives A, and for each agent $i \in N$ a set of potential preference relations $\mathcal{R}_i$ over the alternatives in A.[3] The Gibbard–Satterthwaite Theorem (Theorem 9.8) applies, for example, when each $\mathcal{R}_i$ is the entire set of linear orders on A.

An allocation rule is a function $f\colon \times \mathcal{R}_i \to A$, mapping preferences of the agents into alternatives. It is *strategy-proof* if its use makes it a weakly dominant strategy for agents to truthfully report their preferences. (See Section 9.4). We observe the following principle.

Consider two decision problems $(N, A, \mathcal{R}_1, \ldots, \mathcal{R}_n)$ and $(N, A, \mathcal{R}'_1, \ldots, \mathcal{R}'_n)$, where $\mathcal{R}'_i \subseteq \mathcal{R}_i$ for each $i \in N$. Suppose $f\colon \times \mathcal{R}_i \to A$ is a *strategy-proof* rule for the former problem. Then the restriction of the function f to $(\times \mathcal{R}'_i)$, namely $f|_{\times \mathcal{R}'_i}$, defines a *strategy-proof* rule for the latter problem.

The proof of this is straightforward: on a smaller domain of preferences, *strategy-proofness* is easier to satisfy because it imposes strictly fewer constraints. This simple observation justifies the search for reasonable (or at least nondictatorial) rules for decision problems involving "smaller" domains of preferences than those that yield the Gibbard–Satterthwaite Theorem.

In Section 10.2 we analyze a problem involving a natural domain restriction when agents vote over one-dimensional policies. It is one of the canonical "public good" settings ($\mathcal{R}_i = \mathcal{R}_j$ for all $i, j \in N$) in which interesting, *strategy-proof* rules can be obtained. The analysis here is illustrative of the approach used to characterize such rules in other environments. In Sections 10.3 and 10.4 we analyze matching problems. As opposed to the previous setting, these problems have the feature that each agent cares only about his own private consumption; that is, each $\mathcal{R}_i$ contains only preference relations that are sensitive only to certain dimensions of the alternative space A; hence $\mathcal{R}_i \neq \mathcal{R}_j$ whenever $i \neq j$. These are examples of what are called "private good" problems. Two kinds of matching problems are analyzed, demonstrating the limits of what can be implemented in dominant strategies in such environments.

10.2 Single-Peaked Preferences over Policies

A simple but elegant class of domains involves *single-peaked preferences* over one-dimensional policy spaces. This domain can be used to model political policies, economic decisions, location problems, or any allocation problem where a single point

[3] A preference relation is a weak order on A.

must be chosen in an interval. The key assumption we make is that agents' preferences are assumed to have a single most-preferred point in the interval, and that preferences are "decreasing" as one moves away from that peak.

Formally, the allocation space (or policy space) is the unit interval $A = [0, 1]$. An *outcome* in this model is a single point $x \in A$. Each agent $i \in N$ has a preference ordering $\succeq_i$ (i.e., a weak order) over the outcomes in $[0, 1]$. The preference relation $\succeq_i$ is *single-peaked* if there exists a point $p_i \in A$ (the *peak* of $\succeq_i$) such that for all $x \in A \setminus \{p_i\}$ and all $\lambda \in [0, 1)$, $(\lambda x + (1 - \lambda)p_i) \succ_i x$.[4] Let $\mathcal{R}$ denote the class of single-peaked preferences.

We denote the peaks of preference relations $\succeq_i, \succeq_i', \succeq_j$, etc., respectively by p_i, p_i', p_j, etc. Denote a *profile* (n-tuple) of preferences as $\succeq \in \mathcal{R}^n$.

One can imagine this model as representing a political decision such as an income tax rate, another political issue with conservative/liberal extremes, the location of a public facility on a road, or even something as simple as a group of people deciding on the temperature setting for a shared office. In these and many other examples, the agents have an ideal preferred policy in mind, and would prefer that a decision be made as close as possible to this "peak."

A *rule* $f\colon \mathcal{R}^n \to A$ assigns an outcome $f(\succeq)$ to any preference profile $\succeq$. As before, a rule is *strategy-proof* if it is a dominant strategy for each agent to report his preferences truthfully when the rule is being used to choose a point.

In contrast to the impossibility result of Gibbard (1973) and Satterthwaite (1975), that obtain on the universal domain of preferences, we shall see that this class of problems admits a rich family of *strategy-proof* rules whose ranges include more than two alternatives. In fact, the family of such rules remains rich even when one restricts attention (as we do in this chapter) to rules that satisfy the following condition.

We say that a rule f is *onto* if for all $x \in A$ there exists $\succeq \in \mathcal{R}^n$ such that $f(\succeq) = x$. An *onto* rule cannot preclude an outcome from being chosen *ex ante*. It is not without loss of generality to impose this condition. For instance, fix two points $x, y \in [0, 1]$ and consider a rule that chooses whichever of the two points is preferred to the other by a majority of agents (and where x is chosen in case of a tie). Such a rule is *strategy-proof*, but not *onto*. Similar *strategy-proof* rules can even break ties between x and y by using preference information about other points $x', y', \ldots$, in $[0, 1]$, even though x', etc., are not in the range of the rule.

The *onto* condition is even weaker than what is called *unanimity*, which requires that whenever all agents' preferences have the same peak ($p_i = p_j$ for all i, j), the rule must choose that location as the outcome. In turn, *unanimity* is weaker than *Pareto-optimality*: for all $\succeq \in \mathcal{R}^n$, there exists no point $x \in [0, 1]$ such that $x \succ_i f(\succeq)$ for all $i \in N$.

As it turns out, these three requirements are all equivalent among *strategy-proof* rules.

Lemma 10.1 *Suppose* f *is* strategy-proof. *Then* f *is* onto *if and only if it is unanimous if and only if it is Pareto-optimal.*

[4] The binary relation $\succ_i$ is the strict (asymmetric) part of $\succeq_i$. Under a single-peaked preference relation, preference is strictly decreasing as one moves away from p_i.

PROOF It is clear that Pareto-optimality implies the other two conditions. Suppose f is *strategy-proof* and *onto*. Fix $x \in [0, 1]$ and let $\succeq \in \mathcal{R}^n$ be such that $f(\succeq) = x$. Consider any "unanimous" profile $\succeq' \in \mathcal{R}^n$ such that $p_i' = x$ for each $i \in N$. By *strategy-proofness*, $f(\succeq_1', \succeq_2, \ldots, \succeq_n) = x$, otherwise agent 1 could manipulate f. Repeating this argument, $f(\succeq_1', \succeq_2', \succeq_3, \ldots, \succeq_n) = x, \ldots,$ $f(\succeq') = x$. That is, f is unanimous.

Finally, to derive a contradiction, suppose that f is not Pareto-optimal at some profile $\succeq \in \mathcal{R}^n$. This implies that either (i) $f(\succeq) < p_i$ for all $i \in N$ or (ii) $f(\succeq) > p_i$ for all $i \in N$. Without loss of generality, assume (i) holds. Furthermore, assume that the agents are labeled so that $p_1 \leq p_2 \leq \cdots \leq p_n$.

If $p_1 = p_n$ then unanimity is violated, completing the proof. Otherwise, let $j \in N$ be such that $p_1 = p_j < p_{j+1}$; that is, $j < n$ agents have the minimum peak. For all $i > j$, let $\succeq_i'$ be a preference relation such that both $p_i' = p_1$ and $f(\succeq) \succeq_i' p_i$.

Let $x_n = f(\succeq_1, \ldots, \succeq_{n-1}, \succeq_n')$. By *strategy-proofness*, $x_n \in [f(\succeq), p_n]$, otherwise agent n (with preference $\succeq_n'$) could manipulate f by reporting preference $\succeq_n$. Similarly, $x_n \notin (f(\succeq), p_n]$, otherwise agent n (with preference $\succeq_n$) could manipulate f by reporting preference $\succeq_n'$. Therefore $x_n = f(\succeq)$.

Repeating this argument as each $i > j$ replaces $\succeq_i$ with $\succeq_i'$, we have

$$f(\succeq_1, \ldots, \succeq_j, \succeq_{j+1}', \ldots, \succeq_n') = f(\succeq)$$

which contradicts unanimity. Since a *strategy-proof, onto* rule must be unanimous, this is a contradiction. □

10.2.1 Rules

The central *strategy-proof* rule on this domain is the simple median-voter rule. Suppose that the number of agents n is odd. Then the rule that picks the median of the agents' peaks (p_i's) is a *strategy-proof* rule.

It is straightforward to see why this rule is *strategy-proof*: If an agent's peak p_i lies *below* the median peak, then he can change the median only by reporting a preference relation whose peak lies *above* the true median. The effect of this misreport is for the rule to choose a point even further away from p_i, making the agent worse off. A symmetric argument handles the case in which the peak is above the median. Finally, an agent cannot profitably misreport his preferences if his peak is the median one to begin with.

More generally, for any number of agents n and any positive integer $k \leq n$, the rule that picks the kth highest peak is *strategy-proof* for precisely the same reasons as above. An agent can only move the kth peak further from his own. The median happens to be the case where $k = (n + 1)/2$.

The *strategy-proofness* of such rules stands in contrast to the incentives properties of rules that choose *average*-type statistics. Consider the rule that chooses the average of the n agents' peaks. Any agent with peak $p_i \in (0, 1)$ that is not equal to the average can manipulate the rule by reporting preferences with a more extreme peak (closer to 0 or 1) than his true peak.

This would also hold for any *weighted* average of the agents' peaks, with one exception. If a rule allocated all of the weight to one agent, then the resulting rule simply picks that agent's peak always. Such a *dictatorial* rule is *strategy-proof* and *onto*.

In addition to favorable incentives properties, rules based on order statistics have the property that they require little information to be computed. Technically a rule requires agents to report an entire preference ordering over [0, 1]. The rules we have discussed so far, however, only require agents to report their most preferred point, i.e., a single number. In fact, under the *onto* assumption, this informational property is a consequence of the *strategy-proofness* requirement; that is, *all strategy-proof* and *onto* rules have the property that they can be computed solely from information about the agents' peaks.

To begin showing this, we first observe that the class of "kth-statistic rules" can be further generalized as follows. Consider a fixed set of points $y_1, y_2, \ldots, y_{n-1} \in A$. Consider the rule that, for any profile of preferences $\succeq$, chooses the median of the $2n-1$ points consisting of the n agents' peaks and the $n-1$ points of y. This kind of rule differs from the previous ones in that, for some choices of y and some profiles of preferences, the rule may choose a point that is not the peak of *any* agent's preferences. Yet, for the same reasons as above, such a rule is *strategy-proof.*

It turns out that such rules compose the entire class of *strategy-proof* and *onto* rules that treat agents symmetrically. To formalize this latter requirement, we call a rule *anonymous* if for any $\succeq\, \in \mathcal{R}^n$ and any permutation $\succeq'$ of $\succeq$, $f(\succeq') = f(\succeq)$. This requirement captures the idea that the agents' names play no role in the behavior of a rule. Dictatorial rules mentioned above are examples of rules that are *strategy-proof* and *onto*, but not *anonymous*.

Theorem 10.2 *A rule f is* strategy-proof, onto, *and* anonymous *if and only if there exist $y_1, y_2, \ldots, y_{n-1} \in [0, 1]$ such that for all $\succeq\, \in \mathcal{R}^n$,*

$$f(\succeq) = \text{med}\{p_1, p_2, \ldots, p_n, y_1, y_2, \ldots, y_{n-1}\}. \tag{10.1}$$

PROOF We leave it as an exercise to verify that such a rule satisfies the three axioms in the Theorem. To prove the converse, suppose f is *strategy-proof, onto*, and *anonymous*.

We make extensive use of the two (extreme) preference relations that have peaks at 0 and 1 respectively. Since preferences relations are ordinal, there is only one preference relation with a peak at 0 and only one with a peak at 1. Denote these two preference relations by $\succeq_i^0$ and $\succeq_i^1$ respectively.

(Construct the y_m's.) For any $1 \le m \le n-1$, let y_m denote the outcome of f when m agents have preference relation $\succeq_i^1$ and the remainder have $\succeq_i^0$:

$$y_m = f\left(\succeq_1^0, \ldots, \succeq_{n-m}^0, \succeq_{n-m+1}^1, \ldots, \succeq_n^1\right).$$

Recall that by *anonymity* the order of the arguments of f is irrelevant; if precisely m agents have preference relation $\succeq_i^1$ and the rest have $\succeq_i^0$ then the outcome is y_m. In addition, we leave it to the reader to verify that *stragegy proofness* implies monotonicity of the y_m's: $y_m \leq y_{m+1}$ for each $1 \leq m \leq n-2$. We prove the theorem by showing that f satisfies Eq. (10.1) with respect to this list of y_m's.

Consider a profile of preferences $\succeq \in \mathcal{R}^n$ with peaks $p_1, \ldots, p_n$. Without loss of generality (by *anonymity*) assume that $p_i \leq p_{i+1}$ for each $i \leq n-1$. We wish to show $f(\succeq) = x^* \equiv \text{med}\{p_1, \ldots, p_n, y_1, \ldots, y_{n-1}\}$.

(Case 1: the median is some y_m.) Suppose $x^* = y_m$ for some m. By monotonicity of the peaks and y_m's, since x^* is the median of $2n-1$ points this implies $p_{n-m} \leq x^* = y_m \leq p_{n-m+1}$. By assumption,

$$x^* = y_m = f(\succeq_1^0, \ldots, \succeq_{n-m}^0, \succeq_{n-m+1}^1, \ldots, \succeq_n^1). \tag{10.2}$$

Let $x_1 = f(\succeq_1, \succeq_2^0, \ldots, \succeq_{n-m}^0, \succeq_{n-m+1}^1, \ldots, \succeq_n^1)$. *Strategy-proofness* implies $x_1 \geq x^*$, otherwise agent 1 with preference $\succeq_1^0$ could manipulate f. Similarly, since $p_1 \leq y_m$, we cannot have $x_1 > x^*$, otherwise agent 1 with preference $\succeq_1$ could manipulate f. Hence $x_1 = x^*$. Repeating this argument for all $i \leq n-m$, $x^* = f(\succeq_1, \ldots, \succeq_{n-m}, \succeq_{n-m+1}^1, \ldots, \succeq_n^1)$. The symmetric argument for all $i > n-m$ implies

$$f(\succeq_1, \ldots, \succeq_n) = x^*. \tag{10.3}$$

(Case 2: the median is an agent's peak.) The remaining case is that $y_m < x^* < y_{m+1}$ for some m. (The cases where $x^* < y_1$ and $x^* > y_{n-1}$ are similar, denoting $y_0 = 0$ and $y_n = 1$.) In this case, since the agents' peaks are in increasing order, we have $x^* = p_{n-m}$.

If

$$f(\succeq_1^0, \ldots, \succeq_{n-m-1}^0, \succeq_{n-m}, \succeq_{n-m+1}^1, \ldots, \succeq_n^1) = x^* = p_{n-m} \tag{10.4}$$

then, analogous to the way Eq. (10.2) implied Eq. (10.3), repeated applications of *strategy-proofness* (to the $n-1$ agents other than $i = n-m$) would imply $f(\succeq_1, \ldots, \succeq_n) = x^*$, and the proof would be finished. The remainder of the proof is devoted to showing that indeed Eq. (10.4) must hold.

Suppose to the contrary that

$$f(\succeq_1^0, \ldots, \succeq_{n-m-1}^0, \succeq_{n-m}, \succeq_{n-m+1}^1, \ldots, \succeq_n^1) = x' < x^*. \tag{10.5}$$

(The case $x' > x^*$ can be proven symmetrically.) If agent $(n-m)$ were to report preference $\succeq_{n-m}^0$ instead, f would choose outcome y_m; hence *strategy-proofness* implies $y_m \leq x' < x^*$. See Figure 10.1.

Denote the outcomes that agent $(n-m)$ can obtain by varying his preferences, fixing the others, as[5]

$$O = \{x : \exists \tilde{\succeq}_{n-m} \text{ s.t. } x = f(\succeq_1^0, \ldots, \succeq_{n-m-1}^0, \tilde{\succeq}_{n-m}, \succeq_{n-m+1}^1, \ldots, \succeq_n^1)\}.$$

By definition, $x' \in O$; Case 1 implies $y_m, y_{m+1} \in O$. *Strategy proofness* implies that $x' = \max\{x \in O : x \leq x^*\}$, otherwise by reporting some other preference, agent $(n-m)$ could obtain some $x \in (x', x^*)$, violating *strategy proofness*.

5 The literature on *strategy proofness* refers to this as an option set.

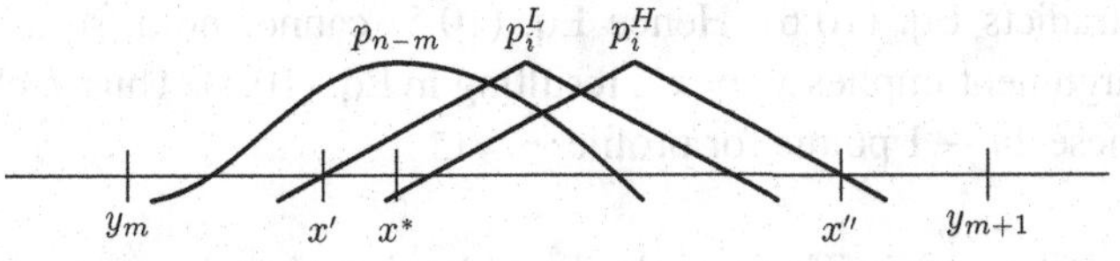

Figure 10.1. Proof of Theorem 10.2. If a *strategy-proof, onto* rule does not pick x^* when it is the median of peaks and y_m's, then a contradiction is reached using preferences with peaks at p_i^L and p_i^H.

Letting $x'' \equiv \inf\{x \in O : x \geq x^*\}$, *strategy proofness* implies $x'' \in O$.[6] To see this, let $\succeq''_{n-m}$ be a preference relation with peak $p''_{n-m} = x''$ and such that $(x'' + \epsilon) \succ''_{n-m} x'$ for some small $\epsilon > 0$. Then *strategy proofness* implies $f(\succeq_1^0, \ldots, \succeq_{n-m-1}^0, \succeq''_{n-m}, \succeq_{n-m+1}^1, \ldots, \succeq_n^1)\} = \hat{x} \in [x'', x'' + \epsilon]$. But if $\hat{x} \neq x''$, then there would exist a misreport resulting in an outcome arbitrarily closer to x'', making agent $(n - m)$ (with preference $\succeq''_{n-m}$) better off. Hence $\hat{x} = x'' = \min\{x \in O : x \geq x^*\}$. With Eq. (10.5), we have $x'' > x^*$.

We have shown that $O \cap (x', x'') = \emptyset$. Let p_i^L be a symmetric preference relation with peak at $p^L = (x' + x'')/2 - \varepsilon$, where $\varepsilon > 0$ is sufficiently small; see Figure 10.1. Similarly let p_i^H be a symmetric preference relation with peak at $(x' + x'')/2 + \varepsilon$. Then *strategy-proofness* implies

$$f(\succeq_1^0, \ldots, \succeq_{n-m-1}^0, \succeq_{n-m}^H, \succeq_{n-m+1}^1, \ldots, \succeq_n^1)\} = x''.$$

By repeated application of *strategy-proofness* (along the lines used in proving Eq. (10.3)), this implies

$$f(\succeq_1^L, \ldots, \succeq_{n-m-1}^L, \succeq_{n-m}^H, \succeq_{n-m+1}^1, \ldots, \succeq_n^1)\} = x''.$$

Lemma 10.1 (Pareto-optimality) implies

$$f(\succeq_1^L, \ldots, \succeq_{n-m-1}^L, \succeq_{n-m}^L, \succeq_{n-m+1}^1, \ldots, \succeq_n^1)\} \geq p_i^L.$$

Therefore, *strategy-proofness* implies

$$f(\succeq_1^L, \ldots, \succeq_{n-m-1}^L, \succeq_{n-m}^L, \succeq_{n-m+1}^1, \ldots, \succeq_n^1)\} = x'' \tag{10.6}$$

otherwise agent $n - m$ could manipulate at one of the two profiles (since ε is small).

On the other hand, *strategy-proofness* implies

$$f(\succeq_1^0, \ldots, \succeq_{n-m-1}^0, \succeq_{n-m}^L, \succeq_{n-m+1}^1, \ldots, \succeq_n^1) = x'$$

by the definition of $\succeq_i^L$. *Strategy-proofness* implies that if agent $(n - m - 1)$ instead reports preference $\succeq^L$, a point must be chosen that is in the interval $[x', x'' - 2\varepsilon]$, otherwise, he could report $\succeq^0$ to gain. By repeated application of this argument, this continues to hold as each agent $1 \leq i \leq n - m - 1$ changes his report from $\succeq_i^0$ to $\succeq_i^L$, so

$$f(\succeq_1^L, \ldots, \succeq_{n-m-1}^L, \succeq_{n-m}^L, \succeq_{n-m+1}^1, \ldots, \succeq_n^1) \in [x', x'' - 2\varepsilon].$$

[6] More generally, *strategy-proofness* alone implies O is closed. For brevity we prove only $x'' \in O$.

This contradicts Eq. (10.6). Hence Eq. (10.5) cannot hold, so $x' \geq x^*$; the symmetric argument implies $x' = x^*$, resulting in Eq. (10.4). Thus f chooses the median of these $2n - 1$ points for profile $\succeq$. □

The parameters (y_m's) in Theorem 10.2 can be thought of as the rule's degree of compromise when agents have extremist preferences. If m agents prefer the highest possible outcome (1), while $n - m$ prefer the lowest (0), then which point should be chosen? A true median rule would pick whichever extreme (0 or 1) contains the most peaks. On the other hand, the other rules described in the Theorem may choose intermediate points (y_m) as a compromise. The degree of compromise (which y_m) can depend on the degree to which the agents' opinions are divided (the size of m).

The *anonymity* requirement is a natural one in situations where agents are to be treated as equals. If one does not require this, however, the class of *strategy-proof* rules becomes even larger. We have already mentioned *dictatorial* rules, which always chooses a predetermined agent's peak. There are less extreme violations of anonymity: The full class of *strategy-proof*, *onto* rules, which we now define, allows agents to be treated with varying degrees of asymmetry.

Definition 10.3 A rule f is a *generalized median voter scheme* (g.m.v.s.) if there exist 2^n points in $[0, 1]$, $\{\alpha_S\}_{S \subseteq N}$, such that

(i) $S \subseteq T \subseteq N$ implies $\alpha_S \leq \alpha_T$,
(ii) $\alpha_\emptyset = 0$, $\alpha_N = 1$, and
(iii) for all $\succeq \in \mathcal{R}^n$, $f(\succeq) = \max_{S \subseteq N} \min\{\alpha_S, p_i : i \in S\}$.

An example is given below. It is worth making two observations regarding Definition 10.3. First, the monotonicity condition (i) is actually redundant. If parameters $\{\alpha_S\}_{S \subseteq N}$ fail this condition, they still define some *strategy-proof* rule via condition (iii). However, the resulting rule could also be defined by an alternate set of parameters $\{\alpha'_S\}_{S \subseteq N}$ that do satisfy condition (i). Second, condition (ii) is present merely to guarantee the rule to be *onto*. Parameters that fail this condition still define a *strategy-proof* rule whose range is $[\alpha_\emptyset, \alpha_N]$.[7]

Consider the rule described by the parameters (α_S's) in Figure 10.2, for the 3-agent case. The reader should first verify the following. If each agent in some set $S \subseteq N$ were to have a preference peak at 1, while each remaining agent (in $N \setminus S$) were to have a preference peak at 0, then the rule would choose α_S as the outcome. In this sense, the α_S parameters reflect a (nonanonymous) degree of compromise at extreme preference profiles, analogous to the y_m parameters of Theorem 10.2.

Without the anonymity condition, some agents – more generally some *coalitions* of agents – are more powerful than others. To see this, consider the profile of preferences represented in Figure 10.2 with peaks p_1, p_2, p_3. Following condition (iii) of Definition 10.3, calculate $\min\{\alpha_S, p_i : i \in S\}$ for each $S \subseteq N$. Beginning with the three

[7] To avoid potential confusion, we point out that, in some of the literature, the term *generalized median voter scheme* also refers to such rules.

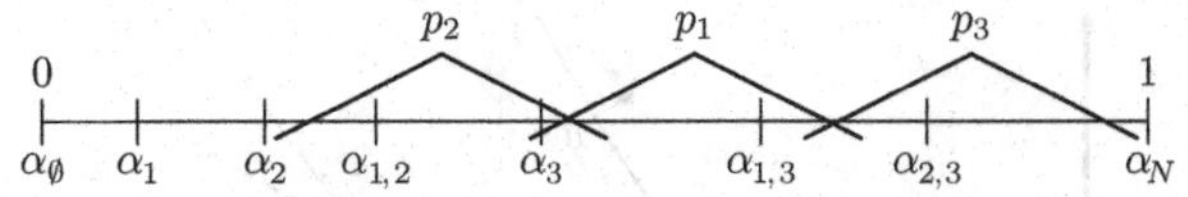

Figure 10.2. An example of a generalized median voter scheme for $n = 3$.

singleton coalitions of the form $S = \{i\}$, these values are α_1, α_2, and α_3, because each p_i is above that agent's corresponding $\alpha_{\{i\}}$. (For peak p_3', the third value would have been p_3' instead.) Since the g.m.v.s. eventually chooses the maximum of these kinds of values (after we also check larger coalitions), agent 3 can be said to have more power than the other two agents, *as a singleton*. A large α_3 corresponds to more instances in which agent 3's peak is a candidate outcome for this rule. A small α_1 corresponds to more instances in which agent 1 has no impact on the outcome (i.e., whenever $p_1 > \alpha_{\{1\}}$).

On the other hand, we also need to calculate these minimum-values for larger coalitions. For the pairs of agents $\{1, 2\}$, $\{1, 3\}$, and $\{2, 3\}$, these values are $\alpha_{\{1,2\}}$, p_1, and p_2 respectively. Coalition $\{1, 2\}$ is the weakest two-agent coalition in the sense that they have the lowest α_S. After checking $S = \emptyset$ (which yields 0) and $S = N$ (yielding a repetition of the value p_2), we calculate the rule's outcome to be the maximum of the 2^n values $\{0, \alpha_1, \alpha_2, \alpha_3, \alpha_{\{1,2\}}, p_1, p_2, p_2\}$ we have obtained, which is $\alpha_{\{3\}}$.

We close by stating the main result of this section. We omit its proof, which has much in common with the proof of Theorem 10.2.

Theorem 10.4 *A rule f is* strategy-proof *and* onto *if and only if it is a generalized median voter scheme.*

10.2.2 Application to Public Good Cost Sharing

Consider a group of n agents who have access to a machine that can convert their labor into some public good. Specifically, suppose that the machine requires the simultaneous labor of all n agents in order to work. The agents are free to jointly decide how many hours of labor, ℓ, to work. Implicit is the requirement that each agent work for ℓ hours, however, since the machine requires all n agents' labor simultaneously. After ℓ hours of labor, the machine outputs $y = Y(\ell)$ units of some public good, where the production function Y is assumed to be an increasing and strictly concave function, with $Y(0) = 0$.

Different agents may have different preferences over how much labor they should provide, in exchange for the public good. Let us suppose that we know nothing about their preferences, other than the fact that they are represented by some utility function $u_i(\ell, y)$ which is strictly increasing in y, strictly decreasing in ℓ, and is quasi-concave.[8] See Figure 10.3.

In this environment, a rule takes as input the reported utility functions of the agents, subject only to the assumptions we have made. It then gives as output a single labor requirement $\ell = f(u_1, \ldots, u_n)$. Each agent is then required to provide ℓ units of labor,

[8] The function $u()$ is quasi-concave if, at each (ℓ, y), the upper contour set $\{(\ell', y') : u(\ell', y') \geq u(\ell, y)\}$ is convex.

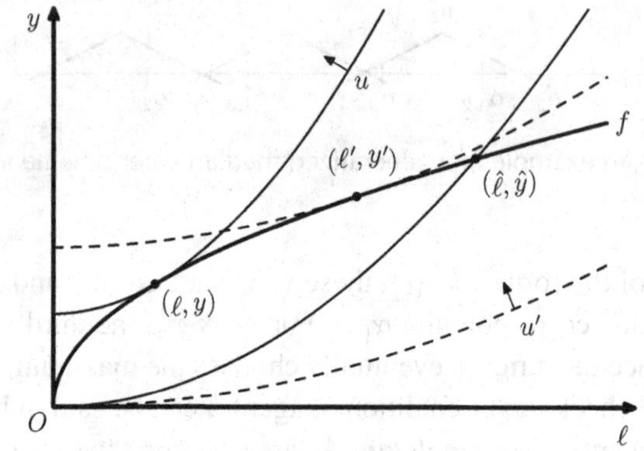

Figure 10.3. An agent with utility function u most prefers the outcome (y, ℓ); one with u' prefers (y', ℓ').

and they enjoy $Y(\ell)$ units of output as a reward. What rules are *strategy-proof* and *onto*?

By assumption, outcomes may only be attained along the graph of Y. Because of the assumptions on Y and on preferences, it is clear that agents have single-peaked preferences over this consumption space. It follows that any *strategy-proof*, *onto* rule for this environment is a generalized median voter schemes operating along the graph of Y.

Proving this is not difficult, but involves some technical details that we omit. First the outcome space is not bounded as we assumed before, although it would certainly be reasonable to bound it by assumption. Second, the preference domain here should be verified to yield all the single-peaked preferences necessary to characterize generalized median voter schemes; e.g., we used *symmetric* single-peaked preferences to construct the proof of Theorem 10.2. Third, one should demonstrate that a *strategy-proof* rule in this environment is invariant to utility information away from the graph of Y. We leave it to the interested reader to verify our claim despite these technicalities.

In this kind of problem, it may be reasonable to add additional requirements to a rule. One that we address is the requirement that an agent should be better off as part of this decision-making group than if he were simply to walk away. Formally, if this public good technology did not exist, each agent would provide no labor ($\ell = 0$), and would enjoy none of the public good ($y = 0$). We say a rule is *individually rational* if for all $U = (u_1, \ldots, u_n)$ and $1 \geq i \geq n$, we have $u_i(f(U), Y(f(U))) \geq u_i(0, 0)$.

What *strategy-proof* and *onto* rules satisfy *individual rationality*? In terms of our earlier model, where agents have single-peaked preferences on [0, 1], that question translates as follows: What g.m.v.s. has the property that, for any preference profile, each agent (weakly) prefers the chosen outcome to the outcome $x = 0$?

The answer is that there is a unique such rule. As an exercise, we leave it to the reader to show that the rule that chooses the minimum peak is the unique *strategy-proof*, *onto* rule that satisfies this individual rationality condition. In terms of this public good model, this corresponds to asking each agent their most preferred labor level ℓ, and choosing the minimum.

10.3 House Allocation Problem

The House allocation problem is a model for understanding the allocation of indivisible goods. It involves a set N of n agents, each owning a unique house and a strict preference ordering over all n houses. The objective is to reallocate the houses among the agents in an appropriate way. A modern version of the same would replace houses by kidneys.

While any possible (strict) preference ordering over the homes is permitted, the set of preferences over allocations is restricted. In particular, an agent is indifferent between all allocations that give her the same house. Therefore the Gibbard–Satterthwaite Theorem does not apply in this setting.

One could select an allocation of homes in a variety of ways, perhaps so as to optimize some function of the preferences and then investigate if the resulting allocation rule is *strategy-proof*. However, this ignores an important feature not present in earlier examples. In this environment, agents control the resources to be allocated. Therefore an allocation can be subverted by a subset of agents who might choose to break away and trade among themselves. For this reason it is natural to focus on allocations that are invulnerable to agents opting out.

Number each house by the number of the agent who owns that house. An allocation is an n vector a whose ith component, a_i, is the number of the house assigned to agent i. If a is the initial allocation then $a_i = i$. For an allocation to be feasible, we require that $a_i \neq a_j$ for all $i \neq j$. The preference ordering of an agent i will be denoted $\succ_i$ and $x \succ_i y$ will mean that agent i ranks house x above house y. Denote by A the set of all feasible allocations. For every $S \subseteq N$ let $A(S) = \{z \in A : z_i \in S \ \forall i \in S\}$ denote the set of allocations that can be achieved by the agents in S trading among themselves alone. Given an allocation $a \in A$, a set S of agents is called a **blocking coalition** (for a) if there exists a $z \in A(S)$ such that for all $i \in S$ either $z_i \succ_i a_i$ or $z_i = a_i$ and for at least one $j \in S$ we have that $z_j \succ_j a_j$. A blocking coalition can, by trading among themselves, receive homes that each strictly prefers (or is equivalent) to the home she receives under a, with at least one agent being strictly better off. The set of allocations that is not blocked by any subset of agents is called the **core**.

The reader will be introduced to the notion of the core in Chapter 15 (Section 15.2) where it will be defined for a cooperative game in which utility is transferable via money (a TU game). The house allocation problem we consider is an example of a cooperative game with nontransferable utility (an NTU game). The definition of the core offered here is the natural modification of the notion of TU core to the present setting.

The theorem below shows the core to be nonempty. The proof is by construction using the top trading cycle algorithm (TTCA).

Definition 10.5 (Top Trading Cycle Algorithm) Construct a directed graph with one vertex for each agent. Insert a directed edge from i to j if house j is agent i's most-preferred one. An edge of the form (i, i) will be called a loop. First identify all directed cycles and loops of this graph. Because preferences are strict and the outdegree of each vertex is exactly one, the set of such cycles and loops is both non-empty and node disjoint. Let N_1 be the set of vertices (agents) incident to these cycles. Each cycle implies a sequence of swaps. For example, suppose $i_1 \to i_2 \to i_3 \to \ldots \to i_r$ is such a cycle. Give house i_1 to agent i_r, house i_r to agent i_{r-1} and so on.

After all such swaps are performed, create a new graph with one vertex for each agent in $N \setminus N_1$. Insert a directed edge from i to j if house j is agent i's most-preferred house among those owned by agents in $N \setminus N_1$. Let N_2 be the set of vertices (agents) incident to the loops and cycles in this graph, and let these agents swap houses as we did with N_1.

Form N_3, etc., similarly. The Top Trading Cycle Algorithm (TTCA) yields the resulting matching.

This algorithm is used to prove the following result.

Theorem 10.6 *The core of the house allocation problem consists of exactly one matching.*

PROOF We prove that if a matching is in the core, it must be the one returned by the TTCA.

Under the TTCA, each agent in N_1 receives his favorite house, i.e., the house ranked first in his preference ordering. Therefore, N_1 would form a blocking coalition to any allocation that does not assign to all of those agents the houses they would receive under the TTCA. That is, any core allocation must assign N_1 to houses just as the TTCA assigns them.

Given this fact, the same argument applies to N_2: Under the TTCA, each agent in N_2 receives his favorite house *not including* those houses originally endowed by agents in N_1. Therefore, if an allocation is in the core and the agents in N_1 are assigned each other's houses, then agents in N_2 must receive the same houses they receive under the TTCA.

Continuing the argument for each N_k proves that if an allocation is in the core, then it is the one determined by the TTCA. This proves that there is at most one core allocation.

To prove that the TTCA allocation is in the core, it remains to be shown that there is no other blocking coalition $S \subseteq N$. This is left to the reader. □

To apply the TTCA, one must know the preferences of agents over homes. Do they have an incentive to truthfully report these? To give a strongly positive answer to this question, we first associate the TTCA with its corresponding direct revelation mechanism. Define the **Top Trading Cycle (TTC) Mechanism** to be the function (mechanism) that, for each profile of preferences, returns the allocation computed by the TTCA.

Theorem 10.7 *The TTC mechanism is* strategy-proof.

PROOF Let π be a profile of preference orderings and a the allocation returned by TTCA when applied to π. Suppose that agent $j \in N_k$ for some k misreports her preference ordering. Denote by π' the new profile of preference orderings. Let a' the allocation returned by TTCA when applied to π'. If the TTCA is not *strategy-proof* $a'_i >^i a_i$. Observe that $a_i = a'_i$ for all $i \in \bigcup_{r=1}^{k-1} N_r$. Therefore, $a'_i \in N \setminus \{\bigcup_{r=1}^{k-1} N_r\}$. However, the TTCA chooses a_i to be agent i's top ranked choice from $N \setminus \{\bigcup_{r=1}^{k-1} N_r\}$ contradicting the fact that $a'_i >^i a_i$. □

If we relax the requirement that preferences be strict, what we had previously called a blocking set is now called a **weakly** blocking set. What we had previously called the core is now called the *strict* core. With indifference, a **blocking** set S is one where *all* agents in S are *strictly* better off by trading among themselves. Note the requirement that all agents be strictly better off. The *core* is the set of allocations not blocked by any set S.

When preferences are strict, every minimal weakly blocking set is a blocking set. To see this, fix a weakly blocking set S. An agent in S who is not made strictly better off by trade among agents in S must have been assigned their own home. Remove them from S. Repeat. The remaining agents must all be allocated houses that make them strictly better off. Hence, when preferences are strict the core and strict core coincide. With indifference permitted, the strict core can be different from the core. In fact, there are examples where the strict core is empty and others where it is not unique. Deciding emptiness of the strict core is polynomial in $|N|$.

Another possible extension of the model is to endow the agents with more than one good. For example, a home and a car. Clearly, if preferences over pairs of goods are sufficiently rich, the core can be empty. It turns out that even under very severe restrictions the core can still be empty. For example, when preferences are separable, i.e., one's ranking over homes does not depend on which car one has.

10.4 Stable Matchings

The stable matching problem was introduced as a model of how to assign students to colleges. Since its introduction, it has been the object of intensive study by both computer scientists and economists. In computer science it used as vehicle for illustrating basic ideas in the analysis of algorithms. In economics it is used as a stylized model of labor markets. It has a direct real-world counterpart in the procedure for matching medical students to residencies in the United States.

The simplest version of the problem involves a set M of men and a set W of women. Each $m \in M$ has a strict preference ordering over the elements of W and each $w \in W$ has a strict preference ordering over the men. As before the preference ordering of agent i will be denoted $\succ_i$ and $x \succ_i y$ will mean that agent i ranks x above y. A **matching** is an assignment of men to women such that each man is assigned to at most one woman and vice versa. We can accommodate the possibility of an agent choosing to remain single as well. This is done by including for each man (woman) a dummy woman (man) in the set W (M) that corresponds to being single (or matched with oneself). With this construction we can always assume that $|M| = |W|$.

As in the house allocation problem a group of agents can subvert a prescribed matching by opting out. In a manner analogous to the house allocation problem, we can define a blocking set. A matching is called **unstable** if there are two men m, m' and two women w, w' such that

(i) m is matched to w,
(ii) m' is matched to w', and
(iii) $w' \succ_m w$ and $m \succ_{w'} m'$

The pair (m, w') is called a **blocking pair**. A matching that has no blocking pairs is called **stable**.

Example 10.8 The preference orderings for the men and women are shown in the table below

$\succ_{m_1}$	$\succ_{m_2}$	$\succ_{m_3}$	$\succ_{w_1}$	$\succ_{w_2}$	$\succ_{w_3}$
w_2	w_1	w_1	m_1	m_3	m_1
w_1	w_3	w_2	m_3	m_1	m_3
w_3	w_2	w_3	m_2	m_2	m_2

Consider the matching $\{(m_1, w_1), (m_2, w_2), (m_3, w_3)\}$. This is an unstable matching since (m_1, w_2) is a blocking pair. The matching $\{(m_1, w_1), (m_3, w_2), (m_2, w_3)\}$, however, is stable.

Given the preferences of the men and women, is it always possible to find a stable matching? Remarkably, yes, using what is now called the deferred acceptance algorithm. We describe the male-proposal version of the algorithm.

Definition 10.9 (Deferred Acceptance Algorithm, male-proposals) First, each man proposes to his top-ranked choice. Next, each woman who has received at least two proposals keeps (tentatively) her top-ranked proposal and rejects the rest. Then, each man who has been rejected proposes to his top-ranked choice among the women who have not rejected him. Again each woman who has at least two proposals (including ones from previous rounds) keeps her top-ranked proposal and rejects the rest. The process repeats until no man has a woman to propose to or each woman has at most one proposal. At this point the algorithm terminates and each man is assigned to a woman who has not rejected his proposal. Notice that no man is assigned to more than one woman. Since each woman is allowed to keep only one proposal at any stage, no woman is assigned to more than one man. Therefore the algorithm terminates in a matching.

We illustrate how the (male-proposal) algorithm operates using Example 10.8 above. In the first round, m_1 proposes to w_2, m_2 to w_1, and m_3 to w_1. At the end of this round w_1 is the only woman to have received two proposals. One from m_3 and the other from m_2. Since she ranks m_3 above m_2, she keeps m_3 and rejects m_2. Since m_3 is the only man to have been rejected, he is the only one to propose again in the second round. This time he proposes to w_3. Now each woman has only one proposal and the algorithm terminates with the matching $\{(m_1, w_2), (m_2, w_3), (m_3, w_2)\}$. It is easy to verify that the matching is stable and that it is different from the one presented earlier.

Theorem 10.10 *The male propose algorithm terminates in a stable matching.*

PROOF Suppose not. Then there exists a blocking pair (m_1, w_1) with m_1 matched to w_2, say, and w_1 matched to m_2. Since (m_1, w_1) is blocking and $w_1 \succ_{m_1} w_2$, in the proposal algorithm, m_1 would have proposed to w_1 before w_2. Since m_1 was not matched with w_1 by the algorithm, it must be because w_1 received a proposal from a man that she ranked higher than m_1. Since the algorithm matches her to m_2 it follows that $m_2 \succ_{w_1} m_1$. This contradicts the fact that (m_1, w_1) is a blocking pair. □

One could just as well have described an algorithm where the women propose and the outcome would also be a stable matching. Applied to the example above, this would produce a stable matching different from the one generated when the men propose. Thus, not only is a stable matching guaranteed to exist but there can be more than 1. If there can be more than one stable matching, is there a reason to prefer one to another? Yes. To explain why, some notation.

Denote a matching by μ. the woman assigned to man m in the matching μ is denoted $\mu(m)$. Similarly, $\mu(w)$ is the man assigned to woman w. A matching μ is **male-optimal** if there is no stable matching ν such that $\nu(m) \succ_m \mu(m)$ or $\nu(m) = \mu(m)$ for all m with $\nu(j) \succ_j \mu(j)$ for at least one $j \in M$. Similarly define **female-optimal**.

Theorem 10.11 *The stable matching produced by the (male-proposal) Deferred Acceptance Algorithm is male-optimal.*

PROOF Let μ be the matching returned by the male-propose algorithm. Suppose μ is not male optimal. Then, there is a stable matching ν such that $\nu(m) \succ_m \mu(m)$ or $\nu(m) = \mu(m)$ for all m with $\nu(j) \succ_j \mu(j)$ for at least one $j \in M$. Therefore, in the application of the proposal algorithm, there must be an iteration where some man j proposes to $\nu(j)$ before $\mu(j)$ since $\nu(j) \succ_j \mu(j)$ and is rejected by woman $\nu(j)$. Consider the first such iteration. Since woman $\nu(j)$ rejects j she must have received a proposal from a man i she prefers to man j. Since this is the first iteration at which a male is rejected by his partner under ν it follows that man i ranks woman $\nu(j)$ higher than $\nu(i)$. Summarizing, $i \succ_{\nu(j)} j$ and $\nu(j) \succ_i \nu(i)$ implying that ν is not stable, a contradiction. □

Clearly one can replace the word "male" by the word "female" in the statement of the theorem above. It is natural to ask if there is a stable matching that would be optimal with respect to both men and women. Alas, no. The example above has two stable matchings: one male optimal and the other female optimal. At least one female is strictly better off under the female optimal matching than the male optimal one and no female is worse off. A similar relationship holds when comparing the two stable matchings from the point of view of the men.

A stable matching is immune to a pair of agents opting out of the matching. We could be more demanding and ask that no subset of agents should have an incentive to opt out of the matching. Formally, a matching μ' **dominates** a matching μ if there is a set $S \subset M \cup W$ such that for all $m, w \in S$, both (i) $\mu'(m), \mu'(w) \in S$ and (ii) $\mu'(m) \succ_m \mu(m)$ and $\mu'(w) \succ_w \mu(w)$. Stability is a special case of this dominance condition when we restrict attention to sets S consisting of a single couple. The set of undominated matchings is called the **core** of the matching game. The next result is straightforward.

Theorem 10.12 *The core of the matching game is the set of all stable matchings.*

Thus far we have assumed that the preference orderings of the agents is known to the planner. Now suppose that they are private information to the agent. As before we can associate a direct revelation mechanism with an algorithm for finding a stable matching.

Theorem 10.13 *The direct mechanism associated with the male propose algorithm is* strategy-proof *for the males.*

PROOF Suppose there is a profile of preferences $\pi = (\succ_{m_1}, \succ_{m_2}, \ldots, \succ_{m_n})$ for the men, such that man m_1, say, can misreport his preferences and obtain a better match. To express this formally, let μ be the stable matching obtained by applying the male-proposal algorithm to the profile π. Let ν be the stable matching that results under the male-proposal algorithm when m_1 reports the preference ordering $\succ_*$ instead, i.e. applied to the profile $\pi^1 = (\succ_*, \succ_{m_2}, \ldots, \succ_{m_n})$. We show that if $\nu(m_1) \succ_{m_1} \mu(m_1)$, then ν is not stable with respect to π_1, which is a contradiction. For notational convenience we write $a \succeq_m b$ to mean $[a \succ_m b$ or $a = b]$.

Let $R = \{m : \nu(m) \succ_m \mu(m)\}$. We show that for any $m \in R$ and $w = \nu(m)$, $m' \equiv \mu(w) \in R$. If $m' = m_1$, we are done. Otherwise, since $w \succ_m \mu(m)$, stability of μ implies $m' \succ_w m$. Stability of ν (for π_1) then implies $\nu(m') \succ_{m'} w$. Therefore $m' \in R$, and we can define $S = \{w : \nu(w) \in R\} = \{w : \mu(w) \in R\}$.

Since $\mu(w) \succ_w \nu(w)$ for any $w \in S$, during execution of the male-proposal algorithm on π, each $w \in S$ rejects $\nu(w) \in R$ at some iteration. Let m be the last man in R to make a proposal during the execution of the male-proposal algorithm. This proposal is made to $w = \mu(m) \in S$ who, by choice of m, must have rejected $\nu(w)$ at some strictly earlier iteration of the algorithm. This means that when m proposes to w, she must reject an outstanding proposal from some $m' \notin R$ such that $m' \succ_w \nu(w)$. Since $m' \notin R$, we have $w \succ_{m'} \mu(m') \succeq_{m'} \nu(m')$. Hence (m', w) form a blocking pair for ν at π^1 (since $m' \neq m_1$). □

The mechanism associated with the male propose algorithm is not *strategy-proof* for the females. To see why, it is enough to consider example. The male propose algorithm returns the matching $\{(m_1, w_2), (m_2, w_3), (m_3, w_1)\}$. In the course of the algorithm the only woman who receives at least two proposals is w_1. She received proposals from m_2 and m_3. She rejects m_2 who goes on to propose to w_3 and the algorithm terminates. Notice that w_1 is matched with her second choice. Suppose now that she had rejected

m_3 instead. Then m_3 would have gone on to proposes to w_2. Woman w_2 now has a choice between m_1 and m_3. She would keep m_3 and reject m_1, who would go on to propose to w_1. Woman w_1 would keep m_1 over m_2 and in the final matching be paired with a her first-rank choice.

It is interesting to draw an analogy between the existence of stable matchings and that of Walrasian equilibrium. We know (Chapter 6) that Walrasian equilibria exist. Furthermore, they are the solutions of a fixed point problem. In the cases when they can be computed efficiently it is because the set of Walrasian equilibria can be described by a set of convex inequalities. The same can be said of stable matchings. The set of stable matchings is fixed points of a nondecreasing function defined on a lattice. In addition, one can describe the set of stable matchings as the solutions to a set of linear inequalities.

10.4.1 A Lattice Formulation

We describe a proof of the existence of stable matchings using Tarski's fixed point theorem. It will be useful to relax the notion of a matching. Call an assignment of women to men such that each man is assigned to at most one woman (but a woman may be assigned to more than one man) a **male semimatching**. The analogous object for women will be called a **female semimatching**. For example, assigning each man his first choice would be a male semimatching. Assigning each woman her third choice would be an example of a female semimatching.

A pair of male and female semimatchings will be called a **semimatching** which we will denote by μ, ν, etc. An example of a semi-matching would consist of each man being assigned his first choice and each woman being assigned her last choice.

The woman assigned to the man m under the semi-matching μ will be denoted $\mu(m)$. If man m is assigned to no woman under μ, then $\mu(m) = m$. Similarly for $\mu(w)$. Next we define a partial order over the set of semimatchings. Write $\mu \succeq \nu$ if

(i) $\mu(m) \succ_m \nu(m)$ or $\mu(m) = \mu(m)$ for all $m \in M$ and
(ii) $\mu(w) \prec_w \nu(w)$ or $\mu(w) = \nu(w)$ for all $w \in W$.

Therefore $\mu \succeq \nu$ if all the men are better off under μ than in ν and all the women are worse off under μ than in ν.

Next we define the meet and join operations. Given two semimatchings μ and ν define $\lambda = \mu \vee \nu$ as follows:

(i) $\lambda(m) = \mu(m)$ if $\mu(m) \succ_m \nu(m)$ otherwise $\lambda(m) = \nu(m)$,
(ii) $\lambda(w) = \mu(w)$ if $\mu(w) \prec_w \nu(w)$ otherwise $\lambda(w) = \nu(w)$.

Define $\lambda' = \mu \wedge \nu$ as follows:

(i) $\lambda'(m) = \mu(m)$ if $\mu(m) \prec_m \nu(m)$ otherwise $\lambda(m) = \nu(m)$,
(ii) $\lambda(w) = \mu(w)$ if $\mu(w) \succ_w \nu(w)$ otherwise $\lambda(w) = \nu(w)$.

With these definitions it is easy to check that the set of semimatchings forms a compact lattice.

Now define a function f on the set of semi-matchings that is nondecreasing. Given a semi-matching μ define $f(\mu)$ to be the following semi-matching:

(i) $f(\mu)(m)$ is man m's most preferred woman from the set $\{w: m \succ_w \mu(w), m = \mu(w)\}$. If this set is empty set $f(\mu)(m) = m$.
(ii) $f(\mu)(w)$ is woman w's most preferred man from the set $\{m: w \succ_m \mu(m), w = \mu(m)\}$. If this set is empty set $f(\mu)(w) = w$.

It is clear that f maps semi-matchings into semi-matchings.

Theorem 10.14 *There is a semi-matching μ such that $f(\mu) = \mu$ and that μ is a stable matching.*

PROOF We use Tarski's theorem. It suffices to check that f is nondecreasing. Suppose $\mu \succeq \nu$. Pick any $m \in M$. From the definition of $\succeq$, the women are worse off under μ than in ν. Thus

$$\{w: m \succ_w \nu(w)\} \subseteq \{w: m \succ_w \mu(w)\}$$

and so $f(\mu)(m) \succ_m f(\nu)(m)$ or $f(\mu)(m) = f(\nu)(m)$. A similar argument applies for each $w \in W$. Thus f is nondecreasing.

Since the conditions of Tarski's theorem hold, it follows that there is a semi-matching μ such that $f(\mu) = \mu$. We show that the semi-matching is a stable matching.

By the definition of a semi-matching we have for every $m \in M$, $\mu(m)$ single valued as is $\mu(w)$ for all $w \in W$. To show that μ is a matching, suppose not. Then there is a pair $m_1, m_2 \in M$, say, such that $\mu(m_1) = \mu(m_2) = w^*$. Since $f(\mu) = \mu$ it follows that w^* is m_1's top-ranked choice in $\{w: m_1 \succ_w \mu(w), m_1 = \mu(w)\}$ and m_2's top ranked choice in $\{w: m_2 \succ_w \mu(w), m_2 = \mu(w)\}$. From this we deduce that $\mu(w^*) = m_3$ where $m_1, m_2 >^{w^*} m_3$. However, $m_3 = \mu(w^*) = f(\mu^*)(w^*)$, which is woman w^*'s top-ranked choice in $\{m: w^* \succ_m \mu(m), \mu(m) = w^*\}$. Since m_1, m_2 are members of this set, we get a contradiction.

To show that the matching μ is stable suppose not. Then there must be a blocking pair (m^*, w^*). Let $w' = \mu(m^*)$ and $m' = \mu(w^*)$, $m' \neq m^*$ and $w^* \neq w'$. Since (m^*, w^*) is blocking, $m^* \succ_{w^*} m'$ and $w^* \succ_{m^*} w'$. Now $w' = \mu(m^*) = f(\mu)(m^*)$, which is man m^*'s top-ranked choice from $\{w : m^* \succ_w \mu(w), m^* = \mu(w)\}$. But this set contains w^*, which is ranked higher by man m^* than w', a contradiction. □

10.4.2 The LP Formulation

One can formulate the problem of finding a stable matching as the solution to a set of linear inequalities. For each man m and woman w let $x_{mw} = 1$ if man m is matched with woman w and zero otherwise. Then, every stable matching must satisfy the following.

$$\sum_{w \in W} x_{mw} = 1 \qquad \forall m \in M$$

$$\sum_{m \in M} x_{mw} = 1 \qquad \forall w \in W$$

$$\sum_{j \prec_m w} x_{mj} + \sum_{i \prec_w m} x_{iw} + x_{mw} \leq 1 \qquad \forall m \in M, w \in W$$

$$x_{mw} \geq 0 \qquad \forall m \in M, w \in W$$

Let P be the polyhedron defined by these inequalities.

The first two constraints of P ensure that each agent is matched with exactly one other agent of the opposite sex. The third constraint ensures stability. To see why, suppose $\sum_{j \prec_m w} x_{mj} = 1$ and $\sum_{i \prec_w m} x_{iw} = 1$. Then man m is matched to a woman, j that he ranks below w. Similarly, woman w is matched to a man she ranks below m. This would make the pair (m, w) a blocking pair.

Theorem 10.15 *P is the convex hull of all stable matchings.*

10.4.3 Extensions

We have been careful to specify that preferences are strict. If we allow for indifference, Theorem 10.7 becomes false. This is because there are instances of the stable matching problem in which no male or female optimal stable matching exists. The other theorems stated above continue to hold in the presence of indifferences.

We also limited ourselves to one-to-one matchings. There are situations where one side of the market wishes to match with more than one agent. The college admissions market is the classic example. Each student can be assigned to at most one college but each college can be assigned to many students. In this more general setup colleges will have preferences over subsets of students. In the absence of any restrictions on these preferences a stable matching need not exist. One restriction on preferences for which the results above carry over with no change in statement or proof is the quota model. Each college has a strict preference ordering over the students and a quota r of students it wishes to admit. Consider two subsets, S and T, of students of size r that differ in exactly one student. The college prefers the subset containing the more preferred student.

A third extension is to relax the bipartite nature of the stable matching problem. The nonbipartite version is called the stable roommates problem. Suppose that a set of N individuals such that $|N|$ is even. A matching in this setting is a partition of N into disjoint pairs of individuals (roommates). Each individual has a strict preference ordering over the other individuals that they would like to be paired with. As before, a matching is unstable if there exists a pair who prefer each other to the person they are matched with. Such a pair is called blocking. Unlike the stable matching problem, stable roommates need not exist as the following four person example illustrates.

$\succ_1$	$\succ_2$	$\succ_3$	$\succ_4$
3	1	2	2
2	3	1	1
4	4	4	4

Each column lists the preference ordering that one agent has over the others. A matching that pairs agent 1 with agent 4 will always be blocked by the pair (1, 2). A matching that pairs 2 with 4 will be blocked by (2, 3). A matching that pairs 3 and 4 will be blocked by (3, 1).

An $O(|N|^2)$ algorithm to determine if a stable matching exists is known. One can also associate a collection of linear inequalities with the stable roommates problem such that the system is feasible if and only if a stable roommates solution exists.

10.5 Future Directions

While the models in this chapter have been studied and extended in a variety of ways, there are plenty of open questions for the creative researcher.

One direction of future research on the single-peaked preference model of Section 10.2 would be to consider choosing multiple alternatives (locations) on an interval (or more general graph) when agents' preferences are single-peaked with respect to the one location that is *closest* to his peak. As an idealized example, when downloading files on the Internet one cares only about the location (distance) of the closest "mirror" site. If a planner can elicit preferences to choose the location of k mirrors on a network, how can this be done in a *strategy-proof* way?

As for the house allocation model of Section 10.3 and the stable matching model of Section 10.4, observe that both models are static in nature. Yet, there are a variety of *dynamic* environments that resemble these models in important ways. As an example, take the problem of allocating kidneys. Until quite recently those needing a kidney transplant would have to wait in a queue (the wait list) for an available kidney that would be an appropriate "fit" or else find a donor fulfilling the appropriate medical conditions.

More recently, however, exchange systems have been implemented which allow kidney patients to "swap" their incompatible (but willing) friends and relatives who are willing to donate a kidney. (Suppose that Alice needs a kidney, and her incompatible friend Bob is willing to donate; also suppose that Carmina and Dijen are in a similar situation. If Alice and Dijen are compatible, and if Carmina and Bob are compatible, then a compatible "swap" can be arranged.) Static versions of such a model have been analyzed by Roth, Sönmez, and Ünver (2004).

Those authors and others have developed a substantial literature around this important problem. If donors and recipients arrive dynamically to such a setting, how should swaps be arranged?

10.6 Notes and References

The canonical results for the single-peaked preference model are provided by Moulin (1980), who proved Theorems 10.2 and 10.4 with the additional requirement that rules take agents' peaks as their only input. Ching (1997) subsequently showed that this requirement is redundant when a rule is *strategy-proof* and *onto*.

Border and Jordan (1983) generalize these conclusions to *multidimensional* models where the outcome space is $\mathbb{R}^k$. They restrict attention to *separable* preferences, i.e., under the assumption that an agent's (relative) preferences over any one dimension are fixed, as we vary any other dimensions of the altnerative. For example with $k = 3$, if $(x_1, x_2, x_3) \succeq_i (x_1', x_2, x_3)$ then separability would imply $(x_1, y_2, y_3) \succeq_i (x_1', y_2, y_3)$. Border and Jordan show that a *strategy-proof*, *onto* rule for separable preferences must be decomposable into k (possibly different) one-dimensional rules. Of course, these one-dimensional rules must be generalized median voter schemes. For further reference on such generalizations, one should consult the survey of Barberà (2001).

Another direction in which these results have been generalized pertains to situations in which agents have single-peaked preferences on graphs. Schummer and Vohra (2004) obtain two types of result, depending on whether the graph contains any cycle. Finally, the book of Austen-Smith and Banks (2005). contains more details on the key results of this literature, and a proof of Theorem 10.4.

The house allocation problem was introduced by Herbert Scarf and Lloyd Shapley (1974). The TTCA is attributed by these authors to David Gale. The idea that the house allocation problem can be used as a model for kidney exchanges is discussed in Roth et al. (2004).

The stable matching problem was introduced by David Gale and Lloyd Shapley (1962). The first algorithm for finding a stable matching was developed a decade earlier in 1951 to match interns to hospitals (Stalnaker, 1953). The intrinsic appeal of the model has inspired three books. The first, by Donald Knuth (1976) uses the stable matching problem as a vehicle to illustrate some of the basic ideas in the analysis of algorithms. The book by Gusfield and Irving (1989) is devoted to algorithmic aspects of the stable matching problem and some of its relatives. On the economics side, the book by Roth and Sotomayor (1991) gives a complete game theoretic treatment of the stable matching problem as well as some of its relatives.

The lattice theoretic treatment of the stable matching problem goes back to Knuth (1976). The proof of existence based on Tarski's fixed point theorem is due to Adachi (2000). In fact, the proposal algorithm is exactly one of the algorithms for finding a fixed point when specialized to the case of stable matchings.

The linear programming formulation of the stable matching problem is due to Vande Vate (1989). The extension of it to the stable room mates problem can be found in Teo and Sethuraman (1998). Gusfield and Irving (1989) give a full algorithmic account of the stable roommates problem.

In parallel, studies have been made of matching models where monetary transfers are allowed. This has inspired models that unify both the stable matching problem as well as matching problems where monetary transfers are allowed. Descriptions can be found in Fleiner (2003) and Hatfield and Milgrom (2005).

Bibliography

H. Adachi. On a characterization of stable matchings. *Economics Letters*, 68:43–49, 2000.

D. Austen-Smith and J. Banks. *Positive Political Theory II: Strategy and Structure*. University of Michigan Press, 2005.

S. Barberà. An introduction of strategy-proof social choice functions. *Soc. Choice Welfare*, 18(4):619–653, 2001.

K. Border and J. Jordan. Straightforward elections, unanimity and phantom voters. *Rev. Econ. Stud.*, 50(1):153–170, 1983.

S. Ching. Strategy-proofness and Âmedian voters. *Intl. J. Game Theor.*, 26(4):473–490, 1997.

T. Fleiner. Some results on stable matchings and fixed points. *Math. Oper. Res.*, 28(1):103–126, 2003.

D. Gale and L.S. Shapley. College admissions and the stability of marriage. *Amer. Math. Monthly*, 69(1):9–15, 1962.

A. Gibbard. Manipulation of voting schemes: A general result. *Econometrica*, 41(4):587–601, 1973.

D. Gusfield and R.W. Irving. *The Stable Marriage Problem: Structure and Algorithms*. MIT Press, 1989.

J.W. Hatfield and P.R. Milgrom. Matching with contracts. *Amer. Econ. Rev.*, 95(4):913–935, 2005.

D. Knuth. *Marriages Stables*. Les Presses de l'Universite de Montreal, 1976.

H. Moulin. On strategy proofness and single peakedness. *Public Choice*, 35(4):437–455, 1980.

A. E. Roth and M. Sotomayor. *Two-Sided Matching: A Study in Game-Theoretic Modelling and Analysis*. Cambridge University Press, 1991.

A. E. Roth, T. Sönmez, and M. U. Ünver. Kidney exchange. *Q. J. Econ.*, 119(2):457–488, 2004.

M. Satterthwaite. Strategy-proofness and arrow's conditions. *J. Econ. Theor.*, 10(2):187–217, 1975.

J. Schummer and R.V. Vohra. Strategy-proof location on a network. *J. Economic Theory*, 104(2):405–428, 2004.

L.S. Shapley and H. Scarf. On cores and indivisibility. *J. Math. Econ.*, 1(1):23–28, 1974.

J. M. Stalnaker. The matching program for intern placement: The second year of operation. *J. Med. Educ.*, 28(1):13–19, 1953.

C. P. Teo and J. Sethuraman. Geometry of fractional stable matchings and its applications. *Math. Oper. Res.*, 23(4):874–891, 1998.

J. H. VandeVate. Linear programming brings marital bliss. *Oper. Res. Lett.*, 8(3):147–153, 1989.

Exercises

10.1 To what extent is Lemma 10.1 sensitive to the richness of the preference domain? For example, does the result hold if the preference domain is even smaller, e.g., containing only *symmetric* single-peaked preferences?

10.2 Suppose that an *anonymous* rule described in Theorem 10.2 has parameters $(y_m)_{m=1}^{n-1}$. Express this rule as a generalized median voter scheme with parameters $(\alpha_S)_{S\subseteq N}$.

10.3 Suppose that a rule f is *strategy-proof* and *onto*, but not necessarily *anonymous*. Fix the preferences of agents 2 through n, $(\succeq_2, \ldots, \succeq_n)$, and denote the outcomes obtainable by agent 1 as

$$O = f(\cdot, \succeq_2, \ldots, \succeq_n) = \{x \in [0,1] : \exists \succeq_1 \in \mathcal{R} \text{ s.t. } f(\succeq_1, \succeq_2, \ldots, \succeq_n)\}.$$

Show that $O = [a, b]$ for some $a, b \in [0, 1]$ (without appealing directly to Theorem 10.4).

10.4 Prove Theorem 10.4.

10.5 *For the case of three agents, generalize Theorem 10.2 to a 3-leaved tree.* Specifically, consider a connected noncyclic graph (i.e., a tree) with exactly three leaves, ℓ_1, ℓ_2, ℓ_3. Preferences over such a graph are single-peaked if there is a peak p_i such that for any x in the graph, and any y in the (unique shortest) path from x to p_i, $y \succeq_i x$. The concepts of *strategy-proofness, onto,* and *anonymity* generalize in the straightforward way to this setting. Describe all the rules that satisfy these conditions for the case $n = 3$. (Hint: first show that when all agents' peaks are restricted to the interval $[\ell_1, \ell_2]$, the rule must behave like one described in Theorem 10.2.) For the nonanonymous case with $n \geq 3$, see Schummer and Vohra (2004).

10.6 Prove that the TTCA returns an outcome in the core of the house allocation game.

10.7 The TTC mechanism is immune to agents misreporting their preferences. Is it immune to agents misreporting the identity of their houses? Specifically, suppose a subset of agents trade among themselves first before participating in the TTC mechanism. Can all of them be strictly better off by doing so?

10.8 Consider an instance of the stable matching problem. Let ν be a matching (not necessarily stable) and μ the male optimal stable matching. Let $B = \{m : \nu(m) >^m \mu(m)\}$. Show that if $B \neq \emptyset$ then there is a $m' \notin B$ and woman w such that (m, w) is a blocking pair for ν.

CHAPTER 11

Combinatorial Auctions

Liad Blumrosen and Noam Nisan

Abstract

In combinatorial auctions, a large number of items are auctioned concurrently and bidders are allowed to express preferences on bundles of items. This is preferable to selling each item separately when there are dependencies between the different items. This problem has direct applications, may be viewed as a general abstraction of complex resource allocation, and is the paradigmatic problem on the interface of economics and computer science. We give a brief survey of this field, concentrating on theoretical treatment.

11.1 Introduction

A large part of computer science as well as a large part of economics may be viewed as addressing the "allocation problem": how should we allocate "resources" among the different possible uses of these resources. An auction of a single item may be viewed as a simple abstraction of this question: we have a single indivisible resource, and two (or more) players desire using it – who should get it? Being such a simple and general abstraction explains the pivotal role of simple auctions in mechanism design theory.

From a similar point of view, "combinatorial auctions" abstract this issue when multiple resources are involved: how do I allocate a collection of interrelated resources? In general, the "interrelations" of the different resources may be combinatorially complex, and thus handling them requires effective handling of this complexity. It should thus come as no surprise that the field of "combinatorial auctions" – the subject of this chapter – is gaining a central place in the interface between computer science and economics.

11.1.1 Problem Statement

The combinatorial auction setting is formalized as follows: There is a set of m indivisible items that are concurrently auctioned among n bidders. For the rest of this chapter we will use n and m in this way. The combinatorial character of the auction comes from the fact that bidders have preferences regarding subsets – bundles – of items. Formally, every bidder i has a valuation function v_i that describes his preferences in monetary terms:

Definition 11.1 A valuation v is a real-valued function that for each subset S of items, $v(S)$ is the value that bidder i obtains if he receives this bundle of items. A valuation must have "free disposal," i.e., be monotone: for $S \subseteq T$ we have that $v(S) \leq v(T)$, and it should be "normalized": $v(\emptyset) = 0$.

The whole point of defining a valuation function is that the value of a bundle of items need not be equal to the sum of the values of the items in it. Specifically for sets S and T, $S \cap T = \emptyset$, we say that S and T are *complements* to each other (in v) if $v(S \cup T) > v(S) + v(T)$, and we say that S and T are *substitutes* if $v(S \cup T) < v(S) + v(T)$.

Note that implicit in this definition are two assumptions about bidder preferences: first, we assume that they are "quasi-linear" in the money; i.e., if bidder i wins bundle S and pays a price of p for it then his utility is $v_i(S) - p$. Second, we assume that there are "no externalities"; i.e., a bidder only cares about the item that he receives and not about how the other items are allocated among the other bidders.

Definition 11.2 An *allocation* of the items among the bidders is $S_1, \ldots, S_n$ where $S_i \cap S_j = \emptyset$ for every $i \neq j$. The *social welfare* obtained by an allocation is $\sum_i v_i(S_i)$. A socially efficient allocation (among bidders with valuations $v_1, \ldots, v_n$) is an allocation with maximum social welfare among all allocations.

In our usual setting the valuation function v_i of bidder i is private information – unknown to the auctioneer or to the other bidders. Our usual goal will be to design a mechanism that will find the socially efficient allocation. What we really desire is a mechanism where this is found in equilibrium, but we will also consider the partial goal of just finding the optimal allocation regardless of strategic behavior of the bidders. One may certainly also attempt designing combinatorial auctions that maximize the auctioneer's revenue, but much less is known about this goal.

There are multiple difficulties that we need to address:

- *Computational complexity:* The allocation problem is computationally hard (NP-complete) even for simple special cases. How do we handle this?
- *Representation and communication:* The valuation functions are exponential size objects since they specify a value for each bundle. How can we even represent them? How do we transfer enough information to the auctioneer so that a reasonable allocation can be found?
- *Strategies:* How can we analyze the strategic behavior of the bidders? Can we design for such strategic behavior?

The combination of these difficulties, and the subtle interplay between them is what gives this problem its generic flavor, in some sense encompassing many of the issues found in algorithmic mechanism design in general.

11.1.2 Some Applications

In this chapter we will undertake a theoretical study and will hardly mention specific applications. More information about various applications can be found in the references mentioned in Section 11.8. Here we will shortly mention a few.

"Spectrum auctions," held worldwide and, in particular, in the united states, have received the most attention. In such auctions a large number of licenses are sold, each license being for the use of a certain band of the electromagnetic spectrum in a certain geographic area. These licenses are needed, for example, by cell-phone companies. To give a concrete example, let us look at the next scheduled auction of the FCC at the time of writing (number 66), scheduled for August 2006. This auction is intended for "advanced wireless services" and includes 1,122 licenses, each covering a 10- or 20-MHz spectrum band (somewhere in the 1.7-GHz or 2.1-GHz frequency range) over a geographic area that contains a population of between 0.5 million to 50 million. The total of the *minimum bids* for all licenses is over 1 billion dollars. Generally speaking, in such auctions bidders desire licenses covering the geographic area that they wish to operate in, with sufficient bandwidth. Most of the spectrum auctions held so far escaped the full complexity of the combinatorial nature of the auction by essentially holding a separate auction for each item (but usually in a clever simultaneous way). In such a format, bidders could not fully express their preferences, thus leading, presumably, to suboptimal allocation of the licenses. In the case of FCC auctions, it has thus been decided to move to a format that will allow "combinatorial bidding," but the details are still under debate.

Another common application area is in transportation. In this setting the auction is often "reversed" – a procurement auction – where the auctioneer needs to *buy* the set of items from many bidding *suppliers*. A common scenario is a company that needs to buy transportation services for a large number of "routes" from various transportation providers (e.g., trucking or shipping companies). For each supplier, the cost of providing a bundle of routes depends on the structure of the bundle as the cost of moving the transportation vehicles between the routes in the bundle needs to be taken into account. Several commercial companies are operating complex combinatorial auctions for transportation services, and commonly report savings of many millions of dollars.

The next application we wish to mention is conceptual, an example demonstrating that various types of problems may be viewed as special cases of combinatorial auctions. Consider a communication network that needs to supply multiple "connection requests" – each requesting a path between two specified nodes in the network, and offering a price for such a path. In the simplest case, each network edge must be fully allocated to one of the requests, so the paths allocated to the requests must be edge-disjoint. Which requests should we fulfill, and which paths should we allocate for it? We can view this as a combinatorial auction: the items sold are the edges of the network. The players are the different requests, and the valuation of a request gives the offered price for any bundle of edges that contains a path between the required nodes, and 0 for all other bundles.

11.1.3 Structure of This Chapter

We start our treatment of combinatorial auctions, in Section 11.2, by leaving aside the issue of representation and concentrating on bidders with simple "single-minded" valuations. For these bidders we address the twin questions of the computational complexity of allocation and strategic incentive compatibility. The rest of the chapter then addresses general valuations. Section 11.3 lays out mathematical foundations and introduces the notion of Walrasian equilibrium and its relation to the linear programming relaxation of the problem. Section 11.4 describes a first approach for computationally handling general valuations: representing them in various "bidding languages." Section 11.5 describes a second approach, that of using iterative auctions which repeatedly query bidders about their valuations. In Section 11.6 we show the limitations of the second approach, pointing out an underlying communication bottleneck. Section 11.7 studies a natural widely used family of iterative auctions – those with ascending prices. Bibliographic notes appear in Section 11.8, followed by a collection of exercises.

11.2 The Single-Minded Case

This section focuses on the twin goals of computational complexity and strategic behavior, while leaving out completely the third issue of the representational complexity of the valuation functions. For this, we restrict ourselves to players with very simple valuation functions which we call "single-minded bidders." Such bidders are interested only in a single specified bundle of items, and get a specified scalar value if they get this whole bundle (or any superset) and get zero value for any other bundle.

Definition 11.3 A valuation v is called *single minded* if there exists a bundle of items S^* and a value $v^* \in \Re^+$ such that $v(S) = v^*$ for all $S \supseteq S^*$, and $v(S) = 0$ for all other S. A single-minded bid is the pair (S^*, v^*).

Single-minded valuations are thus very simply represented. The rest of this section assumes as common knowledge that all bidders are single minded.

11.2.1 Computational Complexity of Allocation

Let us first consider just the algorithmic allocation problem among single-minded bidders. Recall that in general, an allocation gives disjoint sets of items S_i to each bidder i, and aims to maximize the social welfare $\sum_i v_i(S_i)$. In the case of single-minded bidders whose bids are given by (S_i^*, v_i^*), it is clear that an optimal allocation can allocate to every bidder either exactly the bundle he desires $S_i = S_i^*$ or nothing at all $S_i = \emptyset$. The algorithmic allocation problem among such bidders is thus given by the following definition.

Definition 11.4 The allocation problem among single-minded bidders is the following:
INPUT: (S_i^*, v_i^*) for each bidder $i = 1, \ldots, n$.
OUTPUT: A subset of winning bids $W \subseteq \{1, \ldots, n\}$ such that for every $i \neq j \in W$, $S_i^* \cap S_j^* = \emptyset$ (i.e., the winners are compatible with each other) with maximum social welfare $\sum_{i \in W} v_i^*$.

This problem is a "weighted-packing" problem and is NP-complete, which we will show by reduction from the INDEPENDENT-SET problem.

Proposition 11.5 *The allocation problem among single-minded bidders is NP-hard. More precisely, the decision problem of whether the optimal allocation has social welfare of at least k (where k is an additional part of the input) is NP-complete.*

PROOF We will make a reduction from the NP-complete "INDEPENDENT-SET" problem: given an undirected graph $G = (V, E)$ and a number k, does G have an independent set of size k? An independent set is a subset of the vertices that have no edge between any two of them. Given such an INDEPENDENT-SET instance, we will build an allocation problem from it as follows:

- The set of items will be E, the set of edges in the graph.
- We will have a player for each vertex in the graph. For vertex $i \in V$ we will have the desired bundle of i be the set of adjacent edges $S_i^* = \{e \in E | i \in e\}$, and the value be $v_i^* = 1$.

Now notice that a set W of winners in the allocation problem satisfies $S_i^* \cap S_j^* = \emptyset$ for every $i \neq j \in W$ if and only if the set of vertices corresponding to W is an independent set in the original graph G. The social welfare obtained by W is exactly the size of this set, i.e., the size of the independent set. It follows that an independent set of size at least k exists if and only if the social welfare of the optimal allocation is at least k. This concludes the NP-hardness proof. The fact that the problem (of whether the optimal allocation has social welfare at least k) is in NP is trivial as the optimal allocation can be guessed and then the social welfare can be calculated routinely. □

As usual when a computational problem is shown to be NP-complete, there are three approaches for the next step: approximation, special cases, and heuristics. We will discuss each in turn.

First, we may attempt finding an allocation that is approximately optimal. Formally, we say that an allocation $S_1, \ldots, S_n$ is a c-approximation of the optimal one if for every other allocation $T_1, \ldots, T_n$ (and specifically for the socially optimal one), we have that $\frac{\sum_i v_i(T_i)}{\sum_i v_i(S_i)} \leq c$. Perhaps a computationally efficient algorithm will always be able to find an approximately optimal allocation? Unfortunately, the NP-completeness reduction above also shows that this will not be possible. Not only is it known that the finding the maximum independent set is NP-complete, but it is known that approximating it to within a factor of $n^{1-\epsilon}$ (for any fixed $\epsilon > 0$) is NP-complete. Since in our reduction the social welfare was exactly equal to the independent-set size, we get the same hardness here. Often this is stated as a function of the number of items m rather than the number of players n. Since $m \leq n^2$ (m is the number of edges, n is the number of vertices), we get:

Proposition 11.6 *Approximating the optimal allocation among single-minded bidders to within a factor better than* $m^{1/2-\epsilon}$ *is NP-hard.*

As we will see in the next subsection, this level of approximation can be reached in polynomial time, even in an incentive-compatible way (which is the topic of the next subsection).

Second, we can focus on special cases that can be solved efficiently. Several such cases are known. The first one is when each bidder desires a bundle of at most two items $|S_i^*| \leq 2$. This case is seen to be an instance of the weighted matching problem (in general nonbipartite graphs) which is known to be efficiently solvable. The second case is the "linear order" case. Assume that the items are arranged in a linear order and each desired bundle is for a continuous segment of items, i.e., each $S_i^* = \{j^i, j^i + 1, \ldots, k^i\}$ for some $1 \leq j^i \leq k^i \leq m$ (think of the items as lots along the sea shore, and assume that each bidder wants a connected strip of seashore). It turns out that this case can be solved efficiently using dynamic programming, which we leave as an exercise to the reader (see Exercise 11.1).

Third, an NP-completeness result only says that one cannot write an algorithm that is guaranteed to run in polynomial time and obtain optimal outputs on *all input instances*. It may be possible to have algorithms that run reasonably fast and produce optimal (or near-optimal) results on most natural input instances. Indeed, it seems to be the case here: the allocation problem can be stated as an "integer programming" problem, and then the large number of known heuristics for solving integer programs can be applied. In particular, many of these heuristics rely on the linear programming relaxation of the problem, which we will study in Section 11.3 in a general setting. It is probably safe to say that most allocation problems with up to hundreds of items can be practically solved optimally, and that even problems with thousands or tens of thousands of items can be practically approximately solved quite well.

11.2.2 An Incentive-Compatible Approximation Mechanism

After dealing with the purely algorithmic aspect in the last subsection, we now return to handling also strategic issues. Again, we still avoid all representation difficulties, i.e., focusing on single-minded bidders. That is, we now wish to take into account the fact that the true bids are private information of the players, and not simply available to the algorithm. We still would like to optimize the social welfare as much as possible. The approach we take is the standard one of mechanism design: *incentive compatibility*. We refer the reader to Chapter 9 for background, but in general what we desire is an allocation algorithm and payment functions such that each player always prefers reporting his private information truthfully to the auctioneer rather than any potential lie. This would ensure that the allocation algorithm at least works with the true information. We also wish everything to be efficiently computable, of course.

Definition 11.7 Let V_{sm} denote the set of all single-minded bids on m items, and let A be the set of all allocations of the m items between n players. A mechanism for single-minded bidders is composed of an allocation mechanism $f : (V_{sm})^n \rightarrow A$ and payment functions $p_i : (V_{sm})^n \rightarrow \Re$ for $i = 1, \ldots, n$. The mechanism is computationally efficient if f and all p_i can be computed in polynomial time. The mechanism is incentive compatible (in dominant strategies) if for every i, and every $v_1, \ldots, v_n, v_i' \in V_{sm}$, we have that $v_i(a) - p_i(v_i, v_{-i}) \geq v_i(a') - p_i(v_i', v_{-i})$, where $a = f(v_i, v_{-i})$, $a' = f(v_i', v_{-i})$ and $v_i(a) = v_i$ if i wins in a and zero otherwise.

The main difficulty here is the clash between the requirements of incentive compatibility and that of computational efficiency. If we leave aside the requirement of computational efficiency then the solution to our problem is simple: take the socially efficient allocation and let the payments be the VCG payments defined in Chapter 9. These payments essentially charge each bidder his "externality": the amount by which his allocated bundle reduced the total reported value of the bundles allocated to others. As shown in Chapter 9, this would be incentive compatible, and would give the exactly optimal allocation. However, as shown above, exact optimization of the social welfare is computationally intractable. Thus, when we return to the requirement of computational efficiency, exact optimization is impossible. Now, one may attempt using "VCG-like" mechanisms: take the best approximation algorithm you can find for the problem – which can have a theoretical guarantee of no better than $O(\sqrt{m})$ approximation but may be practically much better – and attempt using the same idea of charging each bidder his externality according to the allocation algorithm used. Unfortunately, this would not be incentive compatible! VCG-like payments lead to incentive compatibility if but only if the social welfare is exactly optimized by the allocation rule (at least over some subrange of allocations).

We thus need to find another type of mechanisms – non-VCG. While in general settings almost no incentive compatible mechanisms are known beyond VCG, our single-minded setting is "almost single-dimensional" – in the since that the private values are composed of a single scalar and the desired bundle – and for such settings this is easier. Indeed, the mechanism in Figure 11.1 is computationally efficient, incentive compatible, and provides a $\sqrt{m}$ approximation guarantee, as good as theoretically possible in polynomial time.

This mechanism greedily takes winners in an order determined by the value of the expression $v_1^*/\sqrt{|S_1^*|}$. This expression was taken as to optimize the approximation ratio obtained theoretically, but as we will see, the incentive compatibility result would apply to any other expression that is monotone increasing in v_i^* and decreasing in $|S_i^*|$. The intuition behind the choice of j for defining the payments is that this is the bidder who lost exactly because of i – if Bidder i had not participated in the auction, Bidder j would have won.

Theorem 11.8 *The greedy mechanism is efficiently computable, incentive compatible, and produces a $\sqrt{m}$ approximation of the optimal social welfare.*

The Greedy Mechanism for Single-Minded Bidders:

Initialization:

- Reorder the bids such that $v_1^*/\sqrt{|S_1^*|} \geq v_2^*/\sqrt{|S_2^*|} \geq ... \geq v_n^*/\sqrt{|S_n^*|}$.
- $W \leftarrow \emptyset$.

For i = 1...n do: if $S_i^* \cap \left(\bigcup_{j \in W} S_j^*\right) = \emptyset$ then $W \leftarrow W \cup \{i\}$.

Output:

Allocation: The set of winners is W.

Payments: For each $i \in W$, $p_i = v_j^*/\sqrt{|S_j^*|/|S_i^*|}$, where j is the smallest index such that $S_i^* \cap S_j^* \neq \emptyset$, and for all $k < j, k \neq i$, $S_k^* \cap S_j^* = \emptyset$ (if no such j exists then $p_i = 0$).

Figure 11.1. The mechanism achieves a $\sqrt{m}$ approximation for combinatorial auctions with single-minded bidders.

Computational efficiency is obvious; we will show incentive compatibility and the approximation performance in two separate lemmas. The incentive compatibility of this mechanism follows directly from the following lemma.

Lemma 11.9 *A mechanism for single-minded bidders in which losers pay 0 is incentive compatible if and only if it satisfies the following two conditions:*

(i) **Monotonicity:** *A bidder who wins with bid (S_i^*, v_i^*) keeps winning for any $v_i' > v_i^*$ and for any $S_i' \subset S_i^*$ (for any fixed settings of the other bids).*

(ii) **Critical Payment:** *A bidder who wins pays the minimum value needed for winning: the infimum of all values v_i' such that (S_i^*, v_i') still wins.*

Before we prove the lemma – or actually just the side that we need – let us just verify that our mechanism satisfies these two properties. Monotonicity is implied since increasing v_i^* or decreasing S_i^* can only move bidder i up in the greedy order, making it easier to win. The critical payment condition is met since notice that i wins as long as he appears in the greedy order before j. The payment computed is exactly the value at which the transition between i being before and after j in the greedy order happens.

Note that this characterization is different from the characterization given in Chapter 9 for general single-parameter agents, since single-minded bidders are not considered to have a single parameter, as their private data consists of both their value and their desired bundle.

PROOF We first observe that under the given conditions, a truthful bidder will never receive negative utility: his utility is zero while losing (losers pay zero), and for winning, his value must be at least the critical value, which exactly equals his payment. We will now show that a bidder can never improve his utility by reporting some bid (S', v') instead of his true values (S, v). If (S', v') is a losing bid or if S' does not contain S, then clearly reporting (S, v) can only help. Therefore we will assume that (S', v') is a winning bid and that $S' \supseteq S$.

We next show that the bidder will never be worse off by reporting (S, v') rather than (S', v'). Denote the bidder's payment for the bid (S', v') by p', and for the bid (S, v') by p. For every $x < p$, bidding (S, x) will lose since p is a critical value. By monotonicity, (S', x) will also be a losing bid for every $x < p$, and therefore the critical value p' is at least p. It follows that by bidding (S, v') instead of (S', v') the bidder still wins and his payment will not increase.

It is left to show that bidding (S, v) is no worse than the winning bid (S, v'): Assume first that (S, v) is a winning bid with a payment (critical value) $\widetilde{p}$. As long as v' is greater than $\widetilde{p}$, the bidder still wins with the same payment, thus misreporting his value would not be beneficial. When $v' < \widetilde{p}$ the bidder will lose, gaining zero utility, and he will not be better off.

If (S, v) is a losing bid, v must be smaller than the corresponding critical value, so the payment for any winning bid (S, v') will be greater than v, making this deviation nonprofitable. □

The approximation guarantee is ensured by the following lemma.

Lemma 11.10 *Let OPT be an allocation (i.e., set of winners) with maximum value of $\sum_{i \in OPT} v_i^*$, and let W be the output of the algorithm, then $\sum_{i \in OPT} v_i^* \leq \sqrt{m} \sum_{i \in W} v_i^*$.*

PROOF For each $i \in W$ let $OPT_i = \{j \in OPT, j \geq i \mid S_i^* \cap S_j^* \neq \emptyset\}$ be the set of elements in OPT that did not enter W because of i (in addition to i itself). Clearly $OPT \subseteq \bigcup_{i \in W} OPT_i$ and thus the lemma will follow once we prove the claim that for every $i \in W$, $\sum_{j \in OPT_i} v_j^* \leq \sqrt{m} v_i^*$.

Note that every $j \in OPT_i$ appeared after i in the greedy order and thus $v_j^* \leq \frac{v_i^* \sqrt{|S_j^*|}}{\sqrt{|S_i^*|}}$. Summing over all $j \in OPT_i$, we can now estimate

$$\sum_{j \in OPT_i} v_j^* \leq \frac{v_i^*}{\sqrt{|S_i^*|}} \sum_{j \in OPT_i} \sqrt{|S_j^*|}. \tag{11.1}$$

Using the Cauchy–Schwarz inequality, we can bound

$$\sum_{j \in OPT_i} \sqrt{|S_j^*|} \leq \sqrt{|OPT_i|} \sqrt{\sum_{j \in OPT_i} |S_j|}. \tag{11.2}$$

Every S_j^* for $j \in OPT_i$ intersects S_i^*. Since OPT is an allocation, these intersections must all be disjoint, and thus $|OPT_i| \leq |S_i^*|$. Since OPT is an allocation $\sum_{j \in OPT_i} |S_j| \leq m$. We thus get $\sum_{j \in OPT_i} \sqrt{|S_j^*|} \leq \sqrt{|S_i^*|}\sqrt{m}$, and plugging into Inequality 11.1 gives the claim $\sum_{j \in OPT_i} v_j^* \leq \sqrt{m} v_i^*$. □

11.3 Walrasian Equilibrium and the LP Relaxation

In this section we return to discuss combinatorial auctions with general valuations, and we will study the linear-programming relaxation of the winner-determination problem in such auctions. We will also define the economic notion of a competitive equilibrium with item prices (or "Walrasian equilibrium"). Although these notions appear to be independent at a first glance, we will describe a strong connection between them. In particular, we will prove that the existence of a Walrasian equilibrium is a sufficient and necessary condition for having an integer optimal solution for the linear programming relaxation (i.e., no integrality gap). One immediate conclusion is that in environments where Walrasian Equilibria exist, the efficient allocation can be computed in polynomial time.

11.3.1 The Linear Programming Relaxation and Its Dual

The winner determination problem in combinatorial auctions can be formulated by an integer program. We present the linear programming relaxation of this integer program, and denote it by LPR (in the integer program Constraint (11.6) would be replaced with "$x_{i,S} \in \{0, 1\}$").

The Linear Programming Relaxation (LPR):

$$\textbf{Maximize} \quad \sum_{i \in N, S \subseteq M} x_{i,S}\, v_i(S) \tag{11.3}$$

$$\textbf{s.t.} \quad \sum_{i \in N,\ S | j \in S} x_{i,S} \leq 1 \qquad \forall j \in M \tag{11.4}$$

$$\sum_{S \subseteq M} x_{i,S} \leq 1 \qquad \forall i \in N \tag{11.5}$$

$$x_{i,S} \geq 0 \qquad \forall i \in N, S \subseteq M \tag{11.6}$$

In the integer program, each variable $x_{i,S}$ equals 1 if bidder i receives the bundle S, and zero otherwise. The objective function is therefore maximizing social welfare. Condition 11.4 ensures that each item is allocated to at most one bidder, and Condition 11.5 implies that each player is allocated at most one bundle. Solutions to the linear program can be intuitively viewed as fractional allocations: allocations that would be allowed if items were divisible. While the LP has exponentially (in m) many variables, it still has algorithmic implications. For example, in the case of single-minded bidders only a single variable X_{i,S_i^*} for each bidder i is required, enabling direct efficient solution of the LP. In Section 11.5.2 we will see that, assuming reasonable access to the valuations, the general LP can be solved efficiently as well.

We will also consider the dual linear program.

The Dual Linear Programming Relaxation (DLPR)

$$\textbf{Minimize} \quad \sum_{i \in N} u_i + \sum_{j \in M} p_j \tag{11.7}$$

$$\textbf{s.t.} \quad u_i + \sum_{j \in S} p_j \geq v_i(S) \qquad \forall i \in N,\ \ S \subseteq M \tag{11.8}$$

$$u_i \geq 0, \ \ p_j \geq 0 \qquad \forall i \in N,\ j \in M \tag{11.9}$$

The usage of the notations p_j and u_i is intentional, since we will later see that at the optimal solution, these dual variables can be interpreted as the prices of the items and the utilities of the bidders.

11.3.2 Walrasian Equilibrium

A fundamental notion in economic theory is the notion of a competitive equilibrium: a set of prices where the market clears, i.e., the demand equals the supply. We will now formalize this concept, that will be generalized later in Section 11.7.

Given a set of prices, the *demand* of each bidder is the bundle that maximizes her utility. (There may be more than one such bundle, in which case each of them is called *a* demand.) In this section we will consider a linear pricing rule, where a price per each *item* is available, and the price of each bundle is the sum of the prices of the items in this bundle.

Definition 11.11 For a given bidder valuation v_i and given item prices $p_1, \ldots, p_m$, a bundle T is called a *demand* of bidder i if for every other bundle $S \subseteq M$ we have that $v_i(S) - \sum_{j \in S} p_j \leq v_i(T) - \sum_{j \in T} p_j$.

A Walrasian equilibrium[1] is a set of "market-clearing" prices where every bidder receives a bundle in his demand set, and unallocated items have zero prices.

Definition 11.12 A set of nonnegative prices $p_1^*, \ldots, p_m^*$ and an allocation $S_1^*, \ldots, S_m^*$ of the items is a *Walrasian equilibrium* if for every player i, S_i^* is a demand of bidder i at prices $p_1^*, \ldots, p_m^*$ and for any item j that is not allocated (i.e., $j \notin \cup_{i=1}^n S_i^*$) we have $p_j^* = 0$.

The following result shows that Walrasian equilibria, if they exist, are economically efficient; i.e., they necessarily obtain the optimal welfare. This is a variant of the classic economic result known as the *First Welfare Theorem* but for environments with indivisible items. Here we actually prove a stronger statement: the welfare in a Walrasian equilibrium is maximal even if the items were divisible. In particular, if a Walrasian equilibrium exists, then the optimal solution to the linear program relaxation will be integral.

Theorem 11.13 (The First Welfare Theorem) *Let $p_1^*, \ldots, p_m^*$ and $S_1^*, \ldots, S_n^*$ be a Walrasian equilibrium, then the allocation $S_1^*, \ldots, S_n^*$ maximizes social welfare. Moreover, it even maximizes social welfare over all fractional allocations, i.e., let $\{X_{i,S}^*\}_{i,S}$ be a feasible solution to the linear programming relaxation. Then, $\sum_{i=1}^n v_i(S_i^*) \geq \sum_{i \in N,\, S \subseteq M} X_{i,S}^* v_i(S)$.*

[1] Walras was an economist who published in the 19th century one of the first comprehensive mathematical analyses of general equilibria in markets.

PROOF In a Walrasian equilibrium, each bidder receives his demand. Therefore, for every bidder i and every bundle S, we have $v_i(S_i^*) - \sum_{j \in S_i^*} p_j^* \geq v_i(S) - \sum_{j \in S} p_j^*$. Since the fractional solution is feasible to the LPR, we have that for every bidder i, $\sum_S X_{i,S}^* \leq 1$ (Constraint 11.5), and therefore

$$v_i(S_i^*) - \sum_{j \in S_i^*} p_j^* \geq \sum_{S \subseteq M} X_{i,S}^* \left(v_i(S) - \sum_{j \in S} p_j^* \right). \tag{11.10}$$

The theorem will follow from summing Inequality 11.10 over all bidders, and showing that $\sum_{i \in N} \sum_{j \in S_i^*} p_j^* \geq \sum_{i \in N,\, S \subseteq M} X_{i,S}^* \sum_{j \in S} p_j^*$. Indeed, the left-hand side equals $\sum_{j=1}^m p_j^*$ since $S_1^*, \ldots, S_n^*$ is an allocation and the prices of unallocated items in a Walrasian equilibrium are zero, and the right-hand side is at most $\sum_{j=1}^m p_j^*$, since the coefficient of every price p_j^* is at most 1 (by Constraint 11.4 in the LPR). □

Following is a simple class of valuations for which no Walrasian equilibrium exist.

Example 11.14 Consider two players, Alice and Bob, and two items $\{a, b\}$. Alice has a value of 2 for every nonempty set of items, and Bob has a value of 3 for the whole bundle $\{a, b\}$, and 0 for any of the singletons. The optimal allocation will clearly allocate both items to Bob. Therefore, Alice must demand the empty set in any Walrasian equilibrium. Both prices will be at least 2; otherwise, Alice will demand a singleton. Hence, the price of the whole bundle will be at least 4, Bob will not demand this bundle, and consequently, no Walrasian equilibrium exists for these players.

To complete the picture, the next theorem shows that the existence of an integral optimum to the linear programming relaxation is also a sufficient condition for the existence of a Walrasian equilibrium. This is a variant of a classic theorem, known as "The Second Welfare Theorem," that provided sufficient conditions for the existence of Walrasian equilibria in economies with divisible commodities.

Theorem 11.15 **(The Second Welfare Theorem)** *If an integral optimal solution exists for LPR, then a Walrasian equilibrium whose allocation is the given solution also exists.*

PROOF An optimal integral solution for LPR defines a feasible efficient allocation $S_1^*, \ldots, S_n^*$. Consider also an optimal solution $p_1^*, \ldots, p_n^*, u_1^*, \ldots, u_n^*$ to DLPR. We will show that $S_1^*, \ldots, S_n^*, p_1^*, \ldots, p_n^*$ is a Walrasian equilibrium.

Complementary-slackness conditions are necessary and sufficient conditions for the optimality of solutions to the primal linear program and its dual. Because of the complementary-slackness conditions, for every player i for which $x_{i,S_i^*} > 0$ (i.e., $x_{i,S_i^*} = 1$), we have that Constraint (11.8) is binding for the optimal dual solution, i.e.,

$$u_i^* = v_i(S_i^*) - \sum_{j \in S_i^*} p_i^*$$

Constraint 11.8 thus also shows that for any other bundle S we get

$$v_i(S_i^*) - \sum_{j \in S_i^*} p_i^* \geq v_i(S) - \sum_{j \in S} p_i^*$$

Finally, the complementary-slackness conditions also imply that for every item j for which Constraint (11.4) is strict, i.e., $\sum_{i \in N,\ S | j \in S} x_{i,S} < 1$ – which for integral solutions means that item j is unallocated – then necessarily $p_j^* = 0$. □

The two welfare theorems show that the existence of a Walrasian equilibrium is equivalent to having a zero integrality gap:

Corollary 11.16 *A Walrasian equilibrium exists in a combinatorial-auction environment if and only if the corresponding linear programming relaxation admits an integral optimal solution.*

11.4 Bidding Languages

This section concerns the issue of the *representation* of bids in combinatorial auctions. Namely, we are looking for representations of valuations that will allow bidders to simply encode their valuation and send it to the auctioneer. The auctioneer must then take the valuations (bids) received from all bidders and determine the allocation. Following sections will consider indirect, iterative ways of transferring information to the auctioneer.

Specifying a valuation in a combinatorial auction of m items requires providing a value for each of the possible $2^m - 1$ nonempty subsets. A naive representation would thus require $2^m - 1$ real numbers to represent each possible valuation. It is clear that this would be completely impractical for more than about two or three dozen items. The computational complexity can be effectively handled for much larger auctions, and thus the representation problem seems to be the bottleneck in practice.

We will thus be looking for languages that allow succinct representations of valuations. We will call these *bidding languages* reflecting their intended usage rather than the more precise "valuations languages." From the outset it is clear that due to information theoretic reasons it will never be possible to encode *all* possible valuations succinctly. Our interest would thus be in succinctly representing interesting or important ones.

When attempting to choose or design a bidding language, we are faced with the same types of trade-offs common to all language design tasks: *expressiveness vs. simplicity*. On one hand, we would like our language to express succinctly as many "naturally occurring" valuations as possible. On the other hand, we would like it to be as simple as possible, both for humans to express and for programs to work with. A well-chosen bidding language should aim to strike a good balance between these two goals.

The bottom line of this section will be the identification of a simple langauge that is rather powerful and yet as easily handled by allocation algorithms as are the single minded bids studied in Section 11.2.

11.4.1 Elements of Representation: Atoms, OR, and XOR

The common bidding languages construct their bids from *combinations* of simple *atomic bids*. The usual atoms in such schemes are the single-minded bids addressed in Section 11.2: (S, p) meaning an offer of p monetary units for the bundle S of items. Formally, the valuation represented by (S, p) is one where $v(T) = p$ for every $T \supseteq S$, and $v(T) = 0$ for all other T.

Intuitively, bids can be combined by simply offering them together. Still informally, there are two possible semantics for an offer of several bids. One considers the bids as totally independent, allowing any subset of them to be fulfilled, and the other considers them to be mutually exclusive and allows only one of them to be fulfilled. The first semantics is called an OR bid, and the second is called (somewhat misleadingly) a XOR bid.

Take, for example, the valuations represented by "$(\{a, b\}, 3)\ XOR\ (\{c, d\}, 5)$" and "$(\{a, b\}, 3)\ OR\ (\{c, d\}, 5)$." Each of them values the bundle $\{a, c\}$ at 0 (since no atomic bid is satisfied) and values the bundle $\{a, b\}$ at 3. The difference is in the bundle $\{a, b, c, d\}$, which is valued at 5 by the XOR bid (according to the best atomic bid satisfied), but is valued at 8 by the OR bid. For another example, look at the bid "$(\{a, b\}, 3)\ OR\ (\{a, c\}, 5)$." Here, the bundle $\{a, b, c\}$ is valued at 5 since both atomic bids cannot be satisfied together.

More formally, both OR and XOR bids are composed of a collection of pairs (S_i, p_i), where each S_i is a subset of the items, and p_i is the maximum price that he is willing to pay for that subset. For the valuation $v = (S_1, p_1)\ XOR, \ldots, XOR\ (S_k, p_k)$, the value of $v(S)$ is defined to be $max_{i|S_i \subseteq S}\, p_i$. For the valuation $v = (S_1, p_1)\ OR, \ldots, OR\ (S_k, p_k)$, one must be a little careful and the value of $v(S)$ is defined to be the maximum over all possible "valid collections" W, of the value of $\sum_{i \in W} p_i$, where W is a valid collection of pairs if for all $i \neq j \in W$, $S_i \cap S_j = \emptyset$.

It is not difficult to see that XOR bids can represent every valuation v: just XOR, the atomic bids $(S, v(S))$ for all bundles S. On the other hand, OR bids can represent only *superadditive* bids (for any two disjoint sets S, T, $v(S \cup T) \geq v(S) + v(T)$), since the atoms giving the value $v(S)$ are disjoint from those giving the value $v(T)$, and they will be added together for $v(S \cup T)$. It is not difficult to see that all superadditive valuations can indeed be represented by OR bids by ORing the atomic bids $(S, v(S))$ for all bundles S.

We will be more interested in the *size* of the representation, defined to be simply the number of atomic bids in it. The following basic types of valuations are good examples for the power and limitations of these two bidding languages.

Definition 11.17 A valuation is called *additive* if $v(S) = \sum_{j \in S} v(\{j\})$ for all S. A valuation is called *unit demand* if $v(S) = max_{j \in S}\, v(\{j\})$ for all S.

An additive valuation is directly represented by an OR bid:

$$(\{1\}, p_1)\ OR\ (\{2\}, p_2)\ OR\ \cdots\ OR\ (\{m\}, p_m)$$

while a unit-demand valuation is directly represented by an XOR bid:

$$(\{1\}, p_1)\ XOR\ (\{2\}, p_2)\ XOR\ \cdots\ XOR\ (\{m\}, p_m)$$

where for each item j, $p_j = v(\{j\})$. Additive valuations can be represented by XOR bids, but this may take exponential size: atomic bids for all $2^m - 1$ possible bundles will be needed whenever $p_j > 0$ for all j. (Since an atomic bid is required for every bundle S with $v(S)$ strictly larger than that of all its strict subsets, which is the case here for all S.) On the other hand, nontrivial unit-demand valuations are never superadditive and thus cannot be represented at all by OR bids.

11.4.2 Combinations of OR and XOR

While both the OR and XOR bidding languages are appealing in their simplicity, none of them are expressive enough to succinctly represent many desirable simple valuations. A natural attempt is to combine the power of OR bids and XOR bids. The most general way to allow this general form of combinations is to define OR and XOR as operations on valuations.

Definition 11.18 Let v and u be valuations, then $(v\ XOR\ u)$ and $(v\ OR\ u)$ are valuations and are defined as follows:

- $(v\ XOR\ u)(S) = \max(v(S), u(S))$.
- $(v\ OR\ u)(S) = \max_{R,T \subseteq S,\ R \cap T = \emptyset}\ v(R) + u(T)$

Thus a general "OR/XOR formula" bid will be given by an arbitrary expression involving the OR and XOR operations over atomic bids. For instance, the bid $((\{a, b\}, 3)\ XOR\ (\{c\}, 2))\ OR\ (\{d\}, 5)$ values the bundle $\{a, b, c\}$ at 3, but the bundle $\{a, b, d\}$ at 8. The following example demonstrates the added power we can get from such combinations just using the restricted structure of an OR of XORs of atomic bids.

Definition 11.19 A valuation is called *symmetric* if $v(S)$ depends only on $|S|$. A symmetric valuation is called *downward sloping* if it can be represented as $v(S) = \sum_{j=1..|S|} p_j$, with $p_1 \geq p_2 \geq \cdots \geq p_m \geq 0$.

It is easy to verify that every downward sloping valuations with $p_1 > p_2 > \cdots > p_m > 0$ requires XOR bids of size $2^m - 1$, and cannot be represented at all by OR bids.

Lemma 11.20 *OR-of-XORs bids can express any downward sloping symmetric valuation on m items in size m^2.*

PROOF For each $j = 1, \ldots, m$ we will have a clause that offers p_j for any single item. Such a clause is a simple XOR-bid, and the m different clauses are all connected by an OR. Since the p_j's are decreasing, we are assured that the first allocated item will be taken from the first clause, the second item from the second clause, etc. □

11.4.3 Dummy Items

General OR/XOR formulae seem very complicated and dealing with them algorithmically would appear to be quite difficult. Luckily, this is not the case and a generalization of the langauge makes things simple again. The main idea is to allow XORs to be represented by ORs. This is done by allowing the bidders to introduce *dummy items* into the bids. These items will have no intrinsic value to any of the participants, but they will be indirectly used to express XOR constraints. The idea is that an XOR bid $(S_1, p_1)\, XOR\, (S_2, p_2)$ can be represented as $(S_1 \cup \{d\}, p_1)\, OR\, (S_2 \cup \{d\}, p_2)$, where d is a dummy item.

Formally, we let each bidder i have its own set of dummy items D_i, which only he can bid on. An OR* bid by bidder i is an OR bid on the augmented set of items $M \cup D_i$. The value that an OR* bid gives to a bundle $S \subseteq M$ is the value given by the OR bid to $S \cup D_i$. Thus, for example, for the set of items $M = \{a, b, c\}$, the OR* bid $(\{a, d\}, 1)\, OR\, (\{b, d\}, 1)\, OR\, (\{c\}, 1)$, where d is a dummy item, is equivalent to $((\{a\}, 1)\, XOR\, (\{b\}, 1))\, OR\, (\{c\}, 1)$.

An equivalent but more appealing "user interface" is to let bidders report a set of atomic bids together with "constraints" that signify which bids are mutually exclusive. Each constraint can then be converted into a dummy item that is added to the conflicting atomic bids. Despite its apparent simplicity, this language can simulate general OR/XOR formulae.

Theorem 11.21 *Any valuation that can be represented by OR/XOR formula of size s can be represented by OR* bids of size s, using at most s^2 dummy items.*

PROOF We prove by induction on the formula structure that a formula of size s can be represented by an OR* bid with s atomic bids. We then show that each atomic bid in the final resulting OR* bid can be modified as to not to include more than s dummy items in it.

Induction: The basis of the induction is an atomic bid, which is clearly an OR* bid with a single atomic bid. The induction step requires handling the two separate cases: OR and XOR. To represent the OR of several OR* bids as a single OR* bid, we simply merge the set of clauses of the different OR* bids. To represent the XOR of several OR* bids as a single OR* bid, we introduce a new dummy item x_{ST} for each pair of atomic bids (S, v) and (T, v') that are in two different original OR* bids. For each bid (S, v) in any of the original OR* bids, we add to the generated OR* bid an atomic bid $(S \cup \{x_{ST} | T\}, v)$, where T ranges over all atomic bids in all of the other original OR* bids.

It is clear that the inductive construction constructs an OR* bid with exactly s clauses in it, where s is the number of clauses in the original OR/XOR formula. The number of dummy items in it, however, may be large. However, we can remove most of these dummy items. One can see that the only significance of a dummy item in an OR* bid is to disallow some two (or more) atomic bids to be taken concurrently. Thus we may replace all the existing dummy items with at most $\binom{s}{2}$ new dummy items, one for each pair of atomic bids that cannot be taken together (according to the current set of dummy items). This dummy item will be added to both of the atomic bids in this pair. □

This simulation can be directly turned into a "compiler" that translates OR/XOR formulae into OR* bids. This has an extremely appealing implication for allocation algorithms: to any winner determination (allocation) algorithm, an OR* bid looks just like a regular OR-bid on a larger set of items. But an OR bid looks to an allocation algorithm just like a collection of atomic bids from different players. It follows that any allocation algorithm that can handle single-minded bids (i.e., atomic bids) can immediately also handle general valuations represented as OR* bids or as general OR/XOR formulae. In particular, the various heuristics mentioned in Section 11.2 can all be applied for general valuations represented in these languages.

11.5 Iterative Auctions: The Query Model

The last section presented ways of encoding valuations in bidding languages as to enable the bidders to directly send their valuation to the auctioneer. In this section we consider indirect ways of sending information about the valuation: *iterative auctions*. In these, the auction protocol repeatedly interacts with the different bidders, aiming to adaptively elicit enough information about the bidders' preferences as to be able to find a good (optimal or close to optimal) allocation. The idea is that the adaptivity of the interaction with the bidders may allow pinpointing the information that is relevant to the current auction and not requiring full disclosure of bidders' valuations. This may not only reduce the amount of information transferred and all associated complexities but also preserve some privacy about the valuations, only disclosing the information that is really required. In addition, in many real-life settings, bidders may need to exert efforts even for determining their own valuation (like collecting data, hiring consultants, etc.); such iterative mechanisms may assist the bidders with realizing their valuations by guiding their attention only to the data that is relevant to the mechanism.

Such iterative auctions can be modeled by considering the bidders as "black-boxes," represented by oracles, where the auctioneer repeatedly queries these oracles. In such models, we should specify the types of queries that are allowed by the auctioneer. These oracles may not be truthful, of course, and we will discuss the incentive issues in the final part of this section (see also Chapter 12). The auctioneer would be required to be computationally efficient in two senses: the number of queries made to the bidders and the internal computations. Efficiency would mean polynomial running time in m (the number of items) even though each valuation is represented by 2^m numbers. The running time should also be polynomial in n (the number of bidders) and in the number of bits of precision of the real numbers involved in the valuations.

11.5.1 Types of Queries

Our first step is to define the types of queries that we allow our auctioneer to make to the bidders. Probably the most straightforward query one could imagine is where a bidder reports his value for a specific bundle.

Value query: *The auctioneer presents a bundle S, the bidder reports his value $v(S)$ for this bundle.*

It turns out that value queries are pretty weak and are not expressive enough in many settings. Another natural and widely used type of queries is the *demand query*, in which a set of prices is presented to the bidder, and the bidder responds with his most valuable bundle under the published prices.

Demand query *(with item prices[2]): The auctioneer presents a vector of item prices $p_1, \ldots, p_m$; the bidder reports a demand bundle under these prices, i.e., some set S that maximizes $v(S) - \sum_{i \in S} p_i$.*

How difficult it is for a bidder to answer such a demand query or a value query depends on his internal representation of his valuation. For some internal representations this may be computationally intractable, while for others it may be computationally trivial. It does seem though that in many realistic situations the bidders will not really have an explicit internal representation, but rather "know" their valuation only in the sense of being able to answer such queries.

The first observation that we should make is that demand queries are strictly more powerful than value queries.

Lemma 11.22 *A value query may be simulated by mt demand queries, where t is the number of bits of precision in the representation of a bundle's value.*

PROOF We first show how to answer "marginal value" queries using demand queries: given a bundle S and an item $j \notin S$, compute the marginal value of j relative to S: $v(S \cup \{j\}) - v(S)$ (the items are denoted, w.l.o.g., by $1, \ldots, m$). For all $i \in S$ we set $p_i = 0$, for all $i \notin S \cup \{j\}$, we set $p_i = \infty$, and then run a binary search on p_j. The highest value p_j for which the demand under these prices contains j is the marginal value of j relative to S.

Once we can solve marginal value queries, any value query can be solved by $v(S) = \sum_{j \in S}(v(\{i \in S | i \leq j\}) - v(\{i \in S | i < j\})$. □

Lemma 11.23 *An exponential number of value queries may be required for simulating a single demand query.*

The proof of Lemma 11.23 is left for Exercise 11.3.

11.5.2 Solving the Linear Program

Many algorithms for handling combinatorial auctions or special cases of combinatorial auctions start by solving the linear programming relaxation of the problem, shown in Section 11.3.1. A very useful and surprising property of demand queries is that they allow solving the linear-programming relaxation efficiently. This is surprising since the linear program has an exponential number of variables. The basic idea is

[2] In Section 11.7 we consider more general demand queries where a price of a bundle is not necessarily the sum of the prices of its items.

to solve the dual linear program using the Ellipsoid method. The dual program has a polynomial number of variables, but an exponential number of constraints. The Ellipsoid algorithm runs in polynomial time even on such programs, provided that a "separation oracle" is given for the set of constraints. Surprisingly, such a separation oracle can be implemented by presenting a single demand query to each of the bidders.

Consider the linear-programming relaxation (LPR) for the winner determination problem in combinatorial auctions, presented in Section 11.3.

Theorem 11.24 *LPR can be solved in polynomial time (in n, m, and the number of bits of precision t) using only demand queries with item prices.*[3]

PROOF Consider the dual linear program, DLPR, presented in Section 11.3 (Equations 11.8–11.9). Notice that the dual problem has exactly $n + m$ variables but an exponential number of constraints.

Recall that a separation oracle for the Ellipsoid method, when given a possible solution, either confirms that it is a feasible solution, or responds with a constraint that is violated by the possible solution. Consider a possible solution $(\vec{u}, \vec{p})$ for the dual program. We can rewrite Constraint 11.8 of the dual program as $u_i \geq v_i(S) - \sum_{j \in S} p_j$. Now, a demand query to bidder i with prices p_j reveals exactly the set S that maximizes the RHS of the previous inequality. Thus, in order to check whether $(\vec{u}, \vec{p})$ is feasible it suffices to (1) query each bidder i for his demand D_i under the prices p_j; (2) check only the n constraints $u_i + \sum_{j \in D_i} p_j \geq v_i(D_i)$ (where $v_i(D_i)$ can be simulated using a polynomial sequence of demand queries as was previously observed). If none of these are violated then we are assured that $(\vec{u}, \vec{p})$ is feasible; otherwise, we get a violated constraint.

What is left to be shown is how the *primal* program can be solved. (Recall that the primal program has an exponential number of variables.) Since the Ellipsoid algorithm runs in polynomial time, it encounters only a polynomial number of constraints during its operation. Clearly, if all other constraints were removed from the dual program, it would still have the same solution (adding constraints can only decrease the space of feasible solutions). Now take the "reduced dual" where only the constraints encountered exist, and look at its dual. It will have the same solution as the original dual and hence of the original primal, but with a polynomial number of variables. Thus, it can be solved in polynomial time, and this solution clearly solves the original primal program, setting all other variables to zero. □

11.5.3 Approximating the Social Welfare

The final part of this section will highlight some of the prominent algorithmic results for combinatorial auctions. Some of these results are obtained by solving the LP relaxation. Figure 11.5.2 lists state-of-the-art results for the point in time in which this chapter

[3] The solution will have a polynomial-size support (nonzero values for $x_{i,S}$), and thus we will be able to describe it in polynomial time.

Class	Queries	Approx	IC approx	Lower bound
Gen	Any	$\sqrt{m}$	$\frac{m}{\sqrt{\log m}}$ $\sqrt{m}$ (rand)	$m^{\frac{1}{2}-\epsilon}$ Section 1.6, [NS06]
	Value	$\frac{m}{\sqrt{\log m}}$	$\frac{m}{\sqrt{\log m}}$ [HKDMT04]	$\frac{m}{\log m}$ [BN05a, DS05]
	Demand	$\sqrt{m}$ [BN05a]	$\frac{m}{\sqrt{\log m}}$ $\sqrt{m}$ (rand) [LS05, DNS06]	$m^{\frac{1}{2}-\epsilon}$
SubA	Value	$\sqrt{m}$	$\sqrt{m}$ [DNS05]	$m^{\frac{1}{4}}$
	Demand	2 (rand) [Fei06]	$\sqrt{m}$	2 [DNS05]
XOS	Value	$\sqrt{m}$	$\sqrt{m}$	$m^{\frac{1}{4}}$ [DS06]
	Demand	2 [DNS05] $\frac{e}{e-1}$ (rand) [Fei06]	$\sqrt{m}$ $\log^2 m$ (rand) [DNS06]	$\frac{e}{e-1}$ [DNS05]
SubM	Value	2 [LLN06]	$\sqrt{m}$	$\frac{e}{e-1}$ [KLMM05]
	Demand	2 $\frac{e}{e-1}$-10^{-4} (rand) [FV06]	$\sqrt{m}$ $\log^2 m$ (rand)	$\frac{276}{275}$ [FV06]
Subs	Value	1 [Ber05]	1	
	Demand	1 [GS99, BM97]	1	
***k*Dup**	Demand	$m^{\frac{1}{k+1}}$ [BKV05, DS05]	$k \cdot m^{\frac{1}{k-2}}$ [BGN03]	$m^{\frac{1}{k+1}-\epsilon}$ [BGN03, DS05]
Proc	Any	$\ln n$ [NS06]	-	$\log n$ [Nis02]

Figure 11.2. It describes the best algorithmic results, incentives compatible approximation results and lower bounds which are currently known for different classes of combinatorial-auction valuations. All results apply for a polynomial number of queries of the specified type. Results without references can be trivially derived from other entries in this table. The word "rand" implies that the result is achieved by a randomized algorithm; otherwise, the results correspond to deterministic algorithms only. Results that use ϵ hold for any $\epsilon > 0$. For the simplicity of the presentation, we ignore the constants of the asymptotic results (i.e., we drop the big-Oh and Ω notations). [NS06]: Nisan and Segal, 2006; [BN05a]: Blumrosen and Nisan, 2005; [DS05]: Dobzinski and Schapira, 2005; [LS05]: Lavi and Swamy, 2005; [DNS06]: Dobzinski et al., 2006; [Fei06]: Feige, 2006; [DNS05]: Dobzinski et al., 2005; [DS06]: Dobzinski and Schapira, 2006; [LLN06]: Lehmann et al., 2006; [KLMM05]: Khot et al., 2005; [FV06]: Feige and Vondrak, 2006; [Ber05]: Bertelsen, 2005; [GS99]: Gul and Stacchetti, 1999; [BM97]:Bikhchandani and Mamer, 1997; [BKV05]: Briest et al., 2005; [BGNO3]: Bartal et al., 2003; [Nis02]: Nisan, 2002.

was written. For each class of bidder valuations, we mention the best currently known polynomial-time approximation ratio, the optimal ratio that is currently achievable by ex-post Nash incentive-compatible mechanisms that run in polynomial time, and the best computational hardness result for the algorithmic problem (under standard computational assumptions). We also classify the results according to the queries they use: unrestricted, value queries, or demand queries. In the figure, we refer the reader to the papers that established these results for more details. In particular, a randomized incentive-compatible mechanism that achieves a $O(\sqrt{m})$-approximation for general combinatorial auctions is discussed in Chapter 12. Below are the classes of valuations that we consider and their abbreviations:

Gen – General (unrestricted) valuations.
SubA – Subadditive valuations, i.e., where $v(S \cup T) \leq v(S) + v(T)$ for all S, T.
XOS – All valuations that can be represented by XOR-of-ORs bids with singleton atomic bundles (see Section 11.4).
SubM - Submodular valuations, i.e., where for every two bundles S and T we have that $v(S) + v(T) \geq v(S \cup T) + v(S \cap T)$.
Subs – (Gross-) substitutes valuations, see Definition 11.28 in Section 11.7.
kDup – Combinatorial auctions with k duplicates of each good. Each bidder desires at most a single item of each good.
Proc – Procurement auctions, where a single buyer needs to buy a set of m items from n suppliers. The suppliers have privately known costs for bundles of items. The buyer aims to minimize the total cost paid.

It is known that Gen $\supset$ SubA $\supset$ XOS $\supset$ SubM $\supset$ Subs.

11.6 Communication Complexity

We already saw in Section 11.2.1 that solving the optimal allocation problem is NP-complete even for single-minded bidders and thus certainly for more general types of bidders. However, as mentioned, in practice one can usually solve problems with thousands or tens-of-thousands of items and bids optimally of near-optimally. Will it be possible to do the same for general valuations using some type of queries to the bidders? In other words: is the problem of representing the valuations an obstacle beyond the computational hardness? In this section we provide an affirmative answer: even if the auctioneer had unlimited computational power, then eliciting sufficient information from the bidders as to determine the optimal allocation would require an exponential amount of queries to the bidders – for any query type. We present this lower bound in a very general model – Yao's two-party communication complexity model – and thus it holds for essentially any model of iterative combinatorial auctions with any type of queries. Let us first introduce this model formally.

11.6.1 The Model and Statement of Lower Bound

The lower bound is obtained in Yao's standard model of two-player communication complexity. In this model we consider two players, Alice and Bob, each holding a valuation function. We can restrict ourselves to the special case where the value of each set is either 0 or 1. Thus, the inputs are monotone functions $v_1, v_2 : 2^M \rightarrow \{0, 1\}$. Alice and Bob must embark on a communication protocol whose final outcome is the declaration of an allocation (S, S^c) that maximizes $v_1(S) + v_2(S^c)$. The protocol specifies rules for exchanging bits of information, where Alice's message at each point may depend only on v_1 and on previous messages received from Bob, while Bob's message at each point may depend only on v_2 and on previous messages received from Alice. No computational constraints are put on Alice and Bob – only communication is measured. The main result shows that:

Theorem 11.25 *Every protocol that finds the optimal allocation for every pair of 0/1 valuations* v_1, v_2 *must use at least* $\binom{m}{m/2}$ *bits of total communication in the worst case.*

Note that $\binom{m}{m/2}$ is exponential in m.[4] Since Yao's communication model is very powerful, the lower bound immediately applies to essentially all settings where v_1 and v_2 reside in "different places." In particular, to the case where the bidders reply to queries of the auctioneer (since a protocol with an auctioneer can be converted into one without an auctioneer, by sending all replies directly to each other and having Alice and Bob simulate the auctioneer's queries) and to any larger number of bidders (since the 2-bidder case is a special case where all bidders but two have null valuations.)

11.6.2 The Proof

Fix a communication protocol that for every input valuation pair (v_1, v_2) finds an optimal allocation S, S^c. We will construct a "fooling set": a set of valuation pairs with the property that the communication patterns produced by the protocol must be different for different valuation pairs. Specifically, for every 0/1 valuation v, we define the *dual valuation* v^* to be $v^*(S) = 1 - v(S^c)$. Note that (i) v^* is indeed a monotone 0/1 valuation, and (ii) for every partition (S, S^c), $S \subseteq M$, we have that $v(S) + v^*(S^c) = 1$.

Lemma 11.26 *Let* $v \neq u$ *be arbitrary 0/1 valuations. Then, in a welfare maximizing combinatorial auction, the sequence of bits transmitted on inputs* (v, v^*) *is not identical to the sequence of bits transmitted on inputs* (u, u^*).

Before we prove the lemma, let us see how the main theorem is implied. Since different input valuation pairs lead to different communication sequences, we see that the total possible number of communication sequences produced by the protocol is at least the number of valuation pairs (v, v^*), which is exactly the number of distinct 0/1 valuations v. The number of 0/1 valuations can be easily bounded from below by $2^{\binom{m}{m/2}}$ by counting only valuations such that $v(S) = 0$ for all $|S| < m/2$, $v(S) = 1$ for all $|S| > m/2$, and allowing $v(S)$ to be either 0 or 1 for $|S| = m/2$; there are $\binom{m}{m/2}$ sets of size $m/2$, so the total number of such valuations is exponential in this number. The protocol must thus be able to produce $2^{\binom{m}{m/2}}$ different communication sequences. Since these are binary sequences, at least one of the sequences must be of length at least $\binom{m}{m/2}$.

[4] More precisely, by Stirling's formula, $\binom{m}{m/2} \sim \sqrt{2/(\pi \cdot m)} \cdot 2^m$.

PROOF (of lemma) Assume, by way of contradiction, that the communication sequence on (v, v^*) is the same as on (u, u^*). We first show that the same communication sequence would also be produced for (v, u^*) and for (u, v^*). Consider the case of (v, u^*); i.e., Alice has valuation v and Bob has valuation u^*. Alice does not see u^* so she behaves and communicates exactly as she would in the (v, v^*) case. Similarly, Bob behaves as he would in the (u, u^*) case. Since the communication sequences in the (v, v^*) and the (u, u^*) cases are the same, neither Alice nor Bob ever notices a deviation from this common sequence, and thus never deviates themselves. In particular, this common sequence is followed also on the (v, u^*) case. Thus, the same allocation (S, S^c) is produced by the protocol in all four cases: (v, v^*), (u, u^*), (v, u^*), (u, v^*). We will show that this is impossible, since a single allocation cannot be optimal for all four cases.

Since $u \neq v$, we have that for some set T, $v(T) \neq u(T)$. Without loss of generality, $v(T) = 1$ and $u(T) = 0$, and so $v(T) + u^*(T^c) = 2$. The allocation (S, S^c) produced by the protocol must be optimal on the valuation pair (v, u^*), thus $v(S) + u^*(S^c) \geq 2$. However, since $(v(S) + v^*(S^c)) + (u(S) + u^*(S^c)) = 1 + 1 = 2$, we get that $u(S) + v^*(S^c) \leq 0$. Thus (S, S^c) is not an optimal allocation for the input pair (u, v^*) – contradiction to the fact that the protocol produces it as the output in this case as well. □

More complex lower bounds on communication allow us to prove tight lower bounds for iterative auctions in various setting. The above lower bound on communication can be extended to even approximating the social welfare.

Theorem 11.27 *For every $\epsilon > 0$, approximating the social welfare in a combinatorial auction to within a factor strictly smaller than* $\min\{n, m^{1/2-\epsilon}\}$ *requires exponential communication.*

Note that this is tight: achieving a factor of n is always trivial (by bundling all items together and selling them in a simple single-item auction), and for $n \geq \sqrt{m}$ there exists an $O(\sqrt{m})$ approximation (see Figure 11.5.2). Actually, most of the lower bounds described in Figure 11.5.2 are communication-complexity results.

11.7 Ascending Auctions

This section concerns a large class of combinatorial auction designs which contains the vast majority of implemented or suggested ones: *ascending auctions*. These are a subclass of iterative auctions with demand queries in which the prices can only increase. In this class of auctions, the auctioneer publishes prices, initially set to zero (or some other minimum prices), and the bidders repeatedly respond to the current prices by bidding on their most desired bundle of goods under the current prices. The auctioneer then repeatedly updates the prices by increasing some of them in some manner, until a level of prices is reached where the auctioneer can declare an allocation. There are several reasons for the popularity of ascending auctions, including their intuitiveness,

An item-price ascending auction for substitutes valuations:

Initialization:
For every item $j \in M$, set $p_j \leftarrow 0$.
For every bidder i let $S_i \leftarrow \emptyset$.

Repeat
For each i, let D_i be the demand of i at the following prices:
p_j for $j \in S_i$ and $p_j + \epsilon$ for $j \notin S_i$.
If for all i $S_i = D_i$, exit the loop;
Find a bidder i with $S_i \neq D_i$ and update:
- For every item $j \in D_i \setminus S_i$, set $p_j \leftarrow p_j + \epsilon$
- $S_i \leftarrow D_i$
- For every bidder $k \neq i$, $S_k \leftarrow S_k \setminus D_i$

Finally: Output the allocation $S_1, ..., S_n$.

Figure 11.3. An item-price ascending auction that ends up with a nearly optimal allocation when bidders' valuations have the (gross) substitutes property.

the fact that private information is only partially revealed, that it is clear that they will terminate, and that they may increase the seller's revenue in some settings.

We will describe auctions that belong to two families of ascending auctions. One family uses a simple pricing scheme (item prices), and guarantees economic efficiency for a restricted class of bidder valuations. The second family is socially efficient for every profile of valuations, but uses a more complex pricing scheme – prices for bundles – extending the demand queries defined in Section 11.5.

11.7.1 Ascending Item-Price Auctions

Figure 11.3 describes an auction that is very natural from an economic point of view: increase prices gradually, maintaining a tentative allocation, until no item that is tentatively held by one bidder is demanded by another. Intuitively, at this point demand equals supply and we are close to a Walrasian equilibrium discussed earlier in Section 11.3, which, by the first welfare theorem, is socially efficient.

Of course, we know that a Walrasian equilibrium does not always exist in a combinatorial auction, so this cannot always be true. The problem is that the auction does not ensure that items are not underdemanded: it may happen that an item that was previously demanded by a bidder is no longer so. The following class of valuations are those in which this cannot happen.

Definition 11.28 A valuation v_i satisfies the *substitutes (or gross-substitutes)* property if for every pair of item-price vectors $\vec{q} \geq \vec{p}$ (coordinate-wise comparison), we have that the demand at prices q contains all items in the demand at prices p whose price remained constant. Formally, for every $A \in argmax_S\{v(S) - \sum_{j \in S} p_j\}$, there exists $D \in argmax_S\{v(S) - \sum_{j \in S} q_j\}$, such that $D \supseteq \{j \in A | p_j = q_j\}$.

That is, the only items that could drop from the demand when prices change from $\vec{p}$ to $\vec{q}$ are those whose price has strictly increased. The substitutes property rules out any form of complementarities. For example, a single-minded bidder who is willing to pay 10 for the complete bundle $\{a, b\}$ will demand both items at prices (3, 3), but if the price of b is raised to 8, this bidder will no longer demand any item – contrarily to the requirement of a substitutes valuation. Exercise 11.6 shows that, in general, substitutes valuations must be submodular. It is not difficult to see that this class of valuations contains the classes of additive valuations, unit-demand valuations, and downward-sloping valuations (see Definitions 11.17 and 11.19). With such valuations, the auction maintains the property that every item is demanded by some bidder. The auction terminates when all the bidders receive their demanded bundles, and consequently, the auction converges to a (nearly) Walrasian equilibrium.

Definition 11.29 An allocation $S_1, \ldots, S_n$ and a prices $p_1, \ldots, p_m$ are an ϵ-Walrasian equilibrium if $\bigcup_i S_i \supseteq \{j | p_j > 0\}$ and for each i, S_i is a demand of i at prices p_j for $j \in S_i$ and $p_j + \epsilon$ for $j \notin S_i$.

Theorem 11.30 *For bidders with substitutes valuations, the auction described in Figure 11.3 ends with an ϵ-Walrasian equilibrium. In particular, the allocation achieves welfare that is within $n\epsilon$ from the optimal social welfare.*

PROOF The theorem will follow from the following key claim:

Claim 11.31 *At every stage of the auction, for every bidder i, $S_i \subseteq D_i$.*[5]

First notice that this claim is certainly true at the beginning. Now let us see what an update step for some bidder i causes. For i itself, S_i after the step is exactly equal to D_i (note that the changes in prices of items just added to S_i exactly matches those defining D_i). For $k \neq i$, two changes may occur at this step: first, items may have been taken from S_k by i, and second the prices of items outside of S_k may have increased. The first type of change makes S_k smaller while not affecting D_k. The second type of change does not affect S_k and the substitutes property directly implies that the only items that can be removed from D_k are those whose price strictly increased and are thus not in S_k.

Once we have this claim, it is directly clear that no item that was ever demanded by any player is ever left unallocated; i.e., $\bigcup_i S_i$ always contains all items whose price is strictly positive. Since the auction terminates only when all $D_i = S_i$ we get an ϵ-Walrasian equilibrium. The fact that an ϵ-Walrasian equilibrium is close to socially optimal is obtained just as in the proof of the first welfare theorem (Theorem 11.13). □

Since prices are only going up, the algorithm terminates after at most $m \cdot v_{\max}/\epsilon$ stages, where $v_{\max}$ is the maximum valuation. It may also be useful to view this auction

[5] For simplicity of presentation, the algorithm assumes that D_i is unique. In the general case, the claim is that S_i is contained in some demand bundle D_i, and the auction is required to pick such a D_i.

as implementing a *primal-dual* algorithm. The auction starts with a feasible solution to the dual linear program (here, zero prices), and as long as the complementary-slackness conditions are unsatisfied proceeds by improving the solution of the dual program (i.e., increasing some prices).

Finally, we will address the strategic behavior of the bidders in such ascending auctions. Will strategic bidders act myopically and truthfully reveal their demand in these auctions? If the valuation functions have complementarities, then bidders will clearly have strong incentives not to report their true preferences, due to a problem known as the *exposure problem*: Bidders who bid for a complementary bundle (e.g., a pair of shoes), are exposed to the risk that part of the bundle (the left shoe) may be taken from them later, and they are left liable for the price of the rest of the bundle (the right shoe) that is worthless for them.

However, even for substitutes preferences the incentive issues are not solved. The prices in Walrasian equilibria are not necessarily VCG prices, and therefore truthful bidding is not an ex-post equilibrium.[6] The strategic weakness of Walrasian equilibria is that bidders may have the incentive to demand smaller bundles of items (*demand reduction*), in order to lower their payments. The following example illustrates such a scenario.

Example 11.32 Consider two items a and b and two players, Alice and Bob, with the following substitutes valuations:

	v(a)	**v(b)**	**v(ab)**
Alice	4	4	4
Bob	5	5	10

For these valuations, the auction in Figure 11.3 will terminate at the Walrasian equilibrium prices $p_a = 4$, $p_b = 4$, where Bob receives both items, and earning him a payoff of 2. If Bob placed bids only on a during the auction, then the auction would stop at zero prices, allocating a to Bob and b to Alice. With this demand reduction, Bob improves his payoff to 5.

11.7.2 Ascending Bundle-Price Auctions

As we saw, not every profile of valuations has a Walrasian equilibrium. The next type of auction that we describe will reach an equilibrium that involves a more complex pricing scheme. We start by describing this extended notion of equilibrium, allowing *personalized bundle prices* – a distinct price per each possible bundle and for each bidder. That is, personalized bundle prices specify a price $p_i(S)$ per each bidder i and every bundle S. We can naturally generalize the notion of the demand of bidder i under such prices to $argmax_S(v_i(S) - p_i(S))$.

[6] When we further restrict the class of substitutes valuations such that each bidder desires at most one item ("unit-demand" valuations, see Definition 11.17), then it is known that a similar auction reaches the lowest possible Walrasian-equilibrium prices that are also VCG prices, and hence these auctions are ex-post Nash incentive compatible (see Chapter 9).

A bundle price auction:

Initialization: For every player i and bundle S, let $p_i(S) \leftarrow 0$.

Repeat

- Find an allocation $T_1, ..., T_n$ that maximizes revenue at current prices, i.e., $\sum_{i=1}^{n} p_i(T_i) \geq \sum_{i=1}^{n} p_i(Y_i)$ for any other allocation $Y_1, ..., Y_n$. (Bundles with zero prices will not be allocated, i.e., $p_i(T_i) > 0$ for eve ry i.)
- Let L be the set of losing bidders, i.e., $L = \{i | T_i = \emptyset\}$.
- For every $i \in L$ let D_i be a demand bundle of i under the prices $\overrightarrow{p_i}$.
- If for all $i \in L$, $D_i = \emptyset$ then terminate.
- For all $i \in L$ with $D_i \neq \emptyset$, let $p_i(D_i) \leftarrow p_i(D_i) + \epsilon$.

Figure 11.4. A bundle price auction which terminates with the socially efficient allocation for any profile of bidders.

Definition 11.33 Personalized bundle prices $\overrightarrow{p} = \{p_i(S)\}$ and an allocation $S = (S_1, \ldots, S_n)$ are called a *competitive equilibrium* if:

- For every bidder i, S_i is a demand bundle, i.e., for any other bundle $T_i \subseteq M$, $v_i(S_i) - p_i(S_i) \geq v_i(T_i) - p_i(T_i)$.
- The allocation S maximizes *seller's revenue* under the current prices, i.e., for any other allocation $(T_1, \ldots, T_n)$, $\sum_{i=1}^{n} p_i(S_i) \geq \sum_{i=1}^{n} p_i(T_i)$.

It is easy to see that with personalized bundle prices, competitive equilibria always exist: any welfare-maximizing allocation with the prices $p_i(S) = v_i(S)$ gives a competitive equilibrium. This may be viewed as the Second Welfare Theorem (see Theorem 11.15) for this setting. Even this weak notion of equilibrium, however, guarantees optimal social welfare:

Proposition 11.34 *In any competitive equilibrium* $(\overrightarrow{p}, S)$ *the allocation maximizes social welfare.*

PROOF Let $(\overrightarrow{p}, S)$ be a competitive equilibrium, and consider some allocation $T = (T_1, \ldots, T_n)$. Since S_i is a demand bundle under the prices $\overrightarrow{p_i}$ for every bidder i, we have that $v_i(S_i) - p_i(S_i) \geq v_i(T_i) - p_i(T_i)$. Summing over all the bidders, together with $\sum_{i=1}^{n} p_i(S_i) \geq \sum_{i=1}^{n} p_i(T_i)$, we get that the welfare in the allocation S exceeds the welfare in T. □

Several iterative auctions are designed to end up with competitive equilibria. Figure 11.4 describes a typical one. At each stage the auctioneer computes a tentative allocation that maximizes his revenue at current prices – which we view as the current bids. All the losing bidders then "raise their bids" on their currently demanded bundle. When no losing bidder is willing to do so, we terminate with an approximately competitive equilibrium.

Definition 11.35 A bundle S is an ϵ-*demand* for a player i under the bundle prices $\overrightarrow{p_i}$ if for any other bundle T, $v_i(S) - p_i(S) \geq v_i(T) - p_i(T) - \epsilon$. An

ϵ-*competitive equilibrium* is similar to a competitive equilibrium (Definition 11.33), except each bidder receives an ϵ-demand under the equilibrium prices.

Theorem 11.36 *For any profile of valuations, the bundle-price auction described in Figure 11.4 terminates with an ϵ-competitive equilibrium. In particular, the welfare obtained is within $n\epsilon$ from the optimal social welfare.*

PROOF At each step of the auction at least one price will be raised. Since a bundle price will clearly never exceed its value, the auction will terminate eventually (although this may take exponentially many steps). Since the allocation at each step is clearly revenue maximizing, it suffices to show that, upon termination, each bidder receives an ϵ-demand.

Losing bidders will clearly receive their demand, the empty set, since this is the condition of termination. A winning bidder i gets an ϵ-demand bundle since the auction maintains the property that every bundle T_i with $p_i(T_i) > 0$ is an ϵ-demand. To see this notice that $p_i(T_i) > 0$ implies that at some previous round T_i was the demand of bidder i. At that point, T_i was the exact demand, and thus, an ϵ-demand bundle after the price increment. Since the last time that the bidder demanded (the current) T_i, only prices of other bundles have increased, clearly maintaining the property.

Finally, the near optimality of the social welfare in an approximate competitive equilibrium follows the same arguments as in Proposition 11.34. □

Notice that while the auction always terminates with a (near) optimal allocation, this may require exponential time in two respects: first, the number of stages may be exponential, and, second, each stage requires the auctioneer to solve an NP-hard optimization problem. Of course, we know that this is unavoidable and that, indeed, exponential communication and computation are required in the worst case. Variants of this auction may be practically faster by allowing bidders to report a *collection* of demand bundles at each stage and increase the prices of all of them (in particular, prices of supersets of a reported demand bundle can be, w.l.o.g., maintained to be at least as high as that of the bundle itself.).

The prices generated by this auction are not VCG prices and thus players are not strategically motivated to act myopically and truthfully report their true demand at each stage.[7] One weak positive equilibrium property is achieved when each bidder is committed in advance to act according to a fixed valuation ("proxy bidding"). Then, the auction admits ex-post Nash equilibria, but these equilibria require the participants to possess considerable knowledge of the preferences of the other bidders.

More complex variants of the auction may charge VCG prices from the bidders rather then the equilibrium prices obtained. While this will have the obvious advantage that truthful bidding will be an ex-post Nash equilibrium, it turns out that this will lose some nice properties possessed by the equilibrium prices reached (like resistance to bidder collusion and to false-name bids in some settings).

[7] When bidders have substitutes valuations (Definition 11.28); however, the auction does terminate at VCG prices.

11.8 Bibliographic Notes

This chapter gives only the very basics of the theoretical treatment of combinatorial auctions. Much more information appears in the recently published books (Cramton et al., 2006; Milgrom, 2004). Information about spectrum auctions can be found, for example, in (FCC auctions home page; Cramton, 2002, 2006), and a nice description of industrial applications can be found in (Sandholm, 2006a).

The earliest work on the computational complexity of the winner determination problem in combinatorial auctions is Rothkhof et al. (1998),which contains algorithms for various special cases. Other early work on algorithms for winner determination is due to Sandholm (2002),who also noted the NP-hardness of the problem and of its approximation. The hardness of approximation is based on the hardness of approximation of clique size of Håstad (1999), with the strong version as stated appearing in Zuckerman (2006). Recent surveys on winner determination algorithms appear in (Lehmann et al., 2006b, Muller, 2006; Sandholm, 2006b). The single-minded case was studied in Lehmann et al. (2002) on which Section 11.2.2 is based. Additional results for the single-minded case and generalizations of it can be found in Babaioff et al. (2005) and the references within.

The LP formulation of the problem and the relation of its integrality gap to Walrasian equilibria were studied in Bikhchandani and Mamer (1997) and Bikhchandani and Ostroy (2002).

Bidding languages were studied in a general and formal way in Nisan (2000) on which Section 11.4 is based. Dummy items were suggested in Fujishima et al. (1999). A detailed survey of bidding languages appears in Nisan (2006).

A systematic study of the query model can be found in Blumrasen and Nisan (2005a). The fact that the linear program can be solved in polynomial time using demand queries appears in Nisan and Segal (2006) and Blumfosen and Nisan (2005a). Applications of this fact for various approximation algorithms can be found in Dobzinski et al. (2005), Lavi and Swamy (2000), and Feige and Vondrak (2006). Relations of the query model to machine-learning theory is described in Blum et al. (2004) and Lehaie and Parkes (2004) and the references within.

The analysis of the communication complexity of combinatorial auctions was initiated in Nisan and Segal (2006) on which Section 11.6 is based. A more comprehensive treatment of this subject can be found in the survey (Segal, 2006). A detailed exposition of the theory of communication complexity can be found in Kushilevitz and Nisan (1997).

Ascending item-price combinatorial auctions for the (gross)-substitutes case were first suggested by Demange et al. (1986), extending their use for matching Kelso and Crawford (1982). These were further studied in Bikhchandani and Mamer (1997), Gul and Stacchetti (1999, 2000), Milgrom (2004), and Ausubel (2006). Socially-efficient ascending bundle-price auctions were suggested in Parkes and Ungar (2000) and Ausubel and Milgrom (2002), and hybrid designs that use both item- and bundle prices appear in Kelly and Steinberg (2000) and Cramton et al. (2006). Ausubel and Milgrom (2002) also discussed connections to coalitional games and their core. A detailed study of ascending auctions and their limitations may be found in Blumrosen and Nisan (2005b). A comprehensive survey can be found in Parkes (2006).

Exercise 11.1 is from Rothkhof et al. (1998). A proof for Exercise 11.2 can be found in Muller (2006). Exercise 11.3 is from Blumrosen and Nisan (2005a). Exercise 11.4 is from Dobzinski et al. (2005). Exercise 11.5 is from Nisan (2000). Exercise 11.6 is from Gul and Stacchetti (1999). Exercise 11.7 is from Parkes (2001) and Blumrosen and Nisan (2005b). Exercise 11.8 is from Blumrosen and Nisan (2005b). The algorithm in exercise 11.9 is the classic one for SET-COVER by Lovasz (1975), see also Nisan (2002).

Acknowledgments

The authors thank Shahar Dobzinki, Jason Hartline, and David Parkes for their valuable comments on an earlier draft of this chapter.

Bibliography

L.M. Ausubel. An efficient dynamic auction for heterogeneous commodities. *Amer. Econ. Rev.*, 96(3):602–629, 2006.

L.M. Ausubel and P.R. Milgrom. Ascending auctions with package bidding. *Front. Theor. Econ.*, 1:1–42, 2002.

M. Babaioff, R. Lavi, and E. Pavlov. Mechanism design for single-value domains. In *20th Ntl. Conf. Artificial Intelligence*, pp. 241–247, 2005.

Y. Bartal, R. Gonen, and N. Nisan. Incentive compatible multi unit combinatorial auctions. In *9th Conf. Theor. Aspects of Rationality and Knowledge*, pp. 72–87, 2003.

A. Bertelsen. *Substitutes Valuations and $m^\natural$-Concavity*. M.Sc. Thesis, The Hebrew University of Jerusalem, 2005.

S. Bikhchandani and J.W. Mamer. Competitive equilibrium in an exchange economy with indivisibilities. *J. Economic Theory*, 74:385–413, 1997.

S. Bikhchandani and J.M. Ostroy. The package assignment model. *J. Economic Theory*, 107:377–406, 2002.

A. Blum, J.C. Jackson, T. Sandholm, and M.A. Zinkevich. Preference elicitation and query learning. *J. Mach. Learn. Res.*, 5:649–667, 2004.

L. Blumrosen and N. Nisan. On the computational power of iterative auctions I: demand queries. Discussion paper no. 381, The Center for the Study of Rationality, The Hebrew University, 2005a. An extended abstract in EC'05 contained preliminary results.

L. Blumrosen and N. Nisan. On the computational power of iterative auctions II: Ascending auctions. Discussion paper no. 382, The Center for the Study of Rationality, The Hebrew University, 2005b. An extended abstract in EC'05 contained preliminary results.

P. Briest, P. Krysta, and B. Vöcking. Approximation techniques for utilitarian mechanism design. In *the 37th ACM Symp. Theor. Comp.*, pp. 39–48, 2005.

P. Cramton. In Martin Cave, Sumit Majumdar, and Ingo Vogelsang, eds., *Handbook of Telecommunications Economics. Chapter 14: Spectrum auctions.* Elsevier Science B.V., 2002.

P. Cramton. In P. Cramton, Y. Shoham, and R. Steinberg, eds., *Combinatorial Auctions. Chapter 5. Simultaneous Ascending Auctions.* MIT Press, 2006.

P. Cramton, L.M. Ausubel, and P.R. Milgrom. In P. Cramton, Y. Shoham, and R. Steinberg, eds., Combinatorial Auctions. Chapter 5. The Clock-Proxy Auction: A Practical Combinatorial Auction Design. MIT Press, 2006.

P. Cramton, Y. Shoham, and R. Steinberg (Editors). *Combinatorial Auctions*. MIT Press, 2006.

G. Demange, D. Gale, and M. Sotomayor. Multi-item auctions. *J. Political Econ.*, 94:863–872, 1986.

S. Dobzinski, N. Nisan, and M. Schapira. Approximation algorithms for combinatorial auctions with complement-free bidders. In *37th ACM Symp. Theory Computing*, pp. 610–618, 2005.

S. Dobzinski, N. Nisan, and M. Schapira. Truthful randomized mechanisms for combinatorial auctions. In *38th Annual ACM Symp. Theory of Computing*, pp. 644–652, 2006.

S. Dobzinski and M. Schapira. Optimal upper and lower approximation bounds for k-duplicates combinatorial auctions. Working paper, the Hebrew University, 2005.

S. Dobzinski and M. Schapira. An improved approximation algorithm for combinatorial auctions with submodular bidders. In *Proc. 17th Annual ACM-SIAM Symp. Disc. Algo.*, pp. 1064–1073, 2006.

FCC auctions home page. http://wireless.fcc.gov/auctions.

U. Feige. On maximizing welfare where the utility functions are subadditive. In *38th ACM Symp. Theory of Computing*, pp. 41–50, 2006.

U. Feige and J. Vondrak. Approximation algorithms for allocation problems: Improving the factor of 1-1/e. In *47th Annual IEEE Symp. Foundations of Computer Science*, pp. 667–676, 2006.

Y. Fujishima, K. Leyton-Brown, and Y. Shoham. Taming the computational complexity of combinatorial auctions: Optimal and approximate approaches. In *16th Intl. Joint Conf. Artificial Intelligence*, Stockholm, Sweden, 1999.

F. Gul and E. Stacchetti. Walrasian equilibrium with gross substitutes. *J. Econ. Theor.*, 87:95–124, 1999.

F. Gul and E. Stacchetti. The English auction with differentiated commodities. *J. Econ. Theor.*, 92(3):66–95, 2000.

J. Håstad. Clique is hard to approximate to within $n^{1-\epsilon}$. *Acta Mathematica*, 182, 1999.

R. Holzman, N. Kfir-Dahav, D. Monderer, and M. Tennenholtz. Bundling equilibrium in combinatrial auctions. *Games Econ. Behav.*, 47:104–123, 2004.

F. Kelly and R. Steinberg. A combinatorial auction with multiple winners for universal service. *Management Sci.*, 46:586–596, 2000.

A.S. Kelso and V.P. Crawford. Job matching, coalition formation, and gross substitutes. *Econometrica*, 50:1483–1504, 1982.

S. Khot, R.J. Lipton, E. Markakis, and A. Mehta. Inapproximability results for combinatorial auctions with submodular utility functions. In *1st Workshop on Internet and Network Economics*, pp. 92–101, 2005.

E. Kushilevitz and N. Nisan. *Communication Complexity*. Cambridge University Press, 1997.

S. Lahaie and D.C. Parkes. Applying learning algorithms to preference elicitation. In *5th ACM Conf. Elect. Commerce*, pp. 180–188, 2004.

R. Lavi and C. Swamy. Truthful and near-optimal mechanism design via linear programming. In *46th Annual IEEE Symp. Fdns. of Computer Science*, pp. 595–604, 2005.

B. Lehmann, D. Lehmann, and N. Nisan. Combinatorial auctions with decreasing marginal utilities. *Games Econ. Behav.*, 55(2):270–296, 2006a.

D. Lehmann, R. Müller, and T. Sandholm. In P. Cramton, Y. Shoham, and R. Steinberg, eds., *Combinatorial Auctions. Chapter 12. The Winner Determination Problem.* MIT Press, 2006b.

D. Lehmann, L.I. O'Callaghan, and Y. Shoham. Truth revelation in approximately efficient combinatorial auctions. *J. ACM*, 49(5):577–602, 2002.

L. Lovasz. On the ratio of optimal integral and fractional covers. *Discrete Mathematics*, 13:383–390, 1975.

P. Milgrom. Putting Auction Theory to Work: the simultaneous ascending auction. *J. Political Econ.*, 018(2):245–272, 2000.

P. Milgrom. *Putting Auction Theory to Work*. Cambridge University Press, 2004.

R. Muller. In P. Cramton, Y. Shoham, and R. Steinberg, eds., *Combinatorial Auctions. Chapter 13. Tractable Cases of the Winner Determination Problem.* MIT Press, 2006.

N. Nisan. Bidding and allocation in combinatorial auctions. In *ACM Conf. on Elect. Commerce*, 2000.

N. Nisan. The communication complexity of approximate set packing and covering. In *29th Intl. Colloq. Auto., Langs. Progr.*, pp. 868–875, 2002.

N. Nisan. In P. Cramton, Y. Shoham, and R. Steinberg, eds., *Combinatorial Auctions. Chapter 1. Bidding Languages*. MIT Press, 2006.

N. Nisan and I. Segal. The communication requirements of efficient allocations and supporting prices. *J. Econ. Theor.*, 129(1):192–224, 2006.

D.C. Parkes. *Iterative Combinatorial Auctions: Achieving Economic and Computational Efficiency.* PhD Thesis, Department of Computer and Information Science, University of Pennsylvania, 2001.

D.C. Parkes. In P. Cramton, Y. Shoham, and R. Steinberg, eds., *Combinatorial Auctions. Chapter 3. Iterative Combinatorial Auctions*. MIT Press, 2006.

D.C. Parkes and L.H. Ungar. Iterative combinatorial auctions: Theory and practice. In *17th Ntl. Conf. on Artificial Intelligence*, pp. 74–81, 2000.

M.H. Rothkhof, A. Pekec, and R.M. Harstad. Computationally manageable combinatorial auctions. *Management Sci.*, 44(8):1131–1147, 1998.

T. Sandholm. Algorithm for optimal winner determination in combinatorial auctions. *Artif. Intellig.*, 135:1–54, 2002.

T. Sandholm. Expressive commerce and its application to sourcing. In *Innovative Applications of Artificial Intelligence*, 2006.

T. Sandholm. In P. Cramton, Y. Shoham, and R. Steinberg, eds., *Combinatorial Auctions. Chapter 14. Optimal Winner Determination Algorithms*. MIT Press, 2006.

I. Segal. In P. Cramton, Y. Shoham, and R. Steinberg, eds., *Combinatorial Auctions. Chapter 11. The Communication Requirements of Combinatorial Allocation Problems*. MIT Press, 2006.

D. Zuckerman. Linear degree extractors and the inapproximability of max clique and chromatic number. In *38th Annual ACM Symp. Theory of Computing*, pp. 681–690, 2006.

Exercises

11.1 Consider an auction for items $1,\ldots,m$ where each bidder is single minded and desires an interval of consecutive items, i.e., $S_i = \{j | k_i \leq j \leq l_i)$ where $1 \leq k_i \leq l_i \leq m$. Prove that in this case the socially efficient allocation can be determined in polynomial time.

11.2 Consider combinatorial auctions for m items among n bidders, where each valuation is represented simply as a vector of $2^m - 1$ numbers (a value for each subset of items). Prove that the optimal allocation can be computed in time that is polynomial in the input length: $n(2^m - 1)$. (An immediate conclusion is that when $m{=}O(\log n)$ then the optimal allocation can be computed in polynomial time in n.)
Hint: Use dynamic programming

11.3 Show a class of valuations for bidders in combinatorial auctions for which a single demand query can reveal enough information for determining the optimal allocation, but this task may require an exponential number (in the number of items) of value queries. (This actually proves Lemma 11.23 from Section 11.5.1.)
Hint: Use the fact that the number of distinct bundles of size $\frac{m}{2}$, out of m items, is exponential in m.

11.4 A valuation v is called *subadditive* if for every two bundles S, T, $v(S) + v(T) \geq v(S \cup T)$. Prove that for any $\epsilon > 0$, achieving a $2 - \epsilon$ approximation in a combinatorial auction with sub additive bidders requires exponential communication.
Hint: Construct a reduction from Theorem 11.27 in Section 11.6.

11.5 The *majority* valuation assigns a value of 1 to any bundle of at least $\frac{m}{2}$ items, and 0 to all other bundles. Prove that representing this valuation using an OR^* formula requires size of at least $\binom{m}{\frac{m}{2}}$.

11.6 Prove that every (gross) substitutes valuation is submodular.

11.7 Consider an *anonymous-price* variant of the bundle-price ascending auctions described in Figure 11.4): The same ascending-price process is performed, except that at every stage, all bidders observe the same bundle prices $\{p(S)\}_{S\subseteq M}$. At each stage, the prices of bundles that are demanded by at least one losing bidder are raised by ϵ.

Show that when all the valuations are *super additive* such an auction terminates with the socially efficient allocation. (A valuation is super additive if for every two bundles S,T, $v(S)+v(T)\leq v(S\cup T)$.)

Hint: First show that if bidder i receives the bundle T_i in the optimal allocation, then $v_i(T_i)\geq v_j(T_i)$ for every bidder j.

11.8 Consider a pair of valuations with the following form (where $0<\alpha,\beta<1$ are unknown to the seller):

	v(ab)	v(a)	v(b)
Alice	2	α	β
Bob	2	2	2

Prove that no item-price ascending auction can reveal enough information for determining the socially efficient allocation for such valuations.

11.9 In a *procurement auction* with single-minded bidders, a single buyer needs to buy a set of m items from n possible suppliers. Each supplier i can provide a single set of items S_i for a privately known price v_i. The buyer needs to buy all items, and aims to minimize the total price paid.

(a) Prove that the following greedy algorithm finds a $(1+\ln m)$-approximation to the optimal procurement:
- *Initialize R to contain all m items, and $W\leftarrow\emptyset$.*
- *Repeat until $R=\emptyset$: Choose $j\in argmax_k \frac{v_k}{|R\cap S_k|}$, and let $W=W\cup\{j\}$ and $R=R\setminus S_j$.*

(b) Deduce an incentive-compatible polynomial-time $(1+\ln m)$-approximation mechanism for procurement auctions among single-minded bidders. Show first that the allocation scheme defined by the algorithm is monotone, and identify the "critical values" to be paid by the winning suppliers.

CHAPTER 12

Computationally Efficient Approximation Mechanisms

Ron Lavi

Abstract

We study the integration of game theoretic and computational considerations. In particular, we study the design of computationally efficient *and* incentive compatible mechanisms, for several different problem domains. Issues like the dimensionality of the domain, and the goal of the algorithm designer, are examined by providing a technical discussion on four results: (i) approximation mechanisms for single-dimensional scheduling, where truthfulness reduces to a simple monotonicity condition; (ii) randomness as a tool to resolve the computational vs. incentives clash for Combinatorial Auctions, a central multidimensional domain where this clash is notable; (iii) the impossibilities of deterministic dominant-strategy implementability in multidimensional domains; and (iv) alternative solution concepts that fit worst-case analysis, and aim to resolve the above impossibilities.

12.1 Introduction

Algorithms in computer science, and *Mechanisms* in game theory, are very close in nature. Both disciplines aim to implement desirable properties, drawn from "real-life" needs and limitations, but the resulting two sets of properties are completely different. A natural need is then to merge them – to simultaneously exhibit "good" game theoretic properties as well as "good" computational properties. The growing importance of the Internet as a platform for computational interactions only strengthens the motivation for this.

However, this integration task poses many difficult challenges. The two disciplines clash and contradict in several different ways, and new understandings must be obtained to achieve this hybridization. The classic Mechanism Design literature is rich and contains many technical solutions when incentive issues are the key goal. Quite interestingly, most of these are not computationally efficient. In parallel, most existing algorithmic techniques, answering the computational questions at hand, do not yield the game theoretic needs. There seems to be a certain clash between classic algorithmic techniques and classic mechanism design techniques. This raises many intriguing questions: In what cases this clash is fundamental – a mathematical impossibility? Alternatively, can we "fix" this clash by applying new techniques? We will try to give a feel for these issues.

The possibility of constructing mechanisms with desirable computational properties turns out to be strongly related to the *dimensionality* of the problem domain. In single-dimensional domains, the requirement for game-theoretic truthfulness reduces to a convenient algorithmic monotonicity condition that leaves ample flexibility for the algorithm designer. We demonstrate this in Section 12.2, were we study the construction of computationally efficient approximation mechanisms for the classic machine scheduling problem. Although there exists a rich literature on approximation algorithms for this problem domain, quite remarkably none of these classic results satisfy the desired game-theoretic properties. We show that when the scheduling problem is single-dimensional, then this clash is not fundamental, and can be successfully resolved.

The problem domain of job scheduling has one additional interesting aspect that makes it worth studying: it demonstrates a key difference between economics and computer science, namely the *goals* of algorithms vs. the goals of classic mechanisms. While the economics literature mainly studies welfare and/or revenue maximization, computational models raise the need for completely different objectives. In scheduling problems, a common objective is to minimize the load on the most loaded machine. As is usually the case, existing techniques for incentive-compatible mechanism design do not fit such an objective (and, on the other hand, most existing algorithmic solutions do not yield the desired incentives). The resolution of these clashes has led to insightful techniques, and the technical exploration of Section 12.2 serves as an example.

As opposed to single-dimensional domains, *multi*-dimensionality seems to pose much harder obstacles. In Chapter 9, the monotonicity conditions that characterize truthfulness for multidimensional domains were discussed, but it seems that these conditions do not translate well to algorithmic constructions. This issue will be handled in the rest of the chapter, and will be approached in three different ways: we will explore the inherent impossibilities that the required monotonicity conditions cast on deterministic algorithmic constructions, we will introduce randomness to solve these difficulties, and we will consider alternative notions to the solution concept of truthfulness.

Our main example for a multidimensional domain will be the domain of combinatorial auctions (CAs). Chapter 11 studies CAs mostly from a computational point of view, and in contrast our focus is on designing computationally efficient *and* incentive compatible CAs. This demonstrates a second key difference between economics and computer science, namely the requirement for computational efficiency. Even if our goal is the classic economic goal of welfare maximization, we cannot use Vickrey–Clarke–Groves mechanisms (which classically implement this goal) since in many cases they are computationally inefficient. The domain of CAs captures exactly this point, and the need for computationally efficient techniques that translate algorithms to mechanisms is central. In Section 12.3 we will see how randomness can help. We describe a rather general technique that uses randomness and linear programming in order to convert algorithms to truthful-in-expectation mechanisms. Thus we get a positive answer to the computational clash, by introducing randomness.

In Section 12.4 we return to deterministic settings and to the classic definition of deterministic truthfulness, and study the impossibilities associated with it. Our motivating question is whether the three requirements (i) deterministic truthfulness, (ii) computational efficiency, and (iii) nontrivial approximation guarantees, clash in a fundamental and well-defined way. We already know that single dimensionality does not exhibit such a clash, and in this section we describe the other extreme. If a domain has full dimensionality (in a certain formal sense, to be discussed in the section body), then any truthful mechanism must be VCG. It is important to remark that this result further emphasizes our lack of knowledge about the state of affairs for all the *intermediate* range of multidimensional domains, to which CAs and its different variants belong.

As was motivated in previous chapters, the game-theoretic quest should start with the solution concept of "implementation in dominant strategies," and indeed most of this chapter follows this line of thought. However, to avoid the impossibilities mentioned earlier, we have to deepen our understandings about the alternatives at hand. Studies in economics usually turn to the solution concept of Bayesian–Nash that requires strong distributional assumptions, namely that the input distributions are known, and, furthermore, that they are *commonly* known, and agreed upon. Such assumptions seem too strong for CS settings, and criticism about these assumptions have been also raised by economists (e.g., "Wilson's doctrine"). We have already seen that randomization, and truthful-in-expectation in particular, can provide a good alternative. We conclude the chapter by providing an additional example, of a deterministic alternative solution concept, and describe a deterministic CA that uses this notion to provide nontrivial approximation guarantees.

Let us mention two other types of GT-versus-CS clashes, not studied in this chapter, to complete the picture. *Different models:* Some CS models have a significantly different structure, which causes the above-mentioned clash even when traditional objectives are considered. In online computation, for example, players arrive over time, a fundamentally different assumption than classic mechanism design. The difficulties that emerge, and the novel solutions proposed, are discussed in Chapter 16. *Different analysis conventions:* CS usually employs worst-case analysis, avoiding strong distributional assumptions, while in economics, the underlying distribution is usually assumed. This greatly affects the character of results, and the reader is referred to, e.g., Chapter 13 for a broader discussion.

12.2 Single-Dimensional Domains: Job Scheduling

As a first example for the interaction between game theory and algorithmic theory, we consider single-dimensional domains. Simple single-dimensional domains were introduced in Chapter 9, where every alternative is either a winning or a losing alternative for each player. Here we discuss a more general case. Intuitively, single dimensionality implies that a single parameter determines the player's valuation vector. In Chapter 9, this was simply the value for winning, but less straight-forward cases also make sense:

Scheduling related machines. In this domain, n jobs are to be assigned to m machines, where job j consumes p_j time-units, and machine i has speed s_i. Thus machine i requires p_j/s_i time-units to complete job j. Let $l_i = \sum_{j|\ j \text{ is assigned to } i} p_j$ be the load on machine i. Our schedule aims to minimizes the term $\max_i l_i/s_i$, (the *makespan*). Each machine is a selfish entity, incurring a constant cost for every consumed time unit (and w.l.o.g. assume this cost is 1). Thus the utility of a machine from a load l_i and a payment P_i is $-l_i/s_i - P_i$. The mechanism designer knows the processing times of the jobs and constructs a scheduling mechanism.

Although here the set of alternatives cannot be partitioned to "wins" and "loses," this is clearly a single-dimensional domain.

Definition 12.1 (single-dimensional linear domains) A domain V_i of player i is single-dimensional and linear if there exist nonnegative real constants (the "loads") $\{q_{i,a}\}_{a \in A}$ such that, for any $v_i \in V_i$, there exists $c \in \Re_-$ (the "cost") such that $v_i(a) = q_{i,a} \cdot c$.

In other words, the type of a player is simply her cost c, as disclosing it gives us the entire valuation vector. Note that the scheduling domain is indeed single-dimensional and linear: the parameter c is equal to $1/s_i$, and the constant $q_{i,a}$ for alternative a is the load assigned to i according to a.

A natural symmetric definition exists for value-maximization (as opposed to cost-minimization) problems, where the types are nonnegative.

We aim to design a computationally efficient approximation algorithm, *that is also implementable*. As the social goal is a certain min–max criterion, and not to minimize the *sum* of costs, we cannot use the general VCG technique. Since we have a convex domain, Chapter 9 tells us that we need a "weakly monotone" algorithm. But what exactly does this mean? Luckily, the formulation of weak monotonicity can be much simplified for single-dimensional domains.

If we fix the costs c_{-i} declared by the other players, an algorithm for a single-dimensional linear domain determines the load $q_i(c)$ of player i as a function of her reported cost c. Take two possible types c and c', and suppose $c' > c$. Then the weak monotonicity condition from Chapter 9 reduces to $-q_i(c')(c' - c) \geq -q_i(c)(c' - c)$, which holds iff $q_i(c') \leq q_i(c)$. Hence from Chapter 9 we know that such an algorithm is implementable if and only if its load functions are monotone nonincreasing. Figure 12.1 describes this, and will help us figure out the required prices for implementability.

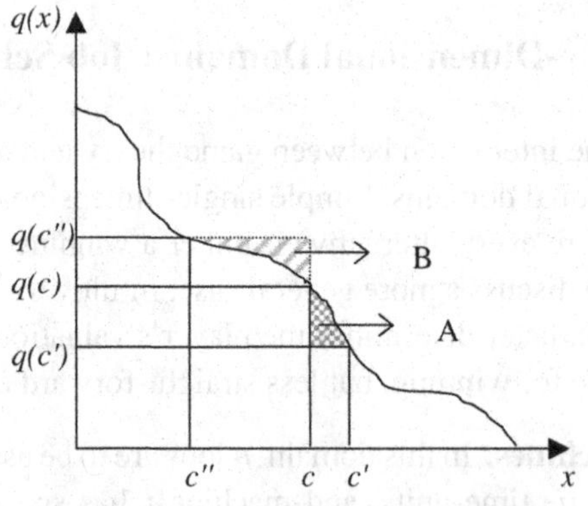

Figure 12.1. A monotone load curve.

Suppose that we charge a payment of $P_i(c) = \int_0^c [q_i(x) - q_i(c)]\,dx$ from player i if he declares a cost of c. Using Figure 12.1, we can easily verify that these prices lead to incentive compatibility: Suppose that player i's true cost is c. If he reports the truth, his utility is the entire area below the load curve up to c. Now if he declares some $c' > c$, his utility will decrease by exactly the area marked by A: his cost from the resulting load will indeed decrease to $c \cdot q_i(c')$, but his payment will increase to be the area between the line $q_i(c')$ and the load curve. On the other hand, if the player will report $c'' < c$, his utility will decrease by exactly the area marked by B, since his cost from the resulting load will increase to $c \cdot q_i(c'')$. Thus these prices satisfy the incentive-compatibility inequalities, and in fact this is a simple direct proof for the sufficiency of load monotonicity for this case.

The above prices do not satisfy individual rationality, since a player always incurs a negative utility if we use these prices. To overcome this, the usual exercise is to add a large enough constant to the prices, which in our case can be $\int_0^\infty q_i(x)\,dx$. Note that if we add this to the above prices we get that a player that does not receive any load (i.e., declares a cost of infinity) will have a zero utility, and in general the utility of a truthful player will be nonnegative, exactly $\int_c^\infty q_i(x)\,dx$. From all the above we get the following theorem.

Theorem 12.2 *An algorithm for a single-dimensional linear domain is implementable if and only if its load functions are nonincreasing. Furthermore, if this is the case then charging from every player i a price*

$$P_i(c) = \int_0^c [q_i(x) - q_i(c)]\,dx - \int_c^\infty q_i(x)\,dx$$

will result in an individually rational dominant strategy implementation.

In the application to scheduling, we will construct a randomized mechanism, as well as a deterministic one. In the randomized case, we will employ truthfulness in expectation (see Chapter 9, Definition 9.27). One should observe that, from the discussion above, it follows that truthfulness in expectation is equivalent to the monotonicity of the *expected* load.

12.2.1 A Monotone Algorithm for the Job Scheduling Problem

Now that we understand the exact form of an implementable algorithm, we can construct one that approximates the optimal outcome. In fact, the optimum itself is implementable, since it can satisfy weak monotonicity (see the exercises for more details), but the computation of the optimal outcome is NP-hard. We wish to construct efficiently computable mechanisms, and hence design a monotone and polynomial-time approximation algorithm. Note that we face a "classic" algorithmic problem – no game-theoretic issues are left for us to handle.

Before we start, let us assume that jobs and machines are reordered so that $s_1 \geq s_2 \geq \cdots \geq s_m$ and $p_1 \geq p_2 \geq \cdots \geq p_n$. For the algorithmic construction, we first need to estimate the optimal makespan of a given instance.

Estimating the optimal makespan. Fix a job-index j, and some target makespan T. If a schedule has makespan at most T, then it must assign any job out of $1, \ldots, j$ to a machine i such that $T \geq p_j/s_i$. Let $i(j,T) = \max\{i \mid T \geq p_j/s_i\}$. Thus any schedule with makespan at most T assigns jobs $1,\ldots,j$ to machines $1,\ldots,i(j,T)$. From space considerations, it immediately follows that

$$T \geq \frac{\sum_{k=1}^{j} p_k}{\sum_{l=1}^{i(j,T)} s_l}. \tag{12.1}$$

Now define

$$T_j = \min_i \max \left\{ \frac{p_j}{s_i}, \frac{\sum_{k=1}^{j} p_k}{\sum_{l=1}^{i} s_l} \right\} \tag{12.2}$$

Lemma 12.3 *For any job-index j, the optimal makespan is at least T_j.*

PROOF Fix any $T < T_j$. We prove that T violates 12.1, hence cannot be any feasible makespan, and the claim follows. Let i_j be the index that determines T_j. The left expression in the max term is increasing with i, while the right term is decreasing. Thus i_j is either the last i where the right term is larger than the left one, or the first i for which the left term is larger than the right one. We prove that T violates 12.1 for each case separately.

Case 1 ($\frac{\sum_{k=1}^{j} p_k}{\sum_{l=1}^{i_j} s_l} \geq \frac{p_j}{s_{i_j}}$): For $i_j + 1$ the max term is received by $\frac{p_j}{s_{i_j+1}}$, Since T_j is the min-max, we get $T_j \leq \frac{p_j}{s_{i_j+1}}$. Since $T < T_j$, we have $i(j,T) \leq i_j$, and $T < T_j = \frac{\sum_{k=1}^{j} p_k}{\sum_{l=1}^{i_j} s_l} \leq \frac{\sum_{k=1}^{j} p_k}{\sum_{l=1}^{i(j,T)} s_l}$. Hence T violates 12.1, as claimed.

Case 2 ($\frac{\sum_{k=1}^{j} p_k}{\sum_{l=1}^{i_j} s_l} < \frac{p_j}{s_{i_j}}$): $T_j \leq \frac{\sum_{k=1}^{j} p_k}{\sum_{l=1}^{i_j-1} s_l}$ since T_j is the min–max, and the max for $i_j - 1$ is received at the right. In addition, $i(j,T) < i_j$ since $T_j = \frac{p_j}{s_{i_j}}$ and $T < T_j$. Thus $T < T_j \leq \frac{\sum_{k=1}^{j} p_k}{\sum_{l=1}^{i_j-1} s_l} \leq \frac{\sum_{k=1}^{j} p_k}{\sum_{l=1}^{i(j,T)} s_l}$, as we need. □

With this, we get a good lower bound estimate of the optimal makespan:

$$T_{\text{LB}} = \max_j T_j \tag{12.3}$$

The optimal makespan is at least T_j for any j, hence it is at least T_{LB}.

A fractional algorithm. We start with a fractional schedule. If machine i gets an α fraction of job j then the resulting load is assumed to be $(\alpha \cdot p_j)/s_i$. This is of course not a valid schedule, and we later round it to an integral one.

Definition 12.4 (The fractional allocation) Let j be the first job such that $\sum_{k=1}^{j} p_k > T_{\text{LB}} \cdot s_1$. Assign to machine 1 jobs $1,\ldots,j-1$, plus a fraction of j in order to equate $l_1 = T_{\text{LB}} \cdot s_1$. Continue recursively with the unassigned fractions of jobs and with machines $2,\ldots,m$.

Lemma 12.5 *There is enough space to fractionally assign all jobs, and if job j is fractionally assigned to machine i then $p_j/s_i \leq T_{\text{LB}}$.*

PROOF Let i_j be the index that determines T_j. Since $T_{\text{LB}} \geq T_j \geq \frac{\sum_{k=1}^{j} p_k}{\sum_{l=1}^{i_j} s_l}$, we can fractionally assign jobs 1, .., j up to machine i_j. Since $T_j \geq p_j/s_{i_j}$ we get the second part of the claim, and setting $j = n$ gives the first part. □

Lemma 12.6 *The fractional load function is monotone.*

PROOF We show that if s_i increases to $s_i' = \alpha \cdot s_i$ (for $\alpha > 1$) then $l_i' \leq l_i$. Let T_{LB}' denote the new estimate of the optimal makespan. We first claim that $T_{\text{LB}}' \leq \alpha \cdot T_{\text{LB}}$. For an instance $s_1'', \ldots, s_m''$ such that $s_l'' = \alpha \cdot s_l$ for all machines l we have that $T_{\text{LB}}'' = \alpha \cdot T_{\text{LB}}$ since both terms in the max expression of T_j were multiplied by α. Since $s_l' \leq s_l$ for all l we have that $T_{\text{LB}}' \leq T_{\text{LB}}''$. Now, if $l_i = T_{\text{LB}} \cdot s_i$, i.e. i was full, then $l_i' \leq T_{\text{LB}}' \cdot s_i' \leq T_{\text{LB}} \cdot s_i = l_i$. Otherwise $l_i < T_{\text{LB}} \cdot s_i$, hence i is the last nonempty machine. Since $T_{\text{LB}}' \geq T_{\text{LB}}$, all previous machines now get at least the same load as before, hence machine i cannot get more load. □

We now round to an integral schedule. The natural rounding, of integrally placing each job on one of the machines that got some fraction of it, provides a 2-approximation, but violates the required monotonicity (see the exercises). We offer two types of rounding, a randomized rounding and a deterministic one. The former is simpler, and results in a better approximation ratio, but uses the weaker solution concept of truthfulness in expectation. The latter is slightly more involved, and uses deterministic truthfulness, but results in an inferior approximation ratio.

Definition 12.7 (A randomized rounding) Choose $\alpha \in [0, 1]$ uniformly at random. For every job j that was fractionally assigned to i and $i + 1$, if j's fraction on i is at least α, assign j to i in full, otherwise assign j to $i + 1$.

Theorem 12.8 *The randomized scheduling algorithm is truthful in expectation, and obtains a 2-approx. to the optimal makespan in polynomial-time.*

PROOF Let us check the approximation first. A machine i may get, in addition to its full jobs, two more jobs. One, j, is shared with machine $i - 1$, and the other, k, is shared with machine $i + 1$. If j was rounded to i then i initially has at least $1 - \alpha$ fraction of j, hence the additional load caused by j is at most $\alpha \cdot p_j$. Similarly, If k was rounded to i then i initially has at least α fraction of k, hence the additional load caused by k is at most $(1 - \alpha) \cdot p_k$. Thus the maximal total additional load that i gets is $\alpha \cdot p_j + (1 - \alpha) \cdot p_k$. By Lemma 12.5 we have that $\max\{p_j, p_k\} \leq T_{\text{LB}}$ and since T_{LB} is not larger than the optimal maximal makespan, the approximation claim follows.

For truthfulness, we only need that the expected load is monotone. Note that machine $i - 1$ gets job j with probability α, so i gets it with probability $1 - \alpha$, and i gets k with probability α. So the expected load of machine i is exactly its fractional load. The claim now follows from Lemma 12.6. □

An integral deterministic algorithm. To be accurate, what follows is not exactly a rounding of the fractional assignment we obtained above, but a similar-in-spirit deterministic assignment. We set virtual speeds, where the fastest machine is set to be slightly faster, and the others are set to be slightly slower, we find a fractional assignment according to these virtual speeds, and then use the "natural" rounding of placing each job fully on the first machine it is fractionally assigned to. With these virtual speeds, the rounding that previously failed to be monotone, now succeeds:

Definition 12.9 (A deterministic algorithm) Given the bids $s_1, \ldots, s_m$, perform:

(i) Set new (virtual) speeds $d_1, \ldots, d_m$, as follows. Let $d_1 = \frac{8}{5}s_1$, and for $i \geq 2$, let d_i be the the closest value of the "breakpoints" $\frac{s_1}{2.5^i}$ (for $i = 1, 2, \ldots$) such that $d_i \leq s_i$.

(ii) Compute T_{LB} according to the virtual speeds, i.e. $T_{\text{LB}} = T_{\text{LB}}(d_i, d_{-i})$.

(iii) Assign jobs to machines, starting from the largest job and the fastest machine. Move to the next machine when the current machine, i, holds jobs with total processing time larger or equal to $T_{\text{LB}} \cdot d_i$.

Note that if the fastest machine changes its speed, then *all* the d_i's may change. Also note that step 3 manages to assign all jobs, since what we are doing is exactly the deterministic natural rounding described above for the fractional assignment, *using the d_i's instead of the s_i's*. As we shall see, this crucial difference enables monotonicity, in the cost of a certain loss in the approximation.

To exactly see the approximation loss, first note that $T_{\text{LB}}(d) \leq 2.5T_{\text{LB}}(s)$, since speeds are made slower by at most this factor. For the fastest machine, since s_1 is lower than d_1, the actual load up to $T_{\text{LB}}(d)$ may be $1.6T_{\text{LB}}(d) \leq 4T_{\text{LB}}(s)$. As we may integrally place on machine 1 one job that is partially assigned also to machine 2, observe (i) that $d_1 \geq 4d_2$, and (ii) by the fractional rules the added job has load at most $T_{\text{LB}}(d)d_2$. Thus get that the load on machine 1 is at most $\frac{5}{4}1.6T_{\text{LB}}(d) \leq 5T_{\text{LB}}(s)$. For any other machine, $d_i \leq s_i$, and so after we integrally place the one extra partial job the load can be at most $2T_{\text{LB}}(d)d_i \leq 2 \cdot 2.5T_{\text{LB}}(s)s_i = 5T_{\text{LB}}(s)s_i$. Since $T_{\text{LB}}(s)$ lower bounds the optimal makespan for s the approximation follows.

To understand why monotonicity holds, we first need few observations that easily follow from our knowledge on the fractional assignment.

For any $i > 1$ and $\beta < d_i$, $T_{\text{LB}}(\beta, d_{-i}) \leq \frac{5}{4}T_{\text{LB}}(d_i, d_{-i})$. Consider the following modification to the fractional assignment for (d_i, d_{-i}): machine i does not get any job, and each machine $1 \leq i' < i$ gets the jobs that were previously assigned to machine $i' + 1$. Since i' is faster than $i' + 1$, any machine $2 \leq i' < i$ does not cross the $T_{\text{LB}}(d_i, d_{-i})$ limit. As for machine 1, note that it is always the case that $d_1 \geq 4d_2$, hence the new load on machine 1 is at most $\frac{5}{4}T_{\text{LB}}(d_i, d_{-i})$.

If a machine $i > 1$ slows down then the total work assigned to the faster machines does not decrease, which follows immediately from the fact that $T_{LB}(d'_i, d_{-i}) \geq T_{LB}(d_i, d_{-i})$, for $d'_i \geq d_i$.

If the fastest machine slows down, yet remains the fastest, then its assigned work does not increase. Let $s'_1 = c \cdot s_1$ for some $c < 1$. Therefore all breakpoints shift by a factor of c. If no speed s_i moves to a new breakpoint then all d's move by a factor of c, the resulting T_{LB} will therefore also move by a factor of c, meaning that machine 1 will get the same set of jobs as before. If additionally some s_i's move to a new breakpoint this implies that the respective d_i's decrease, and by the monotonicity of T_{LB} it also decreases, which means that machine 1 will not get more work.

Lemma 12.10 *The deterministic algorithm is monotone.*

PROOF Suppose that machine i slows down from s_i to $s'_i < s_i$. We need to show that it does not get more work. Assume that the vector d has indeed changed because of i's change.

If i is the fastest machine and it remains the fastest then the above observation is what we need. If the fastest machine changes to i', then we add an artificial breakpoint to the slowdown decrease, where i and i''s speeds are identical, and the title of the "fastest machine" moves from i to i'. Note that the same threshold, T, is computed when the title goes from i to i'. i's work when it is the "fastest machine" is at least $\frac{8}{5}s_i \cdot T$, while i's work when i' is the fastest is at most $2\frac{s_1}{2.5}T < \frac{8}{5}s_i \cdot T$, hence decreases.

If i is not the fastest, but still full, then $d'_i < d_i$ (since the breakpoints remain fixed), and therefore $T_{LB}(d'_i, d_{-i}) \leq \frac{5}{4}T_{LB}(d_i, d_{-i})$. With s_i, i's work is at least $T \cdot d_i$ (where $T = T_{LB}(d_i, d_{-i})$), and with s'_i its work is at most $2 \cdot \frac{5}{4}T\frac{d_i}{2.5} = T \cdot d_i$, hence i's load does not increase.

Finally, note that if i's is not full then by the third observation, since the work of the previous machines does not decrease, then i's work does not increase. □

By the above arguments we immediately get the following theorem.

Theorem 12.11 *There exists a truthful deterministic mechanism for scheduling related machines, that approximates the makespan by a factor of* 5.

A note about price computation is in place. A polynomial-time *mechanism* must compute the prices in polynomial time. To compute the prices for both the randomized and the deterministic mechanisms, we need to integrate over the load function of a player, fixing the others' speeds. In both cases this is a step function, with polynomial number of steps (when a player declares a large enough speed she will get all jobs, and as she decreases her speed more and more jobs will be assigned elsewhere, where the set of assigned jobs will decrease monotonically). Thus we can see that price computation is polynomial-time.

Without the monotonicity requirement, a PTAS for related machines exists. The question whether one can incorporate truthfulness is still open.

Open Question Does there exist a *truthful* PTAS for related machines?

The technical discussion of this section aims to demonstrate that, for single-dimensional domains, the algorithmic implications of the game-theoretic requirement are "manageable," and leave ample flexibility for the algorithmic designer. *Multi*-dimensionality, on the other hand, does not exhibit this easy structure, and the rest of this chapter is concerned with exactly this issue.

12.3 Multidimensional Domains: Combinatorial Auctions

As opposed to single-dimensional domains, the monotonicity conditions that characterize implementability in multidimensional domains are far more complex (see the discussion in Chapter 9), hence designing implementable approximation algorithms is harder. As discussed in the Introduction, this chapter examines three aspects of this issue, and in this section we will utilize randomness to overcome the difficulties of implementability in multidimensional domains. We study this for the representative and central problem domain of Combinatorial Auctions.

Combinatorial Auctions (CAs) are a central model with theoretical importance and practical relevance. It generalizes many theoretical algorithmic settings, like job scheduling and network routing, and is evident in many real-life situations. Chapter 11 is exclusively devoted to CAs, providing a comprehensive discussion on the model and its various computational aspects. Our focus here is different: how to design CAs that are, simultaneously, computationally efficient *and* incentive-compatible. While each aspect is important on its own, obviously only the integration of the two provides an acceptable solution.

Let us shortly restate the essentials. In a CA, we allocate m items (Ω) to n players. Players value *subsets* of items, and $v_i(S)$ denotes i's value of a bundle $S \subseteq \Omega$. Valuations additionally satisfy (i) monotonicity, i.e., $v_i(S) \leq v_i(T)$ for $S \subseteq T$, and (ii) normalization, i.e., $v_i(\emptyset) = 0$. In this section we consider the goal of maximizing the social welfare: find an allocation $(S_1, \ldots, S_n)$ that maximizes $\sum_i v_i(S_i)$.

Since a general valuation has size exponential in n and m, the representation issue must be taken into account. Chapter 11 examines two models. In the *bidding languages* model, the bid of a player represents his valuation in a concise way. For this model it is NP-hard to approximate the social welfare within a ratio of $\Omega(m^{1/2-\epsilon})$, for any $\epsilon > 0$ (if single-minded bids are allowed). In the *query access* model, the mechanism iteratively queries the players in the course of computation. For this model, any algorithm with polynomial communication cannot obtain an approximation ratio of $\Omega(m^{1/2-\epsilon})$ for any $\epsilon > 0$. These bounds are tight, as there exists a deterministic $\sqrt{m}$-approximation with polynomial computation and communication. Thus, for the general case, the computational status by itself is well-understood.

The basic incentives issue is again well-understood: with VCG (which requires the exact optimum) we can obtain truthfulness. The two considerations therefore clash if we attempt to use classic techniques, and our aim is to develop a new technique that will combine the two desirable aspects of efficient computation and incentive compatibility.

We describe a rather general LP-based technique to convert approximation algorithms to truthful mechanisms, by using randomization: given any algorithm to the general CA problem that outputs a c-approximation to the optimal *fractional* social welfare, one can construct a randomized c-approximation mechanism that is truthful in expectation. Thus, the same approximation guarantee is maintained. The construction and proof are described in three steps. We first discuss the fractional domain, where we allocate fractions of items. We then show how to move back to the original domain while maintaining truthfulness, by using randomization. This uses an interesting decomposition technique, which we then describe.

The fractional domain. Let $x_{i,S}$ denote the fraction of subset S that player i receives in allocation x. Assume that her value for that fraction is $x_{i,S} \cdot v_i(S)$. The welfare maximization becomes an LP:

$$\max \quad \sum_{i,S\neq\emptyset} x_{i,S} \cdot v_i(S) \qquad \text{(CA-P)}$$

$$\text{subject to} \quad \sum_{S\neq\emptyset} x_{i,S} \leq 1 \quad \text{for each player } i \qquad (12.4)$$

$$\sum_i \sum_{S:j\in S} x_{i,S} \leq 1 \quad \text{for each item } j \qquad (12.5)$$

$$x_{i,S} \geq 0 \quad \forall i, S \neq \emptyset.$$

By constraint 12.4, a player receives at most one integral subset, and constraint 12.5 ensures that each item is not overallocated. The empty set is excluded for technical reasons that will become clear below. This LP is solvable in time polynomial in its size by using, e.g., the ellipsoid method. Its size is related to our representation assumption. If we assume the bidding languages model, where the LP has size polynomial in the size of the bid (e.g., k-minded players), then we have a polynomial-time algorithm. If we assume general valuations and a query-access, this LP is solvable with a polynomial number of demand queries (see Chapter 11). Note that, in either case, the number of nonzero $x_{i,S}$ coordinates is polynomial, since we obtain x in polynomial-time (this will become important below). In addition, since we obtain the *optimal allocation*, we can use VCG (see Chapter 9) to get:

Proposition 12.12 *In the fractional case, there exists a truthful optimal mechanism with efficient computation and communication, for both the bidding languages model and the query-access model.*

The transition to the integral case. The following technical lemma allows for an elegant transition, by using randomization.

Definition 12.13 Algorithm A "verifies a c-integrality-gap" (for the linear program CA-P) if it receives as input real numbers $w_{i,S}$, and outputs an integral point $\tilde{x}$ which is feasible for CA-P, and

$$c \cdot \sum_{i,S} w_{i,S} \cdot \tilde{x}_{i,S} \geq \max_{\text{feasible } x\text{'s}} \sum_{i,S} w_{i,S} \cdot x_{i,S}$$

Lemma 12.14 (The decomposition lemma) *Suppose that A verifies a c-integrality-gap for CA-P (in polynomial time), and x is any feasible point of CA-P. Then one can decompose x/c to a convex combination of integral feasible points. Furthermore, this can be done in polynomial-time.*

Let $\{x^l\}_{l \in \mathcal{I}}$ be all integral allocations. The proof will find $\{\lambda_l\}_{l \in \mathcal{I}}$ such that (i) $\forall l \in \mathcal{I}$, $\lambda_l \geq 0$, (ii) $\sum_{l \in \mathcal{I}} \lambda_l = 1$, and (iii) $\sum_{l \in \mathcal{I}} \lambda_l \cdot x^l = x/c$. We will also need to provide the integrality gap verifier. But first we show how to use all this to move back to the integral case, while maintaining truthfulness.

Definition 12.15 (The decomposition-based mechanism)

(i) Compute an optimal fractional solution, x^*, and VCG prices $p_i^F(v)$.

(ii) Obtain a decomposition $x^*/c = \sum_{l \in \mathcal{I}} \lambda_l \cdot x^l$.

(iii) With probability λ_l: (i) choose allocation x^l, (ii) set prices $p_i^R(v) = [v_i(x^l)/v_i(x^*)]p_i^F(v)$.

The strategic properties of this mechanism hold whenever the *expected* price equals the fractional price over c. The specific prices chosen satisfy, in addition to that, strong individual rationality (i.e., truth-telling ensures a nonnegative utility, regardless of the randomized choice)[1]: VCG is individually rational, hence $p_i^F(v) \leq v_i(x^*)$. Thus $p_i^R(v) \leq v_i(x^l)$ for any $l \in \mathcal{I}$.

Lemma 12.16 *The decomposition-based mechanism is truthful in expectation, and obtains a c-approximation to the social welfare.*

PROOF The expected social welfare of the mechanism is $(1/c) \sum_i v_i(x^*)$, and since x^* is the optimal fractional allocation, the approximation guarantee follows. For truthfulness, we first need that the expected price of a player equals her fractional price over c, i.e., $E_{\lambda_l}[p_i^R(v)] = p_i^F(v)/c$:

$$E_{\{\lambda_l\}_{l \in \mathcal{I}}}[p_i^R(v)] = \sum_{l \in \mathcal{I}} \lambda_l \cdot [v_i(x^l)/v_i(x^*)] \cdot p_i^F(v)$$

$$= [p_i^F(v)/v_i(x^*)] \cdot \sum_{l \in \mathcal{I}} \lambda_l \cdot v_i(x^l)$$

$$= [p_i^F(v)/v_i(x^*)] \cdot v_i(x^*/c) = p_i^F(v)/c \qquad (12.6)$$

Fix any $v_{-i} \in V_{-i}$. Suppose that when i declares v_i, the fractional optimum is x^*, and when she declares v_i', the fractional optimum is z^*. The VCG fractional prices are truthful, hence

$$v_i(x^*) - p_i^F(v_i, v_{-i}) \geq v_i(z^*) - p_i^F(v_i', v_{-i}) \qquad (12.7)$$

By 12.6 and by the decomposition, dividing 12.7 by c yields

$$\left[\sum_{l \in \mathcal{I}} \lambda_l \cdot v_i(x^{*^l})\right] - E_{\lambda_l}[p_i^R(v_i, v_{-i})] \geq \left[\sum_{l \in \mathcal{I}} \lambda_l \cdot v_i(z^{*^l})\right] - E_{\lambda_l}[p_i^R(v_i', v_{-i})]$$

---

[1] See Chapter 9 for definitions and a discussion on randomized mechanisms.

The left-hand side is the expected utility for declaring v_i and the right-hand side is the expected utility for declaring v_i', and the lemma follows. □

The above analysis is for one-shot mechanisms, where a player declares his valuation up-front (the bidding languages model). For the query-access model, where players are being queried *iteratively*, the above analysis leads to the weaker solution concept of *ex-post Nash*: if all other players are truthful, player i will maximize his expected utility by being truthful.

For example, consider the following single item auction for two players: player I bids first, player II observes I's bid *and then* bids. The highest bidder wins and pays the second highest value. Here, truthfulness fails to be a dominant strategy. Suppose II chooses the strategy "if I bids above 5, I bid 20, otherwise I bid 2." If I's true value is 6, his best response is to declare 5. However, truthfulness is an ex-post Nash equilibrium: if II fixes *any* value and bids that, then, regardless of II's bid, I's best response is the truth.

In our case, if all others answer queries truthfully, the analysis carry through as is, and so truth-telling maximizes i's the expected utility. The decomposition-based mechanism thus has truthfulness-in-expectation as an ex-post Nash equilibrium for the query-access model. Putting it differently, even if a player was told beforehand the types of the other players, he would have no incentive to deviate from truth-telling.

The decomposition technique. We now decompose $x/c = \sum_{l \in \mathcal{I}} \lambda_l \cdot x^l$, for any x feasible to CA-P. We first write the LP P and its dual D. Let $E = \{(i,S) | x_{i,S} > 0\}$. Recall that E is of polynomial size.

$$\begin{array}{llll}
\min \sum_{l \in \mathcal{I}} \lambda_l & \text{(P)} \qquad & \max \frac{1}{c} \sum_{(i,S)\in E} x_{i,S} w_{i,S} + z & \text{(D)} \\
\text{s.t.} & & \text{s.t.} & \\
\sum_l \lambda_l x^l_{i,S} = \frac{x_{i,S}}{c} \quad \forall (i,S) \in E & (12.8) & \sum_{(i,S)\in E} x^l_{i,S} w_{i,S} + z \le 1 \ \forall l \in \mathcal{I} & (12.9) \\
\sum_l \lambda_l \ge 1 & & z \ge 0 & \\
\lambda_l \ge 0 \quad \forall l \in \mathcal{I} & & w_{i,S} \text{ unconstrained} \quad \forall (i,S) \in E. &
\end{array}$$

Constraints 12.8 of P describe the decomposition; hence, if the optimum satisfies $\sum_{l \in I} \lambda_l = 1$, we are almost done. P has exponentially many variables, so we need to show how to solve it in polynomial time. The dual D will help. It has variables $w_{i,S}$ for each constraint 12.8 of P, so it has polynomially many variables but exponentially many constraints. We use the ellipsoid method to solve it, and construct a separation oracle using our verifier A.

Claim 12.17 *If w, z is feasible for D then $\frac{1}{c}\sum_{(i,S)\in E} x_{i,S} w_{i,S} + z \le 1$. Furthermore, if this inequality is reversed, one can use A to find a violated constraint of D in polynomial-time.*

PROOF Suppose $\frac{1}{c} \cdot \sum_{(i,S)\in E} x_{i,S} w_{i,S} + z > 1$. Let A receive w as input and suppose that the integral allocation that A outputs is x^l. We have $\sum_{(i,S)\in E} x^l_{i,S} w_{i,S} \ge \frac{1}{c} \sum_{(i,S)\in E} x_{i,S} w_{i,S} > 1 - z$, where the first inequality follows since A is a

c-approximation to the fractional optimum, and the second inequality is the violated inequality of the claim. Thus constraint 12.9 is violated (for x^l). □

Corollary 12.18 *The optimum of D is 1, and the decomposition* $x/c = \sum_{l\in\mathcal{I}} \lambda_l \cdot x^l$ *is polynomial-time computable.*

PROOF $z = 1, w_{i,S} = 0\ \forall (i, S) \in E$ is feasible; hence, the optimum is at least 1. By claim 12.17 it is at most 1. To solve P, we first solve D with the following separation oracle: given w, z, if $\frac{1}{c}\sum_{(i,S)\in E} x_{i,S}w_{i,S} + z \leq 1$, return the separating hyperplane $\frac{1}{c}\sum_{(i,S)\in E} x_{i,S}w_{i,S} + z = 1$. Otherwise, find the violated constraint, which implies the separating hyperplane. The ellipsoid method uses polynomial number of constraints; thus, there is an equivalent program with only those constraints. Its dual is a program that is equivalent to P but with polynomial number of variables. We solve that to get the decomposition. □

Verifying the integrality gap. We now construct the integrality gap verifier for CA-P. Recall that it receives as input weights $w_{i,S}$, and outputs an integral allocation x^l which is a c-approximation to the social welfare w.r.t. $w_{i,S}$. Two requirements differentiate it from a "regular" c-approximation for CAs: (i) it cannot assume any structure on the weights $w_{i,S}$ (unlike CA, where we have non-negativity and monotonicity), and (ii) the obtained welfare must be compared to the *fractional* optimum (usually we care for the integral optimum). The first property is not a problem.

Claim 12.19 *Given a c-approximation for general CAs, A′, where the approximation is with respect to the fractional optimum, one can obtain an algorithm A that verifies a c-integrality-gap for the linear program CA-P, with a polynomial time overhead on top of A.*

PROOF Given $w = \{w_{i,S}\}_{(i,S)\in E}$, define w^+ by $w^+_{i,S} = \max(w_{i,S}, 0)$, and $\tilde{w}$ by $\tilde{w}_{i,S} = \max_{T\subseteq S,\ (i,T)\in E} w^+_{i,T}$ (where the maximum is 0 if no $T \subseteq S$ has $(i, T) \in E$. $\tilde{w}$ is a valid valuation, and can be succinctly represented with size $|E|$. Let $O^* = \max_{x \text{ is feasible for CA-P}} \sum_{(i,S)\in E} x_{i,S}w_{i,S}$. Feed $\tilde{w}$ to A' to get $\tilde{x}$ such that $\sum_{i,S} \tilde{x}_{i,S}\tilde{w}_{i,S} \geq \frac{O^*}{c}$ (since $\tilde{w}_{i,S} \geq w_{i,S}$ for every (i, S)).

Note that it is possible that $\sum_{(i,S)\in E} \tilde{x}_{i,S}w_{i,S} < \sum_{i,S} \tilde{x}_{i,S}\tilde{w}_{i,S}$, since (i) the left hand sum only considers coordinates in E and (ii) some $w_{i,S}$ coordinates might be negative. To fix the first problem define x^+ as follows: for any (i, S) such that $\tilde{x}_{i,S} = 1$, set $x^+_{i,T'} = 1$ for $T' = \arg\max_{T\subseteq S:(i,T)\in E} w^+_{i,T}$ (set all other coordinates of x^+ to 0). By construction, $\sum_{i,S} \tilde{x}_{i,S}\tilde{w}_{i,S} = \sum_{(i,S)\in E} x^+_{i,S}w^+_{i,S}$. To fix the second problem, define x^l as follows: set $x^l_{i,S} = x^+_{i,S}$ if $w_{i,S} \geq 0$ and 0 otherwise. Clearly, $\sum_{(i,S)\in E} x^l_{i,S}w_{i,S} = \sum_{(i,S)\in E} x^+_{i,S}w^+_{i,S}$, and x^l is feasible for CA-P. □

The requirement to approximate the fractional optimum does affect generality. However, one can use the many algorithms that use the primal-dual method, or a derandomization of an LP randomized rounding. Simple combinatorial algorithms may also satisfy this property. In fact, the greedy algorithm from Chapter 11 for single-minded players satisfies the requirement, and a natural variant verifies a $\sqrt{2} \cdot \sqrt{m}$ integrality-gap for CA-P.

Definition 12.20 (Greedy (revisited)) Fix $\{w_{i,S}\}_{(i,S)\in E}$ as the input. Construct x as follows. Let $(i, S) = \arg\max_{(i',S')\in E}(w_{i',S'}/\sqrt{|S'|})$. Set $x_{i,S} = 1$. Remove from E all (i', S') with $i' = i$ or $S' \cap S \neq \emptyset$. If $E \neq \emptyset$, reiterate.

Lemma 12.21 *Greedy is a $(\sqrt{2m})$-approximation to the fractional optimum.*

PROOF Let $y = \{y_{i,S}\}_{(i,S)\in E}$ be the optimal fractional allocation. For every player i with $x_{i,S_i} = 1$ (for some S_i), let $Y_i = \{\ (i', S) \in E \mid y_{i',S} > 0$ and (i', S) was removed from E when (i, S_i) was added $\}$. We show that $\sum_{(i',S)\in Y_i} y_{i',S}\, w_{i',S} \leq (\sqrt{2}\sqrt{m})w_{i,S_i}$, which proves the claim. We first have

$$\sum_{(i',S)\in Y_i} y_{i',S} w_{i',S} = \sum_{(i',S)\in Y_i} y_{i',S} \frac{w_{i',S}}{\sqrt{|S|}}\sqrt{|S|}$$

$$\leq \frac{w_{i,S_i}}{\sqrt{|S_i|}} \sum_{(i',S)\in Y_i} y_{i',S} \cdot \sqrt{|S|}$$

$$\leq \frac{w_{i,S_i}}{\sqrt{|S_i|}} \sqrt{\left(\sum_{(i',S)\in Y_i} y_{i',S}\right)\left(\sum_{(i',S)\in Y_i} y_{i',S} \cdot |S|\right)} \qquad (12.10)$$

The first inequality follows since (i, S_i) was chosen by greedy when (i', S) was in E, and the second inequality is a simple algebraic fact. We also have:

$$\sum_{(i',S)\in Y_i} y_{i',S} \leq \sum_{j\in S_i} \sum_{(i',S)\in Y_i, j\in S} y_{i',S} + \sum_{(i,S)\in Y_i} y_{i,S} \leq \sum_{j\in S_i} 1 + 1 \leq |S_i| + 1 \qquad (12.11)$$

where the first inequality holds since every $(i', S) \in Y_i$ has either $S \cap S_i \neq \emptyset$ or $i' = i$, and the second inequality follows from the feasibility constraints of CA-P, and,

$$\sum_{(i',S)\in Y_i} y_{i',S} \cdot |S| \leq \sum_{j\in\Omega} \sum_{(i',S)\in Y_i, j\in S} y_{i',S} \leq m \qquad (12.12)$$

Combining 12.10, 12.11, and 12.12, we get what we need:

$$\sum_{(i',S)\in Y_i} y_{i',S} w_{i',S} \leq \frac{w_{i,S_i}}{\sqrt{|S_i|}} \cdot \sqrt{|S_i| + 1} \cdot \sqrt{m} \leq \sqrt{2} \cdot \sqrt{m} \cdot w_{i,S_i} \qquad \square$$

Greedy is not truthful, but with the decomposition-based mechanism, we use randomness in order to "plug-in" truthfulness. We get the following theorem.

Theorem 12.22 *The decomposition-based mechanism with Greedy as the integrality-gap verifier is individually rational and truthful-in-expectation, and obtains an approximation of $\sqrt{2} \cdot \sqrt{m}$ to the social welfare.*

Remarks. The decomposition-based technique is quite general, and can be used in other cases, if an integrality-gap verifier exists for the LP formulation of the problem.

Perhaps the most notable case is multiunit CAs, where there exist B copies of each item, and any player desires at most one copy from each item. In this case, one can verify a $O(m^{\frac{1}{B+1}})$ integrality gap, and this is the best possible in polynomial time. To date, the decomposition-based mechanism is the only truthful mechanism with this tight guarantee.

Nevertheless, this method is not completely general, as VCG is. One drawback is for special cases of CAs, where low approximation ratios exist, but the integrality gap of the LP remains the same. For example, with sub-modular valuations, the integrality gap of CA-P is the same (the constraints do not change), but lower-than-2 approximations exist. To date, no truthful mechanism with constant approximation guarantees is known for this case. One could, in principle, construct a different LP formulation for this case, with a smaller integrality gap, but these attempts were unsuccessful so far.

While truthfulness-in-expectation is a natural modification of (deterministic) truthfulness, and although this notion indeed continues to be a worst-case notion, still it is inferior to truthfulness. Players are assumed to only care about their *expected* utility, and not about the variance, for example. A stronger notion is that of "universal truthfulness," were players maximize their utility for every coin toss. But even this is still weaker. While in classic algorithmic settings one can use the law of large numbers to approach the expected performance, in mechanism design one cannot repeat the execution and choose the best outcome as this affects the strategic properties. Deterministic mechanisms are still a better choice.

12.3.1 A General Overview of Truthful Combinatorial Auctions

The search for truthful CAs is an active field of research. Roughly speaking, two techniques have proved useful for constructing truthful CAs. In "Maximal-in-Range" mechanisms, the range of possible allocations is restricted, and the optimal-in-this-range allocation is chosen. This achieves deterministic truthfulness with an $O(\sqrt{m})$-approximation for subadditive valuations (Dobzinski et al., 2005), an $O(\frac{m}{\sqrt{\log m}})$-approximation for general valuations (Holzman et al., 2004), and a 2-approximation. when all items are identical ("multi-unit auctions") (Dobzinski and Nisan, 2006). A second technique is to partition the set of players, sample statistics from one set, and use it to obtain a good approximation for the other. See Chapter 13 for details. This technique obtains an $O(\sqrt{m})$-approximation. for general valuations, and an $O(\log^2 m)$ for XOS valuations (Dobzinski et al., 2006). The truthfulness here is "universal," i.e., for any coin toss – a stronger notion than truthfulness in expectation. Bartal et al. (2003) use a similar idea to obtain a truthful and *deterministic* $O(B \cdot m^{\frac{1}{B-2}})$-approximation for multiunit CAs with $B \geq 3$ copies of each item. For special cases of CAs, these techniques do not yet manage to obtain constant-factor truthful approximations (Dobzinski and Nisan, 2006 prove this impossibility for Maximal-In-Range mechanisms). Due to the importance of constant-factor approximations, explaining this gap is challenging:

Open Question Does there exist truthful constant-factor approximations for special cases of CAs that are NP-hard and yet constant algorithmic approximations are known? For example, does there exist a truthful constant-factor approximation for CAs with submodular valuations?

For general valuations, the above shows a significant gap in the power of randomized vs. deterministic techniques. It is not known if this gap is essential. A possible argument for this gap is that, for general valuations, every deterministic mechanism is VCG-based, and these have no power. Lavi et al. (2003) have initiated an investigation for the first part of the argument, obtaining only partial results. Dobzinski and Nisan (2006) have studied the other part of the argument, again with only partial results.

Open Question What are the limitations of deterministic truthful CAs? Does approximation and dominant-strategies clash in some fundamental and well-defined way for CAs?

This section was devoted to welfare maximization. Revenue maximization is another important goal for CA design. The mechanism of Bartal et al. (2003) obtains the same guarantees with respect to the optimal revenue. More tight results for multi-unit auctions with budget constrained players are given by Borgs et al. (2005), and for unlimited-supply CAs by Balcan et al. (2005). It should be noted that these are preliminary results for special cases; this issue is still quite unexplored.

12.4 Impossibilities of Dominant Strategy Implementability

In the previous sections we saw an interesting contrast between deterministic and randomized truthfulness, where the key difference seems to be the dimensionality of the domain. We now ask whether the source of this difficulty can be rigorously identified and characterized. What exactly do we mean by an "impossibility," especially since we know that VCG mechanisms *are* possible, in every domain? Well, we mean that nothing *besides* VCG is possible. Such a situation should be viewed as an impossibility, since (i) many times VCG is computationally intractable (as we saw for CAs), and (ii) many times we seek goals different from welfare maximization (as we saw for scheduling domains). The monotonicity characterizations of Chapter 9 almost readily provide few easy impossibilities for some special domains (see the exercises at the end of this chapter), and in this section we will study a more fundamental case.

To formalize our exact question, it will be convenient to use the abstract social choice setting introduced in Chapter 9: there is a finite set A of alternatives, and each player has a type (valuation function) $v : A \to \Re$ that assigns a real number to every possible alternative. $v_i(a)$ should be interpreted as i's value for alternative a. The valuation function $v_i(\cdot)$ belongs to the domain V_i of all possible valuation functions. Our goal is to *implement* in dominant strategies the social choice function $f : V_1 \times \cdots \times V_n \to A$ (where w.l.o.g. assume that $f : V \to A$ is onto A). From chapter 9 we know that VCG implements welfare maximization, for any domain, and that affine maximizers are also always implementable.

Definition 12.23 (Affine maximizer) f is an "affine maximizer" if there exist weights $k_1, \ldots, k_n$ and $\{C_x\}_{x \in A}$ such that, for all $v \in V$,

$$f(v) \in \operatorname{argmax}_{x \in A} \{\Sigma_{i=1}^n k_i v_i(x) + C_x\}.$$

The fundamental question is what other function forms are implementable. This question has remained mostly unexplored, with few exceptions. In particular, if the domain is unrestricted, the answer is sharp.

Theorem 12.24 *Suppose $|A| \geq 3$ and $V_i = \Re^A$ for all i. Then f is dominant-strategy implementable iff it is an affine maximizer.*

We will prove here a slightly easier version of the sufficiency direction. The proof is simplified by adding an extra requirement, but the essential structure is kept. The exercises give guidelines to complete the full proof.

Definition 12.25 (Neutrality) f is neutral if for all $v \in V$, if there exists an alternative x such that $v_i(x) > v_i(y)$, for all i and $y \neq x$, then $f(v) = x$.

Neutrality essentially implies that if a function is indeed an affine maximizer then the additive constants C_x are all zero.

Theorem 12.26 *Suppose $|A| \geq 3$ and for every i, $V_i = \Re^A$. If f is dominant-strategy implementable and neutral then it must be an affine maximizer.*

For the proof, we start with two monotonicity conditions. Recall that Chapter 9 portrayed the strong connection between implementability and certain monotonicity properties. The monotonicity conditions that we consider here are stronger, and are not necessary for all domains. However, for an unrestricted domain, their importance will soon become clear.

Definition 12.27 (Positive association of differences (PAD)) f satisfies PAD if the following holds for any $v, v' \in V$. Suppose $f(v) = x$, and for any $y \neq x$, and any i, $v'_i(x) - v_i(x) > v'_i(y) - v_i(y)$. Then $f(v') = x$.

Claim 12.28 *Any implementable function f, on any domain, satisfies PAD.*

PROOF Let $v^i = (v'_1, \ldots, v'_i, v_{i+1}, \ldots, v_n)$, i.e., players up to i declare according to v'; the rest declare according to v. Thus $v^0 = v$, $v^n = v'$, and $f(v^0) = x$. Suppose $f(v^{i-1}) = x$ for some $1 \leq i \leq n$. For every alternative $y \neq x$ we have $v^i_i(y) - v^{i-1}_i(y) < v^i_i(x) - v^{i-1}_i(x)$, and in addition $v^{i-1}_{-i} = v^i_{-i}$. Thus, W-MON implies that $f(v^i) = x$. By induction, $f(v^n) = x$. □

In an unrestricted domain, weak monotonicity can be generalized as follows.

Definition 12.29 (Generalized-WMON) For every $v, v' \in V$ with $f(v) = x$ and $f(v') = y$ there exists a player i such that $v'_i(y) - v_i(y) \geq v'_i(x) - v_i(x)$.

With weak monotonicity, we fix a player and fix the declarations of the others. Here, this qualifier is dropped. Another way of looking at this property is the following: If

$f(v) = x$ and $v'(x) - v(x) > v'(y) - v(y)$ then $f(v') \neq y$ (a word about notation: for $\alpha, \beta \in \Re^n$, we use $\alpha > \beta$ to denote that $\forall i,\ \alpha_i > \beta_i$).

Claim 12.30 *If the domain is unrestricted and f is implementable then f satisfies Generalized-WMON.*

PROOF Fix any v, v'. We show that if $f(v') = x$ and $v'(y) - v(y) > v'(x) - v(x)$ for some $y \in A$ then $f(v) \neq y$. By contradiction, suppose that $f(v) = y$. Fix $\Delta \in \Re^n$ such that $v'(x) - v'(y) = v(x) - v(y) - \Delta$, and define v'':

$$\forall i,\ z \in A\ :\ v''_i(z) = \begin{cases} \min\{v_i(z)\ ,\ v'_i(z) + v_i(x) - v'_i(x)\} - \Delta_i & z \neq x, y \\ v_i(x) - \dfrac{\Delta_i}{2} & z = x \\ v_i(y) & z = y. \end{cases}$$

By PAD, the transition $v \to v''$ implies $f(v'') = y$, and the transition $v' \to v''$ implies $f(v'') = x$, a contradiction. □

We now get to the main construction. For any $x, y \in A$, define:

$$P(x, y) = \{\alpha \in \Re^n \mid \exists v \in V:\ v(x) - v(y) = \alpha,\ f(v) = x\ \}. \qquad (12.13)$$

Looking at differences helps since we need to show that $\sum_i k_i[v_i(x) - v_i(y)] \geq C_y - C_x$ if $f(v) = x$. Note that $P(x, y)$ is not empty (by assumption there exists $v \in V$ with $f(v) = x$), and that if $\alpha \in P(x, y)$ then for any $\delta \in \Re^n_{++}$ (i.e., $\delta > \vec{0}$), $\alpha + \delta \in P(x, y)$: take v with $f(v) = x$ and $v(x) - v(y) = \alpha$, and construct v' by increasing $v(x)$ by δ, and setting the other coordinates as in v. By PAD $f(v') = x$, and $v'(x) - v'(y) = \alpha + \delta$.

Claim 12.31 *For any $\alpha, \epsilon \in \Re^n$, $\epsilon > \vec{0}$: (i) $\alpha - \epsilon \in P(x, y) \Rightarrow -\alpha \notin P(y, x)$, and (ii) $\alpha \notin P(x, y) \Rightarrow -\alpha \in P(y, x)$.*

PROOF (i) Suppose by contradiction that $-\alpha \in P(y, x)$. Therefore there exists $v \in V$ with $v(y) - v(x) = -\alpha$ and $f(v) = y$. As $\alpha - \epsilon \in P(x, y)$, there also exists $v' \in V$ with $v'(x) - v'(y) = \alpha - \epsilon$ and $f(v') = x$. But since $v(x) - v(y) = \alpha > v'(x) - v'(y)$, this contradicts Generalized-WMON. (ii) For any $z \neq x, y$ take some $\beta_z \in P(x, z)$ and fix some $\epsilon > \vec{0}$. Fix some v such that $v(x) - v(y) = \alpha$ and $v(x) - v(z) = \beta_z + \epsilon$ for all $z \neq x, y$. By the above argument, $f(v) \in \{x, y\}$. Since $v(x) - v(y) = \alpha \notin P(x, y)$ it follows that $f(v) = y$. Thus $-\alpha = v(y) - v(x) \in P(y, x)$, as needed. □

Claim 12.32 *Fix $\alpha, \beta, \epsilon_1, \epsilon_2, \in \Re^n$, $\epsilon_i > \vec{0}$, such that $\alpha - \epsilon_1 \in P(x, y)$ and $\beta - \epsilon_2 \in P(y, z)$. Then $\alpha + \beta - (\epsilon_1 + \epsilon_2)/2 \in P(x, z)$.*

PROOF For any $w \neq x, y, z$ fix some $\delta_w \in P(x, w)$. Choose any v such that $v(x) - v(y) = \alpha - \epsilon_1/2$, $v(y) - v(z) = \beta - \epsilon_2/2$, and $v(x) - v(w) = \delta_w + \epsilon$ for all $w \neq x, y, z$ (for some $\epsilon > \vec{0}$). By Generalized-WMON, $f(v) = x$. Thus $\alpha + \beta - (\epsilon_1 + \epsilon_2)/2 = v(x) - v(z) \in P(x, z)$. □

Claim 12.33 *If α is in the interior of $P(x, y)$ then α is in the interior of $P(x, z)$, for any $z \neq x, y$.*

PROOF Suppose $\alpha - \epsilon \in P(x, y)$ for some $\epsilon > \vec{0}$. By neutrality we have that $\epsilon/4 - \epsilon/8 = \epsilon/8 \in P(y, z)$. By Claim 12.32 we now get that $\alpha - \epsilon/4 \in P(x, z)$, which implies that α is in the interior of $P(x, z)$. □

By similar arguments, we also have that if α is in the interior of $P(x, z)$ then α is in the interior of $P(w, z)$. Thus we get that for any $x, y, w, z \in A$, not necessarily distinct, the interior of $P(x, y)$ is equal to the interior of $P(w, z)$. Denote the interior of $P(x, y)$ as P.

Claim 12.34 *P is convex.*

PROOF We show that $\alpha, \beta \in P$ implies $(\alpha + \beta)/2 \in P$. A known fact from convexity theory then implies that P is convex.[2] By Claim 12.32, $\alpha + \beta \in P$. We show that for any $\alpha \in P$ we have $\alpha/2 \in P$ as well, which then implies the Claim. Suppose by contradiction that $\alpha/2 \notin P$. Thus by Claim 12.31, $-\alpha/2 \in P$. Then $\alpha/2 = \alpha + (-\alpha/2) \in P$, a contradiction. □

We now conclude the proof of Theorem 12.26. Neutrality implies that $\vec{0}$ is on the boundary of any $P(x, y)$; hence, it is not in P. Let $\bar{P}$ denote the closure of P. By the separation lemma, there exists a $k \in \Re^n$ such that for any $\alpha \in \bar{P}$, $k \cdot \alpha \geq 0$. Suppose that $f(v) = x$ for some $v \in V$, and fix any $y \neq x$. Thus $v(x) - v(y) \in P(x, y)$, and $k \cdot v(x) - v(y) \geq 0$. Hence $k \cdot v(x) \geq k \cdot v(y)$, and the theorem follows.

We have just seen a unique example, demonstrating that there exists a domain for which affine maximizers are the only possibility. However, our natural focus is on *restricted* domains, as most of the computational models that we consider do have some structure (e.g., the two domains we have considered in this chapter). Unfortunately, clear-cut impossibilities for such domains are not known.

Open Question Characterize the class of domains for which affine maximizers are the only implementable functions.

Even this question does not capture the entire picture, as, for example, it is known that there exists an implementable but not an affine-maximizer CA.[3] Nevertheless, there do seem to be some inherent difficulties in designing truthful and computationally-efficient CAs.[4] The less formal open question therefore searches for the fundamental issues that cause the clash. Obviously, these are related to the monotonicity conditions, but an exact quantification of this is still unknown.

[2] For $\alpha, \beta \in P$ and $0 \leq \lambda \leq 1$, build a series of points that approach $\lambda\alpha + (1 - \lambda)\beta$, such that any point in the series has a ball of some fixed radius around it that fully belongs to P.

[3] See Lavi et al. (2003).

[4] Note that we have in mind deterministic CAs.

12.5 Alternative Solution Concepts

In light of the conclusions of the previous section, a natural way to advance would be to reexamine the *solution concept* that we are using. In Section 12.3 we saw that randomization certainly helps, but also carries with it some disadvantages. However, in some cases randomization is not known to help, and additionally sometimes we want to stick to deterministic mechanisms. What other solution concepts that fit the worst-case way of thinking in CS can we use?

One simple thought is that algorithm designers do not care so much about actually reaching an equilibrium point – our major concern is to guarantee the optimality of the solution, taking into account the strategic behavior of the players. One way of doing this is to reach a good equilibrium point. But there is no reason why we should not allow the mechanism designer to "leave in" several acceptable strategic choices for the players, and to require the approximation to be achieved *in each of these choices*.

As a first attempt, one is tempted to simply let the players try and improve the basic result by allowing them to lie. However, this can cause unexpected dynamics, as each player chooses her lies under some assumptions about the lies of the others, etc. etc. We wish to avoid such an unpredictable situation, and we insist on using rigorous game theoretic reasoning to explain exactly why the outcome will be satisfactory. The following definition captures the initial intuition, without falling to such pitfalls:

Definition 12.35 (Algorithmic implementation) A mechanism M is an algorithmic implementation of a c-approximation (in undominated strategies) if there exists a set of strategies, D, such that (i) M obtains a c-approximation for any combination of strategies from D, in polynomial time, and (ii) for any strategy not in D, there exists a strategy in D that weakly dominates it, and this transition is polynomial-time computable.

The important ingredients of a dominant-strategies implementation are here: the only assumption is that a player is willing to replace any chosen strategy with a strategy that dominates it. Indeed, this guarantees at least the same utility, even in the worst case, and by definition can be done in polynomial time. In addition, again as in dominant-strategy implementability, this notion does not require any form of coordination among the players (unlike Nash equilibrium), or that players have any assumptions on the rationality of the others (as in "iterative deletion of dominated strategies").

However, two differences from dominant-strategies implementation are worth mentioning: (I) A player might regret his chosen strategy, realizing in retrospect that another strategy from D would have performed better, and (II) deciding how to play is not straight-forward. While a player will not end up playing a strategy that does not belong to D, it is not clear how he will choose one of the strategies of D. This may depend, for example, on the player's own beliefs about the other players, or on the computational power of the player.

Another remark, about the connection to the notion of implementation in undominated strategies, is in place. The definition of D *does not* imply that all undominated strategies belong to D, but rather that for every undominated strategy, there is an *equivalent* strategy inside D (i.e., a strategy that yields the same utility, no matter what the others play). The same problem occurs with dominant-strategy implementations, e.g., VCG, where it is not required that truthfulness should be the *only* dominant strategy, just *a* dominant strategy.

In this section we illustrate how to use such a solution concept to design CAs for a special class of "single-value" players. The resulting auction has another interesting feature: while most mechanisms we have seen so far are direct revelation, in practice indirect mechanisms, and especially ascending auctions (players compete by raising prices and winners pay their last bid) are much preferred. The following result is an attempt to handle this issue as well.

Single-value players. The mechanisms of this section fit the special case of players that desire several different bundles, all for the same value: Player i is *single-valued* if there exists $\bar{v}_i \geq 1$ such that for any bundle s, $v_i(s) \in \{0, \bar{v}_i\}$. That is, i desires any one bundle out of a *collection* $\bar{S}_i$ of bundles, for a value $\bar{v}_i$. We denote such a player by $(\bar{v}_i, \bar{S}_i)$. $\bar{v}_i$ and $\bar{S}_i$ are private information of the player. Since $\bar{S}_i$ may be of size exponential in m, we assume the query access model, as detailed below.

An iterative wrapper. We start with a wrapper to a given algorithmic subprocedure, which will eventually convert algorithms to a mechanism, with a small approximation loss. It operates in iterations, with iteration index j, and maintains the tentative winners W_j, the sure-losers L_j, and a "tentative winning bundle" s_i^j for every i. In each iteration, the subprocedure is invoked to update the set of winners to W_{j+1} and the winning bundles to s^{j+1}. Every active nonwinner then chooses to double his bid (v_i^j) or to permanently retire. This is iterated until all nonwinners retire.

Definition 12.36 (The wrapper) Initialize $j = 0$, $W_j = L_j = \emptyset$, and for every player i, $v_i^0 = 1$ and $s_i^0 = \Omega$. While $W_j \cup L_j \neq$ "all players" perform:

1. $(W_{j+1}, s^{j+1}) \leftarrow \text{PROC}(v^j, s^j, W_j)$.
2. $\forall i \notin W_{j+1} \cup L_j$, i chooses whether to double his value ($v_i^{j+1} \leftarrow 2 \cdot v_i^j$) or to permanently retire ($v_i^{j+1} \leftarrow 0$). For all others set $v_i^{j+1} \leftarrow v_i^j$.
3. Update $L_{j+1} = \{i \in N \mid v_i^{j+1} = 0\}$ and $j \to j+1$, and reiterate.

Outcome: Let $J = j$ (total number of iterations). Every $i \in W_J$ gets s_i^J and pays v_i^J. All others lose (get nothing, pay 0).

For feasibility, PROC must maintain: $\forall i, i' \in W_{j+1}, s_i^{j+1} \cap s_{i'}^{j+1} = \emptyset$.

We need to analyze the strategic choices of the players, and the approximation loss (relative to PROC). This will be done gradually. We first worry about minimizing the number of iterations.

Definition 12.37 (Proper procedure) PROC is proper if (1) **Pareto:** $\forall i \notin W_{j+1} \cup L_j, s_i^{j+1} \cap (\cup_{l \in W_{j+1}} s_l^{j+1}) \neq \emptyset$, and (2) **Shrinking-sets:** $\forall i, s_i^{j+1} \subseteq s_i^j$.

In words, the pareto property implies that the set of winners that PROC outputs is maximal, i.e., that any loser that has not retired desires a bundle that intersects some winner's bundle. The shrinking-sets property says that a player's new tentative bundle must be a subset of the old tentative bundle.

A "reasonable" player will not increase v_i^j above $\bar{v}_i$; otherwise, his utility will be nonpositive (this strategic issue is formally discussed below). Assuming this, there will clearly be at most $n \cdot \log(v_{\max})$ iterations, where $v_{\max} = \max_i \bar{v}_i$. With a proper procedure this bound becomes independent of n.

Lemma 12.38 *If every player i never increases v_i^j above $\bar{v}_i$, then any proper procedure performs at most $2 \cdot \log(v_{\max}) + 1$ iterations.*

PROOF Consider iteration $j = 2 \cdot \log(v_{\max}) + 1$, and some $i_1 \notin W_{j+1} \cup L_j$ that (by contradiction) doubles his value. By Pareto, there exists $i_2 \in W_{j+1}$ such that $s_{i_1}^{j+1} \cap s_{i_2}^{j+1} \neq \emptyset$. By "shrinking-sets," in every $j' < j$ their winning bundles intersect, hence at least one of them was not a winner, and doubled his value. But then $v_{i_1}^j \geq v_{\max}$, a contradiction. □

This affects the approximation guarantee, as shown below, and also implies that the Wrapper adds only a polynomial-time overhead to PROC.

A warm-up analysis. To warm up and to collect basic insights, we first consider the case of *known* single-minded players (KSM), where a player desires *one* specific bundle, $\bar{S}_i$, which is public information (she can lie only about her value). This allows for a simple analysis: the wrapper converts *any* given c-approximation. to a dominant-strategy mechanism with $O(\log(v_{\max}) \cdot c)$ approximation. Thus, we get a *deterministic* technique to convert algorithms to mechanisms, with a small approximation loss.

Here, we initialize $s_i^0 = \bar{S}_i$, and set $s_i^{j+1} = s_i^j$, which trivially satisfies the shrinking-sets property. In addition, pareto is satisfied w.l.o.g. since if not, add winning players in an arbitrary order until pareto holds. For KSM players, this takes $O(n \cdot m)$ time. Third, we need one more property:

Definition 12.39 (Improvement) $\sum_{i \in W_{j+1}} v_i^j \geq \sum_{i \in W_j} v_i^j$.

This is again without loss of generality: if the winners outputted by PROC violate this, simply output W_j as the new winners. To summarize, we use:

Definition 12.40 (The KSM-PROC) Given a c-approximation. A for KSM players, KSM-PROC invokes A with s^j (the desired bundles) and v^j (player values). Then, it postprocesses the output to verify pareto and improvement.

Proposition 12.41 *Under dominant strategies, i retires iff $\bar{v}_i/2 \leq v_i^j \leq \bar{v}_i$.*

(The simple proof is omitted.) For the approximation, the following analysis carries through to the single-value case. Let $S_i|_{s_i^j} = \{s \in S_i \mid s \subseteq s_i^j\}$, and

$$R_j(\vec{v}, \vec{S}) = \{\, (v_i, S_i|_{s_i^j}) | i \text{ retired at iteration } j \,\}, \qquad (12.14)$$

i.e., for every player i that retired at iteration j the set $R_j(\vec{v}, \vec{S})$ contains a single-value player, with value v_i (given as a parameter), and desired bundles $S_i|_{s_i^j}$ (where S_i is given as a parameter). For the KSM case, $R_j(\bar{v}, \bar{S})$ is exactly all retired players in iteration j, as the operator "$|_{s_i^j}$" has no effect. Hence, to prove the approximation, we need to bound the value of the optimal allocation to the players in $\bar{R} = \cup_{j=1}^{J} R_j(\bar{v}, \bar{S})$. For an instance X of single-value players, let $OPT(X)$ be the value of the optimal allocation to the players in X. In particular: $OPT(R_j(\vec{v}, \vec{S})) = \max_{\text{all allocations}(s_1,\ldots,s_n)\ \text{s.t.} s_i \in S_i|_{s_i^j}} \{\sum_{i:\ s_i \neq \emptyset} v_i\}$.

Definition 12.42 (Local approximation) A proper procedure is a c-local-approximation w.r.t a strategy set D if it satisfies improvement, and, for any combination of strategies in D and any iteration j,

Algorithmic approximation $OPT(R_j(v^j, \bar{S})) \leq c \cdot \sum_{i \in W_j} v_i^j$
Value bounds $v_i^j \leq v_i(s_i^j)$, and, if i retires at j then $v_i^j \geq \bar{v}_i/2$.

Claim 12.43 *Given a c-approximation A for single minded players, KSM-PROC is a c-local-approximation for the set D of dominant strategies.*

PROOF The algorithmic approximation property follows since A outputs a c-approximation outcome. The value bounds property is exactly Proposition 12.41. □

We next translate local approximation to global approximation (this is valid also for the single-value case).

Claim 12.44 *A c-local-approximation satisfies* $OPT(\bar{R}) \leq 5 \cdot \log(v_{\max}) \cdot c \cdot \sum_{i \in W_J} \bar{v}_i$ *whenever players play strategies in D.*

PROOF By the value bounds, $OPT(R_j(\bar{v}, \bar{S})) \leq 2 \cdot OPT(R_j(v^j, \bar{S}))$. We have (i) $OPT(R_j(v^j, \bar{S})) \leq c \cdot \sum_{i \in W_j} v_i^j$ by algorithmic approximation, (ii) $\sum_{i \in W_j} v_i^j \leq \sum_{i \in W_{j+1}} v_i^{j+1}$ by improvement, and (iii) $v_i^J \leq \bar{v}_i$ (by the value bounds), and therefore we get $OPT(R_j(\bar{v}, \bar{S})) \leq 2 \cdot c \cdot \sum_{i \in W_J} \bar{v}_i$. Hence $OPT(\bar{R}) \leq \sum_{j=1}^{J} OPT(R_j(\bar{v}, \bar{S})) \leq J \cdot 2 \cdot c \cdot \sum_{i \in W_J} \bar{v}_i$. Since $J \leq 2 \cdot \log(v_{\max}) + 1$, the claim follows. □

For single-minded players, $\bar{R}$ is the set of losing players, hence we conclude:

Theorem 12.45 *Given any c-approximation. for KSM players, the Wrapper with KSM-PROC implements an* $O(\log(v_{\max}) \cdot c)$ *approximation. in dominant strategies.*

A subprocedure for single-value players. Two assumptions are relaxed: players are now multiminded, and their desired bundles are unknown. Here, we define the following specific subprocedure. For a set of players X, let Free(X, s^{j+1}) denote the items not in $\cup_{i \in X} s_i^j$.

Definition 12.46 (1-CA-PROC) Let $M_j = \text{argmax}_{i \in N}\{v_i^j\}$, $GREEDY_j = \emptyset$. For every player i with $v_i^j > 0$, in descending order of values, perform:

Shrinking the winning set: If $i \notin W_j$ allow him to pick a bundle $s_i^{j+1} \subseteq$ Free$(GREEDY_j, s^{j+1}) \cap s_i^j$ such that $|s_i^{j+1}| \leq \sqrt{m}$. In any other case ($i \in W_j$ or i does not pick) set $s_i^{j+1} = s_i^j$.

Updating the current winners: If $|s_i^{j+1}| \leq \sqrt{m}$, add i to any of the allocations $W \in \{W_j, M_j, GREEDY_j\}$ for which $s_i^{j+1} \subseteq$ Free(W, s^{j+1}).

Output s^{j+1} and $W \in \{W_j, M_j, GREEDY_j\}$ that maximizes $\sum_{i \in W} v_i^j$.

Recall that the nonwinners then either double their value or retire, and we reiterate. This is the main conceptual difference from "regular" direct revelation mechanisms: here, the players themselves gradually determine their winning set (focusing on one of their desired bundles), and their price. Intuitively, it is not clear how a "reasonable" player should shrink his winning set, when approached. Ideally, a player should focus on a desired bundle that intersects few, low-value competitors. But in early iterations this information is not available. Thus there is no clear-cut on how to shrink the winning set, and the resulting mechanism does not contain a dominant strategy. This is exactly the point where we use the new notion of algorithmic implementation.

Analysis. We proceed by characterizing the required set D of strategies. We say that player i is "loser-if-silent" at iteration j if, when asked to shrink her bundle by 1-CA-PROC, $v_i^j \geq \bar{v}_i/2$ (*retires if losing*), $i \notin W_j$ and $i \notin M_j$ (*not a winner*), and $s_i^j \cap (\cup_{i' \in W_j} s_{i'}^{j+1}) \neq \emptyset$ and $s_i^j \cap (\cup_{i' \in M_j} s_{i'}^{j+1}) \neq \emptyset$ (*remains a loser after pareto*). In other words, a loser-if-silent loses (regardless of the others' actions) unless she shrinks her winning set. Let D be all strategies that satisfy, in every iteration j:

(i) $v_i^j \leq v_i(s_i^j)$, and, if i retires at j then $v_i^j \geq \bar{v}_i/2$.
(ii) If i is "loser-if-silent" then she declares a valid desired bundle s_i^{j+1}, if such a bundle exists.

There clearly exists a (poly-time) algorithm to find a strategy $st' \in D$ that dominates a given strategy st. Hence, D satisfies the second requirement of algorithmic implementation. It remains to show that the approximation is achieved for *every* combination of strategies from D.

Lemma 12.47 *1-CA-PROC is an $O(\sqrt{m})$-local-approximation w.r.t. D.*

PROOF (sketch). The pareto, improvement, and value-bounds properties are immediate from the definition of the procedure and the set D. The $O(\sqrt{m})$-algorithmic-approximation property follows from the following argument. We need to bound $OPT = OPT(\{(v_i^j, \bar{S}_i|_{s_i^j}) \mid i \text{ retired at iteration } j\})$ by the sum of values of the players in W_{j+1}. We divide the winners in OPT to four sets. Those that are in M_j, $GREEDY_j$, W_j, or in none of the above. For the first three sets the 1-CA-PROC explicitly verifies our need. It remains to handle players in the forth set. First notice that such a player is loser-if-silent. If such a player receives in OPT a bundle with size at least $\sqrt{m}$ we match him to the player with the highest value in M_j. There can be at most $\sqrt{m}$ players in OPT with bundles of size at least $\sqrt{m}$, so we lose a $\sqrt{m}$ factor for these players. If a player, i, in the forth set, receives in OPT a bundle with size at most $\sqrt{m}$, let s_i^* be that bundle. Since he is a loser-if-silent, there exists $i' \in GREEDY_j$ such that $s_{i'}^j \cap s_i^* \neq \emptyset$ and $v_i^j \leq v_{i'}^j$. We map i to i'. For any i_1, i_2 that were mapped to i' we have that $s_{i_1}^* \cap s_{i_2}^* = \emptyset$ since both belong to OPT. Since the size of $s_{i'}^j$ is at most $\sqrt{m}$ it follows that at most $\sqrt{m}$ players can be mapped to i', so we lose a $\sqrt{m}$ factor for these players as well. This completes the argument. □

In the single-value case, $\bar{R}$ does not contain all players, so we cannot repeat the argument from the KSM case that immediately linked local approximation and global approximation. However, Claim 12.44 still holds, and we use $\bar{R}$ as an intermediate set of "virtual" players. The link to the true players is as follows (recall that m denotes the number of items).

Definition 12.48 (First-time shrink) PROC satisfies "first time shrink" if for any $i_1, i_2 \in \{i \;:\; |s_i^j| = m \;\&\; |s_i^{j+1}| < m\}$, $s_{i_1}^{j+1} \cap s_{i_2}^{j+1} = \emptyset$.

1-CA-PROC satisfies this since any player that shrinks his winning bundle is added to $GREEDY_j$.

Lemma 12.49 *Given a c-local-approximation (w.r.t. D) that satisfies first-time shrink, the Wrapper obtains an $O(\log^2(v_{\max}) \cdot c)$ approximation for any profile of strategies in D.*

PROOF We continue to use the notation of Claim 12.44. Let $P = \{(\bar{v}_i, \bar{S}_i) :$ i lost, and $|s_i^J| < m\}$. Players in P appear with all their desired bundles, while players in $\bar{R}$ appear with only part of their desired bundles. However, ignoring the extra bundles in P incurs only a bounded loss:

Claim 12.50 $OPT(P) \leq J \cdot OPT(\bar{R})$.

PROOF Define P_j to be all players in P that first shrank their bundle at iteration j. By "first-time shrink," and since winning bundles only shrink, $s_{i_1}^j \cap s_{i_2}^j = \emptyset$ for every $i_1, i_2 \in P_j$. Therefore $OPT(\bar{R}) \geq \sum_{i \in P_j} \bar{v}_i$: every player i in P_j corresponds to a player in $\bar{R}$, and all these players have disjoint bundles in $\bar{R}$ since the bundles of i are contained in s_i^j. We also trivially have $OPT(P_j) \leq \sum_{i \in P_j} \bar{v}_i$. Thus, for any j, $OPT(P_j) \leq OPT(\bar{R})$, and $OPT(P) \leq \sum_j OPT(P_j) \leq J \cdot OPT(\bar{R})$. □

To prove the lemma, first notice that all true players are contained in $P \cup \bar{R} \cup W_J$: all retiring players belong to $\bar{R} \cup P$ (if a player shrank his bundle then he belongs to P with all his true bundles, and if a player did not shrink his bundle at all then he belongs to $\bar{R}$ with all his true bundles) and all nonretiring players belong to W_J. From the above we have $OPT(P \cup \bar{R}) \leq OPT(P) + OPT(\bar{R}) \leq J \cdot OPT(\bar{R}) + OPT(\bar{R}) \leq 4 \cdot J^2 \cdot c \cdot \sum_{i \in W_J} \bar{v}_i^J$. Since s_i^J contain some desired bundle of player i, we have that $OPT(W_J) = \sum_{i \in W_J} \bar{v}_i$. Thus we get that $OPT(P \cup \bar{R} \cup W_J) \leq 5 \cdot J^2 \cdot \tilde{c} \cdot \sum_{i \in W_J} \bar{v}_i^J$. Since $J \leq 2 \cdot \log(v_{\max}) + 1$ by Lemma 12.38, the lemma follows. □

By all the above, we conclude the following.

Theorem 12.51 *The Wrapper with 1-CA-PROC is an algorithmic implementation of an $O(\log^2(v_{\max}) \cdot c)$-approximation for single-value players.*

This result has demonstrated that if we are less interested in reaching an equilibrium point, but rather in guaranteeing a good-enough outcome, then alternative solution concepts, that are no worse than classic dominant strategies, can be of much help. However, the true power of relaxing dominant strategies to undominated strategies was not formally settled.

Open Question Does there exist a domain in which a computationally efficient algorithmic implementation achieves a better approximation than any computationally efficient dominant-strategy implementation?

12.6 Bibliographic Notes

The connection between classic scheduling and mechanism design was suggested by Nisan and Ronen (2001), that studied unrelated machines and reached mainly impossibilities. Archer and Tardos (2001) studied the case of related machines, and the monotonicity characterization of Section 12.2 is based on their work. Deterministic mechanisms for the problem have been suggested by several works, and the algorithm presented here is by Andelman, Azar, and Sorani (2005). The current best approximation ratio, 3, is given by Kovacs (2005). Section 12.3 is based on the work of Lavi and Swamy (2005). Roberts (1979) characterized dominant strategy implementability for unrestricted domains. The proof given here is based on Lavi, Mu'alem, and Nisan (2004). Generalized-WMON was suggested by Lavi, Mu'alem, and Nisan (2003), which explored the same characterization question for restricted domains in general, and for CAs in particular. Section 12.5 is based on the work of Babaioff, Lavi, and Pavlov (2006). There have been several other suggestions for alternative solution concepts. For example, Kothari et al. (2005) describe an "almost truthful" deterministic FPAS for multiunit auctions, and Lavi and Nisan (2005) define a notion of "Set-Nash" for multi-unit auctions in an online setting, for which they show that deterministic truthfulness obtains significantly lower approximations than Set-Nash implementations.

Bibliography

N. Andelman, Y. Azar, and M. Sorani. Truthful approximation mechanisms for scheduling selfish related machines. In *Proc. of the 22nd Intl. Symp. Theor. Asp. Comp. Sci. (STACS)*, pp. 69–82, 2005.

A. Archer and E. Tardos. Truthful mechanisms for one-parameter agents. In *Proc. of the 42nd Annual Symp. Fdns. of Computer Science*, 2001.

M. Babaioff, R. Lavi, and E. Pavlov. Single-value combinatorial auctions and implementation in undominated strategies. In *Proc. of the 17th Symp. Discrete Algorithms*, 2006.

M. Balcan, A. Blum, J. Hartline, and Y. Mansour. Mechanism design via machine learning. In *Proc. of the 46th Annual Symp. Fdns. of Computer Science*, 2005.

Y. Bartal, R. Gonen, and N. Nisan. Incentive compatible multi-unit combinatorial auctions. In *Proc. of the 9th Conf. Theoretical Aspects of Rationality and Knowledge (TARK)*, 2003.

C. Borgs, J. Chayes, N. Immorlica, M. Mahdian, and A. Saberi. Multi-unit auctions with budget-constrained bidders. In *Proc. of the 6th ACM Conf. Electronic Commerce (ACM-EC)*, 2005.

S. Dobzinski and N. Nisan. Approximations by computationally-efficient vcg-based mechanisms, 2006. Working paper.

S. Dobzinski, N. Nisan, and M. Schapira. Approximation algorithms for combinatorial auctions with complement-free bidders. In *Proc. of the 37th ACM Symp. Theory of Computing*, 2005.

S. Dobzinski, N. Nisan, and M. Schapira. Truthful randomized mechanisms for combinatorial auctions. In *Proc. of the 38th ACM Symp. Theory of Computing*, 2006.

R. Holzman, N. Kfir-Dahav, D. Monderer, and M. Tennenholtz. Bundling equilibrium in combinatorial auctions. *Games Econ. Behav.*, 47:104–123, 2004.

A. Kothari, D. Parkes, and S. Suri. Approximately-strategy proof and tractable multi-unit auctions. *Decis. Support Systems*, 39:105–121, 2005.

A. Kovacs. Fast monotone 3-approximation algorithm for scheduling related machines. In *Proc. of the 13th Annual Eur. Symp. Algo. (ESA)*, 2005.

R. Lavi, A. Mu'alem, and N. Nisan. Towards a characterization of truthful combinatorial auctions. In *Proc. of the 44th Annual Symp. Fdns. of Computer Science*, 2003.

R. Lavi, A. Mu'alem, and N. Nisan. Two simplified proofs for Roberts' theorem, 2004. Working paper.

R. Lavi and N. Nisan. Online ascending auctions for gradually expiring items. In *Proc. of the 16th Symp. on Discrete Algorithms*, 2005.

R. Lavi and C. Swamy. Truthful and near-optimal mechanism design via linear programming. In *Proc. of the 46th Annual Symp. Fdns. of Computer Science*, 2005.

N. Nisan and A. Ronen. Algorithmic mechanism design. *Games and Economic Behavior*, 35:166–196, 2001.

K. Roberts. The characterization of implementable choice rules. In Jean-Jacques Laffont, editor, *Aggregation and Revelation of Preferences*, pp. 321–349, North-Holland, 1979.

Exercises

12.1 (Scheduling related machines) Find an implementable algorithm that exactly obtains the optimal makespan, for scheduling on related machines (since this is an NP-hard problem, obviously you may ignore the computational complexity of your algorithm).

12.2 (Scheduling unrelated machines) In the model of unrelated machines, each job j creates a load p_{ij} on each machine i, where the loads are completely unrelated. Prove, using W-MON, that no truthful mechanism can approximate the makespan with a factor better than 2. Hint: Start with four jobs that have $p_{ij} = 1$ for all i, j.

12.3 A deterministic greedy rounding of the fractional scheduling 12.4 assigns each job in full to the first machine that got a fraction of it. Explain why this is a 2-approximation, and show by an example that this violates monotonicity.

12.4 Prove that 1-CA-PROC of Definition 12.46, and Greedy for multiminded players of Definition 12.20 are not dominant-strategy implementable.

12.5 (Converting algorithms to mechanisms) Fix an alternative set A, and suppose that for any player i, there is a fixed, known subset $A_i \subset A$, such that a valid valuation assigns some positive real number in $[v_{\min}, v_{\max}]$ to every alternative in A_i, and zero to the other alternatives. Suppose $v_{\min}$ and $v_{\max}$ are known. Given a c-approximation algorithm to the social welfare for this domain, construct a randomized truthful mechanism that obtains a $O(\log(v_{\max}/v_{\min}) \cdot c)$ approximation to the social welfare. (Hint: choose a threshold price, uniformly at random). Is this construction still valid when the sets A_i are unknown? (If not, show a counter example).

12.6 Describe a domain for which there exists an implementable social choice function that does not satisfy Generalized-WMON.

12.7 Describe a deterministic CA for general valuations that is not an affine maximizer.

12.8 This exercise aims to complete the characterization of Section 12.4:
Let $\gamma(x, y) = inf\{p \in \Re \mid p \cdot \vec{1} \in P(x, y)\}$. Show that $\gamma(x, y)$ is well-defined, that $\gamma(x, y) = -\gamma(y, x)$, and that $\gamma(x, z) = \gamma(x, y) + \gamma(y, z)$. Let $C(x, y) = \{\alpha - \gamma(x, y) \cdot \vec{1} \mid \alpha \in P(x, y)\}$. Show that for any $x, y, w, z \in A$, the interior of $C(x, y)$ is equal to the interior of $C(w, z)$. Use this to show that $C(x, y)$ is convex.
Conclude, by the separation lemma, that f is an affine maximizer (give an explicit formula for the additive terms C_x).

CHAPTER 13

Profit Maximization in Mechanism Design

Jason D. Hartline and Anna R. Karlin

Abstract

We give an introduction to the design of mechanisms for profit maximization with a focus on single-parameter settings.

13.1 Introduction

In previous chapters, we have studied the design of truthful mechanisms that implement social choice functions, such as social welfare maximization. Another fundamental objective, and the focus of this chapter, is the design of mechanisms in which the goal of the mechanism designer is profit maximization. In economics, this topic is referred to as *optimal mechanism design*.

Our focus will be on the design of profit-maximizing auctions in settings in which an auctioneer is selling (respectively, buying) a set of goods/services. Formally, there are n agents, each of whom desires some particular service. We assume that agents are *single-parameter*; i.e., agent i's *valuation* for receiving service is v_i and their valuation for no service is normalized to zero. A mechanism takes as input sealed bids from the agents, where agent i's bid b_i represents his valuation v_i, and computes an outcome consisting of an allocation $\mathbf{x} = (x_1, \ldots, x_n)$ and prices $\mathbf{p} = (p_1, \ldots, p_n)$. Setting $x_i = 1$ represents agent i being allocated service whereas $x_i = 0$ is for no service, and p_i is the amount agent i is required to pay the auctioneer. We assume that agents have quasi-linear *utility* expressed by $u_i = v_i x_i - p_i$. Thus, an agent's goal in choosing his bid is to maximize the difference between his valuation and his payment.

To make this setting quite general, we assume that there is an inherent cost $c(\mathbf{x})$ in producing the outcome $\mathbf{x}$, which must be paid by the mechanism. Our goal is to design the mechanism, i.e., the mapping from bid vectors to price/allocation vectors so that the auctioneer's profit, defined as

$$\text{Profit} = \sum_i p_i - c(\mathbf{x}),$$

is maximized, and the mechanism is *truthful*.

Many interesting auction design problems are captured within this single-parameter framework. In what follows, we describe a number of these problems, and show that, for most of them, the VCG mechanism (Chapter 9), which maximizes social welfare, is a poor mechanism to use when the goal is profit maximization.

Example 13.1 (single-item auction) We can use the cost function $c(\mathbf{x})$ to capture the constraint that at most one item can be allocated, by setting $c(\mathbf{x}) = 0$ if $\sum_i x_i \leq 1$ and ∞ otherwise. The profit of the Vickrey auction (Chapter 9) is the second highest of the valuations in the vector $\mathbf{v}$. If prior information about agents' valuations is available, then there are auctions with higher profit than the Vickrey auction.

Example 13.2 (digital goods auctions) In a digital goods auction, an auctioneer is selling multiple units of an item, such as a downloadable audio file or a pay-per-view television broadcast, to consumers each interested in exactly one unit. Since the marginal cost of duplicating a digital good is negligible and digital goods are freely disposable, we can assume that the auctioneer has an *unlimited supply* of units for sale. Thus, for digital goods auctions $c(\mathbf{x}) = 0$ for all $\mathbf{x}$.

The profit of the VCG mechanism for digital goods auctions is zero. Indeed, since the items are available in unlimited supply, no bidder places any externality on any other bidder.

Example 13.3 (single-minded combinatorial auction, known bundles) In a combinatorial auction with single-minded agents, each agent has exactly one bun dle of items that he is interested in obtaining. Agent i's value for his desired bundle, S_i, is v_i. We use the cost function $c(\mathbf{x})$ to capture the constraint that each item can be allocated to at most one bidder. Thus, $c(\mathbf{x}) = 0$ if $\forall i, j, S_i \cap S_j \neq \emptyset \rightarrow x_i x_j = 0$, and $c(\mathbf{x}) = \infty$ otherwise.

Example 13.4 (multicast auctions) Consider a network with users residing at the nodes in the network, each with a valuation for receiving a broadcast that originates at a particular node, called the root. There are costs associated with transmitting data across each of the links in the network – the cost of transmitting across link e is $c(e)$. Our problem is then to design an auction that chooses a multicast tree, the set of users to receive the broadcast, and the prices to charge them. In this setting, $c(\mathbf{x})$ is the total cost of connecting all of the agents with $x_i = 1$ to the root (i.e., the minimum Steiner tree cost).

In most nondegenerate instances of this problem the VCG mechanism will run a deficit. One such example is the *public project* setting described in Chapter 9, Section 3.5 which can be mapped to a network with a single link of cost C, where one endpoint is the root and all the users are at the other endpoint.

All of the other examples detailed in Chapter 9, Section 3.5, i.e., *reverse auctions*, *bilateral trade*, *multiunit auctions*, and *buying a path in a network*, as well as many other problems can be modeled in this single-parameter agent framework.

13.1.1 Organization

Our discussion of optimal mechanism design will be divided up into three categories, depending on our assumptions about the agents' private values. On one hand, as is typical in economics, we can assume that agents' private values are drawn from a known prior distribution, the so-called Bayesian approach. Given knowledge of these prior distributions, the Bayesian optimal mechanism is the one that achieves the largest expected profit for these agents, where the expectation is taken over the randomness in the agents' valuations. In Section 13.2, we present the seminal result of Myerson, showing how to design the optimal, i.e., profit-maximizing, Bayesian auction given the prior distribution from which bidders' valuations are drawn.

On the other hand, in many cases, determining these prior distributions in advance may not be convenient, reasonable, or even possible. It is particularly difficult to collect priors in small markets, where the process of collecting information can seriously impact both the incentives of the agents and the performance of the mechanism. Thus, it is of great interest to understand to what extent we are able to to design mechanisms for profit maximization even when we know very little about bidders' valuations. This approach leads us to the more traditional computer science approach of "worst-case analysis." While worst-case analysis could lead to results that are overly pessimistic, we shall see that in many cases we are able to obtain worst-case guarantees that are comparable to the optimal average-case guarantees for valuations from known distributions.

We begin our exploration of worst-case analysis in Section 13.3, where we survey techniques for approximating the optimal mechanism. We give natural mechanisms that approach optimality on large markets and a general formula for their performance as a function of the market size for small markets.

To obtain a theory of optimal mechanisms design without assumptions on the size of the market, we adopt a framework of *relative optimality*. This is motivated by two key observations. First, as we will explain later, there is no truthful mechanism that is best on every input. Second, in the worst case, all the agents' private values could be zero (or negligible) and thus no auction will be able to extract a high profit. In Section 13.4, we describe techniques for designing auctions that always (in worst case) return a profit that is within a small constant factor of some *profit benchmark* evaluated with respect to the agents' true private values.

Finally, in Section 13.5, we consider procurement settings where the auctioneer is looking to buy a set of goods or services that satisfy certain constraints, e.g., a path or a spanning tree in a graph. Specifically, we consider the problem of designing procurement auctions to minimize the total cost of the auctioneer (i.e., maximize their profit) relative to a natural benchmark.

We conclude the chapter with a discussion of directions for future research.

13.1.2 Preliminaries

In this section, we review basic properties of truthful mechanisms.

We will place two standard assumptions on our mechanisms. The first, that they are *individually rational*, means that no agent has negative expected utility for taking part in the mechanism. The second condition we require is that of *no positive transfers* which restricts the mechanism to not pay the agents when they do not win, i.e., $x_i = 0 \rightarrow p_i = 0$.

In general, we will allow our mechanisms to be randomized. In a randomized mechanism, x_i is the probability that agent i is allocated the good, and p_i is agent i's expected payment. Since x_i and p_i are outputs of the mechanism, it will be useful to view them as functions of the input bids as follows. We let $x_i(\mathbf{b})$, $p_i(\mathbf{b})$, and $u_i(\mathbf{b})$ represent agent i's probability of allocation, expected price, and expected utility, respectively. Let $\mathbf{b}_{-i} = (b_1, \ldots, b_{i-1}, ?, b_{i+1}, \ldots, b_n)$ represent the vector of bids excluding bid i. Then with $\mathbf{b}_{-i}$ fixed, we let $x_i(b_i)$, $p_i(b_i)$, and $u_i(b_i)$ represent agent i's probability of allocation, expected price, and expected utility, respectively, as a function of their own bid. We further define the convenient notation $x_i(b_i, \mathbf{b}_{-i}) = x_i(\mathbf{b})$, $p_i(b_i, \mathbf{b}_{-i}) = p_i(\mathbf{b})$, and $u_i(b_i, \mathbf{b}_{-i}) = u_i(\mathbf{b})$.

Definition 13.5 A mechanism is *truthful in expectation* if and only if for all i, v_i, b_i, and $\mathbf{b}_{-i}$, agent i's expected utility for bidding their valuation, v_i, is at least their expected utility for bidding any other value. In other words,

$$u_i(v_i, \mathbf{b}_{-i}) \geq u_i(b_i, \mathbf{b}_{-i}).$$

For single-parameter agents, we restate the characterization of truthful mechanisms which was proven in Chapter 9, Section 5.6.

Theorem 13.6 *A mechanism is truthful in expectation if and only if, for any agent i and any fixed choice of bids by the other agents* $\mathbf{b}_{-i}$,

(i) $x_i(b_i)$ *is monotone nondecreasing.*

(ii) $p_i(b_i) = b_i x_i(b_i) - \int_0^{b_i} x_i(z)\, dz.$

Given this theorem, we see that once an allocation rule $\mathbf{x}(\cdot)$ is fixed, the payment rule $\mathbf{p}(\cdot)$ is also fixed. Thus, in specifying a mechanism we need specify only a monotone allocation rule and from it the truth-inducing payment rule can be derived.

It is useful to specialize Theorem 13.6 to the case where the mechanism is deterministic. In this case, the monotonicity of $x_i(b_i)$ implies that, for $\mathbf{b}_{-i}$ fixed, there is some threshold bid t_i such that $x_i(b_i) = 1$ for all $b_i > t_i$ and 0 for all $t_i < b_i$. Moreover the second part of the theorem then implies that for any $b_i > t_i$, $p_i(b_i) = b_i - \int_{t_i}^{b_i} dz = t_i$. We conclude the following.

Observation 13.1.1 *Any deterministic truthful auction is specified by a set of functions* $t_i(\mathbf{b}_{-i})$ *which determine, for each bidder i and each set of bids* $\mathbf{b}_{-i}$, *an offer price to bidder i such that bidder i wins and pays price* t_i *if* $b_i > t_i$, *or loses and pays nothing if* $b_i < t_i$. *(Ties can be broken arbitrarily.)*

13.2 Bayesian Optimal Mechanism Design

In this section we describe the conventional economics approach of *Bayesian optimal mechanism design* where it is assumed that the valuations of the agents are drawn from a known distribution. The mechanism we describe is known as the Myerson mechanism: it is the truthful mechanism that maximizes the auctioneer's expected profit, where the expectation is taken over the randomness in the agents' valuations.

Consider, for example, a single-item auction with two bidders whose valuations are known to be drawn independently at random from the uniform distribution on $[0, 1]$. In Chapter 9, Section 6.3, it was shown that in this setting the expected revenue of both the Vickrey (second-price) auction and of the first-price auction is 1/3. In fact, it was observed that any auction that always allocates the item to the bidder with the higher valuation achieves the same expected revenue.

Does this mean that 1/3 is the best we can do, in expectation, with bidders of this type? The answer is no. Consider the following auction.

Definition 13.7 (Vickrey auction with reservation price r) The *Vickrey auction with reservation price* r, VA_r, sells the item to the highest bidder bidding at least r. The price the winning bidder pays is the maximum of the second highest bid and r.

It is a straightforward probabilistic calculation to show that the expected profit of the Vickrey auction with reservation price $r = 1/2$ is $5/12$. Thus, it is possible to get higher expected profit than the Vickrey auction by sometimes not allocating the item! This raises the problem of identifying, among the class of all truthful auctions, the auction that gives the optimal profit in expectation. The derivation in the next section answers this question and shows that in fact for this scenario $\text{VA}_{1/2}$ is the optimal auction.

13.2.1 Virtual Valuations, Virtual Surplus, and Expected Profit

We assume that the valuations of the agents, $v_1, \ldots, v_n$, are drawn independently at random from known (but not necessarily identical) continuous probability distributions. For simplicity, we assume that $v_i \in [0, h]$ for all i. We denote by F_i the distribution function from which bidder i's valuation, v_i, is drawn (i.e., $F_i(z) = \mathbf{Pr}[v_i \leq z]$) and by f_i its density function (i.e., $f_i(z) = \frac{d}{dz}F_i(z)$). Since the agents' valuations are independent, the joint distribution from which $\mathbf{v}$ is drawn is just the product distribution $\mathbf{F} = F_1 \times \cdots \times F_n$.

We now define two key notions: *virtual valuations* and *virtual surplus*.

Definition 13.8 The *virtual valuation* of agent i with valuation v_i is

$$\phi_i(v_i) = v_i - \frac{1 - F_i(v_i)}{f_i(v_i)}.$$

Definition 13.9 Given valuations, v_i, and corresponding virtual valuations, $\phi_i(v_i)$, the *virtual surplus* of allocation $\mathbf{x}$ is $\sum_i \phi_i(v_i)x_i - c(\mathbf{x})$.

As the *surplus* of an allocation is $\sum_i v_i x_i - c(\mathbf{x})$, the virtual surplus of an allocation is the surplus of the allocation with respect to agents whose valuations are replaced by their virtual valuations, $\phi_i(v_i)$.

We now show that any truthful mechanism has expected profit equal to its expected virtual surplus. Thus, to maximize expected profit, the mechanism should choose an allocation which maximizes virtual surplus. In so far as this allocation rule is monotone, this gives the optimal truthful mechanism!

Theorem 13.10 *The expected profit of any truthful mechanism, $\mathcal{M}$, is equal to its expected virtual surplus, i.e.,* $\mathbf{E_v}[\mathcal{M}(\mathbf{v})] = \mathbf{E_v}[\sum_i \phi_i(v_i)x_i(\mathbf{v}) - c(\mathbf{x}(\mathbf{v}))]$.

Thus, if the mechanism, on each bid vector $\mathbf{b}$, chooses an allocation, $\mathbf{x}$, which maximizes $\sum_i \phi_i(b_i)x_i - c(\mathbf{x})$, the auctioneer's profit will be maximized. Notice that if we employ a deterministic tie-breaking rule then the resulting mechanism will be deterministic. Theorem 13.10 follows from Lemma 13.11 below, and the independence of the agents' valuations.

Lemma 13.11 *Consider any truthful mechanism and fix the bids $\mathbf{b}_{-i}$ of all bidders except for bidder i. The expected payment of a bidder i satisfies:*

$$\mathbf{E}_{b_i}[p_i(b_i)] = \mathbf{E}_{b_i}[\phi_i(b_i)x_i(b_i)].$$

PROOF To simplify notation, we drop the subscript i and refer simply to the bid b being randomly chosen from distribution F with density function f.

By Theorem 13.6, we have

$$\mathbf{E}_b[p(b)] = \int_{b=0}^{h} p(b)f(b)\,db = \int_{b=0}^{h} bx(b)f(b)\,db - \int_{b=0}^{h}\int_{z=0}^{b} x(z)f(b)\,dz\,db.$$

Focusing on the second term and switching the order of integration, we have

$$\begin{aligned}\mathbf{E}_b[p(b)] &= \int_{b=0}^{h} bx(b)f(b)\,db - \int_{z=0}^{h} x(z)\int_{b=z}^{h} f(b)\,db\,dz.\\ &= \int_{b=0}^{h} bx(b)f(b)\,db - \int_{z=0}^{h} x(z)\,[1 - F(z)]\,dz.\end{aligned}$$

Now, we rename z to b and factor out $x(b)f(b)$ to get

$$\begin{aligned}\mathbf{E}_b[p(b)] &= \int_{b=0}^{h} bx(b)f(b)\,db - \int_{b=0}^{h} x(b)\,[1 - F(b)]\,db.\\ &= \int_{b=0}^{h}\left[b - \frac{1-F(b)}{f(b)}\right]x(b)f(b)db.\\ &= \mathbf{E}_b[\phi(b)x(b)]. \quad \square\end{aligned}$$

13.2.2 Truthfulness of Virtual Surplus Maximization

Of course, it is not immediately clear that maximizing virtual surplus results in a truthful mechanism. By Theorem 13.6, this depends on whether or not virtual surplus maximization results in a monotone allocation rule. Recall that the VCG mechanism, which maximizes the actual surplus, i.e., $\sum_i v_i x_i - c(\mathbf{x})$, is truthful precisely because surplus maximization results in a monotone allocation rule. Clearly then, virtual surplus maximization gives an allocation that is monotone in agent valuations precisely when virtual valuation functions are monotone in agent valuations. Indeed, it is easy to find examples of the converse which show that nonmonotone virtual valuations result in a nonmonotone allocation rule. Thus, we conclude the following lemma.

Lemma 13.12 *Virtual surplus maximization is truthful if and only if, for all i, $\phi_i(v_i)$ is monotone nondecreasing in v_i.*

A sufficient condition for monotone virtual valuations is implied by the *monotone hazard rate* assumption. The hazard rate of a distribution is defined as $f(z)/(1 - F(z))$. Clearly, if the hazard rate is monotone nondecreasing, then the virtual valuations are monotone nondecreasing as well. There is a technical construction that extends these results to the nonmonotone case, but we do not cover it here.

Definition 13.13 Let $\mathbf{F}$ be the prior distribution of agents' valuations satisfying the monotone hazard rate assumption. We denote by $\text{Mye}_{\mathbf{F}}(\mathbf{b})$ the *Myerson mechanism*: on input $\mathbf{b}$, output $\mathbf{x}$ to maximize the virtual surplus (defined with respect to the distribution $\mathbf{F}$).

Thus, for single parameter problems, profit maximization in a Bayesian setting reduces to virtual surplus maximization. This allows us to describe Myerson's optimal mechanism, $\text{Mye}_{\mathbf{F}}(\mathbf{b})$, as follows:

(i) Given the bids $\mathbf{b}$ and $\mathbf{F}$, compute "virtual bids": $b'_i = \phi_i(b_i)$.
(ii) Run VCG on the virtual bids $\mathbf{b}'$ to get $\mathbf{x}'$ and $\mathbf{p}'$
(iii) Output $\mathbf{x} = \mathbf{x}'$ and $\mathbf{p}$ with $p_i = \phi_i^{-1}(p'_i)$.

13.2.3 Applications of Myerson's Optimal Mechanism

The formulation of virtual valuations and the statement that the optimal mechanism is the one that maximizes virtual surplus is not the end of the story. In many relevant cases this formulation allows one to derive very simple descriptions of the optimal mechanism. We now consider a couple of examples to obtain a more precise understanding of $\text{Mye}_{\mathbf{F}}(\mathbf{b})$ and illustrate this point.

Example 13.14 (single-item auction) In a single-item auction, the surplus maximizing allocation gives the item to the bidder with the highest valuation, unless the highest valuation is less than 0 in which case the auctioneer keeps the item. Usually, we assume that all bidders' valuations are at least zero, or they would not want to participate in the auction, so the auctioneer never keeps the item.

However, when we maximize virtual surplus, it may be the case that a bidder has positive valuation but negative virtual valuation. Thus, for allocating a single item, the optimal mechanism finds the bidder with the largest nonnegative virtual valuation if there is one, and allocates to that bidder.

What about the payments? Suppose that there are only two bidders and we break ties in favor of bidder 1. Then bidder 1 wins precisely when $\phi_1(b_1) \geq \max\{\phi_2(b_2), 0\}$. This is a deterministic allocation rule, and thus the payment that a winning bidder 1 must make is the $p_1 = \inf\{b : \phi_1(b) \geq \phi_2(b_2) \wedge \phi_1(b) \geq 0\}$. Suppose that $F_1 = F_2 = F$, which implies that $\phi_1(z) = \phi_2(z) = \phi(z)$. Then this simplifies to $p_1 = \min(b_2, \phi^{-1}(0))$. Similarly, bidder 2's payment upon winning is $p_2 = \min(b_1, \phi^{-1}(0))$, thus we arrive at one of Myerson's main observations.

Theorem 13.15 *The optimal single-item auction for bidders with valuations drawn i.i.d. from distribution F is the Vickrey auction with reservation price $\phi^{-1}(0)$, i.e., $\mathrm{VA}_{\phi^{-1}(0)}$.*

For example, when F is uniform on $[0, 1]$, we can plug the equations $F(z) = z$ and $f(z) = 1$ into the formula for the virtual valuation function (Definition 13.8) to conclude that $\phi(z) = 2z - 1$. Thus, the virtual valuations are uniformly distributed on $[-1, 1]$. We can easily solve for $\phi^{-1}(0) = 1/2$. We conclude that the optimal auction for two bidders with valuations uniform on $[0, 1]$ is the Vickrey auction with reservation price $1/2$, $\mathrm{VA}_{1/2}$.

Example 13.16 (Digital goods auction) Recall that in a digital goods auction, we have $c(\mathbf{x}) = 0$ for all $\mathbf{x}$. Thus, to maximize virtual surplus, we allocate to each bidder such that $\phi_i(b_i) \geq 0$. As in the previous example, the payment a winning bidder must make is his minimum winning bid, i.e., $\inf\{b : \phi_i(b) \geq 0\}$, which is identically $\phi_i^{-1}(0)$.

Notice that with n bidders whose valuations are drawn independently from the same distribution function F, the reserve price for each bidder is $\phi^{-1}(0)$, the solution to $b - \frac{1-F(b)}{f(b)} = 0$. It is easy to check that this is precisely the *optimal sale price* for the distribution F: the take-it-or-leave-it price we would offer each bidder to maximize our expected profit.

Definition 13.17 (optimal sale price) The *optimal sale price* for distribution F is $\mathrm{opt}(F) = \mathrm{argmax}_z\, z(1 - F(z))$.

Summarizing, we obtain:

Theorem 13.18 *The optimal digital goods auction for n bidders with valuations drawn i.i.d. from distribution F is to offer each bidder the price* $\mathrm{opt}(F) = \phi^{-1}(0)$.

13.3 Prior-Free Approximations to the Optimal Mechanism

In the previous section, we saw how to design the optimal mechanism when agents' valuations were drawn from known distributions. The assumption that the valuations are drawn from a known prior distribution makes sense in very large markets. In fact, as we shall see shortly, in large enough markets, a good approximation to the prior distribution can be learned on-the-fly and thus there are prior-free mechanisms that obtain nearly the optimal profit. We discuss these results in the first part of this section.

In small markets, on the other hand, incentives issues in learning an approximation of the prior distribution result in loss of performance and fundamental mechanism design challenges. Thus, new techniques are required in these settings. We develop an approach based on random sampling and analyze its performance in a way that makes explicit the connection between the size of the market and a mechanism's performance.

13.3.1 Empirical Distributions

The central observation that enables effective profit maximization without priors is Observation 13.1.1, which says that a truthful mechanism can use the reported bids of all the other agents in order to make a pricing decision for a particular agent.

Definition 13.19 (empirical distribution) For a vector of bids $\mathbf{b} = (b_1, \ldots, b_n)$, the *empirical distribution* for these bids is $F_{\mathbf{b}}$ satisfying for $X \sim F_{\mathbf{b}}$, $\mathbf{Pr}[X > z] = n_z/n$, where n_z is the number of bids in $\mathbf{b}$ above value z.

We now present a variant on Myerson's mechanism that can be used without any prior knowledge. As we shall see below, this mechanism has interesting interpretations in several contexts.

Definition 13.20 (empirical Myerson mechanism) The *empirical Myerson* mechanism, EM on input $\mathbf{b}$, for each i, simulates $\text{Mye}_{F_{\mathbf{b}_{-i}}}(\mathbf{b})$ to obtain outcome $\mathbf{x}^{(i)}$ and payments $\mathbf{p}^{(i)}$. It then produces outcome $\mathbf{x}$ and $\mathbf{p}$ with $x_i = x_i^{(i)}$ and $p_i = p_i^{(i)}$.

The outcome and payment for agent i in the empirical Myerson mechanism is based on the simulation of $\text{Mye}_{F_{\mathbf{b}_{-i}}}(\mathbf{b})$, and since agent i cannot manipulate $F_{\mathbf{b}_{-i}}$, this mechanism is truthful.

There are two issues that we need to address in order to understand the performance of the EM mechanism. First, we need to see if the outcomes it produces are feasible. The issue is that the allocation to different agents, say i and j, is determined from different information ($\mathbf{b}_{-i}$ versus $\mathbf{b}_{-j}$). As we shall see, this inconsistency will sometimes produce allocations, $\mathbf{x}$, that are not feasible (i.e., $c(\mathbf{x}) = \infty$). Second, in those situations where it does produce feasible allocations, we need to understand how effective the mechanism is at profit maximization. The hope is that, in large markets, $F_{\mathbf{b}_{-i}}$ should be close to $F_{\mathbf{b}}$ and hence the law of large numbers should imply good performance. Again, we will see that this does not hold in general.

We begin by considering the application of EM to digital goods auctions, where there is no feasibility issue.

Definition 13.21 (deterministic optimal price auction) We define the *deterministic optimal* price auction (DOP) as EM applied to the digital goods auction problem.

In the previous section, we saw that if each agent's valuation is drawn from the same distribution F, Myerson's mechanism offers price $\phi^{-1}(0) = \text{opt}(F)$ to each bidder. The deterministic optimal price auction, on the other hand, offers agent i price $\text{opt}(F_{\mathbf{b}_{-i}})$. Using the short-hand notation $\text{opt}(\mathbf{b}) = \text{opt}(F_{\mathbf{b}})$, Observation 13.1.1 allows us to express DOP quite simply as the auction defined by $t_i(\mathbf{b}_{-i}) = \text{opt}(\mathbf{b}_{-i})$. Since $\mathbf{b}_{-i}$ is different for each agent, in general the prices offered the agents are different. Nonetheless, the law of large numbers implies the following result (which is a corollary of Theorem 13.30 proved in the next section).

Theorem 13.22 *For the digital goods setting and n bids* $\mathbf{b}$ *distributed i.i.d. from distribution F with bounded support, the profit of DOP approaches the profit of Myerson in the limit as n increases.*

Unfortunately, the assumption that the input comes from an unknown, but i.i.d. distribution is crucially important to this result as the following example shows.

Example 13.23 With 10 bids at \$10, and 90 bids at \$1, consider the prices $t_i(\mathbf{b}_{-1})$ and $t_i(\mathbf{b}_{-10})$ that DOP offers bidders bidding \$1 and \$10 respectively:

- $\mathbf{b}_{-1}$ is 89 bids at \$1 and 10 bids at \$10, so $\text{opt}(\mathbf{b}_{-1}) = \$10$, and
- $\mathbf{b}_{-10}$ is 90 bids at \$1 and 9 bids at \$10, so $\text{opt}(\mathbf{b}_{-10}) = \$1$.

Thus, bids at \$10 are accepted, but offered price \$1, while bids at \$1 are rejected. The total profit is \$10 whereas the optimal is \$100. This example can be made arbitrarily bad.

What happened in this example is the result of the inconsistency between the distribution $F_{\mathbf{b}_{-i}}$ assumed when choosing a price for agent i, and the distribution $F_{\mathbf{b}_{-j}}$ assumed when choosing a price for agent j. Had we just run $\text{Mye}_{F_{\mathbf{b}_{-i}}}$ or $\text{Mye}_{F_{\mathbf{b}_{-j}}}$ on all bids, all would have been well. Indeed, in this example, we would have chosen either price \$1 for everyone or price \$10 for everyone. Both prices would have been fine.

This problem is not just one with DOP, but with any symmetric deterministic digital goods auction.[1] Indeed, the problem inherent in this example can be generalized to prove the following theorem.

[1] An auction is *symmetric* if the outcome and prices are not a function of the order of the input bids, but rather just the set of bids.

Theorem 13.24 *There do not exist constants β and γ and a symmetric deterministic truthful auction, $\mathcal{A}$, with profit at least* $\text{OPT}/\beta - h\gamma$ *on all bid vectors* $\mathbf{b}$ *with* $b_i \in [1, h]$.

The inconsistency of EM can be more serious than just low profit on some, perhaps unlikely, inputs; if some outcomes are infeasible (i.e., $c(\mathbf{x}) = \infty$ for some $\mathbf{x}$) then EM may result in infeasible outcomes! In the next section we see how these consistency issues can be partially addressed through the use of random sampling.

13.3.2 Random Sampling

Random sampling plays an important role in the design of economic mechanisms. For example, during elections, polls that predict each candidate's ranking affect the results of the elections; and in many settings, market analysis and user studies using a (small) random sample of the population can lead to good decisions in product development and pricing. In this section, we consider a natural extension of the empirical Myerson mechanism that uses random sampling to address the consistency issues raised in the preceding section.

Definition 13.25 (Random sampling empirical myerson) The *random sampling empirical Myerson* mechanism (RSEM) works as follows:

(i) Solicit bids $\mathbf{b} = (b_1, \ldots, b_n)$.
(ii) Partition the bids into two sets $\mathbf{b}'$ and $\mathbf{b}''$ uniformly at random.
(iii) Compute empirical distributions for each set $F' = F_{\mathbf{b}'}$ and $F'' = F_{\mathbf{b}''}$.
(iv) Run $\text{Mye}_{F''}(\mathbf{b}')$ and $\text{Mye}_{F'}(\mathbf{b}'')$.

For digital goods auctions, we can replace Steps iii and iv by their more natural interpretations (facilitated by the short-hand notation $\text{opt}(\mathbf{b}) = \text{opt}(F_{\mathbf{b}})$):

(iii)' Compute the optimal sale prices $p' = \text{opt}(\mathbf{b}')$ and $p'' = \text{opt}(\mathbf{b}'')$.
(iv)' Offer price p' to bidders in $\mathbf{b}''$ and price p'' to bidders in $\mathbf{b}'$.

We refer to the digital goods variant of the random sampling empirical Myerson mechanism as the *random sampling optimal price* auction (RSOP). The randomization in RSOP allows it to bypass the deterministic impossibility for worst case settings leading to the following theorem. (Again, this is as a corollary of Theorem 13.30 which is proven in the next section.)

Theorem 13.26 *For* $\mathbf{b}$ *with* $b_i \in [1, h]$, *the expected revenue of RSOP approaches that of the optimal single price sale as the number of bidders grows.*

Similar results do not necessarily hold for more general settings. It is easy to imagine situations where RSEM also gives infeasible outcomes as the following example illustrates.

Example 13.27 Consider the setting where we are selling a digital good in one of two markets, for convenience, bidders $1, \ldots, i$ are in market A and bidders $i+1, \ldots, n$ are in market B. Due, perhaps, to government regulations, it is not legal to sell the good to bidders in both markets simultaneously. Thus, feasible solutions will have winners either only from market A or only from market B. It is easy to construct settings where RSEM will sell to one market in $\mathbf{b}'$ and the other in $\mathbf{b}''$. The combined outcome, however, is not feasible.

The biggest open problem in prior-free mechanism design is to understand how to approximate the optimal mechanism in more general settings.

13.3.3 Convergence Rates

As we have discussed above, the law of large numbers implies that the profit of the random sampling auction, say in the case of digital goods, is asymptotically optimal as the number of bidders grows. In this section, we study the rate at which the auction approaches optimal performance. The theorem we prove will enable us to obtain a precise relationship between the complexity of the class of outcomes considered by RSOP and its convergence rate. The results in this section will also give us a framework for evaluating the performance of random sampling-based mechanisms in very general contexts.

We make our discussion concrete, using the example of the digital goods auction problem. Recall that RSOP uses a subroutine that computes the optimal sale price for the bids in each partition of the bidders. Suppose that we allowed the auctioneer the ability to artificially restrict prices to be in some set $\mathcal{Q}$. For example, the auctioneer might only sell at integer prices, in which case $\mathcal{Q}$ would be the set of integers. The auctioneer could further limit the set of possible prices, for example, by having $\mathcal{Q}$ be powers of 2. We will see that different choices of $\mathcal{Q}$ will give us different bounds on the convergence rate.

Given $\mathcal{Q}$, we define $\text{RSOP}_{\mathcal{Q}}$ as the random sampling auction that computes the optimal price from $\mathcal{Q}$ on each partition and offers it to bidders in the opposite partition. We make use of the following notation. Let $q(b_i)$ be the payment made by bidder i when offered $q \in \mathcal{Q}$. That is, $q(b_i) = q$ if $b_i \geq q$ and $q(b_i) = 0$ otherwise. Let $q(\mathbf{b}) = \sum_i q(b_i)$. Finally, define $\text{opt}_{\mathcal{Q}}(\mathbf{b}) = \text{argmax}_{q \in \mathcal{Q}}\, q(\mathbf{b})$ as the q that gives the optimal profit for $\mathbf{b}$, and $\text{OPT}_{\mathcal{Q}}(\mathbf{b})$ to be this optimal profit, i.e., $\text{OPT}_{\mathcal{Q}}(\mathbf{b}) = \max_{q \in \mathcal{Q}} q(\mathbf{b})$.

The bounds we give in this section show the rate at which the profit of $\text{RSOP}_{\mathcal{Q}}(\mathbf{b})$ approaches $\text{OPT}_{\mathcal{Q}}(\mathbf{b})$ with some measure of the size of the market. The measure we use is $\text{OPT}_{\mathcal{Q}}$ itself, as this gives us the most general and precise result. Thus, these results show the degree to which $\text{RSOP}_{\mathcal{Q}}$ approximates $\text{OPT}_{\mathcal{Q}}$ as $\text{OPT}_{\mathcal{Q}}$ grows large in comparison to h, an upper bound on the payment of any agent, and the complexity of $\mathcal{Q}$.

Definition 13.28 Given partitions $\mathbf{b}'$ and $\mathbf{b}''$, price q in $\mathcal{Q}$ is *ϵ-good* if

$$|q(\mathbf{b}') - q(\mathbf{b}'')| \leq \epsilon\, \text{OPT}_{\mathcal{Q}}(\mathbf{b})$$

Lemma 13.29 *For* $\mathbf{b}$ *and* h *satisfying* $q(b_i) \leq h$*, for all* i*, if bids* $\mathbf{b}$ *are randomly partitioned into* $\mathbf{b}'$ *and* $\mathbf{b}''$ *then* q *is not* ϵ*-good with probability at most* $2e^{-\epsilon^2 \,\mathrm{OPT}_{\mathcal{Q}}(\mathbf{b})/2h}$.

The proof of this lemma follows from McDiarmid's inequality, see Exercise 13.5. The following is the main theorem of this section. A natural interpretation of h is an upper bound on the highest valuation, i.e., $h = \max_i v_i$.

Theorem 13.30 *For* $\mathcal{Q}$, $\mathbf{b}$*, and* h *satisfying* $q(b_i) \leq h$*, for all* q *and* i*, and* $\mathrm{OPT}_{\mathcal{Q}}(\mathbf{b}) \geq \frac{8h}{\epsilon^2} \ln\left(\frac{2|\mathcal{Q}|}{\delta}\right)$*, with probability* $1 - \delta$ *the profit of* $\mathrm{RSOP}_{\mathcal{Q}}$ *is at least* $(1 - \epsilon)\,\mathrm{OPT}_{\mathcal{Q}}(\mathbf{b})$.

PROOF Assume that $\mathrm{OPT}_{\mathcal{Q}}(\mathbf{b}) \geq \frac{8h}{\epsilon^2} \ln(\frac{2|\mathcal{Q}|}{\delta})$. For random partitioning of $\mathbf{b}$ into $\mathbf{b}'$ and $\mathbf{b}''$, Lemma 13.29 implies that the probability $q \in \mathcal{Q}$ is not $\frac{\epsilon}{2}$-good is at most $\delta/|\mathcal{Q}|$. Using a union bound over all $q \in \mathcal{Q}$, we have that all $q \in \mathcal{Q}$ are $\frac{\epsilon}{2}$-good with probability $1 - \delta$.

Let $q' = \mathrm{opt}_{\mathcal{Q}}(\mathbf{b}')$, $q'' = \mathrm{opt}_{\mathcal{Q}}(\mathbf{b}'')$, and $q^* = \mathrm{opt}_{\mathcal{Q}}(\mathbf{b})$. By definition, $q'(\mathbf{b}') \geq q^*(\mathbf{b}')$ and likewise $q''(\mathbf{b}'') \geq q^*(\mathbf{b}'')$. Thus, $q'(\mathbf{b}') + q''(\mathbf{b}'') \geq q^*(\mathbf{b}) = \mathrm{OPT}_{\mathcal{Q}}(\mathbf{b})$. If all q are $\frac{\epsilon}{2}$-good, certainly q' and q'' are; therefore, $q'(\mathbf{b}'') \geq q'(\mathbf{b}') - \frac{\epsilon}{2}\mathrm{OPT}_{\mathcal{Q}}(\mathbf{b})$ and $q''(\mathbf{b}') \geq q''(\mathbf{b}'') - \frac{\epsilon}{2}\mathrm{OPT}_{\mathcal{Q}}(\mathbf{b})$. Thus, we conclude that our auction profit, which is $q'(\mathbf{b}'') + q''(\mathbf{b}')$ is at least $(1 - \epsilon)\,\mathrm{OPT}_{\mathcal{Q}}(\mathbf{b})$ with probability $1 - \delta$ which gives the theorem. □

Notice that this theorem holds for all ϵ and δ. In particular, it shows how big the optimal profit must be before we can guarantee a certain approximation factor. Of course, in the limit as the optimal profit goes to infinity, our approximation factor approaches one. We refer to the lower bound required of optimal profit, $\mathrm{OPT}_{\mathcal{Q}}$, in the statement of the theorem as the *convergence rate*. Indeed, if the agents' valuations are between 1 and h, the lower bound on the optimal profit can be translated into a lower bound on the size of the market needed to guarantee the approximation.

Let us now consider a few applications of the theorem: Suppose that $\mathcal{Q} = \{1, \ldots, h\}$. Then $|\mathcal{Q}| = h$ and the convergence rate to a $(1 - \epsilon)$-approximation with probability $1 - \delta$ is $O(h\epsilon^{-2} \log(2h/\delta))$. If instead $\mathcal{Q}$ is powers of 2 on the interval $[1, h]$, then $|\mathcal{Q}| = \log h$ and the convergence rate for constant ϵ and δ is $O(h \log\log h)$.

It is worth noting that the particular bids $\mathbf{b}$ that are input to any particular run of $\mathrm{RSOP}_{\mathcal{Q}}$ may further restrict the set of possible prices in $\mathcal{Q}$ that can be selected, say to some subset $\mathcal{Q}'$. We can apply Theorem 13.30 retrospectively to input $\mathbf{b}$ to bound the performance of $\mathrm{RSOP}_{\mathcal{Q}}$ in terms of $|\mathcal{Q}'|$. For example, in the original RSOP auction we consider all real numbers as prices; yet, $\mathrm{opt}(\mathbf{b})$ is always one of the bids. Thus, using $\mathcal{Q}' = \{b_1, \ldots, b_n\}$ and noting that $|\mathcal{Q}'| = n$, tells us that the convergence rate of our original RSOP digital good auction is $O(h\epsilon^{-2} \ln(2n/\delta))$. Even better bounds are possible using a notion called *γ-covers* (Exercise 13.6).

Corollary 13.31 *For $\mathcal{Q}$, $\mathcal{Q}'$, $\mathbf{b}$, and h satisfying $q(b_i) \leq h$ for all q and i, $\text{opt}(\mathbf{b}') \in \mathcal{Q}'$ for all subsets $\mathbf{b}'$ of $\mathbf{b}$, and $\text{OPT}_{\mathcal{Q}}(\mathbf{b}) \geq \frac{8h}{\epsilon^2} \ln(\frac{2|\mathcal{Q}'|}{\delta})$; with probability $1 - \delta$ the profit of* RSOP$_{\mathcal{Q}}$ *is at least* $(1 - \epsilon)\,\text{OPT}_{\mathcal{Q}}(\mathbf{b})$.

Lemma 13.29 and Theorem 13.30 are quite general and can be applied, as written, to a wide variety of unlimited supply auction problems with rich structure on the class of allowable offers, $\mathcal{Q}$. Two examples are *attribute auctions* and *combinatorial auctions*.

13.4 Prior-Free Optimal Mechanism Design

In the previous sections, a number of results on approximating the optimal mechanism in worst-case settings were presented. Unfortunately, these results remain limited in their applicability. For example, what if $\text{OPT}_{\mathcal{Q}}(\mathbf{b})$ is too small, as might happen if the size of the market (i.e., the number of bidders) is too small? In such cases, Theorem 13.30 may give us no guarantee. Thus, a natural question to ask is: what is the best truthful mechanism? Can we design a truthful mechanism for which we can prove nontrivial performance guarantees under any market conditions?

The first observation that must be made is that there is no such thing as an absolute "best" truthful auction. To gain some intuition for this statement, recall that in any truthful auction, the offer price t_i to bidder i is a function of all other bids $\mathbf{b}_{-i}$, but not of b_i. Thus, given any particular auction, which is forced to fix the offer price t_i independently of b_i, (and hence always performs suboptimally for most values of b_i), there is always some input on which a different truthful auction performs better (see Exercise 13.8).

Given that there is no absolute best truthful mechanism on all inputs, we are left with the question of how we can arrive at a rigorous theoretical framework in which we can compare auctions and determine one to be better. The key to resolving this issue is in moving from absolute optimality to relative optimality. Indeed, whenever there is an information theoretic obstacle or computational intractability preventing an absolute optimal solution to a problem we can try to approximate. For example, in the design of online algorithms the objective is to find an online algorithm that performs comparably to an optimal offline algorithm. The notable analogy here is between the game theoretic constraint that a mechanism does not know the true bid values in advance and must solicit them in a truth-inducing manner, and the online constraint that an online algorithm does not have knowledge of the future.

13.4.1 Competitive Framework

The general approach will be to try to design an auction with profit that is always (in worst case) within a small constant factor of some *profit benchmark*.

Definition 13.32 A *profit benchmark* is a function $\mathcal{G} : \mathbb{R}^n \to \mathbb{R}$ which maps a vector of valuations to a target profit.

The following definition captures the intuition that an auction is good if it is always close to a reasonable profit benchmark.

Definition 13.33 The *competitive ratio* of auction $\mathcal{A}$ (defined with respect to an implicit profit benchmark $\mathcal{G}$) is $\beta = \sup_{\mathbf{v}} \frac{\mathcal{G}(\mathbf{v})}{\mathcal{A}(\mathbf{v})}$.

Given a profit benchmark $\mathcal{G}$ the task of an auction designer is to design an auction that achieves the minimum possible competitive ratio. This auction is the *optimal competitive auction* for $\mathcal{G}$.

13.4.2 A Competitive Digital Goods Auctions

In this section, we will see that the RSOP auction that was defined in Section 13.3.2 is in fact a competitive digital goods auction. To make this statement precise, we first need to define the profit benchmark we will be attempting to compete with. In the analysis of online algorithms it is not always best to gauge the performance of an online algorithm by comparing it to an unconstrained optimal offline algorithm. Similarly, in the analysis of truthful auctions, it sometimes makes sense to compare an auction's profit to a profit benchmark that is not necessarily the profit of the optimal algorithm that is given the bidders' true valuations in advance.

For digital goods auctions, natural profit benchmarks, such as (a) the maximum profit achievable with fully discriminating prices (where each bidder pays their valuation) or (b) the maximum profit achievable with a single price, are provably too strong in the sense that no truthful auction can be constant competitive with these benchmarks.

Thus, the profit benchmark we will use is the following.

Definition 13.34 **($\mathcal{F}^{(2)}$)** The *optimal single priced profit with at least two winners* is

$$\mathcal{F}^{(2)}(\mathbf{v}) = \max_{i \geq 2} i\, v_{(i)},$$

where $v_{(i)}$ is the ith largest valuation.

Theorem 13.24 in Section 13.3.1 can be extended to this setting to show:

Corollary 13.35 *No symmetric deterministic truthful auction has constant competitive ratio relative to the profit benchmark* $\mathcal{F}^{(2)}$.

Thus, we turn to randomized auctions where we find the following theorem.

Theorem 13.36 *RSOP is 15-competitive with* $\mathcal{F}^{(2)}$.

We will not prove Theorem 13.36 here as it is primarily a technical probabilistic analysis. We do note, however, that 15 is likely to be a loose upper bound. On the other hand, it is easy to see that RSOP cannot have a competitive ratio better than 4, by considering the bid vector $\mathbf{b} = (\$1, \$2)$. With probability 1/2 both bids end up in the same part and the RSOP profit is 0. Otherwise, with probability 1/2 one bid is in each part. Without loss of generality, $\mathbf{b}' = \{\$1\}$ and $\mathbf{b}'' = \{\$2\}$, then $p' = \$1$ and $p'' = \$2$. Thus, the \$1-bid is rejected (because she cannot pay \$2) and the \$2-bid is offered a price of \$1 which she accepts. The RSOP profit in this case is \$1. The expected profit of RSOP is therefore \$0.50 while $\mathcal{F}^{(2)}(\mathbf{b}) = \$2$, which shows that RSOP is at best 4-competitive. It is conjectured that this two bid input is in fact the worst case and that RSOP has a competitive ratio of 4.

13.4.3 Lower Bounds

Now that we have seen that there exists an auction that has constant competitive ratio to $\mathcal{F}^{(2)}$, it is interesting to ask: what is the *optimal auction* in terms of worst case competitive ratio to $\mathcal{F}^{(2)}$? What is the competitive ratio of this optimal auction? In this section, we approach this question from the other side, by looking for lower bounds on the competitive ratio. Specifically, we discuss a proof that shows that no auction is better than 2.42-competitive.

Theorem 13.37 *No auction has competitive ratio less than 2.42.*

The proof of this theorem involves a fairly complicated analysis of the expected value of $\mathcal{F}^{(2)}(\mathbf{b})$ when $\mathbf{b}$ is generated from a particular probability distribution. We will instead prove a simpler result which highlights the main ideas of the theorem.

Lemma 13.38 *No 2-bidder auction has competitive ratio less than 2.*

PROOF The proof follows a simple structure that is useful for proving lower bounds for this type of problem. First, we consider bids drawn from a particular distribution. Second, we argue that for any auction $\mathcal{A}$, $\mathbf{E_b}[\mathcal{A}(\mathbf{b})] \leq \mathbf{E_b}\left[\mathcal{F}^{(2)}(\mathbf{b})\right]/2$. This implies that there exists a bid vector $\mathbf{b}^*$ such that $\mathcal{A}(\mathbf{b}^*) \leq \mathcal{F}^{(2)}(\mathbf{b}^*)/2$.

We choose a distribution to make the analysis of $\mathbf{E_b}[\mathcal{A}(\mathbf{b})]$ simple. This is important because we have to analyze it for all auctions $\mathcal{A}$. The idea is to choose the distribution for $\mathbf{b}$ so that all auctions obtain the same expected profit. Consider $\mathbf{b}$ with b_i satisfying $\mathbf{Pr}[b_i > z] = 1/z$. Note that whatever the price t_i is that $\mathcal{A}$ offers bidder i, the expected payment made by bidder i is $t_i \times \mathbf{Pr}[b_i \geq t_i] = 1$. Thus, for $n = 2$ bidders the expected profit of any truthful auction is $\mathbf{E_b}[\mathcal{A}(\mathbf{b})] = n = 2$.

We must now calculate $\mathbf{E_b}[\mathcal{F}^{(2)}(\mathbf{b})]$. $\mathcal{F}^{(2)}(\mathbf{b}) = \max_{i \geq 2} i b_{(i)}$ where $b_{(i)}$ is the ith highest bid value. In the case that $n = 2$, this simplifies to $\mathcal{F}^{(2)}(\mathbf{b}) = 2b_{(2)} = 2\min(b_1, b_2)$. We recall that a nonnegative random variable X has $\mathbf{E}[X] = \int_0^\infty \mathbf{Pr}[X \geq z]\, dz$ and calculate $\mathbf{Pr}[\mathcal{F}^{(2)}(\mathbf{b}) > z]$.

$$
\begin{aligned}
\mathbf{Pr_b}[\mathcal{F}^{(2)}(\mathbf{b}) > z] &= \mathbf{Pr_b}[b_1 \geq z/2 \wedge b_2 \geq z/2] \\
&= \mathbf{Pr_b}[b_1 \geq z/2]\, \mathbf{Pr_b}[b_2 \geq z/2] \\
&= 4/z^2.
\end{aligned}
$$

Note that this equation is valid only for $z \geq 2$. Of course for $z < 2$, $\mathbf{Pr}[\mathcal{F}^{(2)}(\mathbf{b}) \geq z] = 1$. Thus,

$$\mathbf{E}_{\mathbf{b}}[\mathcal{F}^{(2)}(\mathbf{b})] = \int_0^\infty \mathbf{Pr}[\mathcal{F}^{(2)}\mathbf{b} \geq z]\, dz = 2 + \int_2^\infty \frac{4}{z^2} dz = 4.$$

For this distribution and any auction $\mathcal{A}$, $\mathbf{E}_{\mathbf{b}}[\mathcal{A}(\mathbf{b})] = 2$ and $\mathbf{E}_{\mathbf{b}}[\mathcal{F}^{(2)}(\mathbf{b})] = 4$. Thus, the inequality $\mathbf{E}_{\mathbf{b}}[\mathcal{A}(\mathbf{b})] \leq \mathbf{E}_{\mathbf{b}}[\mathcal{F}^{(2)}(\mathbf{b})]/2$ holds and there must exist some input $\mathbf{b}^*$ such that $\mathcal{A}(\mathbf{b}^*) \leq \mathcal{F}^{(2)}(\mathbf{b}^*)/2$. □

For two bidders, this lower bound is tight. Indeed, it is trivial to check that for two bidders, the Vickrey auction has competitive ratio 2.

The lower bound proof given above can be generalized by a more complicated analysis to larger n. Such an analysis leads to bounds of $13/6$ for $n = 3$ and eventually to a bound of 2.42 for general n. It is conjectured that these bounds are tight. Indeed they are tight for $n \leq 3$.

13.4.4 The Digital Goods Auction Decision Problem

In the next sections, we derive an auction with a competitive ratio of 4. We do this by defining the notion of a decision problem for mechanism design and reducing the problem of designing a good competitive auction to it.

Definition 13.39 The *digital goods auction decision problem* is: given n bidders, n units of an item, and a target profit R, design a *truthful* mechanism that obtains profit R if possible, i.e., if $R \leq \mathcal{F}(\mathbf{v})$. Here, $\mathcal{F}(\mathbf{v}) = \max_{i \geq 1} i\, v_{(i)}$, where $v_{(i)}$ is the ith largest valuation.

This digital goods auction decision problem is also known as the *profit extraction* problem as its goal is to extract a profit R from a set of bidders. It turns out that this problem is solved by a special case of a general *cost-sharing* mechanism.

Definition 13.40 (ProfitExtract$_R$) The *digital goods auction profit extractor* with target profit R sells to the largest group of k bidders that can equally share R and charges each R/k.

It is straightforward to show that ProfitExtract$_R$ is truthful and obtains a profit of R when $\mathcal{F}(\mathbf{b}) \geq R$ (see Exercise 13.10).

13.4.5 Reduction to the Decision Problem

A classical optimization problem can typically be phrased as follows: "find a feasible solution that maximizes some objective function." The decision problem version of this is: "is there a feasible solution for which the objective function has value at least V?" A standard reduction between the two involves solving the decision problem many times, using binary search over values V. Unfortunately, such an approach will not work for mechanism design as it is not truthful to run several truthful mechanisms and then only take the output of the one that is the most desirable.

The following truthful auction avoids this problem.

Definition 13.41 (RSPE) The *Random Sampling Profit Extraction* auction (RSPE) works as follows:

(i) Randomly partition the bids $\mathbf{b}$ into two by flipping a fair coin for each bidder and assigning her to $\mathbf{b}'$ or $\mathbf{b}''$.

(ii) Compute $R' = \mathcal{F}(\mathbf{b}')$ and $R'' = \mathcal{F}(\mathbf{b}'')$, the optimal profits for each part.

(iii) Run ProfitExtract$_{R'}$ on $\mathbf{b}''$ and ProfitExtract$_{R''}$ on $\mathbf{b}'$.

The intuition for this auction is that ProfitExtract$_R$ allows us treat a set of bidders, $\mathbf{b}$, as one bidder with bid value $\mathcal{F}(\mathbf{b})$. Recall that a truthful auction must just offer a price t_i to bidder i who accepts if her value is at least t_i. This is analogous to trying to extract a profit R from bidders $\mathbf{b}$ and actually getting R in profit when $\mathcal{F}(\mathbf{b}) \geq R$. The RSPE auction can then be viewed as randomly partitioning the bidders into two parts, treating one partition of the bids $\mathbf{b}'$ as a single bid with value $R' = \mathcal{F}^{(2)}(\mathbf{b}')$, the other partition $\mathbf{b}''$ as a single bid with value $R'' = \mathcal{F}^{(2)}(\mathbf{b}'')$, and then running the Vickrey auction on these two "bids." This intuition is crucial for the proof that follows as it implies that the profit of RSPE is the minimum of R' and R''.

Theorem 13.42 *The competitive ratio of RSPE is 4.*

PROOF As we discussed above, the profit of RSPE is $\min(R', R'')$. Thus, we just need to analyze $\mathbf{E}[\min(R', R'')]$.

Assume that $\mathcal{F}^{(2)}(\mathbf{b}) = kp$ has with $k \geq 2$ winners at price p. Of the k winners in $\mathcal{F}^{(2)}$, let k' be the number of them that are in $\mathbf{b}'$ and k'' the number that are in $\mathbf{b}''$. Since there are k' bidders in $\mathbf{b}'$ at price p, $R' \geq k'p$. Likewise, $R'' \geq k''p$. Thus,

$$\frac{\mathbf{E}[\text{RSPE}(\mathbf{b})]}{\mathcal{F}^{(2)}(\mathbf{b})} = \frac{\mathbf{E}[\min(R', R'')]}{kp} \geq \frac{\mathbf{E}[\min(k'p, k''p)]}{kp} = \frac{\mathbf{E}[\min(k', k'')]}{k} \geq \frac{1}{4}.$$

The last inequality follows from the fact that if $k \geq 2$ fair coins (corresponding to placing the winning bidders into either $\mathbf{b}'$ or $\mathbf{b}''$) are flipped then $\mathbf{E}[\min\{\#\text{heads}, \#\text{tails}\}] \geq k/4$.

It is evident that RSPE is no better than 4-competitive via an identical proof to that of the analogous result for RSOP. □

The currently best known competitive auction, which has a competitive ratio of 3.25, is based on generalizing the idea of RSPE: First, the bids are randomly partitioned into three parts, instead of two, with each part being treated as a single bid with value equal to its optimal single price revenue. Then the optimal 3-bidder auction is run on these three "bids."

The random partitioning and profit extraction approach is fairly general. For it to work successfully, it needs to be shown that a profit extractor for the benchmark exists, and that up to constant factors, the benchmark is preserved on a random sample of the agents. Notice that the consistency issue discussed in earlier sections is not relevant if only the agents in one partition win. This approach has been applied successfully to several other settings.

13.4.6 Consensus Estimation and Truthfulness with High Probability

We now look at an alternative reduction to the decision problem and an approach to competitive auctions that does not use random sampling. This approach leads to a truthful digital goods auction that is 3.39-competitive with $\mathcal{F}^{(2)}$. However, rather than presenting that result, we present a more general version of the approach with wider applicability. To achieve this greater level of generality, we will need to relax our solution concept and talk about *truthfulness with high probability*.

Definition 13.43 A randomized mechanism is *truthful with high probability*, say $1 - \epsilon$, if and only if for all i, v_i, b_i, and $\mathbf{b}_{-i}$, the probability that agent i benefits by bidding nontruthfully is at most ϵ, where the probability is taken over the coin flips of the mechanism. In other words, for all i, v_i, b_i, and $\mathbf{b}_{-i}$, $\mathbf{Pr}[u_i(v_i, \mathbf{b}_{-i}) \geq u_i(b_i, \mathbf{b}_{-i})] \geq 1 - \epsilon$.

The techniques presented in this section, when applied to the digital goods auction, result in a mechanism that is truthful with probability $1 - O(1/m)$ where m is the number of winners in $\mathcal{F}^{(2)}$. Thus, as the input instance grows and there are more winners, the probability that nontruthful reporting by the agents is beneficial approaches zero.

Let us first describe the general idea. Consider attempting to design an auction to compete with profit benchmark $\mathcal{G}$. Suppose that there exists a profit extractor for $\mathcal{G}$, ProfitExtract$_{\mathcal{G},R}$, which obtains profit R from $\mathbf{b}$ if $R \leq \mathcal{G}(\mathbf{b})$. Then the mechanism we would like to run is the following:

(i) Compute $R = \mathcal{G}(\mathbf{b})$.
(ii) Run ProfitExtract$_{\mathcal{G},R}$ on $\mathbf{b}$.

This fails of course because, generally, the R computed in Step (i) is a function of an agent's bid and therefore the agent could misreport their bid to obtain an R value that results in a more favorable outcome for them in Step (ii).

On the other hand, it is often the case that a single agent only contributes a small fraction to the profit $\mathcal{G}(\mathbf{b})$. In particular, suppose that there is some ρ such that for all i, $\mathcal{G}(\mathbf{b}_{-i}) \in [\mathcal{G}(\mathbf{b})/\rho, \mathcal{G}(\mathbf{b})]$. In this case $\mathcal{G}(\mathbf{b}_{-i})$ is a pretty good estimate of $\mathcal{G}(\mathbf{b})$. The idea then is to replace Step (i) above with

(i)' Compute $R = r(\mathcal{G}(\mathbf{b}))$.

where the probabilistic function $r(\cdot)$ is a *ρ-consensus β-estimate*:

Definition 13.44 A (randomized) function $r(\cdot)$ is a *ρ-consensus* if for all $V > 0$ with high probability all $V' \in [V/\rho, V]$ satisfy $r(V') = r(V)$.

Intuitively, if $r(\cdot)$ is a ρ-consensus then with high probability $r(\mathcal{G}(\mathbf{b})) = r(\mathcal{G}(\mathbf{b}_{-i}))$ for all i. This will imply that bidder i has very small probability of being able to influence the value of $r(\mathcal{G}(\mathbf{b}))$ and thus we will be able to guarantee truthfulness with high probability.

Definition 13.45 A (randomized) function $r(\cdot)$ is a *β-estimate* if for all $V > 0$ it satisfies $r(V) \leq V$ and $\mathbf{E}[r(V)] \geq V/\beta$.

Intuitively, if $r(\cdot)$ is a β-estimate, then $r(\mathcal{G}(\mathbf{b}))$ is close to, but less than, $\mathcal{G}(\mathbf{b})$. If this is the case, then running ProfitExtract$_{\mathcal{G},R}$ on $\mathbf{b}$, with $R = r(\mathcal{G}(\mathbf{b}))$, will extract a revenue R which is close to $\mathcal{G}(\mathbf{b})$.

Of course, even in Step (i)', R is a function of all the bids, so the resulting auction is not truthful. However, under some mild assumptions[2] it is possible to show that in the case that $r(\mathcal{G}(\mathbf{b}))$ is a consensus no bidder has an incentive to deviate and misreport their valuation. The resulting mechanism is truthful with high probability.

We now show how to construct the function $r(\cdot)$.

Definition 13.46 (r_α) Given $\alpha > 1$, the randomized function $r_\alpha(\cdot)$ picks U uniformly from $[0, 1]$ and is

$$r_\alpha(V) = \text{“}V \text{ rounded down to the nearest } \alpha^{i+U} \text{ for integer } i.\text{”}$$

Straightforward probabilistic analysis can be used to prove the following lemmas.

Lemma 13.47 *r_α is a ρ-consensus with probability* $1 - \log_\alpha \rho$.

Lemma 13.48 *r_α is a β-estimate with $\beta = \frac{\alpha \ln \alpha}{\alpha - 1}$.*

In the most general setting of single parameter agents, given the existence of a profit extractor for a benchmark $\mathcal{G}$, these lemmas can be combined with the *consensus estimate profit extraction* auction (CEPE) described above, to give the following theorem (see Exercise 13.11).

Theorem 13.49 *Given a monotone profit benchmark $\mathcal{G}$ for a single-parameter agent problem specified by cost function $c(\cdot)$ and a monotone profit extractor* ProfitExtract$_{\mathcal{G},R}$, *CEPE is $\frac{\alpha \ln \alpha}{\alpha-1}$-competitive and truthful with probability $1 - \log_\alpha \rho$ on inputs $\mathbf{b}$ satisfing $\mathcal{G}(\mathbf{b}_{-i}) \in [\mathcal{G}(\mathbf{b})/\rho, \mathcal{G}(\mathbf{b})]$.*

13.5 Frugality

We now turn to a radically different class of problems, in which the auctioneer is a *buyer* intent on hiring a team of agents to perform a complex task. In this model, each agent i

[2] What we need here is that the price offered to bidder i by ProfitExtract$_{\mathcal{G},R}$ is monotone in R, that $\mathcal{G}(\mathbf{b})$ is monotone in $\mathbf{b}$, and that $r(V)$ is monotone in V. See Exercise 13.11.

can perform a simple task at some cost $-v_i$ known only to himself. Based on the agents' bids b_i, the auctioneer must select a *feasible set* – a set of agents whose combined skills are sufficient to perform the complex task ($x_i = 1$ if agent i is selected) – and pay each selected agent some amount $-p_i$ (this is negative because we previously defined p_i as a transfer from the agent to the auctioneer). The setting is thus defined by the *set system* of feasible sets $(E, \mathcal{S})$, where E represents the set of agents and $\mathcal{S}$ represents the collection of feasible subsets of E. In terms of our single parameter framework, we have $c(\mathbf{x}) = 0$ if $\{i \mid x_i = 1\} \in \mathcal{S}$, and ∞ otherwise. Several special cases have received a great deal of attention.

Example 13.50 (path auctions) Here the agents own edges of a known directed graph (i.e., E is the set of edges) and the auctioneer wishes to purchase a path between two given nodes s and t (i.e., $\mathcal{S}$ is the set of all s-t paths).

Example 13.51 (spanning tree auctions) Here the agents own edges of a known connected, undirected graph, so again E is the set of edges, and the auctioneer wishes to purchase a spanning tree.

Whereas when the auctioneer was a seller, our goal was to design a mechanism to maximize his profit, here our goal is to design a mechanism to minimize the payments the auctioneer makes, i.e., to hire the team of agents as cheaply as possible. Hence, analyzing the *frugality* of a mechanism – the amount by which it overpays – becomes an important aspect of mechanism design, analogous to profit maximization. We study frugality here using worst-case competitive analysis, as in Section 13.4.

A first observation is that here, unlike the digital goods auctions we focused on in the previous sections, the auctioneer is interested only in a single "object," a feasible set. Thus, at a very high level, these problems are closest in spirit to the single item auction that we discussed in the context of profit maximization. For single-item auctions, in the absence of any prior information about agent's valuations, it is possible to show that the Vickrey auction is optimal, and, of course, achieves a profit equal to the value of the second highest bidder. Thus, a natural first mechanism to consider for hiring-a-team auctions is the VCG mechanism.

Consider a path auction where the graph consists of n parallel edges from s to t. This corresponds exactly to the case where the auctioneer is buying a single item, and the Vickrey mechanism will result in a payment equal to the cost of the second cheapest edge. Compare this to what happens in a graph consisting of two vertex disjoint s-t paths P and P', each with n edges. Suppose that each edge on path P has cost zero, and each edge on path P' has cost one, so that the total cost of path P is zero and of path P' is n. Then the VCG mechanism will purchase path P, and each edge on that path will be paid n, for a total auctioneer payment of n^2. Thus, here the VCG mechanism pays much more than the cost of the second cheapest path. Can we do better? How, in general, does the optimal truthful mechanism (in terms of competitive ratio) depend on the combinatorial structure of the set system?

13.5.1 Competitive Framework

As with our worst-case bounds from the previous section, the first issue that must be addressed to study frugality is the competitive framework and in particular the benchmark for comparison, which in this case is a *cost benchmark*.

We would like the frugality ratio to capture the overpayment of a mechanism with respect to a "natural" lower bound. One natural choice for this lower bound is the minimum payment by a nontruthful mechanism, in which case, the frugality ratio would characterize the cost of insisting on truthfulness.

Consider the mechanism $\mathcal{N}$ which, given the bids $\mathbf{b}$, selects the cheapest feasible set with respect to these bids, and pays each winning agent his bid (ties are broken in favor of the efficient allocation). This mechanism is a *pay-your-bid auction* and is not truthful. However, it does have at least one (full information) pure *Nash equilibrium*, i.e., a bid vector $\mathbf{b}$ such that, for each agent i, given the bids $\mathbf{b}_{-i}$ by all other agents, i maximizes his profit by bidding b_i. A Nash equilibrium can be considered a natural outcome of the mechanism $\mathcal{N}$, and the resulting net payments are thus a good cost benchmark. As we are interested in a lower bound, we define the *cheapest Nash value* $\mathcal{N}(\mathbf{v})$ to be the minimum payments by $\mathcal{N}$ over all of its Nash equilibria.[3]

To illustrate this definition, consider the case of an s-t path auction in which there are k parallel paths, as in our $k = 2$ path example above. Then, $\mathcal{N}(\mathbf{v})$ is precisely the cost of the second-cheapest path – the agents on the cheapest path will raise their bids until the sum of their bids equals the cost of the second-cheapest path, at which point they can no longer raise their bids. None of the other edges have incentive to raise their bids (as they are losing either way), nor to lower their bids, as they would incur a negative profit. Thus, the metric in this case makes perfect sense – it is the cost of the second cheapest solution disjoint from the actual cheapest.

With a cost benchmark in hand, we can now formalize a competitive framework for these problems.

Definition 13.52 The *frugality ratio* of truthful mechanism $\mathcal{M}$ for buying a feasible set in set system $(E, \mathcal{F})$ is

$$\sup_{\mathbf{v}} \frac{\mathcal{M}(\mathbf{v})}{\mathcal{N}(\mathbf{v})},$$

where $\mathcal{M}(\mathbf{v})$ denotes the total payments of $\mathcal{M}$ when the actual private values are $\mathbf{v}$, and $\mathcal{N}(\mathbf{v})$ is the cost benchmark, the cheapest Nash value with respect to the true values $\mathbf{v}$.

13.5.1.1 Bounds on the Frugality Ratio

The example we saw earlier shows that the VCG mechanism does not, in general, have small frugality ratio. There is, however, one class of set systems for which VCG is

[3] Here we consider only Nash eqilibria where nonwinners bid their true value, and ties are broken according to efficiency. We refer the reader to the relevant references for a justification of this restriction.

known to have optimal frugality ratio equal to 1, and is given in the following theorem (see Exercise 13.12).

Theorem 13.53 *VCG has frugality ratio one if and only if the feasible sets of the set system are the bases of a matroid.*

On the other hand, for path auctions, say when there are two parallel paths, each consisting of many agents, VCG can have frugality ratio $\Omega(n)$. The following lower bound shows that this bad case is not unique to the VCG mechanism.

Theorem 13.54 *Consider the path auction problem on a graph G consisting of two vertex disjoint s-t paths, P and P', where $|P| = n$, ($|P|$ is the number of edges on the path P), and $|P'| = n'$. Then any truthful mechanism for buying a path in this graph has frugality ratio at least $\Omega(\sqrt{nn'})$.*

PROOF Define $\mathbf{v}^{(P,i)}$ to be the vector of private values for agents in P, in which edge i on P has cost $1/\sqrt{n}$ (so its value is $v_i = -1/\sqrt{n}$), and all the rest of the edges in P have cost zero. Similarly, let $\mathbf{v}^{(P',j)}$ be the vector of private values for agents in P' in which edge j on P has cost $1/\sqrt{n'}$ and all the rest of the edges have cost zero. Let $\mathcal{M}$ be an arbitrary deterministic truthful path auction applied to this graph. Define a bipartite graph G' with a node for each edge in G and directed edges defined as follows: there is an edge from node i (corresponding to edge i in P) to node j (corresponding to edge j in P') (respectively an edge from j to i), if when running $\mathcal{M}$ on bid vector $(\mathbf{v}^{(P,i)}, \mathbf{v}^{(P',j)})$ path P' wins (resp. P wins).

Since there are nn' directed edges in this graph, there must be either a node i in P with at least $n'/2$ outgoing edges or a node j in P' with at least $n/2$ outgoing edges. In the former case, observe that, by the monotonicity of any truthful mechanism, P' must still win even if all edges in P' bid 0, and the payments to each of the relevant edges equal their threshold bid which is at least $1/\sqrt{n'}$. Thus the total payments are at least $\sqrt{n'}/2$. Since in this case the cheapest Nash equilibrium is $1/\sqrt{n}$, we obtain the desired lower bound. The analysis for the second case proceeds mutatis mutandis. □

The previous lower bound can be generalized to randomized mechanisms. An immediate corollary of this lower bound is that any truthful mechanism has frugality ratio n on a graph consisting of two vertex disjoint paths of length n. Thus, for this graph, VCG achieves the optimal frugality ratio.

On the other hand, if $n' = 1$, the above lower bound on the frugality ratio of any mechanism is $\sqrt{n}$. However, for the case of two parallel paths, one of length 1 and one of length n, VCG has a frugality ratio of n – the worst case is when the long path wins. This raises the question of whether or not there is a better truthful mechanism for this graph.

The answer to this question is "yes." The principle is fairly simple: if a large set is chosen as the winner, each of its elements will have to be paid a certain amount (depending on the other agent's bids). Hence to avoid overpayment, a mechanism should – within reason – give preference to smaller sets. Thus, rather than choosing the cheapest feasible set (i.e., the social welfare maximizing allocation), one could consider weighting the cost of feasible sets by weights that capture the relative sizes of those sets compared to other sets. To obtain a near-optimal mechanism for path auctions, the precise magnitude of these weights should be chosen to balance the worst-case frugality ratio over all potential combinations of winning sets.

To illustrate this, let us return to the graph consisting of two vertex disjoint paths. We can balance the worst-case frugality ratio by choosing the path that minimizes $\sqrt{|P|}c(P)$, where $c(P)$ is the cost of the path P, i.e., $c(P) = -\sum_{i \in P} v_i$. Notice that this mechanism uses a monotone allocation rule and hence is truthful. In this case, if the two paths are P and P', and, say P is chosen, the payments to each edge on P will be upper bounded by $\frac{\sqrt{|P'|}c(P')}{\sqrt{|P|}}$. This is because the threshold bid, and hence the payment, to an edge e on P is the largest value they could bid and still win. Thus, the total payments are

$$|P|\frac{\sqrt{|P'|}c(P')}{\sqrt{|P|}} \leq \sqrt{|P||P'|}c(P').$$

Since $c(P')$ is a lower bound on the cheapest Nash of $\mathcal{N}$, the ratio of payments to cheapest Nash is upper bounded by $\sqrt{|P||P'|}$. The same bound holds when P' is the selected path, resulting in a frugality ratio matching the lower bound to within a constant factor.

These ideas can be generalized to get a mechanism whose frugality ratio is within a constant factor of optimal, for any path auction problem, as well as some other classes of "hiring-a-team" problems. For most set systems, however, the design of a truthful mechanism with optimal or near-optimal frugality ratio is open.

13.6 Conclusions and Other Research Directions

In this chapter, we have surveyed the primary techniques currently available for designing profit-maximizing (or cost-minimizing) auctions in single-parameter settings. Even in the single-parameter setting, finding mechanisms with optimal competitive ratio (for selling problems) or optimal frugality ratio (for buying problems) is challenging and largely open. The situation is much worse once we get to multiparameter problems such as various types of combinatorial auctions. In these settings, numerous new challenges arise. For example, we do not have a nice, clean, simple characterization of truthfulness. Another issue is that it is completely unclear what profit benchmarks are appropriate.

In the rest of this section, we briefly survey a number of other interesting research directions.

Profit Benchmarks. In our discussions of competitive mechanisms, we saw that the profit benchmark of a mechanism was a crucial component of the competitive approach to optimal mechanism design. This raises a fundamental issue (that has yet to be adequately resolved even in simple settings): what makes a profit benchmark the "right" one?

Pricing. In this chapter, we have discussed private-value mechanism design for profit maximization. However, even the public value versions of some of these problems, which are essentially algorithmic pricing problems, are open.

Consider, for example, the problem of pricing links in a network. We are given a graph, and a set of consumer valuations. Each valuation is given as a triple (s_i, t_i, v_i), indicating that consumer i wishes to traverse a path from s_i to t_i and his value for traversing this path (i.e., the maximum price he is willing to pay) is v_i. With no restriction on pricing, the profit-maximizing solution to the public value problem is trivial: charge each consumer his value. However, such a pricing scheme is unreasonable for many reasons, the foremost of which is that this pricing scheme is highly unfair – different customers can get exactly the same product at different prices. An alternative pricing question is the following: define a set of prices for the edges in the graph (think of them as tolls) so as to maximize the total revenue collected. The model is that, for each consumer i, the network will collect the cost of the cheapest path from s_i to t_i with respect to the edge prices set, if that cost is at most v_i. This is just one example of an interesting algorithmic pricing problem that has recently received some attention. The vast majority of interesting combinatorial pricing problems are not well understood.

Derandomization. As we have seen, randomization is a very important tool in the design of competitive auctions. For example, randomization was used in digital goods auctions to skirt around impossibility results for deterministic symmetric auctions. Recently, however, deterministic constant competitive asymmetric digital goods auctions have been discovered. It is an interesting direction for future research to understand the general conditions under which one can derandomize competitive auctions, or design deterministic auctions from scratch. Unfortunately, standard algorithmic derandomization techniques do not work in truthful mechanism design because running the mechanism with the many possible outcomes of a randomized decision making procedure is no longer truthful. Thus, significant new ideas are required.

Fairness. We have focused our attention here on a single goal: profit maximization. In some situations, we desire that the mechanisms we design have other properties. For example, the randomized digital goods auctions that we have seen are not terribly fair – when we run, say, RSOP, some bidders pay a higher price than other bidders, and some bidders lose even though their value is higher than the price paid by other winning bidders. We say that outcomes of this type are not *envy-free*. (An auction is envy-free if after the auction is run, no bidder would be happier with someone else's outcome.)

It turns out that it is not possible to design a truthful, constant-competitive digital goods auction that is envy-free. Thus, alternative approaches have been explored for getting around this impossibility, including relaxing the solution concept to truthfulness with high probability, or allowing the mechanism to have a very small probability of producing a non-envy-free outcome.

More generally, designing auctions that both achieve high profit and are, in some sense, fair is a wide open direction for future research.

Collusion. All of the results presented in this chapter assume no collusion between the agents and indeed do not work properly in the presence of collusion. What can be done in the presence of collusion? For example, for digital goods auctions, it has been shown that it is not possible to design a truthful mechanism that is both profit-maximizing and collusion-resistant. However, using the approach of consensus estimates, it is possible to get around this impossibility with a mechanism that is truthful with high probability.

Bounded communication. How do we design revenue maximizing mechanisms when the amount of communication between the agents and the auctioneer is severely restricted? Bounded communication is particularly relevant in settings such as allocation of low-level resources in computer systems, where the overhead of implementing an auction will by necessity be severely restricted. Most of the work on this topic so far has focused on the trade-off between communication and efficiency. These results, of course, have implications for revenue maximization in a Bayesian setting due to the reduction from revenue maximization to surplus maximization via virtual valuations.

Bundling. Another interesting direction is bundling. It has been proved that in several settings, bundling items together may increase the revenue of the mechanism. However, the limits of this approach are not understood.

Repeated and online Games. Profit maximization (or cost minimization) in mechanism design arises in many settings, including resource allocation, routing and congestion control, and electronic commerce. In virtually every important practical application of mechanism design, the participants are dynamic. They arrive and depart over time, with decisions being made on an ongoing basis. Moreover, in many important applications, the same "game" is played over and over again. Our understanding of online, repeated games from the perspective of profit maximization is limited. For example, sponsored search auctions, discussed in Chapter 28, lead to many interesting open questions of this type.

Alternative solution concepts. Although truthfulness is not a goal in and of itself when the goal is profit maximization, it is a strong and appealing concept: First, truthful mechanisms obviate the need for agents to perform complex strategic calculations or gather data about their competitors. Second, in some cases, especially single-parameter problems, they simplify the design and analysis of protocols. Third, there is no loss of generality in restricting ourselves to truthful mechanisms if our plan is to implement a mechanism with dominant strategies (by the *revelation principle*). Fourth, in a number of settings, the revenue extracted by the natural truthful mechanism is the same as that extracted by natural nontruthful mechanisms (by the *revenue equivalence theorem*). A related point is that there are often natural and appealing variants of truthful mechanisms that achieve the same outcome (e.g., an English auction instead of a second-price auction). Finally, and this is important, *if we do not understand the incentive structure of a problem in a truthful setting, we are going to be very hard-pressed to understand it in any other setting.*

Having said all that, truthful mechanism design also has a number of significant drawbacks. For one thing, people often do not feel that it is safe to reveal their information to an auctioneer. An interesting alternative is to use an *ascending auction*, where published prices can only rise over time, or an *iterative auction*, where the auction protocol repeatedly queries the different bidders, aiming to adaptively elicit enough information about the bidders' preferences to be able to find an optimal or near-optimal outcome. What is the power of ascending and iterative auctions when the auctioneer's goal is profit maximization?

Truthfulness may also needlessly limit our ability to achieve our goals. This is manifested in terms of extreme limitations on the mechanism, exceedingly high competitive ratios, or simply impossibility. In the repeated game setting, these issues are much more severe. Thus, one of the most important directions for future research is to consider alternative solution concepts.

It has been shown that taking a small step away from truthfulness, e.g., to truthfulness with high probability, can enable us to overcome some impossibility results. Other solution concepts that have received consideration in the literature include Nash equilibria, correlated equilibria, and extensions of these. However, very little work has been done concerning the design of profit-maximizing mechanisms using these solution concepts.

In summary, major directions for future research are to figure out the correct solution concepts for use in profit-maximizing auction design, and to develop techniques for designing profit-maximizing mechanisms with respect to these concepts, especially in online and repeated settings. The key desiderata of an equilibrium or solution concept are that (a) there exist mechanisms that in this equilibrium achieve or at least approximate our profit maximization goals (and whatever other goals we may have) and (b) there are simple, rational, i.e., utility-maximizing, strategies for the players that lead to outcomes in this equilibrium.[4]

13.7 Notes

Profit maximization in mechanism design has an extensive history beginning, primarily, with the seminal paper of Myerson (1981) and similar results by Riley and Samuelson (1981). These papers study Bayesian optimal mechanism design in the less restrictive setting of Bayes-Nash equilibrium. However, Myerson's optimal mechanism is precisely the optimal truthful mechanism we present here. This material is by now standard and can be found in basic texts on auction theory (Krishna, 2002; Klemperer, 1999).

The material on approximately optimal mechanism design, including the empirical Myerson mechanism and the random sampling optimal price auction comes from Baliga and Vohra (2003), Segal (2003), and Goldberg et al. (2006). Precise analysis of convergence rates for unlimited supply auction settings is given in Balcan et al. (2005).

The worst-case competitive approach to profit maximization, the proof that no symmetric, deterministic auction is competitive and the RSOP auction were first introduced in Goldberg et al. (1999), Goldberg et al. (2001), and Goldberg et al. (2006). The proof

[4] Alternatively, we can ask that there are simple and reasonable behaviors that the players can follow that lead to outcomes in equilibrium and that the complexity of figuring out how to deviate advantageously is excessive.

of Theorem 13.36 can be found in Feige et al. (2005). The lower bound on the competitive ratio for digital goods auctions is taken from Goldberg et al. (2004). The notion of profit extraction, truthful mechanisms for reducing profit maximization to profit extraction, and the RSPE auction come from Fiat et al. (2002), Deshmukh et al. (2002), and Goldberg and Hartline (2003). The material on cost sharing that is the basis for many of the known profit extractors can be found in Moulin and Shenker (2001). The idea of consensus estimation and truthfulness with high probability come from Goldberg and Hartline (2003), Goldberg and Hartline (2003). Refinements and extensions of these results can be found in Goldberg and Hartline (2005) and Deshmukh et al. (2002). The material on frugality and path auctions is drawn from Archer and Tardos (2002), Elkind et al. (2004), and Karlin et al. (2005).

This survey focused primarily on auctions for digital goods. Further results on profit maximization (and cost minimization) in these and other settings can be found in Goldberg and Hartline (2001), Deshmukh et al. (2002), Fiat et al. (2002), Talwar (2003), Garg et al. (2002), Czumaj and Ronen (2004), Ronen and Tallisman (2005), Balcan et al. (2005), Borgs et al. (2005), Hartline and McGrew (2005), Immorlica et al. (2005), Aggarwal and Hartline (2006), and Abrams (2006).

The research issues surveyed in the conclusions of this chapter are explored in a number of papers. Profit benchmarks are discussed in Goldberg et al. (2006), Deshmukh et al. (2002), Hartline and McGrew (2005), and Karlin et al. (2005); algorithmic pricing problems in Guruswami et al. (2005), Hartline and Koltrun (2005), Demaine et al. (2006), Briest and Krysta (2006), Balcan and Blum (2006), and Glynn et al. (2006); derandomization of digital goods auctions via asymmetry in Aggarwal et al. (2005); fairness in Goldberg and Hartline (2003a); collusion in Schummer (1980) and Goldberg and Hartline (2005); bounded communication in Blumrosen and Nisan (2002) and Blumrosen et al. (in press); and bundling in Palfrey (1983) and Jehiel et al. (in press). Studies of profit maximization in online auctions can be found in Bar-Yossef et al. (2002), Lavi and Nisan (2000), Blum et al. (2004), Kleinberg and Leighton (2003), Hajiaghayi et al. (2004), and Blum and Hartline (2005). Truthfulness with high probability was studied in Archer et al. (2003) and Goldberg and Hartline (2003a, 2005). Alternative solution concepts are explored in Osborne and Rubinstein (1994), Lavi and Nisan (2005), and Immorlica et al. (2005), among others.

Bibliography

Z. Abrams. Revenue maximization when bidders have budgets. In *Proc. 17th ACM Symp. on Discrete Algorithms*, 2006.

G. Aggarwal, A. Fiat, A. Goldberg, J. Hartline, N. Immorlica, and M. Sudan. Derandomization of Auctions. In *Proc. 37th ACM Symp. Theor. Comp.* ACM Press, New York, 2005.

G. Aggarwal and J. Hartline. Knapsack auctions. In *Proc. 17th Annual ACM-SIAM Symp. Discrete Algorithms*, 2006.

A. Archer, C. Papadimitriou, K. Talwar, and E. Tardos. An approximate truthful mechanism for combinatorial auctions with single parameter agents. In *Proc. 14th ACM Symp. on Discrete Algorithms*. ACM/SIAM, 2003.

A. Archer and E. Tardos. Frugal path mechanisms. In *Proc. 13th ACM Symp. on Discrete Algorithms*, pp. 991–999. ACM/SIAM, 2002.

N. Balcan and A. Blum. Approximation algorithms and online mechanisms for item pricing. In *Proc. 8th ACM Conf. on Electronic Commerce*, 2006.

M. Balcan, A. Blum, J. Hartline, and Y. Mansour. Mechanism design via machine learning. In *Proc. 46th IEEE Symp. on Fdns. of Comp. Sci.*, 2005.

S. Baliga and R. Vohra. Market research and market design. *Adv. Theor. Econ.*, 3, 2003.

Z. Bar-Yossef, K. Hildrum, and F. Wu. Incentive-compatible online auctions for digital goods. In *Proc. 13th ACM Symp. on Discrete Algorithms*. ACM/SIAM, 2002.

A. Blum and J. Hartline. Near-optimal online auctions. In *Proc. 16th ACM Symp. on Discrete Algorithms*. ACM/SIAM, 2005.

A. Blum, V. Kumar, A. Rudra, and F. Wu. Online learning in online auctions. *Theoretical Computer Science*, 324:137–146, 2004.

L. Blumrosen and N. Nisan. Auctions with severely bounded communication. In *Proc. 43rd IEEE Symp. on Fdns. of Computer Science*, 2002.

L. Blumrosen, N. Nisan, and I. Segal. Auctions with severely bounded communication. *J. Artificial Intelligence Research*, in press.

C. Borgs, J. Chayes, N. Immorlica, M. Mahdian, and A. Saberi. Multi-unit auctions with budget-constrained bidders. In *Proc. 7th ACM Conf. on Electronic Commerce*, 2005.

P. Briest and P. Krysta. Single-minded unlimited-supply pricing on sparse instances. In *Proc. 17th ACM Symp. on Discrete Algorithms*, 2006.

A. Czumaj and A. Ronen. Towards generic low payment mechanisms for task allocation. In *23rd ACM SIGACT-SIGOPS Symp. on Princ. of Distributed Computing*, 2004.

E. Demaine, U. Feige, M. Hajiaghayi, and M. Salavatipour. Combination can be hard: Approximability of the unique coverage problem. In *Proc. 17th ACM Symp. on Discrete Algorithms*, 2006.

K. Deshmukh, A.V. Goldberg, J.D. Hartline, and A.R. Karlin. Truthful and competitive double auctions. In *Proc. 10th Europ. Symp. on Algorithms*. Springer, 2002.

E. Elkind, A. Sahai, and K. Steiglitz. Frugality in path auctions. In *Proc. 15th ACM Symp. on Discrete Algorithms*. ACM/SIAM, 2004.

U. Feige, A. Flaxman, J. Hartline, and R. Kleinberg. On the Competitive Ratio of the Random Sampling Auction. In *Proc. 1st Workshop on Internet and Network Economics*, 2005.

A. Fiat, A. Goldberg, J. Hartline, and A. Karlin. Generalized competitive auctions. In *Proc. 34th ACM Symp. on Theory of Computing*. ACM Press, 2002.

R. Garg, V. Kumar, A. Rudra, and A. Verma. Coalitional games on graphs: core structures, substitutes and frugality. Technical Report TR-02-60, UTCS, 2002.

P.W. Glynn, P. Rusmevichientong, and B. Van Roy. A non-parametric approach to multi-product pricing. *Oper. Res.*, 54(1):82–98, 2006.

A.V. Goldberg and J.D. Hartline. Competitive auctions for multiple digital goods. In *Proc. 9th Euro. Symp. on Algorithms*. Springer, 2001.

A. Goldberg and J. Hartline. Envy-free auctions for digital goods. In *Proc. 5th ACM Conf. on Electronic Commerce*. ACM Press, 2003.

A.V. Goldberg and J.D. Hartline. Competitiveness via consensus. In *Proc. 14th ACM Symp. on Discrete Algorithms*. ACM/SIAM, 2003.

A. Goldberg and J. Hartline. Collusion-resistant mechanisms for single-parameter agents. In *Proc. 16th ACM Symp. on Discrete Algorithms*, 2005.

A. Goldberg, J. Hartline, A. Karlin, and M. Saks. A lower bound on the competitive ratio of truthful auctions. In *Proc. 21st Symp. on Theoretical Aspects of Computer Science*. Springer, 2004.

A.V. Goldberg, J.D. Hartline, A. Karlin, M. Saks, and A. Wright. Competitive auctions. *Games and Economic Behavior*, 55:242–269, 2006.

A.V. Goldberg, J.D. Hartline, and A. Wright. Competitive auctions and digital goods. Technical Report STAR-TR-99.09.01, STAR Laboratory, InterTrust Tech. Corp., Santa Clara, CA, 1999.

A.V. Goldberg, J.D. Hartline, and A. Wright. Competitive auctions and digital goods. In *Proc. 12th ACM Symp. on Discrete Algorithms*, pp. 735–744. ACM/SIAM, 2001.

V. Guruswami, J. Hartline, A. Karlin, D. Kempe, C. Kenyon, and F. McSherry. On profit-maximizing envy-free pricing. In *Proc. 16th ACM Symp. on Discrete Algorithms*, 2005.

M. Hajiaghayi, D. Parkes, and R. Kleinberg. Adaptive limited-supply online auctions. In *Proc. 6th ACM Conf. on Electronic Commerce*, 2004.

J. Hartline and V. Koltrun. Near-Optimal Pricing in Near-Linear Time. In *Proc. 9th Workshop on Algorithms and Data Structures*. Springer-Verlag, 2005.

J. Hartline and R. McGrew. From optimal limited to unlimited supply auctions. In *Proc. 7th ACM Conf. Electronic Commerce*, pp. 175–182, 2005.

N. Immorlica, D. Karger, E. Nikolova, and R. Sami. First-price path auctions. In *Proc. 7th ACM Conf. on Electronic Commerce*, 2005.

P. Jehiel, M. Meyer ter Vehn, and B. Moldovanu. Mixed bundling auctions. *J. Econ. Theory*, in press.

A. Karlin, D. Kempe, and T. Tamir. Beyond vcg: Frugality in truthful mechanisms. In *Proc. 46th IEEE Symp. on Fdns. of Comp. Sci.*, 2005.

R. Kleinberg and T. Leighton. The value of knowing a demand curve: Bounds on regret for on-line posted-price auctions. In *Proc. 44th IEEE Symp. on Fdns. of Comp. Sci.*, 2003.

P. Klemperer. Auction theory: A guide to the literature. *J. Econ. Surveys*, 13:227–286, 1999.

V. Krishna. *Auction Theory*. Academic Press, 2002.

R. Lavi and N. Nisan. Competitive analysis of incentive compatible on-line auctions. In *The 2nd ACM Conf. Electronic Commerce*, pp. 233–241, 2000.

R. Lavi and N. Nisan. Online ascending auctions for gradually expiring goods. In *SODA 05*, 2005.

H. Moulin and S. Shenker. Strategyproof sharing of submodular costs: budget balance versus efficiency. *J. Econ. Theory*, 18:511–533, 2001.

R. Myerson. Optimal auction design. *Math. Operat. Res.*, 6:58–73, 1981.

M.J. Osborne and A. Rubinstein. *A Course in Game Theory*. MIT Press, Cambridge, MA, 1994.

T.R. Palfrey. Bundling decisions by a multiproduct monopolist with incomplete information. *Econometrica*, 51:463–484, 1983.

J. Riley and W. Samuelson. Optimal auctions. *Amer. Econ. Rev.*, 71:381–92, 1981.

A. Ronen and R. Tallisman. Towards generic low payment mechanisms for decentralized task allocation – A learning based approach. In *Proc. 7th Intl. IEEE Conf. E-Commerce Technology*, 2005.

J. Schummer. Almost dominant strategy implementation. *Games Econ. Behav.*, 48:154–170, 1980.

I. Segal. Optimal pricing mechanisms with unknown demand. *Amer. Econ. Rev.*, 93, 2003.

K. Talwar. The price of truth: Frugality in truthful mechanisms. In *Proc. 20th Annual Symp. on Theoretical Aspects of Computer Science*, 2003.

Exercises

13.1 What is the optimal Bayesian single-item auction when the seller values the item at $v_0 > 0$ and bidder valuations are i.i.d?

13.2 What is the optimal Bayesian auction for a seller with k identical items and $n > k$ bidders with i.i.d. valuations drawn uniformly from $[0, 1]$?

13.3 Consider a discrete setting where bidder i's probability of having valuation v_{ij} is f_{ij}. Derive the virtual valuations in this setting.

13.4 Show that the empirical Myerson mechanism, EM, applied to a single-item auction problem is identically the Vickrey auction.

13.5 The McDiarmid inequality is the following. Let $Y_1, \ldots, Y_n$ be independent random variables taking on values from a set A and $t : A^n \to \mathbb{R}$ a function satisfying

$$\sup_{\mathbf{y} \in A^n, y_i' \in A} |t(\mathbf{y}) - t(y_i', \mathbf{y}_{-i})| \leq c_i$$

for all i. Then for all $\gamma \geq 0$ we have:

$$\mathbf{Pr}\big[|t(Y_1, \ldots, Y_n) - \mathbf{E}[t(Y_1, \ldots, Y_n)]\,| \geq \gamma\big] \leq 2e^{2\gamma^2/\sum_{i=1}^n c_i^2}.$$

Prove Lemma 13.29 using the McDiarmid inequality.

13.6 Given a set of prices $\mathcal{Q}$ and bids $\mathbf{b}$ we say $\mathcal{Q}' \subset \mathcal{Q}$ is a γ*-cover* of $\mathcal{Q}$ on $\mathbf{b}$ if for all $q \in \mathcal{Q}$ there exists q' in $\mathcal{Q}'$ such that

$$\sum_i |q(b_i) - q'(b_i)| \leq \gamma \, \text{OPT}_{\mathcal{Q}}(\mathbf{b}).$$

(a) Prove that if $\mathcal{Q}'$ is a γ-cover of $\mathcal{Q}$ and all $q' \in \mathcal{Q}'$ are ϵ-good then all $q \in \mathcal{Q}$ are $(\epsilon + \gamma)$-good.

(b) Show that $\text{RSOP}_{\mathcal{Q}}$ on input $\mathbf{b}$ such that $\mathcal{Q}'$ is a δ-cover of $\mathcal{Q}$ is a $(1 - \epsilon - \gamma)$-approximation with probability $(1 - \delta)$ when $\text{OPT}_{\mathcal{Q}}(\mathbf{b}) \geq \frac{8h}{\epsilon^2} \ln(\frac{2|\mathcal{Q}'|}{h})$.

(c) For any $\mathbf{b}$ with $b_i \in [1, h]$, find a γ-cover of $\mathcal{Q} = \mathbb{R}$ of size $O(\frac{1}{\gamma} \log \log hn)$.

13.7 Give a deterministic asymmetric auction that is a 2-approximation to the optimal single price sale, $\text{OPT}_{\{1,h\}}(\mathbf{b})$, when $\mathbf{b}$ satisfies $b_i \in \{1, h\}$ for all i and at least two bids have value h.

13.8 Prove that no truthful digital goods auction with 2 bidders is best. In other words, show that for any truthful auction $\mathcal{A}$, there is another auction $\mathcal{A}'$ and an input $\mathbf{v}$ such that the profit of $\mathcal{A}'$ on input $\mathbf{v}$ is higher than that of $\mathcal{A}$.

13.9 Show how to use a β-competitive digital goods auction (against benchmark $\mathcal{F}^{(2)}(\mathbf{v})$) to obtain a β-competitive auction for the limited supply setting where only k identical units are available for sale (use benchmark $\mathcal{F}^{(2,k)}(\mathbf{v}) = \max_{2 \leq i \leq k} i\, v_{(i)}$).

13.10 Prove the correctness of ProfitExtract_R (Definition 13.40): prove that it is truthful and that it always obtains a profit of R when $\mathcal{F}(\mathbf{b}) \geq R$.

13.11 Given a monotone profit benchmark, $\mathcal{G}$; a profit extractor $\text{ProfitExtract}_{\mathcal{G},R}$ for $\mathcal{G}$ that is monotone in R; and a monotone function $r(V)$; consider the mechanism that (a) computes $R = r(\mathcal{G}(\mathbf{b}))$, and (b) runs $\text{ProfitExtract}_{\mathcal{G},R}(\mathbf{b})$.

(a) Prove that if $r(\mathcal{G}(\mathbf{v}_{-i})) = r(\mathcal{G}(\mathbf{v}))$ for particular bidder valuations $\mathbf{v}$ that bidding $b_i = v_i$ is an ex-post-equilibrium, i.e., if $\mathbf{b}_{-i} = \mathbf{v}_{-i}$, then an optimal response for bidder i is to bid $b_i = v_i$.

(b) Prove Theorem 13.49.

13.12 Prove that the VCG mechanism has frugality ratio one for spanning tree auctions.

CHAPTER 14

Distributed Algorithmic Mechanism Design

Joan Feigenbaum, Michael Schapira, and Scott Shenker

Abstract

Most discussions of algorithmic mechanism design (AMD) presume the existence of a trusted center that implements the required economic mechanisms. This chapter focuses on mechanism-design problems that are inherently distributed, i.e., those in which such a trusted center cannot be used. Such problems require that the AMD paradigm be generalized to *distributed algorithmic mechanism design* (DAMD).

We begin this chapter by exploring the reasons that DAMD is needed and why it requires different notions of economic equilibrium and computational complexity than centralized AMD. We then consider two DAMD problems, namely distributed VCG computation and multicast cost sharing, that illustrate the concepts of ex-post Nash equilibrium and network complexity, respectively.

The archetypal example of a DAMD challenge is interdomain routing, which we treat in detail. We show that, under certain realistic and general assumptions, one can achieve incentive compatibility in a collusion-proof ex-post Nash equilibrium without payments, simply by executing the Border Gateway Protocol (BGP), which is the standard for interdomain routing in today's Internet.

14.1 Introduction

To motivate the material in this chapter, we begin with a review of why game theory is relevant to computer science. As noted in the Preface to this book, computer science has traditionally assumed the existence of a central planner who dictates the algorithms used by computational nodes. While most nodes are assumed to be *obedient*, some nodes may malfunction or be subverted by attackers; such *byzantine* nodes may act arbitrarily.

This book's founding premise, in fact its *raison d'être*, is that there are many computational contexts in which there is no central (or cooperative) authority that controls the computational nodes. In particular, the Internet has changed computation from a largely local endeavor to one that frequently involves diverse collections of individuals (or machines acting on their behalf). For example, Web services, peer-to-peer systems, and even the interaction among packets on a wire are all cases in which individuals with no ties to each other, except perhaps a common interest in a document or simultaneous use of a link, find themselves interacting over the Internet.

In such cases, it is often best to treat the computational entities as independent and selfish *agents*, interested only in optimizing their own outcome. As a category of behavior, selfishness lies between the extremes of automatic obedience and byzantine disruption; selfish agents are unwilling to follow a central planner's instructions, but they do not act arbitrarily. Instead, their actions are driven by incentives, i.e., the prospect of good or bad outcomes. The field of mechanism design, described in Chapter 9, has shown how, by carefully constructing economic mechanisms to provide the proper incentives, one can use selfish behavior to guide the system toward a socially desirable outcome.[1] This book is devoted to exploring the interaction of incentives and computing, a topic that has come to be known as Algorithmic Mechanism Design (AMD).

Substituting a decentralized set of incentives for a central planner is a radical departure from traditional algorithm design. However, most work in this new field of AMD assumes the presence of a central computational facility that performs the calculations required by the economic mechanism. In auctions, for example, the agents each have independent goals and desires, but the computation to determine winners and payments is done by the auctioneer, and the hardness of the computation is evaluated using traditional notions of complexity (see, e.g., Chapters 1, 9, 11, and 12). As such, AMD considers novel incentive-related algorithm *design* but uses a standard centralized model of algorithm *execution*.

This combination of decentralized incentives but centralized computation applies in a wide variety of settings, many of which have been described elsewhere in this book. This approach requires transmitting all the relevant information to a single, trusted entity (hereafter called the *trusted center*), which is feasible if (i) such a trusted center exists, and (ii) the communication required to transmit the information and the resulting computational burden on the trusted center are both manageable. However, if either of these two assumptions fails, then a more decentralized approach must be considered.

As we discuss in more detail in Section 14.3 of this chapter, the problem of interdomain routing is one in which a decentralized approach is valuable. The Internet is a collection of smaller networks, called Autonomous Systems (ASes), that are stitched together by the interdomain-routing system to form the fully connected Internet. The interdomain-routing system therefore plays a crucial role in the functioning, even the existence, of the Internet. However, any approach to interdomain routing must address the challenges of trust, scalability, and reliability. The ASes are competing economic entities who want to optimize the routing outcome achieved and minimize the private information revealed; accordingly, they not only act selfishly but are also unwilling to share private information with, or cede control to, any trusted center. Thus, the ASes must distribute the route computation among themselves.

Even if trust were not an issue, scalability would drive the system toward distributed route computation. Centralizing the route computation would involve transmitting the entire AS graph to a central location and updating it whenever the graph changed.

[1] This desired outcome is often defined as the optimum of some global objective function, but a wide variety of social standards can also be used.

Given the considerable size and volatility of the AS graph, such a centralized route computation would be infeasible.

Similarly, the need for reliability, so crucial in the Internet, tends to favor decentralized designs. In a centralized design, the trusted center becomes a single point of failure; the fate of the entire network rests on this single system that could fail or be subverted. As an example of how scalability and reliability can drive the need for decentralization, we note that current intradomain-routing algorithms, which do not span more than one AS and so are designed with the assumption of mutual trust among routers, are almost all distributed.

Thus, there is a need to decentralize not only incentives but also computation; this leads to Distributed Algorithmic Mechanism Design (DAMD), which is the central focus of this chapter. DAMD has the same dual concerns, incentive compatibility, and computational complexity, as AMD, but it differs in two important respects.

The first difference involves the nature of complexity. DAMD's measure of computational complexity is quite different from AMD's, because the computation is distributed. Any measure of the complexity of a distributed algorithm executed over an interconnection network T must consider at least five quantities: the total number of messages sent over T, the maximum number of messages sent over any one link in T, the maximum size of a message, the local computational burden at each node, and the storage required at each node. If a distributed algorithm requires an excessive expenditure of any one of these resources, then its complexity is unacceptable. We will use the term *network complexity* to refer to these, and other, metrics of the difficulty of distributed implementation.

If the interconnection network T is trusted by all the agents and can feasibly serve as the trusted center, then the measure of complexity is the main difference between AMD and DAMD. However, if the distributed computation is done by the agents, then a second difference arises: the strategic nature of the computation itself. In AMD, agents can manipulate a game only by their selection of actions among those described in the *definition* of the economic mechanism; they cannot affect the *computation* of the mechanism, because all outcomes are computed (by the trusted center) from the vector of strategies, according to the definition of the mechanism. If the agents themselves perform the computation using some distributed algorithm, then they have more opportunities to manipulate the outcome, e.g., by misrepresenting the results of a local computation to a neighboring agent or, more drastically, by simply not communicating with that neighboring agent at all, in an attempt to exclude him from the game. Our assumption of selfishness requires that we consider all forms of manipulative behavior when designing the economic mechanism; in particular, this means that we must provide incentives that ensure selfish agents find it in their best interest to perform the distributed computation correctly.

While this chapter discusses the use of incentives to prevent these other forms of manipulation, one can also use cryptographic protocols to replace trusted parties in mechanism computation. This active area of study is covered in Chapter 8 of this volume.

In the next section of this chapter, we briefly discuss two examples of DAMD. Our third section is devoted to an in-depth exploration of the incentive issues in interdomain routing. We conclude with open questions and exercises.

14.2 Two Examples of DAMD

As noted above, DAMD differs from AMD in two respects: the additional ways in which the agents can influence the outcome (referred to hereafter as "computational manipulation") and the measure of computational complexity (the aforementioned "network complexity").

Here, we briefly discuss two examples of DAMD that illustrate these issues. The first is a distributed implementation of a VCG mechanism (see Chapter 9); we will ignore network complexity in this example and focus on how to prevent manipulation of the computation. The second example is sharing the cost of a multicast transmission; it illustrates the notion of network complexity but, because we assume the presence of a trusted computational infrastructure, does not involve computational manipulation.

14.2.1 Distributed Implementation of VCG

We now discuss one way a set of agents can jointly implement a VCG mechanism without fear of manipulation. We start with a set of outcomes O and a collection of agents N, each with his own valuation v_i over those outcomes. In our notation, $\tilde{o}$ is an outcome that maximizes the *total social welfare* of the agents. That is, $\tilde{o} = \text{argmax}_{o \in O} \sum_{i \in N} v_i(o)$, W is the maximum total social welfare value, and W_{-i} denotes the maximum total social welfare of all agents except the i'th. For convenience, we focus on the particular mechanism in which $p_i = W_{-i} - W + v_i(\tilde{o})$, where p_i is the payment by agent i.

We assume that there is no trusted center; i.e., that the computation of the VCG mechanism must be done by the agents themselves. However, we do presume the existence of some central *enforcer* whose responsibility it is to implement the outcome $\tilde{o}$ decided upon by the agents and collect the payments; the enforcer can impose severe penalties if the agents do not agree on an outcome.

To see how a distributed computation can be manipulated, consider a network in which the nodes are connected in a ring, and there is exactly one agent at each node. Assume that the agents are computing a second-price auction of a single good by passing around a message containing the top two bids for that good. If an agent puts his bid on top and puts in a very low bid for the second bid, then he can get the good more cheaply (as long as these fields are not overwritten by some later agents that have higher bids).

More generally, consider any distributed algorithm A, capable of running over an arbitrary number of computational nodes, that takes as input a set of agent valuations and produces the maximizing outcome and the payments. As the preceding example suggests, if we run A over any subset of N to compute $\tilde{o}$, W, and each W_{-i}, then there is the possibility that an agent can manipulate the computation.

One way to avoid this is *replication*: Break the agents into two groups, have them exchange all their valuations, and then have each group compute its own version of $\tilde{o}$ and the p_i. If the two groups agree on the outcomes and payments, then those outcomes and payments are adopted; if not, all agents suffer a severe penalty. Here, an agent plays different roles in the two versions of the computation: In the first, his role is to help compute the outcome and payments; in the other, his role is to provide his valuation so that others may perform this computation. For the first version, an agent i could engage in arbitrary computational manipulation in an attempt to obtain a more favorable p_i or choose an outcome he prefers to the socially optimal one; in the second version, all he could do is lie about v_i. Because the VCG mechanism is strategyproof, the agent will reveal truthfully to the other computational group and therefore, to avoid a severe penalty for inconsistency, will carry out the computation faithfully.

Notice that faithful computation is not a dominant strategy. If, for instance, all the other agents decide to choose a suboptimal outcome, then agent i is better off going along with that choice rather than causing a disagreement (and triggering the severe penalty). However, if all the other agents faithfully execute the prescribed algorithm A, then agent i is best off doing so as well. Thus, the most natural solution concept when considering computational manipulation is not dominant strategies but instead ex-post Nash equilibrium, which was defined in Chapter 9. We will expand on this point further when we discuss interdomain routing in Section 14.3 below.

In this example, we have focused on computational manipulation and ignored network complexity. In our next example, we do the opposite.

14.2.2 Sharing the Cost of a Multicast Transmission

Multicast is an Internet packet-transmission mode that delivers a single packet to multiple receivers. It is accomplished by setting up a shared delivery tree that spans all the receivers; packets sent down this tree are replicated at branch points so that no more than one copy of each packet traverses each link. Because it is far more efficient than traditional unicast transmission (in which packets are sent only to a single destination), multicast is particularly appropriate for distributing popular real-time content, such as movies, to a large number of receivers.

Internet content distribution both provides benefits and incurs cost, which we can model as follows. We assume that there are agents, located at various places in the network, who would derive some utility from receiving the content and that a cost is incurred each time the content is transmitted over a network link. The policy question is how these costs and benefits should be distributed; more specifically, which agents should receive the content, and how much should each agent pay?

To define the problem more precisely, we consider a user population P residing at a set of network nodes N that are connected by bidirectional network links L. The multicast flow emanates from a source node $\alpha_o \in N$; given any set of receivers $S \subseteq P$, the transmission flows through a *multicast tree* $T(S) \subseteq L$ rooted at α_o that spans the nodes at which users in S reside. We make the natural assumption that routing is monotonic, i.e., that $S_1 \subseteq S_2 \Rightarrow T(S_1) \subseteq T(S_2)$.

Each link $l \in L$ has an associated cost $c(l) \geq 0$ that is known by the nodes on each end, and each user i assigns a utility value u_i to receiving the transmission. The total cost $C(S)$ of reaching a set S of receivers is given by $C(S) = \sum_{l \in T(S)} c(l)$, and the net welfare $NW(S)$ of delivering content to this set of receivers is given by $NW(S) = \sum_{i \in S} u_i - C(S)$.

A *cost-sharing mechanism* determines which users receive the multicast transmission and how much each receiver is charged. We let $p_i \geq 0$ denote how much user i

is charged and σ_i denote whether user i receives the transmission; $\sigma_i = 1$ if the user receives the multicast transmission, and $\sigma_i = 0$ otherwise.

The mechanism M is then a pair of functions $M(u) = (\sigma(u), p(u))$. It is important to note that both the inputs and the outputs of these functions are distributed throughout the network; that is, each user inputs his u_i from his network location, and the outputs $\sigma_i(u)$ and $p_i(u)$ must be delivered to him at that location. The practicality of deploying the mechanism on the Internet depends on the feasibility of computing the functions $\sigma(u)$ and $p(u)$ and distributing the results.

In our model, it is the *agents* who are selfish. The routers (represented by tree nodes), links, and other network-infrastructural components are obedient. The cost-sharing algorithm does not know the individual utilities, and so users could lie about them, but once they are reported to the network infrastructure (e.g., by sending them to the nearest router), the algorithms for computing $\sigma(u)$ and $p(u)$ can be reliably executed by the network. Thus, our interest here is in network complexity, not computational manipulation.

Given the selfish nature of agents, the mechanism should be strategyproof, i.e., revealing u_i truthfully should be a dominant strategy. There are two other desirable features one would want in a cost-sharing mechanism: budget balance (the sum of the charges p_i covers the total cost of transmitting the content) and efficiency (the total welfare is maximized). The classic result of Laffont and Green, as reviewed in Chapter 9, implies that no strategyproof mechanism with quasilinear utilities can achieve both budget balance and efficiency[2]; we therefore consider two separate mechanisms, one that achieves budget balance and one that achieves efficiency.

To achieve efficiency, we consider a VCG mechanism called *marginal cost* (MC). Let $\tilde{S}$ denote the largest set that maximizes $NW(S)$ (this is uniquely defined), and let $\widetilde{NW} = NW(\tilde{S})$; similarly, $\widetilde{NW}_{-i}$ is the maximum value over all S of $NW(S - i)$. Then the MC mechanism chooses the receiver set $\tilde{S}$ and sets payments $p_i = \sigma_i u_i - \widetilde{NW} + \widetilde{NW}_{-i}$.

For budget balance, we choose the Shapley Value (SH) mechanism. The mechanism shares the cost of each link equally among all the agents downstream of that link; an agent i is downstream of a link l if $l \in T(\{i\})$. To determine which agents receive the transmission, we first start with $S = P$ and compute the charges. We then eliminate any agent for which the charge exceeds the agent's utility (i.e., $p_i > u_i$) and recursively prune the receiver set until all agents within the set have utilities greater than or equal to their charge. The cross-monotonic nature of these charges (an agent is never charged less after another agent leaves the receiver set) guarantees that the resulting set is well defined, independent of the order in which agents are eliminated. To see why the ordering does not matter, consider the following. We say that an elimination (or pruning) is "legal" if the node to be removed is charged more than its utility; an elimination ordering is "legal" if each individual pruning is legal. We note that, if an agent i is charged more than his utility when the set S of agents remains, then this continues to hold when any subset of S remains (because cross-monotonicity requires

[2] More precisely, the Laffont–Green result reviewed in Chapter 9 shows that the only strategyproof, welfare-maximizing mechanisms with quasi-linear utilities are the VCG mechanisms, which are known not to be budget-balanced. Myerson and Satterthwaite have shown a more general result about the impossibility of achieving efficient and budget-balanced allocations with rational agents; see Chapter 9 for details.

that i's charges are at least as great). This means that the concatenation of any two legal elimination orderings is also a legal elimination ordering (where we ignore duplicate prunings). For example, if $(1, 5, 7, 3)$ and $(7, 2, 5, 8)$ are two legal orderings, then $(7, 2, 5, 8, 1, 3)$ is also legal, as is $(1, 5, 7, 3, 2, 8)$. Thus, if any two subsets S and S' can be arrived at by sequences of legal eliminations, then $S \cap S'$ can also be arrived at by a sequence of legal eliminations.

It is easy to see that both MC and SH are polynomial-time computable by centralized algorithms; so the issue is whether it is hard to implement them in a distributed fashion. Certainly any mechanism can be computed by sending all the valuations to a single node, doing the computation, and then returning the results to each agent. In the worst case, this would require sending $\Omega(|P|)$ bits over some number of links, which is clearly not desirable. It turns out that we cannot do substantially better than this for the SH mechanism.

Theorem 14.1 *Any distributed algorithm, deterministic or randomized, that computes the SH multicast cost-sharing mechanism must send $\Omega(|P|)$ bits over linearly many links in the worst case.*

By contrast, it is possible to compute MC using only two short messages per link and two simple calculations per node. This is done in two phases, the first a bottom-up traversal in which welfare values are computed for each subtree of $T(P)$ and the second a top-down traversal in which membership bits σ_i and cost shares p_i are computed for each $i \in P$. The algorithms are given in Figures 14.1 and 14.2. In these figures, $V(P)$ denotes the node set of tree $T(P)$, $Ch(\alpha)$ the set of children of node α, $res(\alpha)$ the set of users resident at node α, u^α the sum of utilities of users in $res(\alpha)$, c^α the cost of the link connecting α to its parent in $T(P)$, and $T^\alpha(P)$ the union of the subtree rooted at α and the link connecting α to its parent.

The reason that this simple two-phase algorithm suffices is that computing the MC cost share p_i does not require a from-scratch computation of NW_{-i}. Rather, it is enough to compute W^α for every node α in $V(P)$ during the computation of NW. Suppose that

```
At node α ∈ V(P)
    After receiving a message A^β from each child β ∈ Ch(α)
        W^α ← u^α + (Σ_{β∈Ch(α)} A^β) − c^α
        If W^α ≥ 0 then
        {
            σ_i ← 1 for all i ∈ res(α)
            Send W^α to parent(α)
        }
        Else
        {
            σ_i ← 0 for all i ∈ res(α)
            Send 0 to parent(α)
        }
```

Figure 14.1. Bottom-up traversal: Computing welfare values.

Initialize: Root α_o sends W^{α_o} to each of its children.
For each $\alpha \in V(P) - \{\alpha_o\}$
    After receiving message A from $parent(\alpha)$
        //Case 1: $T^\alpha(P) \cap T(\tilde{S}) = \emptyset$.
        //Set σ_i's properly at α and propagate non-membership downward.
        If $\sigma_i = 0$, for all $i \in res(\alpha)$, or $A < 0$, then
        {
            $p_i \leftarrow 0$ and $\sigma_i \leftarrow 0$ for all $i \in res(\alpha)$
            send -1 to β for all $\beta \in Ch(\alpha)$
        }
        //Case 2: $T^\alpha(P) \cap T(\tilde{S}) \neq \emptyset$.
        //Compute cost shares and propagate minimum welfare value downward.
        Else
        {
            $A \leftarrow \min(A, W^\alpha)$
            For each $i \in res(\alpha)$
                If $u_i \leq A$, then $p_i \leftarrow 0$, else $p_i \leftarrow u_i - A$
            For each $\beta \in Ch(\alpha)$
                Send A to β
        }

Figure 14.2. Top-down traversal: Computing membership bits and cost shares.

$i \in res(\beta)$ and that $y_i(u)$ is the smallest W^α of any node α on the path from β to the root of $T(P)$. If $u_i \leq y_i(u)$, then removing i from the set of potential receivers does not change the set of nodes to which the content is delivered. If $u_i > y_i(u)$, then removing i from the set of potential receivers *does* change the set of nodes, and the resulting difference $\widetilde{NW} - \widetilde{NW}_{-i}$ is $y_i(u)$. The proofs of these facts are left as an exercise for the reader.

Theorem 14.2 *MC cost sharing requires exactly two messages per link. There is an algorithm that computes the cost shares by performing one bottom-up traversal of $T(P)$, followed by one top-down traversal.*[3]

More information about AMD for cost sharing can be found in Chapter 15.

14.3 Interdomain Routing

We now turn to the problem of interdomain routing. To provide reachability between hosts, the various ASes that make up the Internet must be interconnected. However, as

[3] The algorithm is provably optimal with respect to the number of messages sent but is not known to be optimal with respect to the maximum size of a message. However, the maximum size of a message is polynomial in $\max_l \text{size}(c(l))$ and $\max_i \text{size}(u_i)$ and polylogarithmic in $|P|$ and $|N|$, and the two local computations required at each node are fast and space-efficient.

we noted earlier, the ASes are economically independent entities (indeed, frequently competitors), and there is no trusted center to which they are all accountable that could assign interdomain routes. Thus, the ASes themselves must compute the routes in a distributed fashion. The route computation scheme must handle three problematic aspects of interdomain routing: (i) there is a large number of ASes; (ii) different ASes have different criteria for choosing one route over another, and these criteria may conflict; and (iii) the collection of ASes and the links between them change frequently. All of these factors make DAMD a highly suitable approach to interdomain routing.

We can formally define the interdomain-routing problem as follows. The network topology is defined in terms of the *AS graph* $G = (N, L)$, where each node in $N = \{1, \ldots, n\}$ corresponds to an AS in the Internet, and each link in L corresponds to a direct connection between a pair of neighboring ASes. Because routing protocols typically compute routes for each destination independently, we can choose a particular destination AS d and let P^i be the set of all loop-free paths from i to d in G that are not removed from consideration.[4] An *interdomain-routing protocol* allocates to each source node $i \in N$ a route $R_i \in P^i$.

We now describe this problem in greater detail, first from the networking perspective and then from the mechanism-design perspective.

14.3.1 Networking Perspective

From a networking or protocol-design point of view, any wide-area routing protocol must fulfill, to some extent, the following requirements:

- For reasons of trust, scale, and robustness, the routing protocol must be *distributed*, carried out by the ASes themselves.
- In order to reduce routing state, the routing protocol must use *destination-based forwarding*; i.e., all routing decisions must be based solely on a packet's destination. Each AS has a single next hop for the destination d, and the resulting *route allocation* $T_d = \{R_1, \ldots, R_n\}$ forms a confluent tree to the destination d.
- The routing protocol should be *adaptive*, adjusting to the current network topology without relying on any *a priori* topology information.
- The routing protocol should be *time-efficient*, *communication-efficient* (in its use of communication between the ASes), and *space-efficient* (in its use of the storage space that each individual AS needs in order to participate in the protocol).

These requirements are satisfied by each of the common routing-protocol designs – namely *distance-vector*, *link-state*, and *path-vector* – although these designs differ in their space requirements. However, interdomain routing has one additional requirement:

- The routing protocol must produce loop-free routes even while individual ASes make *autonomous* decisions about which routes are preferable.

[4] A path from i to d could be "removed from consideration" because it is *filtered* by i or one of i's neighbors or because of link or node failures.

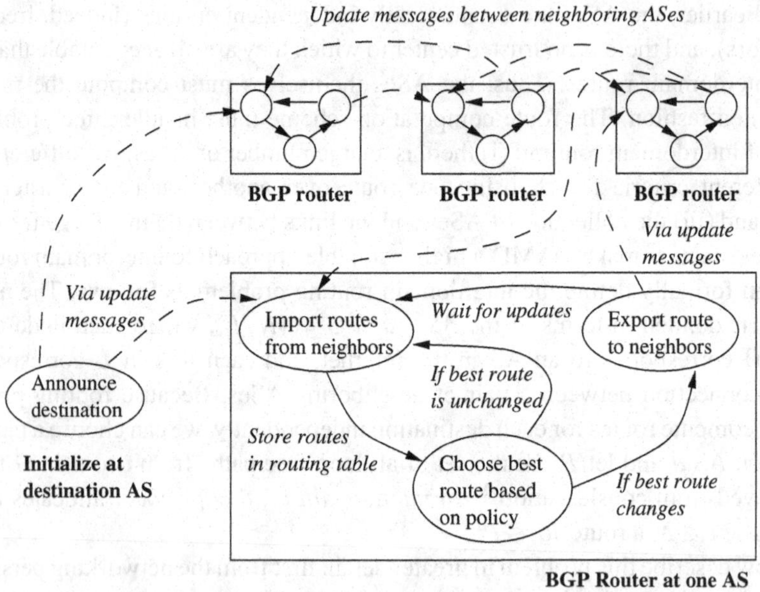

Figure 14.3. Route computation using a path-vector protocol.

Of the common routing-protocol designs, only path-vector satisfies this requirement. As a result, the current standard protocol for Internet interdomain routing, the Border Gateway Protocol (BGP), is a path-vector protocol. To see why path-vector is a suitable design choice, we describe BGP in more detail.

BGP allows adjacent nodes to exchange information through *update messages* that announce newly chosen routes (see illustration in Figure 14.3); a route announcement contains the entire path to the destination (the list of ASes in the path). A path-vector protocol (like most other routing protocols) computes routes to every destination AS independently; so we can focus on routes to a single destination d. The route-computation process is initialized when d announces itself to its neighbors by sending update messages. The rest of the routing tree to d is built recursively, as knowledge of how to reach d propagates through the network via subsequent update messages. We assume that the network is *asynchronous*, meaning that the arrival of update messages along selective links can be delayed.

The routing process at a particular node i has three stages that are iteratively applied:

- **(i)** *Importing routes*: Routes to d are received via update messages from its neighbors. Node i has an *import policy* that specifies which of the routes it is willing to consider. All such importable routes are stored in an internal *routing table*. At any given time, i's internal routing table contains the latest importable routes.
- **(ii)** *Route selection*: If there is more than one route to d in the routing table (i.e., more than one of i's neighbors has announced an importable route to d), node i must choose one (expressing a local preference over routes).
- **(iii)** *Exporting routes*: Whenever there is a change to i's best route, it announces the newly selected route to some or all of its neighbors using update messages. Node i has

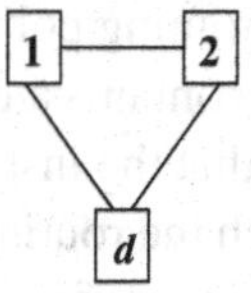

Figure 14.4. When AS 1 prefers route 12*d* to 1*d*, and AS 2 prefers route 21*d* to 2*d*, BGP (or any other path-vector protocol) can oscillate indefinitely.

an *export policy* that determines, for each neighbor j, which routes it is willing to announce to j at any given time.

AS autonomy is expressed through the freedom each AS has in choosing its routes, its import policy, and its export policy. These choices are based on local policy considerations and need not be coordinated with any other AS. The inclusion of the entire path in route announcements allows ASes to avoid routes with loops even while making otherwise arbitrary policy choices. Link-state or distance-vector routing protocols can avoid loops only if all ASes use the same criterion to choose routes and thus do not support autonomy.

One design requirement not explicitly listed here is *convergence*. Clearly the routing protocol should eventually enter a *stable* state in which every node prefers its currently chosen route to all others in its routing table, and all routing tables reflect the current route choices of its neighbors. Moreover, we would like the protocol to be *robust*, converging for every AS graph obtained by removing any set of nodes and links from the original instance.

Unfortunately, while the path-vector form of routing prevents loops, it does not ensure convergence; the routing announcements can enter a persistent oscillatory state. Consider the simple example depicted in Figure 14.4. Both nodes 1 and 2 would rather send traffic through the other source node than send traffic directly to the destination. Let us now simulate the execution of a path-vector protocol in the worst-case scenario: The computation is initialized when d announces itself to its two neighbors, nodes 1 and 2. At this point in time, these direct paths are the only routes available to d. Hence, 1 and 2 will choose the routes $1d$ and $2d$, respectively, and inform each other, via update messages, of their selected routes. Upon receipt of these update messages, nodes 1 and 2 will change their selected routes to, respectively, $12d$ and $21d$. However, now that none of the direct routes is being used, the indirect routes are no longer viable; so 1 and 2 are forced to return to their former routes $1d$ and $2d$, and the oscillation continues indefinitely. Note that, if the network had started with node 1's choosing and announcing $1d$ (having not yet seen an announcement of route $2d$), and then node 2 had chosen $21d$ (having seen route $1d$ announced before it chose and announced its own direct route $2d$), then no further changes would occur, and the network would be in a stable configuration; thus, convergence and oscillations can depend on timing.

A large body of networking research has addressed the problem of providing sufficient conditions on routing policies for the convergence of path-vector protocols. There is an inherent trade-off between the desired autonomy at the local level and robustness (in the sense defined above) at the global level. However, there is a known sufficient condition on policies, called *no dispute wheel*, that guarantees robust convergence while allowing fairly expressive local routing policies. Any network instance on which a path-vector protocol might oscillate contains a dispute wheel and, more importantly, the absence of a dispute wheel means that the instance and every subinstance of it have unique stable route allocations to which the routing protocol converges, i.e., no dispute wheel implies robustness. The following definition provides an equivalent sufficient condition:

Definition 14.3 Define two relations on permitted routes:

(i) Let $R_1 \ominus_1 R_2$ iff R_1 is a subpath of R_2 that ends at d.

(ii) Let $R_1 \ominus_2 R_2$ iff $\exists i \in N : R_1, R_2 \in P^i$, and i prefers R_1 over R_2.

Let $\oslash = (\ominus_1 \cup \ominus_2)^*$ be the transitive closure of $\ominus_1, \ominus_2$. Note that $\oslash$ is inherently reflexive and transitive.

An interdomain-routing instance has *no dispute wheel* iff $R_1 \oslash R_2$ and $R_2 \oslash R_1$ together imply that R_1, R_2 start at the same node. (Informally, this is antisymmetry of $\oslash$ except that ties are allowed in valuations.)

Let us revisit the example in Figure 14.4. Recall that, on this instance, path-vector protocols may oscillate forever. This anomaly is manifested by the following dispute wheel:

$$1d \ominus_1 21d \ominus_2 2d \ominus_1 12d \ominus_2 1d.$$

So far, our discussion of interdomain routing has focused on traditional networking concerns. We now consider the problem from a mechanism-design perspective.

14.3.2 Mechanism-Design Perspective

The policy autonomy in BGP, which was previously allowed to be an arbitrary choice, can be seen as expressing a preference that an AS is selfishly trying to satisfy. To do so, we let each source node i have a private *valuation function* $v_i : S^i \rightarrow R_{\geq 0}$, where S^i is the set of all simple (noncyclic) routes from i to d in the complete graph we get by adding links to G.[5] The valuation function v_i specifies the "monetary value" of each route to source node i. We assume that $v_i(\emptyset) = 0$ and that, for all pairs of routes R_1 and R_2 through different neighboring nodes, $v_i(R_1) \neq v_i(R_2)$.[6] The routing policy of each node i is thus captured by v_i.

While each individual AS is trying to optimize its individual welfare, society as a whole has an interest in reaching a globally desirable outcome. While there are many goals one could choose, we shall focus here on *social-welfare maximization*. A route

[5] Because we do not assume that nodes know the network topology, we cannot assume that they can distinguish valid routes from invalid ones. Thus, the valuation functions are defined over the complete graph to model the possibility of nodes' announcing nonexistent routes.

[6] This assumption is consistent with current interdomain routing: Because at most one route to each destination can be installed in a router's forwarding table, nodes have some way to break ties, e.g., based on the next hop's IP address; so, valuations can be adjusted accordingly to match this. However, because only one route per neighbor is considered at a time, ties in valuation are permitted for routes through the same neighboring node.

allocation T_d maximizes the social welfare if

$$T_d = \text{argmax}_{T=\{R_1,\ldots,R_n\}} \sum_{i=1}^{n} v_i(R_i).$$

If we view a routing protocol from a mechanism-design perspective, it should satisfy the following two requirements:

- If implemented honestly, the protocol should maximize the social welfare.
- The protocol should be incentive-compatible, in that no AS is motivated to deviate from the actions it is asked to perform.

The precise definition of incentive compatibility needed in this setting depends on the nature of the solution concept (or economic equilibrium). We shall now discuss in detail the solution concept that we adopt for interdomain-routing mechanisms. Recall from Section 14.1 that DAMD poses inherently different strategic challenges from AMD, because, in the absence of a trusted center, the computation is performed by the strategic agents themselves. This allows the computational nodes to manipulate the mechanism strategically in ways other than "lying" about their private types. They can, for instance, alter the computation to their own benefit or refuse to pass messages if it suits their needs. In such a scenario, aiming for strategyproofness might be futile, because it is unlikely that there is a single computational behavior that is optimal no matter what the other agents do.

A more suitable solution concept is ex-post Nash equilibrium. The need to settle for ex-post Nash, rather than strategyproofness, can be viewed as the cost of distributing mechanism computation among the agents. We shall now formally define ex-post Nash in a distributed setting: Consider a computational network with n nodes and a set of possible outcomes O. Each node i has a private type $\theta_i \in \Theta_i$ and a utility function $u_i : O \times \Theta_i \rightarrow R$.

Definition 14.4 A *distributed mechanism* d^M is a 3-tuple $d^M = (\Sigma, g, s^M)$, where $\Sigma = (\Sigma_1, \ldots, \Sigma_n)$ is the *feasible strategy space* of the nodes, $g : \Sigma \rightarrow O$ is the *outcome function* computed by the mechanism, and $s^M = (s_1^M, \ldots, s_n^M) \in \Sigma$ is the *prescribed strategy*.

For every node i, $s_i^M \in \Sigma_i$ can be thought of as the algorithm that the mechanism designer intends i to execute. s_i^M is parameterized by the private type θ_i of the node i, with $s_i^M(\theta_i)$ specifying which actions node i should perform in every state of the mechanism and network, given that its type is θ_i.

Definition 14.5 A strategy profile $s^* \in \Sigma$ is an *ex-post Nash equilibrium* of a distributed mechanism $d^M = (\Sigma, g, s^M)$, if

$$u_i(g(s_1^*(\theta_1), \ldots, s_n^*(\theta_n)), \theta_i) \geq u_i(g(s_1^*(\theta_1), \ldots, s_i'(\theta_i), \ldots, s_n^*(\theta_n)), \theta_i)$$

for every node i, for every possible strategy $s_i' \in \Sigma_i$, for every possible θ_i, and for all possible private types $\theta_1, \ldots, \theta_{i-1}, \theta_{i+1}, \ldots, \theta_n$ of the other nodes.

Although weaker than a dominant-strategy equilibrium, ex-post Nash equilibrium is a fairly strong solution concept; it does not require strategic agents to have any knowledge of or to make any assumptions about the private types of other agents. Contrast this with the standard Nash-equilibrium concept, in which agents are assumed to know the private types of other agents; in the interdomain-routing context, this would mean that ASes are assumed to know the local routing policies of other ASes, which is certainly unrealistic.

The ex-post Nash equilibrium solution concept is susceptible to collusion.[7] That is, while it is true that unilateral deviation by an AS from the prescribed strategy profile cannot benefit it, coordinated deviation by several ASes might prove to be beneficial to some. Therefore, if at all possible, we would like our mechanisms to ensure that no deviation by a group of ASes from the prescribed strategy profile is worthwhile. To achieve this, we introduce *collusion-proof ex-post Nash equilibria*. In a collusion-proof ex-post Nash equilibrium, no deviation by a group of agents can strictly improve the outcome of even a single agent in that group without strictly harming another.

14.3.3 A DAMD Approach: Combining the Two Perspectives

To achieve incentive-compatible interdomain routing, we must design a protocol that makes sense from both the networking and the mechanism-design perspectives. The networking requirements point to a path-vector framework combined with a class of routing preferences that guarantees convergence. Mechanism design requires that we incent agents to implement this routing protocol faithfully. Incentive compatibility is often achieved through payments; however, below we show that, under a reasonable set of assumptions about routing policies, one can achieve collusion-proof ex-post Nash equilibrium *without payments* simply by executing BGP.

14.3.3.1 Commercial Internet Routing and the Gao–Rexford Model

There are two types of business relationships that characterize most AS interconnections: *customer-provider* and *peering*. Customer ASes pay their provider ASes for connectivity, and peers are AS pairs that find it mutually advantageous to exchange traffic for free. One advantage of peering is that the two peers need not pay their respective providers to exchange traffic directly. An AS can be in many different relationships simultaneously: It can be a customer of one or more ASes, a provider to others, and a peer to yet others. These agreements are assumed to be relatively long-term contracts that are formed because of various external factors, e.g., traffic patterns and network sizes.

These business relationships naturally induce the following constraints on routing policies, known as the *Gao–Rexford constraints*:

No customer-provider cycles: Let G_{CP} be the digraph with the same set of nodes as G and with a directed edge from every customer to its provider. The Gao–Rexford constraints require that there be no directed cycles in this graph. This requirement is a natural economic assumption, because a cycle in G_{CP} implies that at least one AS is (indirectly) its own provider.

[7] The Nash equilibrium and dominant-strategy equilibrium concepts are also susceptible to collusion.

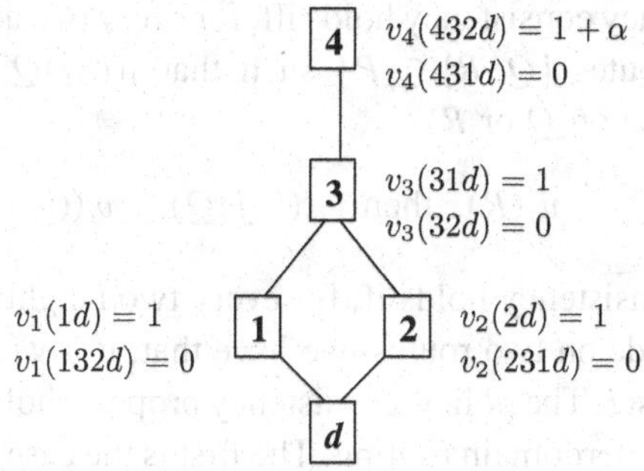

Figure 14.5. A routing instance that satisfies the Gao–Rexford constraints on which every path-vector protocol converges to a route allocation that is arbitrarily far from optimal.

Prefer customers over peers and peers over providers: A *customer route* is a route in which the next-hop AS is a customer. *Provider* and *peer routes* are defined similarly. Because, typically, customers pay providers for service, and peers exchange service for free, the Gao–Rexford constraints require that nodes always prefer (i.e., assign a higher value to) customer routes over peer routes, which are in turn preferred over provider routes.

Provide transit services only to customers: Transit service is carrying packets that originate and terminate at hosts outside the node. ASes are paid to carry customer packets but are not paid to carry peer or provider traffic. The Gao–Rexford constraints require that ASes not carry transit traffic between their providers and peers. ASes should announce all of their customer routes to all of their neighbors and should announce all of their routes to their customers.[8]

These constraints ensure robustness without requiring coordination between ASes. In fact, if all ASes obey the Gao–Rexford constraints, then their valuations cannot induce a dispute wheel.

The Gao–Rexford constraints ensure robust convergence, but in general they do not guarantee that BGP converges to the social-welfare-maximizing route allocation. To see this, consider the example in Figure 14.5. Assume that d is a customer of 1 and 2, that 1 and 2 are customers of 3, that 3 is a customer of 4, and that $\alpha > 0$. Observe that this AS graph satisfies all the Gao–Rexford constraints. The unique stable route allocation (to $1, \ldots, 4$, respectively) is $\{1d, 2d, 31d, 431d\}$. However, the optimal route allocation is $\{1d, 2d, 32d, 432d\}$. This allocation will never be chosen by local decisions, because node 3 would much prefer routing through node 1, a route that is always available for it to choose. Therefore, because the value of α can be arbitrarily high, this implies that the route allocation computed by a path-vector protocol could be arbitrarily far from the welfare-maximizing route allocation.

This problem can be overcome by imposing the *policy-consistency* property.

[8] Note that, in practice, ASes are not obligated to announce *all* customer routes to other ASes but can filter some customer routes by not announcing them to certain neighbors. Indeed, the original Gao–Rexford constraints allow this. For ease of exposition, we disregard this option here. A more general result can be achieved for the more general case, with additional restrictions, as explained in Feigenbaum et al. (2006).

Definition 14.6 Policy consistency holds iff, for every two adjacent nodes $i, j \in N$, and every two routes $\{Q, R\} \subseteq P^j$ such that $\{(i, j)Q, (i, j)R\} \subseteq P^i$[9] (in particular, node i is not on Q or R),

$$\text{if } v_j(Q) \geq v_j(R), \text{ then } v_i((i, j)Q) \geq v_i((i, j)R).$$

Informally, policy consistency holds if, for every two neighboring nodes i, j, such that j is i's next-hop node on two routes, we have that, if j weakly prefers one route over another, then so must i. The policy-consistency property holds in the two most well studied special cases of interdomain routing. The first is the case in which the valuation of a route is solely a function of the route's next hop. (These are called "next-hop policies.") The second is the case in which there is some metric function that assigns a "length" to every link, and every valuation function prefers "shorter" routes (i.e., those with smaller total lengths in this metric). (These are called "metric-based policies.")

We are now ready to state, and prove, the following theorem.

Theorem 14.7 *If the Gao–Rexford constraints and policy consistency hold, then BGP converges to the social-welfare-maximizing route allocation and is incentive-compatible in collusion-proof ex-post Nash equilibrium (without any monetary transfer).*

PROOF We will actually prove a stronger result if the Gao–Rexford constraints, and policy consistency hold BGP actually converges to a solution (an allocation of routes) in which every AS gets its most desired route to the destination. That is, every AS will be assigned a route that maximizes its valuation function. We call this kind of route allocation a *locally optimal* solution. Observe that any locally optimal solution is also globally optimal in that it maximizes the total social welfare. Moreover, locally optimal solutions are *deviation-proof* in that there is no deviation by a group of agents that can strictly improve the outcome of even a single agent. This is far stronger than collusion-proof ex-post Nash equilibrium, which only requires that no deviation by a group of agents can strictly improve the outcome of a single agent in the group without strictly harming another agent in the group.

Because the Gao–Rexford constraints imply that there is no dispute wheel, we are assured (by the result mentioned in Section 14.3.1) that BGP will converge to a unique stable solution. We denote this solution by $T_d = \{S_1, \ldots, S_n\}$, where S_i is the route allocated to node i.

Lemma 14.8 *If the Gao–Rexford constraints hold, and policy consistency holds, then BGP converges to a unique stable, locally optimal route allocation T_d.*

PROOF Consider a node $m \in N$. Let $R = u_k u_{k-1} \ldots u_i \ldots u_0$ be some loop-free route in P^{u_k}, such that $u_k = m$ and $u_0 = d$. By induction, we show for each $u_i \in R$ that S_i, the solution's route for node u_i in T_d, is at least as good as $R_i = u_i \ldots u_0$. If $i = m$, then S_m is at least as good as R; because R and m were chosen arbitrarily, this establishes the local optimality of T_d.

[9] $(i, j)Q$ and $(i, j)R$ are the routes from i to d that have (i, j) as a first link and then follow Q and R, respectively.

Base case. $i = 0$. The induction hypothesis is trivially true, because the only route is the empty one.

Induction step. Assume that the induction hypothesis is true for u_{i-1}, i.e.,

$$v_{u_{i-1}}(S_{i-1}) \geq v_{u_{i-1}}(R_{i-1}). \tag{14.1}$$

Note that u_i does not lie on R_{i-1}, because R is loop-free.

Case I. Assume that $u_i \notin S_{i-1}$. Observe that inequality (14.1) and the meaning of "provide transit services only to customers" imply that u_{i-1} exports S_{i-1} to u_i. Then extend S_{i-1} and R_{i-1} along the edge (u_i, u_{i-1}). $(u_i, u_{i-1})S_{i-1} \in P^{u_i}$; thus, from (14.1) and policy consistency, we have

$$v_{u_i}((u_i, u_{i-1})S_{i-1}) \geq v_{u_i}(R_i). \tag{14.2}$$

T_d is stable; so, S_i is at least as good as any other route at u_i; in particular,

$$v_{u_i}(S_i) \geq v_{u_i}((u_i, u_{i-1})S_{i-1}). \tag{14.3}$$

Combining (14.2) and (14.3) gives

$$v_{u_i}(S_i) \geq v_{u_i}(R_i),$$

which is the induction statement for u_i.

Case II. Assume that $u_i \in S_{i-1}$. We cannot use the policy-consistency argument as in Case I, because extending S_{i-1} to u_i creates a loop. This implies that $u_{i-1} \notin S_i$. Suppose that the induction statement is not true for i, i.e., that $v_{u_i}(R_i) > v_{u_i}(S_i)$. Then $R_i \ominus_2 S_i$. Because $u_{i-1} \notin S_i$ but $u_i \in S_{i-1}$, it must be that $S_i \ominus_1 S_{i-1}$. From the induction hypothesis, $S_{i-1} \ominus_2 R_{i-1}$, and, because $R_i = (u_i, u_{i-1})R_{i-1}$, $R_{i-1} \ominus_1 R_i$. Therefore, we have a cycle in the relation $\oslash$; in particular, we can say that $R_i \oslash R_{i-1}$ and $R_{i-1} \oslash R_i$, but these routes do not start at the same node. This violates the no-dispute-wheel property and shows that the assumption that $v_{u_i}(R_i) > v_{u_i}(S_i)$ leads to a contradiction; recall that the Gao–Rexford constraints are a special case of the no-dispute-wheel property. Therefore, $v_{u_i}(R_i) \leq v_{u_i}(S_i)$, which is the induction statement for u_i. (Recall that there are no ties in valuations.) □

Remark 14.9 Lemma 14.8 holds for every subinstance of the AS graph, because both the Gao–Rexford constraints and policy consistency hold for every subinstance.

Remark 14.10 No dispute wheel implies a unique collusion-proof ex-post Nash solution to which BGP converges. Hence, we are not concerned with the standard problem that arises when multiple equilibria exist, namely whether nodes select the same equilibrium.

14.4 Conclusion and Open Problems

In this chapter, we have reviewed the work that has been done on distributed algorithmic mechanism design, in which the presence of strategic computational agents introduces new incentive and computational challenges for distributed computing. In particular, we have presented in detail some of the known results about DAMD for interdomain routing, which is the best motivated and most extensively studied problem in the area. There are at least two interesting directions for further research.

First, there is the general question of which other problems in networked computation are amenable to the approaches explored in this chapter. Several good candidates have been proposed, i.e., web caching, peer-to-peer file sharing, overlay-network construction, and distributed task allocation. Although both distributed algorithms and incentive compatibility have been considered in the literature about these problems, the results have not been pulled together into a coherent DAMD theory. The construction of such a theory remains a worthy goal.

Second, there are many questions about interdomain routing that have not been fully answered. There is still no complete characterization of the conditions under which BGP converges robustly. ("No dispute wheel" is sufficient but not known to be necessary.) Similarly, the conditions under which collusion-proof ex-post Nash equilibrium is reached simply by executing BGP have not been characterized completely. (Again, the Gao–Rexford and policy-consistency conditions presented in this chapter are sufficient but not known to be necessary.) In fact, necessary and sufficient conditions on AS graphs and routing policies have not yet been obtained for ex-post Nash equilibrium, even if we ignore collusion and allow payments. Both policy consistency and local optimality play an essential role in the main result presented in this chapter, and little is known about what can be obtained without them. In general, the network complexity of BGP is open, even in cases when convergence is assured.

14.5 Notes

Given the distributed and autonomous nature of Internet users, it is no surprise that the networking and distributed-systems literature provides some of the earliest applications of game theory and mechanism design to computer-science problems. These themes were first explored in an early series of papers from Columbia University, e.g., Ferguson (1989), Hsiao and Lazar (1988), Kurose et al. (1985), Kurose and Simha (1989), Mazumdar and Douligeris (1992), and Yemini (1981), which were followed by contributions from Miller and Drexler (1988a, 1988b), Sanders (1986, 1988a, 1988b), and others (Kelly, 1997; Kelly et al., 1998; La and Anantharam 1997; Murphy and Murphy, 1994; Mackie-Mason and Varian, 1995; Shenker, 1990, 1995). Because networking problems are inherently distributed, and network protocols must have reasonable network complexity, these papers were actually early forerunners of DAMD.

Nisan and Ronen were the first to combine algorithmic and economic concerns in a new area of study for which they coined the term "algorithmic mechanism design," and this book is largely an outgrowth of their seminal paper Nisan and Ronen (2001). The extension of AMD to DAMD was first explored in Feigenbaum et al. (2001), which considered the multicast cost-sharing problem described in Section 14.2 and articulated the notion of network complexity; the DAMD agenda was more broadly described soon thereafter in Feigenbaum and Shenker (2002). Subsequent work on DAMD for multicast cost sharing can be found in, e.g., Archer et al. (2004), Adler and

Rubenstein (2002), Fiat et al. (2002), and Feigenbaum et al. (2003). In particular, a generalization of Theorem 14.1 is proven in Feigenbaum et al. (2003).

Distributed VCG computation and the importance of ex-post Nash equilibria in DAMD were first presented by Parkes and Shneidman (2004) and developed further by Petcu et al. (2006).

The BGP specification can be found in Rekhter et al. (2006). The fact that BGP may not converge if there are no constraints on the AS graph or the domains' routing policies was first observed by Varadhan et al. (2000). The example of BGP divergence in Figure 14.4 and the proof that "no dispute wheel" guarantees robust convergence are presented in Griffin et al. (2002). Abstract properties of path-vector protocols are developed in, e.g., Griffin et al. (1999, 2003), Sobrinho (2005). The Gao–Rexford conditions and their implications were first studied in Gao and Rexford (2001) and further developed in, e.g., Gao et al. (2001). Partial results on the network complexity of BGP can be found in, e.g., Karloff (2004).

DAMD was first applied to interdomain routing by Feigenbaum et al. (2005b), who devised a BGP-based algorithm for lowest-cost routing. Computational manipulation by ASes and ex-post Nash equilibrium in BGP-based, lowest-cost routing was first studied by Shneidman and Parkes (2004). Hardness results for more general classes of routing policies can be found in Feigenbaum et al. (2005a, 2006b). A positive result about BGP-based, incentive-compatible routing under the Gao–Rexford and policy-consistency conditions is given in Feigenbaum et al. (2006a) and is the direct precursor of the result presented in Section 14.3. Sobrinho was the first to study policy constraints that guarantee optimality, both global and local; a result that is similar to (but weaker than) Lemma 14.8 is presented in Sobrinho (2005).

For basic background on Internet routing, see Kurose and Ross (2005), Peterson and Davie (2003), or other networking textbooks.

Acknowledgments

We thank Vijay Ramachandran and Rahul Sami for many helpful discussions of interdomain routing. The work of the first author was supported in part by ONR grants N00014-01-1-0795 and N00014-04-1-0725, NSF grant 0428422, HSARPA grant ARO-1756303, and US–Israeli BSF grant 2002065. The work of the second author was supported in part by US-Israeli BSF grant 2002065 and by Israeli Science Foundation grant 169/03. The work of the third author was supported in part by NSF grant 0428422.

Bibliography

A. Archer, J. Feigenbaum, A. Krishnamurthy, R. Sami, and S. Shenker. Approximation and collusion in multicast cost sharing. *Games Econ. Behav.*, 47(1):36–71, 2004.

M. Adler and D. Rubenstein. Pricing multicasting in more practical network models. In *13th Symp. on Discrete Algorithms*, pp. 981–990, ACM/SIAM, New York/Philadelphia, 2002.

J. Feigenbaum, D.R. Karger, V.S. Mirrokni, and R. Sami. Subjective-cost policy routing. In Xiaotie Deng and Yinyu Ye, editors, *First Workshop on Internet and Network Economics*, LNCS 3828:174–183, Springer, Berlin, 2005a.

J. Feigenbaum, A. Krishnamurthy, R. Sami, and S. Shenker. Hardness results for multicast cost sharing. *Theor. Comput. Sci.*, 304(1–3):215–236, 2003.

J. Feigenbaum, C.H. Papadimitriou, and S. Shenker. Sharing the cost of multicast transmissions. *J. Comput. Syst. Sci.*, 63(1):21–41, 2001.

J. Feigenbaum, C.H. Papadimitriou, R. Sami, and S. Shenker. A BGP-based mechanism for lowest-cost routing. *Distr. Comput.*, 18(1):61–72, 2005b.

J. Feigenbaum, V. Ramachandran, and M. Schapira. Incentive-compatible interdomain routing. In *7th Conference on Electronic Commerce*, pp. 130–139, ACM, New York, 2006a.

J. Feigenbaum, R. Sami, and S. Shenker. Mechanism design for policy routing. *Distr. Comp.*, 18(4):293–305, 2006b.

J. Feigenbaum and S. Shenker. Distributed algorithmic mechanism design: Recent results and future directions. In *6th Intl. Workshop on Discrete Algorithms and Methods for Mobile Computing and Communications*, pp. 1–13, ACM, New York, 2002.

A. Fiat, A.V. Goldberg, J.D. Hartline, and A.R. Karlin. Competitive generalized auctions. In *34th Symposium on Theory of Computing*, pp. 72–81, ACM, New York, 2002.

D.F. Ferguson. *The Application of Microeconomics to the Design of Resource Allocation and Control Algorithms*. Ph.D. Thesis, Columbia University, 1989.

L. Gao, T.G. Griffin, and J. Rexford. Inherently safe backup routing with BGP. In *20th INFOCOM*, pp. 547–556, IEEE, Pistacaway, 2001.

L. Gao and J. Rexford. Stable Internet routing without global coordination. *IEEE/ACM Trans. Networking*, 9(6):681–692, 2001.

T.G. Griffin, A.D. Jaggard, and V. Ramachandran. Design principles of policy languages for path vector protocols. In *SIGCOMM '03: Proc. 2003 Conf. Applications, Technologies, Architectures, and Protocols for Computer Communications*, pp. 61–72, ACM, New York, 2003.

T.G. Griffin, F.B. Shepherd, and G. Wilfong. Policy disputes in path-vector protocols. In *7th Intl. Conf. on Network Protocols*, pp. 21–30, IEEE Computer Society, Los Alamitos, 1999.

T.G. Griffin, F.B. Shepherd, and G. Wilfong. The stable paths problem and interdomain routing. *IEEE/ACM Trans. Networking*, 10(2):232–243, April 2002.

M.-T. Hsiao and A.A. Lazar. A game theoretic approach to decentralized flow control of markovian queueing networks. In Pierre-Jacques Courtois and Guy Latouche, editors, *Performance 87', Proc. 12th IFIP WG 7.3 Intl. Symp. Comp. Performance Modelling, Measurement, and Evaluation*, pp. 55–73, North-Holland, Amsterdam, 1988.

H. Karloff. On the convergence time of a path-vector protocol. In *Proc. 15th Symp. on Discrete Algorithms*, pp. 605–614, ACM/SIAM, New York/Philadelphia, 2004.

F.P. Kelly. Charging and rate control for elastic traffic. *Euro. Trans. Telecommuncations*, 8:33–37, 1997.

F.P. Kelly, A. Maulloo, and D. Tan. Rate control in communication networks: Shadow prices, proportional fairness, and stability. *J. Oper. Res. Soc.*, 49(3):237–252, 1998.

J.F. Kurose and K.W. Ross. *Computer Networking: A Top Down Approach Featuring the Internet*. Addison-Wesley, 2005.

J.F. Kurose and R. Simha. A microeconomic approach to optimal resource allocation in distributed computer systems. *IEEE Trans. Comp.*, 38(5):705–717, 1989.

J.F. Kurose, M. Schwartz, and Y. Yemini. A microeconomic approach to decentralized optimization of channel access policies in multiaccess networks. In *5th Intl. Conf. on Distr. Comp. Sys.*, pp. 70–77, IEEE Computer Society, Los Alamitos, 1985.

R.J. La and V. Anantharam. Optimal routing control: Game theoretic approach. In *36th Conf. on Decision and Control*, pp. 2910–2915, IEEE, Piscataway, 1997.

J.K. Mackie-Mason and H. Varian. Pricing the Internet. In Brian Kahin and James Keller, editors, *Public Access to the Internet*, pp. 269–314, MIT Press, Cambridge, 1995.

R.R. Mazumdar and C. Douligeris. A game theoretic approach to flow control in an integrated environment. *J. Franklin Inst.*, 329(2):383–402, 1992.

M.S. Miller and K.E. Drexler. Incentive engineering: For computational resource management. In Bernardo A. Huberman, editor, *The Ecology of Computation*, pp. 231–266. North-Holland, Amsterdam, 1988a.

M.S. Miller and K.E. Drexler. Markets and computation: Agoric open systems. In Bernardo A. Huberman, editor, *The Ecology of Computation*, pp. 133–176. North-Holland, Amsterdam, 1988b.

J. Murphy and L. Murphy. Bandwidth allocation by pricing in ATM networks. In *Broadband Communications II: Proc. 2nd Intl. Conf.*, pp. 333–351, Elsevier, Amsterdam, 1994.

N. Nisan and A. Ronen. Algorithmic mechanism design. *Games Econ. Behav.*, 35(1):166–196, 2001.

D.C. Parkes and J. Shneidman. Distributed implementations of Vickrey-Clarke-Groves mechanism. In *3rd Intl. Joint Conf. on Autonomous Systems and Multiagent Systems*, pp. 261–268, IEEE Computer Society, Los Alamitos, 2004.

A. Petcu, B. Faltings, and D.C. Parkes. MDPOP: Faithful distributed implementation of efficient social choice problems. In *Proc. 5th Intl. Joint Conf. Autonomous Agents and Multiagent Systems*, ACM Press, New York, NY, 2006.

L.L. Peterson and B.S. Davie. *Computer Networks: A Systems Approach*. Morgan Kaufmann, 2003.

Y. Rekhter, T. Li, and S. Hares. A Border Gateway Protocol 4 (BGP-4). RFC 4271, January 2006.

B.A. Sanders. An incentive compatible flow control algorithm for fair rate allocation in computer/communication networks. In *6th Intl. Conf. on Distr. Comp. Syst.*, pp. 314–320, IEEE Computer Society, Los Alamitos, 1986.

B.A. Sanders. An asynchronous, distributed flow control algorithm for rate allocation in computer networks. *IEEE Trans. Comp.*, 37(7):779–787, 1988.

B.A. Sanders. An incentive compatible flow control algorithm for rate allocation in computer networks. *IEEE Trans. Comp.*, 37(9):1067–1072, 1988.

S. Shenker. Efficient network allocations with selfish users. In Peter J. B. King, Isi Mitrani, and Rob Pooley, editors, *Performance '90, Proc. of the 14th IFIP WG 7.3 Intl. Symp. on Computer Performance Modelling, Measurement and Evaluation*, pp. 279–285, North-Holland, Amsterdam, 1990.

S. Shenker. Making greed work in networks: A game-theoretic analysis of switch service disciplines. *IEEE/ACM Trans. Networking*, 3(6):819–831, 1995.

J. Shneidman and D.C. Parkes. Specification faithfulness in networks with rational nodes. In *23rd Symp. on Princ. Distributed Computing*, pp. 88–97, ACM, New York, 2004.

J.L. Sobrinho. An algebraic theory of dynamic network routing. *IEEE/ACM Trans. Networking*, 13(5):1160–1173, 2005.

K. Varadhan, R. Govindan, and D. Estrin. Persistent route oscillations in inter-domain routing. *Comput. Networks*, 32(1):1–16, March 2000.

Y. Yemini. Selfish optimization in computer networks. In *20th Conf. Decision and Control*, pp. 281–285, IEEE, Pistacaway, 1981.

Exercises

14.1 Recall from Chapter 9 that, in a *second-price Vickrey auction* of a single item, the item is sold to the highest bidder, and the price that the winner pays is the second-highest bid. Consider a network in which there is one bidder at each node, and the nodes lie on a cycle. As in Section 14.2, we assume that there is no trusted center to implement an algorithm but that there is a central enforcer that can implement the outcome decided upon by the agents and can impose severe penalties if the agents do not agree on an outcome. Give a distributed algorithm for computing the winner and the price in a second-price Vickrey auction on such a network that has the following properties: (i) it is incentive-compatible in ex-post Nash equilibrium; (ii) it requires no more than two messages to cross each link; and (iii) each message is at most $O(\log m + \log n)$ bits long, where m is the highest bid, and n is the number of bidders. Prove that your algorithm satisfies these three properties

14.2 Prove that, in the MC multicast cost-sharing mechanism, there is a single "largest" receiver set that maximizes NW.

14.3 Prove the correctness of the algorithm given in Section 14.2.2 for computation of MC cost shares.

14.4 A strategyproof mechanism is group strategyproof (GSP) if no coalition of deviating agents can achieve an outcome that is at least as good for all deviating agents and strictly better for at least one. For each of the MC and SH multicast cost-sharing mechanisms, either prove that it is GSP or provide a counterexample.

14.5 Consider a single-item, ascending-price auction with "jump bids." Type θ_i denotes agent i's value for the item. Bids are associated with a "bid price." In round t, the auctioneer announces an "ask price" p^t that is $\epsilon > 0$ above the highest bid received so far. Any agent can bid in round t, as long as the bid is at some price at or above p^t. The provisional winner is the agent with the current highest bid (breaking ties at random). The auction terminates when no agent bids at the current ask price, and the item is then sold to the provisional winner at its final bid price. The information state (p^t, x^t) defines the current ask price p^t and provisional winner $x^t \in \{1, \ldots, n\}$. The following is a straightforward bidding strategy that determines what agent i will do in state (p, x): If $p \leq \theta_i$ and $x \neq i$, then bid p; otherwise, do not bid. Prove that this strategy profile is not an ex-post Nash equilibrium (and *a fortiori* not a dominant-strategy equilibrium).

14.6 Prove that policy consistency is satisfied if all ASes use next-hop policies, or if all use metric-based policies.

14.7 Give an interdomain-routing instance (i.e., an AS graph in which one AS is identified as the destination, each edge is identified as a peer edge or a customer-provider edge, a valuation function is given for each source AS and the import and export policies of each AS are specified) that does not contain a dispute wheel but also does not satisfy the Gao–Rexford constraints. Explain why the Gao–Rexford constraints are not satisfied by this instance.

14.8 Prove that, in the interdomain-routing problem, it is NP-hard to find a route allocation that comes within a constant factor of the maximum social welfare if no restrictions are made on the valuation functions.

CHAPTER 15

Cost Sharing

Kamal Jain and Mohammad Mahdian

Abstract

The objective of cooperative game theory is to study ways to enforce and sustain cooperation among agents willing to cooperate. A central question in this field is how the benefits (or costs) of a joint effort can be divided among participants, taking into account individual and group incentives, as well as various fairness properties.

In this chapter, we define basic concepts and review some of the classical results in the cooperative game theory literature. Our focus is on games that are based on combinatorial optimization problems such as facility location. We define the notion of cost sharing, and explore various incentive and fairness properties cost-sharing methods are often expected to satisfy. We show how cost-sharing methods satisfying a certain property termed cross-monotonicity can be used to design mechanisms that are robust against collusion, and study the algorithmic question of designing cross-monotonic cost-sharing schemes for combinatorial optimization games. Interestingly, this problem is closely related to linear-programming-based techniques developed in the field of approximation algorithms. We explore this connection, and explain a general method for designing cross-monotonic cost-sharing schemes, as well as a technique for proving impossibility bounds on such schemes. We will also discuss an *axiomatic* approach to characterize two widely applicable solution concepts: the Shapley value for cooperative games, and the Nash bargaining solution for a more restricted framework for surplus sharing.

15.1 Cooperative Games and Cost Sharing

Consider a setting where a set $\mathcal{A}$ of n agents seek to cooperate in order to generate value. The value generated depends on the coalition S of agents cooperating. In general, the set of possible outcomes of cooperation among agents in $S \subseteq \mathcal{A}$ is denoted by $V(S)$, where each outcome is given by a vector in $\mathbb{R}^S$, whose i'th component specifies the utility that the agent $i \in S$ derives in this outcome. The set $\mathcal{A}$ of agents along with the function V defines what is called a *cooperative game* (also known as a *coalitional game*) *with nontransferable utilities* (abbreviated as an *NTU game*). A special case, called a *cooperative game with transferable utilities* (abbreviated as a *TU game*), is when the

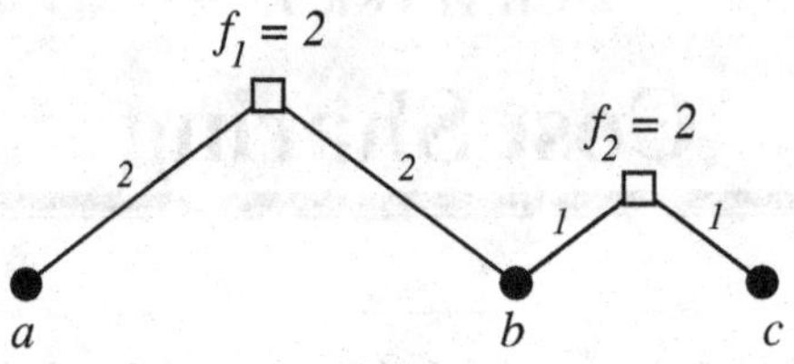

Figure 15.1. An example of the facility location game.

value generated by a coalition can be divided in an arbitrary way among the agents in S. In other words, a TU game is defined by specifying a function v: $2^{\mathcal{A}} \mapsto \mathbb{R}$, which gives the value $v(S) \in \mathbb{R}$ generated by each coalition S. We assume $v(\emptyset) = 0$. The set of all possible outcomes in such a game is defined as $V(S) = \{x \in \mathbb{R}^S\colon \sum_{i \in S} x_i \leq v(S)\}$.

The notion of a cooperative game was first proposed by von Neumann and Morgenstern. This notion seeks to abstract away all other aspects of the game except the combinatorial aspect of the coalitions that can form. This is in contrast with noncooperative games, where the focus is on the set of choices (moves) available to each agent.

Note that in the definition of a cooperative game, we did not restrict the values to be nonnegative.[1] In fact, the case that all values are nonpositive is the focus of this chapter, as it corresponds to the problem of sharing the cost of a service among those who receive the service (this is by taking the value to be the negative of the cost). Again, the cost-sharing problem can be studied in both the TU and the NTU models. The TU model applies to settings where, for example, a service provider incurs some (monetary) cost $c(S)$ in building a network that connects a set S of customers to the Internet, and needs to divide this cost among customers in S. In practice, the cost function c is often defined by solving a combinatorial optimization problem. One example, which we will use throughout the chapter, is the facility location game defined below.

Definition 15.1 In the *facility location game*, we are given a set $\mathcal{A}$ of agents (also known as cities, clients, or demand points), a set $\mathcal{F}$ of facilities, a facility opening cost f_i for every facility $i \in \mathcal{F}$, and a distance d_{ij} between every pair (i, j) of points in $\mathcal{A} \cup \mathcal{F}$ indicating the cost of connecting j to i. We assume that the distances come from a metric space; i.e., they are symmetric and obey the triangle inequality. For a set $S \subseteq \mathcal{A}$ of agents, the cost of this set is defined as the minimum cost of opening a set of facilities and connecting every agent in S to an open facility. More precisely, the cost function c is defined by $c(S) = \min_{\mathcal{F}' \subseteq \mathcal{F}}\{\sum_{i \in \mathcal{F}'} f_i + \sum_{j \in S} \min_{i \in \mathcal{F}'} d_{ij}\}$.

Example 15.2 Figure 15.1 shows an instance of the facility location game with 3 agents $\{a, b, c\}$ and 2 facilities $\{1, 2\}$. The distances between some pairs are marked in the figure, and other distances can be calculated using the triangle

[1] If all values are nonnegative, the problem is called a *surplus sharing* problem.

inequality (e.g., the distance between facility 1 and client c is $2+1+1=4$). The cost function defined by this instance is the following:

$$c(\{a\})=4, \quad c(\{b\})=3, \quad c(\{c\})=3,$$
$$c(\{a,b\})=6, \quad c(\{b,c\})=4, \quad c(\{a,c\})=7, \quad c(\{a,b,c\})=8.$$

Since the monetary cost may be distributed arbitrarily among the agents, it is natural to model the above example as a TU game. An example of a case where the NTU model is more applicable is a network design problem where the cost incurred by an agent i in the set of agents S receiving the service corresponds to the delay this agent suffers. There are multiple designs for the network connecting the customers in S, and each design corresponds to a profile of delays that these agents will suffer. The set of possible outcomes for the coalition S is defined as the collection of all such profiles, and is denoted by $C(S)$. As delays are nontransferrable, this setting is best modeled as an NTU cost-sharing game. For another example of an NTU game, see the housing allocation problem in Section 10.3 of this book.

As most of the work on cost sharing in the algorithmic game theory literature has so far focused on TU games, this chapter is mainly devoted to such games; henceforth, by a cost-sharing game we mean a TU game, unless otherwise stated.

15.2 Core of Cost-Sharing Games

A central notion in cooperative game theory is the notion of *core*. Roughly speaking, the core of a cooperative game is an outcome of cooperation among all agents where no coalition of agents can all benefit by breaking away from the grand coalition. Intuitively, the core of a game corresponds to situations where it is possible to sustain cooperation among all agents in an economically stable manner.

In this section, we define the notion of core for cost-sharing games, and present two classical results on conditions for nonemptiness of the core. We show how the notion of core for TU games can be relaxed to an approximate version suitable for hard combinatorial optimization games, and observe a connection between this notion and the integrality gap of a linear programming relaxation of such problems.

15.2.1 Core of TU Games

Formally, the core of a TU cost-sharing game is defined as follows.

Definition 15.3 Let $(\mathcal{A}, c)$ be a TU cost-sharing game. A vector $\boldsymbol{\alpha} \in \mathbb{R}^{\mathcal{A}}$ (sometimes called a *cost allocation*) is in the *core* of this game if it satisfies the following two conditions:

- **Budget balance:** $\sum_{j\in\mathcal{A}} \alpha_j = c(\mathcal{A})$.
- **Core property:** for every $S \subseteq \mathcal{A}$, $\sum_{j\in S} \alpha_j \leq c(S)$.

Example 15.4 As an example, consider the facility location game of Example 15.2 (Figure 15.1). It is not hard to verify that the vector (4, 2, 2) lies in the core of this game. In fact, this is not the only cost allocation in the core of this game; for example, (4, 1, 3) is also in the core. On the other hand, if a third facility with opening cost 3 and distance 1 to agents a and c is added to this game, the resulting game will have an empty core. To see this, note that after adding the third facility, we have $c(\{a, c\}) = 5$. Now, if there is a vector $\boldsymbol{\alpha}$ in the core of this game, we must have

$$\alpha_a + \alpha_b \leq c(\{a, b\}) = 6$$
$$\alpha_b + \alpha_c \leq c(\{b, c\}) = 4$$
$$\alpha_a + \alpha_c \leq c(\{a, c\}) = 5$$

By adding the above three inequalities and dividing both sides by 2, we obtain $\alpha_a + \alpha_b + \alpha_c \leq 7.5 < c(\{a, b, c\})$. Therefore $\boldsymbol{\alpha}$ cannot be budget balanced.

A classical result in cooperative game theory, known as the Bondareva–Shapley theorem, gives a necessary and sufficient condition for a game to have nonempty core. To state this theorem, we need the following definition.

Definition 15.5 A vector $\boldsymbol{\lambda}$ that assigns a nonnegative weight λ_S to each subset $S \subseteq \mathcal{A}$ is called a *balanced collection of weights* if for every $j \in \mathcal{A}$, $\sum_{S:j\in S} \lambda_S = 1$.

Theorem 15.6 *A cost-sharing game $(\mathcal{A}, c)$ with transferable utilities has a nonempty core if and only if for every balanced collection of weights $\boldsymbol{\lambda}$, we have $\sum_{S\subseteq \mathcal{A}} \lambda_S c(S) \geq c(\mathcal{A})$.*

PROOF By the definition of the core, the game $(\mathcal{A}, c)$ has a nonempty core if and only if the solution of the following linear program (LP) is precisely $c(\mathcal{A})$. (Note that this solution can never be larger than $c(\mathcal{A})$.)

$$\begin{aligned} &\text{Maximize} \quad \textstyle\sum_{j\in\mathcal{A}} \alpha_j \\ &\text{Subject to} \quad \forall S \subseteq \mathcal{A} : \textstyle\sum_{j\in S} \alpha_j \leq c(S). \end{aligned} \tag{15.1}$$

By strong LP duality, the solution of the above LP is equal to the solution of the following dual program:

$$\begin{aligned} &\text{Minimize} \quad \sum_{S\subseteq\mathcal{A}} \lambda_S c(S) \\ &\text{Subject to} \quad \forall j \in \mathcal{A} : \sum_{S:j\in S} \lambda_S = 1 \\ &\qquad\qquad\quad \forall S \subseteq \mathcal{A} : \lambda_S \geq 0. \end{aligned} \tag{15.2}$$

Therefore, the core of the game is nonempty if and only if the solution of the LP (15.2) is equal to $c(\mathcal{A})$. By definition, feasible solutions of this program are balanced collections of weights. Therefore, the core of the game $(\mathcal{A}, c)$ is nonempty if and only if for every balanced collection of weights (λ_S), $\sum_{S\subseteq\mathcal{A}} \lambda_S c(S) \geq c(\mathcal{A})$. □

As an example, the proof of emptiness of the core given in Example 15.4 can be restated by defining a vector $\boldsymbol{\lambda}$ as follows: $\lambda_{\{a,b\}} = \lambda_{\{b,c\}} = \lambda_{\{a,c\}} = \frac{1}{2}$ and $\lambda_S = 0$ for every other set S. It is easy to verify that $\boldsymbol{\lambda}$ is a balanced collection of weights and $\sum_{S \subseteq \mathcal{A}} \lambda_S c(S) < c(\mathcal{A})$.

15.2.2 Approximate Core

As we saw in Example 15.4, a difficulty with the notion of core is that the core of many cost-sharing games, including most combinatorial optimization games based on computationally hard problems, is often empty. Furthermore, when the underlying cost function is hard to compute (e.g., in the facility location game), even deciding whether the core of the game is empty is often computationally intractable. This motivates the following definition.

Definition 15.7 A vector $\boldsymbol{\alpha} \in \mathbb{R}^{\mathcal{A}}$ is in the γ-approximate core (or γ-core, for short) of the game $(\mathcal{A}, c)$ if it satisfies the following two conditions:

- **γ-Budget balance:** $\gamma c(\mathcal{A}) \leq \sum_{j \in \mathcal{A}} \alpha_j \leq c(\mathcal{A})$.
- **Core property:** for every $S \subseteq \mathcal{A}$, $\sum_{j \in S} \alpha_j \leq c(S)$.

For example, in the facility location game given in Example 15.4, the vector $(3.5, 2.5, 1.5)$ is in the $\frac{7.5}{8}$-core of the game. Note that the argument given to show the emptiness of the core of this game actually proves that for every $\gamma > \frac{7.5}{8}$, the γ-core of this game is empty.

The Bondareva–Shapley theorem can be easily generalized to the following approximate version.

Theorem 15.8 *For every $\gamma \leq 1$, a cost-sharing game $(\mathcal{A}, c)$ with transferable utilities has a nonempty γ-core if and only if for every balanced collection of weights $\boldsymbol{\lambda}$, we have $\sum_{S \subseteq \mathcal{A}} \lambda_S c(S) \geq \gamma c(\mathcal{A})$.*

The proof is similar to the proof of the Bondareva–Shapley theorem and is based on the observation that by LP duality, the γ-core of the game is nonempty if and only if the solution of the LP (15.2) is at least $\gamma c(S)$. Note that if the cost function c is subadditive (i.e., $c(S_1 \cup S_2) \leq c(S_1) + c(S_2)$ for any two disjoint sets S_1 and S_2), then the optimal *integral* solution of the LP (15.2) is precisely $c(\mathcal{A})$. Therefore,

Corollary 15.9 *For any cost-sharing game $(\mathcal{A}, c)$ with a subadditive cost function, the largest value γ for which the γ-core of this game is nonempty is equal to the integrality gap of the LP (15.2).*

As it turns out, for many combinatorial optimization games such as set cover, vertex cover, and facility location, the LP formulation (15.2) is in fact equivalent to the standard (polynomial-size) LP formulation of the problem, and hence Corollary 15.9 translates into a statement about the integrality gap of the standard LP formulation of the problem. Here, we show this connection for the facility location game.

We start by formulating the facility location problem as an integer program. In this formulation, x_i and y_{ij} are variables indicating whether facility i is open, and whether agent j is connected to facility i.

$$\begin{aligned} \text{Minimize} \quad & \textstyle\sum_{i\in\mathcal{F}} f_i x_i + \sum_{i\in\mathcal{F}} \sum_{j\in\mathcal{A}} d_{ij} y_{ij} \\ \text{Subject to} \quad & \forall j \in \mathcal{A} : \textstyle\sum_{i\in\mathcal{F}} y_{ij} \geq 1 \\ & \forall i \in \mathcal{F}, j \in \mathcal{A} : \; x_i \geq y_{ij} \\ & \forall i \in \mathcal{F}, j \in \mathcal{A} : \; x_i, y_{ij} \in \{0, 1\}. \end{aligned} \tag{15.3}$$

By relaxing the second constraint to $x_i, y_{ij} \geq 0$ we obtain an LP whose dual can be written as follows:

$$\begin{aligned} \text{Maximize} \quad & \textstyle\sum_{j\in\mathcal{A}} \alpha_j \\ \text{Subject to} \quad & \forall i \in \mathcal{F}, j \in \mathcal{A} : \; \beta_{ij} \geq \alpha_j - d_{ij} \\ & \forall i \in \mathcal{F} : \textstyle\sum_{j\in\mathcal{A}} \beta_{ij} \leq f_i \\ & \forall i \in \mathcal{F}, j \in \mathcal{A} : \; \alpha_j, \beta_{ij} \geq 0 \end{aligned} \tag{15.4}$$

Note that we may assume without loss of generality that in a feasible solution of the above LP, $\beta_{ij} = \max(0, \alpha_j - d_{ij})$. Thus, to specify a dual solution it is enough to give $\boldsymbol{\alpha}$. We now observe that the above dual LP captures the core constraint of the facility location game; i.e., it is equivalent to the LP (15.1).

Proposition 15.10 *For any feasible solution $(\boldsymbol{\alpha}, \boldsymbol{\beta})$ of the LP (15.4), $\boldsymbol{\alpha}$ satisfies the core property of the facility location game.*

PROOF We need to show that for every set $S \subseteq \mathcal{A}$, $\sum_{j\in S} \alpha_j \leq c(S)$, where $c(S)$ is the cost of the facility location problem for agents in S. First we note that for any facility i and set of agents $R \subseteq \mathcal{A}$, by adding the first and the second inequalities of the LP (15.4) for facility i and every $j \in R$ we obtain

$$\sum_{j\in R} \alpha_j \leq f_i + \sum_{j\in R} d_{ij}. \tag{15.5}$$

Now, consider an optimal solution for the set of agents S, and assume $i_1, \ldots, i_k$ are facilities that are open and R_ℓ is the set of agents served by facility i_ℓ in this solution. Summing Inequality (15.5) for every (i_ℓ, R_ℓ) will yield the result. □

By the above proposition, the solution of the dual LP (15.4) (which, by LP duality, is the same as the LP relaxation of (15.3)) is equal to the solution of the LPs (15.1) and (15.2). Furthermore, the optimal integral solution of (15.3) is $c(\mathcal{A})$. Therefore, the integrality gap of (15.3) is the same as that of (15.2) and gives the best budget balance factor that a cost allocation satisfying the core property can achieve. The best known results in the field of approximation algorithms show that this gap (in the worst case) is between $\frac{1}{1.52}$ and $\frac{1}{1.463}$.

15.2.3 Core of NTU Games

We conclude this section with a classical theorem due to Scarf, which gives a sufficient condition for the nonemptiness of the core of NTU games similar to the one given in Theorem 15.6 for TU games. However, unlike in the case of TU games, the condition given in Scarf's theorem is not necessary for the nonemptiness of the core.

Formally, the core of an NTU cost-sharing game $(\mathcal{A}, C)$ is the collection of all cost allocations $\boldsymbol{\alpha} \in C(\mathcal{A})$ such that there is no nonempty coalition $S \subseteq \mathcal{A}$ and cost allocation $\mathbf{x} \in C(S)$ for which $x_j < \alpha_j$ for all $j \in S$. Note that this definition coincides with Definition 15.3 in the case of a TU game. In the following theorem the *support* of a balanced collection of weights $\boldsymbol{\lambda}$ denotes the collection of all sets S with $\lambda_S > 0$.

Theorem 15.11 *Let $(\mathcal{A}, C)$ be a cost-sharing game with nontransferable utilities. Assume for every balanced collection of weights $\boldsymbol{\lambda}$ and every vector $\mathbf{x} \in \mathbb{R}^{\mathcal{A}}$ the following property holds: if for every set S in the support of $\boldsymbol{\lambda}$, the restriction of $\mathbf{x}$ to the coordinates in S is in $C(S)$, then $\mathbf{x} \in C(\mathcal{A})$. Then $(\mathcal{A}, C)$ has a nonempty core.*

The proof of the above theorem, which is beyond the scope of this chapter, uses an adaptation of the Lemke–Howson algorithm for computing Nash equilibria (described in Section 3.4 of this book), and is considered an early and important contribution of the algorithmic viewpoint in game theory. However, the worst case running time of this algorithm (like the Lemke–Howson algorithm) is exponential in $|\mathcal{A}|$. This is in contrast to the proof of the Bondareva–Shapley theorem, which gives a polynomial-time algorithm[2] for computing a point in the core of the game, if the core is nonempty.

15.3 Group-Strategyproof Mechanisms and Cross-Monotonic Cost-Sharing Schemes

The cost-sharing problem defined in this chapter models the pricing problem for a service provider with a given set of customers. In settings where the demand is sensitive to the price, an alternative choice for the service provider is to conduct an auction between the potential customers to select the set of customers who can receive the service based on their willingness to pay and the cost structure of the problem. The goal is to design an auction mechanism that provides incentives for individuals as well as groups of agents to bid truthfully. In this section, we study this problem and exhibit its connection to cost sharing.

We start with the definition of the setting. Let $\mathcal{A}$ be a set of n agents interested in receiving a service. The cost of providing service is given by a cost function c: $2^{\mathcal{A}} \mapsto \mathbb{R}^+ \cup \{0\}$, where $c(S)$ specifies the cost of providing service for agents in S. Each agent i has a value $u_i \in \mathbb{R}$ for receiving the service; that is, she is willing to pay at most u_i to get the service. We further assume that the utility of agent i is given by $u_i q_i - x_i$,

[2] This is assuming a suitable representation for the cost function c, e.g., by a separation oracle for (15.1), or in combinatorial optimization games where statements like Proposition 15.10 hold.

where q_i is an indicator variable that indicates whether she has received the service or not, and x_i is the amount she has to pay. A *cost-sharing mechanism* is an algorithm that elicits a bid $b_i \in \mathbb{R}$ from each agent, and based on these bids, decides which agents should receive the service and how much each of them has to pay. More formally, a cost-sharing mechanism is a function that associates to each vector $\mathbf{b}$ of bids a set $Q(\mathbf{b}) \subseteq \mathcal{A}$ of agents to be serviced, and a vector $\mathbf{p}(\mathbf{b}) \in \mathbb{R}^n$ of payments. When there is no ambiguity, we write Q and $\mathbf{p}$ instead of $Q(\mathbf{b})$ and $\mathbf{p}(\mathbf{b})$, respectively. We assume that a mechanism satisfies the following conditions:

- *No Positive Transfer (NPT)*: The payments are nonnegative (i.e., $p_i \geq 0$ for all i).
- *Voluntary Participation (VP)*: An agent who does not receive the service is not charged (i.e., $p_i = 0$ for $i \notin Q$), and an agent who receives the service is not charged more than her bid (i.e., $p_i \leq b_i$ for $i \in Q$)
- *Consumer Sovereignty (CS)*: For each agent i, there is some bid b_i^* such that if i bids b_i^*, she will get the service, no matter what others bid.

Furthermore, we want the mechanisms to be approximately budget-balanced. We call a mechanism γ-budget-balanced with respect to the cost function c if the total amount the mechanism charges the agents is between $\gamma c(Q)$ and $c(Q)$ (i.e., $\gamma c(Q) \leq \sum_{i \in Q} x_i \leq c(Q)$).

We look for mechanisms, called *group strategyproof mechanisms*, which satisfy the following property in addition to NPT, VP, and CS. Let $S \subseteq \mathcal{A}$ be a coalition of agents, and $\mathbf{u}, \mathbf{u}'$ be two vectors of bids satisfying $u_i = u_i'$ for every $i \notin S$ (we think of $\mathbf{u}$ as the values of agents, and $\mathbf{u}'$ as a vector of strategically chosen bids). Let $(Q, \mathbf{p})$ and $(Q', \mathbf{p}')$ denote the outputs of the mechanism when the bids are $\mathbf{u}$ and $\mathbf{u}'$, respectively. A mechanism is *group strategyproof* if for every coalition S of agents, if the inequality $u_i q_i' - p_i' \geq u_i q_i - p_i$ holds for every $i \in S$, then it holds with equality for every $i \in S$. In other words, there should not be any coalition S and vector $\mathbf{u}'$ of bids such that if members of S announce $\mathbf{u}'$ instead of $\mathbf{u}$ (their true value) as their bids, then every member of the coalition S is at least as happy as in the truthful scenario, and at least one person is happier.

Moulin showed that cost-sharing methods satisfying an additional property termed *cross-monotonicity* can be used to design group-strategyproof cost-sharing mechanisms. The cross-monotonicity property captures the notion that agents should not be penalized as the serviced set grows. To define this property, we first need to define the notion of a cost-sharing *scheme*.

Definition 15.12 Let $(\mathcal{A}, c)$ denote a cost-sharing game. A *cost-sharing scheme* is a function that for each set $S \subseteq \mathcal{A}$, assigns a cost allocation for S. More formally, a cost-sharing scheme is a function $\xi \colon \mathcal{A} \times 2^{\mathcal{A}} \mapsto \mathbb{R}$ such that, for every $S \subseteq \mathcal{A}$ and every $i \notin S$, $\xi(i, S) = 0$. We say that a cost-sharing scheme ξ is γ-budget balanced if for every set $S \subseteq \mathcal{A}$, we have $\gamma c(S) \leq \sum_{i \in S} \xi(i, S) \leq c(S)$.

Definition 15.13 A cost-sharing scheme ξ is *cross-monotone* if for all $S, T \subseteq \mathcal{A}$ and $i \in S$, $\xi(i, S) \geq \xi(i, S \cup T)$.

Mechanism $\mathcal{M}_\xi$
Initialize $S \leftarrow \mathcal{A}$.
Repeat
Let $S \leftarrow \{i \in S : b_i \geq \xi(i, S)\}$.
Until for all $i \in S$, $b_i \geq \xi(i, S)$.
Return $Q = S$ and $p_i = \xi(i, S)$ for all i.

Figure 15.2. Moulin's group-strategyproof mechanism.

The following proposition shows that cross-monotonicity is a stronger property than core.

Proposition 15.14 *Let ξ be an γ-budget-balanced cross-monotonic cost sharing scheme for the cost-sharing game $(\mathcal{A}, c)$. Then $\xi(., \mathcal{A})$ is in the γ-core of this game.*

PROOF We need to verify only that $\xi(., \mathcal{A})$ satisfies the core property, i.e., for every set $S \subseteq \mathcal{A}$, $\sum_{i \in S} \xi(i, \mathcal{A}) \leq c(S)$. By the cross-monotonicity property, for every $i \in S$, $\xi(i, \mathcal{A}) \leq \xi(i, S)$. Therefore, $\sum_{i \in S} \xi(i, \mathcal{A}) \leq \sum_{i \in S} \xi(i, S) \leq c(S)$, where the last inequality follows from the γ-budget balance property of ξ. □

Given a cross-monotonic cost-sharing scheme ξ for the cost-sharing game $(\mathcal{A}, c)$, we define a cost-sharing mechanism $\mathcal{M}_\xi$ as presented in Figure 15.2.

The following proposition provides an alternative way to view the mechanism $\mathcal{M}_\xi$.

Proposition 15.15 *Assume ξ is a cross-monotonic cost sharing scheme for the cost-sharing game $(\mathcal{A}, c)$, and $b_i \in \mathbb{R}^+ \cup \{0\}$ for every $i \in \mathcal{A}$. Then there is a unique maximal set $S \subseteq \mathcal{A}$ satisfying the property that for every $i \in S$, $b_i \geq \xi(i, S)$. The mechanism $\mathcal{M}_\xi$ returns this set.*

PROOF Assume that two different maximal sets S_1 and S_2 satisfy the stated property, i.e., $b_i \geq \xi(i, S_1)$ for every $i \in S_1$ and $b_i \geq \xi(i, S_2)$ for every $i \in S_2$. Then for every $i \in S_1$, $b_i \geq \xi(i, S_1) \geq \xi(i, S_1 \cup S_2)$, where the last inequality follows from cross-monotonicity of ξ. Similarly, for every $i \in S_2$, $b_i \geq \xi(i, S_1 \cup S_2)$. Therefore, the set $S_1 \cup S_2$ also satisfies this property. This contradicts with the maximality of S_1 and S_2.

Let S^* denote the unique maximal set satisfying $b_i \geq \xi(i, S^*)$ for all $i \in S^*$. We claim that $\mathcal{M}_\xi$ never eliminates any of the agents in S^* from the serviced set S. Consider, for contradiction, the first step where it eliminates an agent $i \in S^*$ from the serviced set S. This means that we must have $b_i < \xi(i, S)$. However, since $S^* \subseteq S$, by cross-monotonicity we have $\xi(i, S) \leq \xi(i, S^*)$, and hence $b_i < \xi(i, S^*)$, contradicting the definition of S^*. Therefore, the set Q returned by $\mathcal{M}_\xi$ contains S^*. By maximality of S^*, it cannot contain any other agent, that is, $Q = S^*$. □

We are now ready to prove the following theorem of Moulin.

Theorem 15.16 *If ξ is an γ-budget-balanced cross-monotonic cost-sharing scheme, then $\mathcal{M}_\xi$ is group-strategyproof and γ-budget balanced.*

PROOF Assume, for contradiction, that there is a coalition T of agents that benefits from bidding according to the vector $\mathbf{u}'$ instead of their true values $\mathbf{u}$. Agents in T can be partitioned into two sets T^+ and T^- based on whether their bid in $\mathbf{u}'$ is greater than their bid in $\mathbf{u}$, or not. First, we claim that it can be assumed, without loss of generality, that T^+ is empty, i.e., agents cannot benefit from overbidding. To see this, we start from a bid vector where every agent in T bids according to $\mathbf{u}'$ (and others bid truthfully), and reduce the bids of the agents in T^+ to their true value one by one. If at any step, e.g., when the bid of agent $i \in T^+$ is reduced from u'_i to u_i, the outcome of the auction changes, then by Proposition 15.15, i must be a winner when she bids according to $\mathbf{u}'$, and not a winner when she bids according to $\mathbf{u}$. This means that $u'_i \geq \xi(i, S_i) > u_i$, where S_i is the set of winners when i bids according to $\mathbf{u}'$. However, this means that the agent i must pay an amount greater than her true value in the scenario where every agent in T bids according to $\mathbf{u}'$. This is in contradiction with the assumption that agents in T all benefit from the collusion. By this argument, the bid of every agent in T^+ can be lowered to her true value without changing the outcome of the auction. Therefore, we assume without loss of generality that T^+ is empty.

Now, let S' and S denote the set of winners in the untruthful and the truthful scenarios (i.e., when agents bid according to $\mathbf{u}'$ and $\mathbf{u}$), respectively. As the bid of each agent in $\mathbf{u}'$ is less than or equal to her bid in $\mathbf{u}$, by Proposition 15.15, $S' \subseteq S$. By cross-monotonicity, this implies that the payment of each agent in the untruthful scenario is at least as much as her payment in the truthful scenario. Therefore, no agent can be strictly happier in the untruthful scenario than in the truthful scenario. □

Moulin's theorem shows that cross-monotonic cost-sharing schemes give rise to group-strategyproof mechanisms. An interesting question is whether the converse also holds, i.e., is there a way to construct a cross-monotonic cost-sharing scheme given a group-strategyproof mechanism? The answer to this question is negative (unless the cost function is assumed to be submodular), as there are examples where a cost function has a group-strategyproof mechanism but no cross-monotonic cost-sharing scheme. A partial characterization of the cost-sharing schemes that correspond to group-strategyproof mechanisms in terms of a property called semi-cross-monotonicity is known; however, finding a complete characterization of cost-sharing schemes arising from group-strategyproof mechanisms remains an open question.

15.4 Cost Sharing via the Primal-Dual Schema

In Section 15.2.2, we discussed how a cost allocation in the approximate core of a game can be computed by solving an LP, and noted that for many combinatorial optimization games, this LP is equivalent to the dual of the standard LP relaxation of the problem and the cost shares correspond to the dual variables. In this section, we explain how a technique called the *primal-dual schema* can be used to compute cost shares that not only are in the approximate core of the game, but also satisfy the cross-monotonicity property, and hence can be used in the mechanism described in the previous section. The primal-dual schema is a standard technique in the field of approximation algorithms, where the focus is on computing an approximately optimal primal solution, and the dual variables (cost shares) are merely a by-product of the algorithm.

The idea of the primal-dual schema, which is often used to solve cost minimization problems, is to write the optimization problem as a mathematical program that can be relaxed into an LP (we refer to this LP as the primal LP). The dual of this LP gives a lower bound on the value of the optimal solution for the problem. Primal-dual algorithms simultaneously construct a solution to the primal problem and its dual. This is generally done by initially setting all dual variables to zero, and then gradually increasing these variables until some constraint in the dual program goes tight. This constraint hints at an object that can be *paid for* by the dual to be included in the primal solution. After this, the dual variables involved in the tight constraint are *frozen*, and the algorithm continues by increasing other dual variables. The algorithm ends when a complete solution for the primal problem is constructed. The analysis is based on proving that the values of the constructed primal and dual solutions are close to each other, and therefore they are both close to optimal.[3]

We will elaborate on two examples in this section: submodular games, where a simple primal-dual algorithm with no modification yields cross-monotonic cost-shares, and the facility location game, where extra care needs to be taken to obtain a cross-monotonic cost-sharing scheme. In the latter case, we introduce a rather general technique of using "ghost duals" to turn the standard primal-dual algorithm for the problem into an algorithm that returns a cross-monotonic cost-sharing scheme.

15.4.1 Submodular Games

Let us start with a definition of submodular games.

Definition 15.17 A cost-sharing game $(\mathcal{A}, c)$ is called a *submodular game* if the cost function c satisfies

$$\forall S, T \subseteq \mathcal{A}, \quad c(S) + c(T) \geq c(S \cup T) + c(S \cap T).$$

The above condition is equivalent to the condition of decreasing marginal cost, which says that for every two agents i and j and every set of agents $S \subset \mathcal{A} \setminus \{i, j\}$, the marginal cost of adding i to S (i.e., $c(S \cup \{i\}) - c(S)$) is no less than the marginal cost of adding i to $S \cup \{j\}$ (i.e., $c(S \cup \{i, j\}) - c(S \cup \{j\})$). Recall that we always assume $c(\emptyset) = 0$.

[3] In many primal-dual algorithms, a postprocessing step is required to bring the cost of the primal solution down. However, this step often does not change the cost shares.

Submodular games (also known as *concave* games) constitute an important class of cost-sharing games with many interesting properties. One example in this class is the multicast problem discussed in Section 14.2.2 of this book.

Consider a submodular game $(\mathcal{A}, c)$, and the LPs (15.2) and (15.1) as the primal and the dual programs for this game, respectively. It is not hard to see that by submodularity of c, the solution of the primal program is always $c(\mathcal{A})$, giving a trivial optimal solution for this LP. However, the dual LP (15.1) is nontrivial and its optimal solutions correspond to cost allocations in the core of the game. Let $\boldsymbol{\alpha}$ be a feasible solution of this LP. We say that a set $S \subseteq \mathcal{A}$ is *tight*, if the corresponding inequality in the LP is tight, i.e., if $\sum_{j \in S} \alpha_j = c(S)$. We need the following lemma to describe the algorithm.

Lemma 15.18 *Let $\boldsymbol{\alpha}$ be a feasible solution of the linear program (15.1). If two sets $S_1, S_2 \subseteq \mathcal{A}$ are tight, then so is $S_1 \cup S_2$.*

PROOF Since $\boldsymbol{\alpha}$ is feasible, we have $\sum_{j \in S_1 \cap S_2} \alpha_j \leq c(S_1 \cap S_2)$. This, together with the submodularity of c and tightness of S_1 and S_2, implies

$$\begin{aligned} c(S_1 \cup S_2) &\leq c(S_1) + c(S_2) - c(S_1 \cap S_2) \\ &\leq \sum_{j \in S_1} \alpha_j + \sum_{j \in S_2} \alpha_j - \sum_{j \in S_1 \cap S_2} \alpha_j \\ &= \sum_{j \in S_1 \cup S_2} \alpha_j \end{aligned}$$

Therefore, $S_1 \cup S_2$ is tight. □

Corollary 15.19 *There is a unique maximal tight set. It is simply the union of all the tight sets.*

We are now ready to state the algorithm that computes the cost shares. This algorithm is presented in Figure 15.3. Notice that by Lemma 15.18, when a new set goes tight, the new maximal tight set contains the old one, and therefore once an element $i \in T$ is included in the frozen set F, it will stay in this set until the end of the algorithm. Thus, the cost share α_j at the end of the algorithm is precisely the first time at which the element j is frozen. Furthermore, note that the algorithm never allows $\boldsymbol{\alpha}$ to become an infeasible solution of the LP (15.1), and stops only when the set T goes tight. Hence, the cost shares computed by the algorithm satisfy the budget balance and the core property. All that remains is to show that they also satisfy the cross-monotonicity property.

Theorem 15.20 *The cost sharing scheme defined by the algorithm* SubmodularCostShare *(Figure 15.3) is cross monotone.*

PROOF Let $T_1 \subset T_2 \subseteq \mathcal{A}$. We simultaneously run the algorithm for T_1 and T_2, and call these two runs the T_1-run and the T_2-run. It is enough to show that at any moment, the set of frozen elements in the T_1-run is a subset of that of the T_2-run. Consider a time t (i.e., the moment when all unfrozen cost shares in both runs are

Algorithm SubmodularCostShare

Input: submodular cost sharing game $(\mathcal{A}, c)$
set $T \subseteq \mathcal{A}$ of agents that receive the service

Output: cost shares α_j for every $j \in T$

For every j, initialize α_j to 0.
Let $F = \emptyset$
While $T \setminus F \neq \emptyset$ do
  Increase all α_j's for $j \in T \setminus F$ at the same rate,
    until a new set goes tight.
  Let F be the maximal tight set.

Figure 15.3. Algorithm for computing cost shares in a submodular game.

equal to t), and let $\boldsymbol{\alpha}^l$ and F_l denote the values of the variables and the frozen set at this moment in the T_l-run, for $l = 1, 2$. We have

$$\begin{aligned} c(F_1 \cup F_2) &\leq c(F_1) + c(F_2) - c(F_1 \cap F_2) \\ &\leq \sum_{i \in F_1} \alpha_i^1 + \sum_{i \in F_2} \alpha_i^2 - \sum_{i \in F_1 \cap F_2} \alpha_i^1 \\ &= \sum_{i \in F_1 \setminus F_2} \alpha_i^1 + \sum_{i \in F_2} \alpha_i^2 \\ &\leq \sum_{i \in F_1 \cup F_2} \alpha_i^2, \end{aligned}$$

where the first inequality follows from submodularity of c, the second follows from the tightness of F_l with respect to $\boldsymbol{\alpha}^l$ $(l = 1, 2)$ and the feasibility of $\boldsymbol{\alpha}^1$, and the last follows from the fact that for every $i \in F_1 \setminus F_2$, since $i \in T_1 \subset T_2$ and i is not frozen at time t in the T_2-run, we have $\alpha_i^2 = t \geq \alpha_i^1$. The above inequality implies that $F_1 \cup F_2$ is tight with respect to $\boldsymbol{\alpha}^2$. Since by definition F_2 is the maximal tight set with respect to $\boldsymbol{\alpha}^2$, we must have $F_1 \cup F_2 = F_2$. Hence, $F_1 \subseteq F_2$, as desired. □

15.4.2 The Facility Location Game

We now turn to our second example, the facility location game, and observe how the standard primal-dual scheme for this problem fails to satisfy cross-monotonicity.

Recall the LP formulation (15.3) of the facility location problem, and the observation that one can assume, without loss of generality, that in a solution to this program, we have $\beta_{ij} = \max(0, \alpha_j - d_{ij})$. In designing a primal-dual algorithm for the facility location game, we think of the quantity $\max(0, \alpha_j - d_{ij})$ as the *contribution* of agent j toward facility i, and say that a facility i is *tight* with respect to the dual solution $\boldsymbol{\alpha}$, if the total contribution i receives in $\boldsymbol{\alpha}$ equals its opening cost, i.e., if $\sum_{j \in A} \max(0, \alpha_j - d_{ij}) = f_i$.

Following the general paradigm of the primal-dual schema, let us consider the following algorithm for computing cost shares in the facility location game: initialize the cost shares α_j to zero and gradually increase them until one of these two events occurs: a facility i goes tight, in which case, this facility is opened, and the cost shares of all agents j with positive contribution to i are frozen (i.e., no longer increased); or for an agent j and a facility i that is already opened, $\alpha_j = d_{ij}$, in which case the cost share of j is frozen. This process continues until all cost shares are frozen.

To illustrate this algorithm, consider the facility location game in Example 15.2 (Figure 15.1). In this example, at time 2, facility 2 goes tight as each of b and c makes one unit of contribution toward this facility. Therefore, the cost shares of b and c are frozen at 2. The cost share of the agent a continues to increase to 4, at which point facility 1 also goes tight and the algorithm stops. In this example, the cost allocation (4, 2, 2) computed by the algorithm is budget balanced and satisfies the core property. In fact, it is known that in every instance, with a postprocessing step that closes some of the open facilities, the cost of the primal solution can be brought down to at most 3 times the sum of cost shares, and therefore the cost shares are $\frac{1}{3}$-budget-balanced on every instance of the facility location game. However, unfortunately the cross-monotonicity property fails, as can be seen in the example in Figure 15.1. In this example, if only agents a and b are present, they will both increase their cost share to 3, at which point both facilities go tight and the algorithm stops. Hence, agent a has a smaller cost share in the set $\{a, b\}$ than in $\{a, b, c\}$.

Intuitively, the reason for the failure of cross-monotonicity in the above example is that without c, b helps a pay for the cost of facility 1. However, when c is present, she helps b pay for the cost of facility 2. This, in turn, hurts a, as b stops helping a as soon as facility 2 is opened. This suggests the following way to fix the problem: we modify the algorithm so that even after an agent is frozen, she continues to grow her *ghost* cost share. This ghost cost share is not counted toward the final cost share of the agent, but it can help other agents pay for the opening cost of facilities. For example, in the instance in Figure 15.1 when all three agents are present, even though agents b and c stop increasing their cost share at time 2, their ghost share continues to grow, until at time 3, facility 1 is opened with contributions from agents a and b. At this point, the cost share of agent a is also frozen and the algorithm terminates. The final cost shares will be 3, 2, and 2. The pseudo-code of this algorithm is presented in Figure 15.4. Variables $\boldsymbol{\alpha}'$ in this pseudo-code represent the ghost cost shares.

With this modification, it is an easy exercise to show that the cost shares computed by the algorithm are cross-monotone. However, it is not clear that the budget balance property is preserved. In fact, it is natural to expect that having ghost cost shares that contribute toward opening facilities in the primal solution but do not count toward the final cost shares could hurt the budget balance (see, i.e., Exercise 15.3). For the facility location problem, the following theorem shows that this is not the case.

Theorem 15.21 *The cost allocation computed by the algorithm* FLCostShare *(Figure 15.4) is* $\frac{1}{3}$*-budget balanced.*

Algorithm FLCostShare

Input: facility location game $(\mathcal{A}, c)$ defined by
facility opening costs f_i and distances d_{ij}
set $T \subseteq \mathcal{A}$ of agents that receive the service

Output: cost shares α_j for every $j \in T$

For every j, initialize both α_j and α'_j to 0.
Let $F = \emptyset$.
While $T \setminus F \neq \emptyset$ do
Increase all α_j's for $j \in T \setminus F$ and α'_j's for $j \in T$ at the same rate, until

- for an unopened facility i, $\sum_{j\in T} \max(0, \alpha'_j - d_{ij}) = f_i$:
  in this case, open facility i, and
  add every agent j with a positive contribution toward i to F;
- for an open facility i and an agent j, $\alpha_j = d_{ij}$:
  in this case, add j to F.

Figure 15.4. Algorithm for computing cost shares in the facility location game.

PROOF It is enough to show that for every instance of the facility location problem, it is possible to construct a solution whose cost is at most three times the sum of the cost shares computed by FLCostShare. To do this, we perform the following postprocessing step on the solution computed by FLCostShare. Let t_i denote the time at which facility i is opened by FLCostShare, and order all facilities that are opened by this algorithm in the order of increasing t_i's. We proceed in this order and for any facility i, check if there is any *open* facility i' that comes before i in this order and is within distance $2t_i$ of i. If such a facility exists, we close facility i; otherwise, we keep it open. After processing all facilities in this order, let $\mathcal{F}'$ denote the set of facilities that remain open and connect each agent in T to its closest facility in $\mathcal{F}'$. We now show that $\sum_{j\in T} \alpha_j$ is enough to pay for at least one third of the cost of this solution.

Let S_i denote the set of agents within distance t_i of facility i. First, observe that for any two facilities i and i' in $\mathcal{F}'$, S_i and $S_{i'}$ are disjoint. This is because if there is an agent j in $S_i \cap S_{i'}$, the distance between i and i' is at most $t_i + t_{i'} \leq 2\max(t_i, t_{i'})$, and therefore one of i and i' must have been closed in the above postprocessing step. To complete the proof, it is enough to show two statements. First, we show that for every facility $i \in \mathcal{F}'$, the cost shares of agents in S_i is enough to pay for at least a third of their distances to i (and hence, to their closest facility in $\mathcal{F}'$) plus the opening cost of i. Second, we show that each agent j that is not in $\cup_{i\in\mathcal{F}'} S_i$ can pay for at least one third of its distance to its closest facility in $\mathcal{F}'$.

To prove the first statement, note that for every facility $i \in \mathcal{F}'$, the ghost cost share of every agent contributing to i at the time of its opening is precisely t_i; hence, $\sum_{j\in S_i}(t_i - d_{ij}) = f_i$. Therefore, if we show that for every $j \in S_i$, $\alpha_j \geq t_i/3$, we would get $\sum_{j\in S_i} \alpha_j \geq \frac{1}{3}(f_i + \sum_{j\in S_i} d_{ij})$. Assume, for contradiction, that there is an agent j with $\alpha_j < t_i/3$ and consider the facility i_1 with $t_{i_1} = \alpha_j$ (i.e., the facility whose opening has caused the cost share of j to freeze). There must be a facility $i_2 \in \mathcal{F}'$ that is within distance $2t_{i_1}$ of i_1 (if $i_1 \in \mathcal{F}'$, we can let $i_2 = i_1$). Therefore, the distance between i and i_2 is at most $d_{ij} + d_{i_1 j} + 2t_{i_1} \le t_i + 3\alpha_j < 2t_i$. This contradicts the assumption that $i \in \mathcal{F}'$, since i comes after i_2 in the ordering and $i_2 \in \mathcal{F}'$.

To show the second statement, consider an agent $j \in T \setminus \cup_{i \in \mathcal{F}'} S_i$, and let i be the facility with $t_i = \alpha_j$. There must be a facility i' in $\mathcal{F}'$ that is within distance $2t_i$ of i (i' can be the same as i). Therefore, the distance from j to its closest facility in $\mathcal{F}'$ is at most $d_{ij} + 2t_i \le 3\alpha_j$. □

15.5 Limitations of Cross-Monotonic Cost-Sharing Schemes

As we saw in Section 15.3, a cost-sharing scheme that is cross-monotone also satisfies the core property. As a result, for any combinatorial cost-sharing game, an upper bound on the budget balance factor of cross-monotonic cost-sharing schemes can be obtained using Theorem 15.8 and the integrality gap examples of the corresponding LP. As we will see in this section, for many combinatorial optimization games, the cross-monotonicity property is strictly stronger than the core property, and better upper bounds on the budget balance factor of such games can be obtained using a technique based on the probabilistic method.

The high-level idea of this technique is as follows: Fix any cross-monotonic cost-sharing scheme. We explicitly construct an instance of the game and look at the cost-sharing scheme on various subsets of this instance. We need to argue that there is a subset S of agents such that the total cost shares of the elements of S is small compared to the cost of S. This is done using the probabilistic method: we pick a subset S at random from a certain distribution and show that in expectation, the ratio of the recovered cost to the cost of S is low. Therefore, there is a manifestation of S for which this ratio is low. To bound the expected value of the sum of cost shares of the elements of S, we use cross-monotonicity and bound the cost share of each agent $i \in S$ by the cost share of i in a substructure T_i of S. Bounding the expected cost share of i in T_i is done by showing that for every substructure T, every $i \in T$ has the same probability of occurring in a structure S in which $T_i = T$. This implies that the expected cost share of i in T_i (where the expectation is over the choice of S) is at most the cost of T_i divided by the number of agents in T_i. Summing up these values for all i gives us the desired bound.

In the following, we show how this technique can be applied to the facility location problem to show that the factor $1/3$ obtained in the previous section is the best possible. We start by giving an example on which the algorithm FLCostShare in Figure 15.4 recovers only a third of the cost. This example will be used as the randomly chosen structure in our proof.

Lemma 15.22 *Let $\mathcal{I}$ be an instance of the facility location problem consisting of $m + k$ agents $a_1, \ldots, a_m, a'_1, \ldots, a'_k$ and m facilities $f_1, \ldots, f_m$ each of opening cost 3. For every i and j, the connection costs between f_i and a_i and between*

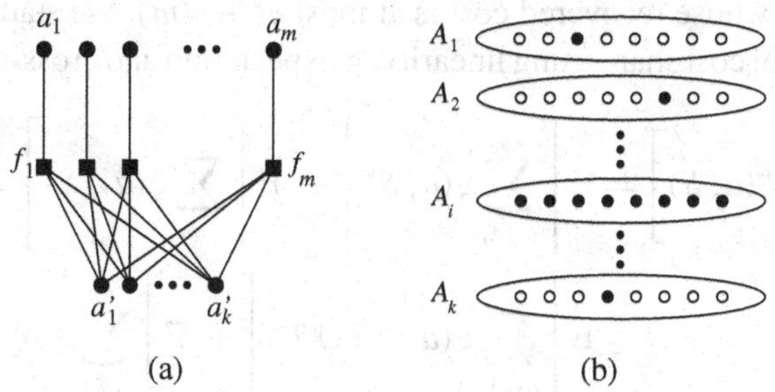

Figure 15.5. Facility location sample distribution.

f_i and a'_j are all 1, and other connection costs are obtained by the triangle inequality. See Figure 15.5a. Then if $m = \omega(k)$ and k tends to infinity, the optimal solution for $\mathcal{I}$ has cost $3m + o(m)$.

PROOF The solution which opens just one facility, say f_1, has cost $3m + k + 1 = 3m + o(m)$. We show that this solution is optimal. Consider any feasible solution that opens f facilities. The first opened facility can cover $k + 1$ agents with connection cost 1. Each additional facility can cover 1 additional client with connection cost 1. Thus, the number of agents with connection cost 1 is $k + f$. The remaining $m - f$ agents have connection cost 3. Therefore, the cost of the solution is $3f + k + f + 3(m - f) = 3m + k + f$. As $f \geq 1$, this shows that any feasible solution costs at least as much as the solution we constructed. □

Theorem 15.23 *Any cross-monotonic cost-sharing scheme for facility location is at most 1/3-budget-balanced.*

PROOF Consider the following instance of the facility location problem. There are k sets $A_1, \ldots, A_k$ of m agents each, where $m = \omega(k)$ and $k = \omega(1)$. For every subset B of agents containing exactly one agent from each A_i ($|B \cap A_i| = 1$ for all i), there is a facility f_B with connection cost 1 to each agent in B. The remaining connection costs are defined by extending the metric, that is, the cost of connecting agent i to facility f_B for $i \notin B$ is 3. The facility opening costs are all 3.

We pick a random set S of agents in the above instance as follows: Pick a random i from $\{1, \ldots, k\}$, and for every $j \neq i$, pick an agent a_j uniformly at random from A_j. Let $T = \{a_j : j \neq i\}$ and $S = A_i \cup T$. See Figure 15.5b for an example. It is easy to see that the set S induces an instance of the facility location problem almost identical to the instance $\mathcal{I}$ in Lemma 15.22 (the only difference is that here we have more facilities, but it is easy to see that the only relevant facilities are the ones that are present in $\mathcal{I}$). Therefore, the cost of the optimal solution on S is $3m + o(m)$.

We show that for any cross-monotonic cost-sharing scheme ξ, the average recovered cost over the choice of S is at most $m + o(m)$ and thus conclude that there is some S whose recovered cost is at most $m + o(m)$. We start by bounding the expected total cost share using linearity of expectation and cross-monotonicity:

$$\begin{aligned}\mathrm{E}_S\left[\sum_{a\in S}\xi(a,S)\right] &= \mathrm{E}\left[\sum_{a\in A_i}\xi(a,S)\right] + \mathrm{E}\left[\sum_{j\neq i}\xi(a_j,S)\right]\\ &\leq \mathrm{E}\left[\sum_{a\in A_i}\xi(a,\{a\}\cup T)\right] + \mathrm{E}\left[\sum_{j\neq i}\xi(a_j,T)\right].\end{aligned}$$

Notice that the set T has a facility location solution of cost $3 + k - 1$ and thus by the budget-balance condition the second term in the above expression is at most $k + 2$. The first term in the above expression can be written as $m\mathrm{E}_{S,a}[\xi(a, \{a\} \cup T)]$, where the expectation is over the random choice of S and the random choice of a from A_i. This is equivalent to the following random experiment: From each A_j, pick an agent a_j uniformly at random. Then pick i from $\{1, \ldots, k\}$ uniformly at random and let $a = a_i$ and $T = \{a_j : j \neq i\}$. From this description it is clear that the expected value of $\xi(a, \{a\} \cup T)$ is equal to $\frac{1}{k}\sum_{j=1}^{k}\xi(a_j, \{a_1, \ldots, a_k\})$. This, by the budget-balance property and the fact that $\{a_1, \ldots, a_k\}$ has a solution of cost $k + 3$, cannot be more than $\frac{k+3}{k}$. Therefore,

$$\mathrm{E}_S\left[\sum_{a\in S}\xi(a,S)\right] \leq m\left(\frac{k+3}{k}\right) + (k+2) = m + o(m), \qquad (15.6)$$

when $m = \omega(k)$ and $k = \omega(1)$. Therefore, the expected value of the ratio of recovered cost to total cost tends to $1/3$. □

15.6 The Shapley Value and the Nash Bargaining Solution

One of the problems with the notion of core in cost-sharing games is that it rarely assigns a unique cost allocation to a game: as illustrated in Example 15.4, the core of a game is often either empty (making it useless in deciding how the cost of a service should be shared among the agents), or contains more than one point (making it necessary to have a second criterion for choosing a cost allocation). In this section, we study a solution concept called the Shapley value that assigns a single cost allocation to any given cost-sharing game. We also discuss a solution concept known as the Nash bargaining solution for a somewhat different but related framework for surplus sharing. In both cases, the solution concept can be uniquely characterized in terms of a few natural axioms it satisfies. These theorems are classical examples of the *axiomatic approach* in economic theory.

Both the Shapley value and the Nash bargaining solution are widely applicable concepts. For example, an application of the Shapley value in combination with the Moulin mechanism to multicasting is discussed elsewhere in this book (see Section 14.2.2). Also, the Nash solution is related to Kelly's notion of proportional fairness discussed in Section 5.12, and the Eisenberg-Gale convex program of Section 6.2.

15.6.1 The Shapley Value

Consider a cost-sharing game defined by the set $\mathcal{A}$ of n agents and the cost function c. A simple way of allocating the cost $c(\mathcal{A})$ among all agents is to order the agents in some order, say $a_1, a_2, \ldots, a_n$, then proceed in this order and charge each agent the marginal cost of adding her to the serviced set. In other words, the first agent a_1 will be charged her stand-alone cost $c(\{a_1\})$, the second agent a_2 will be charged $c(\{a_1, a_2\}) - c(\{a_1\})$, and so on. This method is called an *incremental cost sharing*.

A problem with the method described above is that it is not anonymous, i.e., the ordering of the agents makes a difference in the amount they will be charged. The Shapley value fixes this problem by taking a *random* ordering of the agents picked uniformly from the set of all $n!$ possible orderings, and charging each agent her *expected* marginal cost in this ordering. Since for any agent $i \in \mathcal{A}$ and any set $S \subseteq \mathcal{A} \setminus \{i\}$ with $|S| = s$, the probability that the set of agents that come before i in a random ordering is precisely S is $s!(n-1-s)!/n!$, the Shapley value can be defined by the following formula:

$$\text{For each agent } i, \quad \phi_i(c) = \sum_{s=0}^{n-1} \frac{s!(n-1-s)!}{n!} \sum_{S \subseteq \mathcal{A}\setminus\{i\}, |S|=s} (c(S \cup \{i\}) - c(S)),$$

where $\phi_i(c)$ indicates the cost share of $i \in \mathcal{A}$ in the cost-sharing game $(\mathcal{A}, c)$. As the following example shows, the cost sharing given by the Shapley value need not be in the core of the game, even if the core is nonempty.

Example 15.24 Consider the facility location game defined in Example 15.2. The Shapley values in this game are as follows:

$$\phi_a = \frac{1}{3} \times 4 + \frac{1}{6} \times 3 + \frac{1}{6} \times 4 + \frac{1}{3} \times 4 = \frac{23}{6}$$

$$\phi_b = \frac{1}{3} \times 3 + \frac{1}{6} \times 2 + \frac{1}{6} \times 1 + \frac{1}{3} \times 1 = \frac{11}{6}$$

$$\phi_c = \frac{1}{3} \times 3 + \frac{1}{6} \times 3 + \frac{1}{6} \times 1 + \frac{1}{3} \times 2 = \frac{7}{3}$$

This cost allocation is not in the core of the game, since $\phi_b + \phi_c = \frac{25}{6} > 4 = c(\{b, c\})$. This is despite the fact that, as we saw in Example 15.4, the core of this game is nonempty.

However, for submodular games, it is known that any incremental cost-sharing, and therefore the Shapley value (which is a linear combination of incremental cost-sharing methods), is in the core of the game. In fact, it can be shown that in this class of games, the Shapley value is cross-monotone (see Exercise 15.2), making it useful in the design of group-strategyproof mechanisms using Moulin's mechanism of Section 15.3.[4] This

[4] It is worth noting that since the Shapley value is defined in terms of a formula comprising of exponentially many points of the function $c(\cdot)$, evaluating it is computationally hard in general. However, when the cost function c is submodular, random sampling can be used to approximate the Shapley values to within an arbitrary degree of accuracy.

is used in Section 14.2.2 of this book, in an application to the multicast problem. Many other applications of the Shapley value, as well as various generalizations (to settings such as NTU games or games with nonbinary demands), are extensively studied in the economic literature.

15.6.2 An Axiomatic Characterization of the Shapley Value

In his original paper, Shapley introduced what is now known as the Shapley value as the unique value satisfying the three properties defined below.

Definition 15.25 Fix a set $\mathcal{A}$ of n agents. A *value* is a function that assigns to each cost function c a vector $\phi(c) \in \mathbb{R}^n$ of nonnegative numbers. Three properties of values are defined as follows.

- *Anonymity*: Changing the names of the agents does not change their cost shares. Formally, ϕ satisfies anonymity if for every permutation π of $\mathcal{A}$ and every cost function c, $\phi_{\pi_i}(\pi(c)) = \phi_i(c)$ for every $i \in \mathcal{A}$.
- *Dummy*: An agent who does not add to the cost should not be charged anything. More precisely, if for every set $S \subset \mathcal{A} \setminus \{i\}$, $c(S) = c(S \cup \{i\})$, then $\phi_i(c) = 0$.
- *Additivity*: For every two cost functions c_1 and c_2, $\phi(c_1 + c_2) = \phi(c_1) + \phi(c_2)$, where $c_1 + c_2$ is the cost function defined by $(c_1 + c_2)(S) = c_1(S) + c_2(S)$.

Theorem 15.26 *The Shapley value is the unique value satisfying anonymity, dummy, and additivity.*

The above theorem, whose proof is omitted here, is an example of the *axiomatic* method in the economic theory, whose goal is to find (or prove the nonexistence of) solution concepts that satisfy certain sets of desirable axioms, or characterize known solution concepts in terms of axioms they satisfy. Two other prominent examples of axiomatic results are Nash's theorem on bargaining (presented in the next section; this result is considered a starting point for the axiomatic approach in economic theory), and Arrow's impossibility result in the social choice literature. One example where this framework is applied in computer science is the axiomatic characterization of the *PageRank* algorithm for ranking Web search results.

15.6.3 The Nash Bargaining Solution

The bargaining problem studies a situation where two or more agents need to select one of the many possible outcomes of a joint collaboration. Examples include wage negotiation between an employer and a potential employee, or trade negotiation between two countries. Each party in the negotiation has the option of leaving the table, in which case the bargaining will result in a *disagreement outcome*. More formally, a bargaining game for two players (the case of more players is similar) is given by a set $X \in \mathbb{R}^2$, along with a *disagreement point* $d \in X$. Each point in X corresponds to one outcome of the bargaining, and specifies the utility of each player for this outcome. The point d specifies the utility of each player for the disagreement outcome. As adding or subtracting a value to the utility of an individual does not change her relative preferences, we assume, without loss of generality, that $d = (0, 0)$. Furthermore, we assume that the set X is convex and compact. Note that convexity of X is without loss of generality, if an outcome is allowed to be a probability distribution over *pure* outcomes. Furthermore, we assume X contains at least one point whose coordinates are both positive (i.e., both parties have some incentive to negotiate).

The above model for bargaining was first defined and studied by Nash. Note that an NTU cooperative game can be considered an extension of the bargaining model, where in addition to the outcome of individual deviations (the disagreement point), the outcome of group deviations are also given. Nash's bargaining theorem gives a characterization of a *solution* for the bargaining game in terms of axioms it satisfies. Formally,

Definition 15.27 A solution for the bargaining game (also known as a *social choice function*) is a function that assigns to each set X satisfying the above properties a single point $\phi(X) \in X$. We define four properties of a solution as follows:

- *Pareto Optimality*: $\phi(X)$ is a Pareto optimal point in X, i.e., there is no point $p \in X$ with $p > \phi(X)$, coordinate-wise.
- *Symmetry*: If the set X is symmetric, then $\phi(X) = (u, u)$ for some $u \in \mathbb{R}$.
- *Scale Independence*: The solution is independent of the scale used to measure individual utilities; i.e., if X' is obtained from X by multiplying all utilities of the i'th player by λ_i, then $\phi(X')$ can be obtained from $\phi(X)$ by multiplying the i'th coordinate by λ_i.
- *Independence of Irrelevant Alternatives*: If $Y \subset X$ and $\phi(X) \in Y$, then $\phi(Y) = \phi(X)$.

We now state Nash's bargaining theorem. The proof of this theorem is simple, and is omitted here.

Theorem 15.28 *There is a unique solution for bargaining games satisfying Pareto optimality, symmetry, scale independence, and independence of irrelevant alternatives. This solution assigns to each set X a point (u_1, u_2) maximizing $u_1 u_2$.*

Nash's theorem gives one example of what is called a *collective utility function*. A collective utility function is a function that aggregates the utilities of individuals into a single number indicating the utility of the *society*. Classical examples of collective utility functions are the utilitarian function (which simply adds up the individual utilities), the egalitarian function (which takes the minimum of individual utilities), and the Nash function (which takes the product of the utilities).

15.7 Conclusion

In this chapter, we reviewed some of the basic notions (such as the core, cross-monotonicity, group-strategyproof mechanisms, Shapley value, and the Nash bargaining solution) and classical results on cost and surplus sharing. We observed that the algorithmic questions regarding computing cost shares are closely tied to the LP formulation of the corresponding optimization problem, and explained how standard LP-based techniques developed in the field of approximation algorithms can be used to tackle such questions.

There is also a potential for contributions in the other direction. For many combinatorial optimization problems, thinking in terms of the cost-sharing problem (i.e., the dual problem) instead of the primal can shed new light on the problem. In the facility location example discussed in Section 15.4.2, the proof of Theorem 15.21 gives an approximation algorithm different from the standard primal-dual algorithm for the problem. As it turns out, in this case the algorithm was known before, but Theorem 15.21 gives a new primal-dual interpretation of this algorithm. For the Steiner forest problem, the search for a cross-monotonic cost-sharing scheme has resulted in a new 2-approximation algorithm, and a stronger LP relaxation for the problem. In fact, for most combinatorial optimization problems, LP (15.2) is at least as strong an LP formulation as the standard LP relaxation; i.e., it gives at least as good a lower bound on the value of the optimal solution. These LPs are equivalent for some problems, as we saw in Section 15.2.2 for the facility location problem. However, for many other problems, such as the well-studied Steiner tree problem, this appears not to be the case. Therefore, one possible approach to obtain stronger LP relaxations (which could lead to better approximation algorithms) for such problems is to start from (15.2) and try to relax this program into one that can be solved in polynomial time. In the case of the Steiner tree problem, the integrality gap of LP (15.2) seems to be related to the long open question on the integrality gap of the bidirected LP relaxation of this problem.

Another way the economic approach to cost sharing can contribute to the theory of algorithms is by providing new perspectives and new problems. For example, the axiomatic approach explained in Section 15.6 seems to be a suitable tool for studying properties of heuristic algorithms. One notable example is the axiomatic characterization of the popular web ranking algorithm PageRank. Also, the field of combinatorial optimization almost exclusively deals with problems whose objective is to minimize the total cost, or maximize the total benefit, which, according to the terminology introduced in Section 15.6.3, corresponds to the utilitarian collective utility function. However, the field of social choice suggests other objective functions, which can lead to new challenging algorithmic questions. One notable example is the Santa Claus problem, which seeks to optimize the egalitarian objective in a simple scheduling model. Also, many of the algorithmic results presented in Chapter 5 for Fisher markets (where the Eisenberg–Gale convex program shows that the market equilibrium corresponds to the point maximizing the Nash collective utility function) can be viewed in this light.

15.8 Notes

Sections 15.1 and 15.2. The notion of a cooperative game was first proposed by von Neumann and Morgenstern (1944). The notion of the core was first introduced by

Gillies (1959). Theorem 15.6 was independently discovered by Bondareva (1963) and Shapley (1967). Theorem 15.11 is due to Scarf (1967). Deng et al. (1997) observed the connection between the core of many combinatorial optimization games and the integrality gap of the corresponding LP. Goemans and Skutella (2000) showed this connection for the facility location game, and proved that deciding whether the core of a facility location game is nonempty is NP-complete. The best lower and upper bound on the integrality gap of LP (15.3) are $\frac{1}{1.52}$, due to Mahdian et al. (2006), and $\frac{1}{1.463}$, due to Guha and Khuller (1999) See Immorlica et al. (2006) for an example of a problem modeled using NTU games.

Section 15.3. For a discussion of the NPT, VP, and CS properties of cost sharing mechanisms see Moulin (1999) and Moulin and Shenker (2001). In our definition of group-strategyproof mechanisms, we did not allow side payments between members of a coalition. For a discussion of mechanism design in a setting where collusion with side payments is allowed, see Goldberg and Hartline (2005). This cross-monotonicity property for cost sharing is similar to the population monotonicity property introduced by Thomson (1983, 1995) in the context of bargaining. For cooperative games, this notion was first introduced by Sprumont (1990). The mechanism $\mathcal{M}_\xi$ and Theorem 15.16 are due to Moulin (1999), where he also proves a converse to this theorem for submodular games. Examples on the connection between group-strategyproof mechanisms and cost-sharing schemes, and a partial characterization of such mechanisms are due to Immorlica et al. (2005).

Sections 15.4 and 15.5. For a general introduction to the primal-dual schema from the perspective of approximation algorithms, see the excellent book by Vazirani (2001). The cost-sharing scheme presented in Section 15.4 for submodular games is due to Dutta and Ray (1989). This scheme was formulated as a primal-dual algorithm and generalized to an algorithm that can increase the dual variables at different rates by Jain and Vazirani (2002). Both Dutta and Ray (1989) Jain and Vazirani (2002) also prove several fairness properties of their cost-sharing schemes. The technique of using ghost duals and its application to the facility location problem (algorithm in Figure 15.4) and single-source rent-or-buy problem are due to Pál and Tardos (2003). The proof of their result on the facility location problem (Theorem 15.21) is based on an algorithm that is originally due to Mettu and Plaxton (2000). The first (non-cross-monotonic) primal-dual algorithm for the facility location problem is due to Jain and Vazirani (2001). The probabilistic technique presented in Section 15.5 and its application to several problems including facility location, vertex cover, and set cover are due to Immorlica et al. (2005). Könemann et al. (2007) gave a 1/2-budget-balanced mechanism, together with a matching upper bound for the Steiner forest problem.

Section 15.6. The Shapley value and its axiomatic characterization (Theorem 15.26) are due to Shapley (1953). In the same paper, Shapley shows that for convex games (which correspond to submodular games in the context of cost sharing) the Shapley value is in the core. The application of Shapley values to the multicast problem is due to Feigenbaum et al. (2000) and is explained in detail in Chapter 14. For other applications of the Shapley value, see the book edited by Roth (1988) or the survey by Winter (2002). The generalization of the Shapley value to games with nonbinary demand is due to Aumann and Shapley (1974). See the survey by McLean (1994) for various generalizations to NTU games. The result on the computation of Shapley values for submodular games is due to Mossel and Saberi (2006). The axiomatic result of Arrow is given in Arrow (1959). Axiomatic characterizations of PageRank (Page et al., 1999) are given by Palacois-Huerta and Volij (2004) and by Altman and Tennenholtz (2005). We refer the reader to the excellent survey by Moulin (2002) for further information on the axiomatic approach to cost sharing. Theorem 15.28 is proved in a seminal paper by Nash (1950). See Moulin (1988) for further discussion of this theorem and its generalization to more than two players. See Moulin (1988, 2003) for a discussion of various collective utility functions and social choice rules. For more information on the Santa Claus problem see Bansal and Sviridenko (2006) and Asadpour and Saberi (2006).

Acknowledgment

We would like to thank Anna Karlin, Hervé Moulin, and Nicole Immorlica for their valuable comments.

Bibliography

A. Altman and M. Tennenholtz. Ranking systems: The PageRank axioms. In *Proc. 6th ACM Conf. Electronic Commerce*, pp. 1–8, 2005.

K.J. Arrow. Rational choice functions and orderings. *Econometrica*, 26:121–127, 1959.

A. Asadpour and A. Saberi. An approximation algorithm for max-min fair allocation of indivisible goods. In *Proc. 39th Annual ACM Symp. Theory of Computing*, 2007.

R.J. Aumann and L.S. Shapley. *Values of Non-Atomic Games*. Princeton University Press, 1974.

N. Bansal and M. Sviridenko. The Santa Claus problem. In *Proc. 38th Annual ACM Symp. Theory of Computing*, 2006.

O.N. Bondareva. Some applications of linear programming to cooperative games. *Problemy Kibernetiki*, 1963.

X. Deng, T. Ibaraki, and H. Nagamochi. Algorithms and complexity in combinatorial optimization games. In *Proc. 8th ACM Symp. on Discrete Algorithms*, 1997.

B. Dutta and D. Ray. A concept of egalitarianism under participation constraints. *Econometrica*, 57(3):615–635, May 1989.

J. Feigenbaum, C. Papadimitriou, and S. Shenker. Sharing the cost of multicast transmission. *Proc. 32nd Annual ACM Symp. Theory of Computing*, 2000.

D.B. Gillies. Solutions to general non-zero-sum games. In A. W. Tucker and R. D. Luce, editors, *Contributions to the Theory of Games*, volume IV, pp. 47–85. Princeton University Press, 1959.

M.X. Goemans and M. Skutella. Cooperative facility location games. *Symp. on Discrete Algorithms*, 2000.

A.V. Goldberg and J.D. Hartline. Collusion-resistant mechanisms for single-parameter agents. In *Proc. 16th ACM Symp. Discrete Algorithms*, pp. 620–629, 2005.

S. Guha and S. Khuller. Greedy strikes back: Improved facility location algorithms. *J. Algorithms*, 31:228–248, 1999.

N. Immorlica, K. Jain, and M. Mahdian. Game-theoretic aspects of designing hyperlink structures. In *Proc. 2nd Workshop on Internet and Network Economics (WINE)*, LNCS 4286:150–161, Springer, 2006.

N. Immorlica, M. Mahdian, and V.S. Mirrokni. Limitations of cross-monotonic cost-sharing schemes. In *Proc. 16th ACM Symp. Discrete Algorithms*, 2005.

K. Jain and V.V. Vazirani. Approximation algorithms for metric facility location and k-median problems using the primal-dual schema and Lagrangian relaxation. *J. ACM*, 48:274–296, 2001.

K. Jain and V.V. Vazirani. Equitable cost allocations via primal-dual-type algorithms. In *Proc. 34th Annual ACM Symp. Theory of Computing*, pp. 313–321, 2002.

J. Könemann, S. Leonardi, G. Schäfer, and S. van Zwam. From primal-dual to cost shares and back: A group-strategyproof mechanism for the Steiner forest game. to appear in *SIAM J. Computing*, 2007.

M. Mahdian, Y. Ye, and J. Zhang. Approximation algorithms for metric facility location problems. *SIAM J. Comp.*, 36(2):411–432, 2006.

R.P. McLean. Values of non-transferable utility games. In R.J. Aumann and S. Hart, editors, *Handbook of Game Theory with Economic Applications*, 2:2077–2120. Elseveir Science Publishers B.V., 1994.

R.R. Mettu and G. Plaxton. The online median problem. In *Proc. 41st Symp. on Fdns. of Computer Science*, pp. 339–348, 2000.

E. Mossel and A. Saberi. On efficiently computing the Shapley value of a game. unpublished manuscript, 2006.

H. Moulin. *Axioms of Cooperative Decision Making*. Cambridge University Press, 1988.

H. Moulin. Incremental cost sharing: Characterization by coalition strategy-proofness. *Soc. Choice Welfare*, 16:279–320, 1999.

H. Moulin. Axiomatic cost and surplus sharing. In K. J. Arrow, A. K. Sen, and K. Suzumura, editors, *Handbook of Social Choice and Welfare*, 1:289–357. Elseveir Science Publishers B.V., 2002.

H. Moulin. *Fair Division and Collective Welfare*. MIT Press, 2003.

H. Moulin and S. Shenker. Strategyproof sharing of submodular costs: Budget balance vs. efficiency. *Econ. Theory*, 18:511–533, 2001.

J.F. Nash. The bargaining problem. *Econometrica*, 28:155–62, 1950.

L. Page, S. Brin, R. Motwani, and T. Winograd. The PageRank citation ranking: Bringing order to the web. Technical Report SIDL-WP-1999-0120, Stanford CS Department, 1999.

M. Pál and É. Tardos. Group strategyproof mechanisms via primal-dual algorithms. In *Proc. 44th Annual IEEE Symp. on Fdns. of Computer Science*, pp. 584–593, 2003.

I. Palacois-Huerta and O. Volij. The measurement of intellectual influence. *Econometrica*, 72(3):963–977, May 2004.

A.E. Roth, editor. *The Shapley Value*. Cambridge University Press, 1988.

H.E. Scarf. The core of an n-person game. *Econometrica*, 35(1):50–69, 1967.

L.S. Shapley. A value for n-person games. In H. Kuhn and A.W. Tucker, editors, *Contributions to the Theory of Games*, 2:307–317. Princeton University Press, 1953.

L.S. Shapley. On balanced sets and cores. *Naval Res. Logistics Q.*, 14:453–460, 1967.

Y. Sprumont. Population monotonic allocation schemes for cooperative games with transferable utility. *Games Econ. Behav.*, 2:378–394, 1990.

W.L. Thomson. Problems of fair division and the egalitarian solution. *J. Econ. Theory*, 31:211–226, 1983.

W.L. Thomson. Population-monotonic allocation rules. In W.A. Barnett, H. Moulin, M. Salles, and N.J. Schofield, editors, *Social Choice, Welfare and Ethics*, 2:79–124. Cambridge University Press, 1995.

V.V. Vazirani. *Approximation Algorithms*. Springer-Verlag, Berlin, 2001.

J. von Neumann and O. Morgenstern. *Theory of Games and Economic Behavior*. John Wiley and Sons, 1944.

E. Winter. The Shapley value. In R.J. Aumann and S. Hart, editors, *Handbook of Game Theory*. North-Holland, 2002.

Exercises

15.1 Consider a setting with n agents and m goods where each agent is endowed with a bundle of goods and a linear utility function that specifies the utility that this agent derives from consuming a bundle (this is the same as the linear Arrow–Debreu markets defined in Section 5.10 of this book). The value of a coalition S of agents in this model can be defined as the maximum total utility that agents in S can derive by optimally redistributing their endowments. Model this setting as a TU game. Does this game always have a nonempty core?

15.2 Prove that for submodular cost-sharing games, the Shapley value is cross-monotone.

15.3 In the vertex cover game, agents correspond to edges in a graph, and the cost of a set S of agents is the minimum size of a set of vertices that contains at least one of the endpoints of each edge in S. A simple primal-dual approach gives a 2-approximation algorithm for this problem. Modify this algorithm using the idea of ghost cost shares to obtain a cross-monotonic cost-sharing scheme. Find examples where this scheme fails to extract a constant fraction of the cost of the solution. Use this example, together with the technique explained in Section 15.5, to prove that no cross-monotonic cost-sharing scheme for this game is $\Omega(1)$-budget-balanced.

CHAPTER 16

Online Mechanisms

David C. Parkes

Abstract

Online mechanisms extend the methods of mechanism design to dynamic environments with multiple agents and private information. Decisions must be made as information about types is revealed online and without knowledge of the future, in the sense of online algorithms. We first consider single-valued preference domains and characterize the space of decision policies that can be truthfully implemented in a dominant strategy equilibrium. Working in a model-free environment, we present truthful auctions for domains with expiring items and limited-supply items. Turning to a more general preference domain, and assuming the existence of a probabilistic model for agent types, we define a dynamic Vickrey–Clarke–Groves mechanism that is efficient and Bayes–Nash incentive compatible. We close with some thoughts about future research directions in this area.

16.1 Introduction

The decision problem in many multiagent problem domains is inherently dynamic rather than static. Consider, for instance, the following environments:

- Selling seats on an airplane to buyers arriving over time.
- Allocating computational resources (bandwidth, CPU, etc.) to jobs arriving over time.
- Selling adverts on a search engine to a possibly changing group of buyers and with uncertainty about the future supply of search terms.
- Allocating tasks to a dynamically changing team of agents.

In each of these settings at least one of the following is true: either agents are dynamically arriving or departing, or there is uncertainty about the set of feasible decisions in the future. These dynamics present a new challenge when seeking to sustain good systemwide decisions in multiagent systems with self-interested agents.

This chapter introduces the problem of *online mechanism design* (online MD), which generalizes the theory of computational mechanism design to apply to dynamic problems. Decisions must be made dynamically and without knowledge of future agent types or future decision possibilities, in the sense of online algorithms.

16.1.1 Example: Dynamic Auction with Expiring Items

Consider a dynamic auction model with discrete time periods $T = \{1, 2, \ldots, \}$ and a single indivisible item to allocate in each time period. The type of an agent $i \in \{1, \ldots, N\}$ is denoted $\theta_i = (a_i, d_i, w_i) \in T \times T \times \mathbb{R}_{>0}$. Agent i has arrival time a_i, departure time d_i, value w_i for an allocation of a single unit of the item in some period $t \in [a_i, d_i]$, and wants at most one unit. This type information is all private to an agent. We refer to this as the *canonical expiring items environment.*

The arrival time has a special meaning: it is the first period in which information about the type of this agent can be made available to the auction. (We say "can be made available" because a self-interested agent may choose to delay its report.) Assume quasi-linear utility, with utility $w_i - p$ when the item is allocated in some $t \in [a_i, d_i]$ and payment p is collected from the agent. Consider the following naive generalization of the Vickrey auction to this dynamic environment.

Auction 1. A bid from an agent is a claim about its type, $\hat{\theta}_i = (\hat{a}_i, \hat{d}_i, \hat{w}_i)$, necessarily made in period $t = \hat{a}_i$. Then: in each period t, allocate the item to the highest unassigned bid, breaking ties at random. Collect payment equal to the second-highest unallocated bid in this round.

Example 16.1 Jane sells ice cream and can make one cone each hour. The ice cream melts if it is not sold. There are three buyers, with types (1, 2, 100), (1, 2, 80), and (2, 2, 60), indicating (arrival, departure, value). Buyers 1 and 2 are willing to buy an ice cream in either period 1 or 2 while buyer 3 will only buy an ice cream in period 2. In this example, if every buyer is truthful then buyer 1 wins in period 1 for 80, stops bidding, and buyer 2 wins in period 2 for 60. But buyer 1 can do better. For example, buyer 1 can report type (1, 2, 61), so that buyer 2 wins in period 1 for 61, stops bidding, and then buyer 1 wins for 60 in period 2. Buyer 1 can also report type (2, 2, 80) and delay its bid until period 2, so that buyer 2 wins for 0 in period 1, stops bidding, and then buyer 1 wins for 60 in period 2.

In a static situation the Vickrey auction is (dominant-strategy) truthful because an agent does not affect the price it faces. But, in a sequential setting an agent can choose the auction in which it participates and thus choose the other agents against which it competes and, in turn, the price faced. In fact, if every agent was *impatient* (with $d_i = a_i$), then, prices in future periods are irrelevant and the dominant strategy is to bid truthfully immediately upon arrival. Note also that buyer 1's manipulation relied on a suitable bid from buyer 3 in period 2 and will not always be useful. Nevertheless, this serves to demonstrate the failure of dominant strategy truthfulness.

16.1.2 The Challenge of Online MD

The dynamics of agent arrivals and departures, coupled perhaps with uncertainty about the set of feasible decisions in the future and in general about the state of the environment, makes the problem of online MD fundamentally different from that of standard (offline) MD. Important new considerations in online MD are as follows.

(i) Decisions must be made without information about agent types not yet arrived, coupled perhaps with uncertainty about which decisions will be feasible in future periods.
(ii) Agents can misrepresent their arrival and departure time in addition to their valuation for sequences of decisions. Because of this agent strategies also have a temporal aspect.
(iii) Only limited misreports of type may be available, for instance it may be impossible for an agent to report an earlier arrival than its true arrival.

More generally, online MD can also model settings in which an agent's type is revealed *to itself* over time and with its ability to learn dependent on decisions made by the online mechanism; e.g., a bidder needs to receive a resource to understand its value for the resource.

There are two main frameworks in which to study the performance of online mechanisms. The first is *model-free* and adopts a worst-case analysis and is useful when a designer does not have good probabilistic information about future agent types or about feasible decisions in future periods. The second is *model-based* and adopts an average-case analysis. As a motivating example, consider a search engine selling search terms to advertisers. This is a data-rich environment and it is reasonable to believe that the seller can build an accurate model to predict the distribution on types of buyers, including the process governing arrival and departures.

16.1.3 Outline

In Section 16.2 we present a general model for online MD and introduce the concept of limited misreports. Given this, we define direct-revelation, online mechanisms together with appropriate notions of incentive compatibility. Section 16.3 provides a characterization of truthful online mechanisms in the restricted domain of *single-valued preferences* and gives detailed examples of truthful, dynamic auctions. These auctions are analyzed within the framework of worst-case, competitive analysis. Section 16.4 considers general preference domains, and defines a dynamic Vickrey–Clarke–Groves mechanism, that is efficient and applicable when a model is available and common knowledge to agents. Section 16.5 closes with open problems and future directions.

16.2 Dynamic Environments and Online MD

The basic setting assumes risk neutral agents with quasi-linear utility functions, such that an agent acts to maximize the expected difference between its value from a sequence of decisions and its total payment. Consider discrete time periods $T = \{1, 2, \ldots\}$, indexed by t and possibly infinite. A mechanism makes (and enforces) a sequence of decisions $k = (k^1, k^2, \ldots) \in \mathcal{O}$, with decision k^t made in period t. Let $k^{[t_1,t_2]} = (k^{t_1}, \ldots, k^{t_2})$. The decisions made by a mechanism can depend on messages, such as bids, received from agents as well as uncertain events that occur in the environment.

For example, in sponsored search the realized supply of search terms determines the feasible allocation of user attention to advertisers.

An agent's type, $\theta_i = (a_i, d_i, w_i) \in \Theta_i$, where Θ_i is the set of possible types for agent i, defines a valuation function $v_i(\theta_i, k) \in \mathbb{R}$ on a sequence of decisions k and is private to an agent. Time periods $a_i, d_i \in T$ denote an agent's arrival and departure period and $v_i(\theta_i, k) = v_i(\theta_i, k^{[a_i, d_i]})$; i.e., an agent's value is invariant to decisions outside of its arrival–departure window. In addition to restricting the scope of decisions that influence an agent's value, the arrival period models the first period at which the agent is able to report its type to the mechanism.

The valuation component $w_i \in \mathbb{W}_i$ of an agent's type, where $\mathbb{W}_i$ denotes the set of possible valuations, parameterizes the agent's valuation function and can be more expressive than a single real number. For example, in an online combinatorial auction this needs to convey enough information to define substitutes ("I want item A or item B but not both") or complements ("I only want item A if I also get item B") preferences. Nor does the valuation need to be constant across all periods, for instance an agent could discount its future value in future periods $t > a_i$ by discount factor γ^{t-a_i} for $\gamma \in (0, 1)$.

16.2.1 Direct-Revelation Mechanisms

The family of direct-revelation, online mechanisms restricts the message that an agent can send to the mechanism to a single, direct claim about its type. For the most part we consider "closed" mechanisms so that an agent receives no feedback before reporting its type, and cannot condition its strategy on the report of another agent.

The *mechanism state*, $h^t \in H^t$, where H^t is the set of possible states in period t, captures all information relevant to the decision by the mechanism in that period. Let $\omega \in \Omega$ define the set of possible stochastic events that can occur in the environment, such as the realization of uncertain supply. This does not include the types of agents or any randomization within the mechanism itself. Write $\Omega = \Pi_{t \in T} \Omega^t$ and let $\omega^t \in \Omega^t$ denote the information about ω that is revealed in period t. Similarly, let θ^t denote the set of agent types reported in period t. Given this, it is convenient to define $h^t = (\theta^1, \ldots, \theta^t; \omega^1, \ldots, \omega^t; k^1, \ldots, k^{t-1})$. In practice, the state will be represented by a small, sufficient statistic of this information. The state space $H = \bigcup_t H^t$ may be finite, countably infinite, or continuous. This depends, in part, on whether agent types are discrete or continuous. Let $K(h^t)$ denote the set of all feasible decisions in the current time period, assumed finite for all h^t. Let $I(h^t)$ denote the set of active agents in state h^t, i.e. those agents for which $t \in [a_i, d_i]$.

Definition 16.2 (direct-revelation online mechanism) A direct-revelation online mechanism, $M = (\pi, x)$, restricts each agent to making a single claim about its type, and defines *decision policy* $\pi = \{\pi^t\}^{t \in T}$ and *payment policy*, $x = \{x^t\}^{t \in T}$, where decision $\pi^t(h^t) \in K(h^t)$ is made in state h^t and payment $x_i^t(h^t) \in \mathbb{R}$ is collected from each agent $i \in I(h^t)$.

Decision policy π may be stochastic. The payment policy may collect payments from an agent across multiple periods. For notational convenience, we let

$\pi(\theta, \omega) = (k^1, k^2, \ldots)$ denote the sequence of decisions, and $p_i(\theta, \omega) \in \mathbb{R}$ denote the total payment collected from agent i, given type profile θ and a realization of uncertain events $\omega \in \Omega$.

Example 16.3 Consider the canonical expiring items environment. The state h^t can be defined as a list of reported agent types that are present in period t, indicating whether each agent is already allocated or not. Decision $k \in K(h^t)$ decides whether to allocate the item in the current period to some agent that is present and unallocated.

Limited misreports constrain the strategy space available to agents in direct-revelation, online mechanisms:

Definition 16.4 (limited misreports) Let $C(\theta_i) \subseteq \Theta_i$ for $\theta_i \in \Theta_i$ denote the set of available misreports to an agent with true type θ_i.

In the standard model adopted in offline MD, it is typical to assume $C(\theta_i) = \Theta_i$. We shall assume *no early-arrival* misreports, with $C(\theta_i) = \{\hat{\theta}_i = (\hat{a}_i, \hat{d}_i, \hat{w}_i) : a_i \leq \hat{a}_i \leq \hat{d}_i, \hat{w}_i \in \mathbb{W}_i\}$; i.e., agent i cannot report an earlier arrival because it does not know its type (or know about the mechanism) until a_i. Sometimes, we shall also assume *no late-departure* misreports, which together with no early arrivals provides $C(\theta_i) = \{\hat{\theta}_i = (\hat{a}_i, \hat{d}_i, \hat{w}_i) : a_i \leq \hat{a}_i \leq \hat{d}_i \leq d_i, \hat{w}_i \in \mathbb{W}_i\}$. For example, we could argue that it is not credible to claim to have value for a ticket for a last minute Broadway show after 5 p.m. because the auctioneer knows that it takes at least 2 hours to get to the theater and the show starts at 7 p.m.

We restrict attention to mechanisms that are either dominant-strategy or Bayes–Nash incentive compatible. Let $\theta_{-i} = (\theta_1, \ldots, \theta_{i-1}, \theta_{i+1}, \ldots)$, $\Theta_{-i} = \Pi_{j \neq i} \Theta_j$, and $C(\theta_{-i}) = \Pi_{j \neq i} C(\theta_j)$, and consider misreports $\theta_i \in C(\theta_i)$.

Definition 16.5 (DSIC) Online mechanism $M = (\pi, x)$ is *dominant-strategy incentive-compatible* (DSIC) given limited misreports C if

$$v_i(\theta_i, \pi(\theta_i, \theta'_{-i}, \omega)) - p_i(\theta_i, \theta'_{-i}, \omega) \geq v_i(\theta_i, \pi(\hat{\theta}_i, \theta'_{-i}, \omega)) - p_i(\hat{\theta}_i, \theta'_{-i}, \omega),$$

for all $\hat{\theta}_i \in C(\theta_i)$, all θ_i, all $\theta'_{-i} \in C(\theta_{-i})$, all $\theta_{-i} \in \Theta_{-i}$, all $\omega \in \Omega$.

It will be convenient to also adopt the terminology *truthful* in place of DSIC. The concept of DSIC requires that an agent maximizes its utility by reporting its true type whatever the reports of other agents and for all stochastic events ω. When the decision policy itself is stochastic then DSIC requires that the *expected utility* is maximized from a truthful report, whatever the reports of other agents and (again) for all stochastic events ω. A randomized mechanism (i.e., one with a stochastic policy) is said to satisfy ***strong-truthfulness*** when truthful reporting is a dominant strategy for all random coin flips by the mechanism, and for all external stochastic events ω.

For Bayes–Nash incentive compatibility (BNIC), we assume in addition that all agents know the correct probabilistic model of the distribution on types and uncertain events, and that this is common knowledge.

Definition 16.6 (BNIC) Online mechanism $M = (\pi, x)$ is *Bayes–Nash incentive-compatible* (BNIC) given limited misreports C if

$$\mathbb{E}\{v_i(\theta_i, \pi(\theta_i, \theta_{-i}, \omega)) - p_i(\theta_i, \theta_{-i}, \omega)\} \geq \mathbb{E}\{v_i(\theta_i, \pi(\hat{\theta}_i, \theta_{-i}, \omega)) - p_i(\hat{\theta}_i, \theta_{-i}, \omega)\},$$

for all $\hat{\theta}_i \in C(\theta_i)$, all θ_i, where the expectation is taken with respect to the distribution on types θ_{-i}, and stochastic events ω, and any randomization within the policy.

BNIC is a weaker solution concept than DSIC because it requires only that truth revelation is a best response when other agents are also truthful, and in expectation given the distribution on agent types and on stochastic events in the environment.

16.2.2 Remark: The Revelation Principle

Commonly held intuition from offline MD suggests that focusing on the class of incentive compatible, direct-revelation online mechanisms is without loss of generality. However, if agents are unable to send messages to a mechanism in periods $t \notin [a_i, d_i]$ then this is not true.

Example 16.7 (failure of the revelation principle) Consider the model with no early-arrival misreports but allow for late-departure misreports. Consider two time periods $T = \{1, 2\}$, a single unit of an indivisible item to allocate in either period and an environment with a single agent. Denote the type of the agent (a_i, d_i, w_i) with $w_i > 0$ to denote its value for the item if allocated in period $t \in [a_i, d_i]$. Suppose that possible types are $(1, 1, 1)$ or $(1, 2, 1)$. Consider an indirect mechanism that allows an agent to send one of messages $\{1, 2\}$ in period 1 and $\{1\}$ in period 2. Let ϕ denote a null message. Consider decision policy: $\pi^1(1) = 0, \pi^1(2) = 1, \pi^2(1, z) = \pi^2(2, z) = 0$, for $z \in \{1, \phi\}$, writing the state as the sequence of messages received and decision $k^t \in \{0, 1\}$ to indicate whether or not the agent is allocated in period $t \in \{1, 2\}$. Consider payment policy: $x^1(1) = x^2(1, \phi) = x^2(1, 1) = 0,\ x^1(2) = 3, x^2(2, 1) = -2.01, x^2(2, \phi) = 0$. Type $(1, 1, 1)$ will report message 1 in period 1 because reporting message 2 is not useful and it cannot report messages (2,1). Type $(1, 2, 1)$ will report messages (2,1) and has no useful deviation. This policy cannot be implemented as a DSIC direct-revelation mechanism because type $(1, 2, 1)$ is allocated in period 1 for payment 0.99, and so type $(1, 1, 1)$ (which is unallocated if truthful) will want to report type $(1, 2, 1)$.

The revelation principle fails in this example because the indirect mechanism prevents the agent from claiming a later departure than its true departure. In fact, the revelation principle continues to hold when misreports are limited to no-late departures in addition to no-early arrivals. A form of the revelation principle can also be recovered by introducing simple "heartbeat" messages into a direct-revelation mechanism, whereby an agent still makes a single report about its type but must also send a noninformative heartbeat message in every period $t \in [\hat{a}_i, \hat{d}_i]$.[1] We leave the derivation of this "revelation principle plus heartbeat" result as an exercise.

With this in hand, and in keeping with the current literature on online mechanisms, we will focus on incentive-compatible, direct revelation online mechanisms in this chapter.

16.3 Single-Valued Online Domains

In this section we develop a methodology for the design of DSIC online mechanisms in the restricted domain of *single-valued* preferences. We identify the central role of monotonic decision policies in the design of truthful online mechanisms. The methodology is illustrated in the design of a dynamic auction for two environments: (a) allocating a sequence of expiring items and (b) allocating a single, indivisible item in some period while adapting to information about agent types. Both auctions are model-free and we use competitive analysis to study their efficiency and revenue properties. We close the section with remarks that situate the study of truthful online mechanisms in the context of the wider mechanism design literature.

16.3.1 Truthfulness for Single-Valued Preference Domains

An agent with single-valued preferences has the same value, r_i, whenever any of a set of interesting decisions is made in some period $t \in [a_i, d_i]$, and has value for at most one such decision. For example, in the single-item allocation problems considered earlier an agent's interesting set was all decisions that allocate an item to the agent.

Let $\mathcal{L}_i = \{L_1, \ldots, L_m\}$ describe a language for defining interesting sets for agent i, where $L \subseteq K = \bigcup_h K(h)$, for any $L \in \mathcal{L}_i$, defines a subset of single-period decisions. Let $\succeq_L$ be a partial order defined on $\mathcal{L}_i$. The valuation component $w_i \in \mathbb{W}_i$ of an agent's type, $\theta_i = (a_i, d_i, w_i)$, defines $w_i = (r_i, L_i)$ with $\mathbb{W}_i = \mathbb{R} \times \mathcal{L}_i$. This picks out the interesting set and defines the value on decisions in that set.

Definition 16.8 (single-valued) A single-valued online domain is one where each agent i has a type $\theta_i = (a_i, d_i, (r_i, L_i))$, with reward $r_i \in \mathbb{R}$ and interesting set $L_i \in \mathcal{L}_i$, where type θ_i defines valuation:

$$v_i(\theta_i, k) = \begin{cases} r_i, & \text{if } k^t \in \bigcup_{L: L \succeq_L L_i, L \in \mathcal{L}_i} L \ \text{ for some } t \in [a_i, d_i] \\ 0, & \text{otherwise,} \end{cases} \qquad (16.1)$$

To keep things simple, we assume that *the set of interesting decisions is known by the mechanism* and thus the private information is restricted to arrival, departure, and its value for a decision. We comment on how to relax this assumption at the end of the section. Given the *known interesting-set* assumption, define a partial-order $\preceq_\theta$ on

[1] Thanks to Bobby Kleinberg for suggesting this interpretation.

types:

$$\theta_1 \preceq_\theta \theta_2 \equiv (a_1 \geq a_2) \wedge (d_1 \leq d_2) \wedge (r_1 \leq r_2) \wedge (L_1 = L_2). \tag{16.2}$$

This will be sufficient because we will not need to reason about misreports of interesting set L_i. Consider the following example.

Example 16.9 (known single-minded combinatorial auction) Multiple units of indivisible, heterogeneous items G, are in uncertain supply and cannot be stored from one period to the next. Consider single-valued preferences, where interesting set $L_i \in \mathcal{L}_i$ has an associated bundle $S(L_i) \subseteq G$, and characterizes all single-period decisions that allocate agent i bundle $S(L_i)$, irrespective of the allocation to other agents. Define partial order $L_1 \succeq_L L_2 \equiv S(L_1) \supseteq S(L_2)$ for all $L_1, L_2 \in \mathcal{L}_i$. Agent i with type $\theta_i = (a_i, d_i, (r_i, L_i))$ has value r_i when decision k^t allocates a bundle containing at least $S(L_i)$ items to the agent in some period $t \in [a_i, d_i]$.

The subsequent analysis is developed for *deterministic* policies. We adopt shorthand $\pi_i(\theta_i, \theta_{-i}, \omega) \in \{0, 1\}$ to indicate whether policy π makes an interesting decision for agent i with type θ_i in some period $t \in [a_i, d_i]$, fixing type profile θ_{-i} and stochastic (external) events $\omega \in \Omega$. Since we are often considering auction domains, we may also refer to an interesting decision for an agent as an *allocation* to the agent. The analysis immediately applies to the case of stochastic policies when coupled with strong-truthfulness.[2] We elaborate more on stochastic policies at the end of the section.

Definition 16.10 (critical value) The critical-value for agent i given type $\theta_i = (a_i, d_i, (r_i, L_i))$ and deterministic policy π in a single-valued domain, is defined as

$$v^c_{(a_i,d_i,L_i)}(\theta_{-i}, \omega) = \begin{cases} \min r'_i \text{ s.t. } \pi_i(\theta'_i, \theta_{-i}, \omega) = 1 & \text{for } \theta'_i = (a_i, d_i, (r'_i, L_i)) \\ \infty, & \text{if no such } r'_i \text{ exists,} \end{cases} \tag{16.3}$$

where types θ_{-i} and stochastic events $\omega \in \Omega$ are fixed.

Definition 16.11 (monotonic) Deterministic policy π is monotonic if $(\pi_i(\theta_i, \theta_{-i}, \omega) = 1) \wedge ((r_i > v^c_{(a_i,d_i,L_i)}(\theta_{-i}, \omega)) \Rightarrow \pi_i(\theta'_i, \theta_{-i}, \omega) = 1)$ for all $\theta'_i \succ_\theta \theta_i$, for all θ_{-i}, all $\omega \in \Omega$.

The "strict profit" condition, $r_i > v^c_{(a_i,d_i,L_i)}(\theta_{-i}, \omega)$, is added to prevent weak indifference when $\theta'_i \succ_\theta \theta_i$ and $r'_i = r_i$, and is redundant when $r'_i > r_i$. Say that an arrival-departure interval $[a'_i, d'_i]$ is *tighter* than $[a_i, d_i]$ if $a'_i \geq a_i$ and $d'_i \leq d_i$, and weaker otherwise.

[2] It is convenient for this purpose to consider the random coin flips of a policy as included in stochastic events ω so that no notational changes are required.

Lemma 16.12 *The critical value to agent i is independent of reward r_i and (weakly) monotonically increasing in tighter arrival–departure intervals, given a deterministic, monotonic policy.*

PROOF Fix some $\theta_{-i}, \omega \in \Omega$. Assume for contradiction that $\theta'_i \preceq_\theta \theta_i$ so that $a'_i \geq a_i$ and $d'_i \leq d_i$, but $v^c_{(a'_i,d'_i,L_i)}(\theta_{-i},\omega) < v^c_{(a_i,d_i,L_i)}(\theta_{-i},\omega)$. Modify the reward of type $\theta'_i = (a'_i, d'_i, (r'_i, L_i))$ such that $r'_i := v^c_{(a'_i,d'_i,L_i)}(\theta_{-i},\omega)$ and modify the reward of type $\theta_i = (a_i, d_i, (r_i, L_i))$ such that $r_i := v^c_{(a'_i,d'_i,L_i)}(\theta_{-i},\omega)$. Now, we still have $\theta'_i \preceq_\theta \theta_i$, but $\pi_i(\theta'_i, \theta_{-i}, \omega) = 1$ while $\pi_i(\theta_i, \theta_{-i}, \omega) = 0$ and a contradiction with monotonicity. □

Theorem 16.13 *A monotonic, deterministic decision policy π can be truthfully implemented in a domain with known interesting set single-valued preferences, and no early-arrival and no late-departure misreports.*

PROOF Define payment policy $x^t_i(h^t) = 0$ for all $t \neq \hat{d}_i$, and with

$$x^t_i(h^t) = \begin{cases} v^c_{(\hat{a}_i,\hat{d}_i,L_i)}(\hat{\theta}_{-i},\omega), & \text{if } \pi_i(\hat{\theta}_i,\hat{\theta}_{-i},\omega) = 1 \\ 0, & \text{otherwise} \end{cases} \tag{16.4}$$

when $t = \hat{d}_i$. This critical-value payment is collected upon departure. Fix θ_{-i}, $\theta_i = (a_i, d_i, (r_i, L_i))$, and $\omega \in \Omega$, assume that agent i is truthful, and proceed by case analysis. (a) If agent i is not allocated, $v^c_{(a_i,d_i,L_i)}(\theta_{-i},\omega) > r_i$ and to be allocated, the agent must report some $\theta'_i \succ_\theta \theta_i$, which it can only do with a report $\theta'_i = (a_i, d_i, (r'_i, L_i))$, and $r'_i > r_i$, by limited misreports. But since the critical value is greater than its true value r_i, it will have negative utility if it wins for r'_i. (b) If agent i is allocated, its utility is nonnegative since $v^c_{(a_i,d_i,L_i)}(\theta_{-i},\omega) \leq r_i$ and it does not want to report a type for which it would not be allocated. Consider any report $\theta'_i \in C(\theta_i)$ for which the agent continues to be allocated. But, the critical value for θ'_i is (weakly) greater than for θ_i since it is independent of the reported reward r'_i and weakly increasing for an alternate arrival–departure interval since it must be tighter by limited misreports, and then by appeal to Lemma 16.12. □

We turn now to identifying *necessary* conditions for truthfulness. An online mechanism satisfies *individual rationality* (IR) when every agent has nonnegative utility in equilibrium. This is required when agents cannot be forced to participate in the mechanism.

Lemma 16.14 (critical payment) *In a (known interesting set) single-valued preference domain, any truthful online mechanism that is defined for a deterministic decision policy and satisfies IR must collect a payment equal to the critical value from each allocated agent.*

PROOF Fix θ_{-i} and $\omega \in \Omega$. Payment $p_i(\theta_i, \theta_{-i}, \omega)$, made by agent i contingent on successful allocation, cannot depend on reward r_i because if $p_i(\theta_i, \theta_{-i}, \omega) < p_i(\theta'_i, \theta_{-i}, \omega)$ for $\theta_i = (a_i, d_i, (r_i, L_i))$ and $\theta'_i = (a_i, d_i, (r'_i, L_i))$

and $r_i' \neq r_i$ and $\min(r_i', r_i) \geq v^c_{(a_i,d_i,L_i)}(\theta_{-i}, \omega)$ then an agent with type θ_i' should report type θ_i. Fix type θ_i such that $\pi_i(\theta_i, \theta_{-i}, \omega) = 1$. Now, if $p_i(\theta_i, \theta_{-i}, \omega) < v^c_{(a_i,d_i,L_i)}(\theta_{-i}, \omega)$ then an agent with type $\theta_i' = (a_i, d_i, (r_i', L_i))$ and $p_i(\theta_i, \theta_{-i}, \omega) < r_i' < v^c_{(a_i,d_i,L_i)}(\theta_{-i}, \omega)$ should report θ_i. This is possible even with negative payment $p_i(\theta_i, \theta_{-i}, \omega)$ as long as rewards can also be negative. On the other hand, if $v^c_{(a_i,d_i,L_i)}(\theta_{-i}, \omega) < p_i(\theta_i, \theta_{-i}, \omega)$ then the mechanism fails IR for an agent with type $\theta_i' = (a_i, d_i, (r_i', L_i))$ and $v^c_{(a_i,d_i,L_i)}(\theta_{-i}, \omega) < r_i' < p_i(\theta_i, \theta_{-i}, \omega)$. □

Say that a domain satisfies *reasonable misreporting* when an agent with type θ_i has available *at least* misreports $\theta_i' \in C(\theta_i)$ with $a_i' \geq a_i$, $d_i' \leq d_i$ and any reward r_i'.

Theorem 16.15 *In a known interesting set single-valued preference domain with reasonable misreporting, any deterministic policy π that can be truthfully implemented in an IR mechanism that does not pay unallocated agents must be monotonic.*

PROOF Fix θ_{-i}, $\omega \in \Omega$. Assume, for contradiction, that $\theta_i \prec_\theta \theta_i'$ with $\theta_i = (a_i, d_i, (r_i, L_i))$ and $\theta_i' = (a_i', d_i', (r_i', L_i))$, but $\pi_i(\theta_i, \theta_{-i}, \omega) = 1$, value $r_i > v^c_{(a_i,d_i,L_i)}(\theta_{-i}, \omega)$ and $\pi_i(\theta_i', \theta_{-i}, \omega) = 0$. We must have $p_i(\theta_i, \theta_{-i}, \omega) = v^c_{(a_i,d_i,L_i)}(\theta_{-i}, \omega)$ by Lemma 16.14. Thus, agent i with type θ_i must have strictly positive utility in the mechanism. On the other hand, the agent with type $\theta_i' \succ_\theta \theta_i$ is not allocated, makes nonnegative payment, and has (weakly) negative utility. But, an agent with type θ_i' can report θ_i, which presents a contradiction with truthfulness. □

The restriction that losing agents do not receive a payment plays an important role. To see this, consider a domain with no late-departure misreports, fix θ_{-i}, and consider a single-item valuation with possible types $\Theta_i = \{(1, 1, \$10), (1, 2, \$10)\}$. Policy $\pi_i((1, 1, \$10), \theta_{-i}) = 1$ and $\pi_i((1, 2, \$10), \theta_{-i}) = 0$ is nonmonotonic, but can be truthfully implemented with payments $p_i((1, 1, \$10), \theta_{-i}) = 8$ and $p_i((1, 2, \$10), \theta_{-i}) = -100$.

Monotonic-Late. Theorem 16.13 can be generalized to a domain with arbitrary misreports of departure. For a particular $\theta_{-i}, \omega \in \Omega$ and type $\theta_i = (a_i, d_i, (r_i, L_i))$, define the *critical departure*, $d^c_{(a_i,d_i,L_i)}(\theta_{-i}, \omega)$, as the earliest departure $d_i' \leq d_i$ for which $v^c_{(a_i,d_i',L_i)}(\theta_{-i}, \omega) = v^c_{(a_i,d_i,L_i)}(\theta_{-i}, \omega)$. This is the earliest departure time that agent i could have reported without increasing the critical value. Given this, we say that policy π is *monotonic-late* if it is monotonic and if no interesting decision is made for agent i before its critical departure period. A monotonic-late, deterministic decision policy π can be truthfully implemented in a domain with no early-arrival misreports but arbitrary misreports of departure. Moreover, this requirement of monotonic-late is necessary for truthfulness in this environment.

16.3.2 Example: A Dynamic Auction with Expiring Items

For our first detailed example we revisit the problem of selling an expiring item, such as ice cream, time on a shared computer, or network resources, to dynamically arriving buyers. This is the canonical expiring items environment. Assume for notational convenience that the time horizon is finite. We design a strongly truthful online auction that includes random tie-breaking and satisfies monotonicity (however ties are broken).

We assume no early-arrival and no late-departure misreports. The no late-departure assumption can be readily motivated in physical environments. For ice cream, think about a tour group that will be leaving at a designated time so that it is not credible to claim a willingness to wait for an ice cream beyond that period. For network resources, such as an auction for access to WiFi bandwidth in a coffee house, think about requiring a user to be present for the entire period of time reported to the mechanism. A technical argument for why we need this assumption is also provided below.[3]

Competitive analysis. We perform a worst-case analysis and consider the performance of the mechanism, given a sequence of types that are generated by an "adversary" whose task it is to make the performance as bad as possible. Of particular relevance is the method of *competitive analysis*, typically adopted in the study of online algorithms. The following question is asked: *how effectively does the performance of the online mechanism "compete" with that of an offline mechanism that is given complete information about the future arrival of agent types?* This question is asked in the worst-case, for an adversarially defined input.

Competitive analysis is most easily justified when the designer does not have a good model of the environment. As a motivating example, consider selling a completely new product or service, for which it is not possible to conduct market research to get a good model of demand. Competitive analysis can also lead to mechanisms that enjoy good average-case performance in practice, provide insight into how to design robust mechanisms, and produce useful "lower-bounds." A lower-bound for a problem makes a statement about the best possible performance that can be achieved by *any* mechanism. Online mechanisms are of special interest when their performance matches the lower bound.

In performing competitive analysis, one needs to define: an optimality criterion; a model of the power of the adversary is selecting worst-case inputs; and an offline benchmark, defined with perfect information about the future. We are interested in the efficiency of a dynamic auction for expiring items and adopt as our optimality criterion the value of the best possible offline allocation. This can be computed as follows:

$$V^*(\theta) = \max_{x,y} \sum_{i=1}^{N} y_i w_i \tag{16.5}$$

$$\text{s.t.} \quad \sum_{t=a_i}^{d_i} x_{it} \geq y_i, \quad \forall i \in \{1, \ldots, N\} \tag{16.6}$$

$$\sum_{i:t\in[a_i,d_i]} x_{it} \leq 1, \quad \forall t \in T, \tag{16.7}$$

[3] The requirement of no late departures can be dispensed with, while still retaining truthfulness, in environments in which it is possible to schedule a resource in some period before an agent's reported departure, but withhold access to the benefit from the use of the resource until the reported departure; e.g., in grid computing, jobs can run on the machine but the result then held until reported departure.

where $y_i \in \{0,1\}$ indicates whether bid i is allocated and $x_{it} \in \{0,1\}$ indicates the period in which it is allocated.[4] For our adversarial model, we consider a powerful adversary that is able to pick arbitrary agent types, including the value, arrival, and departure of agents.

Let $z \in \mathcal{Z}$ denote the set of inputs available to the adversary and θ_z the corresponding type profile. Let $\mathrm{Val}(\pi(\theta_z))$ denote the total value of the decisions made by policy π given input θ_z. An online mechanism is *c-competitive for efficiency* if

$$\min_{z \in \mathcal{Z}} \mathbb{E}\left\{\frac{\mathrm{Val}(\pi(\theta_z))}{V^*(\theta_z)}\right\} \geq \frac{1}{c}, \tag{16.8}$$

for some constant $c \geq 1$. Such a mechanism is guaranteed to achieve within fraction $\frac{1}{c}$ of the value of the optimal offline algorithm, whatever the input sequence. The expectation allows for stochastic policies and can also allow for the use of randomization in defining the power of the adversary (we will see this in the next section). Competitive ratio c is referred to as an *upper-bound* on the online performance of the mechanism.

Now consider the following modification to Auction 1:

Auction 2. A bid from an agent is a claim about its type, $\hat{\theta}_i = (\hat{a}_i, \hat{d}_i, \hat{w}_i)$, necessarily made in period $t = \hat{a}_i$.

(i) In each period, t, allocate the item to the highest unassigned bid, breaking ties at random.

(ii) Every allocated agent pays its critical-value payment, collected upon its reported departure.

The auction is the same as Auction 1 except for the payment rule, which now charges the critical value rather than the second price in the period in which an agent wins. We refer to this as a "greedy auction" because the decision policy myopically maximizes value in each period. When every bidder is impatient, then the auction reduces to a sequence of Vickrey auctions (i.e., Auction 1.)

Example 16.16 Consider the earlier example, with three agents and types $\theta_1 = (1, 2, 100)$, $\theta_2 = (1, 2, 80)$, and $\theta_3 = (2, 2, 60)$, and one item to sell in each period. Suppose that all three agents bid truthfully. The greedy allocation rule sells to agent 1 in period 1 and then agent 2 in period 2. Agent 1's payment is 60 because this is the critical value for arrival–departure $(1, 2)$, given the bids of other agents. (A bid of just above 60 would allow the agent to win, albeit in period 2 instead of period 1.) Agent 2's payment is also 60.

Theorem 16.17 *Auction 2 is strongly truthful and 2-competitive for efficiency in the expiring-items environment with no early-arrival and no late-departure misreports.*

[4] Note that the integer program allows the possibility of allocating more than one item to a winning bid but that this does not change the value of the objective and is not useful.

PROOF Suppose that random tie-breaking is invariant to reported arrival and departure. The auction is strongly truthful because the allocation function is monotone: if agent i wins in some period $t \in [a_i, d_i]$ then it continues to win either earlier or in the same period for $w_i' > w_i$, and for $a_i' < a_i$ or $d_i' > d_i$. For competitiveness, consider a set of types θ and establish that the greedy online allocation rule is 2-competitive by a charging argument. For any agent i that is allocated offline but not online, charge its value to the online agent that was allocated in period t in which agent i is allocated offline. Since agent i is not allocated online, it is present in period t, and the greedy rule allocates to another agent in that period with at least as much value as agent i. For any agent i that is allocated offline and also online, charge its value to itself in the online solution. Each agent that is allocated in the online solution is charged at most twice, and in all cases for a value less than or equal to its own value. Therefore the optimal offline value $V^*(\theta)$ is at most twice the value of the greedy solution. □

We now understand that the decision policy in Auction 1 was monotonic but that Auction 1 was not truthful because the payments were not critical-value payments.

It is interesting to note that there is a 1.618-competitive online algorithm for this problem. However, this algorithm is not monotonic and cannot be implemented truthfully. In fact, we have a tight lower bound for the problem of achieving efficiency and truthfulness.

Theorem 16.18 *No truthful, IR, and deterministic online auction can obtain a $(2-\epsilon)$-approximation for efficiency in the expiring items environment with no early-arrival and no late-departure misreports, for any constant $\epsilon > 0$.*

PROOF Fix $\epsilon > 0$, consider $T = \{1, 2\}$ and construct the following three scenarios: (i) Consider agents $\theta_1 = (1, 1, q(1+\delta))$, $\theta_2 = (1, 2, q)$, and choose $0 < \delta < \frac{\epsilon}{1-\epsilon}$ so that $\frac{q(1+\delta)}{q(2+\delta)} < \frac{1}{2-\epsilon}$ and the auction must allocate to both agents to be $(2-\epsilon)$-competitive. Let $q \geq v^c_{(1,1)}(\theta_2)$ (dropping dependence on ω because there are no stochastic events to consider), so that agent 1 must have strictly positive utility since the price is independent of reported value (for truthfulness) and less than or equal to $v^c_{(1,1)}(\theta_{-1})$ for IR. (ii) As in (i) except $\theta_1 \rightarrow \theta_1' = (1, 2, q(1+\delta))$ and a new type $\theta_3 = (2, 2, \infty)$ is introduced. Agent 1 must be allocated else it can report type θ_1. Moreover, agent 1 must be allocated in period 1 because otherwise the mechanism cannot compete when θ_3 arrives. Agent 2 is not allocated. (iii) As in (i) except $\theta_1 \rightarrow \theta_1' = (1, 2, q(1+\delta))$ and $\theta_2 \rightarrow \theta_2' = (1, 1, q)$. The auction must allocate to both agents to be $(2-\epsilon)$-competitive. Further assume that $q > v^c_{(1,1)}(\theta_1')$, which is without loss of generality because if $q = v^c_{(1,1)}(\theta_1')$ then we can repeat the analysis with $q' = \alpha q$ for $\alpha > 1$ replacing q throughout. But now agent 2 with type θ_2' has strictly positive utility since its payment is no greater than its critical value and the auction is not truthful in scenario (ii) because agent 2 can benefit by deviating and reporting θ_2'. □

The following provides a technical justification for why the no late-departure misreports assumption is required in this environment.

Theorem 16.19 *No truthful, IR, and deterministic online auction can obtain a constant approximation ratio for efficiency in the expiring items environment with no early-arrival misreports but arbitrary misreports of departure.*

PROOF Consider M periods. Fix θ_{-i}. Fix $v^c_{(1,1)}(\theta_{-i}) < \infty$ (dropping dependence on ω because there are no stochastic events to consider). First show that any agent with type $\theta_i = (1, M, w_i)$ for $w_i > v^c_{(1,M)}(\theta_{-i})$ must be allocated in period 1. For this, first show that $v^c_{(1,M)}(\theta_{-i}) = v^c_{(1,1)}(\theta_{-i})$. Construct $\theta'_i = (1, M, w'_i)$ with $w'_i = v^c_{(1,1)} + \epsilon$, some $\epsilon > 0$. By truthfulness and thus monotonicity we have $v^c_{(1,M)}(\theta_{-i}) \leq v^c_{(1,1)}(\theta_{-i})$ and agent i must be allocated. Moreover, it must be allocated in period 1 else an adversary can generate $M - 1$ bids $\{(t, t, \beta^{t-1})\}$ for large $\beta > 0$ and $t \in \{2, \ldots, M\}$, all of which must be accepted for the auction to be constant competitive. But in this case the agent should deviate and report $(1, 1, w'_i)$, and be allocated in period 1 with payment $v^c_{(1,1)}(\theta_{-i}) < w'_i$ and have positive utility. Since type $(1, M, w'_i)$ is allocated in period 1, we must have $v^c_{(1,M)}(\theta_{-i}) = v^c_{(1,1)}(\theta_{-i})$ by truthfulness and the critical-payment lemma else type $(1, 1, w'_i)$ can deviate and report $(1, M, w'_i)$ and do better. Consider again type $(1, M, w_i)$, we now have $w_i > v^c_{(1,M)}(\theta_{-i}) \Rightarrow w_i > v^c_{(1,1)}(\theta_{-i})$ and the agent must be allocated in period 1. To finish the proof, now construct type profile $\theta = \{(1, M, q_1), \ldots, (1, M, q_M)\}$ with $q_1, \ldots, q_m$ unique values drawn from $[q, q + \delta]$ for some $q > 0$ and $\delta > 0$. For any i, we must have $v^c_{(1,1)}(\theta_{-i}) < \infty$ else the mechanism is not competitive because the adversary could replace type i with $\theta'_i = (1, 1, w''_i)$ and some arbitrarily large w''_i. We can also assume $q_i \geq v^c_{(1,M)}(\theta_{-i}) \Rightarrow q_i > v^c_{(1,M)}(\theta_{-i})$, which can be achieved by a slight upward perturbation of any value $q_i = v^c_{(1,M)}(\theta_{-i})$. Finally, the online mechanism can allocate at most one of these bids since any bid allocated must be allocated in period 1 and can achieve value at most $q + \delta$ while the efficient offline allocation has value $V^*(\theta) \geq Mq$. Thus, no constant approximation is possible because M can be selected to be arbitrarily large. □

16.3.3 Example: An Adaptive, Limited-Supply Auction

For our second detailed example, we consider an environment with a single, indivisible item to be allocated to one of N agents. Each agent's type is still denoted $\theta_i = (a_i, d_i, w_i) \in T \times T \times \mathbb{R}_{>0}$, with w_i denoting the agent's value for the item. This fits into the known interesting-set model. We assume no early-arrival misreports but will allow arbitrary misreports of departure. Our goal is to define an auction with good revenue and efficiency properties. We will work with a weaker adversarial model than in the setting with expiring items.

We relate this dynamic auction problem to the classical *secretary problem*, a well-studied problem in optimal stopping theory:

The Secretary Problem. An interviewer meets with each from a pool of N job applicants in turn. The total number of applicants is known. Each applicant has a quality and the interviewer learns, upon meeting, the relative rank of each applicant among those already interviewed and must make an irrevocable decision about whether or not to hire the applicant. The goal is to hire the best applicant. By the "random-ordering hypothesis," an adversary can choose an arbitrary set of N qualities but cannot control the assignment of quality to applicant, rather this is sampled uniformly at random and without replacement from the set. The problem is to design a stopping rule that maximizes the probability of hiring the highest rank applicant, in the worst case for all possible adversarially selected inputs. Say that a *candidate* is the most qualified of all applicants seen so far. The *optimal* policy (i.e., the policy that maximizes the probability of selecting the best applicant, in the worst case) is to interview the first $t-1$ applicants and then hire the next candidate (if any), where t is defined by

$$\sum_{j=t+1}^{N} \frac{1}{j-1} \leq 1 < \sum_{j=t}^{N} \frac{1}{j-1}. \tag{16.9}$$

For instance, with $N = 10{,}000$ the optimal t is 3,680, i.e., sample 3,679 applicants and then accept the next candidate. As $N \to \infty$, the probability of hiring the best applicant approaches $1/e$, as does the ratio t/N, and the optimal policy in this big N limit is to sample the first $\lfloor N/e \rfloor$ applicants and then immediately accept any subsequent candidate.

We can reinterpret the secretary problem in the auction context. Bidders, unlike the applicants in the classic model, are strategic and can misrepresent their value and time their entry into the market. Bidders also have both an entry and an exit time. We modify the adversarial model in the secretary problem while retaining the random-ordering hypothesis: an adversary picks a set of values and a set of arrival–departure intervals and agent types are then defined by sampling uniformly at random and without replacement from each set.[5]

In addition to efficiency, we will also consider revenue as an optimality criterion. The auction's revenue for type profile θ is defined as $\text{Rev}(p(\theta)) = \sum_i p_i(\theta)$, where notation $p_i(\theta)$ denotes the (expected) payment by agent i given type profile θ. Notation $\omega \in \Omega$ is suppressed because there are no external stochastic events in the problem. For an offline benchmark we consider the revenue from an offline Vickrey auction and define $R^*(\theta)$ as the second-highest value in type profile θ. An online mechanism is *c-competitive for revenue* if

$$\min_{z \in \mathcal{Z}} \mathbb{E}\left\{\frac{\text{Rev}(p(\theta_z))}{R^*(\theta_z)}\right\} \geq \frac{1}{c}, \tag{16.10}$$

where $z \in \mathcal{Z}$ is the set of inputs available to an adversary, in this case choosing the two sets described above, and the expectation here is taken with respect to the random choice of the sampling process that matches values with arrival–departure intervals.

As we have seen, the optimal policy for the secretary problem has a *learning phase* followed by an *accepting phase*. For a straw-man online auction interpretation, consider: *observe the first $\lfloor N/e \rfloor$ reports and then price at the maximal value received so far, and sell to the first agent to subsequently report a value greater than*

[5] By an averaging argument, our results for randomly ordered inputs imply the same (upper-bound) competitive-ratio analysis when the bids consist of i.i.d. samples from an unknown distribution.

this price. Break ties at random. The following example shows that this fails to be truthful.

Example 16.20 Consider six agents, with types $\theta_i = (a_i, d_i, w_i)$ and $\theta_1 = (1, 7, 6)$, $\theta_2 = (3, 7, 2)$, $\theta_3 = (4, 8, 4)$, $\theta_4 = (6, 7, 8)$, and agents 5 and 6 arriving in later periods. The transition to the accepting phase occurs after $\lfloor 6/e \rfloor = 2$ bids. Agent 4 wins in period 6 and makes payment 6. If agent 1 reports $\theta_1' = (5, 7, 6)$, then it wins in period 5, for payment 4.

The auction is truthful when all agents are impatient ($a_i = d_i$) but fails to be truthful in the general setting with patient agents because the allocation policy is not monotonic with respect to arrival time. Consider instead the following simple variation.

Auction 3. A bid from an agent is a claim about its type, $\hat{\theta}_i = (\hat{a}_i, \hat{d}_i, \hat{w}_i)$, necessarily made in period $t = \hat{a}_i$.

(i) (Learning): In period τ in which the $\lfloor N/e \rfloor th$ bid is received let $p \geq q$ be the top two bid values received so far.
(ii) (Transition): If an agent bidding p is still present in period τ then sell to that agent (breaking ties at random) at price q.
(iii) (Accepting): Else, sell to the next agent to bid a price at least p (breaking ties at random), collecting payment p.

Theorem 16.21 *Auction 3 is strongly truthful in the single-unit, limited supply environment with no early-arrival misreports.*

PROOF Assume that the method used to break ties is independent of the reported departure time of an agent. Fix θ_{-i}. Monotonicity is established by case analysis on type θ_i: (a) If d_i is to the left of the transition, the agent is not allocated and monotonicity trivially holds. (b) If $[a_i, d_i]$ spans the transition, agent i does not trigger the transition, and it wins with $w_i > q$ then there is no tie-breaking and the agent continues to win for an earlier arrival or later departure (because this changes nothing about the price it faces when the transition occurs), and continues to win with a higher value. (c) If arrival, a_i, is after the transition and agent i wins with $w_i > p$ (and perhaps winning a random selection over another agent j arriving in the same period also with $w_j > p$) then it continues to win with an earlier arrival (even one that occurs before the transition because its value will define p), with a later departure (because tie-breaking is invariant to reported departure) and with a higher value. (d) If the agent triggers the transition and wins with $w_i > q$ then its value $w_i = p$, there was no tie to break, and the agent continues to win for an earlier arrival (although at some point the transition will be triggered by the next earliest agent to arrive), for a higher value, and is unaffected by a later departure. The payment is the critical value, namely q in case (b) and (d) and p in case (c). Moreover, the policy is monotonic-late: in case (b) the critical value is infinite for all departures before the transition but constant with respect to departure otherwise and the critical departure period is that of the transition; in cases (c) and (d) the critical value payment is independent of departure time and the critical departure period is equal to the arrival period. □

Example 16.22 Return to the earlier example with six agents and types $\theta_1 = (1, 7, 6)$, $\theta_2 = (3, 7, 2)$, $\theta_3 = (4, 8, 4)$, $\theta_4 = (6, 7, 8)$, with agents 5 and 6 arriving in later periods. The transition to the accepting phase occurs upon the arrival of agent 2. Then $p = 6, q = 2$, and agent 1 wins for 2. Consider instead that $\theta_1' = (1, 2, 6)$. The transition still occurs upon the arrival of agent 2 but now the item is sold in period 6 to agent 4 for a payment of 6. An agent with true type θ_1' does not want to report θ_1 because of the monotonic-late property: although it would win, it would not be allocated until period 3, and this is after its true departure.

Theorem 16.23 *Auction 3 is $e + o(1)$-competitive for efficiency and $e^2 + o(1)$-competitive for revenue in the single-unit, limited supply environment in the limit as $N \to \infty$.*

PROOF Let $\tau = \lfloor N/e \rfloor$. For efficiency, our competitive ratio is at least as great as the probability of selling to the highest value agent. Conditioned on selling at the transition, the probability that we sell to the highest value agent is at least $\frac{\lfloor N/e \rfloor}{N} = 1/e - o(1)$. Conditioned on selling after the transition, the probability of this event is $1/e - o(1)$ according to the analysis of the classical secretary problem. For revenue, our competitive ratio is at least as great as the probability of selling to the highest value agent at a price equal to the second-highest bid. Conditioned on selling at the transition, the probability of this event is $(1/e)^2 - o(1)$ (i.e., the probability that both the highest and second-highest value agents arrive before period τ). Conditioned on selling after the transition, the probability of this event is $(1/e)(1 - 1/e) - o(1)$, i.e., the probability that the second-highest value agent arrives before τ and the highest value agent arrives after τ. The unconditional probability of selling to the highest value agent at the second-highest price is a weighted average of the two conditional probabilities computed above, hence it is at least $(1/e)^2 - o(1)$. □

The random-ordering hypothesis has a critical role in this analysis: there is no constant competitive mechanism in this environment for the adversarial model adopted in our analysis of the expiring items environment.

For the secretary problem it is well known that no stopping rule can achieve asymptotic success probability better than $1/e$. The same lower bound can be established in our setting, even though the mechanism has richer feedback (i.e., it sees numbers not ranks) and even though an allocation to some bidder other than the highest-rank bidder will contribute to expected efficiency. The proof of this result is beyond the scope of this chapter.[6]

16.3.4 Remarks

We end this section with some general remarks that mostly seek to place the study of online mechanisms in single-valued preference domains in the broader context of computational mechanism design.

[6] One shows that for any stopping rule there is some distribution that is hard in the sense that the second-highest value in the sequence is much less than the highest value with high probability. Given this, the expected efficiency ratio of the allocation is determined, to first order, by the probability of awarding the item to the highest bidder.

Ex-post IC. A mechanism is ex-post IC if truth revelation is a best-response contingent on other agents being truthful, and whatever the types of other agents (and thus for all possible futures in the context of online MD). In offline mechanisms the solution concepts of ex-post incentive compatible (EPIC) and DSIC are equivalent with private value types. This equivalence continues to hold for *closed* online mechanisms that provide no feedback to an agent before it submits a bid. However, an online mechanism that provides feedback, for instance prices, or in an extreme case reports of current bids, loses this property. The report of an agent can now be conditioned on the reports of earlier agents, and monotonicity provides EPIC but not necessarily DSIC. Consider again Auction 2 in the expiring items environment, with true types $\theta_1 = (1, 2, 100)$, $\theta_2 = (1, 2, 80)$, and $\theta_3 = (2, 2, 60)$. If the bids are public then a possible (crazy) strategy of agent 3 is to condition its bid as possible: "bid $(2, 2, 1000)$ if a bid of $(1, 2, 100)$ is received or bid $(2, 2, 60)$ otherwise." Agent 1 will now pay 60 if it bids truthfully, but would pay 60 with a bid of $(1, 2, 90)$. Nevertheless, truthful bidding is a best response when other agents bid truthfully.

Simple price-based online auctions. One straightforward method to construct truthful online auctions for known-set, single-valued environments is to define an agent-independent *price schedule* $q_i^t(L, \theta_{-i}, \omega) \in \mathbb{R}$ to agent i for interesting decision set $L \in \mathcal{L}_i$, given stochastic events $\omega \in \Omega$, where $q_i^t(L, \theta_{-i}, \omega)$ defines the price for a decision in set L in period t. Given this, define payment $p_{(a_i,d_i,L_i)}(\theta_{-i}, \omega) = \min_{t \in [a_i,d_i]} q_i^t(L_i, \theta_{-i}, \omega)$ and let $t^*_{(a_i,d_i,L_i)}(\theta_{-i}, \omega)$ denote the first period $t \in [a_i, d_i]$ in which $q_i^t(L_i, \theta_{-i}, \omega) = p_{(a_i,d_i,L_i)}(\theta_{-i}, \omega)$. Then, decision policy π that allocates to agent i with type $\theta_i = (a_i, d_i, (r_i, L_i))$ if and only if $r_i \geq q_i^t(L_i, \theta_{-i}, \omega)$ in some $t \in [a_i, d_i]$, with the allocation period $t \geq t^*_{(a_i,d_i,L_i)}(\theta_{-i}, \omega)$, is monotonic-late and the associated critical-value payment is just $p_{(a_i,d_i,L_i)}(\theta_{-i}, \omega)$. Working with price schedules is quite natural in many domains, although not completely general, as shown in the following example:

> **Example 16.24** Consider the canonical expiring items environment. Fix θ_{-i}, and consider a monotonic-late policy π with critical-value $v^c_{(1,2)}(\theta_{-i}) = 20$, $v^c_{(1,1)}(\theta_{-i}) = v^c_{(2,2)}(\theta_{-i}) = 30$ (dropping dependence on ω because there are no stochastic events to consider). This policy allocates to type $\theta_i = (1, 2, 25)$ in period 2 but not type $\theta_i' = (1, 1, 28)$ or $\theta_i'(2, 2, 28)$. No simple price schedule corresponds to this policy, because it would require $q_i^1(\theta_{-i}) > 28$, $q_i^2(\theta_{-i}) > 28$ but $\min(q_i^1(\theta_{-i}), q_i^2(\theta_{-i})) \leq 25$.

The role of limited misreports. Consider again the above example. The price on an allocation to agent i in period 2 depends on its report: if the agent's type is $\theta_i = (2, 2, w_i)$ then the price is 30 but if the agent's type is $\theta_i = (1, 2, w_i)$ then the price is 20. This is at odds with the principle of "agent-independent prices" that drives the standard analysis of truthful mechanisms. The example also fails *weak-monotonicity*, which is generally necessary for truthfulness.[7]

[7] A social choice function $f : \Theta \to \mathcal{O}$ satisfies weak monotonicity if and only if for any $\theta_i \in \Theta_i$, agent i, and $\theta_{-i} \in \Theta_{-i}$, then $f(\theta_i, \theta_{-i}) = a$ and $f(\theta_i', \theta_{-i}) = b$ implies that $v_i(b, \theta_i') - v_i(b, \theta_i) \geq v_i(a, \theta_i') - v_i(a, \theta_i)$. In

What is going on? In both cases, the reason for this departure from the standard theory for truthful mechanism design is the existence of limited misreports. The auction would not be truthful with early-arrival misreports because an agent with type (2, 2, 28) could usefully deviate and report (1, 2, 28). For limited misreports $C(\theta_i) \subseteq \Theta_i$ that satisfy *transitivity* (which holds for the no-early arrival and no-late departure assumptions that are motivated in online MD), so that $\theta_i' \in C(\theta_i)$ and $\theta_i'' \in C(\theta_i')$ implies $\theta_i'' \in C(\theta_i)$, the payment $p_i(k, \theta_i, \theta_{-i}, \omega)$ collected from agent i conditioned on outcome $k \in \mathcal{O}$, must satisfy $p_i(k, \theta_i, \theta_{-i}, \omega) = \min\{p_i(k, \hat{\theta}_i, \theta_{-i}, \omega) : \hat{\theta}_i \in C(\theta_i), \pi(\hat{\theta}_i, \theta_{-i}, \omega) = k\}$, or ∞ if no such $\hat{\theta}_i$ exists, for all i, all $k \in \mathcal{O}$ and all $\omega \in \Omega$. Limited dependence on the reported type is possible as long as the price is independent across available misreports. For unlimited misreports we recover the standard requirement that prices are agent-independent.

So, the temporal aspect of online MD is both a blessing and a curse: on one hand we can justify limited misreports and gain more flexibility in pricing and in the timing of allocations, on the other hand decisions must be made in ignorance about future types.

Relaxing the known interesting-set assumption. We assumed that the interesting set $L_i \in \mathcal{L}_i$ was known by the mechanism. Domains in which the interesting set is *private information* to an agent can be handled by making the following modifications to the framework:

(i) Require that agent i's domain of interesting sets $\mathcal{L}_i = \{L_1, \ldots, L_m\}$, defines *disjoint* sets so that $L_1 \cap L_2 = \emptyset$ for all $L_1, L_2 \in \mathcal{L}_i$.

(ii) Require that a decision policy π is *minimal* so that it never makes decision $k^t \in L$ for some $L \succ_L L_i$ in some period $t \in [a_i, d_i]$, given reported type $\theta_i = (a_i, d_i, (r_i, L_i))$.

(iii) Extend the partial-order so that

$$\theta_1 \preceq_\theta \theta_2 \equiv (a_1 \geq a_2) \wedge (d_1 \leq d_2) \wedge (r_1 \leq r_2) \wedge (L_1 \succeq_L L_2), \tag{16.11}$$

and adopt this partial order in defining monotonicity.

Given these modifications, the general methods developed above for the analysis of online mechanisms continue to hold. For instance, a monotonic, minimal, and deterministic policy continues to be truthful when combined with critical-value payments, and monotonicity remains necessary for truthfulness amongst minimal, deterministic policies. This is left as an exercise.

The requirement that interesting sets are disjoint can significantly curtail the generality of preference domains that can be modeled. It is especially hard to model substitutes preferences, for instance indifference across a set of items. Suppose that the items are fruit, with $G = \{apple, banana, pear, lime, lemon\}$. With known interesting sets, we can model an agent with a type that defines a value for receiving an item from any subset of the domain G. With unknown interesting sets, we must now assume that there is some partition, for instance into $\{\{apple, pear\}, \{banana\}, \{lime, lemon\}\}$ so that the agent has either the same value for an apple or a pear and no value for anything

the example, when agent i changes its type from (1, 2, 25) to (2, 2, 28) it increases its relative value for an allocation in period 2 over no allocation, but the decision policy switches away from allocating to the agent in period 2.

else, or value for a banana and no value for anything else, or value for a lime and a lemon but no value for anything else.

Stochastic policies. Stochastic decision policies can be important, both algorithmically (many computational methods for online decision use a probabilistic model to sample possible state trajectories) and also to allow for tie breaking while retaining anonymity.

So far we have handled this by requiring *strong*-truthfulness. More generally, a stochastic mechanism is DSIC when truthful reporting maximizes expected utility for an agent (with the expectation defined with respect to randomization in the policy), and for all reports of other agents, and all *external* stochastic events, $\omega \in \Omega$. To handle this, we now $\pi_i(\theta_i, \theta_{-i}, \omega) \in [0, 1]$ to denote the probability that agent i receives an interesting decision ("is allocated"), given type θ_i, types θ_{-i} and (external) stochastic events ω. The appropriate generalization of monotonicity to stochastic policies requires, for every $\theta_i = (a_i, d_i, (r_i, L_i))$, all θ_{-i}, all $\omega \in \Omega$, that

$$\pi_i((a_i, d_i, (r_i, L_i)), \theta_{-i}, \omega) \geq \pi_i((a_i, d_i, (r'_i, L_i)), \theta_{-i}, \omega), \quad \forall r_i \geq r'_i, \tag{16.12}$$

and

$$\int_{x=0}^{r_i} \pi_i((a_i, d_i, (x, L_i)), \theta_{-i}, \omega)\, \mathrm{d}x \geq \int_{x=0}^{r_i} \pi_i((a'_i, d'_i, (x, L_i)), \theta_{-i}, \omega)\, \mathrm{d}x, \tag{16.13}$$

for all $a'_i \geq a_i$, $d'_i \leq d_i$. The critical value payment becomes

$$v^c_{(a_i, d_i, (r_i, L_i))}(\theta_{-i}, \omega) = \pi_i(\theta, \omega) r_i - \int_{x=0}^{r_i} \pi_i((a_i, d_i, (x, L_i)), \theta_{-i}, \omega)\, \mathrm{d}x \tag{16.14}$$

These definitions of monotonicity and critical-value payment reduce to the earlier cases when the policy is deterministic.

Theorem 16.25 *A stochastic decision policy π can be implemented in a truthful, IR mechanism that does not pay unallocated agents in a domain with (known interesting set) single-valued preferences and no early-arrival or late-departure misreports if and only if the policy is monotonic according to (16.12) and (16.13).*

The payment collected from allocated agents is the critical-value payment. The following example illustrates a stochastic policy that satisfies this monotonicity requirement.

Example 16.26 Consider a domain with no early arrival and no late departure misreports, two time periods $T = \{1, 2\}$, fix θ_{-i}, and consider agent i with a single-item valuation and possible types $\Theta_i = \{(1, 1, w_i), (1, 2, w_i), (2, 2, w_i)\}$. For impatient type $(1, 1, w_i)$, consider policy

$$\pi_i((1, 1, w_i), \theta_{-i}) = \begin{cases} 0, & \text{if } w_i \leq 8 \\ \frac{w_i - 8}{2}, & \text{if } 8 < w_i \leq 10 \\ 1, & \text{otherwise.} \end{cases} \tag{16.15}$$

Solving for the critical value payment (16.14), we find

$$v^c_{(1,1,w_i)}(\theta_{-i}) = \begin{cases} 0, & \text{if } w_i \le 8 \\ \frac{w_i^2}{4} - 16, & \text{if } 8 < w_i \le 10 \\ 9, & \text{otherwise.} \end{cases} \tag{16.16}$$

The policy and critical value payment is defined identically for type $(2, 2, w_i)$. For patient type $(1, 2, w_i)$, consider policy

$$\pi_i((1, 2, w_i), \theta_{-i}) = \begin{cases} \frac{w_i}{20}, & \text{if } 0 \le w_i \le 10 \\ \frac{w_i - 5}{10}, & \text{if } 10 < w_i \le 15 \\ 1, & \text{otherwise} \end{cases} \tag{16.17}$$

and the critical value payment, from (16.14), is

$$v^c_{(2,2,w_i)}(\theta_{-i}) = \begin{cases} \frac{w_i^2}{40}, & \text{if } 0 \le w_i \le 10 \\ \frac{w_i^2}{20} - \frac{5}{2}, & \text{if } 10 < w_i \le 15 \\ 8.75, & \text{otherwise.} \end{cases} \tag{16.18}$$

Notice that $\pi_i((1, 1, 10), \theta_{-i}) = 1$ and $\pi_i((1, 2, 10)) = 0.5$, contradicting more simplistic notions of monotonicity, but that truthfulness is retained because $v^c_{(1,1,10)}(\theta_{-i}) = 9$ while $v^c_{(1,2,10)}(\theta_{-i}) = 2.5$. Although type $(1, 2, 10)$ can misreport to $(1, 1, 10)$ and be allocated with certainty, it prefers to report $(1, 2, 10)$ because its expected utility is $(0.5)(10 - 2.5) + (0.5)(0) > (1.0)(10 - 9)$. We leave as an exercise to check that these policies satisfy monotonicity, with $\int_{x=0}^{w_i} \pi_i((1, 2, x), \theta_{-i})dx \ge \int_{x=0}^{w_i} \pi_i((1, 1, x), \theta_{-i})$ for all w_i.

We make a final remark about stochastic policies. In an environment with a probabilistic model that is common knowledge, and that defines both a probability distribution for agent types and for stochastic events $\omega \in \Omega$, we can settle for a weaker monotonicity requirement in which (16.12) and (16.13) are satisfied in expectation, given the model. However, this provides BNIC but not DSIC since monotonicity may not hold out of equilibrium when other agents are not truthful, since the probabilistic model of agent types upon which monotonicity is predicated would then be incorrect.

16.4 Bayesian Implementation in Online Domains

In this section we focus on Bayesian implementation of expected value-maximizing policies in environments in which the designer and every agent has a correct, probabilistic model for types and uncertain events, and this is common knowledge. We consider the goal of value maximization and present a dynamic variation of the offline Vickrey–Clarke–Groves (VCG) mechanism. This will involve computing expected value maximizing sequential decision policies and raise a number of computational challenges. We will see that the dynamic VCG mechanism is BNIC rather than DSIC, with incentive-compatibility contingent on future on-equilibrium play by all participants.

16.4.1 A General Model

A Markov decision process (MDP) provides a useful formalism for defining online mechanisms in model-based environments with general agent preferences. An MDP model $(H, K, \mathcal{P}, R)$ is defined for a set of states H, feasible decisions $K(h)$ in each state, a *probabilistic transition function* $\mathcal{P}(h^{t+1}|h^t, k^t)$ on the next state given current state and decision (with $\sum_{h' \in H^{t+1}} \mathcal{P}(h'|h^t, k^t) = 1$) and a *reward function* $R(h^t, k^t) \in \mathbb{R}$ for decision k^t in state h^t. The Markov property requires that feasible decisions, transitions, and rewards depend on previous states and actions only through the current state. It is achieved here, for example, by defining $h^t \in H^t = (\theta^1, \ldots, \theta^t; \omega^1, \ldots, \omega^t; k^1, \ldots, k^{t-1})$ so that the state captures the complete history of types, stochastic events, and decisions. In practice, a short summarization of state h^t is often sufficient to retain the Markov property.

Given a social planner interested in maximizing total value, then define reward $R(h^t, k^t) = \sum_{i \in I(h^t)} R_i(h^t, k^t)$, with $I(h^t)$ used to denote the set of agents present in state h^t and agent i's reward $R_i(h^t, k^t)$ is defined so that $v_i(\theta_i, k) = \sum_{t=a_i}^{d_i} R_i(h^t, k^t)$ for all sequences of decisions k. For finite time horizons, the expected value of policy π in state h^t is $V^\pi(h^t) = \mathbb{E}_\pi\{\sum_{\tau=t}^{|T|} R(h^\tau, \pi^\tau(h^\tau))\}$, where the expectation is taken with respect to the transition model and given the state-dependent decisions implied by policy π. For infinite time horizons, a standard approach is to define a *discount factor* $\gamma \in (0, 1)$ so that the expected discounted value of policy π in state h^t is $V^\pi(h^t) = \mathbb{E}_\pi\{\sum_{\tau=t}^{\infty} \gamma^{\tau-t} R(h^\tau, \pi^\tau(h^\tau))\}$. This makes sense in a multiagent environment when every agent has the same discount factor γ.

Given MDP value, $V^\pi(h^t)$, then the optimal policy π^* maximizes this value, $V^\pi(h^t)$, in every state h^t. For instance, in the finite time-horizon (no discounting) setting, the *optimal MDP-value function*, V^*, is defined to satisfy recurrence:

$$V^*(h) = \max_{k \in K^t(h)} \left[R(h, k) + \sum_{h' \in H^{t+1}} \mathcal{P}(h'|h, k) V^*(h') \right], \tag{16.19}$$

for all time t and all $h \in H^t$. Given this, the optimal decision policy solves:

$$\pi^*(h \in H^t) \in \arg \max_{k \in K^t(h)} \left[R(h, k) + \sum_{h' \in H^{t+1}} \mathcal{P}(h'|h, k) V^*(h') \right]. \tag{16.20}$$

Of course, the type information within the state is private to agents and we will need to provide incentive compatibility so that the policy has the correct view of the current state.

Example 16.27 The definition of state, feasible decision, and agent type is as in Example 16.3. The transition function $\mathcal{P}(h^{t+1}|h^t, k^t)$ is constructed to reflect a probabilistic model of new agent arrivals, and also the allocation decision. The MDP reward function, $R(h^t, k^t)$, can be defined with $R(h^t, k^t) = w_i$ if decision k^t allocates the item to agent i, for some agent i present in the state, and zero otherwise.

16.4.2 A Dynamic Vickrey–Clarke–Groves Mechanism

For concreteness, consider an environment with a finite time horizon and no discounting, and with the optimal MDP value $V^*(h)$ defined as the total expected reward from state h until the time horizon. We make some remarks about how to handle an infinite time horizon in Section 16.4.3. Consider the following dynamic VCG mechanism.[8] We assume that the decisions and reports in previous periods $t' < t$ are all *public* in period t, although similar analysis holds without this.

Auction 4. The *dynamic VCG mechanism* for the finite time horizon and no-discounting online MD environment works as follows:

(i) Each agent, i, reports a type $\hat{\theta}_i$ in some period $\hat{a}_i \geq a_i$.
(ii) Decision policy: Implement optimal policy π^*, which maximizes the total expected value, assuming the current state as defined by agent reports is the true state.
(iii) Payment policy: In an agent's reported departure period, $t = \hat{d}_i$, collect payment

$$x_i^t(h^t) = v_i(\hat{\theta}_i, \pi^*(\theta^{\leq t}, \omega^{\leq t})) - \left[V^*(h^{\hat{a}_i}) - V^*(h_{-i}^{\hat{a}_i})\right], \qquad (16.21)$$

where $\pi^*(\theta^{\leq t}, \omega^{\leq t})$ denotes the sequence of decisions made up to and including period t based on types $\theta^{\leq t}$ and stochastic events $\omega^{\leq t}$, $V^*(h^t)$ is the optimal MDP value in state h^t, and h_{-i}^t defines the (counterfactual) MDP state constructed to be equal to h^t but removing agent i's type from the state. The payment is zero otherwise.

Agent i's payment is its ex-post value discounted by term $(V^*(h^{\hat{a}_i}) - V^*(h_{-i}^{\hat{a}_i}))$, which is the expected marginal value it contributes to the system as estimated upon its arrival and based on its report. With this, the expected utility to agent i when reporting truthfully is equal to the expected marginal value that it contributes to the multiagent system through its presence.

For incentive-compatibility, we need the technical property of *stalling*, which requires that the expected value of policy π^* cannot be improved (in expectation) by delaying the report of an agent.[9] In addition, we assume an independence property; namely, the probabilistic process defining the arrival of agents other than i is independent of whether or not agent i has arrived.

Theorem 16.28 *The dynamic VCG mechanism, coupled with a policy that satisfies stalling, is Bayes–Nash incentive compatible (BNIC) and implements the expected-value maximizing policy, in a domain with no early-arrival misreports but arbitrary misreports of departure.*

PROOF Consider the expected utility (defined with respect to its information in period a_i) to agent i for misreport $\hat{\theta}_i \in C(\theta_i)$. Let $c \geq 0$ denote the number of

[8] The mechanism is presented in the no early-arrival misreports model but remains BNIC without this assumption.
[9] This is typically reasonable, for example any optimal policy that is able to delay for itself any decisions that pertain to the value of an agent will automatically satisfy stalling.

periods by which agent i misreports its arrival time. The agent's expected utility is

$$\underbrace{\mathbb{E}_{\pi^*}\{v_i(\theta_i, \pi^*(h^{\hat{a}_i}))|\hat{\theta}_i\}}_{\text{(A)}} + \underbrace{\mathbb{E}_{\pi^*}\left\{\sum_{t=a_i+c}^{|T|} R_{-i}(h^t, \pi^*(h^t))\right\}}_{\text{(B)}} - \underbrace{\mathbb{E}_{\pi^*}\{V^*(h_{-i}^{a_i+c})\}}_{\text{(C)}}.$$

Term (A) denotes the expected value to agent i given its misreport. Term (B), which denotes the total expected value to other agents forward from reported arrival, $a_i + c$, given agent i's misreport, corresponds to the expected value of terms $\{-v_i(\hat{\theta}_i, \pi^*(\theta^{\leq \hat{a}_i}, \omega^{\leq \hat{a}_i})) + V^*(h^{\hat{a}_i})\}$ in the payment. Notation R_{-i} denotes the total reward that accrues due to all agents except agent i. Term (C), which denotes the total expected value to other agents forward from period $a_i + c$, but with agent i removed, corresponds to the final term in the payment. Now, add term $\mathbb{E}_{\pi^*}\{\sum_{t=a_i}^{a_i+c-1} R_{-i}(h^t, \pi^*(h^t))\}$ to term (B) and subtract it again from term (C). The adjusted term (C′) is now agent independent (by the independence property) and can be ignored for the purpose of establishing BNIC. Term (A) combined with adjusted term (B′) is the expected value to all other agents forward from period a_i, plus the expected true value to agent i. Agent i's best response is to report its true type (and immediately upon arrival) because the policy π^* is defined to maximize (A)+(B') when the other agents are truthful, i.e. in a Bayes–Nash equilibrium. □

It bears repeating that truth telling is not a dominant strategy equilibrium. We have instead BNIC because the correctness of the policy depends on the center having the correct model for the distribution on agent types. Without the correct model, the policy is not optimal in expectation and an agent with beliefs different from that of the center may be able to improve (its belief about) the expected utility it will receive by misreporting its type and thus misrepresenting the state.[10]

16.4.3 Remarks

We end this section with some general remarks that touch on the computational aspects of planning in model-based environments, and also describe a couple of additional environments in which dynamic VCG mechanisms can be usefully applied.

Computational notes. Many algorithms exist to compute optimal decision policies in MDPs. These include dynamic programming, value iteration, policy iteration, and LP-based methods. However, the state space and action space for real-world online MD problems are large and approximations will typically be required. One appealing method is to couple the VCG mechanism with an online, sampling-based approximation algorithm. Rather than compute *a priori* an entire policy for every possible state one can

[10] Ex-post IR is achieved when the environment satisfies *agent-monotonicity*, which requires that introducing an agent increases the MDP value of any state. The payments collected by the mechanism are nonnegative in expectation (ex ante BB) when the environment satisfies *no positive externalities*, which requires that the arrival of an agent does not have a positive expected effect on the total value of the *other* agents.

determine the next decision to make in state h^t by approximating the decision problem forward from that state. Given an ϵ-approximation, the dynamic VCG mechanism is ϵ-BNIC, in the sense that no agent can gain more than some amount $\epsilon > 0$ (that can be made arbitrarily small) by deviating from truthful reporting, as long as the other agents are truthful and an ϵ-accurate estimate of the optimal MDP value is also available. One class of online, sparse-sampling algorithms work by building out a sample tree of future states based on decisions that could be made by the policy forward to some look-ahead horizon. These algorithms have run time that is independent of the size of the state space but scales exponentially in the number of decisions and in the look-ahead horizon. More recently, a family of *stochastic online combinatorial optimization* algorithms has been proposed that seem especially applicable to online MD environments. The algorithms solve a subclass of MDPs in which the realization of uncertainty is independent of any decision. This is often a natural assumption for truthful dynamic auctions: the allocation decisions made by an IC auction will not affect the reports of agents, and thus the realization of new types is independent of decisions.

Infinite time horizon and discounting. The dynamic VCG mechanism can be extended to handle an infinite time horizon when every agent has a common discount factor. Rather than collect a payment once, upon departure, a payment can be collected from agent i in each period, so as to align its utility stream with the expected, marginal stream of value that it contributes through its presence in the multiagent system.

Coordinated learning. A variant on the dynamic VCG mechanism can be used to support optimal, coordinated learning among a fixed population of self-interested agents. Suppose that in addition to influencing the reward received by an agent in each time period, the decisions made by a mechanism also reveal *information* that an agent can use to update its belief about its type; i.e., types are revealed online. A simple model is provided by a multiagent variation on the classical multi-armed bandits problem. Each agent owns an "arm" and receives a reward when its arm is activated, sampled from a stationary distribution. The reward signals are privately observed and allow an agent to update its model for the reward on its arm. In a setting with an infinite time horizon and discounting, one can use Gittins' celebrated index policy to characterize an efficient online policy that makes the optimal trade-off between exploitation and exploration. In the presence of self-interest, a variant on the dynamic VCG mechanism can provide incentives to support truthful reporting of reward signals by each agent, and thus implement the efficient learning policy.

16.5 Conclusions

We briefly consider some of the many possible future research directions in the area of online mechanism design:

- *Revenue:* Little work exists on the design of revenue-maximizing online mechanisms in model-based environments. For example, the problem of designing an analog to Myerson's optimal auction is only partially solved, even in the very simplest of online settings.

- *Learning by the center:* It is interesting to allow the mechanism to improve its probabilistic model of the distribution on agent types across time, while retaining incentive compatibility along the path of learning, and seek to converge to an efficient or revenue-optimal mechanism.
- *Alternative solution concepts:* Introduce weaker solution concepts than DSIC that avoid the strong common knowledge assumptions that are required to justify BNIC analysis. These could include, for instance, set Nash equilibria, implementation in undominated strategies, or implementation in minimax-regret equilibria and other robust solution concepts.
- *Endogenous information:* Extend online MD to domains in which decisions made by the mechanism affect the information available to agents about their types; i.e., cast online MD as a general problem of coordinated learning by self-interested agents in an uncertain environment.
- *Richer domains:* The current work on *dominant-strategy* implementation is limited to single-valued preference domains with quasi-linear utilities. Simple generalizations, such as to an environment in which some agents want an apple, some a banana, and some are indifferent across an apple and a banana do not satisfy the partition requirement on the structure of interesting sets and remain unsolved. Similar complications occur when one incorporates budget constraints, or generalizes to interdependent valuations. With time, perhaps progress can be made on the problem of online *combinatorial* auctions (and exchanges) in their full generality.

16.6 Notes

Lavi and Nisan (2000) coined the term *online auction* and initiated the study of truthful mechanisms in dynamic environments within the computer science literature. Friedman and Parkes (2003) later coined the term *online mechanism design*. The characterization of monotonicity requirements for truthful online mechanisms in single-valued domains is based on Hajiaghayi et al. (2005), with extensions to single-valued preferences building on Babaioff et al. (2006), see also Chapter 12.[11] Weak-monotonicity and its role in truthful mechanism design are discussed in Bikhchandani et al. (2006).

The discussion of the secretary problem and adaptive truthful auctions in the single-item setting is based on Hajiaghayi et al. (2004); see Babaioff et al. (2007) for a recent extension and (Gilbert and Mosteller, 1966; Dynkin, 1963) for classic references. The discussion of online mechanisms for expiring items is based on Hajiaghayi et al. (2005), and the negative result is due to Lavi and Nisan (2005), who also adopted an alternate solution concept in their analysis; see also (Ng et al., 2003; Porter, 2004; Juda and Parkes, 2006) and Awerbuch et al. (2003). Additional models of dynamic auctions in the computer science literature include unlimited supply, digital goods (Bar-Yossef et al., 2002; Blum et al., 2003; Blum and Hartline, 2005), two-sided auctions with both buyers and sellers (Bredin and Parkes, 2005; Blum et al., 2006), and interdependent

[11] The original paper by Hajiaghayi et al. (2005) mischaracterized the monotonicity requirement that is necessary for the truthful implementation of *stochastic* policies. This was originally brought to the attention of the authors by R. Vohra. The corrected analysis (presented here) is due to M. Mahdian.

value environments (Constantin et al., 2007). For an extended treatment of the single-valued setting, see Parkes and Duong (2007).

Moving to the model-based framework, the discussion of the dynamic VCG mechanism is based on Parkes and Singh (Parkes and Singh, 2003; Parkes et al., 2004). A general presentation in given in Bergemann and Välimäki (2006b), whose work along with that of Cavallo et al. (2006) and Bapna and Weber (2006) pertains to a model of coordinated learning; see also (Bergemann and Välimäki, 2003, 2006a; Athey and Segal, 2007). Pai and Vohra (2006) advance the study of revenue-optimal online mechanisms in model-based environments, and together with Gallien (2006) work to extend Myerson's (1981) optimal auction to dynamic environments; see also Cremer et al. (2007). The observation about the failure of the revelation principle, the example to illustrate the role of nonnegative payments, as well as inspiration for the example of a truthful, stochastic policy are due to Pai and Vohra (2006). For references on online algorithms and methods for solving sequential decision problems, see (Borodin and El-Yaniv, 1998; Van Hentenryck and Bent, 2006; Puterman, 1994; Kearns et al., 1999).

Acknowledgments

Many thanks to Florin Constantin, Bobby Kleinberg, Mallesh Pai, and Rakesh Vohra for providing detailed and constructive comments on an earlier draft, and to my collaborators in this work, including Jonathan Bredin, Ruggiero Cavallo, Florin Constantin, Quang Duong, Eric Friedman, Mohammad Hajiaghayi, Adam Juda, Bobby Kleinberg, Mohammad Mahdian, Chaki Ng, and Satinder Singh. Parkes is supported in part by National Science Foundation grants IIS-0238147, IIS-0534620, and an Alfred P. Sloan Foundation award.

Bibliography

S. Athey and I. Segal. An efficient dynamic mechanism. Technical report, Harvard University and Stanford University, 2007.

B. Awerbuch, Y. Azar, and A. Meyerson. Reducing truth-telling online mechanisms to online optimization. In *Proc. 35th Symp. on Theory of Computing*, 503–510, 2003.

M. Babaioff, N. Immorlica, and R. Kleinberg. Matroids, secretary problems, and online mechanisms. In *Proc. 18th Symp. Discrete Algorithms*, 434–443, 2007.

M. Babaioff, R. Lavi, and E. Pavlov. Mechanism design for single-value domains. In *Proc. 20th Natl. Conf. on Artificial Intelligence*, pp. 241–247, 2005.

A. Bapna and T.A. Weber. Efficient dynamic allocation with uncertain valuations. Technical report, Stanford University, 2006.

Z. Bar-Yossef, K. Hildrum, and F. Wu. Incentive-compatible online auctions for digital goods. In *Proc. 13th ACM-SIAM Symp. Discrete Algorithms (SODA'02)*, 964–970, 2002.

D. Bergemann and J. Välimäki. Dynamic common agency. *J. Econ. Theory*, 11:23–48, 2003.

D. Bergemann and J. Välimäki. Dynamic price competition. *J. Econ. Theory*, 127:232–263, 2006a.

D. Bergemann and J. Välimäki. Efficient dynamic auctions. Cowles Foundation Discussion Paper No. 1584, Yale University, 2006.

S. Bikhchandani, S. Chatterji, R. Lavi, A. Mu'alem, N. Nisan, and A. Sen. Weak monotonicity characterizes deterministic dominant strategy implementation. *Econometrica*, 74:1109–1132, 2006.

A. Blum and J. Hartline. Near-optimal online auctions. In *Proc. 16th Symp. on Discrete Algorithms*, 1156–1163, 2005.

A. Blum, V. Kumar, A. Rudra, and F. Wu. Online learning in online auctions. In *Proc. 14th Symp. Discrete Algorithms*, 137–143, 2003.

A. Blum, T. Sandholm, and M. Zinkevich. Online algorithms for market clearing. *J. ACM*, 53:845–875, 2006.

A. Borodin and R. El-Yaniv. *Online Computation and Competitive Analysis*. Cambridge University Press, 1998.

J. Bredin and D.C. Parkes. Models for truthful online double auctions. In *Proc. 21st Conf. on Uncertainty in Artificial Intelligence*, pp. 50–59, 2005.

R. Cavallo, D.C. Parkes, and S. Singh. Optimal coordinated learning among self-interested agents in the multi-armed bandit problem. In *Proc. 22nd Conf. Uncertainty in Artificial Intelligence (UAI'2006)*, pp. 55–62, Cambridge, MA, 2006.

F. Constantin, T. Ito, and D.C. Parkes. Online auctions for bidders with interdependent values. In *Proc. 6th Int. Conf. on Autonomus Agents and Multiagent Systems (AAMAS 07)* poster paper, 2007.

E.B. Dynkin. The optimum choice of the instant for stopping a Markov process. *Sov. Math. Dokl.*, 4:627–629, 1963.

E. Friedman and D.C. Parkes. Pricing WiFi at Starbucks – Issues in online mechanism design. In *Proc. 4th ACM Conf. on Electronic Commerce (EC'03)*, pp. 240–241, 2003.

J. Gallien. Dynamic mechanism design for online commerce. *Oper. Res.*, 54:291–310, 2006.

J. Gilbert and F. Mosteller. Recognizing the maximum of a sequence. *J. Amer. Statist. Assoc.*, 61(313):35–73, 1966.

M.T. Hajiaghayi, R. Kleinberg, M. Mahdian, and D.C. Parkes. Online auctions with re-usable goods. In *Proc. 6th ACM Conf. on Electronic Commerce (EC'05)*, pp. 165–174, 2005.

M.T. Hajiaghayi, R. Kleinberg, and D.C. Parkes. Adaptive limited-supply online auctions. In *Proc. 5th ACM Conf. on Electronic Commerce (EC'04)*, pp. 71–80, 2004.

P. Van Hentenryck and R. Bent. *Online Stochastic Combinatorial Optimization*. MIT Press, 2006.

A. Juda and D. Parkes. The sequential auction problem on eBay: An empirical analysis and a solution. In *Proc. 7th ACM Conf. on Electronic Commerce (EC'06)*, pp. 180–189, 2006.

M. Kearns, Y. Mansour, and A.Y. Ng. A sparse sampling algorithm for near-optimal planning in large Markov Decision Processes. In *Proc. 16th Int. Joint Conf. on Artificial Intelligence (IJCAI'99)*, pp. 1324–1331, 1999.

R. Lavi and N. Nisan. Competitive analysis of incentive compatible on-line auctions. In *Proc. 2nd ACM Conf. on Electronic Commerce (EC-00)*, 233–241, 2000.

R. Lavi and N. Nisan. Online ascending auctions for gradually expiring goods. In *Proc. 16th Annual ACM-SIAM Symp. on Discrete Algorithms (SODA'05)*, 2005.

R.B. Myerson. Optimal auction design. *Math. of Oper. Res.*, 6:58–73, 1981.

C. Ng, D.C. Parkes, and M. Seltzer. Virtual Worlds: Fast and Strategyproof auctions for dynamic resource allocation. In *Proc. 4th ACM Conf. on Electronic Commerce (EC'03)* short paper, pp. 238–239, 2003.

M. Pai and R. Vohra. Notes on optimal dynamic auctions. Kellogg School of Management, Northwestern University, 2006. Available from the authors.

D.C. Parkes and Q. Duong. An ironing-based approach to adaptive online mechanism design in single-valued domains. In *Proc. 22nd Annual Conf. on Artificial Intelligence*, 2007.

D.C. Parkes and S. Singh. An MDP-based approach to online mechanism design. In *Proc. 17th Annual Conf. on Neural Information Processing Systems (NIPS'03)*, 2003.

D.C. Parkes, S. Singh, and D. Yanovsky. Approximately efficient online mechanism design. In *Proc. 18th Annual Conf. on Neural Information Processing Systems (NIPS'04)*, 2004.

R. Porter. Mechanism design for online real-time scheduling. In *Proc. 5th ACM Conf. on Electronic Commerce (EC'04)*, 61–70, 2004.

M.L. Puterman. *Markov Decision Processes: Discrete Stochastic Dynamic Programming*. John Wiley & Sons, New York, 1994.

Exercises

16.1 Prove that the revelation principle holds with no early-arrival and no late-departure misreports and prove the "revelation principle + heartbeats" result in combination with no early-arrival misreports.

16.2 Consider a (known interesting set) single-valued preference domain with no late-departure misreports. Show that any decision policy π that can be truthfully implemented by an IR mechanism, and does not pay unallocated agents, must be monotonic-early (for a suitable definition of monotonic-early).

16.3 Prove that the approach outlined to constructing truthful online auctions in terms of an agent-independent price schedule $q_i^t(L, \theta_{-i}, \omega)$ induces a monotonic-late decision policy and critical-value payments. How would you modify the construction for an environment with both no early-arrival and no late-departure misreports?

16.4 Construct an example to show that the greedy auction in the expiring items setting has an arbitrarily bad competitive ratio with respect to offline VCG revenue.

16.5 Establish that the self-consistency property on prices in Section 16.3.4, coupled with the condition that a mechanism selects an outcome that maximizes utility for every agent at these prices is sufficient for truthfulness. Prove that the condition reduces to agent-independent prices for unrestrictedxs misreports.

16.6 Prove that modifications (i–iii) in Section 16.3.4 are sufficient to achieve truthfulness with agents with unknown interesting sets, together with no early-arrival and no late-departure misreports and a critical-value payment. What could break if the interesting sets are not disjoint, or if the policy is not minimal?

16.7 Show that the stochastic policy outlined in Example 16.26 satisfies monotonicity conditions (16.12) and (16.13).

16.8 Define a dynamic VCG mechanism that works for infinite time horizon and agents with a common, known discount factor $\gamma \in (0, 1)$.

PART THREE

Quantifying the Inefficiency of Equilibria

CHAPTER 17

Introduction to the Inefficiency of Equilibria

Tim Roughgarden and Éva Tardos

Abstract

This chapter presents motivation and definitions for quantifying the inefficiency of equilibria in noncooperative games. We illustrate the basic concepts in four fundamental network models, which are studied in depth in subsequent chapters. We also discuss how measures of the inefficiency of equilibria can guide mechanism and network design.

17.1 Introduction

17.1.1 The Inefficiency of Equilibria

The previous two parts of this book provided numerous examples demonstrating that the outcome of rational behavior by self-interested players can be inferior to a centrally designed outcome. This part of the book is devoted to the question: *by how much?*

To begin, recall the Prisoner's Dilemma (Example 1.1). Both players suffer a cost of 4 in the unique Nash equilibrium of this game, while both could incur a cost of 2 by coordinating. There are several ways to formalize the fact that the Nash equilibrium in the Prisoner's Dilemma is inefficient. A qualitative observation is that the equilibrium is strictly Pareto inefficient, in the sense that there is another outcome in which all of the players achieve a smaller cost. This qualitative perspective is particularly appropriate in applications where the "cost" or "payoff" to a player is an abstract quantity that only expresses the player's preferences between different outcomes. However, payoffs and costs have concrete interpretations in many applications, such as money or the delay incurred in a network. We can proceed more quantitatively in such applications and posit a specific *objective function*, defined on the outcomes of the game, that numerically expresses the "social good" or "social cost" of an outcome. Two prominent objective functions are the *utilitarian* and *egalitarian* functions, defined as the sum of the players' costs and the maximum player cost, respectively. The Nash equilibrium in the Prisoner's Dilemma does not minimize either of these objective functions.

Introducing an objective function enables us to *quantify* the inefficiency of equilibria, and in particular to deem certain outcomes of a game *optimal* or *approximately* optimal. The primary goal of this part of the book is to understand when, and in what senses, game-theoretic equilibria are guaranteed to approximately optimize natural objective functions. Such a guarantee implies that selfish behavior does not have severe consequences, and thus the benefit of imposing additional control over players' actions is relatively small. Guarantees of this sort are particularly useful in many computer science applications, especially those involving the Internet, where implementing an optimal solution can be impossible or prohibitively expensive.

In the remainder of this section, we discuss different measures that quantify the inefficiency of equilibria. In Section 17.2, we illustrate these concepts and motivate Chapters 18–21 via several examples in network games. Section 17.3 demonstrates how these same concepts provide a comparative framework for mechanism and network design. Section 17.4 concludes with bibliographic notes and suggestions for further reading.

17.1.2 Measures of Inefficiency

Several measures of "the inefficiency of the equilibria of a game" have been considered. All of these measures are defined, roughly, as the ratio between the objective function value of an equilibrium of the game and that of an optimal outcome. To specify such a measure precisely, we must answer the following basic modeling questions.

(1) How are the payoffs or costs of players expressed?
(2) What objective function do we use to compare different outcomes of the game?
(3) What is our definition of "approximately optimal"?
(4) What is our definition of an "equilibrium"?
(5) When there are multiple equilibria, which one do we consider?

We next discuss, at a high level, the most commonly studied answers to all of these questions. We give several examples in Section 17.2.

The answer to the first question will be some concrete payoff that players seek to maximize (such as money earned), or a cost that players aim to minimize (such as network delay). Both cases arise naturally in the applications studied in this book.

Second, we focus primarily on the utilitarian objective function, where the goal is to maximize the sum of players' payoffs or minimize the sum of players' costs. However, we also study the egalitarian objective function in Section 17.2.3 and Chapter 20. We call an outcome of a game *optimal* if it optimizes the chosen objective function. For example, in the Prisoner's Dilemma, the coordinated outcome is optimal for both the utilitarian and egalitarian objective functions. While in principle the measures of inefficiency below make sense for most objective functions, we can only expect the outcome of selfish behavior to approximate an optimal outcome when the objective function is related to the players' objectives.

Third, we quantify the extent to which a given outcome approximates an optimal one according to the ratio between the objective function values of the two outcomes. We consider only nonnegative objective functions, so this ratio is always nonnegative. (By convention, we interpret the ratio $c/0$ as 1 if $c = 0$ and as $+\infty$ if $c > 0$.) This ratio is at least 1 for minimization objectives and at most 1 for maximization objectives. In either case, a value close to 1 indicates that the given outcome is approximately optimal. For example, in the Prisoner's Dilemma, the sum of the players' costs in the Nash equilibrium is 8; since the minimum-possible sum of costs is 4, the corresponding ratio for the equilibrium outcome is 2. As Section 17.4 discusses, this use of a ratio is directly inspired by many similar notions of approximation that have been widely studied in theoretical computer science. While other notions of approximation are possible, almost all work on quantifying the inefficiency of equilibria has followed the approach taken here.

Several equilibrium concepts have been studied in different applications. In this chapter, we confine our attention to Nash equilibria and their analogues in games where the set of players or strategies is not finite. One particularly important issue not addressed in this chapter is the relationship between the inefficiency of equilibria and the ability of players to *reach* an equilibrium. In other words, a bound on the inefficiency of the equilibria of a game is much more compelling if we expect players to learn or converge to one of these equilibria. In many of the games discussed in this part of the book, relatively weak assumptions imply that local, uncoordinated optimization by players leads to an equilibrium outcome in a reasonable amount of time (see Sections 4.7 and 29.3). Some important classes of network games, however, do not admit such convergence results. This fact motivated researchers to define novel notions of "equilibrium outcomes," which include all Nash equilibria but also allow players to wander among a set of unstable outcomes. In some applications, all such equilibria, and not just the Nash equilibria, are guaranteed to be approximately optimal. Chapter 19 briefly discusses some results of this type. See Section 17.4 for further details.

Finally, given a choice of an objective function and an equilibrium concept, a game may have different equilibria with different objective function values; recall, for example, the coordination games of Section 1.1.3. In such games, it is not clear which equilibrium should be compared to an optimal outcome. Section 17.1.3 discusses the two most popular approaches.

17.1.3 The Price of Anarchy and the Price of Stability

The *price of anarchy*, the most popular measure of the inefficiency of equilibria, resolves the issue of multiple equilibria by adopting a worst-case approach. Precisely, the price of anarchy of a game is defined as the ratio between the worst objective function value of an equilibrium of the game and that of an optimal outcome. Note that the price of anarchy of a game is defined with respect to a choice of objective function and a choice of equilibrium concept. For example, as shown in Section 17.2.3 below, the price of anarchy of a game is generally different for different choices of an objective function.

We are interested in identifying games in which the price of anarchy is close to 1; in these games, all equilibria are good approximations of an optimal outcome. We view selfish behavior as benign in such games. Put differently, the benefit provided by (possibly costly or infeasible) dictatorial control over the players' actions is reasonably small.

A game with multiple equilibria has a large price of anarchy even if only one of its equilibria is highly inefficient. The *price of stability* is a measure of inefficiency designed to differentiate between games in which *all* equilibria are inefficient and those in which *some* equilibrium is inefficient. Formally, the price of stability of a game is the ratio between the *best* objective function value of one of its equilibria and that of an optimal outcome. Of course, in a game with a unique equilibrium, its price of anarchy and price of stability are identical. For a game with multiple equilibria, its price of stability is at least as close to 1 as its price of anarchy, and it can be much closer (see Example 17.2 below).

A bound on the price of stability, which ensures only that one equilibrium is approximately optimal, provides a significantly weaker guarantee than a bound on the price of anarchy. Nevertheless, there are two reasons to study the price of stability. First, in some applications, a nontrivial bound is possible only for the price of stability (see Section 17.2.2). Second, the price of stability has a natural interpretation in many network games – if we envision the outcome as being initially designed by a central authority for subsequent use by selfish players, then the best equilibrium is an obvious solution to propose. Indeed, in many networking applications, it is not the case that agents are completely independent; rather, they interact with an underlying protocol that essentially proposes a collective solution to all participants, who can either accept it or defect from it. The price of stability measures the benefit of such protocols. Because of this interpretation, the price of stability is typically studied only for equilibrium concepts that involve no randomization, such as pure-strategy Nash equilibria. For example, since a mixed-strategy Nash equilibrium might randomize only over outcomes that are not (pure-strategy) Nash equilibria, it is not clear how to interpret it as a single proposed outcome for future use by selfish players.

The price of stability thus quantifies the necessary degradation in solution quality caused by imposing the game-theoretic constraint of stability. The goal of seeking a good equilibrium is reminiscent of the general motives of mechanism design (Part II) – designing a game outcome that (approximately) optimizes a social objective function and is also consistent with self-interested behavior.

In this book, we will only quantify the inefficiency of the worst or the best equilibrium of a game. A third interesting approach is to analyze a "typical" equilibrium. Such "average-case analyses" are notoriously difficult to define in a meaningful and analytically tractable way, however, and this approach has not yet been used successfully to study the inefficiency of equilibria.

17.2 Fundamental Network Examples

Even in very simple games, equilibria can be arbitrarily inefficient. For example, consider the Prisoner's Dilemma, and let the players' costs in the Nash equilibrium tend to infinity. For every reasonable objective function, the objective function value of the unique Nash equilibrium is arbitrarily larger than that of the optimal outcome.

Since the inefficiency of equilibria cannot be bounded in general, a natural goal is to identify classes of games in which equilibria are guaranteed to be approximately optimal. Fortunately, this is the case for a wide array of fundamental network models.

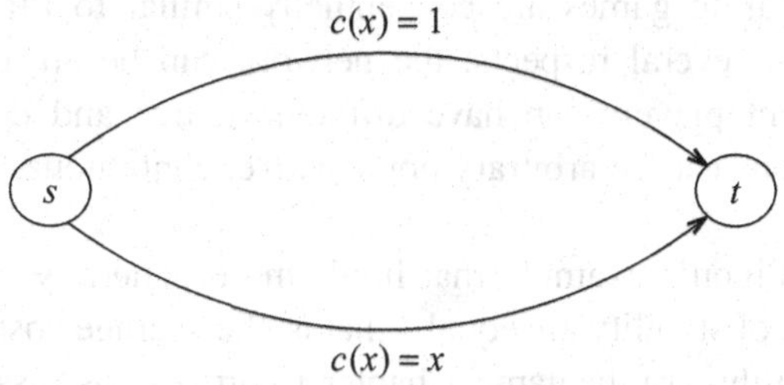

Figure 17.1. Pigou's example. The cost function $c(x)$ describes the cost incurred by users of an edge, as a function of the amount of traffic routed on the edge.

This section illustrates the concepts defined in Section 17.1 by informally introducing four such models. Chapters 18–21 study these and related models in greater depth.

17.2.1 Selfish Routing

We begin with a model of "selfish routing" that is discussed extensively in Chapter 18. We introduce the model via *Pigou's example*, which was first discussed in 1920 by the economist Pigou.

Example 17.1 (Pigou's Example) Consider the simple network shown in Figure 17.1. Two disjoint edges connect a source vertex s to a destination vertex t. Each edge is labeled with a *cost function* $c(\cdot)$, which describes the cost (e.g., travel time) incurred by users of the edge, as a function of the amount of traffic routed on the edge. The upper edge has the constant cost function $c(x) = 1$, and thus represents a route that is relatively long but immune to congestion. The cost of the lower edge, which is governed by the function $c(x) = x$, increases as the edge gets more congested. In particular, the lower edge is cheaper than the upper edge if and only if less than one unit of traffic uses it. We are interested in the price of anarchy of this game.

Suppose that there is one unit of traffic, representing a very large population of players, and that each player chooses independently between the two routes from s to t. Assuming that each player aims to minimize its cost, the lower route is a dominant strategy. In the unique equilibrium, all players follow this strategy, and all of them incur one unit of cost.

To define the optimal outcome, we assume that the objective function is to minimize the average cost incurred by players. In the above equilibrium, this average cost is 1. A simple calculation shows that splitting the traffic equally between the two links is the optimal outcome. In this outcome, half of the traffic (on the upper link) incurs cost 1, while the other half (on the lower link) experiences only 1/2 units of cost. Since the average cost of traffic in this optimal outcome is 3/4, both the price of anarchy and the price of stability in this game equal the ratio $1/(3/4) = 4/3$.

General selfish routing games are conceptually similar to Pigou's example, but are more complex in several respects: the network can be an arbitrarily large directed graph, different players can have different source and destination vertices, and edge cost functions can be arbitrary nonnegative, continuous, and nondecreasing functions.

One property of Pigou's example that holds more generally is that the price of anarchy and the price of stability are equal – that is, the average cost incurred by traffic is the same in all equilibria of the game. Chapter 18 proves this "essential uniqueness" property using a powerful and flexible technique called the *potential function method*. Roughly, a potential function for a game is a real-valued function, defined on the set of possible outcomes of the game, such that the equilibria of the game are precisely the local optima of the potential function. Not all games admit natural potential functions, but most of the ones discussed in this part of the book do. As we will see in Chapters 18 and 19, when a game admits a potential function, there are typically consequences for the existence, uniqueness, and inefficiency of equilibria.

One of the goals of Chapter 18 is to understand how the price of anarchy of a selfish routing game depends on different properties of the network. For example, recall that the price of anarchy in Pigou's example is precisely $4/3$. Does this bound degrade as the network size grows? As the number of distinct source and destination vertices increases? As the edge cost functions become increasingly nonlinear? If players control a nonnegligible fraction of the overall traffic? Chapter 18 provides answers to all of these questions. For example, in every network with affine cost functions (of the form $ax + b$), no matter how large and complex, the price of anarchy is at most $4/3$. With arbitrary cost functions, even with the simple network structure shown in Figure 17.1, the price of anarchy can be arbitrarily large (Exercise 17.1).

17.2.2 Network Design and Formation Games

Chapter 19 studies a diverse set of models of network formation and network design with selfish players. Here we discuss only one, with the goal of illustrating the differences between the price of anarchy and the price of stability.

We define a *Shapley network design game* as follows. Like selfish routing games, such a network design game occurs in a directed graph G. Each edge e of the graph has a fixed, nonnegative cost c_e. There are k players, and each player i is associated with a source vertex s_i and a destination vertex t_i. Player i wants to establish connectivity from its source to its destination, and its strategies are therefore the s_i-t_i paths of G. Given a choice of a path P_i by each player i, we assume that the formed network is simply the union $\cup_i P_i$ of these. The cost of this network is the sum $\sum_{e \in \cup_i P_i} c_e$ of the costs of these edges, and we assume that this cost is passed on to the players in a natural way: the cost of each edge of the formed network is shared equally by the players who use it. More formally, each player i incurs cost c_e/f_e for each edge e of its path P_i, where f_e denotes the number of players selecting paths that contain the edge e. This defines a finite noncooperative game, and we are interested in the inefficiency of the pure-strategy Nash equilibria of this game. We assume that the social objective is to minimize the cost of the formed network.

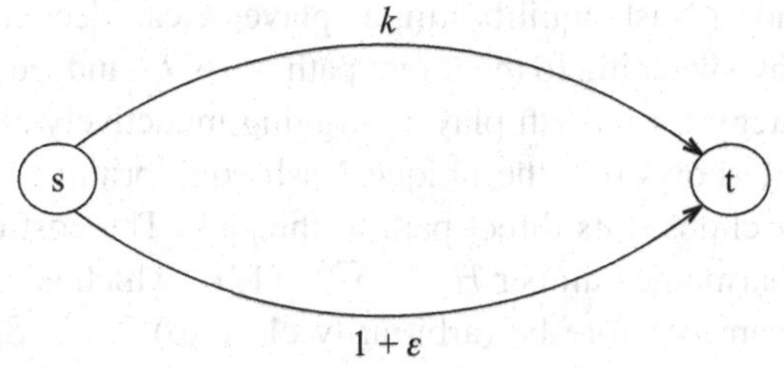

Figure 17.2. Multiple Nash equilibria in Shapley network design games (Example 17.2).

Example 17.2 Consider the network shown in Figure 17.2. There are k players, each with the same source s and destination t. The edge costs are k and $1 + \epsilon$, where $\epsilon > 0$ is arbitrarily small. In the optimal outcome, all players choose the lower edge. This outcome is also a Nash equilibrium. On the other hand, suppose that all of the players choose the upper edge. Each player then incurs cost 1, and if a player deviates to the lower edge, it pays the larger cost of $1 + \epsilon$. This outcome is thus a second Nash equilibrium, and it has cost k.

The price of anarchy of the game in Example 17.2 is roughly the number of players, and we view this as unacceptably large. This example motivates the study of the price of stability of Shapley network design games. Recall from Section 17.1.3 that the price of stability has a natural interpretation in network formation games – it measures the inefficiency of the network that a designer would propose to selfish players (i.e., the best equilibrium).

The price of stability in Example 17.2 is 1. The next example shows that this is not always the case.

Example 17.3 ($\mathcal{H}_k$ example) Consider the network shown in Figure 17.3. There are k players, all with the same sink t, and $\epsilon > 0$ is arbitrarily small. For each $i \in \{1, 2, \ldots, k\}$, the edge (s_i, t) has cost $1/i$. In the optimal outcome, each player i chooses the path $s_i \rightarrow v \rightarrow t$ and the cost of the formed network

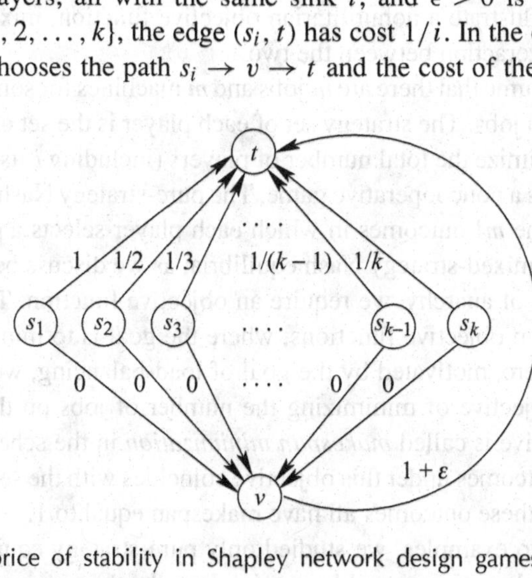

Figure 17.3. The price of stability in Shapley network design games can be at least $\mathcal{H}_k$ (Example 17.3).

is $1 + \epsilon$. This is not a Nash equilibrium, as player k can decrease its cost from $(1 + \epsilon)/k$ to $1/k$ by switching to the direct path $s_k \to t$ – indeed, this direct path is a dominant strategy for the kth player. Arguing inductively about the players $k - 1, k - 2, \ldots, 1$ shows that the unique Nash equilibrium is the outcome in which each player chooses its direct path to the sink. The cost of this outcome is exactly the kth harmonic number $\mathcal{H}_k = \sum_{i=1}^{k}(1/i)$, which is roughly $\ln k$. The price of stability can therefore be (arbitrarily close to) $\mathcal{H}_k$ in Shapley network design games.

Our emphasis on pure-strategy Nash equilibria and Example 17.3 motivate the following two questions.

(1) Does every Shapley network design game possess at least one pure-strategy Nash equilibrium? (Recall from Example 1.7 that not all games have such equilibria.)
(2) What is the largest-possible price of stability in Shapley network design games?

Chapter 19 uses the potential function method discussed in Section 17.2.1 to resolve both of these questions. This method answers the first question in the affirmative, and also shows that the price of stability in every k-player Shapley network design game is at most $\mathcal{H}_k$. In other words, for each value of k, the game in Example 17.3 has the largest-possible price of stability.

Chapter 19 also discusses the price of anarchy and stability in other models of selfish network design and formation.

17.2.3 Scheduling Games

Our next example is a load-balancing scenario, where the goal is to spread several identical "jobs" evenly across a number of identical "machines." This is a very simple type of *scheduling* problem; this and much more general scheduling models have been extensively studied and have numerous applications (see Chapter 20). We focus on this special case to illustrate a nonutilitarian objective function, mixed-strategy Nash equilibria, and the interaction between the two.

Concretely, we assume that there are m jobs and m machines for some integer $m \geq 1$. Players correspond to jobs. The strategy set of each player is the set of machines. Each player i seeks to minimize the total number of players (including i itself) that select its machine. This defines a noncooperative game. The pure-strategy Nash equilibria of this game are precisely the $m!$ outcomes in which each player selects a distinct machine. There are additional mixed-strategy Nash equilibria, as we discuss below.

To study the price of anarchy, we require an objective function. Thus far, we have studied only utilitarian objective functions, where the goal is to minimize the sum of the players' costs. Here, motivated by the goal of load-balancing, we focus primarily on the egalitarian objective of minimizing the number of jobs on the most crowded machine. This objective is called *makespan minimization* in the scheduling literature. The set of optimal outcomes under this objective coincides with the set of pure-strategy Nash equilibria, and these outcomes all have makespan equal to 1.

In the previous two examples, we studied only pure-strategy equilibria, where the objective function value of an equilibrium is clear. In the present application, we also consider mixed-strategy Nash equilibria. Such an equilibrium naturally induces a probability distribution on the set of game outcomes. Specifically, since we assume that the random choices made by distinct players are independent, the probability of a given strategy profile is the product of the probabilities that each player selects its prescribed strategy.

We define the objective function value of a mixed-strategy Nash equilibrium as the expectation, over this induced distribution on the game outcomes, of the objective function value of an outcome. Thus the objective function value of a mixed-strategy Nash equilibrium is its "expected objective function value." As we now show, allowing mixed-strategy Nash equilibria can increase the price of anarchy in scheduling games.

Example 17.4 (Balls and Bins) In the above example with m jobs and m machines, suppose that every player selects a machine uniformly at random. We claim that this defines a mixed-strategy Nash equilibrium. To prove it, adopt the first player's viewpoint. Since each of the other $m - 1$ players chooses a machine uniformly at random, all m machines appear equally loaded. More formally, let X_{ij} denote the indicator random variable for the event that player i selects the machine j. If the first player selects machine j, then it incurs a cost of $1 + \sum_{i>1} X_{ij}$. By linearity of expectation, its expected cost on this machine is $1 + \sum_{i>1} \mathbf{E}[X_{ij}] = 2 - 1/m$. Since this expected cost is independent of the machine j, every pure strategy of the first player is a best response to the mixed strategies chosen by the other players. As a consequence, every mixed strategy of the first player is also a best response (recall Section 1.3.4). This argument clearly applies to the other players as well, and hence this set of mixed strategies forms a Nash equilibrium.

What is the objective function value of this mixed-strategy Nash equilibrium – the expected value of the most heavily loaded machine? We emphasize that this expectation $\mathbf{E}[\max_j\{\sum_i X_{ij}\}]$ is not the same as the maximum expected load, $\max_j\{\mathbf{E}[\sum_i X_{ij}]\}$, which is only 1. Intuitively, the expected number of jobs on the most crowded machine is governed by the severity of the "collisions" that occur when the players select machines in a randomized and uncoordinated way. This nontrivial problem, typically called the *balls into bins* problem, is classical and has been thoroughly analyzed. In particular, the objective function value of the above mixed-strategy Nash equilibrium is $\Theta(\log m / \log\log m)$ as m grows large. (See Chapter 20.)

Collisions due to independent random choices therefore give rise to significant inefficiency: the price of anarchy with respect to pure-strategy Nash equilibria in this example is 1 for every $m \geq 1$, whereas the price of anarchy with respect to mixed-strategy Nash equilibria is $\Omega(\log m / \log\log m)$ as m grows large.

Example 17.4 shows that the price of anarchy can depend fundamentally on the choice of equilibrium concept; recall the fourth question of Section 17.1.2. As an aside, we note that it also illustrates the dependence of the price of anarchy on the choice of objective function. Specifically, consider the utilitarian objective function, where the goal is to minimize the sum of the players' costs. The optimal outcomes again coincide with the pure-strategy Nash equilibria, and all of these have objective function value equal to m. The objective function value of the mixed-strategy Nash equilibrium in Example 17.4 is defined as the expected sum of the players' costs, which by linearity of expectation is the same as the sum of the players' expected costs. The calculation in Example 17.4 shows that each player's expected cost equals $2 - 1/m$, and thus the objective function value of this mixed-strategy Nash equilibrium is precisely $2m - 1$. This is in fact the worst equilibrium of the game (Exercise 17.3), and hence the price of anarchy for the utilitarian objective in this example is only $2 - 1/m$.

We could also consider the objective of minimizing the maximum expected load, instead of the expected maximum load, experienced by a player. Both of these objectives can be viewed as egalitarian objectives, and they assign the same objective function value to every pure strategy profile. In particular, these objective functions have identical optimal values. However, they typically assign different values to a profile of mixed strategies. For example, the maximum expected load experienced by a player in the mixed-strategy Nash equilibrium in Example 17.4 is only $2 - 1/m$. This is the worst equilibrium (as in Exercise 17.3), and the price of anarchy with respect to the maximum expected load of a player is therefore only $2 - 1/m$. An arguably undesirable feature of this objective is that the price of anarchy is small even though, with high probability, the players' random strategy selections produce a pure strategy profile with objective function value $\Omega(\log m / \log\log m)$ times that of optimal.

Returning to the makespan minimization objective considered in Example 17.4, Chapter 20 proves that the price of anarchy is bounded above by $O(\log m / \log\log m)$ in load-balancing games with n jobs and m machines, even when the machines are "nonuniform" in a certain precise sense. Chapter 20 also studies the price of anarchy in several variants of this scheduling game.

17.2.4 Resource Allocation Games

We next study a game that is induced by a natural protocol for allocating resources to players with heterogeneous utility functions. Chapter 21 studies such games in much greater depth.

We consider a single divisible resource – the bandwidth of a single network link, say – to be allocated to a finite number $n > 1$ of competing players. We assume that each player i has a concave, strictly increasing, and continuously differentiable utility function U_i. A *resource allocation game* is defined by the n utility functions $U_1, \ldots, U_n$ and the link capacity $C > 0$. An outcome of such a game is a nonnegative allocation vector $(x_1, \ldots, x_n)$ with $\sum_i x_i = C$, where x_i denotes the amount of bandwidth allocated to player i. We study the utilitarian objective, and are thus interested in maximizing the sum $\sum_i U_i(x_i)$ of the players' utilities.

The *proportional sharing* protocol allocates bandwidth as follows. Each user expresses its interest in receiving bandwidth by submitting a nonnegative bid b_i. The protocol then allocates all of the bandwidth in proportion to the bids, so that each user i receives

$$x_i = \frac{b_i}{\sum_{j=1}^{n} b_j} \cdot C \tag{17.1}$$

units of bandwidth. Player i is then charged its bid b_i. See Section 17.3 and Chapter 21 for a discussion of alternative protocols that have a similar flavor.

We assume that player payoffs are quasilinear in the sense of Section 9.3. In other words, the payoff Q_i to a player i is defined as its utility for the bandwidth it receives, minus the price that it has to pay:

$$Q_i(b_1, \ldots, b_n) = U_i(x_i) - b_i = U_i\left(\frac{b_i}{\sum_{j=1}^{n} b_j} \cdot C\right) - b_i. \qquad (17.2)$$

Assume that if all players bid zero, then all users receive zero payoff. Our restrictions on the utility function U_i ensure that the payoff function Q_i is continuously differentiable and strictly concave in the bid b_i for every fixed vector b_{-i} with at least one strictly positive component (Exercise 17.4). (As usual, b_{-i} denotes the vector of bids of players other than i.)

An *equilibrium* is a bid vector in which every user bids optimally, given the bids of the other users.

Definition 17.5 A bid vector $(b_1, \ldots, b_n)$ is an *equilibrium* of the resource allocation game $(U_1, \ldots, U_n, C)$ if for every user $i \in \{1, 2, \ldots, n\}$,

$$Q_i(b_i, b_{-i}) = \sup_{\tilde{b}_i \geq 0} Q_i(\tilde{b}_i, b_{-i}). \qquad (17.3)$$

The potential function method also applies to resource allocation games. This method can be used to show that, for every resource allocation game, every equilibrium bid vector induces the same allocation. Thus, every equilibrium has equal objective function value. The next example shows that equilibria in resource allocation games can be inefficient.

Example 17.6 Consider a resource allocation game in which the capacity C is 1, the first user has the utility function $U_1(x_1) = 2x_1$, and the other $n - 1$ users have the utility function $U_i(x_i) = x_i$. In the optimal allocation, the first player receives all of the bandwidth and the corresponding objective function value is 2. This allocation does not, however, arise from an equilibrium. To see why, observe that (17.1) implies that the only bid vectors that induce this allocation are those in which only the first player submits a positive bid. Such a bid vector cannot be an equilibrium, as the first player can bid a smaller positive amount and continue to receive all of the bandwidth. (See also Exercise 17.5.)

A similar argument holds whenever the first player's bid is a sufficiently large fraction of the sum of the players' bids: if the first player lowers its bid, its allocation diminishes, but the effective "price per unit of bandwidth" that it pays decreases by a large enough amount to increase its overall payoff. More formally, suppose that $(b_1, \ldots, b_n)$ is an equilibrium, and let B denote the sum of the bids. By Exercise 17.5, at least two of the bids are strictly positive. By definition, the bid b_1 satisfies (17.3). Since the payoff function Q_1 is continuously differentiable and strictly concave in the bid b_1 with b_{-1} fixed (Exercise 17.4), we can compute b_1 by differentiating the right-hand side of (17.3) and setting this derivative to zero. Starting from the defining equation (17.2) of the function Q_i, using that $U_1(x_1) = 2x_1$ and $C = 1$, and calculating, we obtain the condition $2(B - b_1)/B^2 = 1$. For a player $i > 1$, the same calculation yields the condition $(B - b_i)/B^2 = 1$. Subtracting the second equation from the first implies that $2b_1 - b_i = B$ for every $i = 2, 3, \ldots, n$. Adding these $n - 1$ equations together gives $2(n - 1)b_1 - (B - b_1) = (n - 1)B$; solving, we find that the first player's bid is only an $n/(2n - 1)$ fraction of the sum of the bids: $b_1 = nB/(2n - 1)$. In the resulting allocation, the first player obtains only an $n/(2n - 1)$ fraction of the bandwidth. As n grows large, roughly half of the bandwidth is allocated to the first player, while the rest is split equally between the other $n - 1$ players. The objective function value of this allocation is roughly $3/2$, which is only a $3/4$ fraction of the value of the optimal allocation.

Intuitively, inefficiency arises in Example 17.6 because of "market power" – the fact that a single player receives the lion's share of the total bandwidth in the optimal allocation. Indeed, resource allocation games were initially studied under the assumption that no users have nontrivial market power; in this case, equilibria are fully efficient and the price of anarchy is 1. Details are discussed in Chapter 21. Chapter 21 also uses the price of anarchy as a criterion for mechanism and protocol design; we foreshadow this work in the next section.

17.3 Inefficiency of Equilibria as a Design Metric

17.3.1 Motivation

In the previous section, we studied four natural network examples. The game was given and immutable in all of these examples, and the only question involved the quality of its equilibria. While most work on the inefficiency of equilibria has been of this form, the flexibility of the framework presented in Section 17.1.2 begs a more general question: how can we *design* a game, or modify an existing game, to minimize the inefficiency of its equilibria? This question is especially crucial in settings where equilibria are unacceptably inefficient, but directly imposing an optimal solution is impractical.

Example questions of this type include the following. Among a given class of mechanisms, which one induces a game with the best price of anarchy? Quantitatively, what is this best-possible price of anarchy? Given a game and a restricted set of options for influencing its equilibria, which option improves the price of anarchy by the maximum-possible amount? How large is the improvement? Using the measures of inefficiency described in Section 17.1.2, we can rigorously compare the performance of different solutions, and quantify the efficiency loss obtained by an optimal solution.

These goals are conceptually the same as those of algorithmic mechanism design, studied in Part II of this book. However, much of the work we describe below and in the notes (Section 17.4) differs from the bulk of the material in Part II in three technical respects. First, while Part II largely concerns the design of strategyproof mechanisms in which truthful revelation is a dominant strategy for every player, we study the equilibria of mechanisms that are not generally strategyproof. For example, in the proportional sharing mechanism described in Section 17.2.4, the strategy space of a player (nonnegative bids) does not coincide with its type space (utility functions), and no player has a dominant strategy. These differences are typically motivated by practical considerations, as we discuss in Section 17.3.2. Second, some of the research described in Section 17.4 considers games without private preferences. In these cases, the design problem is nontrivial because the mechanism designer lacks full control over the allocation of resources. Optimally influencing traffic in a selfish routing network by pricing the network edges is one example of such a problem. Third, in much of the work discussed in Section 17.4, the problem is not to design a good mechanism from scratch, but rather to leverage a limited amount of power to improve the equilibria of a given game as much as possible.

17.3.2 An Example: The Proportional Sharing Mechanism

We now informally describe one example of how the inefficiency of equilibria can serve as a design metric. Chapter 21 discusses the following result in greater detail, and Section 17.4 discusses additional examples.

Recall the resource allocation games of Section 17.2.4, where n players compete for a divisible link with capacity C. We studied the proportional sharing mechanism, in which each player i submits a bid b_i to the mechanism, the mechanism allocates all of the bandwidth to the players in proportion to their bids, and every player then pays its bid. This mechanism induces a noncooperative game; as proved in Chapter 21, the price of anarchy of every such game is at least $3/4$. We next strive to surpass this efficiency guarantee and ask: how can we modify the mechanism so that the price of anarchy is always even closer to 1?

The answer to this question depends crucially on the class of mechanisms that we are willing to consider. If we impose no restrictions on the allowable mechanisms, then a version of the VCG mechanism (see Chapter 9) always induces a game for which the price of anarchy equals 1. However, this solution is "more complicated" than the proportional sharing mechanism in two ways. First, the communication from the players to the mechanism is more involved; each player must submit a representation of its entire utility function, as opposed to a single bid. Second, the communication from the mechanism back to the players is also more complicated in the following sense. In the proportional sharing mechanism, allocations can be completely summarized by the bids and a single additional parameter, the *price* of bandwidth. To see this, consider a bid vector $(b_1, \ldots, b_n)$ for a link with capacity C. Set a price p equal to B/C, where B is the sum of the bids. The (proportional) allocation to each player i is then simply its bid b_i divided by this price. While the allocations of the VCG mechanism can be similarly interpreted in terms of prices, different players are generally allocated bandwidth according to different prices.

The simplicity of the proportional sharing mechanism – that the communication both to and from the mechanism is limited – makes it particularly suitable for implementation in large communication networks. Is there a mechanism that retains these appealing properties and has strictly smaller worst-case efficiency loss? Chapter 21 shows that the answer is "no" – for an appropriate definition of "bounded communication," every equally simple mechanism can induce a game that has a price of anarchy of at most 3/4. The proportional sharing mechanism is therefore optimal among all mechanisms meeting natural, desirable implementation constraints.

17.4 Notes

The observation that self-interested behavior can lead to a socially inefficient outcome is an old one; see, for example, Dubey (1986), Rapoport and Chammah (1965), and the references therein. The idea of quantifying the inefficiency of equilibria using an objective function and an approximation measure is much newer. The concept of the price of anarchy originated in Koutsoupias and Papadimitriou (1999), where it was called the *coordination ratio*. Koutsoupias and Papadimitriou studied a generalization of the scheduling games described in Section 17.2.3. Papadimitriou (2001) introduced the term "the price of anarchy." The price of stability was first studied in Schulz and Stier Moses (2003); the terminology is from Anshelevich et al. (2004). Several earlier works, and in particular Mason (1985), anticipated these concepts. See also Satterthwaite and Williams (1989) and Moulin and Shenker (2001), who studied additive notions of efficiency loss in mechanism design applications.

The measures of inefficiency discussed in Section 17.1 are similar to and motivated by several well-established concepts in theoretical computer science. One example is the *approximation ratio* of a heuristic for a (typically NP-hard) optimization problem, defined as the worst ratio between the objective function value of the solution produced by the heuristic and that of an optimal solution (Vazirani, 2001). While the approximation ratio measures the worst-case loss in solution quality due to insufficient computational effort, the price of anarchy measures the worst-case loss arising from insufficient ability (or willingness) to control and coordinate the actions of selfish individuals.

The novel notions of "equilibrium outcomes" alluded to in Section 17.1.2 are described in Mirrokni and Vetta (2004) and Goemans et al. (2005). Tennenholtz (2002) also proposed relaxing the assumption that players reach a Nash equilibrium, and examining the consequences for the players' payoffs. The inefficiency of other equilibrium concepts has also been studied; see work by Christodoulou and Koutsoupias (2005) on correlated equilibria (Section 1.5), Andelman et al. (2007) on strong Nash equilibria (Section 1.6), and Hayrapetyan et al. (2006) on equilibria in the presence of coalitions of players.

Pigou's example (Example 17.1) is from Pigou (1920). Selfish routing networks and their equilibria were defined formally by Wardrop (1952) and Beckmann et al. (1956). The potential function method originates in Beckmann et al. (1956) and was later developed by Rosenthal (1973), Monderer and Shapley (1996), Roughgarden and Tardos (2002), and Anshelevich et al. (2004). Shapley network design games were first studied by Anshelevich et al. (2004), and Example 17.3 is from Anshelevich et al. (2004). Example 17.2 was given in an earlier paper by Anshelevich et al. (2003). The scheduling games of Section 17.2.3 and Example 17.4 are due to Koutsoupias and Papadimitriou (1999). See Motwani and Raghavan (1995) for a discussion of the balls into bins problem. The proportional sharing mechanism is due to Kelly (1997), and

Example 17.6 is from Johari and Tsitsiklis (2004). For further references on the four network models of Section 17.2, see Chapters 18–21.

The results mentioned in Section 17.3.2 are from Johari and Tsitsiklis (2006), and are discussed in further detail in Chapter 21. Chapter 21 also covers variants of the VCG mechanism in which users submit only a single bid, rather than an entire utility function. These mechanisms are not (and cannot be) single-price in the sense of Section 17.3.2, however.

We conclude these notes with examples of how measures of inefficiency have been used to compare different mechanisms and different strategies for influencing equilibria in the network models explored in Section 17.2. Several approaches to improving the equilibria of a selfish routing network have been considered, including pricing the network edges, and routing a small fraction of the traffic in a centralized manner. The goal is then to leverage the limited amount of design power to minimize the price of anarchy. For details on this literature, see Roughgarden (2005, Chapters 5–6) and the references therein.

Motivated by the network design games of Section 17.2.2 and Example 17.3, Chen et al. (2007) studied how to design cost-sharing methods to minimize the inefficiency of equilibria in the resulting network game. One of the contributions in Chen et al. (2007) is an analogue of the result described in Section 17.3.2 for resource allocation mechanisms: among all cost-sharing methods that are "oblivious" to the network structure in a certain precise sense, the Shapley cost-sharing method of Section 17.2.2 minimizes the worst-case price of stability. On the other hand, cost-sharing methods that can leverage information about the network topology can outperform Shapley cost-sharing methods (Chen et al., 2007).

Finally, for the scheduling games of Section 17.2.3, Christodoulou et al. (2004) and Immorlica et al. (2005) design machine scheduling policies to improve the inefficiency of equilibria. Informally, such a policy can be used to prioritize one player over another, thereby causing different players to incur different costs on a common machine. As shown in Christodoulou et al. (2004) and Immorlica et al. (2005), even very simple scheduling policies reduce the price of anarchy from logarithmic in the number of machines (Example 17.4) to a small constant.

Bibliography

N. Andelman, M. Feldman, and Y. Mansour. Strong price of anarchy. In *Proc. 18th Symp. Discrete Algorithms*, pp. 189–198, 2007.

E. Anshelevich, A. Dasgupta, J. Kleinberg, É. Tardos, T. Wexler, and T. Roughgarden. The price of stability for network design with fair cost allocation. In *Proc. 45th Annual Symp. on Fdns. of Computer Science*, pp. 295–304, 2004.

E. Anshelevich, A. Dasgupta, É. Tardos, and T. Wexler. Near-optimal network design with selfish agents. In *Proc. 35th Annual ACM Symp. Theory of Computing*, pp. 511–520, 2003.

M.J. Beckmann, C.B. McGuire, and C.B. Winsten. *Studies in the Economics of Transportation*. Yale University Press, 1956.

H. Chen, T. Roughgarden, and G. Valiant. Designing networks with good equilibria. Manuscript, 2007.

G. Christodoulou and E. Koutsoupias. On the price of anarchy and stability of correlated equilibria of linear congestion games. In *Proc. 13th Annual Euro. Symp. Alg.*, pp. 59–70, 2005.

G. Christodoulou, E. Koutsoupias, and A. Nanavati. Coordination mechanisms. In *Proc. 31st Annual Intl. Colloq. on Automata, Languages, and Programming*, volume 3142 of *Lecture Notes in Computer Science*, pp. 345–357, 2004.

P. Dubey. Inefficiency of Nash equilibria. *Math. Operat. Res.*, 11(1):1–8, 1986.

M.X. Goemans, V.S. Mirrokni, and A. Vetta. Sink equilibria and convergence. In *Proc. 46th Annual Symp. on Fdns. of Computer Science*, pp. 142–151, 2005.

A. Hayrapetyan, É. Tardos, and T. Wexler. The effect of collusion in congestion games. In *Proc. 38th Annual ACM Symp. on Theory of Computing*, pp. 89–98, 2006.

N. Immorlica, L. Li, V.S. Mirrokni, and A.S. Schulz. Coordination mechanisms for selfish scheduling. In *Proc. First Annual Intl. Workshop on Internet and Network Economics (WINE)*, LNCS 3828:55–69, 2005.

R. Johari and J.N. Tsitsiklis. Efficiency loss in a network resource allocation game. *Math. Operat. Res.*, 29(3):407–435, 2004.

R. Johari and J.N. Tsitsiklis. Characterization theorems for smooth market-clearing mechanisms. Submitted, 2006.

F.P. Kelly. Charging and rate control for elastic traffic. *Euro. Trans. Telecommunications*, 8(1):33–37, 1997.

E. Koutsoupias and C.H. Papadimitriou. Worst-case equilibria. In *Proc. 16th Symp. Theoretical Aspects of Computer Science*, LNCS 1563:404–413, 1999.

L.G. Mason. Equilibrium flows, routing patterns and algorithms for store-and-forward networks. *Large Scale Systems*, 8:187–209, 1985.

V.S. Mirrokni and A. Vetta. Convergence issues in competitive games. In *Proc. 7th Intl. Workshop on Approximation Algorithms for Combinatorial Optimization Problems (APPROX)*, pp. 183–194, 2004.

D. Monderer and L.S. Shapley. Potential games. *Games Econ. Behav.*, 14(1):124–143, 1996.

R. Motwani and P. Raghavan. *Randomized Algorithms*. Cambridge University Press, 1995.

H. Moulin and S. Shenker. Strategyproof sharing of submodular costs: Budget balance versus efficiency. *Economic Theory*, 18(3):511–533, 2001.

C.H. Papadimitriou. Algorithms, games, and the Internet. In *Proc. 33rd Symp. Theory of Computing*, pp. 749–753, 2001.

A.C. Pigou. *The Economics of Welfare*. Macmillan, 1920.

A. Rapoport and A.M. Chammah. *Prisoner's Dilemma*. University of Michigan Press, 1965.

R.W. Rosenthal. A class of games possessing pure-strategy Nash equilibria. *Intl. J. Game Theory*, 2(1):65–67, 1973.

T. Roughgarden. *Selfish Routing and the Price of Anarchy*. MIT Press, 2005.

T. Roughgarden and É. Tardos. How bad is selfish routing? *J. ACM*, 49(2):236–259, 2002.

M.A. Satterthwaite and S.R. Williams. The rate of convergence to efficiency in the buyer's bid double auction as the market becomes large. *Rev. Econ. Stud.*, 56(4):477–498, 1989.

A.S. Schulz and N.S. Moses. On the performance of user equilibria in traffic networks. In *Proc. 14th Symp. Discrete Algorithms*, pp. 86–87, 2003.

M. Tennenholtz. Competitive safety analysis: Robust decision-making in multi-agent systems. *J. Artificial Intelligence Res.*, 17:363–378, 2002.

V.V. Vazirani. *Approximation Algorithms*. Springer, 2001.

J.G. Wardrop. Some theoretical aspects of road traffic research. In *Proc. Institute of Civil Engineers, Pt. II*, volume 1, pp. 325–378, 1952.

Exercises

17.1 Suppose that we modify Pigou's example (Example 17.1) so that the lower edge has the cost function $c(x) = x^d$ for some $d \geq 1$. What is the price of anarchy of the resulting selfish routing network, as a function of d?

17.2 Suppose we modify the $\mathcal{H}_k$ example (Example 17.3) so that all of the network edges are undirected. In other words, each player i can choose a path from s_i to t that traverses each edge in either direction. What is the price of stability in the resulting Shapley network design game?

17.3 Recall the scheduling game in Example 17.4, with m players and m machines. Prove that the price of anarchy of this game with respect to the utilitarian objective function is precisely $2 - 1/m$.

17.4 Let U_i be a concave, strictly increasing, and continuously differentiable univariate function. Define the function Q_i as in (17.2). Prove that Q_i is continuously differentiable and strictly concave in b_i for every fixed nonnegative vector b_{-i} with at least one strictly positive component.

17.5 Prove that every equilibrium of a resource allocation game (Definition 17.5) has at least two strictly positive components.

CHAPTER 18

Routing Games

Tim Roughgarden

Abstract

This chapter studies the inefficiency of equilibria in noncooperative routing games, in which self-interested players route traffic through a congested network. Our goals are threefold: to introduce the most important models and examples of routing games; to survey optimal bounds on the price of anarchy in these models; and to develop proof techniques that are useful for bounding the inefficiency of equilibria in a range of applications.

18.1 Introduction

A majority of the current literature on the inefficiency of equilibria concerns routing games. One reason for this popularity is that routing games shed light on an important practical problem: how to route traffic in a large communication network, such as the Internet, that has no central authority. The routing games studied in this chapter are relevant for networks with "source routing," in which each end user chooses a full route for its traffic, and also for networks in which traffic is routed in a distributed, congestion-sensitive manner. Section 18.6 contains further details on these applications.

This chapter focuses on two different models of routing games, although the inefficiency of equilibria has been successfully quantified in a range of others (see Section 18.6). The first model, *nonatomic selfish routing*, is a natural generalization of Pigou's example (Example 17.1) to more complex networks. The modifier "nonatomic" refers to the assumption that there are a very large number of players, each controlling a negligible fraction of the overall traffic. We also study *atomic selfish routing*, where each player controls a nonnegligible amount of traffic. We single out these two models for three reasons. First, both models are conceptually simple but quite general. Second, the price of anarchy is well understood in both of these models. Third, the two models are superficially similar, but different techniques are required to analyze the inefficiency of equilibria in each of them.

The chapter proceeds as follows. Section 18.2 introduces nonatomic and atomic selfish routing games and explores several examples. Section 18.3 studies the existence and uniqueness of equilibria in routing games. It also offers a glimpse of the potential function method, a technique that will be developed further in Chapter 19. Section 18.4 proves tight upper bounds on the price of anarchy in nonatomic and atomic selfish routing games. Section 18.5 proposes two ways to reduce the price of anarchy in nonatomic selfish routing games. Section 18.6 concludes with bibliographic notes.

18.2 Models and Examples

18.2.1 Nonatomic Selfish Routing

To introduce nonatomic selfish routing games, we recall the essential features of Pigou's example (Example 17.1 and Figure 17.1). First, we are given a network describing the routes available to the players. In Pigou's example, there are two parallel routes, each a single edge, that connect a source vertex s to a sink vertex t. Each edge has a cost that is a function of the amount of traffic that uses the edge. We assume that selfish players choose routes to minimize the cost incurred; in an equilibrium outcome, all players choose a path of minimum cost. In the equilibrium in Pigou's example, all players choose the second edge, and the cost of this edge in this outcome is 1.

More generally, a selfish routing game occurs in a *multicommodity flow network*, or simply a *network*. A network is given by a directed graph $G = (V, E)$, with vertex set V and directed edge set E, together with a set $(s_1, t_1), \ldots, (s_k, t_k)$ of source–sink vertex pairs. We also call such pairs *commodities*. Each player is identified with one commodity; note that different players can originate from different source vertices and travel to different sink vertices. We use $\mathcal{P}_i$ to denote the s_i–t_i paths of a network. We consider only networks in which $\mathcal{P}_i \neq \emptyset$ for all i, and define $\mathcal{P} = \cup_{i=1}^{k} \mathcal{P}_i$. We allow the graph G to contain parallel edges, and a vertex can participate in multiple source–sink pairs.

We describe the routes chosen by players using a *flow*, which is simply a nonnegative vector indexed by the set $\mathcal{P}$ of source–sink paths. For a flow f and a path $P \in \mathcal{P}_i$, we interpret f_P as the amount of traffic of commodity i that chooses the path P to travel from s_i to t_i. Traffic is "inelastic," in that there is a prescribed amount r_i of traffic identified with each commodity i. A flow f is *feasible* for a vector r if it routes all of the traffic: for each $i \in \{1, 2, \ldots, k\}$, $\sum_{P \in \mathcal{P}_i} f_P = r_i$. In particular, we do not impose explicit edge capacities.

Finally, each edge e of a network has a *cost function* $c_e : \mathcal{R}^+ \to \mathcal{R}^+$. We always assume that cost functions are nonnegative, continuous, and nondecreasing. All of these assumptions are reasonable in applications where cost represents a quantity that only increases with the network congestion; delay is one natural example. When we study the price of anarchy in Section 18.4, we also explore more severe assumptions on the network cost functions. We define a *nonatomic selfish routing game*, or simply a *nonatomic instance*, by a triple of the form (G, r, c).

Next we formalize the notion of equilibrium in nonatomic selfish routing games. Define the cost of a path P with respect to a flow f as the sum of the costs of the constituent edges: $c_P(f) = \sum_{e \in P} c_e(f_e)$, where $f_e = \sum_{P \in \mathcal{P} : e \in P} f_P$ denotes the amount of traffic using paths that contain the edge e. Since we expect selfish traffic to attempt to minimize its cost, we arrive at the following definition.

Definition 18.1 (Nonatomic equilibrium flow) Let f be a feasible flow for the nonatomic instance (G, r, c). The flow f is an *equilibrium flow* if, for every commodity $i \in \{1, 2, \ldots, k\}$ and every pair $P, \tilde{P} \in \mathcal{P}_i$ of s_i–t_i paths with $f_P > 0$,

$$c_P(f) \leq c_{\tilde{P}}(f).$$

In other words, all paths in use by an equilibrium flow f have minimum-possible cost (given their source, sink, and the congestion caused by f). In particular, all paths of a given commodity used by an equilibrium flow have equal cost. Section 18.3.1 proves that every nonatomic instance admits at least one equilibrium flow, and that all equilibrium flows of a nonatomic instance have equal cost.

In Pigou's example, routing all of the traffic on the second link defines an equilibrium flow; only one path carries flow, and the only alternative has equal cost. Splitting the traffic equally between the two links defines a flow that is not an equilibrium flow; the first link carries a strictly positive amount of traffic and its cost is 1, but there is a strictly cheaper alternative (the second link, with cost 1/2).

Remark 18.2 Our description of nonatomic selfish routing games and their equilibria does not parallel that of simultaneous-move games in Chapter 1. For example, we have not explicitly defined the set of players. While more general types of nonatomic games are frequently defined explicitly in terms of player sets, strategy profiles, and player payoff functions, selfish routing games possess special structure. In particular, the cost incurred by a player depends only on its path and the amount of flow on the edges of its path, rather than on the identities of any of the players. Games of this type are often called *congestion games*. Because of this structure, it is sufficient and simpler to work directly with flows in nonatomic selfish routing games.

When we quantify the inefficiency of equilibrium flows in Section 18.4, we consider only the utilitarian objective of minimizing the total cost incurred by traffic. (Other objectives have been studied; see Section 18.6.) Precisely, since the cost incurred by a player choosing the path P in the flow f is $c_P(f)$, and f_P denotes the amount of traffic choosing the path P, we define the *cost* of a flow f as

$$C(f) = \sum_{P \in \mathcal{P}} c_P(f) f_P. \tag{18.1}$$

Expanding $c_P(f)$ as $\sum_{e \in P} c_e(f_e)$ and reversing the order of summation in (18.1) gives a useful alternative definition of the cost of a flow:

$$C(f) = \sum_{e \in E} c_e(f_e) f_e. \tag{18.2}$$

For an instance (G, r, c), we call a feasible flow *optimal* if it minimizes the cost over all feasible flows.

As in Chapter 17, the *price of anarchy* of a nonatomic selfish routing game, with respect to this objective, is the ratio between the cost of an equilibrium flow and that of an optimal flow. We can use the cost of an arbitrary equilibrium flow in lieu of that of a worst equilibrium flow (cf. Chapter 17), since all equilibrium flows of a nonatomic

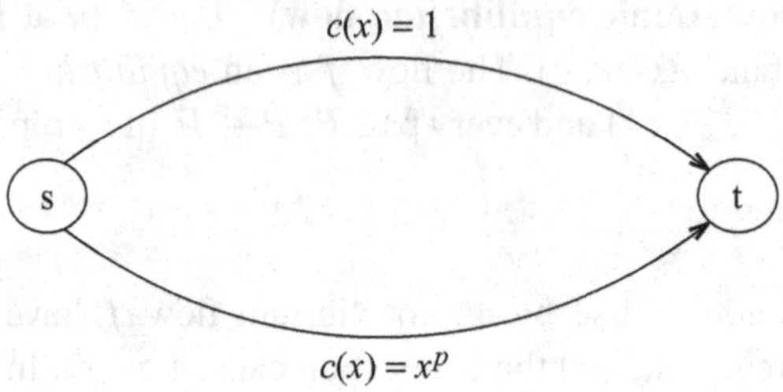

Figure 18.1. A nonlinear variant of Pigou's example (Example 18.3).

instance have equal cost (Section 18.3.1). In Pigou's example, the equilibrium flow routes all of the traffic on the second link and has cost 1. As we will see in Section 18.3.1, the optimal flow splits the traffic equally between the two links and has cost 3/4. The price of anarchy in Pigou's example is therefore 4/3.

We conclude this section with two more important examples of nonatomic selfish routing networks.

Example 18.3 (Nonlinear Pigou's example) The inefficiency of the equilibrium flow in Pigou's example can be amplified with a seemingly minor modification to the network. Suppose that we replace the previously linear cost function $c(x) = x$ on the lower edge with the highly nonlinear one $c(x) = x^p$ for p large (Figure 18.1). As in Pigou's example, the cost of the unique equilibrium flow is 1. The optimal flow routes a small ϵ fraction of the traffic on the upper edge and has cost $\epsilon + (1 - \epsilon)^{p+1}$, where ϵ tends to 0 as p tends to infinity. Precisely, Section 18.3.1 shows that $\epsilon = 1 - (p+1)^{-1/p}$. As p tends to infinity, the cost of the optimal flow approaches 0 and the price of anarchy grows without bound. Exercise 18.1 shows that this rate of growth is roughly $p/\ln p$ as $p \to \infty$.

While the price of anarchy in our final example is no larger than in Pigou's example, it is arguably a more shocking display of the inefficiency of equilibria in selfish routing networks.

Example 18.4 (Braess's Paradox) Consider the four-node network shown in Figure 18.2(a). There are two disjoint routes from s to t, each with combined cost $1 + x$, where x is the amount of traffic that uses the route. Assume that there is one unit of traffic. In the equilibrium flow, the traffic is split evenly between the two routes, and all of the traffic experiences 3/2 units of cost.

Now suppose that, in an effort to decrease the cost encountered by the traffic, we build a zero-cost edge connecting the midpoints of the two existing routes. The new network is shown in Figure 18.2(b). What is the new equilibrium flow?

The previous equilibrium flow does not persist in the new network: the cost of the new route $s \to v \to w \to t$ is never worse than that along the two original paths, and it is strictly less whenever some traffic fails to use it. As a consequence, the unique equilibrium flow routes all of the traffic on the new route. Because of the ensuing heavy congestion on the edges (s, v) and (w, t), all of the traffic now

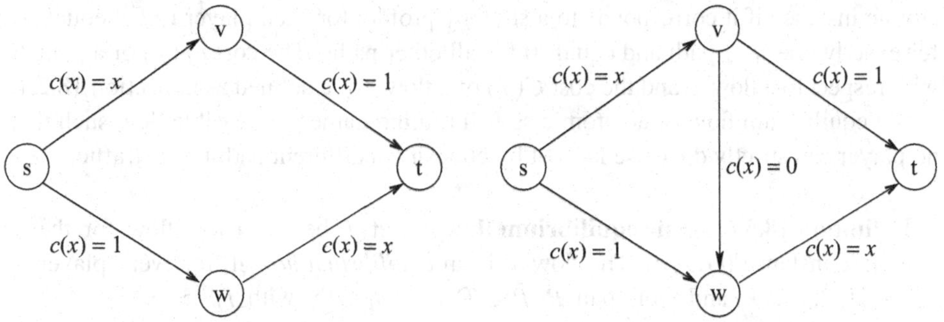

Figure 18.2. Braess's Paradox. The addition of an intuitively helpful edge can adversely affect all of the traffic.

experiences two units of cost. Braess's Paradox thus shows that the intuitively helpful action of adding a new zero-cost edge can increase the cost experienced by all of the traffic!

Braess's Paradox also has remarkable analogues in several physical systems; see Section 18.6 for details.

The optimal flow in the second network of Example 18.4 is the same as the equilibrium flow in the first network. The price of anarchy in the second network is therefore 4/3, the same as that in Pigou's example. This is not entirely a coincidence; in Section 18.4.1 we prove that no nonatomic instance with cost functions of the form $ax + b$ has a price of anarchy larger than 4/3.

While this chapter does not explicitly study Braess's Paradox, we obtain bounds on the worst-case severity of the paradox as a consequence of our results on the price of anarchy (Remark 18.22).

18.2.2 Atomic Selfish Routing

An *atomic selfish routing game* or *atomic instance* is defined by the same ingredients as a nonatomic one: a directed graph $G = (V, E)$, k source–sink pairs $(s_1, t_1), \ldots, (s_k, t_k)$, a positive amount r_i of traffic for each pair (s_i, t_i), and a nonnegative, continuous, nondecreasing cost function $c_e : \mathcal{R}^+ \to \mathcal{R}^+$ for each edge e. We also denote an atomic instance by a triple (G, r, c). The intuitive difference between a nonatomic and an atomic instance is that in the former, each commodity represents a large population of individuals, each of whom controls a negligible amount of traffic; in the latter, each commodity represents a single player who must route a significant amount of traffic on a single path.

More formally, atomic instances are finite simultaneous-move games in the sense of Chapter 1. There are k players, one for each source–sink pair. Different players can have identical source–sink pairs. The strategy set of player i is the set $\mathcal{P}_i$ of s_i–t_i paths, and if player i chooses the path P, then it routes its r_i units of traffic on P. A *flow* is now a nonnegative vector indexed by players and paths, with $f_P^{(i)}$ denoting the amount of traffic that player i routes on the s_i–t_i path P. A flow f is *feasible* for an atomic instance if it corresponds to a strategy profile: for each player i, $f_P^{(i)}$ equals r_i for exactly one s_i–t_i path and equals 0 for all other paths. The cost $c_P(f)$ of a path P with respect to a flow f and the cost $C(f)$ of a flow f are defined as in Section 18.2.1.

An equilibrium flow of an atomic selfish routing game is a feasible flow such that no player can strictly decrease its cost by choosing a different path for its traffic.

Definition 18.5 (Atomic equilibrium flow) Let f be a feasible flow for the atomic instance (G, r, c). The flow f is an *equilibrium flow* if, for every player $i \in \{1, 2, \ldots, k\}$ and every pair $P, \tilde{P} \in \mathcal{P}_i$ of s_i–t_i paths with $f_P^{(i)} > 0$,

$$c_P(f) \leq c_{\tilde{P}}(\tilde{f}),$$

where $\tilde{f}$ is the flow identical to f except that $\tilde{f}_P^{(i)} = 0$ and $\tilde{f}_{\tilde{P}}^{(i)} = r_i$.

We have defined equilibrium flows to correspond to pure-strategy Nash equilibria (see Chapter 1). Flows corresponding to mixed-strategy Nash equilibria have also been studied (see Section 18.6), but we will not consider them in this chapter.

While the definitions of nonatomic and atomic instances are very similar, the two models are technically quite different. The next example illustrates two of these differences. First, different equilibrium flows of an atomic instance can have different costs; as claimed in Section 18.2.1 and proved in Section 18.3.1, all equilibrium flows of a nonatomic instance have equal cost. Second, the price of anarchy in atomic instances can be larger than in their nonatomic counterparts. The following atomic instance has affine cost functions – of the form $ax + b$ – and its price of anarchy is 5/2; in every nonatomic instance with affine cost functions, the price of anarchy is at most 4/3 (Section 18.4.1). We call this the AAE example, after the initials of its discoverers (see Section 18.6).

Example 18.6 (AAE example) Consider the bidirected triangle network shown in Figure 18.3. We assume that there are four players, each of whom needs to route one unit of traffic. The first two have source u and sinks v and w, respectively; the third has source v and sink w; and the fourth has source w and sink v. Each player has two strategies, a one-hop path and a two-hop path. In the optimal flow, all players route on their one-hop paths, and the cost of this flow is 4. This flow is also an equilibrium flow. On the other hand, if all players route on their two-hop paths, then we obtain a second equilibrium flow. Since the first two players each incur three units of cost and the last two players each incur two units of cost, this equilibrium flow has a cost of 10. The price of anarchy of this instance is therefore $10/4 = 2.5$.

Exercise 18.2 explores variants of the AAE example.

Next we study the even more basic issue of the existence of equilibrium flows. Recall that equilibrium flows for atomic instances correspond to pure-strategy Nash equilibria, which do not always exist in arbitrary finite games (see Chapter 1). Do they always exist in atomic selfish routing games? Our second example answers this question in the negative.

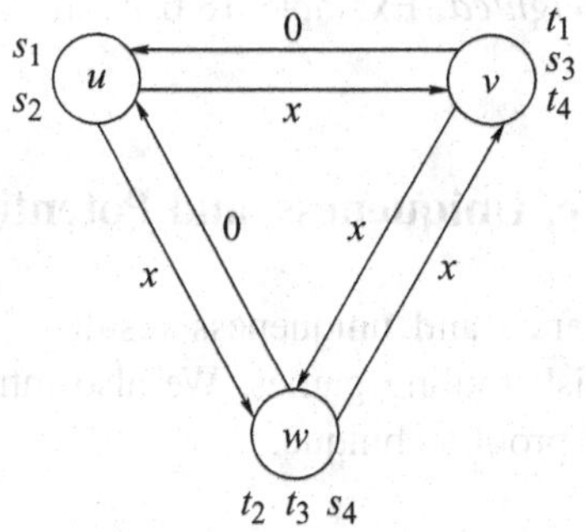

Figure 18.3. The AAE example (Example 18.6). In atomic instances with affine cost functions, different equilibrium flows can have different costs, and the price of anarchy can be as large as 5/2.

Example 18.7 (Nonexistence in weighted atomic instances) Consider the network shown in Figure 18.4. Extend this network to an atomic selfish routing game by adding two players, both with source s and sink t, with traffic amounts $r_1 = 1$ and $r_2 = 2$.

We claim that there is no equilibrium flow in this atomic instance. To prove this, let P_1, P_2, P_3, and P_4 denote the paths $s \to t$, $s \to v \to t$, $s \to w \to t$, and $s \to v \to w \to t$, respectively. The following four statements then imply the claim.

(1) If player 2 takes path P_1 or P_2, then the unique response by player 1 that minimizes its cost is the path P_4.

(2) If player 2 takes path P_3 or P_4, then the unique best response by player 1 is the path P_1.

(3) If player 1 takes the path P_4, then the unique best response by player 2 is the path P_3.

(4) If player 1 takes the path P_1, then the unique best response by player 2 is the path P_2.

We leave verification of (1)–(4) to the reader.

On the other hand, Section 18.3.2 proves that every atomic instance in which all players route the same amount of traffic admits at least one equilibrium flow. We call

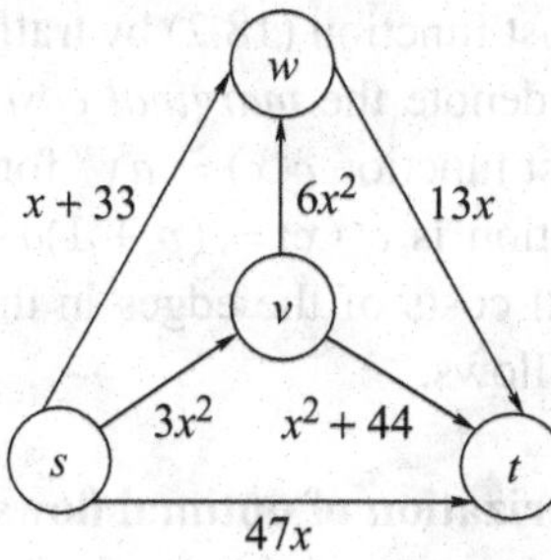

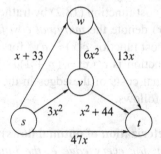

Figure 18.4. An atomic instance with no equilibrium flow (Example 18.7).

instances of this type *unweighted.* Example 18.6 is an unweighted instance, while Example 18.7 is not.

18.3 Existence, Uniqueness, and Potential Functions

This section collects existence and uniqueness results about equilibrium flows in nonatomic and atomic selfish routing games. We also introduce the potential function method, a fundamental proof technique.

18.3.1 Nonatomic Selfish Routing: Existence and Uniqueness

Our next goal is to show that in nonatomic selfish routing games, equilibrium flows always exist and are essentially unique. By "essentially unique," we mean that all equilibrium flows of a nonatomic instance have the same cost. In particular, the price of stability (Section 17.1) and the price of anarchy coincide in every nonatomic instance. Formally, our aim is to prove the following theorem.

Theorem 18.8 (Existence and uniqueness of equilibrium flows) *Let (G, r, c) be a nonatomic instance.*

(a) *The instance (G, r, c) admits at least one equilibrium flow.*

(b) *If f and $\tilde{f}$ are equilibrium flows for (G, r, c), then $c_e(f_e) = c_e(\tilde{f}_e)$ for every edge e.*

Part (b) of the theorem and Definition 18.1 easily imply that two equilibrium flows of a nonatomic instance have equal cost.

We prove Theorem 18.8 with the *potential function method.* The idea of this method is to exhibit a real-valued "potential function," defined on the outcomes of a game, such that the equilibria of the game are precisely the outcomes that optimize the potential function. Potential functions are useful because they enable the application of optimization techniques to the study of equilibria. When a game admits a potential function, there are typically consequences for the existence, uniqueness, and inefficiency of equilibria.

To motivate the potential functions corresponding to nonatomic selfish routing games, we present a characterization of optimal flows in such games. To state this characterization cleanly, we assume that for every edge e of the given nonatomic instance, the function $x \cdot c_e(x)$ is continuously differentiable and convex. Note that $x \cdot c_e(x)$ is the contribution to the social cost function (18.2) by traffic on the edge e. Let $c_e^*(x) = (x \cdot c_e(x))' = c_e(x) + x \cdot c_e'(x)$ denote the *marginal cost function* for the edge e. For example, if $c(x)$ denotes the cost function $c(x) = ax^p$ for some $a, p \geq 0$, then the corresponding marginal cost function is $c^*(x) = (p+1)ax^p$. Let $c_P^*(f) = \sum_{e \in P} c_e^*(f)$ denote the sum of the marginal costs of the edges in the path P with respect to the flow f. The characterization follows.

Proposition 18.9 (Characterization of optimal flows) *Let (G, r, c) be a nonatomic instance such that, for every edge e, the function $x \cdot c_e(x)$ is convex and continuously differentiable. Let c_e^* denote the marginal cost function of the* *edge e. Then f^* is an optimal flow for (G, r, c) if and only if, for every commodity $i \in \{1, 2, \ldots, k\}$ and every pair $P, \tilde{P} \in \mathcal{P}_i$ of s_i–t_i paths with $f^*_P > 0$,*

$$c^*_P(f^*) \leq c^*_{\tilde{P}}(f^*).$$

Proposition 18.9 follows immediately from the first-order conditions of a convex optimization problem with nonnegativity constraints. We omit the details and focus instead on how the proposition leads to a potential function for equilibrium flows in nonatomic instances, and on the implications of this potential function for the existence and uniqueness of equilibrium flows.

Definition 18.1 and Proposition 18.9 immediately imply that equilibrium flows and optimal flows are the same thing, just with respect to different sets of cost functions.

Corollary 18.10 (Equivalence of equilibrium and optimal flows) *Let (G, r, c) be a nonatomic instance such that, for every edge e, the function $x \cdot c_e(x)$ is convex and continuously differentiable. Let c^*_e denote the marginal cost function of the edge e. Then f^* is an optimal flow for (G, r, c) if and only if it is an equilibrium flow for (G, r, c^*).*

For instance, in Pigou's example (Example 17.1), the marginal cost functions of the two edges are $c^*(x) = 1$ and $c^*(x) = 2x$. The equilibrium flow with respect to the marginal cost functions splits the traffic equally between the two links, equalizing their marginal costs at 1; by Corollary 18.10, this flow is optimal in the original network. In the nonlinear variant of Pigou's example (Example 18.3), the marginal cost functions are $c^*(x) = 1$ and $c^*(x) = (p + 1)x^p$; the optimal flow therefore routes $(p + 1)^{-1/p}$ units of traffic on the second link and the rest on the first. In Braess's Paradox with the zero-cost edge added (Example 18.4 and Figure 18.2(b)), routing half of the traffic on each of the paths $s \to v \to t$ and $s \to w \to t$ equalizes the marginal costs of all three paths at 2, and therefore provides an optimal flow.

To construct a potential function for equilibrium flows, we need to "invert" Corollary 18.10: of what function do equilibrium flows arise as the global minima? The answer is simple: to recover Definition 18.1 as an optimality condition, we seek a function $h_e(x)$ for each edge e – playing the previous role of $x \cdot c_e(x)$ – such that $h'_e(x) = c_e(x)$. Setting $h_e(x) = \int_0^x c_e(y)\,dy$ for each edge e thus yields the desired potential function. Moreover, since c_e is continuous and nondecreasing for every edge e, every function h_e is both continuously differentiable and convex.

Precisely, call

$$\Phi(f) = \sum_{e \in E} \int_0^{f_e} c_e(x)\,dx \tag{18.3}$$

the *potential function* of a nonatomic instance (G, r, c). Invoking Proposition 18.9, with each function $x \cdot c_e(x)$ replaced by $h_e(x) = \int_0^x c(y)\,dy$, yields the same condition as in Definition 18.1; we have therefore characterized equilibrium flows as the global minimizers of the potential function Φ.

Proposition 18.11 (Potential function for equilibrium flows) *Let (G, r, c) be a nonatomic instance. A flow feasible for (G, r, c) is an equilibrium flow if and only if it is a global minimum of the corresponding potential function Φ given in* (18.3).

Theorem 18.8 now follows from Proposition 18.11 and routine calculus.

Proof of Theorem 18.8 We first note that, by definition, the set of feasible flows of (G, r, c) can be identified with a compact (i.e., closed and bounded) subset of $|\mathcal{P}|$-dimensional Euclidean space. Since edge cost functions are continuous, the potential function is a continuous function on this set. By Weierstrass's Theorem from elementary mathematical analysis, the potential function Φ achieves a minimum value on this set. By Proposition 18.11, every point at which Φ attains its minimum corresponds to an equilibrium flow of (G, r, c).

For part (b), recall that each cost function is nondecreasing, and hence each summand on the right-hand side of (18.3) is convex. Hence, the potential function Φ is a convex function.

Now suppose that f and $\tilde{f}$ are equilibrium flows for (G, r, c). By Proposition 18.11, both f and $\tilde{f}$ minimize the potential function Φ. We consider all convex combinations of f and $\tilde{f}$ – that is, all vectors of the form $\lambda f + (1 - \lambda)\tilde{f}$ for $\lambda \in [0, 1]$. All of these vectors are feasible flows. Since Φ is a convex function, a chord between two points on its graph cannot pass below its graph. In algebraic terms, we have

$$\Phi(\lambda f + (1 - \lambda)\tilde{f}) \leq \lambda\Phi(f) + (1 - \lambda)\Phi(\tilde{f}) \tag{18.4}$$

for every $\lambda \in [0, 1]$. Since both f and $\tilde{f}$ are global minima of Φ, the inequality (18.4) must hold with equality for all of their convex combinations. Since every summand of Φ is convex, this can occur only if every summand $\int_0^x c_e(y)\, dy$ is linear between the values f_e and $\tilde{f}_e$. In turn, this implies that every cost function c_e is constant between f_e and $\tilde{f}_e$. □

18.3.2 Atomic Selfish Routing: Existence

We now consider equilibrium flows in atomic instances. The AAE example (Example 18.6) suggests that no interesting uniqueness results are possible in such instances, so we focus instead on the existence of equilibrium flows. Similarly, Example 18.7 demonstrates that a general atomic instance need not admit an equilibrium flow. There are two approaches to circumventing this counterexample. The first, taken in this section, is to place additional restrictions on atomic instances so that equilibrium flows are guaranteed to exist. The second approach, discussed in Remark 18.26, is to relax the equilibrium concept so that an equilibrium exists in every atomic instance.

The key result in this section is the following theorem, which establishes the existence of equilibrium flows in atomic instances in which all players control the same amount of traffic.

Theorem 18.12 (Equilibrium flows in unweighted atomic instances) *Let (G, r, c) be an atomic instance in which every traffic amount r_i is equal to a common positive value R. Then (G, r, c) admits at least one equilibrium flow.*

PROOF We obtain Theorem 18.12 by discretizing the potential function (18.3) for nonatomic instances and the proof of Theorem 18.8(a). Assume for simplicity that $R = 1$. Set

$$\Phi_a(f) = \sum_{e \in E} \sum_{i=1}^{f_e} c_e(i) \tag{18.5}$$

for every feasible flow f. Note that Φ_a is the same as the previous potential function Φ for nonatomic instances, except that the integral $\int_0^{f_e} c(x)\,dx$ has been replaced by the sum $\sum_{i=1}^{f_e} c_e(i)$.

Since the atomic instance (G, r, c) has a finite number of players, and each of these has a finite number of strategies, there are only a finite number of possible flows. One of these, call it f, is a global minimum of the potential function Φ_a. We claim that f is an equilibrium flow for (G, r, c). To prove it, assume for contradiction that in f, the player i could strictly decrease its cost by deviating from the path P to the path $\tilde{P}$, yielding the new flow $\tilde{f}$. In other words, we assume that

$$0 > c_{\tilde{P}}(\tilde{f}) - c_P(f) = \sum_{e \in \tilde{P} \setminus P} c_e(f_e + 1) - \sum_{e \in P \setminus \tilde{P}} c_e(f_e). \tag{18.6}$$

On the other hand, consider the impact of player i's deviation on the potential function Φ_a: for edges in $\tilde{P} \setminus P$, the corresponding sum in (18.5) acquires the extra term $c_e(f_e + 1)$; for edges in $P \setminus \tilde{P}$, the corresponding sum sheds the term $c_e(f_e)$; and for edges of $P \cap \tilde{P}$, the corresponding sum remains the same. Thus, $\Phi_a(\tilde{f}) - \Phi_a(f)$ is precisely the third expression of (18.6). Since this expression is negative, the potential function value of $\tilde{f}$ is strictly less than that of f, which contradicts our choice of f. □

Remark 18.13 The proof of Theorem 18.12 establishes a remarkable property of the potential function Φ_a: it "tracks" the change in cost experienced by a deviating player. More formally, for every flow, every player, and every deviation by a player, the change in the player's cost is identical to the change in the potential function. This property has consequences beyond the existence result of Theorem 18.12. For example, it implies that "best-response dynamics" are guaranteed to converge to an equilibrium flow. See Chapter 19 for further details.

Remark 18.14 The proof of Theorem 18.12 did not use any assumptions about the edge cost functions. In particular, it is also valid when cost functions are not nondecreasing. This property will be crucial for some of the network design games studied in Chapter 19, which can be viewed as atomic selfish routing games with *decreasing* cost functions.

The next theorem guarantees the existence of equilibrium flows under a different restriction – affine cost functions. (Recall that a cost function $c_e(x)$ is *affine* if it has the form $a_e x + b_e$; we always assume that $a_e, b_e \geq 0$.)

Theorem 18.15 (Equilibrium flows with affine cost functions) *Let* (G, r, c) *be an atomic instance with affine cost functions. Then* (G, r, c) *admits at least one equilibrium flow.*

The proof of Theorem 18.15 follows the same outline as that of Theorem 18.12, and uses a variant of the potential function method. See Exercise 18.4 for further details.

18.4 The Price of Anarchy of Selfish Routing

18.4.1 Nonatomic Selfish Routing: The Price of Anarchy

This section gives an essentially complete analysis of the price of anarchy in nonatomic selfish routing games. As we know from the nonlinear variant of Pigou's example (Example 18.3), the price of anarchy depends on "nonlinearity" of the network cost functions. Our goal is to show that it depends on nothing else – not the network size, the network structure, nor the number of commodities. More precisely, we show that for every conceivable restriction on the cost functions of a network, the price of anarchy is maximized (over all multicommodity networks) by the network that best "simulates" Pigou's example and its nonlinear variants.

As an aside, we note that the potential function characterization of nonatomic equilibrium flows (Proposition 18.11) already gives a good, but not optimal, upper bound on the price of anarchy. The intuitive explanation is simple: if equilibrium flows exactly optimize a potential function (18.3) that is a good approximation of the objective function (18.2), then they should also be approximately optimal.

Theorem 18.16 (Potential function upper bound) *Let* (G, r, c) *be a nonatomic instance, and suppose that* $x \cdot c_e(x) \leq \gamma \cdot \int_0^x c_e(y)\,dy$ *for all* $e \in E$ *and* $x \geq 0$. *Then the price of anarchy of* (G, r, c) *is at most* γ.

PROOF Let f and f^* be equilibrium and optimal flows for (G, r, c), respectively. Since cost functions are nondecreasing, the cost of a flow (18.2) is always at least its potential function value (18.3). The hypothesis ensures that the cost of a flow is at most γ times its potential function value. The theorem follows by writing

$$C(f) \leq \gamma \cdot \Phi(f) \leq \gamma \cdot \Phi(f^*) \leq \gamma \cdot C(f^*),$$

with the second inequality following from Proposition 18.11. □

Theorem 18.16 implies that the price of anarchy of selfish routing is large only in networks with "highly nonlinear" cost functions. For example, if c_e is a polynomial function with degree at most p and nonnegative coefficients, then $x \cdot c_e(x) \leq (p+1)\int_0^x c_e(y)\,dy$ for all $x \geq 0$. Theorem 18.16 then shows that the price of anarchy in nonatomic instances with such cost functions is at most linear in p.

Corollary 18.17 (Potential function bound for polynomials) *If (G, r, c) is a nonatomic instance with cost functions that polynomials with nonnegative coefficients and degree at most p, then the price of anarchy of (G, r, c) is at most $p + 1$.*

This upper bound is nearly matched by Example 18.3, although the upper and lower bounds differ by roughly a $\ln p$ multiplicative factor (Exercise 18.1). We close this gap using a different and important proof technique, which is driven by *variational inequalities.*

We first formalize a natural lower bound on the price of anarchy based on "Pigou-like examples."

Definition 18.18 (Pigou bound) Let $\mathcal{C}$ be a nonempty set of cost functions. The *Pigou bound* $\alpha(\mathcal{C})$ for $\mathcal{C}$ is

$$\alpha(\mathcal{C}) = \sup_{c \in \mathcal{C}} \sup_{x, r \geq 0} \frac{r \cdot c(r)}{x \cdot c(x) + (r - x)c(r)}, \tag{18.7}$$

with the understanding that $0/0 = 1$.

The point of the Pigou bound is that it lower bounds the price of anarchy in instances with cost functions in $\mathcal{C}$.

Proposition 18.19 *Let $\mathcal{C}$ be a set of cost functions that contains all of the constant cost functions. Then the price of anarchy in nonatomic instances with cost functions in $\mathcal{C}$ can be arbitrarily close to $\alpha(\mathcal{C})$.*

PROOF Fix a choice of $c \in \mathcal{C}$ and $x, r \geq 0$. We can complete the proof by exhibiting a selfish routing network with cost functions in $\mathcal{C}$ and price of anarchy at least $c(r)r/[c(x)x + (r - x)c(r)]$. Since c is nondecreasing, this expression is at most 1 if $x \geq r$; we can therefore assume that $x < r$.

Let G be a two-vertex, two-edge network as in Figure 18.1. Give the lower edge the cost function $c_1(y) = c(y)$ and the upper edge the constant cost function $c_2(y) = c(r)$. By assumption, both of these cost functions lie in $\mathcal{C}$. Set the traffic rate to r. Routing all of the traffic on the lower edge yields an equilibrium flow with cost $c(r)r$. Routing x units of traffic on the lower edge and $r - x$ units of traffic on the upper edge gives a feasible flow with cost $[c(x)x + (r - x)c(r)]$. The price of anarchy in this instance is thus at least $c(r)r/[c(x)x + (r - x)c(r)]$, as desired. □

While Proposition 18.19 assumes that the set $\mathcal{C}$ includes all of the constant cost functions, its conclusion holds whenever $\mathcal{C}$ is *inhomogeneous* in the sense that $c(0) > 0$ for some $c \in \mathcal{C}$ (Exercise 18.5).

We next show that, even though the Pigou bound is based only on Pigou-like examples, it is also an upper bound on the price of anarchy in general multicommodity flow networks. The proof requires the following variational inequality characterization of equilibrium flows.

Proposition 18.20 (Variational inequality characterization) *Let f be a feasible flow for the nonatomic instance (G, r, c). The flow f is an equilibrium flow if and only if*

$$\sum_{e\in E} c_e(f_e)f_e \leq \sum_{e\in E} c_e(f_e)f_e^*$$

for every flow f^* feasible for (G, r, c).

PROOF Fix f and define the function H_f on the set of feasible flows by

$$H_f(f^*) = \sum_{i=1}^{k} \sum_{P\in\mathcal{P}_i} c_P(f)f_P^* = \sum_{e\in E} c_e(f_e)f_e^*;$$

the same reversal of sums used to prove the equivalence of (18.1) and (18.2) shows that these two definitions of $H_f(f^*)$ agree. The value $H_f(f^*)$ denotes the cost of a flow f^* after the cost function of each edge e has been changed to the constant function everywhere equal to $c_e(f_e)$. By the second definition of H_f, the proposition is equivalent to the assertion that a flow f is an equilibrium flow if and only if it minimizes $H_f(\cdot)$ over all feasible flows.

Examining the first definition of H_f shows that a flow f^* minimizes H_f if and only if, for every commodity i, $f_P^* > 0$ only for paths P that minimize $c_P(f)$ over all s_i–t_i paths. Since the flow f satisfies this condition if and only if it is an equilibrium flow, the proof is complete. □

We now show that the Pigou bound is tight.

Theorem 18.21 (Tightness of the Pigou bound) *Let $\mathcal{C}$ be a set of cost functions and $\alpha(\mathcal{C})$ the Pigou bound for $\mathcal{C}$. If (G, r, c) is a nonatomic instance with cost functions in $\mathcal{C}$, then the price of anarchy of (G, r, c) is at most $\alpha(\mathcal{C})$.*

PROOF Let f^* and f be optimal and equilibrium flows, respectively, for a nonatomic instance (G, r, c) with cost functions in the set $\mathcal{C}$. The theorem follows by writing

$$\begin{aligned} C(f^*) &= \sum_{e\in E} c_e(f_e^*)f_e^* \\ &\geq \frac{1}{\alpha(\mathcal{C})}\sum_{e\in E} c_e(f_e)f_e + \sum_{e\in E}(f_e^* - f_e)c_e(f_e) \\ &\geq \frac{C(f)}{\alpha(\mathcal{C})}, \end{aligned}$$

where the first inequality follows from Definition 18.18, applied to each edge e with $x = f_e^*$ and $r = f_e$, and the second inequality follows from Proposition 18.20. □

Proposition 18.19 and Theorem 18.21 show that, for essentially every fixed restriction on the allowable cost functions, the price of anarchy is maximized by Pigou-like examples. Determining the largest-possible price of anarchy in Pigou-like examples (i.e., the Pigou bound) is a tractable problem in many cases. For example, it is precisely $4/3$ when $\mathcal{C}$ is the set of affine cost functions (Exercise 18.6), and more generally is $[1 - p \cdot (p+1)^{-(p+1)/p}]^{-1} \approx p/\ln p$ when $\mathcal{C}$ is the set of polynomials with degree at most p and nonnegative coefficients. In these cases, the maximum price of anarchy (among all multicommodity instances) is achieved by the instances in Examples 17.1 and 18.3. The Pigou bound is also known for several other classes of cost functions; see Section 18.6 for references.

Remark 18.22 (Bounds on Braess's Paradox) Braess's Paradox (Example 18.4) shows that adding edges to a network can increase the cost of its equilibrium flow. Since the equilibrium flow in the original network is a candidate for the optimal flow in the second network, the ratio between the costs of the new and original equilibrium flows is a lower bound on the price of anarchy in the latter network.

On the other hand, Theorem 18.21 and Exercise 18.6 show that the price of anarchy is at most $4/3$ in every network with affine cost functions. Thus, adding edges to a network with affine cost functions cannot increase the cost of its equilibrium flow by more than a $4/3$ factor. Example 18.4 is therefore a worst-case manifestation of Braess's Paradox in networks with affine cost functions. Similar bounds also apply to the physical analogues of Braess's Paradox that are described in Section 18.6.

18.4.2 Atomic Selfish Routing: The Price of Anarchy

We now consider atomic selfish routing games. We again obtain tight bounds on the price of anarchy, at least for polynomial cost functions, but the discrete nature of atomic instances complicates the analysis.

We first note that the potential function method, which gave nontrivial bounds on the price of anarchy for nonatomic instances (Theorem 18.16), cannot be used for atomic instances. The difficulty stems from the non-uniqueness of equilibrium flows in atomic instances (Example 18.6). Recall that a bound on the price of anarchy is a guarantee that *all* equilibrium flows of an instance are nearly optimal. Reviewing the proof of Theorem 18.16, we observe that the potential function method argues about only *one* equilibrium flow – the one with minimum potential function value. As a result, the potential function method is directly useful only for bounding the price of *stability* rather than the price of anarchy. While these two quantities coincide in nonatomic selfish routing games, they are generally different in atomic ones. (See Section 18.6 for results on the price of stability in atomic selfish routing games.)

We instead rely on proof techniques that are partially inspired by the variational inequality of Proposition 18.20. This inequality expresses the fact that equilibrium flows route all traffic on shortest paths, with respect to the induced edge costs. We derive a similar, if more complicated, condition for atomic instances. To keep the proofs as transparent as possible, we focus on atomic instances with affine cost functions. Recall from Theorem 18.15 that every such instance admits at least one equilibrium flow. The analysis can also be extended to other cost functions and other equilibrium concepts; see Remark 18.26 and Section 18.6 for more details.

Our goal is the following theorem.

Theorem 18.23 (The price of anarchy in affine atomic instances) *If* (G, r, c) *is an atomic instance with affine cost functions, then the price of anarchy of* (G, r, c) *is at most* $(3+\sqrt{5})/2 \approx 2.618$.

A variant of the AAE example (Example 18.6) shows that the upper bound in Theorem 18.23 is the best possible if different players can control different amounts of flow (Exercise 18.2(a)). If all of the players control the same amount of flow, then a variant of the following proof gives an improved upper bound of $5/2$, which matches the lower bound furnished by the AAE example (Exercise 18.7).

We build up to Theorem 18.23 in a sequence of steps. We begin with a lemma that follows immediately from the definition of an equilibrium flow.

Lemma 18.24 (Equilibrium condition) *Let* (G, r, c) *be an atomic instance in which each edge* e *has an affine cost function* $c_e(x) = a_e x + b_e$ *with* $a_e, b_e \geq 0$. *Let* f *and* f^* *be equilibrium and optimal flows, respectively, for* (G, r, c). *Let player* i *use the path* P_i *in* f *and the path* P_i^* *in* f^*. *Then*

$$\sum_{e \in P_i} [a_e f_e + b_e] \leq \sum_{e \in P_i^*} [a_e(f_e + r_i) + b_e]. \tag{18.8}$$

Our second step is to combine the inequalities of Lemma 18.24 – one per player – to relate the cost of an arbitrary equilibrium flow to that of an optimal flow.

Lemma 18.25 (Equilibrium inequality) *With the same assumptions and notation as in Lemma 18.24,*

$$C(f) \leq C(f^*) + \sum_{e \in E} a_e f_e f_e^*. \tag{18.9}$$

PROOF For each player i, multiply the inequality (18.8) by r_i. Summing up the resulting k inequalities, we obtain

$$\begin{aligned}
C(f) &\leq \sum_{i=1}^{k} r_i \left(\sum_{e \in P_i^*} a_e(f_e + r_i) + b_e \right) \\
&\leq \sum_{i=1}^{k} r_i \left(\sum_{e \in P_i^*} a_e(f_e + f_e^*) + b_e \right) \\
&= \sum_{e \in E} \left[a_e(f_e + f_e^*) + b_e \right] f_e^*,
\end{aligned}$$

where the equality follows by reversing the order of summation. Since the final expression equals the right-hand side of (18.9), the proof is complete. □

To complete the proof of Theorem 18.23, we upper bound the magnitude of the "error term" in (18.9) relative to the costs of the equilibrium and optimal flows.

Proof of Theorem 18.23 Let f and f^* denote equilibrium and optimal flows, respectively, for the atomic instance (G, r, c). Assume that edge e has the cost function $c_e(x) = a_e x + b_e$ for $a_e, b_e \geq 0$. Apply the Cauchy–Schwarz Inequality to the vectors $\{\sqrt{a_e} f_e\}_{e \in E}$ and $\{\sqrt{a_e} f_e^*\}_{e \in E}$ to obtain

$$\sum_{e \in E} a_e f_e f_e^* \leq \sqrt{\sum_{e \in E} a_e f_e^2} \cdot \sqrt{\sum_{e \in E} a_e (f_e^*)^2} \leq \sqrt{C(f)} \cdot \sqrt{C(f^*)}.$$

Combining this with the Equilibrium Inequality (18.9), dividing through by $C(f^*)$, and rearranging gives

$$\frac{C(f)}{C(f^*)} - 1 \leq \sqrt{\frac{C(f)}{C(f^*)}}.$$

Squaring both sides and solving the corresponding quadratic inequality $x^2 - 3x + 1 \leq 0$, we find that

$$\frac{C(f)}{C(f^*)} \leq \frac{3 + \sqrt{5}}{2} \approx 2.618,$$

as claimed. □

Theorem 18.23 can be extended to atomic instances with cost functions that are polynomials with nonnegative coefficients and degree at most a parameter p. However, the upper bound on the price of anarchy increases with p roughly in proportion to the exponential function p^p – much faster than in nonatomic instances. This exponential dependence is not an artifact of the above proof approach, as nearly matching lower bounds on the price of anarchy are known (Section 18.6).

Remark 18.26 Strictly speaking, the price of anarchy is not always defined in general atomic instances, where equilibrium flows need not exist (Example 18.7). Nevertheless, Theorem 18.23 has been extended to atomic instances with polynomial cost functions in three different ways. First, when such an instance *does* admit at least one equilibrium flow, then all such flows have cost at most $p^{O(p)}$ times that of an optimal flow. Second, by Nash's Theorem (Chapters 1 and 2), every such instance admits a *mixed*-strategy Nash equilibrium, and the expected cost of every such equilibrium is at most $p^{O(p)}$ times that of an optimal flow. Finally, similar upper bounds have been proved for "sink equilibria," an equilibrium concept that always exists in finite games and is motivated by convergence issues.

18.5 Reducing the Price of Anarchy

As we have seen, the price of anarchy can be large in both nonatomic and atomic selfish routing games when cost functions are highly nonlinear. This motivates a question first posed in Section 17.3: how can we design or modify a selfish routing network, without explicitly imposing an optimal solution, to minimize the inefficiency of its equilibria? Can modest intervention significantly reduce the price of anarchy? We briefly discuss two techniques for mitigating the inefficiency of selfish routing in nonatomic instances: influencing traffic with edge taxes (Subsection 18.5.1) and increasing the capacity of the network (Subsection 18.5.2).

18.5.1 Marginal Cost Pricing

Our first approach to reducing the price of anarchy in nonatomic selfish routing games is to use *marginal cost taxes* on the edges of the network. The idea of marginal cost pricing is to charge each network user on each edge for the additional cost its presence causes for the other users of the edge. To discuss this idea formally, we allow each edge e of a nonatomic selfish routing network to possess a nonnegative *tax* τ_e. We denote a nonatomic instance (G, r, c) with edge taxes τ by $(G, r, c + \tau)$. An equilibrium flow for such an instance $(G, r, c + \tau)$ is defined as in Definition 18.1, with all traffic traveling on routes that minimize the sum of the edge costs and edge taxes. Equivalently, it is an equilibrium flow for the nonatomic instance (G, r, c^τ), where the cost function c_e^τ is a shifted version of the original cost function c_e: $c_e^\tau(x) = c_e(x) + \tau_e$ for all $x \geq 0$.

The principle of marginal cost pricing asserts that for a flow f feasible for a nonatomic instance (G, r, c), the tax τ_e assigned to the edge e should be $\tau_e = f_e \cdot c_e'(f_e)$, where c_e' denotes the derivative of c_e. (Assume for simplicity that the cost functions are differentiable.) The term $c_e'(f_e)$ corresponds to the marginal increase in cost caused by one user of the edge, and the term f_e is the amount of traffic that suffers from this increase. We can also interpret the marginal cost tax τ_e using Corollary 18.10: τ_e is precisely the "extra term" in the marginal cost function that is absent from the original cost function. These taxes correct for the failure of selfish users to account for the second, "altruistic" term of the marginal cost function. Formally, Corollary 18.10 easily implies the following guarantee.

Theorem 18.27 *Let (G, r, c) be a nonatomic instance such that, for every edge e, the function $x \cdot c_e(x)$ is convex and continuously differentiable. Let f^* be an optimal flow for (G, r, c) and let $\tau_e = f_e^* \cdot c_e'(f_e^*)$ denote the marginal cost tax for edge e with respect f^*. Then f^* is an equilibrium flow for $(G, r, c + \tau)$.*

Marginal cost taxes thus induce an optimal flow as an equilibrium flow; in this sense, such taxes reduce the price of anarchy to 1. Theorem 18.27 also holds with weaker assumptions on the cost functions; in particular, the convexity hypothesis is not needed. For further discussion of pricing problems in routing games, see Chapter 22.

18.5.2 Capacity Augmentation

Our final result is a novel type of bound on the inefficiency of equilibrium flows in nonatomic selfish routing games with arbitrary cost functions. This bound does not involve the price of anarchy, which is unbounded in such networks (Example 18.3), and instead shows that the cost of an equilibrium flow is at most that of an optimal flow that is forced to route twice as much traffic between each source–sink pair. As we will see, this result implies that in lieu of centralized control, the inefficiency of selfish routing can be offset by a moderate increase in link speed.

Example 18.28 Consider the nonlinear variant of Pigou's example (Example 18.3). When there is one unit of traffic, the equilibrium flow routes all of the flow on the lower edge, while the optimal flow routes ϵ units of flow on the upper edge and the rest on the lower edge (where $\epsilon \to 0$ as $p \to \infty$). When the amount r of traffic to be routed exceeds one, an optimal flow assigns the additional $r - 1$ units of traffic to the upper link, incurring a cost that tends to $r - 1$ as $p \to \infty$. In particular, for every p an optimal flow feasible for twice the original traffic amount ($r = 2$) has cost at least 1, the cost of the equilibrium flow in the original instance.

We now show that the upper bound stated in Example 18.28 for the nonlinear variant of Pigou's example holds in every nonatomic instance.

Theorem 18.29 *If f is an equilibrium flow for (G, r, c) and f^* is feasible for $(G, 2r, c)$, then $C(f) \leq C(f^*)$.*

PROOF Let f and f^* denote an equilibrium flow for (G, r, c) and a feasible flow for $(G, 2r, c)$, respectively. For each commodity i, let d_i denote the minimum cost of an s_i–t_i path with respect to the flow f. Definition 18.1 and the definition of cost (18.1) imply that $C(f) = \sum_i r_i d_i$.

The key idea is to define a set of cost functions $\bar{c}$ that satisfies two properties: lower bounding the cost of f^* relative to that of f is easy with respect to $\bar{c}$; and the new cost functions $\bar{c}$ approximate the original ones c. Specifically, we set $\bar{c}_e(x) = \max\{c_e(f_e), c_e(x)\}$ for each edge e. Let $\bar{C}(\cdot)$ denote the cost of a flow in the instance $(G, r, \bar{c})$. Note that $\bar{C}(f^*) \geq C(f^*)$ while $\bar{C}(f) = C(f)$.

We first upper bound the amount by which the new cost $\bar{C}(f^*)$ of f^* can exceed its original cost $C(f^*)$. For every edge e, $\bar{c}_e(x) - c_e(x)$ is zero for $x \geq f_e$ and bounded above by $c_e(f_e)$ for $x < f_e$, so $x(\bar{c}_e(x) - c_e(x)) \leq c_e(f_e)f_e$ for all $x \geq 0$. Thus

$$\bar{C}(f^*) - C(f^*) = \sum_{e \in E} f_e^*(\bar{c}_e(f_e^*) - c_e(f_e^*)) \leq \sum_{e \in E} c_e(f_e)f_e = C(f). \quad (18.10)$$

In other words, evaluating f^* with cost functions $\bar{c}$, rather than c, increases its cost by at most an additive $C(f)$ factor.

Now we lower bound $\bar{C}(f^*)$. By construction, the modified cost $\bar{c}_e(\cdot)$ of an edge e is always at least $c_e(f_e)$, so the modified cost $\bar{c}_P(\cdot)$ of a path $P \in \mathcal{P}_i$ is always at least $c_P(f)$, which in turn is at least d_i. The modified cost $\bar{C}(f^*)$ therefore equals

$$\sum_{P\in\mathcal{P}} \bar{c}_P(f^*)f_P^* \geq \sum_{i=1}^{k}\sum_{P\in\mathcal{P}_i} d_i f_P^* = \sum_{i=1}^{k} 2r_i d_i = 2C(f). \qquad (18.11)$$

The theorem now follows immediately from inequalities (18.10) and (18.11). □

Another interpretation of Theorem 18.29 is that the benefit of centralized control is equaled or exceeded by the benefit of a sufficient improvement in link technology.

Corollary 18.30 *Let (G, r, c) be a nonatomic instance and define the modified cost function $\tilde{c}_e$ by $\tilde{c}_e(x) = c_e(x/2)/2$ for each edge e. Let $\tilde{f}$ be an equilibrium flow for $(G, r, \tilde{c})$ with cost $\tilde{C}(\tilde{f})$, and f^* a feasible flow for (G, r, c) with cost $C(f^*)$. Then $\tilde{C}(\tilde{f}) \leq C(f^*)$.*

Simple calculations show that Theorem 18.29 and Corollary 18.30 are equivalent; see Exercise 18.8(a).

Corollary 18.30 takes on a particularly nice form in instances in which all cost functions are *M/M/1 delay functions.* Such a cost function has the form $c_e(x) = (u_e - x)^{-1}$, where u_e can be interpreted as an edge capacity or a queue service rate; the function is defined to be $+\infty$ when $x \geq u_e$. (Rigorously allowing infinite costs in this selfish routing model requires some care; we ignore these issues in this chapter.) In this case, the modified function $\tilde{c}_e$ of Corollary 18.30 is $\tilde{c}_e(x) = 1/2(u_e - x/2) = 1/(2u_e - x)$. Corollary 18.30 thus suggests the following design principle for selfish routing networks with M/M/1 delay functions: *to outperform optimal routing, just double the capacity of every edge.*

18.6 Notes

18.6.1 Nonatomic Selfish Routing

Nonatomic selfish routing was first studied in the context of transportation networks. Pigou (1920) informally discussed Pigou's example in his 1920 book, *The Economics of Welfare*, in order to illustrate the inefficiency of equilibria. He also anticipated the principle of marginal cost pricing discussed in Theorem 18.27; indeed, marginal cost taxes are sometimes called *Pigouvian taxes.* The model was first formally defined by Wardrop (1952). For this reason, equilibrium flows in nonatomic selfish routing games are often called *Wardrop equilibria.* We use the term "equilibrium flow" so that the terminology for nonatomic and atomic selfish routing games is the same.

Beckmann et al. (1956) proved a number of fundamental results for the nonatomic model. Theorem 18.8, Proposition 18.9, Corollary 18.10, Proposition 18.11, and Theorem 18.27 were first proved in Beckmann et al. (1956), via proofs essentially identical to the ones given here. Details on first-order conditions for convex programming problems can be found in Bertsekas (1999, Chapter 2). Schmeidler (1973) founded the theory of general noncooperative nonatomic games.

Two decades after nonatomic selfish routing games were first defined, researchers began to use them to model the routing of data through communication networks. Nonatomic selfish routing is immediately relevant for networks that employ so-called *source routing*, meaning that each sender is responsible for selecting a full path of links to the receiver. Assuming that senders seek paths of minimum cost, senders of data in such networks correspond to the users of a selfish routing network.

In large networks such as the Internet, *distributed shortest-path routing* is typically used instead of source routing. In distributed shortest-path routing, each link is given a positive *length*, and data are forwarded along a path of minimum total length to its destination. Shortest-path routing leaves a key parameter unspecified: the length of each edge. A direct correspondence between selfish routing and shortest-path routing exists if and only if the edge cost functions coincide with the lengths used to define shortest paths. In other words, when an x fraction of the overall network traffic is using an edge with cost function $c(\cdot)$, then the corresponding shortest-path routing algorithm should define the length of the edge as the number $c(x)$. If the cost function c is nonconstant, then this is a congestion-dependent definition of the edge length. In this case, shortest-path routing will route traffic exactly *as if* it is a network with selfish routing (or source routing). For details on this equivalence, see the textbook by Bertsekas and Tsitsiklis (1989). See Qiu et al. (2003), for example, for a more recent paper that studies selfish routing from a computer networking perspective.

Braess's Paradox was discovered by Braess (1968). The variant in Example 18.4 was noted by L. Schulman (personal communication, October 1999). For surveys on the large literature inspired by Braess's Paradox, see Roughgarden (2006) and D. Braess's home page (Braess, 2007).

Cohen and Horowitz (1991) noted that Braess's Paradox has startling analogues in physical systems. For instance, Example 18.4 can be simulated in the following system of strings and springs. One end of a spring is attached to a fixed support, and the other end to a very short string. A second identical spring is hung from the free end of the string and carries a heavy weight. Finally, strings are connected, with very little slack, from the support to the upper end of the second spring and from the lower end of the first spring to the weight. Assuming that the springs are ideally elastic, the stretched length of a spring is a linear function of the force applied to it. We can therefore view the network of strings and springs as a selfish routing game, where force corresponds to traffic and physical distance corresponds to cost. Remarkably, severing the very short taut string causes the weight to levitate away from the ground! The rise in the weight is the same as the improvement in the equilibrium flow obtained by deleting the zero-cost edge of Figure 18.2(b) to recover the network of Figure 18.2(a).

The price of anarchy in nonatomic selfish routing games was first studied by Roughgarden and Tardos (2002). The nonlinear variant of Pigou's example (Example 18.3) is from Roughgarden and Tardos (2002), as is Theorem 18.16. Roughgarden and Tardos (2002) also proved the special case of Theorem 18.21 for networks with affine cost functions (where the price of anarchy is at most $4/3$). Roughgarden (2003) introduced the Pigou bound and proved Theorem 18.21 under the same convexity hypothesis used in Theorem 18.9. The solution to Exercise 18.5 can also be found in Roughgarden (2003). A. Ronen (personal communication, March 2002) suggested using the variational inequality in Proposition 18.20, which was first proved by Smith

(1979). Correa et al. (2004) proved Theorem 18.21 without any convexity assumptions. This theorem has been generalized to wider classes of nonatomic games; see Roughgarden (2005a) for a survey, as well as a discussion of the price of anarchy of nonatomic selfish routing games with nonutilitarian objectives.

Finally, Theorem 18.29 is due to Roughgarden and Tardos (2002). A proof of Corollary 18.30 and a counterexample to Theorem 18.29 in atomic instances can be found in Roughgarden (2005a). For extensions of Theorem 18.29 to networks with restricted cost functions, including a solution to Exercise 18.8(e), see Chakrabarty (2004) and Correa et al. (2005).

18.6.2 Atomic Selfish Routing

Atomic selfish routing games were first considered by Rosenthal (1973), who proved Theorem 18.12 with the potential function method. Rosenthal also introduced the concept of "congestion games" (Remark 18.2). Monderer and Shapley (1996) undertook a more general study of "potential games" – games that admit a potential function, which in turn can be used to prove that best-response dynamics converge to an equilibrium (Remark 18.13). Potential games are now studied in their own right; see Voorneveld et al. (1999) and Roughgarden (2005a, Section 4.8) for surveys of this literature.

Rosenthal (1973) showed that equilibrium flows need not exist in weighted multicommodity atomic instances. Example 18.7 is due to Goemans et al. (2005). Fotakis et al. (2005) proved Theorem 18.15 for weighted instances with affine cost functions.

The price of anarchy of atomic instances was first studied by Suri et al. (2007) in the context of the asymmetric scheduling games described in Exercise 18.3 below. Among other results, they proved an upper bound of $5/2$ on the price of anarchy in such games when each player controls one unit of traffic and when all cost functions are affine. This paper also introduced the proof structure used to prove Theorem 18.23 in this chapter.

Awerbuch et al. (2005) significantly generalized the results in Suri et al. (2007). They proved Theorem 18.23, as well as the refinement discussed in Exercise 18.7. The AAE example and the variant in Exercise 18.2(a) are from Awerbuch et al. (2005), as are the exponential (in the degree bound p) upper and lower bounds on the price of anarchy for polynomial cost functions with nonnegative coefficients. For refined versions of these upper and lower bounds, see Olver (2006). Awerbuch et al. (2005) extended all of their upper bounds to mixed-strategy Nash equilibria. Goemans et al. (2005) extended the upper bounds to "sink equilibria," a notion of equilibrium that is motivated by best-response dynamics and that always exists in finite noncooperative games.

For unweighted instances and pure-strategy equilibrium flows, the results in Awerbuch et al. (2005) were obtained independently by Christodoulou and Koutsoupias (2005b). The proofs in Christodoulou and Koutsoupias (2005b) extend without much difficulty to weighted instances and mixed-strategy Nash equilibria. Christodoulou and Koutsoupias (2005b) also studied the price of anarchy with respect to the egalitarian objective (see Section 17.1) and provide solutions to parts (b) and (c) of Exercise 18.2.

Caragiannis et al. (2006) provide a solution to Exercise 18.3(b), as well as numerous other results about the price of anarchy and stability in different classes of asymmetric scheduling instances. For results on the price of stability in atomic selfish routing games, see Anshelevich et al. (2004), Christodoulou and Koutsoupias (2005a), and Caragiannis et al. (2006).

Finally, several researchers have studied selfish routing in the *atomic splittable* model. This model is similar to the atomic selfish routing games studied in this chapter; the key difference is that a player i is permitted to route its r_i units of traffic *fractionally* over the s_i–t_i paths of the network. This model is also different from nonatomic selfish routing games; for example, if there is only one player controlling all of the traffic in the network, then the player will minimize its cost by routing this traffic optimally. More generally, a player takes into account the congestion it causes for its own traffic, while ignoring the congestion it creates for other players.

Equilibrium flows in the atomic splittable model can behave in counterintuitive ways (see Exercise 18.9, taken from Catoni and Pallottino, 1991), and the price of anarchy in this model is not well understood. It was initially claimed that the upper bounds on the price of anarchy for nonatomic instances carry over to atomic splittable ones (Roughgarden, 2005b; Correa et al., 2005), but Cominetti et al. (2006) recently gave counterexamples to these claims in multicommodity networks. Obtaining tight bounds on the price of anarchy in this model remains an important open question.

Bibliography

E. Anshelevich, A. Dasgupta, J. Kleinberg, É. Tardos, T. Wexler, and T. Roughgarden. The price of stability for network design with fair cost allocation. In *Proc. 45th Symp. Fdns. of Computer Science*, pp. 295–304, 2004.

B. Awerbuch, Y. Azar, and L. Epstein. The price of routing unsplittable flow. In *Proc. 37th Symp. Theory of Computing*, pp. 57–66, 2005.

M. J. Beckmann, C. B. McGuire, and C. B. Winsten. *Studies in the Economics of Transportation.* Yale University Press, 1956.

D. P. Bertsekas. *Nonlinear Programming*, 2nd ed. Athena Scientific, 1999.

D. P. Bertsekas and J. N. Tsitsiklis. *Parallel and Distributed Computation: Numerical Methods*, 2nd ed. Prentice-Hall, 1989. Athena Scientific, 1997.

D. Braess. Über ein Paradoxon aus der Verkehrsplanung. *Unternehmensforschung*, 12:258–268, 1968. English translation in Braess (2005).

D. Braess. On a paradox of traffic planning. *Transport. Sci.*, 39(4):446–450, 2005.

D. Braess. `http://homepage.ruhr-uni-bochum.de/Dietrich.Braess/`, Homepage, 2007.

I. Caragiannis, M. Flammini, C. Kaklamanis, P. Kanellopoulos, and L. Moscardelli. Tight bounds for selfish and greedy load balancing. In *Proc. 33rd Annual Intl. Colloq. in Automata, Languages, and Programming*, LNCS 4051:311–322, 2006.

S. Catoni and S. Pallottino. Traffic equilibrium paradoxes. *Transport. Sci.*, 25(3):240–244, 1991.

D. Chakrabarty. Improved bicriteria results for the selfish routing problem. Unpublished manuscript, 2004.

G. Christodoulou and E. Koutsoupias. On the price of anarchy and stability of correlated equilibria of linear congestion games. In *Proc. 13th Euro. Symp. on Algorithms (ESA)*, pp. 59–70, 2005a.

G. Christodoulou and E. Koutsoupias. The price of anarchy of finite congestion games. In *Proc. 37th Symp. on Theory of Computing*, pp. 67–73, 2005b.

J. E. Cohen and P. Horowitz. Paradoxical behavior of mechanical and electrical networks. *Nature*, 352(8):699–701, 1991.

R. Cominetti, J. R. Correa, and N.E.S. Moses. Network games with atomic players. In *Proc. 33rd Intl. Colloq. in Automata, Languages, and Programming*, LNCS 4051:525–536, 2006.

J. R. Correa, A. S. Schulz, and N.E.S. Moses. Selfish routing in capacitated networks. *Math. Operat. Res.*, 29(4):961–976, 2004.

J. R. Correa, A. S. Schulz, and N.E.S. Moses. On the inefficiency of equilibria in congestion games. In *Proc. 11th Conf. on Integer Programming and Combinatorial Optimization*, pp. 167–181, 2005.

D. Fotakis, S. C. Kontogiannis, and P. G. Spirakis. Selfish unsplittable flows. *Theor. Comput. Sci.*, 348(2–3):226–239, 2005.

M. X. Goemans, V. S. Mirrokni, and A. Vetta. Sink equilibria and convergence. In *Proc. 46th Symp. on Foundations of Computer Science*, pp. 142–151, 2005.

D. Monderer and L. S. Shapley. Potential games. *Games Econ. Behav.*, 14(1):124–143, 1996.

N. Olver. *The Price of Anarchy and a Priority-Based Model of Routing*. M.S. thesis, McGill University, 2006.

A. C. Pigou. *The Economics of Welfare*. Macmillan, 1920.

L. Qiu, Y. R. Yang, Y. Zhang, and S. Shenker. On selfish routing in Internet-like environments. In *Proc. SIGCOMM*, pp. 151–162, 2003.

R. W. Rosenthal. The network equilibrium problem in integers. *Networks*, 3(1):53–59, 1973.

T. Roughgarden. The price of anarchy is independent of the network topology. *J. Comput. System Sci.*, 67(2):341–364, 2003.

T. Roughgarden. *Selfish Routing and the Price of Anarchy*. MIT Press, 2005a.

T. Roughgarden. Selfish routing with atomic players. In *Proc. 16th Symp. Discrete Algorithms*, pp. 1184–1185, 2005b.

T. Roughgarden. On the severity of Braess's Paradox: Designing networks for selfish users is hard. *J. Computer System Sci.*, 72(5):922–953, 2006.

T. Roughgarden and É. Tardos. How bad is selfish routing? *J. ACM*, 49(2):236–259, 2002.

D. Schmeidler. Equilibrium points of nonatomic games. *J. Statist. Phys.*, 7(4):295–300, 1973.

M. J. Smith. The existence, uniqueness and stability of traffic equilibria. *Transport. Res., Part B*, 13(4):295–304, 1979.

S. Suri, C. Tóth, and Y. Zhou. Selfish load balancing and atomic congestion games. *Algorithmica*, 47(1): 79–96, 2007.

M. Voorneveld, P. Borm, F. van Megen, S. Tijs, and G. Facchini. Congestion games and potentials reconsidered. *Intl. Game Theory Rev.*, 1(3–4):283–299, 1999.

J. G. Wardrop. Some theoretical aspects of road traffic research. In *Proc. Institute of Civil Engineers, Pt. II*, volume 1, pp. 325–378, 1952.

Exercises

18.1 Recall the nonlinear variant of Pigou's example (Example 18.3). Prove that as the degree p of the cost function of the second link tends to infinity, the price of anarchy tends to infinity as $p/\ln p$.

18.2 This exercise explores lower bounds on the price of anarchy in atomic selfish routing games with affine cost functions.

(a) Modify the players' weights in the AAE example (Example 18.6) so that the price of anarchy in the resulting weighted atomic instance is precisely $(3+\sqrt{5})/2 \approx 2.618$.

(b) Can you devise an unweighted atomic instance with 3 players, affine cost functions, and price of anarchy equal to 5/2? Can you achieve a price of anarchy of $(3+\sqrt{5})/2$ using 3 players and variable weights?

(c) What is the largest price of anarchy in an atomic instance with affine cost functions and only 2 players?

18.3 An *asymmetric scheduling instance* differs from an atomic selfish routing instance in the following two respects. First, the underlying network is restricted to a common source vertex s, a common sink vertex t, and a set of parallel links that connect s to t. On the other hand, we allow different players to possess different strategy sets: each player i has a prescribed subset S_i of the links that it is permitted to use.

(a) Show that every asymmetric scheduling instance is equivalent to an atomic selfish routing game. Your reduction should make use only of the cost functions of the original scheduling instance, plus possibly the all-zero cost function.

(b) [Difficult] Part (a) shows that the worst-case price of anarchy in asymmetric scheduling instances with affine cost functions is at most that in atomic selfish routing games with affine cost functions. Prove that the worst-case price of anarchy is the same in the two models, equal to $5/2$ in unweighted instances and $(3+\sqrt{5})/2$ in weighted instances.

18.4 Prove Theorem 18.15. Make use of the following potential function:

$$\Phi(f) = \sum_{e \in E} \left(c_e(f_e) f_e + \sum_{i \in S_e} c_e(r_i) r_i \right),$$

where S_e denotes the set of players that choose a path in f that includes the edge e.

18.5 A set $\mathcal{C}$ of cost functions is *inhomogeneous* if it contains at least one function c satisfying $c(0) > 0$. Extend Proposition 18.19 to inhomogeneous sets of cost functions.

[Hint: Simulate a Pigou-like example using a more complex network and cost functions drawn only from the given set $\mathcal{C}$.]

18.6 Prove that if $\mathcal{C}$ is the set of nonnegative, nondecreasing, concave cost functions, then the Pigou bound $\alpha(\mathcal{C})$ equals $4/3$.

18.7 Improve the upper bound of Theorem 18.23 for unweighted atomic instances with affine cost functions. Can you match the lower bound provided by the AAE example?

18.8 This exercise studies refinements and extensions of Theorem 18.29.

(a) Deduce Corollary 18.30 from Theorem 18.29.

(b) Show that Theorem 18.29 does not always hold in atomic selfish routing games.

(c) Suppose we define f^* to be a flow feasible for the instance $(G, (1+\delta)r, c)$, where $\delta > 0$ is a parameter. (In Theorem 18.29, $\delta = 1$.) How does the guarantee of Theorem 18.29 change?

(d) Use Example 18.3 to prove that your bound in part (c) is the best possible.

(e) Determine the smallest value of δ such that the following statement is true: for every nonatomic instance (G, r, c) *with affine cost functions*, for every equilibrium flow f for (G, r, c) and optimal flow f^* for $(G, (1+\delta)r, c)$, $C(f) \le C(f^*)$. (Theorem 18.29 implies that the statement holds with $\delta = 1$; the question is whether or not our restriction on the cost functions permits smaller values of δ.)

18.9 Recall the atomic splittable selfish routing model discussed at the end of Section 18.6. Given such a game, we can obtain a new game by replacing a player that routes r_i units of traffic from s_i to t_i by two players that each route $r_i/2$ units of traffic from s_i to t_i. This operation does not change the cost of an optimal flow. Intuitively, since it decreases the amount of cooperation in the network, it should only increase the cost of an equilibrium flow. Prove that this intuition is incorrect: in multicommodity atomic splittable selfish routing networks, splitting a player in two can decrease the price of anarchy.

CHAPTER 19

Network Formation Games and the Potential Function Method

Éva Tardos and Tom Wexler

Abstract

Large computer networks such as the Internet are built, operated, and used by a large number of diverse and competitive entities. In light of these competing forces, it is surprising how efficient these networks are. An exciting challenge in the area of algorithmic game theory is to understand the success of these networks in game theoretic terms: what principles of interaction lead selfish participants to form such efficient networks?

In this chapter we present a number of network formation games. We focus on simple games that have been analyzed in terms of the efficiency loss that results from selfishness. We also highlight a fundamental technique used in analyzing inefficiency in many games: the potential function method.

19.1 Introduction

The design and operation of many large computer networks, such as the Internet, are carried out by a large number of independent service providers (Autonomous Systems), all of whom seek to selfishly optimize the quality and cost of their own operation. Game theory provides a natural framework for modeling such selfish interests and the networks they generate. These models in turn facilitate a quantitative study of the trade-off between efficiency and stability in network formation. In this chapter, we consider a range of simple network formation games that model distinct ways in which selfish agents might create and evaluate networks. All of the models we present aim to capture two competing issues: players want to minimize the expenses they incur in building a network, but at the same time seek to ensure that this network provides them with a high quality of service.

There are many measures by which players might evaluate the quality of a network. In this chapter, we focus primarily on measures of distance (Section 19.2) and connectivity (Section 19.3), rather than measures based on congestion effects (as is done in Chapter 18). We also assume that players have financial considerations. In Sections 19.2 and 19.3, players seek to minimize the construction costs of the networks they create. In Section 19.4, we look at a game with a more sophisticated financial aspect: players represent service providers who set prices for users and seek to maximize their profit, namely their income from users minus the cost of providing the service.

For all of the games we consider, we use Nash equilibrium as the solution concept, and refer to networks corresponding to these equilibria as being *stable*. The models we focus on involve players who can unilaterally build edges, and thus the Nash equilibrium solution concept is appropriate.

To evaluate the overall quality of a network, we consider the *social cost*, or the sum of all players' costs. We refer to the networks that optimize social cost as *optimal* or *socially efficient*. The main goal of this chapter is to better understand the quantitative trade-off between networks that are stable and those that are socially efficient. More precisely, we are interested in bounding the price of anarchy and the price of stability (as defined in Chapter 17). The models we consider in this chapter are network formation games in which these measures are provably small.

In Section 19.2 we consider a local connection game where the nodes of the graph are players who pay for the edges that connect them directly to other nodes (incident edges). In selecting a strategy, players face two conflicting desires: to pay as little as possible, and to have short paths to all other nodes. Our goal here is to bound the efficiency loss resulting from stability. Such connection games have been extensively studied in the economics literature (see Jackson (2006) for a survey) to model social network formation, using edges to represent social relations. The local connection game can also be thought of as a simple model for the way subnetworks connect in computer networks (by establishing peering points), or as modeling the formation of subnetworks in overlay systems such as P2P (peer-to-peer) networks connecting users to each other for downloading files.

We will use a model in which players can form edges to a neighbor unilaterally, and will use Nash equilibrium as our solution concept. This differs from much of the literature in economics, where it is typically assumed that an edge between two players needs the consent or contribution from both players, and where the notion of pairwise stability is used instead of Nash equilibria. We will discuss how the results in Section 19.2 extend to models using pairwise stable equilibria in the notes in Section 19.5.1.

The model we examine was introduced by Fabrikant et al. (2003) and represents the first quantitative effort to understand the efficiency loss of stable networks. In this game, a single parameter α represents the cost of building any one edge. Each player (represented by a node) perceives the quality of a network as the sum of distances to all other nodes. Players aim to minimize a cost function that combines both network quality and building costs: they attempt to minimize the sum the building costs they incur and the distances to all other players. Thus, players use α as a trade-off parameter between their two objectives. This is perhaps the simplest way to model this type of trade-off. While the simplicity of this game makes it easy to evaluate, such a stylized model ignores a number of issues, such as varying costs and possible congestion effects. In Section 19.5.1, we discuss related models that address some of these issues.

In Section 19.3 we study a very different (and also quite simple) model of network design, introduced by Anshelevich et al. (2004), called the global connection game. Whereas players in the game of Section 19.2 only make local choices (which other nodes to link to), players in this game make global decisions, in that they may build edges throughout the network. Unlike the local connection game, this global game attempts to model players who actually build and maintain large-scale shared networks. This model also allows for greater heterogeneity in the underlying graph.

In the global connection game, a player is not associated with an individual node of the networks, but instead has certain global connectivity goals. To achieve these goals, a player may contribute money to any set of edges in the network. As before, we view connectivity as the primary measure of quality. However, players do not desire uniform connectivity; instead, each player has a subset of nodes that it needs to connect, and aims to do so as cheaply as possible. Furthermore, unlike in the local game, players are not concerned with distance, and simply want to connect their terminals.

As in the previous model, players are sensitive to costs. Edge e has a cost $c_e \geq 0$, and players who use e share this cost. In particular, we focus on a *fair sharing rule*; all players using an edge must share its cost evenly. This natural cost-sharing scheme can be derived from the Shapley value, and has many nice properties. We also examine other cost-sharing games, and discuss the role of fair sharing in the price of stability results.

A key technique used in this section is the potential function method. This method has emerged as a general technique in understanding the quality of equilibria. We review this technique in detail in Section 19.3.2. While this technique provides results only regarding the price of stability, it is interesting to note that many of the currently known price of anarchy results (e.g., most of the results in Part III of this book) are for potential games.

In Section 19.4, we consider another potential game; a facility location game with a more sophisticated cost model. In the previous two sections, players simply minimized their costs. Here, edges still have costs, but players also select prices for users so as to maximize net income: price charged minus the cost paid. We again consider a very simplified model in which players place facilities to serve clients, thereby forming a network between the providers and the clients. We show that a socially efficient network is stable (i.e., the price of stability is 1), and bound the price of anarchy.

In the context of facility location games, we also bound the quality of solutions obtained after sufficiently long selfish play, without assuming that players have yet reached an equilibrium. As we have seen in part I of this book, equilibrium solutions may be hard to find (Chapter 2), and natural game play may not converge to an equilibrium (Chapter 4). Thus it is often useful to evaluate the quality of the transient solutions that arise during competitive play. The facility location game considered in this section is one of the few classes of games for which this strong type of bound is known.

19.2 The Local Connection Game

In this section we consider the simple network formation game of Fabrikant et al. (2003), where players can form links to other players. We consider a game with n players, where each player is identified with a node. Node u may choose to build edges from u to any subset of nodes, thereby creating a network. Players have two competing goals; players want to build (and thus pay) for as few edges as possible, yet they also want to form a network that minimizes the distance from their own node to all others. Our main focus in this section is to quantitatively understand the inefficiency that results from the selfish behavior of these network builders.

19.2.1 Model

Players in the local connection game are identified with nodes in a graph G on which the network is to be built. A strategy for player u is a set of undirected edges that u will build, all of which have u as one endpoint. Given a strategy vector S, the set of edges in the union of all players' strategies forms a network $G(S)$ on the player nodes. Let $dist_S(u, v)$ be the shortest path (in terms of number of edges) between u and v in $G(S)$. We use $dist(u, v)$ when S is clear from context. The cost of building an edge is specified by a single parameter, α. Each player seeks to make the distances to all other nodes small, and to pay as little as possible. More precisely, player u's objective is to minimize the sum of costs and distances $\alpha n_u + \sum_v dist(u, v)$, where n_u is the number of edges bought by player u.

Observe that since edges are undirected, when a node u buys an edge (u, v), that edge is also available for use from v to u, and in particular, is available for node v. Thus, at Nash equilibrium at most one of the nodes u and v pay for the connecting edge (u, v). Also, since the distance $dist(u, v)$ is infinite whenever u and v are not connected, at equilibrium we must have a connected graph. We say that a network $G = (V, E)$ is *stable* for a value α if there is a stable strategy vector S that forms G.

The social cost of a network G is $SC(G) = \sum_{u \neq v} dist(u, v) + \alpha|E|$, the sum of players' costs. Note that the distance $dist(u, v)$ contributes to the overall quality twice (once for u and once for v). We will be comparing solutions that are stable to those that are optimal under this measure.

19.2.2 Characterization of Solutions and the Price of Stability

We now characterize the structure of an optimal solution as a function of α. A network is *optimal* or *efficient* if it minimizes the social cost $SC(G)$.

Lemma 19.1 *If $\alpha \geq 2$ then any star is an optimal solution, and if $\alpha \leq 2$ then the complete graph is an optimal solution.*

PROOF Consider an optimal solution G with m edges. We know $m \geq n - 1$; otherwise, the graph would be disconnected, and thus have an infinite cost. All ordered pairs of nodes not directly connected by an edge must have a distance of at least 2 from each other, and there are $n(n-1) - 2m$ such pairs. Adding the remaining $2m$ pairs with distance 1 yields $\alpha m + 2n(n-1) - 4m + 2m = (\alpha - 2)m + 2n(n-1)$ as a lower bound on the social cost of G. Both a star and the complete graph match this bound. Social cost is minimized by making m as small as possible when $\alpha > 2$ (a star) and as large as possible when $\alpha < 2$ (a complete graph). □

Both the star and the complete graph can also be obtained as a Nash equilibrium for certain values of α, as shown in the following lemma.

Lemma 19.2 *If $\alpha \geq 1$ then any star is a Nash equilibrium, and if $\alpha \leq 1$ then the complete graph is a Nash equilibrium.*

PROOF First suppose $\alpha \geq 1$, and consider a star. It turns out that any assignment of edges to incident players corresponds to a Nash equilibrium, but for this result, we need only demonstrate a single solution. In particular, consider the strategy in which player 1 (the center of the star) buys all edges to the other players, while the remaining $n-1$ leaf players buy nothing. Player 1 has no incentive to deviate, as doing so disconnects the graph and thus incurs an infinite penalty. Any leaf player can deviate only by adding edges. For any leaf player, adding k edges saves k in distance but costs αk, and thus is not a profitable deviation. Thus the star is a Nash equilibrium.

Now suppose $\alpha \leq 1$. Consider a complete graph, with each edge assigned to an incident player. A player who stops paying for a set of k edges saves αk in cost, but increases total distances by k, so this outcome is stable. □

There are other equilibria as well, some of which are less efficient (see Exercise 19.6). However, these particular Nash equilibria, in conjunction with the above optimal solutions, suffice to upper bound the price of stability.

Theorem 19.3 *If $\alpha \geq 2$ or $\alpha \leq 1$, the price of stability is 1. For $1 < \alpha < 2$, the price of stability is at most 4/3.*

PROOF The statements about $\alpha \leq 1$ and $\alpha \geq 2$ are immediate from Lemmas 19.1 and 19.2. When $1 < \alpha < 2$, the star is a Nash equilibrium, while the optimum structure is a complete graph. To establish the price of stability, we need to compute the ratio of costs of these two solutions. The worst case for this ratio occurs when α approaches 1, where it attains a value of

$$\frac{2n(n-1)-2(n-1)}{2n(n-1)-n(n-1)/2} = \frac{4n^2-6n+2}{3n^2-3n} < 4/3.$$

□

Exercise 19.3 shows that the complete graph is the unique equilibrium for $\alpha < 1$, so we also have that the price of anarchy is 1 in this range. We now address the price of anarchy for larger values of α.

19.2.3 The Price of Anarchy

The first bound on the price of anarchy for this game was given by Fabrikant et al. (2003), and involves two steps: bounding the diameter of the resulting graph, and using the diameter to bound the cost. We begin with the second step.

Lemma 19.4 *If a graph G at Nash equilibrium has diameter d, then its social cost is at most $O(d)$ times the minimum possible cost.*

PROOF The cost of the optimal solution is at least $\Omega(\alpha n + n^2)$, as we need to buy a connected graph, which costs at least $(n-1)\alpha$, and there are $\Omega(n^2)$ distances, each of which is at least 1. To bound the quality of the solution, consider the distance costs and edge costs separately. The distance cost is at most $n^2 d$, and thus is at most d times the minimum possible.

We now examine edge costs. First we consider *cut edges*, those edges whose removal disconnects G. There are at most $n-1$ cut edges, so the total cost of all cut edges is at most $\alpha(n-1)$, which in turn is at most the optimal solution cost. Now consider the set of all noncut edges paid for by a vertex v. We will argue that there are $O(nd/\alpha)$ such edges, with cost $O(dn)$ for node v, and thus the total cost of all noncut edges is $O(dn^2)$. This will establish that the cost of G is $O(\alpha n + dn^2)$, completing the proof.

Pick a node u, and for each edge $e = (u, v)$ paid for by node u, let V_e be the set of nodes w, where the shortest path from u to w goes through edge e. We will argue that the distance between nodes u and v with edge e deleted is at most $2d$. Thus deleting e increases the total distance from u to all other nodes by at most $2d|V_e|$. Since deleting the edge would save α in edge costs and G is stable, we must have that $\alpha \leq 2d|V_e|$, and hence $|V_e| \geq \alpha/2d$. If there are at least $\alpha/2d$ nodes in each V_e, then the number of such edges adjacent to a node v must be at most $2dn/\alpha$, as claimed.

We now bound the distance between nodes u and v with edge e deleted. Consider Figure 19.1, depicting a shortest path avoiding edge e. Let $e' = (u', v')$ be the edge on this path entering the set V_e. The segment P_u of this path from u to node u' is the shortest path from u to u' as $u' \notin V_e$, and hence deleting e does not affect the shortest path. So P_u is at most d long. The segment P_v from v' to v is at most $d-1$ long, as $P_v \cup e$ forms the shortest path between u and v'. Thus the total length is at most $2d$. □

Using this lemma, we can bound the price of anarchy by $O(\sqrt{\alpha})$.

Theorem 19.5 *The diameter of a Nash equilibrium is at most* $2\sqrt{\alpha}$, *and hence the price of anarchy is at most* $O(\sqrt{\alpha})$.

PROOF From Lemma 19.4, we need only prove that for any nodes u and v, $dist(u, v) < 2\sqrt{\alpha}$. Suppose for nodes u and v, $dist(u, v) \geq 2k$, for some k. The

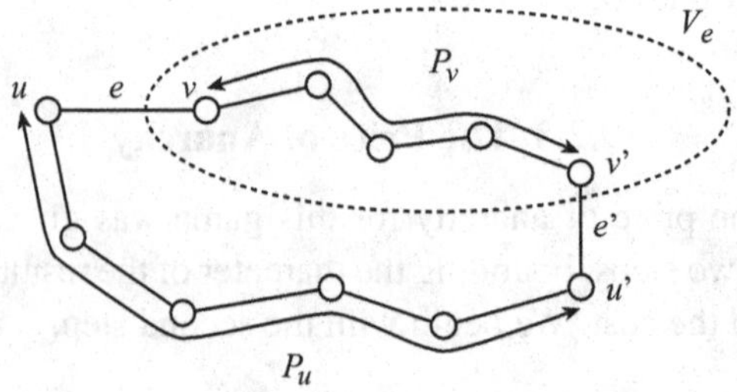

Figure 19.1. Path P_u, $(u', v')P_v$ is the u–v shortest path after edge $e = (u, v)$ is deleted.

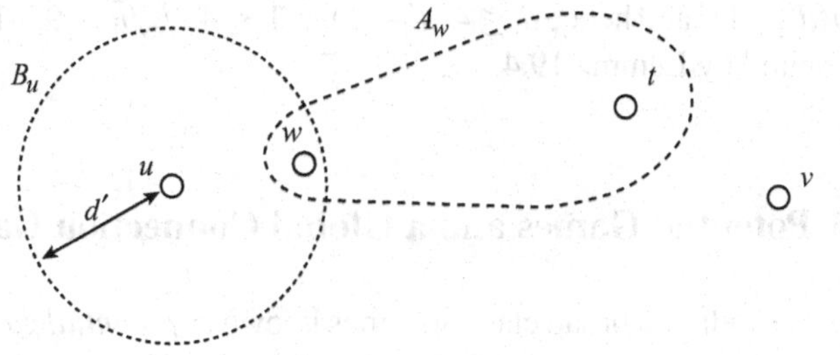

Figure 19.2. Nodes u and v that are at maximum distance d apart. B is the set of nodes at most $d' = (d-1)/4$ away from node u, and A_w is the set of nodes whose shortest path leaves B at w.

main observation is that by adding the edge (u, v), the node u would pay α and improve her distance to the nodes on the second half of the $u - v$ shortest path by $(2k-1)+(2k-3)+\cdots+1 = k^2$. So if $dist(u, v) > 2\sqrt{\alpha}$, node u would benefit from adding the edge (u, v), a contradiction. □

We now show an $O(1)$ bound on the price of anarchy that was given by Lin (2003) (and independently also by Albers et al., 2006) for $\alpha = O(\sqrt{n})$.

Theorem 19.6 *The price of anarchy is $O(1)$ whenever α is $O(\sqrt{n})$. More generally, price of anarchy is $O(1+\alpha/\sqrt{n})$.*

PROOF We again use Lemma 19.4, so all we have to do is improve our bound on the diameter d. Consider nodes u and v with $dist(u, v) = d$. Let $d' = \lfloor (d-1)/4 \rfloor$ and let B be the set of nodes at most d' away from u, as shown on Figure 19.2. Consider how the distance $d(v, w)$ changes for nodes $w \in B$ by adding edge (v, u). Before adding the edge $dist(v, w) \geq d - d'$. After adding (v, u), the distance decreases to at most $d' + 1$. Thus v saves at least $(d - 2d' - 1)$ in distance to all nodes in B, and hence would save at least $(d - 2d' - 1)|B| \geq (d-1)|B|/2$ in total distance costs by buying edge (v, u). If G is stable, we must have $(d-1)|B|/2 \leq \alpha$.

For a node $w \in B$ let A_w contain all nodes t for which the u–t shortest path leaves the set B after the node w. Note that if A_w is nonempty, then w must be exactly at distance d' from u. Therefore, node u would save $|A_w|(d'-1)$ in distance cost by buying edge (u, w). If the network is at equilibrium, then we must have that $|A_w|(d'-1) \leq \alpha$. There must be a node $w \in B$ that has $|A_w| \geq (n - |B|)/|B|$. Combining these, we get that

$$(d'-1)(n-|B|)/|B| \leq \alpha.$$

This implies that $|B|(1+\alpha/(d'-1)) \geq n$, and since $\alpha > d > d'$,

$$|B| \geq n(d'-1)/2\alpha.$$

Combining this with the previous bound of $\alpha \geq (d-1)|B|/2$ yields

$$\alpha \geq (d-1)|B|/2 \geq (d-1)n(d'-1)/4\alpha \geq n(d'-1)^2/\alpha.$$

Thus $\alpha^2 \geq n(d' - 1)^2$ and hence $d \leq 4(d' + 1) + 1 \leq 4\alpha/\sqrt{n} + 9$, which implies the claimed bound by Lemma 19.4. □

19.3 Potential Games and a Global Connection Game

In this section we introduce a broad class of games known as *potential games*. This class encompasses a number of natural and well-studied network-based games. As we will see, potential games possess many nice properties; pure equilibria always exist, best response dynamics are guaranteed to converge, and the price of stability can be bounded using a technique called the *potential function method*. Our motivating example for this class of games is a network formation game called the *global connection game*, which was discussed in Chapter 17. We begin by defining this game, and present some theorems about pure equilibria and the price of stability. We then introduce potential games, and provide generalized results for this broader framework.

The network formation game discussed in Section 19.2 is local in the sense that a player can build links to other nodes, but has no direct means for affecting distant network structure. Such might be the case with social networks or peering relationships in a digital network. The global connection game, in contrast, models players who make global structural decisions; players may build edges throughout the network, and thus consider relatively complex strategies. This game might be more appropriate for modeling the actual construction and maintenance of large-scale physical networks.

Beyond the varying scope of players' strategies, there are two additional features that differentiate these network formation games. First, in exchange for the global connection game's broader strategy space, we consider a relatively simplified player objective function. In particular, we assume that players are unconcerned with their distance to other nodes in the network, and instead want only to build a network that connects their terminals as cheaply as possible. The second notable distinction is that the global connection game supports cooperation, in that multiple players may share the cost of building mutually beneficial links. In the local connection game, an edge might benefit multiple players, and yet the edge's cost is always covered fully by one of the two incident players. We now give a formal description of the global connection game.

19.3.1 A Global Connection Game

We are given a directed graph $G = (V, E)$ with nonnegative edge costs c_e for all edges $e \in E$. There are k players, and each player i has a specified source node s_i and sink node t_i (the same node may be a source or a sink for multiple players). Player i's goal is to build a network in which t_i is reachable from s_i, while paying as little as possible to do so. A strategy for player i is a path P_i from s_i to t_i in G. By choosing P_i, player i is committing to help build all edges along P_i in the final network. Given a strategy for each player, we define the constructed network to be $\cup_i P_i$.

It remains to allocate the cost of each edge in this network to the players using it, as this will allow players to evaluate the utility of each strategy. In principle, there are a vast number of possible cost-sharing mechanisms, each of which induces a distinct network formation game. We will briefly touch on this large space of games at the end of the section, but for now, our primary focus will be on a single cost-sharing mechanism with a number of nice properties, that is both simple and easy to motivate.

In particular, we consider the mechanism that splits the cost of an edge evenly among all players whose path contains it. More concretely, if k_e denotes the number of players whose path contains edge e, then e assigns a cost share of c_e/k_e to each player using e. Thus the total cost incurred by player i under a strategy vector S is given by

$$\text{cost}_i(S) = \sum_{e \in P_i} c_e/k_e.$$

Note that the total cost assigned to all players is exactly the cost of the constructed network. This equal-division mechanism was suggested by Herzog et al. (1997), and has a number of basic economic motivations. Moulin and Shenker prove that this mechanism can be derived from the Shapley (2001) value, and it can be shown to be the unique cost-sharing scheme satisfying a number of natural sets of axioms (see Feigenbaum et al., 2001; Moulin and Shenker, 2001). We refer to it as the *fair* or *Shapley cost-sharing mechanism*. The social objective for this game is simply the cost of the constructed network.

One may view this game as a competitive version of the generalized Steiner tree problem; given a graph and pairs of terminals, find the cheapest possible network connecting all terminal pairs. Indeed, an optimal generalized Steiner tree is precisely the outcome against which we will compare stable solutions in evaluating the efficiency of equilibria. This connection highlights an important difference between this game and routing games; in routing games such as those discussed in Chapter 18, players are sensitive to congestion effects, and thus seek sparsely used paths. But in the global connection game, as with the Steiner forest problem, the objective is simply to minimize costs, and thus sharing edges is in fact encouraged.

The two examples in Chapter 17 provide a few useful observations about this game. Example 17.2 (see Figure 19.3(a)) shows that even on very simple networks, this game has multiple equilibria, and that these equilibria may differ dramatically in quality. There are two equilibria with costs k and 1 respectively. Since the latter is also optimal

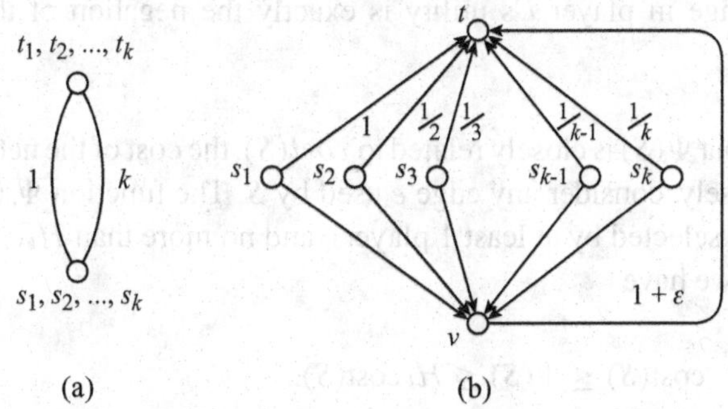

Figure 19.3. An instance of the global connection game with price of anarchy k (a) and an instance with price of stability $\mathcal{H}_k$ (b).

solution, the price of anarchy is k, while the price of stability is 1. It is not hard to show that the price of anarchy can never exceed k on any network (see Exercise 19.9), and thus this simple example captures the worst-case price of anarchy. Our primary goal will be to bound the price of stability in general.

Example 17.3 (see Figure 19.3(b)) shows that the price of stability can indeed exceed 1; this network has a unique Nash equilibrium with cost $\mathcal{H}_k$, the kth harmonic number, while the optimal solution has a cost of $1 + \epsilon$. Thus, the price of stability on this network is roughly $\mathcal{H}_k$. Our aim is to prove that pure equilibria always exist and provide an upper bound the price of stability. Both of these results make use of a *potential function*, which we will formally introduce in Section 19.3.2.

Consider an instance of the global connection game, and a strategy vector $S = (P_1, P_2, \ldots, P_k)$ containing an $s_i - t_i$ path for each player i. For each edge e, define a function $\Psi_e(S)$ mapping strategy vectors to real values as

$$\Psi_e(S) = c_e \cdot \mathcal{H}_{k_e},$$

where k_e is the number of players using edge e in S, and $\mathcal{H}_k = \sum_{j=1}^{k} 1/j$ is the kth harmonic number. Let $\Psi(S) = \sum_e \Psi_e(S)$. While this function does not obviously capture any important feature of our game, it has the following nice property.

Lemma 19.7 *Let $S = (P_1, P_2, \ldots, P_k)$, let $P_i' \neq P_i$ be an alternate path for some player i, and define a new strategy vector $S' = (S_{-i}, P_i')$. Then*

$$\Psi(S) - \Psi(S') = u_i(S') - u_i(S).$$

PROOF This lemma states that when a player i changes strategies, the corresponding change in $\Psi(\cdot)$ exactly mirrors the change in i's utility. Let k_e be the number of players using e under S. For any edge e that appears in both or neither of P_i and P_i', the cost paid by i toward e is the same under S and S'. Likewise, $\Psi_e(\cdot)$ has the same value under S and S'. For an edge e in P_i but not in P_i', by moving from S to S', i saves (and thus increases her utility by) c_e/k_e, which is precisely the decrease in $\Psi_e(\cdot)$. Similarly, for an edge e in P_i' but not in P_i, player i incurs a cost of $c_e/(k_e + 1)$ in switching from S to S', which matches the increase in $\Psi_e(\cdot)$. Since $\Psi(\cdot)$ is simply the sum of $\Psi_e(\cdot)$ over all edges, the collective change in player i's utility is exactly the negation of the change in $\Psi(\cdot)$. □

We also note that $\Psi(S)$ is closely related to $cost(S)$, the cost of the network generated by S. More precisely, consider any edge e used by S. The function $\Psi_e(S)$ is at least c_e (any used edge is selected by at least 1 player), and no more than $\mathcal{H}_k c_e$ (there are only k players). Thus we have

Lemma 19.8 $\text{cost}(S) \leq \Psi(S) \leq \mathcal{H}_k \text{cost}(S)$.

These two lemmas are used to prove the following two theorems, which will follow from Theorems 19.11, 19.12, and 19.13.

Theorem 19.9 *Any instance of the global connection game has a pure Nash equilibrium, and best response dynamics always converges.*

Theorem 19.10 *The price of stability in the global connection game with k players is at most $\mathcal{H}_k$, the kth harmonic number.*

Since the proofs of these two results actually apply to a much broader class of games (i.e., potential games), we now introduce these games and prove the corresponding results in this more general context.

19.3.2 Potential Games and Congestion Games

For any finite game, an *exact potential function* Φ is a function that maps every strategy vector S to some real value and satisfies the following condition: If $S = (S_1, S_2, \ldots, S_k)$, $S'_i \neq S_i$ is an alternate strategy for some player i, and $S' = (S_{-i}, S'_i)$, then $\Phi(S) - \Phi(S') = u_i(S') - u_i(S)$. In other words, if the current game state is S, and player i switches from strategy S_i to strategy S'_i, then the resulting savings i incurs exactly matches the decrease in the value of the potential function. Thus Lemma 19.7 simply states that Ψ is an exact potential function for the global connection game.

It is not hard to see that a game has at most one potential function, modulo addition by a constant. A game that does possess an exact potential function is called an *exact potential game*. For the remainder of this chapter, we will drop the word "exact" from these terms (see Exercise 19.13 for an inexact notion of a potential function). A surprising number of interesting games turn out to be potential games, and this structure has a number of strong implications for the existence of and convergence to equilibria.

Theorem 19.11 *Every potential game has at least one pure Nash equilibrium, namely the strategy S that minimizes $\Phi(S)$.*

PROOF Let Φ be a potential function for this game, and let S be a pure strategy vector minimizing $\Phi(S)$. Consider any move by a player i that results in a new strategy vector S'. By assumption, $\Phi(S') \geq \Phi(S)$, and by the definition of a potential function, $u_i(S') - u_i(S) = \Phi(S) - \Phi(S')$. Thus i's utility can not increase from this move, and hence S is stable. □

Going one step further, note that any state S with the property that Φ cannot be decreased by altering any one strategy in S is a Nash equilibrium by the same argument. Furthermore, best response dynamics simulate local search on Φ; improving moves for players decrease the value of the potential function. Together, these observations imply the following result.

Theorem 19.12 *In any finite potential game, best response dynamics always converge to a Nash equilibrium.*

Note that these two results imply Theorem 19.9.

A less abstract characterization of potential games can be found in a class of games called *congestion games* (Rosenthal, 1973). A congestion game has k players and n resources. Player i has a set S_i of allowable strategies, each of which specifies a subset of resources. Each resource j has a load-dependent cost function $c_j(x)$, indicating the cost incurred by any player i whose chosen strategy includes resource j if there are x such players in total. The total cost charged to player i who chooses a strategy S_i is simply the sum of the costs incurred from each resource in S_i. Thus if the total load on link j is x_j, then i pays $\sum_{j \in S_i} c_j(x_j)$. The Global Connection game is clearly a congestion game; edges are resources, $s_i - t_i$ paths are allowable strategies for player i, and the cost functions are $c_e(x) = c_e/x$.

Rosenthal (1973) proved that any congestion game is a potential game (see Exercise 19.15). Monderer and Shapley (1996) proved the converse; for any potential game, there is a congestion game with the same potential function.

We now present a generic upper bound on the price of stability for an arbitrary potential game.

19.3.3 The Potential Function Method and the Price of Stability

Suppose that we have a potential game G with a potential function $\Phi(S)$ and social cost function $c(S)$. If $\Phi(S)$ and $c(S)$ are similar, then the price of stability must be small. We make this precise in the following theorem.

Theorem 19.13 *Suppose that we have a potential game with potential function Φ, and assume further that for any outcome S, we have*

$$\frac{\text{cost}(S)}{A} \leq \Phi(S) \leq B \cdot \text{cost}(S)$$

for some constants $A, B > 0$. Then the price of stability is at most AB.

PROOF Let S^N be a strategy vector that minimizes $\Phi(S)$. From Theorem 19.11, S^N is a Nash equilibrium. It suffices to show that the actual cost of this solution is not much larger than that of a solution S^* of minimal cost. By assumption, we have that $\frac{\text{cost}(S^N)}{A} \leq \Phi(S^N)$. By the definition of S^N, we have that $\Phi(S^N) \leq \Phi(S^*)$. Finally, the second inequality of our assumption implies that $\Phi(S^*) \leq B \cdot \text{cost}(S^*)$. Stringing these inequalities together yields $\text{cost}(S^N) \leq AB \cdot \text{cost}(S^*)$, as desired. □

Note that this result, taken together with Lemma 19.8, directly implies Theorem 19.10. This technique for bounding the price of stability using a potential function is known as the *potential function method.*

In general, outcomes that minimize the potential function may not be the best Nash equilibrium, and thus this bound is not always tight (see Exercise 19.14). However, in the case of the global connection game, we have seen that the price of stability is at least $\mathcal{H}_k$. Thus, for this class of games, the bound given by the potential function method is the best possible.

Notice that we have essentially already seen the potential function method used in the nonatomic selfish routing game of Chapter 18. For this routing game, all equilibria have the same social value, and hence the price of anarchy and the price of stability are the same. Because of this, Theorem 18.16 is phrased as a statement about the price of anarchy, but we can still view this result as an application the potential function method. In the last section of this chapter, we will see yet another application of this technique for a potential game that models competitive facility location.

We have seen that potential games have pure equilibria, and that the price of stability can be bounded via the potential function method. We now consider the complexity of finding these equilibria in general potential games.

19.3.4 Finding Nash Equilibria in Potential Games

Theorem 19.12 provides an algorithmic means of reaching pure equilibria in potential games. Unfortunately, this theorem makes no claim regarding the rate of this convergence. In some games, best response dynamics always converges quickly, but in many games it does not. In some games, the potential function Φ can be minimized in polynomial time, but in others the minimization problem is NP-hard. To get a better handle on the complexity of finding pure equilibria in potential games, we consider the closely related problem of finding local optima in optimization problems.

The class of *Polynomial Local Search* problems (PLS) was defined by Johnson et al. (1988) as an abstract class of local optimization problems. First, let us define a general *optimization problem* (say a minimization problem) as follows. We have a set of instances I, and for each instance $x \in I$ a set of feasible solutions $F(x)$ and a cost function $c_x(s)$ defined on all $s \in F(x)$. We also have an oracle (or a polynomial-time algorithm) that takes an instance x and a candidate solution s, and checks whether s is a feasible solution ($s \in F(x)$). If it is, the oracle computes the cost of that solution, $c_x(s)$. The optimization problem is to find a solution $s \in F(x)$ with minimum cost $c_x(s)$ for a given instance $x \in I$.

To define a *local optimization problem*, we must also specify a neighborhood $N_x(s) \subset F(x)$ for each instance $x \in I$ and each solution $s \in F(x)$. A solution $s \in F(x)$ is *locally optimal* if $c_x(s) \leq c_x(s')$ for all $s' \in N_x(s)$. The local optimization problem is to find a local optimum $s \in F(x)$ for a given instance $x \in I$. A *local optimization problem is in PLS* if we have an oracle that, for any instance $x \in I$ and solution $s \in F(x)$, decides whether s is locally optimal, and if not, returns $s' \in N_x(s)$ with $c_x(s') < c_x(s)$.

Fabrikant et al. (2004) show that finding a Nash equilibrium in potential games is PLS-complete, assuming that the best response of each player can be found in polynomial time. To see that the problem belongs to PLS, we will say that the neighbors $N_x(s)$ of a strategy vector s are all the strategy vectors s' that can be obtained from s by a single player changing his or her strategy. By definition, a potential function Φ is locally optimal for cost function $c_x(s) = \Phi(s)$ if and only if it is a pure Nash equilibrium, so finding a pure Nash equilibrium is in PLS.

A problem is PLS-complete if it is in PLS and there is a polynomial time reduction from all other problems in PLS such that local optima of the target problem correspond to local optima of the original one. Since the introduction of this class in Johnson et al. (1988), many local search problems have been shown to be PLS-complete, including the weighted versions of satisfiability (Krentel, 1989). The *weighted satisfiability problem* is defined by a formula in conjunctive normal form $C_1 \wedge \ldots \wedge C_n$, with a nonnegative weight w_j for each clause C_j. Solutions s are truth assignments of variables, and the associated cost $c(s)$ is the sum of the weights of the unsatisfied clauses. The neighbors of a truth assignment s are the assignments obtained by flipping a single variable in s.

Here we show via a reduction from this weighted satisfiability problem that finding a pure Nash equilibrium in potential games is PLS complete.

Theorem 19.14 *Finding a pure Nash equilibrium in potential games, where best response can be computed in polynomial time, is PLS complete.*

PROOF We have argued that finding a pure Nash equilibrium in such games is in PLS. To see that the problem is PLS complete, we use a reduction from the weighted satisfiability problem. Consider a weighted satisfiability instance with k variables $x_1, \ldots, x_k$, and n clauses $C_1, \ldots, C_n$ with weight w_j for clause C_j. Our congestion game will have one player for each variable, and one resource for each clause. Player i, associated with variable x_i, has two possible strategies: it can either select the set of resources S_i consisting of all clauses that contain the term x_i, or $\bar{S}_i$, which includes all clauses containing the term $\bar{x}_i$. Selecting S_i corresponds to setting x_i to *false*, while selecting $\bar{S}_i$ corresponds to setting x_i to *true*.

The main observation is that a clause C_j with k_j literals is false if and only if the corresponding element has congestion k_j. Let C_j be a clause with k_j literals and weight w_j. We define the congestion cost of the element j corresponding to the clause C_j as $c_j(\xi) = 0$ if $\xi < k_j$ and $c_j(k_j) = w_j$. For the strategy vector corresponding to the truth assignment s, the potential function has value $\Phi(s) = \sum_j c_j(\xi_j)$, where ξ_j is the number of false literals in C_j. The weight of assignment s is exactly $\Phi(s)$, and thus the equilibria of this game are precisely the local optima of the satisfiability problem. □

19.3.5 Variations on Sharing in the Global Connection Game

We now return to our motivating example, the global connection game. By definition, this game requires that the cost of any built edge be shared equally among all players using that edge. This sharing rule is natural, arguably fair, and as we have seen, implies a number of nice properties. But is this really the best possible sharing rule? Could perhaps another sharing rule induce even better outcomes? We can view this question as a problem of mechanism design, although here we use the term more broadly than in Chapter 9; instead of seeking to elicit "truthful" behavior, we simply want to guarantee that stable outcomes exist and are reasonably efficient.

If we want to design games to induce better outcomes, we must first decide to what extent we will allow ourselves, as mechanism designers, to alter the game. After all, suppose that we define a game in which players receive a large penalty for taking any path that does not conform with a particular optimal solution. Such a game has pure equilibria, and the price of anarchy is trivially 1. But intuitively, this is not a satisfying solution; this game is too restrictive and fails to capture the decentralized spirit of our earlier network formation games. Therefore, our first hurdle is to specify the class of "reasonable" games that are open for consideration.

To this end, Chen et al. (2006) introduce the class of *cost-sharing games*. This class includes the global connection game, as well as similar games with other cost-sharing rules. A cost-sharing game is played on a graph with edge costs and terminals s_i, t_i for each player i. A strategy for player i is an $s_i - t_i$ path. Given a strategy vector S, cost shares are assigned to players on an edge-by-edge basis as specified by a *cost-sharing method* ξ_e for each edge e. In particular, if S_e is the set of players whose path includes e under S, then $\xi_e(i, S_e) \geq 0$ is cost share assigned to i for e. The total cost incurred by player i is the sum of i's cost shares. We require that any cost-sharing method satisfy two basic properties:

- Fairness: For all i, e we have $\xi_e(i, S_e) = 0$ if $i \notin S_e$.
- Budget-balance: For all e we have $\sum_i \xi_e(i, S_e) = c_e$.

A *cost-sharing scheme* specifies a cost-sharing method per edge given a network, a set of players, and a strategy vector. This definition allows cost-sharing schemes to make use of global information, and thus we also consider the special case of *oblivious* cost-sharing schemes, in which cost-sharing methods depend only on c_e and S_e. Note that the Shapley network formation game is an oblivious cost-sharing game, with the cost-sharing method $\xi_e(i, S_e) = c_e/|S_e|$ for $i \in S_e$.

We now return to our question regarding the relative efficiency of the Shapley scheme. In particular, we will show that nonoblivious cost-sharing schemes can provide far better guarantees than the Shapley scheme.

Theorem 19.15 *For any undirected network in which all players seek to reach a common sink, there is a nonoblivious cost-sharing scheme for which the price of anarchy is at most 2.*

PROOF We define a nonoblivious cost-sharing scheme for which players at equilibrium may be viewed as having simulated Prim's MST heuristic for approximating a min cost Steiner tree. Since this heuristic is 2-approximation algorithm, such a scheme suffices. More concretely, if t is the common sink, we order players as follows. Let player 1 be a player whose source s_1 is closest to t, let player 2 be a player whose source s_2 is closest to $\{t, s_1\}$, and so on. Define a cost-sharing method that assigns the full cost of e to the player in S_e with the smallest index. Since player 1 pays fully for her path regardless of the other players' choices, at equilibrium player 1 must choose a shortest path from s_1 to t, and inductively, the remaining players effectively simulate Prim's algorithm as well. □

On the other hand, if we restrict our attention to oblivious schemes, Chen, Roughgarden, and Valiant prove that for general networks, we cannot do better than the Shapley cost-sharing scheme in the worst case. More precisely, they argue that any oblivious cost-sharing scheme either fails to guarantee the existence of pure equilibria or has a price of stability that is at least $\mathcal{H}_k$ for some game. Thus we have an answer to our original question; while there may be nonoblivious schemes that perform better than Shapley cost-sharing, no oblivious scheme offers a smaller price of stability in the worst case. See the notes on this chapter (Section 19.5.2) for a brief discussion of research concerning other cost-sharing approaches.

19.4 Facility Location

In the models we have considered so far, players construct networks so as to achieve certain connectivity-based goals. Intuitively, these goals are meant to capture players' desires to provide service for some implicit population of network users. Given this perspective, we might then ask what happens when we instead view players as financially motivated agents; after all, service providers are primarily concerned with maximizing profits, and only maintain networks for this purpose. This suggests a model in which players not only build networks but also charge for usage, while network users spur competition by seeking the cheapest service available.

We will consider here a pricing game introduced by Vetta (2002) that is based on the facility location problem. In the facility location problem, we want to locate k facilities, such as Web servers or warehouses, so as to serve a set of clients profitably. Our focus here will be to understand the effect of selfish pricing on the overall efficiency of the networks that players form.

We first present Vetta's competitive facility location problem, in which players place facilities so as to maximize their own profit. We then show that this facility location game is a potential game, and prove that the price of anarchy for an even broader class of games is small.

19.4.1 The Model

Suppose that we have a set of users that need a service, and k service providers. We assume that each service provider i has a set of possible locations A_i where he can locate his facility.

Define $A = \cup_i A_i$ to be the set of all possible facility locations. For each location $s_i \in A_i$ there is an associated cost c_{js_i} for serving customer j from location s_i. We can think of these costs as associated with edges of a bipartite graph that has all users on one side and all of A on the other, as shown on Figure 19.4. A strategy vector

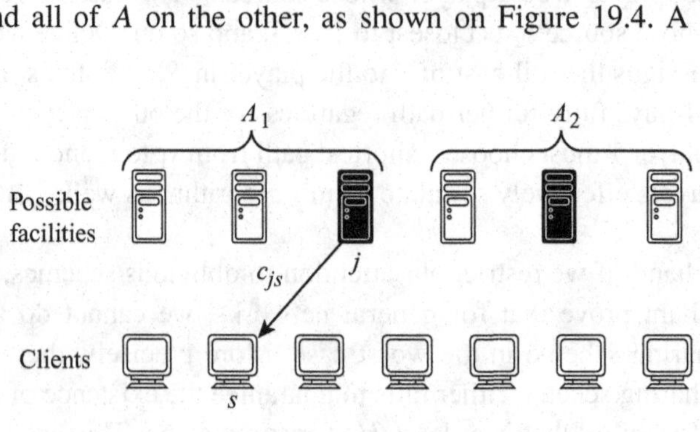

Figure 19.4. The bipartite graph of possible locations and clients. Selected facilities are marked in black.

$s = \{s_1, \ldots, s_k\}$ can be thought of as inducing a subgraph of this graph consisting of the customers and the selected location nodes (marked as black on Figure 19.4).

Our goal is to maximize social welfare, rather than simply minimizing the cost of the constructed network. We assume that customer j has a value π_j for service, and gathers $\pi_j - p$ benefit by receiving service at a price $p < \pi_j$. Locating a facility s_i is free, but that service provider i must pay c_{js_i} to serve client j from location s_i. Doing so generates a profit of $p - c_{js_i}$. If provider i services customer j from location s_i, then this arrangement creates a social value (or surplus) of $\pi_j - c_{js_i}$, the value π_j of service minus the cost c_{js_i} at which the service is provided. Note that this social surplus is independent of the price $p = p_{ij}$ charged; varying p_{ij} simply redistributes welfare between the customer and the provider. We define the *social welfare* $V(S)$ to be the total social value over all providers and customers.

To simplify notation, we assume that $\pi_j \geq c_{js_i}$ for all j, i, and $s_i \in A_i$. To see that this requires no loss of generality, note that decreasing c_{js_i} to be at most π_j does not change the value of any assignment: when $\pi_j < c_{js_i}$ customer j cannot be served from location s_i, while $\pi_j = c_{js_i}$ allows us to serve customer j from location s_i at cost. In either case, the assignment of serving client j from facility s_i results in 0 social value.

To complete the game, we must specify how prices are set and assignments are determined. Given a strategy vector s, we assume that each customer is assigned to a facility that can serve for the lowest cost. The price p_{ij} charged to a customer j using player i's facility s_i is the cost of the second cheapest connection available to j, i.e., $\min_{i' \neq i} c_{js_{i'}}$. Intuitively, this is the highest price i could expect to get away with charging j; charging any more would give some player i' an incentive to undercut i.

Indeed, we can construct an equivalent interpretation of this game in which prices are selected strategically. Consider a three-stage game where both providers and customers are strategic agents. In the first stage, providers select facility locations. In the second stage, providers set prices for users. And, in the last stage, users select a provider for service, and pay the specified price.

As we saw in Chapter 1, subgame perfect equilibrium is a natural solution concept for multistage games. We will use here a further refinement of this concept, the *trembling hand perfect equilibrium* for extensive form games (see Mas-Colell et al., 1995). Assume that with probability $\epsilon > 0$, each player picks a strategy chosen uniformly at random, and chooses a best strategy with the remaining $(1 - \epsilon)$ probability. We use the notion of subgame perfect equilibrium for this ϵ-perturbed game. A *trembling hand perfect equilibrium* is an equilibrium that can be reached as the limit of equilibria in the ϵ-perturbed game as ϵ approaches 0. This stronger notion of stability is required to prevent providers from offering unprofitably low prices and thereby forcing other providers to artificially lower their own prices.

19.4.2 Facility Location as a Potential Game

We start by proving that the facility location game is a potential game.

Theorem 19.16 *The facility location game is a potential game with social value $V(s)$ as the potential function.*

PROOF We need to argue that if a provider i changes her selected location, then the change in social welfare $V(s)$ is exactly the change in the provider's welfare. To show this, we imagine provider i choosing to "drop out of the game" and show that the change in social welfare $V(s)$ is exactly i's profit.

If provider i "drops out," each client j that was served by provider i switches over to his second best choice. Recall that p_{ij} is exactly the cost of this choice. Thus the client will be served at cost p_{ij} rather than c_{js_i}, so the increase in cost is $p_{ij} - c_{js_i}$, exactly the profit provider i gathers from j.

To prove the statement about provider i changing his strategy, we can think of the change in two steps: first the provider leaves the game, and then reenters with a different strategy. The change in social welfare is the difference between the profit of provider i in the two strategies. □

Corollary 19.17 *There exists a pure strategy equilibrium, and furthermore, all efficient outcomes of the facility location game are stable. Thus, the price of stability is 1. Finally, best response dynamics converge to an equilibrium, but this equilibrium may not be socially optimal.*

Our next goal is to prove that the price of anarchy for this facility location game is small. However, it turns out that the proof applies to a much broader class of games, which we present now.

19.4.3 Utility Games

Vetta (2002) introduced the facility location game as one example of a large class of games called *utility games*. In a utility game, each player i has a set of available strategies A_i, which we will think of as locations, and we define $A = \cup_i A_i$. A social welfare function $V(S)$ is defined for all $S \subseteq A$. Observe that welfare is purely a function of the selected locations, as is the case with the facility location game. In defining the socially optimum set, we will consider only sets that contain one location from each strategy set A_i. However, various structural properties of the function $V(S)$ will be assumed for all $S \subseteq A$. For a strategy vector s, we continue to use $V(s)$ as before, and let $\alpha_i(s)$ denote the welfare of player i. A game defined in this manner is said to be a utility game if it satisfies the following three properties.

(i) $V(S)$ is *submodular*: for any sets $S \subset S' \subset A$ and any element $s \in A$, we have $V(S + s) - V(S) \geq V(S' + s) - V(S')$. In the context of the facility location game, this states that the marginal benefit to social welfare of adding a new facility diminishes as more facilities are added.

(ii) The total value for the players is less than or equal to the total social value: $\sum \alpha_i(s) \leq V(s)$.

(iii) The value for a player is at least his added value for the society: $\alpha_i(s) \geq V(s) - V(s - s_i)$.

A utility game is *basic* if property (iii) is satisfied with equality, and *monotone* if for all $S \subseteq S' \subseteq A$, $V(S) \leq V(S')$.

To view the facility location game as a utility game, we consider only the providers as players. We note that the social welfare $V(S) = \sum_j (\pi_j - \min_{a \in S} c_{ja})$ is indeed purely a function of the selected locations.

Theorem 19.18 *The facility location problem is a monotone basic utility game.*

PROOF Property (ii) is satisfied essentially by definition, and we used the equality of property (iii) property in proving Theorem 19.16. To show property (i), notice that adding a new facility decreases the cost of serving some of the clients. The magnitude of this decrease can only become smaller if the clients are already choosing from a richer set of facilities. Finally, adding a facility cannot cause the cost of serving a client to increase, and thus the facility location game is monotone. □

19.4.4 The Price of Anarchy for Utility Games

Since the facility location game is a potential game with the social welfare as the potential function, the price of stability is 1. In fact, this applies for any basic utility game (any utility game with $\alpha_i(s) = V(s) - V(s - s_i)$ for all strategy vectors s and players i). Unfortunately, the increased generality of utility games comes at a cost; these games are not necessarily potential games, and indeed, pure equilibria do not always exist. However, we now show that for monotone utility games that do possess pure equilibria (such as the facility location game), the price of anarchy is at most 2.

Theorem 19.19 *For all monotone utility games the social welfare of any pure Nash equilibrium is at least half the maximum possible social welfare.*

PROOF Let S be the set of facilities selected at an equilibrium, and O be the set of facilities in a socially optimal outcome. We first note that $V(O) \leq V(S \cup O)$ by monotonicity. Let O^i denote the strategies selected by the first i players in the socially optimal solution. That is, $O^0 = \emptyset$, $O^1 = \{o_1\}, \ldots, O^k = O$. Now

$$V(O) - V(S) \leq V(S \cup O) - V(S) = \sum_{i=0}^{n} [V(S \cup O^i) - V(S \cup O^{i-1})].$$

By submodularity (property (i))

$$V(S \cup O^i) - V(S \cup O^{i-1}) \leq V(S + o_i - s_i) - V(S - s_i)$$

for all i. Using property (iii), we can further bound this by $\alpha_i(S + o_i - s_i)$. Since S is an equilibrium, $\alpha_i(S + o_i - s_i) \leq \alpha_i(S)$. Together these yield

$$V(O) - V(S) \leq V(O \cup S) - V(S) \leq \sum_i \alpha_i(S).$$

Finally, property (ii) implies that $\sum_i \alpha_i(S) \leq V(S)$, so $V(O) \leq 2V(S)$, and hence the price of anarchy is at most 2. □

19.4.5 Bounding Solution Quality without Reaching an Equilibrium

For any monotone basic utility game, one can also bound the quality of the solution without assuming that players reach an equilibrium, as was shown in a sequence of two papers by Mirrokni and Vetta (2004) and Goemans et al. (2005).

Theorem 19.20 *Consider an arbitrary solution in a monotone basic utility game. Suppose that at each time step, we select a player at random and make a best response move for that player. For any constant $\epsilon > 0$ the expected social value of the solution after $O(n)$ such moves is at least $1/2 - \epsilon$ times the maximum possible social value.*[1]

PROOF Let S be a state, and O be an socially optimal strategy vector. We will prove that the expected increase in social welfare in one step is at least $\frac{1}{n}(V(O) - 2V(S))$, which implies the claimed bound after $O(n)$ steps.

Let β_i be the maximum possible increase in the value for player i. Thus the expected increase in value is $\frac{1}{n}\sum_i \beta_i$. Selecting strategy o_i is an available move, so $\beta_i \geq \alpha_i(S - s_i + o_i) - \alpha_i(S)$, and by basicness, $\beta_i \geq V(S - s_i + o_i) - V(S - s_i) - \alpha_i(S)$.

The rest of the proof mirrors the price of anarchy proof above. We have

$$V(O) - V(S) \leq \sum_{i=0}^{n} [V(S - s_i + o_i) - V(S - s_i)]$$

as before. We bound $V(S + o_i - s_i) - V(S - s_i) \leq \alpha_i(S) + \beta_i$. Using this with property (ii) yields

$$V(O) - V(S) \leq \sum_i (\alpha_i(S) + \beta_i) \leq V(S) + \sum_i \beta_i.$$

Thus $\sum_i \beta_i \geq V(O) - 2V(S)$, and the expected increase in $V(S)$ is $\frac{1}{n}(V(O) - 2V(S))$. The difference $V(O) - 2V(S)$ is expected to decrease by a factor of $(1 - \frac{2}{n})$ each step. After $n/2$ steps, the difference is expected to decrease by a factor of e, and after $\log(\epsilon^{-1})n$ steps shrinks to an ϵ factor. □

19.5 Notes

19.5.1 Local Connection Game

Network formation games have a long history in the social sciences, starting with the work of Myerson (1977, 1991). A standard example of such games can be found in Jackson and Wolinsky (1996) (see Jackson (2006) for a more comprehensive survey). These network formation games are often used to model the creation of social networks, and aim to capture pairwise relations between individuals who may locally form direct links to one another. In other contexts, these games might model peering relations

[1] The constant in the $O(.)$ notation depends on $\log \epsilon^{-1}$.

between pairs of Autonomous Systems (Johari et al., 2006; Fabrikant et al., 2003), or bilateral contracts between systems as with P2P overlay networks (Chun et al., 2004; Christin et al., 2004). Most network formation games in the economics literature use a bilateral process, in which edges only form between two agents with the consent of both parties, unlike the unilateral process of Section 19.2.

Jackson and Wolinsky (1996) examine the trade-off between efficient and stable networks by studying various network formation games and specifying the conditions under which some (or all) stable outcomes are socially efficient, as done in Section 19.2.2. Section 19.2.3 explores *how* efficient nonoptimal stable outcomes may be.

Corbo and Parkes (2005) study a bilateral variant of local connection game. In the *bilateral network formation game*, two nodes must pay the α cost to form a connecting edge. Thus edges represent bilateral agreements in which players agree to evenly share the edge cost (which is effectively 2α). This contrasts with the unilateral edge formation used in the local connection game. Otherwise, the games are the same; players have the same strategy sets, and evaluate the resulting network in the same manner.

Nash equilibria do not appear to be well-suited for modeling bilateral agreements; for a graph to be stable, we need only ensure that no node wants to drop edges, since a player cannot singlehandedly add an edge. For example, the empty graph is always a Nash equilibrium in the bilateral game, and hence the price of anarchy is very high.

Jackson and Wolinsky (1996) suggest using the notion of *pairwise stable equilibrium*; no user u wants to drop any adjacent edge $e = (u, v)$, and no pair of users u and v wants to add the connecting edge (u, v). This stability concept is closely related to a variant of Nash equilibrium in which we allow coalitions of two players to deviate together (u and v may drop any subset of edges adjacent to them, and possibly add the edge (u, v) connecting them, if this is beneficial to both players). This is the solution concept used in the stable matching problem (see Chapter 10), where the natural deviation for a matching that is not stable is by a "blocking pair": a man and a woman who prefer each other to their current partners.

The optimal network structure is the same as in the unilateral game with edge cost 2α. The proof of Theorem 19.1 can be modified to show that when $\alpha \geq 1$, the star is pairwise stable, and when $\alpha \leq 1$ the complete graph is pairwise stable. Note that in both cases, these networks are also efficient, so the price of stability is 1. One can also extend the bounds of Lemma 19.4 and Theorems 19.5 and 19.6 to bound the quality of a worst pairwise stable equilibrium (see Exercise 19.8).

Andelman et al. (2007) consider the effect of coalitions in the unilateral game. Recall from Chapter 1 that a strong Nash equilibrium is one where no coalition has a joint deviation that is profitable for all members. Andelman et al. show that when $\alpha \in (1, 2)$, there is no stable network resisting deviations by coalitions of size 3, and also that when $\alpha \geq 2$, all strong Nash equilibria have cost at most twice the optimum, i.e., the strong price of anarchy is at most 2.

There are many other natural and relevant variations to the discussed network formation games. One important aspect of the model suggested by Jackson (2006) and Jackson and Wolinsky (1996), is that nodes are not required to reach all other nodes in the network. Instead, node u has a value w_{uv} for connecting to another node v, and this benefit decays exponentially with distance. In this game, pairwise stable equilibria may not be connected.

Chun et al. (2004) introduce a variant of the unilateral network formation game to model overlay networks. They allow the cost incurred by node u for adding a directed edge (u, v) to depend upon v and the degree of v, thereby modeling some congestion effects. The authors also extended the notion of distance beyond hop-count, and consider restricting the set of possible connections available to each player. Using Nash equilibria as their solution concept, they study the quantitative trade-offs between cost, node degree, and path length in an experimental setting. Christin et al. (2004) also use these models, and argue that using approximate (rather than exact) equilibria can improve the predictive power of the model and accommodate small errors in modeling and decision making.

Johari et al. (2006) introduced a related game for modeling bilateral contracts between systems. In this game players form directed edges to carry traffic, and the payments along the links are negotiated, in that players can make offers and demands. Anshelevich et al. (2006) propose a variant of this model with fixed routing that includes both directed links and symmetric peering links, and show that in this model, there exists an efficient solution that is approximately stable in some sense.

Open Problems

We have given a bound of $O(\sqrt{\alpha})$ for the price of anarchy of the local connection game, and improved this bound to $O(1)$ for small α. Also, Albers et al. (2006) proved an $O(1)$ bound for the case $\alpha > 12n \log n$ (see also Exercise 19.7 for the case $\alpha > n^2$). It is an open problem whether a constant bound holds for all values of α.

The local connection game is an extremely simple model of network formation. It would be valuable to understand to what extent the price of anarchy bounds apply to broader classes of games. Albers et al. (2006) extend the price of anarchy bound to games where traffic (which affects distance costs multiplicatively) is not uniform, but edge costs remain uniformly α as before. Unfortunately, these bounds depend on the traffic weights, and are only $O(1)$ when these weights are relatively small ($n^2 w_{\max} \leq \alpha$). Is there a natural characterization of all traffic patterns that support a constant price of anarchy? And, can the price of anarchy results extend to models where edge costs vary over the network?

As mentioned, Christin et al. (2004) argue that approximate equilibria are better models of natural network formation. Can we extend our price of anarchy bounds to approximate equilibria?

So far we have been concerned with the quality of equilibria, and did not consider the network formation process. Does "natural" game play of these local connection games converge to an equilibrium efficiently? Bala and Goyal (2000) show that in their model, game play does converge to an equilibrium in some cases. Is this also true in broader class of games? In cases when natural game play does not converge, or only converges slowly, can one bound the quality of the solution after a "long enough" game play, as we have seen in Section 19.4.5?

The network formation process of Bala and Goyal (2000) is very uniform, and leads to networks with extremely simple structure (such as a cycle, star or wheel).

Newman (2003) and Jackson and Rogers (2006) introduce more complex network-formation process based on a random graph generation process that results in graphs that have a number of real-world network properties, such as the power-law degree distribution, clustering, etc. Unfortunately, this process is exogenous, and not really based on personal incentives. One exciting open challenge is to develop an incentive-based and endogenous model of network formation that generates more heterogenous and realistic networks.

19.5.2 Potential Games and a Global Connection Game

The global connection game is related to a large body of work on cost-sharing (see Feigenbaum et al., 2001; Herzog et al., 1997; and the references therein). Much of this work is not game-theoretic; the network is typically assumed to be fixed, and the goal is to compute cost shares with certain properties. Chapter 15 considers cost sharing in a game-theoretic context by assuming the existence of a central authority who must compute cost shares for nodes, each of which has a private utility for inclusion in the network. Thus, the focus is on developing a cost sharing mechanism that induces nodes to reveal their true valuations.

Our general results for potential games suggest some natural extentions to the global connection game. For example, if we consider the global connection game played on undirected networks, then $\Psi(S)$ is still a potential function. Thus we again have that pure equilibria exist and the price of stability is at most $\mathcal{H}_k$. We can also generalize the global connection game by allowing players to have more than two terminals they wish to connect. In such a game, players would select trees spanning their terminals rather than paths. Again, it is easily verified that $\Psi(S)$ is a potential function, so the same results apply. Furthermore, we assumed that the cost of each edge c_e is independent of the number of users. Consider the case when the cost $c_e(k_e)$ of the edge e depends on the number of players (k_e) that use the edge e. The same analysis also extends to this version, assuming the function $c_e(k_e)$ is concave, that is, the cost exhibits an "economy of scale" property; adding a new user is cheaper when a larger population is using the edge.

Anshelevich et al. (2003) consider an unrestricted variant of the global connection game. In this game, players select not only a path but also cost shares for each edge on that path. If the combined shares for an edge cover its cost, that edge is built. Players are assumed to be unhappy if their path is not fully built, and otherwise aim to minimize their cost shares. This game does not necessarily have pure equilibria, and even when it does, even the price of stability may be $O(k)$. However, in the special case of single source games (all players seek connection to a common terminal), the price of stability is shown to be 1.

Chen and Roughgarden (2006) study a weighted generalization of the global connection game, in which each player has a weight, and costs shares are assigned in proportion to these weights. This turns out not to be a potential game, and further, the authors provide an instance in which no pure equilibrium exists. This paper focuses on finding outcomes that are both approximate equilibria and close to optimal. Another similar weighted game is presented by Libman and Orda (2001), with a different mechanism for distributing costs among users. They do not consider the quality of equilibria, but instead study convergence in parallel networks.

Milchtaich (1996) considers a generalization of congestion games in which each player has her own payoff function. Equilibria are shown to exist in some class of these games even though a potential function may not.

Open Problems

Recall the network shown in Figure 19.3(b), which shows that the price of stability may $\mathcal{H}_k$ for the global connection game. Note, however, that if the edges are undirected, then the price of stability falls to 1. The actual worst-case price of anarchy for undirected graphs remains an open question.

There are a wide variety of cost-sharing schemes, as defined by Chen and Roughgarden (2006), that might be relevant either for practical reasons (such as being more fair), or because they induce better outcomes for certain specific classes of networks. Many such schemes, including weighted fair sharing, do not yield exact potential games. For a large number of these cost-sharing games, the price of anarchy, the price of stability, and even the existence of pure equilibria remain unresolved.

More generally, the class of games we consider aims to model situations where users are building a global shared network and care about global properties of the network they build. Our focus was on requiring connectivity (of a terminal set) and aiming to minimize cost. More generally, it would be valuable to understand which type of utility measures yield games with good price of stability properties. For example, we might consider users who are allowed to leave some terminals unconnected, or who care about other properties of the resulting network, such as distances, congestion, etc.

Potential functions are an important tool in understanding the price of anarchy and stability in games. A recent survey of Roughgarden (2006) shows that one can also understand the price of anarchy analysis of resource allocation problems (see Chapter 21) via the potential function method. Surprisingly, many of the price of anarchy and stability results known to date are for potential games (and their weighted variants); the routing games of Chapter 18, the facility location game of Section 19.4, and the load balancing problems of Chapter 20. In a number of these cases, the analysis of the price of anarchy or stability uses alternative techniques to derive stronger bounds than could have been obtained using the potential function method (e.g., bounding the price of anarchy with multiple equilibria, or analyzing weighted variants of these games). However, one wonders if potential functions still play a role here that we do not fully understand.

19.5.3 Facility Location Game

There is a large body of literature dedicated to understanding the effects of pricing in games. Much of this work focuses on establishing the existence of equilibria, and considering qualitative properties of equilibria (such as whether improved service leads to improved profit, or if selfish pricing leads to socially efficient outcomes).

Our focus with the facility location game is to understand the effect of selfish pricing on the overall efficiency of a network. In many settings, selfish pricing leads to a significant reduction in social welfare, and may also yield models with no pure equilibria. An example of this issue is the pricing game of Example 8 in Chapter 1.

See also Chapter 22 for a discussion of these issues in the context of communication networks.

Our price of anarchy bound requires that social welfare be monotone in the set of facilities selected. It is natural to try to extend this game to a scenario in which facilities cost money: in addition to paying the service cost c_{js_i} for servicing a client j from a facility s_i, the provider also pays an installation cost $f(s_i)$ for building at s_i. Unfortunately, there is no constant bound for the price of anarchy for this case. See Exercise 19.17, which observes that when investment costs are large, noncooperative players do not always make the right investments, and thus equilibria may be far from optimal.

Utility games defined in Section 19.4.3 have a wide range of applications, including routing (Vetta, 2002) (see Exercise 19.18), and a market sharing game introduced by Goemans et al. (2006) in the context of content distribution in ad-hoc networks (see Exercises 19.16 for a special case).

In Section 19.4 we bounded the price of anarchy only for pure equilibria. Recall, however, that general utility games may not have pure equilibria. Theorem 19.19 bounding the quality of equilibria also holds for mixed equilibria (Vetta, 2002) and thus is applicable in a much broader context.

Section 19.4.5 showed that in basic utility games, we can bound the quality of solutions without reaching an equilibrium. Such bounds would be even more valuable for general utility games, as these might not have any pure equilibria. Goemans et al. (2005) provide such bounds for a few other games, including some routing games. Unfortunately, the quality of a solution in a general utility game can be very low even after infinitely long game play, as shown by Mirrokni and Vetta (2004).

Open Problems

Many pricing games fail to have Nash equilibria (Example 8 from Chapter 1) and others have equilibria with very low social value (high price of anarchy and stability). The facility location games give a class of examples where pure Nash equilibria exist, and the price of anarchy is small. It would be great to understand which other classes of pricing games share these features.

It will also be extremely important to understand which other classes of games admit good-quality bounds after limited game play, as shown in Section 19.4.5 for facility location games.

Acknowledgments

We thank Ramesh Johari, Tim Roughgarden, Elliot Anshelevich, and Vahab Mirrokni for their valuable comments and suggestions on an early draft of this chapter.

Bibliography

A. Albers, S. Eilts, E. Even-Dar, Y. Mansour, and L. Roditty. On Nash equilibria for a network creation game. In *Proc. ACM-SIAM Symp. Discrete Algorithms*, pp. 89–98, 2006.

N. Andelman, M. Feldman, and Y. Mansour. Strong Price of Anarchy. In *Proc. ACM-SIAM Symp. on Discrete Algorithms*, 2007.

E. Anshelevich, A. Dasgupta, J. Kleinberg, Tardos, T. Wexler, and T. Roughgarden. The price of stability for network design with fair cost allocatio. In *Proc. IEEE Symp. on Fdns. of Computer Science*, pp. 295–304, 2004.

E. Anshelevich, A. Dasgupta, E. Tardos, and T. Wexler. Near-optimal network design with selfish agents. In *Proc. ACM Symp. Theory of Computing*, pp. 511–520, 2003.

E. Anshelevich, B. Shepherd, and G. Wilfong. Strategic network formation through peering and service agreements. In *Proc. IEEE Symp. on Fdns. of Computer Science*, 2006.

V. Bala and S. Goyal. A Noncooperative Model of Network Formation. *Econometrica* 68(5):1181–1229, 2000.

H.-L. Chen and T. Roughgarden. Network design with weighted players. In *Proc. ACM Symp. on Parallel Algorithms and Architecture*, pp. 29–38, 2006.

H.-L. Chen, T. Roughgarden, and G. Valiant. *Designing Networks with Good Equilibria*, unpublished manuscript, 2006.

N. Christin, J. Grossklags, and J. Chuang. Near rationality and competitive equilibria in networked systems. In *ACM SIGCOMM'04 Workshop on Practice and Theory of Incentives in Networked Systems (PINS)*, August 2004.

B.-G. Chun, R. Fonseca, I. Stoica, and J. Kubiatowicz. Characterizing selfishly constructed overlay networks. In *Proc. IEEE INFOCOM'04*, Hong Kong, March 2004.

J. Corbo and D. Parkes. The price of selfish behavior in bilateral network formation. In *Proc. ACM Symp. Princ. of Distributed Systems*, pp. 99–107, 2005.

A. Fabrikant, A. Luthra, E. Maneva, C. Papadimitriou, and C. Shenker, On a network creation game. In *Proc. ACM Symp. Princ. of Distributed Systems*, pp. 247–351, 2003.

A. Fabrikant, C. Papadimitriou, and K. Talwar. The complexity of pure nash equilibria. In *Proc. ACM Symp. of Theory of Computing*, pp. 604–612, 2004.

J. Feigenbaum, C. Papadimitriou, and S. Shenker. Sharing the cost of multicast transmissions. *J. Comp. and Syst. Sci.*, 63:21–41, 2001.

M. Goemans, L. Li, V. Mirrokni, and M. Thottan. Market sharing games applied to content distribution in ad-hoc networks. In *Proc. ACM Intl. Symp. on Mobile Ad Hoc Networking and Computing*, pp. 1020–1033, 2004.

M. Goemans, V. S. Mirrokni, and S. Vetta. Sink Equilibria and Convergence. In *Proc. IEEE Symp. Fdns. of Comp. Sci.*, pp. 142–154, 2005.

S. Herzog, S. Shenker, and D. Estrin. Sharing the "Cost" of multicast trees: An axiomatic analysis. *IEEE/ACM Trans. on Networking*, Dec. 1997.

M. Jackson. A survey of models of network formation: Stability and efficiency. In G. Demange and M. Wooders (eds), *Group Formation Economics: Networks, Clubs and Coalitions*. Cambridge University Press, Cambridge, UK, in press.

M. Jackson and B. Rogers. Meeting strangers and friends of friends: How random are social networks. In press. *Amer. Econ. Rev.*, 2006.

M. Jackson and A. Wolinsky. A strategic model of social and economic networks. *J. Econ. Theory*, 71(1):44–74, 1996.

R. Johari, S. Mannor, and J. N. Tsitsiklis. A contract-based directed network formation. *Games Econ. Behav.*, 56:201–224, 2006.

D.S. Johnson, C.H. Papadimitriou, and M. Yannakakis. How easy is local search? *J. Computer System Sci.*, 37:79–100, 1988.

M.W. Krentel. Structure in locally optimal solutions. In *Proc. IEEE Fdns. of Comp. Sci.*, pp. 216–221, 1989.

L. Libman and A. Orda. Atomic resource sharing in noncooperative networks. *Telecommunication Systems*, 17:4, 385–409, 2001.

H. Lin. *On the Price of Anarchy of a Network Creation Game*. Unpublished Manuscript December 2003.

A. Mas-Colell, M.D. Whinston and J. R.Green *Microeconomic Theory*. Oxford University Press, 1995.

I. Milchtaich. Congestion games with player-specific payoff functions. *Games Econ. Behav.*, 111–124, 1996.

V.S. Mirrokni and A. Vetta. Convergence issues in competitive games. In *Proc. APPROX 2004*.

V.S. Mirrokni and S. Vetta. Convergence issues in competitive games. In *International Workshop on Approximation Algorithms for Combinatorial Optimization Problems (APPROX)*, Springer, 2004.

D. Monderer and L. Shapley. Potential games. *Games Econ. Behav.*, 14:124–143, 1996.

H. Moulin and S. Shenker. Strategyproof sharing of submodular costs: Budget balance versus efficency. *Econ. Theory*, 18:511–533, 2001.

R.B. Myerson. Graphs and cooperative games. *Math. Operat. Res.*, 2(3), 1977.

R.B. Myerson. *Game Theory: Analysis of Conflict*. Harvard University Press, 1991.

M. Newman. The structure and function of complex networks. *SIAM Review*, 45:167–256, 2003.

R.W. Rosenthal. A class of games possessing pure-strategy Nash equilibria. *Intl. J. Game Theory*, 2:65–67, 1973.

T. Roughgarden. Potential functions and the inefficiency of equilibria. In *Proc. Intl. Congress of Mathematicians (ICM)*, 2006.

A. Vetta. Nash equilibria in competitive societies, with applications to facility location, traffic routing and auctions. In *Proc. IEEE Symp. on Fdns. of Computer Science*, pp. 416–425, 2002.

Exercises

19.1 Consider the local connection game from Section 19.2. In Lemma 19.1, we saw that the star is an optimal solution for $\alpha \geq 2$, and the complete graph is an optimal solution for $\alpha \leq 2$. Prove that if $\alpha \neq 2$, then these are in fact the only optimal solutions.

19.2 Give a complete characterization of all optimal networks for $\alpha = 2$.

19.3 Show that when $\alpha < 1$ the complete graph is the only equilibrium.

19.4 Show that a sufficiently long path cannot be a Nash equilibrium of the local connection game from Section 19.2.

19.5 Show that any path can be a pairwise stable network for a large enough value of α in the bilateral network formation game introduced in Section 19.5.1.

19.6 Construct a Nash equilibrium that is not a star for $\alpha > 2$.

19.7 Show that when $\alpha > n^2$ all Nash equilibria of the local connection game are trees and the price of anarchy is bounded by a constant.

19.8 Prove that the bounds of Lemma 19.4 and Theorems 19.5 and 19.6 are also valid for the worst possible quality of a pairwise stable equilibria of the bilateral version of the game (where an edge needs to be selected, and paid for by both endpoints to be included in G).

19.9 Prove that in the global connection game, the price of anarchy can never exceed k, the number of players.

19.10 Consider the following weighted generalization of the global connection game. For each player i, we have a weight $w_i > 0$. As before, each player selects a single path connecting her source and sink. But instead of sharing edge costs equally, players are now assigned cost shares in proportion to their weight. In particular, for a strategy vector S and edge e, let S_e denote those players whose path contains e, and let $W_e = \sum_{i \in S_e} w_i$ be the total weight of these players. Then player i pays $c_e w_i / W_e$ for each edge $e \in P_i$. Note that if all players have the same weight, this is the original game. Show that, in general, this game does not have an exact potential function.

19.11 In the global network formation game, edge costs reflect fixed building expenses, and thus each player's share for an edge e decreases as more players use e. We might also consider a model with the opposite behavior, i.e., a model in which the cost of using e increases with the number of players. This would be more appropriate for modeling latency or similar effects that make congestion undesirable.

Consider a game played on a network G with k players. Player i has a source s_i and a sink t_i. Each edge $e \in G$ also has a nondecreasing latency function $\ell_e(x)$, indicating the cost incurred by *each* player on e if there are x of these players. A strategy for i is a path from s_i to t_i, and choosing a path P_i incurs a total cost of

$$\text{cost}(P_i) = \sum_{e \in P_i} \ell_e(k_e),$$

where k_e is the number of players using e.

(a) Prove that this game has an exact potential function.

(b) Suppose that we also give each player i an integral weight $w_i \geq 1$.

A strategy for i is a multiset S_i of w_i paths from s_i to t_i. Notice that we do not insist that these paths be disjoint, or even distinct. Costs are now assigned in a natural way; we first compute the cost that each individual path would be charged if each corresponded to a distinct player. Then each player i is charged the sum of the costs of all paths in S_i. Prove that if the latency functions $\ell_e(x)$ are linear for all e, then this game has an exact potential function.

(c) Show that if $\ell_e(x)$ is not linear, then there may not be an exact potential function.

19.12 One problem with using best response dynamics to find pure equilibria in potential games such as the global connection game is that the running time may be exponential. One natural way to deal with this problem is to run best response dynamics, but to consider only moves that provide a substantial decrease in the potential function. In particular, for a constant $\epsilon > 0$, we say a best response move is *substantial* if it decreases the potential function by at least an ϵ/k fraction of its current value. We consider the process of making substantial best response moves until none are available.

(a) Prove that this process terminates in time that is polynomial in n, k, and $\log(\epsilon^{-1})$.

(b) Show that the resulting outcome is not necessarily an approximate equilibrium. That is, show that there may be players who can decrease their costs by an arbitrarily large factor.

19.13 Suppose that we have a game G and a function $\Phi(S)$ mapping game states to reals with the following property: for any strategy vectors $S = (S_1, S_2, \ldots, S_k)$, and any alternate strategy $S'_i \neq S_i$ for some player i, then if $S' = (S_{-i}, S'_i)$, we have that $\Phi(S) - \Phi(S')$ and $u_i(S') - u_i(S)$ share the same sign. Thus $\Phi(S)$ behaves like an exact potential function, except instead of tracking a player's improvement exactly, it simply tracks the direction of the improvement; when a player makes an improving move, the potential function decreases. We call such a function an *ordinal potential function*, and G an *ordinal potential game*.

(a) Prove that if G is an ordinal potential game, then best response dynamics always converge to a Nash equilibrium.

(b) Prove that the converse is also true; if, from any starting configuration, best response dynamics always converge to an equilibrium, then G is an ordinal potential game.

19.14 Give an example of the global connection game for which the best Nash equilibrium does not minimize the potential function Ψ.

19.15 Prove that any congestion game is an exact potential game.

19.16 Consider the following location game. We have an unweighted, undirected network G and k players. Each player selects a node in G as their location. Each node v has one unit of wealth that it uniformly distributes to all players in $N[v]$, the closed neighborhood of v. If there are no players in $N[v]$, this wealth is lost. For example, if v has neighbors u and x, 2 players locate at v, 3 players locate at u, and no one locates at x, then v awards $1/5$ to each of these 5 players. The utility of a player is simply the sum of the value awarded to it by all nodes. We define the social utility of this game as the number of nodes that have at least one player located in their closed neighborhood.

(a) Prove that the price of anarchy of this game can be arbitrarily close to 2.

(b) Prove that this location game is a valid utility game.

19.17 In theorem 19.19 we showed that if the facilities cost 0, then the social welfare of any Nash equilibrium is at least 1/2 of the maximum possible social welfare of any solution. In this problem, we consider a variant where facilities cost money; each possibly facility s_i has a cost $f(s_i)$, to be paid by a player who locates a facility at s_i.

(a) Is the same bound on the quality of a Nash equilibrium also true for the variant of this game that facilities cost money? Prove or give an example where it is not true.

(b) Let F denote the total facility cost of at a Nash equilibrium S, i.e., the sum $\sum_{s_i \in S} f_{s_i}$. Show that we can bound the optimum $V(O)$ by $2V(S) + F$.

19.18 We now consider a variant of the selfish routing game of Chapter 18 with k players. We have a graph G and a delay function $\ell_e(x)$ that is monotone increasing and convex for each edge $e \in E$. Player i has a source s_i and a destination t_i, and must select an $s_i - t_i$ path P_i on which to route 1 unit of traffic. Player i will tolerate up to d_i delay. Player i picks a path from s_i to t_i with minimum delay, or no path at all if this delay exceeds d_i.

(a) Show that this game always has a pure (deterministic) Nash equilibrium.

(b) The traditional way to evaluate such routing games is with the sum of all delays as cost. However, in this version, the cost may be low simply because few players get routed. Thus we can instead consider the value gathered by each player; d_i minus the delay incurred if i does route her traffic, and 0 if she doesn't. By definition, all players routed have nonnegative value. The total value of a solution is simply the sum of player values. Show that this is a utility game.

(c) Is this game a monotone utility game?

CHAPTER 20

Selfish Load Balancing

Berthold Vöcking

Abstract

Suppose that a set of weighted tasks shall be assigned to a set of machines with possibly different speeds such that the load is distributed evenly among the machines. In computer science, this problem is traditionally treated as an optimization problem. One of the classical objectives is to minimize the *makespan*, i.e., the maximum load over all machines. Here we study a natural game theoretic variant of this problem: We assume that the tasks are managed by selfish agents, i.e., each task has an agent that aims at placing the task on the machine with smallest load. We study the Nash equilibria of this game and compare them with optimal solutions with respect to the makespan. The ratio between the worst-case makespan in a Nash equilibrium and the optimal makespan is called the *price of anarchy*. In this chapter, we study the price of anarchy for such load balancing games in four different variants, and we investigate the complexity of computing equilibria.

20.1 Introduction

The problem of load balancing is fundamental to networks and distributed systems. Whenever a set of tasks should be executed on a set of resources, one needs to balance the load among the resources in order to exploit the available resources efficiently. Often also fairness aspects have to be taken into account. Load balancing has been studied extensively and in many variants. One of the most fundamental load balancing problems is *makespan scheduling on uniformly related machines*. This problem is defined by m *machines* with speeds $s_1, \ldots, s_m$ and n *tasks* with weights $w_1, \ldots, w_n$. Let $[n] = \{1, \ldots, n\}$ denote the set of tasks and $[m] = \{1, \ldots, m\}$ the set of machines. One seeks for an assignment $A : [n] \rightarrow [m]$ of the tasks to the machines that is as balanced as possible. The *load* of machine $j \in [m]$ under assignment A is defined as

$$\ell_j = \sum_{\substack{i \in [n] \\ j = A(i)}} \frac{w_i}{s_j}.$$

The *makespan* is defined to be the maximum load over all machines. The objective is to minimize the makespan. If all machines have the same speed, then the problem is known as *makespan scheduling on identical machines*, in which case we shall assume $s_1 = s_2 = \cdots = s_m = 1$.

In computer science, load balancing is traditionally viewed as an algorithmic problem. We design and analyze algorithms, either centralized or distributed, that compute the mapping A. Suppose, however, there is no global authority that can enforce an efficient mapping of the tasks to the machines. For example, in a typical Internet application, tasks might correspond to requests for downloading large files that users send to servers. To maximize the quality of service, each of the users aims at contacting a server with smallest load. This naturally leads to the following game theoretic setting in which we will be able to analyze what happens to the makespan if there is no global authority but selfish users aiming at maximizing their individual benefit decide about the assignment of tasks to machines.

This chapter differs from the other chapters in Part III of this book in two important aspects. At first, the considered objective function, the makespan, is nonutilitarian. At second, our analysis does not only consider pure but also mixed equilibria. By using the makespan as objective function, our analysis simultaneously captures the aspects of efficiency and fairness. By considering mixed equilibria, our analysis explicitly takes into account the effects of uncoordinated random behavior.

20.1.1 Load Balancing Games

We identify agents and tasks, i.e., task $i \in [n]$ is managed by agent i. Each agent can place its task on one of the machines. In other words, the set of *pure strategies* for an agent is $[m]$. A combination of pure strategies, one for each task, yields an assignment $A : [n] \to [m]$. We assume that the *cost* of agent i under the assignment A corresponds to the load on machine $A(i)$, i.e., its cost is $\ell_{A(i)}$. The *social cost* of an assignment is denoted $\text{cost}(A)$ and is defined to be the makespan, i.e., $\text{cost}(A) = \max_{j\in[m]} (\ell_j)$.

Agents may use *mixed strategies*, i. e., probability distributions on the set of pure strategies. Let p_i^j denote the probability that agent i assigns its task to machine j, i.e., $p_i^j = \mathbb{P}[A(i) = j]$. A *strategy profile* $P = (p_i^j)_{i\in[n], j\in[m]}$ specifies the probabilities for all agents and all machines. Clearly, every strategy profile P induces a random mapping A. For $i \in [n]$, $j \in [m]$, let x_i^j be a random variable that takes the value 1 if $A(i) = j$ and 0, otherwise. The expected load of machine j under the strategy profile P is thus

$$\mathbb{E}[\ell_j] = \mathbb{E}\left[\sum_{i\in[n]} \frac{w_i\, x_i^j}{s_j}\right] = \sum_{i\in[n]} \frac{w_i\, \mathbb{E}[x_i^j]}{s_j} = \sum_{i\in[n]} \frac{w_i\, p_i^j}{s_j}.$$

The *social cost of a strategy profile* P is defined as the expected makespan, i.e.,

$$\text{cost}(P) = \mathbb{E}[\text{cost}(A)] = \mathbb{E}\left[\max_{j\in[m]} (\ell_j)\right].$$

We assume that every agent aims at minimizing its expected cost. From point of view of agent i, the expected cost on machine j, denoted by c_i^j, is $c_i^j = \mathbb{E}[\ell_j \mid A(i) = j]$.

For any profile P,

$$c_i^j = \frac{w_i + \sum_{k \neq i} w_k \, p_k^j}{s_j} = \mathbb{E}[\ell_j] + (1 - p_i^j) \cdot \frac{w_i}{s_j}. \qquad (20.1)$$

In general, a strategy profile of a game is a *Nash equilibrium* if there is no incentive for any agent to unilaterally change its strategy. For the load balancing game, such a profile is characterized by the property that every agent assigns positive probabilities only to those machines that minimize its expected cost. This is formalized as follows.

Proposition 20.1 *A strategy profile P is a Nash equilibrium if and only if $\forall i \in [n] : \forall j \in [m] : p_i^j > 0 \Rightarrow \forall k \in [m] : c_i^j \leq c_i^k$.*

The existence of a Nash equilibrium in mixed strategies is guaranteed by the theorem of Nash, see Chapters 1 and 2. A strategy profile P is called *pure* if, for each agent, there exists only one machine with positive probability. A Nash equilibrium in pure strategies is called a *pure Nash equilibrium*. Applying the proposition above to pure profiles and the corresponding assignments yields the following characterization of a pure Nash equilibrium.

Proposition 20.2 *An assignment A is a pure Nash equilibrium if and only if $\forall i \in [n] : \forall k \in [m] : c_i^{A(i)} \leq c_i^k$.*

In words, an assignment is a pure Nash equilibrium if and only if no agent can improve its cost by unilaterally moving its task to another machine. A special property of load balancing games is that they always admit pure Nash equilibria.

Proposition 20.3 *Every instance of the load balancing game admits at least one pure Nash equilibrium.*

PROOF An assignment A induces a *sorted load vector* $(\lambda_1, \ldots, \lambda_m)$, where λ_j denotes the load on the machine that has the j-th highest load. If an assignment is not a Nash equilibrium, then there exists an agent i that can perform an *improvement step*, i.e., it can decrease its cost by moving its task to another machine. We show that the sorted load vector obtained after performing an improvement step is lexicographically smaller than the one preceding it. Hence, a pure Nash equilibrium is reached after a finite number of improvement steps.

Suppose, given any sorted load vector $(\lambda_1, \ldots, \lambda_m)$, agent i performs an improvement step and moves its task from machine j to machine k where the indices are with respect to the positions of the machines in the sorted load vector. Clearly, $k > j$. The improvement step decreases the load on machine j and it increases the load on machine k. However, the increased load on machine k is smaller than λ_j as, otherwise, agent i would not decrease its cost. Hence, the number of machines with load at least λ_j is decreasing. Furthermore, the loads on all other machines with load at least λ_j are left unchanged. Consequently, the improvement step yields a sorted load vector i.e. lexicographically smaller than $(\lambda_1, \ldots, \lambda_m)$. □

Thus improvement steps naturally lead to a pure Nash equilibrium. This issue is also discussed for a broader class of games, so-called potential games, in Chapter 19. Let us remark that this convergence result implies that there exists even a pure Nash equilibrium that minimizes the makespan. Given any optimal assignment, such an equilibrium can be found by performing improvement steps until a Nash equilibrium is reached because improvement steps do not increase the makespan. Thus, for load balancing games with social cost equal to the makespan, it does not make much sense to study the ratio between the social cost in a best Nash equilibrium and the optimal social cost. This ratio is called the "price of stability." It is studied in Chapters 17–19 in the context of other games. In this chapter, we are mainly interested in the ratio between the social cost of the worst Nash equilibrium and the optimal social cost, the so-called the "price of anarchy."

20.1.2 Example of a Load Balancing Game

Suppose that there are two identical machines both of which have speed 1 and four tasks, two *small tasks* of weight 1 and two *large tasks* of weight 2. An optimal assignment would map a small and a large task to each of the machines so that the load on both machines is 3. This assignment is illustrated in Figure 20.1(a).

Now consider an assignment A that maps the two large tasks to the first machine and the two small tasks to the second machine as illustrated in Figure 20.1(b). This way, the first machine has a load of 4 and the second machine has a load of 2. Obviously, a small task cannot improve its cost by moving from the second to the first machine. A large task cannot improve its cost by moving from the first to the second machine either as its cost would remain 4 if it does. Thus assignment A constitutes a pure Nash equilibrium with $\text{cost}(A) = 4$. Observe that all assignments that yield a larger makespan than 4 cannot be a Nash equilibrium as, in this case, one of the machines has a load of at least 5 and the other has a load of at most 1 so that moving any task from the former to the latter would decrease the cost of this task. Thus, for this instance of the load balancing game, the social cost of the worst pure Nash equilibrium is 4.

Clearly, the worst mixed equilibrium cannot be better than the worst pure equilibrium as the set of mixed equilibria is a superset of the set of pure equilibria, but can it really be worse? Suppose that each task is assigned to each of the machines with probability

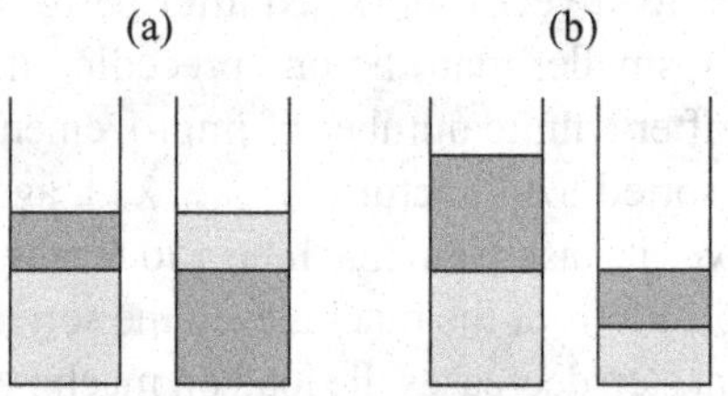

Figure 20.1. (a) Illustration of the optimal assignment of an instance of the load balancing game with two large tasks of size 2 and two small tasks of size 1 as described in the example given in Section 20.1.2. The social cost of this assignment is 3. (b) Illustration of a pure Nash equilibrium for the same instance. The social cost of this assignment is 4, which is the maximum among all pure Nash equilibria for this instance.

$\frac{1}{2}$. This corresponds to a strategy profile P with $p_i^j = \frac{1}{2}$ for $1 \leq i \leq 4, 1 \leq j \leq 2$. The expected load on machine j is thus

$$\mathbb{E}[\ell_j] = \sum_{1 \leq i \leq 4} w_i \, p_i^j = 2 \cdot 2 \cdot \frac{1}{2} + 2 \cdot 1 \cdot \frac{1}{2} = 3.$$

It is important to notice that the expected cost of a task on a machine is larger than the expected load of the machine, unless the task is assigned with probability 1 to this machine. For example, if we assume that task 1 is a large task then Equation 20.1 yields

$$c_1^1 = \mathbb{E}[\ell_1] + (1 - p_1^1)\, w_1 = 3 + \frac{1}{2} \cdot 2 = 4,$$

and, if task 3 is a small task, then

$$c_3^1 = \mathbb{E}[\ell_1] + (1 - p_3^1)\, w_3 = 3 + \frac{1}{2} \cdot 1 = 3.5.$$

For symmetry reasons, the expected cost of each task under the considered strategy profile P is the same on both machines so that P is a Nash equilibrium. The social cost of this Nash equilibrium, cost(P), is defined to be the expected makespan, $\mathbb{E}[\text{cost}(A)]$, of the random assignment A induced by P. The makespan, cost(A), is a random variable. This variable can possibly take one of the four values 3, 4, 5, or 6. There are $2^4 = 16$ different assignments of four tasks to two machines. The number of assignments that yield a makespan of 3 is 4, 4 is 6, 5 is 4, and 6 is 2. Consequently, the social cost of the mixed Nash equilibrium is

$$\text{cost}(P) = \mathbb{E}[\text{cost}(A)] = \frac{1}{16}\,(3 \cdot 4 + 4 \cdot 6 + 5 \cdot 4 + 6 \cdot 2) = 4.25.$$

Thus mixed equilibria can, in fact, be worse than the worst pure equilibrium.

20.1.3 Definition of the Price of Anarchy

Not surprisingly, the example above shows that uncoordinated, selfish behavior can lead to suboptimal assignments. We are interested in the ratio between the social cost (makespan) of a worst-case Nash equilibrium, i.e., the Nash equilibrium with highest social cost, and the social cost of an optimal assignment.

Definition 20.4 (Price of anarchy) For $m \in \mathbb{N}$, let $\mathcal{G}(m)$ denote the set of all instances of load balancing games with m machines. For $G \in \mathcal{G}(m)$, let Nash(G) denote the set of all strategy profiles being a Nash equilibrium for G, and let opt(G) denote the minimum social cost over all assignments. Then the price of anarchy is defined by

$$\text{PoA}(m) = \max_{G \in \mathcal{G}(m)} \max_{P \in \text{Nash(G)}} \frac{\text{cost}(P)}{\text{opt}(G)}.$$

In the following, we study the price of anarchy in load balancing games in four different variants in which we distinguish, as a first criterion, between games with identical and uniformly related machines and, as a second criterion, between pure

Nash equilibria and mixed Nash equilibria. Technically, when considering the price of anarchy for load balancing games with identical machines then we restrict the set $\mathcal{G}(m)$ to instances in which the m machines have all the same speed. When considering the price of anarchy with respect to pure equilibria then the set Nash(G) refers only to pure Nash equilibria rather than mixed equilibria; i.e., we take the maximum only among pure equilibrium assignments rather than among possibly mixed equilibrium strategy profiles.

The motivation behind studying the price of anarchy is to quantify the increase of the social cost due to selfish behavior. With this motivation in mind, does it make more sense to consider pure or mixed equilibria? If one wants to study a distributed system in which agents repeatedly perform improvement steps until they reach a Nash equilibrium, then pure equilibria are the right solution concept. However, there might be other means by which agents come to a Nash equilibrium. In particular, if one views load balancing games as one shot games, then mixed equilibria are a very reasonable solution concept. Moreover, upper bounds about the price of anarchy for mixed equilibria are more robust than upper bounds for pure equilibria as mixed equilibria are more general than pure ones. In this chapter, we consider both of these equilibrium concepts. Our analysis begins with the study of pure equilibria as they are usually easier to handle than mixed equilibria whose analysis requires a bit of probability theory.

20.2 Pure Equilibria for Identical Machines

Our analysis of equilibria in load balancing games begins with the most basic case, namely the study of pure equilibria on identical machines. Our first topic is the price of anarchy. As a second topic, we investigate how long it takes until a pure Nash equilibrium is reached when the agents repeatedly perform "best response" improvement steps.

20.2.1 The Price of Anarchy

In case of pure equilibria and identical machines, the analysis of the price of anarchy is quite similar to the well-known analysis of the greedy load balancing algorithm that assigns the tasks one after the other in arbitrary order giving each task to the least loaded machine. Graham (1966) has shown that the approximation factor of the greedy algorithm is $2 - \frac{1}{m}$. We show that the price of anarchy for pure equilibria is, in fact, slightly better than the approximation factor of the greedy algorithm.

Theorem 20.5 *Consider an instance G of the load balancing game with n tasks of weight $w_1, \ldots, w_n$ and m identical machines. Let $A : [n] \to [m]$ denote any Nash equilibrium assignment. Then, it holds that*

$$cost(A) \leq \left(2 - \frac{2}{m+1}\right) \cdot opt(G).$$

PROOF Let j^* be a machine with the highest load under assignment A, and let i^* be a task of smallest weight assigned to this machine. Without loss of generality, there are at least two tasks assigned to machine j^* as, otherwise, $\text{cost}(A) = \text{opt}(G)$ so that the upper bound given in the theorem follows trivially. Thus $w_{i^*} \leq \frac{1}{2}\text{cost}(A)$.

Suppose there is a machine $j \in [n] \setminus \{j^*\}$ with load less than $\ell_{j^*} - w_{i^*}$. Then moving the task i^* from j^* to j would decrease the cost for this task. Hence, as A is a Nash equilibrium, it holds

$$\ell_j \geq \ell_{j^*} - w_{i^*} \geq \text{cost}(A) - \frac{1}{2}\text{cost}(A) = \frac{1}{2}\text{cost}(A).$$

Now observe that the cost of an optimal assignment cannot be smaller than the average load over all machines so that

$$\begin{aligned}\text{opt}(G) &\geq \frac{\sum_{i\in[n]} w_i}{m}\\ &= \frac{\sum_{j\in[m]} \ell_j}{m}\\ &\geq \frac{\text{cost}(A) + \frac{1}{2}\text{cost}(A)(m-1)}{m}\\ &= \frac{(m+1)\text{cost}(A)}{2m}.\end{aligned}$$

As a consequence,

$$\text{cost}(A) \leq \frac{2m}{m+1}\cdot \text{opt}(G) = \left(2 - \frac{2}{m+1}\right)\cdot \text{opt}(G).$$

□

Observe that the example of a game instance with two identical machines given in Section 20.1.2 has a price of anarchy of $\frac{4}{3} = 2 - \frac{2}{m+1}$, for $m = 2$. Exercise 20.2 generalizes this example. It shows that, for every $m \in \mathbb{N}$, there exists an instance G of the load balancing game with m identical machines and $2m$ tasks that has a Nash equilibrium assignment $A\colon [n] \to [m]$ with

$$\text{cost}(A) = \left(2 - \frac{2}{m+1}\right)\cdot \text{opt}(G).$$

Thus the upper bound on the price of anarchy given in Theorem 20.5 is tight.

20.2.2 Convergence Time of Best Responses

Our analysis about the price of anarchy leaves open the question of how agents may find or compute a Nash equilibrium efficiently. In the existence proof for pure equilibria in Proposition 20.3, we have implicitly shown that every sequence of improvement steps by the agents leads to a Nash equilibrium. However, if players do not converge to an equilibrium in reasonable time, then it might also not matter if the finally reached equilibrium is good. This naturally leads to the question of how many improvement steps are needed to reach a Nash equilibrium. The following result shows that, in case of identical machines, there is a short sequence of improvement steps that leads from any given initial assignment to a pure Nash equilibrium. An agent is said to be *satisfied* if it cannot reduce its cost by unilaterally moving its task to another machine. The *max-weight best response policy* activates the agents one after the other always activating an agent with maximum weight among the unsatisfied agents. An activated agent plays a *best response*; i.e., the agent moves its task to the machine with minimum load.

Theorem 20.6 *Let $A : [n] \rightarrow [m]$ denote any assignment of n tasks to m identical machines. Starting from A, the max-weight best response policy reaches a pure Nash equilibrium after each agent was activated at most once.*

PROOF We claim, once an agent $i \in [n]$ was activated and played its best response, it never gets unsatisfied again. This claim immediately implies the theorem. Our analysis starts with two observations both of which holding only for identical machines. At first, we observe that an agent is satisfied if and only if its task is placed on a machine on which the load due to the other tasks is minimal. At second, we observe that a best response never decreases the minimum load among the machines. As a consequence, a satisfied agent can get unsatisfied only for one reason: the load on the machine holding its task increases because another agent moves its task to the same machine. Suppose that agent k is activated after agent i, and it moves its task to the machine holding task i. Let j^* denote the machine on which i is placed and to which k is moved. For $j \in [m]$, let ℓ_j denote the load on machine j at the time immediately after the best response of agent k. Since the assignment of k to j^* is a best response and as $w_k \leq w_i$ because of the max-weight policy, it follows

$$\ell_{j^*} \leq \ell_j + w_k \leq \ell_j + w_i,$$

for all $j \in [m]$. Hence, after the best response of k, agent i remains satisfied on machine j^* as it cannot reduce its cost by moving from j^* to any other machine. □

Let us remark that the order in which the agents are activated is crucial. For example, if one would always activate an agent of minimum weight among the unsatisfied agents, then there are instances of load balancing games on identical machines where one needs an exponential number of best response steps to reach a pure Nash equilibrium (Even-Dar et al., 2003).

20.3 Pure Equilibria for Uniformly Related Machines

We now switch from identical to uniformly related machines. First, we study the price of anarchy. Then we discuss the complexity of computing equilibria.

20.3.1 The Price of Anarchy

The analysis in Section 20.2.1 shows that, in case of identical machines, the makespan of a pure Nash equilibrium is less than twice the optimal makespan. In this section, we

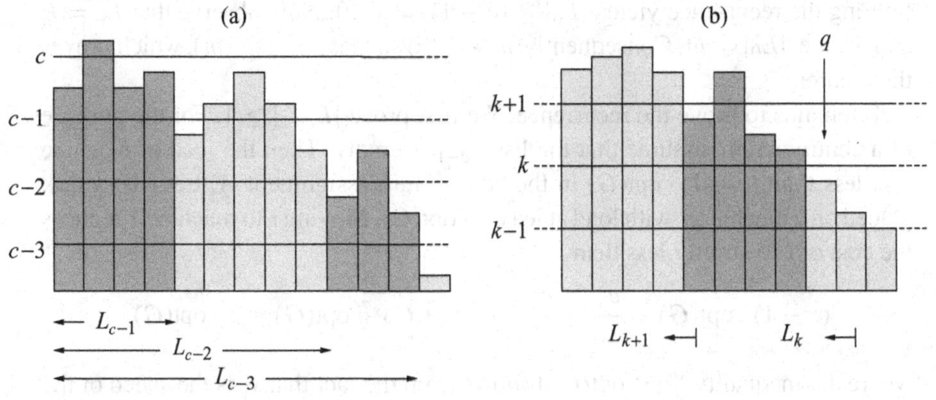

Figure 20.2. (a) Illustration of the definition of the lists $L_{c-1}, L_{c-2}, \ldots, L_0$ from the proof of Theorem 20.7. (b) Illustration of the lists L_k and L_{k+1} and the machine q used in the proof of Lemma 20.8.

show that the makespan of pure equilibria on uniformly related machines can deviate by more than a constant factor. The price of anarchy is bounded, however, by a slowly growing function in the number of machines. Our analysis begins with an upper bound on the price of anarchy followed by the presentation of a family of game instances that match this upper bound up to a small constant factor.

Theorem 20.7 *Consider an instance G of the load balancing game with n tasks of weight $w_1, \ldots, w_n$ and m machines of speed $s_1, \ldots, s_m$. Let $A : [n] \to [m]$ denote any Nash equilibrium assignment. Then, it holds that*

$$\mathit{cost}(A) = \mathcal{O}\left(\frac{\log m}{\log \log m}\right) \cdot \mathit{opt}(G).$$

PROOF Let $c = \lfloor \mathrm{cost}(A)/\mathrm{opt}(G) \rfloor$. We show $c \leq \Gamma^{-1}(m)$, where Γ^{-1} denotes the inverse of the *gamma function*, an extension of the factorial function with the property that $\Gamma(k) = (k-1)!$, for every positive integer k. This yields the theorem as

$$\Gamma^{-1}(m) = \Theta\left(\frac{\log m}{\log \log m}\right).$$

Without loss of generality, let us assume $s_1 \geq s_2 \geq \cdots \geq s_m$, and let $L = [1, 2, \ldots, m]$ denote the list of machines in nonincreasing order of speed. For $k \in \{0, \ldots, c-1\}$, let L_k denote the maximum length prefix of L such that the load of each server in L_k is at least $k \cdot \mathrm{opt}(G)$. Figure 20.2(a) illustrates this definition. We will show the following recurrence on the lengths of these lists.

$$|L_k| \geq (k+1) \cdot |L_{k+1}| \qquad (0 \leq k \leq c-2)$$
$$|L_{c-1}| \geq 1$$

Solving the recurrence yields $|L_0| \geq (c-1)! = \Gamma(c)$. Now observe that $L_0 = L$ and, hence, $|L_0| = m$. Consequently, $m \geq \Gamma(c)$ so that $c \leq \Gamma^{-1}(m)$, which proves the theorem.

It remains to prove the recurrence. We first prove $|L_{c-1}| \geq 1$. For the purpose of a contradiction, assume that the list L_{c-1} is empty. Then the load of machine 1 is less than $(c-1) \cdot \text{opt}(G)$ in the equilibrium assignment A. Let i be a task placed on a machine j with load at least $c \cdot \text{opt}(G)$. Moving i to machine 1 reduces the cost of i to strictly less than

$$(c-1) \cdot \text{opt}(G) + \frac{w_i}{s_1} \leq (c-1) \cdot \text{opt}(G) + \text{opt}(G) \leq c \cdot \text{opt}(G),$$

where the inequality $\frac{w_i}{s_1} \leq \text{opt}(G)$ follows from the fact that s_1 is the speed of the fastest machine. Consequently, agent i is able to unilaterally decrease its cost by moving its task from machine j to machine 1, which contradicts the assumption that A is a Nash equilibrium. Thus, we have shown that $|L_{c-1}| \geq 1$.

Next, we show $|L_k| \geq (k+1) \cdot |L_{k+1}|$, for $0 \leq k \leq c-2$. Let A^* be an optimal assignment, i.e., an assignment whose makespan is equal to opt(G). The following lemma relates the placement of tasks in the equilibrium assignment A to the placement of tasks in the optimal assignment A^*.

Lemma 20.8 *Suppose i is a task with $A(i) \in L_{k+1}$. Then $A^*(i) \in L_k$.*

PROOF If $L \setminus L_k = \emptyset$ then this claim follows trivially. Let q be the smallest index in $L \setminus L_k$, i.e., machine q is one of the machines with maximum speed among the machines $L \setminus L_k$. By the definition of the group L_k, the load of q is less than $k \cdot \text{opt}(G)$, i.e., $\ell_q < k \cdot \text{opt}(G)$. Figure 20.2(b) illustrates the situation.

By the definition of the groups, $A(i) \in L_{k+1}$ implies $\ell_{A(i)} \geq (k+1) \cdot \text{opt}(G)$. For the purpose of a contraction, assume $w_i \leq s_q \cdot \text{opt}(G)$. Then moving task i to machine q would reduce the cost of i to

$$\ell_q + \frac{w_i}{s_q} < k \cdot \text{opt}(G) + \text{opt}(G) \leq \ell_{A(i)},$$

which contradicts the assumption that A is a Nash equilibrium. Hence, every task i with $A(i) \in L_{k+1}$ satisfies $w_i > s_q \cdot \text{opt}(G)$. Now, for the purpose of a contradiction, suppose $A^*(i) = j$ and $j \in L \setminus L_k$. Then the load on j under A^* would be at least

$$\frac{w_i}{s_j} > \frac{s_q \cdot \text{opt}(G)}{s_j} \geq \text{opt}(G)$$

because $s_j \leq s_q$. However, this contradicts that A^* is an optimal assignment. Consequently, $A^*(i) \in L_k$. □

By the definition of L_{k+1}, the sum of the weights that A assigns to a machine $j \in L_{k+1}$ is at least $(k+1) \cdot \text{opt}(G) \cdot s_j$. Hence, the total weight assigned to the machines in L_{k+1} is at least $\sum_{j \in L_{k+1}} (k+1) \cdot \text{opt}(G) \cdot s_j$. By Lemma 20.8 an optimal assignment has to assign all this weight to the machines in L_k such that the load on each of these machines is at most opt(G). As a consequence,

$$\sum_{j\in L_{k+1}} (k+1)\cdot \text{opt}(G)\cdot s_j \le \sum_{j\in L_k} \text{opt}(G)\cdot s_j .$$

Dividing by opt(G) and subtracting $\sum_{j\in L_{k+1}} s_j$ from both sides yields

$$\sum_{j\in L_{k+1}} k\cdot s_j \le \sum_{j\in L_k\setminus L_{k+1}} s_j .$$

Now let s^* denote the speed of the slowest machine in L_{k+1}, i.e., $s^* = s_{|L_{k+1}|}$. For all $j \in L_{k+1}$, $s_j \ge s^*$, and, for all $j \in L_k \setminus L_{k+1}$, $s_j \le s^*$. Hence, we obtain

$$\sum_{j\in L_{k+1}} k\cdot s^* \le \sum_{j\in L_k\setminus L_{k+1}} s^*,$$

which implies $|L_{k+1}|\cdot k \le |L_k \setminus L_{k+1}| = |L_k| - |L_{k+1}|$. Thus, $|L_k| \ge (k+1)\cdot |L_{k+1}|$. This completes the proof of Theorem 20.7. □

We now prove a lower bound showing that the upper bound on the price of anarchy given in Theorem 20.7 is essentially tight.

Theorem 20.9 *For every $m \in \mathbb{N}$, there exists an instance G of the load balancing game with m machines and $n \le m$ tasks that has a Nash equilibrium assignment $A : [n] \to [m]$ with*

$$cost(A) = \Omega\left(\frac{\log m}{\log\log m}\right)\cdot opt(G).$$

PROOF Recall the definition of the gamma function from the proof of Theorem 20.7. We describe a game instance G together with an equilibrium assignment A satisfying

$$\text{cost}(A) \ge \frac{1}{2}\cdot\left(\Gamma^{-1}(m) - 2 - o(1)\right)\cdot \text{opt}(G),$$

which yields the theorem.

Our construction uses $q+1$ disjoint groups of machines denoted $G_0,\ldots,G_q$ with $q \approx \Gamma^{-1}(m)$. More, precisely, we set

$$q = \lfloor \Gamma^{-1}(m/3) - 1\rfloor \ge \Gamma^{-1}(m) - 2 - o(1).$$

For $0 \le k \le q$, group G_k consists of $q!/k!$ machines of speed 2^k each of which is assigned k tasks of weight 2^k. Let us remark that $0! = 1$. The total number of machines in these groups is thus

$$\sum_{k=0}^{q} |G_k| = q!\sum_{k=0}^{q}\frac{1}{k!} \le 3\,\Gamma(q+1) \le m$$

because $\sum_{k=0}^{q}\frac{1}{k!} \le 3$ and $3\Gamma(q+1) \le m$, which follows directly from the definition of q. As m might be larger than the number of the machines in the groups, there might be some machines that do not belong to any of the groups. We assume that these machines have the same parameters as the machines in group G_0; i.e., they have speed $2^0 = 1$ and A does not assign a tasks to them.

We need to show that the described assignment is a Nash equilibrium. An agent with a task on a machine from group G_k has cost k. It can neither reduce its cost by moving its task to a machine in group G_j with $j \geq k$ as these machines have at least a load of k, nor can it reduce its cost by moving its task to a machine in group G_j with $j < k$ as the load on such a machine, after the task moved to this machine, would be

$$j + \frac{2^k}{2^j} = j + 2^{k-j} \geq j + (k - j + 1) = k + 1$$

since $2^t \geq t + 1$, for every $t \geq 1$. Hence, none of the agents can unilaterally decrease its cost. In other words, A is a Nash equilibrium.

The social cost of the equilibrium assignment A is q. Next we show that $\text{opt}(G) \leq 2$ so that the theorem follows. We construct an assignment with load at most 2 on every machine. For each $k \in \{1, \ldots, q\}$, the tasks mapped by A to the machines in group G_k are now assigned to the machines in group G_{k-1}. Observe that the total number of tasks that A maps to the machines in G_k is

$$k \cdot |G_k| = k \cdot \frac{q!}{k!} = \frac{q!}{(k-1)!} = |G_{k-1}|.$$

Hence, we can assign the tasks in such a way that each machine in group G_{k-1} receives exactly one of the tasks that A mapped to a machine in group G_k. This task has a weight of 2^k and the speed of the machine is 2^{k-1}. Hence, the load of each machine in this assignment is at most 2, which completes the proof. □

20.3.2 Algorithms for Computing Pure Equilibria

The proof of Proposition 20.3 reveals that, starting from any initial assignment, a pure Nash equilibrium is reached after a finite number of improvement steps. Theorem 20.6 shows that there exists a sequence of improvement steps of length $O(n)$ in case of identical machines and this sequence can be computed efficiently. However, in the case of uniformly related machines, it is not known whether there always exists a short sequence of improvement steps and whether such a sequence can be efficiently computed like in the case of identical machines. However, the well-known *LPT (largest processing time)* scheduling algorithm allows us to efficiently compute a Nash equilibrium. This algorithm inserts the tasks in a nonincreasing order of weights, assigning each task to a machine that minimizes the cost of the task at its insertion time.

Theorem 20.10 *The LPT algorithm computes a pure Nash equilibrium for load balancing games on uniformly related machines.*

PROOF Let the tasks be numbered from 1 to n in the order of their insertion. Let *time* $t \in \{0, \ldots, n\}$ denote the point of time after the first t tasks have been inserted. We show by an induction that the partial assignment $A : [t] \to [m]$ computed by LPT at time t is a Nash equilibrium. By our induction assumption the tasks $1, \ldots, t-1$ are *satisfied* at time $t-1$; i.e., none of these tasks can improve its cost by a unilateral deviation. When task t is inserted, it might be mapped to a machine $j^* \in [m]$ that holds already some other tasks. We only have to show that these tasks do not get unsatisfied because of the increased load on j^* because of the assignment of task t. Let $i < t$ be one of the tasks mapped to machine j^*. For $j \in [m]$, let ℓ_j denote the load on machine j at time t. Since the assignment of task t to machine j^* minimizes the cost of agent t and as $w_t \leq w_i$,

$$\frac{\ell_{j^*}}{s_{j^*}} \leq \frac{\ell_j + w_t}{s_j} \leq \frac{\ell_j + w_i}{s_j},$$

for all $j \in [m]$. Hence, also at time t, agent i is satisfied on machine j^* as it cannot reduce its cost by moving from j^* to another machine. □

The assignment computed by the LPT algorithm is not only a Nash equilibrium but it also approximates the optimal makespan within a ratio of at most $\frac{5}{3}$ for uniformly related machines and $\frac{4}{3} - \frac{1}{3m}$ for identical machines, see Friesen (1987) and Graham (1966), respectively. As makespan scheduling is NP-hard even on identical machines, one cannot hope for an efficient algorithm that computes an assignment with optimal makespan, unless P $\neq$ NP. However, the polynomial time approximation scheme of Hochbaum and Shmoys (1988) computes an assignment of tasks to uniformly related machines minimizing the makespan within a ratio of $(1+\epsilon)$, for any given $\epsilon > 0$. This assignment is not necessarily a Nash equilibrium. Feldmann et al. (2003a) present an efficient algorithm that transforms any given assignment into an equilibrium assignment without increasing the makespan. This approach is called *Nashification*. Combining the polynomial time approximation scheme with the Nashification approach yields a polynomial time algorithm that computes an equilibrium assignment for scheduling on uniformly related machines minimizing the makespan within a factor of $(1+\epsilon)$, for any given $\epsilon > 0$.

20.4 Mixed Equilibria on Identical Machines

The example with two identical machines presented in Section 20.1.2 shows that the social cost can increase if players make use of randomization. Let us now study this effect systematically. We analyze by how much the price of anarchy is increased when the set of strategies is extended from pure to mixed strategies. First, we consider an extreme case of randomization in which every agent randomizes over all strategies.

20.4.1 Fully Mixed Equilibria

The *support* of an agent is the set of strategies to which the agent assigns positive probability. In a *fully mixed strategy profile* all pure strategies are in the support of every agent. There is exactly one fully mixed strategy profile for load balancing games on identical machines i.e. a Nash equilibrium. In this *fully mixed Nash equilibrium* every player assigns every task with probability $\frac{1}{m}$ to each of the machines, i.e., $P = (p_i^j)$ with $p_i^j = \frac{1}{m}$, for every $i \in [n]$ and $j \in [m]$. The fully mixed Nash equilibrium maximizes the randomization and, hence, seems to be a good candidate to study the effects of randomization.

Our analysis begins with a particularly simple class of load balancing games: Suppose that we have not only identical machines but also identical tasks. That is, we assume that there are m machines of speed 1 and n tasks of weight 1. In the unique fully mixed Nash equilibrium for such a game, each task is assigned to each machine with probability $\frac{1}{m}$. This strategy profile is a Nash equilibrium as the expected cost c_i^j of any task i on any machine j is the same. In particular, Equation 20.1 yields

$$c_i^j = \mathbb{E}[\ell_j] + \left(1 - \frac{1}{m}\right) = 2 - \frac{1}{m}.$$

This setup corresponds to a well-studied balls-and-bins experiment from probability theory in which n balls are assigned independently, uniformly at random to m bins, which is also discussed in Chapter 17. How bad is such a fully mixed Nash equilibrium in comparison to an optimal assignment that distributes the tasks evenly among the machines? An optimal assignment minimizes the makespan, and the optimal makespan is obviously $\lceil \frac{n}{m} \rceil$. The expected makespan of the fully mixed strategy profile corresponds to the expected *maximum occupancy* of the corresponding balls-and-bins experiment, i.e., the expected number of balls in the fullest bin. The following proposition yields a simple formula for this quantity that is exact up to constant factors for any choice of m and n.

Proposition 20.11 *Suppose that $n \geq 1$ balls are placed independently, uniformly at random into $m \geq 1$ bins. Then the expected maximum occupancy is*

$$\Theta\left(\frac{\ln m}{\ln\left(1 + \frac{m}{n} \ln m\right)}\right)$$

Let us illustrate the formula for the expected maximum occupancy given in the proposition with a few examples. If $n \geq m \log m$, then the expected maximum occupancy is $\Theta(\frac{n}{m})$ as, in this case, $\ln\left(1 + \frac{m}{n} \ln m\right) = \Theta\left(\frac{m}{n} \ln m\right)$. If $n \leq m^{1-\epsilon}$, for any fixed $\epsilon > 0$, then the expected maximum occupancy is $\Theta(1)$. Observe, in both of these cases, the ratio between the expected makespan for the fully mixed equilibrium and the makespan of an optimal assignment is $O(1)$. It turns out that this ratio is maximized when setting $m = n$. In this case, the expected maximum occupancy is $\Theta(\log m / \log\log m)$ while the optimal makespan is 1. This yields the following result.

Theorem 20.12 *For every $m \in \mathbb{N}$, there exists an instance G of a load balancing game with m identical machines and $n = m$ tasks that has a Nash equilibrium strategy profile P with*

$$\mathit{cost}(P) = \Omega\left(\frac{\log m}{\log\log m}\right) \cdot \mathit{opt}(G).$$

As the fully mixed Nash equilibrium is the equilibrium that maximizes the randomization, one could guess that this is also the equilibrium that maximizes the ratio between the expected makespan and the optimal makespan for load balancing games. This guess is known as the so-called *fully mixed Nash equilibrium conjecture*. This conjecture is appealing as it would yield a simple characterization of the worst-case Nash equilibrium for load balancing games. Unfortunately, however, the conjecture is wrong. With the help of Proposition 20.11, we can easily construct a counterexample. Let $m = 2^{2k}$, for some $k \in \mathbb{N}$. This way, $\sqrt{m}$ as well as $\log m$ are integers. Now consider the following instance of the load balancing game on m identical machines. Suppose that there are $\sqrt{m}$ *large tasks* of weight 1, and $(m - \sqrt{m}) \cdot \log m$ *small tasks* of weight $\frac{1}{\log m}$. The balls-and-bins analysis above shows that the maximum number of large tasks that are assigned to the same machine by a fully mixed Nash equilibrium is $O(1)$, and the maximum number of small tasks assigned to the same machine is $O(\log m)$. Hence, the expected makespan of the fully mixed Nash equilibrium is $O(1)$. Now consider the following strategy profile: Assign the large tasks uniformly at random to the first $\sqrt{m}$ machines (called group A) and the small tasks uniformly at random to the other machines (called group B). This profile is a Nash equilibrium as Equation 20.1 yields that, for a large task, the expected cost on a machine of group A is less than the expected cost on a machine of group B and, for a small task, the expected cost on a machine of group B is less than the expected cost on a machine of group A. In this equilibrium, the expected maximum occupancy among the large tasks is $\Theta(\frac{\log m}{\log\log m})$, which shows that there is a mixed Nash equilibrium whose expected makespan is larger than the expected makespan of the fully mixed Nash equilibrium by a factor of $\Omega(\frac{\log m}{\log\log m})$.

20.4.2 Price of Anarchy

The fully mixed Nash equilibrium is not necessarily the worst-case Nash equilibrium for every instance of the load balancing game on identical machines. Nevertheless, the following analysis shows that the lower bound on the price of anarchy that we obtained from studying this kind of equilibria is tight.

Theorem 20.13 *Consider an instance G of the load balancing game with n tasks of weight $w_1, \ldots, w_n$ and m identical machines. Let $P = (p_i^j)_{i\in[n], j\in[m]}$ denote any Nash equilibrium strategy profile. Then, it holds that*

$$cost(P) = \mathcal{O}\left(\frac{\log m}{\log\log m}\right) \cdot opt(G).$$

PROOF Without loss of generality, we assume that all machines have speed 1. Recall that $\text{cost}(P) = \mathbb{E}[\max_{j\in[m]}(\ell_j)]$, i.e., $\text{cost}(P)$ corresponds to the expected maximum load over all machines or, in other words, the expected makespan. Our analysis starts with proving an upper bound on the maximum expected load instead of the expected maximum load.

We claim that, for every $j \in [m]$, $\mathbb{E}[\ell_j] \leq (2 - \frac{2}{m+1})\,\text{opt}(G)$. The proof for this claim follows the course of the analysis for the upper bound on the price of anarchy for pure equilibria. More specifically, the proof of Theorem 20.5 can be adapted as follows to mixed equilibria: Instead of considering a smallest weight task i^* placed on a maximum load machine j^*, one defines i^* to be the smallest weight task with positive probability on a machine j^* maximizing the expected load. Also in all other occurrences one considers the expected load instead of the load.

We conclude that the maximum expected load is less than $2\,\mathrm{opt}(G)$. Next we show that the expected maximum load deviates at most by a factor of $\mathcal{O}(\frac{\log m}{\log\log m})$ from the maximum expected load. We use a weighted Chernoff bound in order to show that it is unlikely that there is a machine that deviates by a large factor from its expectation.

Lemma 20.14 (weighted Chernoff bound) *Let $X_1, \ldots, X_N$ be independent random variables with values in the interval $[0, z]$ for some $z > 0$, and let $X = \sum_{i=1}^N X_i$, then for any t it holds that $\mathbb{P}[\sum_{i=1}^N X_i \geq t] \leq (e \cdot \mathbb{E}[X]\,/\,t)^{t/z}$.*

A description how to derive this and other variants of the Chernoff bound can be found, e.g., in Mitzenmacher and Upfal (2005).

Fix $j \in [m]$. Let w denote the largest weight of any task. Applying the weighted Chernoff bound shows that, for every t,

$$\mathbb{P}[\ell_j \geq t] \leq \min\left\{1, \left(\frac{e \cdot \mathbb{E}[\ell_j]}{t}\right)^{t/w}\right\} \leq \left(\frac{2\,e\,\mathrm{opt}(G)}{t}\right)^{t/\mathrm{opt}(G)},$$

because $\mathbb{E}[\ell_j] \leq 2\,\mathrm{opt}(G)$ and $w \leq \mathrm{opt}(G)$. Now let $\tau = 2\,\mathrm{opt}(G)\,\frac{\ln m}{\ln\ln m}$. Then, for any $x \geq 0$,

$$\begin{aligned}\mathbb{P}[\ell_j \geq \tau + x] &\leq \left(\frac{e \ln\ln m}{\ln m}\right)^{2\ln m/\ln\ln m + x/\mathrm{opt}(G)} \\ &\leq \left(\frac{1}{\sqrt{\ln m}}\right)^{2\ln m/\ln\ln m} \cdot e^{-x/\mathrm{opt}(G)} \\ &= m^{-1} \cdot e^{-x/\mathrm{opt}(G)},\end{aligned}$$

where the second inequality holds asymptotically as, for sufficiently large m, $\frac{\ln m}{e \ln\ln m} \geq \sqrt{\log m}$ and $\frac{\ln m}{e\ln\ln m} \geq e$.

Now with the help of the tail bound we can upper-bound $\mathrm{cost}(P)$ as follows. For every nonnegative random variable X, $\mathbb{E}[X] = \int_0^\infty \mathbb{P}[X \geq t]dt$. Consequently,

$$\mathrm{cost}(P) = \mathbb{E}\Big[\max_{j\in[m]} \ell_j\Big] = \int_0^\infty \mathbb{P}\Big[\max_{j\in[m]} \ell_j \geq t\Big]dt\,.$$

Substituting t by $\tau + x$ and then applying the union bound yields

$$\mathrm{cost}(P) \leq \tau + \int_0^\infty \mathbb{P}\Big[\max_{j\in[m]} \ell_j \geq \tau + x\Big]\,dx \leq \tau + \int_0^\infty \sum_{j\in[m]} \mathbb{P}[\ell_j \geq \tau + x]\,dx\,.$$

Finally, we apply the tail bound derived above and obtain

$$\text{cost}(P) \leq \tau + \int_0^{\infty} e^{-x/\text{opt}(G)} dx = \tau + \text{opt}(G),$$

which yields the theorem as $\tau = 2\,\text{opt}(G)\,\frac{\ln m}{\ln \ln m}$. □

20.5 Mixed Equilibria on Uniformly Related Machines

Finally, we come to the most general case, namely mixed equilibria on uniformly related machines. The following theorem shows that the price of anarchy for this case is only slightly larger than the one for mixed equilibria on identical machines or pure equilibria on uniformly related machines. The analysis combines the methods from both of these more restricted cases: First, we show that the maximum expected makespan is bounded by

$$\mathcal{O}\left(\frac{\log m}{\log \log m}\right) \cdot \text{opt}(G)$$

using the same kind of arguments as in the analysis of the price of anarchy for pure equilibria on uniformly related machines. Then, as in the case of mixed equilibria on identical machines, we use a Chernoff bound to show that the expected maximum load is not much larger than the maximum expected load. In fact, this last step loses only a factor of order $\log \log m / \log \log \log m$, which results in an upper bound on the price of anarchy of

$$\mathcal{O}\left(\frac{\log m}{\log \log \log m}\right).$$

After proving this upper bound, we present a corresponding lower bound by adding some randomization to the lower bound construction for pure equilibria on uniformly related machines, which increases also the lower bound by a factor of order $\log \log m / \log \log \log m$ and, hence, yields a tight result about the price of anarchy.

Theorem 20.15 *Consider an instance G of the load balancing game with n tasks of weight $w_1, \ldots, w_n$ and m machines of speed $s_1, \ldots, s_m$. Let P be any Nash equilibrium strategy profile. Then, it holds that*

$$cost(P) = \mathcal{O}\left(\frac{\log m}{\log \log \log m}\right) \cdot opt(G).$$

PROOF As in the case of identical machines, our analysis starts with proving an upper bound on the maximum expected load instead of the expected maximum load. To simplify the notation, we assume $\text{opt}(G) = 1$, which can be achieved by scaling the weights appropriately. Let $c = \lfloor \max_{j \in [m]} (\mathbb{E}[\ell_j]) \rfloor$. We first prove an upper bound on c following the analysis for pure Nash equilibria in Theorem 20.7. Without loss of generality, assume $s_1 \geq s_2 \geq \cdots \geq s_m$. Let $L = [1, 2, \ldots, m]$ denote the list of machines in non increasing order of speed. For $k \in \{0, \ldots, c - 1\}$, let L_k denote the maximum length prefix of L such that the expected load of each server in L_k is at least k. Analogously to the analysis in the proof of Theorem 20.7, one shows the recurrence $|L_k| \geq (k+1) \cdot |L_{k+1}|$, for $0 \leq k \leq c-2$, and $|L_{c-1}| \geq 1$. Solving the recurrence yields $|L_0| \geq (c-1)! = \Gamma(c)$. Thus, $|L_0| = m$ implies $c \leq \Gamma^{-1}(m) = \Theta(\ln m / \ln \ln m)$. Now let

$$C = \max\left\{c+1, \frac{\ln m}{\ln \ln m}\right\} = \Theta\left(\frac{\ln m}{\ln \ln m}\right).$$

In the rest of the proof, we show that the expected makespan of the equilibrium assignment can exceed C at most by a factor of order $\ln \ln m / \ln \ln \ln m$ so that the expected makespan is $\mathcal{O}(\ln m / \ln \ln \ln m)$, which proves the theorem as we assume $\mathrm{opt}(G) = 1$.

As the next step, we prove a tail bound on ℓ_j, for any fixed $j \in [m]$ and, afterward, we use this tail bound to derive an upper bound on the expected makespan. For a machine $j \in [m]$, let $T_j^{(1)}$ denote the set of tasks i with $p_i^j \geq \frac{1}{4}$ and $T_j^{(2)}$ the set of tasks i with $p_i^j \in (0, \frac{1}{4})$. Let $\ell_j^{(1)}$ and $\ell_j^{(2)}$ denote random variables that describe the load on link j only taking into account the tasks in $T_j^{(1)}$ and $T_j^{(2)}$, respectively. Observe that $\ell_j = \ell_j^{(1)} + \ell_j^{(2)}$. For the tasks in $T_j^{(1)}$, we immediately obtain

$$\ell_j^{(1)} \leq \sum_{i \in T_j^{(1)}} \frac{w_i}{s_j} \leq 4 \sum_{i \in T_j^{(1)}} \frac{w_i \, p_i^j}{s_j} = 4\,\mathbb{E}[\ell_j^{(1)}] \leq 4C. \qquad (20.2)$$

To prove an upper bound on $\ell_j^{(2)}$, we use the weighted Chernoff bound from Lemma 20.14. This bound requires an upper bound on the maximum weight. As a first step to bound the weights, we prove a result about the relationship between the speeds of the machines in the different groups that are defined by the prefixes. For $0 \leq k \leq c-2$, let $G_k = L_k \setminus L_{k+1}$, and let $G_{c-1} = L_{c-1}$. For $0 \leq k \leq c-1$, let $s(k)$ denote the speed of the fastest machine in G_k. Clearly, $s(c-1) \geq s(c-2) \geq \cdots \geq s(1) \geq s(0)$. We claim that this sequence is, in fact, geometrically decreasing.

Lemma 20.16 *For $0 \leq k \leq c-4$, $s(k+2) \geq 2\,s(k)$.*

PROOF To prove the claim, we first observe that there exists a task j^* with $w_{j^*} \leq s(k+2)$ that has positive probability on a machine in L_{k+3}. This is because an optimal assignment strategy has to move some of the expected load from the machines in L_{k+3} to machines in $L \setminus L_{k+3}$ and it can only assign those tasks to machines in $L \setminus L_{k+3}$ whose weights are not larger than the maximum speed among this set of machines, which is $s(k+2)$. Now suppose $s(k) > \frac{1}{2}s(k+2)$. The expected load of the fastest machine in $G_k = L_k \setminus L_{k+1}$ is at most $k+1$. Thus the expected cost of j^* on the fastest machine in G_k is at most

$$k+1+\frac{w_{j^*}}{s(k)} < k+1+\frac{2w_{j^*}}{s(k+2)} \leq k+3.$$

This contradicts that the expected cost of j^* in the considered Nash equilibrium is at least $k+3$ as it has positive probability on a machine in L_{k+3}. Thus, Lemma 20.16 is shown. □

Now we apply Lemma 20.16 to prove an upper bound on the weights of the tasks in the set $T_j^{(2)}$.

Lemma 20.17 *For every $j \in [m]$ and $i \in T_j^{(2)}$, $w_i \leq 12\, s_j$.*

PROOF Let i be a task from $T_j^{(2)}$, i.e., $p_i^j \in (0, \frac{1}{4})$. Let $j \in G_k$, for $0 \leq k \leq c-1$. The expected cost of i on j is

$$c_i^j = \mathbb{E}[\ell_j] + \left(1 - p_i^j\right) \frac{w_i}{s_j} \geq k + \frac{3w_i}{4s_j}.$$

Suppose that $k \geq c-3$. In this case, $w_i > 12\, s_j$ implies $c_i^j > k + \frac{3}{4} \cdot 12 \geq c+6$, which contradicts that, under the Nash equilibrium profile, the expected cost of any task on the fastest machine is at most $c+1$. Hence, the lemma is shown for $k \geq c-3$. Now suppose $k \leq c-4$. Let q denote the fastest machine from G_{k+2}. Lemma 20.16 yields $s_q = s(k+2) \geq 2s(k) \geq 2\, s_j$. Hence, the expected cost of i on q is

$$c_i^q = \mathbb{E}[\ell_q] + (1 - p_i^q) \frac{w_i}{s_q} \leq k + 3 + \frac{w_i}{2s_j}.$$

As $p_i^j > 0$, the Nash equilibrium condition yields $c_i^j \leq c_i^q$. Consequently,

$$k + \frac{3w_i}{4s_j} \leq k + 3 + \frac{w_i}{2s_j},$$

which implies $w_i \leq 12\, s_j$ and, hence, completes the proof of Lemma 20.17. □

Let $z = \max_{i \in T_j^{(2)}}(w_i/s_j)$. Lemma 20.17 implies $z \leq 12$. Now applying the weighted Chernoff bound from Lemma 20.14 yields that, for every $\alpha > 0$,

$$\mathbb{P}[\ell_j^{(2)} \geq \alpha C] \leq \left(\frac{e \cdot \mathbb{E}[\ell_j^{(2)}]}{\alpha C}\right)^{\alpha C/z} \leq \left(\frac{e}{\alpha}\right)^{\alpha C/12}$$

since $\mathbb{E}[\ell_j^{(2)}] \leq C$. We define $\tau = 24\, C \ln\ln m / \ln\ln\ln m$. As C is of order $\ln m / \ln\ln m$, it follows that τ is of order $\ln m / \ln\ln\ln m$. Let $x \geq 0$. We substitute $\tau + x$ for αC and obtain

$$\mathbb{P}[\ell_j^{(2)} \geq \tau + x] \leq \left(\frac{eC}{\tau + x}\right)^{(\tau+x)/12} \leq \left(\frac{e \ln\ln\ln m}{24 \ln\ln m}\right)^{2C \ln\ln m / \ln\ln\ln m + x/12}.$$

Observe that $24 \ln\ln m/(e \ln\ln\ln m)$ is lower-bounded by $\sqrt{\ln\ln m}$ and also lower-bounded by e^2. Furthermore, $C \geq \ln m/\ln\ln m$. Applying these bounds yields

$$\mathbb{P}[\ell_j^{(2)} \geq \tau + x] \leq \left(\frac{1}{\sqrt{\ln\ln m}}\right)^{2\ln m/\ln\ln\ln m} \cdot e^{-x/6} = m^{-1} \cdot e^{-x/6}.$$

As a consequence,

$$\begin{aligned}\mathbb{E}\left[\max_{j\in[m]} \ell_j^{(2)}\right] &= \int_0^\infty \mathbb{P}\left[\max_{j\in[m]} \ell_j^{(2)} \geq t\right] dt \\ &\leq \tau + \int_0^\infty \mathbb{P}\left[\max_{j\in[m]} \ell_j^{(2)} \geq \tau + x\right] dx \\ &\leq \tau + \int_0^\infty \sum_{j\in[m]} \mathbb{P}[\ell_j^{(2)} \geq \tau + x] dx.\end{aligned}$$

Now applying our tail bound yields

$$\mathbb{E}\left[\max_{j\in[m]} \ell_j^{(2)}\right] \leq \tau + \int_0^\infty e^{-x/6} dx = \tau + 6. \tag{20.3}$$

Finally, we combine Equations 20.2 and 20.3 and obtain

$$\text{cost}(P) = \mathbb{E}\left[\max_{j\in[m]} \ell_j\right] \leq 4C + \tau + 6 = \mathcal{O}\left(\frac{\log m}{\log\log\log m}\right),$$

which completes the proof of Theorem 20.15. □

Next we show that the upper bound given in Theorem 20.15 is tight by showing that for every number of machines there exists a game instance that matches the upper bound up to a constant factor.

Theorem 20.18 *For every $m \in \mathbb{N}$, there exists an instance G of the load balancing game with m machines and $n \leq m$ tasks that has a Nash equilibrium strategy profile P with*

$$cost(P) = \Omega\left(\frac{\log m}{\log\log\log m}\right) \cdot opt(G).$$

PROOF The starting point for our construction is the game and the Nash assignment A from the proof of Theorem 20.9. We use mixed strategies in only one of the groups, namely in the group G_k with $k = \lceil q/2 \rceil$. Let M denote the number of machines in this group, i.e., $M = q!/k! \geq (q/2)^{\lfloor q/2 \rfloor}$. Observe that $\log M = \Theta(q \log q) = \Theta(\log m)$.

Let T denote the set of tasks mapped by A to one of the machines in G_k. The tasks in T have weight 2^k. Each of these tasks is now assigned uniformly at random to a machine group G_k, i.e., $p_i^j = \frac{1}{M}$, for each $j \in G_k$ and each $i \in T$. For all other tasks the strategy profile P corresponds without any change to the pure strategy profile of assignment A. Observe that the randomization increases the expected cost of the tasks. The expected cost of a task $i \in T$ on a machine

$j \in G_k$ is now

$$c_i^j = \mathbb{E}[\ell_j] + \left(1 - p_i^j\right) \frac{w_i}{s_j} = k + \left(1 - \frac{1}{M}\right) < k + 1.$$

In the proof of Theorem 20.9, we have shown that the cost of a task i of weight 2^k on a machine of group G_j with $j \neq k$ is at least $k + 1$. Thus, the strategy profile P is a Nash equilibrium.

It remains to compare the social cost of the equilibrium profile P with the optimal cost. The structure of the optimal assignment is not affected by the modifications. It has social cost $\text{opt}(G) = 2$. Now we give a lower bound for the social cost of P. This social cost is, obviously, bounded from below by the maximum number of tasks that are mapped to the same machine in the group G_k. Applying Proposition 20.11 with M bins and $N = kM$ balls shows that the expected makespan is

$$\Omega\left(\frac{\ln M}{\ln\left(1 + \frac{1}{k}\ln M\right)}\right) = \Omega\left(\frac{\log m}{\log\log\log m}\right),$$

where the last estimate holds as $k = \Theta(\log m / \log\log m)$ and $\log M = \Theta(\log m)$. This completes the proof of Theorem 20.18. □

20.6 Summary and Discussion

In this chapter, we studied the price of anarchy in load balancing games in four different variants. Table 20.1 summarizes the results about the price of anarchy that we have presented. In the case of pure equilibria on identical machines, the price of anarchy is bounded from above by a small constant term. In all other cases, the price of anarchy is bounded from above by a slowly growing, sublogarithmic function in the number of machines. One might interpret these results as a first game theoretic explanation why the resources in a large distributed system like the Internet that widely lacks global control are shared in a more or less efficient and fair way among different users with different interests, although the considered model is clearly oversimplifying in several aspects.

It is an interesting coincidence that both the price of anarchy for pure equilibria on uniformly related machines as well as the price of anarchy for mixed equilibria

Table 20.1. *The price of anarchy for pure and mixed equilibria in load balancing games on identical and uniformly related machines*

	Identical	Uniformly related
Pure	$2 - \frac{2}{m+1}$	$\Theta\left(\frac{\log m}{\log\log m}\right)$
Mixed	$\Theta\left(\frac{\log m}{\log\log m}\right)$	$\Theta\left(\frac{\log m}{\log\log\log m}\right)$

on identical machines are of order $\log m / \log\log m$. Although both of these models result in essentially the same price of anarchy, the reasons for the increase in the social cost are quite different: In the case of pure equilibria on uniformly related machines, equilibrium assignments correspond to local optima with respect to moves of single tasks. That is, tasks are placed in a suboptimal but nevertheless coordinated fashion. On the contrary, in case of mixed equilibria, the increase in cost is due to collisions between uncoordinated random decisions. If one combines these two effects, then one loses only another very small factor of order $\log\log m / \log\log\log m$, which results in a price of anarchy of order $\log m / \log\log\log m$ for mixed equilibria on uniformly related machines.

Obviously, the price of anarchy for load balancing games as we have defined them in the beginning of this chapter is well understood. As mentioned above, however, this model is very simplistic. To make these results more realistic, one needs to incorporate other aspects from practical application areas like, e.g., more realistic cost functions or other ways to define the social cost. We give pointers to studies of quite a few variants of load balancing games in the bibliographic notes. In Christodoulou et al. (2004), it is made an interesting attempt that adds an algorithmic or constructive element to the analysis of the price of anarchy. The idea behind so-called "coordination mechanisms" is not to study the price of anarchy for a fixed system, but to design the system in such a way that the increase in cost or the loss in performance due to selfish behavior is as small as possible. Similar aspects are also discussed in Chapter 17. We believe that this is a promising direction of research that might result in practical guidelines of how to build a distributed system that does not suffer from selfish behavior but might even exploit the selfishness of the agents.

Besides the price of anarchy, we have studied the question of how agents reach a Nash equilibrium. We have observed that any sequence of improvement steps reaches a pure Nash equilibrium after a finite number of steps. In case of identical machines the max-weight best-response policy reaches an equilibrium in only $O(n)$. In case of uniformly related machines, it is open whether there exists a short sequence of improvement steps that lead from any given assignment to a pure Nash equilibrium. We think that this question is of great importance as Nash equilibria are only of interest if agents can reach them quickly. It is not clear that the only reasonable approach for the agents to reach a Nash equilibrium in a distributed way is to use improvement steps. There might also be other, possibly more strategic or more coordinated behavioral rules that quickly converge to a Nash equilibrium or to an approximate Nash equilibrium. For example, Chapter 29 considers some approaches from evolutionary game theory in the context of routing in networks. It is an interesting research problem to design distributed protocols that ensure that agents reach a Nash equilibrium quickly. Pointers to first results toward this direction can be found in the bibliographic notes.

20.7 Bibliographic Notes

The concept of the price of anarchy was introduced by Koutsoupias and Papadimitriou (1999). In their seminal work, they study load balancing in form of a routing game consisting of two nodes connected by parallel edges with possibly different speeds. Each agent has an amount of traffic that the agent seeks to map to one of the edges such that the load on this edge is as small as possible. In our notation, the parallel edges between the source and the sink correspond to the machines and the pieces of traffic of the agents correspond to the tasks. Let us remark that originally the ratio between the social cost in a worst-case Nash equilibrium and the optimal social cost was called *coordination ratio* but in this chapter we switched to the now commonly used term *price of anarchy*. The game theoretic model underlying the load balancing games is also known as *KP model*.

The results presented in Table 20.1 have been obtained in the following studies. The upper bound of $2 - \frac{2}{m+1}$ on the price of anarchy for pure equilibria in load balancing games with identical machines goes back to the scheduling literature (Finn and Horowitz, 1979), where the same ratio occurs in form of an approximation factor for a local search optimization heuristic. The lower bound on the price of anarchy for mixed equilibria on identical machines is presented in Koutsoupias and Papadimitriou (1999). The analysis for the corresponding upper bound is obtained in Czumaj and Vöcking (2002) and Koutsoupias et al. (2003). Let us remark that the analysis in Czumaj and Vöcking (2002) is tight up to a constant additive term. It shows that the price of anarchy for mixed equilibria in load balancing games on identical machines is $\Gamma^{-1}(m) \pm \Theta(1)$. The upper and lower bounds on the price of anarchy for pure and mixed equilibria in load balancing games with uniformly related machines are from Czumaj and Vöcking (2002) as well. This work also contains a tight characterization of the price of anarchy as a function of the ratio between the speeds of the fastest and the slowest machine.

The existence proof for pure equilibria presented in Section 20.1.1 can be found in Fotakis et al. (2002) and Even-Dar et al. (2003). The result from Section 20.3.2 that the LPT algorithm computes a pure Nash equilibrium is presented in Fotakis et al. (2002) together with several further results about the complexity of computing pure and mixed equilibria in load balancing games. The uniqueness of the fully mixed Nash equilibrium is shown in Mavronicolas and Spirakis (2001). Exercise 20.5 reworks the nice proof for this result. The counterexample to the *fully mixed Nash equilibrium conjecture* presented in Section 20.4.1 is from Fischer and Vöcking (2005). Finally, the results from Section 20.2.2 about the convergence of best response sequences are from Even-Dar et al. (2003).

Let us remark that this chapter does by far not give a complete overview of the rich literature about different variants of games for load balancing or routing on parallel links. We conclude this chapter with a few pointers to further literature. Load balancing games with more general cost functions are considered, e.g., in Caragiannis et al. (2006), Czumaj et al. (2002), Libman and Orda (1999, 2001). Other definitions of the social cost are considered, e.g., in Caragiannis et al. (2006), Gairing et al. (2004a, 2004b) and Suri et al. (2004). Another interesting variant of load balancing games assumes that agents come with subsets of the machines on which they have to place their tasks. The price of anarchy in such a restricted assignment model is investigated in Awerbuch et al. (2003), Gairing et al. (2006), and Suri et al. (2004). The price of anarchy with respect to equilibria that are robust against coalitions is studied in Andelman et al. (2007). An important aspect that we have only touched in this chapter is the complexity of computing Nash equilibria for load balancing games. Further work dealing with the computation of Nash equilibria can be found, e.g., in Even-Dar et al. (2003), Feldmann et al. (2003a), Fotakis et al. (2002), Fischer and Vöcking (2005), and Gairing et al. (2004a). Recent work deals also with the convergence time of distributed load balancing processes in which agents make parallel attempts for improvement steps until they find a Nash equilibrium (Berenbrink et al., 2006; Even-Dar and Mansour, 2005). Another interesting topic is load balancing games with incomplete information that have been considered, e.g., in Beier et al. (2004) and Gairing et al. (2005). Finally, let us remark that the concept of coordination mechanisms has been suggested in Christodoulou et al. (2004) and some further results on this topic can be found in Immorlica et al. (2005).

Several other results for load balancing and routing on parallel links have been collected in the surveys (Czumaj, 2004; Feldmann et al., 2003b; Koutsoupias, 2003).

Bibliography

N. Andelman, M. Feldman, and Y. Mansour. Strong price of anarchy. In *Proc. 18th Annual ACM-SIAM Symp. on Discrete Algorithms*, 2007.

B. Awerbuch, Y. Azar, Y. Richter, and D. Tsur. Tradeoffs in worst-case equilibria. In *Proc. 1st International Workshop on Approximation and Online Algorithms (WAOA)*, pp. 41–52, 2003.

R. Beier, A. Czumaj, P. Krysta, and B.Vöcking. Computing equilibria for congestion games with (im)perfect information. In *Proc. 15th Annual ACM-SIAM Symp. Discrete Algorithms*, pp. 746–755, 2004.

P. Berenbrink, T. Friedetzky, L.A. Goldberg, P.W. Goldberg, Z. Hu, and R.A. Martin. Distributed selfish load balancing. In *Proc. 17th Annual ACM-SIAM Symp. Discrete Algorithms*, pp. 354–363, 2006.

I. Caragiannis, M. Flammini, C. Kaklamanis, P. Kanellopoulos, and L. Moscardelli. Tight bounds for selfish and greedy load balancing. In *Proc. 33rd Intl. Colloq. on Automata, Languages, and Programming*, pp. 311–322, 2006.

G. Christodoulou, E. Koutsoupias, and A. Nanavati. Coordination Mechanisms. In *Proc. 31st Intl. Colloq. on Automata, Languages and Programming*, pp. 345–357, 2004.

A. Czumaj. Selfish Routing on the Internet. Chapter 42 in *Handbook of Scheduling: Algorithms, Models, and Performance Analysis*, edited by J. Leung, CRC Press, Boca Raton, FL, 2004.

A. Czumaj, P. Krysta, and B. Vöcking. Selfish traffic allocation for server farms. In *Proc. 34th Annual ACM Symp. Theory of Computing*, pp. 287–296, 2002.

A. Czumaj and B. Vöcking. Tight bounds for worst-case equilibria. In *Proc. 13th Annual ACM-SIAM Symp. on Discrete Algorithms*, pp. 413–420, 2002.

E. Even-Dar, A. Kesselman, and Y. Mansour. Convergence time to Nash equilibria. In *Proc. 30th International Colloq. on Automata, Languages and Programming*, pp. 502–513, 2003.

E. Even-Dar and Y. Mansour. Fast convergence of selfish rerouting. In *Proc. 16th Annual ACM-SIAM Symp. on Discrete Algorithms*, pp. 772–781, 2005.

R. Feldmann, M. Gairing, T. Lücking, B. Monien, and M. Rode. Nashification and the coordination ratio for a selfish routing game. In *Proc. 30th International Colloq. on Automata, Languages and Programming*, pp. 414–426, 2003a.

R. Feldmann, M. Gairing, T. Lücking, B. Monien, and M. Rode. Selfish routing in non-cooperative networks: a survey. In *Proc. 28th International Symp. on Mathematical Foundations of Computer Science*, pp. 21–45, 2003b.

G. Finn and E. Horowitz. A linear time approximation algorithm for multiprocessor scheduling. *BIT*, 19(3):312–320, 1979.

S. Fischer and B. Vöcking. On the structure and complexity of worst-case equilibria. In *Proc. 1st Workshop on Internet and Network Economics*, pp. 151–160, 2005.

D. Fotakis, S. Kontogiannis, E. Koutsoupias, M. Mavronicolas, and P. Spirakis. The structure and complexity of Nash equilibria for a selfish routing game. In *Proc. 29th Intl. Colloquium on Automata, Languages and Programming (ICALP)*, pp. 123–134, 2002.

D.K. Friesen. Tighter bounds for LPT scheduling on uniform processors. *SIAM J. Computing*, 16(3):554–560, 1987.

M. Gairing, T. Lücking, M. Mavronicolas, and B. Monien. Computing Nash equilibria for scheduling on restricted parallel links. In *Proc. 36th Annual ACM Symp. on Theory of Computing*, pp. 613–622, 2004a.

M. Gairing, T. Lücking, M. Mavronicolas, and B. Monien. The price of anarchy for polynomial social cost. In *Proc. 29th Intl. Symp. on Mathematical Foundations of Computer Science*, pp. 574–585, 2004b.

M. Gairing, T. Lücking, M. Mavronicolas, B. Monien, and M. Rode. Nash equilibria in discrete routing games with convex latency functions. In *Proc. 31st Intl. Colloq. on Automata, Languages and Programming*, pp. 645–657, 2004c.

M. Gairing, T. Lücking, M. Mavronicolas, and B. Monien. The Price of Anarchy for Restricted Parallel Links. *Parallel Process. Lett.*, 16(1):117–132, 2006.

M. Gairing, B. Monien, and K. Tiemann. Selfish routing with incomplete information. In *Proc. 17th Annual ACM Symp. on Parallel Algorithms*, pp. 203–212, 2005.

R.L. Graham. Bounds for certain multiprocessing anomalies. *Bell System Tech. J.*, 45: 1563–1581, 1966.

R.L. Graham. Bounds on multiprocessing timing anomalies. *SIAM J. Appl. Math.*, 17: 263–269, 1969.

D.S. Hochbaum and D.B. Shmoys. A polynomial approximation scheme for scheduling on uniform processors. *SIAM J. Computing*, 17(3):539–551, 1988.

N. Immorlica, L. Li, V.S. Mirrokni, and A. Schulz. Coordination mechanisms for selfish scheduling. In *Proc. 1st Workshop on Internet and Network Economics*, pp. 55–69, 2005.

E. Koutsoupias. Selfish task allocation. *Bulletin of the EATCS (81)*, pp. 79–88, 2003.

E. Koutsoupias, M. Mavronicolas, and P. Spirakis. Approximate equilibria and ball fusion. *Theory of Computing Systems*, 36(6):683–693, 2003.

E. Koutsoupias and C.H. Papadimitriou. Worst-case equilibria. In *Proc. 16th Annual Symp. on Theoretical Aspects of Computer Science*, pp. 404–413, 1999.

L. Libman and A. Orda. The designer's perspective to atomic noncooperative networks. *IEEE/ACM Trans. Networking*, 7(6):875–884, 1999.

L. Libman and A. Orda. Atomic resource sharing in noncooperative networks. *Telecommun. Systems*, 17(4):385–409, 2001.

M. Mavronicolas and P. Spirakis. The price of selfish routing. In *Proc. 33rd ACM Symp. on Theory of Computing*, pp. 510–519, 2001.

M. Mitzenmacher and E. Upfal. *Probability and Computing: Randomized Algorithms and Probabilistic Analysis*. Cambridge University Press, 2005.

S. Suri, C. Toth, and Y. Zhou. Selfish load balancing and atomic congestion games. In *Proc. 16th Annual ACM Symp. on Parallel Algorithms and Architectures*, pp. 188–195, 2005.

Exercises

20.1 Let G be any instance of the load balancing game with three tasks that should be placed on two identical machines. Show that any pure Nash equilibrium for G is optimal, i.e., $\text{cost}(A) = \text{opt}(G)$ for any equilibrium assignment A.
Remark: Interestingly, the example presented in Section 20.1.2 that yields the worst-case price of anarchy for two identical machines uses only four tasks.

20.2 Show, for every $m \in \mathbb{N}$, there exists an instance G of the load balancing game with m identical machines and $2m$ tasks that has a Nash equilibrium assignment $A : [n] \to [m]$ with

$$\text{cost}(A) = \left(2 - \frac{2}{m+1}\right) \cdot \text{opt}(G).$$

Hint: Generalize the example with two machines given in Section 20.1.2.

20.3 Prove that the price of anarchy for pure equilibria on instances of the load balancing game with two tasks and two machines with possibly different speeds corresponds to the golden ratio $\phi = \frac{1}{2}(1 + \sqrt{5})$. That is, show that

a) there is a game instance G admitting an equilibrium assignment A with $\text{cost}(A) = \phi \cdot \text{opt}(G)$.
b) for every game instance G and every equilibrium assignment A for this instance, it holds $\text{cost}(A) \leq \phi \cdot \text{opt}(G)$.

20.4 Consider an instance of the load balancing game with two tasks both of which have weight 1 and two machines, one of speed 1 and the other of speed $s > 0$.

(a) Show that there does not exist a fully mixed Nash equilibrium if $s \leq \frac{1}{2}$ or $s \geq 2$.
(b) Show that there exists a unique fully mixed Nash equilibrium if $\frac{1}{2} < s < 2$. Describe the strategy profile of this equilibrium as a function of s.

20.5 Show that there exists at most one fully mixed Nash equilibrium for every instance of the load balancing game.
Hint: Describe the conditions on the probabilities p_i^j imposed by a fully mixed Nash equilibrium in form of a system of linear equations and show that this system has a unique solution. If all the values for the variables p_i^j in this solution are positive then the solution describes a fully mixed Nash equilibrium. Otherwise, there does not exist a fully mixed equilibrium.

20.6 Suppose that we are given an instance G of the load balancing game with m identical machines and n tasks whose weights are bounded from above by $\alpha \cdot \text{opt}(G)$, for $0 < \alpha < 1$.

(a) Show that $\text{cost}(A) < (1 + \alpha) \cdot \text{opt}(G)$, for every equilibrium assignment A.
(b) Let $\alpha = \frac{1}{\log m}$. Show that $\text{cost}(A) = \mathcal{O}(\text{opt}(G))$, for every equilibrium strategy profile P.

CHAPTER 21

The Price of Anarchy and the Design of Scalable Resource Allocation Mechanisms

Ramesh Johari

Abstract

In this chapter, we study the allocation of a single infinitely divisible resource among multiple competing users. While we aim for efficient allocation of the resource, the task is complicated by the fact that users' utility functions are typically unknown to the resource manager. We study the design of resource allocation mechanisms that are approximately efficient (i.e., have a low price of anarchy), with low communication requirements (i.e., the strategy spaces of users are low dimensional).

Our main results concern the *proportional allocation mechanism*, for which a tight bound on the price of anarchy can be provided. We also show that in a wide range of market mechanisms that use a single market-clearing price, the proportional allocation mechanism minimizes the price of anarchy. Finally, we relax the assumption of a single market-clearing price, and show that by extending the class of Vickrey–Clarke–Groves mechanisms all Nash equilibria can be guaranteed to be fully efficient.

21.1 Introduction

This chapter deals with a canonical resource allocation problem. Suppose that a finite number of users compete to acquire a share of an infinitely divisible resource of fixed capacity. How should the resource be shared among the users? We will frame this problem as an economic problem: we assume that each user has a utility function that is increasing in the amount of the resource received, and then design a mechanism to maximize aggregate utility. In the absence of any strategic considerations, this is a simple optimization problem; however, if we assume that the agents are strategic, we need to design the resource allocation mechanisms to be robust to gaming behavior.

A central theme of this chapter is that *the price of anarchy* can be used as a design metric; i.e., "robust" allocation mechanisms are those that have a low price of anarchy. The present chapter is thus a bridge between two different themes of the book. The first theme is that of *optimal mechanism design* (Part II): given selfish agents, how do we successfully design mechanisms that nevertheless yield efficient outcomes? The second theme is that of quantifying inefficiency (Part III): given a prediction of game theoretic behavior, how well does it perform relative to some efficient benchmark? In this chapter, we use the quantification of inefficiency as the "objective function" with which we will design optimal mechanisms. As we will see, for the resource allocation problems we consider, this approach yields surprising insights into the structure of optimal mechanisms.

The mechanisms we consider for resource allocation are motivated by constraints present in modern communication networks, and similar systems where communication is limited; this precludes use of the traditional Vickrey–Clarke–Groves mechanisms (Chapter 9), which require declaration of the entire utility function. If we interpret the single resource above as a communication link, then we view the mechanism as an allocation policy operating on that link. We wish to design mechanisms that, intuitively, impose low communication overhead on the overall system; throughout this chapter, that scalability constraint translates into the assumption that the players can use only *low-dimensional* (in fact, one-dimensional) strategy spaces.

The remainder of the chapter is organized as follows. In Section 21.2, we introduce the basic resource allocation model we will consider in this chapter, and then introduce a simple approach to allocating the fixed resource: the *proportional allocation mechanism*. In this mechanism, each user submits a bid, and receives a share of the resource in proportion to their bid. We analyze this model under both the assumption that users are price takers (i.e., that they do not anticipate the effect of their strategic decision on the price of the resource); and the assumption that users are price anticipators. The former case yields full efficiency, while in the latter we characterize the price of anarchy. In Section 21.3, we state and prove a theorem showing that in a nontrivial class of "scalable" market mechanisms (in the sense informally discussed above), the proportional allocation mechanism has the lowest price of anarchy (i.e., minimizes the efficiency loss) when users are price anticipating.

In all the mechanisms considered in the first two sections, players have one-dimensional strategy spaces, and the mechanism also only chooses a single price. Because of these constraints, even the highest performance mechanisms suffer a positive efficiency loss, as demonstrated in Section 21.3. In the final section of the chapter, we consider the implications of removing the "single price" constraint. We show in Section 21.4 that if we consider mechanisms with scalar strategy spaces, and allow the mechanism to choose one price per user of the resource, then in fact full efficiency is achievable at Nash equilibrium. The result involves extending the well-known class of Vickrey–Clarke–Groves (VCG) mechanisms to use only a scalar strategy space; for more on VCG mechanisms, see Chapter 9.

21.2 The Proportional Allocation Mechanism

Suppose that R users share a resource of capacity $C > 0$. Let d_r denote the amount allocated to user r. We assume that user r receives a *utility* equal to $U_r(d_r)$ if the allocated amount is d_r; we assume that utility is measured in monetary units. We make the following assumptions on the utility function; we emphasize that *this assumption will be in force for the duration of the chapter*, unless otherwise mentioned.

Assumption 1 For each r, over the domain $d_r \geq 0$ the utility function $U_r(d_r)$ is concave, strictly increasing, and continuous; and over the domain $d_r > 0$, $U_r(d_r)$ is continuously differentiable. Furthermore, the right directional derivative at 0, denoted $U_r'(0)$, is finite. We let $\mathcal{U}$ denote the set of all utility functions satisfying these conditions.

We note that we make rather strong differentiability assumptions here on the utility functions; these assumptions are primarily made to ease the presentation. It is possible to relax the differentiability assumptions (see Notes for details).

Given complete knowledge and centralized control of the system, a natural problem for the network manager to try to solve is the following optimization problem:

SYSTEM:

$$\text{maximize} \sum_r U_r(d_r) \tag{21.1}$$

$$\text{subject to} \sum_r d_r \leq C; \tag{21.2}$$

$$d_r \geq 0, \quad r = 1, \ldots, R. \tag{21.3}$$

Note that the objective function of this problem is the utilitarian social welfare function (cf. Chapter 17); it becomes a reasonable objective if we assume that all utilities are measured in the same (monetary) units. Since the objective function is continuous and the feasible region is compact, an optimal solution $\mathbf{d} = (d_1, \ldots, d_R)$ exists. If the functions U_r are strictly concave, then the optimal solution is unique, since the feasible region is convex.

In general, the utility functions are not available to the resource manager. As a result, we consider the following pricing scheme for resource allocation, which we refer to as the *proportional allocation mechanism*. Each user r gives a payment (also called a *bid*) of w_r to the resource manager; we assume $w_r \geq 0$. Given the vector $\mathbf{w} = (w_1, \ldots, w_r)$, the resource manager chooses an allocation $\mathbf{d} = (d_1, \ldots, d_r)$. We assume the manager treats all users alike—in other words, the network manager does not *price discriminate*. Each user is charged the same price $\mu > 0$, leading to $d_r = w_r/\mu$. We further assume that the manager always seeks to allocate the entire resource capacity C; in this case, we expect the price μ to satisfy

$$\sum_r \frac{w_r}{\mu} = C.$$

The preceding equality can only be satisfied if $\sum_r w_r > 0$, in which case we have

$$\mu = \frac{\sum_r w_r}{C}. \tag{21.4}$$

In other words, if the manager chooses to allocate the entire resource, and does not price discriminate between users, then for every nonzero $\mathbf{w}$ there is a *unique* price $\mu > 0$, which must be chosen by the network, given by the previous equation.

We can interpret this mechanism as a *market-clearing* process by which a price is set so that demand equals supply. To see this interpretation, note that when a user chooses a total payment w_r, it is as if the user has chosen a *demand function* $D(p, w_r) = w_r/p$

for $p > 0$. The demand function describes the quantity the user demands at any given price $p > 0$. The resource manager then chooses a price μ so that $\sum_r D(\mu, w_r) = C$, i.e., so that the aggregate demand equals the supply C. For the specific form of demand functions we consider here, this leads to the expression for μ given in (21.4). User r then receives an allocation given by $D(\mu, w_r)$, and makes a payment $\mu D(\mu, w_r) = w_r$. This interpretation will be further explored in Section 21.3, where we consider other market-clearing mechanisms for allocating a single resource in inelastic supply, with the users choosing demand functions from a family parameterized by a single scalar.

21.2.1 Price Taking Users and Competitive Equilibrium

In this section, we consider a *competitive equilibrium* between the users and the resource manager. A central assumption in the definition of competitive equilibrium is that each user does not anticipate the effect of their payment w_r on the price μ; i.e., each user acts as a *price taker*. In this case, given a price $\mu > 0$, user r acts to maximize the following payoff function over $w_r \geq 0$:

$$P_r(w_r; \mu) = U_r\left(\frac{w_r}{\mu}\right) - w_r. \tag{21.5}$$

The first term represents the utility to user r of receiving a resource allocation equal to w_r/μ; the second term is the payment w_r made to the manager. Observe that this definition is consistent with the notion that all utilities are measured in *monetary* units.

We now say a pair $(\mathbf{w}, \mu)$ with $\mathbf{w} \geq 0$ and $\mu > 0$ is a *competitive equilibrium* if users maximize their payoff as defined in (21.5), and the network "clears the market" by setting the price μ according to (21.4):

$$P_r(w_r; \mu) \geq P_r(\bar{w}_r; \mu) \quad \text{for } \bar{w}_r \geq 0, \;\; r = 1, \ldots, R; \tag{21.6}$$

$$\mu = \frac{\sum_r w_r}{C}. \tag{21.7}$$

The following theorem shows that under our assumptions, a competitive equilibrium always exists, and any competitive equilibrium maximizes aggregate utility.

Theorem 21.1 *There exists a competitive equilibrium* $(\mathbf{w}, \mu)$. *In this case, the vector* $\mathbf{d} = \mathbf{w}/\mu$ *is an optimal solution to SYSTEM.*

PROOF The key idea in the proof is to use Lagrangian techniques to establish that optimality conditions for (21.6)–(21.7) are identical to the optimality conditions for the problem *SYSTEM*, under the identification $\mathbf{d} = \mathbf{w}/\mu$.

Observe that under Assumption 1, the payoff (21.5) is concave in w_r for any $\mu > 0$. Thus considering the first-order condition for maximization of $P_r(w_r; \mu)$ over $w_r \geq 0$, we conclude $\mathbf{w}$ and μ are a competitive equilibrium if and only if

$$U_r'(d_r) = \mu, \quad \text{if } d_r > 0; \tag{21.8}$$

$$U_r'(0) \leq \mu, \quad \text{if } d_r = 0; \tag{21.9}$$

$$\sum_r d_r = C, \tag{21.10}$$

where $d_r = w_r/\mu$. A straightforward Lagrangian optimization shows that the preceding conditions are exactly the optimality conditions for the problem *SYSTEM*, so we conclude $\mathbf{w}$ and μ are a competitive equilibrium if and only if $\mathbf{d} = \mathbf{w}/\mu$ is a solution to *SYSTEM* with Lagrange multiplier μ. Since at least one solution to *SYSTEM* must exist, the proof is complete. □

Theorem 21.1 shows that under the assumption that the users of the resource behave as price takers, there exists a bid vector $\mathbf{w}$ where all users have optimally chosen their bids w_r, with respect to the given price $\mu = \sum_r w_r/C$; and at this "equilibrium," aggregate utility is maximized. However, when the price taking assumption is violated, the model changes into a game and the guarantee of Theorem 21.1 is no longer valid. We investigate this game in the following section.

21.2.2 Price Anticipating Users and Nash Equilibrium

We now consider an alternative model where the users of a single resource are *price anticipating*, rather than price takers. The key difference is that while the payoff function P_r takes the price μ as a fixed parameter in (21.5), price anticipating users will realize that μ is set according to (21.4), and adjust their payoff accordingly; this makes the model a game between the R players.

We use the notation $\mathbf{w}_{-r}$ to denote the vector of all bids by users other than r; i.e., $\mathbf{w}_{-r} = (w_1, w_2, \ldots, w_{r-1}, w_{r+1}, \ldots, w_R)$. Given $\mathbf{w}_{-r}$, each user r chooses w_r to maximize:

$$Q_r(w_r; \mathbf{w}_{-r}) = \begin{cases} U_r\left(\dfrac{w_r}{\sum_s w_s} C\right) - w_r, & \text{if } w_r > 0; \\ U_r(0), & \text{if } w_r = 0. \end{cases} \tag{21.11}$$

over nonnegative w_r. The second condition is required so that the resource allocation to user r is zero when $w_r = 0$, even if all other users choose $\mathbf{w}_{-r}$ so that $\sum_{s \neq r} w_s = 0$. The payoff function Q_r is similar to the payoff function P_r, except that the user anticipates that the network will set the price μ according to (21.4). A *Nash equilibrium* of the game defined by $(Q_1, \ldots, Q_R)$ is a vector $\mathbf{w} \geq 0$ such that for all r:

$$Q_r(w_r; \mathbf{w}_{-r}) \geq Q_r(\bar{w}_r; \mathbf{w}_{-r}), \quad \text{for all } \bar{w}_r \geq 0. \tag{21.12}$$

Note that the payoff function in (21.11) may be discontinuous at $w_r = 0$, if $\sum_{s \neq r} w_s = 0$. This discontinuity may preclude existence of a Nash equilibrium; it is easy to see this in the case where the system consists of only a single user with a strictly increasing utility function. Nevertheless, as long as at least two users are competing, it is possible to show that a unique Nash equilibrium exists, by noting that such an equilibrium solves a version of the *SYSTEM* problem but with "modified" utility functions.

Theorem 21.2 *Suppose that $R > 1$. Then there exists a unique Nash equilibrium $\mathbf{w} \geq 0$ of the game defined by $(Q_1, \ldots, Q_R)$, and it satisfies $\sum_r w_r > 0$. In* *this case, the vector* **d** *defined by*

$$d_r = \frac{w_r}{\sum_s w_s} C, \quad r = 1, \ldots, R, \tag{21.13}$$

is the unique optimal solution to the following optimization problem:

GAME:

$$\text{maximize} \sum_r \hat{U}_r(d_r) \tag{21.14}$$

$$\text{subject to} \sum_r d_r \leq C; \tag{21.15}$$

$$d_r \geq 0, \quad r = 1, \ldots, R, \tag{21.16}$$

where

$$\hat{U}_r(d_r) = \left(1 - \frac{d_r}{C}\right) U_r(d_r) + \left(\frac{d_r}{C}\right)\left(\frac{1}{d_r}\int_0^{d_r} U_r(z)\, dz\right). \tag{21.17}$$

PROOF The proof is similar to the proof of Theorem 21.1. The first key step is to note that at any Nash equilibrium, at least two components of **w** must be positive; this follows from the payoff (21.11) (see Exercise 17.5). Given this fact, the payoff of each user w_r is strictly concave and continuous in w_r so that **w** is a Nash equilibrium if and only if the following first-order conditions hold:

$$U_r'\left(\frac{w_r}{\sum_s w_s} C\right)\left(1 - \frac{w_r}{\sum_s w_s}\right) = \frac{\sum_s w_s}{C}, \quad \text{if } w_r > 0; \tag{21.18}$$

$$U_r'(0) \leq \frac{\sum_s w_s}{C}, \quad \text{if } w_r = 0. \tag{21.19}$$

Note that if we define $\rho = \sum_s w_s / C$ and $d_r = w_r / \rho$, then the preceding conditions can be rewritten as

$$\hat{U}_r'(d_r) = \rho, \quad \text{if } d_r > 0; \tag{21.20}$$

$$\hat{U}_r'(0) \leq \rho, \quad \text{if } d_r = 0; \tag{21.21}$$

$$\sum_r d_r = C. \tag{21.22}$$

Note that these are identical to (21.8)–(21.10), but for the modified objective function (21.14). Since the utility functions $\hat{U}_r(d_r)$ are strictly concave and continuous over $0 \leq d_r \leq C$, the preceding first-order conditions are sufficient optimality conditions for *GAME*. We conclude that **w** is a Nash equilibrium if and only if $\sum_s w_s > 0$, and the resulting allocation **d** solves the problem *GAME* with Lagrange multiplier $\rho = \sum_s w_s / C$. To conclude the proof, observe that *GAME* has a strictly concave and continuous objective function over a compact feasible region, and thus has a unique optimal solution. It is straightforward to verify that this implies uniqueness of the Nash equilibrium as well. □

Note that the preceding theorem gives a form of "potential" for the game under consideration: the Nash equilibrium is characterized as the unique solution to a natural optimization problem. However, the objective function for this optimization problem is not a true (exact or ordinal) potential for the game under consideration; this is because while the objective function (21.14) depends on *allocations*, the users' strategic decisions are *bids*. Notably, this observation is in sharp contrast to the potentials found for routing games in Chapter 18, or for network formation in Chapter 19. For example, we cannot use the objective function (21.14) to conclude that best response dynamics will converge for our game. Nevertheless, the optimization formulation will help us study the price of anarchy of the game in the following section. For later reference, we note the following corollary, which uses a *variational inequality* formulation of the preceding theorem.

Corollary 21.3 *Suppose that* $R > 1$. *Let* $\mathbf{w}$ *be the unique Nash equilibrium of the game defined by* $(Q_1, \ldots, Q_R)$, *and define* $\mathbf{d}$ *according to* (21.13). *Then for any other vector* $\bar{\mathbf{d}} \geq 0$ *such that* $\sum_r \bar{d}_r \leq C$, *there holds:*

$$\sum_r \hat{U}_r'(d_r)(\bar{d}_r - d_r) \leq 0. \tag{21.23}$$

PROOF The stated condition follows easily from (21.20)–(21.22), the optimality conditions for the problem *GAME*. □

21.2.3 Price of Anarchy

We let $\mathbf{d}^S$ denote an optimal solution to *SYSTEM*, and let $\mathbf{d}^G$ denote the unique optimal solution to *GAME*. We now investigate the price of anarchy of this system; i.e., how much utility is lost because the users are price anticipating? To answer this question, we must compare the utility $\sum_r U_r(d_r^G)$ obtained when the users fully evaluate the effect of their actions on the price, and the utility $\sum_r U_r(d_r^S)$ obtained by choosing the point that maximizes aggregate utility. (We know, of course, that $\sum_r U_r(d_r^G) \leq \sum_r U_r(d_r^S)$, by definition of $\mathbf{d}^S$.) As we show in the following theorem, the efficiency loss is exactly 25% in the worst case.

Theorem 21.4 *Suppose that* $R > 1$. *Suppose also that* $U_r(0) \geq 0$ *for all* r. *If* $\mathbf{d}^S$ *is any optimal solution to SYSTEM, and* $\mathbf{d}^G$ *is the unique optimal solution to GAME, then:*

$$\sum_r U_r(d_r^G) \geq \frac{3}{4} \sum_r U_r(d_r^S).$$

Furthermore, this bound is tight: for every $\epsilon > 0$, *there exists a choice of* R, *and a choice of (linear) utility functions* U_r, $r = 1, \ldots, R$, *such that*

$$\sum_r U_r(d_r^G) \leq \left(\frac{3}{4} + \epsilon\right)\left(\sum_r U_r(d_r^S)\right).$$

PROOF Our proof will rely on the following constant β:[1]

$$\beta = \inf_{U \in \mathcal{U}} \inf_{C>0} \inf_{0 \le d, \bar{d} \le C} \frac{U(d) + \hat{U}'(d)(\bar{d} - d)}{U(\bar{d})}. \tag{21.24}$$

Recall the definition of $\mathcal{U}$ in Assumption 1, and of $\hat{U}$ in (21.17).

Our proof involves using Corollary 21.3 to prove that β is a tight bound on the efficiency of Nash equilibria. We first establish that $\beta \ge 3/4$. Note that in (21.24), the quotient is strictly larger than 1 if $d > \bar{d}$, and equal to 1 if $d = \bar{d}$. Thus in computing β we can assume that $d < \bar{d}$ in (21.24). We then have:

$$\begin{aligned} U(d) + \hat{U}'(d)(\bar{d} - d) &= U(d) + U'(d)\left(1 - \frac{d}{C}\right)(\bar{d} - d) \\ &\ge U(d) + \left(1 - \frac{d}{\bar{d}}\right)(U(\bar{d}) - U(d)) \\ &\ge \left(\frac{d}{\bar{d}}\right)^2 U(\bar{d}) + \left(1 - \frac{d}{\bar{d}}\right) U(\bar{d}) \\ &\ge \frac{3}{4} U(\bar{d}). \end{aligned}$$

The first inequality follows since $\bar{d} \le C$ and U is concave. The second inequality follows since U is concave and nonnegative and $d \le \bar{d}$, so $U(d) \ge (d/\bar{d})U(\bar{d})$. Finally, the third inequality follows since $x^2 - x + 1$ is minimized at $x = 1/2$. It follows from (21.24) that $\beta \ge 3/4$.

Next, we show that for any $\delta > 0$, there exists an example where the ratio of Nash aggregate utility to maximum aggregate utility is at least $\beta + \delta$. Our approach is essentially the same as that in Example 17.6. Fix U, $d < \bar{d}$, and let $C = \bar{d}$. Consider the following example. Suppose that $R > 1$ users compete for the resource. Let user 1 have utility function $U_1 = U$, and suppose users $2, \ldots, R$ have *linear* utility functions with slope $\hat{U}'(d)$; i.e., $U_r(d_r) = \hat{U}'(d)d_r = (U'(d)(1 - d/C))d_r$. Let $\mathbf{d}^S$ denote an optimal solution to *SYSTEM* for this model; since one feasible solution involves allocating the entire resource $\bar{d}$ to user 1, we must have $\sum_s U_s(d_s^S) \ge U(\bar{d})$. On the other hand, recall that at any Nash equilibrium at least two users have positive quantities; and since the Nash equilibrium is unique, we conclude that all users $2, \ldots, R$ receive the same positive quantity. Thus as $R \to \infty$, we must have $d_r \downarrow 0$ for $r = 2, \ldots, R$. From (21.20)–(21.21), it follows that the Nash price $\sum_s w_s/C$ must converge to $\hat{U}'(d)$ as $R \to \infty$. Thus, at the Nash equilibrium, user 1 receives an allocation $d + \epsilon$, and all other users receive an allocation $(1 - d - \epsilon)/(R - 1)$, where $\epsilon \to 0$ as $R \to \infty$. The total Nash utility thus converges to $U(d) + \hat{U}'(d)(\bar{d} - d)$. The limiting ratio of Nash aggregate utility to maximum aggregate utility is thus less than or equal to

$$\frac{U(d) + \hat{U}'(d)(\bar{d} - d)}{U(\bar{d})}.$$

[1] A slight subtlety arises in this definition if $U(\bar{x}) = 0$; however, in this latter case we can define β by only taking the infimum over $\bar{x} > 0$. This does not change any of the subsequent arguments.

We conclude that for any $\delta > 0$, there exists a game $(Q_1, \ldots, Q_R)$ in which the ratio of Nash aggregate utility to maximum aggregate utility is at most $\beta + \delta$. By considering the special case in which $U(\hat{d}) = \hat{d}$, $d = 1/2$, and $\bar{d} = 1$, the preceding construction yields a limiting efficiency ratio of exactly 3/4. Combined with the previous argument that $\beta \geq 3/4$, it follows that in fact $\beta = 3/4$.

It remains to show that the bound holds for *every* resource allocation game. Here we simply apply the result of Corollary 21.3. Let $(Q_1, \ldots, Q_R)$ be a resource allocation game where users have utility functions $(U_1, \ldots, U_R)$. Let $\mathbf{d}^S$ be a solution to *SYSTEM*, and let $\mathbf{d}^G$ be a solution to *GAME*. We have

$$\sum_s U_s(d_s^S) \leq \sum_s \frac{1}{\beta}\left(U_s(d_s^G) + \hat{U}_s'(d_s^G)(d_s^S - d_s^G)\right) \leq \frac{1}{\beta}\sum_s U_s(d_s^G).$$

The first inequality follows by the definition of β, and the second follows from Corollary 21.3. Since $\beta = 3/4$, this concludes the proof. □

The preceding theorem shows that in the worst case, aggregate utility falls by no more than 25% when users are able to anticipate the effects of their actions on the price of the resource. Furthermore, this bound is essentially tight. In fact, it follows from the proof that the worst case consists of a resource of capacity 1, where user 1 has utility $U_1(d_1) = d_1$, and all other users have utility $U_r(d_r) \approx d_r/2$ (when R is large). As $R \to \infty$, at the Nash equilibrium of this game user 1 receives a quantity $d_1^G = 1/2$, while the remaining users uniformly split the quantity $1 - d_1^G = 1/2$ among themselves, yielding an aggregate utility of 3/4. On the other hand, the maximum aggregate utility possible is clearly 1, achieved by allocating the entire resource to user 1.

21.3 A Characterization Theorem

In this chapter we ask an axiomatic question: Is the mechanism we have chosen "desirable" among a class of mechanisms satisfying certain "reasonable" properties? Defining desirability is the simpler of the two tasks: we consider a mechanism to be desirable if it minimizes efficiency loss when users are price anticipating. Importantly, we ask for this efficiency property *independent* of the characteristics of the market participants (i.e., their cost functions or utility functions). That is, the mechanisms we seek are those that perform well under broad assumptions on the nature of the preferences of market participants.

How do we define "reasonable" mechanisms? The most important condition we impose is that the strategy space of each market participant should be "simple," which we interpret as *low dimensional*. Formally, we will focus on mechanisms for which the strategy space of each market participant is $\mathbb{R}^+$; i.e., each market participant chooses a scalar, which is a parameter that determines his demand function as input to the market-clearing mechanism. The primary motivation is that if we view such a mechanism to be useful for a communication network setting, information flow is limited; and in particular, we would like to implement a market with as little overhead as possible.

Thus keeping the strategy spaces of the users low dimensional is a reasonable goal.[2] We will show that under a specific set of mathematical assumptions, the proportional allocation mechanism in fact minimizes the worst-case efficiency loss when users are price anticipating.

The class of market mechanisms we will consider is defined as follows. A market mechanism must operate on a particular environment, defined by a triple $(C, R, \mathbf{U})$: $C > 0$ denotes the capacity of the resource; $R > 1$ denotes the number of users sharing the resource; and $\mathbf{U} = (U_1, \ldots, U_R)$ denotes the utility functions of the users, with $U_r \in \mathcal{U}$ (cf. Assumption 1). The following definition captures our notion of a market mechanism.

Definition 21.5 A *smooth market-clearing mechanism* is a differentiable function $D\colon (0, \infty) \times [0, \infty) \to \mathbb{R}^+$ such that for all $C > 0$, for all $R > 1$, and for all nonzero $\boldsymbol{\theta} \in (\mathbb{R}^+)^R$, there exists a unique solution $p > 0$ to the following equation:

$$\sum_{r=1}^{R} D(p, \theta_r) = C.$$

We let $p_D(\boldsymbol{\theta})$ denote this solution.[3]

Note that the market-clearing price is undefined if $\boldsymbol{\theta} = \mathbf{0}$. As we will see below, when we formulate a game between users for a given mechanism D, we will assume that the payoff to all players is $-\infty$ if the composite strategy vector is $\boldsymbol{\theta} = \mathbf{0}$. Note that this is slightly different from the definition in Section 21.1, where the payoff is $U(0)$ to a player with utility function U who submits a strategy $\theta = 0$. We will discuss this distinction further later; we simply note for the moment that it does not affect the results of this section.

Our definition of a smooth market-clearing mechanism generalizes the demand function interpretation of the proportional allocation mechanism. Recall that for that mechanism, each user submits a demand function of the form $D(p, \theta) = \theta/p$, and the link manager chooses a price $p_D(\boldsymbol{\theta})$ to ensure that $\sum_{r=1}^{R} D(p, \theta_r) = C$. Thus, for this mechanism, we have $p_D(\boldsymbol{\theta}) = \sum_{r=1}^{R} \theta_r / C$ if $\boldsymbol{\theta} \neq 0$.

We now generalize *competitive equilibria* and *Nash equilibria* to this setting.

Definition 21.6 Given a utility system $(C, R, \mathbf{U})$ and a smooth market-clearing mechanism D, we say that a nonzero vector $\boldsymbol{\theta} \in (\mathbb{R}^+)^R$ is a *competitive equilibrium* if, for $\mu = p_D(\boldsymbol{\theta})$, there holds for all r:

$$\theta_r \in \arg\max_{\bar{\theta}_r \geq 0} [U_r(D(\mu, \bar{\theta}_r)) - \mu D(\mu, \bar{\theta}_r)]. \tag{21.25}$$

[2] Note that this notion is distinct from "single-parameter domains" as studied in Chapter 9; there it is the true valuations of the agents that are one-dimensional, whereas here the true valuations of the agents may be arbitrary functions. With one-dimensional strategy spaces, we restrict the ability of users to *communicate* information about their valuations to the mechanism.

[3] Note that we suppress the dependence of this solution on C; where necessary, we will emphasize this dependence.

Definition 21.7 Given a utility system $(C, R, \mathbf{U})$ and a smooth market-clearing mechanism D, we say that a nonzero vector $\boldsymbol{\theta} \in (\mathbb{R}^+)^R$ is a *Nash equilibrium* if there holds for all r:

$$\theta_r \in \arg\max_{\bar{\theta}_r \geq 0} Q_r(\bar{\theta}_r; \boldsymbol{\theta}_{-r}). \tag{21.26}$$

where

$$Q_r(\theta_r; \boldsymbol{\theta}_{-r}) = \begin{cases} U_r(D(p_D(\boldsymbol{\theta}), \theta_r)) - p_D(\boldsymbol{\theta}) D(p_D(\boldsymbol{\theta}), \theta_r), & \text{if } \boldsymbol{\theta} \neq \mathbf{0}; \\ -\infty, & \text{if } \boldsymbol{\theta} = \mathbf{0}. \end{cases} \tag{21.27}$$

Notice that the payoff Q_r is $-\infty$ if the composite strategy vector is $\boldsymbol{\theta} = \mathbf{0}$, since in this case no market-clearing price exists.

We are now ready to frame the specific class $\mathcal{D}$ of market mechanisms we will consider in this section, defined as follows.

Definition 21.8 The class $\mathcal{D}$ consists of all functions $D(p, \theta)$ such that the following conditions are satisfied:

(i) D is a smooth market-clearing mechanism (cf. Definition 21.5).

(ii) For all $C > 0$, and for all $U_r \in \mathcal{U}$, a user's payoff is *concave if he is price anticipating*; i.e., for all R, and for all $\boldsymbol{\theta}_{-r} \in (\mathbb{R}^+)^R$, the function:

$$U_r(D(p_D(\boldsymbol{\theta}), \theta_r)) - p_D(\boldsymbol{\theta}) D(p_D(\boldsymbol{\theta}), \theta_r)$$

is concave in $\theta_r > 0$ if $\boldsymbol{\theta}_{-r} = \mathbf{0}$, and concave in $\theta_r \geq 0$ if $\boldsymbol{\theta}_{-r} \neq \mathbf{0}$.

(iii) For all $p > 0$, and for all $d \geq 0$, there exists a $\theta > 0$ such that $D(p, \theta) = d$.

(iv) The demand functions are nonnegative; i.e., for all $p > 0$ and $\theta \geq 0$, $D(p, \theta) \geq 0$.

We pause here to briefly discuss the conditions in the previous definition. The second allows us to characterize Nash equilibria in terms of only first-order conditions. To justify this condition, we note that some assumption of quasiconcavity is generally used to guarantee existence of pure strategy Nash equilibria. The third condition ensures that given a price p and desired allocation $d \in [0, C]$, each player can make a choice of θ to guarantee precisely the allocation d. This is an "expressiveness" condition on the mechanism that ensures that all possible demands can be chosen at any market-clearing price. The last condition is a normalization condition, which ensures that regardless of the bid of a user, he is never required to *supply* some quantity of the resource (which would be the case if we allowed $D(p, \theta) < 0$). The following example gives a family of mechanisms that lie in $\mathcal{D}$.

Example 21.9 Suppose that $D(p, \theta) = \theta p^{-1/c}$, where $c \geq 1$. It is easy to check that this class of mechanisms satisfies $D \in \mathcal{D}$ for all choices of c; when $c = 1$, we recover the proportional allocation mechanism of Section 21.2. The market-clearing condition yields that $p_D(\boldsymbol{\theta}) = (\sum_r \theta_r / C)^{1/c}$. Note that as a result, the *allocation* to user r at a nonzero vector $\boldsymbol{\theta}$ is

$$D(p_D(\boldsymbol{\theta}), \theta_r) = \frac{\theta_r}{\sum_s \theta_s} C.$$

In other words, regardless of the value of c, the market clearing allocations are chosen proportional to the bids. This remarkable fact is a special case of a more general result we establish below: all mechanisms in $\mathcal{D}$ yield market-clearing allocations that are proportional to the bids; they differ only in the market-clearing price that is chosen. The exercises study the price of anarchy of the mechanisms defined in this example using an approach analogous to the proof of Theorem 21.4.

Our interest is in the worst-case ratio of aggregate utility at any Nash equilibrium to the optimal value of *SYSTEM*. Formally, for $D \in \mathcal{D}$ we define a constant $\rho(D)$ as follows:

$$\rho(D) = \inf \left\{ \frac{\sum_{r=1}^{R} U_r(D(p_D(\boldsymbol{\theta}), \theta_r))}{\sum_{r=1}^{R} U_r(d_r)} \;\middle|\; C > 0, R > 1, \mathbf{U} \in \mathcal{U}^R, \right.$$

$$\left. \mathbf{d} \text{ solves } \mathit{SYSTEM}, \text{ and } \boldsymbol{\theta} \text{ is a Nash equilibrium} \right\}.$$

Note that since all $U \in \mathcal{U}$ are strictly increasing and nonnegative, the aggregate utility $\sum_{r=1}^{R} U_r(d_r^S)$ is positive for any utility system $(C, R, \mathbf{U})$ with $C > 0$, and any optimal solution $\mathbf{d}^{\mathbf{S}}$ to *SYSTEM*. Note also that we are considering the ratio over *all* possible Nash equilibria, not just the best one for a given instance; thus, we are studying the price of anarchy, not the price of stability (cf. Chapter 17). However, Nash equilibria may not exist for some utility systems $(C, R, \mathbf{U})$; in this case we set $\rho(D) = -\infty$.

Our main result in this section is the following theorem.

Theorem 21.10 *Let $D \in \mathcal{D}$ be a smooth market-clearing mechanism. Then:*

(i) There exists a competitive equilibrium $\boldsymbol{\theta}$. Furthermore, for any such $\boldsymbol{\theta}$, the resulting allocation $\mathbf{d}$ given by $d_r = D(p_D(\boldsymbol{\theta}), \theta_r)$ solves SYSTEM.

(ii) There exists a concave, strictly increasing, differentiable, and invertible function $B\colon (0, \infty) \to (0, \infty)$ such that for all $p > 0$ and $\theta \geq 0$:

$$D(p, \theta) = \frac{\theta}{B(p)}.$$

(iii) $\rho(D) \leq 3/4$, and this bound is met with equality if and only if $D(p, \theta) = \Delta\theta/p$ for some $\Delta > 0$.

Before continuing to the proof of the theorem, we pause to make several critical comments about the result. Results (i) and (ii) of the theorem are a *characterization* of the types of mechanisms allowed by the constraints that define $\mathcal{D}$. In particular, notice that from (ii), for nonzero $\boldsymbol{\theta}$ we have

$$B(p_D(\boldsymbol{\theta})) = \frac{\sum_{r=1}^{R} \theta_r}{C}. \tag{21.28}$$

Thus we must have

$$D(p_D(\boldsymbol{\theta}), \theta_r) = \frac{\theta_r}{\sum_s \theta_s} C; \tag{21.29}$$

in other words, every mechanism in $\mathcal{D}$ chooses allocations in proportion to the bids. As a result, we conclude that for a given vector $\boldsymbol{\theta}$, when the market clears, mechanisms in $\mathcal{D}$ differ from the proportional allocation mechanism only in the market-clearing price—the allocation is the same. Result (iii) of the theorem is then a price of anarchy result that concerns mechanisms of this form.

We emphasize that the theorem here is distinguished from related work because the allocation rule (21.29) was not assumed in advance. Rather, the result here starts from a set of simple assumptions on the structure of mechanisms to be considered (the definition of the class $\mathcal{D}$), and uses them to *prove* that any mechanism in the class must lead to the allocation in (21.29). (See Notes for details.)

PROOF Throughout the proof we fix a particular mechanism $D \in \mathcal{D}$. Some computational details are left to the reader.

Step 1: A user's payoff is concave if he is price taking. In other words, we will show that for all $U \in \mathcal{U}$ and for all $p > 0$, $U(D(p, \theta)) - pD(p, \theta)$ is concave in θ. The key idea is to use a limiting regime where capacity grows large, so that users that are price anticipating effectively become price taking.

Formally, we first observe that since D must possess a unique market-clearing price regardless of the value of C, $D(p, \theta)$ must be strictly monotonic in p (for fixed $\theta > 0$) where it is nonzero, and either (1) $D(p, \theta)$ is nondecreasing in p for *all* $\theta > 0$, or (2) $D(p, \theta)$ is nonincreasing in p for *all* $\theta > 0$.

To complete the proof of this step, fix $\mu > 0$, and fix $\theta > 0$. Now consider a limit where $R \to \infty$, and $C^R = RD(\mu, \theta)$ is the capacity in the R'th system. It is straightforward to check that if the $R - 1$ users $2, \ldots, R$ submit strategy θ, and the first user submits strategy θ', then the resulting market-clearing price p_D converges to μ as $R \to \infty$, regardless of the value of θ'. This step uses the fact that either (1) or (2) above holds. Applying the fact that player 1's payoff must be concave when he is price anticipating and taking limits as $R \to \infty$, it follows that player 1's payoff is concave when he is price taking for any fixed price $\mu > 0$.

Step 2: There exists a positive function B such that $D(p, \theta) = \theta / B(p)$ for $p > 0$ and $\theta \geq 0$. By Step 1, a player's payoff is concave when he is price taking. By appropriately choosing a linear utility function with very large slope and very small slope, it follows that $D(p, \theta)$ must be concave and convex, respectively, in θ for a given $p > 0$. Thus for fixed $p > 0$, $D(p, \theta)$ is an affine function of θ. Conditions 3 and 4 in Definition 21.8 then imply that the constant term must be zero, while the coefficient of the linear term is positive; thus, $D(p, \theta) = \theta / B(p)$ for some positive function $B(p)$.

Before continuing, we note that the previous step already implies the remarkable fact that for any mechanism $D \in \mathcal{D}$, *the allocation at the market-clearing price is made in proportion to the bids θ.* This follows from the discussion following (21.28) above.

Step 3: For all utility systems $(C, R, \mathbf{U})$, there exists a competitive equilibrium, and it is fully efficient. This step follows primarily because of Condition 3 in Definition 21.8: given a price μ, a user can first determine his optimal choice of quantity, and then choose a parameter θ to express this choice. Formally, suppose that $\mu = p_D(\boldsymbol{\theta})$, and (21.25) holds. Let $d_r = D(\mu, \theta_r)$; then (21.25) implies that the necessary conditions (21.8)–(21.9) hold; these are also sufficient because of Step 1. Furthermore, market clearing implies (21.10) holds. Thus any competitive equilibrium is fully efficient. Existence follows by letting $\mathbf{d}^S$ be a solution to *SYSTEM* with Lagrange multiplier μ, and choosing $\theta_r = d_r/B(\mu)$.

Step 4: For all $R > 1$ and $\boldsymbol{\theta}_{-r} \in (\mathbb{R}^+)^{R-1}$, the functions $D(p_D(\boldsymbol{\theta}), \theta_r)$ and $-p_D(\boldsymbol{\theta})D(p_D(\boldsymbol{\theta}), \theta_r)$ are concave in $\theta_r > 0$ if $\boldsymbol{\theta}_{-r} = \mathbf{0}$, and concave in $\theta_r \geq 0$ if $\boldsymbol{\theta}_{-r} \neq \mathbf{0}$. As in Step 2, this conclusion follows by considering linear utility functions with very large and very small slope, respectively.

Step 5: B is an invertible, differentiable, strictly increasing, and concave function on $(0, \infty)$. We immediately see that B must be invertible on $(0, \infty)$; it is clearly onto, as the right-hand side of (21.28) can take any value in $(0, \infty)$. Furthermore, uniqueness of the market-clearing price in (21.28) requires that B is one-to-one as well, and hence invertible. Since D is differentiable, B must be differentiable as well. Let Φ denote the differentiable inverse of B on $(0, \infty)$; we will show Φ is strictly increasing and convex.

Let

$$w_r(\boldsymbol{\theta}) = p_D(\boldsymbol{\theta})D(p_D(\boldsymbol{\theta}), \theta_r) = \Phi\left(\frac{\sum_{s=1}^R \theta_s}{C}\right)\left(\frac{\theta_r}{\sum_{s=1}^R \theta_s}C\right). \tag{21.30}$$

By Step 4, $w_r(\boldsymbol{\theta})$ is convex in $\theta_r > 0$. By considering strategy vectors $\boldsymbol{\theta}$ for which $\boldsymbol{\theta}_{-r} = \mathbf{0}$, it follows that Φ is convex. Finally, the fact that Φ is strictly increasing follows by differentiating twice and considering the limit where $\theta_r \to 0$, while keeping $\boldsymbol{\theta}_{-r}$ constant and nonzero.[4] This establishes the desired facts regarding B.

Step 6: Let $(C, R, \mathbf{U})$ be a utility system. A vector $\boldsymbol{\theta} \geq 0$ is a Nash equilibrium if and only if at least two components of $\boldsymbol{\theta}$ are nonzero, and there exists a nonzero vector $\mathbf{d} \geq 0$ and a scalar $\mu > 0$ such that $\theta_r = \mu d_r$ for all r, $\sum_{r=1}^R d_r = C$, and the following conditions hold:

$$U_r'(d_r)\left(1 - \frac{d_r}{C}\right) = \Phi(\mu)\left(1 - \frac{d_r}{C}\right) + \mu\Phi'(\mu)\left(\frac{d_r}{C}\right), \quad \text{if } d_r > 0; \tag{21.31}$$

$$U_r'(0) \leq \Phi(\mu), \quad \text{if } d_r = 0. \tag{21.32}$$

In this case $d_r = D(p_D(\boldsymbol{\theta}), \theta_r)$, $\mu = \sum_{r=1}^R \theta_r/C$, and $\Phi(\mu) = p_D(\boldsymbol{\theta})$. Further, there exists a unique Nash equilibrium. The proof of this step is similar to the

[4] While the most direct argument uses twice differentiability of Φ, it is possible to make a similar argument even if Φ is only once differentiable, by arguing only in terms of increments of Φ.

proof of Nash equilibrium characterization in Theorem 21.2; we omit the details, and refer the reader to the Notes section.

Step 7: For any $\epsilon > 0$, there exists a utility systems $(C, R, \mathbf{U})$ such that at any Nash equilibrium $\boldsymbol{\theta}$, the aggregate utility is no more than $3/4 + \epsilon$ of the maximal aggregate utility. Consider a utility system with the following properties. Let $C = 1$. Fix $\mu > 0$, and let $U_1(d_1) = Ad_1$, where $A > \Phi(\mu)$. We will search for a solution to the Nash conditions (21.31) to (21.32) with market-clearing price $\Phi(\mu)$.

We start by calculating d_1 by assuming it is nonzero, and applying (21.31):

$$d_1 = \frac{(A - \Phi(\mu))C}{A - \Phi(\mu) + \mu\Phi'(\mu)}. \tag{21.33}$$

In the spirit of the proof of Theorem 21.4, we will now choose users $2, \ldots, R$ to have identical linear utility functions, with slopes less than A. As we will see, this will be possible if R is large enough.

Formally, let $d = (C - d_1)/(R - 1)$, and (cf. (21.31)) define

$$\alpha = \frac{\Phi(\mu)C + (\mu\Phi'(\mu) - \Phi(\mu))d}{C - d}. \tag{21.34}$$

Let $U_r(d_r) = \alpha d_r$ for $r = 2, \ldots, R$. Note that if

$$\frac{C}{R} \leq \frac{(A - \Phi(\mu))C}{A - \Phi(\mu) + \mu\Phi'(\mu)}, \tag{21.35}$$

then $\alpha \leq A$. This guarantees d_1 must be nonzero at any Nash equilibrium, so that the computation in (21.33) is valid. In turn, letting $d_r = d$ for $r = 2, \ldots, R$, this implies that $(d_1, \ldots, d_R)$ and μ are a valid solution to (21.31)–(21.32), when users have utility functions $U_1, \ldots, U_R$.

Now consider the limiting ratio of Nash aggregate utility to maximal aggregate utility, as $R \to \infty$. We have $d \to 0$, so $\alpha \to \Phi(\mu)$. Furthermore, regardless of R a solution to *SYSTEM* is to allocate the entire resource to user 1, so the maximal aggregate utility is AC. Thus the limiting ratio of Nash aggregate utility to maximal aggregate utility becomes

$$\frac{(A - \Phi(\mu))}{A - \Phi(\mu) + \mu\Phi'(\mu)} + \left(1 - \frac{(A - \Phi(\mu))}{A - \Phi(\mu) + \mu\Phi'(\mu)}\right)\left(\frac{\Phi(\mu)}{A}\right). \tag{21.36}$$

We now want to find the choices of A and μ which minimize this value.

For notational simplicity, we define $x = \Phi(\mu)/A$, and $\Psi(\mu) = \mu\Phi'(\mu)/\Phi(\mu)$. Note that given the convexity and invertibility of Φ, we have $\Psi(\mu) \geq 1$. Then (21.36) is equivalent to

$$F(x; \mu) = \frac{(1 - x)^2}{1 + (\Psi(\mu) - 1)x} + x. \tag{21.37}$$

It is straightforward to establish that the preceding expression is strictly convex in x for fixed μ. Let $G(\Psi(\mu))$ denote the minimal value of $F(x; \mu)$ for $x \in (0, 1)$;

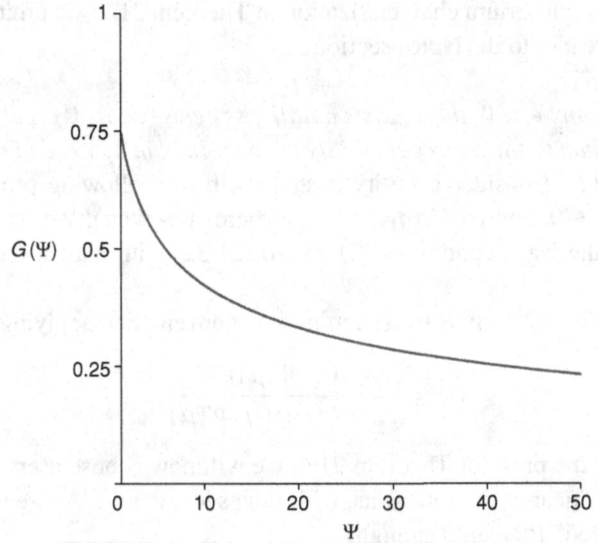

Figure 21.1. The function $G(\Psi)$ defined in (21.38). Note that $G(\Psi)$ is strictly decreasing, with $G(1) = 3/4$.

by differentiating, it follows that $G(\Psi)$ is defined for $\Psi \geq 1$ according to

$$G(\Psi) = \begin{cases} \dfrac{3}{4}, & \text{if } \Psi = 1; \\ \dfrac{2\Psi^2 - 3\Psi\sqrt{\Psi} + \sqrt{\Psi}}{(\Psi - 1)^2\sqrt{\Psi}}, & \text{if } \Psi > 1. \end{cases} \tag{21.38}$$

The function G is plotted in Figure 21.1. It is straightforward to verify that $G(\Psi)$ is continuous and strictly decreasing for $\Psi \geq 1$ so that the worst-case example is given by finding $\mu > 0$ such that $\Psi(\mu)$ is maximized. Furthermore, it is straightforward to check that $G(\Psi) \leq 3/4$, establishing the required claim.

Step 8: For any mechanism other than the proportional allocation mechanism, the worst-case efficiency is strictly lower than 3/4. For the proportional allocation mechanism, we have $\Psi(\mu) = 1$, and we have already established that the efficiency ρ is exactly 3/4. On the other hand, it is straightforward to check that if $B(p)$ is nonlinear, then the maximal value of $\Psi(\mu)$ in the preceding step is strictly greater than 1; and in this case $G(\Psi(\mu))$ is strictly less than 3/4. Thus there exists a game with efficiency ratio strictly lower than 3/4 for such a mechanism. This completes the proof. □

We make several comments regarding the proof. First, notice that every mechanism in the described class allocates in *proportion* to the bids of the players; in this sense all mechanisms in $\mathcal{D}$ are "proportional allocation mechanisms." However, the efficiency loss is minimized exactly when this mechanism charges each user exactly their bid. Second, it is possible to show that the bound constructed in Steps 7–8 of the proof is in fact a tight bound on the price of anarchy of the mechanisms under consideration; it is possible to reformulate this bound so that it depends only on the *elasticity* of the function $B(p)$, i.e., the quantity $\inf_{p>0} pB'(p)/B(p)$. (This is not surprising, since $\Psi(\mu)$ is the elasticity of the function Φ, which is the inverse of B.) It is surprising that the price of anarchy of a general class of such mechanisms can be reduced to this parsimonious calculation.

Finally, we note one potentially undesirable feature of the family of market-clearing mechanisms considered: the payoff to user r is defined as $-\infty$ when the composite strategy vector is $\boldsymbol{\theta} = 0$ (cf. (21.27)). This definition is required because when the composite strategy vector is $\boldsymbol{\theta} = 0$, a market-clearing price may not exist. One possible remedy is to restrict attention instead to mechanisms where $D(p, \theta) = 0$ if $\theta = 0$, for all $p \geq 0$; in this case we can *define* $p_D(\boldsymbol{\theta}) = 0$ if $\boldsymbol{\theta} = 0$, and let the payoff to user r be $U_r(0)$ if $\theta_r = 0$. This condition amounts to a "normalization" on the market-clearing mechanism. It is possible to show that this modification does not alter the conclusion of Theorem 21.10.

21.4 The Vickrey–Clarke–Groves Approach

The mechanisms we considered in the last section had several restrictions placed on them; chief among these are that (1) users are restricted to using "simple" strategy spaces and (2) the mechanism uses only a single price to clear the market. On the other hand, one could consider both generalizations where users are allowed to use more complex strategies, perhaps declaring their entire utility function to the market; and also, where price discrimination is allowed so that each user is charged a personalized per-unit price for the resource.

The best known solution employing both these generalizations is the VCG approach to eliciting utility information (see Notes, and Chapter 9). Such mechanisms allow users to declare their entire utility functions, and then charge users individualized prices so that they have the incentive to truthfully declare their utilities. We review VCG mechanisms in Section 21.4.1.

In this section we are interested in deciding whether the same outcome can be realized preserving restriction (1) above, but removing restriction (2): that is, can mechanisms with "simple" strategy spaces that employ price discrimination achieve full efficiency? In Section 21.4.2 we present an alternate class of mechanisms, inspired by the VCG class, in which users only submit scalar strategies to the mechanism; we call such mechanisms *scalar strategy VCG* (SSVCG) mechanisms. We show that these mechanisms have desirable efficiency properties. In particular, we establish existence of an efficient Nash equilibrium, and under an additional condition, we also establish that all Nash equilibria are efficient.

21.4.1 VCG Mechanisms

In the VCG class of mechanisms, the basic approach is to let the strategy space of each user r be the set $\mathcal{U}$ of possible utility functions, as defined in Assumption 1, and structure the payments made by each user so that the payoff of each user r has the same form as the objective function in *SYSTEM*, (21.1). As VCG mechanisms have been introduced in Chapter 9, we only use this section to fix notation for our subsequent discussion. For each r, we use $\tilde{U}_r$ to denote the declared utility function of user r, and use $\tilde{\mathbf{U}} = (\tilde{U}_1, \ldots, \tilde{U}_R)$ to denote the vector of declared utilities.

Suppose that user r receives an allocation d_r, but has to make a payment t_r; we use the notation t_r to distinguish from the bid w_r of Section 21.2. Then the payoff to user r is

$$U_r(d_r) - t_r.$$

On the other hand, the social objective (21.1) can be written as

$$U_r(d_r) + \sum_{s \neq r} U_s(d_s).$$

Given a vector of declared utility functions $\tilde{\mathbf{U}}$, a VCG mechanism chooses the allocation $\mathbf{d}(\tilde{\mathbf{U}})$ as an optimal solution to *SYSTEM* for the declared utility functions $\tilde{\mathbf{U}}$. For simplicity, let $\mathcal{X} = \{\mathbf{d} \geq 0 : \sum_r d_r \leq C\}$; this is the feasible region for *SYSTEM*. Then for a VCG mechanism, we have

$$\mathbf{d}(\tilde{\mathbf{U}}) \in \arg\max_{\mathbf{d} \in \mathcal{X}} \sum_r \tilde{U}_r(d_r). \tag{21.39}$$

The payments are structured so that

$$t_r(\tilde{\mathbf{U}}) = -\sum_{s \neq r} \tilde{U}_s(d_s(\tilde{\mathbf{U}})) + h_r(\tilde{\mathbf{U}}_{-r}). \tag{21.40}$$

Here h_r is an arbitrary function of the declared utilities of users other than r. In general, we note that mechanisms of this form do not use a single price to clear the market; i.e., the per-unit price paid by user r, $t_r(\tilde{\mathbf{U}})/d_r(\tilde{\mathbf{U}})$, will not be the same for all users. (See also Exercise 21.3.)

For our purposes, the interesting feature of the VCG mechanism is that there exists a dominant strategy equilibrium that elicits the true utility functions from the users, and in turn (because of the definition of $\mathbf{d}(\tilde{\mathbf{U}})$) chooses an efficient allocation. (See Chapter 9 for a formal statement of these results, where it is shown that the VCG mechanism is *incentive compatible*.) In the next section, we explore a class of mechanisms inspired by the VCG mechanisms, but with limited communication requirements.

21.4.2 Scalar Strategy VCG Mechanisms

We now consider a class of mechanisms where each user's strategy is a submitted utility function (as in the VCG mechanisms) except that users are allowed only to choose from a given single parameter family of utility functions. One cannot expect such mechanisms to have efficient dominant strategy equilibria, and we will focus instead on the efficiency properties of the resulting Nash equilibria.

Formally, *scalar strategy VCG* (SSVCG) mechanisms allow users to choose from a given family of utility functions $\overline{U}(\cdot;\theta)$, parameterized by $\theta \in (0, \infty)$.[5] We make the following assumptions about this family.

Assumption 2:

(i) For every $\theta > 0$, the function $\overline{U}(\cdot;\theta) : d \mapsto \overline{U}(d;\theta)$ belongs to $\mathcal{U}$ (i.e., it is concave, strictly increasing, continuous, and differentiable), and is also strictly concave.
(ii) For every $\gamma \in (0, \infty)$ and $d \geq 0$, there exists a $\theta > 0$ such that $\overline{U}'(d;\theta) = \gamma$.[6]

Given $\boldsymbol{\theta}$, the mechanism chooses $\mathbf{d}(\boldsymbol{\theta})$ such that

$$\mathbf{d}(\boldsymbol{\theta}) = \arg\max_{\mathbf{d}\in\mathcal{X}} \sum_r \overline{U}(d_r;\theta_r). \tag{21.41}$$

Since $\overline{U}(\cdot;\theta_r)$ is strictly concave for each r, the solution $\mathbf{d}(\boldsymbol{\theta})$ is uniquely defined. (Note the similarity between (21.39) and (21.41).)

By analogy with the expression (21.40), the monetary payment by user r is

$$t_r(\boldsymbol{\theta}) = -\sum_{s\neq r} \overline{U}(d_s(\boldsymbol{\theta});\theta_s) + h_r(\boldsymbol{\theta}_{-r}). \tag{21.42}$$

Here h_r is a function that depends only on the strategies $\boldsymbol{\theta}_{-r} = (\theta_s, s \neq r)$ submitted by the users other than r. While we do not advocate any particular choice of h_r, a natural candidate is to define $h_r(\boldsymbol{\theta}_{-r}) = \sum_{s\neq r} \overline{U}(d_s(\boldsymbol{\theta}_{-r});\theta_s)$, where $vd(\boldsymbol{\theta}_{-r})$ is the aggregate utility maximizing allocation excluding user r. This leads to a natural scalar strategy analogue of the Clarke pivot mechanism (cf. Chapter 9).

Given h_r, the payoff to user r is

$$P_r(d_r(\boldsymbol{\theta}), t_r(\boldsymbol{\theta})) = U_r(d_r(\boldsymbol{\theta})) + \sum_{s\neq r} \overline{U}(d_s(\boldsymbol{\theta});\theta_s) - h_r(\boldsymbol{\theta}_{-r}).$$

A strategy vector $\boldsymbol{\theta}$ is a *Nash equilibrium* if no user can profitably deviate through a unilateral deviation, i.e., if for all users r there holds:

$$P_r(d_r(\boldsymbol{\theta}), t_r(\boldsymbol{\theta})) \geq P_r(d_r(\theta_r', \boldsymbol{\theta}_{-r}), t_r(\theta_r', \boldsymbol{\theta}_{-r})), \quad \text{for all } \theta_r' > 0. \tag{21.43}$$

We start with the following key lemma, proven using an argument analogous to the proof that truthtelling is a dominant strategy equilibrium of the VCG mechanism (see Chapter 9).

[5] Note that, by contrast with Section 21.3, the choice of bid θ by a user indexes a utility function, rather than a demand function. However, this is not particularly crucial: if a user with utility function U maximizes $U(d) - pd$ (i.e., the user acts as a price taker), the solution yields the demand function $D(p) = (U')^{-1}(p)$. Up to additive constant, the utility function and demand function can be recovered from each other. Thus, equivalently, we could define SSVCG mechanisms where users submit demand functions from a parameterized class. We define our SSVCG mechanisms according to Assumption 2 to maintain consistency with the definition of VCG mechanisms in Section 21.4.1, as well as in Chapter 9.

[6] Since we do not assume differentiability with respect to θ, the only differentiation of $\overline{U}$ is with respect to the first coordinate d, and $\overline{U}'(d;\theta)$ will always stand for the derivative with respect to d.

Lemma 21.11 *Then the vector $\boldsymbol{\theta}$ is a Nash equilibrium of the SSVCG mechanism if and only if for all r:*

$$\mathbf{d}(\boldsymbol{\theta}) \in \arg\max_{\mathbf{d}\in\mathcal{X}} \left[U_r(d_r) + \sum_{s\neq r} \overline{U}(d_s;\theta_s) \right]. \tag{21.44}$$

PROOF Fix a user r. Since θ_r does not affect h_r, from (21.43) user r will choose θ_r to maximize the following effective payoff:

$$U_r(d_r(\boldsymbol{\theta})) + \sum_{s\neq r} \overline{U}(d_s(\boldsymbol{\theta});\theta_s). \tag{21.45}$$

The optimal value of the objective function in (21.44) is certainly an upper bound to user r's effective payoff (21.45). Thus, given a vector $\boldsymbol{\theta}$, if (21.44) is satisfied for all users r, then (21.43) holds for all users r, and we conclude $\boldsymbol{\theta}$ is a Nash equilibrium.

Conversely, given a vector $\boldsymbol{\theta}$, suppose that (21.44) is not satisfied for some user r. We will show $\boldsymbol{\theta}$ cannot be a Nash equilibrium. Since $\mathcal{X}$ is compact, an optimal solution exists to the problem in (21.44) for user r; call this optimal solution $\mathbf{d}^*$. The vector $\mathbf{d}^*$ must satisfy the first-order optimality conditions (21.8)–(21.10), which only involve the first derivatives $U_r'(d_r^*)$ and $(\overline{U}'(d_s^*;\theta_s), s\neq r)$. Suppose now that user r chooses $\theta_r' > 0$ such that $\overline{U}'(d_r^*;\theta_r') = U_r'(d_r^*)$. Then, $\mathbf{d}^*$ also satisfies the optimality conditions for the problem (21.41). Since $\mathbf{d}(\theta_r', \boldsymbol{\theta}_{-r})$ is the unique optimal solution to (21.41) when the strategy vector is $(\theta_r', \boldsymbol{\theta}_{-r})$, we must have $\mathbf{d}(\theta_r', \boldsymbol{\theta}_{-r}) = \mathbf{d}^*$. Thus we have

$$\begin{aligned} P_r(d_r(\boldsymbol{\theta}), t_r(\boldsymbol{\theta})) &< U_r(d_r^*) + \sum_{s\neq r} \overline{U}(d_s^*;\theta_s) + h_r(\boldsymbol{\theta}_{-r}) \\ &= U_r(d_r(\theta_r', \boldsymbol{\theta}_{-r})) + \sum_{s\neq r} \overline{U}(d_s(\theta_r', \boldsymbol{\theta}_{-r});\theta_s) + h_r(\boldsymbol{\theta}_{-r}) \\ &= P_r(d_r(\theta_r', \boldsymbol{\theta}_{-r}), t_r(\theta_r', \boldsymbol{\theta}_{-r})). \end{aligned}$$

(The first inequality follows by the assumption that (21.44) is not satisfied for user r.) We conclude that (21.43) is violated for user r, so $\boldsymbol{\theta}$ is not a Nash equilibrium. □

The following corollary states that there exists a Nash equilibrium which is efficient. Furthermore, at this efficient Nash equilibrium, all users truthfully reveal their utilities in a local sense: each user r chooses θ_r so that the declared marginal utility $\overline{U}'(d_r(\boldsymbol{\theta});\theta_r)$ is equal to the true marginal utility $U_r'(d_r(\boldsymbol{\theta}))$.

Corollary 21.12 *For any SSVCG mechanism, there exists an efficient Nash equilibrium $\boldsymbol{\theta}$ defined as follows: Let $\mathbf{d}^S$ be an optimal solution to SYSTEM. Each user r chooses θ_r so that $\overline{U}'(d_r^S;\theta_r) = U_r'(d_r^S)$. The resulting allocation satisfies $\mathbf{d}(\boldsymbol{\theta}) = \mathbf{d}^S$.*

PROOF By Assumption 2, each user r can choose θ_r so that $\overline{U}'(d_r^S;\theta_r) = U_r'(d_r^S)$. For this vector $\boldsymbol{\theta}$, it is clear that $\mathbf{d}(\boldsymbol{\theta}) = \mathbf{d}^S$, since the optimal solution to (21.41) is uniquely determined, and the optimality conditions for (21.41) involve only the first derivatives $\overline{U}'(d_r(\boldsymbol{\theta});\theta_r)$. By the same argument it also follows that $\mathbf{d}^S$ is an optimal solution in (21.44). Since $\mathbf{d}(\boldsymbol{\theta}) = \mathbf{d}^S$, we conclude that (21.44) is satisfied for all r, and thus $\boldsymbol{\theta}$ is a Nash equilibrium. □

We note that, as in classical VCG mechanisms, there can be additional, possibly inefficient, Nash equilibria, as the following example shows.

Example 21.13 Consider a system with R identical users with strictly concave utility function U. Suppose that user 1 chooses θ_1 so that $\overline{U}'(C;\theta_1) > U'(0)$, and every other user r chooses θ_r so that $\overline{U}'(0;\theta_r) < U'(C)$. Since $U'(C) \leq U'(0)$, it follows that (21.44) is satisfied for all users r. Thus this is a Nash equilibrium where the entire resource is allocated to user 1; however, the unique optimal solution to *SYSTEM* is symmetric, and allocates C/R units of the resource to each of the R users.

The equilibrium in the preceding example involves a "bluff": user 1 declares such a high marginal utility at C that all other users concede. One way to preclude such equilibria is to enforce an assumption that guarantees participation. The next proposition assumes that all users have infinite marginal utility at zero allocation; this guarantees that all Nash equilibria are efficient.

Proposition 21.14 *Suppose that $U_r'(0) = \infty$ for all r. Suppose that $\boldsymbol{\theta}$ is a Nash equilibrium. Then $\mathbf{d}(\boldsymbol{\theta})$ is an optimal solution to SYSTEM.*

PROOF Let $\mathbf{d} = \mathbf{d}(\boldsymbol{\theta})$. The proof follows by noting that all users must have positive allocations at equilibrium if $U_r'(0) = \infty$, from (21.44). Thus at equilibrium, for all users r, s we have $U_r'(d_r) = \overline{U}'(d_s;\theta_s)$. But this in turn implies that $U_r'(d_r) = U_s'(d_s)$ for all r, s, a sufficient condition for optimality for the problem *SYSTEM*. □

Intuitively, for efficiency to hold, we need to have a number of actively "competing" users. In the previous result, this is guaranteed because every user will want strictly positive rate at any equilibrium.

The results of this section demonstrate that by relaxing the assumption that the resource allocation mechanism must set a single price, we can in fact significantly improve upon the efficiency guarantee of Theorem 21.10. It is critical to note that this gain in efficiency occurs only at *Nash equilibria*. The classical VCG mechanisms are unique in that they guarantee efficient outcomes as dominant strategy equilibria; it is straightforward to check that the SSVCG mechanisms described in this section will not have dominant strategy equilibria in general—e.g., the "bluff" example above is one such case.

21.5 Chapter Summary and Further Directions

This chapter considered the allocation of a single resource of fixed supply among multiple strategic users. We evaluated a variety of market mechanisms through Nash equilibria of the resulting resource allocation game. Our key insights are the following:

- **(i)** A simple proportional allocation mechanism, where each user receives a share of the resource in proportion to their bid, ensures full efficiency when users are price takers, and exhibits no worse than a 25% efficiency loss when users are price anticipators.
- **(ii)** In a natural class of mechanisms where users choose one-dimensional strategies, and the market sets a single price, the proportional allocation mechanism minimizes the worst-case efficiency loss when users are price anticipating; i.e., the best possible guarantee here is 75% of maximal aggregate utility.
- **(iii)** This guarantee can be improved if the mechanism is allowed to set one price per user. Using an adapted version of the VCG class of mechanisms, we can construct mechanisms that ensure fully efficient Nash equilibria.

Our investigation also reveals several further directions open for future research, including the following:

- **(i)** For the proportional allocation mechanism, we have proven a bound on the price of anarchy that shows that the ratio of the Nash equilibrium aggregate utility is no worse than 3/4 the maximum possible aggregate utility. For nonatomic selfish routing (cf. Chapter 18), a similar price of anarchy result holds: the ratio of Nash cost to the optimal cost is no worse than 4/3; furthermore, both proofs use the characterization of Nash equilibria as solutions to an optimization problem, with structure similar to the respective efficient optimization problems. These results are suggestive of perhaps a deeper generalization of price of anarchy for games with equilibria characterized as the solution to optimization problems.
- **(ii)** While Theorem 21.10 proves optimality of the proportional allocation mechanism in a reasonable class of mechanisms, the result depends critically on the assumption that all mechanisms in $\mathcal{D}$ yield concave payoffs when agents are price anticipating. Given that some type of quasiconcavity assumption is typically necessary on payoffs to even guarantee existence of Nash equilibria, one might informally expect the result of Theorem 21.10 to hold even if Condition 2 is removed in the definition of $\mathcal{D}$. Whether this is in fact possible remains an open question.
- **(iii)** Our investigation shows, under reasonable assumptions, that with a single market-clearing price a 75% efficiency guarantee is possible, while with one price per user (the scalar strategy VCG approach), full efficiency is possible. This warrants further investigation: what is the exact trade-off between the number of prices and the efficiency guarantee possible? Furthermore, how does increasing the dimensionality of users' strategy affect this efficiency guarantee?

21.6 Notes

21.6.1 Section 20.2

Much of the material in this section is based on Chapter 2 of Johari (2004) and the corresponding paper (Johari and Tsitsiklis, 2004).

The mechanism discussed here was first studied in the context of communication networks by Kelly (1997). (See Chapter 22 for a discussion of the proportional allocation mechanism in congestion control algorithms for communication networks.) Theorem 21.1 is adapted from Kelly (1997), where it is proven in greater generality for an extension of the proportional allocation mechanism to a network context. This theorem is an extension of the classical *first fundamental theorem of welfare economics*; see Mas-Colell et al. (1995, Chapter 16), for details.

The first proof of uniqueness of Nash equilibrium for the proportional allocation mechanism was provided by La and Anantharam (2000). The most general result of existence and uniqueness, and the basis for the result in Theorem 21.2, is due to Hajek and Gopalakrishnan (2002); a less general result was proven by Maheswaran and Basar (2003). The explicit formulation of the problem *GAME* is given by Johari and Tsitsiklis (2004).

The price of anarchy result of Theorem 21.4 is due to Johari and Tsitsiklis (2004). The original proof of this result uses a two-step approach: it is first shown that the worst case is achieved using linear utility functions, and then the efficiency loss calculation is solved directly as a mathematical programming problem. The proof based on the problem *GAME* presented here is due to Roughgarden (2006), who also successfully applies the same method to efficiency loss calculations in several other games.

21.6.2 Section 20.3

Much of the material in this section is based on Chapter 5 of Johari (2004) and Section 4 of Johari and Tsitsiklis (2007).

The most closely related result to this section is presented by Maheswaran and Basar (2004). In their result, they consider mechanisms where each user r chooses a bid w_r, and the allocation is still made proportional to each player's bid. However, rather than assuming that every player pays w_r as in the standard proportional allocation mechanism, Maheswaran and Basar consider a class of mechanisms where the user pays $c(w_r)$, where c is a convex function. They show that in this class of mechanisms, the proportional allocation mechanism (i.e., a linear c) achieves the minimal worst-case efficiency loss when users are price anticipating.

Our work is substantially different, because we do not postulate that the mechanism must use the proportional rule (21.29) in allocating the resource; rather, this emerges as a consequence of rather simple assumptions on our mechanisms. We note that other works on inefficiency of resource allocation mechanisms, including Maheswaran and Basar (2004) and Yang and Hajek (2004), also assume a priori that allocations are made in proportion to users' bids.[7] In this sense, our result lends a rigorous foundation to the

[7] A notable exception is Sanghavi and Hajek (2004), which assumes that users pay their bid, and then designs an allocation rule to minimize worst case efficiency loss.

intuition that the proportional allocation rule (21.29) is a natural choice to determine the allocation among users.

21.6.3 Section 20.4

This section is based on Section 5.2 of the paper by Johari and Tsitsiklis (2007). Simultaneously and independently, a nearly identical formulation was developed by Yang and Hajek (2007). It is worth noting that Yang and Hajek and Maheswaran and Basar had earlier presented a resource allocation mechanism where users receive an allocation in proportion to their bids, but prices are chosen on an individualized basis (Maheswaran and Basar, 2004; Yang and Hajek, 2004); this mechanism can be seen to be a special case of the SSVCG mechanisms (Johari and Tsitsiklis, 2007).

Subsequent to the above work, several papers have presented related constructions of mechanisms that use limited communication yet achieve fully efficient Nash equilibria. Building on earlier work by Semret (1999), Dimakis et al. establish that a VCG-like mechanism where agents submit a pair (price and quantity requested) can achieve fully efficient equilibrium for a related resource allocation game (Dimakis et al., 2006). Stoenescu and Ledyard consider the problem of resource allocation by building on the notion of minimal message spaces addressed in earlier literature on mechanism design, and build a class of efficient mechanisms with scalar strategy spaces (Stoenescu and Ledyard, 2006).

The latter work of Stoenescu and Ledyard recalls perhaps the most related reference (and most seminal) in this area by Reiter and Reichelstein (1988). Their paper calculates the minimal dimension of strategy space that would be necessary to achieve fully efficient Nash equilibria for a general class of economic models known as *exchange economies*. For our model, their bound evaluates to a strategy space per user of dimension $1 + 2/(R(R - 1))$, where R denotes the number of users. This is slightly higher than our result because Reiter and Reichelstein consider a much more general resource allocation problem.

Bibliography

A. Dimakis, R. Jain, and J. Walrand. Mechanisms for efficient allocation in divisible capacity networks. *Proceedings of IEEE CDC*, pp. 1264–1269, 2006.

B. Hajek and G. Gopalakrishnan. Do greedy autonomous systems make for a sensible Internet? Presented at the Conf. Stochastic Networks, Stanford University, 2002.

R. Johari. *Efficiency Loss in Market Mechanisms for Resource Allocation.* PhD thesis, Massachusetts Institute of Technology, 2004.

R. Johari and J.N. Tsitsiklis. Efficiency loss in a network resource allocation game. *Math. Operat. Res.*, 29(3):407–435, 2004.

R. Johari and J.N. Tsitsiklis. Efficiency of scalar-parameterized mechanisms. Management Science and Engineering Working Paper 07-04-6126-34, Stanford University, 2007.

F.P. Kelly. Charging and rate control for elastic traffic. *Euro. Trans. Telecommun.*, 8:33–37, 1997.

R.J. La and V. Anantharam. Charge-sensitive TCP and rate control in the Internet. In *Proc. IEEE INFOCOM*, pp. 1166–1175, 2000.

R.T. Maheswaran and T. Basar. Nash equilibrium and decentralized negotiation in auctioning divisible resources. *Group Decis. Negotiation*, 12(5):361–395, 2003.

R.T. Maheswaran and T. Basar. Social welfare of selfish agents: motivating efficiency for divisible resources. In *Proc. IEEE CDC*, pp. 1550–1555, 2004.

A. Mas-Colell, M.D. Whinston, and J.R. Green. *Microeconomic Theory*. Oxford University Press, Oxford, UK, 1995.

S. Reichelstein and S. Reiter. Game forms with minimal message spaces. *Econometrica*, 56(3):661–692, 1988.

T. Roughgarden. Potential functions and the inefficiency of equilibria. In *Proc. Intl. Congress of Mathematicians*, Vol. III, pp. 1071–1094, 2006.

S. Sanghavi and B. Hajek. Optimal allocation of a divisible good to strategic buyers. In *Proc. IEEE CDC*, pp. 2748–2753, 2004.

N. Semret. *Market Mechanisms for Network Resource Sharing*. PhD thesis, Columbia University, 1999.

T.M. Stoenescu and J. Ledyard. A pricing mechanism which implements a network rate allocation problem in Nash equilibria. 2006. Submitted.

S. Yang and B. Hajek. An efficient mechanism for allocation of a divisible good and its application to network resource allocation. 2004. Preprint.

S. Yang and B. Hajek. VCG-Kelly mechanisms for divisible goods: adapting VCG mechanisms to one-dimensional signals. To appear in *IEEE Journal on Selected Areas in Communications*, 2007.

Exercises

21.1 This exercise, together with the next one, studies the efficiency loss properties of the mechanisms defined in Example 21.9, by following the proof of Theorem 21.4. Suppose that $D(p,\theta) = \theta p^{-1/c}$, where $c \geq 1$. Suppose that given a utility system $(C, R, \mathbf{U})$, a bid vector $\boldsymbol{\theta}$ is a Nash equilibrium, and let the resulting allocation vector be $\mathbf{d}$; i.e., $d_r = D(p_D(\boldsymbol{\theta}), \theta_r)$.

(a) Verify the Nash equilibrium conditions (21.31)–(21.32).

(b) Show that $\mathbf{d}$ is the unique solution to *GAME*, but where $\hat{U}_r$ is defined as follows for each r:

$$\hat{U}_r(d_r) = \int_0^{d_r} \left(\frac{1 - z/C}{1 + (c-1)(z/C)} \right) U_r'(z)\, dz. \qquad \text{(E1.1)}$$

(Hint: rearrange the Nash equilibrium conditions (21.31)−(21.32).*)*

(c) Show that $\hat{U}_r$ satisfies Assumption 1.

21.2 Fix $D(p,\theta) = \theta p^{-1/c}$ and define $\hat{U}$ as in the previous exercise. Define $\beta(D)$ according to (21.24), i.e.,

$$\beta(D) = \inf_{U \in \mathcal{U}} \inf_{C>0} \inf_{0 \leq d, \overline{d} \leq C} \frac{U(d) + \hat{U}'(d)(\overline{d} - d)}{U(\overline{d})}.$$

(a) Show that $\rho(D) \geq \beta(D)$. *(Hint: first construct the variational inequality that identifies the optimality conditions for GAME, then argue as in the proof of Theorem 21.4.)*

(b) Show that $\beta(D) \geq G(c)$.

(c) Using a construction analogous to the proof of Theorem 21.4, show that for any δ there exists a utility system for which the ratio of Nash aggregate utility to the maximum aggregate utility is no more than $G(c) + \delta$. Conclude that $\rho(D) = G(c)$.

21.3 Show by example that a VCG mechanism does not necessarily charge each user the same per-unit price for the resource.

PART FOUR

Additional Topics

CHAPTER 22

Incentives and Pricing in Communications Networks

Asuman Ozdaglar and R. Srikant

Abstract

In this chapter, we study two types of pricing mechanisms: one where the goal of the pricing scheme is to achieve some socially beneficial objective for the network and the other where prices are set by multiple competing service providers to maximize their revenues. For both cases, we present an overview of the mathematical models involved and the relevant optimization and game-theoretic techniques needed to study these models. We study the impact of different degrees of strategic interactions among users and between users and service providers on the network performance. We also relate our models and solutions to practical resource allocation mechanisms used in communication networks such as congestion control, routing, and scheduling. We conclude the chapter with a brief introduction to other game-theoretic topics in emerging networks.

This chapter studies the problem of decentralized resource allocation among competing users in communication networks. The growth in the scale of communication networks and the newly emerging interactions between administrative domains and end users with different needs and quality of service requirements necessitate new approaches to the modeling and control of communication networks that recognize the difficulty of formulating and implementing centralized control protocols for resource allocation. The current research in this area has developed a range of such approaches. Central to most of these approaches is the modeling of end users and sometimes also of service providers as self-interested agents that make decentralized and selfish decisions. This research has two important implications:

(i) The modeling of communication networks consisting of multiple selfish agents requires tools from game theory.

(ii) In the absence of centralized control, the interaction of multiple selfish agents may lead to suboptimal resource allocation.

This chapter will survey and develop existing work focusing on the role of prices, both used as control parameters in the network and set by service providers to increase their revenues. We will identify the different roles that prices may play in communication networks depending on the degree of strategic interactions among users and between users and service providers, and explore their impact on network performance under different scenarios. We will also highlight how the study of large-scale communication networks raises new modeling challenges and develop the mathematical tools that are commonly used in this analysis.

The chapter is organized into three sections: the first two sections correspond to two conceptually different strategic settings, one where pricing is used to achieve some socially beneficial objective, and the other where prices are set by multiple service providers to maximize their revenues. The last section places the material in this chapter in the context of the broader literature, discusses some emerging applications of game theory to communication networks, and suggests a number of areas for future research.

22.1 Large Networks – Competitive Models

In this section, we present a brief overview of the literature on pricing to maximize system utility in a network with a large number of users. This line of research has had a tremendous impact on communication networks, having contributed both to a deeper understanding of network architectures and to the development of new protocols for more efficient use of resources in the Internet. We will end the section with some extensions to wireless networks.

Consider a large network shared by many users, where the goal is to share the network resources in an optimal manner. It may be useful to think of the network as a graph with nodes and links. Each end user in the network is interested in transfering data between a source node and a destination node along a fixed route (or connection). We will use the terms "user," "source," and "connection" interchangeably. The nodes are interconnected by links. The network resources that we consider here are the link bandwidths. The bandwidth of a link is the maximum rate at which it can transmit data between the two nodes at either end of the link. We associate a utility function with each user in the network, and we will refer to a resource allocation scheme as being *socially optimal* if it maximizes the sum of utilities of all users in the network.[1]

A network is modeled as a set of resources indexed by l, called links, with finite capacities c_l. It is shared by a set of sources, indexed by r. Let $U_r(x_r)$ be the utility of source r as a function of its rate x_r (measured in packets per unit time). The utility function U_r is assumed to be a strictly increasing, strictly concave function. Associated with each source is a route that is a collection of links in the network. Let R be a *routing matrix* whose (l, r) entry is 1 if source r's route includes link l and is 0 otherwise. Since there is a one-to-one mapping between users and routes, we will use the same index to denote both a user and its route. For example, an index r can represent both user r and its route. Thus, the notation $l \in r$ indicates that link l is in the route of user r.

[1] In the networking literature, social optimality and fairness are often used interchangeably. For other notions of fairness, see Cho and Goel (2006).

The resource allocation problem can be formulated as the following nonlinear optimization problem (Kelly, 1997):

$$\max_{x \geq 0} \sum_r U_r(x_r), \qquad Rx \leq c, \tag{22.1}$$

where x is the vector of source rates and c is the vector of link capacities. The constraint says that, at each link l, the aggregate source rate $\sum_r R_{lr} x_r$ does not exceed the capacity c_l. If the utility functions are strictly concave, then the above optimization problem has a unique optimal solution, which we refer to as the socially optimal allocation.

To solve this problem directly, we have to the know the utility functions and routes of all the sources in the network. In a large network such as the Internet, this information is not available centrally. One solution to this problem is to devise a mechanism such as the celebrated Vickrey–Clarke–Groves (VCG) mechanism to encourage users to reveal their utilities truthfully (see Chapters 5 and 9). However, such a mechanism is computationally complex to implement and would also require a central authority to solve an optimization problem to compute the prices. Instead, Kelly devised a simple mechanism capable of achieving the optimal allocation of resources in the presence of selfish users (see also Chapter 21). We will describe this scheme in the rest of this section and also show how the pricing motivation also leads to protocols for managing the Internet. Such a scheme was originally proposed in Kelly (1997), Kelly et al. (1998) and variations have been considered in Low and Lapsley (1999), Yaiche et al. (2000), and Kunniyur and Srikant (2002); for a more exhaustive survey of the work in this area, see Srikant (2004).

Given the convexity of (22.1), a vector of rates $\hat{x}$ is optimal if there exists a vector of Lagrange multipliers $\hat{p}$ satisfying the following Karush–Kuhn–Tucker (KKT) conditions:

$$U_r'(\hat{x}_r) = \sum_{l:l \in r} \hat{p}_l, \qquad \forall\, r, \tag{22.2}$$

$$\hat{p}_l \left(\sum_{r:l \in r} \hat{x}_r - c_l \right) = 0, \qquad \forall\, l, \tag{22.3}$$

$$\sum_{r:l \in r} \hat{x}_r \leq c_l, \qquad \forall\, l, \tag{22.4}$$

$$\hat{p}, \hat{x} \geq 0. \tag{22.5}$$

Now, suppose that the network can compute $\hat{p}$ and charges each user r a price per bit of $\hat{q}_r$ where $\hat{q}_r$ is given by

$$\hat{q}_r = \sum_{r:l \in r} \hat{p}_l. \tag{22.6}$$

In vector form, the above relationship can be written as $\hat{q} = R^T \hat{p}$.

If the contribution of each user's flow to the aggregate is negligible, we expect them to take aggregate quantities, in particular prices, as given in their decisions. In this case, we refer to the users as *price takers*. Under this assumption, user r's optimization problem can be expressed as

$$\max_{x_r \geq 0} U_r(x_r) - \hat{q}_r x_r. \tag{22.7}$$

This expression is intuitive since it implies that each user is maximizing his utility minus the marginal cost of his flow, which consists of the sum of the Lagrange multiplier of each link traversed on its route. Clearly the solution to this problem is given by $\hat{x}_r$ in (22.2). The equilibrium under this pricing scheme where each user is charged the sum of the Lagrange multipliers on its path coincides with the socially optimum outcome. There are two key assumptions for this implication: (1) Users are price takers, which is reasonable in the case of a large network such as the Internet and (2) prices are set equal to the Lagrange multipliers to implement the socially optimal allocation. This assumption is reasonable when prices are set by a network controller interested in the overall performance. We will discuss how the situation is different when prices are set by profit-maximizing service providers in the next section.

For the above pricing scheme to work, the network has to be able to compute the Lagrange multipliers. There are two problems associated with this computation:

P1 The network does not know the utility functions of the users.
P2 Even if all the utility functions are known, there is no central authority that knows all the link capacities and the network topology to be able to solve (22.2)–(22.5).

To address (P1)–(P2), we consider the following two-step mechanism. First, each user r announces a bid w_r, which is the price per unit time that it is willing to pay. Then, the network decides to allocate rates to users according to the solution of the following optimization problem:

$$\max_{x \geq 0} \sum_r w_r \log(x_r), \qquad Rx \leq c. \tag{22.8}$$

The solution to the above optimization problem is called a weighted proportionally fair rate allocation. The KKT conditions for the optimization problem (22.8) are given by

$$\frac{w_r}{x_r^*} = \sum_{r:l \in r} p_l^*, \qquad \forall\, r, \tag{22.9}$$

$$p_l^* \left(\sum_{r:l \in r} x_r^* - c_l \right) = 0, \qquad \forall\, l, \tag{22.10}$$

$$\sum_{r:l \in r} x_r^* \leq c_l, \qquad \forall\, l, \tag{22.11}$$

$$p^*, x^* \geq 0, \tag{22.12}$$

where x^* is the solution to (22.8) and p^* is the associated vector of Lagrange multipliers. Furthermore, if the user can be induced to select $w_r = x_r^* U_r'(x_r^*)$, then $x^* = \hat{x}$ and the network problem coincides with the social welfare maximization problem.

To implement the mechanism described above, we have to first design a distributed algorithm to solve (22.8). The algorithm that we design is a dynamic algorithm where each link computes a price as a function of time according to a differential equation. The differential equation is designed so that, in steady state, the price of each link converges to the Lagrange multiplier corresponding to the link's resource constraint. To this end, suppose that each link computes a price according to the differential equation

$$\dot{p}_l = (y_l - c_l)^+_{p_l}, \tag{22.13}$$

where $p_l(t)$ is the instantaneous link price at time t, $y_l = \sum_{r:l \in r} x_r$ is the total arrival rate at link l, and $(a)^+_b$ is equal to $\max(a, 0)$ when $b = 0$ and is equal to a if $b > 0$. Note that the equilibrium of this differential equation is either $y_l = c_l$ or $p_l = 0$ which satisfy one of the KKT conditions (22.10). Each user's computer is hardwired with a program that computes rates according to the equation

$$x_r = \frac{w_r}{q_r}, \tag{22.14}$$

where q_r is the price of route r and is given by $q_r = \sum_{l:l \in r} p_l$.

To implement the above set of equations, it is assumed that the user r's computer is equipped with a protocol to collect q_r, the price of its path, from the network. In networking parlance, equation (22.14) is called a congestion control algorithm since the user reacts to congestion indication in the form of q_r. It is easy to see that if equations (22.13)–(22.14) converge, then their steady-state values satisfy (22.9)–(22.12) and thus, solve the optimization problem (22.8). Indeed the above set of equations converge under some mild assumptions. Let us suppose that the routing matrix R has full row rank, i.e., given a vector q of route prices, the vector of link prices p is uniquely determined by the equation $q = R^T p$. Since x^* is unique, this assumption ensures that p^* is unique. The following identity is useful:

$$q^T x = p^T R x = p^T y.$$

Now, consider the Lyapunov function

$$V(p) = \frac{1}{2}(p - p^*)^T (p - p^*).$$

Differentiating the Lyapunov function, we get

$$\begin{aligned}
\frac{dV}{dt} &= \sum_l (p_l - p_l^*)(y_l - c_l)^+_{p_l} \\
&\overset{(a)}{\leq} \sum_l (p_l - p_l^*)(y_l - c_l) \\
&\leq (p - p^*)^T (y - c) \\
&= (p - p^*)^T (y - y^*) + (p - p^*)^T (y^* - c) \\
&\overset{(b)}{\leq} (p - p^*)^T (y - y^*) \\
&= (p - p^*)^T R (x - x^*) = (q - q^*)^T (x - x^*) \\
&= \sum_r \left(\frac{w_r}{x_r} - \frac{w_r}{x_r^*} \right) (x_r - x_r^*) \\
&\overset{(c)}{\leq} 0,
\end{aligned}$$

where (a) follows from the fact if the projection $(\cdot)^+_{p_l}$ is not active, then the inequality holds as an equality and if the projection is active, the right-hand side of (a) is positive while the right-hand side of the equation above (a) is zero. Inequality (b) follows from the fact that either $y_l^* = c_l$ or $y_l^* < c_l$ and $p_l^* = 0$. Finally, inequality (c) follows from the fact that $1/x_r$ is a decreasing function. Thus, for a fixed set of bids $\{w_r\}$, the system of equations (22.13)–(22.14) converges to the point (x^*, p^*).

The above Lyapunov argument indicates that the congestion control algorithm is stable if w_r is fixed. However, since the price that a user pays is a function of its bid w_r, it is in the interest of the user to vary w_r. How might the user vary w_r? In general, we may expect users to act strategically and take into account the impact of their current bid on the future prices they will face. However, for our purposes here, let us suppose that they ignore these strategic aspects and behave myopically. In this case, they will simply maximize instantaneous net utility, the user's optimization problem to choose w_r is given by

$$\max_{w_r} U_r\left(\frac{w_r}{q_r}\right) - w_r.$$

Thus, the user chooses w_r to satisfy

$$U_r'\left(\frac{w_r}{q_r}\right) = q_r,$$

or equivalently as

$$w_r = x_r U_r'(x_r).$$

The congestion control algorithm then becomes

$$U_r'(x_r) = q_r. \tag{22.15}$$

The equilibrium point of the differential equation (22.13) is then given by (22.9)–(22.12) with w_r replaced by $x_r^* U_r'(x^*)$. In this case, the $x^* = \hat{x}$ where we recall that $\hat{x}$ is the optimal solution of (22.1) and satisfies (22.2)–(22.5). Thus, if the user is price-taking and myopic, then the users' selfish objectives coincide with the social welfare objective of the system. To prove the convergence of (22.13)–(22.15), one can use the same Lyapunov function $V(p)$ as before and proceed along the same lines.

An interesting side benefit of the pricing scheme above is that it provides a natural decomposition of the network functionalities that is useful in designing the architecture of a communication network. The pricing model suggests that the resource allocation functionality should be decomposed into pieces implemented in different parts of the network:

(i) *Congestion control at the end users:* The end users should be equipped with a protocol to adapt their rates in response to congestion feedback (route price) from the network.

(ii) *Congestion indication at the routers:* The routers (the nodes in the graph) in the network should be equipped with a protocol to compute the price of each link that originates from the router. The price is an indicator of congestion on the link.

(iii) *Congestion feedback from the network to the users:* There must be a protocol that allows an end user to collect congestion information from the network. For example, each data packet could contain a field to collect the congestion information. This congestion field could be set to zero at the source and each router on the path can add its price to this field. When the data packet reaches the destination, the congestion field will contain the price of the route. The destination can then send a packet to the source to convey the route price information.

The pricing framework introduced in this section can also be extended to incorporate other functionalities such as scheduling in a wireless network. We will briefly illustrate the extension to wireless networks, using a simple model; for a more general treatment, please see the survey (Lin et al., 2006) and the references within.

In a wireline network, packets can be transferred on all links simultaneously. However, in a wireless network, due to interference and collision, if a packet is scheduled on a link, other links in a neighborhood should be silent to avoid collisions and the resulting packet loss. We refer to a set of links that can be scheduled simultaneously as a *schedule*. Let $M_1, M_2, \ldots, M_n$ be the set of possible schedules in a network. Let f_i be the fraction of time that the network uses schedule M_i. The resource constraints in the network can now be expressed as

$$\sum_{r:l\in r} x_r \leq \sum_{i:l\in M_i} f_i c_l, \tag{22.16}$$

$$\sum_{i=1}^{n} f_i \leq 1, \tag{22.17}$$

$$f, x \geq 0, \tag{22.18}$$

where c_l is the number of packets that can be served by link l if it is scheduled. The goal is to find $\{x_r\}$ and $\{f_i\}$ to maximize $\sum_r U_r(x_r)$. The dual of the problem of maximizing $\sum_r U_r(x_r)$ subject to the constraints (22.16)–(22.18) is

$$\max_{p,\lambda\geq 0} D(p, \lambda),$$

where

$$\begin{aligned} D(p,\lambda) &= \max_{x\geq 0, f\geq 0} \sum_r U_r(x_r) - \sum_l p_l \left(\sum_{r:l\in r} x_r - \sum_{i:l\in M_i} f_i c_l \right) \\ &\quad -\lambda \left(\sum_{i=1}^{n} f_i - 1 \right) \\ &= \max_{x\geq 0} \sum_r U_r(x_r) - \sum_l p_l \sum_{r:l\in r} x_r \qquad (22.19) \\ &\quad + \max_{f\geq 0} \sum_l p_l \sum_{i:l\in M_i} f_i c_l - \lambda \left(\sum_{i=1}^{n} f_i - 1 \right). \qquad (22.20) \end{aligned}$$

It is not difficult to see that the dual objective for the wireline problem would also contain the term (22.19), while (22.20) is unique to the wireless problem. This suggests that the algorithm to compute x and p would be quite similar to the wireline case, but additional computation is necessary to find the optimal value of f. Without using the Lagrange multiplier λ, note that (22.20) can be equivalently written as

$$\max_{\sum_{i=1}^{n} f_i \leq 1, f \geq 0} \sum_{l} p_l \sum_{i:l \in M_i} f_i c_l = \max_{\sum_{i=1}^{n} f_i \leq 1, f \geq 0} \sum_{i} f_i \sum_{l \in M_i} p_l c_l = \max_{i} \sum_{l \in M_i} p_l c_l,$$

where the first equality is a simple interchange of the sums and the second equality follows from the fact that the optimization is a linear program and hence the solution will occur at a corner point. The last maximization problem can be interpreted as follows: pick the schedule that has the largest weighted price where the weights are the link capacities. The update equation at the source remains the same as before and is given by (22.15). It should be noted that while the network picks one of the schedules $M_1, M_2, \ldots, M_n$ to solve (22.15) at each time instant, it turns out that the the long-run fraction of time that each schedule is the optimal solution to the utility maximization problem; the interested reader is referred to Lin et al. (2006) and references within.

The price updates at the links are given by

$$\dot{p}_l = \left(y_l - \sum_{i:l \in M_i} f_i c_l \right)_{p_l}^{+}. \tag{22.21}$$

Note that the above equation does not have to explicitly implemented; it is simply the queue length at link l, which will be automatically maintained by each link. Thus, the only additional implementation required in a wireless network is the computation of the maximum weighted price schedule. This is a computationally hard problem and, in practice, also requires a distributed implementation to be feasible. The problem of low complexity, distributed algorithms to approximate the maximum weighted price schedule is currently open. Assuming that such an algorithm exists, the stability of equations (22.15)–(22.21) can be established using a Lyapunov function approach similar to the wireline case.

22.2 Pricing and Resource Allocation – Game Theoretic Models

The previous section explored how prices can be used as control parameters for allocating resources in communication networks. The analysis was non-game theoretic since users were assumed to be price takers and prices were set as control parameters to achieve the socially optimal allocation. While the framework with prices as control parameters is a useful starting point, it ignores a number of issues that are important for the analysis of resource allocation in large-scale communication networks. First, in a number of settings, where centralized control signals may be impractical or impossible, end users may not face explicit prices. It is therefore important to understand the implications of selfish end-user behavior when the congestion they create and their use of scarce resources are not priced. Second, prices are often set by multiple service providers in control of their administrative domains with the objective of maximizing their (long-run) revenues. In this section, we investigate the implications of profit-maximizing pricing by multiple decentralized service providers. We turn to a discussion of other possible generalizations in the next section.

22.2.1 Pricing and Efficiency with Congestion Externalities

We now construct a model of resource allocation in a network with competing selfish users and profit-maximizing service providers. The central question is whether the equilibrium prices that emerge in such a framework will approximate the prices implementing the socially optimal allocation discussed in the previous section. The class of models incorporating strategic behavior by service providers introduces new modeling and mathematical challenges. These models translate into game-theoretic competition models with negative congestion externalities,[2] whereby the pricing decision of a service provider affects the level of traffic and thus the extent of congestion in other parts of the network. Nevertheless, tractable analysis of pricing decisions and routing patterns are possible under many network topologies.

Models incorporating for-profit service providers have been previously investigated in Basar and Srikant (2002a, 2002b) and Acemoglu and Ozdaglar (2004). Here, we develop a general framework for the analysis of price competition among providers in a congested (and potentially capacitated) network building on Acemoglu and Ozdaglar (2006a, 2006b). We will see that despite its conceptual simplicity, this framework has rich implications. We illustrate some of these, for example, by showing the counterintuitive result that increasing competition among providers can reduce efficiency, which is different from the results of the most common models of competition in economics. Most importantly, we also show that it is possible to quantify the extent to which prices set by competing service providers approximate control role of prices discussed in the previous section. While generally service provider competition does not lead to an equilibrium replicating the system optimum, the extent of inefficiency resulting from price competition among service providers can often be bounded.

We start with a simple example that shows the efficiency implications of competition between two for-profit service providers.

Example 22.1 One unit of traffic will travel from an origin to a destination using either route 1 or route 2 (cf. Figure 22.1). The latency functions of the links, which represent the delay costs as a function of the total link flow, are given by

$$l_1(x) = \frac{x^2}{3}, \qquad l_2(x) = \frac{2}{3}x.$$

It is straightforward to see that the efficient allocation [i.e., one that minimizes the total delay cost $\sum_i l_i(x_i)x_i$] is $x_1^S = 2/3$ and $x_2^S = 1/3$, while the (Wardrop) equilibrium allocation that equates delay on the two paths is $x_1^{\mathrm{WE}} \approx .73 > x_1^S$ and $x_2^{\mathrm{WE}} \approx .27 < x_2^S$. The source of the inefficiency is that each unit of traffic does not internalize the greater increase in delay from travel on route 1, so there is too much use of this route relative to the efficient allocation.

[2] An externality arises when the actions of the player in a game affects the payoff of other players.

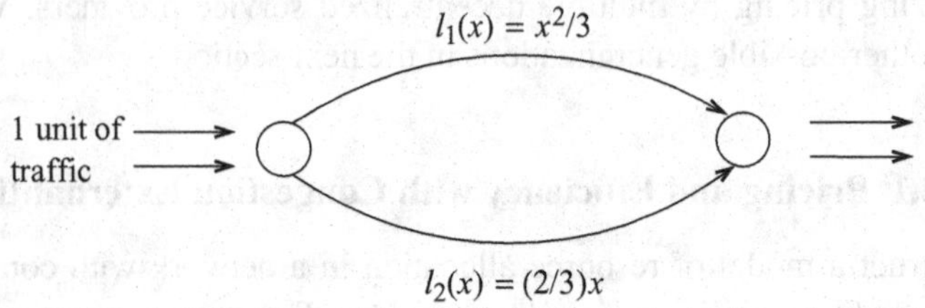

Figure 22.1. A two link network with congestion-dependent latency functions.

Now consider a monopolist controlling both routes and setting prices for travel to maximize its profits. We show below that in this case, the monopolist will set a price including a markup, which exactly internalizes the congestion externality. In other words, this markup is equivalent to the Pigovian tax that a social planner would set in order to induce decentralized traffic to choose the efficient allocation. Consequently, in this simple example, monopoly prices will be $p_1^{\mathrm{ME}} = (2/3)^3 + k$ and $p_2^{\mathrm{ME}} = (2/3^2) + k$, for some constant k. The resulting traffic in the Wardrop equilibrium will be identical to the efficient allocation, i.e., $x_1^{\mathrm{ME}} = 2/3$ and $x_2^{\mathrm{ME}} = 1/3$.

Finally, consider a duopoly situation, where each route is controlled by a different profit-maximizing provider. In this case, it can be shown that equilibrium prices will take the form $p_i^{\mathrm{OE}} = x_i^{\mathrm{OE}}(l_1' + l_2')$ [see Eq. (22.27) in Section 22.2.4], or more specifically, $p_1^{\mathrm{OE}} \approx 0.61$ and $p_2^{\mathrm{OE}} \approx 0.44$. The resulting equilibrium traffic is $x_1^{\mathrm{OE}} \approx .58 < x_1^S$ and $x_2^{\mathrm{OE}} \approx .42 > x_2^S$, which also differs from the efficient allocation. It is noteworthy that although the duopoly equilibrium is inefficient relative to the monopoly equilibrium, in the monopoly equilibrium k is chosen such that all of the consumer surplus is captured by the monopolist, while in the oligopoly equilibrium users may have positive consumer surplus.[3]

The intuition for the inefficiency of the duopoly relative to the monopoly is related to a new source of (differential) monopoly power for each duopolist, which they exploit by distorting the pattern of traffic: when provider 1, controlling route 1, charges a higher price, it realizes that this will push some traffic from route 1 to route 2, raising congestion on route 2. But this makes the traffic using route 1 become more "locked-in," because their outside option, travel on route 2, has become worse. As a result, the optimal price that each duopolist charges will include an additional markup over the Pigovian markup. Since the two markups are generally different, they will distort the pattern of traffic away from the efficient allocation.

22.2.2 Model

We consider a network with I parallel links. Let $\mathcal{I} = \{1, \ldots, I\}$ denote the set of links. Let x_i denote the total flow on link i, and $x = [x_1, \ldots, x_I]$ denote the vector of link

[3] Consumer surplus is the difference between users' willingness to pay (reservation price) and effective costs, $p_i + l_i(x_i)$, and is thus different from the social surplus (which is the difference between users' willingness to pay and latency cost, $l_i(x_i)$, thus also takes into account producer surplus/profits).

flows. Each link in the network has a flow-dependent latency function $l_i(x_i)$, which measures the delay as a function of the total flow on link i. We assume that the latency function l_i is convex, nondecreasing, and continuously differentiable. The analysis can be extended to the case when the links are capacity-constrained as in the previous section; see Acemoglu and Ozdaglar (2006b). We also assume that $l_i(0) = 0$ for all i.[4] We denote the price per unit flow (bandwidth) of link i by p_i. Let $p = [p_1, \ldots, p_I]$ denote the vector of prices.

We are interested in the problem of routing d units of flow across the I links. We assume that this is the aggregate flow of many "small" users and thus adopt the Wardrop's principle (see Wordrop, 1952) in characterizing the flow distribution in the network; i.e., the flows are routed along paths with minimum effective cost, defined as the sum of the latency at the given flow and the price of that path. We also assume that the users have a homogeneous *reservation utility* R and decide not to send their flow if the effective cost exceeds the reservation utility.

More formally, for a given price vector $p \geq 0$, a vector $x^{\mathrm{WE}} \in \mathbb{R}_+^I$ is a *Wardrop equilibrium* (WE) if

$$\begin{aligned} &l_i\left(x_i^{\mathrm{WE}}\right) + p_i = \min_j \left\{l_j\left(x_j^{\mathrm{WE}}\right) + p_j\right\}, \qquad \forall\, i \text{ with } x_i^{\mathrm{WE}} > 0, \\ &l_i\left(x_i^{\mathrm{WE}}\right) + p_i \leq R, \qquad \forall\, i \text{ with } x_i^{\mathrm{WE}} > 0, \\ &\sum_{i \in \mathcal{I}} x_i^{\mathrm{WE}} \leq d, \end{aligned} \tag{22.22}$$

with $\sum_{i \in \mathcal{I}} x_i^{\mathrm{WE}} = d$ if $\min_j\{l_j(x_j^{\mathrm{WE}}) + p_j\} < R$. We denote the set of WE at a given p by $W(p)$.[5]

We next define the social problem and the social optimum, which is the routing (flow allocation) that would be chosen by a planner that has full information and full control over the network. A flow vector x^S is a *social optimum* if it is an optimal solution of the *social problem*

$$\max_{\substack{x \geq 0 \\ \sum_{i \in \mathcal{I}} x_i \leq d}} \sum_{i \in \mathcal{I}} (R - l_i(x_i)) x_i. \tag{22.23}$$

Hence, the social optimum is the flow allocation that maximizes the social surplus, i.e., the difference between users' willingness to pay and total latency. For two links, let x^S be a social optimum with $x_i^S > 0$ for $i = 1, 2$. Then it follows from the definition that

$$l_1\left(x_1^S\right) + x_1^S l_1'\left(x_1^S\right) = l_2\left(x_2^S\right) + x_2^S l_2'\left(x_2^S\right). \tag{22.24}$$

This implies that the prices $x_i^S l_i'(x_i^S)$, i.e., the marginal congestion prices, can be used to decentralize the system optimum [cf. Eq. (22.22)].

[4] This assumption is a good approximation to communication networks where queueing delays are more substantial than propagation delays. We will talk about the efficiency implications of relaxing this assumption in different models.

[5] It is possible to account for additional constraints, such as capacity constraints on the links, by using a variational inequality formulation (see Acemoglu and Ozdaglar, 2006b; Correa et al., 2005).

For a given vector $x \geq 0$, we define the value of the objective function in the social problem,

$$\mathbb{S}(x) = \sum_{i \in \mathcal{I}} (R - l_i(x_i))x_i, \tag{22.25}$$

as the *social surplus*, i.e., the difference between users' willingness to pay and the total latency.

22.2.3 Monopoly Pricing and Equilibrium

We first assume that a monopolist service provider owns the I links and charges a price of p_i per unit bandwidth on link i. The monopolist sets the prices to maximize his profit given by

$$\Pi(p, x) = \sum_{i \in \mathcal{I}} p_i x_i,$$

where $x \in W(p)$. This defines a two-stage dynamic *pricing-congestion game*, where the monopolist sets prices anticipating the demand of users, and given the prices (i.e., in each subgame), users choose their flow vectors according to the WE. We define a vector $(p^{\mathrm{ME}}, x^{\mathrm{ME}}) \geq 0$ to be a *Monopoly Equilibrium* (ME) if $x^{\mathrm{ME}} \in W(p^{\mathrm{ME}})$ and

$$\Pi(p^{\mathrm{ME}}, x^{\mathrm{ME}}) \geq \Pi(p, x), \qquad \forall\, p \geq 0,\ \forall\, x \in W(p).$$[6]

In Acemoglu and Ozdaglar (2006b), it was shown that price-setting by a monopolist internalizes the negative externality and achieves efficiency. In particular, a vector x is the flow vector at an ME if and only if it is a social optimum. This result was extended to a model that incorporates a general network topology in Huang et al. (2006). This is a significant departure from the existing performance results of selfish routing in the literature that assert that the efficiency losses with general latency functions can be arbitrarily bad.

22.2.4 Oligopoly Pricing and Equilibrium

We next assume that there are S service providers, denote the set of service providers by $\mathcal{S}$, and assume that each service provider $s \in \mathcal{S}$ owns a different subset $\mathcal{I}_s$ of the links. Service provider s charges a price p_i per unit bandwidth on link $i \in \mathcal{I}_s$. Given the vector of prices of links owned by other service providers, $p_{-s} = [p_i]_{i \notin \mathcal{I}_s}$, the profit of service provider s is

$$\Pi_s(p_s, p_{-s}, x) = \sum_{i \in \mathcal{I}_s} p_i x_i,$$

for $x \in W(p_s, p_{-s})$, where $p_s = [p_i]_{i \in \mathcal{I}_s}$.

The objective of each service provider, like the monopolist in the previous section, is to maximize profits. Because their profits depend on the prices set by other service

[6] Our definition of the ME is stronger than the standard subgame perfect Nash equilibrium concept for dynamic games. In Acemoglu and Ozdaglar (2006b), we show that the two solution concepts coincide for this game.

providers, each service provider forms conjectures about the actions of other service providers, as well as the behavior of users, which, we assume, they do according to the notion of (subgame perfect) Nash equilibrium. We refer to the game among service providers as the *price competition game*. We define a vector $(p^{\mathrm{OE}}, x^{\mathrm{OE}}) \geq 0$ to be a (pure strategy) *Oligopoly Equilibrium* (OE) if $x^{\mathrm{OE}} \in W(p_s^{\mathrm{OE}}, p_{-s}^{\mathrm{OE}})$ and for all $s \in \mathcal{S}$,

$$\Pi_s\big(p_s^{\mathrm{OE}}, p_{-s}^{\mathrm{OE}}, x^{\mathrm{OE}}\big) \geq \Pi_s\big(p_s, p_{-s}^{\mathrm{OE}}, x\big), \quad \forall\, p_s \geq 0,\ \forall\, x \in W\big(p_s, p_{-s}^{\mathrm{OE}}\big). \tag{22.26}$$

We refer to p^{OE} as the *OE price*.

Analysis of the optimality conditions for the oligopoly problem [cf. (22.26)] allows us to characterize the OE prices (see Acemoglu and Ozdaglar, 2006b). In particular, let $(p^{\mathrm{OE}}, x^{\mathrm{OE}})$ be an OE such that $p_i^{\mathrm{OE}} x_i^{\mathrm{OE}} > 0$ for some $i \in \mathcal{I}$. Then, for all $s \in \mathcal{S}$ and $i \in \mathcal{I}_s$,

$$p_i^{\mathrm{OE}} = \begin{cases} x_i^{\mathrm{OE}} l_i'\big(x_i^{\mathrm{OE}}\big), & \text{if } l_j'\big(x_j^{\mathrm{OE}}\big) = 0 \text{ for some } j \notin \mathcal{I}_s, \\ \min\left\{ R - l_i\big(x_i^{\mathrm{OE}}\big)\ ,\ x_i^{\mathrm{OE}} l_i'\big(x_i^{\mathrm{OE}}\big) + \dfrac{\sum_{j \in \mathcal{I}_s} x_j^{\mathrm{OE}}}{\sum_{j \notin \mathcal{I}_s} \frac{1}{l_j'(x_j^{\mathrm{OE}})}} \right\}, & \text{otherwise.} \end{cases}$$

The preceding characterization implies that in the two link case with minimum effective cost less than R, the OE prices satisfy

$$p_i^{\mathrm{OE}} = x_i^{\mathrm{OE}}\big(l_1'\big(x_1^{\mathrm{OE}}\big) + l_2'\big(x_2^{\mathrm{OE}}\big)\big) \tag{22.27}$$

as claimed before. Intuitively, the price charged by an oligopolist consists of two terms: the first, $x_i^{\mathrm{OE}} l_i'(x_i^{\mathrm{OE}})$, is equal to the marginal congestion price that a social planner would set [cf. Eq. (22.24)] because the service provider internalizes the further congestion caused by additional traffic. The second, $x_i^{\mathrm{OE}} l_j'(x_j^{\mathrm{OE}})$, reflects the markup that each service provider can charge users because of the negative congestion externality (as users leave its network, they increase congestion in the competitor network).

22.2.5 Efficiency Analysis

We investigate the efficiency properties of price competition games that have pure strategy equilibria. [7] Given a price competition game with latency functions $\{l_i\}_{i \in \mathcal{I}}$, we define the efficiency metric at some oligopoly equilibrium flow x^{OE} as the ratio of the social surplus in the oligopoly equilibrium to the surplus in the social optimum [cf. Eq. 22.25 for the definition of the social surplus], i.e., the efficiency metric is given by

$$r_I(\{l_i\}, x^{\mathrm{OE}}) = \frac{\mathbb{S}(x^{\mathrm{OE}})}{\mathbb{S}(x^S)}, \tag{22.28}$$

where x^S is a social optimum given the latency functions $\{l_i\}_{i \in \mathcal{I}}$ and R is the reservation utility. In other words, the efficiency metric is the ratio of the social surplus in an equilibrium relative to the surplus in the social optimum. Following the literature on the "price of anarchy," in particular Koutsoupias and Papadimitriou (1999), we are interested in the worst-case performance of an oligopoly equilibrium, so we look for

[7] This set includes, but is substantially larger than, games with linear latency functions, see Acemoglu and Ozdaglar (2006a).

a lower bound on $r_I(\{l_i\}, x^{\mathrm{OE}})$ over all price competition games and all oligopoly equilibria.

We next give an example of an I link network that has positive flows on all links at the OE and an efficiency metric of 5/6.

Example 22.2 Consider an I link network where each link is owned by a different provider. Let the total flow be $d = 1$ and the reservation utility be $R = 1$. The latency functions are given by

$$l_1(x) = 0, \qquad l_i(x) = \frac{3}{2}(I-1)x, \quad i = 2, \ldots, I.$$

The unique social optimum for this example is $x^S = [1, 0, \ldots, 0]$. It can be seen that the flow allocation at the unique OE is $x^{\mathrm{OE}} = [\frac{2}{3}, \frac{1}{3(I-1)}, \ldots, \frac{1}{3(I-1)}]$. Hence, the efficiency metric for this example is $r_I(\{l_i\}, x^{\mathrm{OE}}) = \frac{5}{6}$.

The next theorem establishes the main efficiency result.

Theorem 22.3 *Consider a general parallel link network with $I \geq 2$ links and S service providers, where provider s owns a set of links $\mathcal{I}_s \subset \mathcal{I}$. Then, for all price competition games with pure strategy OE flow x^{OE}, we have*

$$r_I(\{l_i\}, x^{\mathrm{OE}}) \geq \frac{5}{6},$$

and the bound is tight.

A notable feature of Example 22.2 and this theorem is that the (tight) lower bound on inefficiency is independent of the number of links I and how these links are distributed across different oligopolists (i.e., of market structure). Thus arbitrarily large networks can feature as much inefficiency as small networks.[8]

22.2.6 Extensions

In this subsection, we extend the preceding analysis in two directions: First, we consider elastic traffic, which models applications that are tolerant of delay and can take advantage of even the minimal amounts of bandwidth (e.g., e-mail). We next focus on more general network topologies.

Elastic Traffic

To model elastic traffic, we assume that user preferences can be represented by an increasing, concave, and twice continuously differentiable *aggregate* utility function $u(\sum_{i \in \mathcal{I}} x_i)$, which represents the amount of utility gained from sending a total amount of flow $\sum_{i \in \mathcal{I}} x_i$ through the network.

[8] This result superficially contrasts with theorems in the economics literature that large oligopolistic markets approach competitive behavior. These theorems do not consider arbitrary large markets, but replicas of a given market structure.

We assume that at a price vector, the amount of flow and the distribution of flow across the links is given by the Wardrop's principle (Wardrop, 1952). In particular, for a given price vector $p \geq 0$, a vector $x^* \in \mathbb{R}_+^I$ is a Wardrop equilibrium if

$$l_i(x_i^*) + p_i = u'\left(\sum_{j \in \mathcal{I}} x_j^*\right), \quad \forall\, i \text{ with } x_i^* > 0,$$

$$l_i(x_i^*) + p_i \geq u'\left(\sum_{j \in \mathcal{I}} x_j^*\right), \quad \forall\, i \in \mathcal{I}.$$

We define the social optimum and the efficiency metric as in Eqs. (22.23) and (22.28), replacing $R\sum_{i\in\mathcal{I}} x_i$ (i.e., users' willingness to pay) by $u(\sum_{i\in\mathcal{I}} x_i)$.

It can be shown that for elastic traffic with a general concave utility function, the efficiency metric can be arbitrarily close to 0 (see Ozdaglar, 2006). The two-stage game with multiple service providers and elastic traffic with a single user class was first analyzed by Hayrapetyan, Tardos and Wexler (2005). Using an additional assumption on the utility function (i.e., the utility function has a concave first derivative), their analysis provides nontight bounds on the efficiency loss.[9] Using mathematical tools similar to the analysis in Acemoglu and Ozdaglar (2006b), the recent work (Ozdaglar, 2006) provides a tight bound on the efficiency loss of this game, as established in the following theorem.

Theorem 22.4 *Consider a parallel link network with $I \geq 1$ links, where each link is owned by a different provider. Assume that the derivative of the utility function, u' is a concave function. Then, for all price competition games with elastic traffic and pure strategy OE flow x^{OE}, we have*

$$r_I(u, \{l_i\}, x^{\mathrm{OE}}) \geq \frac{2}{3},$$

and the bound is tight.

Parallel-Serial Topologies

Most communication networks cannot be represented by parallel link topologies, however. A given source-destination pair will typically transmit through multiple interconnected subnetworks (or links), potentially operated by different service providers. Existing results on the parallel-link topology do not address how the cooperation and competition between service providers will impact efficiency in such general networks.

Here, we take a step in this direction by considering the simplest network topology that allows for serial interconnection of multiple links/subnetworks, which is the parallel-serial topology (see Figure 22.2). It was shown in Acemoglu and Ozdaglar (2006a) that the efficiency losses resulting from competition are considerably higher with this topology. When a particular provider charges a higher price, it creates a negative externality on other providers along the same path, because this higher price reduces

[9] For example, they provide the nontight bound of 1/5.064 in general, and the bound of 1/3.125 for the case when latency without congestion is 0.

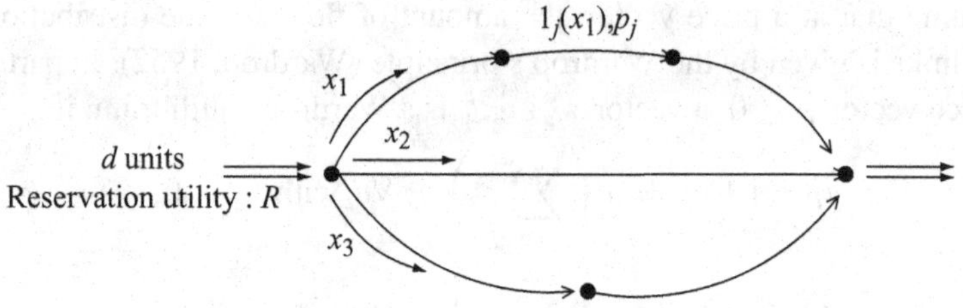

Figure 22.2. A network with serial and parallel links.

the transmission that all the providers along this path receive. This is the equivalent of the *double marginalization* problem in economic models with multiple monopolies and is the source of the significant degradation in the efficiency performance of the network.

In its most extreme form, the double marginalization problem leads to a type of "coordination failure," whereby all providers, expecting others to charge high prices, also charge prohibitively high prices, effectively killing all data transmission on a given path. We may expect such a pathological situation not to arise since firms should not coordinate on such an equilibrium (especially when other equilibria exist). For this reason, we focus on a stronger concept of equilibrium introduced by Harsanyi, the *strict equilibrium*. In strict OE, each service provider must play a strict best response to the pricing strategies of other service providers. We also focus our attention on equilibria in which all traffic is transmitted (otherwise, it can be shown that the double marginalization problem may cause entirely shutting down transmission, resulting in arbitrarily low efficiency, see Acemoglu and Ozdaglar, 2006a).

The next theorem establishes the main efficiency result for this topology.

Theorem 22.5 *Consider a general $I \geq 2$ path network, with serial links on each path, where each link is owned by a different provider. Then, for all price competition games with strict OE flow x^{OE}, we have*

$$r_I(x^{\mathrm{OE}}) \geq \frac{1}{2},$$

and the bound is tight.

Despite this positive result, it was shown in Acemoglu and Ozdaglar (2006a) that when the assumption $l_i(0) = 0$ is relaxed, the efficiency loss of strict OE relative to the social optimum can be arbitrarily large. This suggests that unregulated competition in general communication networks may have considerable costs in terms of the efficiency of resource allocation and certain types of regulation may be necessary to make sure that service provider competition does not lead to significant degradation of network performance.

22.3 Alternative Pricing and Incentive Approaches

The two approaches we have presented so far incorporate many of the important ideas in the role of prices and incentives in communication networks. Nevertheless, a variety of different approaches have also been developed in the literature, and the models presented in the previous two sections leave out several interesting aspects, which can be studied in future work. In this section, we first discuss the previous work on pricing in networks. We then mention several alternative approaches pursued in ongoing work. We conclude with a number of areas for future research.

22.3.1 Previous Work on Pricing

Despite the fact that current Internet access is based on a flat access charge, it has been recognized that the future of the Internet will involve multiple service classes, their use regulated by differentiated prices. The most natural approach to this problem involves the modeling of profit-maximizing service providers as developed in the previous section. Here we discuss some other aspects involved in the use of such prices.

Pricing for Differentiated Services: Service differentiation brings in a clear need for offering incentives to users to encourage them to choose the service appropriate for their needs, hence preventing overutilization of network resources. Pricing mechanisms provide an efficient way to ensure QoS guarantees and regulate system usage. One of the key debates in network pricing area is whether charges should be based on fixed access prices or usage-based prices. While usage-based pricing has the potential to fulfill at least partially the role of a congestion control mechanism, there were criticisms in view of the apparent disadvantages of billing overheads and the resulting uncertainties in networking expenses (see DaSilva, 2000).

A variety of pricing mechanisms have been proposed over the last decade. A well-known usage-based pricing proposal is by Mackie-Mason and Varian (1995), who proposed a "smart market" for resource allocation over a single link. In this scheme, users bid for transmission of each individual packet while the network provides service to packets whose bid exceeds a cutoff level determined by the marginal willingness-to-pay and marginal congestion costs. Users do not pay the price they bid, but rather the market- clearing price which is lower than the bids of all admitted packets. This mechanism resembles the Vickrey auction, and therefore provides users the correct incentives to reveal their true values in their bids. Odlyzko, in his seminal Paris Metro Pricing proposal (1990), suggested partitioning the network into several logical subnetworks. Users choose one of these logical networks for the transmission of their traffic, and this implicitly defines the service level; i.e., higher-priced networks will experience lower utilizations, and therefore will be able to provide a higher service level. Other proposed pricing schemes include *edge-pricing*, which focuses on locally computed charges based on expected values of congestion levels and routes; *expected capacity pricing*, in which users are charged according to the expected capacity the network provisions; and *effective bandwidth pricing*, which proposes the pricing of real-time traffic with QoS requirements, in terms of its "effective bandwidth"; see DaSilva (2000) for an overview of various pricing mechanisms.

First-Best Pricing: There is also a large theoretical literature in both communication networks and transportation networks area that study control mechanisms to induce efficient allocation of resources among competing users. The main focus is to use prices (or tolls) to induce flow patterns that optimize an overall system objective (also referred to as *first-best pricing*). It is well-known that *marginal cost pricing*, i.e., charging individual users for the negative (congestion) externality they impose on other users, achieves the system optimal flows. A number of studies have also characterized the "toll set," i.e., the set of all tolls that induce optimal flows, with the goal of choosing tolls from this set according to secondary criteria, e.g., minimizing the total amount of tolls or the number of tolled routes; see Hearn and Ramana (1998). Other related work focuses on models with heterogeneous users (i.e., users with different congestion-price sensitivities) and studies tolls that induce system optimal flows (see Cole et al., 2003; Fleischer et al., 2004).

22.3.2 Current Research on Pricing and Incentive Models

Many other game-theoretic models are useful in studying communication networks. Instead of providing a comprehensive survey, we now discuss a few models that are of significant practical relevance.

Fixed Pricing and the Marginal User Principle: As mentioned in the previous subsection, for various practical reasons (some of which are perhaps simply legacy reasons), consumers are accustomed to paying a flat-fee (e.g., monthly) for their service. In markets with a flat fee, typically a service provider has some idea of the distribution of the user's utility functions but not the utility function of each individual user.

An important problem therefore is to determine the fixed flat fee that maximizes the service provider revenue and to understand the impact of such a pricing scheme on the allocation of resources. In Acemoglu et al. (2004), we show that in a wireless network the profit-maximizing fixed price is equal to the utility of the marginal user in the network, where the marginal user is defined as a user who is indifferent to joining the network. Since the price and the resource allocation scheme determine the marginal user, they have to be chosen jointly to maximize the network revenue and it has been shown in Acemoglu et al. (2004) that such a resource allocation algorithm and price can be computed by the service provider under certain assumptions on the utility functions.

Incentives for Cooperation in P2P Networks: It is estimated that nearly half the traffic in today's Internet is due to peer-to-peer (P2P) networks. P2P networks are used to typically share large files among users. Some well-known examples of P2P networks are BitTorrent, Gnutella, KaZaa, etc. A P2P network is a collection of a large number of users who contribute some resources (typically, bandwidth, and memory) to not only download files of interest to themselves but to also store and transmit files that may be of interest to others. A P2P network has remarkable scaling properties compared to a Web server that stores many files that can be downloaded by users. A Web server has finite upload bandwidth and therefore, as more users join the network, the bandwidth per user has to decrease. On the other hand, in a P2P network since each user is a potential user as well as a server, as the number of users in the network increases, the capacity of the network also increases to keep up with the demand. In fact, simple analytical models suggest that there is no loss of performance as the number of users increases in a BitTorrent-type network (Qiu and Srikant, 2004). However, such scaling benefits can be achieved only if users cooperate. For example, if all users are only willing to download but refuse to upload files, then the network capacity will not scale with the number of users. Networks such as BitTorrent have some simple built-in incentive mechanisms to combat such problems and these have been studied in Qiu and Srikant (2004). As P2P networks continue to proliferate, it becomes quite important to study incentive mechanisms for such networks. Such issues are studied elsewhere in this book.

Incentives for Cooperation in Wireless Networks: Another form of networking that is expected to see tremendous growth in the near future is multihop wireless networks. In such networks, laptop computer or other mobile radio devices will communicate with each other in a multihop fashion without any infrastructure such as an access point or a base station. For such communication to be feasible, each radio must be willing to forward packets for other users in the network. While on the face of it, the problem appears to be similar to the case of P2P networks, there are some key differences. In a wireless network, since the communication medium is shared, it is possible for a wireless node (say node A) to hear whether a neighbor (call it node B) is being selfish or not. For example, if node A forwards a packet (destined for another node) to node B, then A can listen to see if B forwarded the packet or not. However, if another neighbor of A (say, node C) transmits at the same time as node B, then A will not hear B's transmission and thus, may erroneously assume that B is a selfish user. This is similar to a prisoner's dilemma model with noisy observations of the players' true actions (Piccione, 2002) and has been studied in He et al. (2004) and Mahajan et al. (2005) in a non-game-theoretic setting and in Milan et al. (2006) using game theory. However, the models used for the analysis of cooperation in multihop radio networks are currently quite simplistic and ignore the topological structure of the network. It is an open problem to develop more detailed models of the network and medium-access protocols, and to study the game-theoretic interactions for these more realistic models.

22.3.3 Areas for Future Research

The models presented so far highlight a number of fruitful areas for future research. These include but are not limited to the following topics.

Incentive-compatible Differentiated Pricing: As discussed above, a key role of prices in networks will be in allocating users with different requirements to differentiated services. If the service requirements and other characteristics of users were known by a central controller or service providers, this problem would be similar to those studied above. In practice, however, such information is not available and the market mechanism (i.e., the pricing scheme) has to ensure that individuals choose the services designed for them. This problem can be analyzed as a combination of the competition models developed above and the classical mechanism design approach. In particular, the celebrated Revelation Principle in the mechanism design theory (see Mas-Colell et al., 1995) implies that we can think of direct mechanisms in which individuals truthfully report their types, and are allocated services and charged prices accordingly.

The mathematical formulation then necessitates that a set of incentive-compatibility constraints that make truthful reporting optimal for each user is satisfied. The modeling challenge in this approach lies in combining the competition among service providers and the incentive-compatibility constraints.

Capacity Investments: While the focus of the current literature has been in ensuring the efficiency of the allocation of existing network resources, an arguably more important problem is to ensure that the right amount and type of infrastructure investment and capacity are installed in newly emerging networks. The analysis of this set of problems requires (multi-stage) models in which service providers choose not only prices but also investment levels and capacities.

Simple Pricing Rules: One potential criticism of economic approaches for resource allocation in networks is whether the complicated pricing schemes necessary for achieving socially optimal or profit-maximizing allocations can be computed and implemented in real time. The question of whether simple pricing rules can approximate these objectives and the quantification of the extent of efficiency or profits from such simple rules constitute another area for future research.

Bibliography

D. Acemoglu and A. Ozdaglar. Competition in Parallel-Serial Networks. To appear in *IEEE J. Selected Areas in Commun.*, special issue on Non-cooperative Behavior in Networking, 2006a.

D. Acemoglu and A. Ozdaglar. Competition and efficiency in congested markets. To appear in *Math. Operat. Res.*, 2006b.

D. Acemoglu and A. Ozdaglar. Flow control, routing, and performance from service provider viewpoint. *LIDS report*, WP-1696, May 2004.

D. Acemoglu, A. Ozdaglar and R. Srikant. The marginal user principle for resource allocation in wireless networks. *Proc. of CDC*, 2004.

T. Basar and R. Srikant. A Stackelberg network game with a large number of followers. *J. Optimization Theory Appl.*, 115(3):479–490, December 2002a.

T. Basar and R. Srikant. Revenue-maximizing pricing and capacity expansion in a many-users regime. *Proc. of INFOCOM*, 2002b.

S. Cho and A. Goel. Pricing for fairness: distributed resource allocation for multiple objectives. To appear in *ACM Symp. Theory of Computing*, 2006.

R. Cole and Y. Dodis and T. Roughgarden. Pricing network edges for heterogeneous selfish users. *Proc. of STOC*, 2003.

J.R. Correa, A.S. Schulz and N.S. Moses. On the inefficiency of equilibria in congestion games. *Proc. of IPCO*, pp. 167–181, 2005.

L.A. DaSilva. Pricing for QoS-enabled networks: a survey. *IEEE Communication Surveys and Tutorials*, 3(2):2–8, 2000.

L. Fleischer, K. Jain and M. Mahdian. Tolls for heterogeneous selfish users in multicommodity networks and generalized congestion games. *Proc. of FOCS*, pp. 277–285, 2004.

A. Hayrapetyan, E. Tardos and T. Wexler. A network pricing game for selfish traffic. *Proc. of ACM SIGACT-SIGOPS Symp. Princ. of Distributed Computing*, pp. 284–291, 2005

Q. He, D.Wu and P. Khosla, SORI: A secure and objective reputation based incentive scheme for ad-hoc networks. In *Proc. of IEEE Wireless Communications and Networking Conference (WCNC2004)*, Atlanta, GA, pp. 825–830, 2004.

D.W. Hearn and M.V. Ramana. Solving congestion toll pricing models. In P. Marcotte and S. Nguyen, editors, *Proc. of the Equilibrium and Advanced Transportation Modelling Colloquium*, pp. 109–124, 1998.

X. Huang, A. Ozdaglar and D. Acemoglu. Efficiency and Braess' Paradox under pricing in general networks. *IEEE J. Selected Areas Commun.*, 24(5):977–991, 2006.

F.P. Kelly. Charging and rate control for elastic traffic. *Euro. Trans. on Telecommun.*, 8:33–37, 1997.

F.P. Kelly, A. Maulloo, and D. Tan. Rate control in communication networks: shadow prices, proportional fairness and stability. *J. Operational Research Society*, 49:237–252, 1998.

E. Koutsoupias and C. Papadimitriou. Worst-case equilibria. In: *Proc. 16th Symp. on Theoretical Aspects of Computer Science,* pp. 404–413, 1999.

S. Kunniyur and R. Srikant. A time-scale decomposition approach to adaptive ECN marking. *IEEE Trans. on Automatic Control*, June 2002.

X. Lin, N.B. Shroff and R. Srikant. Cross-layer design in wireless networks: A tutorial. To appear in *IEEE J. Selected Areas Commun.*, June 2006.

S.H. Low and D.E. Lapsley. Optimization flow control–I: basic algorithm and convergence. *IEEE/ACM Trans. on Networking*, 7(6):861–874, December 1999.

J.K. Mackie-Mason and H. Varian. Pricing congestible network resources. *IEEE J. Selected Areas Commun.*, 13(7):1141–1149, 1995.

R. Mahajan, M. Rodrig, D. Wetherall, and J. Zahorjan, Sustaining cooperation in multi-hop wireless networks. In *Proc. Second USENIX Symp. on Networked System Design and Implementation (NSDI 05)*, Boston, MA, May 2005.

A. Mas-Colell, M.D. Whinston, and J.R. Green. *Microeconomic Theory*, Oxford University Press, NY, 1995.

F. Milan, J.J. Jaramillo and R. Srikant. Sustaining cooperation in a multi-hop wireless network with selfish nodes. To appear *Proc. of Workshop on Game Theory for Networks* (GameNets '06), Pisa, Italy, October 2006.

A.M. Odlyzko. Paris Metro Pricing for the Internet. In *Proc. of the 1st ACM Conf. Electronic Commerce*, pp. 140–147, 1999.

A. Ozdaglar. Price competition with elastic traffic. LIDS report, 2006.

M. Piccione. The repeated prisoner's dilemma with imperfect private monitoring. *J. Econ. Theory*, 70–83, 2002.

D. Qiu and R. Srikant, Modeling and performance analysis of BitTorrent-like peer-to-peer networks. *Computer Commmunications Review: Proc. ACM SIGCOMM*, Portland, OR, Sept. 2004.

R. Srikant *The Mathematics of Internet Congestion Control*, Birkhauser, 2004.

J.G. Wardrop. Some theoretical aspects of road traffic research. In: *Proc. of the Institute of Civil Engineers*, II, 1:325–378, 1952.

H. Yaiche, R. Mazumdar, and C. Rosenberg. A game theoretic framework for bandwidth allocation and pricing in broadband networks. *IEEE/ACM Trans. on Networking*, 8(5):667–678, Oct. 2000.

CHAPTER 23

Incentives in Peer-to-Peer Systems

Moshe Babaioff, John Chuang, and Michal Feldman

Abstract

Peer-to-peer (p2p) systems support many diverse applications, ranging from file-sharing and distributed computation to overlay routing in support of anonymity, resiliency, and scalable multimedia streaming. Yet, they all share the same basic premise of voluntary resource contribution by the participating peers. Thus, the proper design of incentives is essential to induce cooperative behavior by the peers. With the increasing prevalence of p2p systems, we have not only concrete evidence of strategic behavior in large-scale distributed systems but also a live laboratory to validate potential solutions with real user populations. In this chapter we consider theoretical and practical incentive mechanisms, based on reputation, barter, and currency, to facilitate peer cooperation, as well as mechanisms based on contracts to overcome the problem of hidden actions.

23.1 Introduction

The public release of Napster in June 1999 and Gnutella in March 2000 introduced the world to the disruptive power of peer-to-peer (p2p) networking. Tens of millions of individuals spread across the world could now self-organize and collaborate in the dissemination and sharing of music and other content, legal or otherwise. Yet, within 6 months of its public release, and long before individual users are threatened by copyright infringement lawsuits, the Gnutella network saw two thirds of its users free-riding, i.e., downloading files from the network without uploading any in return.

Given the large-scale, high-turnover, and relative anonymity of the p2p file-sharing networks, most p2p transactions are one-shot interactions between strangers that will never meet again in the future. It is therefore unsurprising that cooperation is difficult to sustain in these networks. The problem is exacerbated by hidden action due to nondetectable defections, and by the ability of peers to create multiple identities at no cost. It quickly became clear to the p2p developers community that some form of incentives is needed to overcome this free-riding problem.

The subsequent generation of p2p file-sharing networks incorporated incentive mechanisms based on *currency* or *reputation*. For example, in Mojonation, peers earn *mojos* through contributions to others, and use the earned currency to redeem for service from others. In KaZaA, peers build up their reputation scores by uploading, and highly reputed peers receive preferential treatment in their downloads.

The BitTorrent file-sharing system went beyond currency and reputation, and adopted an incentive mechanism based on *barter*. By partitioning large files such as movies and software binaries into small chunks, file-sharing using the BitTorrent protocol necessitates repeat interactions among peers, allowing cooperation to flourish based on *direct reciprocity* rather than *indirect reciprocity*. From a system perspective, there is no need to keep long-term state information, in the form of either reputation or currency. This simplifies the design and improves its robustness against attacks. Empirical studies found much lower levels of free-riding in BitTorrent communities. Yet, theoretical analysis has demonstrated that the BitTorrent protocol can still be manipulated by selfish peers in their favor.

The issue of incentives in p2p systems goes far beyond free-riding in file-sharing networks. Grassroots contribution by autonomous peers are needed to sustain many networked systems, ranging from mobile ad hoc networks and community-based wireless mesh networks, to application layer overlay networks that support anonymous communications and live video streaming. Even interdomain routing over the Internet requires the cooperation of competing network operators.

The strategy space is also far richer than the binary choice of share/not-share in file-sharing networks. Peers make strategic decisions concerning the revelation of *private information*, such as local resource availability, workload, contribution cost, or willingness-to-pay. Peers decide on the amount of exerted effort, given the nonobservability of their *hidden actions*. Peers may adjust their spatial engagement with the network through *strategic network formation*, and temporal engagement through *strategic churning* (arrivals and departures). Finally, peers may choose to manage their own identities and treat the identities of others differently given the availability of cheap pseudonyms.

The increasing prevalence of p2p systems, coupled with the rich strategy space available to the peers, make the problem of *p2p mechanism design* a challenging and broadly relevant topic of study for algorithmic game theory. P2P systems offer a concrete example of strategic behavior in large-scale distributed systems, as well as a live laboratory to validate potential solutions with real user populations. In this chapter, we discuss some p2p incentive mechanisms based on reputation, barter, and currency, as well as mechanisms to overcome the problem of hidden actions. We refer readers to other chapters in this book on the related topics of distributed algorithmic mechanism design (Chapter 14), strategic network formation (Chapter 19), network pricing (Chapter 22), and reputation systems (Chapter 27).

23.2 The p2p File-Sharing Game

A p2p file-sharing system seeks to support efficient and scalable distribution of files by leveraging the upload bandwidth of the downloading peers. In a p2p file-sharing

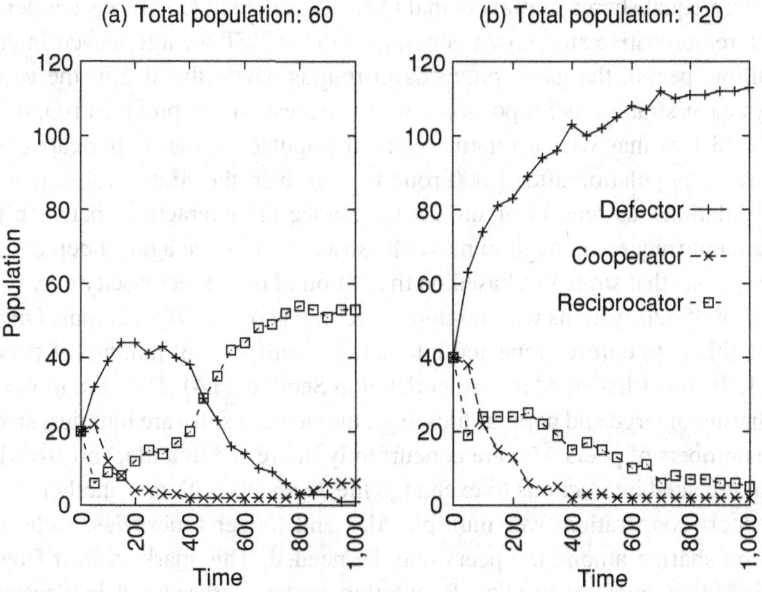

Figure 23.1. The temporal evolution of strategy populations in a p2p file-sharing game. "Time" is the number of elapsed rounds. "Population" is the number of players using a strategy.

system, a peer plays one of two roles. For certain interactions, he is a client who wishes to download a file, and derives benefit from a successful download. For other interactions, he is a server who is requested to upload part or all of a file, and if he agrees he may bear some cost in the form of bandwidth and CPU usage. In such a one-shot game, "free-riding" is a dominant strategy – a player will download when he is a client, and refuse to upload when he is a server.

The interaction between players in a p2p file-sharing system has many characteristics of the Prisoner's Dilemma (PD) game. In the single-shot PD game, players have a dominant strategy to defect, which leads to a socially undesirable equilibrium outcome known as the "tragedy of the commons." In the Iterated Prisoner's Dilemma game, cooperation can be sustained through direct reciprocity (e.g., using the Tit-for-Tat or TFT strategy) since a defection in the current round can lead to retaliation by the other player in a future round. This "shadow of the future" can similarly sustain cooperation in the p2p file-sharing game, where a peer may decide to upload a file to another peer with the expectation that he may wish to download a file from the other peer sometime in the future.

Of course, there is no guarantee that two peers will engage in multiple transactions with each other in their lifetimes. Even if they do, there is no guarantee that they will do so with a proper reversal of client and server roles to facilitate reciprocity or retaliation. In a large dynamic population with random matching of players, the probability of repeat interactions between players may be too small to cast an effective "shadow of the future," and free-riding might prevail.

Figure 23.1, taken from a simulation study of a p2p file-sharing game (Feldman et al., 2004), illustrates the inability of a reciprocative strategy to scale to large populations.

Starting with equal shares of players that (1) always defect, (2) always cooperate, and (3) play a reciprocative strategy (a generalization of TFT for interleaved interactions with multiple peers), the game proceeds in rounds where the size of the population that plays each strategy is proportional to its success in the previous round. We see in Figure 23.1(a) that with a relatively small population, the reciprocative strategy dominates the population after 1,000 rounds. However, the strategy does not scale to larger populations, as seen in Figure 23.1(b), since the interactions between pairs of players are not frequent enough to make the strategy effective against defectors.

This suggests that strategies based on the notion of direct reciprocity may not fit the environment of p2p systems with random matching and large populations. One way to overcome this is to enforce repeated interactions with a small number of peers, as is done in BitTorrent (discussed in further detail in Section 23.4). This design works well for the sharing of large and popular files, e.g., movies and software binaries, since there are large numbers of peers who are concurrently interested in a file, and are willing to engage in repeated interactions to exchange file segments with one another.

To support cooperation over multiple files and longer timescales, some form of information sharing among the peers may be needed. This marks a shift from direct reciprocity to indirect reciprocity. Reputation systems (discussed in Section 23.3) provide a means for a peer to condition his action against his opponent upon the opponent's past actions, not just against the peer himself, but against other peers in the system. This way, a peer may choose to serve a file to another peer on the grounds that the latter had cooperated with other peers in earlier interactions.

Because p2p systems are large, dynamic systems with high turnover rates, peers often interact with strangers with no prior history or reputation. It is therefore very important to think about how one deals with strangers. A tit-for-tat strategy that always cooperates with strangers may encourage newcomers to join the system, but it can be easily exploited by whitewashers who leave and rejoin the system with new identities. The problem arises because a whitewasher is indistinguishable from a legitimate newcomer. Always defecting against strangers is robust against whitewashers, but it discourages newcomers and may also initiate unfavorable cycles of defection. It has been shown that cooperating with strangers with a fixed probability $0 < p < 1$ is not robust against whitewashers. On the other hand, adapting the probability of cooperation with strangers to the frequency of past cooperation by strangers appears to be effective against whitewashers, at least for a sufficiently small turnover rate.

In the next three sections, we will discuss incentive mechanisms for p2p systems based on reputation, barter, and currency.

23.3 Reputation

Reputation has an excellent track record at facilitating cooperation in very diverse settings, from evolutionary biology to online marketplaces like eBay. It is therefore unsurprising that many p2p systems have adopted some form of reputation scheme to reward good behavior and/or punish bad behavior by the peers.

In general, a p2p reputation scheme is coupled with a service differentiation scheme. Contributing peers possess good reputations and receive good service from other peers, while noncontributing peers possess bad reputations and receive poor service from others. For example, peers in the KaZaA file-sharing network build up their reputation scores by uploading files to others, and are rewarded with higher priority when downloading files from others. Similar schemes have been proposed for p2p storage, p2p multicast, and mobile ad hoc networks.

Used in conjunction with other security techniques, a p2p reputation scheme can also be used to identify, isolate, and avoid malicious peers in a system. For example, the Eigentrust algorithm computes global trust values of peers by aggregating local trust values based on the notion of transitive trust, similar to the PageRank algorithm. Peers that introduce inauthentic files into the system receive a low global trust value and will be shunned by others. The Credence system extends the notion of reputation from peers to objects. Reputation scores are maintained for individual objects in the p2p system. These techniques can be used to defend against pollution and poisoning attacks in p2p file-sharing networks.

Reputation systems may be subject to a number of different attacks. Multiple colluding peers may boost one another's reputation scores by giving false praise, or punish a target peer by giving false accusations. The availability of *cheap pseudonyms* in p2p systems make reputation systems vulnerable to *Sybil attacks* and *whitewashing attacks*. In a Sybil attack, a single malicious peer generates multiple identities that collude with one another. In a whitewashing attack, a peer defects in every p2p transaction, but repeatedly leaves and rejoins the p2p system using newly created identities, so that it will never suffer the negative consequences of a bad reputation.

A comprehensive treatment of the design and implementation of reputation systems is provided in a separate chapter of this book. So we will focus our attention to the use of reputation and service differentiation schemes in establishing cooperation in p2p systems. In particular, we will construct a minimalistic model of a p2p system (in Section 23.3.1) to explore its dynamics and resulting equilibria in the absence of any reputation scheme, and see (in Section 23.3.2) how a reputation and service differentiation scheme can improve the performance of the system.

23.3.1 A Minimalist p2p Model

Consider a population of rational peers with heterogeneous willingness to contribute resources to the system. Each peer i has a type θ_i, reflecting his generosity or the maximum cost he is willing to incur in contribution. Each peer makes autonomous decisions whether to contribute or free-ride based on the relationship between the cost of contribution and her type. Since contributors have to carry the load of the system, the contribution cost can be modeled as inversely proportional to the fraction of contributors in the system. Thus, if at present a fraction x of the peers are contributing, the contribution cost is $1/x$, and therefore the decision of a rational peer with type θ_i is:

$$\text{Contribute, if } \theta_i > 1/x;$$
$$\text{Free-ride, otherwise.}$$

Even within this simple framework we can already see some interesting implications. In this "free market" environment where no incentive mechanism is in place,

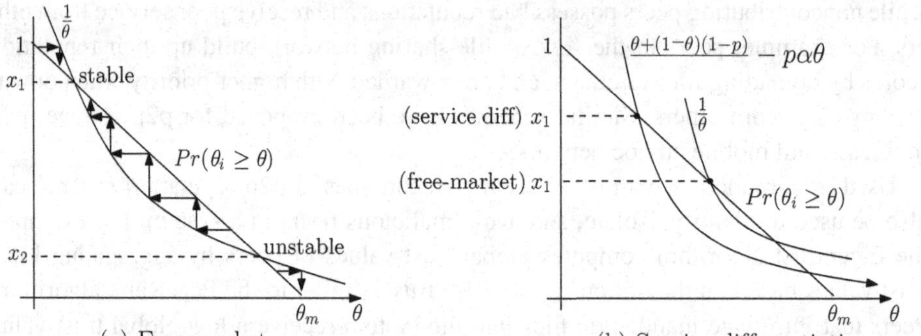

Figure 23.2. (a) The intersection points of the type distribution and cost curves represent two equilibria of the system. The curve $1/\theta$ represents the contribution cost, and $Pr(\theta_i \geq \theta)$ represents the generosity CDF, assuming $\theta_i \sim U(0, \theta_m)$. The higher equilibrium (contribution level x_1) is stable. The point $x = 0$ is an additional equilibrium of the system. (b) Under the service differentiation mechanism, the cost curve shifts from $1/\theta$ to $\frac{\theta+(1-\theta)(1-p)}{\theta} - p\alpha\theta$. Consequently, the attractor (x_1) shifts upward.

the contribution level x in equilibrium is determined as the intersection of the type distribution, $x = Pr(\theta_i \geq \theta)$ with the curve $x = 1/\theta$.

Figure 23.2 shows the equilibria when the generosity type is uniformly distributed between 0 and some maximal value θ_m. There are three equilibria in this system. The first two are the intersection points of the type distribution curve and the cost curve. The third equilibrium is $x = 0$, which always exists. Consider the natural fix-point dynamics of the system, i.e., starting at some initial x, peers arrive at individual decisions, their aggregate decisions define a new x, which leads to a new aggregate decision, and so on. When the system is out of equilibrium, the direction in which the system moves depends on the relative heights of the two curves. If the cost curve is above the type distribution curve, contribution cost is higher than the fraction of users who are willing to contribute at this cost, so the fraction of contributors decreases. For example, in Figure 23.2, this happens for $x < x_2$ or $x > x_1$. Conversely, for $x_1 < x < x_2$, the contribution cost is lower than the willingness to contribute, so contribution level increases. Therefore, $x = x_1$ and $x = 0$ are the two attractors of the fixpoint dynamics. As long as the initial x lies above the lower intersection point (x_2), the process converges to the upper one (x_1). Otherwise, if the initial x is below the lower intersection point, or if there is no intersection; i.e., when there are too many selfish rascals around, then x converges to 0 and the system collapses.

The contribution level of the system, x, is derived by solving the fixpoint equation: $x = Prob(\theta_i \geq 1/x)$. If we consider the case in which the generosity of the peers is uniformly distributed between 0 and θ_m, i.e., $\theta_i \sim U(0, \theta_m)$, then $\text{Prob}(\theta_i \geq 1/x) = 1 - \frac{1}{x\theta_m}$, and the fixpoint equation is $x = 1 - \frac{1}{x\theta_m}$. The solutions are $x_{1,2} = \frac{\theta_m \pm \sqrt{\theta_m^2 - 4\theta_m}}{2\theta_m}$. The larger root x_1 is a stable equilibrium while x_2 is not. θ_m denotes the maximal willingness to contribute resources, and reflects the overall generosity level of the system.

Claim 23.1 *The stable nonzero equilibrium contribution level (x_1) increases in θ_m and converges to 1 as θ_m goes to ∞, but falls to zero when $\theta_m < 4$.*

So far we have been interested only in costs. To understand system performance, we need to consider system benefits as well. We assume that the benefit a peer receives from participation in the system (whether or not she contributes) is proportional to the contribution level in the system, and thus a function of the form αx for some constant $\alpha \geq 1$. We concentrate on cases where α is large, in which $x = 0$ is socially inefficient.

We define the performance of the system, W_S, as the difference between the total benefits received by all peers and the total contribution cost incurred by all peers (noting that free riders incur no costs). Normalizing network size to 1, for $x > 0$ we have

$$W_S = \alpha x - (1/x)x = \alpha x - 1.$$

According to the definition of system performance and Claim 23.1, even if participation can provide high benefits to the peers, the system will still collapse if the maximal generosity is low, since the system performance is limited by the low contribution level. In the next section, we see how a reputation and service differentiation scheme can overcome this problem.

23.3.2 Reputation and Service Differentiation

Now let us introduce an incentive mechanism based upon reputation and service differentiation. Consider a reputation system that can catch free riders with probability p, and a service differentiation policy where identified free riders are excluded from the system. An alternate interpretation is a reputation system that can perfectly distinguish free riders and contributors, used in conjunction with a service differentiation policy where free riders are penalized with a reduced level of service of $1 - p$ times that of a contributor.

Degrading the performance of the free riders has two effects, both of which lead to a higher contribution level. First, since free riders get only a fraction $1 - p$ of the benefits, the load placed on the system decreases to $x + (1 - x)(1 - p)$. Therefore, contribution cost becomes $\frac{x+(1-x)(1-p)}{x}$. Second, the penalty introduces a threat, since peers who free ride know that they will receive reduced service or face the possibility of expulsion.

Let Q, R, and T denote the individual benefit, reduced contribution cost, and threat, respectively. A contributor would realize a performance of $Q - R = \alpha x - \frac{x+(1-x)(1-p)}{x}$ while a free rider would realize a performance of $Q - T = \alpha x - p\alpha x$. Then, the new equilibrium contribution level becomes $x = \text{Prob}(\theta_i \geq R - T)$, and is derived by solving the fixpoint equation: $x = Prob(\theta_i \geq \frac{x+(1-x)(1-p)}{x} - p\alpha x)$.

With the reputation and service differentiation mechanism in place, the system performance now becomes

$$W_S(p) = x(Q - R) + (1 - x)(Q - T) = (\alpha x - 1)(x + (1 - x)(1 - p))$$

Imposing a penalty on free riders, while increasing the contribution level, entails some social loss. The p2p system designer could set the value of p to achieve a target cooperation level. Note that if the penalty is set sufficiently high, the threat T will exceed the contribution cost R, and peers will no longer have any reason to free ride. In this case, no penalty is actually imposed. With no free riders an optimal system performance of $\alpha - 1$ will be achieved.

Claim 23.2 *Under the penalty mechanism, if $p \geq 1/\alpha$, then there exists an equilibrium in which $x = 1$.*

This means that if the benefits of participating in the p2p system are high (α is large), either a service differentiation policy that imposes a small performance penalty on free riders or a mechanism that can catch and exclude free riders with a small probability is sufficient to induce a high level of cooperation (with any maximal generosity level). Otherwise, a more severe penalty or a finer sieve for catching free riders would be necessary.

23.4 A Barter-Based System: BitTorrent

BitTorrent is a popular p2p file-sharing system with incentives as an integral part of its design. It departs from earlier p2p file-sharing systems in that its incentive mechanism is based loosely on direct reciprocity rather than indirect reciprocity.

In BitTorrent, a seeding peer divides a large file into small fixed size pieces, and provides different pieces to different peers, who in turn exchange pieces with one another. A peer can reconstruct the file once it has obtained all the pieces. This technique is known as swarming download or parallel download. To induce peers to upload their pieces, a peer's download rate is influenced by his upload rate through a direct reciprocity or barter scheme.

BitTorrent attempts to alleviate the problem of random matching in large populations (Figure 23.1(b) in Section 23.2) by enforcing repeated transactions among peers. When a peer initiates a file download, it is matched with a small set of around 40 peers who are also downloading or uploading pieces of the same file. The peer selects four or five peers out of the set to connect to as neighbors, and periodically updates the list of neighbors with those peers that provide the best download rates. Through an *opportunistic unchoking* mechanism, a peer occasionally selects a random peer from the set to upload to, with the hope of finding new peers that can provide better download rates than the current neighbors.

With this design, BitTorrent peers engage in multiple interactions with a small number of peers for the duration of a file download period. For the exchange of large files such as movies and software binaries, the number of repeated interactions can be quite large, allowing cooperation to take hold through direct reciprocity. However, the BitTorrent barter scheme does not address cooperation beyond the file download period. As a result, peers have no incentive to serve as a *seeder*, i.e., to continue uploading after their own download is complete. To overcome this problem, a number of BitTorrent communities employ some form of reputation scheme on top of the existing barter scheme, and exclude peers with low contribution levels.

BitTorrent represents the state of the art in p2p file-sharing, and appears to be able to establish cooperative communities in practice. However, several theoretical and experimental studies have revealed flaws associated with its incentive scheme. Through the formalization of *specification faithfulness*, Shneidman et al. (2004) demonstrate that the BitTorrent protocol is vulnerable to a number of rational manipulations by a selfish peer, including (1) pretending to have a lower upload bandwidth while retaining relative order with respect to the upload rate of other peers, so as to reduce its upload rate without compromising its download rate; (2) pretending to be split into multiple nodes (Sybil attack) to increase its chance of being randomly selected for download; (3) replacing identities when it is beneficial to do so (whitewashing attack); and (4) uploading garbage data to boost its upload rate. Therefore, it remains an open question if and how BitTorrent (or any other p2p barter scheme) can be made robust against all forms of rational manipulations.

The Fair, Optimal eXchange (FOX) protocol offers a different, theoretical approach to solving the free-riding problem in p2p file swarming systems. Assuming that all peers are homogeneous with a capacity to serve k requests in parallel, and seeks to minimize its download completion time, FOX runs a distributed, synchronized protocol based on a static structured k-ary tree to schedule the exchange of file blocks between peers. Optimal download completion times can be achieved by all peers if all peers comply with the protocol.

FOX employs a "grim trigger" strategy to enforce compliance. When a peer finds out that its neighbor deviates from the protocol, it can trigger a "meltdown" of the entire system. This threat results in an equilibrium where all rational nodes execute the protocol as specified, since any deviation will lead to an infinite download completion time. However, the equilibrium is not a subgame perfect equilibrium, and the threat is not credible. The protocol has limited practicality since the system is vulnerable to meltdown caused by a single malicious or faulty node.

23.5 Currency

A p2p system can also employ a currency scheme to facilitate resource contributions by rational peers. Generally, peers would earn currency by contributing resources to the system, and spend the currency to obtain resources from the system. MojoNation and Karma are two examples of currency-based p2p systems.

Golle et al. (2001) provide the first equilibrium analysis of a p2p payment system. In the model, each peer makes an independent decision regarding his download and upload amounts. If each peer is charged an amount proportional to the gap between his downloads and uploads, then a unique strict Nash equilibrium exists where all peers would maximize their upload and download amounts.

A more recent work by Friedman et al. (2006) looks at the efficiency of a currency-based p2p system. First, it establishes the existence, for each fixed amount of money supply in the system, a nontrivial Nash equilibrium where all peers play a threshold strategy, given a large enough discount rate. When playing a threshold strategy, a peer will satisfy a request (and earn some money) if his current balance is less than some threshold value, and refuse to satisfy a request if his current balance is above the threshold. By comparing the efficiency of equilibria at different money supply levels, it is possible to determine the money supply level that maximizes efficiency for a system of a given size. It is interesting to note that the effective money supply level can be controlled either via the explicit injection or removal of currency or via changing the price of servicing a request. This means that inflation can be used as a tool to maintain the efficiency of the system as it grows in size.

Robustness against Sybil and whitewashing attacks is still an important requirement for currency-based p2p system design in general. For example, a currency system can still be vulnerable to the whitewashing attack if newcomers are endowed with a positive opening balance, or if the balance is allowed to become negative, even temporarily.

23.6 Hidden Actions in p2p Systems

As we mentioned in the Introduction, strategic behavior in p2p systems goes far beyond free-riding in file-sharing networks. Peers may make strategic decisions on the timing of their arrivals and departures from the network, in selecting which peers to connect to, on whether to truthfully report to the system private information such as costs and valuations, or engage in other ways of manipulating the system protocol or mechanism. In this section, we will consider the issue of hidden action in p2p systems – how peers may behave strategically when their actions are hidden from the rest of the network, and how currency-based incentive mechanisms could be devised to overcome this problem.

Consider the case of p2p file-sharing. In addition to sharing files, the peers in file-sharing networks such as Gnutella and KaZaA are also expected to forward protocol messages to and from their neighbors. For example, when a peer receives a query message from one of its neighbors, it is expected to forward the message to its other neighbors, in addition to responding to the query if it is able to. However, the peer could strategically choose to drop the message or forward the message probabilistically, so as to reduce its message forwarding costs. In many systems, such an action is not easily observable, nor can a defecting node be readily identified, since messages are forwarded on a best-effort basis and the topology is continually changing as peers enter and leave the network. Clearly, such a system would cease to function if all peers strategically decide not to forward any messages. How can the querying node provide incentives for the other nodes to perform the message forwarding task?

The problem of hidden action in message forwarding can be readily generalized to other *peer-to-peer* settings. For example, devices in mobile ad hoc networks (MANETs) strategically drop packets to conserve their constrained energy resources. Internet Service Providers (ISPs) commonly practise *hot potato routing* to avoid the cost of transporting packets over their own networks. Indeed, the problem of hidden action is hardly unique to networks, and has long been studied by economists as the problem of *moral hazard* in contexts ranging from insurance to labor contracts. In the next section, we will apply the principal-agent framework to analyze the efficiency loss due to hidden action, and the design of optimal contracts to induce effort by the agents.

23.6.1 The Principal-Agent Model

A principal employs a set of n agents, N. Each agent $i \in N$ has a set of possible actions $A_i = \{0, 1\}$, and a cost (effort) $c(a_i) \geq 0$ for each possible action $a_i \in A_i$. The cost of low effort is zero while the cost of high effort is $c > 0$, i.e., $c(0) = 0$ and $c(1) = c$. The actions of the agents collectively and probabilistically determine a "contractible" outcome, $o \in \{0, 1\}$, where the outcomes 0 and 1 denote project failure and success, respectively. The principal's valuation of a successful project is given by a scalar $v > 0$, while he gains no value from a project failure. The outcome is determined according to the project *technology*, or a success function $t : A_1 \times \cdots \times A_n \rightarrow [0, 1]$, where $t(a_1, \ldots, a_n)$ denotes the probability of project success when agents adopt the action profile $a = (a_1, \ldots, a_n) \in A_1 \times \cdots \times A_n = A$.

We identify a subclass of technologies that can be represented by *read-once networks*. Read-once networks are given by a graph with two special nodes, a *source* and a *sink*, and each agent i controls a single edge. If an agent exerts low effort, he succeeds with probability γ_i, and if he exerts high effort, the success probability increases to $\delta_i > \gamma_i$. The project succeeds if there is a successful source-sink path, where the technology maps the individual successes and failures of agents (denoted by $x_i = 1$ and $x_i = 0$ respectively) into the probability of project success. Two natural examples are the "AND" and the "OR" technologies. We consider the case in which the technology is anonymous (symmetric in the agents) and is further determined by a single parameter $\gamma \in (0, 1/2)$ that satisfies $1 - \delta_i = \gamma_i = \gamma$ for all i.

The "AND" technology $f(x_1, \ldots, x_n)$ is the logical conjunction of x_i ($f(x) = \bigwedge_{i \in N} x_i$). Thus the project succeeds if and only if all agents succeed in their tasks (shown graphically in Figure 23.3(a)). If m agents exert effort ($\sum_i a_i = m$), then $t(a) = \gamma^{n-m}(1 - \gamma)^m$.

For example, packet forwarding in a mobile ad hoc network can be represented by the AND technology. Each edge on the path is controlled by a single agent who succeeds in forwarding the packet with probability $\gamma \in (0, \frac{1}{2})$ if he exerts low effort ($a_i = 0$), and with probability $1 - \gamma \in (\frac{1}{2}, 1)$ if he exerts high effort ($a_i = 1$). The message is delivered to the final destination if and only if all the individual agents have succeeded in their single-hop deliveries. The sender can only observe whether the message has reached the destination.

The "OR" technology $f(x_1, \ldots, x_n)$ is the logical disjunction of x_i ($f(x) = \bigvee_{i \in N} x_i$). Thus the project succeeds if and only if at least one of the agents succeed in their tasks (shown graphically in Figure 23.3(b)). If m agents exert effort ($\sum_i a_i = m$), then $t(a) = 1 - \gamma^m(1 - \gamma)^{n-m}$.

For example, the practice of *multipath routing* (Ganesan et al., 2001; Xu and Rexford, 2006), where a message is duplicated and sent over multiple paths to a single destination, can be represented by the OR technology if each path is represented by a single agent.[1] Each agent succeeds in forwarding the message with probability $\gamma \in (0, \frac{1}{2})$ if he exerts low effort ($a_i = 0$), and with probability $1 - \gamma \in (\frac{1}{2}, 1)$ if he exerts high effort ($a_i = 1$). The project is considered a success if at least one of the messages is successfully delivered to the destination.

[1] Query message forwarding in p2p file-sharing networks may be modeled by OR-of-AND technology since the messages may be forwarded multiple hops along multiple paths.

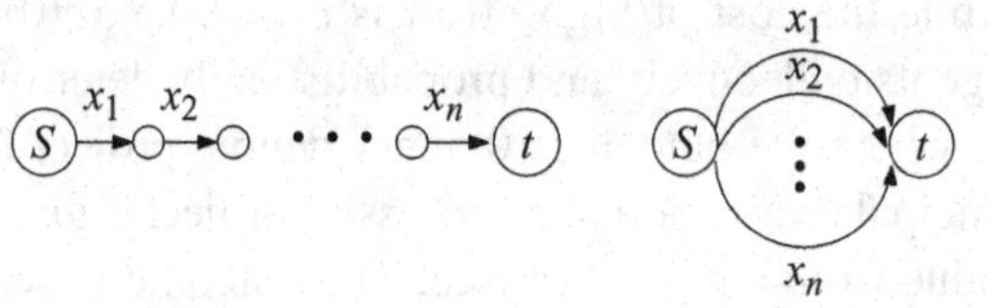

Figure 23.3. Graphical representations of (a) *AND* and (b) *OR* technologies. The project succeeds if there is a successful path from s to t. Each agent controls an edge and succeeds with probability γ with no effort, and with probability $1-\gamma$ with effort.

The principal may design enforceable contracts based on the observable outcome.[2] We impose the *limited liability* constraint, thus negative payments to the agents (or fines paid by agents to the principal) are disallowed. A contract is thus a commitment to pay agent i an amount $p_i \geq 0$ upon project success, and nothing upon project failure.

Given this setting, the agents have been placed in a game, where the utility of agent i under the profile of actions $a = (a_1, \ldots, a_n)$ is given by $u_i(a) = p_i \cdot t(a) - c(a_i)$. Following convention, we denote by $a_{-i} \in A_{-i}$ the vector of the actions of all agents excluding agent i, i.e., $a_{-i} = (a_1, \ldots, a_{i-1}, a_{i+1}, \ldots, a_n)$. The principal's problem is that of designing the contracts p_i for each agent i, so as to maximize his own expected utility $u(a, v) = t(a) \cdot (v - \sum_{i \in N} p_i)$, where the actions $a_1, \ldots, a_n$ are at Nash equilibrium. In the case of multiple Nash equilibria, the principal can choose a desired one and "suggest" it to the agents. While this is a standard assumption, in our setting it is further justified by the fact that the best Nash equilibrium is also a strong equilibrium (i.e., equilibrium in which no subgroup of agents can coordinate a joint deviation such that every member of the subgroup strictly improves his utility), and the unique strong equilibrium in many scenarios.

As we wish to concentrate on motivating agents, rather than on the coordination between agents, we assume that more effort by an agent always leads to a higher probability of success. Formally,

$$\forall i \in N,\ \forall a_{-i} \in A_{-i}\quad t(1, a_{-i}) > t(0, a_{-i})$$

In addition, we assume that $t(a) > 0$ for any $a \in A$.

Definition 23.3 The marginal contribution of agent i, given $a_{-i} \in A_{-i}$ is

$$\Delta_i(a_{-i}) = t(1, a_{-i}) - t(0, a_{-i})$$

$\Delta_i(a_{-i})$ is the increase in success probability due to agent i moving from no effort to effort, given the effort of the others. The best strategy of agent i can be easily determined as a function of the other agents' effort levels, $a_{-i} \in A_{-i}$, and his contract p_i.

[2] An alternate approach is to maintain a trusted clearinghouse to whom agents report intermediate outcomes, and the challenge is to induce the agents to report truthfully (Zhong et al., 2003).

Claim 23.4 *Given a profile of actions a_{-i}, agent i's best strategy is $a_i = 1$ if $p_i \geq \frac{c}{\Delta_i(a_{-i})}$, and is $a_i = 0$ if $p_i \leq \frac{c}{\Delta_i(a_{-i})}$. (In the case of equality the agent is indifferent between the two alternatives.)*

As $p_i \geq \frac{c}{\Delta_i(a_{-i})}$ if and only if $u_i(1, a_{-i}) = p_i \cdot t(1, a_{-i}) - c \geq p_i \cdot t(0, a_{-i}) = u_i(0, a_{-i})$, agent i's best strategy in this case is to choose $a_i = 1$. This allows us to specify the principal's optimal contracts for inducing a given equilibrium.

Claim 23.5 *The best contracts for the principal that induce $a \in A$ as an equilibrium are $p_i = 0$ for agent i who exerts no effort ($a_i = 0$), and $p_i = \frac{c}{\Delta_i(a_{-i})}$ for agent i who exerts effort ($a_i = 1$).*

In this case, the expected utility of agent i who exerts effort is $c \cdot (\frac{t(1,a_{-i})}{\Delta_i(a_{-i})} - 1)$, and 0 for an agent who shirk. The principal's expected utility is given by $u(a, v) = (v - \sum_{i|a_i=1} \frac{c}{\Delta_i(a_{-i})}) \cdot t(a)$.

If $a_i = 1$ in the induced equilibrium a, we say that the principal contracts with agent i. Note that the utility of the principal is lower than in the observable-actions case, as the payment to each agent is higher than the agent cost. In economic terms, the principal can only obtain the "second best" but not the "first best" solution under hidden-actions.[3]

The principal's goal is to determine the profile of actions $a^* \in A$, which gives the highest utility $u(a, v)$ in equilibrium, given his valuation v. Choosing $a \in A$ corresponds to choosing a set S of agents that exert effort ($S = \{i | a_i = 1\}$). The set of agents $S^*(v)$ that the principal contracts with in a^* ($S^*(v) = \{i | a_i^* = 1\}$) is an *optimal contract* for the principal at value v. We will abuse notation and denote $t(S)$ instead of $t(a)$, when S is exactly the set of agents that exert effort in $a \in A$.

A natural yardstick by which to measure this decision is the observable-actions case. When the principal can observe the individual actions of each agent, it can induce effort with a payment $p_i = c_i$ to each agent i. In this case the principal's utility is exactly the social welfare, and so the principal will simply choose the profile $a \in A$ that optimizes the social welfare or global efficiency, $t(a) \cdot v - \sum_{i|a_i=1} c$. The worst case ratio between the optimal principal's utility in this observable-actions case and his optimal utility in the hidden-actions case can be termed the *price of unaccountability*.

Given a technology t, recall that $S^*(v)$ denote the optimal contract in the hidden-actions case and let $S^*_{oa}(v)$ denote an optimal contract in the observable-actions case, when the principal's valuation is v.

Definition 23.6 The *price of unaccountability* $POU(t)$ of a technology t is defined as the worst ratio (over v) between the principal's utility in the observable-

[3] In the case of "AND" technology where $\gamma_i = 0\ \forall i$, it is shown in Feldman et al. (2005) that the principal can obtain the first best. While it is shown for the case in which agents take sequential actions, the same qualitative results also apply to the case of simultaneous actions (as $\Delta_i(a_{-i}) = t(1, a_{-i})$ the expected utility of each agent is 0). It is also shown that the principal achieves the first best either through direct contracts (i.e., the principal contracts with each agent directly) or through recursive contracts (i.e., each agent contracts with its subsequent agent).

actions case and the hidden-actions case:

$$POU(t) = Sup_{v>0} \frac{t(S^*_{oa}(v)) \cdot v - \sum_{i \in S^*_{oa}(v)} c}{t(S^*(v))\left(v - \sum_{i \in S^*(v)} \frac{c}{t(S^*(v)) - t(S^*(v) \setminus \{i\})}\right)}$$

For example, in the packet forwarding example, the POU measures the worst multiplicative loss incurred by the sender due to his inability to monitor the individual actions taken by the intermediate nodes.

23.6.2 Results

We wish to understand how the optimal set of contracted agents should be selected as a function of the principal's valuation of project success. A basic observation is that the optimal contract weakly "improves" with an increase in the valuation v.

Lemma 23.7 **(Monotonicity lemma)** *For any technology t, in both the hidden- actions and the observable-actions cases, the expected utility of the principal at the optimal contracts, the success probability of the optimal contracts, and the expected payment of the optimal contract, are all monotonically nondecreasing with the valuation v.*

For technologies in which the success probability depends only on the number of agents that exert effort (e.g., anonymous *AND* and *OR*), the above implies that the number of contracted agents is a monotonically non-decreasing function of the valuation. We find that the *AND* and *OR* technologies have very different structures on the optimal contracts: *AND* has just a single transition, from 0 agents to n agents, while *OR* has all transitions.

Theorem 23.8 *For any anonymous AND technology with n agents and with $\gamma = \gamma_i = 1 - \delta_i \in (0, \frac{1}{2})$ for all i:*

- *there exists a valuation[4] $v_* < \infty$ such that for any $v < v_*$ it is optimal to contract with no agent, for $v > v_*$ it is optimal to contract with all n agents, and for $v = v_*$, both contracts (0 and n) are optimal.*
- *the price of unaccountability is obtained at the transition point of the hidden-actions case, and is $POU = (\frac{1}{\gamma} - 1)^{n-1} + (1 - \frac{\gamma}{1-\gamma})$*

Notice that the POU is not bounded across the *AND* family of technologies (for various n, γ) as $POU \to \infty$ either if $\gamma \to 0$ (for any given $n \geq 2$) or $n \to \infty$ (for any fixed $\gamma \in (0, \frac{1}{2})$).

This means that in the message forwarding example, the sender will induce either all or none of the agents to exert effort in forwarding a message. Moreover, the loss incurred by the sender due to his inability to monitor the individual actions may be

[4] v_* is a function of n, γ, c.

very large. This suggests a possible role for a network monitoring system, even if it is costly to implement.

Next we consider the OR technology.

Theorem 23.9 *For any anonymous OR technology with n agents and with $\gamma = \gamma_i = 1 - \delta_i \in (0, \frac{1}{2})$ for all i:*

- *there exist finite positive values $v_1 < v_2 < \cdots < v_n$ such that for any v where $v_k < v < v_{k+1}$, contracting with exactly k agents is optimal. (For $v < v_1$, no agent is contracted, for $v > v_n$, all n agents are contracted, and for $v = v_k$, the principal is indifferent between contracting with $k-1$ or k agents.)*
- *the POU for OR technology with any n, c and $\gamma \in (0, \frac{1}{2})$ is upper bounded by $5/2$.*

This means that in the multipath routing example, the sender may induce any number of paths to exert effort in forwarding the message, depending on his valuation of successful message delivery. Moreover, the loss incurred by the sender due to his inability to monitor individual actions is always bounded by a factor of $5/2$.

For general read-once networks, it is not sufficient to determine the number of contracted agents, but the actual *set* of contracted agents. It turns out that computing the optimal contract for any read-once network, is at least as hard as computing the success probability $t(E)$ (the network reliability), which is known to be $\#P$-hard (Provan and Ball, 1983).

Theorem 23.10 *The Optimal Contract Problem for Read-Once Networks is $\#P$-hard (under Turing reductions).*

PROOF SKETCH We will show that an algorithm for this problem can be used to solve the network reliability problem. Given an instance of a network reliability problem $< G, \{\zeta_e\}_{e \in E} >$ (where ζ_e denotes e's probability of success), we define an instance of the optimal contract problem as follows: first define a new graph G', which is obtained by "And"ing G with a new player x, with γ_x very close to $\frac{1}{2}$ and $\delta_x = 1 - \gamma_x$. For the other edges, we let $\delta_e = \zeta_e$ and $\gamma_e = \zeta_e/2$. By choosing γ_x close enough to $\frac{1}{2}$, we can make sure that player x will enter the optimal contract only for very large values of v, after all other agents are contracted. The critical value of v, where player x enters the optimal contract of G', can be found using the algorithm that supposedly finds the optimal contract. At this critical value, the principal is indifferent between the set E and $E \cup \{x\}$. Now, from the expression for this indifference (in terms of $t(E)$ and $\Delta_i^t(E)$), the value of $t(E)$ is derived. □

A natural research problem is to characterize families of technologies whose optimal contracts can be computed in polynomial time. In addition, while there exists fully polynomial time approximation schemes (FPTAS) to various versions of the network reliability problem (Karger, 1995), it remains an open question how well one can approximate the optimal contract problem.

23.7 Conclusion

The fundamental premise of peer-to-peer systems is that of voluntary contribution of resources by individual users. However, there is an inherent tension between individual rationality and collective welfare. Therefore, the design of p2p incentives is of both theoretical and practical interest. In this chapter, we have reviewed different classes of p2p incentive mechanisms based on reputation, barter, and currency. We saw that cooperation can be sustained through barter if the p2p system can enforce repeat transactions among peers. Otherwise, incentive mechanisms based on reputation or currency may be necessary to overcome the free-riding problem. We also discussed the problem of hidden actions in p2p systems, and illustrated the use of contracts to induce the desired behavior by the peers.

Many challenges and open problems remain in the design and evaluation of p2p incentives, of which we highlight two. First, what is the range of possible rational manipulations against a p2p system that are either specific to, or independent of, the type of incentive mechanism in use? For example, we have seen that robustness against Sybil and whitewashing attacks are important design requirements for reputation-, barter-, and currency-based incentive mechanisms. Given a design, can we test its robustness against a comprehensive catalog of rational manipulations? Second, how should we relax the rationality assumption in the analysis and design of p2p systems, to account for heterogeneous populations of peers that may be perfectly rational, bounded rational, altruistic, malicious, and/or faulty? What would be the appropriate solution concepts for p2p systems, and for distributed systems more generally? This appears to call for cross-fertilization with both behavioral economics and computer security.

The ease of deploying p2p systems has led to their flowering in a short period of time. Today, we have a large number of p2p systems of varying scales running real applications of great value to real users. This offers us a unique opportunity to validate, using empirical data taken from real users, different designs and theories on p2p incentives. With hope, this will advance the theory and practice of incentive design for both online and offline systems.

23.8 Bibliographic Notes

Adar and Huberman's (2000) empirical evidence of prevalent free-riding in the Gnutella file-sharing network inspired a concerted study of incentives in p2p systems, leading to the incorporation of incentives in many p2p systems, including those discussed in this chapter: Eigentrust (Kamvar et al., 2003), Credence (Walsh and Sirer, 2005), BitTorrent (Cohen, 2003), FOX (Levin et al., 2006), Mojonation (Wilcox-O'Hearn, 2002), and Karma (Vishnumurthy et al., 2003).

Sybil and whitewashing attacks are introduced in Douceur (2002) and Friedman and Resnick (1998) and further studied in Cheng and Friedman (2005) and Feldman et al. (2006). Strategies for dealing with strangers are explored in Feldman et al. (2004) and Feldman and Chuang (2005). The minimalist p2p model in Section 23.3 is due to Feldman et al. (2006).

The study of hidden actions in p2p systems is initiated in Feldman et al. (2005), Babaioff et al. (2006a, 2006b), and the model in Section 23.6 is due to Babaioff et al. (2006a).

Strategic network formation in p2p systems is studied in Fabrikant et al. (2003), Chun et al. (2004), Albers et al. (2006), and Andelman et al. (2007). while strategic churning is discussed in (Christin and Chuang, 2005).

Bibliography

E. Adar and B.A. Huberman. Free riding on gnutella. *First Monday*, 5(10), October 2000.

S. Albers, S. Elits, E. Even-Dar, Y. Mansour, and L. Roditty. On Nash equilibria for a network creation game. In *ACM-SIAM Symp. on Discrete Algorithms*, pp. 89–98, 2006.

N. Andelman, M. Feldman, and Y. Mansour. Strong price of anarchy. In *ACM-SIAM Symp. on Discrete Algorithms*, 2007.

M. Babaioff, M. Feldman, and N. Nisan. Combinatorial agency. In *ACM Conf. on E-Commerce*, pp. 18–28, 2006.

M. Babaioff, M. Feldman, and N. Nisan. Mixed strategies in combinatorial agency. In *2nd Intl. Workshop on Internet and Network Economics*, 2006.

A. Cheng and E. Friedman. Sybilproof reputation mechanisms. In *ACM SIGCOMM Workshop on the Economics of Peer-to-Peer Systems (P2PECON'05)*, 2005.

N. Christin and J. Chuang. A cost-based analysis of overlay routing geometries. In *IEEE INFOCOM*, 2005.

B.-G. Chun, R. Fonseca, I. Stoica, and J. Kubiatowicz. Characterizing selfishly constructed overlay routing networks. In *INFOCOM*, 2004.

B. Cohen. Incentives build robustness in bittorrent. In *Workshop on Economics of Peer-to-Peer Systems*, 2003.

J.R. Douceur. The Sybil attack. In *Electronic Proc. Intl. Workshop on Peer-to-Peer Systems*, 2002.

A. Fabrikant, A. Luthra, E. Maneva, C. Papadimitriou, and S. Shenker. On a network creation game. In *ACM Symp. Princ. of Distriubted Computing*, 2003.

M. Feldman and J. Chuang. The evolution of cooperation under cheap pseudonyms. In *Proc. 7th Intl. IEEE Conf. on E-Commerce Technology*, 2005.

M. Feldman, J. Chuang, I. Stoica, and S. Shenker. Hidden-action in multi-hop routing. In *ACM Conf. on Electronic Commerce (EC'05)*, pp. 117–126, 2005.

M. Feldman, K. Lai, I. Stoica, and J. Chuang. Robust incentive techniques for peer-to-peer networks. In *ACM Conf. on Electronic Commerce*, 2004.

M. Feldman, C. Papadimitriou, J. Chuang, and I. Stoica. Free-riding and whitewashing in peer-to-peer systems. *IEEE J. Selected Areas in Commun., Special Issue on Price-Based Access Control and Economics of Networking*, 24(5), 2006.

E.J. Friedman, J.Y. Halpern, and I. Kash. Efficiency and Nash equilibria in a scrip system for P2P networks. In *ACM Conf. Electronic Commerce, (EC'06)*, June 2006.

E. Friedman and P. Resnick. The social cost of cheap pseudonyms. *J. Econ. Management Strategy*, 10(2):173–199, 1998.

D. Ganesan, R. Govindan, S. Shenker, and D. Estrin. Highly-resilient, energy-efficient multipath routing in wireless sensor networks. *SIGMOBILE Mob. Comput. Commun. Rev.*, 5(4):11–25, 2001.

P. Golle, K. Leyton-Brown, I. Mironov, and M. Lillibridge. Incentives for sharing in peer-to-peer networks. In *Proc. 3rd ACM Conf. on Electronic Commerce*, 2001.

S.D. Kamvar, M.T. Schlosser, and H. Garcia-Molina. The EigenTrust algorithm for reputation management in P2P networks. In *Proc. 12th Intl. World Wide Web Conference*, May 2003.

D.R. Karger. A randomized fully polynomial time approximation scheme for the all terminal network reliability problem. In *Symp. on Theory of Computing*, pp. 11–17, 1995.

D. Levin, R. Sherwood, and B. Bhattacharjee. Fair file swarming with FOX. In *5th Intl. Workshop on Peer-to-Peer Systems (IPTPS)*, 2006.

J.S. Provan and M.O. Ball. The complexity of counting cuts and of computing the probability that a graph is connected. *SIAM J. Comput.*, 12(4):777–788, 1983.

J. Shneidman, D. Parkes, and L. Massoulie. Faithfulness in Internet Algorithms. In *Proc. SIGCOMM Workshop on Practice and Theory of Incentives and Game Theory in Networked Systems*, 2004.

V. Vishnumurthy, S. Chandrakumar, and E.G. Sirer. KARMA: A Secure Economic Framework for P2P Resource Sharing. In *Workshop on Economics of Peer-to-Peer Networks*, 2003.

K. Walsh and E.G. Sirer. Fighting Peer-to-Peer SPAM and Decoys with Object Reputation. In *Proc. Third Workshop on the Economics of Peer-to-Peer Systems (P2PECON)*, 2005.

B. Wilcox-O'Hearn. Experiences Deploying A Large-Scale Emergent Network. In *Proc. of the Intl. Workshop on Peer-to-Peer Systems*, 2002.

W. Xu and J. Rexford. Miro: Multi-path interdomain routing. In *ACM SIGCOMM*, 2006.

S. Zhong, J. Chen, and Y.R. Yang. Sprite: A simple, cheat-proof, credit-based system for mobile ad-hoc networks. In *22nd Annual Joint Conf. IEEE Comp. Commun. Soc.*, 2003.

Exercises

23.1 Consider the p2p model in Section 23.3.1. The generosity of the peers is now distributed as follows: a fraction ϕ of the peers have their type θ_i uniformly distributed between 0 and θ_m, a fraction $(1-\phi)/2$ are of type $\theta_i = 0$, and the remaining $(1-\phi)/2$ are of type $\theta_i = \theta_m$. How would the resulting equilibrium be different from that of Claim 23.1?

23.2 In the p2p model of Section 23.3.1, suppose that the system designer has full information on each peer's type (i.e., generosity level), and could exclude peers based on their types (rather than based on their behavior, as suggested in Section 23.3.2). Let z denote the fraction of peers who are excluded from the system. Provide an explicit expression, as a function of θ_m and z, for the stable equilibrium in the system under such an exclusion mechanism. Would it always (for any value of θ_m) be beneficial to exclude some nonzero fraction of the population? Explain.

23.3 Provide a proof for Theorem 23.8. Hint: First show that at v_* the principal's utility when contracting with n agents is greater than that when contracting with $1 \leq i < n$ agents. Then, use the monotonicity lemma to show that there must be a single transition for any AND technology. Finally, compute the price of unaccountability.

23.4 Provide a proof for Part 1 of Theorem 23.9, showing that for any OR technology there are n transitions. Hint: Let $v_{i,i+1}$ ($i \in \{0, ..., n-1\}$) be the value of v for which the principal has the same utility from contracting with i agents and with $i+1$ agents. First show that $v_{i,i+1} < v_{i+1,i+2}$ for any $i \in \{0, ..., n-2\}$. Then, show that the above is sufficient to prove the theorem.

23.5 Prove or provide a counterexample to the following claim: For any technology, the number of transitions in the hidden-actions case is equal to the number of transitions in the observable-actions case.

23.6 A strategy profile $a \in A$ is a *strong equilibrium (SE)* if there does not exist any coalition $\Gamma \subseteq N$ and a strategy profile $a'_\Gamma \in \times_{i \in \Gamma} A_i$ such that for any $i \in \Gamma$, $u_i(a'_{-\Gamma}, a_\Gamma) > u_i(a)$. Prove that under the optimal payments that induce the optimal contract S^* in Section 23.6.1, S^* is a strong equilibrium.

CHAPTER 24

Cascading Behavior in Networks: Algorithmic and Economic Issues

Jon Kleinberg

Abstract

The flow of information or influence through a large social network can be thought of as unfolding with the dynamics of an epidemic: as individuals become aware of new ideas, technologies, fads, rumors, or gossip, they have the potential to pass them on to their friends and colleagues, causing the resulting behavior to cascade through the network.

We consider a collection of probabilistic and game-theoretic models for such phenomena proposed in the mathematical social sciences, as well as recent algorithmic work on the problem by computer scientists. Building on this, we discuss the implications of cascading behavior in a number of online settings, including word-of-mouth effects (also known as "viral marketing") in the success of new products, and the influence of social networks in the growth of online communities.

24.1 Introduction

The process by which new ideas and new behaviors spread through a population has long been a fundamental question in the social sciences. New religious beliefs or political movements; shifts in society that lead to greater tolerance or greater polarization; the adoption of new technological, medical, or agricultural innovations; the sudden success of a new product; the rise to prominence of a celebrity or political candidate; the emergence of bubbles in financial markets and their subsequent implosion – these phenomena all share some important qualitative properties. They tend to begin on a small scale with a few "early adopters"; more and more people begin to adopt them as they observe their friends, neighbors, or colleagues doing so; and the resulting new behaviors may eventually spread through the population contagiously, from person to person, with the dynamics of an epidemic.

People have long been aware of such processes at an anecdotal level; the systematic study of them developed, in the middle of the 20th century, into an area of sociology known as the *diffusion of innovations*. The initial research on this topic was empirical (see, e.g., Coleman et al., 1966; Rogers, 1995; Strang and Soule, 1998 for background), but in the 1970s economists and mathematical sociologists such as Schelling (1978) and Granovetter (1978) began formulating basic mathematical models for the mechanisms by which ideas and behaviors diffuse through a population. There are several reasons to seek models that capture observed data on diffusion: in addition to helping us understand, at a fundamental level, how the spread of new ideas "works," such models have the potential to help us predict the success or failure of new innovations in their early stages, and potentially to shape the underlying process so as to increase (or reduce) the chances of success.

In this chapter, we discuss some of the basic models in this area, as well as suggesting some current applications to online information systems. While the overall topic is much too vast even to survey in a brief setting such as this, we hope to convey some of the game-theoretic and algorithmic grounding of the area, and to highlight some directions for future work. We also indicate some of the ways in which large-scale online communities provide rich data for observing social diffusion processes as they unfold, thus providing the opportunity to develop richer models. Further related work is discussed briefly in the Notes at the end of the chapter.

24.2 A First Model: Networked Coordination Games

One of the simplest models for social diffusion can be motivated by game-theoretic considerations. To set the stage for this, notice that many of the motivating scenarios considered above have the following general flavor: each individual v has certain friends, acquaintances, or colleagues, and the benefits to v of adopting the new behavior increase as more and more of these other individuals adopt it. In such a case, simple self-interest will dictate that v should adopt the new behavior once a sufficient fraction of v's neighbors have done so. For example, many new technological, economic, or social practices become more valuable as the number of people using them increases: two organizations may find it easier to collaborate on a joint project if they are using compatible technologies; two people may find it easier to engage in social interaction – all else being equal – if their beliefs and opinions are similar.

Defining the game. Specifically, here is a first model for such situations, based on work of Morris (2000) that in turn builds on earlier work by Blume (1993), Ellison (1993), and Young (1998). Consider a graph $G = (V, E)$ in which the nodes are the individuals in the population, and there is an edge (v, w) if v and w are friends, or otherwise engaged in some kind of social interaction. Sociologists refer to such a graph as a *social network*, a structure in which the nodes are individuals or other social entities (such as organizations), and the edges represent some type of social tie.

We will study a situation in which each node has a choice between two possible behaviors: the "old" behavior, labeled A, and the "new" behavior, labeled B. On each edge (v, w), there is an incentive for v and w to have their behaviors match, which we model as the following coordination game parametrized by a real number q, with $0 < q < 1$.

- If v and w both choose behavior A, they each receive a payoff of q.

- If v and w both choose behavior B, they each receive a payoff of $1-q$.
- If v and w choose opposite behaviors, they each receive a payoff of 0.

Of course, it is easy to imagine many possible generalizations of this simple game, and we will explore some of these in the next section as well as in the exercises at the end of the chapter. But for now, we will keep things deliberately simple.

Node v is playing this game with each of its neighbors in G, and its overall payoff is simply the sum of the payoffs from these separate games. Notice how q (specifically its relation to $1-q$) captures the extent to which the new behavior is preferable to the old behavior at a purely "local" level, taking into account only pairwise interactions.

Suppose that the behaviors of all other nodes are fixed, and node v is trying to select a behavior for itself. If the degree of node v is d_v, and d_v^A of its neighbors have behavior A and d_v^B have behavior B, then the payoff to v from choosing behavior A is qd_v^A while the payoff from choosing behavior B is $(1-q)d_v^B$. A simple computation shows that v should adopt behavior B if $d_v^B > qd_v$, and behavior A if $d_v^B < qd_v$. (To handle ties, we will say that v adopts behavior B if $d_v^B = qd_v$.) In other words, q is a threshold: a node should adopt the new behavior if at least a q fraction of its neighbors have done so. Note that new behaviors for which q is small spread more easily – a node is more receptive to switching to a new behavior B when q is small.

Cascading behavior and the contagion threshold. We can now study a basic model of cascading behavior in G, simply assuming that each node repeatedly updates its choice of A or B in response to the current behaviors of its neighbors. Keeping the model as simple as possible, we assume that each node simultaneously updates its behavior in each of discrete time steps $t = 1, 2, 3, \ldots$. If S is the set of nodes initially adopting the new behavior B, we let $h_q(S)$ denote the set of nodes adopting B after one round of updating with threshold q; we let $h_q^k(S)$ denote the result of applying h_q to S a total of k times in succession – in other words, this is the set of nodes adopting B after k rounds of updating. Note that nodes may switch from A to B or from B to A, depending on what their neighbors are doing; it is not necessarily the case, for example, that S is a subset of $h(S)$.

One of the central questions in such a model is to determine when a small set of nodes initially adopting a new behavior can eventually convert all (or almost all) of the population. We formalize this as follows. First, we will assume that the node set of G is countably infinite, with each node having a finite number of neighbors. (Anything we refer to as a "graph" in this section will have this property.) We say that a node w is *converted* by a set S if, for some k, the node w belongs to $h_q^j(S)$ for all $j \geq k$. We say that a set S is *contagious* (with respect to h_q) if every node is converted by S – that is, if a new behavior originating at S eventually spreads to the full set of nodes.

Now, it is easier for a set S to be contagious when the threshold q is small, so the interesting question is how large a threshold we can have and still observe small sets spreading a new behavior to everyone. We therefore define the *contagion threshold* of the social network G to be the maximum q for which there exists a finite contagious set. Note that the contagion threshold is a property purely of the topology of G – a network with large contagion threshold enables even behaviors that spread sluggishly to potentially reach the full population.

An example and a question. Here is an example to make the definitions more concrete. Suppose that G is a (two-way) infinite path, with nodes labeled $\{\ldots, -2, -1, 0, 1, 2, \ldots\}$, and there is a new behavior B with threshold $q = 1/2$. Now, first, suppose that the single node 0 initially adopts B. Then in time step $t = 1$, nodes 1 and -1 will adopt B, but 0 (observing both 1 and -1 in their initial behaviors A) will switch to A. The system will continue oscillating between even-numbered and odd-numbered nodes adopting B, but no node will ever permanently adopt B.

On the other hand, suppose that the set $S = \{-1, 0, 1\}$ initially adopts B. Then in time step $t = 1$, these three nodes will stay with B, and nodes -2 and 2 will switch to B. More generally, in time step $t = k$, nodes $\{-k, -(k-1), \ldots, k-1, k\}$ will already be following behavior B, and nodes $-(k+1)$ and $k+1$ will switch to B. Thus, every node is converted by $S = \{-1, 0, 1\}$, the set S is contagious, and hence the contagion threshold of G is at least $q = 1/2$. (Note that it would in fact have been sufficient to start with the smaller set $S' = \{0, 1\}$.)

In fact, 1/2 is the contagion threshold of G: given any finite set S adopting a new behavior B with threshold $q > 1/2$, it is easy to see that B will never spread past the rightmost member of S.

It is instructive to try this oneself on other graphs; if one does, it quickly becomes clear that while a number of simple graphs have contagion threshold 1/2, it is hard to find one with a contagion threshold strictly above 1/2. This suggests the following question: *Does there exist a graph G with contagion threshold $q > 1/2$?* We will shortly answer this question, after first resolving a useful technical issue in the model.

Progressive vs. nonprogressive processes. Our model thus far has the property that as time progresses, nodes can switch from A to B *or* from B to A, depending on the states of their neighbors. Many behaviors that one may want to model, however, are *progressive*, in the sense that once a node switches from A to B, it remains with B in all subsequent time steps. (Consider, for example, a professional community in which the behavior is that of returning to graduate school to receive an advanced degree. For all intents and purposes, this is a progressive process.) It is worth considering a variation on our model that incorporates this notion of monotonicity for two reasons. First, it is useful to be able to capture these types of settings; and second, it will turn out to yield useful ways of thinking about the nonprogressive case as well.

We model the progressive contagion process as follows. As before, time moves in discrete steps $t = 1, 2, 3, \ldots$. In step t, each node v currently following behavior A switches to B if at least a q fraction of its neighbors is currently following B. Any node following behavior B continues to follow it in all subsequent time steps. Now, if S is the set of nodes initially adopting B, we let $\overline{h}_q(S)$ denote the set of nodes adopting B after one round of updating in this progressive process, and we let $\overline{h}_q^k(S)$ denote the result of applying $\overline{h}_q$ to S a total of i times in succession. We can then define the notion of *converted* and *contagious* with respect to $\overline{h}_q$ exactly as we did for h_q.

With a progressive process, it seems intuitively that it should be easier to find finite contagious sets – after all, in the progressive process, one does not have to worry about early adopters switching back to the old behavior A and thereby killing the spread of B. In view of this intuition, it is perhaps a bit surprising that for any graph G, the progressive and nonprogressive models have the same contagion threshold (Morris, 2000).

Theorem 24.1 *For any graph G, there exists a finite contagious set with respect to h_q if and only if there exists one with respect to $\overline{h}_q$.*

PROOF Clearly, if S is contagious with respect to h_q, then it is also contagious with respect to $\overline{h}_q$. Hence the crux of the proof is the following: given a set S that is contagious with respect to $\overline{h}_q$, we need to identify a set S' that is contagious with respect to h_q.

Thus, let S be contagious with respect to $\overline{h}_q$. The main observation behind the proof is the following. Since all nodes of G have finite degree, there is a finite set $\overline{S}$ that consists of S together with every node that has a neighbor in S. Since $\overline{h}_q^k(S)$ eventually grows to include every node of G, there exists some ℓ such that $\overline{h}_q^\ell(S)$ contains $\overline{S}$. We define $T = \overline{h}_q^\ell(S)$, and we claim that T is contagious with respect to h_q, which will complete the proof. Thus, intuitively, we watch the nonprogressive process until it "engulfs" the set of initial adopters S, surrounding them with all their possible neighbors; this larger set is then a robust enough point that the process would spread even under the progressive rule from here on.

So why is the set T contagious with respect to h_q? This requires a bit of manipulation of the definitions of h_q and $\overline{h}_q$, although the details are not that complicated. We first note the following fact, whose proof is by induction on j is left an exercise to the reader:

$$\text{For all } X \text{ and all } j, \text{ we have } \overline{h}_q^j(X) = X \cup h_q\left(\overline{h}_q^{j-1}(X)\right). \qquad (24.1)$$

In other words, to get $\overline{h}_q^j(X)$, rather than applying $\overline{h}_q$ to $\overline{h}_q^{j-1}(X)$), we can instead apply h_q and then add in X.

For ease of notation, let S_j denote $\overline{h}^j(S)$, and let T_j denote $\overline{h}^j(T)$. (Recall also that $T = S_\ell$.) Now, suppose $j > \ell$. Then by (24.1) above, we have

$$S_j = S \cup h_q(S_{j-1}). \qquad (24.2)$$

But since S_{j-1} includes T and hence all the neighbors of S, we have $S \subseteq h_q(S_{j-1})$. Hence the "$S \cup$" in (24.2) is superfluous, and we can write $S_j = h_q(S_{j-1})$. By induction, it now follows that for all $j > \ell$, we have

$$h_q^{j-\ell}(T) = h_q^{j-\ell}(S_\ell) = S_j,$$

and hence T is contagious with respect to h_q. □

The contagion threshold is at most 1/2. We now return to our question: does there exist a graph G whose contagion threshold exceeds $1/2$? Thanks to Theorem 24.1, this question has the same answer regardless of whether we consider the progressive or nonprogressive process, and it turns out that the analysis is very easy if we consider the progressive version.

We now show that $1/2$ is in fact an upper bound for all graphs (Morris, 2000). Which can be read as a general statement about contagion on networks: a behavior cannot spread very far if it requires a strict majority of your friends to convince you to adopt it.

Theorem 24.2 *The contagion threshold of any graph G is at most $1/2$.*

PROOF Let $q > 1/2$, and let S be any finite subset of the nodes of G. We show that S is not contagious with respect to $\overline{h}_q$.

Recall our notation that $S_j = \overline{h}_q^j(S)$. For a set of nodes X, we let $\delta(X)$ denote the set of edges with one end in X and the other end not in X, and we let $d(X)$ be the cardinality of $\delta(X)$. Since all nodes in G have finite degree, $d(X)$ is a natural number for any finite set of nodes X.

We now claim that for all $j > 0$ for which $S_{j-1} \subsetneq S_j$, we have $d(S_j) < d(S_{j-1})$. To see this, we account for the difference between the sets $\delta(S_{j-1})$ and $\delta(S_j)$ by allocating it over the separate contributions of the nodes in $S_j - S_{j-1}$. For each node v in $S_j - S_{j-1}$, its edges into S_{j-1} contribute to $\delta(S_{j-1})$ but not $\delta(S_j)$, and its edges into $V - S_j$ contribute to $\delta(S_j)$ but not $\delta(S_{j-1})$. But since $q > 1/2$, and since v decided to switch to B in iteration j, it has strictly more edges into S_{j-1} (i.e., the nodes that had already adopted B) than it has into $V - S_j$. Summing these strict inequalities over all nodes v in $S_j - S_{j-1}$, we have $d(S_j) < d(S_{j-1})$.

Finally, we argue that S is not contagious with respect to $\overline{h}_q$. Indeed, the sequence of numbers $d(S), d(S_1), d(S_2), d(S_3), \ldots$, is strictly decreasing as long as the sets $S, S_1, S_2, \ldots$, remain distinct from one another. But since $d(S)$ is a natural number, and $d(S_j) \geq 0$ for all j, there must be some value k for which the sets stop growing, and $S_k = S_{k+1} = S_{k+2} = \cdots$ from then on. Since S_j is finite for any j, the set S_k in particular is finite, and hence S is not contagious. □

24.3 More General Models of Social Contagion

Thus far, we have been considering a very simple model for cascading behavior in a social network: people switch to a new behavior when a certain threshold fraction of neighbors have already switched; but in our first model this threshold was the same for all nodes, and all neighbors had equal "weight" in raising a node toward its threshold. Clearly a more general model could capture a greater degree of heterogeneity in the population.

It is useful to mention a few preliminary points here. In this section, we will consider graphs that may be either finite or infinite. Also, we will work with directed graphs, enabling us to encode the notion that for two nodes v and w, the influence of v on w may be different from the influence of w on v. (One can model symmetric relationships between a pair of nodes in this case by including edges in both directions between them.) Also, we will consider contagion processes that are progressive, in that a node never switches back from a new behavior to an old behavior; at this end of this section, we will discuss a way to encode nonprogressive processes by a reduction to the progressive case, though by a different means than we saw earlier.

A linear threshold models. In a first generalization of the model, we allow nodes to weigh the influences of their neighbors differently.[1] Furthermore, we assume that each node's threshold – the fraction of neighbors required for it to adopt the new behavior – is chosen uniformly at random. Thus, in the *Linear Threshold Model*, we introduce the following two ingredients.

- We have a nonnegative weight b_{vw} on each edge (w, v), indicating the influence that w exerts on v. We will require that $\sum_{w \in N(v)} b_{vw} \leq 1$, where $N(v)$ denotes the set of nodes with edges to v.
- Each node v chooses a threshold θ_v uniformly at random from $[0, 1]$; this indicates the weighted fraction of v's neighbors that must adopt the behavior before v does.

Now, the (progressive) dynamics of the behavior operates just as it did in the previous section. Some set of nodes S starts out adopting the new behavior B; all other nodes start out adopting A. We will say that a node is *active* if it is following B, and accordingly will say that it has been *activated* when it switches from A to B.

Time operates in discrete steps $t = 1, 2, 3, \ldots$. At a given time t, any inactive node v becomes active if its fraction of active neighbors exceeds its threshold:

$$\sum_{\text{active } w \in N(v)} b_{vw} \geq \theta_v.$$

This in turn may cause other nodes to become active in subsequent time steps, as it did in the model of the previous section, leading to potentially cascading adoption of behavior B.

Note how the different thresholds for nodes indicate different predispositions to adopt B – small θ_v indicates a more liberal approach toward adoption, while a node with large θ_v waits until a greater fraction of its neighbors have already adopted. While we have motivated the model directly in terms of the thresholds, one can also easily derive it from a networked coordination game, in which nodes have different payoff matrices, and different "stakes" in the games with their various neighbors.

A general threshold model. Of course, the Linear Threshold Model is still very simple, in that it assumes influences of neighbors are strictly additive. It would be nice to express the notion that an individual will adopt a behavior when, for example, two of her relatives and three of her coworkers do so – a rule that cannot be expressed as a simple weighted sum.

To handle this richer type of model, we consider the following *General Threshold Model*. Each node v now has an arbitrary function $g_v(\cdot)$ defined on subsets of its neighbor set $N(v)$: for any set of neighbors $X \subseteq N(v)$, there is a value $g_v(X)$ between 0 and 1. We will assume here that this function is *monotone* in the sense that if $X \subseteq Y$, then $g_v(X) \leq g_v(Y)$.[2]

[1] Given the directed nature of the graph, we adopt the following terminological convention: we say here that w is a *neighbor* of v if there is an edge (w, v), and we say that w is an *outneighbor* if there is an edge (v, w).

[2] An interesting issue, which has been the subject of qualitative investigation but much less theoretical modeling, is the question of nonmonotone influence – a node may be motivated to adopt a new behavior once a few friends have done so, but then motivated to abandon it once too many have done so (see e.g., Granovetter, 1978).

Now, the dynamics of adoption proceed just as in the Linear Threshold Model, but with $g_v(\cdot)$ playing the role of the weighed sum. Specifically, each node v chooses a threshold θ_v uniformly at random in $[0, 1]$; there is an initial set S of active nodes; and for time steps $t = 1, 2, 3, \ldots$, each v becomes active if its set of currently active neighbors satisfies $g_v(X) \geq \theta_v$.

This new model is extremely general – it encodes essentially any threshold rule in which influence increases (or remains constant) as more friends adopt. Moreover, the assumption that the threshold is selected uniformly at random (rather than from some other distribution) is essentially without loss of generality, since other distributions can be represented by appropriately modifying the function g_v. We now consider one final class of models, and then discuss some of the intermediate classes of special cases that may hold particular interest.

A cascade model. Thus far, we have formulated models for the spread of a behavior strictly in terms of node thresholds – as some people adopt the behavior, the thresholds of others are exceeded, they too adopt, and the process spreads. It is natural, however, to ask whether we can pose a different model based more directly on the notion that new behaviors are contagious: a probabilistic model in which you "catch" the behavior from your friends. It turns out not to be hard to do this, and moreover, the resulting model is equivalent to the General Threshold Model.

We define the *Cascade Model* to incorporate these ideas as follows. Again, there is an initial active set S, but now the dynamics proceeds as follows: whenever there is an edge (u, v) such that u is active and v is not, the node u is given one chance to activate v. This activation succeeds with some probability that depends not just on u and v, but also on the *set* of nodes that have already tried and failed to activate v. If u succeeds, then v may now in turn try to activate some of its (currently inactive) outneighbors; if u fails, then u joins the set of nodes who have tried and failed to activate v.

This model thus captures the notion of contagion more directly, and also allows us to incorporate the idea that a node's receptiveness to influence depends on the past history of interactions with its neighbors. We make the model concrete as follows. In place of a function g_v, each node v now has an *incremental function* that takes the form $p_v(u, X)$, where u is a neighbor of v and X is a set of neighbors of v not containing u. The value $p_v(u, X)$ is the probability that u succeeds in activating v, given that the set X of neighbors has already tried and failed. For our purposes here, we will only consider functions p_v that are *order-independent*: if a set of neighbors $u_1, u_2, \ldots, u_k$ all try to influence v, then the overall probability of success (as determined by successive applications of p_v) does not depend on the order in which they try.

While the Cascade Model is syntactically different from the General Threshold Model, we now argue that the two are in fact equivalent: One can translate from a set of incremental functions p_v to a set of threshold functions g_v, and vice versa, so that the resulting processes produce the same distributions on outcomes (Kempe et al., 2005).

We now describe the translations in both directions; further detail behind the proofs can be found in Kempe et al. (2005). First, suppose we are given an instance of the General Threshold Model with functions g_v; we define corresponding functions p_v as follows. If a set of nodes X has already tried and failed to activate v, then we know that v's threshold θ_v lies in the interval $(g_v(X), 1]$; subject to this constraint, it is uniformly distributed. In order for u to succeed after all the nodes in X have tried and failed, we must further have $\theta_v \leq g_v(X \cup \{u\})$. Hence we should define the incremental function

$$p_v(u, X) = \frac{g_v(X \cup \{u\}) - g_v(X)}{1 - g_v(X)}.$$

Conversely, suppose that we have incremental functions p_v. Then the probability v is not activated by a set of neighbors $X = \{u_1, u_2, \ldots, u_k\}$ is $\prod_{i=1}^{k}(1 - p_v(u_i, X_{i-1}))$, where we write $X_{i-1} = \{u_1, \ldots, u_{i-1}\}$. Note that order-independence is crucial here, to ensure that this quantity is independent of the way in which we label the elements of X. Hence we can define a threshold function g_v by setting

$$g_v(X) = 1 - \prod_{i=1}^{k}(1 - p_v(u_i, X_{i-1}).$$

This completes the translations in both directions, and hence establishes the equivalence of the two models.

Next we consider some special cases of the Cascade Model that will be of particular interest to us. (Given the equivalence to the General Threshold Model, these could also be written in that framework, though not always as simply.)

(i) First, it is easy to encode the notion that v will deterministically activate once it has k active neighbors: we simply define $p_v(u, X) = 0$ if $|X| \neq k - 1$, and $p_v(u, X) = 1$ if $|X| = k - 1$.

(ii) In contrast, the influence of a node's neighbors exhibits *diminishing returns* if it attenuates as more and more people try and fail to influence it. Thus, we say that a set of incremental functions p_v exhibits diminishing returns if $p_v(u, X) \geq p_v(u, Y)$ whenever $X \subseteq Y$.

(iii) A particularly simple special case that exhibits diminishing returns is the *Independent Cascade Model*, in which u's influence on v is independent of the set of nodes that have already tried and failed: $p_v(u, X) = p_{uv}$ for some parameter p_{uv} that depends only on u and v.

We will see that the contrast between (i) and (ii) above will emerge as a particularly important qualitative distinction: whether the influence of one's neighbors in the social network incorporates some notion of "critical mass" (as in (i)), with a crucial number of adopters needed for successful influence; or whether the strength of influence simply decreases steadily (as in (ii)) as one is exposed more and more to the new behavior. In the next section, we will discuss an algorithmic problem whose computational complexity is strongly affected by this distinction; and following that, we will discuss some recent empirical studies that seek to identify the two sides of this dichotomy in online influence data.

Before this, we briefly discuss a useful way of translating between the progressive and nonprogressive versions of these cascade processes.

Progressive vs. nonprogressive processes (redux). The discussion in this section has been entirely in terms of progressive processes, where nodes switching from the old behavior A to the new behavior B never switch back. There is a useful construction that allows one to study the nonprogressive version of the process by translation to a progressive one on a different graph (Kempe et al., 2003). As it is a very general construction, essentially independent of the particular influence rules being used, we describe it at this level of generality.

Given a graph G on which we have a non-progressive process that may run for up to T steps, we create a larger graph G' built from T copies of G, labeled $G_1, G_2, \ldots, G_T$. Now, let $v^{\langle i \rangle}$ be the copy of node v in the graph G_i; we construct edges $(u^{\langle i-1 \rangle}, v^{\langle i \rangle})$ for each neighbor u of v. As a result, the neighbors of $v^{\langle i \rangle}$ in G' are just the copies of v's neighbors that "live" in the previous time-step. In this way, we can define the same influence rules on G', node-by-node, that we had in G, and study the non-progressive process in G as a progressive process in G': some copies of v in G' will be an active, and other will not, reflecting precisely the time steps in which v was active in G.

24.4 Finding Influential Sets of Nodes

A number of current Internet applications concern domains in which cascading behavior is a crucial phenomenon, and where a better understanding of cascades could lead to important insights. One example is *viral marketing*, where a company tries to use word-of-mouth effects to market a product with a limited advertising budget, relying on the fact that early adopters may convince friends and colleagues to use the product, creating a large wave of adoptions. While word-of-mouth effects have a history in the area of marketing that long predates the Internet, viral marketing has become a particularly powerful force in online domains, given the ease with which information spreads, and the rich data on customer behavior that can be used to facilitate the process.

A second example is the design of search tools to track news, blogs, and other forms of online discussion about current events. When news of an event first appears, it generally spreads rapidly through a network of both mainstream news sources and the larger population of bloggers – as news organizations and individuals learn of the event, they write their own commentary or versions of the story, and subsequent waves can occur as new developments take place. As with our first example, news was studied as a diffusion process long before the appearance of the Internet, but the fact that news sources are now online provides large-scale, time-resolved data for studying this diffusion, as well as the opportunity to build tools that can help people track the development of a news story in real time as it evolves.

There are a number of interesting algorithmic questions related to these processes, and here we focus on a particular one, posed by Domingos and Richardson (2001) – the identification of influential sets of nodes. While this is a natural question in the context of both our examples above, we describe the problem in terms of the viral marketing framework, where it is particularly easy to express the underlying motivation.

The most influential set of nodes. Suppose that we are a firm trying to market a new product, and we want to take advantage of word-of-mouth effects. One strategy would be as follows: we collect data on the social network interactions among our potential customers, we choose a set S of initial adopters, and we market the product directly to them. Then, assuming they adopt the product, we rely on their influence to generate a large cascade of adoptions, without our having to rely on any further direct promotion of the product. The question of how one goes about inferring the social network interactions and building a cascade model for this purpose is an interesting and largely unexplored topic. Here, however, we assume that all this data is provided to us, and we focus on the algorithmic problem that comes next: how do we choose the set S?

We can formulate this question concretely as follows. For any instance of the General Threshold or Cascade Models, there is a natural *influence function* $f(\cdot)$ defined as follows: for a set S of nodes, $f(S)$ is the expected number of active nodes at the end of the process, assuming that S is the set of nodes that are initially active. (We will assume in this section that all graphs are finite, so the processes we are considering terminate in a number of steps that is bounded by the total number of nodes n.) From the marketer's point of view, $f(S)$ is the expected number of total sales if they get S to be the set of initial adopters. Now, given a budget k, how large can we make $f(S)$ if we are allowed to choose a set S of k initial adopters? In other words, we wish to maximize $f(S)$ over all sets S of size k.

This turns out to be a hard computational problem. First, for almost any special case of the models in the previous section – even very simple special cases – it is NP-hard to find the optimal set S. Moreover, one can construct instances of the model for which it is NP-hard even to approximate the optimal value of $f(S)$ to within a factor of $n^{1-\varepsilon}$ for any $\varepsilon > 0$, where again n is the number of nodes (Kempe et al., 2003). We leave the proofs of these statements as exercises to the reader.

Since NP-hardness applies to almost all versions of the model, there is not much we can do about it; instead, we will try to identify broad subclasses of the models that are not susceptible to strong inapproximability results, and for which good approximation results can be obtained.

Submodularity as a route to good approximations. While we will not go into the details of the inapproximability proofs, they rely on constructing a cascade process for which the resulting influence function f has a "knife-edge" property: as one adds nodes to S, one initially gets very little spreading, but once exactly the right set has been added, the process suddenly spreads very widely. And as we will see shortly, this is actually crucial, since influence functions f that grow in a less pathological way allow for good approximation algorithms. The key to this is a property called *submodularity*.

We say that a function f is *submodular* if adding an element to a set Y causes a smaller marginal improvement than adding the same element to a subset of Y. Specifically, f is submodular if for all sets $X \subseteq Y$ and all elements $v \notin Y$, we have

$$f(X \cup \{v\}) - f(X) \geq f(Y \cup \{v\}) - f(Y).$$

Thus, submodularity is a type of diminishing returns property: the benefit of adding elements decreases as the set to which they are being added grows. We also note that all the influence functions arising from our models here are *monotone*, in the sense that $f(\phi) = 0$ and $f(X) \leq f(Y)$ whenever $X \subseteq Y$.

For such a function f, it is natural to hope that a simple "hill-climbing" approach might lead to a good approximation for the optimal value over all k-element sets: since the marginal benefits only decrease as elements are added, it is hard to "hide" a very large optimum. In fact, this is intuition is formalized in the following theorem of Nemhauser, Wolsey, and Fisher (1978).

Theorem 24.3 *Let f be a monotone submodular function, and let S^* be the k-element set achieving the maximum possible value of f. Let S be a k-element set obtained by repeatedly, for k iterations, including the element producing the largest marginal increase in f. (We can think of S as the result of straightforward hill-climbing with respect to the function f.) Then $f(S) \geq (1 - \frac{1}{e}) f(S^*) \geq .63 f(S^*)$.*

This theorem will be our main vehicle for obtaining approximation algorithms for influence maximization: we will identify instances of the Cascade Model for which the influence function is submodular (it is always monotone for the models we consider), and this will allow us to obtain good results from hill-climbing. There is one further wrinkle in our use of Theorem 24.3, however: it is computationally intractable, even in simple special cases, to evaluate the function f exactly. Fortunately, one can adapt Theorem 24.3 to show that for any $\varepsilon > 0$, if one can approximately evaluate f sufficiently accurately (relative to the granularity taken by the values of f, which are integers in our case), this approximate evaluation of f produces a set S such that $f(S) \geq (1 - \frac{1}{e} - \varepsilon) f(S^*)$. As we can achieve such approximate evaluation for the influence functions we are considering here, this will allow us to apply this approximate form of Theorem 24.3.

We now proceed with the search for broad special cases of the Cascade Model for which the influence function f is submodular.

Diminishing returns and submodularity. It is perhaps easier to think first of instances for which the resulting function f is *not* submodular. For example, suppose that every node v has a sharp threshold $\ell > 1$: v requires at least ℓ active neighbors before v itself becomes active. Then it is easy to construct graphs G on which $f(S)$ remains small until a sufficient number of nodes have been included in S, and then it abruptly jumps up; such a function is not submodular.

More generally, instances based on critical mass effects at the level of individual nodes tend not to yield influence functions that are submodular. But is the opposite true? Does diminishing returns at the level of individual nodes imply that the influence function f is submodular? In fact, the following theorem of Kempe, Kleinberg, and Tardos (2003, 2005) establishes a general sense in which this is the case.

Theorem 24.4 *For any instance of the Cascade Model in which all the incremental functions p_v exhibit diminishing returns, the resulting influence function f is submodular.*

An appealing feature of this theorem is the way in which it establishes a "local-to-global" link: if each individual node experiences influence in a way that exhibits diminishing returns, then the network as a whole experiences influence (from an external marketer) in the same way. The search for such cases in which local behavior implies analogous global behavior is a theme throughout social network research, and finding common principles underlying such effects is an interesting general research issue.

The proof of Theorem 24.4, while not long, is a bit intricate; so instead we describe the proof of a special case of this theorem, where the analysis is conceptually very clean, yet still illustrative of some of the issues involved in proving submodularity. Recall that in the Independent Cascade Model, defined in the previous section, we define the incremental functions via $p_v(u, X) = p_{uv}$: in other words, the influence of u on v depends only on u and v, not on the set of other nodes that have already tried and failed to influence v.

Theorem 24.5 *For any instance of the Independent Cascade Model, the resulting influence function f is submodular.*

PROOF Much of the challenge in proving submodularity here is that the computational intractability of our function f also translates into a kind of conceptual intractability: we do not know enough about its structure to simply "plug it in" to the submodular inequality and hope to verify it directly. A much more powerful approach is instead to decompose f into simpler functions, and check submodularity for the parts of this decomposition.

To lay the groundwork for this plan, we start by discussing two useful facts about submodularity. The first is this: if $f_1, f_2, \ldots, f_r$ are submodular functions, and $c_1, \ldots, c_r$ are nonnegative real numbers, then the function f defined by the weighted sum $f(X) = \sum_{i=1}^{r} c_i f_i(X)$ is also submodular. The second fact is actually the identification of a simple, useful class of submodular functions, the following. Suppose that we have a collection of sets $C_1, C_2, \ldots, C_r$, and for a set $X \subseteq \{1, 2, \ldots, r\}$, we define $f(X) = | \cup_{i \in X} C_i|$. For obvious reasons, we will call such a function f a *size-of-union* function. Then it is not hard to verify that any size-of-union function is submodular. As we will see below, such functions will arise naturally in our decomposition of the influence function f.

Now, consider the following alternate way of viewing the Independent Cascade Process. In the standard view, each time a node u becomes active, it flips a coin of bias p_{uv} to determine whether it succeeds in activating v. Now, in the alternate, equivalent view of the process, suppose that for each edge (u, v), we flip a coin of bias p_{uv} *in advance*, planning to only consult the outcome of the coin flip if we ever need to, when u becomes active.

If there are m edges in the graph, then there are 2^m possible collective outcomes of the coin flips. Let α denote a particular one of these 2^m outcomes, and let $f_\alpha(S)$ denote the eventual number of activated nodes, given that S is the initial active set *and* α is the outcome of the coin flips. Unlike f, the function f_α is easy to understand, as follows. For each edge (u, v), we say that it is *live* (with respect to α) if the advance coin flip came up heads. For a node s, we let $R_s^{\langle\alpha\rangle}$ denote the set of all nodes that are reachable from s on paths consisting entirely of live edges. It is now easy to check that a node is eventually activated if and only if it is reachable from some node in S by some path consisting entirely of live edges, and hence

$$f_\alpha(S) = \left| \bigcup_{s \in S} R_s^{\langle\alpha\rangle} \right|.$$

In other words, each f_α is a size-of-union function, and hence submodular.

But this is essentially all we need, since by definition

$$f(S) = \sum_\alpha \text{Prob}[\alpha] \cdot f_\alpha(S).$$

That is, f is a nonnegative weighted sum of submodular functions, and hence f is subdmodular, as desired. □

We close this particular discussion by noting that Theorem 24.4 is not the most general possible formulation of the local-to-global principle we have been discussing. In particular, if all the incremental functions p_v in an instance of the Cascade Model exhibit diminishing returns, then in the equivalent instance of the General Threshold Model, the resulting threshold functions g_v are submodular (a related notion of diminishing returns). However, the converse does not hold: there exist instances of the General Threshold Model with submodular threshold functions g_v for which the equivalent instance of the Cascade Model has incremental functions p_v that do *not* satisfy diminishing returns. (An important example is the Linear Threshold Model, which does not translate into an instance of the Cascade Model with diminishing returns. Despite this, one can show via a separate analysis that influence functions f arising from the Linear Threshold Model are always submodular.)

Thus, the General Threshold Model with submodular threshold functions is strictly more general than the Cascade Model with incremental functions satisfying diminishing returns. Hence the following very recent result of Mossel and Roch (2007), proving a conjecture of Kempe et al. (2003), generalizes Theorem 24.4.

Theorem 24.6 *For any instance of the General Threshold Model in which all the threshold functions g_v are submodular, the resulting influence function f is submodular.*

Further direction: Alternate marketing strategies. We conclude this section by briefly discussing a different strategy through which a marketer could try to take advantage of word-of-mouth effects. Rather than targeting nodes, as we have been discussing thus far, one could instead target edges: each time an individual u buys a product, an incentive is offered for u to recommend the product to a friend v. A number of online retailers have constructed recommendation incentive programs around this idea: for example, each time you buy a product, you are given the opportunity to send an e-mail to a friend with a special offer to buy the product as well; if the friend goes on to buy it, each of you receives a small cash refund (Leskovec et al., 2006a, 2006b).

Strategies of this type have a different flavor from the targeting of nodes: rather than trying to create a large cascade by influencing initial adopters, one tries to create a large cascade in effect by amplifying the force with which influence is transmitted across edges. (Clearly, one still needs some initial adopters as well for this to succeed.)

While there has been empirical work on the outcomes of particular recommendation incentive programs, it is an open question to analyze theoretical models for the result of such incentives for the problem of maximizing influence.

24.5 Empirical Studies of Cascades in Online Data

As we noted at the outset, there has been a huge amount of empirical work on diffusion in social networks over the past half century. A crucial challenge in this research is the fact that the phenomena being studied – the ways in which social network links affect adoption of innovations – are very hard to measure and assess. Most research of this type has focused on small or moderately sized groups, which are then studied in detail, and the resulting analysis has provided fundamental insights into subtle issues such as the characteristics of adopters at different stages of the innovation.

The theoretical models we have been discussing thus far are motivated at a qualitative level by this empirical work, but it remains an important problem to relate the models to real diffusion data at a more precise, quantitative level. One reason why it has been difficult to do this stems from the type of data available: While existing empirical studies can address fairly rich questions at the scale at which they operate, the resulting datasets tend to be too small to provide accurate estimates of basic quantities needed for assessing the validity of the theoretical models – for example, how adoption probability depends on structural properties of a node's network neighbors. What is needed for this task are large datasets tailored to provide answers to such questions with limited noise.

Diffusion data from online communities. Very recently, large online datasets from several sources have produced measurements that raise interesting connections to the theoretical models. One such study was performed on the online blogging and social networking site LiveJournal (Backstrom et al., 2006). LiveJournal has several million members and several hundred thousand user-defined communities; members maintain individual Web pages with personal information, blogs, and – most importantly for our purposes here – lists of their friends in the system and the communities to which they belong.

From the lists of friends, we can construct an underlying social network, with an edge (v, w) if v lists w as a friend. We then treat each community as a behavior that diffuses through this network: since communities grow by acquiring members over time, we can study how a member's likelihood of joining a group depends on the number of friends he or she has in the group.

Here is a concrete way of formulating this question. At two times t_1 and t_2 (a few months apart), snapshots are taken of the social network and community memberships on LiveJournal. Now, for each number $k \geq 0$, consider the set U_k of all pairs (u, C) such that user u did not belong to community C at time t_1, but had u had k friends in C at t_1. We let $P(k)$ denote the fraction of pairs (u, C) in the set U_k for which u had joined C by time t_2. In this way, $P(k)$ serves as an answer to the question: what is the probability of joining a LiveJournal community, given that you had k friends in it at an earlier time?

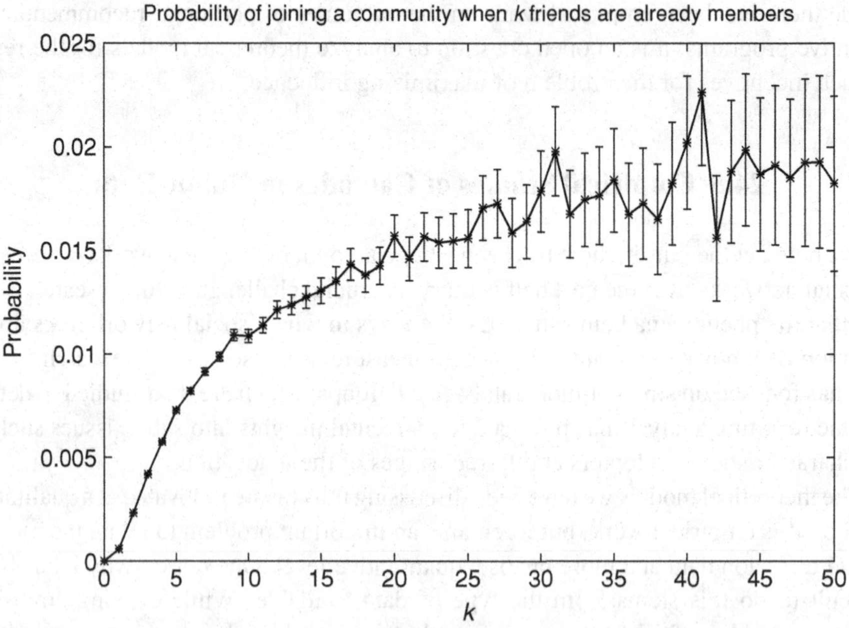

Figure 24.1. The probability of joining a LiveJournal community as a function of the number k of friends in the community at an earlier point in time. Error bars represent two standard errors.

Figure 24.1 shows a plot of $P(k)$ as a function of k for the LiveJournal data. A few things are quickly apparent from the plot. First, the dependence on k is clearly dominated by a diminishing returns effect, in which $P(k)$ grows less quickly as k increases. Indeed, this dependence is quite smooth, with a good fit to a function of the form $P(k) = \varepsilon \log k$ up to moderately large values of k – in particular, this means that $P(k)$ continues increasing even as k becomes fairly large. Finally, there is an initial but significant deviation from diminishing returns for $k = 0, 1, 2$, with $P(2) > 2P(1)$. In other words, having a second friend in a community gives a significant boost to the probability of joining, but after that the diminishing returns effect takes over.

Similar diminishing returns effects have been observed recently in other large-scale datasets that exhibit diffusion-style processes – for example, the probability of publishing a paper at a computer science conference as a function of the number of coauthors who have previously published there (Backstrom et al., 2006); or the probability of purchasing a DVD in a recommendation incentive program run by a large online retailer, as a function of the number of friends who sent an e-mail recommendation (Leskovec et al., 2006). Given how a common effect – diminishing returns – is appearing in large-scale data from such diverse sources, it is an interesting open question to try finding a reasonable mechanism to explain this, potentially including the approximately logarithmic functional form of $P(k)$ in terms of k.

Closer analysis of the LiveJournal data also reveals more subtle effects that contribute to diffusion in a significant way. One that is particularly striking is the connectedness of a person's friends. If we look at the pairs in U_k – recall that this consists of users with k friends in a community they do not initially belong to – it turns out that a user is significantly more likely to join a community if his or her k friends have many edges among themselves than if they do not. In other words, a highly connected set of friends in a community exerts a greater "gravitational force" than a comparable number of friends who are not as well connected among themselves. It is an interesting open question to understand the underlying factors that lead to this effect, to investigate how broadly it applies by considering related datasets, and to think about ways of extending the theoretical models to incorporate effects such as the connectedness of a node's neighbor set.

Relating the empirical and theoretical models. The results shown in Figure 24.1 provide a good means of elaborating on the point made at the start of this section, that diffusion data from online sources, at very large scales, provides both more and less than one finds in classical diffusion studies. It provides less in the sense that we know very little about who individual users on LiveJournal are, what the links between them mean, or what motivates them to join communities. A LiveJournal user may have a link to a close friend, or to someone they have barely met, or simply because they are trying to accumulate as many links on the system as they can. Given this, it is very hard to ask the kind of nuanced questions that one sees in more traditional diffusion studies, which deal with smaller datasets for which they have assembled (often at great effort) a much clearer picture. On the other hand, the fact that the curve in Figure 24.1 is so smooth is precisely the result of having a dataset large enough to contain hundreds of thousands of communities diffusing across a network of millions of users – on a dataset containing just hundreds of individuals, any curve representing $P(k)$ will be extremely noisy. Indeed, given how many different things the links and community memberships on LiveJournal mean to different users, the clean logarithmic form of the resulting curve is perhaps all the more striking, and in need of deeper explanation.

That is a first caveat. A second is that there remains a significant challenge in relating curves like the one in Figure 24.1 to the theoretical models in the earlier sections. The models we discussed there all had a discrete, operational flavor: each node follows a fixed probabilistic rule, and it uses this rule to incorporate information from its neighbors over time. In contrast, the curve in Figure 24.1 is produced by observing the full system at one point in time, and then returning to see what has changed at a later point in time. The dependence of $P(k)$ on k expressed in this way reflects an aggregate property of the full population, and does not imply anything about any particular individual's response to their friends' behaviors. Even for a specific individual, we do not know when (or even if) they became aware of their friends behavior between these two points of time, nor when this translated into a decision by them to act. In particular, this makes it hard to determine how the notion of diminishing returns captured in Figure 24.1 is actually aligned with the formal definition of diminishing returns in Sections 24.3 and 24.4. It is a general and interesting question to explore frameworks that can incorporate this asynchrony and uncertainty about the way in which information flows and is acted on by nodes in a social network, leading to a closer integration of the theoretical and empirical results.

As novel kinds of online information systems continue to proliferate, one sees diffusion processes not just forming part of the underpinnings of the system, but in many cases built directly into the design as well, in settings such as social search, media sharing, or community-based question-answering. As part of this process, extremely rich data are becoming available for studying diffusion processes in online environments, at a large scale and with very fine time resolution. These developments are forming a feedback loop that will inevitably drive the formulation of richer theories, and enable us to pose more incisive questions about the ways in which information, influence, and behaviors of all kinds spread through human social networks.

24.6 Notes and Further Reading

The general topic of diffusion in social networks is discussed in the books by Coleman, Katz, and Menzel (1966), Rogers (1995), and Valente (1995), and the survey by Strang and Soule (1998). Granovetter (1978) and Schelling (1978) provide some of the early mathematical models for these processes. Early game-theoretic formulations of diffusion models were proposed by Blume (1993) and Ellison (1993), and they form part of the focus of a book by Young (1998). The specific model and results in Section 24.2 are from Morris (2000), and further game-theoretic models of diffusion have been explored by Jackson and Yariv (2005). There are also connections at a technical level between the models used in studying diffusion and some of the more graph-theoretic techniques that have been applied to evolutionary game theory; see for example the survey by Lieberman, Hauert, and Nowak (2005) and the paper by Kearns and Suri (2006).

Models for diffusion are also closely related to work the topic of contact processes and particle systems studied in the area of probability (Durrett, 1988; Liggett, 1985), as well as to the long history of work in mathematical epidemiology, which studies the dynamics of biological (as opposed to social) contagion (Bailey, 1975). There has been a recent line of work aimed at relating such probabilistic contagion models more closely to the underlying network structure; see for example the recent work of by Pastor-Satorras and Vespignani (2000), Newman (2002), and Alon, Benjamini, and Stacey (2004).

The problem of finding the most influential set of k individuals, as discussed in Section 24.4, was posed, together with the viral marketing motivation, by Domingos and Richardson (2001). The search for influential nodes in networks of blogs and news sources has been considered by Adar et al. (2004), Gruhl et al. (2004), and Kumar et al. (2004).

The approximation result in Section 24.4 is due to Kempe, Kleinberg, and Tardos (2003, 2005); the general theorem on which it depends, that hill-climbing provides a good approximation for arbitrary monotone submodular functions, is due to Fisher, Nemhauser, and Wolsey (1978). The formulations of the models in Section 24.3 are also from Kempe et al. (2003), with closely related models proposed independently by Dodds and Watts (2004).

Recommendation incentive programs, discussed at the end of Section 24.4, are studied empirically by Leskovec, Adamic, and Huberman (2006) and by Leskovec, Singh, and Kleinberg (2006); the development of theoretical models for such systems remains largely an open question. The study of diffusion processes on LiveJournal discussed in Section 24.5 is from Backstrom, Huttenlocher, Kleinberg, and Lan (2006), where a number of more subtle features of diffusion on LiveJournal are investigated as well. The identification of diminishing returns effects in recommendation incentives is from Leskovec, Adamic, and Huberman (2006).

Bibliography

E. Adar, L. Zhang, L.A. Adamic, and R.M. Lukose. Implicit structure and the dynamics of blogspace. In *Workshop on the Weblogging Ecosystem*, 2004.

N. Alon, I. Benjamini, and A. Stacey. Percolation on finite graphs and isoperimetric inequalities. *Ann. Probability*, 32:1727–1745, 2004.

L. Backstrom, D. Huttenlocher, J. Kleinberg, and X. Lan. Group formation in large social networks: Membership, growth, and evolution. In *Proc. 12th Intl. Conf. on Knowledge Discovery and Data Mining*, 2006.

N. Bailey. *The Mathematical Theory of Infectious Diseases and Its Applications*. Hafner Press, 1975.

L. Blume. The statistical mechanics of strategic interaction. *Games Econ. Behav.*, 5:387–424, 1993.

J. Coleman, E. Katz, and H. Menzel, *Medical Innovations: A Diffusion Study*. Bobbs Merrill, 1966.

P. Dodds and D. Watts. Universal behavior in a generalized model of contagion. *Physical Review Letters*, 92:218701, 2004.

P. Domingos and M. Richardson. Mining the network value of customers. In *Proc. 7th Intl. Conf. on Knowledge Discovery and Data Mining*, pp. 57–66, 2001.

R. Durrett. *Lecture Notes on Particle Systems and Percolation*. Wadsworth Publishing, 1988.

G. Ellison. Learning, local interaction, and coordination. *Econometrica*, 61:1047–1071, 1993.

M. Granovetter. Threshold models of collective behavior. *Am. J. Sociol.*, 83:1420–1443, 1978.

D. Gruhl, D. Liben-Nowell, R.V. Guha, and A. Tomkins. Information diffusion through blogspace. In *13th Intl. World Wide Web Conference*, 2004.

M. Jackson and L. Yariv. Diffusion on social networks. *Economie Publique*, 16:69–82, 2005.

M. Kearns and S. Suri. Networks preserving evolutionary equilibria and the power of randomization. In *Proc. 7th ACM Conference on Electronic Commerce*, 2006.

D. Kempe, J. Kleinberg, and É. Tardos. Maximizing the spread of influence in a social network. In *Proc. 9th Intl. Conf. on Knowledge Discovery and Data Mining*, pp. 137–146, 2003.

D. Kempe, J. Kleinberg, and É. Tardos. Influential nodes in a diffusion model for social networks. In *Proc. 32nd Intl. Colloq. on Automata, Languages and Programming*, pp. 1127–1138, 2005.

R. Kumar, J. Novak, P. Raghavan, and A. Tomkins. Structure and evolution of blogspace. *Comm. ACM*, 47(12):35–39, 2004.

J. Leskovec, L. Adamic, and B. Huberman. The dynamics of viral marketing. In *Proc. 7th ACM Conference on Electronic Commerce*, 2006a.

J. Leskovec, A. Singh, and J.M. Kleinberg. Patterns of influence in a recommendation network. In *Pacific-Asia Conference on Knowledge Discovery and Data Mining*, pp. 380–389, 2006b.

E. Lieberman, C. Hauert, and M. Nowak. Evolutionary dynamics on graphs. *Nature*, 433:312–316, 2005.

T. Liggett. *Interacting Particle Systems*. Springer, 1985.

S. Morris. Contagion. *Review of Economic Studies*, 67:57–78, 2000.

E. Mossel and S. Roch. On the submodularity of influence in social networks. In *Proc. 39th ACM Symp. on Theory of Computing*, 2007.

G. Nemhauser, L. Wolsey, and M. Fisher. An analysis of the approximations for maximizing submodular set functions. *Math. Programm.*, 14:265–294, 1978.

M.E.J. Newman. The spread of epidemic disease on networks. *Phys. Rev. E*, 66:016128, 2002.

R. Pastor-Satorras and A. Vespignani. Epidemic spreading in scale-free networks. *Phys. Rev. Letters*, 86:3200–3203, 2000.

E. Rogers. *Diffusion of innovations*. 4th ed. Free Press, 1995.

T. Schelling. *Micromotives and Macrobehavior*. Norton, 1978.

D. Strang and S. Soule. Diffusion in organizations and social movements: From hybrid corn to poison pills. *Ann. Rev. Sociol.*, 24:265–290, 1998.

T. Valente. *Network Models of the Diffusion of Innovations*. Hampton Press, 1995.

H.P. Young. *Individual Strategy and Social Structure: An Evolutionary Theory of Institutions*. Princeton University Press, 1998.

Exercises

24.1 Prove Claim 24.1 in the proof of Theorem 24.1.

24.2 The first model we considered in Section 24.2 was based on a networked coordination game in which, across each edge (v, w), nodes v and w each receive a payoff of q if they both choose behavior A, they each receive a payoff of $1 - q$ if they both choose behavior B, and they each receive a payoff of 0 if they choose opposite behaviors. Let us call this a *coordination game with parameter q*.

It is natural to ask what happens if we consider a more general kind of coordination game on each edge. Suppose in particular that, on each edge (v, w), node v receives payoff u_{XY} if it chooses strategy X while w chooses strategy Y, for any choice of $X \in \{A, B\}$ and $Y \in \{A, B\}$. Moreover, to preserve the coordination aspect, we assume that it is still better to play matching strategies: $u_{AA} > u_{BA}$ and $u_{BB} > u_{AB}$.

While this is indeed a more general kind of game, prove that the results on the contagion threshold remain the same. Specifically, prove that for any infinite graph G with finite node degrees, and for any choice of payoffs $\{u_{AA}, u_{BA}, u_{AB}, u_{BB}\}$ satisfying $u_{AA} > u_{BA}$ and $u_{BB} > u_{AB}$, there exists a real number q such that the following holds: A finite set S is contagious in G with respect to the coordination game defined by $\{u_{AA}, u_{BA}, u_{AB}, u_{BB}\}$ if and only if it is contagious in G with respect to the coordination game with parameter q.

24.3 **(a)** In Section 24.4, we considered the problem of finding a set S of k nodes that maximizes the expected number of activated nodes $f(S)$. Show that for some class of instances of the General Threshold or Cascade Model, finding the optimal set S is NP-hard.

(b) For some class of instances of the General Threshold or Cascade Model, show that in fact it is NP-hard to approximate the optimal value of $f(S)$ to within a factor of $n^{1-\varepsilon}$ for any $\varepsilon > 0$, where n is the number of nodes.

CHAPTER 25

Incentives and Information Security

Ross Anderson, Tyler Moore, Shishir Nagaraja, and Andy Ozment

Abstract

Many interesting and important new applications of game theory have been discovered over the past 7 years in the context of research into the economics of information security. Many systems fail not ultimately for technical reasons but because incentives are wrong. For example, the people who guard a system often are not the people who suffer the full costs of failure, and as a result they make less effort than would be socially optimal. Some aspects of information security are public goods, like clean air or water; externalities often decide which security products succeed in the marketplace; and some information risks are not insurable because they are correlated in ways that cause insurance markets to fail.

Deeper applications of game-theoretic ideas can be found in the games of incomplete information that occur when critical information, such as about software quality or defender efforts, is hidden from some principals. An interesting application lies in the analysis of distributed system architectures; it took several years of experimentation for designers of peer-to-peer systems to understand incentive issues that we can now analyze reasonably well. Evolutionary game theory has recently allowed us to tie together a number of ideas from network analysis and elsewhere to explain why basing peer-to-peer systems on rings is a bad idea, and why revolutionaries use cells instead. The economics of distributed systems looks like being a very fruitful field of research.

25.1 Introduction

Over the last 7 years, people have realized that security failure is caused at least as often by misaligned incentives as by technical design mistakes. Systems are particularly prone to failure when the person guarding them is not the person who suffers when they fail. The tools and concepts of game theory and microeconomic theory are becoming just as important as the mathematics of cryptography to the security engineer.

In this chapter, we present several live research challenges in the economics of information security, many of which bear on problems in various branches of game theory. We first consider misaligned incentives, and externalities: network insecurity is somewhat like air pollution or traffic congestion, in that people who connect insecure machines to the net do not bear the full consequences of their actions and so do not make a socially optimal investment in protection. Next we examine the role of asymmetric information and the capacity for hidden action: games where one principal has more knowledge of the game state than her opponent, or games where she can make moves that become known only with a certain probability.

The difficulty in measuring information security risks presents another challenge: these risks cannot be better managed until they can be better measured. Auctions and markets can help in various ways to measure the security of software and thereby reduce the information asymmetry prevalent in the software industry. We also examine the problem of insuring against attacks. The local and global correlations exhibited by different attack types largely determine whether an insurance market in the associated risks is feasible.

The structure of computer networks can also have a great impact on player incentives. One topical example is that the effort devoted to censorship resistance in peer-to-peer systems depends upon whether the application design empowers players to choose which files to share or randomly distributes them. This realization enables us to model solidarity in networks that may come under selective attack.

An even more striking example is how network topology can exacerbate the impact of viruses or susceptibility to targeted attacks. The regular networks, or random networks, commonly used in modeling do not behave the same way as real-world networks, which are better approximated by scale-free models. Scale-free networks turn out to be more robust against random failure but more vulnerable to targeted attack. We finally present a model that uses ideas from evolutionary game theory to explore the interaction between attack and defense strategies, and we provide a framework for evaluating strategies in networks where topology matters.

25.2 Misaligned Incentives

One of the observations that drove initial interest in security economics came from banking. In the United States, banks are generally liable for the costs of card fraud; when a customer disputes a transaction, the bank must either show that she is trying to cheat them or refund her money. In the United Kingdom, the banks had a much easier ride: they could often get away with claiming that the ATM system was "secure," so a customer who complained must be mistaken or lying. "Lucky bankers," one might think; yet it turned out that UK banks spent more on security and suffered more fraud. How could this be? Banks appear to have been suffering from a moral-hazard effect: UK bank staff knew that customer complaints would not be taken so seriously, so they became lazy and careless. This situation led to an avalanche of fraud.

Another observation came from the state of the antivirus software market around the year 2000. People were not spending as much money on protecting their computers from infection as would have been ideal. Why not? Well, at that time, a typical virus payload was a service-denial attack against the Web site of a company like Amazon or Microsoft. While a rational consumer might well spend $20 to prevent a virus from trashing his hard disk, he might not do so just to prevent an attack on Bill.

Legal theorists have long known that liability should be assigned to the party that can best manage the risk. Yet everywhere we look, we see online risks that are poorly allocated. The result is privacy failures and even protracted regulatory tussles. For example, the United States has seen widespread debate about medical privacy over the last 10 years: from the passage of the Health Insurance Portability and Accountability Act, through the initial regulations made under the Act by President Clinton, the later regulations made by President Bush, and the recent claims that the law fails to protect health privacy while providing a gold-mine for security vendors. The root problem is that medical information systems are purchased by hospital directors and insurance companies, whose interests in account management, cost control and research are not well aligned with the patients' interests in the privacy of their health records.

25.2.1 Applications of Game Theory

Game theory can provide a means of better understanding the outcome of security decisions made by self-interested individuals. Information security levels often depend on the efforts of many principals, leading to suboptimal security investment whenever decisions are uncoordinated. The level of security investment generally depends on the investor's own costs and benefits, the investment decisions of others, and the manner in which individual investment translates to outcomes. System reliability can depend on the sum of individual efforts, the minimum effort invested, or the maximum effort invested. Programming, for example, might be down to the weakest link (the most careless programmer introducing a fatal vulnerability) while software validation and vulnerability testing might depend on the sum of everyone's efforts. There can also be cases where the security depends on the best effort – the effort of a star cryptanalyst. These different models have interesting effects on whether an appropriate level of defense can be provided and what policy measures are advisable.

A simple model by Varian provides interesting results when players choose their effort levels independently. For the total-effort case, system reliability depends on the agent with the highest benefit-cost ratio, and all other agents free ride. In the weakest-link case, the agent with the lowest benefit-cost ratio dominates, since any additional effort is wasted. Systems become increasingly reliable in the total-effort case as more agents are added, but they become increasingly unreliable in the weakest-link case. What are the implications? One is that software companies should hire more software testers but fewer (more competent) programmers.

Work such as this has inspired other researchers to consider interdependent risk. A recent influential model by Kunreuther and Heal notes that the security of a group often rests on each of its members: an individual taking protective measures creates positive externalities for others that in turn may discourage their own investment. This result has implications far beyond information security. The decision by one apartment owner to install a sprinkler system affects his neighbors' decisions to install their own systems; airlines may decide not to screen luggage transferred from other carriers who are believed to be careful with security; and people thinking of vaccinating their children against a contagious disease may choose to free-ride off the herd immunity instead. In each case, several widely varying Nash equilibrium outcomes are possible, from complete adoption to total refusal, depending on the levels of coordination between independent actors.

25.2.2 Network Effects and Deployment

Game theory is also used to ascertain how network effects impact the level of security investments. In particular, many security technologies face bootstrapping problems. The benefit that these technologies provide to players is dependent upon the number of players that adopt the technology. A bootstrapping problem exists because the cost of the technology is greater than the benefit until a minimum number of players adopt. As a result, each player waits for other players to go first, and the technology is never deployed.

Following the seminal work of Katz and Shapiro, a number of economists have examined the problem of deploying a technology that exhibits network effects. Most of this literature concludes that adoption is a coordination problem. The challenge is to coordinate the different players and to enforce their cooperation. However, the assumptions used in these models do not apply to many security technologies. For example, security technologies that are software-based can often be deployed rapidly, while the economics literature is concerned with coordinating players who must make their decisions far in advance of a slow-moving deployment. Furthermore, security technologies may not provide special benefits to early adopters.

This area is especially topical at the moment. A number of core Internet protocols are considered insecure, such as DNS and routing. More secure protocols exist; the challenge is to bootstrap their adoption. Two examples of security protocols that have already been widely deployed are SSH and IPsec. Both of these protocols overcame the bootstrapping problem because they could provide significant intraorganizational benefits (X session support and VPNs). Adoption was thus driven by organizational needs rather than the benefit that players derived from the global network. The deployment of fax machines also occurred through this mechanism: companies initially bought fax machines to connect their own offices. Limiting the players in a game to the members of some kind of club can also have interesting effects on other aspects of security, as we see below.

25.3 Informational Asymmetries

We now consider two types of informational asymmetries relevant to information security: hidden action, where the difficulty of observing others' actions facilitates certain attacks; and hidden information, where the difficulty of measuring software security has caused vendors to underinvest in quality.

25.3.1 Hidden-Action Attacks

In the theory of asymmetric information, a hidden-action problem arises whenever two parties wish to transact, but one party can take unobservable actions that impact the transaction. The classic example comes from insurance, where the insured party may choose to behave recklessly (which in turn increases the likelihood of a claim) because the insurance company cannot observe her behavior. Crossing to the security domain, this idea generalizes to a class of hidden-action attacks, which are attractive precisely because observation (and therefore punishment) is unlikely.

Computer networks are naturally susceptible to hidden-action attacks. Routers can quietly drop selected packets or falsify responses to routing requests; nodes can redirect network traffic to eavesdrop on conversations; and players in file-sharing systems can hide whether they have chosen to share with others, so some may choose to "free-ride" rather than to help replenish the system. The common element in these examples is that nodes can hide malicious or antisocial behavior from other network elements.

Hidden-action attacks may occur whenever the net utility gain from deviation is greater than the expected penalty enforced when observation is unlikely and less than the expected penalty enforced when observation is likely. (If the expected gain from an attack does not exceed the expected penalty even when actions are likely to remain hidden, then no attack should occur. If the expected gain in attacking exceeds the expected penalty even when observed, then the attack should be launched regardless of whether or not observation is likely.)

In the economics literature, hidden-action problems are dealt with by structuring contracts to induce proper behavior. For example, auto insurers use deductibles to mitigate driver recklessness. By charging customers to file a claim, insurers create an incentive for taking reasonable steps to avoid negative outcomes. The need for observation is eliminated, though not without cost: everyone has to pay, even when the insured did not act recklessly. Mechanism design, as discussed throughout the rest of this book, attempts to create systems that align all of the agents' incentives so that the agents' best interest is to operate as intended. A complementary approach is to alter the topology and structure of the interactions to increase observability.

One telling example comes from peer-to-peer systems. These exploit network externalities to the fullest by having large member populations with a flat topology: joining one creates the potential for collaboration with every other peer in the system. High turnover is also expected; nodes may join and leave the system rapidly. These properties lower the prospects for repeated interactions, which in turn makes cheating more likely. Inexpensive or even costless identities exacerbate the problem of unrepeated interactions while also making penalties harder to implement. In a network with these properties, nodes are predisposed to hidden action.

One solution is to change the network topology. In most peer-to-peer systems, any node can transact with any other on joining the network. While this flat topology maximizes transaction possibilities, it makes repeated transactions unlikely and observation difficult. An alternative is to adopt a network topology based on clubs of nodes with common interests. Here, nodes first transact with other members of their club to establish legitimacy. Once trust has been established inside the cluster, outside transactions can happen through established channels between groups. Such a topology facilitates self-enforcement by establishing a credible threat of observation to forestall hidden action, and by creating long-lived principals (clubs) against whom sanctions hurt.

Social networks can also be used to create better topologies. When honest players can select their friends as neighbors rather than having their neighbors randomly assigned, they minimize the informational asymmetry present during neighbor interactions. This can raise the cost of entry for an attacker as well as align the incentives between normal players. However, social networks can also lead to inefficient outcomes as players may not be exposed to diverse information and isolated players may be marginalized.

25.3.2 Hidden Information: Measuring Software Security

Another information asymmetry in information security is caused by our inability to effectively measure the security of software. Most commercial software contains design and implementation flaws that could easily have been prevented. Although vendors are capable of creating more secure software, the economics of the software industry provide them with little incentive to do so. In many markets, "ship it Tuesday and get it right by version 3" is perfectly rational behavior. Consumers generally reward vendors for adding features, for being first to market, or for being dominant in an existing market. These motivations clash with the goal of writing more secure software, which requires time-consuming testing and a focus on simplicity. Nonetheless, the problems of software insecurity, viruses, and worms are frequently in the headlines; why does the potential damage to vendor reputations not motivate them to invest in more secure software?

Vendors' lack of motivation is readily explained: the software market is a "market for lemons." In a Nobel prize-winning work, economist George Akerlof employed the used car market as a metaphor for a market with asymmetric information. His paper imagines a town in which 50 good used cars (worth \$2,000) are for sale, along with 50 "lemons" (worth \$1,000 each). The sellers know the difference but the buyers do not. What is the market-clearing price? One might initially think \$1,500, but at that price no-one with a good car will offer it for sale; so the market price quickly ends up near \$1,000. Because buyers are unwilling to pay a premium for quality they cannot measure, only low quality used vehicles are available for sale.

The software market suffers from the same asymmetry of information. Vendors may have some intuition about the security of their products, but buyers have no reason to trust them. In some cases, even the vendor might not have a truly accurate picture of its software's security. As a result, buyers have no reason to pay the premium required to obtain more secure software, and vendors are disinclined to invest in protection.

Three broad research approaches have attempted to provide useful measures of the security of software: statistical, market-based, and insurance-based. The former approach relies on the application of reliability growth models to vulnerabilities and is not be discussed here. The latter two approaches are discussed below.

25.3.3 Market-Based Approaches

One possible way to measure the security of software is to rely on a market: let buyers and sellers establish the actual cost of finding a vulnerability in software or merely estimate the security of software according to their own knowledge. For example, banking standards for PIN-entry terminals specify a minimum cost of various kinds of technical compromise.

In the software business, open markets for reports of previously undiscovered vulnerabilities could provide a security metric. The bid, ask, and most recent sale prices in such a market approximate the labor cost to find a vulnerability. These prices can establish which of two products the market deems to have vulnerabilities that are less expensive to find. Alternatively, a vulnerability market of this type could be designed as an auction.

Several organizations are now actively purchasing vulnerabilities, so an open market or auction actually exists. Unfortunately, these organizations are not publishing their prices. Their business model is to provide the vulnerability information simultaneously to their customers and to the vendor of the affected product (in contrast to the previous practice of waiting until after a patch is released and then making the existence of the vulnerability public). The business models of these organizations are thus not socially optimal: they always have an incentive to leak vulnerability information without proper safeguards.

A market for software security derivatives could also enable security professionals to reach a price consensus on the level of security for a product. Contracts could be issued in pairs: the first pays a fixed value if no vulnerability is found in a program by a specific date, and the second pays the same value if vulnerabilities have been found in that program by that date. If these contracts can be issued as desired and traded via some market, then their trading price indicates the consensus opinion on the security of the program. Software security derivatives could thus conceivably be used to hedge risks by software vendors, players, software company investors, and insurance companies.

25.3.4 Insurance-Based Approaches

Another approach to measuring the security of software is to rely on insurers. The argument for insurance is that cyber-insurance underwriters assign premiums based upon a firm's IT infrastructure and the processes by which it is managed. This assessment results in both detailed best practices and, over the long run, a pool of data by which the insurance company can accurately assign a monetary value to the risks associated with certain practices or software. At the moment, however, the cyber-insurance market is both underdeveloped and underutilized. Why should this be?

One reason is the problem of interdependent risk, which takes at least two forms. Firms are 'physically interdependent' because their IT infrastructure is connected via the Internet to other entities – which implies that the work a firm performs to secure itself may be undermined by failures at other firms. Firms are "logically interdependent" because cyber attacks often exploit a vulnerability in a system used by many firms. For example, viruses or worms may have a global impact upon a specific software platform. This interdependence makes certain cyber-risks unattractive to insurers – particularly those where the risk is globally rather than locally correlated, such as worm and virus attacks, and systemic risks such as Y2K. We note in passing that many writers have called for cyber-risks to be transferred to the responsible software vendors; if this were the law, it is unlikely that Microsoft would be able to buy insurance. So far, vendors have succeeded in dumping almost all risk; but this outcome is also far from being socially optimal.

Because a firm's security depends in part on the efforts of others, firms underinvest in both security technology and in cyber insurance. At the same time, insurance companies must charge a higher premium because the risks against which they are insuring are highly correlated: this higher premium may prevent the vast majority of firms from adequately insuring themselves. As a result, cyber insurance markets may lack the volume and liquidity to become economically efficient.

25.4 The Economics of Censorship Resistance

We have seen that misaligned incentives and information asymmetries are important problems in information security that are amenable to a game theoretic analysis. Another such problem is censorship resistance.

Early peer-to-peer systems were oriented toward censorship resistance rather than music file sharing. They put all content into one pot, with the effect that quite different groups would end up protecting each others' free speech – be they Falun Gong members, critics of scientology, or aficionados of sado-masochistic imagery that is legal in California but banned in Tennessee. The question then arises whether such groups might not be better off with their own peer-to-peer systems. Perhaps they would fight harder to defend their own type of dissident, rather than people involved in struggles in which they had no interest and where they might even be disposed to side with the censor. In the file-sharing context, it might make sense to have a constellation of fan clubs, rather than one huge system – as musicians take widely different views of music sharing, remixing and other activities on the fringes of classical copyright practice.

Such questions are also of topical interest to social theorists and policy people, who wonder whether the growing diversity of modern societies is undermining the social solidarity on which modern welfare states are founded. A related question in guerrilla warfare is when combatants should aggregate or disperse.

We find peer-to-peer systems providing a "single pot," with widely and randomly distributed functionality, such as Eternity, Freenet, Chord, Pastry, and OceanStore. Other systems, like the popular Gnutella and Kazaa, allow peer nodes to serve content they have downloaded for their personal use, without burdening them with random files. The comparison between these architectures originally focused on purely technical aspects: the cost of search, retrieval, communications, and storage. However, it turns out that incentives matter here too.

25.4.1 Red–Blue Utility Model

Danezis and Anderson introduced the Red–Blue model to analyze the trade-off between diversity and solidarity in distributed systems. We consider a network of N peer nodes. Each node n_i has a preference among two types of resource, say red and blue; one node might prefer to serve 20% red and 80% blue, while another prefers 80% red and 20% blue and the network overall contains 50% red and 50% blue. A censor who attacks the network tries to impose his own preference, perhaps 80% red and 20% blue. This action may meet the approval of some nodes, but usually not most of them.

We assign to each node n_i a preference for red $r_i \in [0, 1]$ and a preference for blue $b_i = 1 - r_i$ (note that $r_i + b_i = 1$). While each node likes having and serving resources, it prefers to have or serve a balance of resources according to its own preference r_i and b_i. So we define the utility function of a node holding T resources out of which R are red resources and B are blue resources (with $T = R + B$) as

$$U_i(R, B) = -T\left(\frac{R}{T - r_i - 1}\right)\left(\frac{R}{T - r_i + 1}\right). \tag{25.1}$$

This is a quadratic function with its maximum at $R = r_i T$, scaled by the overall number of resources T that the node n_i holds. This utility function increases as the total number of resources does, but is also maximal when the balance between red and blue resources matches the preferences of the node ($R = r_i T$ and $B = b_i T$). When nodes choose the file distribution to serve, their utility is naturally maximized.

Distributed hash tables and architectures such as Eternity, by contrast, scatter the red and blue resources randomly across all nodes n_i. If the system has a total of $\mathcal{R}$ red resources and $\mathcal{B}$ blue resources, we can define a systemwide distribution of resources (r_s, b_s) so that each node in the system holds on average:

$$r_s = \frac{\mathcal{R}}{\mathcal{R}+\mathcal{B}} \qquad b_s = \frac{\mathcal{B}}{\mathcal{R}+\mathcal{B}}. \tag{25.2}$$

Each node n_i has on average a utility equal to $U(r_s T, b_s T)$. The utility each node attains in the random case is always less than or equal to the utility a node has under the discretionary model:

$$U_i(r_i T, b_i T) \geq U_i(r_s T, b_s T). \tag{25.3}$$

$U_i(r_i T, b_i T) = U_i(r_s T, b_s T)$ when $r_s = r_i$ and $b_s = b_i$ – in other words, when the system's distribution of resources aligns with a particular node's preferences. However, this cannot hold true for all nodes unless they share the same preferences. Moreover, it is in every node's self-interest to try to tip the balance of $\mathcal{R}$ and $\mathcal{B}$ toward its own preferences. With a utility function slightly more biased toward serving, the network could be flooded with red or blue files, depending on the dominant preference.

25.4.2 Comparing Censorship Resistance

We model censorship as an external entity's attempt to impose a particular distribution of files r_c, b_c on a set of nodes. The censor's effect is not fixed; rather, it depends on the amount of resistance the affected nodes offer.

Assume a node that is not receiving attention from the censor can store up to T resources. A node under censorship can choose to store fewer resources $(T - t)$ and invest an effort level t to resist censorship. We define the probability that a node successfully fights censorship (and reestablish its previous distribution of resources) as $P(t)$. With probability $1 - P(t)$, the censor prevails and imposes the distribution r_c, b_c.

We first consider the discretionary case, in which nodes select the content they serve. Knowing the nodes' preferences r_i, b_i, the censor's distribution r_c, b_c, the total resource bound T, and the probability $P(t)$ that it defeats the censor, we can calculate the optimal amount of resources a node invests in resisting censorship. The expected utility of a node under censorship is the probability of success, times the utility in that case, plus the probability of failure times the utility in that case:

$$U = P(t)U_i(r_i(T-t), b_i(T-t)) + (1 - P(t))U_i(r_c(T-t), b_c(T-t)). \tag{25.4}$$

Our utility functions U_i are unimodal and smooth, so if the functions $P(t)$ are sufficiently well-behaved, there is a single optimal investment in resistance t in $[0, T]$ by setting $\frac{dU}{dt} = 0$.

We begin with the simplest example, namely where the probability $P(t)$ of resisting censorship is linear in the defensive effort t. Assume that if a node invests all its resources in fighting, it definitely prevails but has nothing left to serve any files. At the other extreme, if it spends nothing on lawyers (or whatever the relevant mode of combat) then the censor prevails for sure. Therefore we define $P(t)$ as

$$P(t) = \frac{1}{T}t. \tag{25.5}$$

By maximizing (25.4) with $P(t)$ defined as in (25.5), we find that the optimal defense budget t_d:

$$t_d = \frac{T}{2}\frac{2U_i(r_c, b_c) - U_i(r_i, b_i)}{U_i(r_c, b_c) - U_i(r_i, b_i)}. \tag{25.6}$$

The node diverts t_d resources from serving files to fighting censorship. We also assume, for now, that the cost of the attack for the censor is equal to the node's defense budget t.

We now turn to the case of Eternity or DHTs where resources are scattered randomly around the network, where each node is expected to hold a mixture of files r_s, b_s. As in the previous example, the utility of a node under censorship depends on its defense budget t, the censor's choice of r_c, b_c, and the system's distribution of files r_s, b_s:

$$U = P(t)U_i(r_s(T-t), b_s(T-t)) + (1 - P(t))U_i(r_c(T-t), b_c(T-t)). \tag{25.7}$$

A similar approach is followed as above to derive the optimal defense budget t for each node:

$$t_s = \frac{T}{2}\frac{2U_i(r_c, b_c) - U_i(r_s, b_s)}{U_i(r_c, b_c) - U_i(r_s, b_s)} \tag{25.8}$$

However, not all nodes are motivated to resist the censor! Some may find that $U_i(r_sT, b_sT) \leq U_i(r_cT, b_cT)$, which means that their utility under censorship increases. This is not an improbable situation: in a network where half the resources are red and half are blue ($r_s = 0.5, b_s = 0.5$) a censor that shifts the balance to $r_c = 0$ benefits the blue-loving nodes, and if they are free to set their own defense budgets then they select $t = 0$.

Who fights censorship harder? The aggregate defense budget, and thus the cost of censorship, is greater in the discretionary model than in the random one, except in the case in which all nodes have the same preferences (in which case equality holds).

For the maximum value of the defense budget t to be positive in the interval $[0, T]$, the following condition must be true:

$$0 < \frac{T}{2}\frac{2U_i(r_c, b_c) - U_i(r_s, b_s)}{U_i(r_c, b_c) - U_i(r_s, b_s)}. \tag{25.9}$$

In other words,

$$2U_i(r_c, b_c) < U_i(r_c, b_c). \tag{25.10}$$

When this is not true, a node maximizes its utility by not fighting at all and choosing $t = 0$. Given these observations, it follows that

$$\forall i \in \mathcal{S}, t_{d_i} \geq t_{s_i} \Rightarrow \sum_{i \in \mathcal{S}} t_{d_i} \geq \sum_{i \in \mathcal{S}} t_{s_i}. \tag{25.11}$$

Whatever the attacker's strategy, it is at least as costly or more so, to attack a network's architecture via the discretionary rather than the random model. Equality holds when for each node, $t_d = t_s$, which in turn means that $r_i = r_s$. This is the case of homogeneous preferences. In all other cases, the cost to censor a set of nodes is maximized when resources are distributed according to their preferences rather than randomly.

25.5 Complex Networks and Topology

The final area of information security that we discuss is the topology of complex networks. Computer networks from the Internet to decentralized peer-to-peer networks are systems of great complexity that emerge from ad hoc interactions of many entities on the basis of simple ground rules that are minimally restrictive. The emergent complexity, coupled with heterogeneity on every relevant scale, is similar to networks found "in the wild" – from the social networks made up from interactions between people to metabolic pathways in living organisms. Recently a discipline of network analysis has emerged at the boundary between sociology and condensed-matter physics. It takes ideas added from other disciplines like graph theory, which provides tools and concepts for modeling and investigating such networks. Our interest here is the interaction of network science with information security; as we shall see, we can build an interesting bridge to evolutionary game theory.

Network topology can strongly influence conflict dynamics. Often an attacker tries to disconnect a network or increase its diameter by destroying nodes or edges, while the defender counters using various resilience mechanisms. Examples include a music industry body attempting to close down a peer-to-peer file-sharing network; a police organization trying to decapitate a terrorist organization; and a totalitarian government conducting surveillance on political activists. Police forces have been curious for some years about whether network science might be of practical use in covert conflicts – whether to insurgents or to counterinsurgency forces.

Different topologies have different robustness properties with respect to various attacks. Albert, Jeong, and Barabási famously showed that certain real-world networks with scale-free degree distributions are more robust to random attacks than targeted attacks. This is because scale-free networks – like many real-world networks – get much of their connectivity from a minority of nodes that have a high vertex order. This resilience makes them highly robust against random upsets; but remove the 'kingpin' nodes, and connectivity collapses.

This is the static case – for example, when a police force becomes aware of a criminal or terrorist network, and sets out to disrupt it by finding and arresting its key personnel. The result of Albert et al. models this well. But what about the dynamic case – where at each round the attacker can remove a certain number of nodes, but the defenders can recruit other nodes to replace them? How do attack and defense interact: what is the interplay of tactics and strategy?

We built a simulation in which a network game is played with a number of rounds. Each round consists of attack followed by node replenishment and adaptation. The attacker can remove a proportion of nodes; his choice of nodes is his strategy. The defenders' strategy lies in the adaptation phase; the way they rewire their network after each round of attack and replenishment. This rewiring must be done using only local knowledge.

An attack strategy is more efficient, for a given defense strategy, if an attacker using it requires a smaller budget to disrupt the network. Similarly, a defense strategy is more efficient if, for a given attack strategy, it compels the attacker to expend a higher budget to achieve network disruption.

We started off by considering the static attacker of Albert et al., whereby high vertex order nodes are removed, and a defense strategy of either random replenishment, forming rings, or forming cliques. In the ring strategy, defenders replace high-order nodes with rings – as in P2P systems such as Chord. In the clique strategy, high-order nodes are replaced with cliques – clusters of nodes all connected to each other.

The results of the initial three simulations are given in Figure 25.1.

Random replenishment (line with circles) in Figure 25.1 provides a calibration baseline. As seen above, it is ineffective: within three rounds the size of the largest connected component has fallen by a half, from 400 nodes to well under 200. The line with crosses shows that rings give only a surprisingly short-term defense benefit. They postpone network collapse from about two rounds to about a dozen rounds. Thereafter, the network is almost completely disconnected.

Cliques (indicated by the caret symbol), on the other hand, work well. A few vertices are disconnected at each attack round, but the network itself remains robustly connected. This may provide some insight into why, although rings have seemed

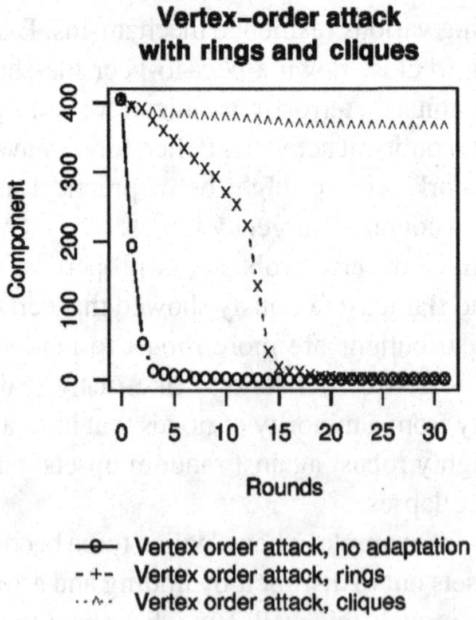

Figure 25.1. Vertex order decapitation attack in rings, cliques, and with no adaptation.

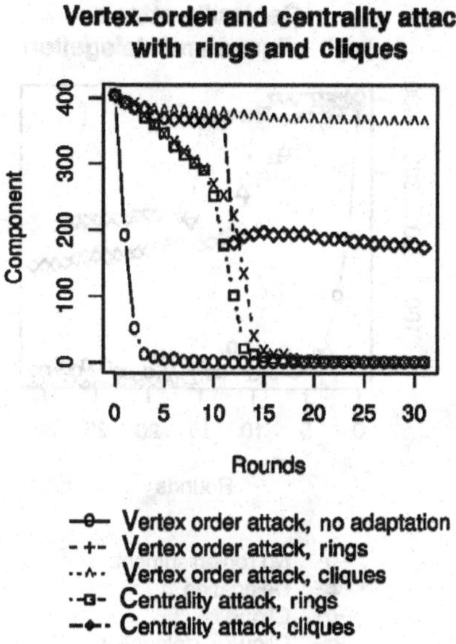

Figure 25.2. Rings and cliques defense under vertex order and centrality attacks.

attractive to theoreticians, those real revolutionary movements that have left some trace in the history books have used a cell structure instead.

We then proceeded through several rounds of attack evolution. As cliques are a good defense against the simple vertex-order attack, we looked for a good way to attack cliques. The best performer we found is an attack based on centrality. We used Brandes' algorithm to select the highest-centrality nodes for destruction at each round. As before, our calibration baseline is random replenishment.

Figure 25.2 shows that the same holds for rings (the squares and crosses): the network collapses completely after about a dozen rounds. Centrality attacks are more effective against cliques; they significantly reduce the size of the largest connected component.

Then, knowing that centrality attacks are powerful, we tried a number of other possible defenses. The most promising at present appears to be a compound defense based on cliques and delegation.

The idea behind delegation is simple. A node that is becoming too well-connected selects one of its neighbors as a "deputy" and transfers some of its links to it. This reflects normal human behavior even in peacetime: busy leaders pass new recruits on to colleagues. In wartime, and with an enemy that might resort to vertex-order attacks, the incentive to delegate is even greater. Thus a terrorist leader who gets an offer from a wealthy businessman to finance an attack might simply introduce him to a young militant who wants to carry one out. The leader need now maintain communications with at most one of the two.

The delegation defense on its own, however, is rather like the ring defense. Network fragmentation is postponed (about 14 rounds with the parameters used here) though not ultimately averted. However, when we form a network and run the delegation strategy for some rounds before attacks start, then run a clique defense as well from

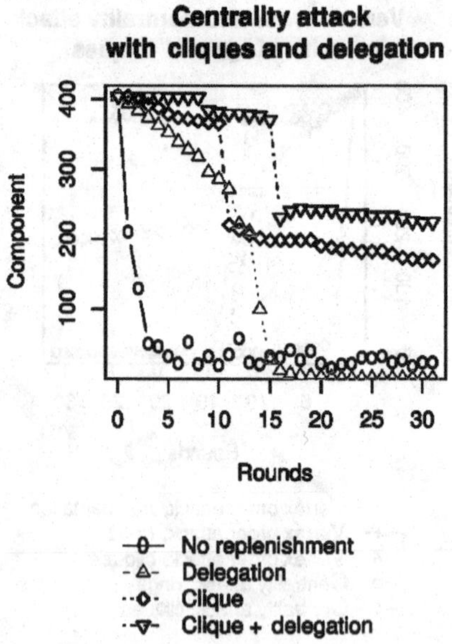

Figure 25.3. Component size: clique, immunization by delegation, and combined clique and delegation defenses against centrality attack.

the initiation of hostilities, this compound strategy works rather better than ordinary cliques. Figure 25.3 shows the simulation results.

Delegation results in shorter path lengths under attack: it postpones and slows down the growth of path length that otherwise results from hub elimination. As a result, equilibrium is achieved later, and with a larger minimum connected component.

Finally, we note that clique formation and delegation do not make the attacks in the earlier rounds of attack evolution any easier. Specifically, the effectiveness of a vertex-order attack depends on the skewness of the distribution of vertex order. Both delegation and clique formation lead to lesser skewness, and this is partly why they are an effective defense against a vertex-order attack in the first place. Hence these defensive manoeuvres will not make the earlier attacks any more effective than in the case where no defense actions are taken.

25.6 Conclusion

Information security has seen a number of interesting applications of game theory over the last 5 years. These have largely taken place in the context of a research program on the economics of security, which has built many cross-disciplinary links and has produced many useful (and indeed delightful) insights from unexpected places.

We have discussed how many information security failures are caused by incentive failures, where the people who guard a system are not the people who suffer when it fails; and how externalities make many security problems somewhat reminiscent of environmental pollution. Some aspects of information security are public goods, like clean air and water. Externalities also play a key role in determining which security products succeed in the market, and which fail.

Games with incomplete information also play an important role: where either information or action is hidden, things can go wrong in interesting ways. Markets, and auctions, can sometimes be used as information-processing mechanisms to tackle the resulting problems; we discussed software dependability and the problems of cyber-insurance.

Finally we looked at effects on distributed system architectures. The designers of early pear-to-pear systems adopted a flat architecture, which promoted free-riding and made attacks easy; later, more successful, systems used a discretionary architecture that mitigated these problems. We now know how to analyze cooperation in heterogeneous distributed systems, and the tools have wider implications for understanding human societies.

The second aspect of architecture is topology. Albert, Jeong, and Barabasi showed that scale-free networks are more robust than random networks against random failure, but more vulnerable to targeted attack; by extending their analysis from the static to the dynamic case, we have shown why revolutionaries organize in cells – and why building peer-to-peer systems based on rings was a bad idea. At the conceptual level, we have provided a framework for analyzing such problems systematically, and started to build a bridge between network analysis and evolutionary game theory.

25.7 Notes

Anderson (2001) was the first security researcher to identify the importance of incentives and economics. In earlier work he described misaligned incentives with respect to ATM security (Anderson, 1994) and the Eternity Service, the first peer-to-peer system designed to offer censorship resistance (Anderson, 1996). With Danezis, he considered the role of economics on censorship resistance (Danezis and Anderson, 2005).

Varian was the first economist to pay attention to information security. He noted that users lacked sufficient incentive to protect themselves from viruses because much of the resulting harm was suffered by others (Varian, 2000). He also created a game-theoretic model to describe the impact of independent security decisions: whether system defense depended on the best effort of the defenders, on their worst effort, or on the sum of their efforts (Varian, 2004).

Kunreuther and Heal extended the result to the case where the security of group rests upon the efforts of interdependent members (Kunreuther and Heal, 2003). Katz and Shapiro (1985) famously noted how network externalities affected the adoption of technology. Akerlof (1970) won a Nobel prize for his articulation of the effect of asymmetric information on markets.

Schechter (2002) was the first to propose vulnerability markets. Ozment (2004) argued that those markets could be better designed as auctions. In joint work, they have proposed statistical measures of software security based upon software engineering approaches (Ozment and Schechter, 2006a). They have also analyzed the bootstrapping problems faced by those who would deploy security technologies (Ozment and Schechter, 2006b).

Banking standards for PIN-entry terminals assume a cost-based analysis of vulnerability (PIN management requirements, 2004). Kannan and Telang have analyzed the social utility of the organizations currently purchasing software vulnerabilities and found it to be less than ideal (Kannan and Telang, 2004). Böhme (2006) has argued that software derivatives are a better tool than markets or auctions for the measurement of software security. With Kataria, he analysed how the interdependence of cyber-risks could cause insurance market failure (Böhme and Kataria, 2006). Hulisi Ogut, Nirup Menon, and Srinivasan Raghunathan showed that the interdependence of cyber-risk results in firms underinvesting in both security and insurance (Ogut et al., 2005).

Crespo and Garcia-Molina (2002) argue for network topologies based on clubs of nodes with common interests. Moore (2005) has noted the security import of hidden-action attacks. Sparrow (1990) surveyed possible applications of social network theory to law enforcement in 1990; a more recent survey is by Ballester, Calvó-Armengol and Zenou (2004). For the debate on whether the diversity of modern societies is undermining the social solidarity on which welfare systems are based, see Goodhart (2004).

Albert, Jeong and Barabási (2000) showed that scale-free network topology being good for robustness against random failure but bad for security against targeted attack. Finally, Nagaraja and Anderson (2006) extended this from the static to the dynamic case.

Bibliography

G.A. Akerlof. The market for "lemons": Quality uncertainty and the market mechanism. *Q. J. Econ.*, 84(3):488–500, 1970.

R. Albert, H. Jeong, and A.l. Barabási. Error and attack tolerance of complex networks. *Nature*, 406(1):387–482, 2000.

R.J. Anderson. Why cryptosystems fail. *Commun. ACM*, 37(11):32–40, 1994.

R. Anderson. The eternity service. In *First Intl. Conf. Theory and Applications of Cryptology, PRAGOCRYPT '96*, 1996.

R. Anderson. Why information security is hard – an economic perspective. In *17th Annual Computer Security Applications Conf.*, December 2001. New Orleans, LA.

R. Böhme. A comparison of market approaches to software vulnerability disclosure. In *Proc. of ETRICS*, LNCS 2995:298–311, Springer, 2006.

R. Böhme and G. Kataria. Models and measures for correlation in cyber-insurance. In *Proc. Fifth Workshop on the Economics of Information Security*, June 2006. Cambridge, UK.

A. Calvó-Armengol, C. Ballester, and Y. Zenou. Who's who in crime networks – wanted the key player. In *IUI Working Paper Series 617*, 2004. The Research Institute of Industrial Economics.

A. Crespo and H. Garcia-Molina. Semantic overlay networks for p2p systems. Technical report, Stanford University, 2002.

G. Danezis and R.J. Anderson. The economics of resisting censorship. *IEEE Security & Privacy*, 3(1):45–50, 2005.

D. Goodhart. Too diverse? *Prospect*, February 2004. http://www.guardian.co.uk/race/story/0,11374,1154684,00.html.

K. Kannan and R. Telang. Economic analysis of market for software vulnerabilities. In *Proc. Third Workshop on the Economics of Information Security*, May 2004.

M.L. Katz and C. Shapiro. Network externalities, competition, and compatibility. *Amer. Econ. Rev.*, 75(3):424–440, June 1985.

H. Kunreuther and G. Heal. Interdependent security. *J. Risk and Uncertainty*, 26(2–3):231–249, March–May 2003.

T. Moore. Countering hidden-action attacks on networked systems. In *Proc. Fourth Workshop on the Economics of Information Security*, June 2005.

S. Nagaraja and R. Anderson. The topology of covert conflict. In *Proc. Fifth Workshop on Economics of Information Security*, June 2006.

H. Ogut, N. Menon, and S. Raghunathan. Cyber insurance and IT security investment: Impact of interdependent risk. In *Proc. Fourth Workshop on the Economics of Information Security*, June 2005.

A. Ozment. Bug auctions: Vulnerability markets reconsidered. In *Proc. Third Workshop on the Economics of Information Security*, May 2004.

A. Ozment and S.E. Schechter. Milk or wine: Does software security improve with age? In *15th Usenix Security Symposium*, July 2006.

A. Ozment and S.E. Schechter. Bootstrapping the adoption of internet security protocols. In *Proc. Fifth Workshop on the Economics of Information Security*, June 2006.

S.E. Schechter. How to buy better testing. In George I. Davida, Yair Frankel, and Owen Rees, editors, *InfraSec*, LNCS 2437:73–87. Springer, 2002.

M. Sparrow. The application of network analysis to criminal intelligence: An assessment of the prospects. *Social Networks*, 13:253–274, 1990.

H. Varian. Managing online security risks. *The New York Times*, June 2000. Available at: http://www.nytimes.com/library/financial/columns/060100econ-scene.html.

H. Varian. System reliability and free riding. In L. Jean Camp and Stephen Lewis, editors, *Economics of Information Security, Advances in Information Security*, 12:1–15. Kluwer Academic Publishers, 2004.

PIN management requirements: PIN entry device security requirements manual, 2004. Available at: http://partnernetwork.visa.com/dv/pin/pdf/Visa_ATM_Security_Requirements.pdf.

CHAPTER 26

Computational Aspects of Prediction Markets

David M. Pennock and Rahul Sami

Abstract

Prediction markets (also known as information markets) are markets established to aggregate knowledge and opinions about the likelihood of future events. This chapter is intended to give an overview of the current research on computational aspects of these markets. We begin with a brief survey of prediction market research, and then give a more detailed description of models and results in three areas: the computational complexity of operating markets for combinatorial events; the design of automated market makers; and the analysis of the computational power and speed of a market as an aggregation tool. We conclude with a discussion of open problems and directions for future research.

26.1 Introduction: What Is a Prediction Market?

Consider the following mechanism design problem called the *information aggregation problem*. Suppose that an individual ("the aggregator") would like to obtain a prediction about an uncertain variable, say the global average temperature in 2020. A number of individuals ("the informants") each hold different and nonindependent sets of information bearing on the outcome of the variable. The goal is to design a mechanism that extracts the relevant information from the informants, aggregates the information appropriately, and provides a collective prediction or forecast. The forecast should ideally be equivalent to the omniscient forecast that has direct access to all the information available to all informants.

A *prediction market*[1] is one mechanism designed to solve the information aggregation problem. The aggregator creates a financial *security* whose payoff is tied to the outcome of the variable. For example, he creates a security that pays $\$x$ dollars if the actual global average temperature in 2020 equals x. The aggregator invites the informants to trade the security however they please. For example, global warming proponents should be willing to buy the security at or above prices equal to today's

[1] Prediction markets are also often referred to as information markets, (Arrow-Debreu) securities markets, contingent claims, contingent contracts, event markets, event futures, event derivatives, and idea futures.

global average temperature, and global warming skeptics should be willing to sell at those prices.[2] The aggregator can view the trading price of the security as a collective forecast for the expected value of the uncertain variable. In fact, as we shall see in Section 26.2.2.3, in some simplified theoretical settings one can prove that the trading price converges to a *rational expectations equilibrium* that mimics the omniscient forecast.

More importantly, in a broad and diverse number of real-world settings in the laboratory, in the field, and in practice, prediction markets seem to yield equal or better forecasts than other methods of information aggregation. Researchers have proposed using prediction markets to help scientists, policymakers, decision makers, the government, and the military. Several companies – from established brands like Google, Microsoft, and Yahoo! to startups like CrowdIQ, InklingMarkets, and NewsFutures – are experimenting with prediction market services in the private sector. The growth of the field is reflected and fueled by a wave of popular press articles and books on the topic, most prominently Surowiecki's "The Wisdom of Crowds."

In this chapter, we focus on algorithmic challenges and constraints associated with implementing a prediction market mechanism. We discuss three areas in which computational constraints are important.

- Effective prediction markets often need to handle combinations of different events or contingent events. However, the number of contingent events grows exponentially in the number of base events. In this situation, the basic functions of listing securities and clearing markets can become computationally intractable. In Section 26.3, we present results on the computational complexity of operating combinatorial markets.
- To increase trading volume, a prediction market operator often acts as a *market maker* who is always ready to trade. However, To limit the exposure of the market maker, it is essential that the market maker adjusts its bid and ask prices after every trade. In Section 26.4, we describe two new designs to automate the price updating process in a way that limits exposure while encouraging informed traders to trade.
- When different traders have complementary information about the value of a security, the market itself ideally performs a computational function: The final trading price should reflect an aggregate of all the traders' initial information. In Section 26.5, we present a simple market model and analyze its computational properties. We derive positive and negative results on when the market will converge to the ideal price, as well as bounds on a measure of convergence time.

In Section 26.2, we set up the problem formally and survey the academic literature on prediction markets.

26.2 Background

26.2.1 Setup and Notation

In this section we formally pose the aggregation problem that prediction markets are designed to address. We begin by introducing a fairly standard model of uncertainty and distributed information.

[2] For simplicity, we ignore the time value of money.

Definition 26.1 Partition model of knowledge: There is a set Ω of possible *states of the world*. At any point of time, the world is in exactly one state $\omega \in \Omega$, but agents do not necessarily know the true state of the world. However, each agent i may have partial information about the true state. Agent i's *information* is represented by a *partition* π_i of Ω; that is, π_i is a collection $\{\pi_{i1}, \pi_{i2}, \ldots, \pi_{ik}\}$ of subsets of Ω such that the different subsets are disjoint and the union of all subsets is Ω. The semantic interpretation is that i can distinguish two states in different subsets π_{i1}, π_{i2} of her partition π_i, but cannot distinguish between two states in the same subset of the partition. In particular, agent i knows in which subset of her partition the true state of the world lies, but does not know which member of that subset is the true state. Given n agents $1, 2, \ldots, n$, their combined information $\hat{\pi}$ is the *coarsest common refinement* of the partitions $\pi_1, \pi_2, \ldots, \pi_n$.

The partition model is often augmented with the assumption that there is a common *prior probability distribution* $\mathcal{P} \in \Delta(\Omega)$, which captures the probability that all agents assign to different states before receiving any information. Once agents obtain their partial information, their *posterior* beliefs follow by conditioning on their information – that is, by restricting prior to the subset of their partition in which the true state lies.

A *forecast* is an estimate of the expected value of some function $f(\omega)$, where f is a commonly known (deterministic or stochastic) function of the state of the world. A special type of function $f : \Omega \to \{0, 1\}$ called an *event* equals one for a particular subset of Ω and zero everywhere else. A *joint forecast* is a joint probability distribution over the values of a number of functions $f_1(\omega), f_2(\omega), \ldots$.

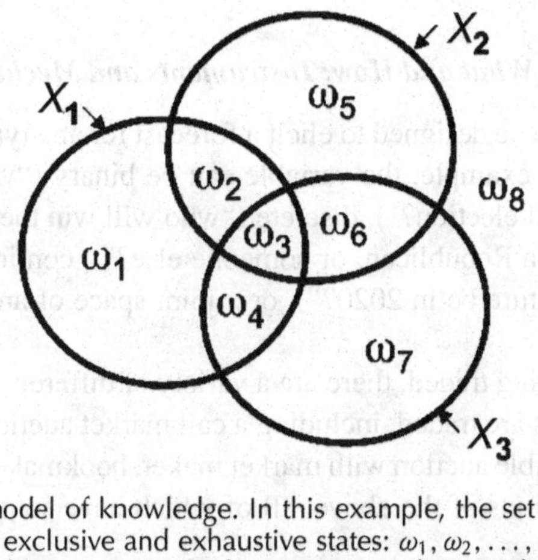

Figure 26.1. Partition model of knowledge. In this example, the set Ω of states of the world contains eight mutually exclusive and exhaustive states: $\omega_1, \omega_2, \ldots, \omega_8$. Subsets of states like X_1, X_2, and X_3 are called *events*. Suppose that agent i can distinguish between states in X_i and states not in X_i, but cannot further distinguish among states. For example, agent 1's partition π_1 is $\{\{\omega_1, \omega_2, \omega_3, \omega_4\}, \{\omega_5, \omega_6, \omega_7, \omega_8\}\}$. In this simple example, the coarsest common refinement of the three agents' partitions is $\hat{\pi} = \Omega$, meaning that the agents' combined information is always sufficient to precisely identify the true state. Often, we may consider the events X_i as the most basic elements of the model, with the ω_i being the implied product space of these base event outcomes. For example, ω_4 in the figure is explicitly indexed as $\omega_{X_1 \bar{X}_2 X_3}$: the future state where X_1 is true, X_2 is false, and X_3 is true.

On its own, an agent's best forecast uses its posterior distribution over Ω, but ignores information that might be obtained via interaction with other agents. The *omniscient forecast* uses the posterior distribution conditioned on all information available to all agents, or $\mathcal{P}$ restricted to the subset of $\hat{\pi}$ in which the true state lies.

In reality, each agent's information is private knowledge that is not directly accessible to any one entity. Thus information aggregation is a problem of mechanism design (see Chapter 9). The goal is to produce a mechanism that incentivizes the agents to reveal their information such that, in equilibrium, the mechanism produces a forecast as close as possible to the omniscient forecast.

A prediction market is one type of information aggregation mechanism. The market contains financial securities whose payoffs are functions of the state of the world. In the simplest case, the market contains a security paying off $f(\omega)$ dollars in state ω. Thus agents are incented through the prospect of financial gain to reveal information bearing on the expected value of $f(\omega)$, and the equilibrium price reached by a number of interacting agents can be viewed as a collective forecast. As we shall see in Section 26.5, even when a single forecast is sought, multiple securities might be required to ensure convergence to equilibrium. In Section 26.3 we explore the computationally challenging case of setting up a market to yield a joint forecast.

26.2.2 Survey of the Field

The field of prediction markets is largely an empirical science, and much of the academic literature focuses on laboratory and field experiments testing the accuracy of predictions in a variety of settings. However, a prediction market is operationally no different than a standard financial market, so a large amount of economic and financial theory applies.

26.2.2.1 What and How: Instruments and Mechanisms

A prediction market can be designed to elicit a forecast for any type of random variable or set of variables. For example, the variable can be binary ("will a Republican win the next US Presidential election?"), discrete ("who will win the next US Presidential election? A Democrat, a Republican, or someone else?"), continuous ("what will the global average temperature be in 2020?"), or a joint space of any combination of the above.

Beyond "what" is being traded, there are a variety of different mechanisms specifying "how" the securities are traded, including a call market auction, continuous double auction, continuous double auction with market maker, bookmaker, parimutuel market, and combinatorial versions of the above, all of which have some empirical record of success.

In a call market auction, all bids are collected over time, then processed together in large batches. The clearing price can be the mth lowest price, the $m+1$st lowest price, or somewhere in between, where m is the number of sellers. A continuous double auction is a continuous version of a call market, where as soon as any trade is acceptable to any two bidders, the trade is immediately executed, usually at the bid price of the least recent bidder. A market maker or bookmaker is a price maker who is nearly always willing to accept both buy and sell orders at some stated (but changing) prices. In a parimutuel market, players compete in a wagering game to earn as large a portion as possible of the total amount of money wagered by all players.

26.2.2.2 Examples and Evaluations

A prediction market cannot surface information that does not exist or is unknown, so the accuracy of a prediction market can only be evaluated in comparison to other information aggregation or forecasting methods. The central empirical question is whether a prediction market aggregates or summarizes information more accurately than other methods.

One of the most cited and most successful prediction markets is the Iowa Electronic Market (IEM). Since 1988, IEM has been operating real-money prediction markets, mostly on the outcomes of political elections. Empirically, on average the market's predictions are more accurate and less volatile than political opinion polls, especially in large US elections. The markets react to new information quickly, sometimes within minutes, and often before the new information becomes widespread. The markets are accurate despite documented evidence that individual traders are often biased and irrational and make mistakes. Several IEM publications support a theory that accuracy derives not from average traders, but from *marginal traders*. Marginal traders are more active, less biased, more successful, and price makers rather than price takers. As long as a few good marginal traders exist, the market as a whole remains accurate despite the poor traders.

Options, futures, and other financial derivatives are contracts whose payoff is a function of some underlying uncertain variable. For example, the payoff of a stock option with strike price k is $max[0, s - k]$, where s is the price of the corresponding stock at some future date. Sports betting markets can also be viewed and analyzed as prediction markets. Several empirical studies verify that derivative prices and sports betting odds constitute accurate forecasts for their underlying variables.

Even play-money markets show a surprising ability to aggregate information. Studies of market games like the Hollywood Stock Exchange, NewsFutures, and the Foresight Exchange report accuracies equal to or better than expert opinions and, remarkably, sometimes on par with equivalent real-money prediction markets.

Experimental economists have tested the aggregation properties of prediction markets in laboratory settings. The experimenter sets up the forecasting problem and carefully controls the information each participant receives. A number of experimental designs reveal when market aggregation seems to work and when it does not. Generally, given enough securities and enough practice, traders in the laboratory often converge to prices close to the omniscient forecasts. Researchers have devised and tested methods for achieving accurate results across as many forecast variables as possible with as few participants as possible.

Economists have also run field tests of markets used to forecast quantities of interest to an organization. For example, a market was tested at Hewlett Packard to project the company's sales volume for particular products. Generally, the market predictions were superior to the official HP forecasts. Other companies, including Microsoft and Google, are now running similar internal prediction markets.

26.2.2.3 Theoretical Underpinnings

There is a fundamental difference between a market for a financial security and a market for a consumer product: the security has no direct consumption value to potential buyers. Buyers want to buy the security only because they believe they can later resell it or cash it out for a higher price. This simple observation invalidates the classical model of demand, in which each trader has a fixed demand curve that describes the quantity demanded at each price. The market provides information about other traders' knowledge and beliefs, which may lead a trader to change her beliefs about the future value of the security. In this manner, *the market prices can lead to changes in the traders' demand curves*! This led to the development of a new theory, the theory of *rational expectations*, that seeks to understand this latter kind of market. The cornerstone of this theory is a new equilibrium concept, the *rational expectations equilibrium*. Intuitively, a rational expectation equilibrium price is a market-clearing price such that traders will not want to change their trades *even after observing the price itself*.

Rational expectations Consider the model of Section 26.2.1: an uncertain world with possible states Ω, and n traders trading in a market for some good. Let $v_i(q_i, \omega)$ denote the ultimate value of q_i units of the good to trader i in state ω. The traders are partially informed: let π_i denote trader i's private information, and assume that there is a common prior distribution $\mathcal{P}$. Furthermore, we assume that all traders are risk-neutral Bayesians. To simplify the exposition, we consider the special case in which the $\hat{\pi} = \Omega$, so the combined information of all agents is sufficient to pinpoint the true state. The equilibrium price is not a simple number as in the case of the competitive equilibrium; instead, it is a mapping $P^* : \Omega \to \Re$ that maps a state of the world to a price.

Definition 26.2 A *rational expectations equilibrium* is a mapping $P^* : \Omega \to \Re$ such that in every state ω, if every trader conditions her demand (or supply) on her private information π_i as well as the price $P^*(\omega)$, the market will clear at a price of exactly $P^*(\omega)$. In other words, it is a self-fulfilling correspondence from states to prices.

This definition is subtle, and needs to be reasoned through carefully. Consider an arbitrary nonconstant mapping P from states to prices. Then, by observing the price $P(\omega)$, an agent who knew the mapping could immediately rule out some states of the world: those that would have resulted in a different price. Thus, any mapping P induces a partition π_P such that anyone observing $P(\omega)$ knows π_P in addition to her initial information. Now, trader i's effective demand curve in state ω will be given by her expected value for the item conditioned on both the price and her private information: $\tilde{v}_i(q_i, \omega) = E[v(q_i, \omega)|\pi_i(\omega), P(\omega)]$. Given the demand and supply curves for the n agents, it is possible to calculate a clearing price $\tilde{v}(\Omega)$. The price mapping P would be a rational expectations equilibrium iff $\tilde{v}(\omega) = P(\omega)$ for all ω. In other words, it is rational for the agents to believe in a price mapping P only if all agents believing in that mapping and acting accordingly would lead to the prices predicted by P.

Researchers have shown the existence of rational expectations equilibria in economies with asymmetric information under fairly general conditions on the value functions $v_i(\cdot, \cdot)$. Furthermore, it has been shown that under generic conditions, these economies admit "fully-revealing" rational expectations equilibria: price correspondences $P^*(\cdot)$ such that $P^*(\omega_1) \neq P^*(\omega_2)$ whenever $\omega_1 \neq \omega_2$. In this case, it follows that the price reveals the combined information of all traders, i.e., $\pi_{P^*} = \hat{\pi}$, the full-information partition. This leads to startling, and sometimes counterintuitive, consequences; we discuss some of these in subsequent sections. We note, however, that the rational expectations literature has been criticized because the definition of a rational expectations equilibrium says nothing about how traders might learn and agree on the equilibrium price mapping P^*. In applying this concept, it is important to keep this in mind, and take the price formation process into account when possible.

Efficient market hypothesis and no-trade theorems. The existence of fully revealing equilibria has led researchers to propose the "efficient market hypothesis." The strong form of this hypothesis states that a security's market price fully reflects all the information relevant to its value. The efficient market hypothesis, with its roots in rational expectations theory, provides a theoretical foundation for why prediction markets are likely to be effective: In a situation in which many traders have a small amount of private information about an event, it states that the prediction market price will reflect the combined information of all traders.

One of the most counterintuitive results of rational expectations theory is the existence of *no-trade theorems*. The key observation is that, in a fully revealing rational expectations equilibrium, the price information captures every agent's private information. Thus, in a fully revealing equilibrium, all agents are conditioning their beliefs on identical information, and hence have identical posterior beliefs. It follows that all agents assign the same expected value to the security, and hence, there will not be any trade in equilibrium. This reasoning can be extended to show that no two rational agents will want to trade with each other even if they are not initially in equilibrium, because the mere willingness of the other party to trade at a given price reveals information that leads to an equilibrium. Several variants of this result, under different conditions, have been shown.

Thus, we seem to have a paradoxical situation in which the final price reflects all the traders' information, but the traders would never want to trade so there is no way for their information to get into the prices! However, the no-trade results are very sensitive to the precise conditions specified – risk-neutrality and common knowledge that all traders are competely rational Bayesians – and even tiny perturbations of these conditions invalidate them. In practice, there are several reasons that can lead an informed trader to expect a profit from trade, such as the existence of irrational traders, traders who are trading to hedge risks, traders who trade for liquidity reasons, or a market maker who is subsidizing the market.

26.3 Combinatorial Prediction Markets

Up to this point, we have concentrated on the economic, strategic, and statistical properties of prediction markets. We now turn our attention to the computational problems that arise in the study of prediction markets. In this section, we consider *combinatorial* markets. These are markets in which the state space is the product space of a number of *base events*. Here, we consider state spaces generated by *Boolean events*: propositions such as, "the price of gasoline is greater than \$3" that may be either true or false in the future world. Suppose that there is some finite set $\mathcal{E}$ of base events, and furthermore, suppose that these events are linearly independent in the sense that the value (`true` or `false`) of any event cannot be determined with certainty even if the value of all other events is known. Then, the state space Ω is of size $2^{|\mathcal{E}|}$, with each state corresponding to a particular assignment of values to the individual events. We use the symbols $X_1, X_2, X_3, \ldots$ to denote the individual Boolean events in $\mathcal{E}$.

Let S_ω be a security that pays \$1 if the eventual state is ω, and pays \$0 otherwise. Classic results on market equilibrium show that a market can be guaranteed to be efficient if it is possible for a trader to express her desire for any such S_ω. This does not necessarily mean that the securities S_ω have to be directly traded in the market, as long as the market has a set of securities such that a trader could construct a portfolio with payoff similar to any S_ω she desires. Such a market is called a *complete* market. Unfortunately, any complete market must have at least $2^{|\mathcal{E}|}$ securities; if the number of base events is large, even listing all the securities may be impossible!

However, this does not mean that it is impossible to achieve efficient hedging or information aggregation in practice. There may be many fewer than $2^{|\mathcal{E}|}$ combinations of events that traders actually care about, or have specific information about. This raises the following questions: (1) Is there a "natural" representation such that realistic events, securities, and buy/sell orders can be represented succintly? (2) Given orders in this representation, is it possible to identify and execute possible trades?

The underlying structure of the state space can be exploited through the use of prediction markets with expressive bidding languages. We distinguish between two forms of expressivity: *combined orders* and *compound orders*.

A combined order allows the trader to specify a collection of securities he or she would like to trade together as a bundle, with limit prices specified for each component security. If the trader cannot obtain all of the securities at prices equal to or better than the specified limits, then the trader prefers not to receive any of the securities. This form of expressivity reduces so-called *execution risk*, where during the course of carrying out a planned series of transactions, the prices of some securities change, thereby reducing or reversing the utility of the earlier trades. If there are $|\mathcal{E}|$ Boolean event securities, then traders can place a combined order for any of the $2^{|\mathcal{E}|}$ possible bundles (subsets) of the securities. When combined orders are allowed, the auctioneer problem is essentially the same as in the combinatorial auction scenario (see Chapter 11). One distinction is that, while bids in combinatorial auctions are generally considered indivisible, bids in a securities market often can be considered divisible, thus simplifying the matching problem. The auctioneer problem of matching combined orders in a securities market is also called *combined value trading*.

A compound order allows the trader to speculate on any compound Boolean expression involving a set $\mathcal{E}$ of base events. If there are $|\mathcal{E}|$ base events, then there are $2^{|\mathcal{E}|}$ possible combinations of outcomes of those events, and there are $2^{2^{|\mathcal{E}|}}$ distinct subsets of those combinations expressible using Boolean formulas. For the remainder of this section, we will focus on compound orders, a strict superset of combined orders.

26.3.1 Compound Prediction Markets

We now describe a concrete representation for compound order securities. The securities are based on Boolean formulas over the set of propositions $\mathcal{E}$; given a formula ϕ, we have a security that pays \$1 *iff* ϕ is true in the eventual state. More generally, we allow *conditional* securities $S_{\phi|\psi}$ based on two formulas ϕ, ψ; this is interpreted as "Make a payoff according to ϕ, conditional on ψ being true." In other words, the owner of security $S_{\phi|\psi}$ is paid \$1 if both ϕ and ψ are true, paid \$0 if ψ is true but ϕ is false, and the security is cancelled (and any money the owner paid for it is refunded) iff ψ is false.

26.3.1.1 Orders

Agents place orders, denoted o, of the form "q units of $S_{\phi|\psi}$ at price p per unit," where $q > 0$ implies a buy order and $q < 0$ implies a sell order. We assume that agents submitting buy (sell) orders will accept any price $p^* \leq p$ ($p^* \geq p$). We distinguish between *divisible* and *indivisible* orders. Agents submitting divisible orders will accept quantity αq for any $0 < \alpha \leq 1$. Agents submitting indivisible orders will accept only exactly q units, or none.

Every order o can be translated into a payoff vector Υ across all states $\omega \in \Omega$. The payoff $\Upsilon^{\langle\omega\rangle}$ in state ω is $q \cdot 1_{\omega\in\psi}(1_{\omega\in\phi} - p)$, where $1_{\omega\in E}$ is the indicator function equaling 1 iff $\omega \in E$ and zero otherwise. Let the set of all orders be $\mathcal{O} = \{o_i\}$ and the set of corresponding payoff vectors be $\mathcal{P} = \{\Upsilon_i\}$.

26.3.1.2 The Matching Problem

The auctioneer's task, called the *matching problem*, is to determine which orders to accept among all orders $o \in \mathcal{O}$. Let α_i be the fraction of order o_i accepted by the auctioneer (in the indivisible case, α_i must be either 0 or 1; in the divisible case, α_i can range from 0 to 1). If $\alpha_i = 0$, then order o_i is considered rejected and no transactions take place concerning this order. For accepted orders ($\alpha_i > 0$), the auctioneer receives the money lost by bidders and pays out the money won by bidders, so the *auctioneer's payoff vector* (or *surplus vector*) is

$$\Upsilon_{\text{auc}} = \sum_{\Upsilon_i \in \mathcal{P}} -\alpha_i \Upsilon_i.$$

Assume that the auctioneer wants to choose a set of orders so that it is guaranteed not to lose any money in any future state, but that the auctioneer does not necessarily insist on obtaining a positive benefit from the transaction (i.e., the auctioneer is content to break even).

Definition 26.3 (Indivisible matching problem) Given a set of orders $\mathcal{O}$, does there exist $\alpha_i \in \{0, 1\}$ with at least one $\alpha_i = 1$ such that $\forall\omega$, $\Upsilon_{\text{auc}}^{\langle\omega\rangle} \geq 0$? In other words, does there exist a nonempty subset of orders that the auctioneer can accept without risk?

Example 26.4 (Indivisible order matching) Suppose $|\mathcal{E}| = 2$. Consider an order to buy one unit of $S_{X_1 X_2}$ at price 0.4 and an order to sell one unit of S_{X_1} at price 0.3. The corresponding payoff vectors are

$$\begin{aligned}\Upsilon_1 &= \left\langle \Upsilon_1^{\langle X_1 X_2\rangle},\ \Upsilon_1^{\langle X_1 \bar{X}_2\rangle},\ \Upsilon_1^{\langle \bar{X}_1 X_2\rangle},\ \Upsilon_1^{\langle \bar{X}_1 \bar{X}_2\rangle} \right\rangle \\ &= \langle 0.6, \quad -0.4, \quad -0.4, \quad -0.4 \rangle \\ \Upsilon_2 &= \langle -0.7, \quad -0.7, \quad 0.3, \quad 0.3 \rangle\end{aligned}$$

The auctioneer's payoff vector (the negative of the component-wise sum of the above two vectors) is

$$\Upsilon_{\text{auc}} = -\Upsilon_1 - \Upsilon_2 = \langle 0.1, 1.1, 0.1, 0.1 \rangle.$$

Since all components are nonnegative, the two orders match. The auctioneer can process both orders, leaving a surplus of \$0.1 in cash and one unit of $S_{X_1 \bar{X}_2}$ in securities.

Now consider the divisible case, where order can be partially filled.

Definition 26.5 (Divisible matching problem) Given a set of orders $\mathcal{O}$, does there exist $\alpha_i \in [0, 1]$ with at least one $\alpha_i > 0$ such that $\forall \omega$, $\Upsilon_{\text{auc}}^{(\omega)} \geq 0$?

The matching problems defined above are decision problems: the task is only to show the existence or nonexistence of a match. We could additionally seek to maximize some objective function – like trading volume or auctioneer expected profit – to choose the best among all possible matches. Here, we restrict our attention to the decision problem formulations.

26.3.1.3 The Computational Complexity of Matching

In this section we examine the computational complexity of the auctioneer's matching problem. Here n is the size of the problem's input, including descriptions of all the buy and sell orders. We also assume that n bounds the number of base securities. We consider four cases based on two parameters:

(i) Whether to allow divisible or indivisible orders.
(ii) The number of securities. We consider two possibilities: (a) $O(\log n)$ base securities yielding a polynomial number of states, or (b) $\Theta(n)$ base securities yielding an exponential number of states.

Theorem 26.6 *The matching problem for divisible orders is*

(i) computable in polynomial-time for $O(\log n)$ base securities.

(ii) co-NP-complete for unlimited securities.

PROOF **Small number of securities with divisible orders.** We can build a linear program based on Definition 26.5. We have variables α_i. For each i, we have $0 \leq \alpha_i \leq 1$. and for each state ω in Ω we have the constraint

$$\text{Payment}(\omega) = \sum_i -\alpha_i \Upsilon_i^{\langle\omega\rangle} \geq 0.$$

Given these constraints, we maximize $\sum_i \alpha_i$. A set of orders has a matching exactly when $\max \sum_i \alpha_i > 0$. With $O(\log n)$ base securities, we can solve this linear program in polynomial time. Note, however, that this approach may not find matchings that have precisely zero surplus.

Large number of securities with divisible orders. With unlimited base securities, the linear program given in Section 26.3.1.3 has an exponential number of constraint equations. Each constraint is short to describe and easily computable given ω. Let $m \leq n$ be the total number of buy and sell orders. By the theory of linear programming, an upper bound on the objective function can be forced by a collection of $m + 1$ constraints. So if no matching exists there must exist $m + 1$ constraints that force all the α_i to zero. In nondeterministic polynomial-time we can guess these constraints and solve the reduced linear program. This shows that matching is in co-NP.

To show co-NP-completeness, we reduce the NP-complete problem of Boolean formula satisfiability to the nonexistence of a matching. Fix a formula ϕ. Let the base securities be the variables of ϕ and consider the single security S_ϕ with a buy order of 0.5. If the formula ϕ is satisfiable, then there is some state with payoff 0.5 (auctioneer payoff -0.5) and no fractional unit of security S_ϕ is a matching. If the formula ϕ is not satisfiable then every state has an auctioneer's payoff of 0.5 and a single unit of S_ϕ is a matching. □

For *indivisible* orders, the matching problem turns out to be even harder to solve. We state the following result; because of space restrictions, we do not reproduce the proof here.

Theorem 26.7 *The matching problem for indivisible orders is*
(i) NP-complete for $O(\log n)$ base securities.
(ii) Σ_2^p-complete for unlimited securities.

26.3.2 Compact Prediction Markets

Compound orders are very general: traders can submit orders for any Boolean expression of base events. Computational limits aside, a market system supporting compound orders effectively implements a complete securities market, as defined above, meaning that all possible mutually agreeable transactions can proceed, supporting a Pareto optimal and economically efficient allocation of securities.

Of course, computational limits are a real practical barrier; matching compound orders can easily become intractable. By limiting the full expressivity of compound orders, computational complexity can be reduced.

One natural restriction takes advantage of any (conditional) independence relationships among base events. Suppose that the statistical dependency structure of the base events is encoded as a Bayesian network. That is, the joint probability distribution over the base events can be factored as follows:

$$\Pr(X_1 X_2 \ldots X_{|\mathcal{E}|}) = \prod_{k=1}^{|\mathcal{E}|} \Pr(X_k \mid \mathbf{pa}(X_k)),$$

where $\mathbf{pa}(X_k)$ is a set of base events with index less than k called X_k's *parents*. The factorization can be depicted as a directed acyclic graph with nodes representing base events and edges from each event in $\mathbf{pa}(X_k)$ to X_k representing direct conditional dependencies.

Now restrict trading to conditional securities of the form $S_{X_j|\mathbf{pa}(X_j)}$, one for each conditional probability $\Pr(X_j|\mathbf{pa}(X_j))$ in the Bayesian network. Each event X_j with $|\mathbf{pa}(X_j)|$ parents corresponds to $2^{|\mathbf{pa}(X_j)|}$ securities, one for each possible combination of outcomes of events in $\mathbf{pa}(X_j)$. A securities market structured in this way contains $O(|\mathcal{E}| \cdot 2^{\max|\mathbf{pa}(X_j)|})$ securities, which can be considerably fewer than the $2^{|\mathcal{E}|}$ securities required for a complete market, if $\max|\mathbf{pa}(X_j)| \ll |\mathcal{E}|$. Call such a market a *BN-structured market.*

Although the need for $2^{|\mathcal{E}|}$ securities cannot be relaxed if one wants to guarantee completeness in all circumstances, there are some restrictive conditions under which a smaller BN-structured securities market may be *operationally complete*, meaning that its equilibrium is Pareto optimal *with respect to the traders involved*. In particular, if all traders' risk-neutral independencies agree with the independencies encoded in the market structure, then the market is operationally complete. For collections of agents all with constant absolute risk aversion (negative exponential utility for money), agreement on *Markov independencies* is sufficient for operational completeness.

26.4 Automated Market Makers

The standard way to organize a market is as a continuous double auction, in which traders arrive asynchronously and place their orders, and a trade takes place if a buyer quotes a higher price than a seller who is present at the same time. In a prediction market organized in this way, a speculator with private information about the security would have to submit her order and wait for another trader to place a matching order.

There are two problems with this scenario. First, the informed trader may not be willing to wait indefinitely for a partner to trade with. If there are few potential traders, they may never even enter the market because they do not expect to find a trading partner. This is the *thin market* problem: a "chicken and egg" scenario where few traders care to participate because other traders are scarce, leading to a potential breakdown of the market. The thin market problem can be especially severe in a combinatorial market because each trader's attention is divided among an exponential number of choices, making the likelihood of a match between traders seem very remote. Second, an informed trader may not want to reveal her willingness to trade (at a given price), because this may tip off other traders, and may prevent her from making a profit. This effect is related to the no-trade theorems discussed in Section 26.2.2.3, and arises because traders are essentially playing a zero-sum game with each other.

Both problems can reduce the incentives for traders to participate, thus reducing the informativeness of prices.

An alternative to using a double auction mechanism is for the market to include a *market maker*. A market maker is an agent who is always ready to trade. Typically, a market maker posts bid and ask prices (which may be identical); then a seller who is willing to sell at the bid price (or a buyer who is willing to pay the ask price) can trade with the market maker. The market maker may later resell the securities it bought to a buyer. In this way, the market maker can effectively engineer a trade between a buyer and a seller who arrive at different times and do not wait.

Of course, one side effect of having a market maker is that the market operator could potentially make a loss. This is not necessarily a negative property; in essence, it is a way of injecting subsidies into the market. The no-trade theorems no longer apply to a market with subsidies, so informed speculators can rationally expect to profit from their trade. However, it is important that the loss be predictable or bounded. To achieve this, the bid and ask prices must be adjusted in a systematic way after every trade; the new prices are computed by an *automated market maker*.

An ideal automated market maker should satisfy three properties: (1) it should run a predictable or bounded loss; (2) informed traders should have an incentive to trade whenever their information would change the price; and (3) after any trade, computing the new prices should be a tractable problem. In this section, we describe two new microstructures for prediction markets that effectively function as automated market makers, and appear to have all these properties.

26.4.1 Market Scoring Rules

Hanson shows how any proper scoring rule, or payment scheme designed to elicit truthful reporting of probabilities, can be converted into an automated market maker. The market maker can be thought of as a sequential shared version of the scoring rule, as we describe later. First, we describe the market maker algorithm in a more conventional light.

Suppose that the market contains $|\Omega|$ mutually exclusive and exhaustive securities. Let q_j be the total quantity of security j held by all traders combined, and let $\vec{q}$ be the vector of all quantities held. The market maker utilizes a *cost function* $C(\vec{q})$ that records the total amount of money traders have spent as a function of the total number of shares held of each security. A trader who wants to purchase δ shares of security j must pay $C(q_1, \ldots, q_j + \delta, \ldots, q_{|\Omega|}) - C(\vec{q})$ dollars. More generally, a trader who wants to buy or sell any bundle of securities (i.e., any *combined order* or *compound order*, as defined in Section 26.3) such that the total number of outstanding shares changes from $\vec{q}_{\text{old}}$ to $\vec{q}_{\text{new}}$ must pay $C(\vec{q}_{\text{new}}) - C(\vec{q}_{\text{old}})$ dollars. Negative quantities encode sell orders and negative "payments" encode sale proceeds earned by the trader. At any time, the going price of security j is $\partial C/\partial q_j$, the cost per share for purchasing an infinitesimal quantity. The full cost for purchasing any finite quantity is the integral of price evaluated from $\vec{q}_{\text{old}}$ to $\vec{q}_{\text{new}}$, or $C(\vec{q}_{\text{new}}) - C(\vec{q}_{\text{old}})$. Once the true outcome becomes known, the market maker pays \$1 per share to traders holding the winning security.

Deriving the cost function associated with a particular scoring rule is straightforward if tedious. The cost function corresponding to the logarithmic scoring rule is

$$C(\vec{q}) = b \ln \left(\sum_j e^{q_j/b} \right)$$

and the price function is $\partial C/\partial q_j = e^{q_j/b} / \sum_k e^{q_k/b}$. The free parameter b controls both the market maker's risk of loss and the effective liquidity of the market. One can show that the maximum possible loss incurred by the maker maker is $b \ln |\Omega|$. But a larger b also means that more shares can be purchased at or near the current price without driving up the price too much, a measure of market liquidity and depth. The logarithmic scoring rule market maker has been implemented in several real-world settings with success, including at InklingMarkets, Net Exchange, and Microsoft.

The cost function corresponding to the quadratic scoring rule is

$$C(\vec{q}) = \frac{\sum_j q_j}{|\Omega|} + \frac{\sum_j q_j^2}{4b} - \frac{(\sum_j q_j)^2}{4b|\Omega|} - \frac{b}{|\Omega|}.$$

The quadratic scoring rule market maker is likely not of much practical interest. The market maker allows traders only to buy a small fixed number of shares of any security. Moreover, as soon as one upper limit is reached on any security, the market maker cannot accept buy orders for other securities. In contrast, the logarithmic scoring rule market maker can accept arbitrarily large quantities of buy or sell orders.

As mentioned, a market scoring rule market maker can be viewed as a sequential shared version of a scoring rule. Conceptually, the market maker begins by setting prices equal to an initial probability estimate. The first trader to arrive agrees to (1) pay the market maker the scoring rule payment associated with the market maker's probability estimate and (2) receive the scoring rule payment associated with the trader's own probability estimate. Myopically, this modified scoring rule still incents the trader to reveal her true probability estimate. The final trader pays the scoring rule payment owed to the second-to-last trader and receives a scoring rule payment from the market maker. The market maker's loss is bounded by the maximum possible payment to the final trader minus the payment from the first trader. One can show that the more conventional cost function formulation of the market maker is equivalent to the sequential shared scoring rule formulation.

26.4.2 Dynamic Parimutuel Markets

A *parimutuel* game is a wagering game where players compete to earn as large a portion as possible of the total pool of money wagered by all players. Again consider a set Ω of mutually exclusive and exhaustive outcomes. Players wagers money on the outcome(s) of their choice. When the true outcome is revealed, players who wagered on the correct outcome split the total pool of money in proportion to the amount they bet. In a sense, the cost of purchasing an equal share of the winnings associated with any outcome is always a constant, say \$1. A dynamic parimutuel market is a dynamic-cost variant of the parimutuel wagering game. As before, traders compete for a share of the total money wagered, however the cost of a single share varies dynamically according to a cost function, thus allowing traders to sell their shares prior to the determination of the outcome for profits or losses. From a trader's perpective, the mechanism acts as a market maker.

A particularly natural cost function is the *share-ratio cost function*, which equates the ratio of prices of any two outcomes with the ratio of number of shares outstanding for the two outcomes. The share-ratio cost function is

$$C(\vec{q}) = \kappa \sqrt{\sum_j q_j^2},$$

where κ is a free parameter. The corresponding price function is $p_j = \kappa q_j / \sqrt{\sum_k q_k^2}$. This cost function is the unique dynamic parimutuel cost function satisfying the ratio constraint $p_j/p_k = q_j/q_k$ for all j and k. Setting $\kappa = 1$ yields a natural version where the price of each outcome is always less than 1, and the payoff per share of each outcome is always greater than 1. The share-ratio cost function is arbitrage-free and ensures that wagers on the correct outcome can never lose money. The market maker initiates the game with an allocation of shares $\vec{q}$ and a corresponding $C(\vec{q})$ dollars, reflecting the market maker's maximum risk of loss.

Besides the different form of the cost function, the main difference between a market scoring rule market maker and a dynamic pari-mutuel market maker is that the former pays a fixed \$1 per share to winning shareholders while the latter pays an equal portion of the total amount wagered to winning shareholders. Because of the added uncertainty surrounding the payoff per share, trading strategies in a dynamic parimutuel market are more complicated, and the interpretation of the price as a forecast is less direct. On the other hand, as a gambling game, the added uncertainty may appeal to risk seeking traders.

26.5 Distributed Computation through Markets

Sections 26.3 and 26.4 concerned algorithmic components of the operation of a prediction market. In this section, we turn that viewpoint inside out, and study the system of market and traders as a computational device (that is perhaps a part of a larger computation)! We construct and analyze a simple model of a prediction market in order to gain insight into two fundamental properties of any computational device: what can it compute? and, how fast does the computation run?

Where is this computation taking place? The traders use their private information to attempt to make profitable trades. Importantly, they observe the market clearing price (or the actual sequence of trades), and *update their beliefs* about the security value. The computation of the market as a whole occurs through the traders' belief-updating processes; this is where a trader takes a signal (the market price) that reflects some information about other traders, and combines it logically with her own private information.

The process by which the market prices adjust is important for another reason: Recall from Section 26.2.2.3 that the rational expectations equilibrium definition does not address the issue of how traders reach the equilibrium price correspondence. We shall see that this can be problematic: With a plausible belief-updating process, the market prices may sometimes get stuck at a noninformative equilibrium, even though a fully revealing equilibrium exists. Thus, we need a better understanding of the dynamics of the price adjustment process. The following model provides some insight.

26.5.1 Boolean Market Model

We model a very simple class of elementary computation problems – computing a Boolean function – and study what can be computed *with a single security*. Initially, suppose that there are n traders, each with a single bit x_i of private information; we use $\mathbf{x}$ to denote the vector $(x_1, \ldots, x_n)$. This model can be translated to a partition model as described in Section 26.2.1: The state space is $\Omega = \{0, 1\}^n$, and each agent i initially has a partition $\pi_i = \{\{\mathbf{x} \in \Omega | x_i = 0\}, \{\mathbf{x} \in \Omega | x_i = 1\}\}$ with two components. We are interested in learning the value of a Boolean function $f : \{0, 1\}^n \to \{0, 1\}$ of the combined information $\mathbf{x}$. To do this, we set up a market in a security F that will pay \$1 if $f(\mathbf{x})$ is ultimately revealed to be 1, and \$0 otherwise. The form of f (the description of the security) is common knowledge among agents. We sometimes refer to the x_i as the *input bits*. At some time in the future after trading is completed, the true value of $f(\mathbf{x})$ is revealed. Note that the traders' combined information is enough to determine the exact value of $f(\mathbf{x})$; thus, if the market is truly efficient, we expect its equilibrium trading price to be equal to $f(\mathbf{x})$.

To have a model that permits analysis, we next need to specify how the market prices are formed, and how the agents bid in the market and react to market information.

26.5.2 Bid Format and Price Formation

Continuous double auctions are complex systems, and there is no standard way to analytically model the price formation process; we use the following linear model that loosely captures the nature of the market, and permits analysis. The market proceeds in synchronous rounds. In each round, each agent i submits a *bid* b_i and a *quantity* q_i. The semantics are that agent i is supplying a quantity q_i of the security and an amount b_i of money to be traded in the market. For simplicity, we assume that there are no restrictions on credit or short sales, and so an agent's trade is not constrained by her possessions. The market clears in each round by settling at a single price that balances the trade in that round: The clearing price is $p = \sum_i b_i / \sum_i q_i$. At the end of the round, agent i holds a quantity q'_i proportional to the money she bid: $q'_i = b_i / p$. In addition, she is left with an amount of money b'_i that reflects her net trade at price p: $b'_i = b_i - p(q'_i - q_i) = pq_i$. Note that agent i's net trade in the security is a purchase if $p < b_i / q_i$ and a sale if $p > b_i / q_i$.

After each round, the clearing price p is publicly revealed. Agents then revise their beliefs according to any information garnered from the new price. The next round proceeds as the previous. The process continues until an equilibrium is reached, meaning that prices and bids do not change from one round to the next.

Here, we make a further simplifying restriction on the trading in each round: We assume that $q_i = 1$ for each agent i. This serves two analytical functions: First, it forces trade to occur. Our model has only rational, risk-neutral, informed traders, and the classic no-trade results would apply. As we have seen, there are several reasons why rational traders would want to trade in practice (subsidies, insurance traders, etc.). This forced trade assumption allows us to capture this practical fact without the complications of explicitly modeling these reasons. Second, the fact that agents know the volume of other agents' trades improves their ability to learn from prices. This perhaps gives our agents too much power; but as we shall see, there are still situations in which the market does not converge to the correct value.

26.5.3 Agent Behavior

We assume that agents are risk-neutral, myopic,[3] and bid truthfully: Each agent in each round bids his or her current valuation of the security, which is that agent's estimation of the expected payoff of the security. Expectations are computed according to each agent's probability distribution. We assume that there is a common prior probability distribution $\mathcal{P}$ over values of $\mathbf{x}$ shared by all agents; the agents use their private information and the observed prices to update their beliefs via Bayes' rule. We also assume that it is common knowledge that all the agents behave in the specified manner.

Example 26.8 Consider a market with two agents, who have private bits x_1 and x_2, respectively. Furthermore, assume that the prior probability distribution is uniform, so that each of the four possible values for $\mathbf{x}$ will have a prior probability of $\frac{1}{4}$. Now, we introduce a security F based on the OR function $f(\mathbf{x}) = x_1 \vee x_2$; that is, F eventually pays \$1 if $f(\mathbf{x})$ is 1. Suppose that agent 1 observed $x_1 = 0$. Then, conditioned on this information, agent 1 believes $P((x_1, x_2) = (0, 0)) = P((x_1, x_2) = (0, 1)) = \frac{1}{2}$. Then agent 1's initial expectation of the value of F is 0.5; hence, in our model, she would bid $b_1 = 0.5$ in the first round of trading. On the other hand, suppose that agent 2 observed $x_2 = 1$. Then, her posterior beliefs would be $P((x_1, x_2) = (0, 1)) = P((x_1, x_2) = (1, 1)) = \frac{1}{2}$. She would know for certain that f is 1, and would bid $b_2 = 1$. The clearing price of the market after the first round would thus be 0.75.

26.5.4 Equilibrium Price Characterization

We now turn to analyzing the equilibrium trading price in the market. Our analysis builds on powerful results from the economic literature on common knowledge of aggregates.

Recall that there is a set of possible states Ω, together with a common prior probability distribution $\mathcal{P}$. As trading proceeds, some possible states can be logically ruled out, but the relative likelihoods among the remaining states are fully determined by the prior $\mathcal{P}$. So the common knowledge after any stage is completely described by the set of states that an external observer – with no information beyond the sequence of prices observed – considers possible (along with the prior). Similarly, the knowledge of agent i at any point is also completely described by the set of states she considers possible.

[3] Myopic behavior means that agents treat each round as if it were the final round: They do *not* reason about how their bids may affect the bids of other agents in future rounds.

We use the notation S^r to denote the common-knowledge possibility set after round r, and S_i^r to denote the set of states that agent i considers possible after round r.

Initially, the set of states considered possible by an external observer is the set $S^0 = \Omega$. However, each agent i also knows the value of her bit x_i; thus, her knowledge set S_i^0 is the set $\{\mathbf{y} \in \Omega | y_i = x_i\}$. Agent i's first-round bid is her conditional expectation of the event $f(\mathbf{x}) = 1$ given that $\mathbf{x} \in S_i^0$. All the agents' bids are processed, and the clearing price p^1 is announced. From his knowledge of the prior and the information structure, the external observer can determine the function $price^1(\mathbf{x})$ that relates the first round price to the true state $\mathbf{x}$. Thus, he can *rule out any vector* $\mathbf{x}$ *that would have resulted in a different clearing price.*

Thus, the common knowledge after round 1 is the set $S^1 = \{\mathbf{y} \in S^0 | \ price^1(\mathbf{y}) = p^1\}$. Agent i knows the common knowledge and, in addition, knows the value of bit x_i. Hence, after every round r, the knowledge of agent i is given by $S_i^r = \{y \in S^r | y_i = x_i\}$. Note that, because knowledge can only improve over time, we must always have $S_i^r \subseteq S_i^{r-1}$ and $S^r \subseteq S^{r-1}$. Thus, after a finite number of rounds, we must reach an equilibrium after which no player learns any further information. We use S^∞ to denote the common knowledge at this point, and S_i^∞ to denote agent i's knowledge at this point. Let p^∞ denote the clearing price at equilibrium.

We now state (without proof) a result that follows immediately from known results on common knowledge of aggregates:

Theorem 26.9 *In the Boolean market, the following conditions must hold at equilibrium:*

$$P(f(\mathbf{y}) = 1 \mid \mathbf{y} \in S^\infty) = p^\infty \tag{26.1}$$

$$\forall i \ \ P\big(f(\mathbf{y}) = 1 \mid \mathbf{y} \in S_i^\infty\big) = p^\infty \tag{26.2}$$

Informally, Theorem 26.9 tells us that, at equilibrium, all agents must have exactly the same expectation of the value of the security, and that this must agree with the expectation of an uninformed observer. Note that they may still have differing knowledge sets, as long as conditioning on their respective knowledge sets yields the same expectation. However, reaching agreement is not sufficient for the purposes of information aggregation. We also want the price to reveal the actual value of $f(\mathbf{x})$. The following example shows that it is possible that the equilibrium price p^∞ of the security F will not be either 0 or 1, and so we cannot infer the value of $f(\mathbf{x})$ from it.

Example 26.10 Consider two agents 1 and 2 with private input bits x_1 and x_2, respectively. Suppose that the prior probability distribution is uniform, i.e., $\mathbf{x} = (x_1, x_2)$ takes the values $(0, 0)$, $(0, 1)$, $(1, 0)$, and $(1, 1)$ each with probability $\frac{1}{4}$. Now, suppose that the aggregate function we want to compute is the *XOR* function, $f(\mathbf{x}) = x_1 \oplus x_2$. To this end, we design a market to trade in a Boolean security F, which will eventually payoff \$1 iff $x_1 \oplus x_2 = 1$.

If agent 1 observes $x_1 = 1$, she estimates the expected value of F to be the probability that $x_2 = 0$ (given $x_1 = 1$), which is $\frac{1}{2}$. If she observes $x_1 = 0$, her expectation is the conditional probability that $x_2 = 1$, which is also $\frac{1}{2}$. Thus, in either case, agent 1 will bid 0.5 for F in the first round. Similarly, agent 2 will also always bid 0.5 in the first round. Hence, the first round of trading ends with a clearing price of 0.5. From this, agent 2 can infer that agent 1 bid 0.5, but this gives her no information about the value of x_1 – it is still equally likely to be 0 or 1. Agent 1 also gains no information from the first round of trading, and hence neither agent changes her bid in the following rounds. Thus, the market reaches equilibrium at this point. As predicted by Theorem 26.9, both agents have the same conditional expectation (0.5) at equilibrium. However, the equilibrium price of the security F does not reveal the value of $f(x_1, x_2)$, even though the combination of agents' information is enough to determine it precisely.

26.5.5 Characterizing Computable Aggregates

We now give a necessary and sufficient characterization of the class of functions f such that, for any prior distribution on $\mathbf{x}$, the equilibrium price of F will reveal the true value of f. We show that this is exactly the class of *weighted threshold functions*:

Definition 26.11 A function $f : \{0, 1\}^n \to \{0, 1\}$ is a **weighted threshold function** iff there are real constants $w_0, w_1, w_2, \ldots, w_n$ such that

$$f(\mathbf{x}) = 1 \text{ iff } w_0 + \sum_{i=1}^{n} w_i x_i \geq 1$$

We now state the following results; because of space restrictions, we do not include the proof. The OR and XOR examples (Examples 26.8 and 26.10) give some insight into these results.

Theorem 26.12 *If f is a weighted threshold function, then, for any prior probability distribution $\mathcal{P}$, the equilibrium price of F is equal to $f(\mathbf{x})$.*

Theorem 26.13 *Suppose $f : \{0, 1\}^n \to \{0, 1\}$ cannot be expressed as a weighted threshold function. Then there exists a prior distribution $\mathcal{P}$ for which the price of the security F does not converge to the value of $f(\mathbf{x})$.*

26.5.6 Convergence Time

The model also enables analysis of the number of rounds it takes for the market to converge. We state (but do not prove) the results here.

Theorem 26.14 *Let f be a weighted threshold function with n inputs, and let $\mathcal{P}$ be an arbitrary prior probability distribution. Then, after at most n rounds of trading, the price reaches its equilibrium value $p^\infty = f(\mathbf{x})$.*

Theorem 26.15 *There is a function $\mathcal{C}_n$ with $2n$ inputs and a prior distribution $\mathcal{P}_n$ such that, in the worst case, the market takes n rounds to reveal the value of $\mathcal{C}_n(\cdot)$.*

26.6 Open Questions

We conclude with some open questions and future work.

Combinatorial Prediction Markets

- Section 26.3 discusses combinatorial prediction markets from the auctioneer's perspective. The bidder's perspective is also interesting to examine. How should bidders choose boolean formulas ϕ, perhaps subject to constraints or penalties on the number or complexity of bids? How should bidders choose quantities and prices?
- Are there less expressive bidding languages that admit polynomial matching algorithms yet are still practically useful and interesting?
- Although exact matching in general is intractable, are there good heuristics that achieve matches in many cases, or approximate a matching? In particular, is there a practically useful logical reduction algorithm for finding matches?
- We can study permutation combinatorics instead of Boolean combinatorics. In this case, the state space Ω consists of all possible orderings of a set of statistics, say finish times in a horse race. Then a high-level bidding language might allow wagers on events like "X_1 will win," "X_1 will finish in the top 3," "X_1 will beat X_2," etc. Are there natural bidding languages with tractable matching problems in this setting?
- Can the auctioneer share the surplus partially or fully with the traders? What are the incentive properties of the resulting mechanisms?
- What is the complexity of finding a match between a single new order and a set of old orders known to have no matches among them? The objective function would be to satisfy as much of the new order as possible, giving the advantage of any price differences to the new order. (This is the standard continuous double auction rule.)
- We may consider a market to be in *computational equilibrium* if no computationally bounded player can find a strategy that increases utility. Can a market achieve a computational equilibrium that is not a true equilibrium? Under what circumstances?

Automated Market Makers

- For every bidding language that admits a polynomial time matching algorithm as defined in Section 26.3, does there exist a corresponding polynomial time market scoring rule market maker algorithm?
- The market makers of Section 26.4 can be considered as simple *online algorithms* (see Chapter 16). Orders arrive one at a time and the market maker must decide to (partially) accept or reject the order under a constraint of bounded worst-case loss. Are there other online algorithms that can accept more orders for the same worst-case bound on loss?

Distributed Computation Through Markets

- The market model in Section 26.5 assumes that the clearing price is known with unlimited precision. Furthermore, the model assumes that none of the traders are misinformed or irrational. What aggregates can be computed even in the presence of noisy prices and traders?

- If the agents have computed the value of the function and a small number of input bits are switched, can the new value of the function be computed incrementally and quickly?
- In the model presented, distributed information is aggregated through a centralized market computation. Can we find a good distributed-computational model of a decentralized market?
- What is the complexity of the computations that agents must do to update their beliefs after each round?
- The model in Section 26.5 directly assumes that agents bid truthfully. Is there a tractable model that assumes only rationality and solves for the resulting game-theoretic solution strategy?
- The negative results in Section 26.5 (Theorems 26.13 and 26.15) examine worst-case scenarios, and thus involve very specific prior probability distributions and initial information states. On the other hand, simulations seem to suggest that almost every threshold function's expected convergence time is near constant, where expectation is taken over the common prior. Can we prove results about average-case convergence?
- Nonthreshold functions can be implemented by combining two or more threshold functions. What is the minimum number of threshold securities required to implement a given function? Are there ways to configure securities to speed up convergence to equilibrium?

26.7 Bibliographic Notes

This section surveys some of the most directly relevant related work; a more extensive bibliography will be made available on the authors' home pages. We also point readers to excellent survey articles on prediction markets by Tziralis and Tatsiopoulos (2006), Wolfers and Zitzewitz (2004, in press), and Berg and Rietz (2003).

A number of studies investigate forecast accuracy and trader behavior on the Iowa Electronic Market, one of the longest-running active prediction markets. Berg et al. (2001) surveys this work. Other empirical studies examine markets on TradeSports.com, an Irish betting exchange (Wolfers and Zitzewitz, 2006; Wolfers et al., 2007; Tetlock, 2004, 2006). Perhaps surprisingly, even play-money market games perform well compared to experts and real-money markets (Chen et al., 2005; Pennock et al., 2001a, 2001b; Servan-Schreiber et al., 2004; Spann and Skiera, 2003; Mangold et al., 2005). The field tests at Hewlett Packard were conducted by Chen and Plott (2002) and Plott (2000). Sunder (1995) reviews a number of laboratory experiments involving prediction markets.

A common concern is that prediction market prices may be manipulated by wealthy traders with ulterior motives. Rhode and Strumpf (2006) analyze manipulation attempts in real markets and find that the effects of manipulations are typically minimal and short lived. Hanson et al. (2006) find that markets appear robust to manipulation in a laboratory setting.

The theory of rational expectations was introduced by Muth (1961) and further developed by Lucas (1972). The article by Grossman (1981) is a good introductory survey. No-trade theorems (Milgrom and Stokey, 1982) have their roots in the theory of common knowledge (Aumann, 1976). Several authors discuss a procedural explanation of rational expectations, showing that repeated announcement of an aggregate statistic of the agents' beliefs will drive the agents to a consensus, if they begin with common priors (Hanson, 1998; Mckelvey and Page, 1986, 1990; Nielsen et al., 1990). The oft-cited *efficient market hypothesis* (Fama, 1970) is rooted in rational expectations theory.

The analysis of combinatorial prediction markets in Section 1.3 follows Fortnow *et al.* (2005). Chen et al. (2007) conduct an analogous study of permutation conbinatorics. Bossaerts et al. (2002) introduce the *combined value trading* framework, providing algorithms for clearing prediction markets when combined orders are allowed.

The description in Section 26.3.2 of compact prediction markets that take advantage of (conditional) independence among events is based on work by Pennock and Wellman (2000, 2005).

Market scoring rules were introduced by Hanson (2003, 2006). Hanson describes how the market scoring rule market maker is especially well suited for combinatorial prediction markets, and discusses some of the associated computational challenges. Scoring rules have long been used to measure forecast accuracy (Savage, 1971; Winkler and Murphy, 1968). Dynamic parimutuel markets were introduced by Pennock (2004).

Section 26.5 follows the work of Feigenbaum et al. (2005). Chen et al. (2006) examine an extended model where aggregate uncertainty remains in equilibrium. Theorem 26.9 follows from a result due to McKelvey and Page; see Nielsen et al. (1990) for more details. The market model is based on a model due to Shapley and Shubik (1977). Ronen and Wahrmann (2005) investigate a slightly different model of *prediction games*, in which a mechanism designer seeks to compute a function of agents' information, but agents incur a cost to access their own information.

Acknowledgments

We thank Yiling Chen for help and contributions. We thank Joan Feigenbaum, Lance Fortnow, Joe Kilian, and Michael Wellman.

Bibliography

R. Aumann. Agreeing to disagree. *Ann. Statist.*, 4:1236–1239, 1976.

J.E. Berg, R. Forsythe, F.D. Nelson, and T.A. Rietz. Results from a dozen years of election futures markets research. In C.A. Plott and V. Smith (eds.), *Handbook of Experimental Economic Results (forthcoming)*. 2001.

J.E. Berg and T.A. Rietz. Prediction markets as decision support systems. *Inform. Systems Frontier*, 5:79–93, 2003.

P. Bossaerts, L. Fine, and J. Ledyard. Inducing liquidity in thin financial markets through combined-value trading mechanisms. *Euro. Econ. Rev.*, 46:1671–1695, 2002.

K.Y. Chen and C.R. Plott. Information aggregation mechanisms: Concept, design and implementation for a sales forecasting problem. Working paper No. 1131, California Institute of Technology, Division of the Humanities and Social Sciences, 2002.

Y. Chen, C.H. Chu, T. Mullen, and D.M. Pennock. Information markets vs. opinion pools: An empirical comparison. In *Proc. Sixth ACM Conf. on Electronic Commerce*, Vancouver, Canada, June 2005.

Y. Chen, L. Fortnow, E. Nikolova, and D.M. Pennock. Betting on permutations. Working Paper, 2007.

Y. Chen, T. Mullen, and C.-H. Chu. An in-depth analysis of information markets with aggregate uncertainty. *Electronic Commerce Res.*, 6(2):201–221, 2006.

E.F. Fama. Efficient capital market: A review of theory and empirical work. *J. Finance*, 25:383–417, 1970.

J. Feigenbaum, L. Fortnow, D.M. Pennock, and R. Sami. Computation in a distributed information market. *Theoretical Computer Science*, 343:114–132, 2005. (A preliminary version appeared in the 2003 ACM Conference on Electronic Commerce).

L. Fortnow, J. Kilian, D.M. Pennock, and M.P. Wellman. Betting boolean-style: A framework for trading in securities based on logical formulas. *Decision Support Systems*, 39(1):87–104, 2005.

S.J. Grossman. An introduction to the theory of rational expectations under asymmetric information. *Rev. Econ. Stud.*, 48(4):541–559, 1981.

R. Hanson. Consensus by identifying extremists. *Theory Decis.*, 44(3):293–301, 1998.

R. Hanson. Shall we vote on values, but bet on beliefs? Working Paper, 2003.

R. Hanson. Logarithmic market scoring rules for modular combinational information aggregation. *J. Predict. Markets*, 1(1), 2006.

R. Hanson, R. Oprea, and D. Porter. Information aggregation and manipulation in an experimental market. *J. Econ. Behav. Organ.*, In press. 2006.

R.E. Lucas. Expectations and the neutrality of money. *J. Econ. Theory*, 4(2):103–24, 1972.

B. Mangold, M. Dooley, G.W. Flake, H. Hoffman, T. Kasturi, D.M. Pennock, and R. Dornfest. The tech buzz game. *IEEE Computer*, 38(7):94–97, July 2005.

R. McKelvey and T. Page. Common knowledge, consensus, and aggregate information. *Econometrica*, 54(1):109–127, January 1986.

R.D. McKelvey and T. Page. Public and private information: An experimental study of information pooling. *Econometrica*, 58(6):1321–1339, 1990.

P. Milgrom and N. Stokey. Information, trade, and common knowledge. *J. Econ. Theory*, 26:17–27, 1982.

J.A. Muth. Rational expectations and the theory of price movements. *Econometrica*, 29(6):315–335, 1961.

L.T. Nielsen, A. Brandenburger, J. Geanakoplos, R. McKelvey, and T. Page. Common knowledge of an aggregate of expectations. *Econometrica*, 58(5):1235–1238, 1990.

D. Pennock. A dynamic parimutuel market for information aggregation. In *Proc. Fourth Annual ACM Conference on Electronic Commerce*, June 2004.

D.M. Pennock, S. Lawrence, C. L. Giles, and F. Nielsen. The real power of artificial markets. *Science*, 291:987–988, February 9 2001a.

D.M. Pennock, S. Lawrence, F.A. Nielsen, and C.L. Giles. Extracting collective probabilistic forecasts from web games. In *Proc. 7th ACM SIGKDD Intl. Conf. Knowledge Discovery and Data Mining*, pp. 174–183, 2001b.

D.M. Pennock and M.P. Wellman. Compact securities markets for Pareto optimal reallocation of risk. In *16th Conf. on Uncertainty in Artificial Intelligence*, pp. 481–488, July 2000.

D.M. Pennock and M.P. Wellman. Graphical models for groups: Belief aggregation and risk sharing. *Decis. Analy.*, 2(3):148–164, 2005.

C.R. Plott. Markets as information gathering tools. *South. Econ. J.*, 67(1):1–15, 2000.

P.W. Rhode and K.S. Strumpf. Manipulating political stock markets: A field experiment and a century of observational data. Working Paper, 2006.

A. Ronen and L. Wharmann. Prediction games. In *Workshop on Internet and Network Economics*, 2005.

L. Savage. Elicitation of personal probabilities and expectations. *J. Amer. Stat. Assoc.*, 66(336):783–801, 1971.

E. Servan-Schreiber, J. Wolfers, D.M. Pennock, and B. Galebach. Prediction markets: Does money matter? *Electronic Markets*, 14(3):243–251, 2004.

L. Shapley and M. Shubik. Trade using one commodity as a means of payment. *J. Political Econ.*, 85:937–968, 1977.

M. Spann and B. Skiera. Internet-based virtual stock markets for business forecasting. *Management Sci.*, 49(10):1310–1326, 2003.

S. Sunder. Experimental asset markets. In J.H. Kagel and A.E. Roth (eds.), *The Handbook of Experimental Economics*, Princeton University Press, pp. 445–500, 1995.

P.C. Tetlock. How efficient are information markets? Evidence from an online exchange. Working Paper, 2004.

P.C. Tetlock. Does liquidity affect securities market efficiency? Working Paper, 2006.

G. Tziralis and I. Tatsiopoulos. Prediction markets: An extended literature review. *J. Prediction Markets*, 1(1), 2006.

R.L. Winkler and A.H. Murphy. Good probability assessors. *J. Appl. Meteorol.*, 7:751–758, 1968.

J. Wolfers, E. Snowberg, and E. Zitzewitz. Partisan impacts on the economy: Evidence from prediction markets and close elections. *Q. J. Econ.*, 122(2), 2007.

J. Wolfers and E. Zitzewitz. Prediction markets. *J. Econ. Perspect.*, 18(2):107–126, 2004.

J. Wolfers and E. Zitzewitz. Using markets to inform policy: The case of the Iraq war. Under Review, 2006.

J. Wolfers and E. Zitzewitz. Prediction markets in theory and practice. In L. Blume and S. Durlauf (eds.), *The New Palgrave Dictionary of Economics*, 2nd ed. Palgrave Macmillan, Houndmills, England, In press.

Exercises

26.1 Describe how the market scoring rule market maker of Section 26.5 can be extended to handle limit orders of the form "buy at most q units of S_ϕ at price less than or equal to p." For simplicity, assume that partially filled limit orders do not remain active in the system.

26.2 A straightforward implementation of a combinatorial market maker, where $\Omega = 2^{\|\mathcal{E}\|}$, requires exponential space to explicitly maintain the vector $\vec{q}$, the number of shares outstanding of each of the $2^{\|\mathcal{E}\|}$ possible outcomes (states). Derive a polynomial-space version of a combinatorial logarithmic market scoring rule market maker, where the input is the list of previously accepted orders and the new order and the output is $C(\vec{q})$. Orders can be either combined orders or compound orders, as defined in Section 26.3.

26.3 Define the *conditional cost function* for the logarithmic market scoring rule as $C_\psi(\vec{q}) = b\ln(\sum_{j:\omega_j\in\psi} e^{q_j/b})$: the same cost function as before but summed only over states in ψ. The conditional cost function can be used to price conditional securities. The cost to buy δ shares of $S_{\phi|\psi}$ is $C_\psi(\vec{q}+\delta\cdot 1_\phi) - C_\psi(\vec{q})$. Also, by Bayes's Rule, we know that the instantaneous price of $S_{\phi|\psi}$ equals the price of $S_{\phi\wedge\psi}$ divided by the price of S_ψ.

(a) Verify that the price of $S_{\phi|\psi}$ defined in this way integrated from 0 to δ equals $C_\psi(\vec{q}+\delta\cdot 1_\phi)$ - $C_\psi(\vec{q})$.

(b) After a trader purchases δ shares of $S_{\phi|\psi}$, what is the new quantity vector $\vec{q}_{\text{new}}$? (Hint: it is *not* $\vec{q}_{\text{old}} + \delta \cdot 1_{\phi}$.)

26.4 Consider the two-agent "OR" market of Example 26.8. Suppose that $X_1 = 0$ and $X_2 = 1$. Prove that bidding truthfully is not a Nash equilibrium. To do so, it suffices to show that if bidder 1 bids truthfully, then bidder 2's optimal bid is not truthful.

CHAPTER 27

Manipulation-Resistant Reputation Systems

Eric Friedman, Paul Resnick, and Rahul Sami

Abstract

This chapter is an overview of the design and analysis of reputation systems for strategic users. We consider three specific strategic threats to reputation systems: the possibility of users with poor reputations starting afresh (*whitewashing*); lack of effort or honesty in providing feedback; and *sybil attacks*, in which users create phantom feedback from fake identities to manipulate their own reputation. In each case, we present a simple analytical model that captures the essence of the strategy, and describe approaches to solving the strategic problem in the context of this model. We conclude with a discussion of open questions in this research area.

27.1 Introduction: Why Are Reputation Systems Important?

One of the major benefits of the Internet is that it enables potentially beneficial interactions, both commercial and noncommercial, between people, organizations, or computers that do not share any other common context. The actual value of an interaction, however, depends heavily on the ability and reliability of the entities involved. For example, an online shopper may obtain better or lower-cost items from remote traders, but she may also be defrauded by a low-quality product for which redress (legal or otherwise) is difficult.

If each entity's history of previous interactions is made visible to potential new interaction partners, several benefits ensue. First, a history may reveal *information about an entity's ability*, allowing others to make choices about whether to interact with that entity, and on what terms. Second, an expectation that current performance will be visible in the future may deter *moral hazard* in the present, that hazard being the temptation to cheat or exert low effort. In other words, visible histories create an *incentive* to reliably perform up to the entity's ability. Finally, because histories reveal information about abilities, entities with higher abilities will be drawn to participate, as they will be distinguishable from those of lower abilities, and respected or rewarded appropriately. In other words, visible histories *avoid problems of adverse selection*.

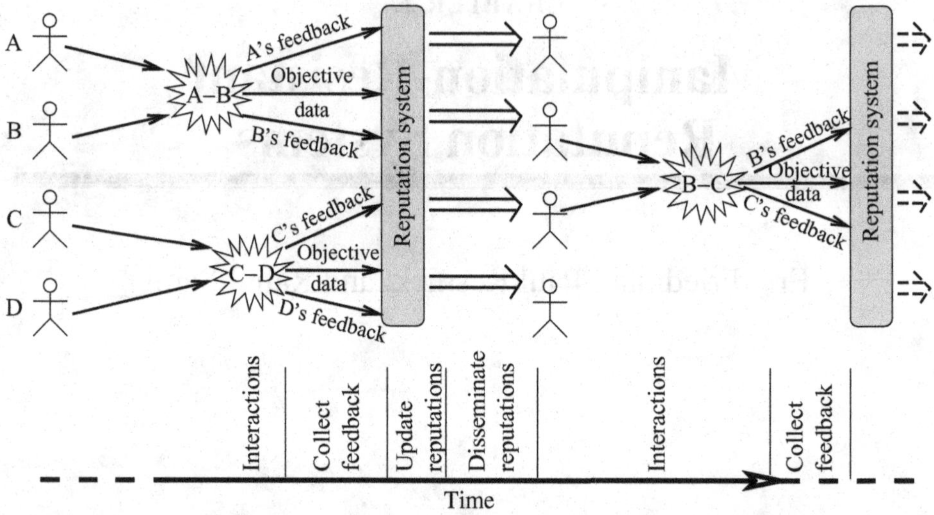

Figure 27.1. Example illustrating reputation system dynamics.

A reputation system collects, maintains, and disseminates *reputations*—aggregated records from past interactions—of each participant in a community. The rapid advance in computational power and communication capacity on the Internet has been a double-edged sword: On one hand, it has enabled the construction of reputation systems that can store, gather, and process large quantities of information. On the other hand, it has allowed more sophisticated attacks on the integrity of the reputation system to be mounted.

Reputation systems have been designed for use in many settings, including online auctions, e-storefronts, and a wide-range peer-to-peer systems. These systems naturally have differing interfaces, and track different aspects of user behavior. However, they all share certain underlying components, which are illustrated in Figure 27.1.

The core of a reputation system involves collecting records of entity A's past behavior, and then disseminating reputation information to others who may potentially interact with A in the future. (We use the term "entity" to denote the real-world entity to which we seek to attach a reputation; typically, this is an individual person, but it could also be an organized group or a firm, or a node in a computer network.) The records are based on both objective information independently collected about interactions and feedback from the entities about each other. The exact nature of both the objective information and the subjective feedback depends on the application. For an online auction, the system may record the agreed sale price and ask the buyer and seller to report their satisfaction with each other's integrity and performance after a trade. In a peer-to-peer system, we might ask each peer to monitor and report how often another peer makes its system available.

In principle, user A's reputation could simply be a concatenation of all records pertaining to A, but in practice, reputations are usually numerical summary values that permit direct comparison between users. Thus, reputation systems include an internal aggregation procedure to convert the reports to reputations. If all reports conform to a common structure, there are two natural dimensions along which to aggregate reports: (1) Aggregating across users by computing a statistic of all other users' reports about A. (2) Aggregation across time by computing a statistic of all past reports. In addition, the aggregation function may use other structure derived from the reports, or from the reputations themselves. In particular, it often relies on some notion of *transitivity of trust*, in the sense that reports from users with high reputation are weighted more heavily than reports from users with low reputation.

Economists have studied models where entities strategically choose actions with an eye toward the histories they will generate. In these models, the link between actions and outcomes is probabilistic (bad actions sometimes lead to good outcomes and vice versa) or outcomes are observed with some error. The analysis of these models is interesting and complex, but beyond the scope of this chapter.

Rather than threats to the informativeness of a user history, we focus our attention on threats to the reputation system itself, the system that collects histories and associates them with entities. When the histories include subjective feedback, that feedback may not be reported or may not be reported honestly. Histories may even include phantom feedback from nonexistent interactions.

A second vulnerability comes from the fact that histories may not be tied directly to entities, but rather to online pseudonyms. In many systems, pseudonyms are cheap, which lead to two threats: an entity may jettison its pseudonym if it accumulates a bad reputation, and an entity may acquire many pseudonyms and have them rate each other favorably in order to inflate their reputations.

To summarize, we consider three threats to the integrity of reputation systems:

(i) *Whitewashing*. An entity may acquire a new pseudonym and start over with a clear reputation.

(ii) *Incorrectly reported feedback*. Entities may not report feedback or may not report it honestly.

(iii) *Phantom feedback*. An entity may provide feedback for interactions that never took place, perhaps using "sock puppet" identities (or sybils) created for the sole purpose of providing such phantom feedback.

We begin in Section 27.2 with a stylized model of interactions over time in a market. Initially, in Section 27.3, we assume that the available objective data about interactions are sufficient to generate informative histories, even without any reporting of subjective feedback. We consider the threat of *whitewashing*, where an entity can start over with a new pseudonym, which will not be linked to the history of actions taken under the previous pseudonym. Reputations can still create an incentive for good behavior, but only if a pseudonym with no history is forced to "pay its dues" in some fashion while it builds up a history of good actions.

Section 27.4 relaxes the assumption of objective data about actions. Feedback about interactions may not be reported correctly. Entities may not report feedback or may not report it honestly, for a variety of reasons, including fear of retaliation, or a desire to be viewed as a nice or skilled evaluator.

One approach is to treat the reporting of feedback about an action as itself an action in some other domain. A history of feedback reports made by an entity can be generated and, suitably aggregated, becomes an entity's reputation as a rater. Just as in any reputation system, rater reputations can deter moral hazard, creating incentives for effort and honest reporting. It may, however, be difficult to assess the quality of subjectively reported feedback. We present a mechanism that does so by comparing it with other subjectively reported feedback.

Section 27.5 takes a second approach. Rather than directly assessing the quality of subjectively provided feedback, it assumes that an entity's reputation as a rater is the same as its reputation as an actor in the original domain. This leads to a notion of transitive trust: if an entity's actions in the original domain lead it to have a positive reputation, the entity is presumed to be a good rater as well, and its ratings are treated as more credible and weighted more highly in computing the reputations of other entities. For example, positive feedback from an eBay member with a good reputation would count more than positive feedback from a member with a bad reputation. This naturally leads to a graph model that represents entities and their feedback about other entities, with actions in the original domain not represented explicitly. Reputations are computed as scores for nodes in the graph, subject to the constraints imposed by the link structure of feedback among entities. We present both possibility and impossibility results on how transitive trust algorithms can handle the threats of incorrectly reported feedback and the problem of phantom feedback from sock puppet entities, the so-called *sybil attack.*

27.2 The Effect of Reputations

Economists have developed many game-theoretic models of the impact of reputations. In this section we present some of the fundamental ideas and technical tools necessary. We begin with an (over)simplified example.

Consider the "prisoners' dilemma," a classic model from the early days of game theory. There are two agents, Alice (A) and Bob (B), who interact. If both agents cooperate (C) then each gains 1 unit of utility, while if they both defect they gain 0; however if one cooperates and the other defects (D), the defector gains 2 and the cooperator loses 1. We summarize this as $\pi_A(C, C) = 1$, $\pi_A(D, D) = 0$, $\pi_A(D, C) = 2$, and $\pi_A(C, D) = -1$. π_B is similarly defined via symmetry.

Clearly the outcome of this game, when played a single time, should be (D, D) since it is a dominant strategy for both agents. In an infinitely repeated game, however, a player may choose C and accept lower payoffs in one round to increase the probability that partners will play C against her in future stage games, and thus increase her future payoffs. We denote the game played in each round as the stage game for that round.

Define the discounted payoff to player i in stage game t to be $\pi_i^t \delta^t$, where π^t is the actual payoff in round t and $0 \leq \delta < 1$ is the discount factor. The idea of a discount factor is that it is somehow preferable to get a payoff in the current round rather than in the next round. If the payoffs are monetary, the possibility of investing the payoff at some interest rate provides a good intuition for why a discount factor is needed.

We will analyze strategy alternatives that consist of decision rules about which action to play in each stage game, contingent on a player's own history and the histories of all other players. The discounted average payoff of a strategy, played infinitely into the future, is defined as

$$\overline{\pi_i} = (1-\delta)\sum_{t=0}^{\infty} \delta^t \pi_i^t.$$

In this infinitely repeated model, consider the Grim strategy: play C unless any player has played D in a previous round. This strategy, pursued by both players, denoted (Grim, Grim), is a Subgame Perfect Nash Equilibrium (SPNE), meaning that, if all players pursue this strategy, there is no stage game at which any player would want to deviate from the strategy.

To prove this is a SPNE, we only need to consider "single deviations" in which an agent only deviates from Grim once and then returns to playing it. This follows from a generalization of the single deviation property in dynamic programming.

Consider a deviation in which Alice plays D in a round 0. Clearly this will lead to (D,D) in all future rounds for Alice (for everyone, in fact), so Alice's discounted average payoff will be $(1-\delta)(2+\delta * 0+\delta^2 * 0+\cdots) = 2(1-\delta)$; however, if she did not deviate, then her payoff would be 1 in every period leading to $(1-\delta)(1+\delta+\delta^2+\cdots) = 1$. Thus, deviating is not advantageous when $1 \geq 2(1-\delta)$ or, equivalently, $\delta \geq 1/2$. Now, this same argument applies to any period $t > 0$ with both sides of the equations multiplied by δ^t.

Thus, when δ is small, the promise of future payoffs is not sufficient to constrain the player's current behavior. This is true in all reputation systems: if the players do not value future payoffs sufficiently, then reputations are of no value.

Other strategies that are "less grim" can also work. For example, punishing for only a small number of periods can lead to a cooperative equilibrium for higher values of δ.

Now consider a group of $N+1$ players with N odd, in which in each round players are paired up at random and play the prisoners' dilemma. In a simple reputational extension of the above analysis we consider reputational-grim, defined as follows: each agent begins with a "good" reputation and keeps it if she plays C against players with good reputations and D against those with bad ones. This reputational-grim strategy, if played by all players, is also an SPNE, for $\delta \geq 1/2$. This is because, from an defector's perspective, the punishments are the same as in the full Grim strategy.

To understand the value of shared reputations, consider an alternative system where a player remembers others' interactions with her but histories are not publicly shared. A natural strategy is to play personalized-Grim, the variant of Grim where a player views the game as being separated into N unrelated games, one with each opponent. In this case, the expected number of rounds between meeting the same opponent is N so a straightforward calculation (see exercises) yields a condition for this to be an SPNE, $\delta \geq 1 - 1/2N$, which is unreasonably close to 1, for large N.

The analysis above applies to situations in which all players have the same ability, but reputations lead them to strategies where they are reliable partners. To operationalize varying player abilities, models allow different players different action sets to choose from in the stage game. For example, a low-ability player might only have action D available (or perhaps in some percentage of stage games have only action D available). A high-ability, honest type might only have action C available. Alternatively, it might take more effort (cost more) for a low type to play C than for the high type. This could arise where C indicates the completion of a high-quality product. (Player types with only one possible action are called "commitment" types in the economics literature.) Players with both types of action available (called "strategic" types in the economics literature) would then want to choose actions that distinguish them from low-ability players and mimic those of high-ability players.

It is also natural to extend the model to situations in which outcomes are only probabilistically linked to actions, or outcomes are reported with random error. This leads to interesting strategic opportunities, including playing C most of the time but sometimes choosing D, which would not be immediately distinguishable from the actions of high-ability honest types who also have bad outcomes only less frequently. The analysis of these models is interesting and complex, but beyond the scope of this chapter. (However, in the following section we will consider random outcomes in a limited way.)

27.3 Whitewashing

One key issue in online reputation systems is the fragility of identity. Agents with bad reputations simply reregister with a new username. This is known as *whitewashing*. It is easy to see that the ability to whitewash will disable the functioning of the reputation systems as described in Section 27.2, as agents will simply choose D and then return with a new identity in the following round.

To prevent this, there needs to be some "initiation fee" upon entry. For example, simply having an upfront cost of f to register will prevent whitewashing as long as the cost is sufficiently high. To compute this f note that the total discounted payoff for deviating once is $\overline{\pi}' = (1-\delta)(2 - f + \delta(1-f) + \delta^2 + \delta^3 \cdots)$ while following reputational grim obtains $\overline{\pi} = (1-\delta)(1 - f + \delta + \delta^2 + \cdots)$. Thus for an SPNE we need $\overline{\pi} \geq \overline{\pi}'$, which implies that $\delta f \geq 1$ or $f \geq 1/\delta$. (Note that we continue to require that $\delta \geq 1/2$ to prevent deviation without whitewashing.)

Unfortunately collecting fees is not always feasible (or politically viable); however, we can create an explicit reputational fee. The key idea is to force the new arrivals to "pay dues" upon arrival. The most efficient way to do this is to allow veterans to defect against newcomers, where newcomers are playing for the first time (apparently) and veterans have played at least once before. Thus, we can define the pay-your-dues (PYD) strategy as: play C against any veteran who has never deviated from PYD, otherwise play D against the veteran. Play D against a newcomer, unless you are a newcomer too, in which case play C.

Intuitively, this leads to the "socially most efficient" SPNE, where social efficiency measures the sums of all players' payoffs. Note, however, that the social efficiency in this equilibrium is less than the maximum social efficiency that could be attained without whitewashing. This follows because the maximum social welfare in a single pair playing the PD is 2 while choosing (D, C) yields a value of $2 - 1 = 1$. (One might consider requiring that newcomers play D against other newcomers, but this obtains a value of 0 and entails further social loss.) Thus, the possibility of whitewashing leads to an unavoidable cost being imposed on society.

Even allowing for whitewashing, PYD leads to an SPNE where every player's average discounted payoff is 1. (You should verify this as in the exercises.) However, we have left out several important details in this model that we discuss in the next section!

27.3.1 A More Dynamic Model

Stepping back, we see that the model we just analyzed has a flaw, since any newcomers in our model are clearly whitewashers. Thus, for that model, always playing D against an agent who arrived after the first period (and personalized-grim otherwise) yields a fully socially efficient SPNE, since (C, C) is played in every interaction.

Thus, it makes sense to extend our model to capture these issues; although the difficulty is retaining tractability. First, we assume αN real newcomers arrive every period and an equal number of veterans depart, where the departing veterans are chosen at random. However, once again this allows us to easily detect whitewashers—if there are more than αN newcomers in any period then the players know that there must be at least one whitewasher. Thus, there is an equilibrium in which players play PYD as long as there are exactly αN newcomers in any period and play D-always if there are ever more. However, it is clear that this equilibrium is extremely fragile, since a single deviation leads to all players defecting forever. Such fragile equilibria are artifacts of the "noiselessness" of the game and the perfect rationality assumptions inherent in game theory.

To make our model more robust, we add some "noise." We assume that in any play of the stage game a player accidently plays D with probability $\epsilon > 0$ and then returns in the following period as a whitewasher. In this model, one can show that PYD leads to the most efficient equilibrium (i.e., the highest fraction of cooperative outcomes (C, C)). Proving that PYD is an equilibrium is intuitively similar to above proofs with the addition of some ideas from dynamic programming, while proving optimality is more difficult and requires a careful stochastic analysis.

The PYD strategy in this stylized model corresponds in more practical settings to a mistrust of newcomers. Until they have proven themselves, veterans do not trust the newcomers sufficiently to allow them to undertake mutually beneficial interactions. If only the veterans could trust the newcomers, the newcomers could start right away to interact in beneficial ways with the veterans. The threat of whitewashing, however, forces a mistrust of newcomers. Because of the threat of whitewashing, in any equilibrium, newcomers must also be penalized at least the amount that a deviator would be penalized.

The only way to improve the treatment of newcomers in an equilibrium with significant cooperation is to make whitewashing difficult, by making it more difficult or expensive for existing participants to get new pseudonyms than it is for newcomers. For example, the organization running the reputation system might require entities to reveal their true names, offer them one free pseudonym, and then restrict the acquisition of addition ones or require a payment for them.

27.4 Eliciting Effort and Honest Feedback

The previous section described models in which feedback was reported automatically and objectively. Any system that actually solicits individual opinions must overcome two challenges. The first is underprovision. Forming and reporting an opinion requires time and effort, yet the information benefits others. The second challenge is honesty. A desire to be nice, or fear of retaliation, may cause a rater to withhold negative feedback. Conflicts of interest or a desire to improve others' perception of them may lead raters to report distorted versions of their true opinions.

An explicit reward system for honest rating and effort may help overcome these challenges. When objective information will be publicly revealed at a future time, individuals' reports can be compared to that objective information. For example, weather forecasts and sports betting odds can be compared to what actually occurs. See Chapter 26 on information markets for algorithms that create incentives for honest revelation of information in such settings.

Here, we develop methods to elicit feedback effectively when independent, objective outcomes are not available. Examples include situations where no objective outcome exists (e.g., evaluations of a product's "quality"), and where the relevant information is objective but not public (e.g., a product's breakdown frequency, which is available to others only if the product's current owners reveal it).

In these situations, one solution is to compare raters' reports to their peers' reports and reward agreement.[1] However, if rewards are made part of the process, dangers arise. If a particular outcome is highly likely, such as a positive experience with a seller at eBay who has a stellar feedback history, then a rater who has a bad experience will still believe that the next rater is likely to have a good experience. If she were to be rewarded simply for agreeing with her peers, she will not report her bad experience. This phenomenon is akin to the problems of herding or information cascades.

We now describe a formal mechanism, the *peer-prediction method*, to implement the process of comparing with peers. The scheme uses one rater's report to update a probability distribution for the report of someone else, whom we refer to as the reference rater. The first rater is then scored not on agreement between the ratings, but on a comparison between the *probabilities* assigned to the reference rater's possible ratings and the reference rater's actual rating. Raters need not perform any complex computations: so long as a rater trusts that the system will update appropriately, she will prefer to report honestly.

Scores can be turned into monetary incentives, either as direct payments or as discounts on future merchandise purchases. In many online systems, however, raters seem to be quite motivated by prestige or privileges within the system. For example, at Slashdot.org, users accumulate "karma" points for various actions and higher karma entitles users to rate others' postings and to have their own postings begin with higher ratings; at ePinions.com, reviewers gain status and have their reviews highlighted if they accumulate points. Similarly, offline point systems that do not provide any tangible reward seem to motivate chess and bridge players to compete harder and more frequently.

[1] Subjective evaluations of ratings could be elicited directly instead of relying on correlations between ratings. For example, the news and commentary site Slashdot.org allows meta-moderators to rate the ratings of comments given by regular moderators. Meta-evaluation incurs an obvious inefficiency, since the effort to rate evaluations could presumably be put to better use in rating comments or other products that are a site's primary product of interest. Moreover, meta-evaluation merely pushes the problem of motivating effort and honest reporting up one level, to ratings of evaluations. Thus, scoring evaluations in comparison to other evaluations may be preferable in certain settings.

27.4.1 A Model

We now consider a model to analyze these issues. A number of raters experience a product and then rate its quality. The product's quality does not vary, but is observed with some idiosyncratic error. After experiencing the product, each rater sends a message to a common processing facility called the center. The center makes transfers to each rater, awarding or taking away points based on the raters' messages. The center has no independent information, so its scoring decisions can depend only on the information provided by other raters. As noted above, points may be convertible to money, discounts or privileges within the system, or merely to prestige. We assume that raters' utilities are linear in points. We also assume that raters are risk neutral, and hence, seek to maximize expected wealth.

We refer to a product's quality as its *type*. Assume the number of product types is finite, and the types are indexed by $t = 1, \ldots, T$. Furthermore, we assume that there is a commonly known prior probability. Let $\Pr_0(t)$ be the commonly held prior probability assigned to the product's being type t. Assume that $\Pr_0(t) > 0$ for all t and $\sum_{t=1}^{T} \Pr_0(t) = 1$.

Let I be the set of raters, where $|I| \geq 3$. I may be (countably) infinite. Each rater has a perception of a product's type, which is called her *signal*. Each rater privately observes her own signal; she does not know any other rater's signal. Let $S = \{s_1, \ldots, s_M\}$ be the set of possible signals, and let S^i denote the random signal received by rater i. Conditional on the product's type, raters' signals are independent and identically distributed; the distribution is represented by function $f(s_m|t) = \Pr(S^i = s_m|t)$, where $f(s_m|t) > 0$ for all s_m and t, and $\sum_{m=1}^{M} f(s_m|t) = 1$ for all t. We assume that this function $f(s_m|t)$ is common knowledge. Furthermore, we assume that the conditional distribution of signals is different for different values of t, so that the signals are informative about the types.

Throughout this section, we use the following simple example as an illustration. There are only two product types, H and L, with prior $\Pr_0(H) = \Pr_0(L) = 0.5$, and two possible signals, h and l. The distribution of the signals, conditioned on the true type, is as follows: $f(h|H) = .85$, $f(l|H) = 0.15$, $f(h|L) = 0.45$, $f(l|L) = 0.55$. Thus, $\Pr(h) = 0.5 * 0.85 + 0.5 * 0.45 = 0.65$.

In the mechanism we propose, the center asks each rater to announce her signal. After all signals are announced to the center, they are revealed to the other raters and the center computes transfers. We refer to this as the *simultaneous reporting game*. Let $x^i \in S$ denote one such announcement, and $x = (x^1, \ldots, x^I)$ denote a vector of announcements, one by each rater. Let $x^i_m \in S$ denote rater i's announcement when her signal is s_m, and $\bar{x}^i = (x^i_1, \ldots, x^i_M) \in S^M$ denote rater i's announcement strategy. Let $\bar{x} = (\bar{x}^1, \ldots, \bar{x}^I)$ denote a vector of announcement strategies. As is customary, let the superscript "$-i$" denote a vector without rater i's component.

Let $\tau_i(x)$ denote the transfer paid to rater i when the raters make announcements x, and let $\tau(x) = (\tau_1(x), \ldots, \tau_I(x))$ be the vector of transfers made to all agents. An announcement strategy $\bar{x}^i$ is a best response to $\bar{x}^{-i}$ for player i if for each m:

$$\forall \hat{x}^i \in S \; E_{S^{-i}}\left[\tau_i\left(\bar{x}^i_m, \bar{x}^{-i}\right) | S^i = s_m\right] \geq E_{S^{-i}}\left[\tau_i(\hat{x}^i, \bar{x}^{-i}) | S^i = s_m\right]. \quad (27.1)$$

That is, a strategy is a best response if, conditional on receiving signal s_m, the announcement specified by the strategy maximizes that rater's expected transfer, where the expectation is taken with respect to the distribution of all other raters' signals conditional on $S^i = s_m$. Given transfer scheme $\tau(x)$, a vector of announcement strategies $\bar{x}$ is a Nash Equilibrium of the reporting game if (27.1) holds for $i = 1, \ldots, I$, and a strict Nash Equilibrium if the inequality in (27.1) is strict for all $i = 1, \ldots, I$.

Truthful revelation is a Nash Equilibrium of the reporting game if (27.1) holds for all i when $x^i_m = s_m$ for all i and all m, Furthermore, truthful revelation is a strict Nash Equilibrium if the inequality is strict. (In other words, if all the other players announce truthfully, truthful announcement is a strict best response.)

Continuing the two-type, two-signal example, suppose that rater i receives the signal l. Recall that $\Pr_0(H) = 0.5$, $f(h|H) = 0.85$, and $f(h|L) = 0.45$, so that $\Pr(s^i_l) = 0.35$. Given i's signal, the probability that rater j will receive a signal h is

$$\Pr(S^j = h|S^i = l) = f(h|H)\frac{f(l|H)\Pr_0(H)}{\Pr(S^i = l)} + f(h|L)\frac{f(l|L)\Pr_0(L)}{\Pr(S^i = l)}$$
$$= 0.85\frac{0.15 * 0.5}{0.35} + 0.45\frac{0.55 * 0.5}{0.35} \cong 0.54.$$

If i had instead observed h, then:

$$\Pr(S^j = h|S^i = h) = f(h|H)\frac{f(h|H)\Pr_0(H)}{\Pr(S^i = h)} + f(h|L)\frac{f(h|L)\Pr_0(L)}{\Pr(S^i = h)}$$
$$= 0.85\frac{0.85 * 0.5}{0.65} + 0.45\frac{0.45 * 0.5}{0.65} \cong 0.71.$$

27.4.2 Peer-Prediction Scoring

We now describe how to assign points to a rater i, based on her report and that of another player j. A *scoring rule* is a function $\mathcal{T}(s|x^i)$ that, for each possible announcement x^i of S^i, assigns a score to each possible value $s \in S$. We cannot directly access the signal s_j, but in a truthful equilibrium, we can use player j's report.

Definition 27.1 A scoring rule is *strictly proper* if the rater maximizes her expected score by announcing her true beliefs.

The literature contains a number of strictly proper scoring rules for eliciting beliefs about the probability of an event. The score can be positive or negative. For example, one proper scoring rule, the *logarithmic scoring rule*, is to penalize the player the log of the probability she assigned to the event that actually occurred. Suppose that there are only two possible events (*h,l*), and a player is asked to report her belief $\hat{p}$ of the probability of event h. The log scoring rule is defined by $\mathcal{T}(h|\hat{p}) = \ln(\hat{p})$, $\mathcal{T}(l|\hat{p}) = \ln(1 - \hat{p})$. If her true belief is that h occurs with probability p, then the expected value of announcement $\hat{p}$ is $p \ln \hat{p} + (1 - p)\ln(1 - \hat{p})$. Setting the first derivative to 0 gives the first-order condition for maximization, which requires $p = \hat{p}$.

In the peer prediction method, for each player we choose a reference rater $r(i)$. The outcome to be predicted is the reference rater's announcement $x^{r(i)}$. Player i does not directly report a probability distribution over the reference rater's report: it is inferred from her own report and the prior probability distribution. Truthful reporting is still a best response if she believes that the reference rater will report honestly.

We write $\mathcal{T}(x^{r(i)}|x^i)$ for $\ln[\Pr_0(S^{r(i)} = x^{r(i)}|S^i = x^i)]$, i.e., the log of the inferred probability that $r(i)$ will see $x^{r(i)}$ given that S^i sees signal x^i. Then, let

$$\tau_i^*\left(x^i, x^{r(i)}\right) = \mathcal{T}\left(x^{r(i)}|x^i\right). \tag{27.2}$$

Proposition 1 *For any mapping r that that assigns to each rater i a reference rater $r(i) \neq i$, truthful reporting is a strict Nash equilibrium of the simultaneous reporting game with transfers τ_i^*.*

PROOF Assume that rater $r(i)$ reports honestly: $x^{r(i)}(s_m) = s_m$ for all m. Since S^i is stochastically informative for $S^{r(i)}$, and $r(i)$ reports honestly, S^i is stochastically informative for $r(i)$'s report as well. For any $S^i = s^*$, player i chooses $x^i \in S$ to maximize

$$\sum_{n=1}^{M} \mathcal{T}\left(s_n^{r(i)}|x^i\right) Pr\left(S_{r(i)} = s_n|S_i = s^*\right). \tag{27.3}$$

Since $\mathcal{T}(\cdot|\cdot)$ is a strictly proper scoring rule, (27.3) is uniquely maximized by announcing $x^i = s^*$. Thus, given that rater $r(i)$ is truthful, rater i's best response is to be truthful as well. □

Since $0 < \Pr(S_{r(i)} = s_n|S_i = s^*) < 1$, $\ln(\Pr(S_{r(i)} = s_n|S_i = s^*)) < 0$; we refer to τ_i^* as rater i's penalty since it is always negative in this case. (By adding a suitably large constant that depends only on the distribution f, it is in principle possible to convert this to a positive score without altering its strategic properties.)

Consider the simple example where rater i received the relatively unlikely signal l ($\Pr(S^i = l) = 0.35$). Even contingent on observing l it is unlikely that rater j will also receive an l signal ($\Pr(S^j = l|S^i = l) = 1 - 0.54 = 0.46$). Thus, if rater i were rewarded merely for matching her report to that of rater j, she would prefer to report h. With the log scoring rule, an honest report of l leads to an expected payoff

$$\ln[\Pr(S^j = h|S^i = l)]\Pr(S^j = h|S^i = l) + \ln[\Pr(S^j = l|S^i = l)]\Pr(S^j = l|S^i = l)$$
$$= \ln(0.54)0.54 + \ln(0.46)0.46 = -0.69.$$

If, instead, she reports h, rater i's expected score is

$$\ln[\Pr(S^j = h|S^i = h)]\Pr(S^j = h|S^i = l) + \ln[\Pr(S^j = l|S^i = h)]\Pr(S^j = l|S^i = l)$$
$$= \ln(0.71)0.54 + \ln(0.29)0.46 = -0.75.$$

As claimed, the expected score is maximized by honest reporting.

The key idea is that the scoring function is based on the updated beliefs about the reference rater's signal, given the rater's report, not simply matching a rater's report to the reference report. The updating takes into account both the priors and the reported signal, and thus reflects the initial rater's priors. Thus, she has no reason to shade her report toward the signal expected from the priors. Note also that she need not perform any complex Bayesian updating. She merely reports her signal. As long as she trusts the center to correctly perform the updating and believes other raters will report honestly, she can be confident that honest reporting is her best action.

Note that while Proposition 1 establishes that there is a truthful equilibrium, it is not unique, and there may be nontruthful equilibria. To illustrate, in the example we have been considering two other equilibria are (1) report h all the time, and (2) report l all the time.[2] While such nontruthful equilibria exist, it is reasonable to think that the truthful equilibrium will be a focal point, especially when communication among raters is limited, or when some raters are known to have a strong ethical preference for honesty. In addition, the center can punish all the raters if it detects a completely uninformative equilibrium such as all h or all l.

A variety of extensions to this base scoring rule have been studied. For example, adding a constant value to the score increases the expected payoff without changing the incentives for honest revelation. Multiplying the score by a constant preserves the incentive for honest revelation but changes the amount of costly effort a rater will want to exert in order to acquire an informative signal. The points that each person earns can be debited from some other participant, so that all scores are settled through transfer payments rather than subsidies from the center. Alternative proper scoring rules to reduce the expected size of payments have also been studied.

The payments can be adapted to a sequential interaction scenario where each rater sees the previous rater's reports before reporting herself. Each rater is scored on the basis of the probability distribution inferred from the common prior beliefs, her own report, *and previous reports*. Since the center will take into account others' reports automatically, it is optimal to report just her own signal.

The most problematic aspect of the scoring mechanism is its reliance on common prior beliefs about the distribution of types and the distribution of signals contingent on types. These are needed to infer from a user's reported signal x_i the probability distribution R for the reference rater's signal, which is used to determine the user's point score. A seemingly attractive alternative is to elicit R directly, but player i may also be a reference rater for some other player, and so x_i must be truthfully elicited to score that other player.

The requirement of common priors can be relaxed somewhat if each player is asked to report her personal priors about the item's type before receiving her information signal about the item, and then to report her signal once she receives it. There still is a requirement of common beliefs about the distribution of signals contingent on types, in order to perform Bayesian updating correctly. One solution would be to define the types empirically according to the distribution of signals they elicit (e.g., type 1 yields 10% h signals; type 2 yields 20%, etc.) Then, the beliefs about distribution of signals contingent on type would, by construction, be commonly held.

Many open questions remain about the peer-prediction method. Can it be extended to situations in which raters vary in their abilities and scores are used both to assess the credibility of raters and to give them incentives for effort and honest reporting? Can the method be extended to situations in which entities choose their interactions partners

[2] To verify the "always play h equilibrium," note that if the reference rater always reports high, the rater expects $\ln(0.54)1 + \ln(0.46)0 = -0.61619$ if she reports l, and $\ln(0.71)1 + \ln(0.29)0 = -0.34249$ if she reports h. Similar reasoning verifies the "always play l equilibrium."

rather than being randomly matched? Can it be made robust to collusion among entities or sybil attacks with fake entities providing confirmatory ratings?

27.5 Reputations Based on Transitive Trust

In this section, we discuss the *transitive trust* approach to dealing with the lack of objective feedback. The foundation of this approach is the postulate that the *credibility of an agent's feedback* is tied to the *credibility of her non-feedback actions.* This assumption enables the construction of reputation systems in the absence of any external signals of interaction outcomes or feedback quality: an entity's reputation is calculated by weighting ratings of the entity according to the raters' credibilities, which are in turn calculated from those raters' reputations. Thus, if we begin with some set of credible agents, we can potentially grow this set transitively: If the currently credible agents have positive feedback about i, i can be included in the set of credible agents. This is a recursive construction; we need to carefully define how to bootstrap the credibility calculation, how to propagate the credibility through the network, and when to terminate the calculation.

One additional simplification is often employed in reputation algorithms, which is to ignore the temporal order in which feedback is received. Now, the feedback can be succinctly expressed in graphical form: At a given point of time, let $t(ij)$ denote the summary feedback (*trust*) that i reports about j, based on interactions between them thus far. We assume that the trust can be expressed as a nonnegative real value. Then, the input to the reputation system can be viewed as a "trust graph" $G = (V, E, t)$, where V is the set of agents, E the set of directed edges, and $t : E \rightarrow \Re^+ \setminus \{0\}$ the weights. (Note that typically the graph will be quite sparse, so for algorithmic considerations we explicitly include E.)

We assume that the reputations computed by our system are numeric values. Then, the reputation aggregation mechanism can be represented as a function from a trust graph to a set of reputation values, $F : G \rightarrow \Re^{|V|}$, where $F_v(G)$ is the reputation value of vertex $v \in V$. The reputation values determine an ordering or ranking of the nodes. A reputation function is trivial if the ranking induced by $F(G)$ is constant over all G; we restrict our attention to nontrivial reputation functions.

This model captures the many reputation systems that have been proposed or used in practice. One important example is PageRank, a mechanism used by Google to rank Web pages. In this case $v \in V$ is a Web page, $(v, w) \in E$ is a directed edge showing that Web page v has a hyperlink to page w and $t(v, w) = 1/Out(v)$, where $Out(v)$ is the outdegree of v. In a peer-to-peer system, $v \in V$ is a peer, $(v, w) \in E$ is a directed edge showing that peer v has interacted with w and $t(v, w)$ represents the degree of trust that v has in w, which can depend on the number, type, and outcomes of v's interactions with w.

There are numerous ways in which the reputations can be computed from the trust graph. We consider a simple version of PageRank, in which the ranking function is given by

$$F_v(G) = \epsilon + (1 - \epsilon) \sum_{v' | (v', v) \in E} F_{v'}(G) t(v', v).$$

Another interesting aggregation function, used in the Advogato system, is the max-flow algorithm, where $F_v(G)$ is the maximum flow from some start node $v_0 \in V$ to v. In the P2P setting it is natural to create personalized reputation functions where each node uses itself as the start node. In the web ranking setting one can simply choose one (or several) "trusted" nodes as the start nodes. Lastly, for comparison, we consider the Pathrank algorithm where $F_v(G)$ is the shortest path from some start node $v_0 \in V$ to v, where the length of an edge is simply the inverse of the trust value.

A reputation system is *monotonic* if adding an incoming edge to v never reduces the rank of v relative to any other node w, i.e., for $E' = E \cup \{uv\}$, $F_v(V, E) > F_w(V, E) \Rightarrow F_v(V, E') > F_w(V, E')$ and $F_v(V, E) \geq F_w(V, E) \Rightarrow F_v(V, E') \geq F_w(V, E')$. All the reputation schemes described above are monotonic. A reputation system is *symmetric* if the function F commutes with permutation of the node names, i.e., the reputations depend only on the graph structure, and not on the labels of the nodes. The simple variant of PageRank described above is symmetric, but the other reputation functions are not: the start node v_0 enjoys a privileged position.

27.5.1 Incentives for Honest Reporting

With the transitive trust model, the incentive problems are particularly acute. Entities are not rewarded or penalized directly for the quality of the ratings they provide, only for the ratings they receive from others. Thus, an entity has no incentive to provide informative feedback. Furthermore, depending on the reputation function F, she may have a strong incentive to provide *incorrect* feedback, so as to influence the credibility of other agents' feedback about herself.

Therefore, we would like a reputation function F in which an agent v cannot strategically choose feedback to boost her own standing. Define a reputation system as *rank-strategyproof* if, for every graph G and every agent $v \in V$, agent v cannot boost her rank ordering by strategic choices of how she rates other agents. This formulation allows an agent to manipulate its own or others' reputation scores as long as it is unable to improve its position in the rank ordering of reputation scores.

It turns out that rank-strategyproofness is very difficult to achieve in symmetric reputation systems: Any nontrivial, monotonic reputation system that is symmetric cannot be rank-strategyproof. For example, in the PageRank ranking system, a node v may be able to improve her rank by dropping an outgoing edge vu to a higher-ranked node u, thereby reducing u's reputation. We refer readers to the references at the end of this chapter for additional results in this vein. We note that this impossibility result does not apply to nonsymmetric reputation systems; the Pathrank function satisfies both the rank-strategyproofness and monotonicity properties.

27.5.2 Sybils and Sybilproofness

Next, we consider robustness to another attack on reputation systems: *sybil attacks*. In a sybil attack, a single agent creates many fake online identities to boost the reputation of its primary online identity. Formally, we assume that a node can create any number of sybil nodes, with any set of trust values between them. In addition, we allow the node to divide incoming trust edges among the sybils in any way that preserves the total trust, $\sum_{v'|(v',v)\in V} t(v', v)$, and manipulate the outgoing trust links in any manner it chooses. Note that many other formulations are possible depending on the specific system being modeled. Most of the results we discuss below hold in many of the other possible formulations.

Definition 27.2 Given a graph $G = (V, E, t)$ and a user $v \in V$, we say that a graph $G' = (V', E', t')$ along with a subset $U' \subseteq V'$ is a **sybil strategy** for user v in the network $G = (V, E, t)$ if $v \in U'$ and collapsing U' into a single node with label v in G' yields G. We can refer to U' as the sybils of v, and denote a sybil strategy by (G', U').

We define two different notions of sybilproofness for reputation functions.

Definition 27.3 A reputation function F is value-sybilproof if for all graphs $G = (V, E)$, and all users $v \in V$, there is no sybil strategy for v, (G', U'), with $G' = (V', E')$ such that for some $u \in U'$, $F_u(G') > F_v(G)$.

Definition 27.4 A reputation function F is rank-sybilproof if for all graphs $G = (V, E)$, and all users $v \in V$, there is no Sybil strategy (G', U') for v (with $G' = (V', E')$) such that, for some $u \in U'$ and $w \in V \setminus \{v\}$, $F_u(G') \geq F_w(G')$ while $F_v(G) < F_w(G)$.

Theorem 27.5 *There is no (nontrivial) symmetric rank-sybilproof reputation function.*

PROOF Given a graph $G = (V, E)$ and reputation function F, let $v, w \in V$ with $F_w(G) > F_v(G)$. Now consider the graph G', which is simply 2 disjoint copies of G, where U is the second copy of G combined with v. By symmetry, there is a node $u \in U$ such that $F_u(G') = F_w(G')$. Thus F is not rank-sybilproof. □

Note that this result does not require the assumption that F is monotonic. In fact, symmetric reputation functions cannot be sybilproof even for an attack with a single sybil.

Definition 27.6 We say that a reputation function is K**-rank-sybilproof** if it is rank-sybilproof for all possible sybil strategies (G', U'), with $|U'| \leq K + 1$.

Theorem 27.7 *There is no symmetric K-rank-sybilproof nontrivial reputation function for $K > 0$.*

PROOF Consider the graphs in the previous example, where $V = \{v = v_1, v_2, \ldots, v_r = w\}$ is the original vertex set and $U = \{u_1, u_2, \ldots, u_r\}$ is the duplicate; let $V' = V \cup U$. Define G^t to be the subgraph of G' with $V^t = V \cup \{u_1, \ldots, u_t\}$ and $G^0 = G$. Then $F_w(G^0) > F_v(G^0)$, while $F_{u_r}(G^r) = F_w(G^r)$ (where u_r is the copy of node $v_r = w$), so there must exist a

t such that $\max_{i \in \{v, u_1, \ldots, u_t\}} F_i(G^t) < F_w(G^t)$, but $\max_{i \in \{v, u_1, \ldots, u_{t+1}\}} F_i(G^{t+1}) \geq F_w(G^{t+1})$. Let m be the node in $\{v, u_1, \ldots, u_t\}$ that achieves the greatest reputation in G^{t+1}. Then either $F_m(G^{t+1}) \geq F_w(G^{t+1})$ or $F_{u_{t+1}}(G^{t+1}) \geq F_w(G^{t+1})$. It follows that the addition of node u_{t+1} is a successful sybil strategy for m in G^t. Hence, F is not 1-rank-sybilproof on all graphs. □

Now, consider PageRank. It is clearly symmetric—changing the labels on the nodes does not change the reputation values. This immediately implies that it is not rank-sybilproof.

One natural approach to overcoming this result is to break the symmetry of the reputation system by using a specific trusted node (or nodes) as a seed. However, care is still needed to achieve robustness against sybil attacks. Here, we consider two simple reputation functions that are provably sybil-resistant.

We first consider the max-flow based ranking mechanism. It is easy to show that it is value-sybilproof.

Theorem 27.8 *The max-flow based ranking mechanism is value-sybilproof.*

PROOF This follows directly from max-flow equals min-cut after noticing that all sybils of $v \in V$ must be on the same side of the cut as v and thus on the other side of the cut from the source s. Thus, no sybil can have a value higher than the min-cut which is equal to $F_v(G)$. □

However, the max-flow based ranking mechanism is not rank-sybilproof, as the example in Figure 27.2 shows. This is because while $v \in V$ cannot increase its own value, it can reduce the value of nodes for which it is on a max-flow path. Nonetheless, there do exist nontrivial rank-sybilproof algorithms. The Pathrank reputation mechanism is one example:

Theorem 27.9 *The Pathrank ranking mechanism is value-sybilproof and rank-sybilproof.*

PROOF It is value sybilproof since sybils cannot decrease the length of the shortest path. Rank-sybilproofness follows from the fact that the only time a node v can affect the value of another node w is if v is on the shortest path from s to w; however, in that case, we must have $F_v(G) > F_w(G)$. □

The basic property that flow-based mechanisms are value sybilproof but not rank-sybilproof can be generalized to include a wide variety generalized flow mechanisms,

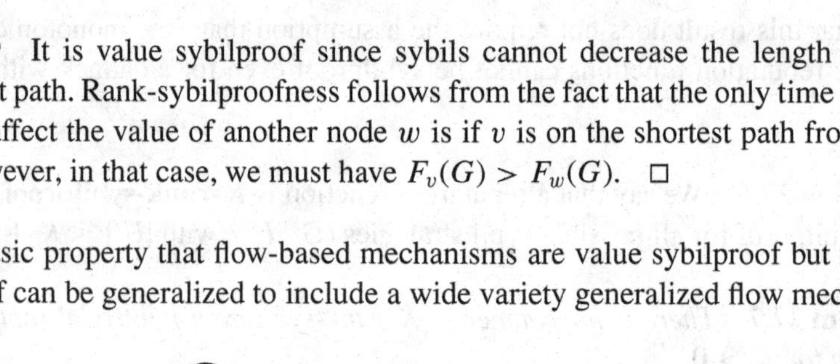

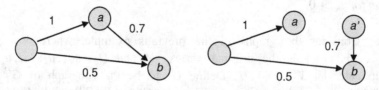

Figure 27.2. Node (a) improves its ranking by adding a sybil (a′) under max-flow.

such as those with "leaky pipes." Similarly, it can be shown that generalized path-based methods are value and rank-sybilproof and only path-based methods are rank-sybilproof in a large class of reputation mechanisms.

Lastly, we note that there are many open questions in this area. For example, while both PageRank and max-flow mechanisms are not rank sybilproof in the worst case, they are very useful reputation systems, and might be less manipulable on average. A precise formulation and analysis of this question is still open. For example, about half the pages on the Web could double their PageRank using only a single sybil.

27.6 Conclusion and Extensions

Reputations provide one of the most successful incentive mechanisms, and reputation systems are widespread on the Internet today. However, many.reputation systems find themselves constantly under attack, and have to resort to fixing strategic problems after they are detected. In particular, many reputation systems are engaged in a constant arms race against attackers, where the systems change their ranking procedure and the attackers experiment until they find a weakness.

We believe that theoretical results on what can and cannot be accomplished by reputation systems, as well as provably secure system designs, would very useful. In this chapter, we have described three components of this theory; several other directions have been explored, and much research remains to be done.

27.6.1 Extensions and Open Problems

Distributed reputation systems. Up to this point, we have considered that users may strategically manipulate the feedback they provide or the identities they use, but we have implicitly assumed that they cannot directly manipulate the way in which the feedback is aggregated or the content of other users' feedback. This is a reasonable assumption as long as the users do not have any control over the communication medium or the server(s) used to compute the reputations. However, many proposed applications of reputation systems are settings, such as peer-to-peer applications or wireless ad hoc networks, in which these assumptions might be violated: there is no neutral trusted party to compute reputations, and users might be able to intercept each other's messages.

This has led many researchers to study *distributed* reputation systems in which the reputations are computed by the users themselves, but measures are adopted to minimize the risk of manipulation. One fundamental technique is to use *replication*: The same computation is performed at multiple nodes, and there are protocols to detect inconsistencies in the results. Similarly, if the users control portions of the communication network, it may be possible to send messages along multiple redundant paths so that no user can block or modify communication between two other users.

Much work remains to be done in this area. In particular, the redundancy technique is vulnerable to collusive attacks; the main design approach is to make these attacks difficult by requiring that a large number of users collude. This may be compromised by the existence of pseudonyms and sybil attacks.

Dynamic attacks. The basic model we have studied assumes that a user has full knowledge of which online identity she is interacting with. In some applications, it may be possible for users to claim credit for an interaction that another user executed, or to freeride by copying another user's actions. For example, if the contribution being measured is the number of puzzles a user solves, or the quality of ratings she gives to online articles, she may be able to garner a high reputation simply by copying another user.

On the other hand, dynamics may restrict the range of attacks in some settings. For example, in a P2P system a peer cannot divide incoming links among its sybils arbitrarily, since one needs an interaction to obtain a link and a low ranked sybil might have difficulty finding (nonsybil) partners.

Metrics and benchmarks. Strategic analysis of reputation systems often takes the form of proving robustness against attacks. While robustness against attacks is certainly desirable, we should not lose sight of the performance of the reputation system. In the extreme, a system in which everybody has zero reputation would be perfectly secure but completely useless. We need to develop metrics (or empirical benchmarks) of how well a particular aggregation method serves the users' information needs. One approach which has been taken is to formulate the performance in terms of an economic welfare measure, but a more direct formulation may be valuable.

Drawing on other social sciences. We have concentrated on economic and game theoretic approaches to reputation. Reputation has also been studied in sociology and social psychology, especially in the form of the broader, but clearly related, notion of *trust*. Insights from this literature are valuable in the design of reputation systems.

Putting it all together. The major challenge in reputation systems is to design a system that coherently puts together all the ideas that have been explored, including accurate feedback elicitation, robustness to whitewashing and sybil attacks, and distributed computation. This remains the key challenge for the reader!

27.7 Bibliographic notes

Below we provide pointers to relevant literature. Our list is meant to provide access to the literature and is certainly not comprehensive, i.e., for each topic we give one or two representative publications from which the reader can iterate the reference finding process.

Several chapters in this book extend our discussion, both providing a more detailed introduction to game theory, and discussing some examples on reputation systems. In particular, Chapter 23 on incentives in peer-to-peer systems includes a detailed discussion on the use of reputation systems in peer-to-peer environments.

There is a large literature on economic models of reputation. The following classic articles provide some foundations: Kreps and Wilson (1982), Milgrom and Roberts (1982), Fudenberg and Levine (1989), and Kandori (1992). Tadelis (1999) considers trading reputations, and shows that it is not always undesirable. Dellarocas (2001) analyzes the economic efficiency of different feedback aggregation mechanisms. For broad overviews of this area, see Dellarocas (2003) and Resnick et al. (2000).

Our presentation of whitewashing follows Friedman and Resnick (2001). That paper includes a detailed proof that no equilibrium can yield substantially more cooperation than the Paying Your Dues equilibrium. Also see Lai et al. (2003), which introduced the term *whitewashing*.

Recently, the robustness of reputation systems to manipulation has attracted considerable research. The peer-prediction method to elicit honest feedback was originally described in an article by Miller et al. (2005). See Cooke (1991, p. 139) and Selten (1998) for a discussion of strictly proper scoring rules. Jurca and Faltings (2006) study modifications to the scoring rule to reduce the total expected payment. Bhattacharjee and Goel (2006) treat the revenues generated by a set of ratings as an objective indicator of the quality of the ratings. They provide an algorithm for dividing the revenues among raters in a way that creates incentives for entities to correct errors in the current community rating consensus.

Maintaining reputations for raters can provide signals about rater quality, in addition to incentives for good performance. Awerbuch and Kleinberg (2005) describe an algorithm that agents can use to learn who the good raters are. Their solution is robust to malicious as well as strategic attackers, provided that there are some altruistic raters who will rate accurately without incentives.

Many researchers have presented transitive-trust approaches to calculating reputations; a general framework using path algebras is described by Richardson et al. (2003). Altman and Tenneholtz (2006) study reputation systems from an axiomatic point of view, and present many possibility and impossibility results of the same flavor found in Section 27.5.1. Chien et al. (2003) prove that PageRank is monotonic. Our presentation of the sybilproofness of reputation systems follows Cheng and Friedman (2005). Many proposed solutions to the sybil attack implicitly or explicitly use the idea of a seed to break the symmetry of the reputations; for example, see Gyöngyi et al. (2004). The Advogato metric proposed by Levien (2004) also falls in this category. An alternative approach is described by Goel et al. (Zhang et al., 2004; Bhattacharjee and Goel, 2005).

Bibliography

A. Altman and M. Tennenholtz. Incentive compatible ranking systems, 2006. Available at: `http://www.technion.ac.il/ alon_a/0incentive.pdf`.

B. Awerbuch and R.D. Kleinberg. Competitive collaborative learning. In *18th Annual Conference on Learning Theory (COLT 2005)*, LNCS 3559:233–248. Springer, 2005.

R. Bhattacharjee and A. Goel. Avoiding ballot-stuffing in ebay-like reputation systems. In *P2PECON '05: Proc. 2005 ACM SIGCOMM Workshop on Economics of Peer-to-Peer Systems*, 2005.

R. Bhattacharjee and A. Goel. Incentive based ranking mechanisms. In *First Workshop on the Economics of Networked Systems (Netecon'06)*, pp. 62–68, 2006. Available at: `http://www.cs.duke.edu/nicl/netecon06/papers/proceedings.pdf`.

A. Cheng and E. Friedman. Sybilproof reputation mechanisms. In *P2PECON '05: Proc. 2005 ACM SIGCOMM Workshop on Economics of Peer-to-Peer Systems*, pp. 128–132, 2005.

S. Chien, C. Dwork, R. Kumar, D. Simon, and D. Sivakumar. Link evolution: Analysis and algorithms. *Internet Math.*, 1(3):277–304, 2003.

R. Cooke. *Experts in Uncertainty: Opinion and Subjective Probability in Science*. Oxford University Press, 1991.

C. Dellarocas. Analyzing the economic efficiency of ebay-like online reputation reporting mechanisms. In *Proc. 3rd ACM Conference on Electronic Commerce*, 2001.

C. Dellarocas. The digitization of word-of-mouth: Promise and challenges of online feedback mechanisms. *Management Sci.*, 49(10):1407–1424, 2003.

D. Fudenberg and D. Levine. Reputation and equilibrium selection in games with a patient player. *Econometrica*, 57:759–778, 1989.

Z. Gyöngyi, H. Garcia-Molina, and J. Pedersen. Combating web spam with trustrank. In *13th Intl. Conf. Very Large Data Bases*, pp. 576–587, 2004.

R. Jurca and B. Faltings. Minimum payments that reward honest feedback. In *Proc. 7th ACM Conference on Electronic Commerce*, pp. 190–199, 2006.

M. Kandori. Social norms and community enforcement. *Rev. Econ. Stud.*, 59(1):63–80, 1992.

D. Kreps and R. Wilson. Reputation and imperfect information. *J. Econ. Theory*, 27(2):253–279, 1982.

K. Lai, M. Feldman, J. Chuang, and I. Stoica. Incentives for cooperation in peer-to-peer systems. In *First Workshop on the Economics of Peer-to-Peer Systems*, 2003.

R. Levien. *Attack-Resistant Trust Metrics*. PhD Thesis, University of California, Berkeley, 2004.

P. Milgrom and J. Roberts. Predation, reputation and entry deterrence. *J. Econ. Theory*, 27(2):280–312, 1982.

N. Miller, P. Resnick, and R. Zeckhauser. Eliciting honest feedback: The peer-prediction method. *Management Sci.*, 51(9):1359–1373, 2005.

P. Resnick and E. Friedman. The social cost of cheap pseudonyms. *J. Econ. Management Strategy*, 10(2):173–199, 2001.

P. Resnick, R. Zeckhauser, E. Friedman, and K. Kuwabara. Reputation systems. *Commun. ACM*, 43(12):45–48, 2000.

M. Richardson, R. Agrawal, and P. Domingos. Trust management for the semantic Web. In *Second International Semantic Web Conference*, LNCS 2870: 351–368. Springer, 2003.

R. Selten. Axiomatic characterization of the quadratic scoring rule. *Exp. Econ.*, 1(1):43–62, 1998.

S. Tadelis. What's in a name? Reputation as a tradeable asset. *Amer. Econ. Rev.*, 89(3), 1999.

H. Zhang, A. Goel, R. Govindan, K. Mason, and B.V. Roy. Making eigenvector-based reputation systems robust to collusion. In *Workshop on Algorithms and Models for the Web Graph (WAW'04)*, 2004.

Exercises

For context, each problem is preceded by the number of the relevant section.

27.1 (27.2) Verify that if the stage game payoff is constant, the (discounted) average payoff per round equals that constant. That is, if $pi_i^t = c$ then $\overline{\pi_i} = c$.

27.2 (27.2) The well-known "tit-for-tat" (TFT) strategy can be defined as: in round i play the strategy that your opponent played in round $i - 1$, starting with C. Show that TFT, played by all players, is not an SPNE for any $\delta < 1$.

27.3 (27.2) Recall our definition of the Grim strategy: play C unless some player has played D in a previous round. Explain why it should not be defined in the apparently equivalent manner: "Play C unless the other player has played D in a previous round." (Hint: SPNE strategies need to optimal even on play paths that should not arise!)

27.4 (27.3) Verify that PYD is indeed an SPNE. In particular, show that deviating from the PYD strategy by playing D instead of C is not profitable when $\delta > 1/2$. (Hint: Argue that, no matter the reputation of the deviator's partner in the next round, she could get a payoff 2 higher if her own reputation is good than if it is bad.)

27.5 (27.3) Compute the equilibrium conditions for personalized-grim. (Hint: Consider each personalized game as a separate game where players only play in some randomly chosen periods.)

27.6 (27.4) Suppose that a rater i can see the ratings of a rater j ($j \neq r(i)$) *before* she submits her rating. Suppose that i was paid off according to the scoring rule $\mathcal{T}(x^{r(i)}|x^i)$ defined in equation 27.2. Construct an example in which honest rating is not always optimal for i.

27.7 (27.4) Consider a situation with two events h and l, in which a player is asked to report her belief $\hat{p}$ about the probability of h. The *quadratic scoring rule* is defined by $\mathcal{T}(h|\hat{p}) = a + 2b\hat{p} - b[\hat{p}^2 + (1-\hat{p})^2]$, $\mathcal{T}(l|\hat{p}) = a + 2b(1-\hat{p}) - b[\hat{p}^2 + (1-\hat{p})^2]$, where a and b are constant parameters. Show that the quadratic scoring rule is a proper scoring rule. Derive upper and lower bounds on the player's score (in terms of the parameters).

27.8 (27.5) Modify the assumptions in the sybilproofness argument for a specific setting and check which of the results are changed. (For example, assume that incoming trust edges cannot be moved, as would be the case for Web page ranking.)

27.9 (27.5) Compute the probability that a sybil changes the rank ordering of two nodes for a randomly generated trust graph for the ranking procedures discussed. (Choose any random model you like and either try to prove a general result or explicitly compute for a small, 3–5 node, graph.)

27.4 (a) Verify that (27.1) is [illegible]. Show that deviating from the [illegible] strategy by playing D instead of C is not profitable when [illegible]. (b) [illegible] intermediate [illegible] payment in the next round [illegible] could be [illegible] 2 higher if [illegible] than [illegible].

27.5 [illegible] the equilibrium [illegible] for [illegible] Consider [illegible] game where players [illegible] in some particularly [illegible].

27.6 (27.4) Suppose that a [illegible] the ratings [illegible] Suppose that [illegible] is paid [illegible] the scoring rule [illegible] in equation 27.[illegible] an example in which [illegible] is not always optimal [illegible].

27.7 (27.5) Consider a [illegible] with two [illegible] in which a player is asked [illegible] the probability of [illegible] the quadratic scoring rule is defined [illegible] where a and b are scaling parameters. Show that the [illegible] is a proper scoring rule. Derive upper and lower bounds on the player's score [illegible] the parameters.

27.8 (27.5) Modify the [illegible] in the [illegible] process [illegible] for a [illegible] and check which of the results are changed [illegible] example [illegible] that [illegible] cannot be [illegible] as would be the case [illegible].

27.9 (27.5) Compute the probability that a small change [illegible] of two [illegible] randomly [illegible] for the [illegible] procedures [illegible]. Choose [illegible] model [illegible] and either try to prove a general result or [illegible] computation [illegible].

CHAPTER 28

Sponsored Search Auctions

Sébastien Lahaie, David M. Pennock, Amin Saberi, and Rakesh V. Vohra

Abstract

One of the more visible means by which the Internet has disrupted traditional activity is the manner in which advertising is sold. Offline, the price for advertising is typically set by negotiation or posted price. Online, much advertising is sold via auction. Most prominently, Web search engines like Google and Yahoo! auction space next to search results, a practice known as *sponsored search*. This chapter describes the auctions used and how the theory developed in earlier chapters of this book can shed light on their properties. We close with a brief discussion of unresolved issues associated with the sale of advertising on the Internet.

28.1 Introduction

Web search engines like Google and Yahoo! monetize their service by auctioning off advertising space next to their standard algorithmic search results. For example, Apple or Best Buy may bid to appear among the advertisements – usually located above or to the right of the algorithmic results – whenever users search for "ipod." These sponsored results are displayed in a format similar to algorithmic results: as a list of items each containing a title, a text description, and a hyperlink to the advertiser's Web page. We call each position in the list a *slot*. Generally, advertisements that appear in a higher ranked slot (higher on the page) garner more attention and more clicks from users. Thus, all else being equal, merchants generally prefer higher ranked slots to lower ranked slots. Figure 28.1(a) shows an example layout of sponsored search results for the query "las vegas travel." Figure 28.1(b) shows the advertisers' bids in the corresponding auction.

Advertisers bid for placement on the page in an auction-style format where the larger their bid the more likely their listing will appear above other advertisements on the page. By convention, sponsored search advertisers generally pay *per click*, meaning that they pay only when a user clicks on their advertisement, and do not pay if their advertisement is displayed but not clicked. Overture Services, formerly GoTo.com and

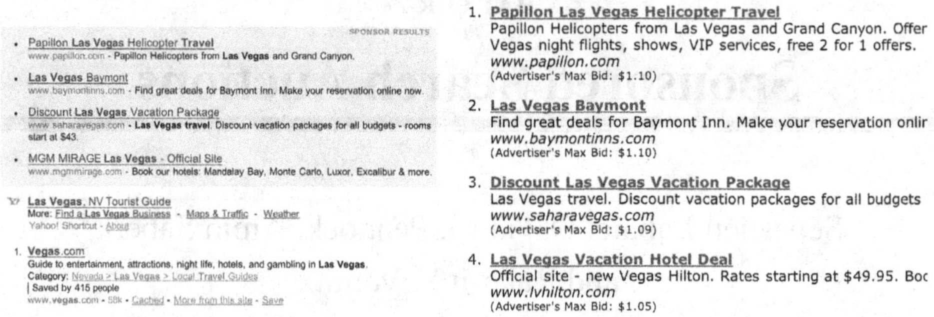
SPONSOR RESULTS
Papillon Las Vegas Helicopter Travel
www.papillon.com - Papillon Helicopters from Las Vegas and Grand Canyon.
Las Vegas Baymont
www.baymontinns.com - Find great deals for Baymont Inn. Make your reservation online now.
Discount Las Vegas Vacation Package
www.saharavegas.com - Las Vegas travel. Discount vacation packages for all budgets - rooms start at $43.
MGM MIRAGE Las Vegas - Official Site
www.mgmmirage.com - Book our hotels: Mandalay Bay, Monte Carlo, Luxor, Excalibur & more.
Las Vegas, NV Tourist Guide
More: Find a Las Vegas Business - Maps & Traffic - Weather
Yahoo! Shortcut - About
1. Vegas.com
Guide to entertainment, attractions, night life, hotels, and gambling in Las Vegas.
Category: Nevada > Las Vegas > Local Travel Guides
| Saved by 415 people
www.vegas.com - 58k - Cached - More from this site - Save
1. Papillon Las Vegas Helicopter Travel
Papillon Helicopters from Las Vegas and Grand Canyon. Offer
Vegas night flights, shows, VIP services, free 2 for 1 offers.
www.papillon.com
(Advertiser's Max Bid: $1.10)
2. Las Vegas Baymont
Find great deals for Baymont Inn. Make your reservation onlir
www.baymontinns.com
(Advertiser's Max Bid: $1.10)
3. Discount Las Vegas Vacation Package
Las Vegas travel. Discount vacation packages for all budgets
www.saharavegas.com
(Advertiser's Max Bid: $1.09)
4. Las Vegas Vacation Hotel Deal
Official site - new Vegas Hilton. Rates starting at $49.95. Boc
www.lvhilton.com
(Advertiser's Max Bid: $1.05)

(a) Search results (b) Advertisers' bids

Figure 28.1. (a) An example display of sponsored search listings above the regular algorithmic listings for the query "las vegas travel." The ordering of sponsored listings is determined via a continuous auction mechanism. (b) The top advertisers' bids (maximum willingness to pay per click) in the auction.

now owned by Yahoo! Inc., is credited with pioneering sponsored search advertising. Overture's success prompted a number of companies to adopt similar business models, most prominently Google, the leading Web search engine today. Sponsored search is one of the fastest growing, most effective, and most profitable forms of advertising, generating roughly $7 billion in revenue in 2005 after nearly doubling every year for the previous 5 years.

The sponsored search industry typically runs separate auctions for each search query: for example, the queries "plasma television" and "investment advice" are associated with two distinct auctions. The entity being sold in each auction is the right to appear alongside the results of that search query. As mentioned, bids are expressed as a maximum willingness to pay per click. For example, a 40-cent bid by HostRocket for "Web hosting" means HostRocket is willing to pay up to 40 cents every time a user clicks on their advertisement. Advertisers may also set daily or monthly budget caps. In practice, hundreds of thousands of advertisers compete for positions alongside several millions of search queries every day. Generally the auctions are continuous and dynamic, meaning that advertisers can change their bids at any time, and a new auction clears every time a user enters a search query. In this way advertisers can adapt to changing environments, for instance by boosting their bids for the query "buy flowers" during the week before Valentine's Day. The search engine evaluates the bids and allocates slots to advertisers. Notice that, although bids are expressed as payments per click, the search engine cannot directly allocate clicks, but rather allocates *impressions*, or placements on the screen. Clicks relate only stochastically to impressions.

Advertising in traditional media is typically sold on a per-impression basis, or according to the (estimated) number of people exposed to the advertisement, in part because of the difficulty of measuring and charging based on the actual effectiveness of the advertisement. Traditional (offline) advertising, and to a large extent banner advertising on the Web, is usually priced via an informal process of estimation and negotiation. The Web's capability for two-way communication makes it easy to track some measures of effectiveness, in particular user clicks. Many advertisers, especially direct marketers looking to close a sale as opposed to brand advertisers, prefer to pay per click rather than per impression, alleviating some of the uncertainty inherent in an impression. More direct performance-based pricing is possible by charging per "action" or per conversion (sale) on the merchant's site.

Search engines are an information gateway to many search and decision-making tasks. Industry surveys report that more than 50% of Web users visit a search engine every day, Americans conduct roughly 6 billion Web searches per month, over 13% of traffic to commercial sites is generated by search engines, and over 40% of product searches on the Web are initiated via search engines. As a result, entire niche industries exist touting services to boost a Web page's ranking on the popular search engines, in part by reverse engineering the search engines' information retrieval algorithms. Research has shown that good placement on a search page leads to high traffic, and eventually an increased financial payoff. Paying for sponsored slots is an alternative means of obtaining prominent positioning. Sponsored search works because users often tolerate or even welcome targeted advertisements directly related to what they are actively searching for. For example, Majestic Research reports that as many as 17% of Google searches result in a paid click, and that Google earns roughly nine cents on average for every search query they process. Today, Internet giants Google and Yahoo! boast a combined market capitalization of over $150 billion, largely on the strength of sponsored search. PricewaterhouseCoopers and the Interactive Advertising Bureau estimate that in 2005, industry-wide sponsored search revenue in the United States reached $5.1 billion, or 41% of total U.S. Internet advertising revenues and 2% of all U.S. advertising revenues. Roughly 85% of Google's $4.1 billion in 2005 revenue and roughly 45% of Yahoo!'s $3.7 billion in 2005 revenue is likely attributable to sponsored search. A number of other companies – including eBay (Shopping.com), FindWhat, InterActiveCorp (Ask.com), LookSmart, and Microsoft (MSN.com) – earn hundreds of millions of dollars in sponsored search revenue annually.

The goal of this chapter is to formally model and analyze various mechanisms used in this domain and to study potential improvements. In Section 28.2, we briefly describe existing mechanisms used to allocate and price sponsored search advertisements. Subsequently in Sections 28.3 and 28.4 we discuss formal models used to analyze the properties of these auctions. Section 28.5 discusses further extensions and open problems.

28.2 Existing Models and Mechanisms

Typically, in sponsored search mechanisms, the advertisers specify a list of pairs of keywords and bids as well as a total maximum daily or weekly budget. Then, every time a user searches for a keyword, an auction takes place among the set of interested advertisers who have not exhausted their budgets.

Focusing on a single auction, let n be the number of bidders and $m < n$ the number of slots. The search engine estimates α_{ij}, the probability that a user will click on the ith slot when it is occupied by bidder j. The quantity α_{ij} is called a *click through rate* (CTR). It is usually presumed for all j that $\alpha_{ij} \geq \alpha_{i+1,j}$ for $i = 1, \ldots, m-1$.[1]

[1] The assumption that clickthrough rate decays monotonically with lower slots is a distinguishing feature of keyword auctions; in particular, it implies that all bidders prefer the first slot to the second, the second slot to the third, etc. This allows for more refined equilibrium analyses than in the more general multi-item case.

The search engine also assigns a weight w_j to each advertiser j. The weight can be thought of as a relevance or quality metric. If agent j bids b_j, his corresponding *score* is $s_j = w_j b_j$. The search engine allocates slots in decreasing order of scores, so that the agent with highest score is ranked first, and so on. We assume throughout that agents are numbered so that agent j obtains slot j. An agent pays per click the lowest bid necessary to retain his position, so that the agent in slot j pays s_{j+1}/w_j. This weighted bid ranking mechanism includes the two most prominent keyword auction designs that have been used in practice: Overture introduced a "rank by bid" mechanism ($w_j = 1$) whereas Google uses a "rank by revenue" mechanism ($w_j = \alpha_{1j}$). Both variants are sometimes called *generalized second price* (GSP) auctions. Prior to 2004, Yahoo! used what is now known as a *generalized first price* (GFP) auction. Agents are ranked by bid but each bidder who secures a slot pays their bid per click.

28.3 A Static Model

The most popular model used to analyze keyword auctions is a static one where the private information of bidder j, the expected payoff from a click, v_j, is one dimensional. The expected payoff to a bidder from not obtaining a slot is assumed to be 0.

Four features of the model deserve comment. The first is its static nature: a substantial departure from reality. Since the study of recurrent auctions is rather daunting, one may be disposed to accept this simplification. Second, the expected payoff per click to a bidder is slot independent. This is tied to the assumption that all bidders prefer the top slot to the second slot to the third slot and so on. Some advertisers believe that the probability of a click being converted into a purchase is lower in the top slot than in the second slot because many clicks on the top slot are made in error, or because a searcher who clicks on a lower-ranked slot is more serious in their intent to purchase. Although the story sounds plausible, conversion-tracking data from Isobar Communications and other sources does not substantiate the hypothesis: in reality the top slot appears to convert about as well as other slots. Third, a bidder's value and CTR for a slot does not depend on the identity of other bidders. It seems plausible that Avis might value the fact that Hertz is not present in any slot when Avis is present. Fourth, CTRs are assumed to be common knowledge. In practice CTRs are estimated by the search engine and can be conditioned on many factors, including user characteristics and page context. Estimating CTRs is a significantly complex machine learning problem for the search engine, including a built-in explore/exploit trade-off. Moreover, bidders' estimates of CTRs may be less accurate since bidders do not have access to the same contextual information available to the search engine. The dynamic nature of the environment means that CTRs can fluctuate dramatically over small periods.

As usual we assume that bidders are risk neutral and that their utility for a slot can be denominated on a common monetary scale. Supplied with copious amounts of salt, let us see where this model takes us.

28.3.1 Revenue Maximization and Efficiency

An auctioneer usually has one of two objectives: revenue maximization or allocative efficiency. In the static model one knows exactly what auction design will achieve either objective.

If the goal is revenue maximization, the classic result of Myerson (described in Chapter 13) applies directly. One simply relabels the allocation variables. In Chapter 13 Section 13.1.12, the allocation variable, $x_j(b)$, is defined to be the expected quantity received by bidder i who bids b. For our setting, $x_j(b)$ becomes the expected click through rate for a bidder who bids b. Basically the generalized Vickrey auction is applied not to the actual values, v_j, but to the corresponding virtual values. The upshot is that the revenue maximizing auction is a generalized Vickrey auction with reserve prices.

If the goal is allocative efficiency, the generalized Vickrey auction will do the trick. The auction is described in Chapters 9 and 11 of this book. The underlying problem of finding the efficient allocation in this case is an instance of the maximum weight assignment problem. For each slot i and bidder j let $x_{ij} = 1$ if bidder j is assigned to slot i and zero otherwise. The object is to choose x_{ij}'s to solve the following:

$$\max \quad \sum_{i=1}^{k}\sum_{j=1}^{n} \alpha_{ij} v_j x_{ij} \tag{28.1}$$

$$\text{s.t.} \quad \sum_{j=1}^{n} x_{ij} \leq 1 \quad \forall i = 1, \ldots, k \tag{28.2}$$

$$\sum_{i=1}^{k} x_{ij} \leq 1 \quad \forall j = 1, \ldots, n \tag{28.3}$$

$$x_{ij} \geq 0 \quad \forall i = 1, \ldots, k, \ \forall j = 1, \ldots, n \tag{28.4}$$

This is equivalent to finding a maximum-weight perfect matching in a bipartite graph and hence can be solved in polynomial time. In fact, because the constraint matrix of this linear program is totally unimodular, it will have an optimal solution that is integral. Any feasible integer solution is called an assignment.

A single computation of the maximum weight assignment is sufficient to determine both the allocation and the generalized Vickrey payments. This is because the Vickrey payments lie in the dual to the above linear program. To write down the dual, let p_i be the dual variable associated with (28.2) and q_j the dual associated with (28.3).

$$\min \quad \sum_{i=1}^{k} p_i + \sum_{j=1}^{n} q_j \tag{28.5}$$

$$\text{s.t.} \quad p_i + q_j \geq \alpha_{ij} v_j \quad \forall i = 1, \ldots, k, \quad \forall j = 1, \ldots, n \tag{28.6}$$

$$p_i, q_j \geq 0 \quad \forall i = 1, \ldots, k, \quad \forall j = 1, \ldots, n \tag{28.7}$$

Here p_i can be interpreted as the expected payment (CTR times price per click) of the bidder obtaining slot i, and q_j as the profit of bidder j. The objective in this program is to minimize the bidders' and auctioneer's profits combined. Among all optimal dual solutions, pick the one that minimizes $\sum_{i=1}^{k} p_i$. The corresponding p_i is the price that the generalized Vickrey auction would set for slot i.

In the special case when the CTRs are bidder independent (i.e., $\alpha_{ij} = \mu_i$) there is a particularly simple algorithm, called the Northwest corner rule, to find the maximum weight assignment. Assign the bidder with the highest value per click to the top slot, the bidder with the second highest value per click to the second slot, and so on. In the Economics literature this is called an *assortative* assignment.

If one objects to the sealed bid nature of the generalized Vickrey auction there are ascending implementations available.

Interestingly, neither of these auctions corresponds to the GFP or GSP auctions. In particular, bidding truthfully is not an equilibrium of either the GFP or GSP auctions. It is interesting to observe that Google's promotional material touts their auction as a modification of Vickrey's sealed bid auction for a single item (which it is) and concluding, therefore, that bidding sincerely is the correct thing to do (which it is not). A similar claim was made with respect to their auction used to sell shares of their IPO. They are not the first and quite possibly not the last to make such claims. For example, the financial services firm Hambrecht, which pioneered the use of auctions to sell IPO's in 1998, says that their auction design is based on the Vickrey auction for a single good. While the Hambrecht auction does specialize to the Vickrey auction for a single good, it does not inherit the attractive properties of the Vickrey auction when applied to multiple units.[2]

To see why one must be careful when generalizing the Vickrey auction to the sale of more than one unit, suppose that there are three bidders with $v_1 > v_2 > v_3$ and two slots. Also, suppose that $\alpha_{ij} = \mu_i$ with $\mu_1 > \mu_2$. If one were to auction off the top slot only, by an English ascending auction, each bidder would remain in as long as at the current price their surplus is nonnegative. So, if the current price on the top slot is p_1, bidder j remains active if $\mu_1(v_j - p_1) \geq 0$. Hence the auction ends at a price p_1 where $\mu_1(v_2 - p_1) = 0$, i.e., $p_1 = v_2$. Now suppose that both slots are available but we will auction off the top slot first followed by the second slot. Let p_1 be the current price of slot 1, $p_2 = 0$ the current price of slot 2. Now bidder j will remain active in the auction for the top slot provided their surplus from the top slot is at least as large the surplus they could get from the second slot (which is currently priced at zero). That is,

$$\mu_1(v_j - p_1) \geq \mu_2(v_j - 0) \Rightarrow p_1 \leq \left(1 - \frac{\mu_2}{\mu_1}\right) v_j.$$

Therefore the auction on the top slot terminates at a price of $(1 - \frac{\mu_2}{\mu_1})v_2 < v_2$. The point is that the presence of a second slot lowers the price at which a bidder on the top slot will drop out of the auction on the top slot. The generalized Vickrey auction incorporates this change in the outside option of a bidder to ensure truthful bidding. The GSP auction does not. The generalized Vickrey auction, however, would allocate the top slot to bidder 1 and charge her $(1 - \frac{\mu_2}{\mu_1})v_2$ and the second slot to bidder 2 and charge her v_3.

As noted above, the GFP and GSP are special cases of what have been called ranking auctions. Bids (the reported v_j's) are weighted (weights are independent of the bids) and then ranked in the descending order. The highest ranked bidder gets the top slot,

[2] All of this reminds one of what is known as the freshman binomial theorem: $(a + b)^n = a^n + b^n$. True for $n = 1$ but not for $n > 2$.

the second highest ranked bidder gets the second slot, and so on. The higher the bid the higher the slot one obtains (other bids held fixed). Since the assignment of bidders to slots is monotonic in the bid (other bids held fixed) it follows from standard results (see Section 9.36 of Chapter 9 for example) that there exists a payment rule that will make truthful bidding an equilibrium of the resulting auction. That payment rule is described, for example, in Section 13.1.2 of Chapter 13. Let $x_j(b|b_{-j})$ denote the expected click through rate for agent j when she bids b, given the profile of other bids is b_{-j}. Then the payment $P_j(b|b_{-j})$ she must make to ensure incentive compatibility is given by

$$P_j(b \mid b_{-j}) = bx(b \mid b_{-j}) - \int_0^b x(t \mid b_{-j})\,dt. \tag{28.8}$$

These ranking auctions are, in general, neither efficient nor revenue maximizing. (Though in the exercises, we explore a special case ranking that is efficient.) The payment rules associated with the GFP and GSP are not such as to induce truthful bidding as an equilibrium.

28.3.2 Equilibrium Properties

The fact that neither the GFP nor GSP is incentive compatible does not imply that they are inefficient or suboptimal in terms of revenue. It is possible that the equilibrium outcomes of both these auctions may be efficient or revenue maximizing. To identify the revenue and efficiency properties of these auctions, it is necessary to determine their equilibria.

The GFP auction does not admit a pure strategy full-information equilibrium but does admit a pure strategy Bayes-Nash symmetric equilibrium. The argument is identical to that of the sealed bid first price auction for a single good. The equilibrium bid functions are monotonic in the value. Therefore the equilibrium allocation of bidders to slots is the same as in the efficient allocation. Hence, by the revenue equivalence theorem, the symmetric equilibrium is efficient.

The efficiency of the GFP (in a Bayesian setting) lends it some appeal but this is where the "static" assumption has bite. In a dynamic setting, the absence of a pure strategy full-information equilibrium encourages bidders to constantly adjust their bids from one period to the next. This produces fluctuations in the bids over time and it has been argued that these fluctuations resulted in significant inefficiencies.

To date nothing is known about the Bayesian equilibrium of the GSP auction. Assume for simplicity that CTRs are bidder-independent, so $\alpha_{ij} = \mu_i$, and that all weights are set to 1. The analysis in this section generalizes straightforwardly to the case where CTRs are separable (i.e., $\alpha_{ij} = \mu_i \beta_j$) and agents are assigned arbitrary weights w_j. These extensions are developed in the exercises.

In this case one can show that the GSP is efficient under full information and a restricted notion of equilibrium called **locally envy-free**. An assignment x is called locally envy-free if there exist prices, $\{p_i\}$, one for each slot, such that for all i, j with $x_{ij} = 1$

$$\mu_i v_j - p_i \geq \mu_{i-1} v_j - p_{i-1} \tag{28.9}$$

and

$$\mu_i v_j - p_i \geq \mu_{i+1} v_j - p_{i+1} \tag{28.10}$$

In words, if bidder j is assigned to slot i, then she prefers slot i to the slot just above her and the slot just below her.

Theorem 28.1 *An assignment x^* is optimal if and only if it is locally envy-free.*

PROOF Suppose first that x^* is locally envy-free and let p^* be the corresponding price vector. It suffices to prove that the assignment x^* is assortative. Let j be such that $x^*_{ij} = 1$ and j' such that $x_{i+1,j'} = 1$. To show that the assignment is assortative, we must show that $v_j \geq v_{j'}$. From the property of being locally envy-free, we have

$$\mu_i v_j - p^*_i \geq \mu_{i+1} v_j - p^*_{i+1}$$

and

$$\mu_{i+1} v_{j'} - p^*_{i+1} \geq \mu_i v_{j'} - p^*_i.$$

Adding them together yields

$$(\mu_i - \mu_{i+1})(v_j - v_{j'}) \geq 0.$$

Since $\mu_i > \mu_{i+1}$ it follows from this inequality that $v_j \geq v_{j'}$.

Now let x^* be an optimal assignment. Let (p^*, q^*) denote an optimal dual solution. It suffices to show that (x^*, p^*) is locally envy-free. Consider a pair (r, j) such that $x^*_{rj} = 1$. Complementary slackness and dual feasibility implies that $\mu_r v_j - p^*_r = q^*_j = \max_i\{\mu_i v_j - p^*_i\}$. Therefore

$$\mu_r v_j - p^*_r \geq \max\{\mu_{r-1} v_j - p^*_{r-1}, \mu_{r+1} v_j - p^*_{r+1}\}.$$

□

Theorem 28.2 *The GSP has a full information equilibrium that yields an allocation that is locally envy-free.*

PROOF Order the bidders so that $v_1 \geq v_2 \geq \ldots \geq v_n$. Let p^*_i be the Vickrey price of slot i. Let bidder 1 bid $b_1 = v_1$ and each bidder $j \geq 2$ bids $b_j = \frac{p^*_{j-1}}{\mu_{j-1}}$. First we show that under the rules of the GSP, bidder 1 is assigned to slot 1, bidder 2 to slot 2, and so on. To do this it suffices to show that $b_{j-1} \geq b_j$. Since the optimal assignment is locally envy-free we have

$$\mu_j v_j - p^*_j \geq \mu_{j-1} v_j - p^*_{j-1}.$$

Therefore

$$\mu_j[v_j - (p_j)/(\mu_j))] \geq \mu_{j-1}[v_j - (p_{j-1})/(\mu_{j-1})] \geq \mu_j[v_j - (p_{j-1})/(\mu_{j-1})]$$

$$\Rightarrow [v_j - (p_j)/(\mu_j))] \geq [v_j - (p_{j-1})/(\mu_{j-1})] \Rightarrow (p_{j-1})/(\mu_{j-1}) \geq (p_j)/(\mu_j)).$$

Which implies $b_{j-1} \geq b_j$.

Hence if each bidder j bids b_j the GSP returns the optimal assignment. It is also easy to see that bidder $j \leq m$ pays p^*_j for their slot. Bidder $j > m$ pays zero.

Since each bidder pays their Vickrey price and receives the slot they would have under the efficient allocation, no bidder has a unilateral incentive to change their bid. Therefore we have an equilibrium that, from Theorem 28.1, is envy-free. □

Absent the recurrent nature of keyword auctions, they are similar to what are known as condominium auctions. In a condominium auction, bidders are interested in purchasing a condominium in a building. The condominiums are identical except for their height above the ground, the side of the building they are located on, etc. If all bidders have identical preferences over the condominiums; i.e., everyone prefers to be on a higher floor, they coincide with keyword auctions.

28.4 Dynamic Aspects

Since these auctions are repeated with great frequency, one should properly model them as repeated games of incomplete information. The set of equilibria of such games is quite rich and complicated, even when restricted to the setting considered here. A full treatment of this case will not be given here. Rather we mention two phenomena that arise in this setting.

One is known as bid rotation. This occurs when competing bidders take turns at winning the auction. In our context this might mean bidders take turns at occupying the top slot. If bidders are short lived, this is unlikely to be a problem, if not, this will lower the auctioneers revenue.

Another possibility that repetition makes possible is vindictive bidding. In the GSP auction one's bid determines the payment of the bidder in the slot above and not one's own. Therefore one can increase the payment of the bidder in the slot above by raising one's bid without affecting one's own payment. This may be beneficial if the bidder in the slot above is a competitor with a limited budget for advertising. In a dynamic environment this encourages a bidder to constantly adjust their bids so as to inflict or avoid damage upon or from their competitor.

Even if one could ignore strategic considerations, a problem remains. The online nature of the auctions in sponsored search complicates the computation of an efficient allocation. Below we describe one model that addresses this difficulty.

28.4.1 The Online Allocation Problem

In this model, the search engine receives the bids of advertisers and their maximum budget for a certain period (e.g., a day). As users search for these keywords during the day, the search engine assigns their advertisement space to advertisers and charges them the value of their bid for the impression of the advertisement.[3] For simplicity of notation we assume that each page has only one slot for advertisements. The objective is to maximize total revenue while respecting the budget constraint of the bidders. Note that in this model bidders pay their bid which is counter to practice. On the other hand, budget constraints that apply across a set of keywords, a real-world feature, are part of the model.

[3] If one scales the bids by the CTR, the model would accommodate pay per click.

Let n be the number of advertisers and m the number of keywords. Suppose that advertiser j has a bid of b_{ij} for keyword i and a total budget of B_j. In this context, it is reasonable to assume that bids are small compared to budgets, i.e., $b_{ij} \ll B_j$.

If the search engine has an accurate estimate of r_i, the number of people searching for keyword i for all $1 \le i \le m$, then it is easy to approximate the optimal allocation using a simple linear program. Let x_{ij} be the total number of queries on keyword i allocated to bidder j. The linear program is

$$
\begin{aligned}
\max \quad & \sum_{i=1}^{m}\sum_{j=1}^{n} b_{ij}x_{ij} & \\
\text{s.t.} \quad & \sum_{j=1}^{n} x_{ij} \le r_i & \forall 1 \le i \le m \\
& \sum_{i=1}^{m} b_{ij}x_{ij} \le B_j & \forall 1 \le j \le n \\
& x_{ij} \ge 0 & \forall 1 \le i \le m, \quad \forall 1 \le j \le n
\end{aligned}
\tag{28.11}
$$

$$
\begin{aligned}
\min \quad & \sum_{j=1}^{n} B_j\beta_j + \sum_{i=1}^{m} r_i\alpha_i & \\
\text{s.t.} \quad & \alpha_i + b_{ij}\beta_j \ge b_{ij} & \forall 1 \le i \le m, \forall 1 \le j \le n \\
& \beta_j \ge 0 & \forall 1 \le j \le n \\
& \alpha_i \ge 0 & \forall 1 \le i \le m
\end{aligned}
$$

By complementary slackness, in an optimal solution, advertiser j is assigned to keyword i if $(1-\beta_j)b_{ij} = \max_{1\le k\le n}(1-\beta_k)b_{ik}$. Using this property, the search engine can use the solution of the dual linear program to find the optimum allocation: every time a user searches for keyword i, the search engine allocates its corresponding advertisement space to the bidder j with the highest $b_{ij}(1-\beta_j)$. In other words, the bid of advertiser j will be scaled down by $1-\beta_j$.

Now β_j represents rate of change of the optimal objective function value of (28.11) for a sufficiently small change in the right-hand side of the corresponding constraint. In other words, if advertiser j's budget were to increase by Δ, the optimal objective function value would increase by $\beta_j\Delta$. Equivalently, it is the opportunity cost of consuming agent j's budget. Hence, if we allocate keyword i to agent now we obtain an immediate 'payoff' of b_{ij}. However, this consumes b_{ij} of the budget, which imposes an opportunity cost of $\beta_j b_{ij}$. Therefore, it makes sense in the optimal solution to (28.11) to assign keyword i to j provided $b_{ij} - \beta_j b_{ij} > 0$.

In practice, a good estimate of the frequencies of all search queries is unavailable. Queries arrive sequentially and the search engine must instantly decide to allocate their advertisement space to bidders without knowledge of the future queries. Therefore, what is needed is a dynamic procedure for allocating bidders to keywords that are queried. We describe one such procedure and analyze its performance within the usual competitive ratio framework. Specifically, we compare the revenue achieved by a dynamic procedure that does not know the r_i's in advance, with the revenue that could be achieved knowing the r_i's advance. The revenue in this second case is given by the optimal objective function value of the program (28.11).

The obvious dynamic procedure to consider is a greedy one: among the bidders whose budgets are not exhausted, allocate the query to the one with the highest bid. It is easy to see that this approach is equivalent to setting all β_j's to 0.

The greedy procedure is not guaranteed to find the optimum solution. It is easy to construct a simple example with two bidders and two keywords in which the revenue of the greedy algorithm is as small as half of the optimum revenue. For example, suppose two bidders each with a budget of \$2. Assume that $b_{11} = 2$, $b_{12} = 2 - \epsilon$, $b_{21} = 2$, and $b_{22} = \epsilon$. If query 1 arrives before query 2, it will be assigned to bidder 1. Then bidder 1's budget is exhausted. When query 2 arrives, it is assigned to bidder 2. This produces an objective function value of $2 + \epsilon$. The optimal solution would assign query 2 to bidder 1 and query 1 to bidder 2, yielding an objective function value of 4. The problem with the greedy algorithm is that, unlike the solution to (28.11), it ignores the opportunity cost of assigning a query to a bidder.

One can prove that the revenue of greedy algorithm is at least half of the optimum revenue for any instance. In the standard terminology of online algorithms, the competitive ratio of greedy algorithm is $1/2$. Can one do better in terms of competitive ratio? Yes. One does so by trying to dynamically estimate the opportunity cost , i.e., the β_j's, of assigning a query to a bidder. This has the effect of spreading the bidders expenditures over time. The effect is called "budget smoothing," and is a feature that some search engines offer their advertisers.

The following modification of the greedy algorithm adaptively updates the β_j's as a function of the bidders spent budget. Let

$$\phi(x) = 1 - e^{x-1}.$$

The algorithm sets $\beta_j = 1 - \phi(f_j)$, where f_j is the fraction of the budget of bidder j, which has been spent.

Algorithm 1. Every time a query i arrives, allocate its advertisement space to the bidder j, who maximizes $b_{ij}\phi(f_j)$, where f_j is the fraction of the bidder j's budget which has been spent so far.

The revenue of this algorithm is at least $1 - 1/e$ of the optimum revenue. It is also possible to prove that no deterministic or randomized algorithm can achieve a better competitive ratio.

Theorem 28.3 *The competitive ratio of Algorithm 1 is* $1 - 1/e$.

We outline the main ideas in the proof of the theorem. Let k be a sufficiently large number used for discretizing the budgets of the bidders. We say that an advertiser is of type j if she has spent within $(\frac{j-1}{k}, \frac{j}{k}]$ fraction of her budget so far. Let s_j be the total budget of type j bidders. For $i = 0, 1, \ldots, k$, define w_i to be the amount of money spent by all the bidders from the interval $(\frac{i-1}{k}, \frac{i}{k}]$ of their budgets.Also define the discrete version of function ϕ,

$$\Phi(s) = 1 - \left(1 - \frac{1}{k}\right)^{k-s}. \tag{28.12}$$

It is easy to see that when k tends to infinity $\Phi(s) \to \phi(\frac{s}{k})$. Let OPT be the solution of the optimal off-line algorithm (i.e., the solution of the optimization program (28.11)). For simplicity, assume that the optimal algorithm spends all of the budget of the bidders. We have the following lemma.

Lemma 28.4 *At the end of the algorithm, this inequality holds:*

$$\sum_{i=0}^{k} \Phi(i)s_i \leq \sum_{i=0}^{k} .\Phi(i)w_i \tag{28.13}$$

PROOF Consider the time that query q arrives. Suppose that OPT allocates q to a bidder of current type t, whose type at the end of the algorithm will be t'. Let b_{opt} and b_{alg} be the amount of money that OPT and the algorithm get from bidders for q. Let i be the type of the bidder that the algorithm allocates the query. We have

$$\Phi(t')b_{\text{opt}} \leq \Phi(t)b_{\text{opt}} \leq \Phi(i)b_{\text{alg}}. \tag{28.14}$$

Now summing the inequality above over all the queries, the left-hand side of (28.14) contributes to the sum $\sum_i \Phi(i)s_i$, and the right-hand side contributes to $\sum \Phi(i)w_i$. So the lemma follows. □

Now, we are ready to prove the Theorem 28.3.

PROOF By definition $w_i \leq \frac{1}{k}\sum_{j=i}^{k} s_j$. Using Lemma 28.4,

$$\sum_{i=0}^{k} \Phi(i)s_i \leq \frac{1}{k}\sum_{i=0}^{k} \Phi(i)\sum_{j=i}^{k} s_j.$$

Changing the order of the sums and computing the sum of the geometric series, we have

$$\begin{aligned}
\sum_{i=0}^{k} \Phi(i)s_i &\leq \frac{1}{k}\sum_{i=0}^{k} \Phi(i)\sum_{j=i}^{k} s_j \\
&\leq \frac{1}{k}\sum_{i=0}^{k}\left(\sum_{j=0}^{i} \Phi(i)\right)s_i \\
&\leq \sum_{i=0}^{k}\left(\frac{i}{k} + \Phi(i) - \Phi(0) + O\left(\frac{1}{k}\right)\right)s_i \\
&\leq \sum_{i=0}^{k}\frac{i}{k}s_i - \left(\Phi(0) - O\left(\frac{1}{k}\right)\right)\sum_{i=0}^{k} s_i + \sum_{i=0}^{k}\Phi(i)s_i,
\end{aligned}$$

which yields

$$\left(\Phi(0) - O\left(\frac{1}{k}\right)\right)\sum_{i=0}^{k} s_i \leq \sum_{i=0}^{k} \frac{i}{k} s_i.$$

Note that as k goes to infinity the left-hand side tends to $(1 - \frac{1}{e})OPT$. The right-hand side is equal to the revenue of the algorithm. So the theorem follows. □

The same algorithm can be applied when multiple advertisement can appear with the result of a query or when advertisers enter at different times. At present, the equilibrium properties of this allocation rule are unknown.

28.5 Open Questions

We close this chapter with a brief review of important issues not directly addressed in this chapter.

While our discussion has focused on existing mechanisms, one should not conclude that there is no room for improvement in their design. For example, there is debate over the role of the budget constraints in these auction. In many cases they do not appear to be hard constraints as bidders frequently adjust them. A bidder can also "expand" their budget simply by lowering their bid and paying less per click. Some argue that the budget constraint is merely a convenient way to express other desires. For example, limiting one's exposure or spreading one's advertising over a longer period. All of this suggests the need for richer bidding models. Ones that might allow bidders to express decreasing marginal value for clicks, or distinct values for traffic from certain geographic regions, demographic profiles, etc., support greater allocative efficiency, though pose a significant burden in terms of computational and elicitation costs.

When advertiser payments are based on user clicks, search engines must invest in the task of detecting and ignoring robot clicks, spam clicks as well as clicks from an advertiser trying to impose costs on their competitor or from an affiliate who actually benefits monetarily from additional clicks. For this reason there is interest in exploring alternate pricing conventions. The most compelling is pay per action or conversion. The advertiser pays only if a click results in a sale, for example. This raises new incentive issues associated with tracking sales.

The models in this chapter, as do most analyses in the literature, assume a monopoly search engine with a static user base. This would be an appropriate model if switching costs for advertisers and users were high. In fact, switching costs for many advertisers are low; many advertisers work with both Google and Yahoo! simultaneously, or work with third-party *search engine marketers* to manage their account across multiple search engines. Switching costs for users are essentially zero: to patronize a different search engine, users need merely type a new address into their web browser.[4] The

[4] Personalization features may begin to introduce moderate switching costs for users. For now, reputation and branding seem to play a major role in search engine loyalty: blind relevance tests show little or no difference in quality among major search engines.

competitive pressures to retain advertisers able to switch advertisement networks or use multiple networks may cause firms to focus less on extracting the maximum revenue from advertisers possible and more on attracting and retaining advertisers. Similarly, search engines must make trade-off decisions between maximizing current period revenue and attracting and retaining users in the long term. For this reason it would be very instructive to understand the properties of keyword auctions in competition with each other.

The major search engines syndicate their advertisements to affiliate search engines and content providers. For example, Google, through its AdSense program, syndicates advertisements to AOL, MySpace, and thousands of other Web sites. The introduction of affiliates greatly complicates the semantics of bidding and allocation.

We have assumed that CTRs are given. In practice, CTRs are learned over time and can depend on a variety of factors such as bidder identity; advertisement identity and content; user characteristics, including demographics, location, and history; and/or page context including other advertisements and algorithmic results. Learning CTRs poses an explore/exploit trade-off: the auctioneer can exploit known high-CTR advertisements, or explore new advertisements or infrequently shown advertisements to uncover even higher-CTR advertisements. The auctioneer's CTR estimate may differ from the bidder's estimate; in particular, the auctioneer usually has more contextual information to learn from.

In this chapter, we have focused on the auctioneer's mechanism design problem. The advertiser's bidding optimization problem is also challenging and the focus of a great deal of commercial and research activity.

28.6 Bibliographic Notes

The growth of paid placement has attracted recent research on this topic. Hoffman and Novak (2000) discuss the trend in Internet advertising toward per-click pricing rather than the traditional per-impression model. A good discussion of the practice of sponsored search is available on the Web at `http://searchenginewatch.com/webmasters/paid.html`.

Computing the explicit form of incentive compatible payments for ranking auctions is carried out in Aggarwal et al. (2006) and Iyengar and Kumar (2006). The Bayesian equilibrium of the GFP is derived in Lahaie (2006). The details of the revenue maximizing auction for (static) slot auctions is derived in Feng (2005) and Iyengar and Kumar (2006). The envy-free analysis of the static model is due to Edelman et al. (in press). A similar analysis can be found in Varian (in press). The latter paper shows how upper and lower bounds on bidders' actual values can be derived given their bids. Feng et al. (2006) explore four ranking algorithms via simulation. All of these results would apply to condominium auctions as well; see Burguet (2005) for a discussion of condominium auctions.

The Northwest corner rule for the assignment problem dates back to Monge (1981). Ascending implementations of the Vickrey auction for the static model can be found in Crawford and Knoer (1981) and Demange, Gale, and Sotomayor (1986) (which is a variant of the Hungarian algorithm for solving the assignment problem). The auction of Demange, Gale, and Sotomayor was dubbed, in Edelman et al. (in press), the generalized English auction.

The online allocation problem studied in Section 28.4.1 is proposed and analyzed by Mehta et al. (2005). This problem is a generalization of the online bipartite matching problem studied by Karp et al. (1990) and Kalyanasundaram and Pruhs (2000). More recently Buchbinder et al. (2006) gave a primal-dual algorithm and analysis for the problem given in Mehta et al. They also extended that framework to scenarios in which additional information is available, yielding improved worst-case competitive factors.

Mahdian et al. (2006) study the online allocation problem when the search engine has a somewhat reliable estimate of the number of users searching for a keyword everyday. Mahdian and Saberi (2006) study multiunit auctions for perishable goods, in a setting where the supply arrives online. They motivate their model by its application to sponsored search. Abrams (2006) and Borgs et al. (2005) design multiunit auctions for budget-constrained bidders, which can be interpreted as slot auctions, with a focus on revenue optimization and truthfulness. For a discussion of vindictive bidding and some of the dynamic aspects of slot auctions see Asdemir (2006) and Zhou and Lukose (2006).

Weber and Zheng (2006) study the implementation of paid placement strategies, and find that the revenue-maximizing search engine design bases rankings on a weighted average of relative quality performance and bid amount. Hu (2003) uses contract theory to show that performance-based pricing models can give the publisher proper incentives to improve the effectiveness of advertising campaigns. Rolland and Patterson (2003) propose a methodology, using expert systems to improve the matching between advertisers and Web users.

Besides the optimal ranking mechanism, the search engine must also choose the number of paid slots by finding the optimal trade-off between sponsorship and user retention. Bhargava and Feng (2002) provide a theoretical model to explain and analyze this trade-off.

The problem of learning CTRs is nontrivial and presents an explore/exploit trade-off. Pandey and Olston (2006) formulate the problem as an appropriate multiarmed bandit optimization; Gonen and Pavlov (2007) derive a bandit optimization algorithm that retains incentive compatibility for bidders.

Several authors explore the advertiser's bidding optimization problem (Borgs et al., 2005; Cary et al., 2007; Kitts et al., 2005; Kitts and LeBlanc, 2004; Rusmevichientong and Williamson, 2006). Kitts et al. (2005) provide evidence that the first slot does not have an appreciably lower conversion rate than the second slot as some advertisers believe.

Bibliography

Z. Abrams. Revenue maximization when bidders have budgets. In *Proc. Symp. on Discrete Algorithms*, Miami, FL, 2006.

G. Aggarwal, A. Goel, and R. Motwani. Truthful auctions for pricing search keywords. In *Proc. 7th ACM Conf. on Electronic Commerce*, Ann Arbor, MI, 2006.

K. Asdemir. Bidding patterns in search engine auctions. In *Proc. 2nd Workshop on Sponsored Search Auctions*, Ann Arbor, MI, 2006.

H.K. Bhargava and J. Feng. Preferential placement in internet search engines. In *Proc. 11th World Wide Web Conf.*, Honolulu, HI, 2002.

C. Borgs, J. Chayes, O. Etesami, N. Immorlica, K. Jain, and M. Mahdian. Bid optimization in online advertisement auctions. Preprint, 2005.

C. Borgs, J. Chayes, N. Immorlica, M. Mahdian, and A. Saberi. Multi-unit auctions with budget-constrained bidders. In *Proc. 6th Conf. Electronic Commerce*, Vancouver, British Columbia, Canada, 2005.

N. Buchbinder, K. Jain, and J. Naor. Online primal-dual algorithms for maximizing ad-auctions revenue. Preprint, 2006.

R. Burguet. The condominium problem; auctions for substitutes. *Rev. Econ. Design*, 9, 2005.

M. Cary, A. Das, B. Edelman, I. Giotis, K. Heimerl, A. Karlin, C. Mathieu, and M. Schwarz. Greedy bidding strategies for keyword auctions. Preprint, 2007.

V.P. Crawford and E.M. Knoer. Job matching with heterogeneous firms and workers. *Econometrica*, 49(2):437–450, 1981.

G. Demange, D. Gale, and M. Sotomayor. Multi-item auctions. *J. Political Econ.*, 94(4):863–872, 1986.

B. Edelman, M. Ostrovsky, and M. Schwarz. Internet advertising and the Generalized Second Price auction: Selling billions of dollars worth of keywords. *Amer. Econ. Review*, In press.

J. Feng. Optimal mechanism for selling a set of commonly ranked objects. Working paper, University of Florida, February 2005.

J. Feng, H.K. Bhargava, and D.M. Pennock. Implementing sponsored search in Web search engines: Computational evaluation of alternative mechanisms. *INFORMS J. Computing*, 2006, In press.

R. Gonen and E. Pavlov. An incentive compatible multi armed bandit mechanism. Preprint, 2007.

D.L. Hoffman and T.P. Novak. How to acquire customers on the Web. *Harv. Busin. Rev.*, 78(3), May–June 2000.

Y.J. Hu. Performance-based pricing models in online advertising. Technical report, Sloan School of Management, MIT, 2003.

G. Iyengar and A. Kumar. Characterizing optimal keyword auctions. In *Proc. 2nd Workshop on Sponsored Search Auctions*, Ann Arbor, MI, 2006.

B. Kalyanasundaram and K.R. Pruhs. An optimal deterministic algorithm for online b-matching. *Theor. Comp. Sci.*, 233(1–2):319–325, 2000.

R. Karp, U. Vazirani, and V. Vazirani. An optimal algorithm for online bipartite matching. In *Proc. 22nd Symp. Theory of Computing*, Baltimore, MD, 1990.

B. Kitts, P. Laxminarayan, B. LeBlanc, and R. Meech. A formal analysis of search auctions including predictions on click fraud and bidding tactics. In *Proc. 1st Workshop on Sponsored Search Auctions at the ACM Conf. on Electronic Commerce*, Vancouver, British Columbia, Canada, 2005.

B. Kitts and B. LeBlanc. Optimal bidding on keyword auctions. *Electronic Markets*, 14(3):186–201, 2004.

S. Lahaie. An analysis of alternative slot auction designs for sponsored search. In *Proc. 7th Conf. on Electronic Commerce*, Ann Arbor, MI, 2006.

M. Mahdian, H. Nazerzadeh, and A. Saberi. Allocating online advertisement space with unreliable estimates. In *Proc. 8th ACM Conf. on Electronic Commerce*, San Diego, CA, 2007.

M. Mahdian and A. Saberi. Multiunit auctions with unknown supply. In *Proc. 7th ACM Conf. on Electronic Commerce*, Ann Arbor, MI, 2006.

A. Mehta, A. Saberi, U. Vazirani, and V. Vazirani. AdWords and generalized on-line matching. In *Proc. 46th Annual Symp. on Fdns. of Comp. Sci.*, 2005.

G. Monge. *Sur la théorie des déblais et des remblais.* Mémoires de l'académie de Paris, 1781.

S. Pandey and C. Olston. Handling advertisements of unknown quality in search advertising. In *Neural Information Processing Systems*, 2006.

E. Rolland and R.A. Patterson. Classification in online pay-for-performance advertising. In *Proc. 13th Annual Workshop On Information Technologies and Systems*, Seattle, WA, 2003.

P. Rusmevichientong and D.P. Williamson. An adaptive algorithm for selecting profitable keywords for search-based advertising services. In *Proc. 7th ACM Conf. on Electronic Commerce*, pp. 260–269, Ann Arbor, MI, 2006.

H.R. Varian. Position auctions. *Intl. J. Industrial Organization*, in press.

T.A. Weber and Z. Zheng. A model of search intermediaries and paid referrals. OPIM Working Paper 02-12-01, Wharton School, April 2002.

Y. Zhou and R. Lukose. Vindictive bidding in keyword auctions. In *Proc. 2nd Workshop on Sponsored Search Auctions*, Ann Arbor, MI, 2006.

Exercises

28.1 Consider the model of keyword auctions where the CTR of agent j in slot i is μ_i. Is every full-information equilibrium of the GSP locally envy-free?

28.2 Consider the model of keyword auctions where the CTR of agent j in slot i is $\mu_i \beta_j$; i.e.; the CTR is separable into a bidder effect β_j and a position effect μ_i. Suppose also that $\mu_1 > \mu_2 > \cdots > \mu_m$. Give a simple algorithm for determining the efficient allocation of bidders to slots. Derive the payment rule implied by the VCG mechanism for this environment.

28.3 In the model of the previous exercise, suppose also that the auctioneer assigns a weight $w_j \equiv w_j(\beta_j)$ to each bidder; weights may depend on the bidder effects, but not on their bids. Suppose bidders are assigned to slots by decreasing order of their scores $w_j b_j$. Use formula (28.8) to derive the payment rule that combined with the allocation rule just described would yield an incentive compatible mechanism.

28.4 Consider the model of keyword auctions where the CTR of agent j in slot i is $\mu_i \beta_j$; i.e., the CTR is separable into a bidder effect β_j and a position effect μ_i. The auctioneer sets weights $w_j = \beta_j$, and a bidder pays the lowest amount necessary to retain his position.

(a) Give the inequalities that characterize a full-information (Nash) equilibrium in this model. Strenghten them to give the inequalities for a locally envy-free equilibrium.

(b) Show that in a locally envy-free equilibrium, bidders are ranked in order of decreasing $\beta_j v_j$.

(c) From among the set of locally envy-free equilibria, exhibit the one that yields the smallest possible revenue to the auctioneer.

28.5 Consider the model of keyword auctions where the CTR of agent j in slot i is μ_i. Give an example of where the GFP auction does not admit a pure strategy full-information equilibrium. For simplicity, you may assume a discretized set of allowable bids.

28.6 Consider the online allocation problem discussed in Section 28.4. Show that the competitive ratio of the algorithm remains the same even if the optimum solution does not exhaust all the budgets.

CHAPTER 29

Computational Evolutionary Game Theory

Siddharth Suri

Abstract

This chapter examines the intersection of evolutionary game theory and theoretical computer science. We will show how techniques from each field can be used to answer fundamental questions in the other. In addition, we will analyze a model that arises by combining ideas from both fields. First, we describe the classical model of evolutionary game theory and analyze the computational complexity of its central equilibrium concept. Doing so involves applying techniques from complexity theory to the problem of finding a game-theoretic equilibrium. Second, we show how agents using imitative dynamics, often considered in evolutionary game-theory, converge to an equilibrium in a routing game. This is an instance of an evolutionary game-theoretic concept providing an algorithm for finding an equilibrium. Third, we generalize the classical model of evolutionary game theory to a graph-theoretic setting. Finally, this chapter concludes with directions for future research. Taken as a whole, this chapter describes how the fields of theoretical computer science and evolutionary game theory can inform each other.

29.1 Evolutionary Game Theory

Classical evolutionary game theory models organisms in a population interacting and competing for resources. The classical model assumes that the population is infinite. It models interaction by choosing two organisms uniformly at random, who then play a 2-player, symmetric game. The payoffs that these organisms earn represent an increase or a loss in fitness, which either helps or hinders the organisms ability to reproduce. In this model, when an organism reproduces, it does so by making an exact replica of itself, thus a child will adopt the same strategy as its parent.

One of the fundamental goals of evolutionary game theory is to characterize which strategies are resilient to small mutant invasions. In the classical model of evolutionary game theory, a large fraction of the population, called the incumbents, all adopt the same strategy. The rest of the population, called the mutants, all adopt some other strategy. The incumbent strategy is considered to be stable if the incumbents retain a higher fitness than the mutants. Since the incumbents are more fit, they reproduce more frequently and the fraction of mutants in the population will eventually go to 0. Put another way, an evolutionarily stable strategy (ESS) is a strategy such that if all the members of a population adopt it, then no mutant strategy could overrun the population. We shall see in Section 29.1.1 that ESS are a refinement of Nash equilibria.

Replication is not the only type of dynamic studied in evolutionary game theory. Imitation is another widely studied dynamic. In imitative dynamics, each agent initially plays some pure strategy. As time goes on, agents interact pairwise. After this pairwise interaction, if one agents sees the other agent earned a higher payoff, the agent with the lower payoff may adopt, or imitate, the strategy of the agent who earned the higher payoff. Imitative dynamics model, for example, a new idea, innovation, or fad spreading through a population of individuals or firms.

In general, there are two main characteristics common to most evolutionary game theoretic models. The first is that the population is infinite. The second is that players adopt a very simple, local dynamic, such as replication or imitation, for choosing and updating their strategies. These dynamics result in the agents learning from the other agents in their environment; they provide a method for an equilibrium strategy to emerge from the population. These types of dynamics explain *how* a population can converge to an equilibrium. For example, Section 18.3.1 shows that equilibria for the nonatomic selfish routing game exists, whereas Section 29.3 will show how agents obeying imitative dynamics can converge to it.

Next we will formally describe the basic model of evolutionary game theory. Then, in Section 29.2, we will analyze the computational complexity of finding and recognizing stable strategies. After that, in Section 29.3, we will see an example of imitative dynamics. We will apply imitative dynamics to the problem of selfish routing and show how agents converge to an equilibrium. Finally, in Section 29.4, we will examine the notion of stable strategies in a context where agents play against their local neighborhood in a graph, as opposed to playing against another agent chosen uniformly at random.

29.1.1 The Classical Model of Evolutionary Game Theory

The classical model of evolutionary game theory considers an infinite population of organisms, where each organism is assumed to be equally likely to interact with each other organism. Interaction is modeled as playing a fixed, 2-player, symmetric game defined by a fitness function F (we emphasize that the same game F is played in all interactions). Let A denote the set of actions available to both players, and let $\Delta(A)$ denote the set of probability distributions or mixed strategies over A, then $F\colon \Delta(A) \times \Delta(A) \to \Re$. If two organisms interact, one playing a mixed strategy s and the other playing a mixed strategy t, the s-player earns a fitness of $F(s|t)$ while the t-player earns a fitness of $F(t|s)$.

In this infinite population of organisms, suppose that there is a $1-\epsilon$ fraction who play strategy s, and call these organisms *incumbents*, and suppose that there is an ϵ fraction who play t, and call these organisms *mutants*. Assume that two organisms are chosen uniformly at random to play each other. The strategy s is an ESS if the expected fitness of an organism playing s is higher than that of an organism playing t, for all $t \neq s$ and all sufficiently small ϵ. Since an incumbent will meet another incumbent with probability $1-\epsilon$ and it will meet a mutant with probability ϵ, we can calculate the expected fitness of an incumbent, which is simply $(1-\epsilon)F(s|s)+\epsilon F(s|t)$. Similarly, the expected fitness of a mutant is $(1-\epsilon)F(t|s)+\epsilon F(t|t)$. Thus we come to the formal definition of an ESS.

Definition 29.1 A strategy s is an *evolutionarily stable strategy (ESS)* for the 2-player, symmetric game given by fitness function F, if for every strategy $t \neq s$, there exists an ϵ_t such that for all $0<\epsilon<\epsilon_t$, $(1-\epsilon)F(s|s)+\epsilon F(s|t) > (1-\epsilon)F(t|s)+\epsilon F(t|t)$.

If one assumes that each organism reproduces asexually, and spawns a number of offspring proportional to its fitness, then stable strategies will be those where the incumbent population will reproduce more than any small mutant invasion. Thus the mutant invasion will have fewer offspring and, in the long run, the fraction of mutants in the population will tend to 0. In fact, a continuous time analysis of the replicator dynamics shows that every ESS is asymptotically stable.

Definition 29.1 holds if and only if either of two conditions on s is satisfied $\forall t \neq s$: (1) $F(s|s) > F(t|s)$, or (2) $F(s|s) = F(t|s)$ and $F(s|t) > F(t|t)$. A consequence of this alternate formulation of an ESS is that for s to be an ESS, it must be the case that $F(s|s) \geq F(t|s)$, for all strategies t. This inequality means that s must be a best response to itself, and thus for any ESS s, the strategy profile (s, s) must also be a Nash equilibrium. This results in another, equivalent way to define an ESS.

Theorem 29.2 *A strategy s is an ESS for a 2-player, symmetric game given by fitness function F, if and only if (s, s) is a Nash equilibrium of F, and for every best response t to s, where $t \neq s$, $F(s|t) > F(t|t)$.*

In general the notion of ESS is more restrictive than Nash equilibrium, and not all 2-player, symmetric games have an ESS.

Next, we give an example of a 2-player, symmetric game called Hawks and Doves, and then solve for its ESS. The game of Hawks and Doves models two organisms fighting over a resource. Obtaining the resource results in a gain of fitness of V, while fighting for the resource and losing results in a fitness decrease of C. If a Hawk plays a Dove, the Hawk will fight for the resource and the Dove will give up. This results in a Hawk earning in increase of fitness of V, and the Dove's fitness staying the same. If two Doves play each other, they split the resource earning them both a fitness increase of $V/2$. If two Hawks play, eventually one will win and one will lose, and it assumed that each organism has a 1/2 chance of being the winner. Figure 29.1 shows the payoff matrix for this game.

The strategy profile (D, D) is not a Nash Equilibrium because one player could unilaterally deviate and play H and increase its payoff from $V/2$ to V. Since (D, D) is

	H	D
H	$(V-C)/2$	V
D	0	$V/2$

Figure 29.1. The game of Hawks and Doves.

not a Nash Equilibrium, D cannot be an ESS. Now, if $V > C$ then H is an ESS. To see this observe that $F(H|H) = (V - C)/2$. Let t be any mixed strategy with probability $p < 1$ of playing H and $1 - p$ of playing D, then $F(t|H) = p\frac{V-C}{2} + (1 - p)0 < (V - C)/2$. Since $F(H|H) > F(t|H)$ for all $t \neq H$, H is an ESS. We leave it as an exercise for the reader (see Section 29.6) to show that if $V \leq C$, the mixed strategy of playing H with probability V/C and D with probability $1 - V/C$ is an ESS. Observe that as $V \to C$, the probability of playing H approaches 1. This coincides with the pure strategy ESS of playing H when $V > C$.

29.2 The Computational Complexity of Evolutionarily Stable Strategies

Next we show the computational complexity of finding an ESS given a 2-player symmetric game is both NP-hard and coNP-hard. To prove this, we will make a reduction from the problem of checking if a graph has a maximum clique of size exactly k. Prior work has shown that this problem is both NP-hard and coNP-hard. Along the way to proving the hardness of finding an ESS, we will see that the problem of recognizing whether a given strategy is an ESS is also coNP-hard.

Next we will give the intuition behind the reduction. The reduction will transform a graph G into a payoff matrix F which will have an ESS if and only if the size of the largest clique in G is not equal to k. The reduction transforms the adjacency matrix of G into the payoff matrix F by replacing all the diagonal entries with the value 1/2, inserting a 0th row with each entry having a constant value, and inserting a 0th column with each entry having the same constant value.

Informally speaking, for a mixed strategy s to be an ESS, incumbents should receive a relatively high payoff when playing other incumbents. In order for a strategy s to have this property for the game F, when s plays itself it must guarantee that the pure strategies chosen will correspond to two adjacent vertices. One can see that having a mixed strategy with support over a clique will achieve this. We will show in Lemma 29.3 that having support over a clique will result in a higher payoff than having support over a dense subgraph that is not a clique. Having the diagonal entries consist of the constant 1/2 will help us prove this. This lemma will allow us to prove that when the size of the maximum clique is greater than k, the uniform mixed strategy corresponding to vertices of the clique will be an ESS. In addition, setting the 0th row and column of F to a carefully chosen constant will give us a pure strategy ESS in the case where the size of the maximum clique is less than k. This constant will also allow us to show that there is no ESS in the case where the size of the maximum clique in G is exactly k.

In describing this reduction, and for the rest of this chapter, we use the notation $F(s|t)$ to denote the payoff of the player playing strategy s when confronted with a player playing strategy t. When we are referring to a specific entry in the payoff matrix of F, we will use the notation $F(i, j)$ to denote the entry in the ith row and jth column. Also, if s is a mixed strategy, we let s_i denote the probability that the pure strategy i is played. (Thus we will use s and t to denote mixed strategies, and i and j to denote indices into these mixed strategies, as well as indices into the payoff matrix F.)

The reduction from a graph $G = (V, E)$ to a payoff matrix F that we consider works as follows.

- for $1 \leq i \neq j \leq n$: $F(i, j) = 1$ if $(i, j) \in E$ and $F(i, j) = 0$ if $(i, j) \notin E$
- for $1 \leq i \leq n$: $F(i, i) = 1/2$
- for $0 \leq i \leq n$: $F(0, i) = F(i, 0) = 1 - 1/(2k)$

To show that F has an ESS if and only if the size of the largest clique in G its not equal to k, we will need the following technical lemma.

Lemma 29.3 *If s is a strategy with $s_0 = 0$, then $F(s|s) \leq 1 - 1/(2k')$, where k' is the size of the maximum clique in G. This holds with equality if and only if s is the uniform distribution over a k'-clique.*

PROOF The proof is by induction on the number of nonedges between the vertices in $G = (V, E)$ corresponding to elements of the support set of s. The base case is when there are 0 such non-edges, which means the vertices corresponding to the support set of s form a k''-clique, where $k'' \leq k$. We assume, without loss of generality, that the vertices in the k''-clique are numbered $1, 2, \ldots, k''$.

$$\begin{aligned}
F(s|s) &= \sum_{i\in[k'']} \sum_{j\in[k'']} s_i s_j F(i, j) \\
&= \sum_{i\in[k'']} \sum_{j\in[k'']} s_i s_j - \sum_{i\in[k'']} s_i^2/2 \\
&= \sum_{i\in[k'']} s_i \sum_{j\in[k'']} s_j - 1/2 \sum_{i\in[k'']} s_i^2 \\
&\leq 1 - 1/(2k'')
\end{aligned}$$

The last inequality comes from the fact that when $||s||_1 = 1$, $||s||_2$ is minimized, and the inequality is tight, only when all of the components of s are equal. Conversely, if s is the uniform distribution over a k'-clique then, the inequality is tight, which is shown as follows,

$$\begin{aligned}
\sum_{i\in[k']} \sum_{j\in[k']} s_i s_j F(i, j) &= 1/k'^2 \sum_{i\in[k']} \sum_{j\in[k']} F(i, j) \\
&= 1/k'^2 [k'^2 - k'/2] \\
&= 1 - 1/(2k').
\end{aligned}$$

For the inductive step, let u and v be two vertices such that $(u, v) \notin E$. We construct a new strategy s' by moving the probability from v to u. So let $s'_u = s_u + s_v$ and $s'_v = 0$, and let the rest of the values of s' be identical to those of s. Since v is no longer in the support set of s, we can use the induction hypothesis to conclude that $F(s'|s') \leq 1 - 1/(2k')$. Let $p = \sum_{(u,w)\in E} s_w$ and let $q = \sum_{(v,w)\in E} s_w$, and without loss of generality assume that $p \geq q$. By writing out the expressions for $F(s'|s')$ and $F(s|s)$ one can show $F(s'|s') = F(s|s) + 2s_v(p - q) + s_u s_v > F(s|s)$. Thus, $F(s|s) \leq 1 - 1/(2k')$, which proves the inductive step. □

Now we will use this lemma to prove the necessary properties of the reduction. The next two lemmas, when taken together, show that if the maximum size clique in G has size not equal to k, then F has an ESS.

Lemma 29.4 *If C is a maximal clique in G of size $k' > k$, and s is the uniform distribution on C, then s is an ESS.*

PROOF By Lemma 29.3, $F(s|s) = 1 - 1/(2k')$. By the construction of the payoff matrix F, $F(0|s) = 1 - 1/(2k) < F(s|s)$. Also, for any $u \notin C$, u is connected to at most $k' - 1$ vertices in C, thus $F(u|s) \leq 1 - 1/k' < F(s|s)$. Thus any best response to s must have support only over C. Furthermore, by Lemma 29.3 the payoff of s against s is maximized when s is the uniform distribution over C. Thus, s is a best response to itself. To prove that s is an ESS, it remains to show that for all $t \neq s$, that are best responses, to s, $F(s|t) > F(t|t)$. Again by Lemma 29.3, $F(t|t) < 1 - 1/(2k')$. Since C is a clique and s and t are distributions with support over C, using the structure of F one can compute that $F(s|t) = 1 - 1/(2k')$. Thus, $F(s|t) > F(t|t)$ and s is an ESS. □

Lemma 29.5 *If the maximum size clique in G is of size $k' < k$ then the pure strategy 0 is an ESS.*

PROOF For any mutant strategy t, $F(t|0) = 1 - 1/(2k) = F(0|0)$, thus 0 is a best response to itself. Next, we show that for any t not equal to the pure strategy 0, $F(0|t) > F(t|t)$. To do so, we first show that we can assume that t places no weight on the pure strategy 0. Let t^* be the strategy t with the probability of playing the pure strategy 0 set to the value 0 and then renormalized. So, $t_0^* = 0$ and for $i \neq 0$, $t^* = t_i/(1 - t_0)$. By writing out the expressions for $F(t|t)$ and $F(t^*|t^*)$, one can show $F(t|t) = (2t_0 - t_0^2)(1 - 1/(2k)) + (1 - 2t_0 + t_0^2)F(t^*|t^*)$. Since $F(0|t) = 1 - 1/(2k)$, $F(0|t) > F(t|t)$ if and only if $F(0|t) > F(t^*|t^*)$. Next, since the maximum size clique in G has size $k' < k$, applying Lemma 29.3 gives $F(t^*|t^*) \leq 1 - 1/(2k') < 1 - 1/(2k) = F(0|t)$. □

The next two lemmas, when combined, show that if the maximum size clique in G has size exactly k, then F has no ESS.

Lemma 29.6 *If the maximum size clique of G is at least k, then the pure strategy 0 is not an ESS.*

PROOF Since $F(0|0) = F(t|0) = 1 - 1/(2k)$ for any strategy t, the pure strategy 0 is a best response to itself. But, if t is the uniform distribution on the maximum clique of G, which has size $k' \geq k$, then by Lemma 29.3 $F(t|t) = 1 - 1/(2k') \geq F(0|t)$. By Theorem 29.2, this means the pure strategy 0 cannot be an ESS. □

Lemma 29.7 *If the maximum size clique of G is at most k, then any strategy for F that is not equal to the pure strategy 0, is not an ESS for F.*

The proof of this lemma uses techniques similar to those used in Lemmas 29.5 and 29.6, so we leave it as an exercise for the reader (see Section 29.6).

Taking Lemmas 29.4, 29.5, 29.6, and 29.7 together, we get the following theorem.

Theorem 29.8 *Given a 2-player, symmetric game F computing whether or not F has an ESS is both NP-hard and coNP-hard.*

Combining Lemmas 29.5 and 29.6 shows that it is coNP-hard to check whether a given strategy is an ESS or not.

Theorem 29.9 *Given a 2-player, symmetric game F and a strategy s, it is coNP-hard to compute whether or not s in an ESS of F.*

PROOF Lemmas 29.5 and 29.6 imply that G has maximum clique of size less than k if and only if the pure strategy 0 is an ESS of F. Since the problem of determining whether a graph has a maximum clique of size less than k is coNP-hard, the problem of recognizing an ESS is also coNP-hard. □

Theorems 29.8 and 29.9 imply that *there exist* games for which, in all likelihood, efficient algorithms for finding and recognizing ESS do not exist. These results are important because if finding an ESS for a given class of games is NP-hard, it is unlikely that a finite population obeying some simple dynamic will quickly converge to it. But, this observation does not mean that one should avoid using models based on ESS. It simply means that to ensure the plausibility of a finite population model, one should check whether it is computationally tractable to find the ESS of the games the model considers. Moreover, this result does not directly imply that an *infinite* population, however, cannot quickly converge to an equilibrium. In fact, the next section explores the convergence time of an infinite population to an equilibrium.

29.3 Evolutionary Dynamics Applied to Selfish Routing

In this section we describe a method for applying evolutionary dynamics to the problem of selfish routing. The model will consider an infinite population of agents, each of which carries an infinitesimally small amount of flow in a network. The agents actions allow them to change the path that they traverse; however, agents will not be allowed to change their paths arbitrarily. The space of actions available to these agents will be governed by simple, imitative dynamics. We show how agents selfishly seeking out low latency paths, while obeying these imitative dynamics, converge to an approximate equilibrium. First, we will formally describe the model which is similar to the nonatomic selfish routing model shown in Section 18.2.1. Then, we will briefly outline a technique that shows, in the limit, these dynamics converge to an equilibrium. Finally, we will analyze the time of convergence to an approximate equilibrium.

29.3.1 The Selfish Routing Model with Imitative Dynamics

Let $G = (V, E)$ be a network with latency functions l_e: $[0, 1] \rightarrow \Re$ defined over each edge. We assume the latency functions are nonnegative, nondecreasing, and Lipschitz continuous. We also assume that there is one unit of flow that is to be routed from a source s to a sink t, and we let P denote the set of s-t paths in G. We also assume that there are infinitely many agents, each of which carries an infinitesimally small amount of flow. Let x_p denote the fraction of flow that is being routed over path p. Thus the vector $\vec{x}$, which is indexed by the paths in P, will describe the flow over G at a given point in time. A flow $\vec{x}$ is *feasible* if it routes 1 unit of flow from s to t. Let $x_e = \sum_{p \ni e} x_p$ be the total *load* of an edge. The total *latency* of an edge is denoted $l_e(x_e)$ and the total latency of a path is the sum of the latencies of the edges in the path, $l_p(\vec{x}) = \sum_{e \in p} l_e(x_e)$. Finally, the average latency of the entire network is $\bar{l} = \sum_{p \in P} x_p l_p(\vec{x})$.

Initially each agent is assumed to play an arbitrary pure strategy. Then at each point in time, each agent is randomly paired with another agent and they compare the latencies of their paths. If the latency of one agent's path is less than the latency of the other agent's path, the agent experiencing higher latency switches to the lower latency path with probability proportional to the difference in latencies. These imitative dynamics model a source node gathering statistics on how long it takes for its packets to reach the destination and changing the route accordingly. In Section 29.3.2 we will describe why these dynamics will continue until the agents reach a Nash flow (also called Wardrop equilibrium), which is a pure strategy Nash equilibrium for this routing game, that we define next.

Definition 29.10 A feasible flow $\vec{x}$ is a Nash flow if and only if for all $p, p' \in P$ with $x_p > 0$, $l_p(\vec{x}) \le l_{p'}(\vec{x})$.

This definition ensures that, at a Nash flow, all s–t paths have the same latency (this is precisely Definition 18.1 when restricted to the single commodity case). If we further restrict the latency functions to be strictly increasing, then Nash flows are essentially ESS. We omit the proof of this since this section focuses on the convergence of the imitative dynamics (we refer the interested reader to Section 29.6 for the appropriate references).

To analyze the convergence of these dynamics to either a Nash flow or an approximate equilibrium, it is necessary to compute the rate of change of the amount of flow over each path. Throughout this section we will use the notation x' to denote the derivative with respect to time of the variable x, that is, $x' = dx/dt$. The following set of differential equations describe the rate of change of the flow over each path.

$$\begin{aligned} x'_p &= -x_p \sum_{q \in P: l_q(\vec{x}) < l_p(\vec{x})} x_q \lambda(\vec{x})[l_p(\vec{x}) - l_q(\vec{x})] \\ &\quad + \sum_{q \in P: l_q(\vec{x}) > l_p(\vec{x})} x_p x_q \lambda(\vec{x})[l_q(\vec{x}) - l_p(\vec{x})] \qquad (29.1) \\ &= \sum_{q \in P} x_p x_q \lambda(\vec{x})[l_q(\vec{x}) - l_p(\vec{x})] \\ &= \lambda(\vec{x}) x_p \left[\sum_{q \in P} x_q l_q(\vec{x}) - l_p(\vec{x}) \sum_{q \in P} x_q \right] \\ &= \lambda(\vec{x}) x_p [\bar{l}(\vec{x}) - l_p(\vec{x})] \qquad (29.2) \end{aligned}$$

In this derivation, the function λ accounts for normalizing factors so that the probabilities are bounded above by 1, and it accounts for the rate at which organisms are paired. The first summation in Equation 29.1 represents the expected number of agents that switch from path p to lower latency paths. The probability than an agent on path p is paired with an agent of path q is equal to the fraction of agents using q, which is x_q. Then the agent using p would switch to q with probability $l_p(\vec{x}) - l_q(\vec{x})$. Multiplying this product by x_p gives the expected number of agents moving from p to a lower latency path q. Similarly, the second summation of Equation 29.1 represents the number of agents that switch to path p from a higher latency path. The rest of the derivation results from straightforward algebraic manipulations.

Intuitively, Equation 29.2 says that paths with below average latency will have more agents switching to them than from them; paths with above average latency will have more agents switching from them than to them. In Section 29.3.3, where we bound the time it takes for the system to converge to an approximate equilibrium, we would like the rate of change of the population to be independent of the scale of the latency functions. Thus we will replace $\lambda(\vec{x})$ by $\bar{l}(\vec{x})^{-1}$ to give a relative rate of change.

While these equations resulted from imitative dynamics, the same equations can be derived from a type of replication dynamic. In the literature, these equations are often called the replicator dynamics. Now that we have defined the model and the dynamics, we will show that the population of agents using imitative dynamics will converge to an approximate equilibrium.

29.3.2 Convergence to Nash Flow

It has been shown that as time goes to infinity, any initial flow that has support over all paths in P will eventually converge to a Nash flow. In this section we give an overview of the technique used to prove this. It is not clear how these techniques could yield a bound on the time to convergence, so we do not go into specific details of the proof. Since this text is focused on *algorithmic* game theory, we shall instead give more attention to another result, shown in Section 29.3.3, that bounds the time of convergence to an approximate equilibrium.

The main vehicle for proving that imitative dynamics converge to a Nash flow is Lyapunov's direct method. This is a general framework for proving that a system of differential equations converges to a stable point, without necessarily knowing how to solve the system of differential equations. Intuitively, this method works by first defining a real valued potential function Φ that measures the potential energy of the system of differential equations. The direct method requires that Φ be defined around a neighborhood of a stable point and vanish at the stable point itself. Then, if one can show that the dynamics of the system cause the potential function to decrease with respect to time (along with a few other technical properties of the potential function), Lyapunov's theorems will imply that if the system reaches the neighborhood of the stable point, the system will converge to the stable point. One drawback to this method is that it provides no guidance for choosing such a potential function.

The argument that applies this method to the system of differential equations described in Equation 29.2 works as follows. First, define Φ over the current flow such that it will measure the total amount of latency the agents are experiencing. We will define just such a function in the next section. Then, show that the imitative dynamics cause Φ to decrease over time, and that Φ will achieve its minimum value at a Nash flow. Applying one of the theorems in the Lyapunov's framework allows one to conclude that if the dynamics ever reach a neighborhood of an equilibrium, they will converge to it. Finally, one has to show this neighborhood of convergence contains any initial, feasible flow with support over all paths in P. This comes from the fact that the dynamics cause the potential of any nonequilibrium flow to decrease and thus move toward an equilibrium. Thus, in this model of selfish routing with imitative dynamics, the Lyapunov framework allows one to show that the system will not get stuck in any local minima and will converge to global minimum from any initial state with support over all paths in P.

29.3.3 Convergence to Approximate Equilibrium

In this section we will give a bound on how long it takes for the population of agents using imitative dynamics to come to an approximate equilibrium.

One might consider using Euclidean distance between the current flow and an equilibrium flow as a measure of approximation. To see intuitively why this is not a suitable metric, consider a network and a flow where an ϵ fraction of the agents uses a path p, which has a latency that is slightly less than the current average latency. If it were essential for an equilibrium to have a large fraction of the population using p, we could take ϵ to be arbitrarily small, which, by Equation 29.2, means we could make x'_p arbitrarily small. Thus the imitative dynamics would cause the population to move arbitrarily slowly to p, and therefore it would take arbitrarily long for the population to approach, in Euclidean distance, a Nash flow. Thus, we define an ϵ-approximate equilibrium next.

Definition 29.11 Let P_ϵ be the paths that have latency at least $(1+\epsilon)\bar{l}$, that is $P_\epsilon = \{p \in P \mid l_p(\vec{x}) \geq (1+\epsilon)\bar{l}\}$, and let $x_\epsilon = \sum_{p \in P_\epsilon} x_p$ be the fraction of agents using these paths. A population $\vec{x}$ is said to be at an ϵ-approximate equilibrium if and only if $x_\epsilon \leq \epsilon$.

This definition ensures at such an equilibrium that only a small fraction of agents experience latency significantly worse than the average latency. In contrast, the definition of a Nash flow requires that all agents experience the same latency (see Definition 29.10).

To prove the convergence of these imitative dynamics to an approximate equilibrium, we will make use of the following potential function. This function is one way to measure the total amount of latency the agents experience.

$$\Phi(\vec{x}) = l^* + \sum_{e \in E} \int_0^{x_e} l_e(u)du \tag{29.3}$$

The integral sums the latency each agent that traverses edge e would experience if the agents were inserted one at a time. Summing this over each edge gives the total latency that each agent would experience if they were entered into the network one at a time. The term l^* denotes the minimum average latency of a feasible flow, $l^* = \min_{\vec{x}} \bar{l}$. We add this term as a technicality that will help prove our bounds on the time convergence to approximate equilibrium. With the exception of the l^* term, this is the same potential function described in Equation 18.3. In the theorem statement below $l_{\max}$ denotes $\max_{p\in P} l_p(\vec{e_p})$ where $\vec{e_p}$ is the vector which puts all of the flow, which is one unit, on path p.

Theorem 29.12 *The imitative dynamics converge to an ϵ-approximate equilibrium within time $O(\epsilon^{-3}\ln(l_{\max}/l^*))$.*

This proof works by analyzing the rate of change of Φ under the imitative dynamics. If the current flow is not at an ϵ-approximate equilibrium, we can lower bound the absolute rate of change of Φ in terms of $\bar{l}$. We then lower bound $\bar{l}$ in terms of Φ, resulting in a differential inequality. Solving it leads to an upper bound on the time it takes for Φ reach an approximate equilibrium.

PROOF We start by computing the derivative with respect to time of the potential function Φ.

$$\Phi' = \sum_{e\in E} x_e' l_e(x_e) = \sum_{e\in E}\sum_{p\ni e} x_p' l_e(x_e)$$

Next we substitute in the imitative dynamics, given by Equation 29.2. After that we simplify the expression with the aim of using Jensen's inequality.

$$\begin{aligned}
\Phi' &= \sum_{e\in E}\sum_{p\ni e} \lambda(\vec{x}) x_p[\bar{l}(\vec{x}) - l_p(\vec{x})] l_e(x_e) \\
&= \lambda(\vec{x}) \sum_{p\in P}\sum_{e\in p} x_p[\bar{l}(\vec{x}) - l_p(\vec{x})] l_e(x_e) \\
&= \lambda(\vec{x}) \sum_{p\in P} x_p[\bar{l}(\vec{x}) - l_p(\vec{x})] l_p(x_p) \\
&= \lambda(\vec{x}) \left(\bar{l}(\vec{x}) \sum_{p\in P} x_p l_p(x_p) - \sum_{p\in P} x_p l_p(\vec{x})^2 \right) \\
&= \lambda(\vec{x}) \left(\bar{l}(\vec{x})^2 - \sum_{p\in P} x_p l_p(\vec{x})^2 \right) \qquad (29.4)
\end{aligned}$$

Jensen's inequality shows that this equation is bounded above by 0.

We would like to upper bound Φ'. To do so, first observe as long as $\vec{x}$ is not at an ϵ-approximate equilibrium, by definition at least an ϵ fraction of the population experiences latency at least $(1+\epsilon)\bar{l}(\vec{x})$. Jensen's inequality also shows that for a fixed value of $\bar{l}(\vec{x})$, the $\sum_{p\in P} x_p l_p(\vec{x})^2$ term is minimized when the less expensive paths all have equal latency which we denote l'. Thus, for the purposes of upper bounding Φ', we assume $\bar{l} = \epsilon(1+\epsilon)\bar{l} + (1-\epsilon)l'$. Plugging this into Equation 29.4 gives

$$\Phi' \le \lambda(\vec{x})[\bar{l}(\vec{x})^2 - (\epsilon((1+\epsilon)\bar{l}(\vec{x}))^2 + (1-\epsilon)l'^2)].$$

Now we substitute in $l' = \bar{l}\frac{1-\epsilon-\epsilon^2}{1-\epsilon}$ and perform some arithmetic giving,

$$\Phi' \leq -\lambda(\vec{x})\frac{\epsilon^3}{1-\epsilon}\bar{l}(\vec{x})^2$$
$$\leq -\lambda(\vec{x})\frac{\epsilon^3}{2}\bar{l}(\vec{x})^2.$$

We also replace $\lambda(\vec{x})$ with $\bar{l}(\vec{x})^{-1}$ to measure the relative rate of change of Φ under the imitative dynamics,

$$\Phi' \leq -\frac{\epsilon^3}{2}\bar{l}(\vec{x}). \tag{29.5}$$

We can bound $\bar{l}$ from below by $\Phi/2$ in the following way,

$$\begin{aligned}\bar{l}(\vec{x}) &= \sum_{p\in P} x_p l_p(\vec{x}) = \sum_{p\in P} x_p \sum_{e\in p} l_e(x_e)\\ &= \sum_{e\in E}\sum_{p\ni e} x_p l_e(x_e) = \sum_{e\in E} x_e l_e(\vec{x})\\ &\geq \sum_{e\in E}\int_0^{x_e} l_e(u)du. \end{aligned} \tag{29.6}$$

The inequality holds because of the assumed monotonicity of the latency functions. Now by the definition of l^*, it is easy to see that $\bar{l} \geq l^*$. Combining this fact with Equation 29.6, we get that $\bar{l} + \bar{l} \geq l^* + \sum_{e\in E}\int_0^{x_e} l_e(u)du = \Phi$. Thus $\bar{l} \geq \Phi/2$. Substituting this into Inequality 29.5, we get the following differential inequality,

$$\Phi' \leq -\epsilon^3\Phi/4.$$

It can be shown via standard methods that any function of the following form is a solution to the above inequality,

$$\Phi(t) \leq \Phi(0)e^{-\epsilon^3 t/4}.$$

Here $\Phi(0)$ is given by the initial boundary conditions. Recall that this inequality only holds as long as $\vec{x}$ is not an ϵ-approximate equilibrium. Thus, $\vec{x}$ must reach an ϵ-approximate equilibrium when Φ reaches its minimum, Φ^*, at the latest. So we find the smallest t such that $\Phi(t) \leq \Phi^*$,

$$t = 4\epsilon^{-3}\ln\frac{\Phi(0)}{\Phi^*}.$$

It is easy to see that $\Phi^* \geq l^*$ and $\Phi(0) \leq 2l_{\max}$, which proves the theorem. □

29.4 Evolutionary Game Theory over Graphs

Next, we will consider a model similar to the classical model of evolutionary game theory described in Section 29.1, but we will no longer assume that two organisms are chosen uniformly at random to interact. Instead, we assume that organisms interact only with those in their local neighborhood, as defined by an undirected graph or network.

As in the classical setting (which can be viewed as the special case of the complete network or clique), we shall assume an infinite population, by which we mean we examine limiting behavior in a family of graphs of increasing size.

Before giving formal definitions, some comments are in order on what to expect in moving from the classical to the graph-theoretic setting. In the classical (complete graph) setting, there exist many symmetries that may be broken in moving to the network setting, at both the group and individual level. Indeed, such asymmetries are the primary interest in examining a graph-theoretic generalization.

For example, at the group level, in the standard ESS definition, one need not discuss any particular set of mutants of population fraction ϵ. Since all organisms are equally likely to interact, the survival or fate of any specific mutant set is identical to that of any other. In the network setting, this may not be true: some mutant sets may be better able to survive than others due to the specific topologies of their interactions in the network. For instance, foreshadowing some of our analysis, if s is an ESS but $F(t|t)$ is much larger than $F(s|s)$ and $F(s|t)$, a mutant set with a great deal of "internal" interaction (i.e., edges between mutants) may be able to survive, whereas one without this may suffer. At the level of individuals, in the classical setting, the assertion that one mutant dies implies that all mutants die, again by symmetry. In the network setting, individual fates may differ within a group all playing a common strategy. These observations imply that in examining ESS on networks we face definitional choices that were obscured in the classical model.

If G is a graph representing the allowed pairwise interactions between organisms (vertices), and u is a vertex of G playing strategy s_u, then the fitness of u is given by

$$F(u) = \frac{\sum_{v \in \Gamma(u)} F(s_u|s_v)}{|\Gamma(u)|}.$$

Here s_v is the strategy being played by the neighbor v, and $\Gamma(u) = \{v \in V : (u, v) \in E\}$. One can view the fitness of u as the average fitness u would obtain if it played each of its neighbors, or the expected fitness u would obtain if it were assigned to play one of its neighbors chosen uniformly at random.

Classical evolutionary game theory examines an infinite, symmetric population. Graphs or networks are inherently finite objects, and we are specifically interested in their asymmetries, as discussed above. Thus all of our definitions shall revolve around an infinite family $G = \{G_n\}_{n=0}^{\infty}$ of finite graphs G_n over n vertices, but we shall examine asymptotic (large n) properties of such families.

We first give a definition for a family of mutant vertex sets in such an infinite graph family to *contract*.

Definition 29.13 Let $G = \{G_n\}_{n=0}^{\infty}$ be an infinite family of graphs, where G_n has n vertices. Let $M = \{M_n\}_{n=0}^{\infty}$ be any family of subsets of vertices of the G_n such that $|M_n| \geq \epsilon n$ for some constant $\epsilon > 0$. Suppose all the vertices of M_n play a common (mutant) strategy t, and suppose the remaining vertices in G_n play a common (incumbent) strategy s. We say that M_n *contracts* if for sufficiently large n, for all but $o(n)$ of the $j \in M_n$, j has an incumbent neighbor i such that $F(j) < F(i)$.

A reasonable alternative would be to ask that the condition above holds for *all* mutants rather than all but $o(n)$. Note also that we only require that a mutant have *one* incumbent neighbor of higher fitness in order to die; one might consider requiring more. In Section 29.6 we ask the reader to consider one of these stronger conditions and demonstrate that our results can no longer hold.

To properly define an ESS for an infinite family of finite graphs in a way that recovers the classical definition asymptotically in the case of the family of complete graphs, we first must give a definition that restricts attention to families of mutant vertices that are smaller than some invasion threshold $\epsilon' n$, yet remain some constant fraction of the population. This prevents "invasions" that survive merely by constituting a vanishing fraction of the population.

Definition 29.14 Let $\epsilon' > 0$, and let $G = \{G_n\}_{n=0}^{\infty}$ be an infinite family of graphs, where G_n has n vertices. Let $M = \{M_n\}_{n=0}^{\infty}$ be any family of (mutant) vertices in G_n. We say that M is *ϵ'-linear* if there exists an ϵ, $\epsilon' > \epsilon > 0$, such that for all sufficiently large n, $\epsilon' n > |M_n| > \epsilon n$.

We can now give our definition for a strategy to be evolutionarily stable when employed by organisms interacting with their neighborhood in a graph.

Definition 29.15 Let $G = \{G_n\}_{n=0}^{\infty}$ be an infinite family of graphs, where G_n has n vertices. Let F be any 2-player, symmetric game for which s is a strategy. We say that s is an ESS with respect to F and G if for all mutant strategies $t \neq s$, there exists an $\epsilon_t > 0$ such that for any ϵ_t-linear family of mutant vertices $M = \{M_n\}_{n=0}^{\infty}$ all playing t, for n sufficiently large, M_n contracts.

Thus, to *violate* the ESS property for G, one must witness a family of mutations M in which each M_n is an arbitrarily small but nonzero constant fraction of the population of G_n, but does not contract (i.e., every mutant set has a subset of linear size that survives all of its incumbent interactions). One can show that the definition given coincides with the classical one in the case where G is the family of complete graphs, in the limit of large n. We note that even in the classical model, small sets of mutants were allowed to have greater fitness than the incumbents, as long as the size of the set was $o(n)$.

In the definition above there are three parameters: the game F, the graph family G, and the mutation family M. Our main results will hold for *any* 2-player, symmetric game F. We will study a rather general setting for G and M: that in which G is a family of random graphs and M is arbitrary. We will see that, subject to conditions on degree or edge density (essentially forcing connectivity of G but not much more), for *any* 2-player, symmetric game, the ESS of the classical settings, and only those strategies, are always preserved. Thus, for the purposes of characterizing stable strategies, the classical method of pairing organisms at random, is equivalent to randomizing the graph.

29.4.1 Random Graphs, Adversarial Mutations

We now proceed to state and prove the random graph result in the network ESS model. We consider a setting in which the graphs are generated via the $G_{n,p}$ model of Erdös and

Rényi. In this model, every pair of vertices is joined by an edge independently and with probability p (where p may depend on n). The mutant set, however, will be constructed adversarially (subject to the linear size constraint given by Definition 29.15). For this setting, we show that for any 2-player, symmetric game, s is a classical ESS of that game, if and only if s is an ESS for $\{G_{n,p}\}_{n=0}^{\infty}$, where $p = \Omega(1/n^c)$ and $0 \leq c < 1$, and any mutant family $\{M_n\}_{n=0}^{\infty}$, where each M_n has linear size. We note that under these settings, if we let $c = 1 - \gamma$ for small $\gamma > 0$, the expected number of edges in G_n is $n^{1+\gamma}$ or larger – that is, just superlinear in the number of vertices and potentially far smaller than $O(n^2)$. It is easy to convince oneself that once the graphs have only a linear number of edges, we are flirting with disconnectedness, and there may simply be large mutant sets that can survive in isolation due to the lack of any incumbent interactions in certain games. Thus in some sense we examine the minimum plausible edge density.

Theorem 29.16 *Let F be any 2-player, symmetric game, and suppose s is a classical ESS of F. Let the infinite graph family $G = \{G_n\}_{n=0}^{\infty}$ be drawn according to $G_{n,p}$, where $p = \Omega(1/n^c)$ and $0 \leq c < 1$. Then with probability 1, s is an ESS with respect to F and G.*

A central idea in the proof is to divide mutants into two categories, those with "normal" fitness and those with "abnormal" fitness. Normal fitness means within a $(1 \pm \tau)$ factor of the fitness given by the classical model, where τ is a small constant greater than 0, and abnormal fitness means outside of that range. We will use the lemma below (provided without proof) to bound the number of incumbents and mutants of abnormal fitness.

Lemma 29.17 *For almost every graph $G_{n,p}$ with $(1-\epsilon)n$ incumbents, all but $\frac{24 \log n}{\tau^2 p}$ incumbents have fitness in the range $(1 \pm \tau)[(1-\epsilon)F(s|s) + \epsilon F(s|t)]$, where $p = \Omega(1/n^c)$ and ϵ, τ and c are constants satisfying $0 < \epsilon < 1, 0 < \tau < 1/6$, $0 \leq c < 1$. Similarly, under the same assumptions, all but $\frac{24 \log n}{\tau^2 p}$ mutants have fitness in the range $(1 \pm \tau)[(1-\epsilon)F(t|s) + \epsilon F(t|t)]$.*

With this lemma we first show that all but $o(n)$ of the population (incumbent or mutant) have an incumbent neighbor of normal fitness. This will imply that all but $o(n)$ of the mutants of normal fitness have an incumbent neighbor of *higher* fitness. The vehicle for proving this is the following result from random graph theory, which gives an upper bound on the number of vertices not connected to a sufficiently large set, U.

Theorem 29.18 *Suppose $\delta = \delta(n)$ and $C = C(n)$ satisfy $\delta pn \geq 3 \log n$, $C \geq 3 \log(e/\delta)$, and $C\delta n \to \infty$. Then almost every $G_{n,p}$ is such that for every $U \subset V$, $|U| = u = \lceil C/p \rceil$ the set $T_u = \{x \in V \setminus U \mid \Gamma(x) \cap U = \emptyset\}$ has at most δn elements.*

This theorem assumes that the size of this large set U is known with equality, which necessitates the union bound argument below. The second main step of the proof uses Lemma 29.17 again, to show that there can be at most $o(n)$ mutants with abnormal fitness. Since there are so few of them, even if none of them have an incumbent neighbor of higher fitness, s will still be an ESS with respect to F and G.

PROOF (Sketch) Let $t \neq s$ be the mutant strategy. Since s is a classical ESS, there exists an ϵ_t such that $(1-\epsilon)F(s|s) + \epsilon F(s|t) > (1-\epsilon)F(t|s) + \epsilon F(t|t)$, for all $0 < \epsilon < \epsilon_t$. Let M be any mutant family that is ϵ_t-linear. Thus for any fixed value of n that is sufficiently large, there exists an ϵ such that $|M_n| = \epsilon n$ and $\epsilon_t > \epsilon > 0$. Also, let $I_n = V_n \backslash M_n$ and let $I' \subseteq I_n$ be the set of incumbents that have fitness in the range $(1 \pm \tau)[(1-\epsilon)F(s|s) + \epsilon F(s|t)]$ for some constant τ, $0 < \tau < 1/6$. Lemma 29.17 shows $(1-\epsilon)n \geq |I'| \geq (1-\epsilon)n - \frac{24 \log n}{\tau^2 p}$. Finally, let

$$T_{I'} = \{x \in V \setminus I' \mid \Gamma(x) \cap I' \neq \emptyset\}.$$

(For the sake of clarity we suppress the subscript n on the sets I' and T.) The union bound gives us

$$\Pr(|T_{I'}| \geq \delta n) \leq \sum_{i=(1-\epsilon)n - \frac{24 \log n}{\tau^2 p}}^{(1-\epsilon)n} \Pr(|T_{I'}| \geq \delta n \text{ and } |I'| = i). \tag{29.7}$$

Letting $\delta = n^{-\gamma}$ for some $\gamma > 0$ gives $\delta n = o(n)$. We will apply Theorem 29.18 to the summand on the-right hand side of Equation 29.7. If we let $\gamma = (1-c)/2$, and combine this with the fact that $0 \leq c < 1$, all of the requirements of this theorem will be satisfied (details omitted). Now when we apply this theorem to Equation 29.7, we get

$$\Pr(|T_{I'}| \geq \delta n) \leq \sum_{i=(1-\epsilon)n - \frac{24 \log n}{\tau^2 p}}^{(1-\epsilon)n} \exp\left(-\frac{1}{6} C \delta n\right) \tag{29.8}$$
$$= o(1).$$

This is because Equation 29.8 has only $\frac{24 \log n}{\tau^2 p}$ terms, and Theorem 29.18 gives us that $C \geq (1-\epsilon)n^{1-c} - \frac{24 \log n}{\tau^2}$. Thus we have shown, with probability tending to 1 as $n \to \infty$, at most $o(n)$ individuals are not attached to an incumbent which has fitness in the range $(1 \pm \tau)[(1-\epsilon)F(s|s) + \epsilon F(s|t)]$. This implies that the number of mutants of approximately normal fitness, not attached to an incumbent of approximately normal fitness, is also $o(n)$.

Now those mutants of approximately normal fitness that *are* attached to an incumbent of approximately normal fitness have fitness in the range $(1 \pm \tau)[(1-\epsilon)F(t|s) + \epsilon F(t|t)]$. The incumbents that they are attached to have fitness in the range $(1 \pm \tau)[(1-\epsilon)F(s|s) + \epsilon F(s|t)]$. Since s is an ESS of F, we know $(1-\epsilon)F(s|s) + \epsilon F(s|t) > (1-\epsilon)F(t|s) + \epsilon F(t|t)$, thus if we choose τ small enough, we can ensure that all but $o(n)$ mutants of normal fitness have a neighboring incumbent of higher fitness.

Finally by Lemma 29.17, we know that there are at most $o(n)$ mutants of abnormal fitness. So even if all of them are more fit than their respective incumbent neighbors, we have shown all but $o(n)$ of the mutants have an incumbent neighbor of higher fitness. □

Next we briefly outline how to prove a converse to Theorem 29.16. Observe that if in the statement of Theorem 29.16 we let $c = 0$, then $p = 1$, which in turn, makes $G =$

$\{K_n\}_{n=0}^{\infty}$, where K_n is a clique of n vertices. Then for any K_n all of the incumbents will have identical fitness and all of the mutants will have identical fitness. Furthermore, if s is an ESS for G, the incumbent fitness will be higher than the mutant fitness. Finally, one can show that as $n \to \infty$, the incumbent fitness converges to $(1-\epsilon)F(s|s) + \epsilon F(s|t)$, and the mutant fitness converges to $(1-\epsilon)F(t|s) + \epsilon F(t|t)$. In other words, s must be a classical ESS, providing a converse to Theorem 29.16.

29.5 Future Work

Most evolutionary game-theoretic models consider an infinite population of agents. These agents usually obey some simple dynamic such as imitation or replication. Typical results in these models show that in the limit (as time goes to infinity) the population converges to an equilibrium. A major open problem in the intersection of evolutionary game theory and theoretical computer science is to analyze a population of n agents, who obey one of these dynamics, and bound the time of convergence to an equilibrium. The notions of equilibrium and stability might have to be adapted to this new finite setting. Results along these lines would yield simple, distributed algorithms that agents could implement and converge to an equilibrium in a bounded (and hopefully short) amount of time. This would provide contribution beyond proving the existence of equilibria, and beyond showing that an infinite population will eventually converge to it. It will show that a population of a given size will converge to a stable equilibrium within a certain amount of time.

To start on this endeavor, the simplest models could consider n agents, where each agent could interact with each other agent. One example of such a problem would be to analyze a selfish routing model, such as the one described in Section 29.3, except with n agents, as opposed to infinitely many, and show a strongly polynomial time bound for their convergence. After baseline models such as this have been developed and studied, one might then try to find dynamics that result in these agents converging to an equilibrium that maximizes an appropriate notion of social welfare. Another extension would be to consider models where agents are arranged in a graph and can only interact with agents in their local neighborhood. One could then analyze not only the effect of the graph topology on equilibrium, as was done in Section 29.4, but also how it affects the convergence time.

It may turn out that hardness results stand in the way of such progress. Then one could try to bound the time of convergence to an approximate equilibrium, or simply bound the amount of time the population spends far away from an equilibrium. Also results such as the one given in Section 29.2 imply that there exist games for which it is hard to compute equilibria. There still could be many well-motivated classes of games for which arriving at an equilibrium is computationally tractable.

29.6 Notes

The motivation for evolutionary game theory and the description of the model, definitions, and dynamics were inspired by Smith (1982), Osborne and Rubinstein (1994), Weibull (1995), Hofbauer and Sigmund (1998), Kontogiannis and Spirakis (2005), and Kearns and Suri (2006). The Hawks and Doves game and its motivation come from Smith (1982), Osborne and Rubinstein (1994), Weibull (1995), and Alexander (2003).

The section on the computational complexity of ESS comes from Nisan (2006), which extended work by Etessami and Lochbihler (2004). Lemma 29.3 is a slight modification of a lemma in Motzkin and Straus (1965). Papadimitriou and Yannakakis (1982) show the problem of determining whether or not a graph has a maximum clique of size k is coD^p-hard. We will not define the complexity class coD^p here, but simply state that it contains both NP and coNP. Etessami and Lochbihler (2004) show that finding a strategy that is close in ℓ_p norm to and ESS takes super-polynomial time unless P=NP. They also show that finding an ESS is in Σ_2^P, and that finding a regular ESS is NP-complete. In addition, they prove that counting the number of ESS and counting the number of regular ESS are both #P-hard.

Most of Section 29.3 comes from Fischer and Vöcking (2004) and Fischer (2005). For more details regarding the convergence of the imitative dynamics to a Nash flow, see those two references. We refer the reader to Brauer and Nohel (1969) for an excellent introduction into the Lyapunov framework. For a more extensive and technical treatment see Bhatia and Szegö (1970). For applications of the Lyapunov framework to other evolutionary game theoretic models and dynamics, see Weibull (1995) and Hofbauer and Sigmund (1998). There are many other places where evolutionary game theory is studied in conjunction with imitative dynamics, for example see Björnerstedt and Schlag (1996) and Schlag (1998) and chapter 4 of Weibull (1995).

There is a nice sequence of papers that continues the work of Fischer and Vöcking (2004) shown in Section 29.3. Fischer and Vöcking (2005) consider a similar model where agents may have stale information regarding the latencies of other paths. Fischer et al. (2006) consider a model where agents switch paths in a round based fashion.

Section 29.4 comes from Kearns and Suri (2006) . Vickery (1987) first noticed that a constant number of mutants may have higher fitness than the incumbents who are playing an ESS. Theorem 29.18 is Theorem 2.15 from Bollobás (2001) . In Kearns and Suri (2006), the authors give a pair of results dual to Theorem 29.16 and its converse. They show that if the graph is chosen adversarially, subject to some density restrictions, and the mutants are chosen randomly then ESS are preserved.

Acknowledgments

The author gives many thanks to Michael Kearns, Simon Fischer, Berthold Vöcking, Larry Samuelson, Huanlei Ni, and Eyal Even-Dar for very helpful comments on an earlier draft of this chapter.

Bibliography

J. M. Alexander. Probability and evolutionary game theory. London School of Economics and Political Science, July 2003.

N.P. Bhatia and G.P. Szegö. *Stability Theory of Dynamical Systems*. Springer-Verlag, 1970.

J. Björnerstedt and K.H. Schlag. On the evolution of imitative behavior. Discussion Paper B-378, University of Bonn, 1996.

B. Bollobás. *Random Graphs*. Cambridge University Press, 2001.

F. Brauer and J.A. Nohel. *The Qualitative Theory of Ordinary Differential Equations*. W.A. Benjamin, Inc., 1969.

K. Etessami and A. Lochbihler. The computational complexity of evolutionarily stable strategies. Technical Report TR04-055, Electronic Colloquium on Computational Complexity, 2004.

S. Fischer. Evolutionary game theory. Informatik 1, RWTH Aachen University, July 2005.

S. Fischer, H. Räcke, and B. Vöcking. Fast convergence to Wardrop equilibria by adaptive sampling methods. In *Proc. 38th Symp. Theory of Computing*, pp. 653–662, 2006.

S. Fischer and B. Vöcking. On the evolution of selfish routing. In *Proc. 12th Annual Euro. Symp. on Algorithms*, pp. 323–334, 2004.

S. Fischer and B. Vöcking. Adaptive routing with stale information. In *Proc. 24th Annual ACM SIGACT-SIGOPS Symp. Princ. of Distributed Comput.*, pp. 276–283, 2005.

J. Hofbauer and K. Sigmund. *Evolutionary Games and Population Dynamics*. Cambridge University Press, 1998.

M. Kearns and S. Suri. Networks preserving evolutionary equilibria and the power of randomization. In *Proc. 7th ACM Conf. on Electronic Commerce*, 2006.

S. Kontogiannis and P. Spirakis. Evolutionary games: An algorithmic view. In O. Babaoglu, M. Jelasity, A. Montresor, C. Fetzer, S. Leonardi, A. van Moorsel, and M. van Steen, eds., *Self-star Properties in Complex Information Systems: Conceptual and Practical Foundations*, pp. 97–111. Springer-Verlag, 2005.

T.S. Motzkin and E.G. Straus. Maxima for graphs and a new proof of a theorem of Turan. *Can. J. Math.*, 17:533–540, 1965.

N. Nisan. A note on the computational hardness of evolutionary stable strategies. Technical Report TR06-076, Electronic Colloquium on Computational Complexity, 2006.

M.J. Osborne and A. Rubinstein. *A Course in Game Theory*. The MIT Press, 1994.

C.H. Papadimitriou and M. Yannakakis. The complexity of facets (and some facets of complexity). In *Proc. 14th Symp. Theory of Computing*, pp. 255–260, 1982.

K.H. Schlag. Why imitate and if so, how? *J. Econ. Theory*, 78:130–156, 1998.

J.M. Smith. *Evolution and the Theory of Games*. Cambridge University Press, 1982.

W.L. Vickery. How to cheat against a simple mixed strategy ESS. *J. Theor. Biol.*, 127:133–139, 1987.

J.W. Weibull. *Evolutionary Game Theory*. The MIT Press, 1995.

Exercises

29.1 Find the ESS of Prisoners Dilemma.

29.2 In the game of Hawks and Doves, given by Figure 29.1, if $V \leq C$, show that V/C is a mixed strategy ESS. (Hint: Use the fact that for any mixed Nash equilibrium, s^* with support $s_1, s_2, \ldots, s_k$, $F(s_1|s^*) = F(s_2|s^*) = \cdots = F(s_k|s^*) = F(s^*|s^*)$).

29.3 Consider a 2×2-symmetric game with four arbitrary constants for payoffs. Characterize the ESS for such a game in terms of the payoffs. Use this to conclude that any 2×2-symmetric game has an ESS.

29.4 Give an example of a game that has a Nash Equilibrium but no ESS.

29.5 Prove Lemma 29.7.

29.6 Show that $\sum_{p \in P} x'_p = 0$, where x'_p is defined by Equation 29.2. Using this, conclude that if, in the selfish routing model of Section 29.3, the imitative dynamics initially start with a feasible flow, then for all time the flow remains feasible.

29.7 Show that there exists a game such that with high probability for a family of random graphs with $p = \Omega(1/n^c)$ and $0 \leq c < 1$, an adversary can construct a mutant set such that there will exist at least one mutant with higher fitness than all of its incumbent neighbors.

Index

AAE example, 466–467, 476
aborting games, 188, 190
adaptive behavior, 81
adaptive limited-supply auction, 424–427
adoption as coordination problem, 636
adverse selection, 677
advertisements. *See* sponsored search auctions
affiliate search engines, 712
affine maximizer, 228, 317, 320
affinely independent, 57
agents. *See* players
aggregation of preferences. *See* mechanism design
aggregation problem, 651–655
algorithmic mechanism design. *See also* mechanism design; distributed algorithmic mechanism design
allocation in combinatorial auction, 268, 270–272
AMD. *See* algorithmic mechanism design
"AND" technology, 603–606
announcement strategies, 685–686
anonymous games, 40
anonymous rules, 247, 250
approximate core, 389–391
approximate equilibria, 45, 138, 143, 167
ApproximateTreeNash, 166–168, 176
approximation mechanisms, computationally efficient
  alternative solution concepts, 321–327
  dominant strategy, impossibilities of, 317–320
  history, 327
  multidimensional domains, 310–317
  overview, 301–303
  single-dimensional domains, 303–310
  submodularity, 623–624
  theorems, 305, 307, 309, 315, 318, 324
Arrow–Debreu market model, 103, 104, 121–122, 136
Arrow's theorem, 212–213, 239
artificial equilibrium, 61
ascending auctions, 289–294
ascending price auction, 126
assortative assignment, 704
asymmetries in information security, 636–639
atomic bids, 280, 282
atomic selfish routing, 461, 465–468, 470–472, 475–477, 482–483
atomic splittable model, 483
attribute auction, 344
auctions
  adaptive, limited-supply, 424–427
  ascending, 289–294
  bidding languages, 279–283
  call market, 654–655
  combinatorial. *See* combinatorial auctions
  competitive framework, 344–345
  convergence rates, 342–344
  deterministic optimal price, 340
  digital goods, 332, 338, 340, 345–346
  dynamic, with expiring items, 412, 420–424
  examples in mechanism design, 209–210, 220–221
  first price (Bayesian analysis), 20, 234–236
  frugality, 350–354
  iterative, 283–287
  known single-minded combinatorial, 418
  lower bounds, 346–347
  profit maximization, 331–332, 336

auctions (*cont.*)
random sampling optimal price (RSOP) auction, 341–342
random sampling profit extraction, 348–349
single-item, 332, 337
sponsored search auctions. *See* sponsored search auctions
symmetric, 340
truthful combinatorial, 316–317
Vickrey auction. *See* Vickrey auction
automated market makers, 662–665, 670
autonomous systems (ASes), 364–365, 370–371, 373–379, 487, 507
axiomatic method, 404

backward induction, 69
balanced flow, 111–116, 119
balls into bins problem, 451–452, 530
bandwidth-sharing game, 6–7, 452–455, 587, 588
banking and security, 634, 647
barter-based system, 600–601
basis matrix, 65
battle of the sexes game, 7, 12
Bayes' rule, 667
Bayesian first price auction, 20
Bayesian-Nash implementation, 233–237, 416, 431–436
Bayesian network structured market, 662
Bayesian optimal mechanism design, 333, 335–338, 357
behavior strategy, 67
sequence form, 71
best response
in graphical games, 162
and learning in games, 18
max-weight best response policy, 524
and Nash equilibrium, 30–31, 54, 497
in peer-to-peer networks, 605
polyhedron, 57–59
for identical machines, 522–524
in reputation systems, 686
in strict incomplete information games, 223
best response polyhedron, 57
BGP. *See* Border Gateway Protocol (BGP)
bid format and price formation, 666–667
bid vector, 453–454
bidders
bidding languages, 279–283
in combinatorial auctions, 267–268
exposure problem, 292
iterative auctions (query model), 283–287
single-minded, 270–275, 295, 323–324, 332
single-value, 322
sponsored search auctions. *See* sponsored search auctions
bidding languages, 279–283, 295, 310
bilateral network formation game, 507
bilateral trade, 220–221
bimatrix game, 30, 54–57, 62, 152
binding inequality, 57–59
BitTorrent, 570, 589, 596, 600–601
blocking coalition, 253–255
blocking pair, 255, 256, 507
blogs, 622, 627, 630
BNIC. *See* Bayes-Nash incentive-compatible
Bondareva–Shapley theorem, 388, 389, 391, 407
Boolean circuit, 41, 43
Boolean events, 658, 661
Boolean market model, 666, 668
bootstrapping problems, 636, 647, 689
Borda count, 211
Border Gateway Protocol (BGP), 372, 374, 376, 378–379, 381
bounded communication, 356
Braess's Paradox, 464–465, 475, 481
Brandes' algorithm, 645
brittle and nonbrittle comparators, 43
broadcast and secure channels, 185, 201
Brouwer's fixpoint theorem, 32, 41–43
budget balanced, 22, 392, 393, 501
budget constraints. *See* sponsored search auctions
bundle-price ascending auctions, 292–295
bundles of items. *See* combinatorial auctions
bundling, 356

call market auction, 654–655
capacity augmentation, 479–480
capacity investments, 590
Cascade Model, 620–621, 624–625
cascading behavior in networks
contagion threshold, 615–616
finding influential sets of nodes, 622–627
general social contagion, 618–622
history, 630–631
networked coordination games, 614–618
online data empirical studies, 627–630
overview, 613–614
theorems, 617, 618, 624–626
CE. *See* correlated equilibrium
cell structure, 644–645
censorship resistance, 640–643
centrality attacks, 645
CEPE auction. *See* consensus estimate profit extraction (CEPE) auction

CES. *See* constant elasticity of substitution (CES)
cheap pseudonyms, 597, 679, 683
"cheap talk" preamble phase, 188
Chernoff bound, 532, 533–535
chicken game, 45–46
churn, 594
Clarke pivot rule, 219–221, 561
clearing prices. *See* market clearing prices
click through rate (CTR), 701–704, 707, 712
clique strategy, 644–646, 721–722
coalition game. *See* cooperative game theory
coalition-proof equilibrium, 192
coalitions of agents, 250, *See also* collusions
coarsest common refinement, 653
Cobb-Douglas functions, 139, 143, 146, 155
collective utility function, 405
collusion-proof ex-post Nash equilibria, 376
collusions, 189, 191, 199, 356, 597
combinatorial auctions
  alternative solution concepts, 321–327
  applications of, 269–270
  ascending auctions, 289–294
  bidding languages, 279–283
  communication complexity, 287–289
  computationally efficient mechanisms. *See* approximation mechanisms
  definitions and problem, 267–269
  history, 295–296
  iterative auctions (query model), 283–287
  linear programming relaxation, 275–277
  multidimensional domains, 310–317
  single-minded case, 270–275, 332, 418
  theorems, 273, 277, 278, 282, 285, 288, 289, 291, 294
  truthful, 316–317
  Walrasian equilibrium, 277–279
combinatorial prediction markets, 657–662, 670
combined value trading, 658, 672
combining expert advice. *See* external regret
  Internet routing, 376–379
commitment types, 682
common value model, 238
communication complexity in combinatorial auctions, 287–289, 295
communications networks
  alternative pricing and incentive approaches, 587–590
  efficiency analysis, 583–584
  future research, 589–590
  large networks (competitive models), 572–578
  monopoly pricing and equilibrium, 582
  oligopoly pricing and equilibrium, 582–583
  overview, 571–572
  pricing and efficiency with congestion externalities, 579–582
  pricing and resource allocation theoretic models, 578–579, 584–587
  theorems, 584, 585
compact prediction markets, 661–662
competitive analysis, 344–345, 351, 352–354, 413, 417, 421
competitive auctions, 345–349, 355
competitive digital goods auction, 345–346
competitive equilibrium
  definition, 292
  large communications networks, 572–578
  price takers, 546–547
  smooth market-clearing mechanism, 552
  social welfare, 293
competitive ratio, 345–348, 354, 357, 358, 422, 425
complementary slackness, 74
complementary slackness conditions, 104, 109
complements *vs.* substitutes, 268, 290, 292
complete information models, 239
completely labeled, 58, 59, 61–63, 66
complex networks and topology, 643–646
compound prediction markets, 659–661
computational aspects of prediction markets. *See* prediction markets
computational evolutionary game theory
  classical evolutionary model, 718–720
  computational complexity of evolutionarily stable strategies, 720–723
  evolutionary dynamics applied to selfish routing, 723–728
  future research, 733
  graphs, 728–733
  history, 733–734
  overview, 717–718
  theorems, 719, 723, 727, 731
computational indistinguishability, 185
computational manipulation example, 366–367
computationally efficient mechanisms. *See* approximation mechanisms
computer science and game theory, 363–364
computer science *vs.* economics, 301–303
concave games. *See* submodular games
conditional equilibrium, 164, 176
conditional securities, 659
Condorcet's paradox, 211
congestion control algorithm, 576–577
congestion games, 41, 463, 482, 497–498, 579–582
consensus, 349–350

consensus estimates, 356
consensus estimate profit extraction (CEPE) auction, 350
constant elasticity of substitution (CES), 139, 149–151, 155
constant sum games, 89–90
constraint satisfaction programming (CSP), 169
consumer demand and constant elasticity of substitution, 149–150
consumer sovereignty (CS), 392
consumer surplus, 580
contact process, 630
contagion threshold, 615–618, 620
contingent claims/contracts. *See* prediction markets
continuous double market, 654, 662, 666–667
convergence, 342–344, 373, 523–524, 669; *see also* learning
  rates, 342–344, 523–524
  times, 669
convex program, 104, 105–109, 112
convex programming for market equilibria
  approximate equilibrium, 138
  definitions, 136–137
  equilibrium *vs.* optimization, 139–140
  exchange economies and weak gross sustainability, 142–148
  Fisher model with homogeneous consumers, 141–142
  gross substitutability, 138
  limitations, 150–152
  models with production, 152–155
  overview, 135–136, 155–156
  tâtonnement process, 137–138, 144, 147
  utility function special forms, 139, 148–150
cooperative game theory
  barter-based system, 600–601
  and cost sharing, 21–22, 385–387
  graphical games, 177
  overview, 20–21
  in peer-to-peer networks, 588–589, 593, 596
  reputation as incentive, 596–600
  strong Nash equilibrium, 21
  in wireless networks, 589
coordination game, 7–8, 614–618
coordination ratio. *See* price of anarchy
core, 22, 387–391, 402
correctness and privacy properties, 184, 194–195, 197
correlated equilibrium
  approximating, 48
  definition, 46, 47, 90
  ex ante, 196
  in graphical games, 161–163, 169–175
  Markov networks, 170–174
  mediators, removing, 192–195
  vs. Nash equilibria, 47–48
  overview, 14–16, 45–47
  regret minimization, 88–92
  in succinct games, 48–49
  and swap regret minimization, 90–91
cost benchmark, 352
cost function, 462, 663–665
cost matrix, 4, 5, 8
cost-sharing
  and cooperative games, 385–387
  core, 387–391
  facility location game, 397–402
  and fair division, 21–22, 347
  games, 501
  group-strategyproof mechanisms and cross-monotonic schemes, 391–394
  history, 406–408
  limitations of cross-monotonic schemes, 400–402
  mechanism, 392
  multicast transmission mechanism, 367–370
  overview, 405–406
  primal-dual schema, 394–400
  Shapley value and Nash bargaining solution, 402–405
  submodular game, 395–397
  theorems, 388, 389, 391, 394, 396, 398, 401, 404, 405
costs. *See also* prices
  censorship, 642–643
  defense *vs.* attack, 644
  defining, 9
  function, 9–10
Credence system, 597
critical payment, 274, 419, 430–431
critical values, 229
cross-monotonic cost-sharing schemes, 391–394, 396–397, 400–402
cryptography
  game theory influences on, 197–202
  game theory notions and settings, 187–189
  history, 203–204
  influence on game theory, 191–197
  multiparty computation, 181–182, 185–187
  multiparty computation *vs.* games, 189–191
  overview, 202
  security of multiparty computation, 182–185
CS. *See* consumer sovereignty
currency-based p2p systems, 594, 601–602

DAMD. *See* distributed algorithmic mechanism design

decision making in uncertain environment, 79–81. *See also* regret analysis
decision policy, 414
decomposition-based mechanism, 312–314
deferred acceptance algorithm, 256–258
degenerate games, 56, 65–66
delegation defense, 646
demand bundle, 284, 292–294
denial of service attacks, 634
derandomization, 355
design metric and inefficiency of equilibria, 454–456
design of scalable resource allocation mechanisms. *See* scalable resource allocation mechanisms
deterministic algorithm, 308–309
deterministic optimal price auction, 340
dictatorship, 214, 247
diffusion of innovations, 613–614, 622, 627–630
digital goods auctions
  competitive model, 345–346
  consensus estimation and truthfulness with high probability, 349–350
  convergence rates, 342–344
  decision problem, 347
  definition, 332
  theorems, 340
  and virtual surplus, 338
diminishing returns, 621, 624–626, 628
direct reciprocity, 594
direct-revelation online mechanisms, 414–416
disagreement outcome, 404–405
discrete tâtonnement process, 144, 147
dispute wheel, 373–374, 378–380
distance-vector, 371
distributed algorithmic mechanism design (DAMD)
  vs. algorithmic mechanism design, 365, 380
  combining networking and mechanism design perspectives, 376–379
  history, 380–381
  interdomain routing, 374–376
  multicast transmission cost-sharing, 367–370
  networking perspective, interdomain routing, 371–374
  open problems, 380
  overview, 363–365, 379–380
  theorems, 369, 370, 378
  of Vickrey–Clarke–Groves mechanisms, 366–367
distributed computation through markets, 665–669, 670–671
distributed mechanism, 375
distributed reputation systems, 693
distributed shortest-path routing, 481
divisible matching problem, 660–661
divisible *vs.* indivisible orders, 659
dominant strategies, 10–12, 91–92, 222–225, 317–320
dominant strategy incentive-compatible (DSIC), 415, 428, 430, 436
dominated strategy, 60
DOP auction. *See* deterministic optimal price auction
double marginalization problem, 586
DSIC. *See* dominant strategy incentive-compatible
dual growth process, 109–110
duopoly pricing, 580
dynamic aspects of sponsored search auctions, 707–711
dynamic attacks in reputation systems, 694
dynamic environments and online mechanism design, 413–417
dynamic parimutuel markets, 664–665
dynamic VCG mechanism, 433–434
dynamics of regret minimization, 99

early-arrival misreports, 415, 430
early stopping, 190
economics *vs.* computer science, 301–303
effective bandwidth pricing, 587
efficiency in sponsored search auctions, 703–705
efficient market hypothesis, 657, 672
egalitarian function, 443
Eigentrust algorithm, 597
Eisenberg–Gale program
  combinatorial algorithms, 104
  convex, 105–108, 155
  Nash bargaining solution, 402
  primal-dual schema, 109
elastic traffic, 584–585
elasticity of substitution, 139
elections and mechanism design, 209, 211–212
electronic market design, 210
Ellipsoid method, 156
empirical distribution, 339–341
empirical Myerson mechanism, 339–341
empty threats, 195–196, 201
envy-freedom, 355, 712
epidemic. *See* cascading behavior in networks
equilibria
  approximate, 45
  artificial, 61
  atomic flow, 466

equilibria (*cont.*)
  Bayesian-Nash, 235
  complexity of finding, 16, 29–31
  computational, 191
  correlated, 14–16, 45–49
  equilibrium price, 23, 25, 108–109, 135
  finding. *See* finding equilibria
  graphical games. *See* graphical games
  for identical machines, 522–524, 529–533
  inefficiency. *See* inefficiency of equilibria
  via labeled polytopes, 57–60
  of markets. *See* market equilibria
  Nash. *See* Nash equilibrium
  nonatomic flow, 463
  noncooperatively computable, 198
  vs. optimization, 139–140
  price characterization, 667–669
  reduced strategic form, 69–70
  regret analysis. *See* regret analysis
  sequence form, 73–74
  in sponsored search auctions, 705–707
  subgame perfect, 19–20, 68–69
  for uniformly related machines, 524–529, 533–537
  Wardrop. *See* Wardrop equilibria
Euler's identity, 142
evolutionarily stable strategy (ESS), 718–723, 729–731, 734
evolutionary game theory. *See* computational evolutionary game theory
ex ante correlated equilibrium, 196
ex-post incentive compatible. *See* incentive compatible mechanisms
ex-post Nash equilibrium, 375–376, 377–379
ExactTreeNash, 168, 177
exchange economy, 136, 142–148, 566
exchange model. *See* Arrow–Debreu model
exclusivity, 197
existence and uniqueness in atomic selfish routing, 470–472
existence and uniqueness in nonatomic selfish routing, 468–470
expected capacity pricing, 587
exporting routes in BGP, 372–373
exposure problem, 292
expressiveness *vs.* simplicity in language, 279
extensive game, 40, 54, 66–68, 188–189, 195–197
external regret
  in constant sum games, 89–90
  generic reduction to swap regret, 92–94
  minimization of, 82–88
  model, 81–82
  overview, 80–81
  and partial information model, 94–96
externality, 273, 579

facet, 57
facility location game
  and cost sharing, 386–387, 389–390
  and network formation games, 502–506
  open problems, 510–511
  primal-dual scheme and cross-monotonicity, 397–402
  Shapley values and, 403
fair division, 21–22
Fair, Optimal eXchange (FOX) protocol, 601
fair sharing rule, 489
fairness, 184, 194, 355, 501, 572, 581, 584, 639
faulty parties, 182–184, 186
FCC auctions, 269
feedback in reputation systems, 683–689
file-sharing game, 594–596, 640
finding equilibria
  PPAD, 36–39
  complexity, 16
  correlated equilibrium, 45–49
  Lemke–Howson algorithm, 33–36
  NP-completeness and Nash equilibrium, 31–33
  overview, 29–31, 49–50
  reduction to Brouwer, 41–45
  succinct game representations, 39–41
first price auction (Bayesian analysis), 234–236, 335
first welfare theorem, 103, 277
Fisher's model
  Arrow–Debreu model and, 121–122
  concave utilities, 131
  exchange model with proportional endowments, 140
  with homogeneous consumers, 141–142
  linear case, 104, 105–108, 121, 131
  linear utilities, 121–122, 131
fitness function, 718–719, 729–732
fixed pricing, 588
fixpoint. *See* Brouwer's fixpoint theorem
flat fees, 588
flow, 462, 463, 465, 468–470, 723
forecast, 653–654. *See also* prediction markets
formation games and network design. *See* network formation games
FPTAS. *See* fully polynomial time approximation schemes
fractional allocations
  algorithm, 306–307
  domain, 311
  load function, 307

optimum, 314–315
free-market environment, 597–598
free-riding, 595, 597, 599, 601, 608, 637, 647
frugality, 350–354
full information model, 81
fully mixed equilibria, 529–533
fully mixed Nash equilibrium conjecture, 531
fully polynomial time approximation schemes (FPTAS), 607

gadgets, 42–43
game theory
computational evolutionary. *See* computational evolutionary game theory
and computer science, 363–364
cryptography, influences on, 197–202
efficiency, 191
and information security, 635–636
vs. issues in cryptography, 189
and multiparty computation. *See* multiparty computation (MPC)
notions and settings, 187–189
and regret minimization, 88–92
game tree, 54, 68, 70, 72–74
games. *See also* specific game names and types
aborting, 188, 190
battle of the sexes, 7–12
Bayesian, 20
best response and learning in, 18, 30–31
compactly represented, 9–10
cooperative, 20–22
cooperative and cost sharing, 385–387
coordination, 7–8, 614–620
cost sharing, 501
definition, 3, 88
graphical. *See* graphical games
ISP routing, 4–5
matching pennies, 8–9
pricing, 14, 502
prisoners' dilemma, 3–6, 443–444, 446–447, 595, 680, 681
repeated and online, 356
routing. *See* routing games
routing congestion, 7–8, 96–99
simultaneous move, 9
standard form, 9–10
succinct representations of, 39–41
tragedy of the commons, 6–7, 595
transferable utility, 21, 385–386, 387–391
two-person zero-sum, 16–18, 73
ultimatum, 19–20
with turns, 18–20
Gao–Rexford conditions, 376–380
general equilibrium theory, 22–23, 103
General Threshold Model, 619–620, 626
generalized first price (GFP) auctions, 702, 704–705
generalized median voter scheme (g.m.v.s.), 250, 251
generalized second price (GSP) auctions, 702, 704–706
generalized-WMON, 318–319
Gibbard–Satterthwaite theorem, 213–215, 243, 244
Gittins' index policy, 435
global connection game, 488–489, 494–498, 500–502, 509–510
global trust values, 597
goods. *See* market equilibria
government policy and mechanism design, 210, 221
graphical exchange economies, 176–177, 178
graphical games
complexity of finding Nash equilibrium, 40
computational benefits, 160
correlated equilibrium, 161–163, 169–175
definitions, 161–163
future research and open problems, 177
interdisciplinary benefits, 160
Markov networks, 170–174
Nash equilibrium in, 160–161
Nash equilibrium in tree graphical games, 164–169
overview, 159–161, 177–178
structural benefits, 160
greedy algorithms, 83–84, 315, 522
greedy auctions, 273–274, 422, 709
Green-Laffont, 368
grim-trigger strategy, 601, 681, 683
gross substitutability, 138, 145
group-strategyproof mechanisms, 391–394
GS. *See* gross substitutability
GSP auctions. *See* generalized second price (GSP) auctions

ham sandwich problem, 38
Hawks and Doves game, 719–720, 734
hidden actions, 239, 594, 602–609, 636–638, 648
hill-climbing, 623–624, 630
hiring-a-team auctions, 351
hiring, secretary problem, 424–425, 427
honest-but-curious parties, 182, 186, 197
honest parties, 182, 183
hot potato routing, 602
house allocation problem, 253–255, 262, 263

IC. *See* incentive compatible mechanisms
idea futures. *See* prediction markets
ideal model, 183
identity,682. *See also* reputation systems
IDoWDS, 200–202
imitative dynamics of selfish routing model, 723–726, 734
importing routes in BGP, 372
improvement step, 519–520, 522–524, 528
incentive compatible differentiated pricing, 589–590
incentive compatible mechanisms
  approximation in ascending auctions, 286
  characterizations of, 225–226
  direct characterization, 226
  interdomain routing, 375
  mechanisms with money, 217–218
  price uniqueness, 230–231
  randomized mechanisms, 231–233
  scalable resource allocation mechanisms, 560
  single-minded bidders, approximation, 272–275
  single-parameter domains, 228–230
  social choice, 214, 215
  weak monotonicity, 226–227
  weighted Vickrey–Clarke–Groves mechanisms, 227–228
incentives and information security. *See* information security
incentives for honest reporting, 690
incentives in communication networks. *See* communications networks
incentives in peer-to-peer networks. *See* peer-to-peer networks (P2P)
incomplete information games, 187–188, 222–223, 647
incremental cost-sharing, 403
incremental function, 620, 621, 624–626
incumbents, 717, 718, 720, 729–732
Independent Cascade Model, 621, 625
independent private values, 222–223
indirect reciprocity, 594, 596
individual rationality (IR), 219, 252, 333,419; *see also* voluntary participation
indivisible matching problem, 659–660
indivisible order matching, 660, 661
inefficiency of equilibria
  communications networks. *See* communications networks
  as a design metric, 454–456
  examples, 446–452
  history, 456–457
  measures of, 444–445
  in network formation games. *See* network formation games
  overview, 443–444
  price of anarchy, 445
  price of stability, 446
  in resource allocation. *See* scalable resource allocation mechanisms
  in routing games. *See* routing games
  in selfish load balancing. *See* selfish load balancing
inequalities
  binding, 57–59
  characterizing equilibrium, 154
  correlated equilibrium, 46
  irredundant, 57
  Jensen's, 727
infinite time horizon and discounting, 434
influential sets of nodes, 622–627, 630
information aggregation problem, 651–655
information cascades, 684
information markets. *See* prediction markets
information-measuring software security, 638
information security
  censorship resistance economics, 640–643
  complex networks and topology, 643–646
  informational asymmetries, 636–639
  insurance-based approaches to information security, 639
  misaligned incentives, 634–636
  overview, 633–634, 646–647
  in reputation systems, 678
information set, 54, 67
initiation fee, 682
integer pivoting, 63–65
integrality gap, 314–316
interdependent values, 238–239
interdomain routing
  combining networking and mechanism design perspectives, 376–379
  introduction, 370–371
  mechanism design perspective, 374–376
  networking perspective, 371–374
internal regret. *See* swap regret
Internet Service Providers (ISPs), 4–5, 587, 602
invisible hand, 217
Iowa Electronic Market (IEM), 655, 671
irrelevant information sets, 70–72
IR. *See* individual rationality
item-price ascending auctions, 290–292, 295
iterated deletion of weakly dominated strategies (IDoWDS), 200–202
iterative auctions (query model), 283–287
iterative wrapper, 322

Jensen's inequality, 727
job scheduling problem, 302–310
joint deviation. *See* coalitions of agents
joint forecast, 653

K-rank-sybilproof, 691–692
k-resiliency, 191–194, 200
Karush-Kuhn-Tucker (KKT) conditions, 104, 106, 107, 109–110, 125, 128, 140, 141, 573, 575
Kelly's model, 104–105, 124–125, 402
keyword auctions. *See* sponsored search auctions
kidney matching model, 262, 263
KKT conditions. *See* Karush-Kuhn-Tucker (KKT) conditions
known interesting-set assumption, 429–430
known single-minded combinatorial auction, 332
known single-minded (KSM) players, 323–324, 418
KP model. *See* load balancing games
Kuhn's theorem, 71

labels, 57–60
labeled polytopes and equilibria, 57–60
Lagrangian function and multipliers, 173, 547, 556, 573–575, 578
large actions spaces and regret minimization, 98
largest processing time (LPT) algorithm, 528–529
late-departure misreports, 415, 423, 430
latency function, 96, 97, 584, 724,726; *see also* cost function
lattice formulation, 259–260, 263
LCP. *See* linear complementarity problem
leaders, 43
learning. *See also* regret analysis
  coordinated learning, 435
  response and learning, 18, 30–31, 54
Lemke–Howson algorithm, 33–36, 59, 61–63, 391
Lemke's algorithm, 74
Leontief functions, 139, 152
LH algorithm. *See* Lemke–Howson algorithm
liability, in information security, 634–636
limited misreports, 415, 419, 420, 423, 428–430
linear complementarity problem, 74
linear exchange economies, 149
linear programming relaxation, 260–261, 275–278, 284–285, 388, 395, 406
Linear Threshold Model, 619, 626
link-state, 371, 373
Lipschitz continuous, 723–725
LiveJournal, 627–630
load balancing games
  defining price of anarchy, 521–522
  example, 520–521
  history, 538–540
  introduction to, 518–520
  mixed equilibria on identical machines, 529–533
  mixed equilibria on uniformly related machines, 533–537
  overview, 517–518, 537–538
  price of anarchy, 521–522
  pure equilibria for identical machines, 522–524
  pure equilibria for uniformly related machines, 524–529
local connection game, 489–494, 506–509
local effect games, 41
local game matrices, 162
local neighborhood equivalence, 170–171
local-to-global link, 624, 626
locally envy-free, 705–707
locally optimal solutions, 378
logarithmic scoring rule, 686, 687
loser-if-silent, 325
low communication, 544, 551–552
low-dimensional strategies, 544, 551–552, 564
lower bounds, 287–289, 346–347, 421
LP formulation. *See* linear programming relaxation
Lyapunov function, 575–576, 725–726, 734

MAB. *See* partial information model
makespan minimization, 305–310, 450, 452, 517, 518, 525–530
malicious parties, 182
manipulation-resistant reputation systems. *See* reputation systems (manipulation-resistant)
marginal cost (MC), 368–370, 468
marginal cost pricing, 478–480, 588
marginal traders, 655
marginal utility, 562
market-based approaches to information security, 638–639
market clearing prices
  bid format and price formation, 666
  definition, 23–24, 105
  equilibrium price characterization, 668–669
  proportional allocation mechanism, 545–546
  rational expectations equilibrium, 656
  in resource allocation, 555–557
  smooth market-clearing mechanism, 552–553
  and Walrasian equilibrium, 277

market equilibria
  Arrow–Debreu model, 121–122
  auction-based algorithm, 122–124
  balanced flows, 111–115
  combinatorial algorithms for, 103–105
  convex programming limitations, 150–152
  convex programming models with production, 152–155
  convex programming techniques for, 135–141, 155–156
  exchange economies and weak gross sustainability, 142–148
  finding tight sets, 117–118
  Fisher model with homogeneous consumers, 141–142
  Fisher's linear case and Eisenberg–Gale convex program, 105–108
  graphical exchange economies, 176–177
  and mechanism design, 209
  open problems, 109
  overview, 22–23, 131
  prices as equilibrium prices, 108–109
  in resource allocation markets, 124–125
  simple algorithm, 23–26
  single-source multiple-sink markets algorithm, 126–131
  utility functions for, 148–150
market maker, 652, 654–655, 662–665, 670
market power, 454
market predictions. *See* prediction markets
market scoring rules, 663–664
marketing. *See* cascading behavior in networks; sponsored search auctions
Markov decision process, 432, 435
Markov networks, 170–174
Markov process, 93
matching. *See* stable matching problem
matching pennies game, 8–9
matching problem, 659–661
matrix form, 9–10
matroid, 353
maximal Nash subset, 66
maximum aggregate utility, 550–551
maximum flow, 112–114, 690, 692
MC. *See* marginal cost (MC)
McDiarmid's inequality, 343
MDP. *See* Markov decision process model
measures of inefficiency, 444–445
mechanism design
  Bayesian-Nash implementation, 233–237
  Clarke pivot rule, 219–220
  combinatorial auctions. *See* combinatorial auctions
  complete information models, 239
  computationally efficient mechanisms. *See* approximation mechanisms
  definition, 209
  direct characterization of incentive compatible mechanisms, 226
  distributed algorithmic. *See* distributed algorithmic mechanism design
  examples and applications, 209–211
  hidden actions, 239
  history, 239–240
  implementation in dominant strategies, 222–225
  incentive compatible, 217–218, 225–226
  interdependent values, 238–239
  online. *See* online mechanism design
  price uniqueness, 230–231
  randomized mechanisms, 231–233
  risk aversion model, 238
  single-parameter domains, 228–230
  social choice, 211–215
  theorems, 213, 214, 219, 227–230, 232, 236
  Vickrey auction, 216–217
  Vickrey–Clarke–Groves mechanisms, 218–219
  weak monotonicity, 226–227
  weighted Vickrey–Clarke–Groves mechanisms, 227–228
mechanism design and profit maximization
  Bayesian optimal mechanism design, 335–338
  examples and applications, 331–332
  frugality, 350–354
  history, 357–358
  overview, 331–334
  prior-free approximations to the optimal mechanism, 339–344
  prior-free optimal mechanism design, 344–350
  open problems, 354–357
  theorems, 334, 336, 338, 340, 341, 343, 345, 346, 348, 353
  truthful mechanisms, 333–334
mechanism design without money
  future research and open problems, 262
  history, 263
  house allocation problem, 253–255
  lattice formulation, 259–260
  overview, 243–244
  single-peaked preferences over policies, 244–252
  stable matchings, 255–262
  theorems, 247, 251, 254, 256–258, 260, 261
median voter rule, 246
mediated games, 188

mediators, removing in correlated equilibrium, 192–195
minimax theorem, 89–90
misreports, 415, 419, 420, 423, 428–430
mixed strategy
bimatrix games and best response, 54
graphical games, 162, 167
introduction to, 8–9
in load balancing games, 518, 529–537
vs. pure strategies, 520–522
mixed strategy Nash equilibria, 13, 450–452
mobile ad hoc networks (MANETs), 602
model-free *vs.* model-based frameworks, 413
monopoly pricing and equilibrium, 580, 582
monotone algorithm for job scheduling, 305–310
monotone hazard rate, 337
monotonicity
cross-, 392–393
deterministic policy, 418
in facility location problems, 505
in peer-to-peer networks, 606, 619, 623–624
progressive cascading behavior, 616–617
single-minded bidders, 274
weak, 226–227, 304–305, 307–309, 318–319, 428
Moulin's theorem, 392–394, 402, 403, 407, 408
MPC. *See* multiparty computation
multi-armed bandits problem (MAB). *See* partial information model
multicast cost-sharing, 332, 367–370
multicommodity flow network, 462
multidimensional domains, 302, 310–317
multiparty computation (MPC)
cryptographic influences on game theory, 191–197
existing results, 185–187
game theory influences on cryptography, 197–202
game theory notions and settings, 187–189
vs. games, 189–191
generalizations, 182
history, 203–204
overview, 181–182, 202
rational, 199–202
security of, 182–185
theorems, 185, 193, 199
multipath routing, 603
multiplayer games. *See also* graphical games; specific multiplayer games
definitions, 161–163
graphical, 159–161
multiplication game, 42
mutants, 717, 718, 722, 729–732
Myerson's mechanism, 337–339, 341–342, 357, 435, 703
myopic behavior, 667

Nash bargaining solution, 404–405
Nash equilibrium
aggregate utility, 550–551
Bayesian-Nash implementation, 233–237
and bimatrix games, 54–57, 152
is a combinatorial problem, 31
computational, 191
and correlated equilibrium, 14–15, 163
in degenerate games, 66
and evolutionarily stable strategy, 719–720
finding. *See* finding equilibria
and frugality, 352
in games with turns, 18–20
games without, 13–14
in graphical games, 160–162
inefficiency of equilibria, 446
k-resiliency, 194
and Lemke–Howson algorithm, 33–36, 61–63
mixed strategy, 13, 529–533
in network formation games, 488
and NP-completeness, 31–33
in potential games, 497, 499–500
in resource allocation games, 547–549
pure strategy, 12–13, 55, 519, 520, 528–529, 724
and regret minimization, 96–99
selfish routing, evolutionary dynamics of, 725–726
in Shapley network design games, 449–450
smooth market-clearing mechanism, 552–553
strong, 21
subgame perfect, 19–20, 68–69, 681–683
with succinct game representations, 39–41
symmetric, 30–31, 34
theorems, 13, 17, 34, 47
in tree graphical games, 164–169
in two-person zero-sum games, 16–18
without full information (Bayesian games), 20
Nashification, 529
NashProp, 161, 164, 168–169, 177–178
NCC. *See* noncooperatively computable (NCC)
NE. *See* Nash equilibrium
network complexity, 365, 367–370, 380, 381
network congestion games, 41
network formation games
and facility location, 502–506
global connection games, 500–501
local connection games, 489–494, 506–509

network formation games (*cont.*)
  Nash equilibrium in potential games, 499–500
  open problems, 508–511
  overview, 448–450, 487–489
  potential function method and price of stability, 498–499
  potential games and congestion games, 497–498
  potential games and global connection games, 494–497, 509–510
  theorems, 491–493, 497, 498, 500, 501, 503, 505, 506
neutrality, 318, 320
no dispute wheel, 373–374, 378–380
no positive transfer (NPT), 392
no-trade theorems, 657, 663, 672
nonatomic selfish routing, 461–465, 468–470, 472–475, 478, 480–482, 499
noncooperatively computable (NCC), 197–199
nondegenerate, 56, 60
nondirect revelation, 223–224
nonlinear Pigou's example, 464, 479
nonoblivious cost-sharing scheme, 501
nonprogressive *vs.* progressive processes, 616–617, 621–622
nontransferable utilities (NTU) in cooperative games, 385–386, 391,405. *See also* house allocation problem
nonutilitarian, 518
normal form games, 161; *see also* standard form
Northwest corner rule, 704, 712
NP-completeness and Nash equilibrium, 31–33, 271, 623, 661, 720, 723
NTU. *See* nontransferable utilities

oblivious cost-sharing schemes, 501
oligopoly pricing and equilibrium, 582–583, 586
one-dimensional strategies, 564
one-shot simultaneous move games, 9
online allocation problem, 707–711
online mechanism
  adaptive, limited supply auction, 424–427
  challenge of, 412–413
  dynamic auction with expiring items, 420–424
  dynamic environments, 413–417
  dynamic Vickrey–Clarke–Groves mechanism, 433–434
  ex-post incentive compatible, 428
  future research, 435–436
  history, 436–437
  known interesting-set assumption, 429–430
  Markov decision process model, 432
  overview, 411–413
  planning in model-based environments, 434–435
  simple-price-based online auctions, 428
  stochastic policies, 430–431
  theorems, 419, 420, 422, 423, 426, 427, 430, 433
  truthfulness for single-value preference domains, 417–420
onto condition, 245, 247, 249–252, 263
operationally complete market, 662
opportunistic unchoking mechanism, 600
opportunity cost, 708–709
optimal contract, 605–607
optimal sale price, 338, 341, 342
optimal single price profit, 345, 348
optimal stopping theory, 424–425
optimization program in sponsored search engines, 710
optimization *vs.* equilibrium, 139–140
option set for strategy-proofness, 248
OR bids, 280–283
"OR" technology, 603–604, 606, 607, 669
organisms, in evolutionary game theory, 717–718

P2P. *See* peer-to-peer networks (P2P)
PageRank, 404, 406, 408, 597, 689–690, 692
pairwise stable equilibrium, 507, 615, 729
parallel information sets, 70
parallel-serial topologies, 585–586
Pareto-optimality, 103, 245, 249, 662
parimutuel games, 664–665
partial information model, 81, 94–96
parties in multiparty computation, 182–184, 193–194
partition model of knowledge, 653
path auctions, 351, 353, 354
path-vector, 371–373
Pathrank algorithm, 690
pay per click, 699, 701, 703, 707, 711
pay-your-dues (PYD) strategy, 682–683, 695
payment policy, 414–415, 422
payoffs
  in bimatrix games, 54, 55
  defining, 9
  evolutionarily stable strategy, 720–721
  and inefficiency, 444, 453
  in parimutuel games, 665
  with risk-neutral players, 13
  in scalable resource allocation mechanisms, 555
  sequence form, 72–73

payoff matrix, 8, 12, 15
peer-prediction scoring, 686–689
peer-to-peer networks (P2P)
  barter-based system, 600–601
  and censorship resistance, 640
  currency as incentive, 601–602
  pricing and incentive models, 588–589
  file-sharing game, 594–596
  hidden actions, 602–608, 637
  history, 608–609
  open problems, 608
  overview, 593–594, 608
  reputation as incentive, 596–600, 678
  theorems, 607
peering, 377
perfect information, 67
perfect recall, 54, 71
perfect security, 184
phantom feedback, 679
Pigou's example, 447–448, 456, 462–464, 469, 472–474, 479
Pigouvian taxes, 480, 580; *see also* marginal cost pricing
pivoting, 63–65
players. *See also* bidders; specific games
  leaders, 43
  limited information, 20
  loser-if-silent, 325
  in multiplayer games. *See* graphical games
  payoffs. *See* payoffs
  in peer-to-peer networks, 596
  price anticipating, 547–549
  price takers, 546–547, 573, 574
  risk-neutral, 13
  and transferable utility, 21–22
  in two-person zero-sum games, 16–18
policy-consistency, 377–379
pollution game, 5–6
polyhedra, 53, 57
polynomial local search (PLS) problems, 499–500
polynomial parity argument (directed case). *See* PPAD
polynomial weights (PW) algorithm, 86–88
polytopes, 57–60, 65
population and strategy, 595–596, 613–614, 618–622. *See also* computational evolutionary game theory
positive association of differences (PAD), 318, 319
potential function method, 448, 468, 469, 471, 472, 482, 489, 494, 496
potential games
  congestion games, 497–498
  facility location games, 503–504
  global connection games, 494–497, 509–510
  Nash equilibrium, 499–500
  price of stability, 498–499
PPAD, 36–39, 151–152, 156
PPAD-complete, 16, 41–42, 44, 45
prediction markets
  automated market makers, 662–665
  combinatorial, 657–662
  definition, 651–652
  distributed computation, 665–669
  history, 671–672
  open problems, 670–671
  setup and notation, 652–654
  survey of field, 654–657
  theorems, 660, 661, 668, 669
preference ordering, 9
prices
  equilibrium, 123
price anticipating users (in resource allocation games), 547–549
price characterization, 667–669
price competition game, 583
price correspondences, 657
price discriminate, 545
price formation, 666–667
price of anarchy
  of atomic selfish routing, 459, 463–466, 468–470, 473–479, 480–481
  coordination ratio, 456
  definition, 445, 517, 520–522
  facility location games, 504–505, 511
  fully mixed Nash equilibrium, 531–533
  in global connection games, 495
  in local connection games, 491–494
  mixed equilibria on uniformly related machines, 533
  of nonatomic selfish routing, 463–464, 472–477, 481, 447–448
  of the proportional sharing mechanism, 455–456
  pure equilibria for identical machines, 522–523
  pure equilibria for uniformly related machines, 524–528
  pure *vs.* mixed equilibria, 537–538
  reducing in routing games, 478–480
  of scalable resource allocation mechanisms, 549–551, 558–559
  in scheduling games, 451
  utility games, 505, 507
price of stability, 446–449, 490–491, 495, 498–499, 520
price of unaccountability (POU), 605–607

price takers (in resource allocation games), 546–547, 573, 574, 576
prices
  automated market makers, 662–665
  in communications networks. *See* communications networks
  for differentiated services, 587–588
  equilibrium, 23, 25, 108–109, 135; *see also* market equilibria
  and information security, 638
  market clearing, 23, 24, 105, 106, 122; *see also* market clearing prices
  in sponsored search auctions, 699–701
  uniqueness of, 230–231
pricing game, 14, 502
primal-dual schema, 104, 109–110, 126, 291, 394–400, 407
Prim's algorithm, 501
principal-agent model in peer-to-peer networks, 602–606
prior distribution, 333, 337, 339
prior-free mechanism design, 344–350
  convergence rates, 342–344
  empirical distributions, 339–341
  random sampling, 341–342
prior probability distribution,653; *see also* Bayesian-Nash implementation
Prisoners' dilemma, 3–6, 443–444, 446–447, 595, 680, 681
privacy and correctness properties, 184, 194–195, 197
probabilistic functions, 182, 186, 201, 620, 679
procurement auction, 220, 269
profit benchmark, 333, 344–345, 349, 350, 354
profit extraction problem, 347
profit extractor, 347–350, 358
profit maximization and mechanism design
  Bayesian optimal mechanism design, 335–338
  in communications networks, 579–582
  examples and applications, 331–332
  frugality, 350–354
  history, 357–358
  overview, 331–334
  prior-free approximations to the optimal mechanism, 339–344
  prior-free optimal mechanism design, 344–350
  future research, 354–357
  theorems, 334, 336, 338, 340, 341, 343, 345, 346, 348, 350, 353
progressive *vs.* nonprogressive processes, 616–617, 621–622
proportional allocation mechanism, 544–551, 558, 564
proportional fairness, 125
proportional sharing, 452, 455–456
pseudonyms, 597, 679, 683
public good cost sharing, 251–252
pure strategy Nash equilibrium, 12–13, 55, 466, 519, 520, 528–529, 724
PW algorithm. *See* polynomial weights (PW) algorithm

quadratic scoring rule market maker, 664
quality of service (QoS), 587
query model (iterative auctions), 283–287, 310

random ordering, 403, 424, 427
random replenishment, 644
random sampling empirical Myerson, 341–342
random sampling optimal price (RSOP) auction, 341–346, 355, 357
random sampling profit extraction auction, 348–349
randomized-greedy (RG) algorithm, 83, 84
randomized incentive compatible mechanisms, 231–233
randomized rounding, 307–308
randomized scheduling algorithm, 307–308
randomized strategies, 8–9; *see also* mixed strategies
randomized weighted majority (RWM) algorithm, 85–86
rank-strategyproof, 690
rater reputations, 679–680, 684–688, 695
rational expectations equilibrium, 652, 656–657, 672
rational multiparty computation, 199–202
realization plan, 71–74
reciprocity, 594, 600
recommendation incentive programs, 626–627, 630
Red-Blue utility model, 640–641
reduced strategy, 69–70
reductions, 41–45
regret analysis
  external regret minimization, 82–88
  generic reduction from external to swap regret, 92–94
  lower bounds, 87–88
  model, 81–82
  overview, 80–81, 99
  partial information model, 94–96
  regret minimization and game theory, 88–92
  regret minimization strategies in routing games, 96–99

theorems, 82–85, 87, 88
relative optimality, 333; *see also* competitive analysis
replicator dynamics, 727
reputation as incentive, 594, 596–600, 678
reputation systems (manipulation-resistant)
dynamics, 678
effect of, 680–683
eliciting effort and honest feedback, 683–689
history, 694–695
importance of, 677–680
meta-evaluation, 684
metrics and benchmarks in reputation systems, 694
open problems and extensions, 693–694
sybilproofness, 690–693
theorems, 691, 692
and transitive trust, 689–693
whitewashing, 682–683
residency matching, 255
resilient equilibrium, 191–192
resource allocation markets, 124–125, 452–454,573. *See also* communications networks; scalable resource allocation mechanisms
revelation principle, 12, 224–225, 231, 234, 356, 416–417, 589
revenue equivalence, 236–237, 356, 705
revenue maximization. *See* profit maximization and mechanism design
reverse auction, 220
ring structure, 644–645, 647
risk aversion model, 238
risk-neutral, 13
Roberts theorem, 228
rock-paper-scissors game, 44, 45
routing congestion game, 7–8, 96–99; *see also* routing games
routing games
atomic selfish routing, 465–468, 482–483
Braess's Paradox, 464–465, 475, 481
existence and uniqueness, 468–470
vs. global connection games, 495
history, 480–483
network formation games. *See* network formation games
nonatomic selfish routing, 462–465, 480–482
nonexistence in weighted atomic instances, 467
overview, 461–462
Pigou's example, 447–448, 456, 462–464, 469, 472–474, 479
potential function, 470–472
price of anarchy in atomic selfish routing, 475–477
price of anarchy in nonatomic selfish routing, 472–475
reducing the price of anarchy, 478–480
theorems, 468, 471, 472, 476, 478, 479
routing matrix, 572, 575
routing protocol, 371–379
routing security, 636
RSEM. *See* random sampling empirical Myerson
RSOP auction. *See* random sampling optimal price (RSOP) auction
RSPE auction. *See* random sampling profit extraction auction
RWM algorithm. *See* randomized weighted majority (RWM) algorithm

satisfiability, 31–33, 500, 524, 529
scalable resource allocation mechanisms
characterization theorem, 551–559
history, 565–566
overview, 543–544, 564
proportional allocation, 544–551
theorems, 546, 547, 549, 554
Vickrey–Clarke–Groves approach to, 559–563
scalar strategy VCG mechanisms, 559–563
scale-free networks, 643, 648
scheduling games. *See* load balancing games
scheduling related machines, 303–304, 450–452, 577
scoring peer-prediction, 686–689
second-price auction. *See* Vickrey auction
second welfare theorem, 278
secret-sharing, 186–187, 200, 201
secretary problem, 424–425, 427
secure and broadcast channels, 185
securities markets. *See* prediction markets
security. *See* information security
security of multiparty computation, 182–185, 190
security parameters, 185
seeder, 600
selfish load balancing. *See* load balancing games
selfish routing, 447–448, 723–728; *see also* routing games
semihonest parties, 182
sequence form, 70–74
sequential decision problem, 431, 437
serial connection, 585–586
service differentiation, 598–600
Shamir secret-sharing scheme, 186, 187, 201
Shapley cost-sharing mechanism, 495

Shapley network design game, 448–450; *see also* network formation games
Shapley value, 22, 368–369, 402–405, 407–408, 489, 501
signal, 685, 687, 688
simple polytope, 60
simple pricing rules, 590
simultaneous move game, 9
simultaneous reporting game, 685
single-dimensional domains, 303–310; *see* single-parameter domains
single-item auction, 332, 335, 337, 338, 351
single-minded bidders, 270–275, 295, 323–324, 332
  greedy mechanism for single-minded bidders, 273–274
single-parameter domains, 228–230, 303–310, 350, 354, 356, 417–420
single-peaked preferences, 244–252
single-source multiple-sink markets algorithm, 126–131
single-value players, 322, 324–325
single-valued preference domains. *See* Single parameter domains
slots, 699
smart market, 587
Smith, Adam, 217
smooth market-clearing mechanism, 552–554
social choice
  Arrow's theorem, 212–213
  Condorcet's paradox, 211
  Gibbard–Satterthwaite theorem, 213–215
  and mechanism design, 209, 210
  and mechanisms with money, 216–222
  voting methods, 211–212
social choice function, 212–215, 225–226, 237, 405
social cost, 488, 490–491, 518, 520–522, 528
social network, 614–618, 622–625, 627, 637, 643, 630
social welfare function, 212–213, 215, 218
socially efficient networks, 488, 490, 682–683
sock puppet identities. *See* phantom feedback; Sybil attacks
software security, 638
solution concepts
  correlated equilibrium, 14–15
  dominant strategy, 10–12
  mixed strategy Nash equilibrium, 13
  pure strategy Nash equilibrium, 12–13
source routing, 481, 603
spanning tree auctions, 351
sparse games, 40
specification faithfulness, 601
spectrum auctions, 269, 295
SPNE. *See* subgame perfect equilibrium
sponsored search auctions
  discussion of practice, 712
  dynamic aspects of, 707–711
  equilibrium properties, 705–707
  history, 712–713
  models and mechanisms, 701–702
  open problems, 711–712
  overview, 699–701
  static model, 702–707
  theorems, 706, 709
stable matching problem
  college student matching, 255, 261
  deferred acceptance algorithm, 256–258
  extensions, 261–262
  lattice formulation, 259–260
  LP formulation, 260–261
  overview, 255
stalling, 433
standard form, 9–10
statistical security, 184
Steiner forest problem, 406, 407, 495
Stirling's formula, 288
stochastic policies, 430–431
strategic and privacy equivalence, 196
strategic form. *See* standard form
strategic network formation, 594, 609; *see also* network formation games
strategic voting, 211–212
strategy proof mechanism. *See* truthfulness
strategy-proof rules, 243–251, 258, 262, 263, 690
strategy, 9, 10, 12, 18, 556, 561
strict equilibrium, 586
strict incomplete information, 222–223
strict quasi-concavity, 137
strong Nash equilibrium, 21
strong truthfulness, 415, 430
subgame perfect equilibrium, 19–20, 68–69, 681–683
subgames, 54
submodular function, 624–626, 630
submodular games, 395–397, 403, 504
submodularity, 623–626
substitutes *vs.* complements, 139, 268, 290, 292
succinct game representations, 39–41, 48–49
supply and demand, 135; *see also* market equilibria
support, 31, 34–36, 54
surplus sharing problem,386; *see also* cost sharing

surplus vector, 112, 121, 659–660
surplus, 119–121, 335–337,583. *See also* market equilibria
swap regret
  definition, 80–82
  and dominated strategies, 91–92
  generic reduction from external to, 92–94
  minimization and correlated equilibrium, 90–91
swarming download, 600, 601
Sybil attacks, 597, 601, 602, 608, 679, 680, 690–693
symmetric game, 30, 40, 45–46, 340

Tarski's fixed point theorem, 259–260
tâtonnement process, 137–138, 144, 147
TCP congestion control, 104–105
thin market problem, 662
tit-for-tat strategy, 595, 596
top trading cycle mechanism, 254
traffic light example, 14–15
tragedy of the commons, 6–7, 595
transferable utilities (TU) in cooperative games, 21–22, 385–391
transitivity of trust, 679, 680, 689–693
tree graphical games, 164–169
TreeNash, 164–167, 176
trembling hand perfect equilibrium, 503
trusted parties, 182, 190
truthful with high probability
truthfulness
  adaptive limited-supply auction, 425–426
  automated market makers, 662–665
  in canonical expiring items environment, 412
  combinatorial auctions, 312–314
  and dominant strategy incentive-compatible, 415
  with high probability, 349–350
  and profit maximization, 356–357
  single-valued preference domains, 417–420
TU. *See* transferable utilities
two-person zero-sum games, 16–18, 73
two-player game equilibrium computation
  bimatrix games and best response, 54–57
  degenerate games, 65–66
  extensive games, 66–68
  further reading for, 75
  integer pivoting, 63–65
  via labeled polytopes, 57–60
  Lemke–Howson algorithm, 61–63
  overview, 53–54, 75–76
  reduced strategic form, 69–70
  sequence form, 70–73

ultimatum game, 19
uniqueness of prices, 230–231
unit demand, 280
upper envelope, 57, 59
users. *See* players
utilitarian function, 443
utility, 331, 334, 357
utility function
  Cobb-Douglas, 139, 143, 146, 155
  definition, 9–10
  gross substitutability, 138, 145
  in information security, 640–641
  Leontief, 139, 152
  market equilibria, 131, 148–150
  maximizing with convex programs, 106
  for scalable resource allocation mechanisms, 544–545, 556
  special forms of, 139

valuation, 12, 20, 216–222, 238–240, 268, 331–334, 335–339, 355, 356, 374
value queries, 284
variational inequalities, 473–474
VCG mechanism. *See* Vickrey–Clarke–Groves mechanisms
vertex-order attacks, 644–646
Vickrey auction, 11–12, 216–217, 220, 335, 422, 703–704
  reserve price, 338
Vickrey–Clarke–Groves mechanisms
  and Clarke pivot rule, 219, 221
  competitive communications network problems, 573
  definition, 218–219
  distributed implementation of, 366–367
  in dynamic environments, 434–435
  and frugality, 352–353
  incentive compatible approximation, 273
  marginal cost, 368–370
  multidimensional domains and combinatorial auctions, 311
  scalable resource allocation mechanisms, 559–564
  and Walrasian equilibrium, 292
  with scaler strategies, 559–563
  weighted, 227–228
viral marketing, 622–623, 626–627, 630
virtual surplus, 336, 337, 338
virtual valuation, 335–336, 338
voluntary participation (VT), 392, 608; *see also* individual rationality
voting and mechanism design, 209, 211–215, 246

voyeurism, 197

Walras' Law, 137, 147
Walrasian equilibrium, 277–279, 290–292, 121–122
Walrasian model. *See* Arrow–Debreu model
Wardrop equilibria, 480, 579–581, 724; *see also* equilibria nonatomic flow
Wardrop model of traffic flow, 96–98,585; *see also* selfish routing
weak gross substitutability, 131
weak gross sustainability (WGS), 138, 142–148
weak monotonicity, 226–227, 304–305, 307–309, 318–319, 428
weighted-packing problem, 271
threshold function, 669
weighted Vickrey–Clarke–Groves mechanisms, 227–228
WGS. *See* weak gross sustainability (WGS)
whitewashing attacks, 597, 601, 602, 608, 679, 682–683, 695
winner's curse, 238
wireless networks, 577, 588, 589
"The Wisdom of Crowds", 652
WMON. *See* weak monotonicity
worst-case analysis, 333, 357, 558; *see also* competitive analysis

XOR bids, 280–283, 668

Zermelo's algorithm, 69
zero-sum games, 16–18, 73, 662

Printed in the United States
By Bookmasters